SHEFFIELD UNITED FOOTBALL CLUB

WHO'S WHO

Denis Clarebrough and Andrew Kirkham

Published by **The Hallamshire Press**
for and on behalf of **Sheffield United Football Club**

Photographs courtesy of Sheffield Newspapers,
Sheffield United Football Club and from the Denis Clarebrough collection

Typesetting and design
Hallamshire Publications Limited

Printed in Great Britain by
Cromwell Press, Trowbridge

British Library Cataloguing in Publication Data:
A catalogue record for this book is available from the British Library

ISBN 978-1-874718-69-7

CONTENTS

To research and produce such an extensive work of reference has inevitably been a long job and our deepest gratitude therefore must be to our wives Maureen and Alison for their patience and encouragement.

Acknowledgements

The authors wish to warmly acknowledge the many hundreds of people who have helped to supply the detailed information in this book. They include former players of Sheffield United, past and present staff and numerous supporters. We are particularly grateful to former Directors, Derek Dooley, Albert Jackson, Frank O'Gorman, and Dick Wragg, all of whom, sadly, have died. Also John Hassall and former United Secretaries, David Capper and the late Arnold Newton, Managers Ken Furphy, Dave Bassett and Neil Warnock and Coach Reg Wright. We also express our gratitude to the all those members of Sheffield United staff who have helped in the production of this book. In particular to Andy Pack for providing the more recent photos and to John Garrett who has been responsible in these last few years for adding an enormous amount to our knowledge of United's history and for the collection on behalf of the Club of a wide variety of written and photographic evidence and other ephemera including shirts and medals which is now available for display.

We also thank the large number of former players and their relatives who have been generous in sharing their memories of players and games.

An enormous number of United supporters have helped in the preparation of this book. We thank them all and in particular, Gary Armstrong, Dave Burkinshaw, Eric Dawson, Derek Goodison, the late Peter Harvey, Chris Kentzer, Darren White and Beryl and Peter Whitney.

We are also delighted to pay a warm tribute to the enormous number of football historians and statisticians for their generosity in time and willingness to share their vast knowledge of soccer. In particular, we thank Dr Geoff Allman, Ian Barnsley, Stuart Basson, Mike Blackstone, Graham Blackwood, Tony Bluff, Arthur Bower, John Brodie, Tony Brown, Mick Cooper, Jim Creasy, John Cross, Peter Cullen, Mike Davage, Gareth Davies, Jason Dickinson, Gareth Dykes, Leigh Edwards, Keith Farnsworth, Jon Farrelly, Grenville Firth, Mick French, Terry Frost, Harry Glasper, Andrew George, George Glass, Bob Goodwin, Frank Grande, Malcolm Hartley, Graham Hayes, Keith Howard, Derek Hyde, David Instone, Steve Jarvis, Mike Jay, Paul Joannou, Trefor Jones, Jeff Kent, John Litster, Malcolm K Macdonald, Simon Marland, Gerald Mortimer, Donald and Ian Nannestad who publish *Soccer History*, Michael Norton, Richard Owen, Barry Pearson, the late Jack Retter and Geoff Sadler, Charles Robinson, the Rev Nigel Sands, Phil Sherwin, Ken Smales, Jarrod Smith, WR (Bill) Smith, John Staff, David Steel, John A Steele, Paul Taylor, Ben Thacker, Roger Walsh, Barry Watson, David Watson, Ian Watts, Peter Windle, David Woods, Gerry Wostenholme and Robert Wray.

We would also wish to thank for their assistance, the staff of the local studies departments of several of our local libraries including Barnsley, Chesterfield, Doncaster, Gainsborough, Rotherham and Worksop but in particular, of course, Sheffield. We would also wish to thank Lorna Parnell and her colleagues at the headquarters of The Football League and James Hopegill Smith of the Sheffield & Hallamshire Football Association.

Last, and by no means least, we acknowledge our debt to our publisher Pauline Climpson of Hallamshire Publications Limited for her patient, helpful and careful assistance.

Foreword

In my business travels around the world, I am so often explaining to corporate audiences that football clubs are companies with shareholders but have peculiar responsibilities that can never be ignored. It is clubs such as ours that represent not only supporters who can be based far and wide but more particularly the local communities they serve along with the town and city they represent. History and heritage mean so much and if you trace the roots back in the *Who's Who* of Sheffield United they do, of course, start before the evolution of our world famous football club to the creation in 1855 of Bramall Lane—established before organised football was born—through to Sheffield United Cricket Club, Yorkshire County Cricket Club and the formation of a stadium that has hosted so many sports at national and international levels.

We are lucky to have such a rich history at the 'home of football' and to be able to call upon Denis and Andrew to research, write and present in such an interesting format Sheffield United's *Who's Who* is fortune indeed.

Denis began watching the Blades along with his father prior to the Second World War and became a regular season ticket holder in 1946. He began writing in the club programme from 1983 producing his first book on Sheffield United in 1989 and has since written two other books and co-authored with Andrew *The Complete Record of Sheffield United FC 1889–1999.*

Andrew has likewise been a Blade supporter kicking off in the mid 1950s, again initially being taken by his father. His first season ticket was a Christmas gift in 1954—although he must have received it in August well prior to the festive celebrations! He became interested in football statistics after acquiring the paperback book *Sixty Seasons of League Football* by R.C. Churchill around 1960. Andrew has also written in our programme since 1984, made minor contributions to Denis's first book and was co-author of *The Complete Record of Sheffield United 1889–1999.*

The time, commitment, effort and passion that our two authors have contributed to this fascinating *Who's Who* is testimony to their skills, ability and dedication.

The Blades are fortunate indeed to have such characters around.

Enjoy the read and to all Sheffield United supporters, recognise what a great Club we really are.

Up the Blades!

Kevin McCabe
Chairman

Preface

We suspect that this is the most comprehensive Football Club Who's Who ever published. Only those who have prepared similar books can be aware of the thousands of hours that are necessary to research, check and present a really accurate and comprehensive book of this type and the frustration of knowing that it can never be 'complete' and certainly not one hundred per cent accurate. We are happy therefore, if you find or suspect errors and omissions, that you contact us through Sheffield United and we would encourage any one of you with a desire for football historical research to seek help from a local studies library.

We made our task more difficult by taking the decision to include all those former players who appeared in non-competitive (ie friendly or club) first team fixtures and being rather generous in our definition of 'first team'. To compound the agony, we have also added a separate section of players who never played for United's first team but were signed by or linked in some way to United and later played football at a senior level (usually Football League) with another club. Other sections cover Directors, Managers, Staff and other people with close links to the Club.

For those seeking further information on former United players, please contact Denis Clarebrough.

Introduction

The people of Great Britain should be proud of the fact that organized sport was, to an overwhelming extent, created and presented to the rest of the world by our nation and no sport offers a better example than the world's greatest game of football. The city of Sheffield led the way in the mid 1850s with the formation of the Sheffield Football Club and the creation of the enormous Bramall Lane cricket ground which became the home of the Yorkshire County Cricket Club and the venue for so many other sports, in particular football, and from 1889, the home ground of the Sheffield United Football Club.

In preparing a Who's Who of the Sheffield United Football Club, we have been very conscious of those nineteenth century pioneers who created *Sheffield United* many years before the Football Club was formed. We would also like to stress the importance of the concept of a football *club* which brings together the players who represent the club but also the committee or directors who run the club, the staff and loyal supporters both near and far away.

A football club Who's Who is a work of reference and should best be used in conjunction with a detailed club history or record and for the Blades, we would hope that the *Complete Record of Sheffield United Football Club1889-1999*—work is in progress on a new edition—or the centenary history, *Sheffield United Football Club, The First 100 Years* are available to put a player's career in context with the United teams and staff of the time and the matches they played.

Any book of this type must be judged in part by the accuracy of the hundreds of thousands of 'facts' that it contains and we do offer words of caution. The historian and statistician seek those facts through a multitude of sources and then attempt, after countless checks and balances, to present an accurate and balanced result but we are well aware that errors will be present in original or early sources and will have been repeated many times.

Until the quite recent past, we have been mainly dependent for information for a book of this type on the written word and human memory and the possibility of error is larger than one might expect. What we might term official records should be treated as a source of probable rather than certain truth. This soon becomes obvious when, for instance, the information from a birth certificate or census return is compared with a death certificate.

A valuable source of information has been the records of the Football League but although 'official', they are, particularly in the early years, far from accurate and anyone approaching them with the idea that they were collated by diligent and accurate clerks is in for a rude awakening. Sheffield United, for instance, if the League records are to be believed, played one game with eight men—and we assure you they had eleven—and on several occasions played two goalkeepers and the records frequently go sadly awry when United had two or more players with the same or a similar surname.

Newspapers and football annuals and magazines are another obvious source of information but although, pre-1920, they offer extensive match reports and comment, the current cult of personality and celebrity was in general, shunned. A perfect example is W Robertson who was United's first centre forward (striker): he played in every game in that first season and set up records galore but we don't know his first name, where or when he was born and little about his playing career before he came to Sheffield and, when he left United, as far as the newspapers were concerned, he just disappeared.

Newspapers however, are a major source of information and the Sheffield and other local papers in particular but we feel it is necessary to add that a multiplicity of sources doesn't always add to the clarity of the situation. The newspapers that we have found available for study were: *The Sheffield Telegraph* (to 1986), its sister evening paper, *The Star*, and the Saturday *Green 'Un* (1907–1939, 1947–2008), also *The Sheffield Independent* (to 1938) and the evening paper, *The Sheffield Mail* (1919–28). Recourse has also been made to the local newspapers covering South Yorkshire, North Derbyshire, North Nottinghamshire and Gainsborough but the quality and quantity of these resources vary enormously.

Further information has been gathered from the official Sheffield United programme which was first published in 1897 and every first team copy and most of the reserve issues have been studied. United were one of the earliest clubs to issue a programme but one has to admit that until comparatively recent times, the programme was not a first class record of the week by week changing events at Bramall Lane.

The Chairman and staff of the Sheffield United Football Club and a huge number of former players have been very supportive and we are particularly grateful for the permission given to Denis Clarebrough, the club historian, to see official minute books of the Football Committee from 1896 to quite recent times and some lists of players which give details of when they were signed and released. Sadly, any minute books or similar official documentation relevant to the years before 1896 are missing. One can only surmise that they may have been destroyed during the Sheffield Blitz of 1940, either at the ground which was badly damaged, or perhaps, in the offices of a Sheffield solicitor.

The final but massive source of information comes from people who in the main are football enthusiasts though a few are family historians and they include a number who have been surprised to find a professional footballer among their antecedents.

Dr Samuel Johnson, in compiling his famous dictionary, poked fun at himself and his fellow '*compilers and lexicographers*' by including in his definition, a '*harmless drudge, a hack*'. The contemporary football historian or statistician can only offer his deepest gratitude to those who have gone before, first producing simple football guides and records and in more recent years, the immense publications such as the *Sky Sports Football Yearbooks* (formerly *Rothman's*), *Football League Players' Records 1888–1939* by Michael Joyce (published by Soccer Data Publications) and also *The PFA Premier and Football League Players' Records* and *The PFA Footballers' Who's Who* (formerly *The Official PFA Footballers' Factfile*) edited and compiled by Barry J Hugman.

An even greater debt is owed to the many football club historians who willingly share their detailed local knowledge with their fellow enthusiasts. One result of their work is that only a handful of clubs in membership of the Football League are now without a detailed club history and yet none were available thirty years ago. A particular mention should be given to Jim Creasy for his enormous general research and for providing the link between football historians and for bringing the information into a shared pool and also to Tony Brown for similar work and also bringing research to a wider audience through his many publications.

In conclusion, we hope those of you who read or refer to this book, whether Unitedites or not, will find information that is new to you but also bring to mind, not just the great and famous players from the past, but those all but forgotten, reviving memories of your own or reminding you of the tales of old days at the Lane that you listened to when young.

We would, however, like to stress that opinions expressed in this book are from an extensive range of sources including interviews with former players recalling their old colleagues or opponents and games but responsibility lies with the authors and not necessarily with the Sheffield United Football Club.

Denis Clarebrough
Andrew Kirkham
September 2008

Introduction to the Players' and Managers' Sections

Those listed in the main list of players include anyone who has played in at least one competitive game for United, including minor cup competitions (eg AIC, SCC, YHC) and the competitive games in WW1 and WW2.

For each player the surname is listed first (with possible alternative spellings) then the forenames (if known) and commonly used nicknames. The used forename is in bold.

The player's position is listed and if the player commonly played in more than one position these are also listed, with his most usual position first. The abbreviations used are:

G	Goalkeeper
CD	Central defender
CF	Centre Forward
CH	Centre half
D	Defender
FB	Full back
IF	Inside forward
IR/IL	Inside right/left
LH	Left half back
L(W)B	Left (wing) back
MF	Mid field
OR/OL	Outside right/left
RH	Right half back
R(W)B	Right (wing) back
WH	Wing half

The dates following the position are the years of his first team debut and final appearance – not necessarily those of his time with United.

Height and weight are given where known. Different sources give different values even for height. An average is used if the values are close. Sometimes a range is given.

Place and date of birth are given if known and similarly place and date of death if relevant and if known. For some players, their date of birth or death is known only within a three month period

JFM	January February March
AMJ	April May June
JAS	July August September
OND	October November December

The player's career is then listed with dates if known. The dates of the player joining and leaving United are given as exactly as possible. Main sources are United's records and the registration lists of the Football League, which until c1906 might use the 'date posted' or 'date received' and then 'date eligible', and similar lists held by the Football Association. Other sources include newspaper reports, contracts and football programmes and in many cases, no single 'correct' date can be given. A player may have 'signed' but the contract date might not tally with the day of signature or the registration date with the relevant League or Association. Also, particularly in United's early years, the club might hold a player's FL registration for some time before he 'signed' and retain him long after his contract had ended. When a player left or joined another club the month and year are given if known.

The player's debut for United is given. The sequence, if relevant, is first appearance in any game, first full appearance in any game, first competitive appearance, first full competitive appearance, first appearance in a major cup competition (FAC or FLC), first full appearance in a major cup competition, first League appearance, first full League appearance. For a player's last game the above sequence is followed in reverse.

The player's appearances for United are listed at the end of each player's section. The figures in brackets (as elsewhere) are substitute appearances. In these listings FL includes Football League and Premier League appearances; AMC includes FLT, GC, SVT; FMC includes SM, ZDS.

In the 'Managers Section' the 'League Record' listed at the end is the Manager's record as United's manager.

Abbreviations used but not already listed above are:

39–40	The three FL games played at the start of the 1939–40 season subsequently declared void due to the outbreak of the Second War
ABD	Abandoned
AIC	Anglo Italian Cup
amat	amateur
AMC	Associate Members Cup
App(s)	Appearance(s)
ASC	Anglo Scottish Cup
AWS	Auto Windscreen Shield
BC	Birmingham Cup
BM	Benefit or testimonial match
c	circa (approximately)
CC	Sheffield & Hallamshire Football Association County Cup
CIT	Cyprus International Football Tournament (1974)
CL	Central League
CM	Charity match
cs	Close season
FA	Football Association
FAC	Football Association Cup
FL	Football League
FLN	Football League North (1945-46)
FLT	Football League Trophy
FMC	Full Members Cup
Fr	Friendly match (known as a 'club game' 1889 to c1900)
GC	Football League Group Cup
GI	Gibraltar International Soccer Festival (1976)
gl, gls	goal(s)
jnr	junior
LC	Football League Cup (including its various sponsored successors)
MCL	Midland Counties League
mgr	manager
nc	non-contract
NL	Northern League
PL	Premier League
PO	Football League Play off
pro	Professional
SCC	Sheffield Challenge Cup
SM	Simod Cup
SVT	FL Sherpa Van Trophy
sub	substitute
TEX	Texaco Cup
TM	Test match
trib	fee set by a tribunal
UCL	United Counties League
WC	Watney Cup
WCC	Wharncliffe Charity Cup
WW1	First World War (1915-19) competitions
WW2	Second World War (1939-46) competitions
YHC	Yorkshire & Humberside Cup
YTS	Youth Training Scheme
ZDS	FL Zenith Data Systems Trophy

The Directors

ARGALL Simon

Operations Director

Simon joined Sheffield United in 2006 from a Leisure and Hotel background. He comes from a family steeped in Football history as he is the great great grandson of William Suddell—founding father of the Preston North End Football Club. He is a member of the plc board.

ATKIN Edward Thomas

A member of the Ground Committee from 1863–93

Several other members of the Atkin family became United directors though their interest was more often on the cricket side. They were electroplate manufacturers and owned the Truro Works.

ATKIN E Senior

Club and Football Chairman 1955–57

Elected to the Board in 1929, Senior Atkin, taking advantage of the outbreak of war in the summer of 1939, was responsible for draining the ground which for many years had been one of the worst in the country in wet conditions. The managing director of the silversmiths, Atkin Brothers, his reputation was that of a blunt Yorkshireman who didn't call a spade, a spade but 'a bloody shovel'.

He became the Chairman in 1955 and will always be remembered as the man who gave Joe Mercer the job of managing United, much to the chagrin of the other directors who were all but presented with a *fait accompli*. Nor could they have been pleased to hear the Chairman declare that he knew 'damn all about football but this lot know a damn sight less'. Serious disputes were inevitable though Atkin held on to the position of Chairman until May 1957 when he was replaced by Leslie Lewis. Atkin died in 1968 at the age of eighty one.

BEAN Sean Mark (originally Shaun).

Born in Sheffield in 1958, the actor and film star, best known perhaps for his portrayal of Sharpe, a TV series about a soldier in the Napoleonic wars, and for the lead role in the (1996) football film *When Saturday Comes*. He became a director in April 2002 and resigned in November 2007.

BEEDEN Walter Musgrove

A Thrybergh building contractor, Beeden was a director from 1920 until his resignation in 1923 but rejoined the board in 1933. He died in February 1947.

BINGHAM Arthur

Arthur Bingham was a Committee member prior to 1899 when he was elected to the first board. His death was reported in 1912. Sir Albert Edward Bingham of Ranby House, Retford, was a member of the board 1910–19.

BOARD Maurice

A chartered accountant and director from 1959 to 1976; he was a vice-chairman under Dick Wragg and a vice-president. Born in 1913, he died in July 1991.

BOTT Tom

Football Chairman 1913–21

A native of Birmingham and a Sheffield wholesale fishmonger, Tom Bott devoted countless hours to United's cause in the period of the Club's greatest triumphs, in particular, being the 'director in charge' when the team went away for cup-tie training. In the period 1899–1902, United fought their way through to three FA Cup Finals, winning the trophy in 1899 and 1902. Although he was never the 'team manager', his influence and encouragement was no doubt invaluable. He became the chairman of the Football Committee in 1913 on the death of Charles Stokes and held the post until 1921. He died in October 1925.

BREALEY Reginald (Reg) John

Chairman 1981–1990 and 1993–95

A Lincolnshire businessman, Reg Brealey joined the board as Financial Director in June 1980 and became the Chairman eleven months later after the club was relegated to the Fourth Division. Facing record trading losses and debts of over £1 million, he appointed Ian Porterfield as the new manager and provided funds for new players and started the climb back from the lowest level of the Football League. Brealey proposed and backed a new share issue sufficient to give him control over the club and he later put forward sweeping imaginative £20 million plans for development of the ground but these were rejected by the socialist City Council. He was also defeated when he contested what he believed were excessive police charges. He encouraged new ideas such as the travel club, a United newspaper and the Junior and Senior Blades and he saw the need to widen the club's sources of revenue but, burdened by problems with his other businesses and frustrated by the Sheffield City Council, he lost his enthusiasm and desire.

He threatened to leave the club (1986–87) and was involved in a battle for control which led to his resignation in December 1990. The club's debts were now over £3 million and financial problems worsened. 'Reg' reluctantly returned on 29 June 1993 to stabilize the club's finances and to seek a buyer for his controlling interest in the club. Matters seemed to be settled in July 1995 in favour of Mike McDonald but it was not until 22 September that Brealey stood down though he remained on the board until 7 December.

Believed at one time to be a director of fifty companies and the chairman of ten, Brealey was declared bankrupt in October 1998. His brother, **Len Brealey** was also a club director in 1993.

BURNLEY John

A senior partner in a firm of chartered surveyors, he joined the plc board in February 2005.

CAPPER Simon

Financial Director and plc Company Secretary 2008

Simon joined the United board in 2007, replacing Mark Fenoughty. He had previously worked for Kevin McCabe in his business empire prior to being invited to bring his expertise and experience on board at Bramall Lane.

CATTELL Alfred

Football Chairman 1930–33

Born in Cottesmore (Rutland) in 1857, he was associated with United for more than forty years and became the chairman in 1930 on the retirement of Walter Sissons. A Welsh rugby international and a member of the teaching profession, he moved to Sheffield and played rugby with a group of men who founded the Sheffield Rugby Club. The head of St Paul's School until 1892, he became a wholesale fruit merchant and served as the Lord Mayor of Sheffield. He died in September 1933.

His brother, the **Rev Edward Cattell** was the head of Duchess Road School and a United director from 1912 and also played cricket for the Club.

CLEGG Sir J Charles
Club Chairman 1899–1936 and President 1924–37

Born in Sheffield on 15 June 1850, he became a partner in the family firm of solicitors and was the Sheffield Official Receiver in Bankruptcy. A fine athlete and footballer, he played for Broomhall, Sheffield Club, the Wednesday and Sheffield Albion. He played in the first official Scotland versus England international in 1872 and refereed the 1882 and 1892 FA Cup Finals. A local councillor for ten years, he gave that up to concentrate on football and was the first president of the Sheffield & Hallamshire Football Association and held the office until his death (1887–1937). Known as the 'Napoleon of football', he was a member of the FA Council from 1886, chairman from 1890 and president from 1923 until his death and was the first man to be knighted for services to football (1927).

A formidable, highly principled administrator, total abstainer from alcohol and tobacco, he led the fight both in Sheffield and in the councils of the FA against professionalism and betting. His conduct was governed by strict morality which he summed up in a speech in 1911 when he said that 'no one had ever got lost on a straight road and that was the path that the (Football) Association must travel'.

When the authorities at Bramall Lane began to formulate their ideas for the formation of a football club, which would use the best amateur players in the town assisted by a small nucleus of professional players, Clegg was sympathetic to the idea and offered advice but he had also to bear in mind that, as president of the local association, he was responsible for all the clubs in the area.

He became the chairman and later president of both United and the Wednesday, holding board meetings normally on the same evening. The United one was usually held first and was frequently brief and there were many hurried journeys across the city. Clegg's position in the game and strict views often limited the actions of the two city clubs compared to others who were more likely to 'bend the rules' and one minor consequence was that United regularly received invitations from the FA to tour overseas but rejected them (until 1936) as they involved playing on Sundays. Clegg, of course, was ultimately responsible for both the invitation and the refusal. He died in Sheffield, 26 June 1937 at the age of eighty seven.

His brother, **Sir William Edwin Clegg** played for the Wednesday from 1870 to 1890 and for England against Scotland in 1873 and against Wales in 1879. He turned his attentions to local government serving as the Lord Mayor of the city in 1898 and on the council for forty years until his death in 1932.

COLOMBOTTI Carlo
plc Chairman 1998–99

A London-based lawyer with Italian and Welsh roots, he became the plc chairman in November 1998 after agreeing to purchase a significant part of Mike McDonald's controlling shareholding. The deal was never completed and his position was never secure after his plan to raise capital through a share issue collapsed. He had made a loan to the club of £750k and this was paid off with interest in October 1999 at the time of his resignation.

CONNELL Arthur

A director from 1958 to 1973 and Yorkshire CCC chairman, he was a senior member of the cricket committee which came to an end when the last match was played at the Lane.

COPESTAKE Frank
Football Chairman 1952–56

Elected to the board in 1925, he became the chairman in October 1952 on the death of George Marlow and held the post until ill-health brought about his resignation in the summer of 1956. He died in January 1957.

DODWORTH Maurice

Had been a committee member and director for more than thirty years when he died in 1908. His son **George Dodworth** served as a director from 1909 until 1922. Both were primarily concerned with cricket matters.

DONCASTER Basil

A member of the Sheffield firm, Daniel Doncaster & Son, he was a keen amateur sportsman who joined the board in 1944.

DOOLEY Derek
Commercial Manager, Associate and Managing Director and Football Chairman 1999–2006

Born in Sheffield 13 December 1929, Derek played as an amateur for the YMCA, Lincoln City (two FL appearances scoring two goals during the 1946–47 season) and Denaby United and trained on two evenings a week at Bramall Lane. Tall and fast with a powerful shot, he became a professional with Sheffield Wednesday and though his playing career was disrupted by National Service, he became a prolific scorer in the 'A' team and reserves but had little success when given opportunities in the first team. A change of fortune came in October 1951 and he finished that season with an astonishing record-breaking 47 goals in 31 League and Cup appearances and after a hesitant beginning in the former First Division, the goals began to flow again (16 in 29).

We will never know how great a player Derek might have been for his leg was broken in a match at Preston and had to be amputated. Later, he worked as a fund raiser for Wednesday and was the team manager from 1971 until his controversial Christmas Eve sacking in 1973.

He became United's Commercial Manager in November 1974 and joined the board as a full-time associate director in April 1983—he was the second paid director in the Football League—and became the Managing Director and Chief Executive in January 1986. He twice served as acting chairman; the second occasion coming after his official retirement in 1992 and he left the board in 1996 only to return in November 1999 as chairman of the Football Club. A plc director from 2000 to 2003, he was also the acting chief executive and football club chairman, finally retiring in 2006.

A man of great integrity, Derek provided experience, knowledge, trust and wisdom over a long period for an all too often unsettled and divided board, finding common ground and taking the club forward. A United vice-president, Derek was made a freeman of the city in 1993 and was awarded an MBE in the 2003 New Year's honours list and was a fine ambassador for football in general and Sheffield United in particular. A legend in Sheffield, he died at home on 5 March 2008.

DUDLEY Michael (Mick) Douglas

A lifelong Blade originally from the Gleadless Valley area of the City, he was Chairman of Moss House Group, a computer company based in Mosborough on the outskirts of Sheffield. Dudley joined the plc board in 2000, becoming Deputy Chairman of the plc Board in 2006.

ELLISON Michael J

Chairman 1855–91, President 1891–98

Michael Ellison was the son of, and became the agent in Sheffield for, the Duke of Norfolk. In 1854 he was the chief instigator and driving force behind the idea to create a new and first class cricket ground at Bramall Lane which would be the home ground for six of the leading clubs in the town. Opened in 1855, it would also be used for other sports which the middle and professional classes were taking up with enthusiasm and the original 477 proprietors and regular patrons began to refer to themselves as members of the Sheffield United Cricket Club although no team bearing that name took the field until 1892.

Ellison was the chairman of the committee which managed the ground and he also set in motion what was necessary to create an official Yorkshire County Cricket Club which was run from Sheffield with Ellison becoming the first President in 1863. He was not enthusiastic about football but once the decision had been made, in 1889, to form the Sheffield United Football Club, he ably defended it in his capacity as Chairman and President. He died 12 July 1898.

FENOUGHTY Mark Thomas

After working for Leicester City, Mark became United's Finance Director in July 2003, working also as Chief Operations Officer and later Secretary of the plc until June 2007.

GRAHAM Ernest S

Club Chairman 1949–59

Ernest Graham was a city councillor, alderman and Lord Mayor and a director of United from 1935 to 1959 when he was made president. He had succeeded George Platt as the club chairman in 1949.

GREEN David

Appointed to the Sheffield United Board of Directors in July of 2005. Born in Rotherham, he is the Managing Director of Barlborough-based Greenpiling, which was founded in 2000.

HAIGH David

A Wincobank coal merchant and agent, who became the secretary of the Hallamshire FA from its formation in 1878 and was the first secretary of the Sheffield & Hallamshire FA in 1887 holding the position until 1904. A member of the committee which organized the new United football club in 1889, he was always held chiefly responsible for the initial, and generally failed, policy to use Scottish players. An FA councillor, an FL vice-president and a United director when the new limited company was set up in 1899, his official standing in football and connection with United ended abruptly in 1904.

HASHIMI Sam

A young Iraqi-born businessman introduced to the club as a potential purchaser by chairman Reg Brealey in March 1990. He was touted as the new chairman but some directors were suspicious that all his plans and wealth were not totally grounded in fact and the doubts were soon confirmed and 'Samantha', as he was later known, disappeared from United's view.

HASSALL John

Chairman 1974–81

Born in 1927, Hassall was a Sheffield builder who joined the board in May 1963 and became the chairman, replacing Dick Wragg, in August 1974. Hassall has the unenviable reputation as the man who took the Blades down from the old First Division to the Fourth but he was essentially a victim of problems, mainly financial, that would have defeated most men in spite of all his hard work and enthusiasm.

Debts, mainly a consequence of the erection of the new South Stand, were threatening to cripple the club and he made an early decision to bring in Derek Dooley to lead the commercial side of the club. Relegation in 1976 and again in 1979 reinforced the difficulties. Neither the directors nor new managers Jimmy Sirrel, Harry Haslam and Martin Peters could solve the deepening financial crisis.

It was Hassall who brought Reg Brealey onto the board to deal with the club's finances which had deteriorated further. When internal work on the new South Stand had to be paid for, it was Brealey's decision to personally pay these debts but possibly without the agreement and knowledge of the board. A few days later, United were relegated to the old Fourth Division and Hassall resigned from the board and Reg Brealey was in control of the club.

HAWKE Martin Bladen

President 1899–1917

Born in 1860, Lord Hawke, the famous Yorkshire cricket captain and president was a member of the United board until his resignation as president in 1917.

HINCHLIFFE Stephen

A headline making, flamboyant local businessman who acquired a plethora of high street commercial names. He had joined the United board in August 1992 and appeared to be a saviour in waiting and future chairman. He resigned in 1993, returned in December 1995 as vice-chairman but resigned again seven months later. Faced with a Department of Trade & Industry investigation, his financial problems eventually led to a five-year jail sentence.

JACKSON Albert

A Chartered Surveyor and Sheffield United Director from 1970 to 1990. His tenure was through some of the most turbulent times in United history, seeing the departure of Cricket, the building of the South Stand and the fall and rise of the Club through the Divisions. He died in Sheffield in July 2008.

JACKSON F S

The Hon Sir Frank Stanley Jackson was a fine Yorkshire and England cricketer who was a United director until 1909 and later president of the MCC and the Yorkshire CCC.

LAVER Arnold

A local man who had built up his successful timber firm from his Royal Flying Corps gratuity. He joined the board in June 1941 and provided some necessary opposition when Senior Atkin was the rather overbearing chairman. He was offered that position in 1960 but preferred a less visible though invaluable part in the affairs of United and was content to be vice-chairman. A Lloyds underwriter and insurance company chairman, he died in November 1971 at the age of 72.

LAVER Arnold (Alan) Hastings

President 1997

Born in 1923, 'Alan' Laver joined the board in July 1976 and was a great help to the club during the most difficult period of United's history, twice serving as acting chairman (October 1992 and October 1995). Appointed president in February 1997, he died in May of that year. His son, and the third generation of the family to serve the club, **Andrew James Laver** joined the board in 1998 and has provided the support that led to Kevin McCabe taking the club forward.

LAWRENCE George Herbert

A razor blade ('Laurel') manufacturer who joined the board in 1934 and paid for a cover over the Shoreham Street Kop and improvements to the bowling green. He also funded the open-air swimming baths at Hathersage and visits to the Derbyshire village always featured in United's late 1930's pre-season training. On the night of the Sheffield blitz, in December 1940, he drove into Sheffield from his home in Hathersage and was killed along with twelve of his staff.

LAWRENCE Richard (Dick)

Like his contemporary (George), Dick Lawrence also joined the board in June1934. A former Midland League footballer, he died in 1959.

LEWIS Leslie

Club Chairman 1957–60

An accountant and keen amateur sportsman, he joined the board in 1941 and became chairman of the finance committee. He became club chairman in 1957 replacing Senior Atkin but resigned in October 1960 for business reasons though he remained a director until 1963.

McCABE Kevin Charles

plc Chairman from 1998 and Football Chairman 2008

Brought up in Duchess Road, close to Bramall Lane, he became a quantity surveyor in the construction industry before setting up his own business in 1976. A very successful property developer, he became a United director in December 1995 and became the club chairman in March 1998 after Mike McDonald's resignation.

His massive investment in United and careful and steady development has brought about remarkable changes in the development of the ground at Bramall Lane, the training ground at Shirecliffe and the general future of Sheffield United as a football club. His influence has far exceeded that of any other chairman since Charles Stokes created the football club in 1889. He has gradually transformed the football club with practical and innovative ideas. Success on the field as a football club is the hub and focus but it is aided by being at the heart of an expanding property, leisure and services business both in the UK and overseas.

His period in office coincided with that of Neil Warnock as the football manager for seven years followed by the disappointing Bryan Robson and the revival under Kevin Blackwell. The Chairman has also raised the idea of a 'head of football' with overall supervision of football matters as the club becomes more globally focused and in 2008 became the chairman of the Football Club as well as the plc.

Kevin's sons **Simon** and **Scott** joined the football club board of directors in 2006 and 2007 respectively.

McDONALD Anthony Michael (Mike)

Club Chairman 1995–98 and plc from 1997–99

The head of Texas Holdings, a Manchester-based private company, McDonald had failed to win control of Manchester City before turning his attention to Sheffield United. After protracted negotiations and premature announcements, he became a director on 19 October 1995 and finally took control of the club from Reg Brealey and became Chairman by 2 December 1995.

Determined to take United into the Premiership, work began and was completed on the new John Street stand and he replaced manager Dave Bassett with Howard Kendall. Money was provided and there was a rapid turnover of new players, the threat of relegation was averted and there was a new spirit of enthusiasm in the United half of the city. In the next season, McDonald made United a plc and the club challenged for promotion but hopes were dashed by defeat in the Wembley Play-off Final against Crystal Palace. Mike McDonald had fulfilled his promise to the previous chairman but that Wembley defeat had massive effects on the future of the club.

Nigel Spackman replaced Kendall and more money was invested in new players but, all too soon, injury problems blighted hopes of a return to the Premier League and quality players were sold. Spackman's resignation and growing spectator unrest led to McDonald standing down as chairman of the football club in March 1998 though he remained chairman of the plc until November 1998 when the Texas group shares were sold to Carlo Columbotti's 'Blades Italia'. He returned briefly as plc chairman in October 1999 but finally left the board on 23 November 1999.

MARLOW George E

Football Chairman 1949–52

A Sheffield builder, city councillor and later alderman, George Marlow became a director in November 1923 and Football committee chairman in 1949 on the resignation of Albert Platt. Illness in the latter part of 1951 led to his death in September 1952 and the election as chairman of Frank Copestake.

MELLING Frank

Born in the city in 1919 and a graduate of the University, he qualified as an architect. He played football for Norton Woodseats, Sheffield Club, Yorkshire Amateurs and, as an amateur during the war, for the Wednesday. He played in the 1943 war-time North Cup Final and turned down the offer of a professional contract. He played cricket for United from 1949 and was a Yorkshire committee member and a United director from June 1954, leading the opposition in their unsuccessful battle to keep cricket at the Lane. He died in October 2004.

NEAL Arthur
Born in 1862, he was a committee member from about 1893. He chaired the meeting in 1899 which decided to make an offer to the Duke of Norfolk on behalf of the proprietors to purchase the Bramall Lane ground and to make the Club, a limited liability company. A lawyer, city alderman, the Liberal MP for Hillsborough and vice-president of the local FA, he died in January 1933.

O'GORMAN Frank
A consultant surgeon at the Northern General Hospital until 1975, he had joined the board in 1963, leaving in 1982. Born in 1910, he died in Sheffield in December 1992.

PLANT John
A director of Chesterfield Football Club until 1993 when he joined the United board and supported Reg Brealey's decision to sell Brian Deane. He resigned in October 1996.

PLATT Albert J
Football Chairman 1933–49, Club Chairman 1936–58
President 1949–58
Born in Sheffield, he played football for Attercliffe and trained as a chartered accountant. Elected to the board in 1913, he became chairman of the football committee in 1933 and was successful over the next fourteen years in paying off the large club debts, loans and mortgage on the ground. Elected club president in 1949 and a life president in 1957, he died in October 1958 at the age of 79.

PRICE George
Born in 1899, he joined the board in 1957. A mining engineer who played cricket for Swinton and Sheffield Collegiate, he and Arnold Laver led the opposition that led to the downfall of the chairman, Senior Atkin.

PROCTOR Bernard
A director of several companies, he joined the board in 1993. The chairman of the plc from November 1999, he stood down in 2002. He provided, with Alan Laver and Derek Dooley, an oft-needed stabilizing influence through some difficult periods.

PYE Frederick
A former part-time professional footballer, manager and businessman who had been the chairman of Stockport County and vice-chairman of Manchester City, he was a friend of Mike McDonald and briefly a member of the board from January 1997 to November 1998.

ROBINSON Terry
Football Chairman 2006–08
An experienced football administrator who joined the United board in January 2002 after over eighteen years as the Chairman and chief executive at Gigg Lane. Initially sharing the duties of Football Executive, he became the club Vice-chairman in 2004 and Chairman from May 2006 to the summer of 2008 when he took over control of the United subsidiary, Ferencvaros in Hungary.

ROCKETT Jason
Chief Executive and director
A former professional footballer (b. London 26 September 1969) with Rotherham and Scarborough where he made over two hundred appearances before his playing career was brought to an end by a knee injury in 1998. He had qualified as a chartered surveyor and was a director of the Scarborough Development Group before joining United in September 2005 as Chief executive. He became a plc director in November 2005.

SISSONS Walter
Football Chairman 1920–30
A chartered accountant, he was the club auditor for 14 years before he joined the board in 1899. He first chaired the finances and general purposes committee and the football committee from December 1920 to 1930. He died in August 1934.

SMITH Joseph
Football Chairman 1920
A football committee member from 1891, he became the vice-chairman of the football committee in 1913 and chairman in June 1920 but resigned six months later when the board decided to sign Joe Kitchen just four months after he had been sold to Rotherham County. Smith resigned as a director but was persuaded to return six months later.

STEER Chris
Vice-Chairman of the Football Club 2006–
Chairman of Pyramid Carpets, a well-known Sheffield family business based in the Woodseats area. He joined the Football Club Board of Directors in January 2002 and became Vice Chairman in 2006.

STERLAND Jim
Born in 1898, he was a Labour councillor, Lord Mayor and a director from 1967 until 1977.

STOKES Charles
Football Chairman 1889–1913

Charles Stokes can be thought of as the founder of the Sheffield United Football Club. Born in Sheffield in 1847, he played football for the Heeley, Milton and Broomhall clubs and, in 1867, he was a founder member and player for the Wednesday Football Club and the new Sheffield Football Association.

He became a member of the Bramall Lane Bowling Club in 1869 and was invited to join the ground committee in 1875 and the Yorkshire CCC committee two years later. A dental surgeon who lived at Cecil House, Highfields, he was the first treasurer in 1887 of the new Sheffield & Hallamshire FA.

Stokes was aware that there were United committee members who enjoyed football as well as cricket and he had considered that it would be possible to form a new Sheffield football club based at Bramall Lane. He took advantage of the success of the FA Cup semi-final held at the ground in March 1889 which produced record gate receipts and was mainly instrumental in calling, that same month, a special meeting of the Bramall Lane Ground Committee. He had rallied support for the idea and secured a narrow majority in favour of a motion to form a football club. He became the first chairman of the new football committee though Michael Ellison remained the Club chairman until his death in 1898 when that position was taken by Charles Clegg.

Stokes, with Ellison's support, prevented the closure of the new football section in the first couple of years and was responsible in early 1891 for bringing players in from Preston North End and establishing a more professional attitude to the football club. He died 8 October 1913 aged 66 when his son **Percy** joined the board. **Harry Stokes**, born in 1865, joined the board in 1933 and served until his death in 1954.

TOMLINSON Joseph (Joe)

Born in the mid 1850s, he was a forward who captained the Heeley Football Club and represented the Sheffield Association on several occasions. He became a qualified referee and served as the vice-president of Heeley FC and as a committee member working in an administrative capacity for the S&HFA. A fine cricketer, he also served on the committee of the Yorkshire CCC.

He was a founding member of the new United football club which he and many others regarded as the successor of the declining Heeley club and, after severing his formal links with Yorkshire and the S&HFA, he gave most of his time to working for United. He was, for instance, regarded as a good judge of a player and did a great deal of scouting. He died 6 May 1925, just eleven days after United won the FA Cup for the fourth time. **Thomas (Tommy) Arthur Tomlinson**, played for Heeley at full back in the 1880s and also served on the United committee until his death in 1896 at the age of 38.

WATTERSON Mike

A snooker promoter and former Chesterfield director, Watterson was a member of the board June-November 1980.

WHITE Stewart

The head of a land reclamation group and the father of David, the United forward, Stewart was co-opted onto the board in July 1996 with a special interest in youth development. He resigned in December 1999.

WILLEY Harvey 'Harry' Broughton

A player with Collegiate both at cricket and football, Harry also played for Sheffield Club and served as their secretary for over 35 years. A manufacturer, he became a United director in 1914 and served until his death in November 1933.

WOOLHOUSE Paul G

Chairman 1990–92

A local businessman dealing in metals, he became a director in March 1986 at the age of 36. He became the United chairman in December 1990, when it was reported that he had acquired, from Reg Brealey, a controlling interest in the share capital and he took the position of Chief Executive from Derek Dooley in August 1992. Two months later he stood down because of 'temporary financial problems' which left him unable to meet the installments due to purchase the Brealey shares. In May 1993, he was dismissed from the post of Chief Executive and soon lost his position on the board, the controlling interest remaining with the Brealey family. Declared bankrupt in the December, he has since been sought by the police.

WRAGG Richard 'Dick'

Football Chairman 1960–68, Chairman 1968–1974
President 1974–92

Born 23 May 1910, Dick Wragg was a Builders' Merchant in Darnall. He joined the board in 1953 and became the Football Chairman in 1960. The only United Chairman, other than Charles Clegg, to play a prominent role in national football affairs, he was an FA Councillor from 1963, joined the international committee in 1969 and became the chairman. A member of UEFA, he joined the FL management committee in 1971.

Determined to raise United's profile as a football club, he ended the club's tradition of separate committees in 1968 and put pressure on John Harris, the manager, to move away from a policy of 'home grown' players though Wragg was also responsible for the sale of Mick Jones and Alan Birchenall. Wragg will be mainly remembered however for grasping the nettle of the removal of cricket from the Lane. Pressure from shareholders who advocated a four sided football ground began in 1967 and the board took the decision in the summer of 1971.

Dick Wragg was chosen as the club President in 1974 and was the first to remain on the board. He died in Sheffield, 6 November 1992.

His son, **Michael A Wragg** served on the board from November 1983 until May 1993.

YATES H Blacow FRCS

Football Chairman 1957, Club Chairman 1960–68

Born in Preston and a medical student at Cambridge, he came to Sheffield in 1921, working in the Royal Hospital and played football for Sheffield Club. He joined the board in March 1938 and succeeded Senior Atkin as Football Committee Chairman. He became Club Chairman in October 1960 before resigning for domestic reasons in 1968. His death was announced in November 1969.

The Managers

BASSETT David (Dave 'Harry')

Manager 21 Jan 1988 to 12 Dec 1995
b. Stanmore, nr Edgware, Middlesex 4 Sep 1944

Hayes. Chelsea 1962 amateur/ Wycombe W./ Hayes/ Watford 1965 amateur/ Hendon. Walton & Hersham/ Wimbledon player and coach 1974–81, mgr Jan 1981–84/ Crystal Palace mgr May 1984/ Wimbledon mgr 1984–87 manager. Watford mgr May 1987.
United: Manager 21 Jan 1988 to 12 Dec 1995
Crystal P mgr Feb 1996 to Feb 97/ Nottingham Forest general mgr then mgr May 1997 to Jan 1999/ Barnsley mgr May 1999 to Dec 2000 / – / Leicester City mgr,director of football, mgr Oct 2001 to Apr 2002/ Southampton ast mgr, briefly mgr cs to Dec 2005/ Millwall coach 2006/ Leeds U asst mgr Oct 2007–Jan 08

Dave Bassett was an amateur international with Walton & Hersham. He had played earlier with Hayes, Chelsea and Watford at youth level and then with Hendon. He became a professional with Southern League Wimbledon who entered the Football League in 1977 and was their captain during their first season, making 35 FL appearances as a defender. He later acted as their coach and assistant manager and then, from 1981, as manager as they climbed from the Fourth to the First (now PL) Division. In May 1984, he was the manager of Crystal Palace for four days before realizing it was a mistake and returning to Wimbledon.

'Harry' had a brief and unsuccessful spell as the manager of Watford and was forty-three when he replaced Billy McEwan in the managerial chair at the Lane. A bright and breezy, enthusiastic Londoner, he expected and demanded the same total commitment and honest endeavour from the players that had been a feature of his own play. He was honest, won respect and got the best from the players and will be remembered as one of United's most popular managers—though some players and supporters had misgivings as to the 'long ball' style of football that Bassett used.

Initially he was unsuccessful. United were in a Second Division relegation battle when he arrived and, as at Watford, he tried to do too much, too quickly. In the short time available, his decision was to sell Martin Kuhl and to use the money to bring in new players and there was a quite remarkable turnover of players. The changes may have been necessary but United were relegated.

There was however, a totally different atmosphere at the Lane. Bassett was an excellent communicator and used the media to the Club's advantage and also brought tremendous enthusiasm and excitement to the players, staff and spectators which had been lacking for many years.

More players were sold, the chief of which was Beagrie, as Bassett continued to put together his own team. United now had an exciting pair of strikers in Tony Agana and Brian Deane and they were an ideal pair to finish off the chances that were provided by United's stirring attacking style of play as they returned to the Second Division.

Dave Bassett's teams took the game to the opposition playing at a fast and furious pace and in the opponent's half; speed was of essence and crosses into the box had to be quick and frequent. With the right forwards, 'Harry's game' was exciting to watch and new forwards, Brian Deane, Tony Agana and Ian Bryson thrived on the opportunities which were presented and the addition of Bob Booker in mid-field proved to be inspirational. The BBC made the 'United' television series during the 1989–90 season and there was a happy ending, United securing a second promotion after a thrilling 5–2 victory at Leicester.

Attendances began to rise as United rose from the Third to the old First Division but money remained tight and battles to avoid relegation earned Bassett the nickname of 'Harry Houdini'. 'Harry' increased the number of players and new players included, Beesley, Pemberton, Hoyland, Vinnie Jones, Marwood, Hodges, Gayle and Gage. United had finished thirteenth, ninth and fourteenth but the final positions were misleading for each season had seen United involved in a relegation battle and tragedy lay ahead. The First Division had become the Premier League in 1992. Alan Kelly, Nilsen and Flo had been signed but Brian Deane was sold against the manager's advice. Bassett told the chairman that United would be relegated and they were—in the dying minutes of the final game at Chelsea—in very unfortunate circumstances.

In Bassett's defence, the financial constraints that had dogged the club for decades, but which had become critical from about 1973, remained throughout the period when he was at the Lane. No doubt, there was a lot of truth in his grim joke that the only promise that the Chairman and Board kept, was that there would be no money. It must not be forgotten that the Club, for the first time in many years, had had some comparative success in the FA Cup reaching the sixth round in 1990, the fifth in 1992 and the semi-final in 1993. 'Harry' soldiered on but the continuing financial problems and the lack of progress on the development of the old John Street stand site had a demoralising effect on the club. In 1995, Mike McDonald eventually replaced Reg Brealey as the Club Chairman, which gave grounds for a more optimistic outlook but Bassett informed McDonald, that he was 'stale' and could no longer motivate the players and felt that it was time to go. He was probably correct.

Bassett later managed Crystal Palace, Nottingham Forest and Barnsley and worked in a more advisory capacity with Southampton, Leicester City and Leeds United.

His only appearance as a player during his time with United was in the Paul Stancliffe Benefit match:

16 Mar 1992 United XI 1 Malmo (Sweden) 6 (BM)

League Record:	P	W	D	L	F	A	%W
	338	127	87	124	481	460	37.6

BLACKWELL Kevin Patrick

Assistant manager Dec 1999 to cs 2003
Manager 14 Feb 2008, 3 year contract 3 May 2008
b. Luton 21 Dec 1958

Cambridge Utd app/ Bedford T/ Barton Town/ Middlesex Wanderers/ Barnet/ Boston Utd (£5000) 1980/ Barnet 1986/ Scarborough Nov 1986/ Notts County Nov 1989/ Torquay Utd Jan 1999/ Huddersfield T Aug 1993/ Plymouth Argyle Aug 1995/ – / Bury coach Oct 1998/ **United asst mgr Dec 1999**/ Leeds Utd asst mgr cs Jun 2003, mgr Jun 2004 to Sep 2006/ – / Luton Town mgr Mar 2007 to Jan 2008/ – /
United: mgr 14 Feb 2008

Goalkeeper and bricklayer, Kevin Blackwell was an apprentice with Cambridge United and played in non-League football for Bedford Town, Barton Town, Middlesex Wanderers, Barnet, Boston United and Barnet again. He was twice on the losing side at Wembley, with Barton in the FA Vase final in 1978 and with Boston in the FA Challenge Trophy in 1985, when he saved a penalty. In November 1986 he joined Neil Warnock, on loan at Scarborough, the beginning of a long association.

At the end of his first season, Scarborough were promoted and Kevin (now transferred for £2,000), made his FL debut in Scarborough's first ever League game, at home to Wolves on 15 August 1987. He made 44 appearances before following Neil to Notts County (no apps), Torquay United (18), Huddersfield Town (5) and Plymouth Argyle (24). He had undertaken coaching duties at Huddersfield and Plymouth and when Neil left Plymouth in Feb 1995, Kevin stayed on in a coaching role. He re-joined Neil at Bury in Oct 1998 as assistant manager and that was his role when the pair moved to the Lane although he was still registered as a player. His one appearance for United was on tour as a substitute:

14 May 2000 Tobago XI 1 United 3 (Fr)

Kevin was on the subs bench for three games in 2000–01 and one the following season. Had he played he would have been the oldest player to make a League appearance for the Blades.

Kevin left the Lane in the summer of 2003 to become the assistant manager to Peter Reid at Leeds United and ended a seventeen-year association with Neil Warnock and in June 2004 he became manager. Relegated from the Premier League, Leeds were in severe financial difficulties but they reached the Championship play-offs in 2006 only for Blackwell to be sacked in September. He became the manager of Luton Town in March 2007 who faced similar problems. He was unable to avoid relegation and, in the following season, Luton went into administration with the manager helping some of the younger players with funds from his own pocket. He stayed on for a while but was dismissed in January 2008.

Kevin was appointed United's manager until at least the end of the season following Bryan Robson's departure from the Lane. United were sixteenth in the League table and he set about rebuilding the team's confidence. His fourth game in charge was a dismal home defeat by Charlton, a display which Kevin referred to amongst other things, as 'dross'. Following this defeat, there was a frank exchange of views in the dressing room and there was a steady improvement in the standards of play and results, so much so that United had an outside chance of the play-offs going into the final game but, above all, he had raised the spirits of the supporters as well as the morale of the players. In the summer of 2008 his position was made permanent when he signed a 3-year contract.

League Record:	P	W	D	L	F	A	%W
(to cs 2008)	14	8	3	3	22	15	57.1

BRUCE Stephen (Steve) Roger

Player-Manager July 1998 to May 1999
CD 1998 (player) 6' 0" 12st 6
b. Corbridge, Northumberland, 31 December 1960

Wallsend Boys Club/ Gillingham app (Jul 1977) to pro Oct 1978/ Norwich City (c£130k) Aug 1984/ Manchester United (c£825k) Dec 1987/ Birmingham City Jun 1996 (free)
United: Player-manager 1 Jul 1998 to 17 May 1999.
Debuts: 23 Jul 1998 E'Quip Romagna 1 United 1 (Fr)
8 Aug 1998 United 2 Swindon Town 1
Last game: 28 Nov 1998 United 0 Sunderland 4
Huddersfield T mgr May 1999 to Oct 2000/ Wigan Athletic mgr Apr 2001/ Crystal Palace mgr May to Dec 2001/ Birmingham mgr Dec 2001/ Wigan Athletic mgr from Nov 2007

Steve Bruce had made his FL debut with Gillingham at Blackpool on 18 August 1979 and was a player that Ian Porterfield had hoped to bring to the Lane. He represented England at youth and B level, played for the Football League and won medals galore with Norwich and Manchester United. Many considered that he was the best central defender not to win a full cap.

Steve had been a magnificent whole-hearted central defender but he had no managerial experience when he came to the Lane. When he joined the Blades as player-manager he had made 723(4) League appearances and he became the club's first current manager to play for the club other than in friendly games. At first, there were still glimpses of the former commanding figure but age, injuries and sciatica soon ended his playing career. He claimed that he accepted the appointment as United's player-manager with a promise that money would be made available to strengthen the team but he had been misled and the Club's financial position dictated that more players would have to be sold than purchased.

Gareth Taylor and Dean Saunders were the first to go and Borbokis, Holdsworth and Stuart followed. Rob Kozluk and Jonathan Hunt were brought in but Oliver Tebily, another recent newcomer, was sold during the close season. It was said of Bruce that he had a 'big heart' but the enforced sale of players and lack of clear leadership from above proved too much and led to a seemingly inevitable resignation.

Appearances		Apps	Gls
	FL	10	0
	LC	1	0
	Total	11	0

League Record:	P	W	D	L	F	A	%W
(as manager)	46	18	13	15	71	66	39.1

DAVISON John Edward (Teddy)

Secretary-Manager, June 1932 to June 1952
b. Gateshead 2 September 1887
d. Wortley (Sheffield) February 1971

Gateshead Town, Sheffield Wednesday Apr 1908 tp cs 1926/ Mansfield Town player-mgr then mgr Jun 1926/ Chesterfield mgr Dec 1927
United: Secretary-Manager, 15 Jun (1 Jul) 1932 to 31 Jun 1952
Chesterfield mgr, then chief scout 1952–1958

Although Teddy Davison's height was only about 5' 7" he became an excellent goalkeeper with the Wednesday, making 424 League and Cup appearances and winning one England cap.

Davison was the manager of Chesterfield when they were promoted to the Second Division in 1931 and, one year later, he was appointed as United's first Secretary-Manager. He succeeded John Nicholson as the Secretary of United but Davison was the first individual to be the Football Manager of the club. National financial constraints were severe and Sheffield, like many other northern cities suffered severely and Davison was forced to sell Jimmy Dunne, United's leading goal scorer, they were relegated for the first time in their history in 1934.

The introduction of 'Jock' Dodds and the growing maturity of Smith, Hooper, Jackson and Johnson revitalized the team which reached the Cup Final in 1936 and narrowly missed out on promotion in that same season

and again in 1938. Davison gradually made some excellent additions to the team by the development of young players through the 'A' (third) team—Cox, Carr and Settle—but he will always be remembered for signing Jimmy Hagan from Derby County in November 1938. Davison was forced to sell Dodds but he brought in Hampson, Reid and Henson and, in May 1939, United returned to the First Division taking the second promotion position by one point from local rivals, Wednesday.

The destruction by German bombs of much of the John Street stand—United's only seated area—was a terrible blow but the youth policy continued in the war years and the fruits were evident during the 1945–46 season when United won the League North championship and also in the following season when United challenged strongly for both the League and the Cup.

That fine team was broken up and Davison made several ill-fated moves in the transfer market. United were relegated in 1949 but Davison had sown some of the seeds of recovery by signing Hawksworth, Ringstead and Browning.

Davison decided in 1952 that a younger man was needed at the Lane and he recommended to the Board that they appoint Reg Freeman, the manager of Rotherham United, as his successor and he was able to pass on an excellent first team to the new man.

League Record:	P	W	D	L	F	A	%W
	546	226	129	191	939	862	41.4

FREEMAN Reginald (Reg) Vincent

Manager Aug 1952 to Aug 1955
b. New Brighton 20 Dec 1893
d. Wickersley (Rotherham) 4 Aug 1955.

Northern Nomads 1919–1920/ Oldham Athletic Jan 1921/ Middlesbrough Apr 1923 (£4,000)/ Rotherham United Aug 1930, player-mgr Jan 1934–35, manager 1935 to Aug 1952.
United: Manager Aug 1952 to Aug 1955

Reg Freeman had been a stylish full-back before becoming a manager with Rotherham United and he began to put together an excellent team towards the end of the war. The good work continued and Rotherham were promoted to the old Second Division for the first time in their history in 1951.

It was something of a surprise when Freeman moved to Bramall Lane in August 1952 after more than twenty years at Millmoor. Teddy Davison, the United manager, had spoken of retirement and had suggested to the Football Committee that Freeman might be the man to replace him. Both men were very similar in background and temperament. It was said of Freeman that he was 'one of nature's gentlemen' and his quiet but authoritative opinions won the respect of the players. Freeman worked closely with his players, always available with

advice and encouragement and the number of young players that blossomed under his guidance is tribute enough to his warmth and decency.

The new manager led United to the Second Division Championship at the end of his first season playing fine attacking football. The illness of Len Browning, during the following season, was a severe blow but United clung on to their place in the old First Division and gradually, younger players—Coldwell, Grainger, Hodgkinson and Iley—were introduced into the team.

Sadly for United, Freeman's health was deteriorating and, taken ill in 1955 on a close season tour, he was forced to return home and died later that summer. His death in August 1955 was a tragedy for the Club and football had lost an astute manager.

League Record:	P	W	D	L	F	A	%W
	126	53	28	45	236	231	42.1

FURPHY Kenneth (Ken)

Manager Dec 1973 to Oct 1975
b. Stockton, 28 May 1931

Everton Nov 1950/ Runcorn Dec 1951/ Darlington Aug 1953, becoming youth team coach/ Workington player-mgr Jul 1962/ Watford player-mgr Nov 1964, Blackburn Rovers mgr Aug 1971
United: Manager 7 Dec 1973 to 6 Oct 1975
New York Cosmos mgr Jan 1976/ Miami Toros coach(1976–77)/ Ipswich Town scout 1977/ Detroit Express coach 1977–80/ Washington Diplomats coach 1981/ Bermuda mgr/ Cleveland Force mgr

Ken Furphy had had a long and successful career as a defender in the lower divisions of the League, making 416(6) FL appearances. He gained the reputation as a first class coach and managed Workington, Watford and Blackburn Rovers before joining United.

He faced very difficult problems at Bramall Lane, taking over an ageing first team with poor reserves at a time when little money was available for new players because of the financial restraints forced on the club as a consequence of building the new South Stand. Geoff Salmons was sold but money was found to purchase Jim Brown and Tony Field and the team did better than expected in his first full season, narrowly failing to qualify for the UEFA Cup.

The opening of the new stand in 1975 had seemed to the supporters to be the start of a promising new era in United's history. Furphy had signed Chris Guthrie, a centre forward who, it was thought, would score the goals from the excellent passes of Tony Currie and the centres of Alan Woodward but the idea failed. The team made a wretched start to that 1975–76 season and Furphy was sacked at the beginning of October. Few noticed that the manager had also signed another striker, a young man called Keith Edwards.
Furphy may have played for United as a substitute in New Zealand:
1 June 1975 Taranaki XI 0 United XI 5 (Fr)

League Record:	P	W	D	L	F	A	%W
	78	27	22	29	85	100	34.6

HARRIS John

Manager 13 March 1959 to Dec 1973
(General Manager 1968–69)
Senior Executive Dec 1973 to June 1977
b. Glasgow 30 June 1917
d. Sheffield 24 July 1988

Swindon Town/ Swansea Town Aug 1934/ Tottenham Hotspur Feb 1939/ Wolverhampton W. May 1939/ Chelsea (£8,000) Aug 1945/ Chester player manager then mgr Jul 1956
United: Manager from 13 March/20 Apr 1959 to Aug 1968. General Manager from Aug 1968 to Aug 1969, then Manager to Dec 1973. Senior Executive, Dec 1973 to June 1977
Sheffield Wednesday (1977) Chief scout

John Harris, a centre half or full back, was the son of a famous Newcastle United centre forward. A war-time Scottish international, John was the captain of Chelsea when they won the First Division Championship in 1955 and had been the manager at Chester where he brought his total of League appearances to 381. The news of his appointment came in March 1959 but it was April before John moved to the Lane.

Harris is the longest serving post-war United manager although his time in office was broken by the 1968–69 season when Arthur Rowley acted as Team manager, with Harris taking a new position of General manager.

A teetotal, non-smoking, quiet bachelor, 'gentleman John' was a man of integrity, respected throughout the game. He was a fine manager but perhaps his ambitions, and consequently, his achievements, were more limited than they might have been.

Harris inherited an excellent team from Joe Mercer and he changed very little, wisely retaining Archie Clark as chief scout and unofficial assistant manager. Willie Hamilton, a brilliant but undisciplined player, was replaced by Keith Kettleborough and Len Allchurch was signed in March 1961 to play a massive part in the successful push for promotion in 1961. The Blades also fought their way to the semi-final stage of the FA Cup after two previous sixth round defeats.

Harris had inherited one team; now, he created a second. He introduced young local players that he and Archie Clark had brought to the Lane and, by the mid-sixties, the United First Division team consisted almost entirely of young home-grown players who, he claimed, would promote loyalty and team spirit. Len Badger and Bernard Shaw were at full-back, midfield players included Tony and Barry Wagstaff, Ken

Mallender, Reg Matthewson, Frank Barlow and David Munks with forwards Alan Woodward, Mick Jones and Alan Birchenall and soon, only goalkeeper Alan Hodgkinson remained from the old team. Gil Reece, a £10k signing from Newport County, was the only notable exception.

The team had continued on a reasonably successful path up to about 1964 but the cup fighting qualities of old had disappeared and although United retained their place in the First Division, attendances were very disappointing and, sadly for United, Archie Clark died early in 1967. Dick Wragg, the Football Committee chairman was ambitious for the club; supporters, it was claimed, wanted fresh faces and headline news of transfer dealings. Money, however, was required to pay for the new Bramall Lane stand and new players and it must have been a shock to Harris when the Club sold Mick Jones to Leeds United and Alan Birchenall to Chelsea.

Harris signed Willie Carlin and Colin Addison as their immediate replacements, and also a potential star in Tony Currie but United were relegated. The manager admitted that he had kept players too long and that more discipline was needed. Harris suggested that he might become the General Manager, seeking new players in the Second, Third and Fourth Divisions and that Andy Beattie, his new assistant manager, who was four years older than Harris, would be the Team manager. The Board, approved the idea, but chose Arthur Rowley as the Team manager.

Harris took back his old position one year later and profited from Rowley's signings and it is this third Harris team of the early 1970s, when Currie and Woodward were at their best, that most people will remember when Harris's name is mentioned. Strengthened by the signing of Billy Dearden and Trevor Hockey, it was a fine team playing exciting, attractive, attacking football and brought a new enthusiasm to United's supporters. Promotion was secured in 1971 but there was no strength in depth. Harris, seemingly, had lost interest in developing young players and, as ever, was reluctant to back his judgement in the transfer market. He stepped down in 1973 in favour of a 'track suit' manager and accepted a rather vague title of Senior Executive.

League Record:	P	W	D	L	F	A	%W
	567	234	138	195	824	770	41.3

HASLAM Harry

Manager 26 Jan 1978 to 16 Jan 1981
b. Manchester 30 July 1921
d. Biggleswade 11 September 1986

Rochdale amat May 1945/ Oldham Athletic May 1946/ Brighton & Hove Albion Sep 1947/ Leyton Orient Jul1948/ Guilford City Oct 1949/ Hastings U player-asst mgr/ Eastbourne mgr/ Gillingham coach/ Barry Town mgr 1954–59/ Tonbridge mgr 1959–68/ Fulham scout/ Luton Town scout, coach, manager. May 1972 to Jan 1978
United: Manager 26 Jan 1978 to 16 Jan 1981. Public relations to Jun 1981

Harry Haslam replaced Jimmy Sirrel and caretaker-manager Cec Coldwell when he was appointed in January 1978. He had played only 9 FL games, as a full back, and was an engaging cheerful character with an eye for raw talent and an excellent reputation for 'wheeling and dealing' in the transfer market. United's debts were still huge and success for Haslam depended on repeating the profitable deals that he had achieved with Luton Town, his previous club.

He brought in Danny Bergara from Luton as his assistant but, sadly, failed to persuade David Pleat to also join the coaching staff. Haslam set to work with enthusiasm and showed that he still had an eye for a promising young player, bringing in Imre Varadi but was less successful when signing Guy, Renwick, Keeling and Finnieston.

Haslam will chiefly be remembered, however, for signing the Argentinian Alex Sabella and for the inevitably doomed attempt to bring the 16-year-old Maradona to the Lane but he had to sell young players of promise—Varadi, Edwards and Stainrod—and in 1979 United, for the first time, sank into the Third Division. A good start was made in the new season but the new signings failed to inspire and Hamson, Benjamin and Sabella were sold.

The 1980–81 season also began well. Haslam deserves praise for the well intentioned plan to sign former World Cup star Martin Peters with the idea that he would eventually take the managerial chair and he had also signed Hatton, Houston and Trusson. Results began to go badly wrong towards the end of September and there were some awful performances after Christmas. Haslam was ill and handed over the reins to Peters; United's plight was serious but not desperate.

Haslam's policies failed at Bramall Lane. In the end, he probably had made a small profit on his transfer deals but the club had been relegated to the Third Division and, when Peters took over, he proved unsuited to the position of manager and United were relegated again.

League Record:	P	W	D	L	F	A	%W
	134	46	30	58	179	197	34.3

HEATH Adrian Paul

Player and Assistant Manager Dec 1995 to Mar 1996
Manager June 1999 to 23 Nov 1999
MF 1995–96 5' 6" 10st 1
b. Stoke-on-Trent 11 January 1961

Stoke City from app Jan 1979/ Everton (£700k) Jan 1982/ Espanol, Spain (£600k) Nov 1988/ Aston Villa (£360k) Aug 1989/ Manchester City (£300k) Feb 1990/ Stoke City (£50k) Mar 1992/ Burnley (free) Aug 1992
United: 13/15 Dec 1995, player and asst mgr to 7 Mar 1996
Debut: 23 Dec 1995 Stoke City 2 United 2 (sub)
Last game: 10 Feb 1996 Crystal Palace 0 United 0 (sub)
Burnley (free) player-mgr Mar 1996 to June 1997/ Everton (1997–98) coach/ Sunderland (1998–99) coach
United: Manager, 13/15 June 1999 to 23 Nov 1999
Sunderland coach 1999 to Oct 2002)/ – / Coventry City asst mgr May 2004, mgr 6–23 Jan 2005, 17 Jan to 19 Feb 2007

The England U21 and B international made his League debut with Stoke City on 1 April 1978 as a substitute at home to Cardiff City. His full debut came on 7 October 1978 at Fulham and he had made 481(54) League appearances when his playing career ended. He had made more than 200 League appearances for Everton, where he won League Championship and FA Cup winners medals, and over 100 for both Stoke City and Burnley.

A small but clever attacking midfield player, Adrian Heath's playing days were coming to an end when he joined United on a free transfer to act as an assistant to the new manager Howard Kendall. Heath made five substitute appearances in a brief three month stay before taking the managerial position with Burnley.

He returned three years later following the resignation of Steve Bruce but Heath also had to agree to the release of players including Tebily, Dellas, Lee Morris, Alan Kelly and Marcello with Marcus Bent as his single significant signing. Morale throughout the club was at a low ebb and the manager resigned a few months later after a succession of poor results which had ended with a dreadful home defeat by Port Vale.

Appearances		Apps	Gls
	FL	0 (4)	0
	FAC	0 (1)	0
	Total	0 (5)	0

League Record:	P	W	D	L	F	A	%W
(as manager)	19	4	5	10	21	33	21.1

KENDALL Howard

Manager Dec 1995 to June 1997
b. Ryton-on-Tyne, 22 May 1946

Preston N.E May 1963/ Everton (£80k) Mar 1967/ Birmingham City (£180k) Feb 1974/ Stoke City (£40k) player-coach Aug 1977/ Blackburn Rovers player-mgr June 1979/ Everton player-mgr May 1981 to June 1987/ Athletico Bilbao, Spain(1987–89) coach/ Manchester City mgr Dec 1989/ Everton mgr Nov 1990 to Dec 1993/ Greece/ Notts County mgr Jan to April 1995
United: Manager 13 Dec 1995 to 24/27 Jun 1997
Everton mgr Jun 1997 to Jul 98/ Jerez, Spain mgr Nov 1998 (unable to take up appointment)/ Ethnikos Piraeus (Greece) 1998–99

Howard Kendall was a fine midfield player who had made 611(2) League appearances but, surprisingly, was never capped. He was an experienced, successful manager though his career appeared to be in decline when Chairman Mike McDonald brought him to the Lane to succeed Dave Bassett with United in the last but one position in the table.

One of his first decisions (puzzling to most supporters) was to sell Nathan Blake to Bolton Wanderers but it was followed by an extraordinary root and branch reconstruction of the team involving an amazing number of transfer moves. By the end of the season, United had used a record number of players though the net outlay on transfer fees was small. Howard was 'a players man' engendering a good spirit among the team and his man-management skills were excellent. Kendall also made an immediate change to the style of play. Gordon Cowans was an influential figure in midfield and for the first time for some years, ripples of applause could be heard around the ground, as the supporter's expressed their pleasure in United's passing and general play. The League position remained perilous for some time but the tide turned and United rose rapidly away from the danger zone.

Optimism was understandably high when the 1996–97 began. The new John Street stand was opened and attendances rose but, sadly, results didn't match up to the expectations. Cowans had not been retained and the midfield no longer ran smoothly and many would argue this decision of the Manager proved fatal. Kendall was given the green light to strengthen the team. There was a net outlay over the financial year of about £3 million but the policy, inevitably risky, failed. Serious injuries to Vonk, Short, Whitehouse and Ebbrell were a factor and although United did reach the play-off final, the expensive plan for promotion failed and Kendall returned to Everton.

League Record:	P	W	D	L	F	A	%W
	71	31	24	16	105	67	43.7

McEWAN William (Billy) Johnston McGowan

Coach, Acting Manager March 1986
Manager May 1986 to Jan 1988
b. Cleland, Wishaw. 20 June 1951

Hibernian 1969 Blackpool May 1973/ Brighton & H A Feb 1974/ Chesterfield Nov 1974/ Mansfield Town Jan 1977/ Peterborough United Nov 1977/ Rotherham United player coach Jul 1979
United: Sep 1984 coaching staff. Acting manager from 27 Mar 1986, manager from 21 May 1986 to 2 January 1988
Rotherham United mgr Apr 1988 to Jan 1991/ Scarborough asst-mgr 1991–2/ Darlington mgr May 1992 to Oct 1993/ Derby County coaching staff, assistant manager, twice acting manager, coach, 1993–2004/ York City mgr Feb 2005 to Nov 2007/ Mansfield T mgr July 2008

A Scottish Youth and U23 international, Billy McEwan made 290(11) FL appearances as a midfield player. He had shown an aptitude for coaching at Millmoor and it was Ian Porterfield who brought McEwan to the Lane with the youth team as his particular responsibility and he was a success with the best squad of young players since the 1960s. Committed and dedicated, he took over as caretaker manager when Porterfield was sacked in March 1986 and accepted the full managerial position at the end of the season.

McEwan brought down the average age of the team with new signings but still the quality of the football was a disappointment and the average attendance in the new manager's first full season fell below ten thousand for the first time—other than some war years—since 1897. McEwan gradually introduced more of United's own young players but attendances continued to fall. Relegation became a serious threat and at the turn of the year and after three successive defeats, culminating with a 0-5 defeat at home against Oldham, McEwan was sacked. He made four appearances with United:

Debut: 8 May 1986 Chesterfield 2 United XI 1 (Moss BM)
Two (Fr) games (12 and 15 May 1986) in the Channel Islands and
Last game: 23 Nov 1986 Hallam 3 United XI 5 (Fr)

League Record:	P	W	D	L	F	A	%W
	79	25	22	32	89	111	31.6

MERCER Joseph (Joe) OBE

Manager 18 Aug 1955 to 25 Dec 1958
b. Ellesmere Port, 9 August 1914
d. Hoylake 9 August 1990

Ellesmere Port Town/ Everton amat 1931, pro Sep 1932/ Arsenal (£7,000) Nov 1946, retired through injury 1954
United: appointed Manager 18 Aug 1955 to 25 Dec 1958.
Aston Villa mgr Dec 1958 to Jul 1964/ – / Manchester City mgr Jul 1965, general mgr Oct 1971,/ Coventry City general mgr Jun 1972–75, director Apr 1975 to Jul 1981/ England (1974) Caretaker manager

Joe Mercer was the left half in the Everton First Division Championship side of 1939 and captain of Arsenal when they won the First Division title in 1948 and 1953 and the F A Cup in 1950. He was awarded five England caps immediately prior to the outbreak of war in 1939 and captained England on many occasions during the war.

Mercer's football career had been an illustrious one (he had made 411 League appearances) but it presented a problem when he accepted the manager's job at the Lane for he had little experience of less than brilliant players. Another problem was his lack of any managerial experience, and furthermore, those distinguished years with two famous clubs were a poor preparation for a club struggling to survive in the First Division.

Joe was appointed as the new United manager by the Chairman, Senior Atkin, two days before the season began, the other directors being totally unaware of Atkin's negotiations with Mercer. At half-time in their first game, United were losing three nil (they lost 2–4) and, a few days later, Ernest Jackson, the trainer, resigned. Joe now knew he had serious problems to face. Hodgkinson and Graham Shaw were National Servicemen and rarely available, Jack Cross, the centre forward had to be transferred and Hagan and Joe Shaw had problems with injuries. United were immediately involved in a relegation battle and nearly escaped that fate but, at the end of Mercer's first season, they went down.

Mercer made mistakes but he would admit and learn from them. The signing of Malcolm Barrass is an example. Joe preferred a big traditional centre half and a hat trick by big Tommy Briggs of Blackburn finally convinced him to drop Joe Shaw and buy Barrass but the new man was way past his best and Shaw returned to the side.

Mercer was a genial man and had excellent contacts in the game but he had to sell players before he could buy new. Grainger and Iley went and he tried to sell Graham Shaw but he brought some fine players to the Lane—Hodgson, Hamilton, Lewis, Summers, Russell, Pace and Simpson for instance—and he worked hard in coaching those players who would listen and learn.

He created and coached the famous United defence that served the club so well in spite of their lack of inches. Hodgkinson; Coldwell and Graham Shaw; Richardson, Joe Shaw and Summers are the names that will be remembered for many a long day.

In the end, however, Mercer was impatient: he was looking for a 'big' club and his choice was Aston Villa. In later years, Joe found delight in reminding people that his first season there, also ended in relegation, but of course, more days of glory lay ahead. He had a short successful period in charge of England for seven games in 1974 and was later awarded the OBE for his services to football. During his time with United he played in nine friendly or benefit games (see 'Other Players' section).

League Record:	P	W	D	L	F	A	%W
	149	63	32	54	268	229	42.3

PETERS Martin Stanford MBE

Player 1980–81, Manager 1981
MF 1980–81 5' 11" 11st 10
b. Plaistow 8 November 1943

West Ham United app May 1959, pro Nov 1960/ Baltimore Bays/ Tottenham Hotspur (£200k) Mar 1970/ Norwich City (£60k) Mar 1975
United: Player-coach 31 Jul 1980, Manager 18 Jan 1981 to 30 May 1981
Debuts: 2 Aug 1980 United 2 Hull City 1 (ASC)
9 Aug 1980 Sheffield Wednesday 2 United 0 (LC)
16 Aug 1980 Carlisle United 0 United 3
Last games: 17 Jan 1981 United 0 Gillingham 1
22 Mar 1981 Truro City XI 1 United 9 (BM Keith Solomon)
Gorleston Town 1981–82

Martin Peters, a schoolboy and youth international, made his FL debut with West Ham United on 20 April 1962 at home to Cardiff City. In November 1962 he won his first U23 cap and in 1965 gained a European Cup-Winners Cup winners' medal. He gained his first full England cap in May 1966 and his move to Spurs was for a British record fee. After a distinguished playing career during which he earned 67 England caps and scored one of the England goals in the 1966 World Cup Final, this quiet, intelligent player seemed certain to become a first class soccer manger.

It appeared to be an astute move of Harry Haslam to bring him to the Lane as a player and coach and groom him to take over the managerial chair at the Lane. On moving to the Lane he had played 697(1) League games, scoring 171 goals. The immediate aim was promotion but early in October after some poor results and disappointing personal performances, Peters was reported as saying 'we have no divine right to go up' and that it was difficult for him to 'play well in the Third Division' as the players around him 'do not play like First Division players'.

Haslam became ill and Peters took over earlier than perhaps had been planned but though United's position was perilous, it was far from critical and with sixteen fixtures remaining, there was time to make changes and influence the players. Martin brought in the experienced Don Givens and United should never have been relegated but they were and it was Givens who missed the penalty kick that sent them down. Peters had failed and he took the honourable step and resigned.

After a time playing with Gorelston Town he worked for a fruit machine manufacturer and then teamed up with Geoff Hurst at a motor insurance repair company.

Appearances		Apps	Gls
	FL	23 (1)	4
	LC	2	0
	ASC	2	0
	Total	27 (1)	4

League Record: (as manager)	P	W	D	L	F	A	%W
	16	3	6	7	20	25	18.8

PORTERFIELD John (Ian)

Manager 1981–86
b. Dunfermline 11 February 1946
d. Surrey 11 September 2007

Raith Rovers 1964/ Sunderland (£38k) Dec 1967/ Reading (loan) 1976, Sheffield Wednesday (£15k) Jul 1977 player, player-coach/ Rotherham United mgr Dec 1979
United: Manager 6 June1981 to 27 March 1986
Aberdeen mgr Nov 1986 to May 1988/ Chelsea asst mgr Nov 1989/ Reading mgr Nov 1989 to Apr 1991/ Chelsea mgr Jun 1991 to Feb 1993/ Zambia national coach 1993/ Ittihead, (Saudi Arabia) summer 1994 / – / Bolton Wanderers assistant manager Jan 1996 to May 1996/ Worthing mgr cs 1996/ Zimbabwe national coach Oct 1996/ Oman national coach/ Trinidad & Tobago national coach 2000/ Kumasi Asante Kotoko (Ghana) coach 2002/ Busan I'Park (club side in South Korea) 2003 to Aug 2006/ Armenia national coach Aug 2006-Sep 2007

An attacking mid-field player, who made 325(15) FL appearances, Ian Porterfield will always be remembered for the goal he scored that won the FA Cup for Sunderland in the 1973 Final but with mixed feelings by United supporters.

It was Reg Brealey, the new chairman at the Lane after United had slipped into the Fourth Division, who offered Ian Porterfield the vacant managerial position. Porterfield had just led Rotherham United to the Third Division Championship but he accepted Brealey's offer of an attractive salary, what was reported to be an unusually long contract and money to strengthen the team. The plan was a return to the First Division in five years.

Keith Edwards returned and other good signings included Waugh and Colin Morris and the championship was won with some style and two years later United were back in the Second Division where they remained for the remainder of Porterfield's time with United.

He was sacked in January 1986 and was deeply shocked. He claimed that his net outlay on players in taking the Club up two divisions had been less than £450k and that 'I have done miracles for this club', probably making the point that Brealey had not made available quite as much money as Porterfield expected. Inevitably, there was another side to the affair.

He had brought in some good players; Stancliffe and Cockerill for example but money had been wasted and the manager had been over reliant in the end on older players who were, in general, past their best. It was said that Porterfield was a fine coach but not good at man management and many players were unhappy working under him. A manager and board of directors also have to realise, that in professional football, the customer is king, and there were too many unhappy spectators at the Lane. Attendance figures were very disappointing and in Porterfield's final season, the average—war-time years apart—was the lowest in the twentieth century.

After leaving United, he managed in the UK before having several posts abroad. Early in 2007 he was diagnosed with colon cancer and died while still manager of Armenia. He was the first Premier League manager to be sacked (by Chelsea in 1993) and so far, the last person to succeed Sir Alex Ferguson as a manager.

League Record:	P	W	D	L	F	A	%W
	213	94	55	64	351	275	44.1

ROBSON Bryan OBE

Manager 2007–08
b. Witton Gilbert, Chester-le-Street 11 January 1957

West Bromwich Albion from app Aug 1974/ Manchester United (£1.5m) Oct 1981/ Middlesbrough (free) player-mgr May 1994, mgr 1997-Dec 2000, joint with Terry Venables Dec 2000 to Jun 2001/ – / Bradford City mgr 24 Nov 2003 to Jun 2004/ – / West Bromwich Albion mgr 9 Nov 2004 to 18 Sep 2006/ – /
United: manager 22 May 2007 to 14 Feb 2008

Bryan Robson was one of the finest mid-field players; capable of making the most resolute winning tackles deep in his own half, then a penetrating almost instantaneous pass and, almost unseen, bursting forward to score spectacularly at the other end. The ideal box to box player, 'Captain Marvel' as he became known, played his last game on 1 January 1997, ten days before his fortieth birthday, having played 543 (25) League games and scored 114 goals. He had won 90 England caps as well as those at youth, U21 and B level.

Great footballers don't necessarily make good managers but Robson was initially a success. Well supported financially as the player-manager (manager 1997) at Middlesbrough, he twice took the Boro to the Premier League—with relegation in between—and three defeated cup final appearances. He was unable to keep struggling Bradford City in Division One but in 2004–05 he saved his first love, West Bromwich Albion from relegation; the first time that a club which was bottom of the Premiership at Christmas had has stayed up but he failed when relegation loomed twelve months later.

After eight months out of the game, he moved to the Lane following United's relegation and Neil Warnock's departure. He brought in some new players; James Beattie for a record fee, Gary Naysmith, the Scottish International left back, Lee Hendrie and Billy Sharp, the former United player. Bryan was not a universally popular choice amongst the fans and matters did not go well on the field. He tried to introduce a more methodical passing game but there were some poor performances, for example at Scunthorpe and Bristol and, despite the useful loan signings of Gary Cahill and Phil Bardsley, the side struggled for consistency.

The team played with a lack of confidence and the crowd became increasingly restless as the season progressed. Gary Speed and Ugo Ehiogu were signed and Martin and Cotterill came on loan but the club couldn't rise from a position of mid-table mediocrity. Lacklustre performances at Hillsborough and against the bottom clubs, Colchester and Scunthorpe, the latter, a goalless draw against 10 men for much of the game, led to a car-park demonstration and widespread criticism. United were in 16th place in the League table and seven points from a relegation place. Robson met with the chairman Kevin McCabe during the following week and was offered an alternative post as overseeing the restructuring of the footballing side but he declined this and resigned.

League Record:	P	W	D	L	F	A	%W
	32	9	12	11	34	36	28.1

ROWLEY George **Arthur**

Manager 1968–69
b. Wolverhampton 21 April 1926
d. Shrewsbury 18 December 2002

Wolverhampton W amat 1942/ West Bromwich Albion amat Mar 1944, pro May 1944/ Fulham Dec 1948/ Leicester City (£12k) Jul 1950/ Shrewsbury Town (£7,000) player-mgr then mgr Jun 1958 to Jul 1968
United: Manager, 11 July 1968 to 6 August 1969
Southend United mgr Mar 1970 to May 1976, then scout/ Telford asst mgr/ – / Oswestry Town mgr Jul 1979 to Oct 1980

Arthur Rowley is the Football League's record goal-scorer with 434 goals, in 619 League games. A big, burly forward, good with his head and with a powerful shot, he scored the bulk of his goals with Leicester City and Shrewsbury Town.

In the 1968 close season, the United Board decided to appoint a 'team manager' while retaining John Harris as the 'General Manager' but, 'within a fortnight', they suspected that they had probably made a mistake and the players were disappointed with the new man who seemed strangely quiet and reserved. 'He wasn't positive enough' was a typical comment and he preferred the racecourse to the training ground.

There was a considerable turnover in players. Rowley wasted no time in moving players on, particularly, in some cases, if he thought their attitude was wrong and no United manager has shown such excellent judgment in signing new players for very reasonable fees. Carlin, Mallender, Tony and Barry Wagstaff, Munks and Bernard Shaw were sold and the newcomers—Hemsley, Powell, Colquhoun, Tudor and Flynn—would go on to play a large part in the promotion season of 1970–71. The team, on many occasions, played attractive football under Rowley but the results were inconsistent and he was sacked after just one year. John Harris, who had kept a low profile and his thoughts to himself, would be the man to profit from the turnover of players.

League Record:	P	W	D	L	F	A	%W
	42	16	11	15	61	50	38.1

SIRREL James (Jimmy)

Manager 1975–77
b. Glasgow 2 February 1922

Celtic 1945/ Bradford PA May 1949/ Brighton & Hove Albion Aug 1951/ Aldershot player then trainer Aug 1954/ Brentford trainer and acting mgr Sep 1967/ Notts County mgr Nov 1969
United: Manager 16/21 October 1975 to 27 September 1977
Notts County mgr, then general mgr, then director, then mgr Oct 1977 to May 1987/ Derby County chief scout 1990

Jimmy Sirrel, an inside forward who made 98 FL appearances and 13 League appearances with Celtic, had his first managerial post at Brentford where he helped keep the club going and reduce their overdraft significantly. At Notts County he achieved two promotions taking the club into the Second Division for the first time in 15 years and gaining a reputation as an astute and hard working manager.

He arrived at the Lane with the team firmly entrenched at the bottom of the old First Division and, with no money available, he was unable to bring about any improvement and another seventeen games went by before a victory was achieved.

Sirrel was enthusiastic but the players lost interest when they found that his training sessions almost totally consisted of practice matches in which the first team forwards played the defence or the Central League team consistently defeated the first team. Eddy, Field and Garbett left for America and age and injuries were catching up with Badger (who moved to Chesterfield) Dearden and Hemsley. The Club's financial position made it almost impossible to seriously strengthen the team and the addition of Paul Garner and Jimmy Johnstone to the squad did little to help matters.

Tony Currie had to be sold but Sirrel failed to find a solution to the extremely difficult financial problems. Keith Edwards, Tony Kenworthy, Gary Hamson and Simon Stainrod showed promise but United had sunk to next to the bottom of the Second Division when Sirrel was dismissed.

League Record:	P	W	D	L	F	A	%W
	78	20	22	36	88	131	25.6

SPACKMAN Nigel James

Player-Coach July 1996, Assistant Manager
Caretaker Manager 1997, Manager 1997–98
MF/D 1996–97 6' 1" 13st 2
b. Romsey, Hants. 2 December 1960

Andover Aug 1979/ Bournemouth (free) May 1980/ Chelsea (£40k) Jun 1983/ Liverpool (£400k) Feb 1987/ Queens Park Rangers (£500k) Feb 1989/ Glasgow Rangers (£500k) Nov 1989/ Chelsea (£485k) Sep 1992
United: (free) 8 July 1996 as Player-coach and Assistant manager, Caretaker-manager 27 June 1997, Manager 15 August 1997, resigned 2 March 1998 (His registration as a player was retained).

Debuts: 18 Jul 1996 Sarawak (Malaysia) 1 United 2 (sub Fr)
23 Jul 1996 Sabah FC (Malaysia) 0 United 0 (Fr)
17 Aug 1996 Reading 1 United 0
Last games: 4 May 1997 Charlton Athletic 0 United 0
26 May 1997 Crystal Palace 1 United 0 (PO at Wembley)
25 July 1997 Arjang (Sweden) 1 United 8 (as mgr, Fr)
30 Jul 1997 Forde IL (Norway) 0 United 4 (as mgr, Fr)
England U18 (asst coach), scout, TV/ Barnsley mgr Jan to Oct 2001/ TV and radio/ Millwall mgr May to Sep 2006/ TV and radio

Nigel Spackman began his very successful playing career when he made his League debut with Bournemouth on 16 August 1980 at York City. In his first season at Chelsea, he helped them to the Second Division Championship and then played regularly in the top flight both North and South of the border. He won a Championship medal with Liverpool in 1988 and several League and Cup medals with Rangers.

He came to United as an experienced top class mid-field player and as Howard Kendall's assistant but unfortunately he never played consistently well. He was given the manager's job when Kendall left and received almost instantaneous praise when the team, which now included a previous reserve player, Wayne Quinn and new signings, Brian Deane, Paul McGrath, Vas Borbokis and Nicky Marker, made a promising start to the new season. Sadly for United and the new manager, this didn't last. Serious injuries to Dane Whitehouse, David White and Michel Vonk and the enforced retirement of McGrath were the initial blows but serious problems lay ahead.

The club had made huge losses and carried a large staff on high wages. Decisions had been taken in the past two years on the assumption that the Blades would now be members of the Premier League with all its attendant benefits but now the coat had to be cut according to the cloth. The relationship between Spackman and the Chairman, Mike McDonald and his Chief Executive, Charles Green who was increasingly powerful, worsened and soon the manager, who was also unhappy with Steve Thompson's role, was seemingly only responsible for coaching and picking the team.

The enforced sales of Tiler, Ward, Deane, Fjortoft and Hutchinson with Spackman bringing in Saunders, Marcelo, Stuart and Ford undoubtedly weakened the team and Willie Donachie, the chief coach left to join Manchester City. Morale in the club was very low and Spackman resigned.

Nigel had made two friendly appearances for United when he was the manager and he ended his playing career with 502(28) League appearances, including those in Scotland.

Appearances		Apps	Gls
	FL	19 (4)	0
	PO	1	0
	FAC	1	0
	LC	2	0
	Total	23 (4)	0

League Record:	P	W	D	L	F	A	%W
(as manager)	34	15	13	6	50	37	44.1

THOMPSON Steven (Steve) Paul

Player 1988–89, Player Coach 1997
Manager and Assistant Manager 1998
CD/MF 1989 6' 1" 14st 4
b. Sheffield, 28 July 1955.

[United] trial/ Frecheville, Worksop Town/ Boston United/ Lincoln City (£15k) Apr 1980/ Charlton Athletic (£25k) Aug 1985/ Leicester City (£40k) Jul 1988
United: (£15–20k) 11 Nov 1988 to Aug 1989
Debuts: 17 Jan 1989 Wrexham 2 United 1 (SVT)
21 Jan 1989 United 4 Gillingham 2
Last game: 29 Apr 1989 Fulham 2 United 2
Lincoln City player Aug 1989 acting mgr, manager Nov 1990 to May 1993/ Newcastle United coach/ Doncaster Rovers asst mgr/ Southend United. (acting mgr, mgr Feb to Jun 1995/ Notts County. Team mgr 1995to Jul 1997
United: July 1997 coaching staff, 9 Mar 1998 appointed manager to the end of the season, assistant manager July to 16 Nov 1998.
Scouting/ Cambridge United mgr Dec 2004 to May 2005/ radio work/ Notts County Jun 2006 to Oct 2007

Steve Thompson had a trial at the Lane as a youngster but was released and moved into non-League football. At the age of 25 he joined Lincoln City, making his FL debut at home to Peterborough United on 16 August 1980. He immediately became a regular in the first team and after over 150 appearances he moved to Charlton where he was an important member of the promotion side of 1986. There followed a successful season in the top flight including a trip to Wembley in the Simod Cup final.

He then moved to Leicester but was languishing in the reserves and had made no first team appearances when he was signed by Dave Bassett as extra cover for the defence. Steve, a tough, uncompromising defender played regularly in the second half of the season in an ultimately successful return to Division Two and, promotion being achieved, he returned to Lincoln.

Injuries limited his appearances and in November 1990 he retired as a player, with 295(1) career League appearances and began a career in management and coaching, successfully saving the Imps from relegation in his first season. After leaving Lincoln he had various coaching and assistant managerial roles and a spell as manager of Southend, saving the club from relegation.

In 1997, he returned to the Lane as a coach, assisting Willie Donachie. It was a period of turmoil at the Lane. Donachie moved to Oldham in February and a few weeks later, Nigel Spackman resigned and Thompson was given the position of team manager until the end of the season.

The team responded with fine performances against Coventry City in the sixth round of the FA Cup but was not good enough to overcome Newcastle United in the semi-final. Paul Devlin, Ian Hamilton and Chris Wilder had been signed before the transfer deadline but faced with a backlog of fixtures, United took only six points from their last seven fixtures and were fortunate to qualify for the play-offs. Facing Sunderland, the team made a valiant effort but fortune denied them a place in the final and United decided against giving Thompson the position of manager, engaging Steve Bruce.

Appearances		Apps	Gls
	FL	20	1
	FAC	2	0
	AMC	1	0
	Total	23	1

League Record:	P	W	D	L	F	A	%W
(as manager)	12	4	4	4	19	17	33.3

WARNOCK Neil

Manager 1999–2007
b. Sheffield 1 December 1948

Swallownest MW/ Chesterfield pro Jul 1968/ Rotherham United Jun 1969/ Hartlepool United Jul 1971/ Scunthorpe United (£3,250) Feb 1972/ Aldershot Mar 1975/ Barnsley Oct 1976/ York City May 1978/ Crewe Alexandra Dec 1978/ Burton Albion Aug 1979/ – / Todwick mgr/Gainsborough Trinity pl-mgr cs 1980/ Burton Albion mgr Jan 1981 to Feb 1986/ – / Scarborough mgr cs 1986 to Jan 1989/ Notts County mgr Jan 1989/ Torquay United 'consultant-mgr' Feb 1993, mgr March to May 1993/ Huddersfield Town mgr cs 1993/ Plymouth Argyle mgr cs 1995/ Oldham Athletic mgr Feb 1997/ Bury mgr cs 1998
United: Manager 1 Dec 1999 to 16 May 2007
Crystal Palace mgr from Oct 2007

Neil Warnock made 296 (33) FL appearances as a quick, enthusiastic and in his words, 'brainless' winger in the lower divisions. Towards the end of his career he went part-time, working as a salesman, a greengrocer and, later, opened a chiropody business in Sheffield while managing Gainsborough Trinity and then Burton Albion.

He began his managerial career in non-League football and his first major success was in 1986 when Scarborough became the first club to be automatically promoted to the Football League. He subsequently achieved two promotions with Notts County, one with Huddersfield and one with Plymouth, all via the play-offs and had been offered the chance to manage Chelsea when he was with Notts County.

He moved to the Lane in December 1999 with Kevin Blackwell as his assistant after Adrian Heath's resignation following a poor start to the season. A life-long Blades supporter, he said that managing United was for him, the best job in football. A great motivator and a man who knew the importance of a 'good dressing room', he immediately sparked an improvement and relegation was easily avoided with basically the players that had started the season, with Michael Brown being the most significant import.

His time in charge, if on occasions frustrating, was never dull. His tactics were very similar to those of Dave Bassett and could be dismissed as the pursuit of results more than style but sport is about results. Inevitably, both Bassett and Warnock had their critics because of the type of football they employed but judged by results, both football and financial, and keeping in mind the situation of the club when they were appointed, they were good managers.

A successful Warnock team was exciting to watch. Speed and determination were essential throughout the team with the game played in the opponent's half of the field. He preferred two strikers but would work with one and would usually have two or three more attacking players on the bench, often at the expense of a substitute goalkeeper. Neil's team selections were sometimes 'surprising' and his animated presence on the touchline was a Warnock trademark. A qualified referee, other referees were frequently criticised and although Warnock was often in trouble, he was often correct in what he said. Until his final season, he was allowed very little money but, under Kevin McCabe, the financial basis of the club improved. Every season bar one, 2004–05, the average attendance improved and the Club's positions in the second tier were chronologically: 16, 10, 13, 3, 8, 8 and 2.

Young players were given a chance and three in particular, Jagielka, Montgomery and Tonge, blossomed. Some of the players he brought in lasted only a short time but others, such as Keith Curle, Peter Ndlovu, Paul Peschisolido, Robert Page, Chris Morgan, David Kelly and Stuart McCall had a big influence. It was McCall's arrival that was instrumental in one of the most exciting seasons in United's history with two semi-final appearances and a play-off final. Sadly the final at Cardiff was a massive disappointment and it was the only time, up to then, that Warnock had failed in the play-offs.

His long time associate, Kevin Blackwell, departed for Leeds during the summer of 2003 and many felt that Warnock would be less effective without him. David Kelly took over as assistant manager and just over 12 months later he left to be replaced by Stuart McCall. Following the euphoria of 2002–03 the following two seasons were a disappointment despite finishing eighth on both occasions. 2004 saw the arrival of three former Owls: Leigh Bromby, Alan Quinn and Derek Geary and they were to play a significant role the following season.

It was widely felt that 2005–06 was Warnock's last chance to achieve his dream of taking 'his' club to the Premiership. He brought in Paul Ifill, Neil Shipperley and David Unsworth and United made their best ever start to a season. Despite a poor spell after Christmas, promotion was achieved with three games to go. The only expensive signing was Rob Hulse although Mikele Leigertwood, Christian Nade and Colin Kazim-Richards were also added to the staff. United deserved to stay up but didn't and the 'Tevez Affair' left all associated with United with the feeling of being cheated. Nevertheless, three days after the defeat by Wigan in the final game, Warnock resigned, having been in charge for one more League game than Dave Bassett. For all his faults, he had done a tremendous amount for Sheffield United.

Neil made one appearance in United's colours in Dane Whitehouse's testimonial match:

14 May 2001 Blades All Stars XI (Sub BM)

League Record:	P	W	D	L	F	A	%W
	339	140	90	109	442	401	41.3

THE PLAYERS

ABLETT Gary Ian

CD 1996 6' 2" 12st 2
b. Liverpool 19 November 1965

Liverpool app to pro Nov 1983/ Derby County (L) Jan 1985/ Hull City (L) Sep 1986/ Everton (£750k) Jan 1992
United: (L) 1 Mar 1996 to cs 1996
Debut: 2 Mar 1996 Birmingham City 0 United 1
Last game: 4 May 1996 United 1 Port Vale 1
Birmingham City (£390k) Jun 1996/ Wycombe Wanderers (L) Dec 1999/ Scunthorpe United (trial)/ Blackpool Jan 2000

Initially a Liverpool apprentice, Gary Ablett won two League Championship medals and the FA Cup whilst at Anfield, also gaining England U21 and B caps, although he made his FL debut on 30 January 1985 whilst on loan at Derby, at home to Bournemouth. The left sided defender could not hold a regular place and moved across the city to Goodison for £750k in January 1992, gaining another FA Cup winner's medal.

He was brought to Bramall Lane by Howard Kendall in March 1996 on a three month loan deal. A calm and reliable left side defender, he played a key role in the final 12 games of the season (of which eight were won and only one lost), helping to guide United away from the possibility of relegation to a respectable ninth in the table. It was expected that he might sign permanently for the Blades but instead he moved to Birmingham City. Following a serious knee injury in February 1999 he lost his place and eventually joined Blackpool, on a free, in January 2000, retiring six months later.

Appearances:		Apps	Gls
	FL	12	0
	Total	12	0

ADDISON Colin

IF/ CF/ LH 1967–70 5' 11" 11st 11
b. Taunton 18 May 1940

York City amateur 1956–pro Jul 1957/ Nottingham Forest (£12k) Jan 1961/ Arsenal (£45k) Sep 1966
United: 29 Nov 1967 to 14 Oct 1971
Debut: 2 Dec 1967 West Ham U 3 United 0
Last game: 5 Dec 1970 Luton T 2 United 1
Hereford United (£3000) Oct 1971 as player-mgr/ Durban City mgr Jan 1975/ Notts County asst mgr Dec 1975–Oct 1976/ Newport County mgr Jan 1977–May 1978/ West Bromwich Albion asst mgr Jul 1978–1979/ Derby County mgr May 1979–Jan 1982/ Newport County mgr Jan 1982–May 1985/ coach Kuwait, Qatar/ Celta Vigo(Spain) mgr Apr 1986–Aug 1987/ West Bromwich Albion asst mgr Sep 1987–Oct 1988/ Athletico Madrid (Spain) asst mgr, mgr Oct 1988–Jun 1989/ Cadiz FC (Spain) mgr Mar–Jul 1990/ Hereford United mgr Jul 1990–May 1991/ El Arabi(Kuwait) mgr 1992/ Cadiz FC mgr 1993–94/ Club Deportivo Badajoz (Spain) mgr 1995/ Merthyr Tydfil mgr 1996–98/ Scarborough mgr 1999/ Yeovil Town mgr 2000/ Swansea City mgr 2001/ Forest Green Rovers mgr Sep 2002–Dec 2003/ Barry Town mgr Feb–Aug 2004

Colin Addison moved from Taunton to York at the age of 11, becoming a York City full time professional at the start of the 1957–58 season and made his FL debut on 14 September 1957 at home to Bury. He moved to Nottingham Forest for £12k (a record fee for York) in January 1961 and then to Arsenal.

He asked for a transfer from Highbury and the Blades assistant manager, Andy Beattie who had been Colin's manager at the City Ground, persuaded the former Forest player to move to the Lane. He joined the Blades in December 1967 for a fee of £40k but, although he was a very intelligent player, he was unable to solve United's relegation and goal scoring problems. He had begun his career as an inside forward but played at centre forward for much of his time at Bramall Lane, laying the ball off for others. He began the 1970–71 promotion season as a regular member of the side but moved to the left half position before losing his place to Frank Barlow and Trevor Hockey, Bill Dearden taking over the centre forward spot.

In October 1971 he moved to Hereford United as their player manager and he was involved in their famous FA Cup run and their entry into the Football League before pursuing a long and generally successful career in management and coaching.

Appearances:		Apps	Gls
	FL	93 (1)	22
	FAC	6	2
	LC	5	0
	CC	3 (1)	1
	WC	2	1
	ABD	1	0
	Total	110 (2)	26

ADEY Wilfred (Wilf)

LB/ RB 1932 5' 8½" 11st 6
b. Featherstone 6 July 1909
d. Worksop February 1975

Thurcroft Church/ Thurcroft Main Colliery/ Huddersfield T (trial) Aug 1930/ Thurcroft Main Colliery/ Norton Woodseats
United: 2 Sep 1931 to 30 May 1934
Debut: 7 May 1932 United 1 Blackpool 3
Last game: 1 Oct 1932 Wolverhampton W 5 United 1
Barnsley cs1934/ Carlisle United Oct 1936/ Aberdeen May 1938

Wilf Adey's two first team opportunities ended in heavy defeats but his playing career improved when he was transferred, with fellow reserve defender Bill Anderson, to Barnsley. He went on to make over 170 League appearances with Barnsley, Carlisle and Aberdeen, finishing his career with three games in the 1939–40 season with the Scottish club and making four appearances with Carlisle and one for Barnsley in that first war-time season.

Appearances:		Apps	Gls
	FL	2	0
	Total	2	0

AGANA Patrick Anthony (Tony) Olozinka

Striker 1988–91 6' 0" 12st 2
b. Bromley 2 October 1963

Charlton Athletic(schoolboy)/ Welling United/ Weymouth/ Watford Aug 1987
United: 16 Feb 1988 to 8 Nov 1991
Debut: 20 Feb 1988 United 1 Barnsley 0
Last game: Nov 1991 Manchester United 2 United 0
Notts County (£680k) Nov 1991/ Leeds United (L) Feb 1992/ Hereford United Mar 1997/ Cliftonville/ Leek Town/ Guisley

Tony Agana worked for an insurance company while playing for Welling United and when the firm moved to Poole, he became a part-time professional with Weymouth, playing as a winger and winning one England semi professional cap in his three years there. He joined Watford in August 1987, signed by Dave Bassett and made his FL debut, at nearly 24 years of age, on 15 August, at home to Wimbledon.

When Bassett moved to Bramall Lane, Tony was one of his first signings along with Peter Hetherston in an exchange deal for Martin Kuhl and a cash adjustment. Tony scored on his debut but Bassett's many team changes failed to stave off relegation. In the following season, Tony immediately struck up a fine striking partnership with Brian Deane and between them they scored 60 FL and Cup goals. Tony had tremendous pace, could twist and turn at speed and was able to hold the ball and bring others into play. United gained promotion and the partnership continued in the following season, Tony scoring twice in the 5–2 victory at Leicester which clinched promotion back to the top flight.

Injuries and loss of pace became a problem for the player and he missed an increasing number of games and it was a surprise when, in November 1991, Notts County, managed by Neil Warnock, paid a County record fee for him of £680k. Tony moved on a free transfer to Hereford United where his two goals in the vital last game of the 1996–97 season were not enough to keep Hereford in the League. Recently he has been involved on match days with Corporate Hospitality at Bramall Lane.

Appearances:		Apps.	Gls
	FL	105 (13)	42
	PO	0 (1)	0
	FAC	14	5
	LC	12	3
	AMC 3	1	
	FMC	1	0
	YHC	4 (1)	1
	Total	139 (15)	52

AKINBIYI Adeola (Ade) Oluwatoyin

Striker 2006–07 6' 1" 12st 9
b. Hackney 10 October 1974

Norwich City from trainee Feb 1993/ Hereford United (L) Jan 1994/ Brighton & Hove Albion (L) Nov 1994/ Gillingham (£250k) Jan 1997/ Bristol City (£1.2m) May 1998/ Wolverhampton Wanderers (£3.5m) Sep 1999/ Leicester City (£5m) Jul 2000/ Crystal Palace (£2.2m+) Feb 2002/ Stoke City (L) Mar 2003, free Sep 2003/ Burnley (£600k) Feb 2005
United: (£1.75m) 26 Jan 2006 to 3 Jan 2007
Debut: 1 Feb 2006 United 0 Derby County 1
Last games: 16 Sep 2006 United 1 Reading 2
24 Oct 2006 United 2 Birmingham City 4 (LC)
Burnley (£750k) Jan 2007

Ade Akinbiyi made his FL debut whilst on loan at Hereford United. He came on as a sub on 22 January 1994 at home to Crewe Alexandra and he scored on his full debut two weeks later at home to Bury. He played for a variety of clubs, including Leicester City whilst they were in the Premiership, but his most successful spells were with the lower Division clubs. He made one appearance for Nigeria, in a friendly against Greece in 1999 and although called up on other occasions he did not honour the invitation. He was a Neil Warnock target in February 2005 but he signed for Burnley instead. However, a year later he signed for the Blades, for a club record fee, rising to a possible £1.75m, and scored on his debut.

Ade's main assets were his strength and speed and he was capable of scoring spectacular goals such as the one he scored at Hillsborough but he also missed easier chances and he was never consistent. Following United's promotion to the Premiership, he soon lost his place to Danny Webber, although he did score on his final appearance against Birmingham in the League Cup. He returned to Burnley where by 2008 he reached a career total of 136 League goals in 373(95) games.

Appearances:		Apps	Gls
	FL	12 (6)	3
	LC	2	1
	Total	14 (6)	4

ALDERSON John (Jack) Thomas

G 1925–28 6' 1" 13st 7
b. Crook 28 November 1891
d. Sunderland 17 February 1972

Crook Town/ Shildon Athletic/ Middlesbrough (amateur) cs1912/ Newcastle United (£30) Jan 1913/ WW1 guest: Crystal Palace/ Crystal Palace (£50) Jan 1919/ Pontypridd Jul 1924

United: (£500) 8 May 1925 to cs1929
Debut: 5 Sep 1925 United 2 Huddersfield Town 3
Last game: 29 Sep 1928 Bury 4 United 0
Exeter City 28 May 1929/ Torquay United Nov 1930/ Crook Town Mar 1931/ Worcester City Sept 1931 to cs1932

After signing for Middlesbrough as an amateur, Jack Alderson became a professional with Newcastle United but made just one FL appearance on 15 January 1913 at home to Woolwich Arsenal. He served in the Army during the First War, based at Woolwich, playing occasionally for Crystal Palace and signing for them in 1919. He was an ever present in their championship winning side of 1920–21 and won an England cap in 1923 but a dispute with Palace over a benefit led to him playing for non-league Pontypridd during the 1924–25 season.

United had won the F A Cup in 1925 but Sutcliffe, the goalkeeper, was regarded as no better than adequate. Jack had a reputation as spectacular rather than sound but had earned an excellent reputation as a penalty saver but there was a doubt about his age and the United Football Committee sanctioned his purchase at a transfer fee of £500 if he was not over thirty years of age. The responsibility for verifying the matter lay with John Nicholson, the United Secretary and the fee was paid to Palace who held his FL registration. The press reported that Alderson was twenty nine, which was far from the truth!

Jack had a fine physique and was certainly fit but the United players thought he was 'a bit dotty'. He often kicked the ball when it seemed more sensible to use his hands and would entertain the crowd by touching the ground without bending his knees. A bit of a character was our Jack.

Appearances:		Apps	Gls
	FL	122	0
	FAC	11	0
	CC	3	0
	ABD	1	0
	Total	137	0

ALLCHURCH Leonard (Len)

OR 1961–65 5' 5½" 11st 0
b. Swansea 12 September 1933

Swansea Town amateur Nov 1949 to pro Oct 1950
United: (£12.5k) 16 Mar 1961 to 5 Sept 1965
Debut: 25 Mar 1961 Leeds United 1 Sheffield United 2
Last games: 10 Apr 1965 United 0 Wolverhampton W 2 (FL)
2 Jun 1965 United 1 Blackpool 2 (Fr in New Zealand)
Stockport County (£5500) Sep 1965/ Swansea City Jul 1969/ Haverfordwest cs 1971

Welsh Schoolboy international Len Allchurch made his FL debut with Swansea Town on 28 April 1951, at home to Grimsby Town, and made 272 FL appearances—some with his elder brother Ivor—with his home town team before joining the Blades.

It was an inspired signing by the United manager John Harris, who had made an earlier offer of £12k that had been rejected. United's promotion challenge to Division One was faltering and Len made an immediate impact, scoring on his debut and adding five more goals in the final seven games, taking United back to the top flight. Playing on the right wing, he was quick thinking, two-footed, with fine ball good control and a deceptive body swerve. He was a good finisher and created many openings for others and although small, he was well able to resist a challenge and he held a proud record of never receiving a booking or caution throughout his FL career. He gained four Welsh caps whilst with United to add to the seven he gained with Swansea.

He moved to Stockport County in September 1965 and won a Division Four Championship medal the following season, returning to Swansea in July 1969 and helping them to gain promotion from Division Four. He played his final game for the 'Swans' in April 1971, almost 20 years after his debut, and then rejoined Ivor at Haverfordwest. He became a hotelier in Swansea before running a leather goods business.

Appearances:		Apps	Gls
	FL	123	32
	FAC	12	2
	LC	9	2
	CC	2	1
	Total	146	37

ALLISON Wayne (Chief) Anthony

Striker 2002–04 6' 1" 12st 6
b. Huddersfield 16 October 1968

Halifax Town Jul 1987/ Watford Jul 1989 (£250k)/ Bristol City Aug 1990(£300k)/ Swindon Town Jul 1995 (£475k)/ Huddersfield Town Nov 1997(£800k)/ Tranmere Rovers Sep 1999 (£300k)
United: (free) 30 Jul 2002 to 25 Jun 2004
Debuts: 31 Jul 2002 Scarborough 0 United 0 (Fr. sub)
10 Aug 2002 Coventry C 2 United 1 (sub)
17 Aug 2002 United 1 Walsall 1
Last game: 9 May 2004 Preston NE 3 United 3
Chesterfield Jul 2004 to Feb 2008/ Chester C coach Aug 2008

Wayne Allison made his FL debut with Halifax Town, coming on as a substitute and scoring at home to Wolves, on 17 March 1987. Four days later, he made his full debut at home to Torquay and again found the net and went on to provide excellent service for five more clubs in the lower divisions.

He joined United in the close season of 2002 at the age of 33 and initially took second place to Iffy Onuora. Following Iffy's injury Wayne, nicknamed 'the Chief', was a regular in the side, being used as a target man where he used his strength, bulk and experience to hold the ball up for others.

More than half his appearances were from the subs bench but he scored some vital goals, particularly in his first season when United reached the play off final and both cup semi finals. In the 2003–04 season, Wayne made 25 sub appearances in the League, a record for a United player in a single season. He undoubtedly gave of his best in whatever role was asked of him and he accepted an extension to his contract for 2004–05 but, with the influx of other strikers, it was agreed that he move to Chesterfield for the start of the season.

He continued to play for the Spireites and in the autumn of 2007, he reached a career total of 750 FL appearances.

Appearances:		Apps	Gls
	FL	29 (44)	7
	PO	0 (2)	0
	FAC	4 (4)	2
	LC	7 (1)	1
	Total	40 (51)	10

ALLOTT H and/or Richard (Dick)

OR 1915

Silverwood/ Chelsea
United: WW1 guest
Only game: 4 Sep 1915 Lincoln City 7 United 3 (WW1)
WW1 guest: Barnsley, Rotherham County, Grimsby Town Denaby U (1920–21)

Brought up in Rawmarsh or Silverwood near Rotherham, Allott had two seasons as a Chelsea reserve player but was a guest player for United in the first game of the 1915–16 war-time season. He played as a guest for several clubs during the First War and was playing for Denaby United during the 1920–21 season.

Appearances:		Apps	Gls
	WW1	1	0
	Total	1	0

ALMOND John (Jack)

IF/ CF 1896–1901 5' 10½" 11st 6
b. Darlington 6 November 1876

Bishop Auckland/ Darlington (by 1894–95)
United: 5 May 1896 to cs 1901
Debut: 19 Sep 1896 United 3 Sunderland 0
Last game: 30 Apr 1901 West Brom A 0 United 2
Gainford (Darlington)/ Millwall Athletic Nov 1901 to cs 1903/ Leeds City ? Oct 1904/ Bradford City Jan 1905/ Doncaster Rovers Mar 1905 to cs 1906

There is still much to be discovered about the life and the death of Jack Almond. In 1897, according to press reports, he inherited from his father, a Yorkshire brewer, six or twelve thousand pounds at a time when the average wage was a little over £2 per week. Almond was twenty one but his wealth didn't prevent him from playing an important part in United's League and Cup successes of 1898 and 1899 and his FA Cup winning medal was sold at auction in 2008.

As a player, he was 'always working, clever with his head' and had a fine sense of positional play and passed the ball well but his play was never dashing or bustling and didn't always appeal to spectators. He lost his form in 1901 and wasn't chosen for the Cup Final and seemingly gave up the game as a professional and took a pub in Gainford, a village west of Darlington and was reported to be playing for the local team. Jack soon returned to senior football with Millwall and played until at least 1906. He was reported as working at the Doncaster locomotive works in 1910 but nothing is certain after that.

There is a mystery over the place and year of his death. A 'John Almond, age 35', died in Liverpool in 1912 but two Sheffield newspapers commented on his presence at a Blades match in Leeds in April 1931 and it was reported that he was the assistant manager of the Griffin Hotel in Leeds and would soon control a residential hotel in Bangor.

Appearances:		Apps	Gls
	FL	109	19
	FAC	13	2
	ABD	3	0
	Total	125	21

ANDERSON Edward Totty

Forward 1906 5' 8" 11st 5
b. Newcastle on Tyne JFM 1884

Willington Athletic
United: 16 May 1905 to cs1906
Only game: 17 Feb 1906 United 1 Derby County 0
Queens Park Rangers 1906

Edward Anderson failed to impress at the Lane and ended his playing career at a senior level with nineteen Southern League games for Queens Park Rangers.

Appearances:		Apps	Gls
	FL	1	0
	Total	1	0

ANDERSON Peter Thomas

OR/WH 1978–79 5' 9½" 11st 0
b. Hendon 31 May 1949

Hendon Town/ Luton Town Feb 1971/ Royal Antwerp (£70k) 1975/ San Diego Sockers Apr May1978/ Tampa Bay Rowdies Jun to Aug 1978

United: (£5000) 12 Sep 1978 to 30 May 1979
Debuts: 23 Sep 1978 (sub) West Ham United 2 United 0
30 Sep 1978 (full) United 0 Luton Town 1
Last game: 5 May 1979 Cambridge United 1 United 0
Tamapa Bay Rowdies Aug 1979 to Sep 1980/ Millwall player-mgr Dec 1980 to Dec 1982

Peter Anderson made his FL debut with Luton Town, on 13 February 1971 at home to Watford but financial problems forced Luton to sell him and, after a period in Belgium and the USA, he was no doubt happy to rejoin his old manager, Harry Haslam at the Lane. A talented attacking player down the right flank, Anderson will be best remembered for his two goals in a televised match against Sunderland including a 'Goal of the Day'. Sadly, the season ended with relegation and his contract was cancelled.

Appearances:		Apps	Gls
	FL	28 (2)	12
	FAC	2	0
	LC	1	0
	Total	31 (2)	12

ANDERSON Walter (Wattie)

Forward 1899–1901 5' 8" 12st 0
b. Thornaby on Tees, October-December 1879
d. Lambeth 2 March 1904

Darlington/ Thornaby Utopians
United: 10 May 1899 to 28 Dec 1901
Debuts: 23 Oct 1899 United 7 Kaffirs 2 (Fr)
18 Nov 1899 Preston North End 0 United 1
Last game: 19 Oct 1901 Small Heath 5 United 1
Woolwich Arsenal Dec 1901/ Plymouth Argyle cs 1903

Walter Anderson made his FL debut as an outside right with United and, although he stayed at Bramall Lane for three seasons, he only played in three other League fixtures and in three friendlies with the first team, all at centre forward.

He played 28 FL games scoring 10 goals for Woolwich Arsenal and moved on to Southern League Plymouth Argyle but was taken ill after a game at Fulham and died a few days later.

Appearances:		Apps	Gls
	FL	4	0
	Total	4	0

ANDERSON William (Bill)

LB/ RB 1933–35 5' 11" 12st 8
b. High Westwood (Newcastle on Tyne) 12 January 1913
d. Radcliffe on Trent 19 February 1986

Medomsley Jrs (Durham)/ Nottingham Forest (trial Aug 1931/ Chopwell Institute Oct 1931
United: (£150) 6 Feb 1932 to 30 May 1935
Debuts: 27 Apr 1933 Derry C 3 United 0 (Fr)
14 Oct 1933 Wolverhampton Wanderers 3 United 2
Last game: 9 Mar 1935 Plymouth A 2 United 0
Barnsley (£170) May 1935 to cs1936/ Bradfod PA (trial 1937)/ Barrow (trial 1937)

A schoolboy international, Bill Anderson played in the same County Durham junior team as 'Jock' Dodds. A resolute and robust reserve defender, he was transferred to Barnsley but his leg was broken in a match against Forest in 1935 and that effectively ended his days as a player.

He qualified as a masseur but any thoughts of a return to the world of football were interrupted until 1945 by the outbreak of the Second War. He became the Lincoln City trainer in 1945, quickly moving on to the position of manager and proved to be one of the very best, achieving promotion and keeping Lincoln City in the Second Division for many years. City's fortunes declined in the sixties and Anderson was forced out in 1966 and worked as assistant-manager for Nottingham Forest until 1975.

Appearances:		Apps	Gls
	FL	23	0
	FAC	1	0
	CC	3	0
	Total	27	0

ANGELL Brett Ashley Mark

Striker 1996 6' 2" 13st 11
b. Marlborough 20 August 1968

Portsmouth (nc) Aug 1986/ Cheltenham Town/ Derby County (£40k) Feb 1988/ Stockport County (£30k) Aug 1988/ Southend United (£100k) Jul 1990/ Everton (L) Sep 1993/ Everton (£500k) Jan 1994/ Sunderland (£600k–750k) Mar 1995
United: (L) 30 Jan 1996 to 28 Feb 1996
Debut: 31 Jan 1996 Luton Town 1 United 0
Last game: 28 Feb 1996 Norwich C 0 United 0
West Bromwich Albion (L) Mar 1996/ Stockport County (L) Aug 1996, (£120k) Nov 1996/ Notts County (L) Dec 1999/ Preston NE (L) Feb 2000/ Walsall Jul 2000/ Rushden & Diamonds Feb 2002/ Port Vale Aug 2002/ Queens Park Rangers Nov 2002

A well built bustling striker and consistent goal scorer in the lower levels of the Football League. Brett Angell made his FL debut with Stockport County on 22 October 1988 at Scarborough. He moved to Southend United and helped them to gain promotion in 1991. Moves to Everton and then Sunderland proved unsuccessful and it was whilst at Sunderland that he moved, on loan, to Bramall Lane to fill the strikers role, vacant since the departure of Nathan Blake.

United's manager, Howard Kendall, had earlier had Brett on loan at Everton and did not regard him as a Premier League player but considered him suitable for United's immediate requirements and so, after six games and two goals he returned to the North East. In August of 1996 he rejoined Stockport County where he helped the club to the semi finals of the Coca Cola Cup and promotion to Division One. There followed moves to several clubs before Brett's League career ended at Queens Park Rangers with a career record of 164 goals in 398(67) games. He later had a spell as youth team coach at Portsmouth.

Appearances:		Apps	Gls
	FL	6	2
	Total	6	2

ANNAN Walter Archibald (Archie)

RB/ LB 1904–05 5' 10" 11st 10
b. Carnwath (Lanarkshire) 23 March 1877

West Calder Aug 1899/ Edinburgh St Bernard's May 1900/ Sunderland Apr 1902
United: 22 Dec 1903 (£200) to 29 Apr 1905
Debut: 9 Jan 1904 Everton 2 United 0
Last games: 11 Feb 1905 United 1 Newcastle United 3
18 Feb 1905 Leeds City 2 United 2 (Fr)
Bristol City Apr 1905/ Burslem Port Vale Jul 1911/ Mid Rhondda player-mgr Aug 1912/ Bristol City Coach Mar 1921

Archie Annan began his FL career at Sunderland, making just one appearance at home to Notts County on 4 April 1903. His first United appearance was on Christmas Day in a reserve game against the Wednesday. He spent 16 months with United, playing mainly at left back. A strong player with a powerful kick, he was placed on the transfer list in the close season of 1904 but it was twelve months later when he transferred to Bristol City.

At Ashton Gate, he played for six seasons and was ever present for the first two. He won a Second Division championship medal in 1906 and a losers medal in the 1909 FA Cup Final. When his football days were over, he served for a time in the Bristol police force.

Appearances:		Apps	Gls
	FL	27	0
	FAC	1	0
	Total	28	0

ANTHONY Graham John

M 1993–97 5' 7" 10st 5
b. South Shields 9 August 1975

United: Jul 1993 to 24 Mar 1997
Debuts: 27 Jul 1993 Bradford C 3 United 0 (Fr)
5 Oct 1994 United 3 Ancona 3 (AIC)
21 Feb 1995 United 2 Burnley 0 (sub)
20 Sep 1995 United 2 Bury 0 (LC)
Last game: 1 Feb 1997 Swindon T 2 United 1
BK IFK Vaasa (Finland) (L) summer 1995/ Scarborough (L) Mar 1996/ Bury(L)/
Swindon Town (nc) Mar 1997/ Plymouth Argyle (nc) Aug 1997/ Carlisle United Nov 1997/ Barrow Aug 2000/ Workington (£2000) cs 2006

Graham Anthony joined United as a trainee in July 1991 but found it difficult to make the breakthrough into the first team squad. He made just three FL appearances, all as a substitute and his full FL debut was with Scarborough on 24 February 1996.

Good passing was a feature of his game and he played regularly for three years with Carlisle United and then, from August 2000, with Barrow where he was twice 'Player of the Year' before moving to Workington. He runs a guest house in Cumbria.

Appearances:		Apps	Gls
	FL	0 (3)	0
	LC	1	0
	AIC	2	0
	Total	3 (3)	3

ARCHER William (Bill) Henry

CH 1941–45
b. Scunthorpe 5 February 1914
d. Scunthorpe 17 October 1992

Scunthorpe & L Utd?/ Gainsborough Trinity (1932–38)/ Grantham Town
United: 8 Feb 1941 to 23 Aug 1945
Debut: 4 Jan 1941 Grimsby Town 3 United 2 (WW2, at Scunthorpe)
Last game: 26 May 1945 Sheffield Wednesday 4 United 2 (WW2)
Lincoln C (small fee) Aug 1945/ Doncaster Rovers 10 Oct 1945 to cs 1949/ Scarborough to cs 1950

United had tried to sign Bill Archer before the outbreak of the First War but he refused to give up his job. He had played 280 games for Gainsborough Trinity in his five seasons there and was awarded a benefit match.

Bill was a typical burly stopper centre half, difficult to deceive and pass who became a regular United player during the War. It may be that Lincoln City had signed Archer in 1939 but Grantham and Lincoln had not retained him and perhaps he was a free agent. In the event, his first game was as a guest player but he was quickly registered with the FL as a United player and he made more than 140 appearances for the Blades before he was transferred to Lincoln City in 1945. A few weeks later he joined Doncaster Rovers, finally making his FL debut on 31 August 1946 at home to Rochdale but that was his only appearance of the season. After 13 appearances towards the end of the following season his FL career came to an end.

He became a partner in a plant hire and engineering business and a director and chairman of Scunthorpe United and recommended Kevin Keegan to United but he was thought too small.

Appearances:		Apps	Gls
	WW2	131	0
	CC	10	0
	Total	141	0

ARMSTRONG Christopher (Chris)

MF/ WB 2003– 5' 10" 10st 8
b. Newcastle on Tyne 5 August 1982

Bury trainee to pro Mar 2001 Oldham Athletic Oct 2001 (£200k)
United: 6 Jul/ 1 Aug 2003 (£100k)
Debuts: 23 Jul 2003 Frechville CA 0 United 9 (Fr)
9 Aug 2003 United 0 Gillingham 0
Blackpool (L) 14 Oct 2005 to 20 Nov 2005

Chris Armstrong had been a youngster on Bury's books when Neil Warnock was their manager. He made his FL debut with Bury at Northampton on 13 January 2001 but soon moved on to Oldham Athletic.

An England youth International, he was signed by Warnock for United in the close season of 2003 and was a regular in the squad though he made most of his appearances from the bench, either on the left side of midfield or as a left wing back. After some encouraging performances, where he showed speed and good use of the ball, he underwent a cartilage operation in December 2003 and, after nearly two seasons out of the game, it did seem his career would be ended.

After a loan spell at Blackpool in October 2005 Chris had to decide whether to play on or accept £250k insurance pay out. He decided to play on and soon became a regular in the promotion side of 2005–06, playing on the left in various roles. A key member of the side in the 2006–07 Premiership campaign, Chris won a Scotland B cap in November 2007 but missed the end of the season through injury.

Appearances:		Apps	Gls
	FL	76 (19)	6
	FAC	3 (1)	0
	LC	4 (1)	0
	Total	83 (21)	6

ARNOTT Kevin William (Ossie)

M 1982–87 5' 10" 11st 13
b. Bensham (Gateshead) 28 September 1958

Sunderland Sep 1976/ Blackburn Rovers(L) Nov 1981
United: **(Free) 22 May 1982 to May 1987**
Debuts: **3 Aug 1982 Raith Rovers 0 United 3 (Fr)**
14 Aug 1982 United 1 Grimsby Town 3 (FLT)
28 Aug 1982 Portsmouth 4 United 1
Last game: **28 Feb 1987 Grimsby Town 1 United 0**
Blackburn Rovers (L) 6 Nov 1982 to 15 Mar 1983/ Rotherham United (L) Mar 1983
Vasalund (Sweden) Jun 1987/ Chesterfield (L) Nov 1987/ Vasalund Mar 1988/ Chesterfield Aug 1988 to Jan 1990/ Sweden/ Gateshead Nov 1990 / – / Nykarbley (Finland) 1992–94/ Hebburn FC 1994/ Jarrow Roofing CA player coach 1995 then asst. manager

An England Youth international, Kevin Arnott was a stylish midfielder with ball control, vision and a great right foot. He began his career as a Sunderland apprentice, signing as a professional before making his FL debut at Leicester on 15 January 1977. He played a key role in Sunderland's promotion to the top flight in 1979–80 but played less well under new manager, Alan Durban. Following a loan spell at Blackburn in 1981 he was on the transfer list at a £350k fee but came to the Lane on a free transfer.

Ian Porterfield, United's manager and a former team-mate, signed Kevin for the start of the 1982–83 campaign but he was not an immediate success, spending the second half of the season on loan with Blackburn Rovers and Rotherham United. The following season he played a key role in United's promotion from the old Division Three. Described by Porterfield as the 'architect', he was a great provider when the team was playing well and became the first Blade to be ever-present in a 46 game League season. In 1987 he moved to Vasalund in Sweden who allowed him to play indoor soccer in Dallas (USA) and then at Saltergate, initially on loan, during the Swedish close season. He returned to England and spent three seasons at Chesterfield until his FL career was ended by a knee injury, playing his final FL game, of 356(7), in December 1990. He later worked in his family building business in South Wearside.

Appearances:		Apps	Gls
	FL	120 (1)	12
	FAC	9	1
	LC	13	1
	AMC	5 (1)	0
	FMC	4	1
	Total	151 (2)	15

ASABA Carl Edward

Striker 2001–03 6' 2" 13st 5
b. Westminster 28 January 1973

Dulwich Hamlet/ Brentford Aug 1994/ Colchester United (L) Feb 1995/ Reading (£800k) Aug 1997/ Gillingham (£600k) Aug 1998
United: **(£92.5k+) 8 Mar 2001 to 6 Aug 2003**
Debut: **10 Mar 2001 United 1 Nottingham F 3**
Last games: **26 May 2003 United 0 Wolves 3 (PO Final, Cardiff)**
2 Aug 2003 United 2 Middlesbrough 3 (Fr) (sub)
Stoke City Aug 2003/ Millwall Aug 2005 to cs 2006/ Leeds United (trial), Leicester City (trial)/ retired Jun 2006

Carl Asaba made his FL debut whilst on loan at Colchester United, scoring the winner at Barnet on 18 February 1995. Signed by Neil Warnock in the hope he would prove to be the '20 goals a season striker', Carl never quite lived up to expectations. Fast, good on the ball and hard working, he perhaps lacked that extra sharpness in front of goal and he had spells out through injury. He looked better playing off a front man but he was often used, less successfully, in that role. His 11minute hat-trick, including two penalties at the Withdean Stadium gave the Blades an improbable victory over Brighton in October 2002 and when he moved to Stoke in 2003, coinciding with Steve Kabba's injury, it left United short of a striker for much of that season.

When he retired from League football he had scored 101 FL goals in 239(71) appearances.

Appearances:		Apps	Gls
	FL	52 (15)	23
	PO	3	0
	FAC	2 (1)	0
	LC	6 (1)	1
	Total	63 (17)	24

ASH Michael (Micky)

IF 1962–65 5' 5" 11st 0
b. Sheffield 4 September 1943

United: **apprentice pro 4 Nov 1960 to 25 Sep 1965**
Debuts: **23 May 1962 St. Louis CYO(USA) 1 United 4 (Fr sub)**
21 Dec 1963 Chelsea 3 United 2
Last games: **28 Dec 1963 United 1 Nottingham Forest 2**
2 Jun 1965 Blackpool 2 United 1 (Fr. In New Zealand)
Scunthorpe United (£2500) Sep 1965/ New York Generals(USA) May 1967/ Atlanta Chiefs(USA) 1968–70/ Boca Juniors(Argentina) 1970–72/ River Plate(Argentina) 1972–74

Micky Ash joined United's ground staff in 1959 and played for England at both schoolboy and youth level. He signed professional forms in November 1960 but, despite being at Bramall Lane for a further five years, he made just three first team appearances, all at inside right and scored on his final appearance. At the end of the following season, he moved to Scunthorpe United and subsequently played in both North and South America.

Micky, whose son played for Rotherham United and Scarborough, ran a computer business in the States.

Appearances:

	Apps	Gls
FL	3	1
Total	3	1

ASHMORE Alfred Maxwell (Max)

G 1957 6' 0" 11st 6
b. Woodhouse (Sheffield) 11 September 1937

United: 24 Aug 1957 to 30 Jun 1961
Only game: 14 Dec 1957 United 0 Leyton Orient 2
Bradford City Jul 1961/ Chesterfield Oct 1962/ Heanor Town cs 1963/ Matlock Town May 1967

Max Ashmore joined United as an amateur during the 1955–56 season. He played just 12 competitive games for his three clubs (all in the League), one for United, nine for Bradford City and two for Chesterfield before moving into non-league football. He later worked in Sheffield.

Appearances:

	Apps	Gls
FL	1	0
Total	1	0

ASHTON Edward (Teddy, Tubby and Mucker)

OL 1936–38 5' 5½" 12st. 0
b. Kilnhurst 19 January 1906
d. Kilnhurst AMJ 1978

Kilnhurst Bible Class/ Rotherham Utd(trial)/ Kilnhurst WMC/ Kilnhurst Athletic/ Mexborough Town Jan 1926/ Barnsley (£200) Nov 1927
United: 29/ 31 Oct 1936 to cs (31 May?) 1938
Debut: 31 Oct 1936 United 5 Aston Villa 1
Last game: 2 Apr 1938 Bradford PA 5 United 1
Carlisle United (free) Aug 1938

A miner and part-time professional with Mexborough, Teddy Ashton made his FL debut for Barnsley on 9 April 1928 at Nottingham Forest and played more than 300 games, scoring seventy goals, for the Oakwell club before moving to Bramall Lane. A big hearted, strong winger he was slow and past his best with United. He served in the army during the early part of the Second War but then returned to his old job as a miner.

Appearances:

	Apps	Gls
FL	35	4
FAC	3	1
CC	1	0
Total	39	5

ATKIN William (Bill) H

G 1939

Thorne Colliery
United: 17 Nov 1938 to cs1946
Debuts: 2 Mar 1940 United 1 Huddersfield Town 3 (Fr)
9 Mar 1940 Chesterfield 5 United 0 (WW2)
Last game: 22 Mar 1940 United 0 Grimsby Town 2 (WW2)

Bill Atkin was signed in 1938, United making a £25 donation to his colliery club. Described as a Bentley man, he played four first team games in goal for the Blades; one friendly and three in the war-time East Midland League.

Appearances:

	Apps	Gls
WW2	3	0
Total	3	0

ATKINS Robert (Bob) Gary

CD 1981–85 6' 0½" 12st 2
b. Leicester 16 October 1962

Leicester City apprentice/ Enderby Town
United: 21 Jul 1982 after a trial during the 1981–82 season to 29 Mar 1985
Debuts: 7 Dec 1981 Barrow 0 United 1 (Fr)
14 Aug 1982 United 1 Grimsby Town 3 (FLT)
28 Aug 1982 Portsmouth 4 United 1
Last games: 1 Jan 1985 United 3 Birmingham C 4
5 Jan 1985 Watford 5 United 0
Preston North End (L) 15 Feb 1985, transfer 29 Mar 1985 to cs 1991

Referred to frequently as 'Atkin', Bob Atkins played for Enderby Town in a pre-season fixture against a United reserve team and came to the Lane for a trial. A strong wholehearted defender, he will always be remembered by Blades' fans for his magnificent vital last minute winning goal at Millmoor in April 1984. He moved to Preston, firstly on loan, in a joint transfer deal with Gary Brazil, and made 198(2) FL appearances for the club.

Appearances:

	Apps	Gls
FL	36 (4)	3
FAC	1	0
LC	6 (1)	0
AMC	4 (1)	0
CC	1	0
Total	48 (6)	3

BADGER Leonard (Len)

RB 1962–76 5' 7½" 10st 9
b. Sheffield 8 June 1945

United: appr signed 20 Aug 1962 to 7 Jan 1976
Debuts: 23 May 1962 St Louis CYC All Stars 1 United 4 (Fr) (sub)
30 May 1962 Edmonton City 0 United 7 (Fr)
23 Oct 1962 Bury 3 United 1 (LC)
26 Apr 1963 United 2 Leyton Orient 0
Last game: 13 Dec 1975 United 1 Manchester United 4
Chesterfield Jan 1976 (£3000)

Len Badger rose through United's junior ranks from Coleridge Road School where he played at right half or inside right but Sheffield Boys used him in his future right back position. He won England schoolboy and youth caps and made his first team debut on tour at the age of sixteen. Towards the end of the 1963–64 season he became the regular right back, replacing Cec Coldwell, a position he held until 1975. He made regular appearances for the England U23 side and three for the Football League, and many felt he was worthy of a full cap but it was not to be. Despite being rather small in stature Len was a fine, polished full back with a calm authority. He always tried to use the ball well, was quick in recovery and he was always prepared to attack—he did play as an inside forward for fourteen games in 1972. He was made captain by John Harris in 1966 but relinquished the position to Eddie Colquhoun in 1968.

Soon after the arrival of Jimmy Sirrel, Len was sold to Chesterfield (46 FL app), managed by his former mentor Joe Shaw. Two serious injuries ended Len's career in 1978 and he became a publican in the Chesterfield area.

Appearances:		Apps	Gls
	FL	457 (1)	7
	FAC	24	0
	LC	29 (1)	0
	ASC	8	1
	CC	18	0
	ABD	2	0
	WC	3	0
	Total	541 (2)	8

BAGNALL Samuel (Sam)

OR 1913–14 5' 7" 11st 8
b. Neepsend (Sheffield) OND 1892

Clowne Rising Star/ Chesterfield Town Oct 1912
United: (£152 10s 0d though United informed the FL in 1919 that the fee had been £350). 25/26/29 Apr 1913 to cs 1914
Debut: 27 Sep 1913 United 1 Blackburn Rovers 1
Last game: 3 Jan 1914 Manchester City 2 United 1
South Liverpool cs 1914/ Welbeck Colliery Dec 1916

Sam Bagnall was fast but lacked confidence and it was once written that he was a 'better sprinter than footballer'. He was wounded in his left shoulder and arm in France in 1916 and discharged from the army.

Appearances:		Apps	Gls
	FL	7	1
	Total	7	1

BAILEY Thomas Graham

RB 1948–49 5' 9½"
b. Dawley (Telford) 22 March 1920

Donnington W/ Huddersfield Town June 1936 (amat), Mar 1937 (pro)
WW2 guest: Bradford PA, Bradford C
United: 13 Mar 1948 to 31 Jul 1950
Debut: 17 Apr 1948 United 0 Huddersfield Town 1
Last game: 4 May 1949 Manchester United 3 United 2

Graham Bailey first played for Huddersfield Town in 1940, and was a regular throughout the Second War when he also made six appearances for the Bradford clubs. His FL debut came on 31 August 1946 at home to Blackpool and he made 33 FL appearances for Town. He came to the Lane with George Hutchinson in a largely unsuccessful exchange for Albert Nightingale. It was ironic that the bulk of his appearances for United came in a relegation season when Huddersfield escaped the same fate with a final day victory. His final season with United was spent with the reserve team.

Appearances:		Apps	Gls
	FL	20	0
	FAC	2	0
	CC	1	0
	Total	23	0

BAINES Reginald (Reg)

CF 1933 5' 11" 12st 0
b. York 3 June 1906
d. Tel Aviv (Israel) 21 October 1974

York City Aug 1924/ Selby Town/ Scarborough/ Selby Town cs 1930/ York City Jul 1931
United: (£500) 4 May 1933 to 15/17 Nov 1934
Debut: 26 Aug 1933 United 0 Tottenham Hotspur 0
Last game: 2 Dec 1933 West Bromwich Albion 3 United 0
Doncaster Rovers (£300) Nov 1934/ York City May 1937/ Barnsley May 1938/ Halifax Town May 1939

Reg Baines had played for York City in their Midland League days as an eighteen year old and returned there in 1931, making his FL debut and scoring on 3 October 1931 at Carlisle United. A bustling, determined player with a good shot, he had scored 58 goals in 71 FL appearances when he was signed by Teddy Davison, United's manager.

He made his debut with the reserves two days after signing but began the new season in the first team as Jimmy Dunne was at first unfit and a month later had been transferred to Arsenal. Baines had been signed as a useful reserve and United were happy when he insisted on retaining his job as a foreman in a York chocolate factory where he eventually worked for fifty years. It had always been unlikely that he would have been an adequate replacement for Dunne and although he did reasonably well, United signed Bill Boyd and his days as a First Division player were over.

In a FL career of 203 appearances, Reg scored 130 goals, an excellent record but the top level had proved a step too far. He died whilst on holiday in Tel Aviv, Israel, in 1974.

Appearances:		Apps	Gls
	FL	10	5
	CC	1	1
	Total	11	6

BAIRSTOW William (Billy)

(other variations on the name:
Bairstoe, Bairsto, Baisto, Baristo, Bastoe and Bastow)

OR/OL/IR/IL 1890–92
b. Sheffield
d. Barnsley

Engineer Wanderers, Sheffield (1889)
United: Mar 1890 to cs 1892
Debuts: 3 Mar 1890 United 2 Newton Heath 1 (Fr)
20 Sep 1890 United 3 Rotherham Town 0 (MCL)
Last game: 31 Mar 1892 Attercliffe 0 United 2 (WCC) at Olive Grove
Penistone Oct 1892/Ardsley/Barnsley St Peters cs 1893 to 1895–96

Billy Bairstow joined United in March 1890 towards the end of the club's first season, playing in ten friendly fixtures on the left wing. The following season he was a regular in the MCL fixtures and local cup competitions as well as continuing to play in a significant number of friendly fixtures but now mainly on the right wing. In his final season (1891–92) he played just five games, but none in the Northern League which the club had now joined, nor did he play in any FA cup games in his time at Bramall Lane. After his move to Barnsley St Peters he was a regular in their side for two seasons and finally made an appearance in the FA Cup. His death was attributed to typhoid fever.

Appearances:		Apps	Gls
	MCL	14	3
	SCC	6	5
	WCC	2	1
	Total	22	9

BAKER George Samuel (Sam)

IL 1943–44

Chesterfield/ Youlgreave 1942–43
United: 11 Oct 1943 to cs 1946
Debut: 16 Oct 1943 Nottingham Forest 4 United 0 (WW2)
Last game: 6 May 1944 United 2 Rotherham United 3 (CC)
WW2 guest: Chesterfield(1943–44), Notts County

Sam Baker had been a Chesterfield player but had not featured in the first team. Described as coming from the Tupton district of Chesterfield, he was a thoughtful, stylish inside left, serving with the fire service when he came to the Lane. He was registered by United with the FL for the 1944–45 and 1945–46 season but may not have played for the club at any level in those two seasons.

Appearances:		Apps	Gls
	WW2	16	6
	CC	1	0
	Total	17	6

BALL John (Jack)

IL 1918–20 5' 8½" 12st 0
b. Hazel Grove 29 September 1899
d. Coventry December 1989

Silverwood Colliery
United: Nov 1918 and May 1919 to May 1921
Debuts: 16 Nov 1918 Grimsby Town 2 United 2 (WW1)
30 Aug 1919 Manchester City 3 United 3
Last game: 23 Oct 1920 Aston Villa 4 United 0
Bristol Rovers May 1921/ Wath Athletic cs 1922/ Bury (£350) May 1923/ West Ham United May 1929/ Coventry City May 1930/ Stourbridge cs 1931/ Hinckley Athletic Sept 1931 to cs1932

Jack Ball may have played an occasional game for Rotherham Town in the early years of the First World War but he was playing for Silverwood Colliery when United gave him a first team opportunity. It was not until May 1919, when registrations by the FL for the first post-war season began, that he became officially a United player and the club recognised this fact in August by making a £10 donation to the Colliery team.

He was a strong player with a powerful shot but United released him and, after a less than successful season with Bristol Rovers, he was playing in the Midland League when Bury, then a Second Division side, signed him. Twelve months later, his new club were promoted and he went on to win an England cap. He ended his career having scored 110 FL goals in 269 games, mainly with Bury.

Appearances:		Apps	Gls
	FL	6	0
	WW1	8	4
	Total	14	4

BARBER

OL 1890

Sheffield FC
United: guest
Only game: 27 Sep 1890 United 0 Long Eaton Rangers 1 (MCL)

Almost certainly, this was Mr A D Barber, a member of the Sheffield Club who also played for the amateur eleven in a pre-season practice match against the United professionals

Appearances:		Apps	Gls
	MCL	1	0
	Total	1	0

BARCLAY Robert (Bobby)

IR 1931–37, 1944–45 5' 8" 10st 10
b. Scotswood 27 October 1906
d. Huddersfield 13 July 1969

Scotswood United Church/ Bell's Close Amateurs/ Allendale/ Scotswood/ Derby County 9 Feb 1927
United: (£3500) 5 Jun 1931 to 15/16 Mar 1937
Debut: 29 Aug 1931 United 1 Portsmouth 2
Last game: 13 Mar 1937 United 5 Chesterfield 0
Huddersfield Town Mar 1937 to cs 1946
WW2 guest: Barnsley, Bradford PA, Sheff Utd, Bradford City, York City, Crewe Alexandra, Oldham Ath
United: WW2 guest
First game: 4 Nov 1944 United 3 Grimsby Town 1
Last game: 17 Mar 1945 Derby County 3 United 2
Hurst FC (Cheshire County League) 2 Jul 1946

Bobby Barclay made his FL debut with Derby County at Newcastle on 15 December 1928 and he scored 26 League and Cup goals in 64 appearances before moving to the Lane. He was a clever, unselfish player who could thread his way through a defence in a seemingly effortless style. He was cool and methodical and yet could move with rapier like darts and a fine body swerve taking the ball with supreme confidence right up to his opponent. He wasn't a good shot however and his play perhaps lacked a little fire. His subtle footwork and constructive passing earned him three England caps and he was a key figure in the excellent United 1936 Cup Final forward line which lacked only a first class left winger. Bobby scored in his final FL game for United as he also did on his last guest appearance in 1945.

He was transferred to Huddersfield Town, with Eddie Boot, for a joint fee of £7000 in March 1937 and was yet again on the losing side when Town were defeated in the 1938 Cup Final. When the War ended, he finished his playing days with Hurst in the Cheshire League before returning to Leeds Road as an assistant trainer and was also a coach in Holland. He had scored 109 goals in 368 FL appearances.

Appearances:		Apps	Gls
	FL	231	67
	FAC	18	3
	CC	7	2
	WW2	8	5
	Total	264	77

BARDSLEY Philip (Phil) Anthony

LWB 2007–08 5' 11" 11st 8
b. Salford 28 June 1985

Manchester United from trainee Jul 2003/ Royal Antwerp (Belgium) (L) Jan to May 2004/ Burnley (L) Mar 2006/ Glasgow Rangers (L) Aug 2006/ Aston Villa (L) Jan 2007
United: (L) 15 Oct 2007 to Jan 2008
Debut: 20 Oct 2007 United 1 Preston North End 1
Last game: 1 Jan 2008 Wolverhampton Wanderers 0 United 0
Sunderland (£2m) Jan 2008

Phil Bardsley made his League debut with Manchester United on 24 September 2005 at home to Blackburn Rovers, after having played in the League, FA and European Cups. He spent various spells on loan and joined United on that basis as Bryan Robson sought to tighten the defence following Derek Geary's injury. Phil played impressively during his time at the Lane, defending well, being comfortable on the ball and dangerous when coming forward.

It seemed that Phil was going to join United on a permanent basis but in due course he returned to Old Trafford and signed for Sunderland.

Appearances:		Apps	Gls
	FL	16	0
	Total	16	0

BARKE John Lloyd

CH 1934–37 5' 10½" 12st 0
b. Nuncargate (Notts) 16 December 1912
d. Kirkby in Ashfield 7 March 1976

Annesley Colliery/ Chesterfield(amateur)/ East Kirkby Welfare/ Bleak Hall United/ Mansfield Town(trial)/ Scunthorpe & Lindsey United Jul 1932
United: 27 May 1933 to 1 May 1937
Debuts: 30 Apr 1934 United 6 Shamrock Rovers 4 (Duggan Cup)
20 Apr 1935 Hull City 0 United 3
Last game: 2 Jan 1937 Newcastle United 4 United 0
Mansfield Town (£80) 26 June 1937/ WW2 guest: Notts C Denaby United cs 1947/ Sutton T 1950/ Ilkeston Town 1951/ Belper Town 1952/ Heanor Town 1953 to 1954

Essentially a rather crude reserve player at the Lane, John Barke gave yeoman service to Mansfield Town as a hard working, tough tackling half back, making 117 FL appearances. He was the acting manager at Field Mill towards the end of the War and then had a succession of non-League player-manager appointments until he was forty.

Appearances:		Apps	Gls
	FL	6	0
	CC	1	0
	Total	7	0

BARKER Thomas (Tom) G

LH 1941–44

Norfolk Juniors
United: 17 Oct 1941 (amateur), 4/5/8 Dec 1941 (pro) to 4 May 1946
Debut: 18 Oct 1941 Barnsley 2 United 1 (WW2)
Last game: 6 May 1944 United 2 Rotherham United 3 (CC)

Tom Barker was reported to be from the Mexborough area, working at the Osborn factory in Sheffield and to have had trials with Wolves and Barnsley. Most of Tom's appearances came in season 1941–42 when he played in more than half the games. He was playing in the A team in his final season.

Appearances:		Apps	Gls
	WW2	24	0
	CC	2	0
	Total	26	0

BARLOW Frank Charles

MF 1965–72 5' 9½" 11st 9
b. Mexborough 15 October 1946 (or Sheffield ?)

United: jnr 1963, pro 27 Aug/1 Sep 1965 to 9 Aug 1972
Debuts: 6 Dec 1965 Arsenal 6 United 2 (sub)
25 Mar 1966 Stoke City 2 United 0
Last game: 29 Mar 1972 Chelsea 2 United 0
Chesterfield (£15k) Aug 1972 to 1976, coach Sep 1976, caretaker mgr 1976, mgr Sep 1980 to Jun 1983/ Scunthorpe United mgr Aug 1984–Mar 1987/ various coaching roles/ Nottingham Forest Jan 2005 coach, caretaker mgr 2006/ Hull City coach, caretaker mgr 2 days Jun 2006, to Oct 2006 / – / Bradford City coach Feb 2007/ Wigan asst mgr Jun 2007, caretaker mgr Nov 2007

Educated at Mexborough Grammar School, Frank Barlow was one of several Don & Dearne Schoolboys spotted by scout Archie Clark and signed by John Harris. An outstanding young footballer, Frank captained the England Schoolboys team and opted for a career in football rather than taking a university chemistry course.

He made his first team debut at Highbury as a substitute, coming on with United trailing 5–1, when David Munks' leg was broken. In April 1966, he appeared to have secured a permanent place in the mid-field of the first team but he lacked pace, power and self-belief and never revealed the quality that many expected and he lost his place with Munks and Barry Wagstaff usually preferred. Frank could play in both defensive and attacking midfield roles but only in season 1969–70 could he be said to have been a regular member of the side. He was a thoughtful and honest player, often more successful in away matches where his anticipation and tackling could be used to shackle a dangerous opponent and to provide extra cover for the defence but his playing career was ultimately disappointing.

He moved to Chesterfield (140(1) FL app) for what was at the time, a record fee for the Saltergate club but gave up playing in 1976 after a series of knee problems and became Chesterfield's first team coach. After managing Chesterfield and Scunthorpe United he then had a long career in the game, mainly as a coach or assistant manager with Barnsley, Sheffield Wed, Birmingham City, Bristol City and Walsall being among the clubs he served and in 2005 he became joint acting manager of Nottingham Forest after the departure of Gary Megson. There followed other coaching roles and 2 days as caretaker manager at Hull City while they awaited the arrival of their new manager.

In 2007 he had a brief spell as caretaker manager of Premiership side Wigan and became First Team coach on Steve Bruce's arrival.

Appearances:

	Apps	Gls
FL	116 (5)	2
FAC	5	0
LC	9	0
CC	7 (1)	1
WC	0 (1)	0
Total	137 (7)	3

BARNES David

LB 1989–94 5' 10" 11st 1
b. Paddington 16 November 1961

Coventry City appr Aug 78, pro May 1979/ Ipswich Town May1982/ Wolves (£35k) Oct 1984/ Aldershot (£17k) Aug 1987
United: (£52k) United 11 Jul 1989 to 13/14 Jan 1994
Debuts: 23 Jul 1989 TuS Celle 2 United 2 (Fr) (sub)
24 Jul 1989 TSV Havelse 0 United 6 (Fr)
9 Aug 1989 Scarborough 1 United 3 (YHC)
19 Aug 1989 West Bromwich Albion 0 United 3
Last games: 2 Oct 1993 Southampton 3 United 3
5 Oct 1993 United 2 Blackpool 0 (LC)
Watford (£50k) Jan 1994/ Colchester United Aug 1996 to Mar 1997

David Barnes was a Barnardo Boy and grew up in the Felixstowe area. He became a Coventry City apprentice making his FL debut at Bolton Wanderers, on 15 April 1980 and in that same year he helped England win the UEFA International Youth Tournament. A move to Ipswich was not a success and his time with Wolves was worse as they were relegated from Division Two to Division Four and a transfer to Aldershot must have been a reality shock for a player whose football career had begun so brightly.

A fine left sided defender, two footed and comfortable on the ball, David was signed by Dave Bassett soon after the Blades had been promoted to Division Two. Apart from injuries, he was a regular in the side for two seasons and was an important member of the team which took the Blades back to the top level of English football and fought successfully to keep them there. Bassett wasn't satisfied however and David rejected a move to Bristol City and there were contract disputes in the 1991–92 season. The arrival of Tom Cowan in 1991 and Roger Nilsen in 1993 made his position less secure and led to a transfer to Watford. Knee injuries ended his career in March 1997 having played 288(4) FL games.

Appearances:

	Apps	Gls
FL	82	1
FAC	14	0
LC	6	0
FMC	4	0
YHC	1	0
Total	107	1

BARNES Phillip (Phil) Kenneth

G 2004–06 6' 1" 11st 1
b. Sheffield 2 March 1979

Rotherham United from trainee Jun 1997/ Blackpool (£100k) Jul 1997
United: (free) 2 Jul 2004 to 29 Jun 2006
Debuts: 19 Jul 2004 Tavistock 2 United 5 (Fr)
26 Feb 2005 United 1 Rotherham United 0
Last game: 7 Jan 2006 United 1 Colchester United 2 (FAC)
Torquay United (L) Feb 2005/ Queens Park Rangers (L) Feb 2006
Grimsby Town (fee undisclosed) Jun 2006

Phil Barnes made his FL debut with Rotherham United, at home to York City, on 26 April 1997. After a lengthy spell at Blackpool where he made over 150 first team appearances, he jumped at the chance to join the club he had supported as a boy as cover for Paddy Kenny. His opportunities were limited and during his first season other 'keepers were brought in on loan when Paddy was injured. During the 2005–06 season, Phil played only in Cup games and it was not surprising that he was allowed to leave in the summer of 2006.

He joined Grimsby where he was ever present in his first season with the Mariners and by the end of 2007–08 he had a total of 238 FL appearances.

Appearances:		Apps	Gls
	FL	1	0
	FAC	1	0
	LC	3	0
	Total	5	0

BARNES William (Billy) Edwin

IR/IL/OL 1899–1902 5' 9" 11st
b. Stratford (East London) 28 July 1877
d. Letchworth 26 January 1962

Leyton and Thames Ironworks (amateur)
United: Apr 1899 to May 1902
Debuts: 17 Apr 1899 Brentford 2 United 5 (Fr)
30 Dec 1899 United 5 Everton 0
Last games: 26 Apr 1902 United 2 Southamton 1 (FACF)
28 Apr 1902 Derby County 3 United 1
West Ham United May 1902 (Joint transfer with W. Biggar)/ Luton Town cs1904/ Queens Park Rangers cs1907/ Southend United 25 June 1913

An east London amateur forward with Leyton, Billy Barnes also assisted the Thames Ironworks club. With a fine burst of speed, good ball control and a good shot, Barnes joined United and became a professional player; Leyton asked United for a £10 donation but were refused. Billy scored twice on his FL debut but his first team opportunities were limited because of the quality of the existing first team players but he was a good player to have in reserve.

His place in the history of the game changed when Walter Bennett, the United international forward, was injured in the 1902 Cup Final. United had drawn with Southampton and Barnes was brought in for the replay and scored the winning goal. United travelled back to Sheffield on the Monday, stopping off at Derby to play the final FL game of the season and it proved to be Billy's final game for the club for he returned to London almost immediately.

He had received a message stating 'family claims rendering it desirable that he should play in future nearer his home in Leytonstone' and a rapid transfer to West Ham United was arranged. One strange result of these events is that no photograph of the United Cup winning team appears to have been taken. The 'Cup winning' team photograph that appears in all publications is the team that appeared in the first drawn game and Barnes is the 'unseen' hero. At one time his Cup medal was stolen but it was bought by United and presented to his son. Happily, it is now on display at Bramall Lane.

Billy returned to London—where the family had a silversmiths business—and had a long career in the Southern League making over 330 appearances before moving to Spain in the close season of 1914 to work as a coach with Athletico Bilbao. He returned to England to enlist in the army but returned to Spain as a coach from 1918 to 1921.

Appearances:		Apps	Gls
	FL	23	7
	FAC	2	1
	ABD	1	0
	Total	26	8

BARNSHAW Robert (Bob) James (or John)

CH 1913–14 5' 10" 11st 7
b. Hebburn 14 March 1889
d. Watford 30 January 1974

Hebburn Argyle/ Pelaw/ Sheffield Wednesday Nov 1910 to cs 1911/ Hebburn Argyle
United: (£10 plus £50 plus £30) 1 May 1913 to 19 May 1914
Debut: 1 Nov 1913 Bolton Wanderers 3 United 1
Last game: 14 Mar 1914 Chelsea 2 United 0
WW1 guest: Sheff U reserves/ Leeds C/ Darlington Forge Albion
Watford (£50) 20 May 1914 to cs 1921 Aberdare Athletic June 1922 to cs 1922

Bob Barnshaw was a Wednesday player but a knee injury brought his career at Owlerton to an end before he had played for the first team and it was nearly a year later before he began to play again with his former club, Hebburn Argyle. Wednesday had retained his FL registration however, and United paid their city rivals £10 to secure his transfer as well as a £50 donation to the Hebburn club with a promise of a further £30 if he secured a place in the first team.

One of the old style centre halves, playing a more forward role, Bob had a hard shot but was transferred at the end of the season only returning to play a few games for our reserves at the start of the War time 1915–16 season. He also played as a 'guest' for Leeds City on Christmas Day 1916 and also assisted the Darlington Forge team.

Appearances:		Apps	Gls
	FL	3	0
	Total	3	0

BARNSLEY Andrew (Andy)

D 1986–88 6' 0" 11st 7
b. Sheffield 9 June 1962

Frecheville Community Assoc/ Denaby United/ Rotherham United Jun 1985
United: (£25–35k) 12 Jul 1986 to 14/15 Dec 1988
Debuts: 1 Aug 1986 United 1 Seville 1 (Fr)
23 Aug 1986 United 1 Shrewsbury Town 1
Last games: 10 Sep 1988 Gillingham 2 United 1
5 Nov 1988 Huddersfield Town 3 United 2 (sub)
13 Dec 1988 United 2 Chester City 2 (SVT)
Rotherham United (£30k) 14 Dec 1988/ Carlisle United Aug 1991/ Buxton cs1993/ Frickley Athletic cs1994

Andy Barnsley was 21 before he became a professional. An apprentice engineer in Sheffield, he was playing for Denaby United when Rotherham United offered him a game in their Reserves. Manager Norman Hunter offered him a one year contract and Andy made his FL debut at Bolton, on 17 August 1985.

At the end of the year he joined the Blades and in his first two seasons Andy was a regular in the side, playing mainly at right back but with a spell in a more central defensive role. When United were relegated to Division Three, Dave Bassett offered Andy a new contract but he decided to move back to Rotherham, helping the Millers to win the Division Four Championship. A move to Carlisle was followed by a spell in non-League football, which came to an end with a broken leg. He made 231(12) FL appearances. He still lives in Sheffield and is a financial sales manager.

Appearances:		Apps	Gls
	FL	73 (4)	0
	PO	2	0
	FAC	6 (1)	0
	LC	3	0
	AMC	2	0
	FMC	3	0
	YHC	0 (1)	0
	Total	89 (6)	0

BARNWELL John

WH/IF 1970–71 5' 8" 11st 7
b. Newcastle 24 December 1938

Bishop Auckland 1954/ Arsenal Nov 1956/ Nottingham Forest (£30k) Mar 1964
United: (£20k) 24 Apr/ 1 May 1970 to 18 Jan 1972
Debuts: 25 Apr 1970 Sheffield Wednesday 3 United 3 (BM)
1 Aug 1970 Aldershot 0 United 6 (WC)
15 Aug 1970 Orient 3 United 1
Last game: 16 Jan 1971 Bolton W 2 United 1
Hereford U asst mgr/Peterborough United asst mgr to mgr May 1977–Nov 1978/ Wolverhampton Wanderers mgr Nov 1979–Jan 1982 / – / Saudi Arabia/ AEK Athens mgr/ Notts County mgr Jun 1987–Dec 1988/ Walsall mgr Jan 1989–Mar 1990 / – / Northampton Town mgr Sep 1993–Dec 1994 / – / Grantham T mgr Feb to Jul 1996

John Barnwell began his career at Arsenal making his FL debut at Sunderland on 13 April 1957 and won England caps at youth and U23 level. An intelligent player with good control, passing ability and flair, John moved to Nottingham Forest but was injury prone in his last two seasons and the decision by United to sign him was unwise. His playing days ended early in 1972 when his contract was cancelled after a FL career of 319(8) appearances.

He turned to coaching and also had spells as a manager with various clubs before becoming the Chief Executive of the League Managers Association in the summer of 1996.

Appearances:		Apps	Gls
	FL	9	2
	FAC	1	0
	CC	1	0
	WC	2	0
	Total	13	0

BARRASS Malcolm (Matt) Williamson

CH 1956–57 5' 11½" 13st
b. Blackpool 15 December 1924

Ford Motors (Manchester)/ Wolves(trial)/ Bolton Wanderers amateur Aug, pro Nov 1944
United: (£4160) 27/28 Sep 1956 to 30 Jun 1958
Debut: 29 Sep 1956 United 1 West Ham United 0
Last game: 19 Jan 1957 Bristol City 5 United 1
Wigan Athletic player-mgr cs 1958 to 1 Jan 1959/ Nuneaton Borough mgr c1959–60/ Pwlleli trainer 1961/ Hyde U trainer 1962

The son of a Blackpool, Wednesday and Manchester City inside forward, Malcolm Barrass played over 400 games for Bolton Wanderers, gaining three full England caps and playing in a Victory international and twice for the Football League. He began his career in 1944, during the Second War, as a forward, and made his FL debut for Bolton at home to Stoke City, on 11 September 1946, scoring twice. He moved to wing half but was at his best as a centre half, playing in that position for England and in the memorable 1953 'Matthews' FA Cup Final.

He was brought to the Lane by Joe Mercer to replace Joe Shaw at centre half as Mercer judged that Shaw was not tall or powerful enough for that position. It was a decision which soon proved to be wrong for Malcolm was past his best and was now too slow and ponderous. After several poor displays including being left chasing shadows by John Ateyo, the Bristol City forward, he was dropped and spent the last fifteen months of his time with United in the reserve team.

After a short period in management, he became a sales representative in the Bury area whilst acting as trainer firstly at Pwllheli and then Hyde United.

Appearances:		Apps	Gls
	FL	18	0
	FAC	3	0
	Total	21	0

BARRETT Earl Delisser

D 1998 5' 10" 11st 7
b. Rochdale 28 April 1967

Manchester City from trainee Apr 1985/ Chester C(L) Mar 1986/ Oldham Athletic (£35k) Nov 1987/ Aston Villa (£1.7m) Feb 1992/ Everton (£1.7m) Jan 1995

United: (L) 16 Jan 1998 to 23 Feb 1998
Debut: 17 Jan 1998 United 1 Wolves 0
Last game: 22 Feb 1998 Birmingham City 2 United 0
Sheffield Wednesday Feb 1998/ retired Dec 1999

Earl Barrett made his FL debut whilst on loan at Chester City, away to Mansfield Town on 4 March 1986. A fine consistent full and occasional wing-back, he suffered injury problems but during his career he gained 3 full England caps as well as caps at U21, B level and he also represented the Football League.

He was signed on a month's loan by Nigel Spackman when Vas Borbokis was unavailable and performed well both at full back and centre back. He signed for a second month and there were suggestions that he might join the Blades on a permanent basis but he moved on a free transfer to Sheffield Wednesday only to suffer a knee injury in October which ended his career.

After retiring, with 401(10) FL appearances, he worked with young people in the community and was involved with various campaigns to eradicate racism from football. He appeared in 'Celebrity Stars in their Eyes' as Marvin Gaye and became Events Organiser with Manchester City.

Appearances:		Apps	Gls
	FL	5	0
	Total	5	0

BARRETT P

(other variations of the name are Barrell? (FL), Barratt and Barritt)

OR 1918

United: guest
Debut: 30 Nov 1918 Bradford City 0 United 0 (WW1)
Last game: 28 Dec 1918 United 0 Hull City 0 (WW1)

An air mechanic with the Flying Corps, the Telegraph reported that 'he shaped quite well' but later grumbled that he held the ball too long. He may have been the P J Barritt, a 'native of Rotherham', a winger who played for Rotherham County reserves in the 1919–20 season and he may have played once for Bury in 1918 and for Bradford (Oct–Dec 1917) and for Bradford City (Apr 1917 and 1917–18).

Appearances:		Apps	Gls
	WW1	6	0
	Total	6	0

BARTON Harold

OR 1934–43 5' 8½" 11st 8 to 12st
b. Leigh 3 August 1910
d. Sheffield JAS 1969

Whitegate Juniors(Blackpool)/ Prescot Aug 1927/ Stockport C (trial)/ Liverpool Nov 1928

United: (£1600) 15/18 Jun 1934 to Mar 1944 or 8 Oct 1945
Debut: 25 Aug 1934 Port Vale 2 United 0
Last games: 29 Apr 1939 Coventry City 0 United 3
8 May 1939 United 0 Sheffield Wednesday 0 (CC)
30 Oct 1943 United 1 Barnsley 0 (WW2)
WW2 guest: Bradford (1939–40, 1940–41), Chesterfield (1939–40), Lincoln City (1940–41), Rotherham United (1943–44, 1944–45), Sheffield Wednesday (1943–44)
Denaby U Oct 1946

Harold Barton made his FL debut with Liverpool on 9 October 1929 at home to Blackburn Rovers and went on to make 106 FL and Cup appearances and score 29 goals for the club. Normally an outside right, he scored all four goals at Chesterfield playing at centre forward in a cup-tie and scored a hat trick against Everton in a League match. He lost his place in the Liverpool team to Nieuwenhuys, a South African player, and was signed by Teddy Davison for United in the close season of 1934.

Two footed and very fast, he had good ball control and he could pass an opponent on both sides with ease and his shooting was both hard and accurate. An ideal winger you might think but Barton had his weaknesses and there were many in the crowd who were not slow to voice their opinions. Some said he was moody and others, more bluntly, that he 'disappeared' if his opponent didn't play in the spirit of the old Corinthians. Barton asked for a transfer in December 1935 but came back

to play well as United reached the Cup Final and it was from one of his fine centres, that Jock Dodds headed the ball against the cross-bar.

United accepted an offer from Spurs of £2500 for Harold in May 1936 but he remained at the Lane and he was offered to Bradford in 1938 at the same price. He put in another transfer request after crowd abuse in January 1939 but again came back as United returned to the First Division though he may not have been surprised in the close season to learn that the only significant signing of that summer was an outside right.

Barton worked in Sheffield during the war. He made occasional appearances for United in the first season but none in 1940–41 returning to play regularly from September 1941 until October 1943 when he began to play as a guest for Rotherham. More mature by now, he was a superb winger and a good man with a spot kick as he proved with a hat trick of penalties for the Millers at Barnsley. When he gave up playing, he became a publican in Sheffield and a regular as a spectator at the Lane.

Appearances:		Apps	Gls
	FL	184	41
	FAC	19	5
	CC	11	1
	WW2	76	27
	Total	290	74

BATES Francis (Frank) George

G 1917–19 5' 8½" 11st 7
b. Eckington OND 1890
d. Chesterfield 6 August 1947

Staveley Lowgates/ Eckington Red Rose (5 seasons)/ Beighton Recreation/ Eckington Rovers cs 1917
United: **Guest player between Nov 1917 and Jan 1919**
Debut: **24 Nov 1917 United 1 Huddersfield Town 0 (WW1)**
Last games: **1 Jan 1919 Barnsley 2 United 2 (WW1)**
4 Jan 1919 Hull City 4 United 0 (WW1 abd)
WW1 guest: Crystal P
Beighton Rec/ Barnsley Aug 1920/ Scunthorpe & L Utd cs 1921

Frank Bates played regularly for United during the 1917–18 season when Ernest Blackwell injured his collar bone and also in the early part of the last wartime season of 1918–19. It was also reported that he had assisted Crystal Palace during his army service. Frank made his FL debut for Barnsley on 13 November 1920 at home to Clapton Orient and made eight FL and Cup appearances.

Appearances:		Apps	Gls
	WW1	22	0
	Abd	1	0
	Total	23	0

BATTERSBY Anthony (Tony)

F 1993–95 5' 11½" 11st 8
b. Doncaster 30 August 1975

United: **Youth trainee to pro 5 Jul 1993 to 8 Jan 1996**
Debuts: **14 Dec 1992 Worksop 3 United 1 (sub BM)**
6 Sep 1994 Piacenza 2 United 2 (sub AIC)
12 Sep 1995 United 2 Charlton Athletic 0 (sub)
17 Sep 1995 Barnsley 2 United 2
Last game: **23 Dec 1995 Stoke City 2 United 2**
Southend (L) 23 Mar 1995/ BKI (Fin) (L) cs 1995/
Notts County Jan 1996 (£150/200k)/Bury (L) Mar 1997, May (£120/125k)/ Lincoln City Aug 1998 (£75k)/ Northampton Town (L) Sep 1999/ Boston United Oct 2002/ Hucknall Town/Rushden & Diamonds Feb 2003/ Stevenage Borough Mar 2003/ Gravesend & Northfleet/ Cambridge City/Kings Lynn/ Grays Aug 2005/ AFC Wimbledon Mar 2006/ Chelmsford City Jul 2006/ Welling United (L)/ Stamford cs 2007/ Corby T Feb 2008

Tony made his FL debut whilst on loan at Southend, coming on as a sub at Bristol City on 25 March 1995 and making his full debut at home to Burnley on 8 April. A very promising, long striding forward, his career never reached the level expected when he was a youngster. Unusually, his first three goals in the FL came with three different clubs. He went on to make 170(84) FL appearances, roughly half of them for Lincoln, scoring 41 goals before moving into non-League football.

Appearances:		Apps	Gls
	FL	3 (7)	1
	LC	1 (1)	0
	AIC	2 (1)	1
	Total	6 (9)	2

BATTY William (Billy)

IL 1907–10 5' 9½" 10st
b. Killamarsh (NE Derbys) 13 July 1886 or Chapeltown, nr Sheffield or Ormskirk.
d. 1974?

Thorncliffe c1904/ Mortomley 1905–06/ High Green Swifts/
United: **amat 14 Apr 1906, pro May 1907 to 3/4/7 Apr 1910**
Debut: **28 Sep 1907 United 4 Blackburn Rovers 2**
Last game: **2 Apr 1910 Bury 2 United 0**
WW1 guest: Darfield, Doncaster R (1915), Barnsley (1915–16)
Bristol City (£275) Apr 1910/ Lincoln City cs 1911/ Swindon Town May 1912
Barnsley June 1922 (player-coach)

A stylish inside forward, Batty scored on his debut with United but never looked likely to hold a regular place with the first team. He made five appearances with Bristol City and then joined Lincoln City who were then in the CL. He was more successful with Swindon (110 SL appearances, 44 goals) and played for the Southern League. He returned to south Yorkshire in 1915 and resumed his old job as a miner and made 21appearances for Barnsley in 1915–16. He played again for Swindon after the war before ending his FL career with one match with Barnsley in a season when he was engaged as a player-coach.

Appearances:		Apps	Gls
	FL	38	7
	FAC	2	1
	Total	40	8

BAXTER Lee Stuart

G 2003 6' 1" 13st 6
b. Helsingborg, Sweden 17 July 1975

Apprentice Blackburn Rovers/ Hiroshima/ Vissel Kobe/ AIK Solna Stockholm/ Malmo
United: 4 Dec 2003(L)
Only game: 6 Dec 2003 Burnley 3 United 2
IFK Goteborg/ Bodens/ Malmo 2005/Landskrona BoIS 2006–07/AIK Stockholm goalkeeper coach 2008

With no senior goalkeepers available, Lee Baxter was signed only two days before the game at Burnley, along with Alan Fettis. To the surprise of many, Lee began the game but, after two crucial errors, both leading to goals, he was substituted at half time, thus Lee and Fettis, both goalkeepers, made their club debuts in the same game. This was not only Lee's only appearance for United but also in English football. He left the club later that month, returning to Sweden.

Appearances:		Apps	Gls
	FL	1	0
	Total	1	0

BEAGRIE Peter Sydney

Forward 1986–88 5' 8½" 9st 10 to 10st
b. North Ormesby 28 November 1965

Guisborough/ Middlesbrough jnr to pro Sep 1983
United: (£35k) 8/11/16 Aug 1986 to 29 Jun 1988
Debuts: 16 Aug 1986 York City 1 United 1 (Fr)
23 Aug 1986 United 1 Shrewsbury Town 1 (sub)
25 Aug 1986 West Bromwich A 1 United 0
Last games: 7 May 1987 Huddersfield Town 0 United 2
18 May 1987 United 1 Bristol City 1 (PO)
Stoke City (£210/215k) Jun 1988/ Everton (£750k) Nov 1989/ Sunderland (L) Sep 1991/ Manchester City (£1.1m) Mar 1994/ Bradford City (£50k) Jul 1997/ Everton (L) Mar 1998/ Wigan Athletic Feb 2001/ Scunthorpe United Jul 2001/ Grimsby T Jul 2006/ retired Oct 2006

Peter Beagrie made his FL debut as a substitute with Middlesbrough on 2 October 1984 at Oldham and his full debut at Grimsby on 22 December. He was signed for United by Billy McEwan—the fee set by a tribunal—and he was virtually ever-present for two seasons with United, usually on the left wing.

Tricky and quick with two good feet, he provided searching crosses and he also possessed a fierce shot and was a good header of the ball. An England Under 21 and B international, Peter would celebrate his goals with a back-flip somersault but although he had all the skills, tackled and worked hard, he was a frustrating player, often ignoring the simple ball, delaying his centres and confusing his colleagues. This, and his inconsistency was too much for new manager Dave Bassett and Peter was sold to Stoke City—£160k to United, the remainder to Middlesbrough—following United's relegation at the end of the 1987–88 season.

Peter went on to have a long career in the game, playing beyond the age of 40 and scoring 90 goals in 581(89) FL games. Recently he has also acted as a pundit on TV.

Appearances:		Apps	Gls
	FL	81 (3)	11
	PO	2	0
	FAC	5	0
	LC	5	0
	FMC	2	0
	Total	95 (3)	11

BEARD Mark

RB/MF 1995–98 5' 10" 11st 3
b. Roehampton 8 October 1974

Wimbledon (schoolboy)/ Millwall trainee to pro Mar 1993
United: (£117.5k) 16/18 Aug 1995 to cs 1998
Debuts: 19 Aug 1995 United 0 Tranmere Rovers 2 (sub)
26 Aug 1995 Oldham Athletic 2 United 0
Last games: 4 Mar 1997 United 3 Port Vale 0
24 Jan 1998 Ipswich Town 1 United 1 (FAC)
3 Mar 1998 United 0 Ipswich Town 1 (sub)
7 Mar 1998 Coventry City 1 United 1 (FAC sub)
Southend United (L) 24 Oct 1997
Southend United Jul 1998/ Kingstonian cs 2000/ Southend United Oct 2001/ Kingstonian June 2003/ San Pedro (Spain) player coach/ Banstead 2005/ Stevenage Borough Jun 2006 to May 2007/ St Albans City player mgr

Mark made his FL debut with Millwall, the club where he began his career as a trainee, on 2 October 1993 at home to Watford. He was signed by Dave Bassett, just after the start of the 1995–96 season, and had a good run in the side, generally as a right wing back but occasionally in midfield. A determined defender, he then struggled to hold a regular place and was placed on the transfer list at the start of the 1996–97 season. He featured little during the following two seasons before being given a free transfer.

In due course, after 168(51) FL appearances, Mark moved into non-League football and had the honour of being on the winning side when Stevenage won the FA Trophy in 2007, the first club side to win a cup at the new Wembley.

Appearances:		Apps	Gls
	FL	22 (16)	0
	FAC	2 (2)	0
	LC	2 (1)	0
	Total	26 (19)	0

BEATTIE James Scott

Striker 2007– 6' 1" 12st 0
b. Lancaster 27 February 1978

Blackburn Rovers from trainee Mar 1995/ Southampton (£1m) Jul 1998/ Everton (£6m) Jan 2005
United: (£4m) 4 Aug 2007
Debut: 11 Aug 2007 United 2 Colchester United 2

James Beattie began his career with Blackburn Rovers, making his League debut on 12 October 1996 at home to Arsenal. He had a successful move to Southampton where he made over 200 League appearances scoring once in roughly every three games and won five England U21 caps and five full caps. His move to Everton was less successful and in 2006–07 the goals were hard to come by.

United's new manager Bryan Robson paid the club's record fee for James at the start of the 2007–08 season and he was an immediate success. He scored United's first goal of the season in the opening game and reaching 22, all in the League, making him the first United player to

exceed 20 goals since 1989–90. He worked hard for the team and was effective both in the air and on the ground. He scored six times from the penalty spot and was very dangerous from free kicks, scoring a fine goal to equalise against Wednesday at the Lane and reached his 100th League goal.

Appearances:		Apps	Gls
	FL	36 (3)	22
	FAC	2	0
	Total	38 (3)	22

BEAUMONT Percy

CH 1917–21 5'10" 11st to 11st 7
b. Mexborough 3 September 1897
d. Mexborough 10 November 1967

Mexborough Rovers and or Town
United: Apr 1917 and 1 May 1919(pro) to cs 1921
Debuts: 1 Apr 1917 Rotherham C 0 United 1 (WW1)
20 Oct 1919 United 0 Blackburn Rovers 0
Last game: 26 Feb 1921 United 0 Derby County 1
Barnsley cs 1921 free/ Southend United May 1926/ Mexborough Athletic Aug 1927 to c1930

Percy was a pale faced, hard working player who may have played one or two games for the reserve team before his first team debut and probably appeared as 'Smith' on five occasions in October and November 1918. When 'normal' football resumed in 1919, he never fulfilled his early war time promise and was transferred to Barnsley where he made 138 FL appearances and then added 30 more for Southend United.

Appearances:		Apps	Gls
	FL	34	3
	FAC	3	0
	WW1	25	1
	Total	62	4

BECKETT Luke John

Striker 2004–05 5' 11" 11st 6
b. Sheffield 25 November 1976

Barnsley trainee to pro Jun 1995/ Chester City Jun 1998/ Chesterfield (£75k) Jul 2000/ Stockport County (£100k) Dec 2001
United: (£50k) 15 Nov 2004 to 30 Jun 2006
Debuts: 27 Nov 2002 United 3 Wolverhampton Wanderers 3 (sub)
5 Mar 2005 Cardiff City 1 United 0
Last game: 12 Mar 2005 Stoke City 2 United 0 (sub)
Huddersfield Town(L) 14 Jan 2005 / Oldham Athletic(L) Mar 2005 and Jul 2005 to cs 2006
Huddersfield Town (undisclosed) 30 Jun 2006

Although Luke began his career with Barnsley, he made his FL debut after his move to Chester City, at home to Leyton Orient on the 8 August, the opening day of the 1998–99 season.

When he was signed by Neil Warnock, he had not played for a while due to injury and in his first two months at the club he made just one brief substitute appearance before being loaned to Huddersfield Town to regain match fitness. On his return he made a few appearances before moving on loan to Oldham Athletic, where he returned, again on loan, for 2005–06. Some United supporters felt that he had deserved a better opportunity at the Lane but the general feeling was that the Championship or Premier League would be a step too far.

During the close season he made a permanent move to Huddersfield Town and it was reported that United had made a profit of £100k on the original deal. During his loan spells and after his return on a permanent basis to Huddersfield his goalscoring record was impressive and by 2008 he had totalled 145 FL goals in 308(44) games, United being the only club he has not scored for.

Appearances:		Apps	Gls
	FL	1 (4)	0
	Total	1 (4)	0

BECTON Francis (Frank)

IL/CF 1898–99 5' 6½" 10st 2
b. Preston (or Liverpool) OND 1873
d. Preston 6 November 1909

Fishwick Ramblers(Preston)/ Preston North End c1891/ Liverpool (£100) Mar 1895
United: (c£200) 6 Oct 1898 to Jun 1899
Debut: 22 Oct 1898 United 1 Preston North End 1
Last games: 14 Jan 1899 Stoke 4 United 1
2 Feb 1899 Burnley 2 United 1 (FAC)
Bedminster June 1899/ Preston N E Sep 1900/ Swindon Town Aug 1901/ Nelson cs1902/ Swindon T 1902/ Ashton Town cs 1903

Frank Becton made his FL debut with Preston North End on 21 November 1891 at West Bromwich Albion. Capped twice by England, he had played for the Football League and had a Second Division championship medal with Liverpool. He was a clever, creative player with good ball control and a deadly shot but his transfer was a gamble, for he came to Sheffield with a reputation 'by no means clean' and for 'the trouble he caused his masters'.

There were reports that marriage had improved his behaviour but sadly, from United's point of view, not for long. He was thrown out of the Rising Sun on Hermitage Street for drunkenness, he missed training, he was insolent before the United Committee and they suspended him. It had been a poor return for the transfer fee and high wages paid.

He moved on from club to club with poor health bringing his playing days to an end, with 86 FL goals in 196 games, before he died from tuberculosis.

Appearances:		Apps	Gls
	FL	11	3
	FAC	2	0
	Total	13	0

BEER William (Billy) John

RH/IR/OR/CF/RB/CH 1897–1901 5'10" 11st 3 to 12st.
b. Saltburn 4 January 1879

Poolsbrook United/ Staveley Town/ Chesterfield Town Apr 1897
United: 26 May 1897 (FL registration as 'Bier') and Apr 1898 to 30 Jan 1902
Debuts: 6 Nov 1897 United 2 Corinthians 2 (Fr)
19 Apr 1898 Victoria U(Aberdeen) 1 United 0 (Fr)
26 Sep 1898 United 2 Newcastle United 2
Last games: 12 Oct 1901 United 0 Sunderland 1
21 Dec 1901 United 1 Glasgow Rangers 0 (Fr)
Small Heath (£1000 for Beer and C Field) Jan 1902 to 1910

Often known as 'Beers', Billy may have been brought up in Monkwearmouth before his parents moved to Poolsbook in north east Derbyshire. Reported as a promising right half, he made five Midland League appearances for Chesterfield in April 1897 but United had also spotted his potential and secured his FL registration.

Billy was one of those rare players to move successfully from wing half to inside forward. He was not a great artist with the ball but a big, strong all round player. He could take knocks, was difficult to dispossess, was good in the air and had a powerful shot and was at his best in cup-ties and scored in both the semi-final and Final of 1899. He missed the 1901 Cup Final and knee troubles led United to agree to his transfer with Charlie Field to Small Heath.

They made their debut at the Lane and no doubt there were some red faces among the United directors as the Birmingham side ran out winners by four goals to one. Beer gave his new club excellent service with 250 FL and Cup appearances. A gifted musician and church organist, he retired in 1910 moving to Australia where he worked as a sheep farmer, returning to England in 1920 and becoming a licensee in Birmingham. He was invited to take over the manager's role of Birmingham in May 1923, finally resigning in March 1927 and returning to the licensing trade. Some publications record that he died in March 1941 but a midlands newspaper mentioned his 75th birthday in 1954.

Appearances:		Apps	Gls
	FL	73	15
	FAC	16	6
	ABD	2	0
	Total	91	21

BEESLEY Paul

CD LB 1990–95 6' 1" 11st 11 to 12st 6
b. Liverpool (Wigan?) 21 July 1965

Marine/ Wigan Athletic Sep 1984/ Leyton Orient (£175k) Oct 1989
United: (£300–375k) 4/10 Jul 1990 to 2/4 Aug 1995
Debuts: 27 Jul 1990 Kramfors Alliansen (Swe) 1 United 5 (Fr)
29 Aug 1990 Derby County 1 United 1
Last games: 6 May 1995 United 3 Grimsby Town 1
31 Jul 1995 Sundal (Nor) 0 United 2 (Fr)
Leeds United (£250k) Aug 1995/ Manchester City (£500k) Feb 1997/ Port Vale (L) Dec 1997/ West Bromwich Albion (L) Mar 1998/ Port Vale Aug 1998/ Blackpool May 1999/ Chester City Jul 2000 (player-coach)/ Ballymena United Aug 2001/ Stalybridge Celtic Oct 2001/ Buxton 2003–04

Paul Beesley began his FL career with Wigan Athletic, making his debut on 29 September 1984 at home to York City. From the start of the 1986–87 season he was firmly established and in 1989 he joined Leyton Orient for what was their record transfer fee.

He was signed by Dave Bassett following United's return to the top flight in 1990 and was, for the most part, a regular in the four seasons he spent at the Lane. A reliable central defender, he was good in the air and in the tackle, although prone to the occasional error. He initially took over from Paul Stancliffe and in his second season formed a useful partnership with Brian Gayle. He was unlucky to miss the 1993 Wembley FAC semi-final but by then, he was no longer an automatic choice and subsequently, often filled the left-back role. Although very dependent on his left foot and lacking a bit of pace, Paul played within his limitations and gave United excellent service, being strong, dependable and consistent.

His move to Leeds for £250k caused some surprise and after two seasons there he moved quickly between other clubs as his football career

wound down with a final total of 437 (19) League appearances before moving into non-League football.

Appearances:		Apps	Gls
	FL	162 (6)	7
	FAC	9 (2)	1
	LC	12 (1)	0
	FMC	3	1
	Total	186 (9)	9

BELL Charles (Charlie) Thomas

CH 1966 6' 3½" 11st 9 to 12st 3
b. Sheffield 21 March 1945

United: jnr Aug 1971 to part time pro 23/24 Jan 1964, full 3 May 1965 to 25 May 1968
Debut: 22 Oct 1966 Aston Villa 0 United 0
Last game: 5 Nov 1966 Sunderland 4 United 1
Chesterfield June 1968/ Jan 1974/ Rotherham United coach 1974–78/ Stockport County coach 1978–79

Charlie Bell was a tall slim defender who made his CL debut in September 1964. With hindsight, he was unlucky with United in that his only first team opportunities were at centre forward where he scored on his final appearance. Chesterfield, his next club, gave more thought to his physique and weight training brought increased weight and strength and made him a better player and he was a Fourth Division championship winner at Saltergate and made 148(3) appearances.

Appearances:		Apps	Gls
	FL	3	1
	LC	1	0
	Total	4	1

BELL Harold

IL 1918 5' 9" 10st 10
b. Sheffield

Craven Sports
United: guest
Only game: 16 Mar 1918 United 0 Wednesday 5 (WW1)
WW1 guest: Wednesday (Apr to Nov 1917), Bradford (Dec 1917 to cs 1919)
Barnsley Sep 1919/ Bristol Rovers Aug 1920/ Castleford Town Jul 1921

Harold Bell made eleven 'guest' appearances for the Wednesday and then played regularly for Bradford until the close season of 1919. He played just this single game for United, twice hitting the Wednesday crossbar.

After the War he joined Barnsley where he made his FL debut on 4 October 1919 at home to Rotherham County and scored six times in his sixteen FL and Cup appearances. He moved to Bristol Rovers in the club's first season in the Football League but played only twice before being released and moving into non-League football.

Appearances:		Apps	Gls
	WW1	1	0
	Total	1	0

BELL William (Billy) Todd

LH 1927 5' 9½" 11st 3
b. North Seaton (Northumberland)
1 January 1905 or 17 March 1905

Blyth Spartans
United: (£150 rising to £200) 12/15 Dec 1925 to 8 Jun 1928
Debut: 7 Feb 1927 United 1 Liverpool 4
Last games: 19 Mar 1927 United 0 Leicester City 3
28 Nov 1927 Sheffield Wednesday 3 United 1 (CC)
Grimsby Town (£300) 8 Jun 1928/ Hull City May 1932 to May 1933

Billy Bell came to United as a hard shooting forward but his first team appearances were all at left half, making his first team debut in the same match as Jack Pickering. Grimsby Town converted him to a full back but he was always essentially a reserve player and played only 20 FL games in total.

Appearances:		Apps	Gls
	FL	5	0
	CC	1	0
	Total	6	0

BENJAMIN Ian Tracey

Forward 1978–79 5' 11" 13st 1
b. Nottingham 11 December 1961

United: App 8 May 1978 (pro 26 May 1979) to 29/31 Aug 1979
Debuts: 30 Aug 1978 United 1 River Plate (Arg) 2 (Fr sub)
21 Apr 1979 Cardiff City 4 United 0 (sub)
8 May 1979 United 2 Leicester City 2
Last game: 25 Aug 1979 Chester City 1 United 1
West Bromwich Albion (£125k) Aug 1979/ Notts County Feb 1982/ Peterborough United Aug 1982/ Northampton Town Aug 1984/ Cambridge United Oct 1987/ Chester City Jul 1988/ Exeter City Feb 1989/ Southend United Mar 1990/ Luton Town Nov 1992/ Brentford Sep 1993/ Wigan Athletic Sep 1994/ non-League playing, coaching, managing

Ian Benjamin was an extremely gifted schoolboy with skill and pace who made reserve team appearances when he was fifteen, and gained England youth caps. The first United black player in modern times and a younger brother of the Notts County and Chesterfield defender, Tristram Benjamin, Ian had a long career in the game. He made 452 (34) FL appearances for his various clubs and scored 126 goals, mainly in the lower divisions but he never lived up to that early promise or the remarkable fee paid for his transfer by West Brom.

After his FL career ended at Wigan in 1994–95 he had spells in non-League football, playing for Kettering, Chelmsford City and Raunds Town before managing Corby Town, Warboys Town, Soham Town Rangers and Wisbech Town. He then became a postman in Kettering and then worked in the tool hire business.

Appearances:		Apps	Gls
	FL	4 (1)	3
	LC	1 (1)	0
	ASC	3	0
	Total	8 (2)	3

BENNETT Ian Michael

G 2004–05, 2006 6' 0" 12st 10
b. Worksop 10 October 1971

QPR (trainee)/ Newcastle United pro Mar 1989/ Peterborough United Mar 1991/ Birmingham City (£325k) Dec 1993
United: (L) 9 Dec 2004 to 9 Jan 2005
Debut: 11 Dec 2004 Rotherham United 2 United 2
Last game: 1 Jan 2005 United 0 Wigan Athletic 2
Coventry City (L) Feb 2005/ Leeds United (free) Jun 2005
United: (£100k) from 27 Jul 2006
Debuts: 29 Jul 2006 Scunthorpe U 1 United 0 (Fr)
16 Sep 2006 United 1 Reading 2

Although having been a trainee with Queens Park Rangers and a pro with Newcastle United, Ian did not make his FL debut until his move to Peterborough United, keeping a clean sheet at home to Bournemouth on 8 April 1992. He had a long spell with Birmingham (285(2) FL appearances.

He moved to United on a month's loan after Paddy Kenny's three game suspension following a sending-off at Millwall. Despite his lack of first team action at the time he played well and saved a penalty in United's 2–1 win at Coventry on Boxing Day 2004. Ian returned as cover for Kenny after the club's promotion to the Premiership but played only a handful of games, missing one opportunity with a broken finger. He was unlucky again in 2007–08, taking over from the injured Kenny only for Ian himself to be injured.

Appearances:		Apps	Gls
	FL	13 (1)	0
	LC	3	0
	Total	16 (1)	0

BENNETT Jesse

RB 1929 5' 10" 11st 7 to 12st 0
b. Dronfield Woodhouse OND 1903
d. Sheffield 1985?

Dronfield Woodhouse (1926–27)
United: 26 Apr 1928 to 5 May 1932
Debut: 12 Oct 1929 Blackburn Rovers 0 United 1
Last game: 14 Dec 1929 Aston Villa 5 United 1
Coventry City (c£150) May 1932/ Northampton Town cs 1933 to1936 / – / Folkestone Town Sep 1937 to ? / – / Norton Woodseats Sept 1940

Jesse was mentioned as both 'John' and 'Jim' in the Sheffield newspapers and as a 'sure tackler'. He made 90 FL appearances in total for the three clubs.

Appearances:		Apps	Gls
	FL	9	0
	CC	1	0
	Total	10	0

BENNETT Thomas (Tom)

RH/OR 1902–03

Heeley Friends
United: 30 Mar 1900 to cs 1903
Debuts: 3 May 1902 Wednesday 3 United 0 (CM)
25 Oct 1902 Notts County 1 United 1
Last games: 14 Feb 1903 West Bromwich A 3 United 3
4 Apr 1903 Northampton Town 0 United 1 (Fr)
Doncaster Rovers cs 1903 to cs 1904

Tom was a part time reserve player who was more at home in the Midland League with Doncaster Rovers scoring a dozen goals in the 1903–04 season.

Appearances:		Apps	Gls
	FL	2	0
	Total	2	0

BENNETT Walter (Cocky)

OR/IR 1896–1905 5' 7½" 12st 1 to 13st 4
b. Mexborough April 1874
d. Denaby 6 April 1908

Mexborough
United: (£10 or £40) 19/25 Jan 1896 to 13 Apr 1905
Debut: 22 Feb 1896 West Bromwich A 1 United 0
Last game: 18 Mar 1905 Aston Villa 3 United 0
Bristol City (£50) 1905 to cs 1907/ Denaby United cs 1907 until his death in 1908

Walter Bennett came from a football family and his brother William ('Mick') Bennett had played for the Wednesday in the disastrous 1890 Cup Final. Walter had a great 1895–96 season with Mexborough and Derby County tried to secure his transfer. Nevertheless, a writer in a local newspaper was not impressed when United secured Walter's signature commenting that '£10 seems a long price to pay'.

'Cocky' never looked like an athlete; he was a heavy, thick-set man with a listless walk and sombre in appearance and yet he was a remarkable winger. He had one of the hardest shots in the game and full-time training and a two stone loss of weight left him with a good turn of speed. He could dribble, centre well and was adept at meeting centres from the left and was a vital member of the great United team that was a dominant force in English football between 1897 and 1904. He was the leading scorer in the Championship side of 1897–98, gained a winners' medal in the 1899 FA Cup Final, scoring United's first ever FA Cup Final goal, a losers' medal in 1901 and he appeared in the first game of the 1902 Final, missing the replay through injury.

He could be moody and introspective and trainers and colleagues were kept well aware of the 'ailments' and problems that Walter suffered from. It was said that he was 'not as surly as he looked' but a poor playing partner was made well aware of his failings. On his day, 'Cocky' was irresistible and thoroughly deserved the honours that came his way.

He was placed on the transfer list in 1903 but persuaded United to re-sign him. He seemed to be well past his best but he signed for Bristol City(48 app, 22 gl) and secured a Second Division Championship medal with his new club in 1906. He returned to south Yorkshire but he was killed as a result of a roof fall at Denaby Main Colliery in April 1908 at the age of thirty three.

Appearances:		Apps	Gls
	FL	195	59
	FAC	37	11
	ABD	2	0
	Total	234	70

BENNIE Peter

OR 1893
b. Carluke (Scotland) ?
d. Scotland 1921

Airdrieonians
United: 24 Oct 1893 to probably May 1894
Debut: 23 Oct 1893 United 5 Rotherham Town 3 (Fr)
Only game: 4 Nov 1893 Derby County 2 United 1
Royal Albert 1894/ Wishaw Thistle May 1896/ Slamannan Oct 1898

Peter Bennie became a director of Airdrieonians and the family name is synonymous with the Scottish club.

Appearances:		Apps	Gls
	FL	1	0
	Total	1	0

BENSON Edgar C

LB 1892

Sheffield Club
United: Registered with FL Aug 1892 to cs 1895
Debuts: 27 Dec 1889 United 3 Casuals 3 (Fr)
11 Apr 1892 United 2 Sunderland Albion 1 (NL)
Last game: 21 Apr 1892 United 1 Casuals 3 (Fr)
Sheffield Club to at least 1896

Edgar Benson was one of several amateur players from the Sheffield Club who assisted United in their early years. He must have been one of the better ones as United registered him with the FL from August 1892 until the close season of 1895 though no doubt it would only have been in a dire emergency that he would have been called upon. In his one competitive game for United, the Sheffield Independent, referred to him as 'Smith'. He played regularly for Sheffield Club making just five appearances in those years for United. In later years he was the secretary of Lindrick Golf Club.

Appearances:		Apps	Gls
	NL	1	0
	Total	1	0

BENSON Robert (Bob) William

RB/LB 1905–13 5' 9½" 12st 8
b. Whitehaven 9 February 1883
d. Highbury, London 19 February 1916

Dunston V/ Shankhouse/ Swalwell/ Newcastle United (£150) Dec 1902/ Southampton (£150) Sep 1904
United: (£150) 3 May 1905 to 18 Nov 1913
Debut: 2 Sep 1905 Bolton Wanderers 1 United 2
Last game: 20 Sep 1913 Bradford City 2 United 1
Woolwich Arsenal (£600) Nov 1913

Bob Benson's FL debut came with his only game for Newcastle United, away at Liverpool on 7 March 1903 before he joined Southampton who were members of the Southern League.

He was bought by United for a low fee because Southampton thought, incorrectly, that Newcastle United had retained his FL registration which the Blades would have had to pay. He was an imposing figure and an excellent player. Sturdily built with fair hair, he was a 'tower of strength' for United, a fine tackler and volleyer and good in the air. He will particularly be remembered for his penalty kicks, jogging forward from his normal defensive position before breaking into a run and shooting after a colleague had put the ball on the spot.

He took over the captaincy from Bernard Wilkinson but lost his place in the United team to Jack English through injury and asked for a transfer. His weaknesses were minuscule in relation to his strengths but he could be nervous and moody and there were occasional lapses such as when trying to dribble his way out of trouble and he didn't do himself justice on his single international appearance against Ireland. He also represented the Football League and went on an FA tour of South Africa.

He moved to Highbury and his last FL appearance was as a centre forward, where he had never played before, and he scored twice. He took no part in the game when war time football took over, becoming a munitions worker but volunteered to play one game although he had not trained that season. It proved too much of a strain and he died in the dressing room after walking off the pitch having 'burst a blood vessel'. He was buried in his Arsenal shirt.

Appearances:		Apps	Gls
	FL	273	20
	FAC	10	1
	ABD	2	0
	Total	285	21

BENSTEAD Graham Mark

G 1989–90 6' 2" 12st 12
b. Aldershot 20 August 1963

Wimbledon(amat)/ Queens Park Rangers app to pro Jul 1981/ Norwich City (£10k) Mar 1985 Colchester United (L) Aug 1987
United: (L) 22 Mar 1988, (£35k) 19 Jul 1988 to 30 Jul 1970
Debut: 26 Mar 1988 United 4 Ipswich Town 1
Last games: 22 Apr 1989 United 2 Brentford 2
27 Jan 1990 United 1 Watford 1 (FAC)
Brentford (c£65k) Jul 1990/ Kettering (L) Nov 93/ Rushden & Diamonds (1995–7)/ Kingstonian (L) cs 1997/ Kettering (player coach)/ Brentford (player coach) Jul 1997/ Basingstoke/ Chertsey Town (L) Mar 1999/ Farnborough (player coach) 2002–03 / – / Stevenage Boro asst mgr May to Oct 2004

An England youth international, Graham Benstead began his professional career at Queens Park Rangers. Although he was there for four seasons, he made just one appearance, on 8 January 1983 in the FA Cup at West Bromwich Albion. His FL debut came with Norwich City, where he was second string to Chris Woods, on 6 April 1985 at Arsenal.

Graham was signed by Dave Bassett, shortly after his arrival at Bramall Lane and replaced Andy Leaning for the end of the 1987–88 season which saw the Blades relegated. He was almost ever-present until the end of the following season when he was replaced by Simon Tracey who became the first choice in 1989–90. In his 47 FL games for the Blades, Graham made an impressive four penalty saves but was regarded as weak on crosses.

After a spell with Brentford, he moved to Kettering where he gained three England semi-professional caps. He played for various non-League clubs and, after leaving Basingstoke, he joined Farnborough Town as their goalkeeping coach, playing on occasions. At the end of the 2002–03 season, he moved to Stevenage Borough, becoming their assistant manager in May 2004 but in October he stepped down due to business commitments. He made 194 FL appearances.

Appearances:		Apps	Gls
	FL	47	0
	PO	2	0
	FAC	8	0
	LC	5	0
	AMC	2	0
	YHC	6	0
	Total	70	0

BENT Marcus Nathan

Striker 1999–2000 6' 2" 12st 4
b. Hammersmith 19 May 1978

Brentford trainee to pro Jul 1995/ Crystal Palace (£150k) Jan 1998/ Port Vale (£375k) Jan 1999
United: 27/28 Oct 1999 (£300 000) to 24 Nov 2000
Debut: 30 Oct 1999 United 0 Huddersfield Town 1
Last game: 21 Nov 2000 United 1 Fulham 1
Blackburn Rovers (£1.3 to £2m) Nov 2000/ Ipswich Town (£3m) Nov 2001/ Leicester City (L - season) Sep 2003/ Everton (£450k) Jun 2004 / Charlton A (£2m) Jan 2006/ Wigan A (L) Aug 2007/ Birmingham C Jul 2008

Marcus Bent made his FL debut with Brentford, the club where he began his career as a trainee, on 4 November 1995 at home to Shrewsbury Town. Following his move to Crystal Palace, he gained two England U21 caps, playing in the Toulon Tournament.

He was signed for United by Adrian Heath shortly before his resignation. He quickly became popular with the fans, being fast with good ball control and the ability to beat an opponent. He scored goals with both his head and his feet and under Neil Warnock's guidance, he increased his work rate. Unfortunately, there was open hostility between Bent and Paul Devlin and the goals dried up during the following season. There were also disputes over wages and whether he held on to the ball too long and because of his attitude to younger players. The solution came with a transfer to Blackburn for a fee which delighted United and included a sell-on clause.

After leaving United, he played for a variety of clubs but latterly, he was troubled by hamstring problems. He came to the fore again on loan with Wigan where he became one of only a few players to score for six different Premiership clubs. By 2008, he had scored 90 League goals in 330 (102) games.

Appearances:

	Apps	Gls
FL	48	20
FAC	3	1
LC	5	3
Total	56	24

BETTNEY Christopher (Chris) John

Forward 1996–97 5' 10" 10 st 10 to 11st 4
b. Chesterfield 27 October 1977

United: from trainee 1 May 1996 to cs 1999
Debut: 27 Aug 1996 United 4 Sheffield Wednesday 1 (sub Fr)
19 Apr 1997 Tranmere Rovers 1 United 1 (sub)
Last game: 19 Aug 1997 United 0 Everton 4 (Fr)
Hull City 26 Sep 1997(L) to cs 1998)
Chesterfield Jul 1999/ Rochdale Nov 1999/ Macclesfield (nc) Jul 2000/ Worksop Town Oct 2000/ South Normanton?/ Staveley MW?/ Ilkeston?/ Alfreton Town 2002/ Rushden & D 2002/ Alfreton (2004–5)/ – / Harrogate T from cs2006/ Bradford PA Jun 2008c

Chris was originally a mid-field player, with a good engine and pace, though one footed. Manager Dave Bassett gave him an opportunity as a forward and he went on to play 47 (23) FL games with his various clubs before moving into the non-League game.

Appearances:

	Apps	Gls
FL	0 (1)	0
Total	0 (1)	0

BIBBO Salvatore (Sal)

G 1994–95 6' 2" 13st 0
b. Basingstoke 24 August 1974

Bournemouth/ Crawley Town Aug 1992
United: 18 Aug 1993 to 31 Jun 1996
Debut: 5 Oct 1994 United 3 Ancona (Ita) 3 (AIC)
Last games: 15 Nov 1994 Cesena (Ita) 1 United 4 (AIC)
18 May 1995 Viterbese (Ita) 3 United 1 (Fr)
Chesterfield (L) Feb 1995/ Ards (L) Mar 1996
Reading Aug 1996 to June 1998/ Basingstoke/Millwall/ Havant & Waterlooville Nov 1999/ Bath City cs 2000 / – / Reading goalkeeping coach part time, full time 2006

Salvatore Bibbo never made a FL appearance with the Blades as he was in the shadow of Simon Tracey and Alan Kelly. He was agile but lacked strength and composure and his first FL match was a substitute appearance whilst on loan at Chesterfield at home to Bury on 4 March 1995. He made 7 FL appearances for Reading, his full FL debut coming at Barnsley on 28 August 1996. The following season, he played for Reading at Bramall Lane in their 0–1 FA Cup defeat but later moved into non-League football and then returned to Reading as a coach.

Appearances:

	Apps	Gls
AIC	2	0
Total	2	0

BIGGAR Frederick William (Billy)

G 1900–02 6' 1½" 13st 2
b. Mexborough 16 October 1874 or Blaydon OND 1877
d. Croydon 11 July 1935

Birtley to pro 1 Mar 1900
United: 5/6 Mar 1900 to May 1902
Debut: 31 Mar 1900 Nottingham Forest 4 United 0
Last game: 12 Apr 1902 United 1 Newcastle United 0
West Ham United May 1902/ Fulham cs 1903/ Watford May 1904/ Rochdale May 1910 to cs 1917 (trainer from Aug 1916)/ Leyland Motors 1919–20/ Third Lanark trainer 1920–22

Billy Biggar was signed by United as understudy to Bill Foulke though he failed to shine when given a first team opportunity. His name may have been registered at birth as Biggers but he used Biggar as a surname and it led to harmless fun for he was a big chap but certainly not bigger than Bill Foulke. He gave Watford good service and may have made an odd appearance for Rochdale in the Christmas period of 1916.

Appearances:

	Apps	Gls
FL	14	0
Total	14	0

BIRCHENALL Alan (Sherman, Birch) John

Striker 1964–67 5' 11½" 11st 13
b. East Ham 22 August 1945

Notts County (amat)/ Bulwell Forest Villa/ Thorneywood Athletic
United: 1/12 Jun 1963 to 29/30 Nov 1967
Debut: 2 Sep 1964 Stoke City 0 United 1
Last game: 25 Nov 1967 United 0 Leicester City 0
Chelsea (£100k) Nov 1967/ Crystal Palace (£100k) Jun 1970/ Leicester City(£100k) Sep 1971/ Notts County(L) Mar 1976/ San Jose Earthquakes(L) Apr 1977/ Notts County Sep 1977/ Memphis Rogues Apr 1978/ Blackburn Rovers Sep 1978/ Luton Town Mar 1979/ Hereford United Oct 1979/ Trowbridge Town Jan 1980 (player manager)

Alan Birchenall's family moved to Nottingham when he was four years old. He came under the wing of Notts County but found it difficult to get the time off work to train and began playing for Thorneywood, a leading Nottingham junior club and it was there that he was watched by Archie Clark, United's chief scout. Signed by John Harris, Alan took a time to settle but then became a prolific scorer in the 1963–64 NIL side and became one of the group of youngsters who formed the bulk of the club's First Division side in the mid-sixties.

Alan made his FL debut in a victory at Stoke after just eight games with the CL team and three days later, he scored twice in United's 2–0 victory at Hillsborough and netted nine goals in his first twelve First Division games. A strong forward with a good shot and a fine header of the ball, Alan formed an exciting and dangerous striking partnership with Mick Jones—they had played together for Notts Boys—and it was a bitter blow when he was sold to Chelsea soon after Mick had been sold to Leeds United. The first United player to be substituted in a FL match (September 1965 at Fulham), Alan gained two England U23 caps whilst with United and two more with Chelsea.

A cheerful extrovert character who always played well in the games against the Wednesday, 'Birch' is also remembered for the playful kiss he exchanged at the Lane with Tony Currie while playing for Leicester City. He returned to the midlands club when his playing days ended, with a total of 74 FL goals in 447(11) games, and took a commercial role and became the PR man as well as running a footwear business and the Griffin Inn in nearby Swithland.

Appearances:		Apps	Gls
	FL	106 (1)	31
	FAC	8	2
	LC	6	2
	CC	3	2
	Total	123 (1)	37

BIRD Donald (Don/Bill/Dickie) William Carlton

OL 1935–36 5' 8" 11st 6
b. Llandrindod Wells 5 January 1908
d. Newton Abbot 24 February 1987

Llandrindod Wells/ Cardiff City 1930/ Bury May 1931/ Torquay United Jun 1932/ Derby County (£250) Jun 1934
United: 24 Dec 1935 to 8 Oct 1936
Debut: 26 Dec 1935 United 4 Swansea Town 1
Last game: 5 Sep 1936 United 2 Newcastle United 1
Southend United(£250 or £500) Oct 1936 to cs 1937

Don Bird made his FL debut with Cardiff City on 21 April 1930 at Reading. He was a clever, intelligent but rather moody player, signed by United as yet another inevitably failed attempt to replace Fred Tunstall. Don had a strong though not always accurate shot and was capable of delivering fine centres and corner kicks. He scored one of United's goals in the 1936 F A Cup semi-final—some thought it was intended as a cross—and was unlucky not to be chosen for the Cup Final and he also scored in his final game for the Blades.

His playing career came to an end in April 1937 after 115 FL games when he suffered a severe facial injury. He later became a director of Torquay United.

Appearances:		Apps	Gls
	FL	13	3
	FAC	4	1
	CC	1	0
	Total	18	4

BIRKS Leonard (Len)

LB 1924–31 5' 10" 11st 8
b. Fenton (Stoke-on-Trent) 6 October 1896
d. Shirehampton (Bristol) 22 March 1975

Butt Lane Star/ Port Vale May 1920
United: 21/23/24 Oct 1924(£2,300) to 27 Feb 1931
Debut: 25 Oct 1924 United 3 Preston North End 0
Last game: 19 Feb 1931 Blackburn Rovers 2 United 1
Plymouth Argyle (£1500) Feb 1931/ Bristol City Sep 1933/ Yeovil & Petters United Aug 1934/ Bristol City coach Aug 1935

Len Birks made his FL debut for Port Vale at Blackpool on 5 March 1921 and made 102 League and Cup appearances for the Staffordshire club.

A clever tackler and good ball distributor, he was signed by United at a time when it was thought that Ernest Milton, the regular first team left back, was coming towards the end of his career but Birks was slow to settle with United and failed to win a place in the team that went on to win the FA Cup. Len wasn't consistent for he was one of those players who often had a poor game if he made an early error but he gave the Blades good service and played particularly well in the Cup semi-finals of 1928. His FL career ended with 375 appearances.

Appearances:		Apps	Gls
	FL	195	0
	FAC	16	0
	CC	8	0
	ABD	1	0
	Total	220	0

BISBY John Charles (Charlie)

IL 1905 5' 8½" 10st 7 to 11st
b. Rotherham JFM 1877
d. Doncaster 1945

Highthorne 1902
United: 16 Mar 1905 to 3 May 1906
Only game: 30 Sep 1905 Birmingham 2 United 0
Grimsby Town May 1906 to cs1908 / – / Denaby United Feb 1909

United made a grant of £5 to Highthorne when John Bisby was signed. Described as 'vigorous and dashing'—the last word prone to over use in those Edwardian days—he was never more than a competent reserve player. He made 7 FL appearances with Grimsby Town and he was referred to as 'Charlie' with Denaby and was still playing for them in 1911.

Appearances:		Apps	Gls
	FL	1	0
	Total	1	0

BLACK Kingsley Terence

Winger 1995 5' 8½" 10st 11
b. Luton 22 June 1968

Luton Town jnr to pro Jul 1986/ Nottingham Forest (£1.5m) Sep 1991
United: (L) 2 Mar 1995 to May 1995
Debut: 25 Mar 1995 United 1 Reading 1
Last game: 6 May 1995 United 3 Grimsby Town 1
Millwall (L) Sep 1995/ Grimsby Town (£25k) Jul 1996/ Lincoln City (L) Oct 2000/ Lincoln City Jul 2001/retired Oct 2002

Kingsley Black made his FL debut with Luton Town, the club where he began his career as a junior, on 26 September 1987 at Queens Park Rangers. Whilst there, he gained a League Cup winners' medal and, despite having been an England Schoolboy International, he won the first of his 30 Northern Ireland caps. With Forest, he gained a ZDS Cup winners medal and later an AWS winners medal with Grimsby Town.

In March 1995 he was signed by Dave Bassett on loan, to boost United's fading play-off chances. A skilful player but hardly dynamic, he stayed to the end of the season, scoring in his final game but United finished four points adrift of their target.

He ended his career with Lincoln City having played 338 (79) FL games.

Appearances:		Apps	Gls
	FL	8 (3)	2
	Total	8 (3)	2

BLACK Russell Palmer

Striker 1984–86 5' 9" 11st 6
b. Dumfries 29 July 1960

Gretna
United: (£1500) 1 Jul 1984 to 30 Jun 1986
Debut 29 Jul 1984 Vanesborg(Swe) 1 United 4 (sub Fr)
17 Nov 1984 United 0 Manchester City 0
Last game: 19 Apr 1986 Blackburn Rovers 6 United 1
Dundee(L) 30 Aug 1985/
Halifax Town Aug 1986 to cs 1988/ Gretna

Russell Black was signed, with Don Peattie, from Gretna, the Scottish borders club. The two forward were not quite good enough though Russell did score on his only appearance on loan with Dundee and did reasonably well with Halifax (63(9) app, 14 gl). He later did some coaching in Australia.

Appearances:		Apps	Gls
	FL	10 (4)	0
	Total	10 (4)	0

BLACK Thomas (Tommy) Robert

Striker 2004 5' 7" 11st 4
b. Chigwell 26 November 1979

Arsenal trainee to pro Aug 1999/ Carlisle United (L) Aug 1999/ Bristol City (L) Dec 1999/ Crystal Palace (£250k+) Jul 2000 to cs 2007
United: (L) 17 Sep 2004 to Oct 2004
Debuts: 18 Sep 2004 Wigan Athletic 4 United 0 (sub)
21 Sep 2004 Wrexham 2 United 3 (LC)
25 Sep 2004 United 1 Coventry City 1
Last game: 2 Oct 2004 Brighton & Hove Albion 1 United 1
Gillingham (L) Jan to May 2006/ Bradford C (L) Nov 2006/ Southend Utd (free) Jul 2007

Tommy Black began his career with Arsenal and made one substitute appearance in the PL at Everton on the 29th of April 2000 but his full FL debut had been while on loan with Carlisle at Mansfield Town on 28 August 1999.

Injuries to United players, in particular to Andy Liddell, prompted Neil Warnock to sign Tommy on a month's loan in September 2004. He played as a wide attacking midfielder to create opportunities for others but although he scored on his full FL debut, he only showed brief flashes of the zestful, incisive play that had made him such a favourite at Selhurst Park and he returned to Palace a few days early.

By 2008, he had made 129 (71) FL appearances.

Appearances:		Apps	Gls
	FL	3 (1)	1
	LC	1	0
	Total	4 (1)	1

BLACKWELL Ernest

GK 1916–24 5' 9" 11 to 12st
b. Sheffield 19 July 1894
d. 16 October 1964

Atlas & Norfolk/ United (trial)/ Scunthorpe & Lindsey United 1913–14
United: 2/4 May 1914 to cs 1925 (retired)
Debuts: 12 Feb 1916 United 3 Nottingham Forest 1 (WW1)
1 Nov 1919 Manchester United 3 United 0
Last game: 13 Sep 1924 United 2 Aston Villa 2
WW1 guest: Wednesday (Feb 1917), Crystal Palace (1918), Leicester Fosse (Feb 1919) v United

Ernest Blackwell was United's reserve goalkeeper in the period when Harold Gough held the first team spot. He had made his first team debut during the First World War and joined the Navy in 1918. A cousin of Sam Hardy, the England keeper, and a brother of Harry Blackwell, the Scunthorpe, Aberdeen, Orient and Preston keeper, Ernest was a committed Christian and lay preacher and occasionally missed fixtures which clashed with the religious festivals. He was an adequate reserve keeper and happy to play at that level and the highlight of his career was playing in the 1923 Cup semi-final.

Troubled by injuries and his health affected by appendicitis, he was warned in June 1924 that a kick in the abdominal area could have potentially disastrous results and he was forced to retire, United making him a grant of £500 to assist him with a business venture.

Appearances:		Apps	Gls
	FL	47	0
	FAC	9	0
	CC	5	0
	WW1	31	0
	Total	92	0

BLAIR John

CH 1897–98
b. Glasgow

Benburb (Glasgow)/ Grimsby Town cs1895/ Stalybridge Rovers
United: Apr and 11 May 1897 (£15 to Grimsby T) to cs 1898
Debut: 1 Sep 1897 United 2 Derby County 1
Last game: 12 Apr 1898 United 1 Newton Heath 4 (Fr)
Gravesend/ New Brompton Jul 1901 to cs 1902

John Blair was a Scottish junior international who played once in the FL for both Grimsby and United, his FL debut being with Grimsby on 2 September 1895 at Arsenal. United gave him a first team opportunity at the start of the new season because Tommy Morren was ill and he played twice against the Corinthians but he wasn't regarded as good enough and was released at the end of the season.

He had better fortune in the Southern League and played regularly for one season at left half for New Brompton.

Appearances:

	Apps	Gls
FL	1	0
Total	1	0

BLAIR John Guthrie

IR 1927–29 5' 11" 12st 3
b. Neilston (Renfrew) 23 August 1905
d. Kilmarnock 1 January 1972

Neilston Victoria/ Third Lanark 1922 or 1923/ Tottenham Hotspur Apr 1926
United: (£3000) 24 Nov 1927 to May 1929
Debut: 26 Nov 1927 United 3 Cardiff City 4
Last game: 17 Nov 1928 United 2 Everton 1
Fordsons (Cork) Nov 1929/ other Republic of Ireland teams

A goal scoring inside forward, John Blair made his FL debut, and scored, whilst with Spurs at home to Everton on 28 August 1926 and later scored on his United debut. He was thought by many to be a future international but Spurs, after he had been sent off twice, lost faith with him.

He was a clever, two footed player who, although strong and broad shouldered, lacked pace, vigour and discipline and lost his place in the United team. In April 1929, he failed to turn up to play and was suspended. Transfer listed by United—he was not given a free transfer until1934—and probably, to all intents and purposes, blacklisted, he played in the Republic of Ireland until at least 1932.

Appearances:

	Apps	Gls
FL	26	7
FAC	8	0
Total	34	7

BLAKE Nathan Alexander

Striker 1994–95 5' 11" 13st 2
b. Cardiff 27 January 1972

Chelsea trainee/ Cardiff City Aug 1990
United: (£300k) 17 Feb 1994 to 23 Dec 1995
Debuts: 22 Feb 1994 Ipswich Town 3 United 2 (sub)
16 Mar 1994 United 1 Queens Park Rangers 1
Last game: 16 Dec 1995 Ipswich Town 1 United 1
Bolton Wanderers (£1.25m and Mark Patterson valued at c£500k) Dec 1995/ Blackburn Rovers (£4.25m) Oct 1998/ Wolves (£1.4m) Sep 2001/ Leicester City Aug 2004/ Leeds United (L) Jan 2005/ retired Jul 2005/ Newport Co Aug to Oct 2006

Nathan began his FL career with Cardiff City making his debut as a defender at Bristol Rovers on 24 March 1990. He joined the Blades in February 1994 to boost the club's chances of staying in the Premiership. He immediately impressed with his skill and strength on the ball, although, to the surprise of many supporters, he was often only used as a substitute and his five goals in 12 appearances didn't prevent relegation. Part of the truth was that he was overweight and a player of moods and it was felt that he had insufficient work rate and commitment. He continued to score goals during the following season but was sold to Bolton Wanderers after playing just 45 minutes for new manager Howard Kendall. While he was at the Lane, he won his first five Welsh caps having previously been capped at youth, U21 and B levels.

He continued to score goals in the top two Divisions, averaging better than a goal every four games, United receiving, approximately, a further quarter of a million when he was transferred to Blackburn Rovers. After a successful time with Wolves, he had brief spells with Leicester and Leeds before retiring. He had scored 145 League goals in around 450 games. Some time after announcing his retirement he joined Newport County but left after a few games to concentrate on his property development business.

Appearances:

	Apps	Gls
FL	55 (14)	34
FAC	1	0
LC	3 (1)	1
AIC	1	0
Total	60 (15)	35

BLAKEMAN Alec George

CF/IR 1948
b. Oxford 11 June 1918
d. Deddington 1994

Oxford City/ Brentford May 1946
United: (£4000) 5 Nov 1948 to 5 Feb 1949
Debut: 6 Nov 1948 United 3 Preston North End 2
Last game: 4 Dec 1948 United 1 Middlesbrough 0
Bournemouth (£2000) 5 Feb 1949 to May 1950

A prisoner of war, who had worked in salt mines in Poland, Alec Blakeman made his FL debut with Brentford, at Arsenal, on 12 October 1946. He scored twice and did so the following week against Preston North End but, not surprisingly, he couldn't maintain that level adding only three more goals in his next 40 games.

Signed by Teddy Davison, Alec was not lacking in confidence in his own ability but he never looked as if he would solve United's lack of goals and he asked for a transfer. Transferred to Bournemouth, he scored 8 more FL goals in 25 games.

Appearances:

	Apps	Gls
FL	5	0
Total	5	0

BLOUNT Mark

Defender 1994–95 5' 10" 12st 0
b. Derby 5 January 1974

Derby County/ Gresley Rovers cs 1993 (Tranmere R - trial)
United: Feb 1994 (£12.5k) to 4 Mar 1996
Debuts: 6 Sep 1994 Piacenza 2 United 2 (AIC)
18 Feb 1995 Southend United 1 United 3
Last games: 30 Sep 1995 United 2 Ipswich Town 2
3 Oct 1995 Bury 4 United 2 (LC)
18 Nov 1995 Sunderland 2 United 0 (sub)

Scarborough Mar 1996 (trial)/ Peterborough United (nc) Mar 1996/ Gresley Rovers/ Burton Albion cs1997/ Worcester City (L?)/ Alfreton Town cs 2003

Mark played with determination but struggled to come to terms with First Division football and was one of the many players who left the Lane when Howard Kendall became the manager. He made 4(1) FL appearances with Peterborough.

Appearances:		Apps	Gls
	FL	11 (2)	0
	LC	2	0
	AIC	2	0
	Total	15 (2)	0

BLUFF Edgar Underwood

IR/IL/OR/CF 1905–07 5' 6½" 11st 6
b. Attercliffe (Sheffield) AMJ 1882
d. Nottingham 2 July 1952

High Hazels(Sheffield)/Yorkshire Light Infantry/ 1st Army Corps/ Reading (trial) Jan 1903/ Southampton Apr 1904
United: (£300) 7 Sep 1905 to 12 Dec 1907
Debut: 23 Sep 1905 United 4 Sunderland 1
Last game: 23 Nov 1907 United 0 Notts County 1
Birmingham 13 Dec 1907/ St Helens Town Sept 1908

Edgar Bluff joined the Yorkshire Light Infantry in 1900 and served for four years until Southern League Southampton paid for his discharge from the army. He was a first team regular in 1904–05 and was selected as first reserve for England (v Ireland) in 1905.

An energetic forward with good ball control and scoring record, Edgar had made a fine start as a professional player. It was later reported that he had been reluctant to join United but he scored on his debut and made a reasonable start at the Lane but then faded and was suspended in October 1907 for not carrying out training instructions. A move to Birmingham (9 FL apps) failed to solve his problems. He was still playing with St Helens in the 1909–10 season.

Appearances:		Apps	Gls
	FL	65	16
	FAC	3	0
	Total	68	16

BOLAM Robert (Bob) Coltman

OR/OL 1920–21 5' 8" 11st 7
b. Tynemouth AMJ 1896
d. Gateshead 20 June 1964

Lewin's Temperance (Birtley) Nov 1919/ Birtley
United: (£100) 22/23 Jan 1920 to May 1922
Debut: 7 Feb 1920 West Bromwich Albion 0 United 2
Last game: 1 Oct 1921 Newcastle United 2 United 1
Darlington June 1922/ South Shields Aug 1923/ Queens Park Rangers May 1924 to May 1925/ – / Lewin's Temperance Aug 1929/ Birtley Nov 1929

Bob Bolam may have scored on his United debut and he certainly made a capital start with United, mention being made that he was a tricky, go ahead player, with a good turn of speed but his form soon fell away. Transfer listed at £100, this was quickly changed to a free. He has a small part in soccer history for in 1924, while with QPR, he took advantage of a poorly drafted new corner kick rule and dribbled the ball from the corner before passing to a colleague who scored. He retired from football in 1926 having played 79 FL games (5 goals) and joined an insurance business.

Appearances:		Apps	Gls
	FL	33	2
	FAC	1	0
	Total	34	2

BOLSOVER Henry or Harry

G 1894

Sheffield Club
United: 16 Mar 1894 to cs 1894
Debut: 21 Apr 1894 Derby County 2 United 0 (UCL)
Last game: 26 Apr 1894 Wednesday 0 United 1 (WCC)
Sheffield Club/ Sheffield Wednesday Mar 1900/ Sheffield Club to at least cs 1904

An amateur goalkeeper with Sheffield Club, he may be Joseph Harry Bolsover who was born in Sheffield JFM 1874. He played two games for United but did manage to win a medal, his second and last game being the final of the Wharncliffe Charity Cup, which United won. He went on to play two FL games with Wednesday, his FL debut being on 12 March 1900 at home to Burton Swifts and he was a member of the Sheffield Club team which won the Amateur Cup in 1904.

Appearances:		Apps	Gls
	UCL	1	0
	WCC	1	0
	Total	2	0

BOLTON Joseph (Joe)

LB/MF 1983–86 5' 11½" 12st 11
b. Birtley 2 February 1955

Sunderland App to pro Feb 1972/ Middlesbrough (£200k) Jul 1981
United: (free) 1 Aug 1983 to 30 Jun 1986
Debuts: 2 Aug 1983 Grantham Town 1 United 5 (Fr)
3 Sep 1983 Lincoln City 0 United 2
Last games: 3 May 1986 Crystal Palace 1 United 1
15 May 1986 Jersey XI 1 United 5 (Fr)
Rotherham United 30 June 1986 trial/ Matlock Town

Joe made his FL debut with Sunderland at home to Watford on 17 April 1972. He went on to play over 300 first team games for the Roker Park club, during which time he became a cult hero and he was a regular member of the side which won the Second Division title in 1976.

After two years with Middlesbrough he joined United, signed by his former colleague, Ian Porterfield, and he gave the Blades three years sterling service. He was a no nonsense defender who did not shirk a tackle. A knee injury ended his career towards the end of the 1985–86 season having played 432(9) FL games, and he failed to secure a contract at Millmoor. He had a season and a half with Matlock before he was forced to retire and became a lorry driver.

Appearances:		Apps	Gls
	FL	109	3
	FAC	6	0
	LC	11	3
	FMC	1	0
	AMC	3	0
	Total	130	6

BONE James (Jim)

Striker 1973–74 5' 9½" 11st 8
b. Bridge of Allan 22 September 1949

Bannockburn/ Airth Castle Rovers/ Partick Thistle May 1968/ Norwich City (£30k) Feb 1972
United: (£113,333) 21/22 Feb 1973 to 18/20 Feb 1974
Debut: 24 Feb 1973 Leicester City 0 United 0
Last game: 9 Feb 1974 Norwich City 2 United 1
Celtic (£25k plus 20% of any future sale) Feb 1974/ Arbroath Jan 1975(£7,000)/ St Mirren Jan 1978/ Toronto Blizzard May to Aug 1979/ Hong Kong Rangers June 1982/ Heart of Midlothian Aug 1983/ Arbroath player-mgr Mar 1985 St Mirren asst. mgr Dec 1986/ Airdrie mgr May 1989 to May 1991/ Power Dynamos (Zambia) mgr/ coach in S Africa/ St Mirren mgr May 1992/ East Fife mgr 1996–98/ Dunfermline coach 1998 / – / Ross County asst. mgr 2003–04/ Partick Th asst mgr 2005, caretaker mgr Mar to May 2007/ Chester C mgr Dec 2007 to Feb 2007

Jim Bone attended a rugby playing school but played football with his friends. An electrician by trade, he had trials with several clubs but was told he was too small before Partick Thistle gave him a contract. He made his Scottish League debut when only 18 years old on 7 September 1968 away to Rangers and went on to win a League Cup winners medal with Thistle. He moved to Norwich City, making his FL debut on 4 March 1972 at Birmingham City and gained two Scottish caps but, after just one year, he moved to the Lane.

Jim was signed by John Harris in an exchange deal with United's Trevor Hockey; the clubs valuing Bone at £73,333 and Hockey at £40k. A strong, dangerous forward with a good shot, he soon moved back to Scotland saying that his style of play didn't suit the English First Division. He wanted to be a 'target man' and his opinions led to clashes with his managers and inevitable transfers but he was always a proven goal scorer.

He remained in football with a long career in coaching and management.

Appearances:		Apps	Gls
	FL	30 (1)	9
	ASC	2	0
	CC	1	2
	Total	33 (1)	11

BOOKER Robert (Bob)

D/MF 1988–91 6' 2" 12st 4
b. Watford 25 January 1958

Bedmond Social/ Brentford Oct 1978/ Barnet (L) c1978
United: 23 Nov 1988 (free) to 19 Nov 1991
Debut: 26 Nov 1988 United 3 Bristol City 0
Last game: 5 Oct 1991 Leeds United 4 United 3
Brentford Nov 1991/ Harrow Borough/ Brentford coaching staff / Brighton & Hove Albion Oct 2000 asst mgr to Sep 2006/ Pease Pottage coach cs 2006

Bob Booker began his career at Brentford, making his FL debut on 14 October 1978 at Watford and gave the club great service making over 250 FL appearances for the Bees. A free transfer, in view of his long and excellent work for Brentford, had been part of his contract but he was thirty years old with knee injury problems so he was both surprised and delighted when he was signed by Dave Bassett in November 1988 to take Simon Webster's mid-field position after Simon's leg was broken.

A strong, wholehearted, totally committed all round player, he took a little time to win over some of the crowd but none could deny his enthusiasm, determination and team spirit as Bob assisted the Blades in gaining promotion to Division Two and then Division One. He was captain on that happy day at Leicester in 1990 when the last hurdle was cleared.

Although a midfielder when he arrived, Bob was willing to play anywhere—and he played in most positions from full back to striker—and it was fitting that his last goal for United, which came at QPR, secured United's place in the top Division. He had become a cult hero and cries of 'Ooh Aah, Bob Bookaah' were regularly heard from the United fans and even after his move back to Brentford, he was often seen at United's games, sitting with the crowd.

A knee injury brought his career to an end, having made 313(66) FL appearances, and he went into coaching and spent several years as assistant manager at Brighton, having had two spells as caretaker manager. More recently, he has enjoyed success with Pease Pottage, a small club in Sussex.

Appearances:		Apps	Gls
	FL	91 (18)	13
	FAC	8 (2)	0
	LC	3 (1)	0
	FMC	3 (1)	1
	AMC	3	0
	YHC	1	0
	Total	109 (22)	13

BOOT Edmund (Eddie)

LH 1935–37, 1941 5' 11" 11st 0
b. Laughton Commom 13 October 1915
d. Dewsbury August 1999

Laughton Common/ Denaby United June 1934
United: trial 8/10 Oct 1935, 2 Nov 1935 to 15/16 Mar 1937
Debuts: 21 Oct 1935 United 3 Rotherham United 0 (CC)
16 Nov 1935 Charlton Athletic 1 United 1
Last game: 13 Mar 1937 United 5 Chesterfield 0
WW2 guest: 24 May 1941 Everton 3 United 3 (WW2)
Huddersfield Town Mar 1937 as a player until cs 1952

A Dinnington Colliery miner, Eddie was a stylish player with good ball control who passed the ball with cool judgement. United doubted his strength and sold him to Huddersfield Town but they were wrong.

Boot joined Town in March 1937 along with Bobby Barclay for a joint fee of £7000 and both appeared in the 1938 FA Cup Final which Town lost to a last minute penalty goal. Eddie had a fine football brain but he was also a tenacious tackler. He played throughout the war for Huddersfield and made one guest appearance for United in May 1941 at Everton.

He made 305 FL appearances for Town and more than 200 during the war before he joined the coaching staff in April 1952 though he still played occasionally for the reserve team. He became the manager in January 1960, following the legendary Bill Shankly and kept the post until his resignation in Sept 1964. He was appointed chief scout at Scunthorpe in February 1965.

Appearances:		Apps	Gls
	FL	41	0
	FAC	4	0
	CC	2	0
	WW2	1	0
	Total	48	0

BOOTH J W

OL/OR 1918–19
b. c1897

Great Central Railway (Sheffield)
WW1 guest: Sheffield Wednesday (Dec 1916)
United: guest 1918–19
Debut: 7 Sep 1918 United 5 Huddersfield Town 1 (WW1)
Last game: 1 Feb 1919 Barnsley 2 United 0 (WW1)
Scunthorpe & Lindsey United Oct 1919/ Welbeck Colliery/
Creswell Colliery 1922

Booth played for both Wednesday and United during the First War. He turned out on Boxing Day 1916 for the Wednesday but had more opportunities with United. He became a professional with Scunthorpe in the Midland League but was reinstated as an amateur in 1922.

Appearances:		Apps	Gls
	WW1	17	1
	Total	17	1

BOOTH William (Billy)

CH 1908 5' 9½" 11st to 11st 10
b. Sheffield 9 May 1886
d. JFM 1963

Thorpe Hesley Church
United: 24 Mar 1905 to cs1908 (FL registration retained to cs 1915)
Only game: 25 Jan 1908 Blackburn Rovers 3 United 3
Brighton & Hove Albion May 1908/ Castleford Town cs1920/
Worthing 1925–26

A player who began work as a collier, Billy played regularly for United's reserves but came to the fore with Brighton who were then in the Southern League. He was a stalwart of the Brighton side, playing in more than 350 games. He made two appearances for the Southern League against the FL and, in 1913, was a travelling reserve for England against Ireland in Belfast. During the First War he served in the Footballers' Battalion and was no doubt surprised to find that United still had him on their transfer list at £50 at the end of the 1918–19 season. His son, Sammy, was a professional with Port Vale, Cardiff City and Brighton.

Appearances:		Apps	Gls
	FL	1	0
	Total	1	0

BORBOKIS Vassilios (Vas)

RWB 1997–99 5' 11" 12st 0
b.Serres, Greece 10 February 1969

Apollon Limassol 1989/ AEK Athens Jul 1993/ Aris Salonika?
United: 24 Jun/1 Jul 1997 (£750k (?) to AEK) to 12 Mar 1999
Debuts: 18 Jul 1997 Sheffield FC 0 United 3 (Fr)
10 Aug 1997 United 2 Sunderland 0
Last games: 16 Jan 1999 United 1 Bolton Wanderers 2
27 Jan 1999 United 4 Cardiff City 1 (FAC)
Derby County (valued at £1.1m in a part exchange) Mar 1999/ PAOK Salonika (£200k) Dec 1999/ AEK Athens Jul 2002 to cs 2005/ Anorthosis Famagusta (Cyprus) 2005–06

Vas's signing was negotiated by Howard Kendall just before his resignation, and finalised by new manager Nigel Spackman. A newspaper later reported later that the fee was probably less than in the contemporary accounts. He scored on his FL debut, the first of many excellent displays as a right wing back. He was a very talented player but defensively not a good tackler, and he played twice for Greece whilst with United. Speedy, two footed with a fierce shot, he was a regular in the side, although he had problems when with the Greek squad over completing his national service which was postponed to the end of the season. He carried on the following season as he had left off but, after being injured against Cardiff City in the FA Cup (which was to be his final game), he asked if he could return to Greece but Steve Bruce, the United manager, refused. He went anyway. He was fined, put on the transfer list and moved to Derby County as part of the deal that brought Jonathan Hunt, Rob Kozluk and 'close to £500k' to Bramall Lane. After a short spell with the Rams, during which time he broke his jaw, he returned to play in Greece.

Appearances:

	Apps	Gls
FL	55	4
PO	1	1
FAC	9	1
LC	9	3
Total	74	9

BOTTOM Arthur Edwin

IF/CF 1948–54 5' 9½" 11st 10
b. Sheffield 28 February 1930

Sheffield YMCA
United: 8 May 1946(amateur), 12 Apr 1947(pro) to 16/19 Jun 1954
Debut: 23 Oct 1948 United 2 Stoke City 2
Last games: 19 Apr 1954 United 1 Sunderland 3
27 Apr 1954 Northampton Town 1 United 1 (BM)
York City (£2500) Jun 1954/ Newcastle United (£4500) Feb 1958/ Chesterfield (£5000) Nov 1958/ Boston United cs 1960/ Alfreton Town to c1963

Born near to the ground and a ball boy at the Lane, Arthur was a strong forward with a powerful shot but was described in the Telegraph, after scoring a hat trick in January 1953, as 'sluggish in movement and thought'. At his best on heavy grounds, he was difficult to dispossess but made only occasional appearances in the high scoring United team of those days and his future as a footballer seemed to be very limited.

Transferred to York City, he made an impressive start, scoring a hat trick on his debut. He was one of the stars in City's run to the FA Cup semi-final of 1955, scoring the equaliser in the first game at Hillsborough before Newcastle won the replay, 2–0, at Roker Park. Even more forceful than in his days with United, he scored 105 FL and Cup goals in 158 appearances for York and his six goals in his first five appearances in Newcastle's colours went a long way towards saving them from relegation. In total, he scored 115 goals in his 205 FL appearances.

Appearances:

	Apps	Gls
FL	24	7
FAC	3	2
CC	4	0
Total	31	9

BOULDING Michael Thomas

Striker 2002 5' 10" 11st 4
b. Sheffield 8 February 1976

Hallam/ Mansfield Town Aug 1999/ Grimsby Town Aug 2001/ Aston Villa Jul 2002
United: (L) 27 Sep 2002 to 1? Nov 2002
Debuts: 28 Sep 2002 United 1 Watford 2 (sub)
1 Oct 2002 United 4 Wycombe Wanderers 1 (LC)
5 Oct 2002 Wolverhamton W 1 United 3
Last game: 30 Oct 2002 Derby County 2 United 1
Grimsby Town (free) Jan 2003/ Barnsley (£50k) Feb 2004 to cs 2005/ Cardiff City (L) Mar 2005/ Crewe Alexandra (trial) Jul 2005 / – / Rotherham United Mar 2006/ Mansfield T Aug 2006 to cs2008/ Bradford C Jul 2008

Sheffield born and a Unitedite, Michael Boulding was a good tennis player, holding an ATP singles ranking between 1996 and 1999, and it was not until 1999 that he decided to concentrate on football as a career. He made his FL debut with Mansfield Town as a substitute on 7 August 1999 at Brighton, his first start coming at home to Shrewsbury on 24 September. After a season with Grimsby Town, his future looked bright when he was signed by Aston Villa but the Villa quickly let him join United on a one month's loan, with a view to a permanent move.

Michael scored on his debut in the League Cup against Wycombe Wanderers and, after some encouraging performances, mainly playing as a wide attacking player, his loan was extended but shortly after, he suffered ankle ligament damage in the game at Derby County and returned to Villa Park. When fit, he moved back to Grimsby Town on loan before making the move permanent but his career has been dogged by injuries.

He spent much of 2005–06 away from football before joining Mansfield after a brief spell at Rotherham. He scored over 20 goals in 2007–08, bringing his total to 76 goals in 187(78) FL games, but they were insufficient to keep Town in the League.

Appearances:

	Apps	Gls
FL	3 (3)	0
LC	1	1
Total	4 (3)	1

BOURNE Jeffrey (Jeff) Albert

Striker 1979–80 5' 10" 12st 0
b. Linton (Burton on Trent) 19 June 1948

Linton United/ Burton Albion/ Derby County Jan–Jun 1969/ Dallas Tornado (L) Apr 1976/ Crystal Palace (£30k) Mar 1977/ Dallas Tornado Mar 1978/ Atlanta Chiefs Mar 1979
United: (£35k) 6 Sep 1979 to 28 Feb 1980
Debut: 8 Sep 1979 Hull City 3 United 1
Last game: 26 Feb 1980 United 1 Chester 1
Atlanta Chiefs Mar 1980/ Seattle Sounders Jul 1980/ Wichita Wings 1982/ Gresley Rovers, coach, 1986 to June 1987

Jeff Bourne made his FL debut with Derby County at Burnley on 24 April 1971 and although he did not feature in the following season when Derby were Champions, he did make 17 appearances in 1974–75 when they were Champions again. A neat, thoughtful player with good ball control and a good finisher, Jeff was one of Harry Haslam's many signings. After a brief time with United, he played for various clubs in the North American Soccer League.

Appearances:		Apps	Gls
	FL	25 (1)	11
	FAC	2	0
	ASC	3	0
	Total	30 (1)	11

BOURNE Richard (Dickie) Arthur

OL 1900–02
b. c1881
d. 1944?

Roundel (Sheffield) 1899
United: 22 Feb 1900 to 6 Jun 1902
Debut: 8 Dec 1900 United 2 Newcastle United 0
Last game: 15 Feb 1902 United 1 Small Heath 4
Barnsley (£25) June 1902/ Preston North End Apr 1903/ Clapton Orient (£100) May 1905/ West Bromwich Albion (£135) Feb 1907/ Walsall Jul 1908 as player/trainer to cs1909

Dickie Bourne was a United reserve player, signed from an Attercliffe team, who scored on his debut but rarely troubled goalkeepers in the rest of his career. He was a Second Division medal winner with Preston and finished his career having made 154 FL appearances, scoring 10 goals.

Appearances:		Apps	Gls
	FL	8	1
	Total	8	1

BOUSATTA Dries

MF 2003–04 5' 8" 10st 6
b. Amsterdam 23 December 1972

Ajax Amsterdam/ Stormvogels Telstar/ FC Haarlem/ FC Utrecht/ AZ 67 Alkmaar to Jan 2002/ SC Excelsior Rotterdam to Jul 2003 / – /
United: 5 Nov 2003 to 24 Mar 2004
Debuts: 9 Dec 2003 United 2 Walsall 0 (sub)
15 Feb 2004 United 1 Colchester United 0 (FAC)
13 Mar 2004 Watford 0 United 2
Last games: 20 Mar 2004 United 2 Bradford City 0
23 Mar 2004 United 1 Derby County 1 (sub)
Karriereende/ Emirati Al Shaab (UAE) Sep 2004

Dries Bousatta had won three full caps for Holland while playing for Ajax but he was a free agent when he signed for United until the end of the season. His opportunities were limited although in his role as an attacking right sided midfielder he showed that he had good control and that he could produce searching crosses. He could not be described as forceful and on his final appearance, he came on as a substitute and was himself substituted after only 14 minutes. Although his substitution was for tactical reasons, it was mutually agreed, the following day, to terminate his contract early but he agreed have a scouting role for the club in Holland.

Appearances:		Apps	Gls
	FL	3 (3)	0
	FAC	1	0
	Total	4 (3)	0

BOWER Kenneth (Ken)

OL 1944

United: 27 Feb 1945(amateur) to cs 1946
Debut: 28 Apr 1945 United 1 Burnley 1 (WW2)
Last game: 19 May 1945 United 1 Sheffield Wednesday 3 (WW2)
Possibly: Darlington cs(?)1946, Jan 1947(pro)/ Rotherham United Jul 1949/ Frickley Coll Aug 1951/ Scarborough 1952–54 / – / S Kirkby Colliery (1957–59)/ ?

Described as 'from Skelmanthorpe', Ken Bower played only four games for United, two of which were against Sheffield Wednesday and it was against them that he scored his one United goal. He played with the 'A' team during the 1945–46 season and was then released.

He may be the centre forward, born in Huddersfield, 18 March 1926, who joined Darlington and made his FL debut at home to Stockport County on 16 November 1946, going on to score 45 goals in 102 FL appearances for the Quakers and Rotherham.

Note also that both Denaby and Scunthorpe U had inside forwards reported as 'Bowers' playing in season 1946–47 and a Rotherham born K Bower died in Huddersfield in August 2002.

Appearances:		Apps	Gls
	CC	1	0
	WW2	3	1
	Total	4	1

BOWES John Thomas

IL/OL 1896–97
b. Middlesbrough OND 1876

Darlington 1894
United: 26 Apr 1896 to cs 1897
Debuts: 12 Dec 1896 Manchester City 1 United 3 (Fr)
23 Jan 1897 United 1 Wolverhampton W 3
Last games: 15 Apr 1897 Stoke 2 United 0
21 Apr 1897 Clowne 2 United 7 (Fr)
Darlington cs 1897 to Oct 1901

One of the many players signed from the Darlington and Middlesbrough area in the 1890's, John may have scored on his friendly debut; accounts are confused as to whether it was an own goal.

Appearances:		Apps	Gls
	FL	4	1
	Total	4	1

BOYD William (Willie) Gillespie

CF 1933–35 5' 8" 11st 0
b. Cambuslang 27 November 1905
d. Bristol 14 December 1967

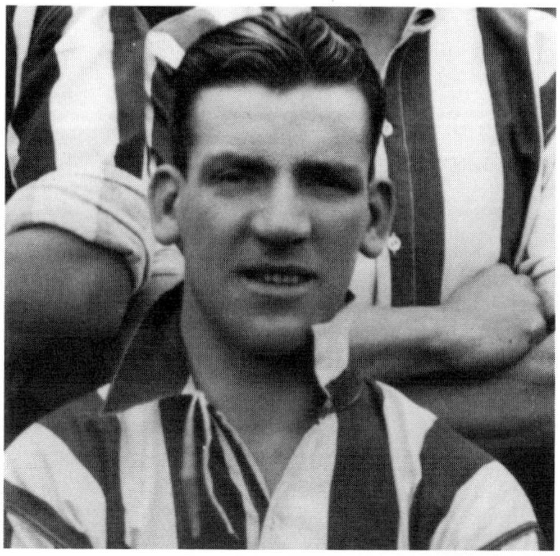

Regent Star (Rutherglen)/ Rutherglen Glencairn/ Royal Albert 1926/ Larkhall Thistle Aug 1927/ Clyde June 1930
United: (£2250) 12/14 Dec 1933 to 7/9 Feb 1935
Debut: 16 Dec 1933 Derby County 5 United 1
Last games: 19 Jan 1935 United 1 Swansea Town 1
26 Jan 1935 West Bromwich Albion 7 United 1 (FAC)
Manchester United (£1750) Feb 1935/ Tunbridge Wells R Aug 1935/ Workington Dec 1935/ Luton Town Dec 1935/ Southampton June 1936/ Weymouth Aug 1937/ Workington 1938–39/ Nuneaton Borough June 1939

Willie Boyd was free-scoring centre forward with Clyde and won two Scottish caps in 1931 and also represented the Scottish League on three occasions.

Signed by Teddy Davison, in his brief time with United, he continued to score frequently, missing just seven games and scoring at a rate of nearly one goal in every one and a half games in which he played. These included a hat trick against the Wednesday and four goals against Bradford City.

A quick, nippy forward who could shoot with both feet, he was full of grit and adept at finding space and timing his runs. Sadly, Willie had problems and was difficult to control both on and off the field. Alcohol was the chief and he lacked the necessary discipline that is expected from a professional footballer. He rarely stayed long with any club in spite of his undoubted talents and the fact that he scored three goals in his last match with Manchester United says a lot about this man of mixed qualities, who scored 52 goals in 80 FL games.

Appearances:

	Apps	Gls
FL	42	30
FAC	3	1
CC	4	1
Total	49	32

BOYLE Peter

LB 1898–1904 5' 9" 12st to 12st 10
b. Mountain Park, Carlingford, Co Louth, 26 April 1876
d. Doncaster 24 June 1939

Coatbridge/ Gaelic FC/ Albion Rovers June 1895/ Sunderland Dec 1896
United: 1 Dec 1898 (£175) to 9 May 1904
Debut: 17 Dec 1898 United 2 Sunderland 0
Last game: 9 Apr 1904 Wednesday 3 United 0
Motherwell (£100) 9 May 1904/ Clapton Orient May 1905 to Apr 1906 / – / Wigan Town Aug 1907/ Chorley Nov 1907/ Eccles Borough Dec 1907 / – / Brodsworth Colliery/ York City player-mgr Aug to Dec 1912/ Brodsworth Colliery player-coach to 1914? / – / Abertillery? manager cs1919/ Brodsworth Colliery mgr-coach

Peter Boyle's family had moved from Ireland to Scotland when he was a child and he came to England when he was twenty to join Sunderland where he made his FL debut at home to Blackburn Rovers on 19 December 1896.

He joined United in 1898 as the club needed a replacement for Bob Cain who had signed for Spurs. The high point of Boyle's career came with United, particularly in the FA Cup in which he made thirty four appearances and gained winners medals in 1899 and 1902 and a runners-up medal in 1901. While at Bramall Lane, he won 5 caps for Ireland, becoming the club's first Irish international and would have won more had he not rejected several invitations in order to play for United. He was described as a 'robust' (occasionally 'dirty') defender with a 'devil may care' attitude, a fine tackler, a superb kicker and a determined opponent.

His relationship with United deteriorated in 1903, Boyle angry that he hadn't received a benefit and he was twice suspended for 'misconduct' before being transferred for a 'nominal' fee, United making him a grant of £10 in lieu of benefit.

He had said that he wanted to return to Scotland but a year later, he was back in England with Clapton Orient and played in their first FL fixture and bringing his FL appearances to 190. After his playing career came to an end, he worked as a miner at Brodsworth colliery and coached the colliery team and later became a manager. His son, Tommy, gained an FA Cup winners' medal in 1925 with United.

Appearances:

	Apps	Gls
FL	150	1
FAC	34	0
ABD	3	0
Total	187	1

BOYLE Thomas (Tommy)

IR/IL 1922–28 5' 9½" 11st 6 to 12st.
b. Sunderland 21 January or 27 February 1897
or Sheffield 1899

Bullcroft Colliery
United: (£125 donation) 13/14 Oct 1921 to 14/15 Mar 1929
Debut: 14 Jan 1922 Middlesbrough 1 United 1
Last game: 17 Nov 1928 United 2 Everton 1
Manchester United (£2000) Mar 1929/ Macclesfield Town May 1930/ Northampton Town Jul 1930/ Scarborough player-mgr May 1935 to cs1936

Tommy Boyle, like his father Peter, gained an FA Cup winner's medal with United. He was a strong, hard working, two footed player who could dribble and, like his father, he wasn't afraid to use his weight. Tommy had a hard shot but he but he wasn't particularly quick. He gave a poor display on his first team debut and found it difficult to establish himself in the first team but his play improved; in particular his heading ability and he began to find the back of the net more regularly. It was principally these factors which led to him being selected, rather than Tommy Sampy, for the Cup Final.

After leaving United, he a brief spell with Manchester United (17 FL app, 6 gl) and it is a comment on how times have changed that the Old Trafford club initially paid half the amount with the remainder to be paid by the end of September with the addition of 5% interest. Tommy then spent five seasons with Northampton Town (142 FL app, 35 gl) before becoming player-manager at non-League Scarborough for just one season. He was successful but chose to retire and became the landlord of the Plough Inn at nearby Scalby.

Appearances:		Apps	Gls
	FL	127	38
	FAC	6	2
	CC	4	0
	Total	137	40

BRADDOCK Joseph (Joe)

CF 1945

United: 11 Jan 1945 (amateur) to cs1945
Only game: 28 Apr 1945 United 1 Burnley 1 (WW2)

A tall centre forward with a local works team, Joe Braddock scored a few goals with the reserves but the first team was a step too far.

Appearances:		Apps	Gls
	WW2	1	0
	Total	1	0

BRADFORD David William

MF 1974–76 5' 5" 9st 8
b. Manchester 22 February 1953

Blackburn Rovers app to pro Aug 1971
United: (£10k) 8/9 Jul 1974 to 18 Feb 1977
Debuts: 17 Jul 1974 Lechia (Poland) 0 United 0 (Fr)
6 Aug 1974 United 4 Manchester City 2 (TX sub)
28 Sep 1974 United 1 Liverpool 0
Last game: 2 Oct 1976 United 1 Burnley 0
Peterborough United (L) Oct 1976
West Bromwich Albion (£6000) Feb 1977/ Detroit Express 1979–80/ Washington Diplomats 1981/ Coventry City Oct 1981/ Tulsa Renegades 1982/ Seattle Sounders 1983/ Tulsa Renegades 1984

On Manchester City's books as a boy but released, David Bradford wrote to several clubs asking for a trial and was taken on by Blackburn Rovers, making his FL debut at home to Rotherham United on the opening day of the season, 14 August 1971.

Bradford was one of several players that United's manager, Ken Furphy, brought from a former club. Furphy's comment, while at Blackburn, that David would be the first million pound player never looked likely and, though he was a hard working player, he struggled to win the support of the fans and a regular first team place. He was transferred to West Bromwich Albion but failed to win a place in the League side and then re-joined Furphy in the United States and played regularly for seven seasons. His FL career total of appearances was a disappointing 122 (12).

Appearances:		Apps	Gls
	FL	54 (6)	2
	FAC	2 (1)	0
	LC	3	1
	TEX	0 (2)	0
	ASC	5	0
	CC	5	0
	Total	69 (9)	3

BRADLEY Gordon

G 1942 5' 11" 11st 10
b. Scunthorpe 20 May 1925
d. Poole May 2006

Scunthorpe United (amat)/ Leicester City Nov 1942
United: WW2 guest
Debut: 5 Dec 1942 United 6 Mansfield Town 2 (WW2)
Last game: 12 Dec 1942 Mansfield Town 4 United 3 (WW2)
WW2 guest: Grimsby Town, Notts County, Lincoln City
Notts County Feb 1950/ Cambridge United Aug 1958/ Glentoran 1959 to c1962

Gordon Bradley made his two appearances for United as a guest player soon after signing for Leicester City during the Second World War. He represented the RAF against the Irish League and he also played in inter-service tournaments. He made his FL debut for the Foxes on 21 December 1946 at West Bromwich Albion and was on the losing for Leicester in the 1949 FA Cup final. Whilst with Notts County, he was ever present for two seasons and on one occasion he scored a goal when playing in an outfield position after injuring a hand. As well as his prowess as a goalkeeper, he was Leicestershire table tennis champion and also played lawn tennis professionally, coaching for the Irish LTA after his soccer career of 261 FL appearances was over.

Appearances:		Apps	Gls
	WW2	2	0
	Total	2	0

BRADSHAW Albert Ernest

G 1896–99 5' 10" 10st 0
b. Staveley JAS 1872 or Chesterfield JAS 1875

Eckington Works
United: 15 May 1895 to 15/21 May 1899
Debuts: 18 Jan 1896 Old Carthusians 0 United 2 (Fr)
20 Jan 1896 United 2 Wolverhampton Wanderers 0 (BC)
25 Jan 1896 Blackburn Rovers 1 United 0
Last game: 11 Mar 1899 United 3 Bolton Wanderers 0
New Brighton Tower May 1899 to cs 1901

Albert Bradshaw was living in Staveley when United signed him as an understudy to Bill Foulke and although he saved a penalty kick on his FL debut, he had few first team opportunities. He made 27 FL appearances for the New Brighton club before they folded.

Appearances:		Apps	Gls
	FL	5	0
	FAC	1	0
	BC	1	0
	Total	7	0

BRADSHAW Carl

D/MF 1989–94 6' 0" 11st to 11st 8
b. Sheffield 2 October 1968

Sheffield Wednesday app to pro Aug 1986/ Barnsley(L) Aug 1986/ Manchester City (part Varadi exchange deal) Sep 1988
United: (L) 5/7 Sep, (£50k) 2/5 Oct 1989 to 28 Jul 1994
Debuts: 16 Sep 1989 Plymouth Argyle 0 United 0 (sub)
30 Sep 1989 Sunderland 1 United 1
Last games: 7 May 1994 Chelsea 3 United 2
16 Jul 1994 Toggaen (Swe) 1 United 5 (Fr)
Norwich City (£450–500k) Jul 1994/ Wigan Athletic Oct 1997/ Scunthorpe United Jul 2001/ Alfreton Town Jul 2002 to cs 2005

An England youth international and younger brother of fellow professional Darren, Carl Bradshaw, a Unitedite, began his career with Sheffield Wednesday but made his FL debut, whilst on loan with Barnsley at home to Crystal Palace on 23 August 1986. He scored in that game and also scored on his debut with Wednesday later that season.

Dave Bassett brought him to the Lane, a move made permanent after an initial period on loan and during his five seasons at Bramall Lane he played in a variety of roles. Originally a right winger, he was used as a hard working, hard tackling midfield player but converted to a wing back in the 1993–94 season when he was also team captain.

Whilst at Norwich City, he was involved in a late night fracas with a taxi driver which resulted in a brief custodial sentence for Carl and he also had injury problems. Following a spell with Wigan Athletic, who reached the Division Two play-offs, and with Scunthorpe United, he moved into non-League football with Alfreton Town and became a building worker in Sheffield. He made 327(69) FL appearances.

Appearances:		Apps	Gls
	FL	122 (25)	8
	FAC	12 (1)	3
	LC	10 (1)	2
	FMC	4	0
	Total	148 (27)	13

BRADY Joseph (Joe)

OR/IF/OL 1892–93

Renton
United: 14 Aug 1892 to cs 1893
Debuts: 12 Sep 1892 United 1 Woolwich Arsenal 0 (Fr)
14 Jan 1893 Newcastle United 1 United 1 (NL)
4 Feb 1893 United 1 Sunderland 3 (FAC)
Last game: 8 Apr 1893 Stoke 1 United 3 (Fr)

Joe Brady joined United in the club's initial season in the Football League. He played in two competitive games and also in 10 friendly matches, scoring in his first, against Woolwich Arsenal but never played in any of the Second Division fixtures. It is possible that he had played earlier in England with Gainsborough Trinity(December 1888) and against United for Lincoln City in October 1890.

Appearances:		Apps	Gls
	FAC	1	0
	NL	1	0
	Total	2	0

BRAWN William (Billy) Frederick

OR 1900–01 6' 1" 13st 5
b. Wellingborough 1 August 1878
d. Brentford 18 August 1932

Wellingborough St. Marks/ Wellingborough Town Aug 1893/ Northampton Town Jul 1895
United: (£125 + a match) 25 Jan 1900 to 23 Dec 1901
Debut: 3 Mar 1900 Aston Villa 1 United 1
Last game: 19 Oct 1901 Small Heath 5 United 1
Aston Villa Dec 1901/ Middlesbrough (£600) Mar 1906/ Chelsea (£180) Nov 1907/ Brentford Aug 1911 to cs 1913
WW1 guest: Brentford, Tottenham H (1 app)

United gave £125 and played a game at Northampton to secure Billy Brawn's signature who became a professional when he joined the Blades at £2.50 per week. He made his debut in the same match as Bert Lipsham and he scored the consolation goal in his final appearance. He was tall and heavy for a winger and had a long raking stride but he only came to the fore after moving to Villa Park where he won two England caps in 1904 and an FA Cup winner's medal in 1905.

His playing days as a professional ended in 1913, with 258 FL appearnces, though he did make a few war time appearances for the Bees and turned out in 1918 for Tottenham when they arrived at Griffin Park with only nine players. He became a licensee in Brentford but returned to football from 1919 to 1921 as advisory manager of Brentford and later became a director of the club.

Appearances:		Apps	Gls
	FL	14	4
	Total	14	4

BRAYSHAW Walter (Wally)

IL 1919–20 5' 7½" 10st 9
b. Mexborough or Denaby c1899
d. Sheffield 17 June 1935

Mexborough West End/ Mexborough Loco 1918/ Mexborough Rovers/ Denaby United
United: **26 Apr (amat), 1 May 1919(pro) to 30 Apr 1920**
Debuts: **26 Apr 1919 Rotherham County 0 United 4 (WW1)**
26 Dec 1919 Bradford Park Avenue 1 United 0
Last game: **17 Jan 1920 Liverpool 2 United 0**
Exeter City May 1920 to cs1921/ Denaby United cs1921/ Mexborough cs1922/ Wath cs1923/ Denaby United June 1924/ Blackburn Rovers Apr 1925/ Southend United May 1926/ Denaby United Jan 1928/ Wombwell Athletic Jul 1929/ Wombwell Town cs1931

Brought up in Attercliffe (Sheffield), Walter Brayshaw was chosen to play for England Boys in Cardiff but missed the opportunity, possibly because of the expense involved. He made an explosive start with United, scoring a hat trick on his war time debut. He had a good shot and passed the ball reasonably well but playing in the FL really proved to be a step too far. He had a season with Exeter City—their first in the Football League—and later with Blackburn and Southend—but with limited results and a FL career total of 31 appearances and 5 goals.

He lived most of his life in his home town but died in the Sheffield Infirmary.

Appearances:		Apps	Gls
	FL	4	0
	FAC	1	0
	WW1	1	3
	Total	6	3

BRAZIL Gary Nicholas

MF/WF 1980–85 5' 11" 10st 2
b. Tunbridge Wells 19 September 1962

Crystal Palace (app)
United: **trial 6 May; 6/11 Aug 1980 to 29 Mar 1985**
Debuts: **4 Mar 1980 United 9 Select XI 1 (BM, sub)**
17 Jan 1981 United 0 Gillingham 1 (sub)
7 Feb 1981 United 2 Reading 0
Last game: **23 Mar 1985 United 2 Leeds United 0**
Port Vale(L) Aug 1984
Preston North End (L) Feb, (£12.5k) 29 Mar 1985, / Mansfield T(L) / Newcastle United (£250k) Feb 1989/ Fulham (L) Sep 1990, (£110k) Nov 1990/ Cambridge United (nc) Aug 1996/ Barnet Sep 1996/ St Albans C/ Slough Town Jan 1997/ Notts County youth manager Jan 1999, acting manager Oct 1999–May 2000, Aug 2001–Jan 2002, then youth development coach/ Doncaster R youth coach May 2004 / FA apprentices (PL) scheme Jul 2004/ Fulham coach 2006

Released by Crystal Palace after failing to reach the first team, Gary Brazil was signed for United by Harry Haslam. An intelligent, left side attacking player, he lacked weight, power and perhaps pace but could pass and strike a ball well and was calm in front of goal. He played regularly from October 1982 but less frequently in the promotion season of 1983–84.

Transferred to Preston with Bob Atkin for £35k, Gary established himself as a striker and was the Player of the Season in Preston's promotion season of 1986–87. He made 166 FL appearances (58 goals) for North End and subsequently, 214 (14 goals) for Fulham, ending his playing career with 438 (53) FL appearances and 121 goals. He moved into coaching and was twice the caretaker manager of Notts County.

Appearances:		Apps	Gls
	FL	39 (23)	9
	FAC	4 (5)	1
	LC	4 (1)	0
	AMC	1 (1)	0
	CC	2	1
	Total	50 (30)	11

BRELSFORD Charles(Charlie) Henry

RB 1918–19 5' 8" 10st 6
b. Darnall (Sheffield) OND 1880

Kilnhurst Town/ Buxton/ Sheffield Wednesday Mar 1912
United: **WW1 guest**
Debut: **28 Dec 1918 United 0 Hull City 0 (WW1)**
Last game: **1 Mar 1919 United 1 Nottingham Forest 1 (WW1)**
WW1 guest: Barnsley v Wednesday Oct 1918
South Shields Jul 1919/ Castleford Jan 1921/ Mansfield Town Aug 1923 to Sept 1926

A tenacious defender, Charles, a younger brother of United's Bill Brelsford, made his FL debut for Wednesday on 9 Nov 1912 at home to Oldham but played only six FL games in total. His two appearances for United were as a guest during the First War and he probably also played in an unofficial game against Wednesday at Tankersley on the 27th of December 1918. A broken leg brought his playing days to an end.

Appearances:		Apps	Gls
	WW1	2	0
	Total	2	0

BRELSFORD William (Bill or Beau) Henry

RH/CH 1909–22 5' 6½" to 5' 8" 11st 9 to 12st 7
b. Darnall (Sheffield) JFM 1885
d. Sheffield 25 March 1954

Attercliffe United 1902–4/ Tinsley Park Jul 1904/ Lodge Inn/ Rawmarsh Albion/ Doncaster Rovers cs1907
United: 30 Apr 1909 to cs 1924 and cs1925 to 1929
Debut: 1 Sep 1909 Middlesbrough 0 United 2
Last games: 29 Oct 1921 United 2 Bradford City 0
11 Oct 1922 Hartlepool United 0 United 2 (BM)
Taunton (?) or Torquay United (?) cFeb 1925/ United training staff June 1925 to Sept 1939

Bill Brelsford was the eldest of four brothers who were all professional footballers. Bill was supposed to have a trial with Wednesday but it never took place but Tom, Charlie (see above) and Ben all played for Wednesday. The births of Charles and Bill were registered as 'Brailsford'.

United made Doncaster Rovers a grant of £20 when they signed Bill and he went on to become one of the club's most determined and hard working players and a member of the 1915 FA Cup winning team. Very strong both in the air and on the ground, Bill was a 'battler' and if there was a 'dust-up', he was usually in the thick of it and he was suspended for six weeks in 1916 after fighting Glennon (four weeks suspension) of Wednesday. A consistent player and prodigious worker, he was a master of the shoulder charge but his passing was never better than adequate.

Bill was an assistant trainer at the Lane for many years and United kept his FL registration until 1929 so that he could have played in a dire emergency. He was the first team trainer between 1932 and 1935 and he later became the kennel master at Darnall greyhound track.

Appearances:		Apps	Gls
	FL	277	1
	FAC	19	0
	CC	2	0
	ABD	1	0
	WW1	118	1
	Total	417	2

BREWSTER John Robert

RB 1964
b. Creswell 19 August 1942

United: jnr to pro 22 Apr/2 May 1960 to Jun 1964
Only game: 29 Apr 1964 Rotherham United 0 United 2 (CC)
Torquay United cs 1964/ Poole Town

John Brewster was a hard working reserve wing half and yet his single 'senior' appearance for the Blades was at right back in a County Cup fixture in a season when the clubs had agreed to field 'reserve elevens'. John joined Torquay United, making his FL debut on 22 August 1964, the opening day of the campaign at home to Bradford City but after 21 games he moved into non-League football.

Appearances:		Apps	Gls
	CC	1	0
	Total	1	0

BRIDGEWATER William (Billy)

IR/CF 1890–91
b. Parkgate (Rotherham) 14 September 1866
d. Doncaster 21 March 1941

Rawmarsh U 1885–6/ Doncaster Rovers Jan 1886/ Newton Heath 1887–88/ Oldham Olympic Athletic 1887–88/ Gainsborough Trinity 1887–88/ Doncaster Rovers Nov 1888 to Oct 1889/ Hexthorpe Wanderers 1888–89/ Rotherham Town (trial Mar 1889) and Oct 1889 to Aug 1890
United: 1 Sep 1890 to cs 1891
Debuts: 1 Sep 1890 United 9 Sheffield Club 0 (Fr)
13 Sep 1890 Burton Wanderers 1 United 1 (MCL)
4 Oct 1890 Derby Junction 0 United 1 (FAC)
Last game: 13 Apr 1891 Burslem Port Vale 3 United 1 (MCL)
Doncaster Rovers cs 1891 to at least 1893–94/ Hexthorpe W 1893–94

Billy Bridgewater scored a hat trick in his first game for United, making his debut with Teddy Cross, another Rotherham Town player. Billy was a lively character with a 'bit of a temper' but he had more than average ability and intelligence. He had played for the local Association in 1889 and retained his links with United, acting as a scout in 1900.

He was also a professional boxer but injuries brought about retirement in both sports. He opened a gym in Doncaster and became a boxing and wrestling promoter there and the manager of two British boxing champions.

Appearances:		Apps	Gls
	FAC	4	0
	MCL	18	9
	Total	22	9

BRIGHT Samuel (Sam)

RH/CH 1900–02
b. Clowne OND 1875

Clowne Rovers Aug 1899
United: 1 May 1900 to cs 1903
Debut: 3 Nov 1900 Notts County 2 United 4
Last games: 29 Mar 1902 United 0 Wolverhampton W 0
1 Apr 1902 Tottenham Hotspur 3 United 2 (Fr)
Bradford City Jul 1903/ Worksop T Jul 1905/ Shirebrook Moores Athletic Aug 1906 to at least 1908–09

Sam Bright had limited first team opportunities with United but did make six appearances in Bradford City's first Football League season.

Appearances:		Apps	Gls
	FL	3	0
	Total	3	0

BRODDLE Julian Raymond

D 1982 5' 9" 11st 3
b. Laughton 1 November 1964

United: Dec 1978 to app May 1981, pro 1 Nov 1982 to 23 Aug 1983
Debut: 2 Jan 1982 United 2 Halifax Town 2
Last game: 21 May 1982 United 3 Sheffield Wednesday 2 (CC)
Scunthorpe United Aug 1983/ Barnsley Sep 1987/ Plymouth Argyle (£70k) Jan 1990/ St Mirren(£50k) Dec 1990/ Scunthorpe United(L) Sep 1992/ Partick Thistle c Jan 1993/ Raith Rovers Jul 1993

When Julian played against Halifax Town on 2 January 1982 he became the youngest player to make a League appearance for United, a record he held until it was broken by Steve Hawes in 1995. Although he made only three senior appearances for the Blades, Julian made over 200 FL appearances in England before moving on to Scotland. There he gained a Scottish League Cup Winners' medal when Raith Rovers defeated Celtic on penalties in November 1994 and in 1995, he gained promotion to the SPL.

He became a driving instructor in Dunfermline but then returned to England, reports suggesting he is a member of the Greater Manchester police force.

Appearances:		Apps	Gls
	FL	1	0
	CC	2	0
	Total	3	0

BRODERICK Mortimer

IR 1950–51
b. Cork 1 September 1923

Cork Athletic
United: (£5000) 30 Jun 1950 to 31 Jul 1951
Debut: 14 Oct 1950 Grimsby Town 2 United 2
Last game: 23 Mar 1951 Brentford 3 United 1
Crusaders(Cork) Dec 1951/ Cork Athletic, United retaining his FL registration until 10 Mar 1952

United signed Mortimer Broderick and Patrick O'Sullivan after they had played for the League of Ireland against the Football League in February 1950. United didn't profit from the transfers though Mortimer, a small, neat forward, did at least make two FL appearances. He had also played against the Irish League before moving to the Lane. A story that one United player loved to tell was that the Irishman, when checking his football pools coupon on the coach home after his debut at Blundell Park, asked if anyone knew Grimsby Town's result!

Appearances:		Apps	Gls
	FL	2	0
	Total	2	0

BROMAGE George

OL 1921–24 5' 8" 11st 4
b. Derby JFM 1899

Derby County/ Doncaster Rovers cs1920
United: 10 May 1921 to May 1924
Debuts: 17 May 1921 Barnsley 2 United 3 (CC)
17 Feb 1923 United 7 Birmingham 1
Last game: 12 Apr 1924 United 0 Huddersfield Town 2
Buxton Jul 1924/ Shirebrook

George Bromage came from a Derbyshire football family (qv William Bromage) with strong links to both Derby County and Doncaster Rovers and he played for both clubs before joining United. He had been a reserve player with Derby County and had played in the Midland League with Doncaster Rovers.

His debut for United was at Hillsborough in a replay against Barnsley in the inaugural year of the Sheffield & Hallamshire FA County Cup competition but he had to wait nearly two years before he could make his FL debut in a 7–1 victory against Birmingham. With Fred Tunstall as the first team outside left, opportunities were limited and George didn't look good enough and was given a free transfer.

Appearances:		Apps	Gls
	FL	5	1
	CC	2	0
	Total	7	1

BROMAGE William (Billy)

OL/IL 1906–08 5' 7½" 11st 6
b. Derby 31 March 1881

Derby Hills Ivanhoe/ Derby County c1900/ Gainsborough Trinity Sep 1902/ Whitwick White Cross 1903–4
United: 27 Apr/1 May 1904 to cs 1910
Debut: 10 Feb 1906 Everton 3 United 2
Last games: 26 Sep 1908 Blackburn Rovers 0 United 1
5 Oct 1908 Wednesday 0 United 0 (CM)
Doncaster Rovers cs 1910 to cs 1913/ Leicester area local football/ Derby County trainer 1918–Aug 1945

A brickburner by trade and living in Derby, Billy Bromage made his FL debut with Gainsborough Trinity (19 FL app) at home to Blackpool on 20 September 1902. He left the Lincolnshire club because they couldn't afford to pay summer wages and he rejected their offer of work in a foundry. He was a tricky and conscientious player but spent most of his six seasons with United in the reserves, taking a benefit in a Midland League fixture against Chesterfield.

He was one of six brothers, all professionals and his son Sidney was on United's books for the 1937–38 season.

Appearances:		Apps	Gls
	FL	30	5
	FAC	2	0
	Total	32	5

BROMBY Leigh

LWB/CD 2004–08 6' 0" 11st 8
b. Dewsbury 2 June 1980

Liversedge/ Sheffield Wednesday Jul 1998/ Mansfield Town(L) Dec 1999/ Norwich City(L) Feb 2003
United: 1 Jul 2004 to 31 Jan 2008
Debuts: 16 Jul 2004 Weymouth 3 United 5 (Fr)
7 Aug 2004 Burnley 1 United 1
Last game: 29 Jan 2008 United 1 Watford 1
Watford (£600k rising possibly to £850k) Jan 2008

A schoolboy England International, Leigh Bromby made his FL debut whilst on loan to Mansfield Town at Barnet on 18 December 1999. Having been released by neighbours Wednesday at the end of the 2003–04 campaign, Leigh signed for the Blades, along with former team-mate Alan Quinn.

He was not fully involved in the pre-season games but, due to Simon Francis' last minute illness, Leigh was called into action in his unaccustomed role as left wing back in the opening game of the season. The former central defender improved the physical side of his game and showed that he was good in the tackle, strong in the air, read the game well and was quick to recover. He regularly reverted to his former position as a central defender and his long throw was frequently used to good effect.

An ever present in his first season, injury brought his run of 80 consecutive FL appearances to an end and knee ligament damage meant Leigh missed the end of the promotion campaign and lost a regular place in the team. His contract ran until the summer of 2008 and Bryan Robson, who had stiffened the defence by bringing in Cahill and Bardsley on loan, transferred Leigh to Watford. By the summer of 2008 he had made 233(7) FL appearances.

Appearances:

	Apps	Gls
FL	104 (5)	6
FAC	8	0
LC	7 (1)	0
Total	119 (6)	6

BROOK Harold

IF/CF/WH 1940–54 5' 9½" 10st 12 to 11st 6
b. Sheffield 15 October 1921
d. Sheffield 9 November 1998

Woodbourn Alliance/ Fulwood
United: 1939(amat), 26 Apr 1940, 3/5 Apr 1943 to Jul 1954
Debuts: 14 Sep 1940 Lincoln City 9 United 2 (WW1
5 Jan 1946 Huddersfireld Town 1 United 1 (FAC)
31 Aug 1946 United 0 Liverpool 1
Last games: 26 Apr 1954 United 2 Aston Villa 1
8 May 1954 Rotherham United 2 United 4 (CC)
WW2 guest: Manchester United, Queens Park Rangers
Leeds United (£600) 1 Jul 1954/ Lincoln City Mar 1

Harold Brook played for Sheffield Boys at both cricket and football and signed amateur forms for United in 1939. He made his first team debut as a left back in a disastrous war time defeat at Lincoln but service at RAF Weeton near Blackpool, meant that he played little serious football though he began to play more as a forward. He had a successful period with Manchester United as a guest player during the 1943–44 season and also made one appearance during the following season for QPR at Highbury, but played only occasionally for United before 1946.

He returned to the Lane playing an important part in the League North Championship team. He was a fast, two footed inside forward with a fierce shot that required little back lift. He could also play at wing half and appeared to have a fine future in the game but, plagued by knee injuries, he was rather slow to mature. 'The trouble with football', he confided, is that by the time you know how to play, you are too old'. This was not quite true, in his case. He captained the 1952–53 Second Division Championship team which had a superb forward line of Ringstead, Hagan, Browning, Brook and Hawksworth and played a vital role in the Leeds United team which won promotion in 1956.

Harold had scored on what turned out to be his final appearance for the Blades in May 1954. The medical opinion in Sheffield was that his football career was over but a specialist called in by Leeds United thought he might last six months. In fact, his knee never gave him any trouble whatsoever and he scored 47 FL and Cup goals for his new club in 103 games.

'Brooky', with Jimmy Hagan, had a sports goods shop on London Road and after he finished playing he was very successful as a newsagent and was a captain and president of Dore & Totley Golf Club.

Appearances:

	Apps	Gls
FL	229	89
FAC	20	9
CC	8	3
WW2	29	10
Total	286	111

BROOKES ('Brooks') John Arthur

OR/OL/RH 1891–94
b. Sheffield JFM 1871

United: 1891 to cs 1895
Debut: 28 Nov 1891 South Bank 0 United 5 (NL)
Last games: 31 Mar 1892 Attercliffe 0 United 2 (WCC)
31 Jan 1894 Lincoln C 1 United 0 (Fr)

John Brookes (or 'Brooks') played just three games for the Blades and possibly one friendly. He may have scored on his debut but reports are unclear whether it was an 'own goal' and the 1894 appearance against Lincoln could have been M Brookes, another United player who made no other first team appearances.

Appearances:		Apps	Gls
	NL	1	0
	SCC	1	0
	WCC	1	0
	Total	3	0

BROOKS (Brookes) Joseph (Joe)

LB 1907–11 5' 11" 12st 12 to 13st
b. Stalybridge c1883

Stalybridge Rovers/ Glossop cs 1900, pro cs1902/ Watford Aug 1903
United: 18/20 Apr 1907 (£275) to cs 1912
Debut: 16 Nov 1907 Bristol City 3 United 2
Last game: 2 Dec 1911 United 1 Tottenham Hotspur 2
Stalybridge Celtic Aug 1912 to cs 1920/ c1921 Hurst (mgr)

Joe Brooks made his FL debut with Glossop, at home to Walsall on 2 March 1901 and became a professional at the end of that season. A first class athlete and amateur cycling champion and as hard as nails, the former Watford captain who continued to live in Stalybridge, quickly settled in at the Lane and formed an excellent full-back partnership with Bob Benson. Relations between club and player deteriorated after an injury and he demanded a free transfer which was eventually granted.

Appearances:		Apps	Gls
	FL	126	0
	FAC	2	0
	ABD	1	0
	Total	129	0

BROWN Arthur Samuel

CF 1902–08 5' 9" 11st 9
b. Gainsborough 6 April 1885
d. Gainsborough 27 June 1944

Gainsborough Church Lads Brigade/ Gainsborough Trinity 1902
United: 21 May 1902 (£350) to 23 Jun 1908
Debut: 25 Oct 1902 Notts County 1 United 1
Last game: 7 Mar 1908 Wednesday 2 United 0
Sunderland (£1600) Jun 1908/ Fulham Oct 1910/ Middlesbrough May 1912 to retire 1912

Arthur Brown was a grammar school boy in Gainsborough where his family ran a business as builders' merchants and monumental masons. Just before his seventeenth birthday, he began his FL career with Gainsborough Trinity, making his debut on 5 April 1902. His talents were obvious and a little more than a month later, he signed for United. An immediate success, he gained two England caps, the first in February 1904 whilst only 18 years old making him United's youngest international and he still holds the United record for the most League appearances and goals as a teenager.

Arthur was quick of mind and body; an opportunist and a wonderful shot who led the forward line with intelligence and he had the rare ability to stop dead in his tracks leaving opponents stranded.

He was never a 'soccer slave'. He was probably the youngest player of his age to take a benefit and made use of the transfer system to his own advantage. His move to Sunderland in 1908 was a controversial and rather underhand affair and an FA enquiry into the affair led to the player paying the costs as his evidence was deemed unsatisfactory. Arthur had threatened to give up football unless he was transferred back to Gainsborough Trinity and allowed to return to work in the family business but eventually he joined Sunderland and no more was heard of the need to work in his home town. Family legend has it that the houses in Gainsborough that he later owned were purchased from the contents of an envelope collected at Darlington railway station. The fee United received (£1600, perhaps £1800) was, at the time, a record.

After spells with Sunderland and Fulham, he moved to Middlesbrough, making just 4 appearances before retiring through injury, having totalled 132 goals in 276 FL games. He became a Special Constable, earning a long service medal, and was a good billiards player and cricketer playing in the Bassetlaw League with Gainsborough Britannia. His brother Fred would later play for United.

Appearances:		Apps	Gls
	FL	178	100
	FAC	9	4
	Total	187	114

BROWN Douglas (Duggie) Alexander

CF/IL/OL 1979–80 5' 9" 12st 4
b. Poole 21 March 1958

Airdrie Academicals/ Chapel Hill BC/ Aberdeen/ Clydebank
United: 2 Mar 1979 to 18 Oct 1980
Debut: 3 Mar 1979 Oldham Athletic 1 United 1
Last game: 3 May 1980 Grimsby Town 4 United 0

An engineering fitter, Duggie Brown played with plenty of enthusiasm but, though he had a reasonable scoring record with Aberdeen Reserves, he was far from successful in a short spell with Clydebank or with United. He left to work for his father, a former professional who was a building sub-contractor.

Appearances:		Apps	Gls
	FL	17 (8)	2
	LC	1	1
	ASC	4 (1)	2
	Total	22 (9)	5

BROWN Frederick (Fred)

IR/IL/OR 1915–23 5' 7" (or 5' 10") 11st 7 to 12st.
b. Gainsborough 28 June 1895
d. Gainsborough 6 November 1960

Gainsborough Trinity 1913–19
United: War guest and 5/7 Aug 1919 to May 1923
Debuts: 25 Dec 1915 Grimsby T 2 United 1 (WW1 guest)
6 Sep 1919 United 3 Manchester City 1
Last games: 28 Oct 1922 Stoke 4 United 0
23 Apr 1923 Barnsley 3 United 1 (CC)
Brighton & Hove Albion May 1923/ Gillingham June 1924/ Gainsborough Trinity Jun 1927 to cs 1928

Fred, a younger brother of United's former centre forward, Arthur, played as a guest during the First War while working at the Hadfield's factory in Sheffield on munitions. He spent part of the War period in the army and became a United professional on his discharge. Strong and skilful with good ball control, he scored on his Blades' League debut but lacked the speed and fine shooting of his brother.

He made a further 114 FL appearances, scoring 29 goals, for Brighton and Gillingham.

Appearances:		Apps	Gls
	FL	38	8
	FAC	2	0
	CC	4	0
	WW1	55	12
	Total	99	20

BROWN George (Gee Gee) Gravar

OL 1908 5' 7" 11st 2
b. Kirkley (Suffolk) 17 January 1880

Kirkley/ Dulwich Hamlet/ Woolwich Arsenal/ Stoke Aug 1904 pro/ Norwich City Oct 1905/ Millwall Athleti May 1906/ Gainsborough Trinity May 1907
United: (£600 for Brown and Kitchen) 26/29 Mar 1908 to cs 1909
Debut: 12 Sep 1908 Sunderland 3 United 1
Last game: 14 Sep 1908 United 0 Liverpool 2

George made his FL debut with Stoke (8 FL app) at home to Derby County on 1 September 1904. He was probably a 'make-weight' when transferred from Gainsborough Trinity (18 FL app) to United with Joe Kitchen the main target. His United FL debut was a disaster, missing a rail connection at York and taking the field two minutes late with the match in progress. Supposedly fast and tricky, the Sheffield Independent reported that he 'held the ball too long' and it was soon evident that he wasn't good enough and he was not retained at the end of the season.

In 1925 he was the caretaker of the British Seaman's Institute in Tarragona, Spain. He returned to England before the Spanish Civil War and was the Clerk of works on various airfields that were being built.

Appearances:		Apps	Gls
	FL	2	0
	Total	2	0

BROWN James (Jim) Grady

G 1974–78 5' 10" 11st 13
b. Coatbridge 11 November 1952

Bargeddie Amateurs/ Albion Rovers cs 1969/ Chesterfield (c£7500) Dec 1972
United: (c£80k) 14 Mar 1974 to 17 Mar 1979
Debut: 16 Mar 1974 Manchester City 0 United 1
Last games: 29 Apr 1978 United 0 Cardiff City 1
30 Aug 1978 United 1 River Plate (Arg) 2 (Fr)
Detriot Express (£27.5k) Mar 1979/ Washington Diplomats cs 1981/ Chicago Sting Dec 1982/ UNITED 25 Mar 1982 to cs 1982/ Chesterfield nc Nov 1982/ Cardiff City Dec 1982/ Kettering Town 1983/ Chesterfield Jul 1983/ Matlock Town Jan 1989/ Saltergate FC to Feb 1990

Jim Brown's debut match with Chesterfield was unusual in that it was played twice because his FL registration was lost in the post and, as a result, the match at Blackburn, on 26 December 1972 had to be replayed in March! His official FL debut was therefore on 30 December at home to Bournemouth.

Jim was signed for United by Ken Furphy who was unhappy with the displays in goal of both Connaughton and Hope following the serious injury to Tom McAlister. He made his debut along with Tony Field, at Maine Road and gave many fine displays. Though understanding with his defenders could be occasionally lacking, Jim was an extremely agile keeper and won a full Scotland cap in 1975, having previously made four U23 appearances.

He played for several clubs in the US and on the transfer deadline day of 1982 rejoined United as cover for Keith Waugh, making just one reserve appearance. One of few goalkeepers to have scored two goals—for Washington Diplomats in 1981 and Chesterfield in 1983—Jim took over commercial duties at Saltergate, while still a player, in 1986 and continued in that role until at least 2008.

Appearances:		Apps	Gls
	FL	170	0
	FAC	6	0
	LC	7	0
	CC	8	0
	ASC	12	0
	Total	203	0

BROWN Michael Robert

MF 1997–2003 5' 9" 11st 8
b. Hartlepool 25 January 1977

Lion Hillcarter FC/ Manchester City, YT, pro Sep 1994/ Hartlepool United (L) Mar 1997/ Portsmouth(L) Nov 1999
United: (L) 17 Dec 1999, (£400k) 14 Jan 1999 to 31 Dec 2003
Debut: 19 Dec 1999 United 2 Blackburn Rovers 1
Last game: 13 Dec 2003 United 2 Watford 2
Tottenham Hotspur (£500k) Dec 2003/ Fulham (£1.5m) Jan 2006/ Wigan Ath Jul 2007

Michael began his professional career with Manchester City, making his FL debut as a substitute on 26 August 1995 at Queens Park Rangers (he was sent off during the game), his full debut coming four days later at home to Everton. He gained four U21 England caps whilst at Maine Road and was City's 'Player of the Year' for the 1997–98 season.

Michael had gained a reputation as a 'big-time Charlie' and played for Portsmouth in Neil Warnock's first game in charge of United but Michael was Neil's first signing and throughout his first three and a half seasons with United, his displays steadily improved. Playing in midfield, he worked tremendously hard, having the speed and ability to beat an opponent both in the centre of the field and down the flanks. His passing was searching and accurate and his long range shooting produced many goals. Without doubt 2002–03 was his best season. As United progressed to two semi-finals and the play-off final, Michael contributed 22 goals, and, as many people remarked, he could have had a 'Goal of the Season' competition to himself.

The following season was an anticlimax. Amid speculation about his future (he would be out of contract at the end of the season), his appearances were limited by injury and suspension and in the January transfer window he moved to Tottenham Hotspur. He continued to play in the Premiership and by summer 2008 had totalled 329(43) League appearances but scored only twice since leaving the Lane.

Appearances:		Apps	Gls
	FL	146 (5)	27
	FAC	6	3
	LC	13 (1)	3
	PO	3	2
	Total	168 (6)	35

BROWNING Leonard (Len) James

CF 1951–53 6' 2" 11st 8
b. Doncaster 30 March 1928

Headingley Rangers/ Leeds United Aug 1946
United: 23 Nov 1951 (£14,000) to 30 Jun 1956
Debut: 24 Nov 1951 Unlted 2 Doncaster Rovers 1
Last game: 26 Sep 1953 Aston Villa 4 United 0
East End Park(Leeds)

Len Browning made his FL debut with Leeds United at Charlton Athletic on 25 September 1946. He made 97 FL appearances for Leeds, scoring 42 goals before signing for the Blades to complete the fine forward line that brought the Second Division Championship to the Lane in 1953.

Tall and skilful with his head and with good ball control, he was a fine leader of the line, distributing the ball accurately and with intelligence but for some time, although playing well, he couldn't score. Relief finally came in a re-played cup-tie against West Ham on the day that King George V1 died when Len's header from a corner kick hit the under side of the bar and fell just over the line.

His professional career ended in October 1953 due to tuberculosis though he remained a United player until the close season of 1956 and a benefit match was arranged on his behalf in October of that year. In 1957 he resumed playing with East End Park in Leeds before a broken leg ended his playing days. He later worked as a representative and as a technician in All Saints' College, Horsforth and has done hospitality work at Elland Road on match days.

Appearances:		Apps	Gls
	FL	65	25
	FAC	8	3
	CC	1	1
	Total	74	29

Dr BROWN-SIM James (Jim)

CF 1908
b. Nottingham JAS 1884
d. Oadby (Leicestershire)) 13 November 1957

Queens Park
United: 5/6 Nov 1908 to cs 1910
Only game: 7 Nov 1908 Notts County 3 United 1
Sheffield FC 1908–09

Dr James Brown-Sim had made 27 Scottish League appearances for Queens Park and scored 14 goals before linking up with United. He showed a few nice touches in his single appearance but 'never seemed to be able to do the right thing'. He toured the USA with the Pilgrims, an occasional amateur team, in the autumn of 1909 and remained registered as a United amateur while playing for Sheffield Club until the close season of 1910.

Appearances:		Apps	Gls
	FL	1	0
	Total	1	0

BRUCE Stephen (Steve) Roger

See 'Managers' section

Appearances:		Apps	Gls
	FL	10	0
	LC	1	0
	Total	11	0

BRYSON James Ian (Jock) Cook

OL/LMF 1988–93 5' 10½" 11st 11 to 12st 10
b. Kilmarnock 26 November 1962

Hurlford Juniors/ Kilmarnock Oct 1981
United: trial, signed (£40k) 18/24 Aug 1988 to 12 Aug 1993
Debuts: 1 Aug 1988 Ljusdals (Sweden) 1 United 4 (Fr)
22 Aug 1988 Halifax Town 0 United 1 (YHC)
27 Aug 1988 Reading 1 United 3
Last games: 10 Mar 1993 United 0 Norwich City 3
16 Mar 1993 United 2 Blackburn Rovers 2 (FAC)
17 Apr 1993 United 1 Blackburn Rovers 3 (sub)
2 Aug 1993 Ullensalker (Norway) 1 United 5 (Fr)
Barnsley (£20k) Aug 1993/ Preston North End (£42.5k) Nov 1993/ Rochdale Jul 1997 to cs1999/ Bamber Bridge

Ian was a part time professional with Kilmarnock, working on a farm as his 'day job' when he was given a trial by Dave Bassett. He had made his Scottish League debut at home to Hamilton Academicals on 16 January 1982 and in 214 SL appearances he had scored 40 goals.

Ian became an integral part of the side for the next five years, including two promotions and an FA Cup run, although he missed out on the semi-final at Wembley against Sheffield Wednesday in 1993. It was Ian who scored two goals in United's first win back in the old First Division (3–2 against Forest after 16 games without a victory). He played mainly as an outside left but latterly in a more withdrawn role. He was a strong, hardworking, conscientious player, good in the air with a powerful shot who could cross the ball well and was dangerous in meeting centres from the opposite wing.

Ian captained the 1996 Preston Third Division championship side and, after retiring, he became a coach at Preston North End's centre of Excellence and worked for the Press Association. He made 338(38) FL appearances scoring 59 goals.

Appearances:		Apps	Gls
	FL	138 (17)	36
	FAC	18 (4)	4
	LC	11 (2)	1
	FMC	4	2
	AMC	3	1
	YHC	3	0
	Total	177 (23)	44

BUCKLEY Patrick (Pat or Paddy) McCabe

OL 1968–71 5' 5½" 11st 5
b. Leith 12 August 1946

Preston Athletic/ Hibernian 1961/ Third Lanark 1961/ Wolverhampton Wanderers (£10k or £17k) Feb 1964
United: 12 Jan 1968 (£30k) to 6 Jun 1972
Debut: 13 Jan 1968 Arsenal 1 United 1
Last games: 19 Apr 1969 Oxford United 1 United 0
20 Apr 1970 United 2 Doncaster Rovers 0 (CC)
16 Jan 1971 Bolton Wanderers 2 United 1 (sub)
Rotherham United Jun 1972(free) to May 1973/ Pan Hellenic (Australia)/ Frickley C cs1974

The son of a Scottish international, Pat Buckley made his Scottish League debut for Third Lanark when he was fifteen. He moved to England, making his FL debut with Wolves at home to Birmingham City on 30 September 1964 soon after his 18th birthday. A tricky player, forever troubled by injuries, he never fulfilled his early promise.

When his playing days ended, Paddy held managerial and coaching posts with Goole Town, Sheffield Club, Retford Town, Kiveton Park and Alfreton Town (1990).

Appearances:		Apps	Gls
	FL	9 (6)	2
	FAC	1	0
	CC	2 (1)	0
	Total	12 (7)	2

BUCKLEY William (Bill) E

CH 1944–45
b. c1923
d. 2006

Worrall United
United: 12 Jan 1944 (am), 12 Feb 1944 (pro) to 30 Jun 1949
Debut: 10 Apr 1944 Barnsley 5 United 1 (WW2)
Last game: 21 Apr 1945 Burnley 2 United 0 (WW2)
Stocksbridge Works to cs 1958

A tall centre half, Bill Buckley had a trial with the reserve team in December 1943. He played for the British Army in Brussels against the Belgian Army in 1948 but never played for United's first team in his last four seasons with the club.

Appearances:		Apps	Gls
	WW2	2	0
	Total	2	0

BUDDERY Harold

CF 1915–17 5' 9" 11st 7
b. Sheffield 6 October ? 1889
d. Sheffield 23 August 1962

Denaby United/ Doncaster Rovers 1912/ Portsmouth May 1913
United: WW1 guest
Debut: 18 Dec 1915 United 5 Huddersfield Town 1 (WW1)
Last game: 6 Jan 1917 Rotherham County 2 United 0 (WW1)
WW1 guest: Barnsley, Bradford PA, Huddersfield Town, Rotherham County, Wednesday
Southend United Nov 1921 to cs 1922 / – / Rotherham T Oct 1924

Harold Buddery played regularly for Pompey in the Southern League but his FL debut came when the Third Division was formed in 1920 playing in their third ever League game at Swansea Town on 4 September 1920.

During the First War he played only occasional games for Portsmouth, but did make guest appearances for various clubs. A hard working player with United, he went six games without scoring and then bagged a hat trick.

Appearances:

	Apps	Gls
WW1	25	9
Total	25	9

BUET E

LH 1918

United: WW1 guest
Only game: 6 Apr 1918 Barnsley 1 United 1 (WW1)

Nothing is known about this player, who made one guest appearance during the First World War. The Football League records give his name as E Buet. Various local papers give his name as 'Batesmead', 'Bewet' and 'Beylet'. Rotherham County fielded a right half reported as 'Bluer' in March and April 1916.

Appearances:

	Apps	Gls
WW1	1	0
Total	1	0

BULLOCK Darren John

MF 2001 5' 9" 12st 10
b. Worcester 12 January (or February) 1969

Nuneaton Borough/ Huddersfield Town (£55k) Nov 1993/ Swindon Town (£400k) Feb 1997/ Bury (£150k) Feb 1999/ Rushden & Diamonds(L) Mar 2000
United: Trial 21st and (L)22 Mar 2001 to 8 May 2001
Debuts: 21 Mar 2001 Scarborough 1 United 3 (trial, Fr)
1 Apr 2001 Sheffield Wednesday 1 United 2
Last game: 17 Apr 2001 United 1 Wimbledon 0
Worcester City Oct 2001

Darren Bullock began his FL career when Neil Warnock signed him for Huddersfield Town and gave him his debut on 20 November 1993 at Blackpool and it was Neil who signed him for United, on loan, on deadline day in March 2001. Described by his manager as a 'likeable rogue', he made a few promisingly combative displays, including his debut in the Sheffield 'derby' but a hernia injury ended his hopes of a permanent deal and he returned to Bury.

When he moved into non-League football he had made 233(20) career FL appearances.

Appearances:

	Apps	Gls
FL	6	0
Total	6	0

BURGIN Edward (Ted)

G 1949–57 5' 9" 11st 7
b. Bradfield/Stannington (Sheffield) 29 April 1927

Marshall's Sports, Alford Town
United: Trial from 30 Mar 1949, signed pro 25 Apr 1949 to 19/21 Dec 1957
Debut: 1 Sep 1949 Swansea Town 1 United 0
Last games: 6 Apr 1957 Doncaster Rovers 1 United 0
2 May 1957 Boston United 2 United 3 (BM)
Doncaster Rovers (£3,000) Dec 1957/ Leeds United Mar 1958/ Rochdale Jan 1961/ Glossop player-mgr Jul 1966/ Buxton/ Oswestry/ Wellington Town/ Burton Albion

Ted Burgin wrote to United for a trial without mentioning that he was less than average height and played in goal. His ability however, was immediately obvious. Very agile—the players called him 'the cat'—and the fittest player on the books, he was outstanding at punching the ball and incredibly quick off his line. Ted was a great keeper but his career record of over twenty fractures while pointing to his bravery, also indicate that he hadn't the technical excellence of, for instance Alan Hodgkinson, who succeeded him in the United goal.

Ted wasn't the easiest man to manage; he was too outspoken for his own good and there were inevitable disputes with managers, trainers or directors leading to transfer requests and for a time, he became a part timer and spoke of emigration. There were also the occasional off-days—a 7–2 defeat by Rotherham United for example after a dust up with manager Joe Mercer—but these were quickly forgiven by the supporters. He was a member of the 1952–53 Second Division Championship team and went on the FA tour of Australia in 1951 and won England B caps and was in the 1954 World Cup squad as Gil Merrick's deputy.

His career at the Lane ended in December 1957. A medical report after an operation on a finger and a broken arm gave no guarantee of success and after a further injury in a December reserve game, Ted was transferred to Doncaster Rovers. More misfortunes were to come his way before he moved to Rochdale where he played in the 1962 League Cup Final. In all, he made 551 FL appearances before moving into non-League football.

Appearances:

	Apps	Gls
FL	281	0
FAC	20	0
CC	13	0
Total	314	0

BURKE John

OL/MF 1981–82 5' 7" 10st 8
b. Motherwell 10 August 1962

Fir Park B C/ Motherwell cs 1979
United: 16 Jun 1980 to 7 Mar 1983
Debuts: 1 Aug 1981 Queen of the South 1 United 1 (sub Fr)
7 Dec 1981 Barrow 0 United 1 (Fr)
17 May 1982 Barnsley 0 United 0 (CC)
Last game: 21 May 1982 United 3 Sheffield Wednesday 2 (CC)
Exeter City (nc) Mar 1983/ Chester City (nc) Aug 1983/ Motherwell

A Scottish Schoolboy international, John Burke had not played a League or Cup game for Motherwell and only played two competitive games for United but he did win a medal, scoring the winning goal in the County Cup final against Sheffield Wednesday. He made his FL debut following his move to Exeter City on 19 March 1983 at Walsall but managed only six FL appearances in total and made no League or Cup appearances for Motherwell when he returned to Scotland.

Appearances:		Apps	Gls
	CC	2	1
	Total	2	1

BURKINSHAW Ralph (Roy)

OR/IR 1919 5' 8½" 12st 0
b. Kilnhurst/Mexborough 26 March 1898
d. Mexborough JAS 1951

Sheffield Wed (amateur)
WW1 guest: Mexborough/ Barnsley 1915–17/ Wath Athletic/ Mexborough Town Apr 1916/ Sheffield Wednesday 1918–19
United: WW1 guest
Debut: 1 Jan 1919 Barnsley 2 United 2 (WW1)
Last game: 1 Feb 1919 Barnsley 2 United 0 (WW1)
South Shields Aug 1919/ Northampton Town 1919–20/ Wath Athletic May 1920/ Gainsborough Trinity Oct 1920/ Bury Nov 1920/ Bradford City Jul 1925/ Wrexham Jul 1930/ Scarborough Jul 1932/ Mexborough Athletic Sep 1933/ Denaby United cs 1934

Ralph Burkinshaw (newspaper reports frequently refer to him as 'Roy' or 'Ron') was the youngest of three brothers to play League football. Jack and Laurie both played before the First War for Wednesday but Ralph's career began during the War and he came to the fore with Barnsley particularly during the 1916–17 season when he made 31 appearances and scored 18 goals. Given an opportunity by Wednesday, he was a disappointment and although he scored on his debut for the Blades, United were not impressed sufficiently to sign him when the war ended.

After the War he joined South Shields who were newly elected to Division Two and he made his FL debut in the club's first ever League game at Fulham on 30 August 1919. Although playing only once more for South Shields he went on to make 105 League appearances for Bury, 166 for Bradford City and 64 for Wrexham. He later was a publican, a crane driver and worked at a local bakery.

Appearances:		Apps	Gls
	WW1	5	1
	Total	5	1

BURLEY Adam Gareth

M 1999–2001 5' 10" 12st 6
b. Sheffield 27 November 1980

Sheffield Wednesday junior
United: trainee 1997 to pro 1/5 Jul 1999 to Jul 2002
Debuts: 16 Jul 1999 Doncaster Rovers 0 United 1 (sub, Fr)
10 Aug 1999 United 3 Shrewsbury Town 0 (sub. LC)
4 Sep 1999 United 3 Crystal Palace 1 (sub)
Last games: 9 Sep 2000 Birmingham City 1 United 0 (sub)
17 Jul 2001 Sheffield FC 0 United 7 (sub, Fr)
Burton Albion (L) Jan 2001/ Scarborough(L) Jan 2002
Stocksbridge Park Steels trial Aug 2002/ – / Gainsborough Trinity Aug 2003/ Worcester C Feb 2006

An attacking left sided player and former Sheffield Boys player, Adam Burley was on United's books for some time but made only six competitive appearances, all as a substitute and then moved into non-League football. He did make the starting line-up once in a friendly fixture in Tobago.

Appearances:		Apps	Gls
	FL	0 (3)	1
	LC	0 (3)	0
	Total	0 (6)	1

BURRIDGE John ('Budgie')

G 1984–87 5' 11" 13st 3
b. Workington 3 December 1951

Workington app to pro Jan 1970/ Blackpool (L) Apr to (£10k) May 1971/ Aston Villa (£100k) Sep 1975/ Southend United (L) Jan 1978/ Crystal Palace (£65k) Mar 1978/ Queens Park Rangers (£200k) Dec 1980/ Wolverhampton Wanderers (£75k) Aug 1982/ Derby County(L) Sep 1984
United: (£15k) 24 Oct 1984 to 31 Jul/11 Aug 1987
Debut: 27 Oct 1984 United 3 Wimbledon 0
Last games: 9 May 1987 Portsmouth 1 United 2
13 May 1987 Glossop 0 United 3 (Fr)
Southampton (£25k) Aug 1987/ Newcastle United (£25k) Oct 1989/ Hibernian cs 1991/ Newcastle United Aug 1993/ Scarborough Oct 1993/ Lincoln City (nc) Dec 1993/ Enfield Feb 1994/ Aberdeen Mar 1994/ Barrow Sep 1994/ Dumbarton Oct 1994/ Falkirk Nov 1994/ Manchester City Dec 1994/ Notts County Aug 1995/ Witton Albion Oct 1995/ Darlington Nov 1995/ Grimsby Town Dec 1995/ Gateshead Jan 1996/ Northampton Town Jan 1996/ Queen of the South Mar 1996/ Blyth Spartans player manager Jul 1996/ Scarborough(L) Dec 1996/ Blyth Spartans to cs 1998

John Burridge was signed by Ian Porterfield to take the place of Keith Waugh in the United goal and played in one of the least successful and least enjoyable periods in United's history. A flamboyant, popular, character who played to the crowd (though he would deny it), 'Budgie' was very fit and agile, vocal and a good organiser at the back but, surprisingly, not altogether reliable or confident with a high ball in a crowded goal area.

John probably made a record number of moves between clubs including some not listed above where he was a non-playing substitute. He had made his FL debut, aged seventeen, with Workington, at home to Newport County, on 8 May 1969 and gave a superb display on his debut in the First Division for Blackpool at Everton but, in reality, his career, although long and full of interest, never reflected those early moments.

In season 1995–96 he was registered with four FL clubs but played for only Darlington, becoming their oldest ever player at the age of 44. After moving to Blyth Spartans as player manager, he returned briefly to Scarborough, playing his last first class game on 10 December 1996, at home to Notts County in the Auto Windscreens Shield, at the age of 45. In 1998 he became the national manager in Oman.

Appearances:		Apps	Gls
	FL	109	0
	FAC	6	0
	LC	6	0
	FMC	4	0
	Total	125	2

BURTON Ernest

OR 1943
b. Sheffield 2 September 1921

Atlas & Norfolk(Sheffield)
United: 17 Sep 1943 (amat) to cs?
Only game: 4 Dec 1943 Mansfield 0 United 0 (WW2)
Sheffield Wednesday Nov 1947/ York City Aug to Oct 1948/ Matlock Town/ Retford Town/ Selby Town

Ernest Burton made one appearance for Lincoln City at Rotherham a fortnight before his one game for United.in the 1943–44 season and his 3 FL appearances were with York City, his debut coming on 23 Aug 1948, at Southport. His son, Ken, also played for the Wednesday.

Appearances:		Apps	Gls
	WW2	1	0
	Total	1	0

BUSBY Vivian ('Viv') Dennis

CF 1980 6' 0" 12st 1
b. High Wycombe 19 June 1949

Terries (High Wycombe/ Wycombe Wanderers 1966)/ trials QPR and Fulham/ Luton Town Jan 1970/ Newcastle United (L) Dec 1971 to Feb 1972/ Fulham (£25k) Aug 1973/ Norwich City (£50k) Sep 1976/ Stoke City (£50k) Nov 1977/ Tulsa Roughnecks (L) cs1979
United: (L) 3 Jan to 2 Feb 1980
Debut: 5 Jan 1980 Chesterfield 2 United 1
Last games: 19 Jan 1980 United 1 Hull City 1
26 Jan 1980 United 2 Leeds United 1 (Fr)
Tulsa R Mar to Nov 1980/ Blackburn Rovers (£40k) Feb 1981/ York City player-coach May 198/ – / Hartlepool United mgr Feb 1993 to Nov 1993 / – / Swindon Town youth coach to cs 2004/ Sheffield Wednesday girls & women's football co-ordinator/ York City asst mgr Sep 2004, mgr Nov 2004 to Feb 2005 / – / Gretna academy mgr/ Workington asst mgr Sep 2007

Viv Busby made his FL debut with Luton Town at home to Rotherham United on 27 March 1970. Fast with good ball control his goals helped take Fulham to the 1975 Cup Final. His short loan spell with United consisted of three FL games and finished with a friendly, but he did score on his debut.

Later he became an assistant manager at York and Sunderland, the manager of Hartlepool United and held many scouting and coaching posts including working under Howard Kendall for United at the end of 1995 before acting as Fulham's reserve team manager from December 1999 until March 2000. It was reported in October 2000 that he was suffering from leukaemia but he was able to resume working in football with Swindon and Sheffield Wednesday and was York City's caretaker manager in 2004 and has since worked at Gretna and Workington.

Appearances:		Apps	Gls
	FL	3	1
	Total	3	1

BUTCHER L

CF 1941

United: WW2 guest
Only game: 8 Feb 1941 Preston North End 4 United 1 (WW2)

Little is known about Butcher who played just once for United during the Second War when the club was a man short but he probably was the forward who scored for Fullwood, a Preston local side in March 1941. The Football League referred to him as 'an airman based near Preston' and a Preston newspaper refers to him as 'Butler'.

Appearances:		Apps	Gls
	WW2	1	0
	Total	1	0

BUTLIN Barry Desmond

Striker 1979–81 5' 11½" 11st 10
b. Rosliston (Derbyshire) 9 November 1949

Derby County jnr to pro Jan 1967/ Notts County(L) Jan to Oct 1969/ Luton Town (£50k) Nov 1972/ Nottingham Forest (£122k) Oct 1974/ Brighton & Hove Albion(L) Sep 1975/ Reading(L) Jan 1977/ Peterborough United Aug 1977
United: (£15k) 26 Jul/Aug 4 1979 to 31 Jul 1981
Debuts: 4 Aug 1979 Cambridge United 1 United 0 (ASC)
11 Aug 1979 United 1 Doncaster Rovers 1 (LC)
18 Aug 1979 United 2 Swindon Town 1
Last game: 28 Feb 1981 United 2 Huddersfield Town 2

Barry Butlin began his career at Derby County making his FL debut at home to Carlisle United on 18 November 1967. He made few appearances for Derby in his time there, but was a regular for Notts County in his extended loan period in 1969. When he moved to Luton Town, the £50k they paid was, at the time, the highest fee Derby County had received for a player.

He had been one of Harry Haslam's first signings at Luton and he would not be the last former Hatter to come to United. A thoughtful though hardly dynamic striker, he led the line well but lacked pace. He was a regular in his first season at Bramall Lane but his goal tally (7 from 35 appearances) was disappointing and he was no more successful during the following season when United sank into the Fourth Division. He ended his career with 80 goals in 284(17) FL appearances.

He later became secretary of Derby County Former Players' Association.

Appearances:		Apps	Gls
	FL	50 (3)	12
	FAC	5	0
	LC	2 (1)	0
	CC	1	0
	TEX	8	1
	Total	66 (4)	13

CADAMARTERI Daniel (Danny) Leon

Striker 2004–05 5' 7" 11st 12
b. Cleckheaton 12 October 1979

Everton trainee to pro Oct 1996/ Fulham(L) Nov 1999/ Bradford City Feb 2002/ Leeds United Jul 2004
United: (£50k) 30 Sep 2004 to 13 Jun 2005
Debut: 2 Oct 2004 Brighton & Hove Albion 1 United 1
Last game: 12 Mar 2005 Stoke City 2 United 0
Bradford City (free) Jun 2005 to May 2006/ Grays Athletic Dec 2006/ Leicester City (free) Jan 2007/ Doncaster Rovers (L) Mar 2007/ Huddersfield Town Jun 2007

Danny Cadamarteri began his League career with Everton, making his League debut at home to Chelsea as a substitute on 11 May 1997, the final day of the season. His full debut, and his first League goal, came at home to Barnsley on 20 September 1997 but he was always on the fringe of the Everton team for five years (93 app, 13 gl). Following a loan spell at Fulham and two years at Bradford City, he moved to Leeds United on a free transfer in the close season of 2004. Unfortunately, his relationship with the manager (Kevin Blackwell) was poor and after a few weeks and one sub appearance in the FLC, they were ready to part company.

Neil Warnock signed him for United after a private game against Leeds on a two year deal as the Blades were short of fit strikers. Danny made an immediate impact with his speed, trickery and hard shooting and was perhaps a little unlucky to score only once in his first few games. Later in the season he was in and out of the side, most of his appearances being from the bench. He was transfer listed at the end of the season and he joined Bradford City after it was mutually agreed to terminate his contract.

During the latter half of 2006 he served a six month ban for failing a drug test and after one game for Grays Athletic he joined Leicester City and then Doncaster on loan. He joined Huddersfield Town in the summer of 2007, and by the following summer he had played 138(97) FL games but his career has been a series of setbacks and his scoring record disappointing.

Appearances:		Apps	Gls
	FL	14 (7)	1
	FAC	1	0
	Total	15 (7)	1

CADETTE Richard Raymond

Striker 1987–88 5' 8" 11st 3
b. Hammersmith 21 March 1965

Wembley/ Leyton Orient Aug 1984/ Southend United Aug 1985
United: (£130k) 20 Jul 1987 to 18/22 Jul 1988
Debuts: 25 Jul 1987 Chesterfield 1 United 1 (Fr)
15 Aug 1987 United 0 Bournemouth 1
Last games: 7 May 1988 Huddersfield Town 0 United 2
18 May 1988 United 1 Bristol City 1 (PO)
Brentford (£77.5k) Jul 1988/ Bournemouth (L) Mar 1990/ Falkirk (£50k) Jan 1992/ Millwall (L) Oct, (£135k) Nov 1994/ Shelbourne/ Clydebank to Sep 1997/ Millwall youth coach/ Tooting & Mitcham mgr Nov 2002 to May 2006

Richard Cadette made his FL debut for Leyton Orient on 25 August 1984, the opening day of the season, at Brentford. Having scored 49 goals in 90 FL appearances for Southend he moved to the Lane. He was fast but never looked like justifying the fee paid by manager McEwan. He claimed that the 'long ball' tactics used by Dave Bassett and subsequently at Brentford led to his move north of the border. In the FL he scored 86 goals in 225(33) games.

He was voted Scottish First Division Player of the Year for 1993–94 with Falkirk and, after retiring, he became youth coach at Millwall's Academy. His time as manager of Tooting & Mitcham came to an end when he just missed promotion in successive seasons.

Appearances:		Apps	Gls
	FL	26 (2)	7
	PO	2	0
	FAC	2	0
	LC	1	0
	Total	31 (2)	7

CAHILL Gary James

CD 2007 6' 2" 12st 6
b. Dronfield 19 December 1985

Aston Villa from trainee Dec 2003/ Burnley (L) Nov 2004
United: (L) 19 Sep 2007 to 18 Dec 2007
Debut: 22 Sep 2007 Crystal Palace 3 United 2
Last game: 15 Dec 2007 United 1 Barnsley 0
Bolton Wanderers (£5m) Jan 2008

Locally born Gary Cahill made his FL debut whilst on loan with Burnley, on 13 November 2004 at home to Notts Forest. In 2006–07 he played regularly for Villa once he had recovered from an injury on the pre-season tour. He joined United on a three month loan as new manager Bryan Robson sought to strengthen the centre of defence.

Gary made an impressive start and improved as he immediately became a regular in the side. Good in the air and confident when in possession he scored the vital winning goal at Stoke. It was hoped that a permanent move or another loan spell could be arranged but in the January transfer window, he signed for Bolton.

Appearances:		Apps	Gls
	FL	16	2
	Total	16	2

CAIN Robert (Bob)

FB 1891–98 5' 7" 12st-12st 8
b. Slamannan 13 February 1866

Airdrieonians (am)/ Glasgow Rangers (am)/ Everton (pro) cs 1889/ Bootle cs 1890

United: cs 1891 to 2 May 1898
Debuts: 1 Sep 1891 United 5 Middlesbrough Ironopolis 1 (Fr)
12 Sep 1891 Sunderland Albion 2 United 4 (NL)
24 Oct 1891 United 4 Lincoln City 1 (FAC)
3 Sep 1892 United 4 Lincoln City 2
Last games: 11 Apr 1898 United 2 West Bromwich Albion 0
30 Apr 1898 Liverpool 1 United 0 (Fr)

Tottenham Hotspur May 1898/ Albion Rovers Sep 1899/ Small Heath Oct/Nov 1899

Bob Cain made his FL debut with Everton on 2 November 1889 in the 8–0 home victory over Stoke. He joined United before the club had joined the Football League and in his first season played 66 games, mainly friendly matches but also NL and FA Cup fixtures. In 1892 United became members of the Football League Second Division and Bob played in our first ever FL game. He was a regular member of the side until the summer of 1898 and in his final three seasons, he was ever present in the FL games, culminating in United being League Champions.

Bob was a big man though he only took a size five in boots. His game 'was strength personified'. He kicked 'brilliantly without a semblance of effort' and 'tackled shrewdly and generally fairly' and twenty years later, many considered him the best left back that Sheffield had ever seen though others thought Peter Boyle his equal.

When he moved to Tottenham he had made 106 consecutive FL appearances and was the first United player to reach the 100 consecutive appearances mark and not until Derek Pace in the 1960s was his feat equalled by an outfield player.

His move to Tottenham, for which he was paid £70, infuriated United for the London club were not members of the Football League and no transfer fee had to be paid. Bob lived to regret the move which came soon after his benefit. He didn't settle in the south and asked United to take him back but his request was rejected and his playing career soon ended and he returned to his previous job as a miner.

Appearances:		Apps	Gls
	FL	164	3
	TM	1	0
	FAC	14	0
	ABD	1	0
	NL	21	0
	UCL	12	0
	SCC	2	0
	WCC	3	0
	BC	2	0
	Total	220	3

CALDER William (Billy) L

OL/OR/IL 1889–91
b. Scotland
d. late May 1936

United: Dec 1889 to Dec 1891
Debuts: 9 Dec 1889 United 1 Everton 10 (Fr)
26 Dec 1889 United 1 Doncaster Rovers 1 (WCC)
18 Jan 1890 United 2 Burnley 1 (FAC)
Last games: 28 Nov 1891 South Bank 0 United 5 (NL)
5 Dec 1891 United 1 Gainsborough Trinity 0 (FAC)
15 Dec 1891 Mount St Mary's 1 United 8 (Fr)

Gainsborough Trinity Jan 1892/ Barnsley St Peters Sep 1893/ Doncaster Rovers 25 May 1895 to perhaps 1897–98

Billy Calder's first two appearances may have been in friendly matches (23 and 25 November) as a trialist under the alias of 'W Jones'. Reported as from Edinburgh and a smart little outside left, he settled in Doncaster and acted as the honorary manager of the reformed Rovers from 1920 to 1922.

Appearances:		Apps	Gls
	FAC	7	2
	NL	1	0
	MCL	12	2
	SCC	5	3
	WCC	2	0
	Total	27	7

CALVERLEY Alfred

OL/OR 1944 5' 7" 11st 2
b. Huddersfield 24 November 1917
d. 1991

Huddersfield Town am to pro Oct 1943
United: WW2 guest player
Debut: 18 Nov 1944 United 6 Notts County 0 (WW2)
Last game: 25 Nov 1944 Notts County 1 United 0 (WW2)
WW2 guest: Bradford City, Darlington, Leeds United, Sheffield Utd, Sheffield Wednesday, Clapton Orient and Coventry City
Mansfield Town Jun 1946/ Arsenal (£2500) Mar 1947/ Preston North End (£1500) Jul 1947/ Doncaster Rovers (£4000) Dec 1947 to May 1953

Alfred Calverley began his career with Huddersfield during the Second War. He played a few times for Town, but also played as a guest player for other clubs while serving in the RASC.

When League football re-started in 1946 he had moved to Mansfield Town, where he made his FL debut on the opening day of the season, 31 August 1946, at home to Crystal Palace. The £2500 received when Alfred moved to Arsenal was a record for Mansfield at the time. Injury ended his career whilst at Doncaster, having played 196 FL games, 142 for Rovers.

Appearances:		Apps	Gls
	WW2	2	0
	Total	2	0

CALVERT Clifford (Cliff) Alastair

LB/RB/MF 1975–79 5' 10" 12st 4
b. Dunnington (York) 21 April 1954

Dunnington/ York City jnr, appr to pro Jul 1972
United: (£38,888) 18/19 Sep 1975 to 28 Feb 1979
Debut: 20 Sep 1975 West Ham United 2 United 0
Last game: 24 Feb 1979 United 0 Millwall 2
Toronto Blizzard Mar 1979/ Dallas Tornado 1981/ Toronto Blizzard 1982–84

A York City England Youth International, Cliff Calvert made his FL debut on 26 March 1973 at home to Plymouth Argyle. He moved to Bramall Lane as replacement for Len Badger for, at the time, a York City record fee, but this was not the ideal time to move to the Lane as United suffered one of their worst seasons.

He was a quick and capable defender but he did not establish himself as a regular in the side until the 1977–78 season and in the spring of 1979 he moved to North America.

Appearances:		Apps	Gls
	FL	78 (3)	5
	FAC	3	0
	LC	1	1
	TEX	2 (3)	0
	CC	7	2
	Total	91 (6)	8

CAMMACK Francis John

OR 1920 5' 5" 10st 0
b. Prescot 14 April 1900
d. Weston May 1984

Hallam
United: 29/30 Sep 1920 to cs 1921
Debut: 23 Oct 1920 Aston Villa 4 United 0
Last game: 27 Nov 1920 United 0 Chelsea 1
Houghton Main Colliery/ Worksop Town Aug 1922/ Scunthorpe & Lindsey United cs 1924/ Mansfield Town/ Mexborough Athletic Feb 1925

Undoubtedly quick, Francis Cammack's brief first class career consisted of his six successive games for United during which he was never on the winning side. Thereafter he played in non-League football.

Appearances:		Apps	Gls
	FL	6	0
	Total	6	0

CAMMACK Stephen (Steve) Richard

Striker 1972–75 5' 10" 11st 9
b. Sheffield 20 March 1954

United: app 31 Jul 1969, pro 12 May 1971 to 23 Jan 1976
Debut: 29 Mar 1972 Chelsea 2 United 0
Last games: 29 Nov 1975 Ipswich Town 1 United 1
27 Dec 1975 Newcastle United 1 United 1 (sub)
Chesterfield (£11k) Jan 1976/ Scunthorpe United (£15k) Sep 1979/ Lincoln City Jul 1981 (£20k+)/ Scunthorpe United (£3000) Mar 1982/ Port Vale (L) Dec 1985/ Stockport County Jan 1986/ Scarborough Oct 1986/ Worksop Town Nov 1986/ Harworth Colliery/ Heanor Town/ Wombwell Town player-coach Feb 1991

From Wybourn School, Steve Cammack played for Sheffield Boys and became an England youth international. Quick and sharp in the penalty area, he made his reserve team debut a week before his seventeenth birthday but he never quite fulfilled his early promise.

He had a successful time in the lower divisions scoring a career 143 FL goals in 381(38) games. Steve had a particularly successful time at Scunthorpe and is still the club's leading League goal scorer with 110 goals.

He spent some time in non-League football before entering the licensing trade.

Appearances:		Apps	Gls
	FL	21 (15)	5
	LC	1 (1)	0
	CC	1	0
	TEX	3 (1)	0
	Total	26 (17)	5

CAMPBELL Andrew (Andy) Paul

Striker 1998–99 5' 11" 11st 7
b. Stockton 18 April 1979

Middlesbrough trainee to pro Jul 1996
United: (L) 10 Dec 1998 to 13 Jan 1999,
then (L) 25 Mar 1999 to May 1999
Debut: 11 Dec 1998 Bury 3 United 3
Last game: 20 Apr 1999 Grimsby Town 1 United 2
Bolton Wanderers (L) Mar 2001/ Cardiff City (£950k) Feb 2002/ Doncaster Rovers (L) Jan 2004/ Oxford United (L) Aug 2005/ Dunfermline Jan 2006/ Halifax Town Aug 2006

Andy Campbell, an England youth international, became the first 16 year-old to appear in the Premiership. He made his League debut as a substitute for Middlesbrough, at home to Sheffield Wednesday, on 5 April 1996, just 13 days before his 17th birthday. He made his full debut shortly afterwards, at Anfield, on 27 April.

His first loan spell with United was restricted to five games by injury, but he returned in March until the end of the season. He was very fast and direct, both down the centre and out wide, scoring both goals in his final game for the Blades but although manager Steve Bruce was keen to sign him permanently, he returned to Middlesbrough.

Despite a promising start to his career on Teeside, he was injury prone and made only 76(78) League appearances, scoring 19 goals, during his career.

Appearances:		Apps	Gls
	FL	11	3
	Total	11	3

CAMPBELL Robert (Bobby) McFaul

Striker 1977–78 6' 0" 12st 7
b. Belfast 13 September 1956

Aston Villa app to pro Jan 1974/ Halifax Town (L) Feb 1975/ Huddersfield Town (£5000) Apr 1975

United: (£10k) Jul 1977 (FL 11/13 Aug 1977) to 14 Jun 1978
Debuts: 30 Jul 1977 Torquay United 1 United 1 (Fr)
6 Aug 1977 Oldham Athletic 2 United 3 (ASC)
20 Aug 1977 Tottenham Hotspur 4 United 2
Last games: 29 Apr 1978 United 0 Cardiff City 1
11 May 1978 United 2 Rotherham United 1 (CC)
Vancouver Whitecaps (Canada) 14 Jun 1978/ Huddersfield Town Sep 1978/ Halifax Town Oct 1978/ Brisbane City (Australia) May 1979/ Bradford City Dec 1979/ Derby County (£70k) Aug 1983/ Bradford City (£35k) Nov 1983/ Wigan Athletic (£25k) Oct 1986/ Guiseley Jul 1988

Bobby Campbell began his career at Aston Villa, making his FL debut as a substitute on 20 April 1974 at home to Sunderland. His full debut came a week later at Carlisle United. A strong and determined Northern Ireland youth international, Bobby quickly acquired a reputation for poor discipline which United's manager Jimmy Sirrel was well aware of but couldn't tame. Cec Coldwell and Harry Haslam were no more successful and the latter was in charge when Bobby, having failed to remember that the kick off at Craven Cottage was in the morning, took the field in not complete control of his senses.

Later Bobby gained two full caps whilst with Bradford City where he was a great success and immensely popular and was a member of the Irish World Cup squad in 1982. He ended his FL career with 179 goals in 457(190) games, well above half of which were with Bradford.

Appearances:		Apps	Gls
	FL	35 (2)	11
	LC	1	0
	TEX	4	3
	CC	1	0
	Total	41 (2)	14

CARLIN William (Willie)

MF 1967–68 5' 5½" 9st 6
b. Liverpool 6 October 1940

Liverpool amat to part time pro May 1958/ Halifax Town Aug 1962 (£1500)/ Carlisle United Oct 1964 (£10k)
United: 19/23 Sep 1967 (£40k) to 26 Aug 1968
Debut: 23 Sep 1967 United 2 Newcastle United 1
Last game: 24 Aug 1968 United 1 Millwall 0
Derby County (£60k) Aug 1968/ Leicester City (£35k) Oct 1970/ Notts County (£18k) Sep 1971/ Cardiff City Nov 1973 to May 1974

An England schoolboy and youth international, Willie Carlin began his career with Liverpool, making his FL debut, and his only appearance for the Reds, on 10 October 1959 at home to Brighton & Hove Albion.

Signed by John Harris, he joined United from Carlisle and immediately impressed, not only by scoring on his debut but with his work rate and passing in midfield. Sadly his skills did not keep United in the top division and, with the arrival of Arthur Rowley, a transfer was always likely as there had been previous ill feeling between the pair. Willie moved to Derby County who paid what was, at the time, a record fee for his new club.

After retiring, Willie, who had won championship medals with Carlisle, Derby and Leicester and promotion with Notts County and made 424(3) FL appearances, became a newsagent and later had a bar and restaurant in Majorca before returning to live in Derbyshire.

Appearances:		Apps	Gls
	FL	36	3
	FAC	4	0
	CC	2	0
	Total	42	3

CARNEY David Raymond

MF 2007– 5' 10" 12st 5
b. Sydney 30 November 1983

Everton junior/ Oldham Athletic Aug 2003/ Halifax Town cMar 2004/ Hamilton Academicals c Oct 2004 to Feb 2005/ Sydney FC Mar 2005
United: (£46.5k) 4 Aug 2007
Debuts: 14 Aug 2007 United 3 Chesterfield 1 (LC)
18 Sep 2007 Blackpool 2 United 2 (sub)
6 Oct 2007 Bristol City 2 United 0

At the age of 16, David Carney came to England and signed for Everton after impressing in a trial match. He played in youth and reserve games alongside Wayne Rooney, including losing to Aston Villa in the 2002 FA Youth Cup final. Failing to gain a contract, he left Goodison and had spells with Oldham, where he made one sub appearance in the League Cup, Halifax and Hamilton Academicals where he made his Scottish League debut on 13 November 2004 at home to Queen of the South.

He returned to Australia and, after a trial, signed for the newly formed A League side Sydney FC. He was an immediate success and despite interest from and trials with various European clubs in the summer of 2006, he decided to stay with Sydney. In August 2006 he gained his first cap and in the summer of 2007, he accepted an offer from Bryan Robson to the Lane.

The pace of the English game meant David took some time to settle and he found it difficult to win a regular first team place. He played mainly on the left of midfield and scored a well taken one at Colchester.

In February 2008 he was presented with the Australian Four-Four-Two magazine's 'Player of the Year' award.

Appearances:		Apps	Gls
	FL	18 (3)	2
	FAC	1 (1)	1
	LC	3	0
	Total	22 (4)	3

CARR Darren John

D 1988–90 6' 2" 13st 7
b. Bristol 4 September 1968

Bristol Rovers trainee to pro Aug 1986/ Newport County (L) Oct 1987/ Newport County (£3000) Jan 1988
United: (£8000) 7/10 Mar 1988 to 20 Dec 1990
Debut: 19 Apr 1988 United 1 Plymouth Argyle 0
Last games: 13 May 1989 Bristol City 2 United 0
5 Mar 1990 Barnsley 0 United 1 (sub FAC)
Plymouth Argyle (trial) cs 1990
Crewe Alexandra (L) Sep 1990, (£35k) c20 Dec 1990/ Chesterfield (£30k) Jul 1993/ Gillingham (£7500) Aug 1998/ Brighton & Hove Albion (£25k) Jul 1999/ Rotherham United (L) Nov 2000/ Lincoln City (L) Jan 2001/ Carlisle United (L) Feb 2001/ Dover Athletic Oct 2001/ Rushden & Diamonds Jan 2002 to Mar 2002/ Bath City cs 2002

Darren Carr made his FL debut whilst still 17 years old with Bristol Rovers on 3 May 1986, the final day of the season, at Gillingham. He was one of Dave Bassett's many signings in 1988 but played only three games before United were relegated. Darren failed to establish himself in the side but did play a part in the 1988–89 promotion campaign, playing in the penultimate game of the season which clinched promotion and in the final game at Bristol. This was to be Darren's final FL game for United before he left at the end of the following season.

He later moved to Chesterfield where he was a member of the side which was unfortunate to lose to Middlesbrough in the FA Cup semi-final in 1997 and ended his FL career with 282(26) appearances.

Appearances:		Apps	Gls
	FL	12 (1)	1
	FAC	7 (1)	0
	LC	1	0
	AMC	1	0
	YHC	1	0
	Total	22 (2)	1

CARR Franz Alexander

RW 1993–94 5' 7" 10st 12
b. Preston 24 September 1966

Blackburn Rovers app to pro Jul 1984/ Nottingham Forest (£100k) Aug 1984/ Sheffield Wednesday (L) Dec 1989/ West Ham United (L) Mar 1991/ Newcastle United (£250k) Jun 1991
United: 12 Jan 1993 (L), (£120k to c£180k) 8 Apr 1993 to 11 Oct 1994
Debut: 16 Jan 1993 United 3 Ipswich Town 0
Last games: 16 Apr 1994 United 1 Aston Villa 2
14 Jul 1994 Baden (Sweden) 0 United 1 (Fr)
Leicester City (L) Sep, 11 Oct 1994 (£100k)/ Aston Villa (£250k) Feb 1995/ Reggiana (Italy) Oct 1996/ Bolton Wanderers Oct 1997/ West Bromwich Albion Feb 1998/ Grimsby Town (trialist)/ Runcorn

An England youth international, Franz Carr made his FL debut after moving to Forest, on 12 October 1985 at Aston Villa and went on to win nine U21 Caps.

Dave Bassett signed him when United were in the Premiership. He played mainly as a right winger and when on song, his pace and skill caused problems but he was injury prone and never held a permanent place in the side.

After the club's relegation, he spent some of the close season in Portugal on trial but he then moved to Leicester City. Undoubtedly, the best part of his career had been with Forest where he made 122(9) of his 184(33) League appearances.

Appearances:		Apps	Gls
	FL	18	4
	AIC	1	1
	Total	19	5

CARR Joseph (Joe)

LB 1937–39 5' 9½" 11st 5
b. Sheffield 1918/19
d. Dunkirk (France) 31 May 1940, age 21

Atlas & Norfolk
United: amat 11 Jan 1936, pro 12/14 Feb 1936 to his death in 1940
Debut: 9 Oct 1937 United 1 Blackburn Rovers 1
Last games: 6 May 1939 United 6 Tottenham Hotspur 1
8 May 1939 United 0 Sheffield Wednesday 0 (CC)
2 Sep 1939 Leeds United 0 United 1 (FL Div 1)
30 Mar 1940 United 4 Sheffield Wed 3 (WW2)
WW2 guest: Bradford PA, Mansfield Town 1939

A Sheffield Boys player who went to work at Firth Browns, the fair haired Joe Carr secured a regular first team place in December 1938 in the season which saw United promoted to Division One. He played in the vital 6–1 over Spurs, which put United in second spot and rivals Wednesday into third place. He played in the opening games of the 1939–40 season before the Second War began and he also played in the first five friendlies following the Declaration of War. Subsequently, Joe made nine guest appearances for Bradford PA and one for Mansfield Town. In October 1939, he was called up, joining the Royal Artillery, and was killed at Dunkirk.

His tragic death robbed United of a fine full back of immense promise who was cool under pressure and always tried to use the ball.

Appearances:		Apps	Gls
	FL	26	0
	FAC	4	0
	39/40	3	0
	CC	2	0
	WW2	2	0
	Total	37	0

CARRIGAN Patrick (Pat)

CH 1930–33 5' 10" 12st 0
b. Wyndedge, Motherwell 5 July 1898
d. Leicester 4 December 1957

Douglas Water Thistle/ Leicester City Oct 1923
United: 12/15 Mar 1930 (£1750) to 6 May 1933
Debut: 15 Mar 1930 Leeds U 2 United 2
Last games: 29 Oct 1932 Blackburn Rovers 3 United 0
18 Apr 1933 United 2 Sheffield Wednesday 1 (BM)
Southend United Sep 1933/ Hinckley United Nov 1933

Pat Carrigan made his FL debut with Leicester City, on 2 January 1924 at Bury. He had two good seasons at Filbert Street, playing 75 FL games, but then lost his first team place. A rugged, uncompromising centre half, Pat's heading was good but he lacked pace and his distribution on the ground was only moderate and he failed to solve United's central defensive problems.

He failed to make the first team at Southend before moving into non-League football.

Appearances:		Apps	Gls
	FL	52	0
	FAC	5	0
	CC	2	0
	Total	59	0

CAS Marcel

D 2003 6' 1" 12st 8
b. Breda (Netherlands) 30 April 1972

Groen-Wit '58/ Advendo/ NAC/ Unitas 30/ SC Gastel/ RBC Roosendaal Aug 1995/ Notts County Jul 2001
United: 4 Feb 2003 to 7 Jul 2003
Debuts: 18 Feb 2003 United 1 Reading 3 (sub)
7 Apr 2003 Wimbledon 1 United 0
Last game: 4 May 2003 Watford 2 United 0
Grimsby Town Jul 2003/ Roosendaal Jan 2004/ FC Den Bosch Jun 2004 to cs 2006

Having played for various clubs in Holland, Marcel Cas moved to England in July 2001 and made his FL debut with Notts County on 11 August 2001 at Port Vale. This was the opening day of the season and he made a memorable start, scoring County's first goal and went on to make over 50 appearances.

He signed for United (after a two-week trial) until the end of the season and after six intermittent appearances, three as sub, he was released. After a brief spell at Grimsby he returned to Holland but had to retire n 2006 due to a serious injury.

Appearances:		Apps	Gls
	FL	3 (3)	0
	Total	3 (3)	0

CASEY Paul

RB 1980–82 5' 8" 10st 6
b. Rinteln, Germany 6 October 1961

Netherton United
United: app 5 Aug 75, pro 28 May 1979 to 22 Jun 1982
Debuts: 26 Jan 1980 United 2 Leeds United 1 (sub Fr)
8 Mar 1980 Millwall 1 United 1
Last games: 17 Apr 1982 Aldershot 1 United 1
17 May 1982 Barnsley 0 United 0 (CC)
Boston United cs 1982/ Lincoln City Mar 1988/ Boston United cs 1991 to c1996

Paul Casey came into the United first team as a quick and tenacious midfield player before moving to right back. After leaving Bramall Lane he moved to non-league Boston United where he gained a runners-up medal in the 1985 FA Trophy final.

He moved to Lincoln City but he missed the end of what turned out to be his final season when he was given a custodial sentence for grievous bodily harm in March 1991. On his release, he returned to Boston.

Appearances:		Apps	Gls
	FL	23 (2)	7
	CC	4	0
	Total	27 (2)	7

CASSIDY Patrick

IR 1907 5' 11½" 12st 0
b. Willington Quay JAS 1886

North Shields Athletic
United: 29 Apr 1907 to cs 1908
Only game: 12 Oct 1907 United 1 Birmingham 0
South Shields/ Bradford City Apr 1911/ Cardiff City May 1912 to cs1920/ Willington St Aidans Aug 1922

Patrick Cassidy was a powerful looking man who played once for United and made four further FL appearances with Bradford City. He later gave excellent service to Cardiff City in the Southern League being a regular at half back.

Appearances:		Apps	Gls
	FL	1	0
	Total	1	0

CAWLEY Thomas (Tom) Edward

CF 1917 5' 9½" 12st 0
b. Sheffield 21 November 1891
d. Sheffield 15 February 1980

Sheffield Club 1911/ Sheffield Wednesday amat 1911, pro 1912/ Leeds City Feb 1914
United: WW1 guest
Debut: 14 Apr 1917 Wednesday 2 United 1 (WW1)
Last game: 5 May 1917 United 1 Wednesday 2 (Fr)
Rotherham County Jun 1919/ Worksop Town May 1922/ Scunthorpe & Lindsey United cs1925 to cs1926

The son of a famous Wednesday player, Tom Cawley played one competitive game for United followed by two friendly games, all as a guest player during the First War. He scored twice in the friendly against Rotherham County, the club he later joined.

Although he had joined Leeds City before the outbreak of war, he did not play a FL game for the club. He made some appearances for City during the War also for Wednesday and Rotherham County but his FL debut came after his transfer to Rotherham County. He played in County's first game after League football re-started, on 30 August 1919, and scored County's first goal in their 2–0 home defeat of Nottingham Forest.

Appearances:		Apps	Gls
	WW1	1	0
	Total	1	0

CAWTHORNE Harold (Harry) Henry

RH/LH 1927–29 5ft 10½" 12st
b. Darnall, Sheffield AMJ 1900
d. Sheffield OND 1966

Darnall OB/ Handsworth/ Woodhouse/ Huddersfield Town Oct 1919
United: (£2300) 25 Feb 1927 to cs1929
Debut: 26 Feb 1927 United 3 Cardiff City 1
Last games: 5 Jan 1929 Newcastle United 4 United 2
12 Jan 1929 Burnley 2 United 1 (FAC)
Connah's Quay Jul 1929/ Mansfield Town Oct 1929/ Manchester Central Oct 1929/ Middlewich Mar 1930/ Kettering Aug 1930/ Denaby United Jan–Dec 1931/ Woodhouse Alliance

Although Harry Cawthorne joined Huddersfield Town in 1919, his FL debut was not until 18 March 1922, at Tottenham Hotspur. A big, strong, hard working and versatile player, he was a Championship winner with Huddersfield but he was less successful at the Lane as his growing lack of pace was exposed and his playing career petered out in non-League football.

He later was a licensee on the southern edge of Sheffield at Woodhouse and at Halfway.

Appearances:		Apps	Gls
	FL	27	0
	FAC	1	0
	ABD	1	0
	Total	29	0

CHAFER John

CF 1940

Thrybergh
United: cs 1939 to cs 1940
Only game: 25 May 1940 United 3 Doncaster Rovers 0 (WW2)
Thrybergh/ Rotherham United 1944–45/ Denaby United cs 1946

John Chafer made only one first team appearance for United though later he made sixteen appearances for Rotherham, scoring four goals in the 1944–45 season.

Appearances:		Apps	Gls
	WW2	1	0
	Total	1	0

CHANDLER Albert (Bert)

RB/LB 1926–29 5' 10½" 11st 12
b. Carlisle 15 January 1897
d. Carlisle 28 January 1963

Dalston Beach R/ Army football/ Derby County Aug 1919/ Newcastle United (£3250) Jun 1925
United: 28/30 Oct 1926 (£2620 or £2625) to May 1929
Debut: 30 Oct 1926 Leicester City 2 United 2
Last game: 1 Apr 1929 United 1 Leeds United 1
Mansfield Town Apr 1929(never played)/ Northfleet Nov 1929/ Manchester Central Feb 1930/ Holme Head (Carlisle) cs 1930/ Queen of the South cs 1931

After serving in the army during the First World War—he was commissioned in the Machine Gun Corps and survived a gas attack in 1918—Albert Chandler signed for Derby County. He was a regular for four seasons making his FL debut on Christmas Day 1919 at home to Arsenal and 169 FL appearances in total.

He was a strong player, ramrod stiff in appearance, with a good sliding tackle and a touch of class about him. Sadly, he had gambling problems and his final season was poor on the field and disastrous off it. In June 1928 he was censured for not paying in, as the local secretary of the Players' Union, the subscriptions he had collected. Consequently he was blacklisted by the Football League as a player whose 'registration is to be refused' and so his last FL game in England was with United.

Appearances:		Apps	Gls
	FL	70	0
	FAC	7	0
	CC	2	0
	ABD	1	0
	Total	80	0

CHANTREY Robert (Bob)

IR 1918

Kilnhurst Town
United: WW1 guest
One game: 12 Oct 1918 Birmingham 4 United 1 (WW1)

The FL record his name incorrectly as 'Shanley'. Described in local newspapers as 'from Treeton', Bob Chantrey had played occasionally for the United reserve team in the seasons of 1915–16 and 1916–17 and was responsible for bringing Ernest Milton, who would play in the 1925 Cup Final team, to the Lane as they had played together at Kilnhurst. Bob also made one appearance in the 1916–17 season for Rotherham County.

Appearances:		Apps	Gls
	WW1	1	1
	Total	1	1

CHAPMAN Herbert

IR/CF 1902–03 5' 7" 11st 10
b. Kiveton Park, Sheffield 19 January 1878
d. Hendon 6 January 1934

Kiveton Park May 1896/ Ashton North End Aug 1896/ Stalybridge Rovers Jul 1897/ Rochdale Oct 1897/ Grimsby Town May 1898/ Swindon Town May 1899/ Sheppey United Nov 1899/ Worksop Oct 1900/ Northampton Town 20 Jul 1901
United: 3/14 May 1902 (paying a small fee to Grimsby T) to May 1903
Debut: 1 Sep 1902 United 2 Wednesday 3
Last games: 28 Feb 1903 Bolton Wanderers 1 United 0
14 Apr 1903 Bohemians(Dublin) 3 United 3 (Fr)
Notts County (£300) May 1903/ Northampton Town May 1904/Tottenham Hotspur Mar 1905/ Northampton Town player-mgr Apr 1907/ Leeds City mgr Jun 1912–Oct 1919/ Huddersfield Town secretary Sept 1920, mgr 31 Mar 1921/ Arsenal mgr Jun 1925 to his death Jan 1934

Herbert Chapman signed for United at the Wednesday ground after watching his brother Harry, an outstanding inside forward, play against United. A mining engineer, Herbert had moved from club to club as his engineering career had developed. His FL debut had been with Grimsby Town on 3 September 1898 at Manchester City but he spent most of his playing career with Southern League clubs and made only 38 FL appearances.

In his early years, he had played mainly as an amateur but was a professional with Northampton and United. A sturdily built, energetic player, he passed the ball beautifully but lacked pace and wasn't a great goal scorer.

He will always be remembered however, for his career as a manager. He introduced new tactical methods and established the managers' role as being in complete control of team matters. He first led Northampton Town to a Southern League Championship but for a time he was suspended from Football, being caught up in the Leeds City illegal payments scandal in 1919. He worked as a manager in the oil and coke business in Selby but was finally exonerated and returned to football management. He went on to win the First Division championship twice with Huddersfield Town and twice with Arsenal, also winning the FA Cup with both clubs.

Appearances:		Apps	Gls
	FL	21	2
	FAC	1	0
	Total	22	2

CHARLES Frederick (Fred)

IF/various 1911–18 5' 6" 11st

Doncaster Rovers cs 1907/ Mexborough cs 1909
United: 3 May 1910 to cs1912
Debut: 27 Mar 1911 United 2 Middlesbrough 1
Last game: 16 Sep 1911 Bradford City 1 United 0
Castleford Town cs1912 to cs1915
United: WW1 guest
Debut: 11 Dec 1915 Bradford C 1 United 2 (WW1)
Last game: 28 Sep 1918 Notts County 5 United 2 (WW1)
WW1 guest: Grimsby Town, Notts County, Birmingham, Hull City

Reported as a twenty year old when he came to the Lane, Fred Charles played seven FL games for United in 1911 and then joined Castleford. He returned to play for United occasionally during the First War from December 1915 to September 1918. He was also a war time guest player on one occasion only for Grimsby Town, Notts County, Birmingham and Hull City when the clubs were a man short against United.

Appearances:		Apps	Gls
	FL	7	0
	WW1	27	6
	Total	34	6

CHARLES Stephen (Steve)

OL/CF/various 1980–84 5' 9" 11st 12
b. Sheffield 10 May 1960

Sheffield University 1978
United: 14 Jan (pro)1980 to 31 Oct/ 2 Nov 1984
Debut: 12 Jan 1980 Exeter City 3 United 1
Last game: 20 Oct 1984 Oxford United 5 United 1
Wrexham (£10–15k) Oct/Nov 1984/ Mansfield Town (£15k) Jul 1987/ Scunthorpe United (L) Nov 1992/ Scarborough Feb 1993/ Stalybridge Celtic Aug 1996/ Boston United cSep 1997/ Gainsborough Trinity cs 1999/ Boston United Oct 1999/ Matlock Town cs 2001 to cs 2003 / – / Gainsborough Tr mgr Dec 2007

Steve Charles was an England schoolboy international who turned down a professional offer from Wednesday, choosing a soccer scholarship in the USA. He made his debut for United as an amateur player, becoming a professional two days later. A Sheffield University student, he later gained degrees in mathematics and marketing.

A left footed, hard working and enthusiastic player, Steve was used mainly as an attacking player, either on the left or in the centre, but also played in midfield and occasionally as an attacking full back. He was a regular member of the United side which won the Division Four Championship in 1982 and a Welsh Cup winner in1986 with Wrexham.

He was one of the rare players to make over 100 League appearances for four League clubs (all but Scunthorpe), including more than 200 for Mansfield, and he made 592(19) in total. He played non-League football into his 40s.

Appearances:		Apps	Gls
	FL	112 (11)	10
	FAC	9 (1)	1
	LC	12	1
	CC	4	0
	ASC	1	0
	AMC	6	2
	Total	144 (12)	14

CHEESEMUR Frederick (Fred/Frank) Harold

IL 1930–34 5' 11" 11st 1
b. Wandsworth 16 January 1908
d. Folkestone August 1987

Columbia Gramophone Works/ Dartford 1926/ Arsenal May 1927/ Charlton Athletic Dec 1928/ Gillingham May 1929
United: (£1750) 9 Dec 1930 to 5 May 1934
Debut: 20 Dec 1930 United 4 Middlesbrough 2
Last game: 26 Dec 1933 Birmingham 4 United 2
Southend United Jul 1934/ Folkestone Aug 1936

Fred Cheesemur scored on his FL debut with Gillingham at home to Walsall on 31 August 1929 and had scored 19 goals in 55 appearances when he joined United.

At the Lane, it was soon obvious that, although he could pass with accuracy, he lacked speed and, although he played several games in season 1930–31, he was selected just once in each of the following two seasons and for handful of games in 1933–34. He subsequently played 31 more games for Southend.

Appearances:		Apps	Gls
	FL	17	2
	Total	17	2

CHISHOLM Jack ('Jumbo') Richardson

CH 1949 5' 11½" 13st 0
b. Edmonton 9 October 1924
d. Waltham Forest September 1977

Tottenham Hotspur from jnr Oct 1941/ Brentford Oct 1947
United: (£15.2k) 15/16 Mar 1949 to 21/24 Dec 1949
Debut: 19 Mar 1949 Chelsea 1 United 0
Last game: 17 Dec 1949 United 1 Coventry City 1
Plymouth Argyle (£12,612) 24 Dec 1949 to retire 1954 / – / Helston mgr/ Finchley mgr/ Romford mgr

Jack Chisholm made his war debut for Spurs in 1942 and quickly established a first team place as a powerful, stylish, constructive centre half and he also made guest appearances for Fulham and Millwall. Army service and serious knee injuries nearly ended his career and he was nearly 23 years old before he made his FL debut at home to West Bromwich Albion on 23 August 1947. He was also a good cricketer playing for Bedfordshire with one game for Middlesex and later for Devon.

Signed by Teddy Davison in 1949 with United deep in a relegation battle, he was bow-legged and slow and never moved far from his own penalty area but he was a good talker, organising the defence and difficult to get past. He gave of his best but United dropped into the Second Division. He was undoubtedly a character who appealed to the majority of supporters and he was made captain of the team but the players were less enthusiastic. Jack's refusal to live in Sheffield and subsequent transfer request left a situation that was only resolved when he moved to Plymouth where he added 175 more FL appearances to his final total of 247.

In Devon, he attained legendary status until his retirement as a player. After a spell managing Helston and failing as a publican, he returned to north London managing Finchley and Romford and a betting shop in Edmonton.

Appearances:		Apps	Gls
	FL	21	1
	Total	21	1

CHRISTOPHER John (Jack) William

CF 1943–44
b. probably Sheffield

Atlas & Norfolk
United: (amat) 24 Jul 1943, (pro) 28 Sep, 2 Oct 1943 to 24 Nov 1947
Debut: 25 Sep 1943 United 3 Rotherham United 1 (WW2)
Last game: 29 Apr 1944 Rotherham United 1 United 0 (CC)
Buxton (1948–49) / – / Witton A/ Goole T cs 1953

Three of John Christopher's four appearances were against Rotherham United and his one goal was against the Millers. He missed the second half of his debut suffering from concussion after a collision with the goalkeeper. A good header of the ball, he also made one guest appearance for Mansfield Town. He played regularly for the reserves in 1944–45.

Appearances:		Apps	Gls
	CC	1	0
	WW2	3	1
	Total	4	1

CHURCHILL Trevor

G 1942 6' 0½" 12st 7
b. Barnsley 20 November 1923

Loughborough College
United: (amat) 20/23 May 1942 to 13 Apr 1945
Debut: 25 May 1942 Chesterfield 1 United 2 (CM)
Last game: 5 Sep 1942 Halifax Town 3 United 2 (WW2)
Yorkshire Amateurs/ Dartford Aug 1946/ Reading amat Sep, pro Oct 1946/ Leicester City Aug 1947/ Rochdale Jan 1949/ Swindon Town May 1953/ Tonbridge cs1954/ Hitchin Town coach May 1955

The son of a Barnsley policeman, Trevor Churchill rejected a possible link up with Wolves in order to train as a teacher. He played a few games for United before he joined the Navy. After the war, he played for Reading, making his FL debut as an amateur, on 14 September 1946 at QPR.

Although he made no first team appearances for Leicester he made 110 FL appearances for Rochdale, contributing to his total of 131.

Appearances:		Apps	Gls
	WW2	3	0
	Total	3	0

CLARKE Benjamin (Ben)

RB 1935–37 5' 8" 11st 4
b. Dungannon 6 August 1911 or 1913
d. Dungannon October 1981

Portadown
United: (£1000) Apr and 17/23 May 1935 to 5 Aug 1937
Debut: 27 Apr 1935 United 2 Nottingham Forest 1
Last game: 1 May 1937 West Ham United 1 United 0
Exeter City Aug 1937/ Carlisle United cs 1939/ Coleraine 1940–41 player-mgr/ Dungannon local football

An Irish amateur international, Ben Clarke was never a regular member of the side in his three seasons with United. Transfer listed in May 1937, he moved to Exeter on a free transfer though the Devon club agreed to pay United £500 if they transferred him to a League club (an agreement probably cancelled when the 1939–40 season was abandoned). He had reached 52 FL appearances—including two with Carlisle U—before the outbreak of war, during which he worked in an ammunition factory.

Appearances:		Apps	Gls
	FL	10	0
	CC	2	0
	Total	12	0

CLARKE T B A

CF 1889–90

Wentworth
United: occasional, Dec 1889 to Dec 1890
Debuts: 23 Dec 1889 Casuals 1 United 0 (Fr)
13 Sep 1890 Burton Wanderers 1 United 1 (MCL)
4 Oct 1890 Derby Junction 0 United 1 (FAC)
Last games: 25 Oct 1890 Burton Swifts 2 United 1 (FAC)
30 Dec 1890 United 7 Casuals 0 (Fr)
Sheffield Club 1890

An amateur player and a Cambridge University graduate, 'Mr Clarke' often captained United in those early days and played for the Sheffield Association against Glasgow in January 1890. He was a committee member during the 1891–92 season.

Fourteen of Clarke's nineteen appearances for United were in friendly games, but he did score the only goal in his first FA Cup game for the club.

Appearances:		Apps	Gls
	FAC	2	1
	MCL	3	0
	Total	5	1

CLARKE William Henry

RB/LB 1902–03 5' 10" 12st 0
b. Kettering JFM 1880

Kettering Town/ Kettering St Mary's/ Kettering Town/
United: May 1902 to May 1903
Debuts: 29 Sep 1902 Kettering Town 2 United 1 (Fr)
20 Dec 1902 United 2 Aston Villa 4
Last game: 7 Mar 1903 United 1 Middlesbrough 3
Northampton Town May 1903/ Southampton Apr 1905 to Oct 1908

William Clarke made his United debut against his former club in a friendly match at Kettering, United charging no expenses (receipts £48) in lieu of a fee for the player and Herbert Winterhalder. In his four games with United, including two friendlies, William was never on the winning side. After leaving Bramall Lane, he moved to Southern League clubs Northampton Town and then to Southampton where his health deteriorated and a serious knee injury in 1907 led to him leaving the game in October 1908.

Appearances:		Apps	Gls
	FL	2	0
	Total	2	0

CLAY William

LB/RB 1903–04 5' 7½" 10st 3
b. Belfast 1882 or 1883

Belfast Celtic
United: (£75) 3/4 Jun 1903 to 8 Mar 1905
Debuts: 5 Oct 1903 United 1 Wednesday 3 (CM)
10 Oct 1903 United 3 Notts County 1
Last game: 23 Apr 1904 West Bromwich Albion 3 United 3
Belfast Celtic/ Leeds City May 1905/ Derry Celtic cs1906

When he was with Belfast Celtic, William Clay played for the Irish League against the Football League and was a reserve for Ireland. He was a skilful player but not good enough for a regular first team place and severe injuries ended his playing career. Whilst with Leeds City his one first team appearance was in the FA Cup.

Appearances:		Apps	Gls
	FL	7	0
	Total	7	0

CLIFF Philip (Phil) Robert

OL/IL/OR 1967–70 5' 8½" 10st 7
Rotherham 20 November 1947

United: 13 May 1963(app) 18/25 Nov 1965 to 8 Feb 1971
Debuts: 28 Jan 1967 Charlton Athletic 0 United 1 (FAC)
28 Mar 1967 Leeds United 2 United 0 (sub)
4 Apr 1967 West Ham United 0 United 2
Last game: 31 Mar 1970 United 3 Millwall 1
Chesterfield (£7.5k) 8 Feb 1971/ Worksop Town cs1973

Phil Cliff wasn't lacking in technical ability and scored both goals in a Fifth Round FA Cup victory at West Ham in 1968 but he wasn't forceful enough to command a regular place and his last game against Millwall was his sole appearance that season.

During his time at Chesterfield he made 29 FL appearances.

Appearances:

	Apps	Gls
FL	16 (6)	5
FAC	2	2
LC	1	0
CC	3	2
Total	22 (6)	9

CLINCH Thomas (Tommy) H

LB/RB 1899–1900 5' 10" 12st 4
b. Bolton JFM 1875
d. Bolton 27 April 1956

Chorley/ Nelson/ Halliwell Rovers May 1897
United: 12 Jun 1899 to 24 May 1900
Debuts: 23 Oct 1899 United 7 Kaffirs 2 (Fr)
6 Nov 1899 West Bromwich Albion 1 United 2
Last game: 13 Apr 1900 Blackburn Rovers 3 United 3
Reading 24 May 1900/ Notts County May 1904 to cs1905

Tommy Clinch was a player who tackled and kicked strongly, had fair pace and 'knew the game thoroughly' but United perhaps could see future trouble in store and let him go. Before his playing days ended, he did, in fact, receive a six months ban from the Football Association. He made 94 Southern League appearances for Reading but a serious injury with Notts County, after 6 FL appearances, ended his football career. He served in the First World War and then worked in a Bolton mill.

Appearances:

	Apps	Gls
FL	9	0
Total	9	0

COCKERILL Glenn

IR 1984–85 6' 0" 12st 4
b. Grimsby 25 August 1959

Ritz Club (Louth)/ Louth United/ Lincoln City Nov 1976/ Swindon Town (£100k) Dec 1979/ Lincoln City (£40k) Aug 1981
United: (£140k) 20/21 Mar 1984 to 15/17 Oct 1985
Debut: 27 Mar 1984 Scunthorpe United 1 United 1
Last game: 12 Oct 1985 Grimsby Town 0 United 1
Southampton (£225k) 15–17 Oct 1985/ Leyton Orient Dec 1993/ Fulham Jul 1996/ Bashley Aug 1997/ Brentford (nc) Nov 1997/coach or asst mgr/ Woking mgr Sep 2002 to Mar 2007

Glenn Cockerill's father Ron was a Huddersfield and Grimsby professional and his brother John also played for the Lincolnshire club. Glenn made his FL debut as a substitute with Lincoln City on 5 February 1977 at home to Northampton Town, his full debut coming at Tranmere on 23 April.

Signed by manager Ian Porterfield to strengthen United's push for promotion, Glenn had a great engine and he provided the extra drive and enthusiasm which provided more opportunities for forwards Colin Morris and Keith Edwards.

He went on to have a long career in the game making 680(34) FL appearances, including nearly 300 for Southampton. At Brentford, he took on the role of assistant manager and he was then coach or assistant manager at Fulham, Crystal Palace and Woking, where he took the position of manager until March 2007.

It is reported that he is now a full time painter.

Appearances:

	Apps	Gls
FL	62	10
FAC	1	0
LC	6	1
Total	69	11

COCKROFT Joseph (Joe)

LH 1948–49 5' 7½" 11st 0
b. Barnsley 20 June 1911
d. 12 February 1994

Yorkshire Paper Mills/ Ardsley/ Wombwell Jan 1931/ Rotherham United Feb 1931/ Gainsborough Trinity Jul 1932/ West Ham United Mar 1933/
WW2 guest: Dartford, Chesterfield, Huddersfield T, Sheffield Wednesday
Sheffield Wednesday 24 Nov 1945
United: (£2000) 5/6/8 Nov 1948 to 31 Jun 1949
Debut: 6 Nov 1948 United 3 Preston North End 2
Last games: 22 Jan 1949 United 0 Huddersfield Town 0
29 Jan 1949 United 0 Wolverhampton Wanderers 0 (FAC)
Wisbech (player-mgr) cs1949/ Goole 1952

After an unsuccessful trial with Barnsley, Joe Cockroft made his FL debut with Rotherham United on 11 April 1931 at home to Hartlepools United. After a time with non-League Gainsborough Trinity he moved to West Ham United and became a stylish left half, setting a club record by playing 217 consecutive League and Cup games. When war was declared in 1939, he continued to play for the Hammers and was a guest for Dartford but his house was wrecked in 1940 and he moved back to South Yorkshire, working in the Sheffield steel works of Edgar Allen. He played for Chesterfield, once for Huddersfield and regularly for Sheffield Wednesday, signing for them at the end of the War.

Signed by Teddy Davison, his transfer to United was remarkable. Few players had moved between United and Wednesday and Joe, at thirty seven years of age, was making his first appearance in the First Division though this wasn't, as it turned out, a record. The move wasn't however, a great success. Joe was a skilful player and a qualified coach but the relegation struggle in which United were involved was too demanding and he was unfortunate in failing with two penalty kicks and lost his place in the side to Joe Shaw.

After a period with Wisbech Town, he entered the licensing trade and then worked as a printer.

Appearances:

	Apps	Gls
FL	12	0
FAC	2	0
Total	14	0

COLDWELL George Cecil (Cec)

RB 1952–66 5' 10½" 11st 12
b. Dungworth (Sheffield) 16 January 1929

Marshall's Sports/ Norton Woodseats
United: 12/14 Sep 1951 to 30 Jun 1968 as player and to 20 Jul 1983 as a coach
Debut: 26 Apr 1952 Southampton 0 United 1
Last games: 5 Nov 1966 Sunderland 4 United 1
12 Nov 1966 United 1 Blackpool 1 (sub)
also 22 Mar 1981 Truro City XI 1 United 9 (BM sub)

Cec Coldwell was the United captain when promotion to the First Division was achieved in 1961. He was one of the most reliable and dedicated players to have served the club and, when his playing days were over, he remained at the Lane as trainer and coach until 1983 and acted as caretaker manager on two occasions.

He had attended evening training sessions at the Lane but failed to impress and rejected an offer from Bradford City before finally accepting professional terms with United, the club making a grant which eventually became £100 to Norton Woodseats. Cec was twenty two years old and, although strong and determined, he appeared stiff and not a natural footballer and few rated his chances but he 'worked tremendously hard to make himself a top class player'.

Slowly he improved but he didn't have any regular first team games until Fred Furniss was injured in 1953 and it was not until 1955 that he became the established right back. He learned a lot from managers Freeman and Mercer and it was the latter who put together and coached the famous United defensive formation of Alan Hodgkinson in goal, Coldwell and Graham Shaw as full-backs behind Brian Richardson, Joe Shaw and Gerry Summers.

Cec was never a stylish player in the way of Graham and Joe Shaw but he was a first class, dedicated, professional player. He was difficult to beat, his tackling strong and decisive; he was quick to recover and his positional play and covering first rate and he used the ball simply but effectively. He took over the captaincy in 1957 and retained the position until Joe Shaw took over in 1964. His last appearance was the only time he appeared as a substitute.

He was retained as a player until 30 June 1968, although by then he was fully employed as a junior coach. John Harris appointed him as first team coach in the summer of 1969 and he retained that position until 1983 and had two periods of acting manager in October 1975 and from September 1977 to January 1978. Sportsmanlike against an opponent, helpful to his colleagues, modest in demeanour and dedicated as a professional player, he later was a newsagent in Sheffield and ran a post office in Cheshire.

Appearances:

	Apps	Gls
FL	409 (1)	2
FAC	41	0
LC	10	0
CC	17	0
Total	477 (1)	2

COLE George Douglas (Doug)

CH 1937 5' 10½" 11st 6
b. Hessle 2 July 1916
d. Stannington (Sheffield) 30 January 1959

Sheffield Wednesday Oct 1935
United: 6/8 May 1937 to 6 May 1939
Only game: 13 Nov 1937 Swansea Town 3 United 5
Chester May 1939 to season 1947–48/ Stalybridge Celtic

A young Wednesday reserve defender, Doug Cole made one appearance for United before joining Chester shortly before the outbreak of the Second World War. He played fairly regularly with Chester until January 1944 and again towards the end of the War when he also made guest appearances for Rochdale and Plymouth Argyle. When League football restarted he made 20 appearances for Chester.

He later worked in the office equipment business.

Appearances:

	Apps	Gls
FL	1	0
Total	1	0

COLLEY Douglas

CF 1944

United: 8 Sep 1944 (amat)
Only game: 9 Sep 1944 United 2 Nottingham Forest 0 (WW2)

Reported as 'out of is depth', Douglas Colley was also a fast bowler with Atlas & Norfolk, the Sheffield steel firm.

Appearances:

	Apps	Gls
WW2	1	0
Total	1	0

COLLINDRIDGE Colin

OL/CF 1939–50 5' 10½" 11st 3
b. Barugh Green(Barnsley) 15 November 1920

Barugh Green/ Wombwell Main 1936–37/ Wolverhampton Wanderers (month trial)/ Rotherham United (amat) 1937–38/ Barugh Green
United: 5 Dec 1938 (am) pro 12/13 Jan 1939 to 11/17 Aug 1950
Debuts: 29 Apr 1939 Rotherham U 2 United XI 1 (BM)
23 Sep 1939 Huddersfield Town 1 United 2 (Fr)
21 Oct 1939 United 3 Nottingham Forest 0 (WW2)
7 Jan 1946 United 2 Huddersfield Town 0 (FAC)
31 Aug 1946 United 0 Liverpool 1
Last game: 8 Apr 1950 Brentford 1 United 0
WW2 guest: Chesterfield (1940–41), Notts County (1942–45), Lincoln City (1944–45)/ Oldham A 1945–46
Nottingham Forest Aug 1950 (£12.5k)/ Coventry City Jun 1954/ Bath City Jul 1956/ Arnold St Mary's

Colin Collindridge had first played for the reserves in February 1939 and made his first team debut for United soon after the outbreak of the Second War, quickly taking over the first team outside left position left vacant when Bobby Reid returned to Scotland. Fast and strong with a powerful left foot and a fine header of the ball, he was a threat to any defence. He was working in his old job as a miner but switched in the 1941 close season to the RAF and was employed as an armourer.

Colin had made one guest appearance for both Chesterfield and Lincoln City and about thirty five for Notts County when he was recalled

by United for the War Cup North competition early in 1944 and scored a thrilling breakaway goal in the semi-final at Villa Park. He returned to the Lane in December 1945 and, playing at centre forward, played a massive part in securing the Football League North Championship. It was also the season when Colin finally, after seven years with United, made his first class debut when he scored in the FA Cup against Huddersfield Town. He scored a hat trick in vain in the next round against Stoke City and also scored a hat trick for Oldham Athletic in the first of his last two appearances as a guest player.

His FL debut came in August 1946 against Liverpool and he was a major force for United in that excellent first post-war season. He was called on more and more to play at centre forward, despite his wish to feature on the left wing. In the close season of 1950, after rejecting a transfer offer from Preston North End, he moved to Nottingham Forest where he won a Third Division Championship medal at the end of his first season. Despite the war he managed to total 327 League appearances, scoring 103 goals. He was later involved in the catering trade and lives near Newark.

Appearances:		Apps	Gls
	FL	142	52
	FAC	10	6
	CC	3	1
	WW2	77	36
	Total	232	95

COLLINS Neill William

CD 2006 6' 3" 13st 0
b. Irvine 2 September 1983

Queens Park from jnr Mar 2001/ Dumbarton Jul 2002/ Sunderland (£25k) Aug 2004/ Hartlepool United (L) Aug 2005
United: (L) 18 Feb 2006 to 16 Mar 2006
Debut: 18 Feb 2006 Sheffield Wednesday 1 United 2
Last game: 25 Feb 2006 United 2 Queens Park Rangers 3
Wolverhampton Wanderers (£150k) Nov 2006

Neill's career began in Scotland where he was a part timer, studying for a Sports degree. He made his League debut, as a sub, with Queens Park on 24 March 2001. His English League debut came with Sunderland, during their promotion season, on 31 August 2004 at Reading.

A Scottish U21 international, Neill Collins was signed by Neil Warnock on loan to the end of the season, because of an injury crisis amongst the central defenders. Having signed on the morning of the Hillsborough derby he gave an impressive display in the 2–1 victory. He played just one more game before the regular defenders were fit and after one month, following the departure of Sunderland's manager Mick McCarthy, he was recalled to the Stadium of Light. He subsequently moved to Wolverhampton where he played regularly.

Appearances:		Apps	Gls
	FL	2	0
	Total	2	0

COLQUHOUN Edmund (Eddie) Peter Skiruing

CH 1968–78 6' 0" 12st 5
b. Prestonpans (Edinburgh) 29 March 1945

Prestonpans YMCA/ Edinburgh Norton/ Bury from jnr Mar 1961/ West Bromwich Albion (£25k) Feb 1967
United: (£27.5k) 16 Oct 1968 to Dec 1978
Debut: 19 Oct 1968 Huddersfield Town 1 United 0
Last game: 14 Mar 1978 United 1 Stoke City 2
Detroit Express (L) Mar 1978, (Tr) Mar 1979 to 1980/ Washington Diplomats Apr 1981 to summer 1982

After moving to England to join Bury, Eddie Colquhoun made his FL debut on 19 October 1963 at home to Grimsby Town. Coached by Bob Stokoe, he made great strides and was signed by West Brom's manager, Jimmy Hagan. Eddie was denied a Cup Final appearance in his second season when his leg was broken but gained Scottish caps at youth and U23 level but he was unable to get his place back in the Albion team and accepted an offer from Arthur Rowley to join the Blades.

Strong and very quick, he was difficult to beat, very good in the air and tackled and played with determination and with John Flynn as his partner, they formed a real bulwark at the heart of the defence. Appointed captain in the week following his debut, he went on to miss just 15 FL games in his first seven seasons with the Blades. Whilst at the Lane he gained his nine Scottish Caps.

He moved to the NASL in 1978, being a regular for Detroit Express for three seasons, under coach Ken Furphy. In 1981 he moved, with Furphy, to Washington Diplomats. Despite his time in the USA he still managed 487(3) FL appearances. Later, he ran a Post Office in Conisborough.

Appearances:

	Apps	Gls
FL	360 (3)	21
FAC	13	0
LC	20	0
CC	15	2
TEX	7	0
ASC	8	0
WC	5	0
ABD	2	0
Total	430 (3)	23

COMMON Alfred (Alf)

IR/CF 1901–04 5' 8" 13st 0
b. Millfield, Co. Durham 25 May 1880
d. Darlington 3 April 1946

South Hylton 1896/ Jarrow 1897/ Sunderland Aug 1900/
United: **(£325/£350) 24 Oct 1901 to 5 Jun 1904**
Debut: **2 Nov 1901 Wednesday 1 United 0**
Last games: **23 Apr 1904 West Bromwich Albion 2 United 2**
30 Apr 1904 Bradford City 0 United 4 (Fr)
Sunderland (£520) Jun 1904/ Middlesbrough (£1000) 16 Feb 1905/ Woolwich Arsenal (£100) Aug 1910/ Preston North End (£250) Dec 1912/ retired 1914

Alf Common was one of the most famous players of his day though this was in large part because he was involved in notorious transfer deals. He was the first player to be transferred for over £500 and in a sensational move, a few months later, he became the first player to be sold for one thousand pounds.

He had made his FL debut with Sunderland on 15 September 1900 at Wolverhampton Wanderers and came to the Lane, for a large fee by the standards of the time, early in the following season. A strong, aggressive forward, he moved surprisingly quickly for such a burly figure. He had great stamina, played with contagious enthusiasm and his close ball control and powerful shooting made him a very dangerous forward. Whilst with United he was awarded two England caps, played for the Football League and won a FA Cup Winners' medal in 1902, scoring in the first drawn game against Southampton.

In the close season of 1904 he asked for a move back to Sunderland because of 'business interests' and United felt forced to agree although they claimed that other clubs were willing to pay more money than Sunderland. His move to Middlesbrough a few months later, 'business interests' apparently forgotten, was sensational news. The transfer and fee were regarded as obscene and led to attempts to limit fees and Common was referred to as the 'wandering Jew of football' and yet he would still be awarded one further cap and total 389 FL appearances.

After retiring from football, he was a licensee in Darlington for many years.

Appearances:

	Apps	Gls
FL	67	21
FAC	12	3
Total	79	24

CONNAUGHTON Patrick John

G 1973–74 5' 11" 10st 12
b. Wigan 23 September 1949

Manchester United from app Oct 1966/ Halifax Town(L) Sep 1969/ Torquay United (L) Oct 1971
United: **(£15k) 30 Sep/2 Oct 1972 to 28 Jun 1974**
Debut: **27 Oct 1973 Liverpool 1 United 0**
Last game: **12 Jan 1974 United 2 Tottenham Hotspur 2**
Port Vale Jun 1974/ Altrincham Jan 1980

An England youth international, John Connaughton began his professional career at Old Trafford where he made three FL appearances for the club; the first being at Bramall Lane in a 1–1 draw on 4 April 1972. His FL debut had come earlier while on loan at Halifax Town away to Tranmere Rovers on 18 October 1969.

A serious injury to Tom McAlister gave him a first team opportunity at the Lane but he didn't satisfy, leading to the recall of John Hope and the signing of Jim Brown.

His longest spell of success was with Port Vale where he played 191 games and was voted 'Player of the Year' in 1975. With Altrincham, he was on the losing side, to Enfield, in the FA Trophy final.

Appearances:

	Apps	Gls
FL	12	0
FAC	1	0
CC	1	0
Total	14	0

CONNOR Edward (Ted/Teddy)

OR 1911 5' 7½" 10st 4
b. Salford OND 1890
d. Barton (Stretford) 19 January 1955

Altrincham/ Walkden Central/ Pendlebury Lincoln City (amat) Nov 1907/ Eccles Borough Feb 1908/ Manchester United May 1909
United: **(£300) 8 Jun 1911 to 5 Jul 1912**
Debut: **2 Sep 1911 Oldham Athletic 2 United 3**
Last game: **9 Dec 1911 Manchester United 1 United 0**
Bury Jul 1912/ Exeter City cs 1919/ Rochdale Jul 1920/ Nelson/ Chesterfield Oct 1921/ Saltney Athletic Dec 1921/ Chesterfield Apr 1922

Edward Connor made his FL debut as an amateur with Lincoln City at Hull City on Christmas Day 1907 although he had played earlier, on 23 November, at Glossop but that game was abandoned due to bad light.

He played for Manchester United (15 app) and was on their transfer list at a fee of £750 but came to the Lane after the League reduced this to £300. A quick two footed player who centred accurately, he failed to solve United's outside right problem and was transfer listed at £150 and was sold, with Billy Peake, to Bury.

Edward played regularly for Bury until 1917 and occasionally in 1918 and made possible guest appearances for Stoke and Manchester City. After he retired he scouted for Manchester United and was a member of the Old Trafford office staff for many years.

Appearances:		Apps	Gls
	FL	14	0
	Total	14	0

CONROY Steven (Steve) Harold

G 1974–84 5' 11" 12st 10
b. Chesterfield 19 December 1956

United: from 10 Jul 1972 and app Jun 1974 to 13 Feb 1983
Debuts: 7 Jun 1974 Apoel (Greece) 0 United 4 (CIT sub)
23 Aug 1977 United 2 Hull City 0
Last games: 4 Dec 1982 Wigan Athletic 3 United 2
18 Apr 1984 United 1 Ipswich Town 1 (BM)
Leeds Utd (L) Oct 1981/
Rotherham (nc) Feb 1983/ Rochdale Jun 1983/ Rotherham United Jan to Dec 1985

Steve Conroy played for North East Derbyshire, Chesterfield and England Boys before joining the Lane ground-staff. He held a regular first team place from August 1978 but lost it because of a broken arm in a match at St Mirren in December 1979. He was back playing for the reserve team in March and returned to the first team a year later, in the season when United were relegated to the Fourth Division.

He continued to be dogged by injuries and these brought his playing career to an end. His final game in a United shirt, a benefit match for Les Tibbott, took place after he had signed for Rotherham United, although he made no first team appearances during his second spell at Millmoor.

He was later involved in part time coaching at the Lane.

Appearances:		Apps	Gls
	FL	104	0
	FAC	6	0
	LC	9	0
	ASC	11	0
	AMC	1 (3)	0
	CC	4	0
	Total	135 (3)	0

COOK A

OL 1918–19

United: WW1 guest
Debut: 9 Nov 1918 United 6 Lincoln City 1 (WW1)
Last game: 8 Mar 1919 Leeds City 2 United 1 (WW1)
Wath Athletic Aug 1919

Referred to as 'well built' and 'the youngster from the 'Mexborough district', Cook or 'Cooke' may have been on the books of Doncaster Rovers and played a few games for Rotherham County in 1916 before assisting United in these war-time games.

Appearances:		Apps	Gls
	WW1	3	0
	Total	3	0

COOK Herbert (Bert)

IL 1910 and 1915–16 5' 8" 9st 10
b. Sheffield c1888

Worksop/Thorpe Hesley
United: 28 Apr 1908 to cs 1912
Debut: 19 Sep 1910 United 2 Liverpool 0
Last games: 1 Oct 1910 United 0 Nottingham Forest 1
3 Oct 1910 Wednesday 2 United 0 (CM)
Doncaster Rovers Jun 1912/ Chesterfield May 1913/ Mexborough Town cs1914
United: WW1 guest
Debut: 4 Sep 1915 Lincoln C 7 United 3 (WW1)
Last game: 4 Mar 1916 Hull City 5 United 2 (WW1)
Halifax T 1919–20 / – / Sheffield Old Boys (1926)

Bert Cook played his three FL games and one friendly, in 1910. A fair haired, part time player who worked for Mappin & Webb, he turned down the offer of full-time terms and joined Doncaster and then Chesterfield where he had the misfortune to break his leg.

He returned to play two games for United during the First War before joining the Royal Flying Corps and played twice for Watford.

It is not certain that he is the same player who later, with United's permission, made six appearances for Chesterfield (March and April 1916 and April 1917).

Appearances:		Apps	Gls
	FL	3	1
	WW1	2	0
	Total	5	1

COOK William (Bill)

RB 1912–27 5' 7½" 10st 8 to 12st 0
b. Usworth (Co. Durham) 2 March 1890
d. Sheffield 24 May 1974

Hebburn Argyle
United: (c£80) 13/16 Apr 1912 to May 1929
Debut: 28 Sep 1912 Bradford City 3 United 1
Last games: 17 Mar 1926 Arsenal 4 United 0
8 Jan 1927 United 2 Arsenal 3 (FAC)
Worksop Town Aug 1929 as player/coach

An FA Cup winner with United in 1915 and 1925, Bill Cook played football with a smile and no fuss. He could kick a ball with either foot, untroubled at whatever angle it came to him. A steady, composed, tactical player and as hard as steel, he lacked pace but his positional play and anticipation more than compensated.

Despite playing more than 250 FL games for United and more than 300 in total, Bill never scored a goal. Probably his best chance was against Bradford Park Avenue in 1915 when he took a penalty kick but it was saved. He did claim a goal in junior football but admitted it went through the goal on an adjoining pitch!

He played at right back in all his games but for one war time game when he switched to left back. A miner in the early part of the war, he served in the Northumberland Fusiliers and the Royal Field Artillery and was awarded the DCM in 1918. He played little war time football but did turn out for Hebburn Argyle and in February 1919 with Darlington Forge.

Strange to relate, in his playing days, he lived in the North East but moved to Sheffield when he gave up the game, first keeping a shop and then the George Hotel in Boston Street and from April 1935, worked for at least twenty years at Metro-Vickers.

Appearances:		Apps	Gls
	FL	264	0
	FAC	33	0
	CC	5	0
	WW1	21	0
	ABD	1	0
	Total	324 (7)	0

COONEY Joseph (Joe)

OL/IL 1918

Silverwood
United: WW1 guest
Debut: 26 Oct 1918 United 1 Rotherham County 0 (WW1)
Last game: 2 Nov 1918 Lincoln City 2 United 1 (WW1)
Mexborough FC Apr 1918 / – / Maltby Main (1924–27)

Described as 'from Rawmarsh' and a 'Silverwood youth', Joe Cooney was playing for Silverwood in 1916 and made three war time appearances for Grimsby Town in the latter half of that year. Joe may have scored in the last of his two appearances for United. Press reports suggest either he or E Cutts scored United's goal. He also assisted Rotherham County in November 1918.

Appearances:		Apps	Gls
	WW1	2	0
	Total	2	0

COOP James (Jim) Yates

OL 1947–48 5' 7½" 10st 10
b. Horwich 17 September 1927
d. Doncaster March 1996

Brodsworth Main Colliery
United: 24 Jan (Utd records)/ 9 May 1946 (£150) to 11 Jul 1949
Debut: 8 Nov 1947 United 1 Derby County 2
Last game: 11 Dec 1948 Newcastle United 3 United 2
York City (£750) Jul 1949/ Goole Town Jul 1951/ Frickley Colliery Aug 1952

Jim Coop made a guest appearance for Shrewsbury Town in an away fixture against Denaby United (Midland League) on the 25 March 1946. He had a useful left foot and a fair turn of speed but never looked likely to succeed at the top level and made just thirteen senior appearances for York after leaving United. He later worked at Askern Colliery.

Appearances:		Apps	Gls
	FL	9	1
	Total	9	1

COOPER Richard David

MF 1982–85 5' 10" 10st 8
b. Brent (London) 7 May 1965

United: from 8 Jun 1981 to 30 Jun 1985
Debuts: 21 May 1982 United 3 Sheffield Wednesday 2 (CC sub)
8 May 1983 Bradford City 2 United 0 (sub)
14 May 1983 Orient 4 United 1
Last games: 13 Apr 1985 United 0 Carlisle United 0
11 May 1985 Brighton & Hove Albion 1 United 0 (sub)
Lincoln City Aug 1985/ Exeter City Jul 1987/ Weymouth Mar 1989/ Yeovil Town Nov 1990 to c1995

Richard Cooper failed to make any significant impression in his few first team opportunities and was released by manager Porterfield, joining Lincoln City initially on a non-contract basis. He made a total of 114(15) FL appearances before moving into non-League football.

Appearances:		Apps	Gls
	FL	2 (4)	0
	FAC	1	0
	CC	0 (1)	0
	Total	3 (5)	0

CORK Alan Graham

Striker 1992–94 6' 0" 12st 0
b. Derby 4 March 1959

Derby County from jnr Jul 1977/ Lincoln City (L) Sep 1977/ Wimbledon Feb 1978

United: 9 Mar 1992 to Aug 1994
Debuts: 11 Mar 1992 Sheffield Wednesday 1 United 3 (sub)
14 Mar 1992 United 1 Manchester United 2
Last game: 3 May 1994 Oldham Athletic 1 United 1

Fulham Aug 1994 player, youth development and asst mgr/ Swansea City asst mgr Oct 1997, mgr Oct 1997–Jun 1998/ Chesham United mgr/ Brighton & H A asst mgr Apr 1999/ Cardiff City assistant, then manager Oct 2000–Feb 2002/ Leicester City asst mgr Jun 2002 to Oct 2004/ Coventry City coach Jan 2005 to Jan 2007/ Bolton W scout

Although Alan Cork began his professional career at Derby County, he did not play a League game for the club, making his League debut whilst on loan at Lincoln City away to Oxford United on 14 September 1977. He then joined Wimbledon where he gained an FA Cup Winners medal and played in all four divisions, making well over 400 League appearances.

Alan was another of Dave Bassett's signings from their days together at Wimbledon. Although he was 33 years old and past his best, he was a regular in the United squad for the 1992–93 season, often being used as a substitute. During the club's FA Cup run, which reached the semi final, he grew a beard, refusing to shave it off whilst United were still in the competition. Defeat came at Wembley against the Owls but Alan had the honour of scoring United's goal, only the second Blade to score for United at the famous old stadium. His appearances were less frequent during the following season but in his final appearance he scored the goal in the 1–1 draw at Oldham Athletic which seemed enough to keep United in the Premier League. It was not to be, as in the next and final game, defeat at Chelsea saw the club relegated. Alan left in the close season and after a time at Fulham, where he brought his League career totals to 155 goals in 393(111) games, he began his long career as a coach and manager.

Appearances:		Apps	Gls
	FL	25 (29)	7
	FAC	5 (1)	2
	LC	2 (2)	0
	Total	32 (32)	9

COTTERILL David Rhys George Best

MF 2008 5' 10" 10st 11
b. Cardiff 4 December 1987

Bristol City from trainee Jan 2005/ Wigan Athletic (£2m) Aug 2006

United: (L) 8 Feb 2008 to May 2008
Debut: 9 Feb 2008 United 0 Scunthorpe United 0
Last game: 4 May 2008 Southampton 3 United 2
United: (undisclosed) 31st Jul 2008

David Cotterill made his League debut with Bristol City as a substitute on 30 October 2004 at home to Colchester United, his full debut coming at Colchester on 19 February 2005. A Wales Youth international, he gained U21 and full caps whilst with City and continued to do so after his move to Wigan.

Having played few games for Wigan during 2007–08 he joined United on loan until the end of the season. He featured in all the available League games and, growing in confidence, used his pace and control to attack the opposition and his centres created opportunities in the penalty area.

In July he joined United on a permanent basis.

Appearances:		Apps	Gls
	FL	15 (1)	0
	Total	15 (1)	0

COWAN Thomas (Tom)

LB 1991–93 5' 8½" 11st 10
b. Bellshill 28 August 1969

Motherwell (amat)/ Netherdale BC/ Clyde Jan 1988/ Glasgow Rangers Feb 1989 (£100k)

United: (£350k) 11Jul/ 1 Aug 1991 to 24 Mar 1994
Debuts: Jul/Aug 1991 pre season tour of Sweden
(first game uncertain)
17 Aug 1991 Norwich City 2 United 2
Last game: 18 Sep 1993 Leeds United 2 United 1
Stoke City (L) Oct 1993/ Notts County (L) Mar 1994
Huddersfield Town (L) Mar 1994, transfer (£200k) 6 Jul 1994/ Burnley (£20k) Mar 1999/ Cambridge United (L) Feb 2000, free Jul 2000 / Peterborough United (L) Jan 2002/ York City Jul 2002 to / Dundee Aug 2003/ Carlisle United Nov 2003 / Barrow cs 2005/ Workington Dec 2005/ Hucknall Town Oct 2006/ Stalybridge Celtic Mar 2007/ Hyde United cs 2007/ Retford Town (L) Jan 2008

Tom Cowan made his Scottish League debut with Clyde on 15 October 1988, away to Airdrieonians. Dave Bassett failed in a bid to secure his transfer but was more successful in securing him from Rangers. His precise debut with the Blades is unknown. He played in the friendly games on 6 August 1991 but probably in some of the tour games before that.

An enthusiastic left wing back, his speed was an asset and he was excellent in the air but he could be a little impetuous. Tom was a regular member of the side for two seasons competing for his place with David Barnes. In October 1994, the arrival of Roger Nilsen saw an end to Tom's career with United and after a loan spell with Stoke City where he rejected a transfer, he moved to Huddersfield Town. Whilst with the Terriers, he wrote a book about his experiences when he was out of the game for some time with a career threatening injury.

Despite this injury he totalled 316(8) FL games and a further 28(5) League games in Scotland. His two seasons with Carlisle saw the club relegated to the Conference and then promoted back to the Football League. Tom then continued to play for various non-League clubs, also being involved in some media work. He had a spell at Gretna FC, running the Community Scheme whilst continuing to play south of the border. When he returned to the Sheffield area he worked as an electrician, finally retiring from playing in January 2008. He then joined the fire service and became involved in media work.

Appearances:		Apps	Gls
	FL	45	0
	FAC	2	0
	LC	5	0
	FMC	1	0
	Total	53	0

COWANS Gordon Sidney

MF 1996 5' 7" 10st 6
b. Cornforth (Co Durham) 27 October 1958

Aston Villa from app Sep 1976/ Bari (Italy) (£500k) Jul 1985/ Aston Villa (£250k) Jul 1988/ Blackburn Rovers (£200k) Nov 1991/ Aston Villa Jul 1993/ Derby County (£80k) Feb 1994/ Wolverhampton Wanderers (£20k)Dec 1994
United: 29 Dec 1995 to Jul 1996
Debuts: 6 Jan 1996 Arsenal 1 United 1 (FAC)
13 Jan 1996 Tranmere Rovers 1 United 1
Last game: 4 May 1996 United 1 Port Vale 1
Bradford City Jul 1996/ Stockport County Mar 1997/ Burnley (nc) Aug 1997/ Aston Villa 1998 (coach)

Gordon Cowans made his FL debut with Aston Villa as a substitute on 7 February 1976 at Maine Road, his full debut coming just over a year later, on 12 February, at Ipswich Town. In his first spell with Villa he helped them win the League Championship, the European Cup and the European Super Cup. During his career he won full England caps as well as at U21 and B level.

Gordon joined United as one of Howard Kendall's early singings. Though he was now 37 years old, he worked tirelessly in midfield using his experience and ability both creatively and as a ball winner. It was perhaps no mere coincidence that United lost only two of the 20 FL games in which he was involved. At the end of the season, he moved to Bradford City, newly promoted to Division One. He ended his playing career at Burnley, having totalled 567(27) League appearances, not including his games in Italy. He then returned to Villa and became youth coach.

Appearances:		Apps	Gls
	FL	18 (2)	0
	FAC	3	0
	Total	21 (2)	0

COX Albert Edward Harrison ('Coxy')

LB/RB 1935–52 5' 9½" 10st 10 to 11st 0
b. Treeton 24 June 1917
d. Rotherham 4 April 2003

Treeton United/ Woodhouse Mill Welfare
United: 22/24 Apr 1935 to 30 Jun 1952
Debut: 20 Feb 1936 United 1 Blackpool 1

Last games: 1 Mar 1952 Rotherham United 3 United 1
8 Mar 1952 United 0 Chelsea 1 (FAC)
10 May 1952 Rotherham United 1 United 3 (CC)
WW2 guest: Fulham, Barnsley
Halifax Town Jul 1952 to cs 1954/ United training staff 1956–57 to 1960–61

Albert Cox's first game for United was at right back, his second at left back and his fourth was the 2–1 victory in the 1936 FA Cup semi-final. He went on to become a great favourite at the Lane and was a member of the United team which won promotion to Division One in 1939.

Albert was never a stylish player but he was two footed, fast and quick to recover. A happy go lucky character but always urging his team-mates on to greater effort, 'Coxy' was a hard tackler and in particular, an expert in a sliding tackle and played with great energy and enthusiasm.

He enlisted in the Signals Regiment during the war serving in Egypt, France and Germany and played 18 games for Fulham (1943–44) and made one appearance for Barnsley during the 1945–46 season. After the war, he formed a fine full-back partnership with Fred Furniss playing regularly until 1952. He subsequently played 54 FL games for Halifax and in due course, he returned to a coaching role at the Lane.

Later, he kept the Brunswick Hotel at Woodhouse, had a general store in Treeton and did some scouting for John Harris.

Appearances:		Apps	Gls
	FL	267	5
	FAC	25	0
	CC	10	0
	WW2	31	1
	Total	333	6

CRADDOCK Jody Darryl

CB 1999 6' 1" 12st 4
b. Bromsgrove 25 July 1975

Christchurch/ Cambridge United Aug 1993/ Sunderland (£300k) Jul 1997/
United: (L) 27 Aug 1999 to Oct 1999
Debut: 28 Aug 1999 United 2 Ipswich Town 2
Last game: 23 Oct 1999 Swindon Town 2 United 2
Wolverhampton Wanderers (£1.75m) Aug 2003/ Stoke City (L) Aug 2007

Jody Craddock made his FL debut with Cambridge United on 11 December 1993 at home to Stockport County. Transferred to Sunderland, he was loaned United, initially on for a month but then extended to two. Jody played impressively at centre back. There was talk of a permanent move but injuries and suspensions at Sunderland resulted in a recall to the Stadium of Light. He moved to Molineux after Wolves gained promotion to the Premiership, having beaten United at Cardiff in May 2003.

By 2008 he had made 434(20) League appearances.

Appearances:		Apps	Gls
	FL	10	0
	Total	10	0

CRAWFORD Gavin

IF 1890–91 5' 9" 11–12st.
b. Galston, nr Kilmarnock 24 January 1869
d. Plumstead (London) 2 March 1955

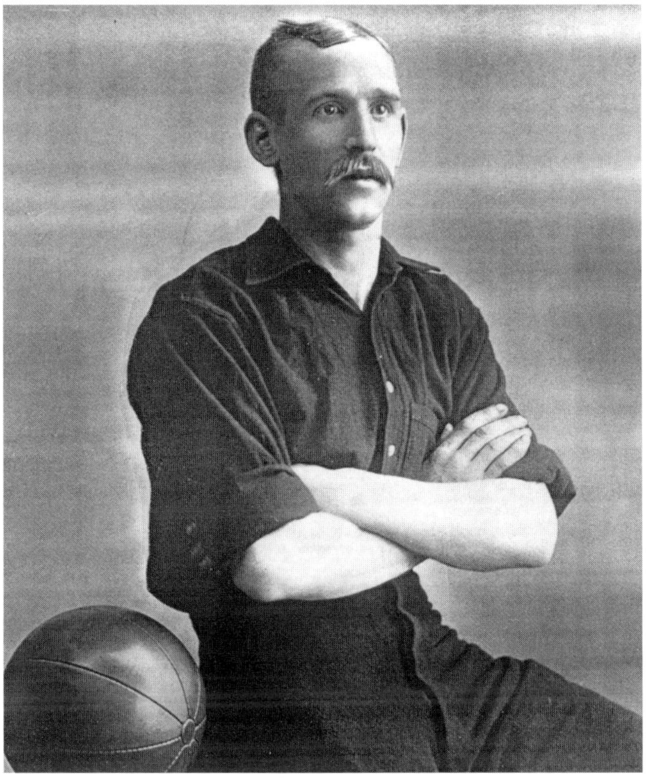

Ash Lea FC/ Fairfield Rangers (Glasgow) 1887
United: Autumn 1890 to cs 1891
Debuts: 8 Dec 1890 United 3 Middlesbrough Ironopolis 2 (Fr)
21 Feb 1891 United 0 Derby Midland 1 (MCL)
Last games: 13 Apr 1891 Burslem Port Vale 3 United 1 (MCL)
25 Apr 1891 Stockton 3 United 0 (Fr)
Woolwich Arsenal 1891/ Millwall Athletic 1898/ Queens Park Rangers May 1899

A tricky, constructive forward and a Scottish Junior Cup winner, Gavin Crawford spent half a season at the Lane but went on to play over three hundred games for the Arsenal. One of the first Arsenal professional players, his first appearance for the club was in a friendly match against United in September 1891. His FL debut finally came on 11 September 1893 when he scored in the 4–0 home victory against Walsall Town Swifts in what was Arsenal's third ever League game and later he captained the side. After retiring in 1899 he later became the Charlton groundsman working until 1947.

Appearances:		Apps	Gls
	MCL	5	4
	SCC	2	0
	WCC	1	0
	Total	8	4

CRAWFORD Peter Graeme

G 1969–70 6' 1" 12st 7
b. Falkirk 7 August 1947

Denny BC/ Bo'ness United/ East Stirling £200
United: 10/11Sep 1968 (£10k) to 25 Sep 1968 and 1Nov 1968 to Oct 1971
Debuts: 1 Jun 1969 Napoli (Italy) 3 United 3 (Fr)
6 Sep 1969 United 1 Norwich City 0
Last game: 30 Sep 1970 Portsmouth 1 United 5
Mansfield Town (L) Jul 1971
York City (L) Oct, signed Nov 1971/ Scunthorpe United Aug 1977/ York City Jan 1980/ Rochdale Sep 1980/ Scarborough cs 1983 to 1984/ Goole Town Sep 1989/ – / Copmanthorpe (York) coach/ – / Alfreton Town asst mgr cs1989 to Dec 1990

A trainee manager at a paper mill before signing for United, Graeme Crawford was an understudy to Alan Hodgkinson and managed just two competitive appearances in his three seasons at Bramall Lane. He made 235 FL appearances with York equalling a League record—since broken—by keeping eleven consecutive clean sheets. More than five years after his retirement, at the age of 42 he played in an FA Cup tie for Goole Town.

Appearances:		Apps	Gls
	FL	2	0
	Total	2	0

CREIGHTON R

G 1889–91

Sheffield Club
United: occasional games, Nov 1889 to Apr 1891
Debut: 9 Nov 1889 Staveley 7 United 0 (Fr)
Only competitive game: 13 Apr 1891 Burslem Port Vale 3 United 1 (MCL)

A Sheffield Club amateur player, he is also recorded as 'Crichton'. In his three games for United, Creighton conceded 12 goals, nine in his two friendly games.

Appearances:		Apps	Gls
	MCL	1	0
	Total	1	0

CROOT Frederick (Freddie) Richard

OL/IL 1905–07 5' 8" 11st 7 to 12st 2
b. Rushden 1886
d. Rushden 5 July 1958

Wellingborough (Aston Villa amat)
United: 2 May 1905 to 3 May 1907
Debuts: 13 Sep 1905 Gainsborough Trinity 0 United 8 (Fr)
28 Oct 1905 Nottingham Forest 4 United 1
Last game: 20 Apr 1907 United 0 Aston Villa 0
Leeds City (£350) 3–11 May and 31 May 1907 to Mar 1918 / – / Clydebank 1919–20

Freddie Croot was noted for his fine centres and described as a 'gentleman on and off the field'. His only goal for United was scored on his debut in a friendly game at Gainsborough but he gave Leeds City excellent service, scoring 38 goals in 218 FL games.

Appearances:		Apps	Gls
	FL	8	0
	FAC	1	0
	Total	9	0

CROSS Edward (Teddy) E

RH/RB 1890–91
b. Northwich?

Northwich Victoria/ Rotherham Town cs 1889
United: cs 1890 to cs 1891
Debuts: 1 Sep 1890 United 9 Sheffield Club 0 (Fr)
13 Sep 1890 Burton Wanderers 1 United 1 (MCL)
4 Oct 1890 Derby Junction 0 United 1 (FAC)
Last games: 17 Jan 1891 United 1 Notts County 9 (FAC)
13 Apr 1891 Burslem Port Vale 3 United 1 (MCL)
25 Apr 1891 Stockton 3 United 0 (Fr)
Northwich Victoria May 1891/ Rotherham T 1892/ Chesterfield Sep 1893 to 23 Mar 1894/ Rotherham Town Sep 1894

Teddy Cross played as a full-back in Rotherham Town's first Midland League fixture in 1889 and he was certainly popular there as the local paper described him as the 'little champion'. His season with Chesterfield ended with dismissal when he failed to turn up for the Easter fixtures but in his third spell with the Rotherham Club, he made two FL appearances, his first away at Crewe Alexandra on 22 September 1894.

Appearances:		Apps	Gls
	FAC	5	0
	MCL	16	0
	SCC	4	0
	WCC	1	0
	Total	26	0

CROSS John (Jack)

CF 1954–55 5' 10½" 12st 0
b. Bury 5 February 1927
d. Poole (Dorset) 19 February 2006

Blackpool (am)/ Hendon/ Guildford City/ Bournemouth Jun 1947/ Northampton Town (£5500/£6500) Oct 1953
United: (£11k) 2/3 Feb 1954 to 29 Sep/3 Oct 1955
Debut: 6 Feb 1954 Huddersfield T 2 United 2
Last game: 1 Sep 1955 Charlton Athletic 3 United 2
Reading (£2600) Oct 1955/ Headington United Mar/Apr 1957/ Weymouth 1958/ Poole

Jack Cross made four appearances for Blackpool (1944–45) before he joined the Coldstream Guards and played as a guest in the London area. He was 22 when he signed for Bournemouth, becoming a professional and making his FL debut at home to Swansea Town on 23 August 1947. He completed a five year accountancy degree course at Bournemouth before moving to Northampton.

Recommended by Jack Pickering, our former international forward, Cross moved to the Lane when it became obvious that Len Browning, our centre forward who had contracted tuberculosis, was unlikely to play again. Jack led the line well, had a good shot and turn of speed and settled quite well in the First Division. He scored in his first three games for United and on his final appearance but shocked United in September 1954 when he accepted a position at Harwell with the UK Atomic Energy Authority.

Appearances:		Apps	Gls
	FL	44	16
	CC	2	2
	Total	46	18

CROXON William (Billy) James F

OR/IR 1892–94
b. West Ham JFM 1871
d. Sheffield OND 1949

Royal Arsenal Mar and Apr 1891/ Millwall 1891–92/ Ilford
United: 5 Nov 1892 to 31 Aug 1894
Debuts: 10 Nov 1892 Casuals 1 United 2 (Fr)
19 Nov 1892 Darwen 3 United 1
Last games: 26 Dec 1893 West Bromwich Albion 3 United 1
12 Mar 1894 United 0 Woolwich Arsenal 2 (Fr)
Rotherham Town 31 Aug 1894

Billy Croxon made few first team appearances in his two seasons at Bramall Lane but he did subsequently play 9 FL games for Rotherham Town. He later worked as a clerk in a Sheffield school and played cricket for Shiregreen.

Appearances:		Apps	Gls
	FL	3	0
	NL	1	0
	Total	4	0

CRYAN Colin

CD 2000–03 5' 10" 13st 4
b. Dublin 23 March 1981

United: from 1 Jul 2000 to cs 2004
Debuts: 19 Sep 2000 United 3 Colchester United 0 (LC sub)
23 Sep 2000 Crystal Palace 0 United 1 (sub)
Last games: 13 Sep 2003 Nottingham Forest 3 United 1 (sub)
23 Sep 2003 United 0 Queens Park Rangers 2 (LC sub)
Scarborough (L) Oct 2002/ Scarborough (L) Oct 2003
Scarborough Jul 2004/ Lincoln City Jul 2005/ Boston United Jan 2007/ Droylsden Aug 2007

A regular in the reserves for several seasons and captain for the 2003–04 season, Colin Cryan was a Republic of Ireland U21 international but he failed to make the breakthrough into the first team squad, all his competitive appearances being from the subs bench. He had two loan spells with the Conference side Scarborough and was involved in their FA Cup run in 2003–04. At the end of that season he was released by United and joined Scarborough on a permanent basis.

In the summer of 2005 he joined Lincoln and finally made his full FL debut on 6 August 2005 at home to Northampton. After moving to Boston, he played in their final 15 League games before they were relegated from the League.

Appearances:		Apps	Gls
	FL	0 (5)	0
	LC	0 (3)	0
	Total	0 (8)	0

CULLEN David Jonathan (Jon)

MF 1998–99 6' 0" 12st 0
b. Bishop Auckland 10 January 1973

Doncaster Rovers from YT Sep 1991–93/ Spennymoor United / – / Eppleton CU/ Whitley Bay/ Perth (Australia)/ Morpeth Town 1996–97/ Hartlepool United £1000 Mar 1997
United: (£250k) 26 Jan 1998 to 3/4 Mar 2000
Debut: 27 Jan 1998 United 1 Huddersfield T 1 (sub)
Last game: 9 Mar 1999 Portsmouth 1 United 0 (sub)
Shrewsbury T (L) Aug 1999/ Halifax T (L) Dec 1999/
Peterborough United (£35k) Mar 2000/ Carlisle United(L) Mar 2001/ Darlington Aug 2002/ Spennymoor United Oct 2002/ Morpeth Town Feb 2003/ Halifax Town Jul 2003/ Spennymoor United Oct 2003/ Sunderland Nissan/ Newcastle Blue Star/ Sunderland Nissan/ Morpeth Town Jan 2008

Jon Cullen made his FL debut with Doncaster on 11 May 1991 at Gillingham. After a year out of the game and a period of non-League football he moved to Hartlepool United and, in January 1998, was signed by Nigel Spackman.

He made just four substitute FL appearances in his time with United though he did make the starting line-up in a friendly fixture at the start of the 1998–99 season, scoring in a 2–0 win. Other than loan spells at Shrewsbury Town and Halifax Town, Jon spent his time in the reserves before joining Peterborough United in March 2000 and he featured in their play-off final against Darlington at Wembley. He completed 108(18) FL appearances before moving into non-League football playing in particular for various clubs in the north east.

Appearances:		Apps	Gls
	FL	0 (4)	0
	Total	0 (4)	0

CULLIP Daniel (Danny)

CD 2004–05 6' 1" 12st 7
b. Bracknell 17 September 1976

Oxford United from trainee Jul 1995/ Fulham Jul 1996/ Brentford (£75k) Feb 1998/ Brighton & Hove Albion (£50k) Sep 1991
United: (£250k) 17 Dec 2004 to 3 Aug 2005
Debut: 18 Dec 2004 United 2 Cardiff City 1

Last games: 8 Mar 2005 United 4 Crewe Alexandra 0
26 Jul 2005 Matlock T 1 United XI 2 (Fr)
Watford(L) Mar 2005
Nottingham Forest Aug 2005/ Queens Park Rangers Jan to Dec 2007/ Gillingham (nc) Feb to May 2008

Danny Cullip made no FL appearances for his first club Oxford, making his FL debut with Fulham on 17 August 1996 at home to Hereford United. However, it was with Brighton that he had the longest spell of his career playing 216(10) FL games.

Danny was signed by Neil Warnock, in December 2004, to strengthen the central defence and bring the leadership qualities that he had shown when captaining Brighton. The fee was staged to rise to a possible £400k. A no nonsense defender, he had a run of 13 games but he didn't fit in nor respond to problems in the way that the manager had expected and, after a few games out through injury, he moved on loan to Watford on 'deadline' day.

After moving to Forest for a 'nominal' fee, he moved again to QPR but after a take-over, his contract was terminated in December 2007. By 2008, after a spell at Gillingham, he had made over 350 League appearances.

Appearances:		Apps	Gls
	FL	11	0
	FAC	4	1
	Total	15	1

CUNNINGHAM John

IL/OL 1897–98 5' 5" 11st 3
b. Glasgow c1873
d. 1910

Glasgow Benburb/ Celtic (trial) May 1889/ Burnley Nov 1889/ Glasgow Hibernian Dec 1889/ Celtic 1890/ Partick Thistle 1892/ Hearts Oct 1892/ Rangers 1892/ Glasgow Thistle Mar 1893/ Preston North End Sep 1893
United: 3/11 May 1897 to 20 Jun 1898
Debut: 4 Oct 1897 United 5 Blackburn Rovers 2
Last games: 11 Apr 1898 United 2 West Bromwich Albion 0
30 Apr 1898 Liverpool 1 United 0 (Fr)
Aston Villa (£125) Jun 1898/ Newton Heath Oct 1898/ Wigan County Jun 1899/ Barrow Aug 1901 to cs1903?

John Cunningham's League debut in Scotland was with Celtic on 29 Apr 1891 at home to Third Lanark. His FL debut came with Preston North End on 9 September 1893 at Burnley.

United gave him his debut after they had completed the first six games of the 1897–98 season. A clever, stylish player, he would head for the opposition goal, 'wriggling, twisting like an eel' and his late goal in a crucial match at Villa Park was one of the most vital in United's successful Division One Championship campaign. Surprisingly, after such a success, Jack informed United that he wanted to go home to Wigan but accepted a transfer to the Villa.

Despite the large transfer fee paid by Villa, he failed to make a FL appearance for them and United rejected an offer to take him back at half the price they had received and he joined Newton Heath. After playing 90 FL games in total, he then moved into non-League football, where he played in Barrow's first ever game.

Appearances:		Apps	Gls
	FL	24	7
	FAC	2	0
	Total	26	7

CURLE Keith

CD/LB 2000–02 6' 1" 12st 12
b. Bristol 14 November 1963

Bristol Rovers from app Nov 1981/ Torquay United (£5000) Nov 1983/ Bristol City (£10k) Mar 1984/ Reading Oct 1987/ Wimbledon (£350k) Oct 1988/ Manchester City (£2.5m) Aug 1991/ Wolverhampton Wanderers Aug 1996
United: (free) 10 Jul 2000 to Jun 2002
Debuts: 18 Jul 2000 Tideswell 0 United 8 (Fr)
5 Sep 2000 Lincoln City 1 United 0 (LC)
21 Oct 2000 Norwich City 4 United 2 (sub)
24 Oct 2000 United 1 Stockport County 0
Last game: 1 Apr 2002 United 0 Wimbledon 1

Tranmere Rovers (trial) cs2002/ Barnsley (free) Aug 2002 to Oct 2002/ Mansfield Town mgr Dec 2002 to Dec 2004/ Chester City magr Apr 2005 to Feb 2006/ United scout/ Torquay United chief coach (mgr) Feb to May 2007/Crystal Palace coach, asst mgr Oct 2007

Keith Curle's professional career began with Bristol Rovers where he made his FL debut on 29 August 1981 at home to Chester. During his career, Keith played for the Football League and gained England B caps and three full caps, the latter whilst with Manchester City.

He was signed by Neil Warnock towards the end of his playing career to stiffen and guide the defence and became in effect if not by title, a senior coach. Keith, by then was lacking in pace but he used his intelligence and experience and 'every trick in the book to spoil and disrupt' and was a regular member of the defence for two seasons, playing in the centre alongside first Sean Murphy and then Robert Page. He also had spells as a left back.

He later went into management with Mansfield Town, where he continued to play for a time, and then Chester City and had a short spell at Torquay but was unable to stave off relegation from the League. He was controversially sacked as Mansfield manager in December 2004 after allegations that he bullied a youth-team player. However, in August 2006, Keith won a case for wrongful dismissal against the club and was awarded undisclosed damages. He rejoined Neil Warnock, as first team coach, when Neil became manager of Crystal Palace.

When Keith retired from playing he had made 675(30) League appearances.

Appearances:		Apps	Gls
	FL	53 (4)	1
	FAC	1	0
	LC	3	0
	Total	57 (4)	1

CURRAN Edward (Terry)

IL/OL/OR 1982–83 5' 10" 12st 4
b. Kinsley (Hemsworth) 20 March 1955

Doncaster Rovers from jnr Sep 1973/ Nottingham Forest Aug 1975/ Bury (L) Oct 1977/ Derby County (£50k) Nov 1977/ Southampton (£65k) Aug 1978/ Sheffield Wednesday (£85k) Mar 1979
United: £100k (trib) 28 Jul 1982 to Sep 1983
Debuts: 3 Aug 1982 Raith Rovers 0 United 3 (Fr)
14 Aug 1982 United 1 Grimsby T 3 (FLT)
28 Aug 1982 Portsmouth 4 United 1
Last game: 7 May 1983 United 0 Lincoln City 1
Everton (L) Dec 1982
Everton (c£95k) Sep 1983/ Orebro (Sweden) Apr 1985/ Huddersfield Town Jul 1985/ Panionis (Greece) Jul 1986/ Hull City (trial) Oct 1986/ Sunderland Nov 1986/ Matlock Town (trial) Jul 1987/ Grantham Sep 1987/ Grimsby Town Oct 1987/ Chesterfield (nc) Mar 1988/ Goole Town (player-mgr) cs to Nov 1988, mgr Nov 1989 to Mar 1992/ – / Mossley mgr Nov-Dec 1992

The first of Terry Curran's many clubs was Doncaster Rovers where he made his FL debut on 29 September 1973 at Gillingham.

He was a tricky and hugely talented player but temperamental and no manager could control him and, in a seemingly desperate attempt to enjoy life, he was, in the eyes of most people, his own worst enemy. He was at his best with the Wednesday, playing under Jack Charlton and it was during that period that he first appeared in a United shirt, playing in John Flynn's benefit match on 15 November 1980.

Signed by Ian Porterfield for United, the fee set by a tribunal, Terry was a huge disappointment apart from a fine display at Stoke when he was probably aware that other managers were watching him. He infuriated Porterfield and Everton's manager, Howard Kendall, when he rejected a transfer in February 1983 though he did eventually sign for the Liverpool club.

After playing for Chesterfield (his 13th FL club) Terry moved into non-League football as the player manage at Goole Town before injuries ended his playing days. A failure as a manager, he was more successful later in business, buying a café on the A1, setting up a pallet business, expanding the cafe into a motel, then an Italian restaurant before selling up in 2001.

Appearances:		Apps	Gls
	FL	31 (2)	3
	FAC	4	0
	LC	4	0
	AMC	3	0
	Total	42 (2)	3

CURRIE Anthony (Tony or TC) William

IL/IR 1968–76 5' 11" 12st 10
b. Edgware 1 January 1950

QPR (school)/ Chelsea (trial)/ Watford from amat Sep 1965 to pro May 1967
United: 1/2 Feb 1968 (£26,500) to 8 Jun 1976
Debut: 26 Feb 1968 United 3 Tottenham Hotspur 2
Last games: 4 May 1976 United 1 Birmingham City 1
7 May 1976 United 1 Doncaster Rovers 2 (CC)
27 May 1976 Wolverhampton Wanderers 4 United 1 (GI)
Leeds United (£264.6k/£245k) Jun 1976/ Queens Park Rangers (£400k) Aug 1979/ Vancouver Whitecaps (£40k) May 1983/ Toronto N/ Chesham United/ Southend United/ Torquay United (nc) Feb 1984/ Hendon/ Dunstable/Goole Town (player-coach) to Dec 1987

Tony Currie was one of United's greatest all time players. He began his illustrious career with Watford, where he made his debut as a substitute in a League Cup fixture at Stoke on 13 September 1967, three days before his FL debut at home to Bristol Rovers when he scored twice. In his 17(1) FL appearances for Watford, he scored nine goals including two hat tricks and won England youth honours.

United had been watching his progress and an agreement was made on a fee and that his transfer would be deferred until the Hertfordshire club were knocked out of the FA Cup. As it happened, it was the Blades who knocked Watford out and it was to the credit of their chairman that he stood by the deal, even though the player's value had risen sharply.

Tony scored on his debut for the Blades and, although the club were surprisingly relegated at the end of the season, he went on to become the star of the very talented team which took the club back to the top division in 1971. He took on the role of an attacking midfield player and this gave him the scope to display his massive talents to the full. Tremendous ball control, passing and dribbling skills were backed up with great strength so that it was almost impossible to knock him off the ball. He also had great vision and distribution and it was no surprise that he won representative honours with the England U23 and the Football League and was awarded seventeen England caps (seven with United).

As his career developed with United, so did the flamboyance of his play, which reflected the spirit of those years; he sat on the ball to annoy Arsenal—a deserved retribution for a similar act by Alan Ball—he blew kisses and waved to the United fans on the terrace while dribbling the ball down the field and took advantage of a tumble with Alan Birchenall to exchange kisses. It was marvellous entertainment but, inevitably, not always in the eyes of the critic or manager, what the situation demanded.

Ken Furphy, the United manager from December 1973, made 'TC' captain hoping it would bring a more responsible attitude to his play in general and attention to marking and playing to instructions in particular and Don Revie, when he became the England manager, made it plain that players like Tony, Frank Worthington and Stan Bowles would have little to hope for as far as he was concerned.

No players, however great, are free from criticism. There were accusations that Currie was 'lazy', a 'poor trainer' and that he should have scored more goals but, for all but a handful of Unitedites, to recall Tony in a Blades shirt is to feel pure joy and perhaps hear, in the distance, the songs 'Rose Garden' and 'You can do magic'.

During his approximately eight and a half seasons with United, he played an average of about 45 competitive games per season. He played 136 consecutive League games (only Jack Smith and Alan Woodward, and recently Phil Jagielka, have achieved a higher total) and in three seasons he was ever present in League games.

After leaving the Lane he had a successful time with Leeds followed by a spell at QPR when he captained the team in the re-play of the 1982 FA Cup Final and also played in North America. On his return he was involved briefly with a few lower division clubs, bringing his total of FL appearances to 525(3), scoring 80 goals.

In February 1988, Tony returned to the Lane to work in the Football in the Community scheme and he made one further appearance in Paul Stancliffe's benefit match:
16 Mar 1992 United XI 1 Malmo (Sweden) 6 (sub BM).
He has received two benefits, countless tributes and in February 2008, he was given the role of Club Ambassador.

Appearances:

	Apps	Gls
FL	313	54
FAC	10 (1)	2
LC	22	3
TEX	7	3
ASC	2	0
CC	16	2
WAT	5	4
ABD	2	0
Total	377 (1)	68

CURRY Robert (Bob)

Forward 1943–45 5' 8" 12st 0
b. Gateshead 2 November 1918
d. Halstead (Essex) 23 June 2001

Gateshead/ Sheffield Wednesday Oct 1936 to cs 1939/ Gainsborough Trinity Jun 1939 (WW2 guest: Bradford PA, Sheffield Wednesday)
United: 18 Sep 1943 to cs 1945
Debut: 2 Oct 1943 Rotherham United 2 United 3 (WW2)
Last game: 31 Mar 1945 Bradford City 4 United 3 (WW2)
WW2 guest: Lincoln C, Leeds U, Mansfield T and Fulham (?)
Gainsborough Tr cs 1945/ Colchester United Jul 1946/ Clacton Town (player-coach and manager) Jun 1951/ Halstead (manager) 1954–60

Bob Curry made his FL debut with Sheffield Wednesday, playing just one game for them on 18 September 1937 at Villa Park, although the Owls had failed to register him with the League and were subsequently fined. A member of the TA, Bob was called up on the outbreak of war but made two appearances for Bradford (PA) before he sailed for France. Wounded in France in 1940, he was discharged from the Army and took up work in Sheffield and played for Lopham Street and returned to Hillsborough as a guest player.

A thoughtful inside forward with a good shot, he scored both on his debut for United and on his final appearance. He netted twice as a guest player with Leeds United (18 Mar 1944) and played against United in December 1944 as a guest for Mansfield Town.

He joined Colchester United and helped them to League status making his second appearance in the FL twelve years after his first, and going on to make 32 FL appearances for the club. A joiner by trade he later worked for his son.

Appearances:

	Apps	Gls
WW2	20	6
Total	20	6

CURTIS John Charles Keyworth

RWB 2003 5' 10" 11st 9
b. Nuneaton 3 September 1978

Manchester United from YT Oct 1995/ Barnsley (L) Nov 1999/ Blackburn Rovers (£2.25m) Jun 2000
United: (L) 3 Mar 2003 to cs 2003
Debuts: 4 Mar 2003 Grimsby Town 1 United 4 (sub)
15 Mar 2003 Stoke City 0 United 0
Last games: 4 May 2003 Watford 2 United 0
26 May 2003 Wolverhampton Wanderers 3 United 0 (PO)
Leicester City Aug 2003/ Portsmouth Feb 2004/ Preston North End (L) Oct–Nov 2004/ Nottingham Forest Feb 2005/ Queens Park Rangers Jun to Dec 2007

John Curtis made his League debut with his first club, Manchester United, on 25 October 1997 at home to Barnsley and also, whilst at Old Trafford, gaining England caps at schoolboy, youth, U21 and B level.

He was signed by Neil Warnock in March 2003 on loan from Blackburn Rovers until the end of the season, as an extra defender following the clubs tiring schedule of Cup games. He quickly slotted into his right wing back role and was involved in 15 of the final 17 games of the season, including the FA Cup semi-final against Arsenal and helped the Blades reach the play-offs. He was involved in the dramatic games against Nottingham Forest and the disappointment of the defeat against Wolves.

John subsequently had short spells at various clubs winning a regular place with Nottingham Forest. He was not retained in the summer of 2007 and joined QPR but had his contract terminated by the new club owners.

Appearances:

	Apps	Gls
FL	9 (3)	1
PO	3	0
FAC	1	0
Total	13 (3)	1

CUTBUSH William John

RB 1977–81 5' 8" 10st 10
b. Malta 28 June 1949

Tottenham Hotspur from app Sep 1966/Fulham Jul 1972
United: 10/11 Mar 1977(L), Tr (£10k) 8/11 Apr 1977 to 31 Jul 1981
Debuts: 12 Mar 1977 Burnley 1 United 0 (sub)
19 Mar 1977 United 2 Nottingham Forest 0
Last game: 21 Apr 1981 United 1 Fulham 2
Wichita Wings (L) (NASL indoor soccer) cs1979?

Despite spending six seasons at White Hart Lane, John Cutbush failed to make a competitive appearance in the first team. His FL debut came after his move to Fulham, on 16 August 1972 away at Reading. John played for Fulham in the 1975 FA Cup Final, gaining a losers' medal and made a total of 131(30) FL appearances.

John was signed by Jimmy Sirrel during what was a less than moderate period in United's history. A player of undoubted skill and some pace, he lacked the confidence that he had shown in his early years at Fulham. Relegation followed in 1979 and again in 1981, though John missed the dismal final game against Walsall.

Appearances:

	Apps	Gls
FL	126 (3)	1
FAC	3	0
LC	5	0
ASC	13	0
CC	5	0
Total	152 (3)	1

CUTTS E

IF 1918–19

United: 1915 to cs 1919
Debut: 21 Sep 1918 United 2 Notts County 2 (WW1)
Last games: 23 Nov 1918 United 3 Grimsby Town 1 (WW1)
4 Jan 1919 Hull City 4 United 0 (ABD WW1)
Rotherham Town 1919 to at least Oct 1922/ Treeton Reading Room

Described as a local player from Treeton, Cutts first played for the United reserve team in the 1915–16 season. Although credited with just one goal for United, he may have scored on three other occasions but different press reports leave matters uncertain. He played for Rotherham Town after being released by United and reverted to amateur status in October 1922.

Appearances:

	Apps	Gls
WW1	9	1
Total	9	1

DALE Cyril

OR 1945

St George's Church (Sheffield)
United: amat 9 Sep 1944, pro 1/3 Mar 1945 to 4 May 1946
Debuts: 3 Mar 1945 United 2 Polish RAF XI 1 (Fr)
10 Mar 1945 Lincoln City 2 United 1 (WW2)
Last game: 9 May 1945 United 2 Sheffield Wednesday 0 (WW2)
Gainsborough Tr cs 1946/ Buxton c 1948–49

A clever, local eighteen year old, Cyril scored both goals (one a penalty) on his debut against the Polish RAF XI but didn't appear to have enough drive and determination to succeed as a top class full time professional.

Appearances:	Apps	Gls
CC	2	1
WW2	6	1
Total	8	2

DAVIDSON Ross James

RB 1994–95 5' 8½" 11st 7
b. Chertsey 13 November 1973

Walton & Hersham
United: 25 Jun 1993 (fee dependent on appearances) to 26 Mar 1996
Debuts: 24 Aug 1994 United 1 Udinese 2 (AIC)
6 May 1995 United 3 Grimsby Town 1
Last game: 7 Oct 1995 United 0 Derby County 2
Chester City Jan 1996 (L), Mar 1996/ Barnet Nov 1999 (L)/ Shrewsbury Town Mar 2000/ Ashford Town (Middlesex) Jul 2001 to cs 2005

Ross Davidson was unable to break through to become a regular member of the first team. After a trial with Blackpool (July 1995) and a loan spell with the Preston reserve team, he went on loan to Chester City, before making the move permanent and going on to make over 100 FL appearances for the club.

Appearances:	Apps	Gls
FL	2	0
AIC	2	0
Total	4	0

DAVIES David Walter

CF/IF 1913–15 5' 7½" 11st 4
b. Treharris 1 October 1888

Merthyr Town amat 1908–09 / – / Treharris 1910–11/ Oldham Athletic (£180) May 1912/ Stockport County Mar 1913
United: (£350) 25/26 Apr 1913 to May 1915
Debut: 26 Dec 1913 Aston Villa 3 United 0
Last game: 19 Apr 1915 Tottenham Hotspur 1 United 1
Cardiff City (1915–16)/ Millwall Athletic (1919)/ Merthyr Town (1919–20)/ Treharris Albion (1920–21)

David Davies made his FL debut with Oldham Athletic, against United at Bramall Lane on 7 September 1912. He gained two Welsh caps, the first whilst with Treharris and the second with Oldham Athletic. A former miner, he was a hard working, clever player and a 'trier' but 'lacks the finer points of the game'. At the end of the 1914–15 season he returned to South Wales and his work in the mines.

Appearances:	Apps	Gls
FL	27	9
FAC	3	0
Total	30	9

DAVIES Frederick (Fred) H

IF/WH 1891–94

Ardwick
United: cs1891 to cs1895
Debuts: 29 Oct 1891 Grimsby Town 5 United 1 (Fr)
12 Mar 1892 United Strollers 2 Wednesday Wndrs 1 (SCC)
18 Apr 1892 Stockton 1 United 1 (NL)
3 Sep 1892 United 4 Lincoln City 2
Last games: 7 Apr 1894 Preston North End 3 United 0
21 Apr 1894 Derby County 2 United 0 (UCL)
10 Sep 1894 United 4 Rotherham Town 2 (Fr)
Baltimore (USA)

Fred Davies was reported as having played for Ardwick but he doesn't appear to have featured in any serious competitive game. He may also have played for Birmingham St George in the 1890–91 season.

He first played for United in the 1891 pre-season practice match but had few first team opportunities in his first season. He was one of the eleven to play in United's first ever Football League game, at home to Lincoln City on 3 September 1892 and he began to play 'quite well' in the team which took United into the First Division. That level was perhaps a step too far and he sailed to the United States in October 1894 with other former Ardwick players 'to teach football'. He was one of the British players who signed for Baltimore in the new American League of Pro Football though the first season was not completed.

Appearances:	Apps	Gls
FL	16	6
FAC	2	0
NL	5	1
UCL	3	0
WCC	1	0
SCC	1	0
ABD	1	0
Total	29	7

DAVIES Joseph (Joe)

IR 1894–95 5' 6½" 11st 0
b. Chirk 1866
d. Wrexham 7 October 1943

Chirk/ Everton Oct 1888/ Chirk 1889–91/ Ardwick Feb 1891
United: 24/25 Jan 1894 to 7 Nov 1895
Debuts: 18 Apr 1894 Ardwick 0 United 2 (Fr)
29 Sep 1894 United 3 Nottingham Forest 2
Last games: 21 Sep 1895 Bury 1 United 0
23 Oct 1895 Gainsborough Trinity 2 United 0 (Fr)

Manchester City 8 Nov 1895/ Millwall Athletic May 1896/ Reading May 1898/Manchester City May 1900/ Stockport County Aug 1901/Chirk cs 1902 to 1905

A former miner, Joe Davies made his FL debut with Everton, during the Football League's first season, at West Bromwich Albion on the 1 December 1888. A 'splendid shot with good ball control', Joe won three of his eleven Welsh caps with United in 1895. He was suspended by United in September 1895 for 'lodging in a public house' and transferred, with Hugh Morris and Bob Hill, to Manchester City but was only there for a few months before moving to play in the Southern League. He made most (29) of his total of 74 FL appearances with Stockport.

Appearances:		Apps	Gls
	FL	12	4
	FAC	3	2
	UCL	3	1
	Total	18	7

DAVIS Claude

CD 2006–07 6' 3" 14st 4
b. Kingston, Jamaica 6 March 1979

Portmore United (Jamaica)/ Preston North End (L) Aug 2003, signed Mar 2004
United: (£2.5m) 14/15 Jun 2006 to 6/25 Jul 2007
Debuts: 21 Jul 2006 Inverness Caledonian Thistle 0 United 3 (Fr)
19 Sep 2006 United 1 Bury 0 (LC)
23 Sep 2006 Arsenal 3 United 0
Last games: 14 Apr 2007 United 3 West Ham United 0
13 May 2007 United 1 Wigan Athletic 2 (sub)
Derby County (£3m) Jul 2007

More keen on basketball then soccer as a youngster, Claude Davis captained Portmore United (previously known as Hazard United) to the League title in 2002–03. During that summer he moved to Preston, initially on loan, but then signed permanently. He made his FL debut at West Bromwich Albion on 25 August 2003 and became an increasingly important member of the side. In 2005–06 he was voted 'Player of the Season'.

Following United's promotion to the Premiership he was signed by Neil Warnock, who described him as 'an athlete, a great battler', for a club record fee.

A cartilage operation delayed his competitive debut, which finally came in the League Cup. Good in the air and strong, if unorthodox in the tackle and quick to recover, he could use the ball well. He was, however, prone to occasional misjudgements, some of which were costly and he also suffered from various leg injuries which kept him sidelined. By the end of the season he was used mainly as a substitute. A Jamaican international with 47 caps, injuries prevented him gaining any more when he was with United although he was called into the squad on occasions.

Following United's relegation, he moved to newly promoted Derby County, rejoining his former Preston manager Billy Davies but went on to experience relegation for the second successive season.

Appearances:		Apps	Gls
	FL	18 (3)	0
	LC	1	0
	Total	19 (3)	0

DAVIS George

HB 1928–30 5' 9" 11st 4
b. Sheffield 10 February 1907
d. Bournemouth? May 1990

Norton Woodseats
United: 1 Sep 1927(am), 26 Jan 1928(pro) to cs 1931 and 9 Oct 1934 to 4 May 1935
Debut: 26 Dec 1928 United 6 Manchester United 1
Last game: 5 Apr 1930 United 2 Portsmouth 3
Rotherham United Jul 1931 to cs 1934 / – / United Oct 1934–cs 1935

George Davis played for Sheffield and Yorkshire Boys before joining Norton Woodseats. He played only six games for United but went on to make 55 FL appearances for the Millers and then returned to the Blades acting as a player-coach with the third team. A part timer and a printer by trade, Davis was 'a bit crude' but also an enthusiastic 'ninety minute man.' Later he became captain and president of the Hallowes Golf Club at Dronfield.

Appearances:		Apps	Gls
	FL	6	0
	Total	6	0

DAVISON Aidan John

G 1999 6' 1" 13st 12
b. Sedgefield (Co Durham) 11 May 1968

Billingham Synthonia/ Notts County Mar 1988/ Orient (L)/ Bury (£6000) Oct 1989/Chester (L)/ Blackpool (L)/ Millwall Aug 1991/ Bolton Wanderers (£25k) Jul 1993/ Ipswich (L)/ Hull City (L) Nov 1996/ Bradford City Mar 1997/ Grimsby Town Jul 1997
United: (free) 5/6 Aug 1999 to 14/16 Mar 2000
Debut: 21 Aug 1999 Manchester City 6 United 0 (sub)
Last game: 4 Sep 1999 United 3 Crystal Palace 1
Bradford City 3 Dec 1999(L), 14/16 Mar 2000 (nominal)/ Grimsby Town (free) Aug 2003/ Colchester U (free) Jul 2004

The much-travelled goalkeeper, Aidan Davison made his FL debut with Notts County, his one appearance for the club, at Preston North End on 15 April 1989. Capped three times by Northern Ireland, he was signed by United as cover for Simon Tracey after Alan Kelly had been transferred. Aidan's first appearance was a baptism of fire: Simon Tracey was sent off with the score 0–1 and Aidan conceded five more goals in his appearance as a substitute—the worst start by a United 'keeper, although the whole team was culpable. His one other appearance was due to Simon Tracey's suspension following the sending off.

Aidan continued his travels and by 2008 had made over 350 League appearances.

Appearances:		Apps	Gls
	FL	1 (1)	0
	Total	1 (1)	0

DAVISON Robert (Bobby)

Striker 1992, 1993–94 5' 9" 11st 9
b. South Shields 17 July 1959

Red Duster/ Seaham Colliery Welfare/ Huddersfield Town (£1000) Jul 1980/ Halifax Town (£20k) Aug 1981/ Derby County (£80k) Dec 1982/ Leeds United (£350k) Nov 1987/ Derby County (L) Sep 1991
United: (L) 5/6 Mar 1992
Debut: 11 Mar 1992 Sheffield Wednesday 1 United 3
Last game: 2 May 1992 Wimbledon 3 United 0
Leicester City (£50k) Aug 1992
United: (L) 28 Sep, (free) 4 Nov 1993 to 14 Oct 1994
Debut: 5 Oct 1993 United 2 Blackpool 0 (LC)
Last games: 3 Sep 1994 Tranmere Rovers 2 United 1
13 Sep 1994 United 0 Sunderland 0 (sub)
18 Oct 1993 Blackburn Rovers 0 United 0
5 Oct 1994 United 3 Ancona 3 (AIC)
Rotherham United (free) Oct 1994/ Hull City (L) Nov 1995/ Halifax Town cs 1996/ Guiseley player-coach 1997, player-mgr 1998, player 2000/ Bradford City coach/ Derby County coach cs 2002/ – / Bradford City spring 2003 youth coach, asst-mgr Jun 2004 to Jun 2007/ – / Ferencvaros coaching advisor Feb 2008, coach Apr 2008

Bobby Davison began his professional career at Huddersfield Town, making his FL debut on 30 August 1980 at Rotherham. He quickly moved to Halifax Town where he showed he had the knack of scoring goals, with 29 in 63 appearances. After successful spells at Derby County (where he made over 200 appearances) and Leeds United, he moved to United, on loan for the final two months of the 1991–92 season.

Quick in movement and anticipation, he became an instant hero by scoring two goals on his debut, giving United a 3–1 victory at Hillsborough and a League double over the Owls. It was hoped he would make a permanent move but he moved to Leicester City.

Bobby rejoined the Blades in September 1993 but was unable to gain a regular place in the side and, just over 12 months later, he moved to Rotherham United and then Hull City. On retiring from League football he had scored 170 goals in 423(30) FL appearances.

He gained experience in non-League football and worked for the Midas Group who were a United sponsor and then became a coach with Bradford City and later assistant manager. In February 2008 Bobby took up the position of advisory coach with Ferencvaros as United became more involved with the Hungarian club and in April, he took over the coaching role.

Appearances:		Apps	Gls
	FL	15 (8)	5
	LC	2	1
	AIC	2	0
	Total	19 (8)	6

DAWS Anthony (Tony)

F 1986–87 5' 8" 11st 10
b. Sheffield 10 September 1966

Man United (app)/ Notts County from app Sep 1984
United: 19 Aug 1986 (trial}, Nov 1986 to 30 Jun 1987
Debuts: 1 Aug 1986 United 1 Seville (Spain) 1 (Fr, sub)
4 Nov 1986 Blackburn Rovers 1 United 0 (FMC, sub)
8 Nov 1986 Blackburn Rovers 0 United 2
Last game: 14 Feb 1987 Millwall 1 United 0
Scunthorpe United Jul 1987/ Grimsby Town (£50k) Mar 1993/ Lincoln City (£50k) Feb 1994/Halifax Town Mar 1996(L)/ Scarborough Aug 1996/ Altrincham Feb 1997/ coaching

An England schoolboy and youth international, Tony Daws made his FL debut with Notts County at Birmingham City on 9 March 1985. On moving to United, although he was small and slight, he was quick and direct and made an impact on his League debut, scoring both goals in a 2–0 win at Blackburn. After a brief run in the side, he lost his place and was transferred to Scunthorpe United where he made over 180 FL appearances. After short spells with other clubs he was forced to retire in 1997, having scored 81goals in 239(36) FL appearances.

He joined the coaching staff at Bramall Lane as a part time Youth Development Officer and ran his own coaching centres and, in 2000, he became the assistant academy and under-19 coach but moved to neighbours Sheffield Wednesday in 2004. Tony has also worked as a pundit on BBC Radio Humberside, commentating on Scunthorpe United's games and in May 2005 he returned to Glanford Park as youth team coach.

Appearances:		Apps	Gls
	FL	7 (4)	3
	FAC	1	0
	FMC	0 (1)	0
	Total	8 (5)	3

DAY Mervyn Richard

G 1992 6' 2" 15st 1
b. Chelmsford 26 June 1955

West Ham United from app Mar 1973/ Leyton Orient (£100k) Jul 1979/ Aston Villa (£25k) Aug 1983/ Leeds United (£30k) Jan 1985 to May 1993/ Luton Town (L) Mar 1992
United: (L) 1 to 4 May 1992
Only game: 2 May 1992 Wimbledon 3 United 0
Carlisle United Jul 1993 as player, coach, manager (Jan 1996 to Sept 1997/ Charlton Athletic coach then asst mgr to 1998 to May 2006/ West Ham United asst mgr Dec 2006

Mervyn Day, and England youth and U23 international, began his long career (642 League games) with West Ham United, making his FL debut at home to Ipswich Town on 27 August 1973 at the age of 18 years and 2 months.

His loan spell with United, with Simon Tracey and Mel Rees both injured, was for the final game of the 1991–92 season. United lost 0–3 but Mervyn did save a John Fashanu penalty.

After a spell as manger of Carlisle United he moved to Charlton Athletic as goalkeeping coach and then has worked as Alan Curbishley's assistant manager.

Appearances:		Apps	Gls
	FL	1	0
	Total	1	0

DEANE Brian (Deano) Christopher

Striker 1988–93, 1997–98, 2006 6' 3" 12st 7 to 14st.
b. Leeds 7 February 1968

Yorkshire Amateurs/ Doncaster Rovers from jnr Dec 1985
United: (£40k) 19 Jul 1988 to 14 Jul 1993
Debuts: 26 Jul 1988 Skegness Town 1 United 8 (Fr)
13 Aug 1988 Bradford City 0 United 1 (YHC)
27 Aug 1988 Reading 1 United 3
Last games: 8 May 1993 United 4 Chelsea 2
15 May 1993 Trinidad & Tobago 1 United 1 (Fr)
Leeds United (£2.7or £2.9m) Jul 1993
United: (£1.5m) 29 Jul 1997 to 15/16 Jan 1998
Debuts: 24 Jul 1997 Tistedalen 1 United 4 (Fr)
10 Aug 1997 United 2 Sunderland 0
Last game: 10 Jan 1998 Sunderland 4 United 2

Benfica(Portugal. £1m. (£200k to Leeds U) Jan 1998/ Middlesbrough (£3m) Oct 1998/ Leicester City (£150k) Nov 2001/ West Ham United Oct 2003/ Leeds United 2004/ Sunderland/ Perth Glory(Australia) to Oct 2005
United: 1 Jan 2006 to cs 2006
Debut: 21 Jan 2006 United 3 Brighton 1 (sub)
Last game: 30 Apr 2006 United 1 Crystal Palace 0 (sub)

After trials with Leeds, Barnsley, Notts County and Bradford, Brian Deane began his career with Doncaster Rovers. He completed a college course and began full-time training which 'toughened him up' and led to his FL debut at home to Swansea City on 4 February 1986. Very tall and slim with 'spindly legs' and improving ball control, it was said that 'it was like watching Bambi on ice' but it was sufficient to draw the attention of Dave Bassett, the United manager.

In his first spell with United, Brian's all round strength, powerful shooting, excellent heading and the ability to bring others into play made him a really excellent striker. He struck up an immediately successful partnership with Tony Agana and their goals (46 in 1988–89 and 31 in 1989–90) were a major factor in restoring United from the Third to the First (top) Division. Brian was United's leading scorer in (League and Cup) each season and will always be known nationally as the scorer of the first Premier League goal and first penalty when he scored twice in the opening game against Manchester United.

Reg Brealey resumed the position of chairman in the summer of 1993 and sold Brian to Leeds United. Dave Bassett agreed to stay but told the chairman that his decision would result in relegation and he was proved correct. Brian returned to the Lane under the new regime of chairman Mike McDonald and manager Nigel Spackman but the optimism of summer turned to winter gloom when players, including Brian, were sold.

Brian was a player who missed very few games; he was awarded three England caps while with United and returned to the Lane for a third spell in 2006. He almost scored on his third debut and made a final cameo appearance in the last game of the season, promotion having been achieved. Brian retired from playing but has occasional involvement with United.

Appearances:		Apps	Gls
	FL	221 (2)	93
	FAC	24 (1)	11
	LC	20	13
	FMC	2	2
	YHC	3 (2)	0
	Total	270 (5)	119

DEARDEN William (Billy)

CF 1970–75 5' 10½" 10st 13 to 11st 3
b. Oldham 11 February 1944

Oldham Athletic from jnr Sep 1963/ Crewe Alexandra Dec 1966/ Chester City (£3000) Jun 1968
United: (£10k) 17/21 Apr 1970 to 16 Jul 1976
Debuts: 23 Apr 1970 United 0 Barnsley 0 (CC)
22 Aug 1970 United 2 Swindon Town 1
Last game: 13 Dec 1975 United 1 Manchester United 4
Chester City (L) 20 Feb 1976, Jul 1976/ Chesterfield Aug 1977 to cs1979 then coach to cs 1983/ Mansfield cs1983 coach, asst mgr, caretaker mgr/ Port Vale asst mgr Jul 1994/ Mansfield Town mgr Jun 1999/ Notts mgr Jan 2002 to Jan 2004/ Blackpool asst mgr Jun 2004/ Milton Keynes Dons coach Sep 2005 to Jun 2006 / – / Mansfield Town mgr Dec 2006 to Mar 2008

Billy Dearden was an apprentice plumber in his early days at Oldham Athletic where he made his FL debut on 1 September 1964 at home to Peterborough United. He showed potential at times, playing mainly at outside right but his career, partly because of injuries, failed to take off.

At the age of 26, Billy was signed by John Harris, who quickly switched him to centre forward where he was to play nearly all his games for United. There had been plenty of criticism and little praise in the past but now, playing at this higher level, Bill was determined to prove his critics wrong.

He had great pace, was difficult to mark and was a good finisher but above all, he had tremendous courage, ignoring knocks and he played on, in spite of serious cartilage problems, when United returned to the top flight in 1971.

He was the top scorer for the following two seasons and recorded a hat trick against Bobby Moore's West Ham in February 1972 but cartilage problems began to take their toll. His final game for United was in the dreadful 1975–76 season, although he did score the United goal in the home defeat by Manchester United.

He returned to Chester, initially on loan, and, after moving to Chesterfield (where he had trained during his second spell with Chester) he finally retired at the end of the 1979–80 season, having scored 101 goals in 384(21) FL games.

By then he was on Chesterfield's coaching staff and became youth team coach. In 1983 he moved to Mansfield Town for eleven years, being caretaker manager for a short time. After a time at Port Vale working under John Rudge he returned to Mansfield as manager and in January of 2002 he took charge of Notts County, parting company by 'mutual agreement' two years later. After two coaching roles he returned to Mansfield as manager but he was dismissed in March 2008 as the club was fighting (unsuccessfully) to stay in the Football League.

Appearances:

	Apps	Gls
FL	170 (5)	61
FAC	7	2
LC	15	5
TX	3	1
CC	4	2
WC	3 (2)	1
ABD	2	0
Total	204 (7)	72

De GOEY Leendert (Len)

OR, MF 1979–80 5' 11" 11st 5
b. Amsterdam (Holland) 29 February 1952

Telstar 1975–76/ Sparta Rotterdam cs 1976/
United: (£125k) 1 Aug 1979 to 30 Jul or Oct 1980
Debuts: 11 Aug 1979 United 1 Doncaster Rovers 1 (LC)
18 Aug 1979 United 2 Swindon Town 1
Last game: 3 May 1980 Grimsby Town 4 United 0
Deventer Go Ahead Eagles (£70k or 'small') 1980 to 1982

A stylish, constructive player, usually playing wide on the right, Len De Goey, who had been signed by Harry Haslam, fitted in well as the team led the Third Division promotion race. However, his form deteriorated along with rest of the team and he seemed to lack the necessary determination when it was most required. He returned to Holland after one season.

Appearances:

	Apps	Gls
FL	33	5
FAC	1	0
LC	2	0
ASC	3	0
Total	39	5

DELLAS Traianos (Tri)

MF etc 1997–99 6' 4" 15st
b. Thessaloniki or Monastiri (Greece) 31 January 1976

Aris Thessalonika 1993–94/ Panserraikos(L) 1994–96/ Aris Thessalonika 1996–97
United: (£300k rising to £700k) 6/7/13 Aug 1997 to cs 1999
Debut: 29 Nov 1997 United 1 Crewe Alexandra 0
Last game: 9 May 1999 Ipswich Town 4 United 1
AEK Athens (free) cs 1999/ Perugia (Italy) cs 2001/ AS Roma 2002 to 2005 / – / AEK Athens cs2005

Signed by Steve Bruce, the 21-year-old Tri Dellas showed, at times, the potential to be a very good player. Soon after he joined United, he required micro-surgery for a back injury and, although showing immense potential, he never produced consistent performances. In May 1998, he captained Greece in the UEFA U21 championships.

With United he was used in a variety of roles: centre back, wing back, mid-field and even centre forward, but, partly through various injuries, he failed to find a regular place in the side. A commanding figure with a great stride, he was two footed, comfortable in possession and could use the ball well. His three United goals were memorable, one being an unstoppable 35 yard drive against Portsmouth and the other two turning a likely defeat into a 3–2 victory at Tranmere, when he came on as a late substitute.

Homesick after two seasons with United, he returned to Greece, winning his first full cap in 2001 and becoming an integral part of the Greek side which, in 2004, surprisingly won the European Championship, Tri scoring the goal which gave them victory in the semi-final. He left Roma as a free agent but missed several months of football through injury before rejoining AEK and played for Greece in the 2008 European Championship.

Appearances:

	Apps	Gls
FL	14 (12)	3
PO	0 (1)	0
FAC	0 (2)	0
LC	2	0
Total	16 (15)	3

DEMPSEY Mark James

MF 1986–88 5' 8" 10st 4
b. Manchester 14 January 1964

Manchester United from May 1980, app Jan 1982/ Swindon Town (L) Jan 1985
United: (L) 5/20 Aug, (£25k) 2 Sep 1986 to 19 Oct 1988
Debuts: 5 Aug 1986 Skegness Town 1 United 11 (Fr sub)
8 Aug 1986 Matlock Town 0 United 2 (Fr)
23 Aug 1986 United 1 Shrewsbury Town 1
Last game: 9 Apr 1988 Birmingham City 1 United 0
Chesterfield (L) Sep 1988

Rotherham United (£15k) Oct 1988 / Macclesfield Town cs 1991/Buxton Nov 1993/ Altrincham Mar 1994/ Buxton Nov 1994/ Frickley Athletic player-mgr Jan 1995/ Gainsborough Trinity Feb 1997/ Maltby MW Aug 1997/ Alfreton Town player-mgr Sep 1997 to Apr 1998/ Redcliffe Borough Jul 1998/ Manchester United Academy coach c2002

Mark Dempsey began his career at Old Trafford making just one League appearance (7 December 1985) and a substitute appearance in the European Cup Winners Cup. His FL debut came after his European appearance while on loan with Swindon Town on 26 January 1985 at home to Tranmere Rovers.

Signed by Billy McEwan, Mark was a regular member of the side for his two seasons at Bramall Lane. He had good technique but made it clear that he wasn't happy with the style of play that Dave Bassett employed. After leaving Bramall Lane he gained a Division Four Championship medal with the Millers before moving into non-League football. He had a spell as player manager of Frickley Athletic and later held a similar position with Alfreton Town. Currently he coaches in the Manchester United Academy.

In his youth, he had also been an actor, appearing in the children's TV programme, 'Murphy's Mob'.

Appearances:		Apps	Gls
	FL	60 (3)	8
	FAC	4 (1)	1
	LC	4	2
	FMC	2	0
	Total	70 (4)	11

DENIAL Geoffrey (Geoff)

LH 1952–54 6' 0" 11st 0
b. Stocksbridge 31 January 1932

Oaks Fold
United: Jun 1959 (amat) to pro 22/25 Jan 1952 to 30 Jun 1956
Debut: 15 Nov 1952 Notts County 0 United 3
Last game: 13 Sep 1954 United 1 Cardiff City 3
Headington (Oxford) United (£250) Sept 1956

A product of Southey Green School and Oaks Fold, the United nursery side, Geoff Denial played nine of his ten FL games in a seven week spell in 1952–53, United's Second Division Championship season. Although he was at the club for two further seasons, he made only two more appearances, one of those being in a friendly. He appeared to have a first class future in the game but lost his way while completing his National Service in the Army.

After moving to Headington United as a part timer, he became an influential player in the club's rise to Football League status as Oxford United and he was their captain when the club converted to full-time professionalism in 1959. He was still there in 1962–63 when he played six times in Oxford United's first FL season, the new League club paying a £250 transfer fee.

Appearances:		Apps	Gls
	FL	10	0
	FAC	1	0
	Total	11	0

DERRY Shaun Peter

MF/D 1998–2000 5' 10" 10st 13
b. Nottingham 6 December 1977

Notts County from trainee Apr 1996
United: (£680k/700k/£750k) 26 Jan 1998 to 16 Mar 2000
Debut: 27 Jan 1998 United 1 Huddersfield Town 1
Last game: 11 Mar 2000 Port Vale 2 United 3
Portsmouth (£300k+ £300k+ £100k) Mar 2000/ Crystal Palace (£600k) Aug 2002/ Nottingham Forest (L) Dec 2004/ Leeds United(£250k) Feb 2005/ Crystal Palace (L) Nov 2007, signed (£300k) Jan 2008

Shaun Derry's career with Notts County began as a ten year old and he made his FL debut at home to York City on 12 March 1996.

A strong, determined, hard tackling, hard working player, he was signed by Nigel Spackman and in his second game, took over in goal at Fratton Park and kept a clean sheet. In March 1998 he made a substitute appearance for a FL U21 eleven. He was sold to Portsmouth by Neil Warnock, in his first season at the Lane, the original fee of £300k rising by another hundred thousand when Pompey escaped relegation.

There followed various moves before Shaun, who had missed half the previous season at Leeds through injury, rejoined Warnock at Crystal Palace shortly after the latter became manager. Soon after the move, Shaun topped 350 career League appearances.

Appearances:		Apps	Gls
	FL	62 (10)	0
	FAC	7	1
	LC	4	0
	Total	73 (10)	1

DEVLIN Paul (Dev) John

OR/M/F 1998–2002 5' 8½" 10st 5 to 11st 5
b. Birmingham 14 April 1972

Tamworth 1989–90/ Armitage 1990/ Stafford Rangers 1990/ Notts County (£40,000) Feb 1992/ Birmingham City Mar 1996
United: (£200k+) 13 Mar 1998 to 8 Feb 2002
Debuts: 14 Mar 1998 United 4 Reading 0 (sub)
13 Apr 1998 Swindon Town 1 United 1
Last game: 3 Feb 2002 Norwich City 1 United 2
Notts County(L) Oct 1998

Birmingham City (L) 8 Feb, (£200k) 8 May 2002/ Watford Sep 2003/ Walsall(L) Feb 2006/ Bohemians Jul 2006 to Aug 2006/ Tamworth Sep 2006 to Oct 2006/ Sutton Coldfield Town/ Halesowen Town Feb 2007 to Jan 2008/ Rugby Town asst mgr Jan 2008 (1 week)

Paul Devlin made his FL debut with Notts County, managed at the time by Neil Warnock, coming on as a substitute at home to Luton Town on 26 September 1992. He made his full debut three days later at Tranmere. Neil knew he was 'a likeable rogue' but admired his battling qualities. Transferred to Birmingham, he was their top scorer and 1996–97 Player of the Year.

Paul was signed by Steve Thompson for United in the season when United lost narrowly to Sunderland in the play-off Semi-finals. A fast and direct player, raiding down the right flank, 'Dev' had a good shot and could put across a good, firm centre but he often promised more than he delivered. With Neil Warnock in charge, the rogue element remained and Devlin and Marcus Bent were not the best of team-mates and he was not the easiest player to manage.

Unsettled at the start of the 2001–02 season, he was placed on the transfer list and had a frequent place on the subs bench and, failing to impress, he was sold to Birmingham where, in less than a year from October 2002, he had 10 Scottish caps. After two more League clubs, he moved into non-League football having scored 88 League goals in 434(69) appearances.

Appearances:		Apps	Gls
	FL	122 (25)	24
	PO	2	0
	FAC	8	1
	LC	9 (3)	4
	Total	141 (28)	29

DE VOGT Wilko

G 2001–03 6' 3" 12st 13
b. Breda (Holland) 17 September 1975

NAC Breda
United: 10 Jul/ 7 Aug 2001 to 31 Jan 2003
Debuts: 23 Jul 2001 Bodmin Town 0 United 9 (Fr)
29 Sep 2001 United 2 Norwich City 1
Last games: 6 Apr 2002 United 3 Watford 0
25 Jan 2003 United 4 Ipswich Town 3 (FAC)
RBC Roosendaal (free) Feb 2003/ RKC Waalwijk cs 2003/ TOP Oss cs 2004

Wilko de Vogt made his debut in the Netherlands with NAC Breda in May 1997. He was signed by United, after a delay because of injury, as cover for Simon Tracey in what was regarded as a season's trial. He played only when Simon was unavailable. He dealt competently with crosses but never looked like becoming the first choice keeper. He left the club early by mutual agreement and eventually joined TOP Oss in 2004 becoming their regular goalkeeper.

Appearances:		Apps	Gls
	FL	5 (1)	0
	FAC	3	0
	Total	8 (1)	0

DEWIS George Ranger

CF 1944–45 5' 10" 12st 0
b. Burbage 22 January 1913
d. Hinckley 23 October 1994

Stoke Golding/ Nuneaton Town 1933/ Leicester City Nov 1933
United: (Guest) Dec 1944 to Mar 1945
Debut: 25 Dec 1944 Sheffield Wednesday 1 United 2 (LWCQ WW2)
Last game: 10 Mar 1945 Lincoln City 3 United 1 (LWCQ WW2)
WW2 guest: Chesterfield (1941–42), Leeds United (1943–44), Sheff Utd, Bury Town (1945–46) and Yeovil & Petters U (1945–46)
Yeovil Town cs 1950/ Leicester City cs 1951 (training, coaching staff and kitman to 1983)

A centre forward whose play was based on strength and ability in the air, George Dewis spent all of his peacetime professional League career with Leicester City, making his FL debut on 9 December 1933 at home to West Bromwich Albion and scoring 45 goals in 116 FL games. A consistent goal scorer, his best years were lost to the Second World War when he served in the Army and also played as a guest for various clubs including United, scoring on his debut at Hillsborough. He was Leicester's leading scorer in the first post-war season but his best days were over. After one season with Yeovil, he returned to Filbert Street, initially as a coach and then as trainer to youth and reserve teams and finally as kit man until 1983.

Appearances:		Apps	Gls
	WW2	3	3
	Total	3	3

DICKINSON Martin John

MF 1988 5' 10" 12st 3
b. Leeds 14 March 1963

Leeds United from app May 1980/ West Bromwich Albion Feb 1986
United: (free) Jul 1988 to Jun 1989
Debuts: 26 Jul 1988 Skegness Town 1 United 8 (Fr)
16 Aug 1988 Doncaster Rovers 0 United 0 (YHC)
Last game: 24 Sep 1988 Brentford 1 United 4 (sub)
Retired Jun 1989

Martin Dickinson began his career with Leeds United, making his FL debut on 2 April 1980 at home to Middlesbrough. He made 100(3) FL appearances for Leeds and 46(4) for West Bromwich Albion before moving to Bramall Lane.

Martin was signed by Dave Bassett who hoped that his experience would boost United's chances of promotion to the top flight but after played in the pre-season games, he suffered a neck injury in a car accident and, after one substitute appearance, he was advised to retire on medical grounds.

Appearances:		Apps	Gls
	FL	0 (1)	0
	YHC	1	0
	Total	1 (1)	0

D'JAFFO Laurent

Striker 2000–02 6' 0" 13st 5
b. Aquitaine (France) 5 November 1970

Montpellier/ Niort/ Red Star Paris/ Ayr United Oct 1997/ Bury Jul 1998/ Stockport County (£100k) Aug 1999
United: (£175k) 4 Feb 2000 to c13 Jul 2002
Debuts: 12 Feb 2000 Crystal Palace 1 United 1 (sub)
11 Mar 2000 Port Vale 2 United 3
Last game: 21 Apr 2002 Birmingham City 2 United 0

Aberdeen (free) Jul 2002 to cs 2003/ Benin/ Mansfield Town Mar 2004/ Skonto Riga (Latvia) Jun 2004

A strong forward with good heading ability and al round technique, Laurent D'Jaffo never produced what he was capable of and he presented attitude and fitness problems. When he left Aberdeen, Laurent was without a club but played for Benin in the African Nations Cup early in 2004 and after leaving Mansfield Town he was still in the Benin World Cup squad.

After retiring, having made a total 141(36) League appearances in England and Scotland, Laurent acted as a football agent and assisted Neil Warnock with scouting.

Appearances:		Apps	Gls
	FL	45 (24)	11
	FAC	1 (2)	0
	LC	0 (2)	1
	Total	46 (28)	12

DOANE Benjamin (Ben) Nigel David

RWB 1999–2003 5' 10" 12st 0
b. Sheffield 22 December 1979

United: from trainee (1996–97), pro 15 Jul 1998 to cs 2003
Debuts: 27 Jul 1999 York City 0 United 3 (sub, Fr)
24 Aug 1999 Shrewsbury Town 0 United 3 (sub, LC)
20 Nov 1999 Stockport Country 1 United 1 (sub)
7 Dec 1999 Whitby Town 1 United 3 (Fr)
21 Apr 2001 Grimsby Town 1 United 3
Last game: 7 Apr 2003 Wimbledon 1 United 0
Kettering T (L) Jan 2000/ Mansfield Town(L) Jan 2003/ retired May 2003

Ben Doane was not able to maintain a consistent place in the first team. In October and November of 2001 he was a regular for eight games but he lost his place following a suspension after being sent off at Walsall. He made a few appearances in the following season but in April, he suffered a bad ankle injury which ended his professional career of 30(4) FL appearances.

Appearances:		Apps	Gls
	FL	19 (4)	1
	LC	1 (2)	0
	Total	20 (6)	1

DOBSON Samuel (Sammy)

IR/IL 1891–93
b. Preston

Crewe A 1889–90/Preston North End cs 1890
United: c14 Mar 1891 to Oct 1893
Debuts: 21 Mar 1891 Royal Arsenal 1 United 1 (Fr)
23 Mar 1891 United 2 Burton Wanderers 2 (MCL)
3 Sep 1892 United 4 Lincoln City 2
Last games: 15 Oct 1892 United 2 Darwen 0
29 Oct 1892 Middlesbrough Ironopolis 1 United 0 (NL)
16 Sep 1893 Leicester Fosse 4 United 1 (Fr)
Retired

Sammy Dobson made his senior debut scoring for Crewe Alexandra in a Football Alliance fixture against Walsall Town Swifts in September 1889. His FL debut was with Preston North End, scoring in the 3–1 win at Derby County on 20 September 1890 and he also played for North End in the ill-fated 1890 National Baseball League.

He was one of the three Preston North End players signed through the instigation of United's chairman Charles Stokes in February and March 1891—Billy Hendry and Jack Drummond were the other two—to improve and bring a more professional attitude to the club. Sammy was a regular in 1891–92 and played in United's first ever Football League match but managed only five more FL appearances, scoring in his final one.

A fine shot, he was selected for an England trial in February 1892 but couldn't play because of illness. He remained on United's retained list until 1895 though it had seemed likely, when he returned to Preston in October 1893, that injuries had ended his playing career. Later, he was employed at Deepdale as a groundsman.

Appearances:		Apps	Gls
	FL	6	1
	FAC	5	3
	NL	18	11
	MCL	5	1
	SCC	1	2
	WCC	2	1
	Total	37	19

DOCHERTY James (John)

CF/IR 1894–95

Motherwell
United: 13 Nov 1894 to 24 Oct 1895
Debuts: 24 Nov 1894 Linfield Athletic 1 United 5 (Fr)
15 Dec 1894 Derby County 4 United 1
Last game: 19 Oct 1895 Wolverhampton Wanderers 4 United 1
Bury Oct 1895/ Motherwell May 1896

John Docherty made his Scottish League debut with Motherwell in the early part of the 1894–95 season but after just three first team appearances he signed for United and scored on his League debut, albeit in a 1–4 defeat. Reported as a good leader of the line and also good with his head, he was too slow. Signed by Bury, he made four FL appearances with the Lancashire team before returning to Motherwell though he doesn't appear to have played again for their first team.

Appearances:		Apps	Gls
	FL	17	9
	FAC	1	0
	UCL	3	1
	Total	21	10

DOCHERTY John ('Doc')

OR 1961–65 5' 5" 9st 5
b. Glasgow 29 April 1940

St Roch's (Glasgow)/ Brentford Jul 1959
United: (£4000+£2000 promotion and 20 games)
8/9/11 Mar 1961 to 10 Dec 1965
Debut: 11 Mar 1961 Brighton & Hove Albion 0 United 0
Last game: 30 Oct 1965 United 1 Chelsea 2

Brentford (£10k) Dec 1965/ Reading (£10.2k) Feb 1968/ Brentford Mar 1970/ QPR player-coach Jul 1974/ Brentford mgr Jan 1975/ Cambridge United coach 1976, mgr Jan 1978 to Sep 1983/ Brentford asst mgr Feb 1984/ Millwall mgr Jul 1986/ Bradford City mgr Mar 1990 to cs 1991/ Slough Town mgr Nov 1993/ Millwall mgr Feb to cs1997/ Inverness Caledonian Thistle coach cs 1997, brief mgr Jan 2006, coach

Educated at St Mungo's Academy and spotted playing in Glasgow junior football by the Brentford manager, Malcolm MacDonald, John Docherty made his FL debut at Torquay on the 14 September 1960 and soon established a regular place in the team at outside right.

John was signed for United by John Harris shortly before the FA Cup semi-final against Leicester City and as the battle for promotion with Ipswich came to a climax. Harris may have thought that 'Doc' would solve the problem right wing position and played him at the end of the week at Brighton but he wasn't good enough and Harris moved quickly to sign Welsh international Len Allchurch who filled the position in the final games of the season leading to promotion.

A traditional tricky winger but a little lacking in pace and thrust, United's acquisition of Allchurch must have been a blow to the young Scot who came to believe that no matter how he played, a regular first team place would be denied. In truth, he never looked likely to hold down the first team spot. It wasn't until September of 1964 that he played in more than six successive games and, after a run of 13 games early in the 1965–66 season, scoring from the spot in his final game, he was replaced by Alan Woodward.

John was a clever and intelligent player and a clinical scorer from the penalty spot—perhaps his only failure came when he hit the post in a reserve match against Bury—and it was no surprise that he built a long career as a coach and manager. In his FL career he scored 84 goals in 337(5) appearances.

Appearances:		Apps	Gls
	FL	41	9
	LC	3	1
	CC	3	3
	Total	47	13

DODDS Ephraim (Jock)

CF/IL 1934–39 5' 11½" 12st 4 to 12st 10
b. Grangemouth (Stirling) 7 September 1915
d. Blackpool 23 February 2007

Shell-Mex/ Medomsley Juniors/ Huddersfield Town amat Jun 1932, pro Feb 1933
United: 7/9 May 1934 to 10/13 Mar 1939
Debut: 15 Sep 1934 United 0 Burnley 0
Last game: 4 Mar 1939 Sheffield Wednesday 1 United 0
Blackpool (£10k) Mar 1939
WW2 guest: Manchester United, Fulham, West Ham United
Shamrock Rovers cs 1946/ Everton (£7750) Nov 1946/ Lincoln City (£6000) Oct 1948 to Jun 1950

Brought up from the age of twelve in County Durham, 'Jock' Dodds played for the County Schoolboys as a defender, moving into the forward line when he left school. He joined Huddersfield Town as a sixteen year old but was given a free transfer after a couple of seasons which had included a short loan spell with Lincoln City.

Teddy Davidson, the United manager, watched 'Jock's' last reserve appearance for Town who were cutting their wage bill and saw his potential. It was said that the player 'could hardly stand on his left foot let alone shoot with it', but Jock was prepared to return to the training ground in the afternoon to improve his game. After scoring a hat trick in a reserve game, he was given his FL debut in September 1934 at inside left but things began to come together early in 1935 when he was moved to centre forward and he ended that season and each succeeding one, as leading scorer.

With short quick strides and a deceptive body swerve, Jock, a powerfully built man with deep reserves of energy and stamina, was a difficult man to stop. He became two footed and his heading was both powerful and clever and his 'ball control and speed are wonderful' for a big fellow. United gave a good account of themselves in the 1936 Cup Final against Arsenal having the agony of seeing Jock, although pushed in the back, thundering a header against the bar and they just missed out on promotion.
Everton and Bolton in 1935, Liverpool, Aston Villa and Blackpool in 1937, WBA and Sunderland in 1938, were among the clubs who sought

his transfer but matters came to a head in 1939 when Jock asked for a move because, he would claim, of problems with his mother's health. United received a record fee from Blackpool and fortunately, promotion was still achieved.

Jock set all sorts of scoring records during the war. In five and a half seasons he scored over two hundred and fifty goals including eight in one game and a hat trick in less than three minutes and he made ten appearances for Scotland, scoring a hat trick against England.

When the war ended, he rebelled against the maximum wage, playing in the Republic of Ireland and in June 1950 he was expelled from the Football League over his role as a recruiting agent for the Colombian club Millionarios (the Colombian League was not affiliated to FIFA). Later he spent many years as a successful businessman in many varying ventures—hotel, a rock factory, night clubs—occasionally troubling and no doubt amusing the Blackpool Constabulary who were regular visitors, both on duty and off. He was a great footballer and a real character and at the time of his death, the oldest surviving Cup Final player.

Appearances:		Apps	Gls
	FL	178	113
	FAC	17	10
	CC	8	7
	Total	203	130

DONALD (see Donald FRASER)

DONIS Georgios (George)

RW 1999 6' 0" 12st 6
b. Greece 22 October 1969

PAS Giannina 1990–92/ Panathinaikos 1992/ Blackburn Rovers Jul 1996/ AEK Athens Sep 1997
United: 25 Mar 1999 to 4 Jun 1999
Debuts: 3 Apr 1999 Barnsley 2 United 1 (sub)
17 Apr 1999 United 2 QPR 1
Last game: 9 May 1999 Ipswich Town 4 United 1
Huddersfield Town (free) Jun 1999 to Jul 2000/ Ilisiakos coach cs 2000/ Larissa coach cs 2002

George Donis moved to England from Greece in 1996, making his English League debut for Blackburn Rovers at home to Tottenham Hotspur on 17 August 1996. After one season, he returned to AEK Athens but left the club as a free agent in 1999 after a court ruled in his favour regarding a financial dispute with the club. Several clubs were reportedly interested in the Greek International's services and Steve Bruce signed him for United in the transfer deadline week, at least until the end of the season. Quick, tricky and powerfully built, he played in United's final few games, scoring in the last one, but he was not retained and was signed by Bruce who had moved on to Huddersfield. Although a 'Bosman' free transfer, it was reported the cost of the three year contract would be about £1m but, after one season, he failed to return for pre-season training, claiming he had received call-up papers for the Greek Army.

He soon moved into coaching in Greece and has been very successful with both his clubs, being voted 'Coach of the Year' in 2006 and 2007.

Appearances:		Apps	Gls
	FL	5 (2)	1
	Total	5 (2)	1

DONNELLY James (Jimmy)

IR/OR 1902–07 5' 8½" 11st 8
b. South Bank JAS 1879
d. 1959?

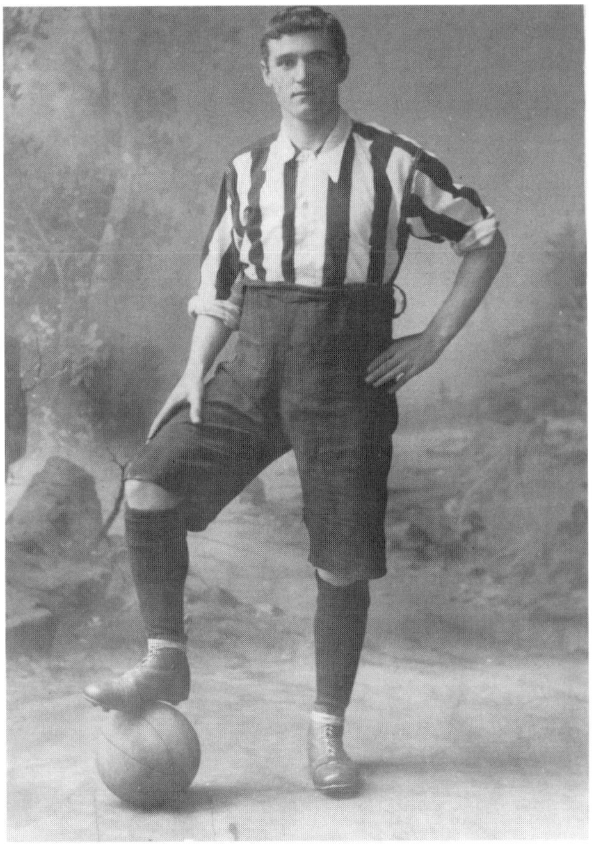

South Bank/ Darlington St Augustine's 1901–02
United: 5 Nov 1902 (after trial) to 1 May 1907
Debuts: 1 Nov 1902 United 1 Lincoln City 1 (Fr)
21 Mar 1903 United 3 Wolverhampton Wanderers 0
Last games: 5 Jan 1907 United 2 Bolton Wanderers 1
12 Jan 1907 Everton 1 United 0 (FAC)
Leicester Fosse (£150) May 1907/ Darlington cs 1910 to cs1914

Jimmy Donnelly, who was probably an amateur with St Augustine's, came as a fast winger and first played on trial in a friendly game but had to wait until March to make his FL debut when he made up for lost time by scoring twice. He made few appearances in the following season and proved to be better at inside forward than on the wing and missed just one game in 1904–05. A clever player who passed the ball well, he was a regular during the following campaign but lost his place to Bluff in 1907.

He was transferred to Leicester Fosse, a move he came to regret, though he assisted them to promotion and in 1908, scored their first ever goal in the top flight. When he played for non-League Darlington, the club reached the last 16 of the FA Cup and he played in the side which beat United on the way.

Appearances:		Apps	Gls
	FL	89	23
	FAC	4	0
	Total	93	23

DORNAN Peter

M 1976 6' 0½" 12st 0
b. Belfast 30 June 1953

Bangor/ Linfield
United: (£30k) 3 Dec 1976 to 31 Dec 1976
Debut: 11 Dec 1976 Plymouth Argyle 0 United 0
Last game: 28 Dec 1976 United 2 Bolton Wanderers 3 (sub)
Linfield/ Swindon Town Feb to Jul 1979/ Linfield

Peter Dornan, a Northern Ireland schoolboy international and later a hockey international, had gained a law degree at Queens University in Belfast when he was signed by United. A thoughtful mid-field player, he struck the bar in his first game but told Cec Coldwell, the United trainer and coach that if he couldn't 'have a Guinness before a match', then he would 'pack it in,' adding later that, 'I could not put up with eating, drinking and sleeping football'.

He returned to Ireland and Linfield returned the transfer fee. Three years later he made one substitute appearance for Swindon and played in a handful of reserve games before no doubt convincing himself that his 1976 opinion of the life of a professional player had been correct.

He spent nine seasons with Linfield, playing in European competitions, and is now a solicitor in Belfast.

Appearances:		Apps	Gls
	FL	1 (2)	0
	Total	1 (2)	0

DOWNES Christopher (Chris) Bryan

MF 1988 5' 10" 10st 8
b. Sheffield 17 January 1969

United: from YT 1 Jul 1985, 30 Jun 1987 to 30 May 1989
Debuts: 12 Jan 1988 Portsmouth 2 United 1 (sub FAC)
5 Nov 1988 Huddersfield Town 3 United 2
Last games: 8 Nov 1988 Aldershot 1 United 0
5 Dec 1988 Wrexham 1 United 1 (sub SVT)
Scarborough(L) Mar 1988
Stockport County Jun 1989/ Crewe Alexandra Aug 1991/ Hyde United Oct 1991/ Buxton

Chris Downes may have made his debut as a substitute in a pre-season friendly at Scunthorpe in August 1987 but his first serious fixture came when he played as a substitute in an FA Cup tie at Fratton Park. All his four appearances for United were away from Bramall Lane and his hopes of a long career in football were damaged when he was at Stockport by a long term viral infection. He made a total of 15(2) FL appearances, scoring one goal before moving into non-League football.

Appearances:		Apps	Gls
	FL	2	0
	FAC	0 (1)	0
	AMC	0 (1)	0
	Total	2 (2)	0

DOWNES Walter (Wally) John

MF 1988 5' 10" 10st 11
b. Hammersmith 9 June 1961

Wimbledon from app Jan 1979/ Newport County(L) Dec 1987
United: (nc) 3 Feb 1988 to May 1989
Debuts: 6 Feb 1988 Stoke City 1 United 0 (sub)
19 Mar Leeds United 5 United 0
Last games: 7 May 1988 Huddersfield Town 0 United 2
18 May 1988 United 1 Bristol City 1 (PO)
Non-league/ Millwall Feb 1990 coaching/ Crystal Palace coaching 1991 to May 1993/ United coaching U21 1993 to Dec 1995/ Bury youth coach 1996/ Lincoln City coaching/ Brentford coach, manager Jun 2002 to Mar 2004/ Reading coach 2004

Wally Downes, a nephew of boxer Terry Downes, started his career with Wimbledon, where he made his FL debut at home to York City on 11 May 1979, a game which clinched promotion for the Dons. It was at Wimbledon that he met up with Dave Bassett and it was Dave who brought Wally to Bramall Lane, soon after his own arrival as manager, to add bite and experience to midfield in what turned out to be an unsuccessful attempt to avoid relegation.

His 11 appearances (eight ended in defeat) were a disaster. United were relegated via the play-offs and the attempt to add bite saw him dismissed twice and the second, against Bradford City, was probably one of the crudest 'tackles' ever seen on the ground.

A pre-season ankle injury meant he had to retire and he took up a coaching role, initially with Millwall then with Crystal Palace. Wally then returned to the Lane as a coach, initially for the U21s, but left when Bassett resigned. He subsequently became Steve Coppell's assistant at Brentford and in June 2002 took over as manager but in March 2004, after a poor run of results, he was dismissed and rejoined Coppell as a coach at Reading.

Appearances:		Apps	Gls
	FL	6 (3)	1
	PO	2	0
	Total	8 (3)	1

DRAKE Alonzo

IL/CF 1903-07 5' 10" 12st 0
b. Parkgate (Rotherham) 16 April 1884
d. Honley, Huddersfield 14 February 1919

Parkgate/ Doncaster Rovers 1902–03
United: 23/25 Jun 1903 to 13 Dec 1907
Debut: 31 Oct 1903 United 1 Aston Villa 2
Last game: 9 Nov 1907 United 1 Wednesday 3
Birmingham (£700) Dec 1907/ Queens Park Rangers Aug 1908/ Huddersfield Town Sep 1909 to Dec 1914/ Rotherham Town

Alonzo Drake made his FL debut with Doncaster Rovers, on 15 February 1902, scoring in the 2–1 win at Stockport County. Having joined United he was a regular in the side for the three seasons 1904–07. Although described as a 'hard working dashing' player, capable of fine passing, many United and later, Birmingham supporters, considered him lazy, thinking he dallied too long on the ball, and he suffered abuse from the crowd. His best spell was with United and in total he played 142 FL games in total scoring 34 goals.

He also played cricket for Yorkshire as an all rounder. Not only was he one of the few players to take 10 wickets in an innings (and the first Yorkshire bowler to do so), but also one of very few to take four wickets in successive balls. A heavy smoker, Alonzo was twice rejected by the army following the outbreak of war and his health declined and he died in 1919. He played in 157 matches with a batting average of 21.7 and he took 480 wickets at an average of 18.0.

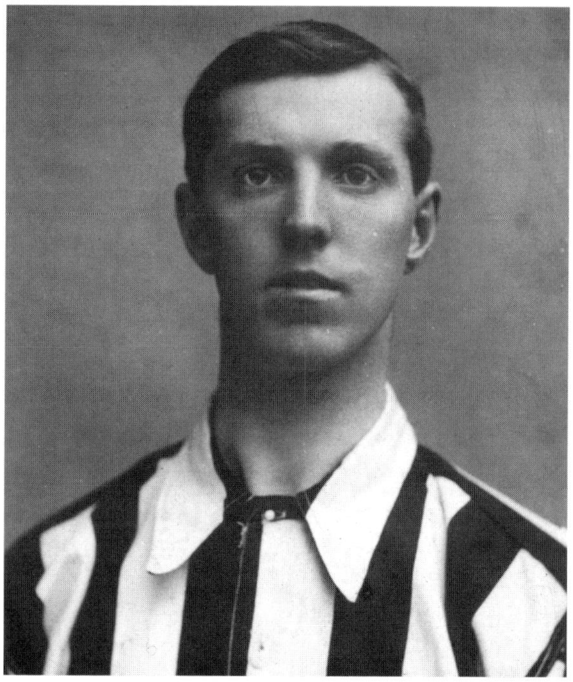

Appearances:		Apps	Gls
	FL	95	20
	FAC	3	0
	Total	98	20

DRAPER James Walter

IR/CF 1895–97
b. Kimberley(Notts) JFM 1878

Kimberley Sep 1895
United: 29 Oct 1895 to cs 1897
Debut: 16 Nov 1895 Aston Villa 2 United 2
Last game: 6 Mar 1897 Wolverhampton Wanderers 1 United 1
Ilkeston Town Aug 1897 to at least Mar 1899/ Kimberley Mar 1901/ Ilkeston T Sep 1901/ Kimberley 31 Jan 1902

Despite scoring in his first three games for United, James Draper was unable to keep a regular place in the side and spent most of his career in non-League football.

Appearances:		Apps	Gls
	FL	12	3
	FAC	1	0
	Total	13	3

DRUMMOND John (Jack)

OL/OR/ IL/CF 1891–94
b. Edinburgh 15 March 1869?

Partick Thistle/ Preston North End May 1890
United: Feb 1891 to cs 1894
Debuts: 14 Feb 1891 Derby C 3 United 2 (Fr)
28 Feb 1891 Derby Junction 1 United 3 (MCL)
3 Sep 1892 United 4 Lincoln City 2
Last games: 7 Apr 1894 Preston North End 3 United 0
21 Apr 1894 Derby County 2 United 0 (UCL)
26 Apr 1894 Wednesday 0 United 1 (WCC)
Liverpool cs 1894/ Barnsley St Peters Oct 1895 to 1897

Jack Drummond was apprenticed as a shipyard carpenter and worked in the Dumbarton yards until he was nearly seventy eight. He played for Partick Thistle as early as 6 April 1889 in a friendly fixture at home to Dykebar and made his FL debut with Preston North End, scoring in the 3–0 home defeat of West Bromwich Albion on 13 September 1890.

One of three Preston players—Hendry and Dobson were the others—signed in February and March 1891 to improve the standards of play, Jack was an energetic player with a tremendous shot and could operate on either wing, at first on the left with United and then on the right. He played in United's first League game against Lincoln City and was a regular in that first season, scoring a superb goal in the Test match at Nottingham against the old Accrington club to take United into the First Division. The ground was in a terrible state and Drummond was just about the only player to keep his feet, attributing this to the black lead that he had applied to the soles of his boots to stop the mud sticking.

He joined Liverpool in the summer of 1894 and twelve months later, returned to South Yorkshire and played for Barnsley in the Midland League for two seasons and may have played in Huddersfield in 1898 as the association game attempted to gain a foothold in an area dominated by rugby.

Appearances:

	Apps	Gls
FL	40	9
TM	1	1
FAC	7	0
NL	25	10
MCL	5	1
UCL	5	1
WCC	3	2
SCC	2	0
ABD	1	0
Total	89	24

DRYDEN John (Jack) R

OL 1935–36 5' 8½" 11st 6
b. Broomhill (Northumberland) 21 August 1908
d. Ashington 16 September 1975

Pegswood U/ Ashington Aug 1930/ Aberdeen Mar 1931/ Newcastle United (£175) Aug 1932/ Exeter City May 1934
United: (free) 23/25 May 1935 to 2 May 1936
Debut: 31 Aug 1935 United 1 Leicester City 2
Last game: 11 Apr 1936 Port Vale 1 United 1
Bristol City (free) cs 1936/ Burnley May 1938/ Peterborough United cs 1939
WW2 guest: Aberdeen, Burnley 1939–40, 1945–46), Charlton (1939–43), Clapton Orient (1941–3), Lincoln (1942–3), Plymouth (1945–6), Walsall (1939–41) and York (1941–2)

Jack Dryden made one appearance for Aberdeen in March 1931 and his FL debut for Newcastle United was on 21 January 1933 at home to Leicester City.

A fast, skilful player with a hard shot, he moved to Bramall Lane on a free transfer and his first game was a defeat but Jack then scored four goals in his next three games. He lost his place in November and played just twice more before moving to Bristol City where he had two successful seasons, ending his FL career with 26 goals in 113 games.

He joined the RAF in 1939 and played as a guest player for several clubs.

Appearances:

	Apps	Gls
FL	19	5
Total	19	5

DUFFIELD Peter ('Duff')

Forward 1987–93 5' 6" 10st 4
b. Middlesbrough 4 February 1969

Middlesbrough from Jun 1984, app Nov 1986
United: Jul 1987(trial), 13 Aug (nc), 20 Aug 1987 to 24 Sep 1993
Debuts: 17 Oct 1987 United 2 Leicester City 1 (sub)
11 Nov 1987 United 4 Manchester United 1 (Fr)
17 Nov 1987 Shrewsbury Town 2 United 0
Last games: 10 Dec 1989 Swindon Town 0 United 2
25 Sep 1990 Northampton Town 0 United 1 (LC)
7 Sep 1991 Oldham Athletic 2 United 1 (sub)
9 Aug 1993 United 0 Sheffield Wednesday 1 (BM)
Halifax Town(L) Mar 1988/ Rotherham United(L) Mar 1991/ Blackpool(L) Jul 1992/ Crewe Alexandra(L) Jan 1993/ Stockport County(L) Mar 1993

Hamilton Academicals (£15k+),Sep 1993/ Airdrie (£135k), Jul 1995/ Raith Rovers (£150k), Mar 1996/ Morton Nov 1997/ Falkirk Jan 1999/ Darlington (L) Jan 1999/ York City Jul 2000/ Boston United Jan 2003/ Carlisle United 2004/ Alfreton Town cs 2004/ Frickley Athletic (L) player coach Mar 2006/ Retford United player-asst mgr Jun 2006, mgr cs 2007

Peter Duffield began his career with Middlesbrough where he led the NIL scoring charts. Danny Bergara, the United coach, had spotted his potential and he was signed after a trial and may have made his debut at Scunthorpe as a substitute in a pre-season friendly in August 1987.

Although he was small, he was strong and enjoyed playing up front, either as the lone striker or feeding off a taller target man. He had a great sense of anticipation and space and was a clinical finisher with either foot and always had a superb record from the penalty spot. He had just established himself in the side when Billy McEwan resigned and Dave Bassett arrived at Bramall Lane. Peter was not involved for the rest of the season which saw United relegated but was a regular in the side, sometimes as a substitute, during the following season, scoring 11 goals, and was the first United sub to be substituted.

When United returned to Division Two, Peter became a fringe player and was unlucky to break his leg at Swindon, his challenge for the ball producing a goal which is credited to either Peter or the Swindon defender Gittens.

This was Peter's final League start for the Blades although he remained with the club for a further three and a half years. Much of that time he was elsewhere on loan and when he finally left Bramall Lane, it was for Scotland. He was eventually sold to Hamilton for £15k and a 15% sell on fee but three years later, no cheque had arrived at the Lane.

There were many more clubs and injuries but always goals. During this period, the goal scoring ability brought him an average of one goal for every three games. Doubtless, many of his goals were from the penalty spot. His record with United was seven successes and no failures.

Peter moved into non-League football after he had made 338(99) League appearances in England and Scotland, scoring 142 goals.

Appearances:

	Apps	Gls
FL	34 (24)	14
FAC	6 (2)	1
LC	2 (5)	2
FMC	1 (2)	2
AMC	2	1
YHC	2 (1)	0
Total	47 (34)	20

DUNCAN James

IL/OR/OL 1889–92
b. Scotland

Dundee Strathmore 1889/Boys of Dundee
United: summer 1889 to cs 1890
Debuts: 7 Sep 1889 Nottingham Rangers 4 United 1 (Fr)
5 Oct 1889 Scarborough 1 United 6 (FAC)

Last game: 22 Mar 1890 Rotherham T 1 United 0 (SCCF)
Nottingham F? 1890–91
United: Dec? 1891 to cs 1892
Debut: 12 Dec 1891 Walsall Town Swifts 2 United 0 (Fr)
Last games: 18 Apr 1892 Stockton 1 United 1 (NL)
10 Oct 1892 United 4 Gainsborough Tr 0 (Fr)

James Duncan, who had played for Forfarshire against an All Scotland team, was one of the Scottish players who joined the new United Football Club in 1889 and he played at inside left in United's first ever game at Nottingham Rangers.

During that first season, he played in 46 out of 57 first team games, most of which were friendly fixtures, scoring 11 goals. He played in all five forward positions but mainly at inside left or outside right.

He made no appearances during the following season and may have returned to Scotland but he may be the J Duncan who played for Forest in 3 friendly matches and two Football Alliance fixtures between December 1890 and April 1891.

The J Duncan who played quite regularly for United—virtually all friendly games—from December 1891 to the end of the season received no comment as to his previous history. It was reported in November 1892 that he had returned to Scotland though United retained his League registration for the 1892–93 season.

Appearances:

	Apps	Gls
FAC	7	1
NL	2	1
SCC	7	1
WCC	2	0
Total	18	3

DUNNE James (Jimmy and Snowy)

CF 1926–33 5' 9½" 11st 10
b. Ringsend (Dublin) 3 September 1905
d. Dublin 14 November 1949

Shamrock Rovers Nov 1923/ New Brighton Oct/Nov 1925
United: (£500) 19/20 Feb 1926 to 30 Sep/2 Oct 1933
Debut: 27 Sep 1926 Derby County 1 United 0
Last games: 23 Sep 1933 United 0 Portsmouth 1
27 Sep 1933 Belfast Celtic 3 United 0 (Fr)
Arsenal (£8,250) Oct 1933/ Southampton (£1,000) Jul 1936/ Shamrock Rovers Jun 1937 player then coach/ Bohemians coach 1942/ Shamrock Rovers coach 1947

Jimmy Dunne had played Gaelic football as a youth but he played soccer in the Curragh where he had been interned after joining the IRA. He joined Shamrock Rovers and moved to England, joining New Brighton after a one month trial and scoring on his FL debut at home to Rochdale on 7 November 1925.

He signed for United in February 1926 after being watched by Ernest Needham but for more than three years, he was no more than a useful reserve. He received encouragement from fellow Irishman, Billy Gillespie and was selected for Ireland early in 1928. However it wasn't until 1929 when he scored two goals in an end of season game at Fratton Park and scored a hat trick at Leicester in September that he established himself as a regular member of the first team.

Jimmy Seed, the Wednesday captain, described Jimmy as 'the ideal centre forward'. His ball control was excellent, he had pace, a fine shot in both feet and terrific power in heading and he was quick of thought and, so often, first to a free kick or centre. Many of these came from Fred Tunstall on United's left wing and the catch phrase 'Tunnie-Dunnit' became a regular headline in the Sheffield sport pages. Nicknamed 'Snowy' because of his fair hair, he was United's leading scorer in four successive seasons (1929–33) and his total of 41 League goals in 1930–31 and five more in the FA Cup is still the club record. He scored 15 hat tricks (12 in League games), including 4 goals in a game four times and 5 in a friendly fixture. Only Harry Johnson and Alan Woodward have scored more League goals for the Blades.

Herbert Chapman, the Arsenal manager made an offer in March 1932 of £10k for Jimmy which United bravely rejected but, as the Depression of the early 1930's grew more severe, the club was forced to sell. Jimmy was never happy in London and played in only 28 FL games for the Gunners and United tried to bring him back to the Lane in February 1935 but discovered that he had cartilage problems.

Jimmy was awarded 22 Irish caps but chose on some occasions to play for United. He died at the early age of 44 and is buried in Dean's Grange cemetery in Dublin. The gravestone carries a photograph of this great centre forward in his United colours.

Appearances:

	Apps	Gls
FL	173	143
FAC	10	11
CC	7	13
Total	190	167

DYER Bruce Antonio

Striker 2006 6' 0" 11st 3
b. Ilford 13 April 1975

Watford from trainee Apr 1993/ Crystal Palace (£1.1m) Mar 1994/ Barnsley (£700k) Oct 1998/ Watford (free)/ Stoke City (free) Aug 2005/ Millwall (L) Nov 2005
United: (free) 26/27 Jan 2006 to 5 Jun 2006
Debut: 14 Feb 2006 United 1 Reading 1
Last game: 22 Apr 2006 Luton Town 1 United 1
Doncaster Rovers (free) Jun 2006 to Jan 2008/ Bradford City (L) Jan 2007/ Rotherham United (L) Sep 2007/ Chesterfield Mar to cs 2008

Bruce Dyer made his League debut with Watford as a substitute on 17 April 1993 at home to Birmingham City; his full debut coming at home to Barnsley on 21 August. He became the first million pound teenage player when he was transferred to Crystal Palace and he had a successful spell with them and with Barnsley.

When he arrived at the Lane, he was very experienced, having made nearly 400 League appearances and had scored over 100 goals. Neil Warnock had been impressed with his attitude and signed him as cover for the strikers as United's promotion push began to falter. Strong and hard working, Bruce scored on his debut but his opportunities were limited and at the end of the season, he moved on and in due course played for two more South Yorkshire clubs. In January 2008 he agreed to settle his contract and leave Doncaster and moved to Saltergate. He was released at the end of the season having reached a total of 119 goals in 340(128) League appearances.

In September 2007 he had played for the Montserrat National side in the 0–4 defeat at Ashford Town.

Appearances:

	Apps	Gls
FL	3 (2)	1
Total	3 (2)	1

EADES John Thomas C

LB 1906 5' 9½" 11st 7
b. Worcester AMJ 1881

Goldthorpe Institute
United: 19 Apr 1906 to Apr 1907
Debut: 8 Dec 1906 United 0 Newcastle United 0
Last game: 15 Dec 1906 Aston Villa 5 United 1
Rotherham Town Apr 1907

Little is known of John Eades whose two appearances for United at left back constituted his first class career.

Appearances:

	Apps	Gls
FL	2	0
Total	2	0

EBBRELL John Keith

MF 1997 5' 9½" 11st 11
b. Bromborough 1 October 1969

Everton from YT Nov 1986
United: (£1m) 26 Feb/ 4 Mar 1997 to Jan 1999
Only game: 29 Mar 1997 United 2 Reading 0
Retired

John Ebbrell gained England caps at schoolboy, youth, U21 and B level whilst with Everton where he made his FL debut at home to Newcastle United on 27 August 1988, going on to make 207(10) League appearances. He had seemed destined for full caps but never quite fulfilled his potential.

When John, a Howard Kendall signing, moved to Bramall Lane, there were some doubts about his fitness because of an ankle problem and in his only first team game, his pass led to United's first goal but he lasted only to half time when he retired with a rib injury. His ankle problem persisted and despite three further operations and various attempts at a come-back, he finally retired in January 1999. He was an expensive signing and when all costs were taken into consideration, it was estimated that United had paid £38k for each of those 45 minutes.

He subsequently worked for a Sports Management company.

Appearances:

	Apps	Gls
FL	1	0
Total	1	0

ECKHARDT Jeffrey (Jeff) Edward

Defender 1984–87 5' 11" 11st 6
b. Sheffield 7 October 1965

United: from jnr Apr 1982, pro 16 Jul 1984 to 20 Nov 1987
Debuts: 2 May 1984 Hull City 1 United 0 (AMC)
30 Mar 1985 Crystal Palace 1 United 3
Last game: 17 Nov 1987 Shrewsbury Town 2 United 0
Fulham (£40k) Nov 1987/ Stockport County (£50k) Jul 1994/ Cardiff City (£30k),Aug 1996/Newport County Jul 2001/ Merthyr Tydfil cs 2004/ Newport County (L) 2005/ Risca United coach Aug 2006, mgr Jan 2007

Jeff Eckhardt stayed on at Newfield School to complete his sixth form studies before signing professional forms. A solid and dependable defender though perhaps not quite tall enough for centre half, he improved when playing with the experienced Ken McNaught and also performed well at right back.

He went on to have a long career in the game, latterly as a part timer, playing 503(22) FL games and scoring 48 goals. He then moved into non-League football in South Wales and was playing occasionally into his 40s.

Appearances:

	Apps	Gls
FL	73 (1)	2
FAC	2	0
LC	2	0
FMC	4	0
AMC	1	0
Total	82 (1)	2

EDDY Keith

MF 1972–76 5' 11" 11st 10
b. Barrow 23 October 1944

Holker OB/ Barrow June 1962/ Watford (£1500) Jul 1966
United: (£50k) 1 Aug 1972 to 30 Jan 1976
Debuts: 5 Aug 1972 Bristol Rovers 0 United 0 (sub WC)
12 Aug 1972 Birmingham City 1 United 2
Last game: 10 Jan 1976 Coventry City 1 United 0
New York Cosmos (£15k) Jan 1976 to 1978?/ coaching in Canada including Toronto Blizzard Mar 1979 to 1982

Keith Eddy made his FL debut with Barrow on the 8 September 1962 at Torquay United. Ken Furphy, Workington's manager, recognised his talents and when Furphy took over at Watford he signed Keith who captained the club to an FA Cup semi-final and promotion to Division Two.

Signed by John Harris for United, his first touch of the ball was a successful penalty kick in the Watney Cup Final shoot-out at Bristol Rovers.

A calm commanding mid-field player who used the ball shrewdly and accurately, Eddy took some time to settle and when his former manager, Ken Furphy, took over at the Lane, he somewhat controversially nominated Keith as United's penalty taker ahead of Alan Woodward.

Furphy had given Tony Currie the captaincy but Eddy took the position in February 1975.

He left in the January of the disastrous 1975–76 season and it was a 'great loss to the club.' He rejoined Furphy in the USA, playing for New York Cosmos and later worked as a coach in Canada and became a successful businessman in the USA.

During his career in England he made over 100 FL appearances for Barrow and United and 240 for Watford, totalling 479(3).

Appearances:		Apps	Gls
	FL	113 (1)	16
	FAC	5	1
	LC	6	3
	TEX	4	0
	ASC	3	1
	CC	3	0
	WC	0 (1)	0
	Total	134 (2)	21

EDGHILL Richard Arlon

LWB 2003 5' 9" 11st 5
b. Oldham 23 September 1974

Manchester City from trainee Jul 1992 to cs 2002/ Birmingham City (L) Nov 2000/ Wigan Athletic Oct 2002 to Jan 2003
United: (nc) 17 Jan 2003 to end Feb 2003
Only game: 18 Feb 2003 United 1 Reading 3 (sub)
Queens Park Rangers (free) Aug 2003/ Bradford City (free) Aug 2005/ Macclesfield Town (free) Jul 2007 to May 2008

Richard Edghill was an experienced defender who had made his League debut with Manchester City on 20 September 1993 at Wimbledon. With Manchester City, he gained England caps at U21 and B level and played over 200 League and Cup games for City.

He signed for United on a non-contract basis in January 2003 and replaced Wayne Quinn, with 20 minutes remaining, in his one Blades' appearance. He was released after one month and in due course joined Queens Park Rangers. He missed some time with Bradford due to a broken leg but after moving to Macclesfield he had reached 261(22) FL appearances by the summer of 2008.

Appearances:		Apps	Gls
	FL	0 (1)	0
	Total	0 (1)	0

EDGLEY (Edgeley) Frank

IF/CF 1904–05 5' 9" 12st 8
b. Crewe JAS 1880
d. Hartlepool 16 October 1910

Crewe Alexandra cs 1900
United: 2 May 1903 to cs 1905
Debut: 12 Mar 1904 Liverpool 3 United 0
Last games: 11 Feb 1905 United 1 Newcastle United 3
18 Feb 1905 Leeds City 2 United 2 (Fr)
Fulham cs 1905/ Reading Oct 1906/ Hartlepools United cs 1908 to his death Feb 1910

Frank Edgley had played regularly for Crewe Alexandra's first team in the Lancashire and then Birmingham & District Leagues from 1900 to 1903, once scoring six goals against Haydock.

A vigorous player with a strong shot, he appears in United's wage books and FL records as 'Edgeley'. He was a prolific scorer for the reserves netting over eighty goals but he didn't impress with the first team and was transferred to Fulham.

He was more successful in the Southern League and with Hartlepools United in their first season where, once more, he was a prolific scorer. His sudden death in his second season was due to appendicitis.

Appearances:		Apps	Gls
	FL	5	0
	Total	5	0

EDWARDS Keith

Striker 1976–78, 1981–86 5' 8½" 10st 3
b. Middlesbrough 16 July 1957

Mddlesbrough junior football
United: trial 6 Aug, 22/26 Sep 1975 to 7 Aug 1978
Debuts: 3 Jan 1976 Leicester City 3 United 0 (FAC)
28 Feb 1976 United 0 Queens Park Rangers 0 (sub)
13 Mar 1976 United 1 Wolverhampton Wanderers 4
Last games: 29 Apr 1978 United 0 Cardiff City 1
11 May 1978 United 2 Rotherham United 1 (CC)
29 Jul 1978 DFC Nordstern, (Basle) 1 United 3 (Fr)
Hull City (£55k) Aug 1978
United: (£95/100k) 24,25 Sep 1981 to 5/6 Aug 1986
Debut: 26 Sep 1981 United 1 Scunthorpe United 0
Last games: 3 May 1986 United 1 Crystal Palace 1
1 Aug 1986 United 1 Seville(Spain) 1 (Fr)
Leeds United (£125k) Aug 1986/ Aberdeen (£60k) Sep 1987/ Hull City (£60k) Mar 1988/ Stockport County (£50k) Jul 1989/ Huddersfield Town (L) Mar to cs 1990/ Huddersfield Town Aug 1990 to Oct 1991/ Plymouth Argyle(L) Dec 1990/ Stafford Rangers Jan 1992/ Stalybridge Celtic Aug 1992/ Alfreton Town Oct 1992 to cs1993

Keith Edwards had trials with Wolves, Leeds and the Orient before Ken Furphy signed him for United in the summer of 1975 after pre-season games with the junior and reserve teams. His first team debut came in the disastrous 1975–76 season but he didn't become a regular until March 1977, scoring eleven goals in eight successive games and being top scorer for the season. Despite his obvious goal scoring ability, Harry Haslam sold Keith to Hull City in August 1978 but three seasons later Ian Porterfield persuaded him to return, for a fee fixed by a tribunal. In 1981–82 Keith scored 35 FL goals in 41 appearances, a post war record for the club, as United became Champions of the old Division Four. Dropped in 1982 in an unhappy season for the team and Keith personally, he responded with three goals as a substitute but returned to form in the following season, scoring 33 FL goals (41 in League and cup competitions). When he left for Leeds United, having fittingly scored in his final FL appearance, only Harry Johnson and Alan Woodward had scored more League goals for the club.

He was a superb craftsman with all the skills and a joy to watch. He had fine anticipation and the ability to find space and lose his marker, timing his runs as if it was the most natural thing in the world and he owed much to Colin Morris on the United right flank who provided so many of those opportunities. He was a clinical finisher, accurate with both feet and an excellent header. He had confidence in his ability and admitted to 'being a bit greedy and selfish' near goal and yet he limited his scoring opportunities, taking countless corner and free kicks for United, enjoying the responsibility and the opportunity to use his abilities to the full. In the FL he scored just over 250 goals in 505(39) appearances.

A superb footballer but… Keith was sometimes criticised for his work rate and he was not the most enthusiastic trainer and he was never tested at the highest levels of the game and one can argue pointlessly as to how he would have fared in the old First Division. United fans of the time can remember his 'Pele' goal against Bristol Rovers in April 1984 when he dummied the keeper and a defender, Keith going to the left and the ball to the right, a perfection of timing that had to be seen to be believed. At moments like that, it really is a beautiful game.

He went on to play for various other clubs, including Ian Porterfield's Aberdeen and a second spell with Hull City. He returned to the Lane to play in Paul Stancliffe's benefit match:
16 Mar 1992 United XI 1 v Malmo (Sweden) 6 (sub BM)

When he finished playing, he worked as a radio pundit and for a cancer research charity.

Appearances:

	Apps	Gls
FL	247 (14)	143
FAC	19	10
LC	14 (3)	10
ASC	4	4
FMC	2	0
AMC	6	3
CC	1 (1)	0
Total	293 (18)	170

EGAN Thomas William

CF/IR 1895–96
b. Chirk AMJ 1872
d. Tibshelf (Derbyshire) OND 1946

Chirk 1889/ Fairfield (Manchester) 1892/ Ardwick Nov 1893/ Burnley Mar 1894/ Ashton North End 30 May 1895
United: 19/21 Nov 1895 to 19 Aug 1896
Debut: 30 Nov 1895 Preston North End 4 United 3
Last games: 7 Apr 1896 Small Heath 2 United 1
14 Apr 1896 Hibernian 1 United 1 (Fr)
Lincoln City Aug?/Oct 1896 to Apr 1987/ Birdwell Nov 1897/ Altofts Oct 1898/ Darwen Jun 1899/ Royston United Aug 1901/ Stockport County Sep to Oct 1901//Chirk 1903

William Egan made his FL debut (his one Welsh Cap was awarded with Chirk) with Ardwick (now Manchester City) on 2 December 1893 at Liverpool and he made a total of 48 FL appearances for his various clubs.

Reported as 'Regan' in one Sheffield paper and described over the years as tricky, a good shot and with a fair speed, those supposed qualities were not enough for United to retain him very long. He settled in Derbyshire, returning to his former work as a miner. Two sons, Harry and Douglas, were both professional footballers.

Appearances:

	Apps	Gls
FL	15	4
FAC	3	0
BC	4	3
ABD	1	0
Total	23	7

EGGLESTON Arthur

IL/WH 1937–44 5' 10½" 11st 3 to 11st 12
b. Chopwell 4 January 1910
d. Sheffield 21 December 1990

Spen Black & White Sep 1929/ Bury Mar 1930/ Plymouth Argyle Jul 1935
United: 11/14 May 1937 to 31 Jul 1948
Debut: 28 Aug 1937 United 2 Nottingham Forest 1
Last games: 6 May 1939 United 6 Tottenham Hotspur 1
1 Jan 1944 Rotherham United 7 United 2 (WW2)
Reserve player until 1947 and coach to 1952

A former colliery worker, Arthur made his FL debut with Bury at Barnsley on 6 December 1931. A constructive, calm player with a strong shot, Arthur could play anywhere but was best at wing half and had scored 47 FL goals in 145 games for his two previous clubs.

Signed by Teddy Davison, he scored on his United debut and his final FL appearance for the club was in the vital 6–1 home defeat of Spurs, which clinched promotion at the expense of neighbours Wednesday. He was one of the players whose career was curtailed by the Second War, joining the Army in September 1940 and serving in the Artillery. He played with decreasing frequency with the first team until 1944 and, when demobilised, was essentially a player-coach with the reserves in the first post-war season of 1946–47 and a full-time coach thereafter until 1952 although his player registration had been retained until 1948.

Appearances:

	Apps	Gls
FL	24	2
CC	2	0
WW2	37	7
Total	63	9

EHIOGU Ugochuku (Ugo)

CD 2008– 6' 2" 14st 10
b. Hackney 3 November 1972

West Bromwich Albion from trainee Jul 1989/ Aston Villa (£40k) Jul 1991/ Middlesbrough (£8m) Oct 2000/ Leeds United (L) Nov 2006/ Rangers (free) Jan 2007
United: (free) 18 Jan 2008
Debut: 29 Jan 2008 United 1 Watford 1

Ugo Ehiogu made his FL debut with his first club, West Brom, as a substitute on 22 September 1990 at Hull City. His full debut, at home to Arsenal on 24 August 1991, came after he had joined Aston Villa. He made well over 200 appearances for Villa, gaining 15 England U21caps, one B and the first of his four full caps, before moving to Middlesbrough where he made over 100 more appearances. During 2006–07 however, despite a loan spell with Leeds and a move to Rangers, he played few games but his career appearance record was 360(20) League games, including nine in Scotland.

When he moved to the Lane, he had not played since September. Signed by Bryan Robson, who had been his manager at Middlesbrough, as cover for the central defence, he worked on his fitness before making his debut. Good in the air and accurate in the tackle, he used his experience and anticipation to cover for his lack of pace.

Appearances:

	Apps	Gls
FL	5 (5)	0
Total	5 (5)	0

ENGLISH John (Jack) Cogal

LB 1913–16 5' 8" 11st 4 to 11st 7
b. Hebburn 13 December 1886?
d. Northampton 21 January 1953

Hebburn Argyle Sep 1907/ Wallsend Park Villa/ Preston North End May 1910/ Watford (less than £100) Aug 1912
United: (£500) 14/18 Apr 1913 to May 1923
Debut: 8 Sep 1913 Tottenham Hotspur 2 United 1

Last games: **26 Apr 1915 Bolton Wanderers 0 United 1**
11 Mar 1916 United 2 Rotherham County 3 (WW1)
WW1: **Hebburn A, South Shields, Palmer & Co**
Darlington mgr Dec 1919 (player 1919–21) to May 1928/ Nelson mgr cs 1928/ Northampton Town mgr Jan 1931 to Feb 1935/ Exeter City mgr Oct 1935 to 1939/ Darlington mgr Mar 1945 to cs 1946

Jack English made his FL debut some six months after joining Preston North End on 2 January 1911 at Blackburn Rovers and, after less than a season with Watford, he moved to Bramall Lane.

It was reported that he was twenty four which was probably unlikely but United's secretary, John Nicholson, was always loath to ask to see a birth certificate and the Secretary must also have been aware that English had an independent spirit as he insisted on securing a two year contract. He was a neat, intelligent, polished player with a good sense of anticipation and passed the ball accurately and he grasped the opportunity to secure his place when Bob Benson was injured. In January 1914, he represented the North v England and was selected to play against Wales in March but instead played for United in a replayed Cup-tie. He gained an FA Cup winners' medal in the 'Khaki' Final of 1915.

During the First War, he worked in the shipyards and, along with Bill Cook, played for Hebburn Argyle in 1916 and in 1917 for South Shields.

In June 1919, Jack requested a free transfer so that he could become the manager of the Darlington Forge Albion club which, later that summer, became the new Darlington FC. United, not surprisingly, rejected the idea and at the end of the year Sunderland, who had initially offered United £1000 for the player, agreed to pay £1250. English asked for fifty per cent of the increase and the FA was informed and it was clear that other financial demands from the player infringed the regulations of the FL.

In his first spell as manager of Darlington, the club joined the Football League and in 1925 were promoted to the old Second Division (for two seasons) for the only time in their history. English went on to manage various clubs including Northampton where his son Jack English remains as the leading goal scorer.

Appearances:		Apps	Gls
	FL	55	0
	FAC	14	0
	WW1	4	0
	Total	73	0

EPWORTH James

OR 1941

Tinsley Park
United: **5 Nov 1938 (am), 18/20 May 1939 (pro) to cs 1946**
Only game: **15 Feb 1941 United 2 Rotherham United 3 (WW2)**

Although registered as a United player for almost eight years, including the period of the Second World War, James Epworth made just one first team appearance and that was a match played at Hillsborough soon after the Sheffield blitz when Bramall Lane had to be closed due to bomb damage. At that time he was employed in Sheffield and playing for Lopham Street and he would also make one guest appearance for Rotherham United in the 1943–44 season.

Appearances:		Apps	Gls
	WW2	1	0
	Total	1	0

EVANS John (Jack)

OL 1923–24 5' 8½" 11st 0
b. West Bromwich JAS 1903

West Bromwich Bush Rangers/ Wednesbury Old Athletic Jul 1920/ Walsall Sep 1921/ Shrewsbury Town Jul 1922
United: **(£300) 6/8 May 1923 to 16 Jun 1924**
Debut: **20 Oct 1923 United 2 Burnley 1**
Last game: **15 Mar 1924 United 0 Huddersfield Town 2**
Stoke (£300) Jun 1924/ Nantwich May 1925/ Shrewsbury Town cs 1925–cs26/ Stalybridge Connaughts

John Evans' single appearance for Walsall was his FL debut at Barrow on 2 February 1922 during the first season of the newly formed Division 3(N). After a season with non-League Shrewsbury Town he joined United, Shrewsbury receiving a record fee. He was the second leading scorer in the CL but, at the end of the season, he was transferred to Stoke City. There he made 12 FL appearances, bringing his career total to 15.

Appearances:		Apps	Gls
	FL	2	0
	Total	2	0

EVANS Robert (Bob) Ernest

OL 1908–18 5' 10½" 11st 10
b. Chester 19 October 1885
d. Saltney (Chester) 28 November 1965

Saltney Ferry/ Bretton 1900/ Saltney Works 1902/ Wrexham cs 1905/ Aston Villa (£30) Mar 1906
United: **(c.£900) 2/3 Oct 1908 to cs 1920**
Debut: **3 Oct 1908 United 3 Bradford City 0**
Last games: **26 Apr 1915 Bolton Wanderers 0 United 1**
26 Dec 1918 United 3 Wednesday 0 (WW1)
WW1 local football, Tranmere Rovers
Crichton Athletic 1920/ Sandycroft/ Saltney Ferry/ Connah's Quay Mar 1921/ Brookhirst to 1924

Bob Evans is one of a very limited number of players who won senior international caps for two countries. He won the first two of his 10 Welsh caps whilst with non-League Wrexham, adding four further caps with Aston Villa, where he had made his FL debut on 3 November 1906 at Preston North End.

A joint transfer deal of £1100 brought Bob and Peter Kyle to the Lane in 1908 and he gained four more Welsh caps before the United Secretary discovered that Bob had been born on the English side of the border. He went on to win four caps for his 'new' country whilst at Bramall Lane. His Welsh parents had moved a short distance back into Wales just three weeks after he was born and the player always regarded himself as Welsh.

A centre forward in his early days with Wrexham, Bob became a left winger with a long raking stride who could centre and shoot with power

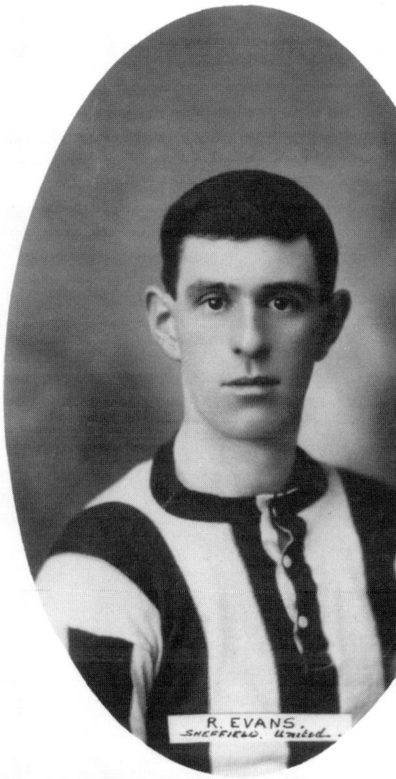

and often scored from a narrow angle. In the right mood, he was a fine player though the 'Green 'Un' in November 1914 wished 'he would go in more and not make arriving a second too late, a sort of science'. His penultimate first class game for United was the 1915 FA Cup Final where he gained a winners' medal. Two days later, he played in the final FL game before the competition was suspended due to the First War.

During the First War he worked as a carpenter in a shipyard at Saltney, playing for the works team and occasionally for Tranmere Rovers. He appeared for United in two Christmas games against Wednesday in 1918 but a few days later, in a works game, he broke his leg, ending hopes of his playing again for the Blades. He was finally released in the close season of 1920 and returned to the Chester area. After a spell playing in local football, he worked for Shell Mex in Ellesmere Port and trained local junior sides.

Appearances:		Apps	Gls
	FL	204	38
	FAC	12	0
	WW1	2	0
	ABD	2	1
	Total	220	39

EVANS Stewart John

F 1980–81 6' 3½" 11st 5 to 13st 0
b. Matlby 15 November 1960

Rotherham United from app Nov 1978/ Gainsborough Trinity
United: **(£4000) 6 Nov 1980 to 10 Mar 1982**
Debuts: **17 Nov 1980 United 8 Select XI 4 (sub John Flynn BM)**
6 May 1981 United 0 Rotherham United 2 (CC)
Last game: **15 Aug 1981 United 2 Doncaster Rovers 1 (LGC)**
Wimbledon Mar 1982/ West Bromwich Albion Aug 1986/ Plymouth Argyle Mar 1987/ Rotherham United Nov 1988/ Torquay United (L) Mar 1991/ Crewe Alexandra Sep 1991/ Denaby United cs 1994 to 1998–99/ Maltby Main/ Parkgate cs 1999 to manager cs 2002

Stewart Evans failed to make a FL appearance for either Rotherham or the Blades and was released by Ian Porterfield at both clubs. Tall with a strong left foot but a little ungainly, it was not until he joined Wimbledon and became much stronger, that his career prospered.

Stewart went on to make 175 FL appearances for the Dons and 248(49) in his career. He was signed by Wimbledon manager Dave Bassett and made his FL debut on 20 March 1982 at Exeter City. He played in Divisions Four, Three and Two for the Dons and left when they had been promoted to the top flight, moving to West Bromwich Albion who had been relegated to Division Two. Stewart had scored for Wimbledon against United and repeated the feat with West Brom and Plymouth.

Appearances:		Apps	Gls
	AMC	1	0
	CC	1	0
	Total	2	0

EVES Melvyn (Mel) James

Striker 1984–86 5' 11" 11st 8
b. Wednesbury 10 September 1956

Wolverhampton Wanderers from appr Jul 1973, pro Jul 1975/ Huddersfield Town (L) Mar 1984
United: **trial 13 Dec 1984 to 27 Mar 1985, 28 Mar 1985 to 30 Jun 1986**
Debut: **15 Dec 1984 United 1 Brighton & Hove Albion 1**
Last game: **8 Apr 1986 Barnsley 2 United 1**
Gillingham Aug 1986/ Mansfield Town (L) Oct 1987/ Man C/ West Bromwich Albion Dec 1988/ Cheltenham Town (L) Dec 1988/ Walsall/ Telford United 1989–90/ Cheltenham Town 1993–94 / – / Willenhall Town mgr Feb 2006 to Nov 2007

Mel Eves made his name with Wolves where he made 180 FL appearances, making his FL debut on 26 November 1977 at home to Ipswich Town. A fast and dangerous, attacking player, he won an England B cap and a League Cup winners' medal with Wolves but was prone to injury, which limited his career to 223(20) FL appearances.

He was brought to Bramall Lane by Ian Porterfield on a three month trial with a further fortnight extension and then signed on a free transfer because Mel had a history of Achilles tendon injuries. Mel played well for United, scoring nine important goals in 17 games in that first season as United struggled against relegation but an undiagnosed hernia problem made the following one a nightmare and ended his stay at the Lane.

Mel made thirty more FL appearances with Gillingham and Mansfield but further League football proved to be impossible and, after some time in non-League soccer, he became a players' agent with his own company specialising in financial investments.

Appearances:		Apps	Gls
	FL	25 (1)	10
	FAC	1 (1)	0
	Total	26 (2)	10

FALCONER William (Willie) Henry

MF/D 1993–94 6' 1" 12st 10
b. Aberdeen 5 April 1966

Lewis United/ Aberdeen 9 Apr 1982/ Watford (£300k) Jun 1988/ Middlesbrough (£305k Aug 1991/
United: **(£425k) 10/12 Aug 1993 to 9 Feb 1994**
Debut: **14 Aug 1993 United 3 Swindon Town 1**
Last games: **18 Dec 1993 Wimbledon 2 United 0**
1 Jan 1994 United 2 Oldham Athletic 1 (sub)
Celtic (£350/£375k) Feb 1994/ Motherwell (£200k) Jan 1996/ Dundee Jul 1998/ Clydebank Aug 2001/ St Johnstone Aug 2001/ Grimsby Town Mar 2002/ Clyde cs 2002

Willie Falconer made his Scottish League debut as a substitute on 23 April 1983 at home to Celtic and his FL debut in England came with Watford on 27 August 1988 at home to Birmingham City. After two seasons with Middlesbrough, he was signed by Dave Bassett just before the opening day of the 1993–94 season going straight into the side and scoring the club's first League goal of the campaign.

An attacking midfield player and a former Scottish international at school and youth level, he appeared in every game until Boxing Day but lost his place soon after. His play was rarely better than adequate and his transfer to Celtic caused little surprise. He continued to play for several Scottish clubs and, after a brief return to England with Grimsby Town (1 FL appearance), he retired after one more season with Clyde. He had played over 450 League games north and south of the border.

Appearances:		Apps	Gls
	FL	21 (2)	3
	LC	2	0
	Total	23 (2)	3

FARROW George Henry

LH 1948 5' 10" 12st 13
b. Whitburn 4 October 1913
d. Whitburn 9 December 1980

Whitburn (Aldershot trial Aug 1929)/ Stockport County Oct 1930/ Wolverhampton Wanderers Jan 1932/ Bournemouth Jul 1933/ Blackpool Jun 1936
WW2 guest: Blackburn Rovers, Liverpool, Manchester United, and Rochdale (all 1940–41)
United: **5 Jan 1948 to 31 Jul 1948**
Debut: **17 Jan 1948 United 4 Grimsby Town 1**
Last game: **Barnsley 2 United 0 (CC)**
Bacup Borough player-mgr Aug 1948/ Whitburn St. Marys/ Whitburn FC

George Farrow made his FL debut with Stockport County on 25 December 1931 at home to Carlisle United and had a long and successful career making 106 FL appearances for Bournemouth and 148 for Blackpool where he also appeared over 150 times during the Second World War.

The decision in January 1948 by Teddy Davison, the United manager, to exchange the determined, energetic Walter Rickett for Farrow turned out to be one of the worst he ever made. George had been a fine player; a strong tackler, capable of long accurate passes and a long throw but he was thirty four and he had lost his place in the Blackpool team to Hugh Kelly. Farrow moreover, refused to move to Sheffield and no doubt lost motivation as Blackpool and Rickett made progress to the 1948 Cup Final.

On leaving football he worked in the Whitburn area, where he lived after his retirement.

Appearances:		Apps	Gls
	FL	1	0
	CC	1	0
	Total	2	0

FATHI Ahmed

MF 2007 5' 9" 11st 5
b. Egypt 11 October 1984

Ismaily (Egypt)
United: **trial Dec 2006, (£700k) 24 Jan 2007 to 11 Sep 2007**
Debuts: **10 Feb 2007 United 2 Tottenham Hotspur 1 (sub)**
24 Feb 2007 Liverpool 4 United 0
Last games: **3 Mar 2007 United 1 Everton 1**
14 Aug 2007 United 1 Nottingham Forest 0 (Fr)
Al-Ahly (Egypt) (£675k) Sep 2007/ Kazma (Kuwait) (L) Sep 2007

Ahmed Fathi had a trial with Arsenal in 2004 and with United in December 2006. Signed by Neil Warnock, he was the first Egyptian player to move from his home club to the Premiership. Already an international, he became United's first Egyptian international when he played and scored against Sweden before his United debut.

Because of the form of the other midfielders he had little opportunity whilst at the Lane but he 'had an eye for a pass' and looked comfortable on the ball. Although playing in some pre-season games Ahmed was not part of Bryan Robson's plans, the manager feeling his style of play did not suit what was required in the Championship, and he returned to the Egyptian top flight, but due to transfer window restrictions he initially played for three months on loan in Kuwait.

During his time at the Lane he gained three international caps and early in 2008, playing as a wing back, he was part of the Egyptian team which won the Africa Cup of Nations.

Appearances:		Apps	Gls
	FL	2 (1)	0
	Total	2 (1)	0

FAULKNER Stephen (Steve) Andrew

D 1973–77 6' 3" 13st 5
b. Sheffield 18 December 1954

United: **from app 9/12 Aug 1971, pro 2 Feb 1972 to 30 Jun 1978**
Debuts: **20 Mar 1973 United 1 Sheffield Wed 1 (Badger BM)**
17 Apr 1973 United 4 Doncaster Rovers 2 (CC)
23 Apr 1973 Manchester United 1 United 2
Last game: **12 Mar 1977 Burnley 1 United 0**
Stockport County (L) Mar 1978
York City Jul 1978 to 1981/ Frickley Athletic / Rowntree Mackintosh (York)

Steve Faulkner played for Sheffield Boys before joining United as an apprentice. Although his height gave him an advantage as a defender, he never made the breakthrough to becoming a regular in the first team and his various appearances were spread over four seasons. After leaving Bramall Lane he went on to make over 100 FL and Cup appearances for York City before moving into non-League football.

Appearances:		Apps	Gls
	FL	14 (2)	0
	FAC	1	0
	LC	1	0
	CC	2 (1)	0
	Total	18 (3)	0

FAZACKERLEY Stanley (Stan) Nicholas

IR/IL/CF 1913–20 5' 11½" 11st 7
b. Ashton on Ribble (Preston) 3 October 1891
d. Ridgeway (Sheffield) 20 June 1946

Lane Ends United/ Preston North End Aug 1909(trial)/ – / Accrington Stanley 1910?–12 (Charlestown [Boston League] USA summer (1911)/ Hull City (£50) Apr 1912
United: **(£1000) 15 Mar 1913 to 5/6 Nov 1920**
Debut: **21 Mar 1913 Sunderland 1 United 0**
Last game: **30 Oct 1920 United 0 Aston Villa 0**
WW1 guest: Preston North End, Blackpool, Chelsea
Everton Nov 1920 (£4000) / Wolverhampton Wanderers Nov 1922/ Kidderminster Harriers Mar 1925/ Derby County (£2500) Aug 1925 to Apr 1926

Stan Fazackerley made his FL debut with Hull City at home to Clapton Orient on 20 April 1912 and his immediate success in the League (he scored 19 goals in 29 games) led United to pay a record fee of £1000 for the twenty one year old inside forward. His presence in the team played a large part in United reaching the semi-final of the F A Cup in 1914 and winning the trophy in 1915 when Stan scored one of United's three goals.

Tall and slim in build, almost graceful in movement, he dribbled skilfully and was also difficult to shake off the ball. He was cool in front of goal and a good header of the ball and his clever ball control and extraordinary trickery, which occasionally baffled his colleagues as well as opponents, made him a fine player. It was said that he didn't enjoy physical battles though his skill usually kept him out of trouble and he usually came off the most muddy of fields with his shirt immaculate.

There was friction between United and the player in the 1915–16 season when he played for Preston North End without permission and he also appeared as a guest player for Blackpool and later Chelsea after he had joined the Royal Field Artillery. In 1920 he toured South Africa with the FA but played poorly for United on his return and requested a transfer and was sold to Everton for £4000, a near record fee for those days though Stan's part in the move led to an FA enquiry.

Two years later, he was transferred to Wolverhampton Wanderers where he won a Division 3(N) Championship medal and finally to Derby County where he was soon forced to retire on medical advice.

Appearances:		Apps	Gls
	FL	105	43
	FAC	14	4
	WW1	24	11
	Total	143	58

FEATHERSTONE George

IR 1908–09 5' 7½" 11st 0 to 11st 6
b. Stockton (registered Middlesbrough) JFM 1885

Darlington St Hildas 1902–03/ Darlington 1903–04/ Stockton
United: 25/27 Feb 1908 to cs1909
Debut: 29 Feb 1908 United 2 Woolwich Arsenal 2
Last game: 9 Apr 1909 Aston Villa 3 United 0
Brighton & Hove Albion cs 1909/ Hartlepools United cs 1910 to cs 1911

George had gained an FA Amateur Cup runner's-up medal with Stockton in 1907 and was reported as 22 years old when signed by United. He scored on his FL debut and began to score quite regularly but after just over a season at the Lane, he moved on to Southern League Brighton. He played there for just one season before returning to junior football, somewhat surprisingly, as his 9 goals in 22 outings had helped the South coast club to the Southern League Championship.

Appearances:		Apps	Gls
	FL	29	11
	Total	29	11

FENOUGHTY Thomas (Tom)

IL/IR/OL/CF 1964–69 5' 10" 10st 7
b. Dalton (Rotherham) 7 June 1941

Manchester Univ/ Sheffield FC
United: (amat) 1960–61 and (FL) 8 Nov 1963, (part time pro) 10/15 Sep 1964, (full-time) 8 Aug 1966 to 30 Jun 1969
Debut: 29 Feb 1964 Ipswich Town 1 United 0
Last games: 7 Sep 1968 Norwich City 2 United 0
16 Apr 1969 United 9 Barnsley 0 (sub CC)
Chesterfield Jul 1969 to cs1972 / – / Matlock Town player, player manager 1976, manager

The son of a professional footballer and a graduate of Manchester University in pharmacy, Tom Fenoughty was at Bramall Lane for six seasons and was the last amateur to appear for United in a League match. He was twenty five when he became a full-time professional, signing a few days after breaking his nose and dislocating his elbow in a CL game.

A thoughtful, constructive player, he played mainly at inside forward. Most of his appearances came between January 1966, when Kettleborough was sold to Newcastle United, and March 1967 but he was never sure of his place in the team. He scored in his final appearance in a Blades shirt, coming on as a substitute in a County Cup game against Barnsley and was given a free transfer.

He moved to Chesterfield making over 100 FL appearances for the club and winning a Fourth Division championship medal. He retired in 1973, returning to pharmacy but also playing for, and then managing, Matlock Town. In 1975 he played at Wembley, alongside his brothers Mick and Nick (both former United reserve players) in the Matlock side that won the FA Trophy, Tom scoring one of the goals which beat Scarborough 4–0.

Appearances:		Apps	Gls
	FL	47 (3)	4
	FAC	2	0
	LC	3	1
	CC	1 (2)	1
	Total	53 (5)	6

FENWICK(E) Richard A

G 1890–91

Sheffield Club
United: amateur, occasional games, Jan 1890 to Sep 1892
Debuts: 25 Jan 1890 United 3 Derby Midland 1 (Fr)
21 Feb 1891 United 0 Derby Midland 1 (MCL)
Last game: 21 Sep 1891 United 4 Bolton Wanderers 3 (Fr)
Sheffield Club

Richard Fenwick was an amateur keeper with Sheffield Club who occasionally assisted United. Although he played just one competitive game, he appeared in 13 friendly fixtures, including four games in United's first season. He also turned out for the reserves in his final season and assisted Doncaster Rovers and played in some of the first soccer games in Leeds, Wakefield and Bradford.

Appearances:		Apps	Gls
	MCL	1	0
	Total	1	0

FETTIS Alan William

G 2003 6' 1" 12st 10
b. Belfast 1 February 1971

Ards/ Hull City (£50k) Aug 1991/ West Bromwich Albion (L) Nov 1995/ Nottingham Forest (£250k) Jan 1996/ Blackburn Rovers (£300k) Sep 1997/ York City Mar 2000/ Hull City Jan 2003
United: (L) 5 Dec 2003 to Feb 2004
Debuts: 6 Dec 2003 Burnley 3 United 2 (sub)
9 Dec 2003 United 2 Walsall 0
Last game: 13 Dec 2003 United 2 Watford 2
Grimsby Town (L) Mar 2004/ Macclesfield Town Jul 2004/ Bury Jun 2006/ Derby County goalkeeping coach May 2007

Alan Fettis joined Hull City from Irish football and made his FL debut on17 August 1991 at Reading. He quickly established himself, becoming a Northern Ireland international adding full caps to those gained at schoolboy, youth and B level. Whilst with the Tigers he scored two goals, once as an outfield substitute and once when he was selected to start as an outfield player. His transfers to more senior clubs were not too successful as much of his time was spent in the reserve teams but he re-established himself with York City.

Alan joined United on loan at the same time as another keeper, Lee Baxter. Paddy Kenny was injured and Paul Gerrard's three month loan had expired. Baxter was chosen to play against Burnley but, having conceded three goals, two with basic errors, he was substituted and Alan came on in the second half, resulting in two goalkeepers making their debuts for the club in the same game. Alan played in two more games before Paddy Kenny resumed.

After 375(7) League appearances he moved into coaching.

Appearances:		Apps	Gls
	FL	2 (1)	0
	Total	2 (1)	0

FICKLING Ashley

D 1991–94 5' 10" 11st 8
b. Sheffield 15 November 1972

United: from jnr, pro Jul 1991 to 22/23 Mar 1995
Debuts: 2 Apr 1990 Combined Services 0 United XI 0 (Fr, Catterick)
23 Apr 1991 Lincoln City 2 United 0 (sub BM)
8 Oct 1991 United 1 Wigan Athletic 0 (LC)
Last game: 15 Nov 1994 Cesena 1 United 4 (AIC)
Darlington (L) Nov 1992/ Darlington (L) 9 Aug 1993/ Bradford C trial 1994
Grimsby Town Mar 1995/ Darlington (L) Mar 1998/ Scunthorpe United Jul 1998/ Scarborough Jul 2001 to Mar 2003/ – / Sheffield Wednesday physio Feb 2007

An England choice at schoolboy and U18 level, Ashley Fickling was slow to progress with United and didn't make a FL appearance for the club but he went on to make over 100 such appearances in the lower divisions, including three separate loan spells with Darlington. It was in his first loan spell with Darlington that he made his FL debut, at home to Barnet on 28 November 1992.

Transfer listed in February 1995, he moved to Grimsby Town with the possibility of a fee dependent on appearances. He later moved into non-League football with Conference side Scarborough.

He trained as a physiotherapist and, after working on a non-permanent basis for Sheffield Wednesday with the youth team, Ashley joined the club on a permanent basis in February 2007.

Appearances:		Apps	Gls
	FAC	2 (1)	0
	AICc	3	0
	Total	5 (1)	0

FIDLER John (Joe) Edward

LB 1904 5' 9" 11st 12
b. Sheffield JFM 1885

South Street New Connection Sunday School
United: 18 Feb 1903 to May 1905
Debut: 2 Jan 1904 United 1 Small Heath 1
Last game: 26 Nov 1904 Blackburn Rovers 2 United 4
Fulham May 1905/ Queens Park Rangers May 1906/ Woolwich Arsenal (£50) Feb 1913/ Port Vale cs 1914 / – / Turton Platts

A stocky, strong tackling full back with a bit of a temper, Joe Fidler made just two appearances for United and had to leave the field on his United debut with a cut head. He was only a reserve player with Fulham but played more than 190 games for Southern League Queens Park Rangers, representing the Southern League against the Scottish League in 1912.

Arsenal paid United £50 for his FL registration and his playing career at a senior level ended with Port Vale. He joined the Army in January 1915 but was discharged later that year and returned to work in Sheffield and play in local football finally being reinstated as an amateur by the FA in 1923 and playing for Turton Platts, a Sheffield factory team.

Appearances:		Apps	Gls
	FL	2	0
	Total	2	0

FIELD Anthony (Tony)

OL 1974–76 5' 7" 10st 5
b. Halifax 6 July 1946

Illingworth Utd/ Halifax Town from jnr Jul 1963/ Barrow Aug 1966/ Southport Mar 1968/ Blackburn Rovers £15,000 Oct 1971
United: (£76,666) 14 Mar 1974 to 13 Feb 1976
Debut: 16 Mar 1974 Manchester City 0 United 1
Last game: 7 Feb 1976 United 0 Everton 0
New York Cosmos Feb 1976/ Memphis Rogues 1978 to 1981

Tony Field made his FL debut with Halifax Town at Brighton on 11 April 1964. There were few highlights and little glamour in the early years of his playing career in the Third and Fourth Divisions but he was a consistent goal scorer and Ken Furphy, who had been his manager at Blackburn, brought him to the Lane. By then Tony had scored 105 FL goals in 287(10) games.

Tony made his debut at Maine Road on the same day as Jim Brown and achieved far more in the old First Division than most people expected. He was quick and tricky, difficult to mark and dispossess and a good finisher and will be particularly remembered for a goal against Ipswich Town in August 1974 when he left four defenders in a daze after a corkscrew run into the penalty area.

After leaving Bramall Lane he moved to the USA and played for the New York Cosmos numbering among his team-mates Pele and Beckenbauer and was managed for the third time by Ken Furphy. It must have seemed a far cry from those early days in the lower reaches of the Football League.

Appearances:		Apps	Gls
	FL	63 (3)	13
	FAC	2	1
	LC	4	0
	TEX	3	0
	ASC	1 (2)	0
	CC	2	1
	Total	75 (5)	15

FIELD Charles (Oakey) William Frederick

IL/IR 1898–1901 5' 6" 10st 7
b. Hanwell (Brentford) JFM 1879

Hanwell/ Royal Ordnance Factory/ Brentford Aug 1896
United: 4 May 1898 to 30 Jan 1902
Debut: 10 Sep 1898 Notts County 2 United 2

Last games: 30 Nov 1901 Wolverhampton Wanderers 1 United 1
21 Dec 1901 United 1 Glasgow Rangers 0 (Fr)
Small Heath Jan 1902 to 1906 / – / Brentford 16 Nov 1907 to cs 1908

Charlie Field became a professional when he joined United and was one of those rare players to score two goals on his debut. A hard working, clever little player with a good goal scoring record, he was at his best on dry grounds. He was rather unlucky in that Jack Almond was preferred to him for the FA Cup Final at the end of his first season but he did play in the 1901 Final when United were defeated by Tottenham Hotspur.

He was transferred with Billy Beer to Small Heath in 1902 and both players no doubt enjoyed their debuts in a convincing victory at Bramall Lane. Injuries appeared to have ended his days as a player in 1906 though he did return to Brentford for a few months in 1907 before retiring at the end of the season and setting up a business in the town.

Appearances:

	Apps	Gls
FL	54	19
FAC	7	0
Total	61	19

FINNIESTON Stephen (Steve) James

CF 1978–79 5' 11" 11st 3
b. Edinburgh 30 November 1954

Chelsea from app Dec 1971/ Cardiff City(L) Oct 1974
United: (£90k) 5 Jun 1978 to 29 Feb 1980 (contract cancelled)
Debuts: 26 Jul 1978 Servette (Geneva, Switzerland) 5 United 0 (Fr)
5 Aug 1978 Oldham Athletic 1 United 0 (ASC)
19 Aug 1978 United 1 Orient 2
Last game: 5 May 1979 Cambridge United 1 United 0
Addlestone/ Weybridge Town/ Hartney Witney to 1983

A Scottish youth international, Steve Finneston joined Chelsea from school at Weybridge and was a prolific goal scorer in junior and reserve football. He made his FL debut whilst on loan at Cardiff City on 16 October 1974 at home to York City and played for the Chelsea first team later that season. Although he was hindered by injuries, he scored 34 goals in 80 FL games for the London club.

He was signed by Harry Haslam and perhaps it was a known gamble on his fitness for there were members of the staff who suspected that he was a 'crock'. Sadly for the club and player, injuries blighted his season which ended in relegation and forced his retirement, although he did play in non-League football until his late 30s. He spent 20 years selling building materials and later became a postman.

Appearances:

	Apps	Gls
FL	23	4
LC	2	0
ASC	2	2
Total	27	6

FINNIGAN Denis Vincent

CH 1960–67 5' 11" 11st 11
b. Sheffield 23 March 1940
d. Sheffield 4 December 1994

Doncaster R (trial)
United: amateur, then part time pro 24/27 Apr 1959 to 26 Sep 1968
Debuts: 30 Jan 1960 United 3 Nottingham Forest 0 (FAC)
6 Feb 1960 Bristol City 2 United 2
Last game: 22 Apr 1967 Leicester City 2 United 2
Chesterfield (£900/£1400) Sep 1968/ Buxton Jun 1970

A loyal and reliable club-man, Denis was a part timer with United, working as an administrator for the local Regional Hospital Board and also rising to the rank of lieutenant in the Territorial Army. He spent most of his time at Bramall Lane in the reserves, playing the occasional game when Joe Shaw and later, Reg Matthewson and Ken Mallender were unavailable or 'rested'. He occasionally played at centre forward in the reserves and had a spell in 1964 when he scored fifteen goals including a hat trick of headers against Aston Villa.

On moving to Chesterfield, he remained a semi-professional but had two short periods in the first team in his two seasons at Saltergate, playing 27 games (10 in the Fourth Division Championship season), before being released in 1970. Later, Denis assisted in coaching with several local clubs including Worksop, Hallam, Waterworks, United (1982–83) and Wednesday.

Appearances:

	Apps	Gls
FL	14	0
FAC	2	0
LC	6	0
CC	8	0
Total	30	0

FITZGERALD Scott Brian

D 1995 6' 0" 12st 7
b. Westminster 13 August 1969

Wimbledon from trainee Jul 1989
United: (L) 23 Nov 1995 to Dec 1995
Debut: 25 Nov 1995 United 0 Reading 0
Last game: 26 Dec 1995 United 1 Birmingham City 1
Millwall (L) Oct 1996/ Millwall (£50k) Jul 1997/ Colchester United Oct 2000/ Brentford (L) Mar 2004/ Brentford (L) Mar 2004, signed Mar 2004, youth team mgr cs 2005/ Walsall (L) Feb 2006/ Brentford mgr Nov 2006 to Apr 2007 / – / Gillingham youth team mgr Jul 2007/ Millwall youth team mgr Dec 2007

Scott Fitzgerald, who won Republic of Ireland caps at U21and B level, made his FL debut as a substitute with Wimbledon on 28 April 1990 at home to Tottenham Hotspur but his full debut did not come until the opening day of the 1991–92 season.

His loan move to Bramall Lane was Dave Bassett's last 'signing' and Scott's loan move ended when Howard Kendall signed Michael Vonk. Scott was an intelligent player but insufficiently physical for a central defender. He had a successful spell with Colchester and ended his career at Brentford with a total of 338(16) FL appearances. He moved into coaching with the youth team before a spell as manager but he was sacked after Brentford were relegated. He reverted to youth team coaching at other clubs.

Appearances:

	Apps	Gls
FL	6	0
Total	6	0

FJORTOFT Jan-Aage

Striker 1997–98 6' 3" 13st 4 to 14st 3
b. Aasund (Norway) 10 January 1967

Hamar Jan 1987/ Lillestrom Jan 1988/ Rapid Vienna 1989/ Swindon Town (£500k) Jul 1993/ Middlesbrough (£1.3m) Mar 1995
United: (£700k) 31 Jan 1997 to 16 Jan 1998
Debut: 1 Feb 1997 Swindon Town 2 United 1
Last games: 20 Dec 1997 Bury 1 United 1
13 Jan 1998 United 2 Bury 1 (FAC)
Barnsley (£680–800k) Jan 1998/ Eintracht Frankfurt (£450–400k) Nov 1998/ Stabaek 2001/ Lillestrom May 2002

Jan-Aage Fjortoft began his career in Norway in 1987 and moved to England in 1993, making his League debut with Swindon Town at Bramall Lane on 14 August. A Norwegian international and proven goal scorer, he had excellent ball control, was difficult to dispossess and a clinical finisher.

Signed by Howard Kendall for United with 17 games remaining in the 1996–97 season, his 10 goals played a key role in achieving the play-offs and his 'aeroplane' goal celebrations became a regular feature. He added one more to his tally against Ipswich Town but was unable, as were the rest of the team, to find the net against Palace in the Final. By January in the following season he had scored nine goals in 17 games and it was a shock when he was then sold to Barnsley, shortly after Brian Deane had left for Benfica.

After retiring from the game in the summer of 2002 he worked for Norwegian television before taking up the position of managing director of Lillestrom in December 2004.

Appearances:		Apps	Gls
	FL	30 (4)	19
	PO	3	1
	FAC	1 (1)	2
	LC	2 (1)	1
	Total	36 (6)	23

FLEMING William (Billy)

IL 1893–94
b. 1871

Darlington
United: cs1893 to cs 1894
Debut: 2 Sep 1893 Everton 2 United 3
Last games: 26 Mar 1894 United 1 Burnley 0
26 Apr 1894 Wednesday 0 United 1 (WCCF)
Paisley Abercorn/ Bury Jan 1896/ Tottenham Hotspur Nov 1896

One of the many players that United signed in the 1890s from the north east, Billy Fleming made his debut in the club's first fixture in the original First Division and one report credits him with United's second goal. He played less well as the season advanced and moved to Scotland at the end of the season.

Subsequently he joined Bury who paid a small fee to United. His career with Spurs was short and somewhat mysterious. After scoring three goals in five games he was suspended by the club for reasons still unknown, and he left the club immediately.

Appearances:		Apps	Gls
	FL	21	6
	FAC	1	0
	UCL	3	0
	WCC	1	0
	Total	26	6

FLITCROFT Garry William

MF 2006 6' 0" 12st 2
b. Bolton 6 November 1972

Manchester City from trainee Jul 1991/ Bury (L) Mar 1992/ Blackburn Rovers (£3.2m) Mar 1996
United: 12 Jan 2006 to cs 2006
Debuts: 21 Jan 2006 United 3 Brighton & Hove Albion 1 (sub)
11 Feb 2006 Plymouth Argyle 0 United 0
Last game: 11 Mar 2006 Coventry City 2 United 0

Garry Flitcroft, an England youth and U21 international with Manchester City, made his FL debut while on loan at Bury on 7 March 1992 at Chester. Tenacious, hard working and determined, he captained both City and Rovers, playing over 100 League games for Manchester City and nearly 250 for Blackburn, where he was sent off after only a few minutes of his debut.

He was signed by Neil Warnock as midfield cover as United battled for promotion in 2006. He had played only twice for Rovers during the season and he made only a handful of appearances for United, partly due to the form of Michael Tonge and partly due to a persistent knee injury. The injury forced his retirement in the close season.

Appearances:		Apps	Gls
	FL	3 (3)	0
	Total	3 (3)	0

FLO Jostein

Striker 1993–95 6' 4" 13st 12
b. Eid (Norway) 3 October 1964

Stryn 1980/ Molde 1986/ Lierse (Belgium) 1990–91/ Sogndal (Norway) cs 1991
United: (£475k) 10/13 Aug 1993 to 29 Jan 1996
Debut: 21 Aug 1993 Everton 4 United 2
Last games: 2 Dec 1995 Derby County 4 United 2
9 Dec 1995 United 0 Huddersfield 2 (sub)
Stromgodset (Norway) 1996 to 2002

Jostein Flo began his career in Norway with his local club Stryn. Whilst with Molde he played for Norway in the Olympic Games qualifiers and his international career began whilst he was with Sogndal.

Signed by Dave Bassett, he was seen by many as a replacement for Brian Deane, not an enviable position. He started with three goals in his first four games but a tally of nine in 32 games in the season when United dropped out of the Premier League was seen as disappointing. He was a regular for the following season, again with fewer goals than hoped for, and his final game coincided with Dave Bassett's last match in charge though his departure was partly due to the fact that another appearance would have added a further increment on his transfer fee.

Jostein, for the most part, had the support of the fans: they appreciated his hard work but referees tended to dislike what many regarded as a quite fair use of his height, strength and bulk. He seemed to Bassett to be an ideal target man but many of his critics noticed that he was used by Norway as a right side player and that he lacked the pace,

close control and quickness and finishing ability in the goal area to be a big goal scorer.

In his time at the Lane he amassed 23 caps for Norway, scoring five goals. After leaving United on a free transfer, he continued to play for Norway, finishing with a total of 53 caps and 11 goals. He retired in 2002 and took up a marketing position with Stromsgodset for whom he had played successfully for six seasons. He subsequently became director of football.

Appearances:		Apps	Gls
	FL	74 (10)	19
	FAC	1 (1)	0
	LC	4	3
	Total	79 (11)	22

FLOOD John Gerard

RW/MF 1978–81 5' 7" 9st. 8 to 10st 4
b. Glasgow 25 December 1960

United: from amat 28 Jun 1977, pro 11 Oct 1978 to 20 Feb 1981
Debuts: 27 Feb 1978 Hastings United 1 United 0 (Fr) sub
23 Oct 1978 Winterton R 1 United 1 (Fr)
28 Feb 1979 Wrexham 4 United 0
Last game: 31 Jan 1981 Oxford United 2 United 0
Airdrieonians Feb 1981/ Partick Thistle cs 1988/ Kirkintilloch Rob Roy 1992/ mgr Kilsyth Rangers/ Wishaw Juniors mgr 2002–05

John Flood was a tricky traditional Scottish winger and one of a very small number to join United as a youngster but he wasn't forceful enough and never established himself as a regular first team player in his three seasons with United. He did score one of United's quickest ever goals, scoring after an estimated fifteen seconds against Wimbledon in April 1980 but he moved back to Scotland in the relegation year of 1981.

During his time there he was a regular first team player, playing mainly as a forward or attacking midfielder and in his seven seasons with Airdrieonians, John was twice the club's leading scorer, albeit with 11 goals.

Appearances:		Apps	Gls
	FL	16 (3)	1
	FAC	0 (1)	0
	LC	1	1
	ASC	3 (1)	1
	CC	0 (1)	0
	Total	20 (6)	3

FLYNN John Edward

D 1969–78 6' 0" 11st 0 to 11st 11
b. Workington 20 March 1948

West Coronation Boys' Club/ Workington from jnr Sep 1967
United: (£5000) 17/18 Jul 1969 to 3 Jul 1978
Debuts: 27 Jul 1969 Haarlem (Holland) 0 United 0 (Fr)
1 Nov 1969 United 4 Blackburn Rovers 0
Last games: 29 Apr 1978 United 0 Cardiff City 1
11 May 1978 United 2 Rotherham United 1 (CC)
Rotherham United Jul 1978/ Spalding United 1980–82

John Flynn made his first team debut with Workington as a seventeen-year-old amateur, coming on as a substitute at Oldham on 27 December 1966. His full debut came at home to Bradford City on 9 September 1967 but at the end of the season he was given a free transfer. A move to South Africa was delayed by a car accident and he was then offered a contract by the new manager for the 1968–69 season.

He was spotted by United's then general manager, John Harris and became the last of several excellent signings made by Arthur Rowley. Initially, after two pre-season games, he was kept out of the side by Dave Powell but Dave's proneness to injury meant John gradually had more first team opportunities and was a regular in the side from April in the promotion year of 1971 to May 1978.

Playing alongside Eddie Colquhoun, they formed a formidable partnership. John was strong and quick in the tackle and excellent in the air and he always played with courage and determination. He was a threat in the opposition's penalty area at corner kicks and although scoring only 10 goals for the Blades, John did manage to find the net in his final game, against Rotherham United, the club he moved to shortly afterwards. After a total of 250(9) FL games he had a period with Spalding, before working in the probation and community services.

Appearances:		Apps	Gls
	FL	185 (5)	8
	FAC	6	0
	LC	14 (1)	0
	TEX	9	0
	CC	10 (1)	2
	WC	2	0
	Total	226 (7)	10

FOLEY Steven (Steve)

MF 1985–87 5' 7" 11st 3 to 12st 0
b. Kirkdale, Liverpool 4 October 1962

Liverpool from 16 to app Sep 1980/ Fulham (L) Dec 1983/ Grimsby Town Aug 1984 to cs 1985
United: Jul 1985(trial), 8/20 Aug 1985 to 18/24 Jun, 9 Jul 1987
Debuts: 30 Jul 1985 Skegness Town 0 United 3 (Fr)
3 Sep 1985 United 5 Rotherham United 1 (LC)
7 Sep 1985 Norwich City 4 United 0
Last game: 4 May 1987 United 0 Ipswich Town 0
Swindon Town (£35k tribunal, increased to £43k) Jun 1987/ Stoke City (£30–60k) Jan 1992/ Lincoln City Jul 1994/ Bradford City Aug to Oct 1995/ Barrow/ Morecambe Jan to Mar 1996

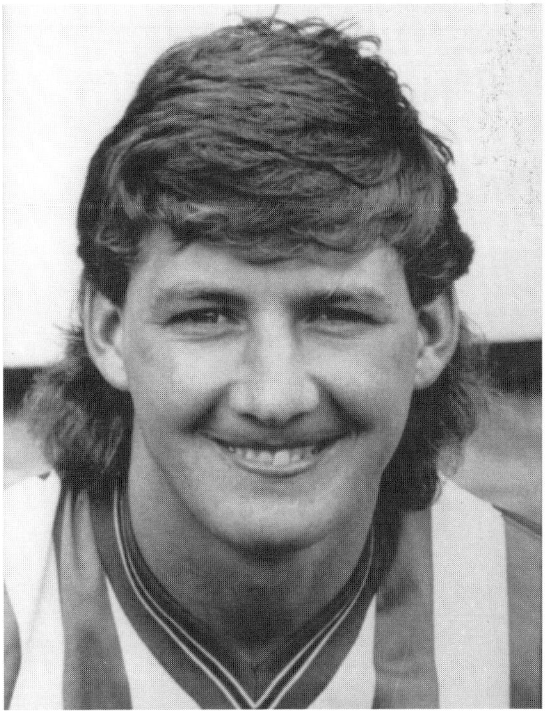

Although coming through the junior ranks at Anfield, Steve Foley did not make a competitive first team appearance for the Reds. His FL debut came whilst briefly on loan at Fulham, away to Oldham Athletic on 17 December 1983. After a season with Grimsby Town, his contract was terminated by mutual consent.

Signed by Ian Porterfield, he was a regular member of the side for two seasons with United, particularly in 1986–7, playing in midfield. Quick and sharp in action, he scored some useful goals.

After a wages dispute with United, Steve moved on and went on to make a total of 352(23) FL appearances, including more than 100 with both Swindon Town and Stoke City, before moving into non-League football.

Appearances:		Apps	Gls
	FL	56 (10)	14
	FAC	5	1
	LC	5	3
	FMC	2 (1)	0
	Total	68 (11)	18

FORAN Mark James

CD 1994–95 6' 4" 13st 12 to 14st 3
b. Aldershot 30 October 1973

Millwall from trainee Nov 1990
United: (£25k) 27/28 Aug 1994 to 8 Feb 1996
Debuts: 14 Jul 1994 Winterhur(Sweden) 1 United 1 (Fr)
27 Sep 1994 United 1 Stockport County 0 (LC)
18 Feb 1995 Southend United 1 United 3
Last games: 9 Dec 1995 United 0 Huddersfield Town 2
26 Dec 1995 United 1 Birmingham City 1 (sub)
Rotherham United (L) Aug 1994/ Wycombe Wanderers (L) Aug 1995
Peterborough United (£40k) Feb 1996/ Lincoln City (L) Jan 1997/ Oldham Athletic (L) Mar 1997/ Crewe Alexandra (£45/25k) Dec 1997/ Bristol Rovers (£75k) Aug 2000/ Telford United Aug 2002/ Northwich Victoria Jul 2003/ Ashton United cs 2005 to cs 2006

Brought to Bramall Lane by Dave Bassett, Mark Foran was never the most mobile or the quickest of defenders and never established himself in the first team and his move to another club was no surprise.

At his various League clubs Mark clocked up just over 105(16) FL appearances.

Appearances:		Apps	Gls
	FL	10 (1)	1
	LC	1	0
	AIC	0 (1)	0
	Total	11 (2)	1

FORBES Alexander (Alex) Rooney

LH/CF/IF 1944–48 5' 10½" 12st 0
b. Dundee 21 January 1925

Ashdale Boys' Club/ Dundee NE
United: (£40 which was increased to £105) 27/29 Sep and 2 Oct 1944 to 19/21 Feb 1948
Debuts: 30 Sep 1944 United 1 Barnsley 0 (WW2)
5 Jan 1946 United 1 Huddersfield Town 1 (FAC)
31 Aug 1946 United 0 Liverpool 1
Last game: 17 Jan 1948 United 4 Grimsby Town 0
Arsenal Feb 1948 (£16k)/ Leyton Orient Aug 1956 (£3500/free)/ Fulham Sep 1957/ Gravesend & Northfleet Aug 1958/ Sligo Rovers Nov 1960

A letter arrived at Bramall Lane in the summer of 1944 recommending a Scottish goalkeeper. Teddy Davison, the manager, replied that a centre forward would be more welcome and received a reply that a young man who had just had a trial with Aberdeen might be worth looking at. An invitation was offered and the red-haired Alex Forbes with his boots in a brown paper parcel arrived at Bramall Lane and he became a United player after a trial against Barnsley Reserves.

Alex playing at centre forward had raw talent, speed, plenty of spirit and some skill but although he scored six goals in his first half dozen games, it was soon obvious that he wasn't good enough and he was no more successful when playing at inside forward. He did however, have the determination to improve and he was one of a very small band who returned to the training ground in the afternoon. In November of the following season, Alex was tried at left half against Everton and played well in a convincing United victory. Facing him in the Everton team was Joe Mercer and after the match, Alex sought his advice; Mercer would not forget the young Scottish lad who went on to play a large part in helping United win the League North Championship that season. Good in the air, his anticipation and distribution were first class and his fiery temper, strong tackling and seemingly limitless energy made him a formidable opponent and it was no surprise when he gained his first Scottish Cap against England, in April 1947. He went on to win five with United and fourteen in all.

Encouraged by Arsenal stars Archie Macauley and Joe Mercer, Alex asked for a transfer and moved to Arsenal in February 1948, winning a

Championship medal in 1953 and gaining FA Cup winners and losers medals in 1950 and 1952 respectively. Cartilage problems ended his Arsenal career and he then played for a variety of FL (totalling 290 games) and non-league clubs. After leaving Sligo Rovers in 1962 he became youth team coach at Arsenal before moving to South Africa where he coached (Highlands Park) and later managed Johannesburg Rangers.

Appearances:

	Apps	Gls
FL	61	6
FAC	9	0
CC	1	2
WW2	53	9
Total	124	17

FORD David

OL/IR 1971–73 5' 7½" 10st 7
b. Sheffield 2 March 1945

Sheffield Wednesday from amat 1961, app Jan 1963/ Newcastle United Dec 1969
United: (exchange) 27/28 Jan 1971 to May 1973
Debut: 6 Feb 1971 United 2 Luton Town 1
Last games: 9 Dec 1972 United 1 Manchester City 1
20 Mar 1973 United 1 Sheffield Wednesday 1 (BM)
Halifax Town Aug 1973 to cs 1976

Sheffield Schools 100yd champion and an England U23 international, David made his FL debut as Sheffield Wednesday's first substitute, on 23 October 1965 at home to Sunderland. His full debut came a week later at Aston Villa and later that season, he played and scored in the FA Cup Final.

A fast and dangerous attacking player on the left flank and a good finisher, David never recovered his old form after a serious car accident in 1967. His transfer to Newcastle United in exchange for Jackie Sinclair in 1969 was not successful, nor was his move to Bramall Lane in 1971.

He was signed by John Harris—on the same day as Trevor Hockey from Birmingham—along with John Hope in an exchange deal with John Tudor moving to Newcastle. The move was a successful one for United in that promotion was achieved but David, who came with a leg strain, could never command a regular place in the United team. His final appearance in a Blades' shirt was in Len Badger's benefit game against the Wednesday and he scored against his former club before being given a free transfer.

After playing for Halifax Town, David ran a successful plumbing and heating business in Sheffield and at one time ran the Wednesday Executive Club. He had appeared in 245(15) FL games and scored 42 goals.

Appearances:

	Apps	Gls
FL	21 (6)	2
LC	2	0
TEX	2	0
CC	1	3
ABD	1	0
Total	27 (6)	5

FORD Robert (Bobby) John

MF 1997–2002 5' 8" 11st 0
b. Bristol 22 September 1974

Oxford United from trainee Oct 1992
United: (£400k) 28 Nov 1997 to Aug 2002
Debuts: 29 Nov 1997 United 1 Crewe Alexandra 0 (sub)
6 Dec 1997 United 2 Norwich City 1
Last games: 1 Apr 2002 United 0 Wimbledon 1
3 Aug 2002 Linfield 1 United 5 (sub Fr)
Oxford United Aug 2002 / – / Bath City Jan 2004 to Nov 2005

Bobby Ford began and ended his FL career with Oxford United, making his debut as a substitute at home to Stoke City on 10 October 1993; his full debut coming later that season on 12 February at home to Charlton Athletic.

After playing more than 100 games for Oxford, he joined the Blades, signed by Nigel Spackman, and was a regular member of the side for three and a half seasons. Generally playing as an attacking midfielder, he did on occasions fill a defensive role as a wing back and, whatever position he was asked to play, he was always a busy, hard working and committed player with good passing ability but lacking power and finishing ability.

He returned to Oxford United in 2002 and after the end of the season he took a break from football before joining non-League Bath City. Troubled by injuries, he finally retired in November 2005.

Appearances:		Apps	Gls
	FL	138 (17)	6
	PO	2	0
	FAC	14 (4)	0
	LC	10 (2)	1
	Total	164 (23)	7

FORD S

OR 1918 5' 8½" 10st 12
b. Sheffield

Nunnery Colliery
WW1: Wednesday, United, Lincoln C (against United), Rotherham County
United: WW1 guest
Only game: 2 Nov 1918 Lincoln City 2 United 1 (WW1)
Barnsley cs 1919 to cs1920

Ford made ten war time appearances for the Wednesday in 1918 and 1919 in different forward positions, two for Rotherham County and also assisted Lincoln City but made just one appearance for United. He signed for Barnsley after the war but didn't appear in the first team.

Appearances:		Apps	Gls
	WW1	1	0
	Total	1	0

FOREMAN Matthew (Matt)

D 1992–94 6' 0" 12st 1
b. Gateshead 15 February 1975

United: from trainee 5 Jul 1993 to 22/26 Mar 1996
Debuts: 14 Dec 1992 Worksop Town 3 United 1 (sub BM)
24 Aug 1994 United 1 Udinese 2 (sub AIC)
Last games: 6 Sep 1994 Piacenza 2 United 2 (AIC)
15 Nov 1994 Cesena 1 United 4 (sub AIC)
Scarborough Mar 1996/ Tarwa (New Zealand)/ Durham City Aug 1996

Matt Foreman was unable to make the breakthrough into the first team at Bramall Lane, his only senior competitive games coming in the Anglo-Italian tournament which manager Bassett didn't take seriously.

He eventually made his FL debut after moving to Scarborough, on 23 March 1996 as a substitute at Barnet, his full debut coming on 2 April at Lincoln City. He left at the end of the season, and after a brief time abroad, moved into non-League football.

Appearances:		Apps	Gls
	AIC	1 (2)	0
	Total	1 (2)	0

FORSTER William (Bill) E

RH 1903–05 5' 9" 12st 2
b. c1882

North Wingfield May 1901/ Grassmoor Red Rose Aug 1902
United: 8/9 Jan 1903 to 3 May 1906
Debut: 21 Nov 1903 Bury 0 United 1
Last game: 7 Oct 1905 United 3 Everton 2
Crystal Palace cs 1906/ Grimsby Town May 1908 to May 1909

The Grassmoor club received a donation of £25 and the receipts from a reserve match at the Lane when United signed Bill Forster. A robust, determined player, he made just nine FL appearances for United and Grimsby Town, but in his two seasons with Southern League Crystal Palace, he played a total of 60 games in the Southern League and FA Cup.

Appearances:		Apps	Gls
	FL	4	0
	FAC	2	0
	Total	6	0

FORTE Jonathan Ronald James

F 2002–06 6' 2" 12st 2
b. Sheffield 25 July 1986

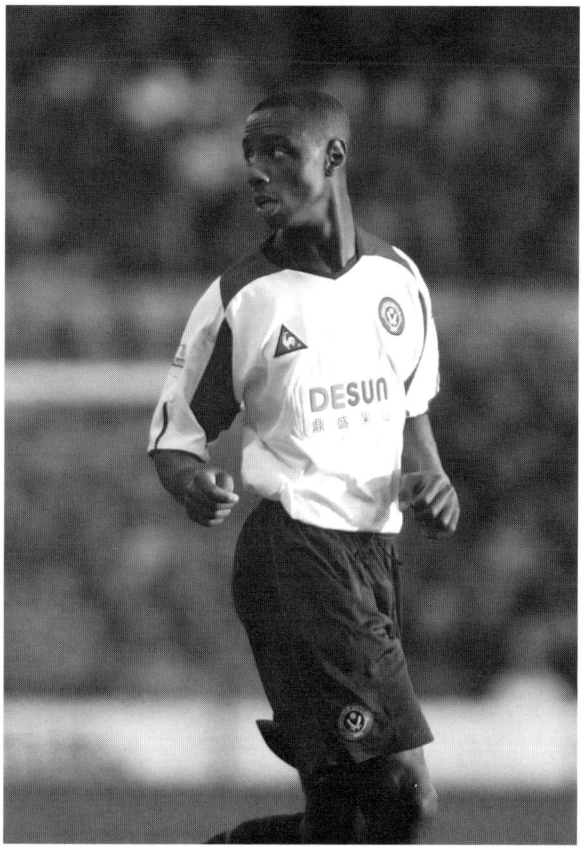

United: from trainee 7 Jul 2004 to 4/5 Jul 2007
Debuts: 3 Aug 2002 Linfield 1 United 5 (sub Fr)
25 Jan 2004 Nottingham Forest 0 United 3 (sub FAC)
28 Jan 2004 Derby County 2 United 0 (sub)
24 Feb 2004 Crewe Alexandra 0 United 1
Last games: 30 Apr 2004 United 0 Millwall 1
25 Oct 2005 Reading 2 United 0 (LC)
22 Apr 2006 Luton Town 1 United 1 (sub)
Doncaster R (L) 31 Aug to Oct, 18 Nov to Dec 2005/ Rotherham U (L) 9 Jan 2006/ Doncaster R (L) 21 Jul 2006
Scunthorpe United Jul 2007

Jonathan Forte came through the United academy and gained England caps at U16 level. He made a great impression on his senior competitive debut, aged 17, in the FA Cup, using his pace to run at and beat defenders and produce telling crosses but he lacked the necessary physical strength to see off a challenge. His FL debut came shortly after but for the rest of the season and the following one most of his appearances were from the bench.

In the 2005–06 season, he had loan spells with Doncaster Rovers and Rotherham United to give him more competitive experience. He spent nearly all the following season on an extended loan at Doncaster, being a regular in the side and scoring an early goal in the Johnstone's Paint Trophy final which Rovers won.

In the summer of 2007, he moved to Scunthorpe, as part of the deal that saw Billy Sharp return to the Lane, and was a regular in their squad as they fought an unsuccessful battle against relegation and by the summer had made a total of 68(65) FL appearances.

Appearances:		Apps	Gls
	FL	2 (28)	1
	FAC	0 (4)	0
	LC	3 (2)	0
	Total	5 (34)	1

FOULKE William (Bill/Billy) Henry

G 1894–1905 6' 2½" 12st 5 (1894)
to over 19st (1899) and 22?st
b. Dawley(Shropshire) 12 April 1874
d. Sheffield 1 May 1916

Blackwell
United: c19 Apr 1894 to 19 Aug 1905
Debut: 1 Sep 1894 United 2 West Bromwich Albion 1
Last games: 19 Nov 1904 United 0 Aston Villa 3
15 Apr 1905 Hull City 3 United 1 (Fr)
Chelsea (£30/£50) Aug 1905/ Bradford City 4 Apr 1906 to Nov 1907

Bill Foulke is one of the most famous and legendary goalkeepers of all time and separating the truth from the half-truth or fantasy isn't easy.

His name appears on his birth certificate as 'Foulk' but there were numerous variations used in the area of Shropshire where he was born and in his playing days, newspapers and programmes generally used 'Foulke' or 'Foulkes', Bill preferring the former and his mother the latter, which she regarded as superior.

Bill's father, a miner, had brought the family to Blackwell, a Derbyshire village where Bill also worked as a miner and played in goal for the village team. Recommended by a referee, United signed him after watching him play in a local cup-tie for Blackwell, beating off competition from Derby County and Nottingham Forest.

Bill was exceptionally tall by the standards of those days but in his first two seasons, he was also slim weighing a modest 12st 5 when he came to United. It was soon apparent that he was an exceptional keeper and a remarkable character, full of confidence, authority and humour. Let there be no doubt as to his ability; more than one of his contemporaries called him the greatest ever and season on season, he is always statistically among the very best in the League.

Bill used his height, weight, strength and agility to maximum effect but he soon became aware that he was an 'attraction' and began to play to the gallery though not to the detriment of his playing ability or the team. He became a 'character' and 'showman', drawing more spectators through the turnstiles and he was happy to inform all and sundry that the opposition as well as United should pay his wages which were soon, only exceeded by Ernest Needham, the United and future England captain. Bill would deliberately kick and fist the ball enormous distances, as much to astonish the spectators as to help United's cause and would pick up the ball with one hand as though it was a size more suited to cricket or tennis.

To opposition supporters, he was a stage villain and the United directors found themselves admonishing their normally genial giant for 'leaping the railings' and persuading him that he 'must restrain his inclination to argue with the spectators' (1895). He was of course, sometimes the victim and a brave referee lectured the Wednesday crowd in 1897 for throwing stones at Foulke and he was attacked by the Notts County crowd in 1898. As his weight and reputation grew, every centre forward regarded the home fixture against United as the charging challenge of the season. Bill was usually ready for them. He fell on top of Bell, the Everton forward and carried him from the field like a baby and used the momentum of Allan of Liverpool to send him spinning on his way and upside down—though the United players were less amused by the award of a penalty kick but, as a team-mate would later say, Bill was 'a good sort… just like a big boy for fun'.

The Football Association and other 'bigwigs' feared a player like Bill. He was chosen just once by England (Bramall Lane in 1897) and by the Football League (1898) but was a League Championship winner in 1898, FA Cup winner in 1899 and 1902 and runner-up in 1901 and a useful cricketer, making four appearances for Derbyshire.

Bill was past his best by 1905 but he added to his legendary status by playing in Chelsea's first season (34 games) before an attack of 'rheumatic gout' forced his retirement while playing for Bradford City (22 games).

He remained a celebrated and ever popular figure in Sheffield, keeping a pub and later a grocery store and maintaining an enthusiastic following of horse racing and professional athletics. He acted as a referee in local handicap races and probably won more money than he lost with his inside knowledge.

Contrary to legend, Bill died in a Sheffield nursing home and not penniless in Blackpool though he probably did, while on holiday, offer his services to a fairground stall for the public to 'score a goal against Bill Foulke'.

Appearances:

	Apps	Gls
FL	299	0
FAC	41	0
UCL	5	0
BC	3	0
ABD	4	0
Total	352	0

FOUNTAIN John (Jack)

LH 1951–56 5' 7½" 11st 3
b. Leeds 27 May 1932

Ashley Road Methodist (Leeds)
United: (£20) 31 Oct/3 Nov 1949 to 10/12 Jan 1957
Debuts: 31 Jan 1951 Mansfield Town 2 United 1 (FAC)
3 Feb 1951 Leeds United 1 United 0
Last games: 14 Jan 1956 Manchester United 3 United 1
6 Feb 1956 United 4 Heart of Midlothian 2 (Fr)
Swindon Town (£1500) Jan 1957/ York City Aug 1960 to Apr 1964

Jack Fountain's eight years at Bramall Lane were spent mainly in the reserves as a part time player though he lost nearly two years (1951–53) serving in the RAF on National Service. He signed full-time in June 1953 and 20 of his 31 FL appearances came in season 1954–55. He lacked speed but went on to have five good seasons as a determined, hard working, hard tackling midfielder with Swindon Town and York City, where he was captain for a while. He amassed 242 FL appearances in total.

Sadly, his career ended in disgrace when he was found guilty of match fixing whilst with York City. The football betting scandal was exposed by the Sunday People in April 1964 and resulted in Jack receiving a 15 month prison sentence.

Appearances:		Apps	Gls
	FL	31	0
	FAC	2	0
	CC	3	0
	Total	36	0

FRAIN David

MF 1986–88 5' 8" 10st 9
b. Sheffield 11 October 1962

Nottingham F(14–16 years)/ Dronfield United
United: 6/7 Sep 1985 to Jun 1988
Debut: 31 Mar 1986 United 1 Sunderland 0
Last game: 6 Feb 1988 Stoke City 1 United 0
Rochdale Jul 1988/ Stockport County (£50k) Jul 1989/ Mansfield Town (L) Sep 1994/ Stalybridge Celtic Apr 1995
Coaching/mgr: Stalybridge C Apr 1996/ Alfreton Town Oct 1996/ Hallam Feb 1999/ Worksop Mar 1999/ Heeley Red Lion 1999–2000 / – / Alfreton T to Jun 2005 / – / Staveley Miners Welfare asst mgr Jan 2006 to Nov 2006

David Frain was on Nottingham Forest's books as a 14 to 16 year old right winger and played for Sheffield Boys and then for Rowlinson YC and Dronfield United. He was twenty three and an apprentice plumber before he had the chance of a career as a professional player and although he had been signed by Ian Porterfield, his first team debut did not come until Billy McEwan had taken over.

Playing down the right side as a neat, thoughtful, attacking midfielder he had good ball control. He was given a good run in the side at the start of both the 1986–87 and 1987–88 seasons but he lacked pace and, after playing just one game under Dave Bassett, he was given a free transfer.

David joined his old coach, Danny Bergara, at Rochdale and again at Stockport County where he played 187 FL games and reached a career total of more than 250 FL appearances before moving into non-League football as a player, coach and manager.

Appearances:		Apps	Gls
	FL	35 (9)	6
	LC	3 (2)	0
	FMC	2	0
	Total	40 (11)	6

FRANCE Gary

F 1974 5' 10" 12st 2
b. Whitwell (Derbyshire) 18 June 1955

United: from app 6 Jun 1971, pro Jun 1973 to 7 Feb 1975
Debut: 20 Apr 1974 United 1 Queens Park Rangers 1
Last game: 31 Aug 1974 United 3 Ipswich Town 1 (sub)

Gary France played quite often for the reserves but his one goal for the first team was scored in an end of season friendly game in Cyprus. He was given a free transfer in November 1974 and his contract was paid up to February in the following year.

Appearances:		Apps	Gls
	FL	1 (1)	0
	Total	1 (1)	0

FRANCIS John Andrew

Striker 1988–90 5' 8" 12st 13
b. Dewsbury 21 November 1963

Ardsley Celtic/ Emley (Halifax Town (trial) Feb 1985)
United: trial Sep 1988. (£5,000 + £5,000 after 25 app) 15 Sep 1988 to 22/24 Jan 1990
Debuts: 13 Sep 1988 Scarborough 1 United 2 (YHCF)
17 Sep 1988 United 6 Chester City 1 (sub)
12 Nov 1988 United 1 Fulham 0
Last game: 13 Jan 1990 Ipswich Town 1 United 1
Burnley (£90k) Jan 1990/ Cambridge United (£95k) Aug 1992/ Burnley (£70k) Mar 1993/ Scunthorpe United Aug 1996/ Halifax Town Oct 1996/ Emley (L)/ Farsley Celtic Feb 1997/ Guisley/ Lancaster City/ Whitby Town/ Ossett Town/ Bradford PA/ Harrogate Town 2000/ Garforth Town Sep 2001/ Eccleshill United cs 2002

John Francis made his FL debut as a substitute during his brief period as a trialist with Halifax Town, on 26 February 1985 at home to Northampton Town; his full debut coming on 22 March at home to Chester City. He returned to Emley and in 1988 was a member of their losing side in the FA Vase final at Wembley.

He had written to United in Billy McEwan's time as manager but no action was taken until Dave Bassett moved to Bramall Lane. Signed at the age of twenty four, his appearances for some time were mainly from the bench. Injuries to Tony Agana meant more opportunities for John in his second season but in January he moved to Burnley, United making a significant profit.

John's speed caused problems for the opposition but he lacked power and strength and his final pass or shot could be disappointing. Nevertheless there were moments to remember especially a fine winning goal against Brighton in September 1989 and he finished his first class career with 174(83) FL appearances, scoring 45 goals. He continued to play in non-League football for a variety of clubs and the list above is not necessarily complete nor in the correct order. More recently, he has been coaching school children.

Appearances:		Apps	Gls
	FL	14 (28)	6
	FAC	0 (1)	0
	LC	0 (2)	0
	FMC	1 (1)	1
	AMC	2 (1)	0
	YHC	3	1
	Total	20 (33)	8

FRANCIS Simon Charles

RWB 2004–06 6' 0" 12st 6
b. Nottingham 16 February 1985

Bradford City from trainee May 2003
United: (£200k) 16 Mar 2004 to 13 Jun 2006
Debut: 27 Mar 2004 Cardiff City 2 United 1

Last games: **12 Apr 2005 Nottingham Forest 1 United 1**
25 Oct 2005 Reading 2 United 0 (LC)
22 Apr 2006 Luton Town 1 United 1 (sub)
Grimsby Town (L) 26 Sep 2005/ Tranmere Rovers (L) 18 Nov 2005
Southend United (£70k) Jun 2006

Simon Francis, an England youth international, made his FL debut with Bradford City on 16 November 2002 at Nottingham Forest and he immediately became a regular in the side.

In March 2004, with City in financial difficulties, Simon moved to the Lane and made a promising start as a right wing back playing with confidence and good control. Scheduled to be in the starting line-up for the following season, he was taken ill with glandular fever and when recovered, he suffered medial ligament damaged. Unable to break into the squad in 2005, although some felt he should have been given more of a chance, he went on loan to Grimsby and Tranmere and in February 2006, he represented the Football League in a match against an Italian Seria B eleven. Unable to gain a place in United's side, he moved to Southend United where he, at last, was a regular first team player and by the summer of 2008 had made over 150 FL appearances in total.

Appearances:		Apps	Gls
	FL	6 (6)	0
	FAC	0 (1)	0
	LC	2	0
	Total	8 (7)	0

FRANKS Colin James

D/MF/CF 1973–79 6' 0½" 12st 8 to 13st 0
b. Wembley 16 April 1951

Boreham Wood/ Uxbridge/ Wealdstone c1968/ Watford amat Mar 1968, pro Jul 1969
United: (£55,555) 19 Jun 1973 to Feb 1979
Debuts: **31 Jul 1973 Roda (Heerlen, Holland) 1 United 4 (sub Fr)**
3 Aug 1973 Wuppertaler SV (WG) 2 United 1 (Fr)
18 Sep 1973 United 0 Dundee United 0 (Tex)
29 Sep 1973 Southampton 3 United 0
Last game: **24 Feb 1979 United 0 Millwall 2**
Toronto Blizzards Feb 1979/ Edmonton Drillers Jun to Aug 1982

Colin Franks made his FL debut with Watford on 13 September 1969 at home to Aston Villa and made 112 FL appearances for the club.

He became the fifth former Watford player signed for United by John Harris. A strong running, powerful utility player, Colin never really fulfilled his potential. His goals tally was disappointing and, though regarded by some as a fast player, his speed was only obvious over a long run and Ken Furphy, his manager at Watford and at the Lane, thought his approach to the game was poor.

After leaving Bramall Lane he moved to Toronto with Chris Calvert, joining former team-mate Keith Eddy and playing in the NASL for four years, moving part way through his final season from Toronto to Edmonton before electing to settle in Canada.

Appearances:		Apps	Gls
	FL	139 (11)	7
	FAC	6	0
	LC	7 (1)	1
	CC	7	2
	TEX	11	0
	Total	170 (12)	10

FRASER Donald

HB/CF 1889–90
b. Scotland

United: Aug 1889 to cs 1890
Debuts: **7 Sep 1889 Nottingham Rangers 4 United 1 (Fr)**
5 Oct 1889 Scarborough 1 United 6 (FAC)
Last games: **18 Jan 1890 United 2 Burnley 1 (FAC)**
17 Mar 1890 Staveley 2 United 1 (WCC)
29 Mar 1890 Doncaster Rovers 1 United 1 (Fr)

Donald Fraser was one of several Scots who answered United's advertisement for players for their first season. He played until December under the pseudonym of 'Donald' and had the honour of playing in the club's first ever game at Nottingham Rangers and, a month later, he scored in the club's first ever FA Cup game at Scarborough. As well as the nine competitive Cup matches, 'the little Scotchman' also played in 30 friendly games.

Appearances:		Apps	Gls
	FAC	5	3
	SCC	3	1
	WCC	1	0
	Total	9	4

FRENCH P Archibald

IR 1898 5' 9" c11st 2

Airdrieonians
United: 8 Dec 1897 to cs1898
Debut: **1 Jan 1898 Notts County 1 United 3**
Last game: **12 Apr 1898 United 1 Newton Heath 4 (Fr)**
/ – / Albion Rovers 7 Aug 1899

Reported to be from Burnbank and 'about 21', Archibald French, although appearing in only one competitive fixture for United, would be able to say that he had played for the English League Champions, as 1897–98 was the season United finished top of the old Division One.

Appearances:		Apps	Gls
	FL	1	0
	Total	1	0

FREW Joseph (Joe)

IL 1895

Stevenston Thistle (Ayrshire)
United: 28 Oct 1895 to 18 Dec 1895
Debut: **2 Nov 1895 Stoke City 4 United 0**
Last game: **23 Nov 1895 United 2 Nottingham Forest 1**
Glossop North End Dec 1895/ Stevenston Thistle Sep 1898/ Wishaw Thistle Aug 1899/ Stevenston Thistle Nov 1900 to at least Oct 1902

The contemporary Sheffield newspapers reveal little about Joe Frew who had a remarkably short career with United before joining Glossop, the small but ambitious Derbyshire club though Joe left them before they were elected to the Football League.

Appearances:		Apps	Gls
	FL	4	1
	Total	4	1

FROGGATT Aubrey G

G 1941

Doncaster R 1940/ Grimethorpe Rovers
United: 27/31 Dec 1941 to cs 1942
Only game: **27 Dec 1941 Nottingham Forest 3 United 3 (WW2)**

Aubrey Frogatt was an amateur player who had appeared in the Doncaster Rovers public practice match in August 1940 and turned out for United as a late replacement for Fred White.

Appearances:		Apps	Gls
	WW2	1	0
	Total	1	0

FULFORD John H or W

CF 1940
b. c1919
d. c1941 in an RAF raid on Brest in France

Sheffield University/ Corinthians
United: amateur guest
Debut: 22 Mar 1940 Grimsby Town 2 United 0 (WW2)
Last game: 23 Mar 1940 Rotherham United 0 United 4 (WW2)

A former pupil of King Edward VII School (Sheffield) and medical student at Sheffield University, John's two games for United were on successive days at Easter 1940. John and his brother were both killed in action while serving in the RAF.

Appearances:		Apps	Gls
	WW2	2	0
	Total	2	0

FURLONG Paul Anthony

Striker 2002 6' 0" 13st 8
b. Wood Green 1 October 1968

Enfield/ Coventry City (£130k) Jul 1991/ Watford (£250k) Jul 1992/ Chelsea (£2.3m) May 1994/ Birmingham City (£1.5m) Jul 1996/ Queens Park Rangers (L) Aug 2000
United: (L) 5/8 Feb 2002 for one month
Debut: 9 Feb 2002 United 4 Portsmouth 3
Last game: 2 Mar 2002 United 3 Stockport County 0
Queens Park Rangers (L) Aug 2002, (free) Sep 2002/ Luton Town (free) Aug 2007/ Southend United Jun 2008

Paul Furlong was nearly 23 years old when he moved into League football, making his FL debut with Coventry City, as a substitute at home to Manchester City, on 17 August 1991; his full debut came a week later at Queens Park Rangers. He had come to prominence with Enfield and while he was there, he played for England at semi-professional level. He had a successful time with his first four clubs, making well over 100 appearances for Birmingham.

During his brief loan spell with United, which ended early through injury, the powerful striker scored twice on his debut, the second and winning goal from a penalty kick in injury time. The following season, nearing 34 years old, he joined Queens Park Rangers for a second time and, in 2007–08 and aged 39, he joined troubled Luton and passed the 500 League games mark, having scored over 170 goals.

Appearances:		Apps	Gls
	FL	4	2
	Total	4	2

FURNISS Frederick (Fred)

RB 1941–55 5' 8½" 11st 4 to 11st 9
b. Sheffield 10 July 1922

Hampton Sports/ Woodbourn Alliance and Fulwood Amateurs
United: amat 2 Apr 1941 to pro 16/19 Jan 1943 to 30 Jun 1955
Debuts: 24 May 1941 Everton 3 United 3 (WW2)
5 Jan 1946 Huddersfield Town 2 United 2 (FAC)
31 Aug 1946 United 0 Liverpool 1
Last game: 5 Feb 1955 Sheffield Wednesday 1 United 2
Chesterfield (£400) Aug 1955/ Worksop Aug 1956

A pupil at Phillimore Road School, Fred Furniss played for Sheffield and Yorkshire Boys with Harold Brook. He signed amateur forms with United and made his debut at Everton in a match which was played against a background of air-raid sirens and anti-aircraft gunfire. He worked at Hamptons and then as a Bevin Boy at Orgreave Colliery where, after a near miss from a coal tub, he decided that the Army, in the form of the Royal Artillery offered more safety.

He became a regular in the first team in October 1943, a position he held until 1954. He was an excellent full-back; fast and a good tackler with a fine sense of anticipation. He used the ball well but above all, he was reliable and consistent. Nearly all his appearances were at right back but he also acted as a wing back (in the days before the term was used), using his speed to support his forwards. He had a very good record as a penalty taker, missing just two of seventeen in competitive games and played in both the League North Championship (1945–46) and the 1952–53 Second Division Championship teams.

In 1955 he finally lost his place to Cec Coldwell and moved to Chesterfield where he played and coached with the reserves. After playing in non-League football with Worksop, he continued to play in local football until the age of fifty five after which he refereed Sunday games for youngsters. He was a keen snooker and bowls player and continued to attend United's matches well into the new millennium.

Appearances:		Apps	Gls
	FL	279	14
	FAC	24	0
	CC	17	1
	WW2	113	3
	Total	433	18

FURNISS (FURNESS) Samuel (Sam)

CH 1921 5' 10" 11st 0 to 11st 5
b. Sheffield 9 March 1895
d. Sheffield 11 March 1977

United: Aug 1919 to 12 May 1921
Debut: 22 Jan 1921 Middlesbrough 2 United 2
Last game: 7 Feb 1921 Preston North End 2 United 0
Bristol Rovers May 1921/ Swindon Town May 1924 to cs 1927 / – / Boston Town Oct 1927/ Scarborough cs1928

Sam was known almost entirely throughout his playing career with United as 'Furniss' though he appears in the Football League records are 'Furness'. Transferred to Bristol with John Ball after he had made just three appearances for United, Sam, playing mainly at right half, went on to play 126 FL games for Bristol Rovers (90) and Swindon Town (36) in the old Division 3(South) before moving into non-League football.

Appearances:		Apps	Gls
	FL	3	0
	Total	3	0

GABRIELI Emanuele

D 2004 5' 11" 12st 8
b. L'Aqila (Italy) 31 December 1980

Chieti/ Cavese
United: 1 Oct 2004 to 31 Jan 2005
Only game: 17 Oct 2004 Gillingham 1 United 3 (sub)
Boston United Feb 2005/ Italy

After a month's trial, which included a private fixture against Leeds United, Emanuele Gabriele was signed in October on a four month contract. He was a regular in the reserves and scored three times but made just one substitute appearance for the first team. He moved to Boston United in February but played just four games and when his contract came to a close, he returned to Italy.

Appearances:		Apps	Gls
	FL	0 (1)	0
	Total	0 (1)	0

GADSBY Kenneth (Ken) John

LB 1945 5' 9" 11st 10
b. Chesterfield 3 July 1916

Middlecliffe Rovers/ Scarborough/ Leeds United Oct 1934 to cs 1948
WW2 guest: Sheffield Wednesday (1 app) 1943/ Sheff United/ Yeovil Town 1945–46
United: WW2 guest
Only game: 26 May 1945 Sheffield Wednesday 4 United 2 (CC/LN WW2)
Kings Lynn cs 1948

Ken Gadsby made his FL debut in a 1–7 defeat at Everton on 3 March 1937. When the Second World War broke out, he was being thought of as a possible England player and had toured South Africa with the FA in 1939. Ken was serving with the RASC when he appeared once for Wednesday in 1942–43 and in this one game for United.

Appearances:		Apps	Gls
	CC	1	0
	Total	1	0

GAGE Kevin William

RB/LB 1991–95 5' 9½" 12st 11
b. Chiswick 21 April 1964

Wimbledon from Jun 1980, pro Jan 1982/ Aston Villa (£100k) Jul 1987
United: (L)14/15 Nov 1991, (£150–175k) 15/17 Feb 1992 to 27/28 Mar 1996
Debut: 23 Nov 1991 Tottenham Hotspur 0 United 1
Last game: 4 Nov 1995 United 4 Portsmouth 1
Preston North End Mar 1996/ Chesterfield (trial) Aug 1997/ Hull City 19 Sep 1997

An England Youth international, Kevin Gage made his FL debut with Wimbledon when just 17 years of age on 2 May 1981 at home to Bury. Having made more than 100 FL appearances for both the Dons and Aston Villa, he lost his place when Ron Atkinson, their new manager, brought in new players.

Kevin joined United, signed by his former Wimbledon boss Dave Bassett, and went on to reach a century of games for his third club. He scored on his debut against Spurs and he became a regular in the side for the remainder of the season and the following one. He played mainly as a right wing back, being solid in defence and creating opportunities coming forward. Season 1993–94 saw him in and out of the side but he was again a regular and '1995 Player of the Year' in the following season. Kevin lost his place when Mark Beard was signed in August 1995 and he moved on a free transfer to Preston North End and, after a trial in August with Chesterfield, signed for Hull City. He totalled 385(46) League games.

He did return to Bramall Lane in the new millennium, as one of the former players involved with match day hospitality and is involved in the licensing trade in Dronfield.

Appearances:		Apps	Gls
	FL	107 (5)	7
	FAC	10 (2)	0
	LC	6	0
	AIC	1	0
	Total	124 (17)	7

GALBRAITH Dugald

OR/IL/IR 1889–90
b. Scotland

Dundee local football
United: Aug 1889 to cs 1890
Debuts: 7 Sep 1889 Nottingham Rangers 4 United 1 (Fr)
5 Oct 1889 Scarborough 1 United 6 (FAC)
Last games: 1 Feb 1890 Bolton Wanderers 13 United 0 (FAC)
17 Mar 1890 Staveley 2 United 1 (WCC)

Reported to be 'from Dundee', Dugald Galbraith made 45 appearances in total for United, 31 of them being in friendly games. He played in the club's first 23 games, including our first FA Cup game at Scarborough in which he scored our first ever FA Cup goal and missed just two of United's first 47 games.

(An unknown forward with the same surname played one FL game for Notts C in December 1888 but contemporary newspapers don't link the two players).

Appearances:		Apps	Gls
	FAC	7	4
	SCC	5	1
	WCC	2	0
	Total	14	5

GALLACHER ('Gallagher') Hugh (Paddy)

OL/IL/CF 1893–94
b. Galston 11 May 1870
d. Girvan 20 May 1941

Maybole (Ayrshire)/ Celtic May 1889/ Preston North End Sep 1890
United: 27/28 Jan 1893 to Aug 1894
Debut: 6 Feb 1893 United 3 Burton Swifts 1
Last games: 7 Apr 1894 Preston North End 3 United 0
14 Apr 1894 Wednesday 1 United 1 (UCL)
Leicester Fosse Aug 1894 to cs1896/ Nelson 1896/ New Brompton May 1897 to May 1899

Hugh Gallacher joined Celtic in 1889 and played just one League game for the club, their second such game and the first at home, on 30 August 1890 against Cambuslang. Hugh made his FL debut with Preston on 17 September 1890 at home to Bolton Wanderers, and his six goals that season made him North End's top scorer.

The second United player to be signed by transfer under the Football League's registration system, he made an immediate impact on joining United, scoring twice on his debut and playing in the final nine games and the successful promotion-deciding Test Match. He missed just one game in United's first season in the top flight before moving on to Leicester Fosse. Described by George Waller, United's famous trainer, as a 'fine outside left', the player would usually chew an ounce of twist tobacco during the game.

Appearances:		Apps	Gls
	FL	38	7
	TM	1	0
	FAC	1	0
	NL	2	1
	UCL	5	0
	WCC	1	0
	Total	48	8

GALLIMORE George

OL/IL/CF 1908–10 5'8½" 11st 7
b. Hanley 10 August 1886 or 1888
d. Stoke 1949

Ashwood Villa/ East Vale (Hanley Swifts)/ Stoke Apr 1903
United: 17 Jun 1908 to Jul 1910
Debut: 1 Sep 1908 Bury 1 United 2
Last game: 2 Apr 1910 Bury 2 United 0
Birmingham Jul 1910/ Leek Town Sep 1911 to May 1913/ East Vale

George Gallimore signed for Hanley Swifts but the transfer was declared illegal and he joined the old Stoke club. He made his FL debut with Stoke on 16 January 1904 against United at Bramall Lane and scored in the 1–1 draw.

In 1908 Stoke had financial problems and dropped out of the League and George, (who had made 77 FL appearances) along with Albert Sturgess, were signed by United. It was reported that George was fast and could put across an accurate centre but he was unable to keep a regular place in the side, playing just five games in his second season. He returned to the Midlands, joining Birmingham, where he played regularly until December when he lost his place and after one season, he moved into non-League football.

Appearances:		Apps	Gls
	FL	16	2
	ABD	1	0
	Total	17	2

GAMBLE ('Gambles') Frank

IF 1893 and 1895
b. Sheffield JAS 1870 or OND 1871

Heeley 1891 and 1892–93
United: 30 Sep 1892 to cs 1893
Only game: 30 Jan 1893 United 1 Stockton 3 (NL)
Worksop Town cs1893 to cs 1894
United: cs 1894 to 14 May 1896
Debut: 7 Oct 1895 United 1 Sunderland 2
Last game: 9 Nov 1895 United 1 Everton 2
Oldham County May 1896/ Worksop Town Nov 1896/ Ilkeston Town Jan 1897/ Wombwell Town Aug 1898/ Mexborough Town Jul 1899 to1900/

Frank Gamble's story is far from clear. 'F Gamble' or 'Gambles' was playing for Heeley between February 1891 and April 1892 when he was joined by 'A Gamble', perhaps a relative and a former Sheffield Club player and a player reported as 'Gambles' played for Wednesday's reserves in September 1890.

'F Gamble' is described as 'from Worksop' and 'a Heeley player' when United registered him with the Football League in 1892. He spent most of that season with the reserves or with his old club. It is probable that it was the same man registered in 1894. In the end, United lost all the four games in which Gamble played and his goose was finally cooked when he missed a train to a fixture in Birmingham and only played once for the reserves after that.

Appearances:		Apps	Gls
	FL	3	0
	NL	1	0
	Total	4	0

GANNON James (Jim) Paul

CD 1989 6' 2" 13st 2
b. Southwark 7 September 1968

Dundalk
United: 27 Apr 1989 (£50k) to 7 Mar 1990
Debuts: 31 Jul 1989 Skegness Town 0 United 4 (Fr)
10 Aug 1989 United 1 Rotherham United 1 (YHC)
Last games: 14 Aug 1989 Halifax Town 1 United 0 (YHC)
4 Dec 1989 Bourne Town 0 United 2 (Fr)
Halifax Town(L) Feb 1990
Stockport County (£40–70k) Mar 1990/ Notts County (L) Jan 1994/ Crewe Alexandra Dec 2000 to cs 2001/ Shelbourne Jul 2001/ Dundalk mgr Jun 2004/ Stockport County mgr Jan 2006

Jim Gannon moved with his Irish parents to Dublin when he was fifteen and played for Dundalk. A former private in the Irish army, he was signed by Dave Bassett and made his FL debut while on loan at Halifax Town on 24 February 1990 at Maidstone United. Jim made just four first team appearances, two in friendlies, for United and then was transferred to Stockport County where he had a distinguished career of nearly 500 first team games.

After a total of 359(35) FL appearances he returned to Ireland, completed his accountancy exams whilst playing for Shelbourne and then moved into management, taking Stockport into League One in 2008.

Appearances:		Apps	Gls
	YHC	2	0
	Total	2	0

GANNON John Spencer

MF 1989–96 5' 8½" 11st 10
b. Wimbledon 18 December 1966

Wimbledon from app Dec 1984, pro Feb 1985/ Crewe Alexandra (L) Dec 1986
United:: **(L) 23 Feb 1989, signed Jun 1989 to 7/8 Mar 1996**
Debuts: **25 Feb 1989 United 4 Blackpool 1 (sub)**
15 Apr 1989 Northampton Town 1 United 2
Last game: **13 Jan 1996 Tranmere Rovers 1 United 1**
Middlesbrough (L) 5 Nov 1993 to Jan 1994
Oldham Athletic (nominal fee/£10k) Mar 1996/ – / Mansfield Town Football in the Community Officer to Dec 2002, asst mgr/ Chester City asst mgr to Feb 2006/ Notts County asst manager Jun 2006 to Oct 2007/ Leeds U coaching Nov 2007 to Jan 2008

John Gannon was an England U16 player who had trials in the 1983–84 season with the Irish youth squad. A nephew of Eddie Gannon, the former Wednesday and Irish international, John made his FL debut with Wimbledon on 8 May 1986 at Bradford City and scored in the 1–1 draw.

After 16 appearances with the Dons and 15 on loan with Crewe, he joined United. Signed by his former Wimbledon boss Dave Bassett, initially on loan, he came on for his debut as an 80th minute substitute. He was cautioned after his first tackle, took an excellent corner with his first kick and scored (89 minutes) with his second. One can hardly imagine a more crowd-pleasing debut but, although John always tackled hard, covered and distributed the ball well with his left foot, he lacked pace and took some time to win the support of the crowd. Busy, industrious and determined, he played an important mid-field role in taking United back to the old First Division in 1990, a position they retained until the unfortunate relegation in 1994. Loaned out that season, he returned to play in 13 of the last 14 games and more were won than lost in those last few months.

After appearing in over two hundred League and Cup games for the Blades, his one season at Oldham Athletic was blighted by a knee injury and he was released in April 1997 and forced to give up the game as a player. In 1997 he instituted a scheme of football academies for five to thirteen year olds and teamed up at Mansfield with his former playing colleague, Keith Curle and has worked as a coach or assistant manager.

Appearances:		Apps	Gls
	FL	162 (12)	6
	FAC	14	0
	LC	13 (1)	0
	FMC	4	0
	AIC	2	1
	YHC	1	1
	Total	196 (13)	8

GARBETT Terry Graham

MF/CF 1974–75 5' 9" 11st 12
b. Lanchester (Co Durham) 9 September 1945

Pelton Fell/ Stockton/ Middlesbrough Aug 1963/ Watford (£7000) Aug 1966/ Blackburn Rovers (£20k) Sep 1971
United: **(£30/35k) 31 Jan 1974 to 13 Feb 1976**
Debut: **5 Feb 1974 United 1 Wolverhampton Wanderers 0**
Last game: **8 Nov 1975 Aston Villa 5 United 1**
New York Cosmos (£9000) Apr 1976 to Sep 1979 / – / Coach University of S. Carolina

Terry Garbett made his FL debut with Middlesbrough on 7 September 1965 at Ipswich Town and having played seven games that season he moved to Watford where he had a successful five seasons, scoring 46 goals in 200 FL games. He moved to Blackburn and was brought to Bramall Lane by Ken Furphy, his manager at his two previous clubs.

An industrious player, he failed to win the crowd's backing and never looked good enough for the top flight of English football. On leaving United he and Tony Field teamed up yet again with Furphy in the United States, United receiving £9000. After his four seasons with New York Cosmos he became a coach in the USA.

Appearances:		Apps	Gls
	FL	26 (5)	0
	LC	3 (2)	0
	TEX	1 (1)	0
	CC	1 (1)	0
	Total	31 (9)	0

GARDNER Charles Richard (Dick)

IR 1937 5' 9½" 11st 4
b. Birmingham 22 December 1912
d. Birmingham January 1997

Evesham Town/ Birmingham (am) Sep 1932/ Notts County May 1933/ Stourbridge Aug 1934/ Manchester United May 1935
United: **(£1400) 8 May 1937 to 7 May 1938**
Debut: **6 Sep 1937 United 2 Bury 1**
Last games: **30 Oct 1937 Plymouth Argyle 2 United 0**
5 May 1938 Boston United 1 United 2 (Fr)
Stourbridge Aug 1938

Dick Gardner had failed to impress Birmingham, Notts County and Aston Villa (Stourbridge acted as a nursery club for Villa) but finally made his FL debut with Manchester United on 28 December 1935 at home to Plymouth Argyle. After 16 games in two seasons, he moved to Bramall Lane where his twelve competitive appearances were in successive games and he played in one friendly game about six months later. A clever, scheming player, he lacked pace and though he was placed on United's transfer list, he moved into non-League football.

Appearances:		Apps	Gls
	FL	11	1
	CC	1	0
	Total	12	1

GARNER Paul

LB/MF/OL/OR 1975–84 5' 8½" 10st 8
b. Doncaster 1 December 1955

Harworth CI/ Huddersfield Town from app Apr 1971, pro Dec 1972
United: **(L) 13 Nov 1975, (£59,555) 10 Dec 1975 to 13 Sep 1984**
Debut: **15 Nov 1975 United 1 Leicester City 2**
Last games: **12 May 1984 United 2 Newport County 0**
15 Aug 1984 Mansfield Town 2 United 1 (Fr)
Gillingham (L) 2 Sep 1983
Mansfield Town (free) Sep 1984 to cs 1989

An England youth international, Paul Garner made his FL debut with Huddersfield Town on 23 April 1973 at Hull City and made nearly 100 FL appearances for Town before moving to Bramall Lane. Huddersfield were then in Division Four and United in Division One, albeit looking fairly certain to be relegated.

Paul was Jimmy Sirrel's first signing and went on to play for United in all four Divisions. He was a regular member of the side from November 1975 and although United were relegated, Paul offered hope for the future, being enthusiastic, tackling keenly and using his speed constructively on the flanks. A serious car accident in August 1977 meant that he missed most of that season but he played regularly during the relegation seasons of 1978–79 and 1980–81.

Under Ian Porterfield, he went on to gain a Division Four Championship medal and, for the second half of the season, was a key member of the promotion side of 1983–84. He grew to feel that he wasn't wanted by Porterfield and moved on a free transfer to Mansfield. Sadly, he suffered a succession of injuries which brought his playing days to an end in 1989 (with 451(12) FL games to his credit) though insurance money allowed him to become an insurance agent in Sheffield before buying a milk round in north Derbyshire.

Appearances:

	Apps	Gls
FL	248 (3)	7
FAC	14	1
LC	8 (1)	0
TEX	15	0
AMC	4	2
CC	8	1
Total	297 (4)	11

GAUDIE Ralph

CF 1897–98 5' 7" 11st 2
b. Guisborough JFM 1876
d. 1938

South Bank
United: 27 Nov 1897 (am), 1 Feb 1898 (pro) to 9 Aug 1898
Debuts: 6 Nov 1897 United 2 Corinthians 2 (Fr)
1 Jan 1898 Notts County 1 United 3
Last games: 11 Apr 1898 United 2 West Bromwich Albion 0
30 Apr 1898 Liverpool 1 United 0 (Fr)
Aston Villa (£150) Aug to Dec 1898/ Dudley T?/ South Africa/ Woolwich Arsenal Oct 1899 to cs 1901/ South Africa/ Manchester United Aug 1903 to cs 1904/ Darlaston May 1904/ Stourbridge 1906–08

Ralph Gaudie's debut for United was on trial and he played at full-back. Although he only appeared in six competitive matches for United, he played a significant part in winning the League Championship. He scored twice on his debut and played well in the vital match at Villa Park in spite of breaking his nose.

At the end of that season he moved to Aston Villa but after five games he was taken ill. He went out to South Africa to see his brother and to recuperate and on his return was unhappy with Villa's terms. He thought of returning to the Cape or seeking a Southern League side but eventually joined the Arsenal and was the club's leading scorer in his two seasons there, including a hat trick in Arsenal's record win (12–0 against Loughborough Town). He became ill again and went to South Africa and worked as a journalist, eventually returning to play (7 app) for Manchester United.

Appearances:

	Apps	Gls
FL	6	2
Total	6	2

GAYLE Brian Wilbert

CD 1991–96 6' 1" 13st 12
b. Kingston (Jamaica) 6 March 1965

Wimbledon from app Oct 1984/ Manchester City (£325–345k) Jul 1988/ Ipswich Town (£330k) Jan 1990
United: (£700k) 5/17 Sep 1991 to cs 1996
Debut: 17 Sep 1991 United 1 Notts County 3
Last games: 2 Sep 1995 West Bromwich Albion 3 United 1
4 May 1996 United 1 Port Vale 1 (sub)
Exeter City 14 Aug 1996/ Rotherham United Oct 1996/ Bristol Rovers(L) Mar 1997/ Shrewsbury Town Dec 1997 to cs 1999 / – / Telford United Mar 2000 to May 2001

Brian Gayle made his FL debut with Wimbledon on 27 March 1985 at home to Shrewsbury Town and then played for Manchester City and Ipswich Town.

He had made 196 FL appearances for the three clubs when he rejoined his former Wimbledon boss, Dave Bassett, at Bramall Lane on the 5 September 1991. The transfer became an extraordinary affair when it appeared that United were unable to find the money to complete the club's then record transfer fee and Bassett dipped into his own pocket with a loan to enable Brian to begin his Blades' career.

Playing as a central defender, he was a regular for his first two seasons, although several games were missed due to knee problems. For this reason he missed the first half of the 1993–94 season and in his final season (1995–96), his only appearance after August, was a farewell cameo as a substitute in the final game.

Brian captained United and led by example, being good in the air and always playing with determination and spirit. A good organiser, he was dangerous at set pieces but his most memorable goal was into his own net, over the head of Mel Rees in the game which secured Leeds United the Championship. Despite arthritic knee problems, he continued playing in the lower divisions for three more seasons, appearing in a total of 422(10) League games before moving into non-League football.

Appearances:

	Apps	Gls
FL	115 (2)	9
FAC	10	1
LC	9	0
FMC	1	1
Total	135 (2)	11

GEARY Derek (Del) Peter

LWB 2004– 5' 6" 10st 8
b. Dublin 19 June 1980

Cherry Orchard/ Sheffield Wednesday Nov 1997/ Stockport County (free) Aug 2004
United: (£25k+£25k) 22 Oct 2004
Debut: 29 Oct 2004 Crewe Alexandra 2 United 3

Derek Geary made his FL debut with neighbours Wednesday as a substitute on the 30 September 2000 at Gillingham; his full debut coming on the final day of that season (6 May) at home to Crewe Alexandra. He made 104 FL appearances for the Owls and was then transferred to Stockport County (13 FL app) as Wednesday strove to reduce their wage bill.

He was signed by Neil Warnock, who had seen him playing for Stockport's reserves, as an extra defender but was soon playing on a regular basis and he scored his first ever goal at Millwall in December 2004 after more than 150 senior appearances. He played a significant role in United's promotion season but it seemed his opportunities would be limited in the Premiership. Given his chance however, his speed and work rate stood him in good stead and he began to eliminate from his play, the 'silly free kicks and bookings' and had the energy to get well forward and supply good crosses and he was one of the few successes in a season which ended with disappointment.

Derek missed much of the 2007–08 season through injury although, when he did play, he gave his all and remained a firm favourite with the fans.

Appearances:		Apps	Gls
	FL	77 (9)	1
	FAC	9 (1)	0
	LC	6 (1)	0
	Total	92 (11)	1

GERRARD Paul William

G 2003, 2007 6' 2" 14st 4
b. Heywood 22 January 1973

Oldham Athletic from trainee Nov 1991/ Everton (£1 M) Jul 1996/ Oxford United(L) Dec 1998/ Ipswich Town(L) Nov 2002
United: (L) 29 Aug 2003 to Nov 2003
Debut: 30 Aug 2003 United 2 Coventry City 1
Last game: 29 Nov 2003 United 2 Preston North End 0
Nottingham Forest Mar 2004 to Aug 2006
United: 19/20 Sep 2006 to cs 2008
Debut: 1 Jan 2007 Middlesbrough 3 United 1
Last game: 13 Jan 2007 United 1 Portsmouth 1
Blackpool (L) 24 Jan 2008

Paul Gerrard made his FL debut with Oldham Athletic on 5 December 1992 at Queens Park Rangers. Having gained his place, he played for the rest of the season, Oldham just avoiding being relegated from the top Division and during his time at Boundary Park he gained 18 U21 England caps. After moving to Everton, he found it difficult to break into the first team and only in seasons 1999–2001 did he play more than 13 games.

He moved to Bramall Lane on loan for three months after Paddy Kenny was injured at Crystal Palace and made an immediate impact, being voted 'Man of the Match' on his debut. During his time with United, he produced a series of competent displays but left when his loan expired. He later moved to Nottingham Forest, signing permanently after a loan spell and was a regular in their 2004–05 campaign.

In September 2006, he returned to train with United after being released by Forest in the summer. He signed a four month contract as cover for Paddy Kenny and Ian Bennett, no loan keepers being allowed in the Premiership, and when Bennett broke a finger and Kenny strained his groin, Paul was called into action despite having had little League action for some time. He was released at the end of the season but then re-signed but having made no appearances by January he was loaned to Blackpool until the end of the season. He wasn't called upon and United released him at the end of the season. He had made 317(3) League appearances.

Appearances:		Apps	Gls
	FL	18	0
	FAC	1	0
	Total	19	0

GETLIFF(E) William Henry

(also 'Catliff', 'Gatliffe', 'Getcliffe')

F 1891–2
b. Shustoke (Warwickshire) 1869
d. Shireoaks (Worksop) 1955

Darnall (Sheffield)
United: Jan 1891 to cs 1892
Debuts: 2 Jan 1891 United 2 Linthouse (Glasgow) 1 (Fr)
17 Jan 1891 United 1 Notts County 9 (FAC)
Last game: 27 Feb 1892 Kilnhurst 0 United 4 (SCC)

'Getliff' (Getliffe in the 1881 census) was the spelling used in general by this amateur player who 'declined professional terms, preferring to carry on teaching.' He played eight games for United, six being friendlies, playing in four forward positions and scoring three goals. He played just one game in the 1891–92 season, being called into action because United played two first team games on the same day.

He was Headmaster of St Lukes School, Shireoaks for thirty one years and also served as President of the Bassetlaw (cricket) League, a game he had played in his earlier years for Owlerton.

Appearances:		Apps	Gls
	FAC	1	0
	SCC	1	0
	Total	2	0

GIBSON John (Jock) Rutherford

RB/LB 1929–33 5' 10½" 12st 2
b. Philadelphia (USA) 23 March 1898
d. Luton July 1974

Netherburn/ Blantyre Celtic/ Sunderland Nov 1920/ Hull City May 1922
United: (£3000) 13/14 Mar 1929 to 6 May 1933
Debut: 16 Mar 1929 Blackburn Rovers 1 United 1
Last games: 11 Feb 1933 United 0 Wolverhampton Wanderers 0
18 Apr 1933 United 2 Sheffield Wednesday 1 (BM)
Luton Town (£250) May 1933 to cs1934/ Vauxhall Motors, Luton Oct 1934

Born in the USA of Scottish parents, John Gibson moved back to Scotland when he was two, living in Lanarkshire though some of his boyhood was spent in Sheffield. He made his FL debut with Sunderland on 20 November 1920 at Everton but then made 210 FL appearances with Hull City before moving to United.

Always immaculate, 'Jock' had a good turn of speed, tackled well, particularly when the wet grounds suited his sliding tackle and he used the off-side law cleverly but there were periods when he was hesitant and lacked confidence, particularly with his left foot.

On leaving football, with 291 FL appearances, he worked as an inspector for Vauxhall Motors in Luton, retiring in 1964.

Appearances:		Apps	Gls
	FL	74	0
	FAC	3	0
	CC	3	0
	Total	80	0

GIBSON Sidney (Sid) George

OR 1928–32 5' 8 11st 11
b. Walgrave (Northants) 20 May 1899
d. West Ham 5 July 1938

Kettering Town/ Nottingham Forest (£500) Oct 1921
United: (£5000) 12/14/15 Sep 1928 to 7 May 1932
Debut: 15 Sep 1928 United 3 Cardiff City 1
Last game: 16 Jan 1932 United 3 Derby County 1
Retired May 1932 / – / Southend United asst mgr, scout Jan 1935 / – /
West Ham Utd chief scout 1937–38

Sid Gibson made his FL debut with Nottingham Forest on 22 October 1921 at West Ham United. He went on to make 252 FL appearances for Forest, being a regular in the side for six seasons and winning a Second Division Championship medal in 1922.

The transfer fee, when he joined United shortly after the start of the 1928–29 campaign, was a record for both clubs. United were hoping that he would replace the ageing David Mercer but it soon became apparent that his best days were perhaps behind him. Sid was a player of undoubted talent; stylish, fast and clever and also a good marksman, though he often passed the ball rather than shooting himself.

With United, he was inconsistent, lacking confidence and appearing hesitant, and soon lost the support of a section of the crowd. He will, however, be remembered in United's history, for a fine display in the 5–1 victory at Old Trafford in May 1930 which saved United from relegation.

A serious knee injury sustained against Derby County in January 1932 and further knee injuries, three weeks later, in a reserve match against Birmingham, forced him to retire at the age of 33, with 358 FL appearances. He received £350 from the League and a similar guaranteed benefit match against the Wednesday in 1933. A fine pianist and church organist, he was only thirty nine when he died.

Appearances:		Apps	Gls
	FL	106	22
	FAC	7	4
	CC	5	3
	Total	118	29

GIJSBRECHTS ('GYSBRECHTS') David (Davy)

CD 1999–2000 6' 1" 13st 8
b. Heusden (Belgium) 20 September 1972

SK Ranst/ Beringen FC/KV Mechelen/ KSC Lokeren cs 1997
United: (£200k) 6 Aug 1999 to 10 Jan 2002
Debuts: 21 Aug 1999 Manchester City 6 United 0 (sub)
21 Sep 1999 Preston North End 3 United 0 (LC)
26 Oct 1999 Wolverhampton Wanderers 1 United 0
Last games: 29 Apr 2000 Norwich City 2 United 1
18 Jul 2000 Tideswell 0 United 8 (Fr)
VK Beringen

With 228 league appearances and one international cap in Belgium to his credit, David 'Gysbrechts' (the spelling used by United) was signed by Adrian Heath as cover for Shaun Murphy and Lee Sandford but never seemed happy with the physical demands of football in England and was also injury prone.

His debut as a substitute was in a 0–6 defeat at Maine Road and his full debut was in the 0–3 reverse at Preston in the League Cup. He subsequently had a run of five games, the last one being Neil Warnock's first match in charge. Thereafter Davy appeared only intermittently and usually as a substitute. After playing in the first pre-season friendly of the 2000–01 season a knee injury kept him sidelined (other than one reserve appearance) for the whole season and he left the club, returning to Belgium, in the autumn of 2001.

Appearances:		Apps	Gls
	FL	9 (8)	0
	FAC	1	0
	LC	1	0
	Total	11 (8)	0

GILHOOLY Patrick (Paddy)

IR 1900–01 5' 7½" 11st 6
b. Blackwood/Draffan (Lanark) 6 July 1876
d. Cleland 20 February 1907

Vale of Avon Juveniles/ Larkhall Thistle/ Cambuslang Hibernian/
Celtic Oct 1896
United: 10 Sep 1900 to 14 Jun 1901
Debut: 29 Sep 1900 United 1 West Bromwich Albion 1
Last game: 13 Apr 1901 Newcastle United 3 United 0
Tottenham Hotspur Jun 1901/ Brighton & Hove Albion May 1904 to 1905

Paddy Gilhooly made his League debut with Celtic on 28 November 1896 at home to Hibernian. He was a regular member of the side and played for the Scottish League against the Football League in 1898. A clever inside forward or winger with a good goal-scoring record, he lacked speed and his early enthusiasm for the game faded.

It was not one of United's most well thought out signings. He came to the Lane in a joint transfer with Tommy Turnbull for a 'hefty sum' which was also reported to be £150. John Nicholson, the United Secretary, said that the figure was incorrect but refused to reveal the true amount. The move south was described as an 'undoubted failure' and, after less than a season with United he signed for Southern League Spurs where his three seasons were spent mainly in the reserves. After less than a season with Brighton, ill health forced his retirement. In January 1907 he went into hospital for a 'serious operation' but, according to one report, was found to be very ill and went home to Cleland where he died at the age of 31.

Appearances:		Apps	Gls
	FL	15	3
	Total	15	3

GILLESPIE Keith Robert

RW 2005– 5' 10" 11st 3
b. Bangor (N Ireland) 18 February 1975

Manchester United from trainee Feb 1993/ Wigan Athletic (L) Sep 1993/
Newcastle United (£l m) Jan 1995/ Blackburn Rovers (£2.25 m) Dec 1998/
Wigan Athletic(L) Dec 2000/ Leicester City Jul 2003/ Leeds United (trial)
United: (free) 5 Aug 2005
Debuts: 2 Aug 2005 Scarborough 3 United XI 2 (Fr)
6 Aug 2005 United 4 Leicester City 1 (sub)
23 Aug 2005 United 1 Boston United 0 (LC)
29 Aug 2005 Crewe Alexandra 1 United 3

Although Keith began his career with Manchester United, he made his League debut whilst on loan at Wigan Athletic on 4 September 1993 at Doncaster Rovers. For most of his career he played in the Premiership but after Leicester City were relegated in 2004, he was released.

Keith had a trial with Leeds United but it came to nothing. Craig Short, a former colleague, recommended him to Neil Warnock and, after a two week trial with United, he was signed on a one year appearance related contract. He was initially used as a substitute and quickly showed his ability to beat the opposition and provide searching crosses, and his commitment so impressed Neil Warnock that Keith was offered a two-year deal in September. Initially, he wasn't an automatic choice and he failed to score during his first season but, on United's return to the Premiership, Keith worked hard, both in a defensive role as well as going forward and secured a regular place. He finally scored his first Blades' goal against his former club, Manchester United and also gained one unenviable record. Having come on as a substitute at Reading he was dismissed after a few seconds before play had been restarted, probably the fastest sending off in history and certainly a record for United.

After being first choice at the start of the 2007–08 season, his performances were disappointing and from January, he was used mainly as a substitute.

A Northern Ireland international with 62 caps before he came to the Lane, his regular international appearances while with United included the first victory against England since 1927 and by the summer of 2008 he had reached 81 caps.

Appearances:		Apps	Gls
	FL	58 (38)	4
	FAC	2 (1)	0
	LC	2 (1)	0
	Total	62 (40)	2

GILLESPIE William (Billy)

IL/IR/CF/OL 1911–31 5' 8½" 10st 8 to 11st 10
b. Kerrykeel (Co.Donegal) 6 August 1891
d. Bexley 2 July 1981

Derry Institute 1906–10/ Linfield Apr 1910/ Leeds City May 1910
United: (£500) 22 Dec 1911 to 17 Jun 1932
Debut: 26 Dec 1911 Newcastle United 2 United 2
Last game: 31 Aug 1931 Blackpool 2 United 0
Derry City manager Jun 1932 to Jun 1940

Billy Gillespie scored two goals for an Irish junior international team at Hampden Park and was given a trial by Linfield against Belfast Celtic. He was about to sign as a professional for Linfield when the Leeds City manager, who had seen the game in Scotland, persuaded Billy and his father, that Leeds would be the better choice. It was there that he made his FL debut on 3 September 1910 at home to Blackpool.

Billy, playing mainly in the reserves with Leeds, was unhappy with his lack of progress and moved to Bramall Lane 17 months later, scoring on his United debut. He was then regarded as a striker and initially played in a variety of forward positions, although mainly inside forward. He gained his first Irish cap in February 1913, scoring both goals in his country's first victory over England and in the following season, he played a key role when Ireland won the home international championship for the first time, scoring against both Wales and England.

The first major setback in his career came when he broke his leg at Sunderland in the first game of the 1914–15 season and he missed the remainder of the season and United's victory over Chelsea in the 'Khaki' FA Cup Final.

He returned from active service as a gunner in the First World War having lost most of his hair and made the inside left spot his own, playing a more constructive, rather than striking role. 'Gilly', as the players called him, had fine ball control, a natural body swerve and, although never fast, he had a deceptively long raking stride which took him away from many an opponent and he had a good goal scoring record, though virtually never with his head. He used his head, he would say, 'to save his legs'.

Billy took over the captaincy in 1923 from the more demonstrative George Utley and led the Blades to the FA Cup semi-final and to the 1925 FA Cup Final triumph and in 1928 to the semi-final again. He was a master strategist and constructive player and his long and short passing were both shrewd and accurate and he was, first and foremost, a team player. Superbly supported from behind by left half George Green, he had in Fred Tunstall and Harry Johnson, the near ideal players to take advantage of his intelligent, measured passes, particularly after the change in the off-side law.

He began coaching the younger players in the 1930–31 season and, after his final first team game, he coached United's new 'A' (third) team until appointed as the manager of Derry City. He returned to Sheffield during the Second World War, working at Hadfields and moved to Bexley in 1948 where he died aged eighty-nine.

He will be remembered as one of United's and Ireland's greatest players. Only Jack Pickering played for United for a longer period and Billy gained 25 caps for Ireland, and on at least eight other occasions he was selected for his country but chose to play for the Blades. His final international appearance in 1930 came nearly eighteen years after his first and his 13 goals for Ireland remained a record until recent years.

Appearances:		Apps	Gls
	FL	448	127
	FAC	44	10
	WW1	56	19
	CC	14	5
	ABD	1	0
	Total	563	161

GILMARTIN L

LB/RB 1889–90
b. Scotland

United: cs 1889 to cs 1890
Debuts: 28 Sep 1889 United 0 Birmingham St George 4 (Fr)
5 Oct 1889 Scarborough 1 United 6 (FAC)
Last games: 1 Feb 1890 Bolton Wanderers 13 United 0 (FAC)
22 Mar 1890 Rotherham Town 1 United 0 (SCCF)

Gilmartin, playing at left back or right back, appeared in 41 games in United's first season, including 26 friendlies. He played in the club's first game at Bramall Lane (his debut) and in the first FA Cup game at Scarborough. He played in the finals of the Sheffield Challenge Cup and the Wharncliffe Charity Cup but was a runner-up on both occasions.

Appearances:		Apps	Gls
	FAC	7	0
	SCC	6	0
	WCC	2	0
	Total	15	0

GIVENS Daniel (Don) Joseph

IR 1981 6' 0" 12st 2
b. Limerick 9 August 1949

Dublin Rangers 1964/ Manchester United from app Dec 1966/ Luton Town Apr 1970/ Queens Park Rangers (£40k) Jul 1972/ Birmingham City (£165k) Aug 1978/ Bournemouth (L) Mar–Apr 1980
United: (£15k) 11 Mar 1981 to 31 Jul 1981
Debut: 14 Mar 1981 United 3 Charlton Athletic 2
Last games: 2 May 1981 United 0 Walsall 1
6 May 1981 United 0 Rotherham United 2 (CC)
Neuchatel Xamax (Switzerland) Jun 1981 to May 1987/ Arsenal youth coach 1997/ Republic of Ireland U21 coach 2000 to Jan 2003 and again from Oct 2007

Don Givens gained 56 Republic of Ireland caps before his brief spell with United. He had made his FL debut as a substitute with Manchester United at Crystal Palace on 9 August 1969 and his full debut came 10 days later at Everton. An intelligent forward with an excellent goal scoring record, he had made 397 FL appearances with his various clubs before he moved to Bramall Lane, signed by Martin Peters on a short term contract to bolster the midfield in an effort to avoid relegation.

He scored on his United debut but he will always be remembered for missing the last minute penalty (his final kick in League football in England) which meant United, not Walsall, were relegated to Division Four. It should not be forgotten however, that John Matthews, the designated penalty taker, declined the vital task and that Don accepted the responsibility.

He moved to Switzerland in the close season following United's relegation where he played, coached and acted as assistant manager, although hip problems curtailed his playing career. On retiring he returned to Ireland before becoming a youth coach with Arsenal and manager of the Irish Republic Under 21 team. He had two brief spells as acting manager of the Republic of Ireland team following Mick McCarthy's resignation and later that of Steve Staunton.

Appearances:		Apps	Gls
	FL	11	3
	CC	1	0
	Total	12	3

GLOVER Dean Victor

MF 1986 5' 10" 11st 13
b. West Bromwich 29 December 1963

Aston Villa from app Dec 1981
United: (L) 17 Oct 1986 to 16 Nov 1986
Debut: 18 Oct 1986 United 0 Huddersfield Town 0
Last game: 15 Nov 1986 United 3 Stoke City 1
Middlesbrough (£50k) Jun 1987/ Port Vale (£200k) Feb 1989/ Kidderminster Harriers Aug 1998 / – / Port Vale coach and asst mgr to 2003 / – / Port Vale asst mgr Mar 2004, caretaker mgr Sep to Nov 2007, asst mgr

Dean Glover began his career with Aston Villa and made his FL debut on 19 January 1985 at Coventry City. In an attempt to strengthen United's midfield, Billy McEwan signed Dean on a one month loan and after five games he returned to Villa.

After a spell with Middlesbrough, Dean moved to Port Vale and served them well, though in his later years, he suffered ankle problems. After retiring from playing, with a career total of nearly 450 FL games, he joined the Vale coaching staff.

He was dismissed as a cost cutting exercise when Vale went into administration but later returned and had a brief, if not too successful, spell as caretaker manager. He was also involved with Stone Dominoes, a football club concentrating on the development of young players.

Appearances:		Apps	Gls
	FL	5	0
	Total	5	0

GOONEY William Harry

RH/LH 1930–35 5' 10½" 10st 8
b. Sheffield 8 October 1910
d. Blackpool 11 June 1978

Grimesthorpe Wesleyans/ Norton Woodseats 1926–27
United: 15 Jun 1925 (cancelled), pro 15 Oct 1927 to 4 May/ 5 Jun 1935
Debut: 8 Sep 1930 Leicester City 2 United 2
Last game: 4 May 1935 Brentford 3 United 1
Plymouth Argyle (£300) Jun 1935/ Luton Town Feb to May 1936

Educated at Newhall CM School and a brilliant player as a youngster, Harry Gooney captained both Sheffield and England Boys but never fully fulfilled his early promise. United registered him as a player as soon as he left school but this had to be cancelled as he was under age. Worried that they might lose him to another club, he was given a job by United as an 'office boy' though he trained with the players. He also played for Grimesthorpe Wesleyans and Norton Woodseats until he was seventeen.

Harry later felt that he was plunged too early into tough and rough local football, particularly as many opponents felt it was their job to literally bring him down to earth. He was never a strong player and his development was also held back by three bouts of pneumonia and he was nearly twenty before this gifted young player made his first team debut. He was capable of fine football but lacking both strength and stamina, particularly on the heavy grounds which were so common in those days, he gave too many indifferent displays. He asked for a transfer in 1933 which wasn't granted and, when appointed as team captain in August 1934, he resigned the position in January.

United finally agreed to release him but there was no happy ending and after leaving Bramall Lane, he played just 18 more FL games. He was injured in his final League appearance with Luton Town at Kenilworth Road; the game ended scoreless but two days later, Luton scored thirteen goals.

There was much disappointment and sadness in the Gooney story. Football gave way to life on the dole before he finally found employment, eventually working for 33 years with the Sheffield Electricity Department.

Appearances:		Apps	Gls
	FL	132	2
	FAC	10	0
	CC	6	0
	Total	148	2

GORDINE Barry

G 1968 5' 9" 10st 10
b. Stepney 1 September 1948

Bexley United 1964/ Gravesend & Northfleet 1966
United: **am Nov 1967 to pro 6/10 Jun 1968 to 21 May 1969**
Debut: **15 May 1968 Doncaster Rovers 1 United 1 (CC)**
Last game: **17 May 1968 Doncaster Rovers 3 United 1 (CC)**
Oldham Athletic (L) 12 Dec 1968, transfer (£3,500) May 1969/ Southend United Aug 1971/ Brentford Oct 1974

Barry had played for London Schools and joined Bexley United whilst in his sixth form. Determined to become a professional, he wrote to every Football League club and was taken on by United, initially on amateur forms, turning professional some six months later. Although spending only a brief time with United, Barry did go on to make 83 appearances with Oldham Athletic, making his FL debut at Watford on 14 December 1968. He returned to the south of England in 1971 but played only reserve team football.

Barry had to retire after being injured while with Brentford. He became involved in the Leisure Centre industry before moving to Reading, firstly as Academy goalkeeping coach and later as reserve and first team coach and Football in the Community manager. He left in 2006 and later moved to Buxton, becoming involved in goalkeeping coaching in the Oldham area.

Appearances:		Apps	Gls
	CC	2	0
	Total	2	0

GORAM Andrew (Andy) Lewis

G 1998 5' 11" 12st 6
b. Bury 13 April 1964

West Bromwich Albion jnr/ Oldham Athletic Aug 1981/ Hibernian (£325k) Oct 1987/ Glasgow Rangers (£1m) Jun 1991/ Notts County Sep 1998
United: **7 Sep 1998 to 3 Nov 1998/12 Jan 1999**
Debut: **8 Sep 1998 United 3 Grimsby Town 2**
Last game: **31 Oct 1998 Port Vale 2 United 3**
Motherwell Jan 1999/ Manchester United (£100k) Mar 2001/ Boreham Wood Jul 2001/ Coventry City Sep 2001 to Feb 2002/ Oldham Athletic Mar 2002/ Queen of the South 2002 / – / Elgin City 2003 / – / Airdrie United goalkeeping coach Mar 2006/ Clyde goalkeeping coach Feb 2007

Although he started his football career with West Bromwich Albion, Andy Goram made his FL debut with Oldham Athletic at home to Charlton Athletic on 4 May 1982. After nearly 200 FL games with the Latics, he moved to Scotland, returning South after eleven years.

His move to Bramall Lane came soon after his final game for Scotland and was as cover for the injured Simon Tracey and Alan Kelly but he moved on when they were fit again.

He made two Premiership appearances with Manchester United and then he moved to Coventry City, after trials with Hamilton Academicals and Blackpool. On leaving Oldham Athletic for the second time, after nearly 600 career League games and more then 750 games in total, both North and South of the border, he joined Motherwell as goalkeeping coach.

Not only was he a fine goalkeeper in his prime, winning 43 Scottish caps, he also represented Scotland at cricket and played as a wicket keeper/batsman for various Lancashire clubs. As well as coaching, Andy is an after dinner speaker.

Appearances:		Apps	Gls
	FL	7	0
	LC	2	0
	Total	9	0

GOUGH Harold C

G 1913–24 5' 10½" 12st 6 to 13st 3
b. Newbold (Chesterfield) 31 December 1890
d. Castleford AMJ 1970

Spital Olympic/ Bradford Park Avenue Mar 1910/ Castleford Town Aug 1911
United: **(£40) 30 Apr 1913/ 7 Aug 1913 to Jan 1925 but retained until 3 or 4 Jan 1927**
Debut: **1 Sep 1913 United 1 Tottenham Hotspur 4**
Last games: **3 May 1924 West Bromwich Albion 3 United 1**
10 May 1924 Wednesday 0 United 2 (CC)
WW1 Guest with Leeds City, Hibernian
Castleford Town Jan 1925/ Harrogate Town Oct 1926/ Oldham Athletic Feb (£500) Jan 1927/ Bolton Wanderers (£25) Dec 1927/ Torquay United Jun 1928 to cs1930

Harold Gough made his FL debut with Bradford Park Avenue on 11 February 1911 at home to Bolton Wanderers but after just three FL appearances he joined Midland League side Castleford Town. Two years later, after a fine display against United Reserves, he moved to Bramall Lane.

Gough stepped straight into the first team when Ted Hufton, later to play for West Ham United and England, broke his nose in the pre-season practice match. Harold was an immediate success—in spite of the score on his debut—and appeared in the 1914 Cup semi-final and in 1915 gained an FA Cup Winners' medal when United defeated Chelsea.

He was described as 'brilliant and stable', allowing nothing to worry him. An expert at coming out to meet an onrushing forward, he was agile, physically strong, punching with power and able to kick the ball over the halfway line with either foot. During the First War he worked at Fryston Colliery and later served in the navy. He gained one England cap, against Scotland, in 1920 but suffered a bruised hand and wasn't at his best and he also toured South Africa with the FA in 1920.

In the summer of 1924, he took over the Railway Hotel in Castleford which was against the terms of his contract, although he claimed he was unaware of this. Perhaps he had never read the standard United contracts but they did clearly state that he must 'not engage in any business which the Directors might deem unsuitable'. In effect this meant the player should not run licensed premises. United, rather than putting him on the transfer list, referred the matter to the FA who cancelled his player registration. It was restored in January 1925, but living in Castleford with a high transfer fee of £2400 on his head, he could only play non-League football and while Harold was playing for Castleford, his successor at Bramall Lane, Charles Sutcliffe, won an FA Cup Winners' medal in the 1925 Final.

The transfer fee was reduced to £1150 in November 1925 and eventually to £500 but he didn't return to League football until 1927 when he joined Oldham Athletic and then Bolton Wanderers. After two final seasons with Torquay United, injury brought his playing days to an end and he returned to Castleford having made 309 FL appearances.

Appearances:		Apps	Gls
	FL	242	0
	FAC	19	0
	WW1	70	0
	CC	4	0
	Total	335	0

GOULD Walter (Wally)

OL 1958–59 5' 7½" 10st 12
b. Thrybergh (Rotherham) 25 September 1938

Rotherham United jnr/ Rawmarsh Welfare
United: (£500) 27/28 Mar 1958 to 16/18 Feb 1961
Debut: 13 Sep 1958 United 0 Huddersfield Town 0
Last games: 30 Apr 1959 Ipswich Town 1 United 0
4 May 1959 Wednesday 1 United 4 (CC)
York City £2000) Feb 1961/ Brighton & Hove Albion (£4000) Jan 1964/ Durban United (SA) Feb 1968/ Hellenic (Cape Town, SA) 1969 player, asst player-mgr/East London Utd (SA) 1974 player-mgr / – / Chelmsford 1975–77/ Stoke City 1977–1983 coaching staff

Strong and direct, two footed and reasonably quick, Wally Gould scored in the first minute of his debut for United Reserves. Signed by Joe Mercer, he had stiff competition for the outside left position held by Bill Hodgson and Ronnie Simpson and was transferred to York City by John Harris.

He was more successful with York and Brighton, making over 300 League and Cup appearances and later played and coached in South Africa, lining up with the former England players, George Eastham and Johnny Byrne. He returned to England and played with Chelmsford while becoming a licensee but shortly afterwards, he joined Stoke City as a coach under George Eastham, Alan Durban and Richie Barker. He became a painter and decorator and now lives in Spain.

Appearances:		Apps	Gls
	FL	5	1
	CC	1	0
	Total	6	1

GOULDING Stephen (Steve)

RB/LB 1971–77 5' 8" 10st 9
b. Mexborough 21 January 1954
d. March 1985

United: from 7/11 Apr 1969 (sch), app 12 May 1971, pro May 1974 to 7 May 1977
Debut: 13 Nov 1971 United 2 Coventry City 0
Last games: 4 May 1976 United 1 Birmingham City 1
24 Jan 1977 Newcastle United 3 United 1 (FAC)

A product of Conisborough Northcliffe School, Steve Goulding was one of a large number of boys brought to the Lane from the Don & Dearne Schoolboys team though it had been expected that he would sign for the Wednesday. A forward as a boy, United tried him out as a mid-fielder before he settled on the full back position and he had a good run in the first team at the beginning of the 1972–73 season under John Harris.

Steve was quick and a good tackler but not good enough for the First Division in the eyes of manager Ken Furphy who had succeeded Harris and the player spent most of his time at the Lane in the reserves. Called into first team action for a Cup-tie at Newcastle in 1977, he suffered a knee injury and was given a free transfer at the end of the season. Sadly, he took his own life a few years later.

Appearances:		Apps	Gls
	FL	28	0
	FAC	1	0
	LC	6	0
	TEX	5	0
	ASC	2	0
	CC	4	0
	WC	2	0
	Total	48	0

GRAHAM Frederick Todd

IR 1937
b. Tynemouth 24 March 1912
d. Whitley Bay 31 July 1973

Wolverhampton Wanderers
United: 5/6 Feb 1937 to 1 May 1937
Debut: 29 Mar 1937 Leicester City 1 United 2
Last game: 3 Apr 1937 Coventry City 2 United 0

Although he began his career with Wolverhampton Wanderers, Fred Graham did not make any League or FA Cup appearances for the club. His move to Bramall Lane was a brief success when he scored on his United debut, but he was given a free transfer at the end of the season and his two games and one goal for the Blades were the sum total of his FL career.

Appearances:		Apps	Gls
	FL	2	1
	Total	2	1

GRAINGER Colin

OL 1953–57 5' 9" 10st 8
b. Havercroft, nr Wakefield 10 June 1933

South Elmsall/ Wrexham 1949, to pro Oct 1950
United: (£2500) 26 Jun 1953/14 Jul 1953 to 5/8 Feb 1957
Debut: 14 Nov 1953 United 1 Charlton Athletic 1
Last game: 2 Feb 1957 United 0 Blackburn Rovers 2
Sunderland (c£17k) Feb 1957/ Leeds United (£13.5k) Jul 1960/ Port Vale (£6000) Oct 1961/ Doncaster Rovers Aug 1964/ Macclesfield Town cs 1966 to Oct 1966

Colin Grainger had worked as a car mechanic and engineer before joining the Wrexham ground staff, prompted by his cousin Dennis who also played for the Welsh club. He made his FL debut on 24 February 1951 at home to Hartlepool United but due to his National Service in the South

of England, he had made only five FL appearances when he was signed for United by Reg Freeman, who had managed Colin's brother Jack at Millmoor.

Although extremely quick, Colin made only three appearances in his first season and he gave little indication of what was to come. At the start of his second season, now fitter, stronger and benefiting from extra training and practice in the afternoons, he was given an extended run in the side. At the end of that season, manager Reg Freeman died and Joe Mercer took over and under his guidance, Colin improved and, despite United's relegation to the Second Division, he gained the first of his England caps in 1956, scoring twice against Brazil. Colin went on to win five more caps with United and one more after his move to Sunderland and he also represented the Football League on three occasions.

His time with United was probably when he was at his best although he also did well with Sunderland. He was tremendously fast with good ball control, passing the opposing full backs on either side and his centres were quick and accurate. He was also a good shot, dangerous when cutting inside and scored many fine goals with his head, adept at meeting balls from the opposite wing. Inevitably with such a quick player, he suffered several injuries including a serious one when playing for England against Wales. This perhaps affected his confidence but memories of this fine player moving at speed with remarkable balance will linger long in the memories of those who were privileged to see him at his peak.

He was transferred to Sunderland by Joe Mercer for £16k, with Sammy Kemp moving to the Lane as part of the deal, and he eventually played 325 FL games, scoring 54 goals. Colin also worked with great success as a professional singer, particularly in the clubs in the North of England. When his playing career was over, he was also employed as a regional manager for a cash register company and later worked for a wine and spirits company and acted as a scout for Neil Warnock.

Appearances:		Apps	Gls
	FL	88	26
	FAC	7	1
	CC	3	0
	Total	98	27

GRAINGER Dennis

OR 1945 5' 7" 11st 0
b. Royston (Barnsley) 5 March 1920
d. Duckmanton, nr Chesterfield 6 June 1986

Frickley C/ South Kirby/ Southport Oct 1938
United: WW2 guest
Only game: 19 May 1945 United 1 Sheffield Wednesday 3 (CC)
WW2 guest: Doncaster Rovers, Millwall, Walsall, Rotherham United, Lincoln City
Leeds United (c£1000) 29 Sep 1945/ Wrexham Dec 1947/ Oldham Athletic Jun 1951/ Bangor City Aug 1952/ Flint Town Aug 1953

Dennis Grainger was one of those players who made his FL debut in a game that 'never was', playing for Southport in the opening game of the 1939–40 season at Darlington on the 26 August. Because of the outbreak of the Second War, League football was abandoned and the few games played are not usually included in official statistics.

Dennis, a cousin of Colin Grainger, played once as a guest for United soon after the war in Europe had ended and scored.

After the War he moved to Leeds United where he made a second FL debut on the opening day of the 1946–47 season at Preston North End on the 31 August. Despite losing seven years of his career to the War, he went on to make 138 FL appearances and later was a licensee at Duckmanton, near Chesterfield.

Appearances:		Apps	Gls
	CC	1	1
	Total	1	1

GRANT Edward(Eddie) Anthony

RH 1951 6' 0" 13st 6
b. Greenock 1 October 1928

Hibernian/ Weymouth
United: 11/16 May 1950 to Jan 1952
Debut: 18 Apr 1951 Barnsley 1 United 1
Last game: 5 May 1951 Doncaster Rovers 1 United 1
Kilmarnock(trial) Feb 1952/ Grimsby Town Jul 1952/ Corby Town cs 1954/ cs 1955 Wisbech/ Kings Lynn cs 1956

Eddie Grant made his four appearances in the final games of the 1950–51 season. A thoughtful player, who passed the ball well, he lacked pace and fire. He made the decision in the autumn of 1951 to return to Scotland and run his late father's business and United gave him a free transfer although they may have been surprised when he soon returned to football in England.

Appearances:		Apps	Gls
	FL	4	0
	Total	4	0

GRATTON Dennis

CH 1952–59 5' 9" 10st 12 to 11st 7
b. Bramley (Rotherham) 21 April 1934

Thurcroft/ Worksop Town cs 1951
United: 5 Aug/1 Oct 1952 to 12/28 Sep 1959
Debuts: 14 Dec 1955 Royal Signals 1 United 7 (Fr)
27 Dec 1955 Luton Town 2 United 1
Last game: 11 Apr 1959 Stoke City 1 United 2
Lincoln City (c£5000) Sep 1959/ Boston United Aug to Nov 1961/ Worksop Town cs 1962

Dennis Gratton came to the Lane on an eight week trial before becoming a part time player with United. His seven seasons at the Lane were spent mainly in the reserves, being second choice to Howard Johnson and then Joe Shaw. His lack of height and power were disadvantages but he was reliable and a good tackler. He asked for a transfer in 1958 and left a year later and had two successful seasons with Lincoln City, making 45 FL appearances. After retiring from the professional game he worked as a miner.

Appearances:		Apps	Gls
	FL	6	0
	CC	2	0
	Total	8	0

GRAY Andrew (Andy) David

Striker 2004–05 6' 1" 13st 0
b. Harrogate 15 November 1977

Leeds United from trainee Jul 1995/ Bury(L) Dec 1997/ Nottingham Forest (£175k) Sep 1998/ Preston NE(L) Feb 1999/ Oldham Athletic(L) Mar 1999/ Bradford City Aug 2002
United: (nominal) 27 Feb 2004 to 10 Aug 2005
Debut: 28 Feb 2004 Reading 2 United 1
Last game: 6 Aug 2005 United 4 Leicester City 1
Sunderland (£750k/£1m) Aug 2005/ Burnley(L) Mar 2006, (£750k+£100k to United) Jun 2006/ Charlton Ath (L) Jan 2008, signed Jan 2008

Andy Gray, son of former Leeds player Frank, made his League debut with Leeds United, as a substitute, on 13 January 1996 at home to West Ham United; his full debut coming at Queens Park Rangers on 6 March. After three loan spells and two other clubs he moved to Bramall Lane in February 2004 from Bradford City, a club in financial difficulties at the time, for what was reported to be a nominal fee.

Signed by Neil Warnock, Andy scored seven goals in fourteen games for United and managed a total of 47 FL games in total that season (33 for City and 14 for United).

A hard working and committed player, he missed few games in 2004–5, playing as a lone striker for much of the season, a role which many felt was not the best use of his talents. He finished as top scorer with 15 goals, a testimony to his efficiency in converting chances, and he was an excellent penalty taker. Having gained two Scottish Caps before moving to Bramall Lane he was called into the squad whilst with United but did not play.

After just one appearance in August 2005 he was sold to Sunderland, giving him the opportunity to play in the Premiership. He had scored in his first three and last two League games for the Blades and recorded the strange achievement of scoring on the first day of the new season for both United and Sunderland. The move to the North East was a dismal failure but his goal scoring touch returned when he moved to Burnley.

He ended 2007–08, after moving to Charlton, with 78 goals in 284(58) League games.

Appearances:		Apps	Gls
	FL	56 (2)	25
	FAC	5	1
	LC	2	2
	Total	63 (2)	28

GREEN George Henry

LH/LB/RB 1923–34 5' 9½" 11st 5 to 12st 0
b. Leamington Spa 2 May 1901
d. Kineton 1 March 1980

Leamington St Johns/ Leamington Imperial/ Leamington Town/ Nuneaton Borough Aug 1921
United: (£300 +£100) Apr or 2/4 May 1923 to 5 May 1934
Debut: 25 Aug 1923 Manchester City 2 United 1
Last game: 29 Jan 1934 United 2 Sunderland 0
Leamington Town Jul 1934 (player-mgr) to 1937

George Green worked as a turner and fitter and was playing for Nuneaton Borough when he was signed by United's John Nicholson, a transfer later described as 'secured under rather peculiar circumstances' which probably involved a woman, though no complete explanation was ever given. Signed as a right half, George was asked to play left half in a pre-season practice match and immediately struck up an understanding with the left wing pairing of Tunstall and Gillespie. It was as at left half that George played the vast majority of his games for United including his debut, which coincided with the opening of Manchester City's Maine Road ground.

George was a regular member of the United side for nine seasons, playing in the FA Cup winning side of 1925 and winning eight England caps, the first in 1926. He was a strong and determined player, a fine tackler and a crisp and accurate passer of the ball and had the knack of 'appearing to do the obvious' but, with great skill and speed, he would lose his opponent and move another way. Above all, he was calm, consistent and reliable, playing with courage and determination, an example being the 5–7 home defeat by Blackburn Rovers when a dislocated shoulder was put back without anaesthetic, George returning and finishing the game.

In the 1930s, Green often played at full-back and he took over the captaincy in 1931 and it was a sad coincidence that United were relegated, for the first time, at the end of his final season.

He became the player manager of Leamington and later became a publican. He was a great sporting all-rounder and a competent violinist, which led to his nickname of 'Fiddler' among the other players.

Appearances:		Apps	Gls
	FL	393	10
	FAC	29	0
	CC	15	0
	ABD	1	0
	Total	438	10

GREEN Harold (Harry)

LH 1926–27 5' 11" 12st 0
b. Sedgley (Staffordshire) 3 August 1904
d. Wolverhampton OND 1975

Coseley Amateurs/ Redditch United
United: (£150) 6 Mar 1925 to 31 May 1927
Debut: 17 Apr 1926 Bolton Wanderers 2 United 1
Last game: 4 May 1927 Bradford Park Avenue 4 United 1 (Fr)
Nottingham Forest (£100) 27 Aug 1927/ Halifax Town Aug 1928/ Hereford United Aug 1929/ Kidderminster Harriers Jul 1930

Although he played for three League clubs, Harry Green made a total of only six FL appearances.

Appearances:		Apps	Gls
	FL	1	0
	Total	1	0

GREENSILL Edwin

IF 1901–02
b. Rotherham JAS 1877

Swallownest Rovers Jun 1896/ Swallownest Bible Class Sep 1896/ Ulley Church Aug 1898/ Royston Utd Sep 1899
United: 3 May 1900 to 20 Nov (?) 1902
Debut: 12 Oct 1901 United 0 Sunderland 1
Last games: 7 Apr 1902 United 2 Bolton Wanderers 0
29 Sep 1902 Kettering Town 2 United 1 (Fr)
Gainsborough Trinity Nov or Dec 1902/ Thornhill United Jul 1904/ Aughton Jun 1905

Edwin Greensill scored in both his final League game and in his final appearance (a friendly) for United and made 34 FL appearances for Gainsborough Trinity before returning to play in his home town with Thornhill United.

Appearances:		Apps	Gls
	FL	4	1
	Total	4	1

GREENWOOD Wilson

OL 1895 5' 6" 11st 0
b. Halifax JAS 1871
d. Padiham JFM 1943

Blue Star (Burnley)/ Brierfield/ Accrington
United: 25 Jan 1895 to 8 Jun 1895
Debut: 9 Feb 1895 United 3 Stoke 0
Last game: 25 Mar 1895 United 3 Leicester Fosse 2 (UCL)
Rossendale 1895/ Nelson Feb 1896/ Rochdale Jun 1896/ Warmley Nov 1897/ Grimsby Town May 1898/ Newton Heath Oct 1900–01

Wilson Greenwood had joined Accrington soon after they had resigned from the Football League and he only made one FL appearance for United. He returned to north-east Lancashire but United retained his FL registration and, three years later, transferred him and Tom Jenkinson to Grimsby Town for the princely sum of £10. He spent two successful seasons with Grimsby Town scoring 13 goals in 36 League and Cup games during his first season. His move to Newton Heath, where he made just three appearances, was not a success.

Appearances:		Apps	Gls
	FL	1	0
	UCL	1	0
	Total	2	0

GROVES George Jasper

LH/RH/various 1889–95 'small' 9st 7
b. Nottingham 19 October 1868
d. Newmarket 18 February 1941

Heeley (1888)/ Sheffield Club (by Nov 1888–91) / Wednesday/ Bolton W
United: Amateur. Guest Nov 1889 to 1891, signed by Mar 1891 to cs1896. League registration 19 Dec 1892 to cs 1893, 1894–95, 1895–96 and 1902–03
Debuts: 5 Nov 1889 United 0 Preston North End 2 (Fr)
18 Oct 1890 Lincoln City 2 United 1 (MCL)
15 Nov 1890 United 3 Matlock 0 (FAC)
Last game: 19 Oct 1895 Wolverhampton Wanderers 4 United 1
Woolwich Arsenal, Vampires and other London amateur clubs

'Mr Groves', as he was usually referred to in the press, was a Sheffield Club amateur player in the late 1880s. He may also have played for Heeley and occasionally for the Wednesday. In United's first season, he played in the friendly fixtures against Preston and Everton but began to play regularly in the second season, when he played in 38 games. He resigned from the Sheffield Club early in 1891 and was then regarded by the local Association as a United player.

Described as a small, very active player, who never flinched, and a good tackler, he had usually captained United and was a member of the Committee (1891–92). His work as a journalist, which included cricket and horse racing, frequently took him away from Sheffield and one can only guess at the number of clubs he may have played for. He assisted Gainsborough Trinity (Christmas 1891) and Bolton Wanderers held his Football League registration until it was transferred to United (19 Dec 1892) though he didn't play FL or FAC matches for them. He thus became the first United player to be transferred from another League club.

He moved to London in late 1891or 1892 and assisted Woolwich Arsenal and several amateur clubs and he made only occasional appearances in United's colours. The professional game, in any case, had changed and there were few opportunities for an amateur and so, it was remarkable that George's final first team appearance for United turned out to be his FL debut in 1895.

In total, he made 59 first team appearances for United, the majority during the 1890–91 season.

Appearances:		Apps	Gls
	FL	1	0
	FAC	3	0
	NL	1	0
	MCL	10	0
	SCC	4	0
	WCC	1	0
	Total	20	0

GROVES James Albert

RB 1903–06 5' 8½" 10st 8
b. South Bank July 1883

Grangetown/ South Bank/ Lincoln City Jun 1903
United: (more than £300) 13 Apr 1904 to Aug 1907
Debut: 16 Apr 1904 United 1 Sunderland 2
Last game: 1 Dec 1906 Preston North End 2 United 1
Middlesbrough Aug 1907 to cs1910 / – / Wingate Albion 1912

Albert Groves made his FL debut with Lincoln City at home to Grimsby Town on 5 September 1903. He moved to United just before the end of that season and in February 1905 he played in an international North v South trial match but failed to win a full cap. He had a 'good turn of speed' and could use the ball well if a short pass was required but generally tended to balloon the ball and was lacking in physique. On moving to Middlesbrough, he found his chances limited and played only intermittently.

Appearances:

	Apps	Gls
FL	62	0
FAC	3	0
Total	65	0

GUTHRIE Christopher (Chris) William

CF 1975–77 6' 1" 13st 5 to 13st 10
b. Hexham 7 September 1953

Newcastle United from app Dec 1970/ Southend United (£10k) Nov 1972
United: (£87,222) 2/6 May 1975 to 26 Jul 1977
Debuts: 24 May 1975 Al Shabab(Kuwait) 1 United 2 (Fr)
2 Aug 1975 United 3 Blackburn Rovers 1 (ASC)
16 Aug 1975 United 1 Derby County 1
Last games: 5 Mar 1977 Blackburn Rovers 1 United 0
19 May 1977 United 0 Rotherham 1 (CC)
Swindon Town (£22k) Jul 1977/ Fulham (£65k) Sep 1978/ Millwall (£100k) Feb 1980–retired Mar 1982//Roda JC, Holland 1982/ Willem II, Holland 1982/ Witney player manager Jul 1982/ Helmond Sport(Holland) 1983/ Seiko, Hong Kong Feb 1984/ Blyth Spartans Apr 1985/ Racing White, Holland Sep 1985/ Ashington commercial manager/ Newcastle United kit-mgr 1989–Oct 1993

Chris Guthrie, an England schoolboy international, made his FL debut with Newcastle United at home to Manchester United on 23 October 1971, shortly after his eighteenth birthday. After just three appearances for Newcastle he moved to Southend United and, in his three seasons there, he scored 35 goals in 108 FL appearances.

He moved to Bramall Lane at the end of the 1974–75 season. United had finished sixth in the old First Division and Chris was brought in by Ken Furphy to add weight and height to the attack and, in particular, to take advantage of the clinical passing of Currie and Woodward's superb centres. Sadly for United, Chris was not a natural finisher and rarely found space near goal; the season went from bad to worse and United were relegated, though Chris did finish second top scorer with nine goals. He was capable of an occasional fine header and he scored with three in a League Cup-tie at Halifax but it was said that he preferred fishing to football.

Towards the end of the following season, Chris, who had lost his place to the young Keith Edwards, was transferred to Swindon Town. He remained in football in England and abroad and returned to Newcastle United as kit-man but was perhaps happiest as an international fly fisherman.

Appearances:

	Apps	Gls
FL	58 (2)	15
FAC	2	0
LC	3	3
CC	8	5
ASC	6	0
Total	77 (2)	23

GUY Michael (Mike) James

OR/IR/CF 1978–79 5' 9" 11st 2
b. Limavady 4 February 1953

Sligo Rovers/ Coleraine
United: (£15k) 3 Mar 1978 to 20 Sep 1979
Debuts: 14 Mar 1978 United 1 Stoke City 2 (sub)
10 Apr 1978 Worksop Town XI 0 United 0 (Fr)
8 Aug 1978 Bolton Wanderers 1 United 0 (ASC)
16 Sep 1978 United 4 Burnley 0
Last games: 8 May 1979 United 2 Leicester City 2
31 Jul 1979 United 1 Mansfield Town 0 (ASC)
Crewe Alexandra Sep 1979 to cs1981/ Ballymena United

Mike Guy was Harry Haslam's first signing after a trial which included three appearances in the reserve team. Mal Donaghy, a future international, also played in the first of these which resulted in a ten nil defeat but it was Mike who was signed. Playing mainly down the right flank, he scored on his full United League debut but played only intermittently in his eighteen months at Bramall Lane. In his two seasons with Crewe he topped 50 FL appearances but then returned to Ireland.

Appearances:

	Apps	Gls
FL	12 (6)	2
FAC	1	0
ASC	2 (1)	0
CC	1	1
Total	16 (7)	3

GYSBRECHTS (see GIJSBRECHTS)

HAGAN James (Jimmy)

IL/IR/OR 1938–57, 1965, 1967 5' 9" 10st 10 to 11st 2
b. Washington (Co Durham) 21 January 1918
d. Sheffield 27 February 1998

Washington Colliery/ Unsworth Colliery/ Liverpool, amateur Dec 1932/ Derby County amateur May 1933, pro Jan 1935/
United: (£2925) 3/4 Nov 1938 to 30 Jun 1958
Debut: 5 Nov 1938 Swansea Town 1 United 2
Last games: 14 Sep 1957 Derby County 2 United 0
29 Mar 1965 United 5 All Star XI 6 (Joe Shaw BM)
26 Apr 1967 United 3 Sheffield Wednesday 2 (Graham Shaw BM)
WW2 guest: Aldershot, Huddersfield T (1939–40), Shrewsbury Town (1 appearance 1945–46)
Blackpool (guest 1958 cs overseas tour)/ Peterborough United, manager, Aug 1958 to Oct 1962/ West Bromwich Albion, manager, Apr 1963 to May 1967/ Man C scout/ Benfica, coach, Mar 1970 to Sep 1973/ Kuwait coaching 1973 to1975/ Sporting Lisbon, coach 1976/ Oporto, coach 1976/ Boavista, coach

The son of a former professional footballer Alf Hagan, Jimmy, a schoolboy international, joined Liverpool when he was fourteen, but the Football League ruled that he was too young to be on their ground staff and he returned home to the North East. A few months later, rules ignored, he joined Derby County where he made his FL debut at home to Everton on 28 December 1935, shortly before his eighteenth birthday. Derby frequently fielded an all international forward line but Jimmy was still able to make 30 FL appearances in the following three years.

Signed by Teddy Davison in November 1938, he was immediately influential in United's promotion that season and scored a hat trick in the vital final game. During the Second War Jimmy was an army physical training instructor adding weight and strength to his brilliant ball skills and, as a consequence, he became a regular in the superb wartime England team, making 16 appearances.

He returned to Bramall Lane in 1946 but the insecurity of professional football led him to refuse United's terms and, for a time, he became a part time player, training in the evening. In 1948 he gained his one England cap against Denmark and was a member of FA touring teams to Canada and Australia. He also gained an England B cap and represented the Football League but was otherwise ignored by the English selectors despite almost perpetual arguments in his favour in the press. Jimmy captained the Blades for three seasons but relinquished this position after relegation in 1949 only taking the post again for a short period in 1951 and he was a key member of the 1952–53 Second Division championship side. In February 1951, neighbours Wednesday offered a then record fee of £32,500 for Jimmy but, ever his own man, he refused to move, stating he would finish his career with United.

There can be no doubt that 'Sir James' was one of the greatest players, if not the greatest, to play for the Blades and he was consistent both in the supreme quality of his play and in the fact that he missed very few games. New opponents were surprised by his strength on the ball and although not the fastest of players, his speed of thought was super-fast, occasionally it has to be added, too demanding for his colleagues. He had perfect ball control, was two footed and able to shoot with power with either foot, scoring an average of one goal every three games. He had a trick for every occasion and was very difficult to dispossess. He could head the ball, but it was not a major part of his game. He took few penalties, missing as many as he scored and, although capable of superb free kicks over a wall of players, he usually left it to others as if to say 'enough is enough'.

For twenty years his wonderful skills and genius delighted United's supporters, never more so than his ability to collect a high ball with an outstretched foot, as though he had a claw on the end of his boot and instantly wheel away in one sweet movement, in perfect control of the ball. Jimmy could be stubborn and idiosyncratic and Reg Freeman, one of Jimmy's managers at the Lane, said of him, that at teams talks he would agree politely and then ignore it all on Saturday and some of his colleagues at times would wish for a more straightforward and predictable partner.

The quality of his play remained high to the end and in April 1957, when he was thirty nine, Jimmy destroyed a Liverpool team desperate for points for promotion. After retiring, he moved into management and in his first post he guided Peterborough United into the Football League. He then managed West Bromwich Albion where he fell out with some of the players over training in cold weather. He managed Benfica and Sporting Lisbon in Portugal and, when his statue was unveiled at Bramall Lane, the famous Portuguese star, Eusebio, was present to pay tribute to a great football man.

Appearances:		Apps	Gls
	FL	361	117
	FAC	28	5
	CC	15	11
	39–40	3	1
	WW2	35	17
	Total	442	151

HAIDONG Hao

Striker 1999, 2006 5' 10" 11st 0
b. Qingdao, China 9 May 1970

Bayi (army team/ Dalian Shide 1997
United: 23 Dec 2004 to cs 2007
Debuts: (trial) 7 Dec 1999 Whitby Town 1 United 3 (Fr)
17 Jul 2005 Zhejiang Greentown 0 United 3 (Fr)
Last game: 7 Jan 2006 United 1 Colchester United 2 (sub FAC)

Haidong's first appearance for the Blades was in December 1999 as a trialist in a hastily arranged friendly with Whitby Town, immediately after Neil Warnock's arrival as manager. He scored and, a year later, he returned for a second trial. Hao was regarded as being one of the best strikers in the Jia A but also one of the most controversial figures in Chinese soccer. He helped Dalian Shide to their Championship titles in 1997 and 1998 but, spitting at a referee resulting in a year's ban, a broken arm and a public slanging match with the Chinese coach, meant he missed many club and international games. More goals for Dalian in 2001 earned him a recall to the national side for China's second round of World Cup qualifying matches, during which he helped the side qualify for Korea/Japan 2002. Overall, he made 115 appearances for China.

He joined United for a nominal fee of £1, his role being to play but also to coach at United's Academy and to be a high profile figure in helping United become involved in China. His signing was delayed because of a court case in China and when he arrived he was not match fit and then developed ankle problems. He eventually played in the first team during the Club's 2005 pre-season tour of China where he attracted much attention. His injury problems persisted but he finally played in a competitive game in January 2006 when curious supporters had a brief glimpse of his undoubted skill but, disappointingly, he returned to China.

Appearances:		Apps	Gls
	FAC	0 (1)	0
	Total	0 (1)	0

HALL Ellis

CH 1915 5' 9½" 12st 7
b. Ecclesfield 22 June 1889
d. Loughborough OND 1949

Ecclesfield/ Hull City Jan 1906/ Millwall Athletic?/ Hastings & St Leonards/ Mexborough? Feb 1908/ Stoke May 1908/ Huddersfield Town May 1910/ South Shields Jun 1912
United: WW1 guest
Only game: 4 Sep 1915 Lincoln City 7 United 3 (WW1)
WW1 guest: Derby County/ Grimsby Town/ Goole Town/ Huddersfield Town
Hamilton Academicals Jun 1919/ Millwall trial Jun 1922/ Halifax Town Aug 1922/ Rochdale Nov 1925/ Consett Jul 1927

A war time guest player for United, Ellis Hall had made his FL debut for Hull City at Blackpool on 14 March 1906 when only 16 years old. In a career that spanned over twenty years, he made over 100 appearances, as a centre half, for both Hamilton Academicals and then Halifax Town. His brothers Ben, Fred and Harry were also professional footballers.

Appearances:		Apps	Gls
	WW1	1	0
	Total	1	0

HALL George (Noggs) William E

LH/RH 1932–35 5' 9" 10st 10 to 11st
b. Worksop 5 September 1912
d. Mansfield February 1989

Worksop Town/ Bradford City (trial)
United: 11/12 Apr 1932 to 4 May 1935
Debut: 8 Oct 1932 United 3 Newcastle United 1
Last games: 23 Mar 1935 Newcastle United 4 United 1
1 May 1935 Chesterfield 1 United 2 (BM)
Coventry City Jun 1935/ Newport County May 1936/ Bristol City May 1937 to cs 1939/ Scarborough cs1939/ (WW2 guest player Lincoln City)
Scarborough player mgr Aug 1946/ coach in Holland Aug 1947/ Scarborough trainer

George Hall made a good impression when he was given a first team opportunity with United. He was described as a player 'who never knows when he is beaten' and 'playing like a veteran'. He was a near ever present from October 1932 to March 1933 but, having lost his place to veteran George Green and then Harry Gooney, he made only four more appearances before United released him in 1935. He played in just one minor cup-tie with Coventry but made 41 more FL appearances with his other clubs.

Appearances:		Apps	Gls
	FL	22	0
	CC	1	0
	Total	23	0

HALL Harry

CF 1914–15 5' 8½" 11st 7
b. Newark OND 1893

Gainsborough Trinity/ Newark/ Long Eaton Rangers/ Long Eaton St Helens
United: (£65) 26/29 Apr 1913 to Sep 1915
Debut: 14 Mar 1914 Chelsea 2 United 0
Last game: 4 Sep 1915 Lincoln City 7 United 3 (WW1)
WW1 guest: Nottingham Forest ?(Oct 1917)
Long Eaton cs 1919/ Worksop Town/ Ilkeston United Oct 1920/ Sheffield Wednesday (£300) Dec 1920 to Feb 1922/ Lincoln City/ Gainsborough Trinity/ Newark Town Aug 1922/ Long Eaton St Helens/ Grantham Town Feb 1924/ Ransome & Marles Aug 1927

Harry Hall's peace time appearances all came towards the end of the 1913–14 season and included the FA Cup semi-final replay against Burnley but he never played for the first team again apart from the first match of the war time 1915–16 season when he played at right half.

A well built player, he became one of the few players to play for both Sheffield's senior clubs when he joined the Wednesday in 1920 but though he made 31 FL and Cup appearances, he scored only a single goal.

Appearances:		Apps	Gls
	FL	5	0
	FAC	1	0
	WW1	1	0
	Total	7	0

HALL Paul Anthony

Striker 1999–2000 5' 8½" 10st 4
b. Manchester 3 July 1972

Torquay United from trainee Jul 1990/ Portsmouth (£70k) Mar 1993/ Coventry City (£300k) Aug 1998/ Bury (L) Feb 1999
United: (L) 17/18 Dec 1999 to 18 Jan 2000
Debuts: 19 Dec 1999 United 2 Blackburn Rovers 1 (sub)
3 Jan 2000 Grimsby Town 2 United 2
Last game: 15 Jan 2000 Walsall 2 United 1 (sub)
West Bromwich Albion (L) Feb 2000/ Walsall (free) Mar 2000/ Rushden & Diamonds (free) Oct 2001/ Tranmere Rovers (free) Mar 2004/ Chesterfield (free) Jun 2005/ Walsall (free) Jun 2007/ Wrexham Jan 2008/ Newport County Jul 2008

Paul Hall made his FL debut with Torquay United on 14 November 1989, as a substitute, at home to Gillingham, his first start coming at Burnley on 6 March 1990. His move to Portsmouth was a success and in his five seasons there he made nearly 200 appearances. After moving to Coventry City, he failed to establish himself in the first team and went out on loan.

He played for United in a wide attacking role and scored on his only start, in the club's first game of the new millennium at Grimsby Town. His career continued with lower division clubs and at each one he was a regular member of the side. Fast and tricky and in his later years, cool in front of goal, he has made 538(108) FL appearances in his career, scoring over 100 goals and gained over 40 caps for Jamaica.

Appearances:		Apps	Gls
	FL	1 (3)	1
	Total	1 (3)	1

HALLIWELL Jonathan Clifford (Cliff)

LH/RH 1921–26 5' 8" 11st 0 to 11st 7
b. Sheffield 20 May 1898
d. Sheffield June 1984

Darnall Old Boys
United: 28/30 Apr 1920 to cs1926
Debuts: 17 May 1921 Barnsley 2 United 3 (CCSF at Hillsborough)
8 Oct 1921 Burnley 2 United 1
Last game: 13 Mar 1926 United 3 Notts County 1
Bournemouth & Boscombe Athletic (£50) Aug 1926 to retired May 1932

Described as 'tricky' and 'dainty', Cliff Halliwell was never more than a useful reserve player and suffered when the grounds were heavy. Twelve of his 27 appearances came in his second season (1921–22) and thereafter, he played only a few times for the first team each season.

He was a more established player with Bournemouth, making 217 FL appearances in his six seasons there but a knee injury brought his career to an end. He then returned to Sheffield where he was briefly the landlord of the Old Crown Inn before spending 38 years at the Firth Vickers steelworks. He had served in the Royal Navy during the First War.

Appearances:		Apps	Gls
	FL	25	0
	CC	2	0
	Total	27	0

HALLS John

LWB 2008 6' 0" 12st 4
b. Islington 14 February 1982

Arsenal from trainee Jan 2000/ Colchester United (L) Jan 2002/ KSK Beveren (Belg) (L) Jul 2002/ Stoke City (L) Oct 2003, (£100k) Jan 2003/ Reading(£250k) Jan 2006 to cs 2008/ Preston NE (L) Nov 2007/ Crystal Palace (L)

United: (L) 14 Mar 2008 to cs
Debuts: 22 Mar 2008 Barnsley 0 United 1 (sub)
25 Mar 2008 Ferencvaros 0 United 1 (Fr)
29 Mar 2008 Preston North End 3 United 1
Last game: 4 May 2008 Southampton 3 United 2

John Halls, an England youth international, made three League Cup substitute appearances for Arsenal and his FL debut came whilst on loan with Colchester on 19 January 2002 at home to Chesterfield. He spent the 2002–03 season on loan in Belgium before two productive years at Stoke. His move to Reading was less successful, making occasional appearances when the club clinched promotion to the Premiership and he played only in League Cup games in 2006–07.

After two loan spells in 2007–08 he joined United, initially on a one month loan, later extended to the end of the season, as defensive cover. When called upon he acquitted himself well both as a right wing back, being accurate in the tackle and producing useful crosses when coming forward and, in an emergency, as a central defender.

Appearances:		Apps	Gls
	FL	5 (1)	0
	Total	5 (1)	0

HAMILTON Derrick (Des) Vivian

MF 1998 5' 10½" 12st 13
b. Bradford 15 August 1976

Bradford City from YT Jun 1994/ Newcastle United (£1.5m+) Mar 1997

United: (L) One month from 16 Oct 1998
Debut: 17 Oct 1998 United 1 Barnsley 1
Last game: 10 Nov 1998 Wolverhampton Wanderers 2 United 1

Huddersfield Town (L) Feb 1999/ Norwich City (L) Mar 2000/ Tranmere Rovers (L) Oct 2000/ Tranmere Rovers (L) Jan 2001/ Cardiff City Jul 2001/ Grimsby Town (L) Mar 2003, (free) Jul 2003/ Barnet Mar–Jul 2004

Des Hamilton made his FL debut with Bradford City on 3 May 1994 at home to Barnet. After 88 FL appearances for City, he moved to Newcastle United for a fee of £1.5m+ but in his four seasons there he played just twelve times in the Premiership. Although he gained an England U21 cap it was estimated that Newcastle had paid out about £8,000 for each appearance.

He also made five loan moves, the first bringing him to Bramall Lane where in played six times in a midfield role and manager Steve Bruce may well have signed him, appreciating that he was a versatile player and was still only twenty two, but sufficient funds were not available. A skilful player but hardly dynamic, he returned to St James's Park and more loan spells, his final League outings were with Grimsby Town, bringing his total to 138(43), before moving to the then non-league club Barnet.

Des returned to Bradford and played for Campion, a local amateur club.

Appearances:		Apps	Gls
	FL	6	0
	Total	6	0

HAMILTON Ian (Chico) Michael

OL/IF 1976–78 5' 9½" 11st 1
b. Streatham 31 October 1950

Chelsea from app May 1966, pro Jan 1968/ Southend United (£5000) Sep 1968/ Aston Villa (£40k) Jun 1969

United: (£30–40k) 19 Jul 1976 to Feb 1978
Debuts: 1 Aug 1976 PSV Eindhoven (Holland) 1 United 1 (Fr)
7 Aug 1976 United 0 Newcastle United 1 (ASC)
21 Aug 1976 Luton Town 2 United 0
Last games: 14 Jan 1978 United 1 Bolton Wanderers 5
28 Jan 1978 Swindon Town 2 United 3 (Fr)

Minnesota Kicks (£35k) Feb 1978/ San Jose Earthquakes 1982/ Sheffield area local football 1983/ Worksop Town/ Rotherham United Community Development Officer

Chico Hamilton made his FL debut, and scored, for Tommy Docherty's Chelsea at Tottenham Hotspur on 18 March 1967 at the age of 16 years and 138 days, making him the club's youngest player to make a FL appearance. Dave Sexton, who replaced Docherty as manager, wasn't so impressed with the 'cheeky' young man and eight months after he had signed professional forms, Chico was transferred to Southend United.

Docherty, who was now the manager of Aston Villa, signed Chico again, and in his seven seasons at Villa Park, the player made over 200 FL appearances. An England youth international, he won a Third Division Championship medal in 1972 and a League Cup medal in 1975.

Chico was a very clever, predominately left footed, attacking player but this was not the best period to be at Bramall Lane. The team spirit under the United manager Jimmy Sirrel was generally poor and Ian was one of the first players to be moved on by Harry Haslam as he began his wheeling and dealing. Ian had played 281(28) FL games but now spent five seasons playing in the North American Soccer League. He returned to Sheffield and recently was reported to be involved in an after-school club in Sheffield.

Appearances:		Apps	Gls
	FL	55 (5)	13
	FAC	3	0
	LC	2	0
	CC	2	0
	ASC	6 (1)	2
	Total	68 (5)	15

HAMILTON Ian Richard

MF 1998–2000 5' 9" 11st 3
b. Stevenage 14 December 1967

Southampton from app Dec 1985/ Cambridge United Mar 1988/ Scunthorpe United Dec 1988/ West Bromwich Albion Jun 1992

United: (£325k) 26 Mar 1998 to 18 Aug 2000
Debut: 28 Mar 1998 United 2 Port Vale 1

Last games: 21 Aug 1999 Manchester City 6 United 0
24 Aug 1999 Shrewsbury Town 0 United 3 (LC)
7 Dec 1999 Whitby Town 1 United 3 (Fr)
29 Apr 2000 Norwich City 2 United 1 (sub)
Grimsby Town (L) 4 Nov 1999
Bristol C trial Aug 2000/ Notts County Aug 2000/ Lincoln City Nov 2001/ Woking Oct 2002 to cs 2003

Ian Hamilton began his professional career with Southampton but made his FL debut after his move to Cambridge United, scoring with a splendid 25–yard shot in the 1–0 home win over Darlington on 1 April 1988.

He was an experienced player when Steve Thompson brought him to Bramall Lane as deadline day approached, having played 145 League games for Scunthorpe and 240 for West Bromwich Albion. The hard working midfielder was a regular in the side for the following twelve months but, after starting a few games under Adrian Heath, he lost his place and under Neil Warnock he made only a few substitute appearances.

In all, he had made over 500 League appearances before moving into non-league football with Woking.

Appearances:		Apps	Gls
	FL	38 (7)	3
	PO	2	0
	FAC	2 (3)	0
	LC	6	1
	Total	48 (10)	4

HAMILTON William (Willie) Murdoch

IR/IL 1956–60 5' 8½" 10st 0 to 10st 8
b. Airdrie 16 February 1938
d. Canada October 1976

Drumpellier Amateurs
United: 30 Jan/1 Feb 1956 to 18 Feb 1961
Debuts: 26 Sep 1956 Worksop Town 1 United 0 (CM)
2 Feb 1957 United 0 Blackburn Rovers 2
Last game: 27 Dec 1960 United 0 Sunderland 1
Middlesbrough (£13.5k) Feb 1961/ Heart of Midlothian (£3000) Jun 1962/ Hibernian (£6000) Oct 1963/ Aston Villa (£25k) Aug 1965/ Exeter City 1967/ Heart of Midlothian Aug 1967 to 1969/ South Africa/ Ross County 1970

Willie Hamilton joined United when Joe Mercer was the manager. A hugely talented young player with superb ball control, he had a keen football brain, awareness and was a fine passer of the ball. Sadly however, he lacked the temperament and determination to fulfil his potential. United's staff and playing colleagues tried their utmost to guide his development but failed to generate much sense of dedication, application and determination in this 'likeable rogue'. There were wonderful moments such as a goal in February 1959 against Barnsley, when he left three opponents dumbfounded in a thirty yard run but there should have been so much more. His most consistent season was that of 1959–60 when he missed just five games but John Harris, who had replaced Mercer as United's manager, gave up on Hamilton and he was sold to Middlesbrough.

Playing with Brian Clough, he scored on his debut with Middlesbrough but that was the only bright moment (10 app, 1gl) and he was no doubt happy to return to Scotland where he was immensely popular with Hearts' fans. He won a Scottish League Cup medal in 1962 and later gained one Scottish cap with Hibernian and also made two appearances for the Scottish Football League. After two years with Aston Villa, he played in South Africa before returning to Scotland. He died in Canada at the age of 38. It was a tragic waste of a great talent.

Appearances:		Apps	Gls
	FL	79	21
	FAC	9	0
	CC	4	0
	Total	92	21

HAMMOMD Walter Harry

IF/CF/HB 1891–97 5' 6½" 11st 9
b. Chorlton JAS 1868
d. Bolton December 1921

Edgehill/ Everton 1889
United: cs1891 to cs 1897
Debuts: 1 Sep 1891 United 5 Middlesbrough Ironopolis 1 (Fr)
12 Sep 1891 Sunderland Albion 2 United 4 (NL)
24 Oct 1891 United 4 Lincoln City 1 (FAC)
3 Sep 1892 United 4 Lincoln City 2
Last games: 16 Apr 1897 Bolton Wanderers 0 United 2
30 Apr 1897 Combined Suffolk XI 1 United 4 (Fr)
New Brighton Tower 26 Aug 1897/ Leicester Fosse May 1900 to cs1901

Harry Hammond made his FL debut with Everton, his only FL appearance for the club, as a fullback on 8 March 1890 at home to West Bromwich Albion.

He moved to United, who were new members of the NL, in 1891 and was a consistent goal scorer and, the next season, Harry played in the club's first Football League fixture and scored United's first League hat trick in the 4–2 victory over Lincoln City. Throughout his time at Bramall Lane he was a determined centre forward and led the scoring charts in three of the club's first four League campaigns. He became the first of only two United players to score five goals in a competitive match, doing so in a 8–3 League defeat of Bootle. Although credited with 49 FL goals, he may well have been the first United player to reach 50 as he was the possible scorer of several un-attributable goals.

Harry was also the first United player to be sent off in a FL match. Fearing for his life and showing more discretion than valour, he fled from the Crewe ground and 'hid' at the railway station until the United party arrived! Always hard working and enthusiastic, in 1894 he played for the Football League against the Irish League.

He moved in 1897 to the newly formed New Brighton Tower. After one season, in which they won the Lancashire League, the club were elected to the FL and Harry scored in their first FL game. He missed much of his one season with Leicester Fosse due to his contracting typhoid fever and, after leaving football, he became a publican in Bolton and reportedly died whilst playing billiards.

Appearances:		Apps	Gls
	FL	108	49
	TM	1	0
	FAC	15	2
	NL	24	13
	UCL	13	3
	SCC	4	2
	WCC	3	0
	ABD	2	0
	Total	170	69

HAMPSON Harold

IF 1938–42 5' 7½" 11st 8
b. Little Hulton (Lancashire) 8 June 1918
d. Southport 24 June 1942

Walkden Methodists/ Everton amateur or trial Dec 1935/ Walkden Methodists 1936/ Southport amateur Sep 1936, pro Nov 1936

United: (£2,250) 4/6 Jun 1938 to 24 Jun 1942
Debut: 27 Aug 1938 Nottingham Forest 0 United 2
Last games: 6 May 1939 United 6 Tottenham Hotspur 1
30 Aug 1939 Preston North End 0 United 0
18 Apr 1942 United 2 Bradford Park Avenue 1 (WW2)
WW2 guest: Swindon Town and Southport

Harold Hampson made his FL debut with Southport at home to Port Vale on 31 October 1936. A younger brother of Jimmy, the Blackpool and England striker who had drowned in January 1938, Harold was just twenty when he joined United.

A sound, consistent, hard working player and a good shot, he was influential in the promotion season of 1938–39 and scored the first goal in the 6–1 defeat of Spurs which clinched promotion in the final game of the season. Called up for army service in July 1939, he played in the first two games of the 1939–40 season, scoring one of the first goals of the season after five minutes, but, because of the War, the season was terminated and these games do not always appear in player's records.

In the early part of the War, he served with the British Expeditionary Force and was evacuated from Dunkirk by barge. He played no serious football in the 1940–41 season but played again for United from November 1941 but in June 1942, a small swelling on his neck led to complications and he died in a Southport hospital from septicaemia.

Appearances:		Apps	Gls
	FL	39	13
	FAC	4	0
	CC	2	0
	39–40	2	1
	WW2	14	5
	Total	61	19

HAMSON Gary

IL/OL 1976–79 5' 9" 10st 2 to 10st 12
b. Nottingham 24 August 1959

Ilkeston Town

United: app 27 Jul 1976, pro Nov 1976 to 30 Jul 1979
Debut: 30 Oct 1976 Cardiff City 0 United 2
Last game: 8 May 1979 United 2 Leicester City 2

Leeds United (£140k) Jul 1979/ Bristol City Jul 1986/ Port Vale Dec 1986 to youth coach Aug 1988/ retired Jul 1989

When Gary Hamson made his FL debut for United, he became the youngest player to make a FL appearance (aged 17 years 67 days) for the Club. Although he later lost the record to Julian Broddle, Gary still holds the club record for the most appearances as a teenager. An attacking left sided midfielder with a cultured left foot, he passed the ball well but was somewhat lacking in pace. A regular member of the first team for two and a half seasons, he is remembered for a superb winning shot against Liverpool in the League Cup match in August 1978.

When United were relegated to the Third Division in 1979, Gary was transferred to Leeds United. He was still only nineteen and went on to make 292 FL appearances before an ankle injury with Port Vale ended his playing career in March 1989 and, after a year as youth coach with the Staffordshire club, he left and became a builder.

Appearances:		Apps	Gls
	FL	107 (1)	8
	FAC	5	0
	LC	3	1
	ASC	7	0
	CC	1	0
	Total	123 (1)	9

HANDLEY George Albert (see also Hanson)

OL 1918–19 5' 8" 10st 3
b. Totley, (Sheffield) JFM 1886
d. Bradford AMJ 1952

Hallam/ United (trial)?/ Chesterfield Town Jan 1905/ Bradford City (£250) Oct 1906/ Southampton May 1911/ Goole Town player-mgr Apr 1912/ Bradford City Dec 1913/ Barrow Jul 1914
United: WW1 guest
Debut: 28 Sep 1918 Notts County 5 United 2 (WW1)
Last games: 26 Apr 1919 Rotherham County 0 United 4 (WW1)
17 May 1919 Hull City 0 United 2 (CM)
Bradford City May 1919/ Bruhl FC (St Gallen, Switz) coach Apr to Oct? 1922

George Handley, who had played for Sheffield Boys, made his FL debut with Chesterfield on 4 March 1905 at home to Leicester Fosse. A fine outside left who centred well and was a good shot, he scored 30 goals in 103 FL appearances in his three spells with Bradford City but he also played for Southern League Southampton and two northern non-League clubs.

His appearances for United were as a guest player during the First War when he served in the Royal Flying Corps (RAF). It was reported that in March 1919, he wasn't sure which club he belonged to, so he went along to Valley Parade to find out and was subsequently re-registered with the FL by the Bradford club. He must have returned to service life after a short coaching spell in Switzerland as he was reported to be serving at Coal Aston (on the Sheffield/Derbyshire border) in November 1922.

His appearances below include one as 'Hanson'.

Appearances:		Apps	Gls
	WW1	18	3
	Total	18	3

HANSBURY Roger

G 1987 5' 11" 12st 0
b. Barnsley 26 January 1955

Norwich City from app Jan 1973/ Cambridge United (L) Nov 1977/ Bolton W (L)/ Orient (L) Dec 1978/ Eastern AA (Hong Kong) Dec 1981/ Burnley Jul 1983/ Cambridge United Jul 1985/ Birmingham City Mar 1986
United: (L) Oct to Nov 1987
Debut: 17 Oct 1987 United 2 Leicester City 1
Last game: 4 Nov 1987 West Bromwich Albion 4 United 0
Wolverhampton Wanderers (L) Mar 1989/ Colchester United (L) Aug 1989/ Cardiff City Oct 1989 to Feb 1991

Roger Hansbury made an inauspicious start to his FL career, making his debut at the age of 19 in Norwich City's 0–4 defeat at Fulham on 21 September 1974. His brief loan spell with United came to an end at West Bromwich Albion when he was injured and Paul Stancliffe went into goal, conceding two of the goals. However, his most important work for United had occurred in May 1984 when, as the Burnley keeper, he had prevented Hull City scoring a third goal which would have denied promotion to the Blades. He played League football for nine clubs during 18 seasons making 377 FL appearances.

He has worked at a sports centre and has run a greeting cards shop in the West Midlands.

Appearances:		Apps	Gls
	FL	5	0
	Total	5	0

HANSON

(probably a newspaper error for G A Handley)

OL 1919

United: WW1 guest
Only game: 26 Apr 1919 Rotherham County 0 United 4 (WW1)

Hanson's only game was as a guest player in the First War but is almost certainly a newspaper error for 'Handley'.

Appearances:		Apps	Gls
	WW1	1	0
	Total	1	0

HARDINGE Harold Thomas William (Walter or Wally)

IL/IR 1907–13 5' 6½" to 5' 7½" 10st 13 to 12st 7
b. Greenwich 25 February 1886
d. Cambridge 8 May 1965

Eltham/ Tonbridge/ Maidstone United/ Newcastle United May 1905
United: (£350) 2/3 Dec 1907 to Jun 1913
Debut: 7 Dec 1907 United 2 Preston North End 0
Last game: 12 Apr 1913 United 2 Manchester United 1
Woolwich Arsenal (£500) Jun 1913, retired cs 1921
Tottenham Hotspur reserve coach 1935

'Walter' Hardinge, as he was usually known, made his FL debut with Newcastle United on 1 September 1905 at Sunderland and made eight more appearances in the FL before he moved to Bramall Lane in December 1907.

He played regularly in the United first team for six seasons, scoring on his debut and again in his final game for the club. He was an intelligent and stylish inside forward who dribbled well and had a good shot on the run but he was also a player of moods who had too many off days. Many regarded him as the key player in the team but if he 'had been as consistent in his form as he was clever with ball', there would have been fewer spells in the reserve team. He was probably rather fortunate to be capped against Scotland at Hampden Park in 1910 but there were several approaches to United for his services.

Arsenal made their third approach in 1910 and terms were agreed, including a generous settlement for the player, but Walter changed his mind and refused to go and he refused transfers to Bolton Wanderers and Spurs in 1912. Transfer listed in 1913 with a fee of £1000, United eventually accepted a fee of half that amount and though the FL registered a transfer in May, it was not until June, and after the intervention of the FA, that the player finally agreed to move. Soccer slaves there may have been, but Walter—like George Utley who joined United five months later—was certainly not one of them.

He was also a first class cricketer, playing for Kent until 1933. An opening bat and slow left arm bowler, he was voted a Wisden 'Player of the Year' in 1915, and he played 623 first class matches, scoring 33,519 runs at an average of 36.5 and taking 371 wickets at an average of 26.5. He was also a double international, playing for England against Australia at Headingley in 1921.

During the First World War, he served in the Royal Naval Air Service as a Chief Petty Officer and he chaired a meeting in December 1918 that led to the formation of the Professional Football Players and Trainers Union. After his football playing days were over, with 210 FL appearances to his credit, he joined, and became a director of, the sports outfitters and publishers John Wisden & Co.

Appearances:		Apps	Gls
	FL	147	45
	FAC	5	1
	ABD	2	0
	Total	154	46

HARLEY Jonathan (Jon)

LWB/MF 2002, 2003, 2004–05 5' 9" 11st 9
b. Maidstone 26 September 1979

Chelsea from trainee Mar 1997/ Wimbledon (L) Oct 2000/ Fulham (£3.5m) Aug 2001
United: (L) 30 Oct 2002 to 2 Jan 2003
Debuts: 2 Nov 2002 Nottingham Forest 3 United 0 (sub)
9 Nov 2002 United 0 Ipswich Town 0
Last game: 28 Dec 2002 United 0 Coventry City 0
United: (L) 16 Sep 2003 to 16 Oct 2004
Debut: 16 Sep 2003 United 5 Rotherham United 0
Last game: 4 Oct 2003 United 0 Sunderland 1
West Ham United (L) Jan 2004/
United: (free) 21 Jun/ 4 Aug 2004 to 28/30 Aug 2005
Debuts: 16 Jul 2004 Weymouth 3 United 5 (Fr)
7 Aug 2004 Burnley 1 United 1
Last game: 20 Aug 2005 United 2 Preston North End 1
Burnley (L) 27 to 29 Aug, Transfer (£70k rising to £150k) Aug 2005/
Watford (free) Jul 2008

Jon Harley was the first player to join the Blades on three separate occasions, albeit that the first two moves were on loan and he was always a popular figure at the Lane. He began his career with Chelsea, making his League debut 5 April 1998 at Derby County and while he was at Stamford Bridge, he gained England international caps at youth and U21 level. After a loan spell at Wimbledon, an expensive move to Fulham followed but he was unable to secure a regular first team place.

Harley moved on loan to Bramall Lane to cover for the injured Rob Ullathorne and immediately impressed both as a quick defender, tackling well and with anticipation and also prominent in attack, possessing a hard shot, which was particularly dangerous at free kicks. His second loan spell was equally encouraging but ended after five games due to injury. After regaining fitness he was loaned to West Ham United and scored for them with a superb long range effort against United at Bramall Lane.

Jon joined United on a permanent basis during the summer of 2004 with perhaps no fee involved and he missed just two games during the season, playing as a left wing back or on the left side of midfield. Although producing solid performances, some thought his standards were not so high during the second half of the season and when David Unsworth joined United, it was decided to accept a transfer offer from Burnley, where he has now made over 100 League appearances and over 250 in total.

Appearances:		Apps	Gls
	FL	61 (1)	3
	FAC	5	0
	LC	5	0
	Total	71 (1)	3

HARMSTON Michael (Mick) James

LB 1968–69 6' 0" 11st 10
b. Sheffield 7 April 1950

United: from 14/18 Oct 1965, pro 7 May/Jul 1967 to 30 Jun 1971
Debuts: 10 Sep 1968 United 2 Sheffield Wednesday 2 (Hodgkinson BM)
14 Sep 1968 United 1 Oxford United 2
Last games: 17 Mar 1969 Preston North End 2 United 2
2 Aug 1969 De Graafschap (Hol) 0 United 3 (Fr)
Southend United(L) 29 Dec 1970
Worksop Town/ Matlock Town/ Buxton/ Worksop Town 1978–79/ Spalding United player-mgr c1981/ player and player-mgr Sheffield Club

A Sheffield Boys player, Mick Harmston was a strong, powerful defender but he failed to make the transition to regular first team League football and during his loan spell with Southend United, he made just one appearance. However, he had a good career at non-League level. Now in sales, he has also acted as a scout for Southampton.

Appearances:		Apps	Gls
	FL	5	0
	Total	5	0

HARRIS Bernard

RB/LB 1924–27 5' 9½" 11st 0 to 11st 7
b. Greenock West or Sheffield 14 March 1901
d. Leeds 1 March 1987

Upperthorpe Comrades (Sheffield)/ Gainsborough Trinity 1920/ Rotherham County Sep 1922
United: (£2000) 14 May 1923 to 25 Oct 1928
Debut: 8 Sep 1924 United 1 Cardiff City 0
Last game: 7 May 1927 Birmingham 2 United 3
Luton Town (£250) Oct 1928/ Queens Park Rangers Jun 1929/ Llanelli Jul 1932/ Swindon Town Jun 1933/ Margate Jul 1934/ Ramsgate c1936

Bernard Harris made his FL debut with Rotherham County on 30 September 1922 at home to South Shields. A skilful, two footed and quick full-back, Harris appeared to have a good future in the game.

Sunderland were rumoured to have offered £4000 for him but true or false, United's offer of £2000 was a big sum for those days. Sadly, his playing career was ruined by injuries; torn ligaments in a reserve fixture wrecked his first season and although he spent five seasons with United, injuries hindered his progress and it was only in the 1926–27 season that he had a regular spell in the first team. He missed most of the following season after a cartilage operation and was transfer listed at £1500. United had to let him go in the end for just £250 but he was more fortunate in the Third Division making 104 FL appearances with Luton, QPR and Swindon.

Appearances:		Apps	Gls
	FL	44	0
	CC	2	0
	Total	46	0

HARRISON G

G 1918

United: WW1 guest
Only game: 6 Apr 1918 Barnsley 1 United 1 (WW1)

When Ernest Blackwell, the United goalkeeper's, train was delayed during the First War, Lieutenant Harrison, described as a 'Barnsley officer', stepped into the breach and played as a guest player for United. He may have been the same man as, or related to, the 'Lieutenant J Harrison' who played twice as a forward for Barnsley and once at centre half for Rotherham County in November 1918.

Appearances:		Apps	Gls
	WW1	1	0
	Total	1	0

HARRISON John (Jack or Jacky) Richardson

IL 1930–31 5' 8"? 11st 0
b. Rhyl AMJ 1908
d. Rhyl 2 August 1966

Rhyl Athletic/ Llandudno Junction/ Rhyl Athletic/ Manchester City Feb 1929
United: (£350) 7/11 Jun 1930 to cs 1931
Debut: 30 Aug 1930 Birmingham 3 United 1
Last game: 21 Mar 1931 United 0 Huddersfield Town 2
Brighton & Hove Albion (£200) Aug 1931 to cs1934/ Northwich Victoria Nov 1934

Jack Harrison won junior international honours with Llandudno Junction and was regarded as a very fast forward 'with a cannon-ball shot' but he found League football a more difficult game.

He made his FL debut with Manchester City on 19 October 1929 at home to West Ham United and scored in his second and final game. In his season with United, Jack made intermittent appearances for the first team before moving on to Brighton & Hove Albion where he broke his collar bone in a reserve game and didn't make his first team debut until April 1933. After a few appearances, he was released in 1934 and after leaving the professional game, he returned to the plumbing trade. Jack made only 12 FL appearances in five years but scored five goals for his three clubs.

Appearances:		Apps	Gls
	FL	5	1
	CC	1	0
	Total	6	1

HARROP James (Jimmy)

LH/CH 1921 5' 9½" 11st 9
b. Heeley (Ecclesall Bierlow, Sheffield) 5 February 1884
d. Sheffield 25 May 1954

Meersbrook Alliance 1898/ Heeley St Peters/ Kent Road Mission/ Ranmoor Wesleyans/ Wednesday amat 1904, pro Apr 1905/ Denaby United May 1906/ Rotherham Town May 1907/ Liverpool (£75) Jan 1908/ Aston Villa (£600) May 1912
WW1 guest: Sheffield Wednesday
United: (£1500) 10 Mar 1921 to cs1922
Debut: 12 Mar 1921 United 2 Bolton Wanderers 2
Last game: 12 Nov 1921 United 1 Chelsea 2
Burton All Saints (player) Aug 1922, (player-coach) cs 1923

A Sheffield grinder by trade, Jimmy, who had played for Wednesday's reserves, made his FL debut with Liverpool on 18 January 1908 at home to Bolton Wanderers and went on to make 133 appearances for the club before moving to Aston Villa where he made a further 153 FL appearances. With Villa, he won an FA Cup winners' medal in 1913 but missed the honour of captaining Villa to a further triumph in 1920 through injury. Unfortunate not to be capped by England, he played twice for the Football League.

'Among the brainiest of half-backs, bringing intelligence to bear' in both attack and defence, he was 37 years old when he joined United in March 1921and his experience and calm demeanour, chatting and singing before a game, were no doubt helpful as the team successfully struggled to avoid relegation. His job was done and after eight games at the start of the next season, he played only for the reserves. Transfer listed with a fee of £250, he then moved into non-League football.

A works manager in Sheffield, Jimmy was a noted angler and keen golfer. He lived in Edale in north Derbyshire and was buried there.

Appearances:		Apps	Gls
	FL	14	0
	Total	14	0

HARTFIELD Charles (Charlie) Joseph

MF/D 1991–95 6' 0" 12st 3 to 13st 8
b. Lambeth 4 September 1971

Arsenal from trainee Sep 1989
United: (free) 1/6 Aug 1991 to 28 Nov 1997
Debut: 31 Aug 1991 Crystal Palace 2 United 1
Last games: 16 Nov 1996 Port Vale 0 United 0
29 Jan 1997 Manchester City 0 United 0 (sub)
Fulham (L) 5 Feb 1997
Swansea City Nov 1997 to cs 1999/ Lincoln City (L) Sep 1998 and Mar 1999/ Telford United Oct 1999/ Sheffield FC Nov 2000/ Caernarfon Town Aug 2002/ Halifax Town Nov 2002/ Ilkeston Town 2003/ Buxton 2003–04

Although England youth international Charlie spent two seasons as a professional with Arsenal, his FL debut was delayed until he signed for United. The strong, hard tackling midfielder was in and out of the side for his first three seasons but he played more regularly in the 1994–95 season after losing weight. Charlie could get himself into trouble with referees and was sent off three times whilst with United, one of those occasions in the game against Udinese in the Anglo-Italian Cup when two other United players (and Dave Bassett) were dismissed. He missed the 1995–96 season with a cruciate ligament injury and made only three appearances in his final season before his release in the summer of 1997.

He had trials with various clubs before joining Swansea City on a non-contract basis but after two seasons, he moved into non-League football. In 2001 he appeared as a prison footballer in the film 'Mean Machine' in which former team mate Vinny Jones had a major role. Hartfield was unlucky with injuries but was his own worst enemy in his private life; an addiction to gambling costing him both career and family.

Appearances:		Apps	Gls
	FL	45 (11)	1
	FAC	4 (1)	0
	LC	2 (1)	0
	AIC	1	0
	Total	52 (13)	1

HARTLE Barry

OL/IL 1960–66 5' 8½" 10st 3
b. Salford 8 August 1939

Watford Aug 1956
United: (£2,750) 13/16 Jun 1960 to 26 Jul 1966
Debuts: 3 Oct 1960 Dundee United 1 United 1 (Fr)
29 Oct 1960 Middlesbrough 3 United 1
Last game: 30 Apr 1966 United 0 West Bromwich Albion 0
Carlisle United (£14.9k) Jul 1966/ Stockport County Sep 1967/ Oldham Athletic Jun 1970/ Southport Jul 1971/ Macclesfield Town cs 1972/ Buxton 1974/ Witton Albion 1975/ Hyde United 1976–1977

A Salford Grammar School boy, Barry Hartle spent four seasons at Watford after being spotted playing in a local park and made his FL debut on 13 December 1958 at Shrewsbury Town. He was a key member of their 1959–60 promotion side and was then signed by United's manager, John Harris.

Barry made only three competitive appearances in his first season with United but thereafter, with United promoted to Division One, he played a little more frequently in the first team, either as a left winger or at inside left but usually only when Billy Hodgson or Ronnie Simpson were unavailable.

A skilful rather than a powerful player, it was only in 1964–65 that he really established himself with 39 of a possible 42 appearances. He moved on to Carlisle United in the summer of 1966 and, after spells with three other League clubs and having made just over 300 FL appearances, he moved into non-League football. He later became a postman and then a taxi driver.

Appearances:		Apps	Gls
	FL	101	16
	FAC	6	1
	LC	6	2
	CC	4	2
	Total	117	21

HARWOOD Richard Andrew

IR 1978 5' 7" 10st 12
b. Sheffield 13 September 1960

United: from 28 Jun 1977, app Jul 1978 to 31 Jul 1980
Debut: 7 Oct 1978 United 3 Sunderland 2
Last games: 14 Oct 1978 Millwall 1 United 1
16 Dec 1978 United 2 Cardiff City 1 (sub)
Scarborough Aug 1980

Richard Harwood's three FL appearances with United were the sum total of his Football League career and he moved into non-League football.

Appearances:		Apps	Gls
	FL	2 (1)	0
	LC	1	0
	Total	3 (1)	0

HATTON Robert (Bob) James

Striker 1980–82 5' 11" 12st 0
b. Hull 10 April 1947

Hull City (amat)/ Wath Wanderers/ Wolverhampton Wanderers from jnr Nov 1964/ Bolton Wanderers Mar 1967/ Northampton Town Oct 1968/ Carlisle United (£8,000) Jul 1969/ Birmingham City (£82.5k) Oct 1971/ Blackpool (£50k) Jul 1976/ Luton Town Jul 1978
United: (£75/100k) 14 Jul 1980 to 1 Dec 1982
Debuts: 31 Jul 1980 Chesterfield 1 United 0 (ASC)
9 Aug 1980 Sheffield Wednesday 2 United 0 (LC)
16 Aug 1980 Carlisle United 0 United 3
Last games: 13 Nov 1982 United 0 Southend United 1
20 Nov 1982 Hull City 1 United 1 (FAC)
Cardiff City (free) Dec 1982 to May 1983/ Dundalk (Ireland)/ Lodge Cotterill FC (Birmingham)

Bob Hatton had a nomadic career as a professional footballer, playing for nine clubs but only making more than 100 FL appearances for one of them—Birmingham City, where the fee was a record for the club. He had made his FL debut with Wolverhampton Wanderers, scoring in the home win over Portsmouth on 8 October 1966.

Cool in front of goal with quick reactions and difficult to shake off the ball, Bob had an excellent goal scoring record and worked hard for the team. It is said that his motto was 'Give me three chances and I will score from one'. His 215 FL goals in 617 games suggest he lived up to it.

Signed by Harry Haslam for United who were then in Division Three, both Bob and the Club made a good start to the 1980–81 season. He scored twice on his FL debut and the Blades were soon top of the League but, although Bob scored 18 FL goals in 44 games, United's performances deteriorated and they were relegated after the final game against Walsall. United won the Fourth Division championship in the following season when Bob formed a dangerous partnership with Keith Edwards. The two strikers worked well together, Edwards scoring 35 FL goals with Bob (he missed just one game) netting 15 but, in the following season, Bob lost his place to Alan Young and moved to his final club, Cardiff City.

After retiring from the game, he worked on local radio whilst working in the insurance business and financial management for the PFA in the Midlands.

Appearances:		Apps	Gls
	FL	92 (3)	34
	FAC	6	2
	LC	7	3
	ASC	3	2
	AMC	4 (1)	1
	CC	2	1
	Total	114 (4)	43

HAWES Steven(Steve) Robert

MF 1995–97 5' 8" 11st 10
b. High Wycombe 17 July 1978

United: trainee Jul 1994, 1/2 Mar 1996 to 20 Feb 1998
Debuts: 18 May 1995 Viterbese (Italy) 3 United 1 (Fr)
2 Sep 1995 West Bromwich Albion 3 United 2 (sub)
7 Oct 1995 United 0 Derby County 2
Last game: 29 Jan 1997 Manchester City 0 United 0 (sub)
Doncaster Rovers(L) 18 Sep 1997
Doncaster Rovers Feb 1998/ Hull City Jul 1998/ Altrincham Nov 1999/ Worksop Town 2002/ Stocksbridge Steels cs2004/ Altrincham cs2005/ Stocksbridge Steels Oct 2005/ Worksop Town cs 2007/ Sheffield FC Feb 2008

When Steve Hawes made his FL debut for the Blades, he became, at the time (17 years, 47 days) the youngest player to make a FL appearance for the club. A calm and thoughtful mid-field player who captained the Junior team, he failed to make the breakthrough into the first team squad.

He moved to Doncaster Rovers, firstly on loan, and then was transferred to Hull City. The combative Steve started the 1998–99 season in the Tigers' first team but gradually faded out of the picture, having totalled 27(7) FL appearances. He moved to Altrincham where he experienced the club's last-day-of-the-season relegation from the Conference and extended his career as a non-League player.

Appearances:		Apps	Gls
	FL	1 (3)	0
	Total	1 (3)	0

HAWKSWORTH Derek Marshall

OL/CF/OR/IL 1950–58 5' 10" 10st 11 to 11st 2
b. Bradford 16 July 1927

Manningham Mills 1942/ East Bierley/ Bradford United/ Bradford Park Avenue (amat) Apr 1943
WW2 guest: Colchester U Dec 1945 followed by Services football in India.
Huddersfield Town (amat) Apr 1948/ Bradford City amateur Jun 1948, pro Oct 1948
United: (£12.5k) 9/11 Dec 1950 to 26 May 1958
Debut: 16 Dec 1950 Blackburn Rovers 0 United 2
Last game: 26 Apr 1958 Leyton Orient 0 United 1
Huddersfield Town (player exchange R Simpson +£6000) May 1958/ Lincoln City (£3000) Feb 1960/ Bradford City (£3000) Jan 1961/ Nelson Aug 1962–cs1963

After serving with the RAF in India during the Second War, Derek Hawksworth signed for Huddersfield Town but only as an amateur. He signed professional forms when he moved to Bradford City, whose manger, David Steele, had managed Park Avenue where Derek had played during the War. He made his FL debut with City on 21 August 1948 at Barrow.

Teddy Davison signed Derek for United (a record fee for Bradford City) and, playing at outside left, he scored on his debut. He went on to be a key member of the United side for more than seven seasons and Derek and Alf Ringstead (outside right) were one of the most dangerous pair of wingers in United's history and played a massive part in securing the Second Division championship in 1953.

A natural right footed player, Derek initially played at outside left, where he made good use of his pace, ability to beat a man and frequently, after cutting inside, finishing with a good right footed shot or centre. He was also strong, difficult to knock off the ball and able to take knocks and was often used at centre forward. During his time with United, he did play in all the forward positions although he was probably at his best on the left wing. He also played for the Football Association against the Army (November 1951) and was also selected for England B against France (May 1952).

He was transferred to Huddersfield Town in 1958 in a move which brought left winger Ronnie Simpson to the Lane and was signed on a third occasion by David Steele when he moved to Lincoln City. In total, he made 465 FL appearances and scored 144 goals. Later, he returned to his native city of Bradford to run a newsagents shop.

Appearances:		Apps	Gls
	FL	255	88
	FAC	17	6
	CC	14	9
	Total	286	103

HAWLEY Frederick (Fred)

CH 1913–18 5' 11" 12st to 12st 8
b. Darlington 28 October 1890
d. Derby 27 May 1954

Shelton United/ Leys Recreational/ Derby Midland/ Ripley Town
United: (£70) 10 Jan 1913 to 23 May 1919
Debut: 15 Mar 1913 United 4 Derby County 1
Last games: 26 Apr 1915 Bolton Wanderers 0 United 1
23 Feb 1918 Nottingham Forest 0 United 0 (WW1)
WW1 guest: Derby County (1915–16, 1919), Notts County (1917, 1917–18), Birmingham (1918)
Coventry City (£350) May 1919/ Birmingham (£250) Jan 1920/ Swindon Town May 1920/ Bristol City Mar 1923/ Brighton & Hove Albion (£350) Jun 1925/ Queens Park Rangers May 1926/ Loughborough Corinthians Apr 1928–May 1929

Fred Hawley wasn't the first United player to be vague about the date and place of his birth. His age was given as twenty when he signed and Derby or Ripley often appear in print as the birthplace but, when later questioned, he spoke of the 'north country' and coming to Derby as a small child and ignored the matter of his age.

A strong centre half, he actually made his debut for United in 1913 at centre forward. He soon established himself as a regular member of the first team, adding bite to the defence though he was less good in bringing the ball forward. He was rather unlucky with United in that he missed the two FA Cup semi-finals of 1914 through injury and was one of the two reserves for the 1915 FA Cup Final side.

A munitions worker in Coventry during the First World War, he was able to play for United on a fairly regular basis during the first two seasons and also assisted other clubs. Despite missing four seasons due to the War, Fred still made 305 FL appearances for his various clubs.

Appearances:		Apps	Gls
	FL	57	1
	FAC	8	0
	WW1	39	0
	Total	104	1

HAWTHORNE Mark David

MF 1994 5' 8½" 10st 12/11st 8
b. Glasgow 31 October 1973

Crystal Palace from jnr Jun 1992
United: 16 Aug 1994 to 23 Jan 1995
Debut: 6 Sep 1994 Piacenza 2 United 2 (AIC)
Last game: 15 Nov 1994 Casena 1 United 4 (AIC)
Walsall Jan 1995/ Torquay United Mar 1995/ Hayes cs 1997/ Crawley Town Sep 1997/ Slough Town cs 1998/ Crawley Town Nov 2000/ Slough Town cs 2001/ Carshalton Athletic Nov 2002 to Jun 2004 / – / Worthing Sep 2004/ Burgess Hill Town Jan 2005/ Horsham 2005 to present

Having begun his professional career with Crystal Palace, where he made no first team competitive appearances, Mark had to content himself with just three Anglo-Italian games with United, scoring in his final appearance.

He had been signed by Dave Bassett, as a non-contract player, but after two seasons, he moved to Walsall, but again failed to make the first team. He met with more success with Torquay United and finally made his FL debut as a substitute at Fulham on 25 March 1995, his full debut coming on 15 April 1995 at Hartlepool United. He went on to make 43(15) appearances for Torquay before moving into non-League football in the South of England.

Appearances:		Apps	Gls
	AIC	3	1
	Total	3	1

HAYLES Barrington (Barry) Edward

Striker 2004 5' 9" 13st 0
b. Lambeth 17 May 1972

Willesden Hawkeye 1990/ Stevenage Borough Jul 1993/ Bristol Rovers (£250k) Jun 1997/ Fulham (£2.1m) Nov 1998
United: (free) 26 Jun 2004 to 1 Sep 2004
Debuts: 13 Jul 2004 Matlock Town 4 United 3 (Fr)
7 Aug 2004 Burnley 1 United 1
Last games: 20 Aug 2004 Preston North End 0 United 1
24 Aug 2004 United 4 Stockport County 1 (LC)
Millwall Sep 2004/ Plymouth A (£100k) Aug 2006/ Leicester City Jan 2008/ Cheltenham (L) Aug 2008

Barry Hayles, who gained semi-professional caps for England, moved into League football at the age of 25, making his debut with Bristol Rovers on 9 August 1997 at home to Port Vale. After six seasons with Fulham, he moved to Bramall Lane on a free transfer ready for the 2004–05 season. Neil Warnock was looking for a '20-goals-a-season' striker and Hayles, strong, quick, a good finisher and difficult to knock off the ball looked to be a likely candidate. After only a few games however, for reasons that were not divulged, Barry moved on to Millwall.

Although he failed to score for the Blades, the Jamaican international had, by the summer of 2008, scored 109 goals in 298(78) League games.

Appearances:		Apps	Gls
	FL	4	0
	LC	1	0
	Total	5	0

HEATH Adrian Paul

For details see 'Managers' section

Appearances:		Apps	Gls
	FL	0 (4)	0
	FAC	0 (1)	0
	Total	0 (5)	0

HEATON James Michael (Mick)

LB/RB 1965–70 5' 6" 10st 11
b. Sheffield 15 January 1947
d. Oswaldtwistle (Lancashire) 11 April 1995

United: app 24 Apr 1962, pro 13 Sep/14 Nov 1964 to 7 Oct 1971
Debuts: 23 May 1965 Blackpool 3 United 0 (Fr in New Zealand)
15 Oct 1966 United 2 Sunderland 0 (sub)
17 May 1968 Doncaster Rovers 3 United 1 (CC)
4 Jan 1969 Mansfield Town 2 United 1 (FAC)
11 Jan 1969 United 2 Portsmouth 0
Last games: 31 Oct 1970 United 2 Carlisle United 2
3 Nov 1970 Barnsley 3 United 2 (CC)
Blackburn Rovers (£6,750) Oct 1971/ retired/ Blackburn Rovers coach 1978, asst manager/ Everton coach to 1987 / – / Blackburn R Community Manager 1988 / – / Workington manager Dec 1988 to Oct 1989// Manchester City assistant manager 1990

A hard working never-say-die left back and former Sheffield and Yorkshire Boys player, Mick Heaton made his CL debut in October 1963 but he never quite had the quality or speed to maintain a regular place in United's first team.

It was future United manager, Ken Furphy who took him to Blackburn Rovers and he was immediately installed at right back and was a regular member of the Rovers first team for four seasons, captaining the side to the Division Three Championship in 1974–75. The following season, he suffered a knee injury which, despite an attempted comeback, ended his playing career.

He opened a local sports shop before returning to Ewood Park as reserve team coach and then, when Howard Kendall took over, as first team coach. He moved, with Kendall, to Goodison Park, but, when Kendall moved to Spain, Mick returned to run the Community programme at Blackburn. After a brief spell as manager of non-League Workington in 1989, he returned to Blackburn but in 1990 he joined up again with Howard Kendall as assistant manager at Manchester City.

He was working as a scout for Blackburn Rovers when he was killed in a road accident in 1995.

Appearances:

	Apps	Gls
FL	31 (3)	0
FAC	1	0
LC	3	0
CC	4	0
Total	39 (3)	0

HEDLEY George Albert

CF/IF 1898–1903 5' 10" 12st 0 to 12st 4
b. South Bank 20 July 1876
d. Wolverhampton 16 August 1942

South Bank
United: amat 10/11 Sep 1896, pro 6 May 1898 to May 1903
Debut: 26 Mar 1898 West Bromwich Albion 2 United 0
Last games: 28 Feb 1903 Bolton Wanderers 1 United 0
6 Apr 1903 West Yorkshire XI 5 United 8 (Fr)
Southampton May 1903/ Wolverhampton Wanderers May 1906 to cs1912
Bristol City manager Apr 1913 to May 1915

George Hedley was registered with the FL as a United amateur for nearly two years before he played his first game for the club. He finally came to Sheffield in 1898 as United closed in on securing the First Division championship and played in two of the last four games. He was chosen for the vital match at Bolton but his employer refused to let him play. His father was not keen on the young man becoming a professional player but finally relented and United forwarded £10 to the South Bank club 'for their kindness'.

George became a regular member of the first team for the following four seasons, leading the line well with good ball control, dribbling skills and general fine play, but he was not the most prolific of goal scorers, in part due to the fact that he 'was unselfish to a fault'. He played in three FA Cup finals for United, winning in 1899 and 1902, when he scored in the replay, but losing to Spurs in 1901. In his final season, he lost his place to the up and coming youngster Arthur Brown and it was also thought that damaged heart muscles would end his career. With United, he gained his one England Cap against Ireland at the Dell in 1901and he represented the Football League, scoring in the 2–2 draw against the Scottish League in 1900.

He moved to Southern League Southampton (no transfer fee being needed between Southern and FL clubs) and, after three successful seasons there, winning a Championship medal in 1904, he returned to the FL, signing for Wolves. He made nearly 200 appearances for Wolves, gaining another FA Cup winners medal in 1908, before hanging up his boots, returning to the game for two years as manager of Second Division Bristol City.

After his time as a manager, George became a licensee in Bristol and later, he ran a boarding house in Wolverhampton.

Appearances:

	Apps	Gls
FL	120	33
FAC	32	6
ABD	3	0
Total	155	39

HEELEY Charles Jones

LB 1902
b. Ecclesall (Sheffield) OND 1880

United: 24 Sep 1900 to cs 1907
Only game: 26 Dec 1902 United 7 Bolton Wanderers 1

Charles Heeley is possibly unique in that his single first team game in English football was in the First Division and ended in a 7–1 victory. A fairly regular reserve team player until 1906, he was a part timer and appeared in both full-back positions. He was transfer listed in 1904 and probably reverted to amateur status in October 1905.

Appearances:		Apps	Gls
	FL	1	0
	Total	1	0

HEFFERNAN Thomas (Tom) Patrick

RB 1983–85 6' 2" 12st 7
b. Dun Laoghoire (Dublin} 30 April 1955

Dun Laoghoire Celtic/ Tottenham Hotspur Oct 1977/ Bournemouth May 1979
United: (L) 25 Aug, (£20k) 5 Sep 1983 to 30 Jun 1985
Debuts: 29 Aug 1983 Bradford City 0 United 1 (LC)
3 Sep 1983 Lincoln City 0 United 2
Last games: 13 May 1985 Huddersfield Town 2 United 2
31 May 1985 Dallas Americans (USA) 0 United 2 (Fr)
Bournemouth Jul 1985/ Swanage Town & Herston Jul 1988/ Bournemouth 'Poppies'/ Downton/ Sturminster Marshall/ Hamworthy Engineering/ Parley Sports

Although his first professional club was Spurs, it wasn't until his free transfer move to Bournemouth that Tom Heffernan made his FL debut at Rochdale on 18 August 1979. He was a regular in the Bournemouth side and became their captain before his move to Bramall Lane

In his two season spell with United, he proved to be a capable defender and missed just seven competitive games out of a possible 105 and he was a key member of the defence when the club gained promotion to Division Two in 1984.

He returned to Bournemouth but injuries brought his playing career in the FL to an end, having played 292(7) games, in February 1988. He moved into non-League football, playing for a variety of clubs whilst working as a van driver for Allied Bakeries in Bournemouth. He later returned to Ireland becoming a painter and decorator.

Appearances:		Apps	Gls
	FL	82	5
	FAC	6	0
	LC	7	0
	AMC	3	0
	Total	98	5

HEMMINGFIELD A

CH 1890

Ecclesfield 1887/ Attercliffe 1889/ Doncaster Rovers cs1890
United: Oct or Nov 1890 to cs 1891
Debut: 14 Mar 1891 United 4 Kilnhurst 1 (SCC)
Last game: 21 Mar 1891 United 1 Doncaster Rovers 2 (SCCF)

Hemmingfield (also 'Hemingfield') had played as a professional for both Attercliffe and Doncaster Rovers before joining United. On the two occasions that he played for the United first team, the club had two fixtures on the same day (a friendly and a Sheffield Challenge Cup tie). He played in the cup games but failed to gain a winners' medal as United lost to Doncaster in the final.

Appearances:		Apps	Gls
	SCC	2	0
	Total	2	0

HEMMINGS A

CH 1895

Bucknall
United: trialist
Only game: 11 Mar 1895 United 2 Nottingham Forest 6 (UCL)

Playing at centre half, Hemmings gave 'a poor display' in his single appearance on trial in a United Counties League game

Appearances:		Apps	Gls
	UCL	1	0
	Total	1	0

HEMSLEY Edward (Ted) John Orton

LB/WH 1968–77 5' 8½" 11st 5
b. Norton (Stoke-on-Trent) 1 September 1943

Shrewsbury Town Jul 1961
United: (£27.5) 21/22 Aug 1968 to 30 Jun 1977
Debut: 24 Aug 1968 United 1 Millwall 0
Last game: 5 Mar 1977 Blackburn Rovers 1 United 0
Doncaster Rovers Jul 1977

Ted Hemsley was brought up in Shropshire and made his mark at football and cricket at Bridgnorth Grammar School. His FL debut with Shrewsbury Town came when he was seventeen on 29 April 1961 at Bradford City.

Arthur Rowley had been the Shrewsbury player-manager and when he took over as United's manager, Ted was one of the first players he signed. He was brought in as a reliable, tough tackling midfield player and it was there that he played in his first season. In November 1969, he was given an opportunity at left back, taking the place of Mick Heaton, and Ted made the position his own. He was a key member of the side that won promotion to the top flight in 1971 and he held his first team pace until 1975 when a stomach injury led to the introduction of Paul Garner.

Unitedites often recall Ted Hemsley as the player who missed the shoot-out penalty in the Watney Cup final of 1972 but he should be remembered as a committed and consistent full back. He was strong and decisive in the tackle, difficult to pass and his covering and marking were excellent. Voted the Supporters' Club 'Player of the Year' in 1973, he ended his soccer career, at Doncaster Rovers, having played more than 500 FL games.

A fine cricketer, he first played for Worcestershire in 1963, making his Championship debut in 1966 and continued to play county cricket until 1982. Ted played 243 first class matches, scoring 9740 runs at an average of 29.3 and he took 70 wickets at an average of 35.7 and was the last man to play both cricket and football at County and League level at Bramall Lane. He later ran a turf accountant business in Dronfield and has been involved in Bramall Lane hospitality on match days.

Appearances:		Apps	Gls
	FL	247	7
	FAC	10 (1)	0
	LC	17	2
	TEX	4	0
	ASC	1	0
	CC	8	0
	WC	5	1
	ABD	2	0
	Total	294 (1)	10

HENDERSON Charles

IR 1896
b. Hartlepool AMJ 1872 or Durham April 1870

South Bank 1891/ Grimsby Town Apr 1892/ Leith Athletic Feb 1893/ Bolton Wanderers cs 1894/ Wolverhampton Wanderers (£20) May 1895
United: 11 May 1896 to cs 1897
Debuts: 2 Sep 1896 Lincoln City 0 United 1 (Fr)
5 Sep 1896 United 1 Burnley 0
Last games: 5 Dec 1896 United 1 West Bromwich Albion 0
19 Dec 1896 Gainsborough Trinity 2 United 2 (Fr)
New Brighton Tower 26 Aug 1897/ South Bank/ Dundee Harp 1898?/ Edinburgh Thistle 1899–1901?

Charles Henderson made his FL debut with Grimsby Town in the club's first ever FL match on 3 September 1892 at home to Northwich Victoria. After a period with Leith Athletic, he moved to Bolton Wanderers where he was the club's top scorer in the 1894–95 season. Perhaps his most successful season was the following one with Wolves when he was ever present and appeared in the FA Cup Final, albeit on the losing side, against the Wednesday.

On moving to Bramall Lane in 1896, he began reasonably well, described as 'cool and steady, passing accurately' and he played in the first 13 FL games but made just one more appearance before moving on to play in New Brighton Tower's inaugural season.

Appearances:		Apps	Gls
	FL	14	4
	Total	14	4

HENDERSON Michael (Mick) Robert

MF/D 1982–84 5' 10" 11st 6
b. Gosforth, Newcastle 31 March 1956

Sunderland app Jul 1972, pro Apr 1974/ Watford (£125k) Nov 1979/ Cardiff City Mar 1982
United: (free) 21 Jul 1982 to 14 Jan 1985
Debuts: 3 Aug 1982 Raith Rovers 0 United 3 (Fr)
14 Aug 1982 United 1 Grimsby Town 3 (FLT)
28 Aug 1982 Portsmouth 4 United 1
Last game: 26 Dec 1984 Fulham 1 United 0
Chesterfield Jan 1985, player-coach 1987, to Feb 1989, coach, caretaker manager Oct 1988, player Nov to Feb 1989/ Matlock Town Sep 1989 / – / Sheffield local football

Mick Henderson made his FL debut with Sunderland, away to York City, on 1 November 1975. He moved to Watford for £125k, the only time he moved for a fee, and, after a brief period with Cardiff City who were relegated, he joined United.

A strong, hard tackling, two footed player but rather short of speed, Mick was signed by Ian Porterfield on a free transfer and made team captain as one of several new players who were added to the squad after United's promotion from Division Four. He was a regular member of the side, firstly as a defender and then in midfield until February 1984 but after promotion to Division Two had been secured, he found it more difficult to hold down a first team place and in January he moved to neighbours Chesterfield.

At Saltergate, his determined approach helped win the Fourth Division championship and he also took on a coaching role and, for a few weeks acted as caretaker manager. Given a free transfer in February 1989, he promptly broke his leg in a reserve match which brought his career as a FL player to an end. After retiring from football, having made 342(7) FL appearances, he joined the South Yorkshire Police force.

Appearances:		Apps	Gls
	FL	65 (2)	0
	FAC	11	0
	LC	6	0
	AMC	5	0
	Total	87 (2)	0

HENDRIE Lee Andrew

MF 2007– 5' 10" 11st 1
b. Birmingham 18 May 1977

Aston Villa from trainee May 1994/ Stoke City (L) Sep 2006/ Stoke City (L) Jan 2007
United: (free) 19 Jul 2007
Debuts: 4 Aug 2007 United 1 Nottingjam Forest 0 (Fr)
11 Aug 2007 United 2 Colchester United 2
Leicester City (L) 28 Feb 2008

Youth international Lee Hendrie made his League debut with Aston Villa, as a substitute, on 23 December 1995 at QPR, his full debut coming on 19 March 1996 at home to Middlesbrough. He went on to make 251 League appearances (27 gls) for Villa and gained one full England cap as well as those at B and U21 level. With a history of indiscretions that wouldn't have pleased his manager, he was out of the first team during 2006–07 and spent much of the season on loan at Stoke (28 app, 3gls).

Released at the end of the season, Lee was signed by new manager Bryan Robson but, being troubled by injuries, he was unable to get a consistent run in the side. By the time he returned the side was struggling and, although he showed glimpses of his potential as a hard working, energetic attacking midfielder, he failed to impress many in the crowd. He scored a fine winning goal against QPR but against Watford, he was substituted at half time and moved on loan to Leicester.

Appearances:

	Apps	Gls
FL	7 (5)	1
FAC	1	0
LC	1	0
Total	9 (5)	2

HENDRY William (Billy) Harold

CH 1891–95 5' 9½" 11st 0 to 13st 8
b. Newport on Tay (Fife) 1869
d. Kidderminster 4 May 1901

Dundee Wanderers 1886/ West Bromwich Albion May 1888/ Kidderminster Harriers Mar 1889/ Stoke Aug–Dec 1889/ Kidderminster Harriers early 1890?/ Preston North End early 1890
United: Feb 1891 to 30 May 1895
Debuts: 28 Feb 1891 Derby Junction 1 United 3 (MCL)
24 Oct 1891 United 4 Lincoln City 1 (FAC)
3 Sep 1892 United 4 Lincoln City 2
Last games: 26 Dec 1894 Blackburn Rovers 3 United 2
25 Mar 1895 United 3 Leicester Fosse 2 (UCL)
16 Apr 1895 Rotherham Town 3 United 2 (Fr)
Dundee May 1895/ Bury May 1896/ West Herts (Watford) trial Mar 1898/ Brighton United May 1898/ Shrewsbury Jul 1899 until his death

One of the most important though rarely remembered players in United's history; Billy Hendry left his native Scotland so that he could become a professional footballer. A centre forward in those days, he made his FL debut for West Bromwich Albion in their first ever FL match at Stoke on the Football League's first day, 8 September 1888. The following season saw him change to a central mid-field role, playing for Stoke and then for Preston North End and United.

It was said that it was the United Chairman, Charles Stokes, who was responsible for bringing Billy and two other Preston players to the Lane. North End dominated English football at that time and Stokes reasoned that an infusion of three of their players would bring a more professional attitude to United. He was correct and Billy was the key man, moving to United who were then, midway through their second season.

A stocky, cool, neat and effective player with fine control and superb heading ability, he captained the team and his inspirational leadership and ability on the field and all round knowledge of the game were soon apparent. United moved on to play in the NL and in 1892 were elected to the new Second Division of the Football League and Billy had the distinction of playing in United's first ever FL game just as he had done earlier with West Bromwich Albion.

The first United player to have a benefit, he had a 'strong personality' and was an influential figure with the Committee who 'set great value on his opinions as to the arrangement and formation of the team'. After just one season in the League, United gained promotion to Division One. Billy had a great part to play in developing the natural talents of Ernest Needham and he helped to lay the foundations of the team which gained so much success at the turn of the century.

An injury at Leith Athletic in a New Year's Day friendly in 1895 appeared to have brought his career as a top class player to an end and, after four more games, he left United and returned to Scotland.

He played for Dundee before returning south of the border and saw FL action again with Bury but died in 1901 of heart disease. More than forty years later, there were some elderly followers of the game who believed that, in view of his all round qualities, he was the best footballer that Sheffield had ever seen.

Appearances:

	Apps	Gls
FL	69	2
TM	1	0
FAC	8	0
NL	23	0
MCL	7	0
UCL	6	1
SCC	2	0
WCC	4	0
ABD	1	0
Total	121	3

HENRY Nicholas (Nick) Ian

MF 1997–99 5' 6" 10st 10
b. Liverpool 21 February 1969

Oldham Athletic from school Jan 1985, pro Jul 1987/ Halmstad (Sweden) (L) Mar 1988
United: **(exchange, valued c£500k) 28 Feb 1997 to 25 Mar 1999**
Debut: **7 Mar 1997 Barnsley 2 United 0**
Last games: **9 Jan 1999 Swindon Town 2 United 2**
23 Jan 1999 Notts County 3 United 4 (FAC)
27 Feb 1999 Norwich City 1 United 1 (sub)
Walsall (free) Mar 1999/ Tranmere Rovers Jul 1999/ Scarborough Jul 2002, mgr Jun 2004 to Oct 2005

Nick Henry made his FL debut with Oldham Athletic on 19 September 1987 at Hull City and went on to make play more than 300 FL and Cup games for the Latics in spite of suffering from a serious illness and injuries early in his career.

He joined United in an exchange deal, with Doug Hodgson joining the Lancashire team. Signed by Howard Kendall in early March 1997, his determined, energetic play helped the team reach the play-offs but Nick was sent-off in the semi-final second leg at Portman Road and he didn't play at Wembley. His hard tackling also had a down-side in that whilst making only twenty-one appearances in total for the Blades, he was sent off three times.

A back problem and hamstring injury limited him to one appearance the following season and, when he finally played again in November 1998, he broke his hand. Thereafter, he was in and out of the side and usually on the bench and he moved on to Walsall near the 1999 deadline day. Having played 369(17) FL games, he moved into non-League football with Scarborough where he was manager for sixteen months. Later he took a pub in Scarborough.

Appearances:		Apps	Gls
	FL	13 (3)	0
	PO	2	0
	FAC	2 (1)	0
	Total	17 (4)	0

HENSON George Horace

CF 1939–40 5' 10½" 12st 7
b. Stony Stratford 25 December 1911
d. Stony Stratford 25 April 1988

Wolverton Town/ Northampton Town amateur Nov 1932, pro Aug 1933/ Wolverhampton Wanderers (£1,700) Nov 1934/ Swansea Town (£850) May 1936/ Bradford PA (£400) Jun 1937
United: **(£3,000) 9/10 Mar 1939 to 4 May 1946**
Debut: **11 Mar 1939 United 1 Swansea Town 2**
Last games: **6 May 1939 United 6 Tottenham Hotspur 1**
2 Sep 1939 Leeds United 0 United 1 (1939–40)
11 May 1940 United 1 Barnsley 0 (WW2)
WW2 guest: Northampton T, Watford, Bedford Town
Bedford Town cs1946/ Stony Stratford by 1949 to 1951

A prolific scorer for Wolverton, George Henson made his FL debut with Northampton Town, scoring in the 2–2 draw at home to Norwich City on 30 September 1933.

He was signed by Teddy Davison, the United manager, to fill a gap that would result from the expected transfer of Jock Dodds to Blackpool and he moved to Bramall Lane having scored 62 goals in 132 games for four FL clubs. A powerful player with a fierce shot and with the enthusiasm that gave opponents no peace, George had scored six goals in one match for Bradford and his hat trick against United in April 1938 that had cost United promotion hadn't been forgotten.

It proved to be a good decision, the new man scoring on his United debut and adding a further four including a brace in the vital last match of the season which United needed to win to pip Wednesday for promotion.

George played in the three games at the start of the 1939–40 campaign, scoring United's final goal before the outbreak of the Second War. He then returned south and worked as a fitter in Bedford and made only three further appearances in United's colours.

Appearances:		Apps	Gls
	FL	10	5
	39–40	3	1
	CC	1	0
	WW2	3	1
	Total	17	7

HETHERSTON Peter

RW 1988 5' 9" 10st 7
b. Bellshill 6 November 1964

Rancel/ Bargeddie United 1983/ Falkirk Dec 1984/ Watford (£63k) Jul 1987
United: **(£50k) 19 Feb 1988 to 28 Jul 1988**
Debut: **20 Feb 1988 United 1 Barnsley 0**
Last games: **23 Apr 1988 United 0 West Bromwich Albion 0**
15 May 1988 Bristol City 1 United 0 (PO)
Falkirk Jul 1988/ Raith Rovers (£20k) cs 1991/ Aberdeen (over £200k) Jun 1994/ Airdrieonians (£100k) Mar 1996/ Partick Thistle Aug 1997/ Raith Rovers Aug 1999, player/mgr Dec 2000 to Dec 2001)/ Albion Rovers mgr May 2002 to Dec 2003/ Queen of the South Feb to Jun 2003

Peter made his League debut in Scotland with Falkirk on 29 December 1985 at home to East Fife. Having made around 70 appearances for Falkirk he moved south, making his FL debut with Watford as a substitute at home to Chelsea on 26 September 1987, his full debut coming on 17 October at Southampton.

He had been signed by Dave Bassett and, when 'Harry' moved to Bramall Lane, Peter was part of an exchange deal in which Tony Agana came to the Lane and Martin Kuhl moved to Watford. A clever, right sided attacking player, he was unfortunate on more than one occasion not to score but at the end of the season he felt he would be happier in Scotland and returned there, making more than 200 League appearances before retiring. He won the First Division Championship with Raith Rovers in 1992–93 and a League Cup winner's medal with Aberdeen in 1995. As manager of Albion Rovers he was in trouble for criticising a female referee.

Appearances:		Apps	Gls
	FL	11	0
	PO	1	0
	Total	12	0

HEWITT Gerald (Gerry)

RH 1957 5' 7" 10st 4
b. Sheffield 28 January 1935
d. 20 August 2007

United: **from jnr 10/13 Jul 1954 to 24 Jun 1958**
Debuts: **26 Jan 1957 United 3 Leeds United 1 (Fr)**
2 Feb 1957 United 0 Blackburn Rovers 2
Last game: **16 Feb 1957 United 0 Bristol Rovers 0**
Workington Jun 1958

Gerry Hewitt made just two FL appearances with United and had the misfortune to concede an own goal on his debut. He was transferred to Workington but failed to make a first team outing for the Cumbrian club.

Appearances:		Apps	Gls
	FL	2	0
	Total	2	0

HEWITT Ronald (Ron)

G 1945 6' 0"
b. Chesterfield 25 January 1924

Youlgreave
United: amateur 27 May 1944, pro 31 Oct/2 Nov 1944 to 4 May 1946
Debuts: 3 Mar 1945 United 2 Polish RAF XI 1 (Fr)
10 Mar 1945 Lincoln City 3 United 1 (WW2)
Last game: 17 Mar 1945 Derby County 3 United 2 (WW2)
WW2 guest: Shrewsbury T(1 app 1945–46)
Lincoln City Aug 1946/ Worksop Town Aug 1949/ Grantham cs 1952/ Spalding United 1957

A native of Barrow Hill near Chesterfield and a miner, Ron Hewitt made three war time appearances for the Blades before joining Lincoln City in 1946. A broken wrist meant that he missed virtually all that season and he didn't make his FL debut until 23 October 1948 at Fulham, two years after his move to Lincoln City. He made just three first team appearances for the City, conceding eleven goals and then moved into non-League football.

Appearances:		Apps	Gls
	WW2	2	0
	Total	2	0

HIBBERD William

OL 1898

United: 17 Aug 1898 to cs 1899 (see below)
Only game: 3 Dec 1898 United 1 Blackburn Rovers 1
Sheffield Club (1901–02)/ Wycliffe(1903–04)/ Mexborough T?/ Doncaster's Sports?

William Hibberd made just one first team appearance for United and a few for the reserves although he was registered by United with the FL for seasons 1902–03, 1903–04 and 1904–05.

Appearances:		Apps	Gls
	FL	1	0
	Total	1	0

HILL Colin Frederick

MF/RWB 1989–92 5' 11" 12st 11
b. Uxbridge 12 November 1963

Glebe Athletic/ Park Lane/ Hillingdon/ Arsenal amateur Dec 1979 pro Jul 1981/ Brighton & Hove Albion (L) Jan 1986/ Maritimo (Madeira) cs 1986/ Colchester United Oct 1987
United: (£85k) 1 Aug 1989 to 26 Mar/31 Jul 1992
Debuts: 9 Aug 1989 Scarborough 1 United 3 (sub YHC)
10 Aug 1989 United 1 Rotherham United 1 (YHC)
19 Aug 1989 West Bromwich Albion 0 United 3
Last games: 18 Jan 1992 United 1 Norwich City 0
26 Jan 1992 Charlton Athletic 0 United 0 (FAC)
15 Feb 1992 Chelsea 1 United 0 (sub FAC)
17 Feb 1992 United 4 New Zealand 2 (Fr)
17 Mar 1992 Leek Town 3 United XI 1 (sub Fr)
Leicester City (L) Mar 1992, (£200k, £34.5k to Colchester) Jul 1992/ Trelleborg (Sweden) cs 1997/ Northampton Town Nov 1997 to retired Jun 1999

Colin Hill made his FL debut with Arsenal on 20 April 1983 at Norwich City. After a time abroad in Portugal, he returned to England, joining Colchester United and it was from that club that Dave Basset signed him. Colin had made 46 FL appearances for Arsenal and 69 for Colchester.

Colin joined United after the club's promotion to the old Division Two and, playing as a right wing back, he missed only three League games in the season which led to United returning to the top Division in 1990. A solid and reliable defender, Colin now played more in midfield and central defence, scoring his one goal for the club in the 2–2 draw at Norwich City in August 1991. His appearances became less frequent and, after a period on loan, he was transferred to Leicester City.

After a brief spell in Sweden, he ended his career with Northampton Town, having played 376(20) League games and scoring just two goals. Colin, who had an Irish father, won 27 Northern Ireland caps of which the first six came when he was with United.

Appearances:		Apps	Gls
	FL	77 (5)	1
	FAC	10 (2)	0
	LC	5	0
	FMC	3	0
	YHC	1 (1)	0
	Total	96 (8)	1

HILL Michael (Mick) Richard

CF/IF 1967–69 6' 0" 11st 10
b. Hereford 3 December 1947
d. Hereford 23 June 2008

Cardiff City/ Bethesda Athletic 1965
United: (£500) 16/20 Sep 1965 to 17/20 Oct 1969
Debut: 22 Apr 1967 Leicester City 2 United 2
Last games: 9 Nov 1968 United 0 Carlisle United 1
13 Sep 1969 Birmingham City 2 United 1 (sub)
Ipswich Town (£30/33k) Oct 1969/ Colchester United (L)/ Crystal Palace (£35k) Dec 1973/ Cape Town City (South Africa) Feb 1976

The son of a former Cardiff City winger and spotted by a scout, Mick Hill joined United as a 17 year old but he had to wait nineteen months to make his first team scoring debut in a 2–2 draw against Leicester City. He became a regular member of the side from October 1967 and scored six goals in 24 FL outings but after being in and out of the side during the following season, he moved to Ipswich Town where he won two Welsh caps. Sadly, he was in dispute with both Bobby Robson and Jim Smith (who had taken him on loan at Colchester but never gave him a first team opportunity) and after a period with Crystal Palace, he moved to South Africa. In all, he made 148 FL appearances scoring 33 goals.

Appearances:		Apps	Gls
	FL	35 (2)	9
	FAC	3	1
	CC	4	2
	Total	42 (2)	12

HILL Robert (Bob)

CF/IF/OR 1892–95 5' 6½" 11st 12
b. Forfar 3 July 1867
d. Redcar 3 October 1938

Black Watch/ Glentoran/ Linfield cs 1890
United: 11 Feb 1893 to 7/9 Nov 1895
Debuts: 11 Feb 1893 United 4 Nottingham F 3 (Fr)
4 Mar 1893 Ardwick 2 United 3
Last games: 7 Oct 1895 United 1 Sunderland 2
23 Oct 1895 Gainsborough Trinity 2 United 0 (Fr
Ardwick (Manchester City) Nov 1895 to cs 1897/ Watford St Mary's Feb 1898 to cs 1898/ Millwall Oct 1898/ Brighton United May 1899/ Dundee Mar 1900/ Forfar Athletic Aug 1901

Bob Hill was a soldier in the Black Watch Regiment who showed potential as a footballer. He made one appearance for Glentoran in a friendly match but it was Linfield who bought him out of the army and secured his signature and he was successful in winning two Irish Cup and Championship medals with the Belfast club.

He came for a trial with United and scored in a friendly match against Forest under the pseudonym of 'Jones'. An intelligent and well respected forward, he established himself in the first team towards the end of the 1892–93 season, playing in the Test Match which clinched promotion to the top Division. He was a frequent member of the first team for the following two seasons but, despite having started 1895–96 as a regular, he moved to Ardwick (now Manchester City) in November 1895 with Joe Davies and Hugh Morris.

Appearances:		Apps	Gls
	FL	58	18
	TM	1	0
	FAC	2	1
	NL	1	2
	UCL	5	0
	WCC	1	0
	Total	68	21

HILL Roy

RB 1975
b. Sheffield

Simplex MW
United: 10 Oct 1973 to 8 Jun 1976
Debuts: 8 Apr 1975 Barnsley 3 United 3
(Testimonial abandoned due to snow)
Last game: 16 Sep 1975 United 5 Rotherham United 0 (CC)

A Hinde House School and Sheffield Boys player, Roy Hill became an apprentice professional when he was sixteen. In his one competitive first team appearance, Roy helped the Blades to progress to the final of the County Cup but he was not chosen for that game. He 'left the club' in November 1975 but returned in March only to be given a free transfer at the end of April 1976.

Appearances:		Apps	Gls
	CC	1	0
	Total	1	0

HILL Walter

LH/RH/FB 1892–96

Grimethorpe
United: cs 1891 (FL 12 Jun 1892–cs 1896) to cs1899
Debuts: 1 Jan 1892 United 4 Rotherham Town 3 (Fr)
23 Jan 1892 United 4 Doncaster Rovers 0 (SCC)
30 Apr 1892 Middlesbrough Ironopolis 2 United 1 (NL)
10 Sep 1892 Bootle 2 United 0
Last games: 4 Feb 1896 Burnley 5 United 0
10 Feb 1896 Walsall 2 United 5 (BC)
19 Dec 1896 Gainsborough Trinity 2 United 2 (Fr)

Although he was with United for eight seasons, Walter spent most of the time in the reserves and never played more than five consecutive games for the first team. He did play in about 30 friendly games as well as those listed below and was a Sheffield Challenge Cup winner with the reserves in April 1899.

Appearances:		Apps	Gls
	FL	15	0
	NL	1	0
	UCL	2	0
	SCC	3	0
	WCC	2	0
	BC	2	0
	Total	25	0

HITCHEN Henry (Harry)

RH/CF/CH 1948–53 6' 0" 12st 6 to 12st 12
b. Liverpool 22 October 1922
d. Whiston 9 April 1993

Formby/ New Brighton Aug 1946 (ama), Sep 1946 (pro)
United: (£4000) 11/13 May 1948 to 20 May 1953
Debut: 25 Sep 1948 Portsmouth 3 United 0
Last games: 24 Jan 1953 United 3 Barnsley 0
31 Jan 1953 United 1 Birmingham City 1 (FAC)
22 Apr 1953 Buxton v United XI (BM)?
Bury May 1953

Because of the Second War in which he saw service in Burma, China and Egypt with the Royal Marine Commandos, Harry Hitchen was just turned 24 years old when he made his FL debut with New Brighton on 26 October 1946 at home to Hull City.

Signed by Teddy Davison, his transfer to United in 1948 may have been the biggest fee received by the Cheshire club. Harry's normal position was at centre half or wing half but his debut was at centre forward and was not a success and it was not until February 1949, after a famous County Cup victory at Hillsborough, that Harry (and Joe Shaw) became regular first team players. United were relegated but he kept his place for three seasons, being an ever-present in 1951–52, playing mainly at right half but with occasional appearances at centre half and a few at centre forward.

A careful, stern, hard tackling player though rather stiff and lacking pace, he was made team captain, but in his final season at Bramall Lane, when United took the Second Division title, he fractured his leg and played in only sixteen games. At the end of the season he moved to Bury but played only twice.

Appearances:		Apps	Gls
	FL	154	15
	FAC	13	0
	CC	5	0
	Total	172	15

HOBSON James (George or Judd)

OR 1908–09 5' 8½" 10st 7
b. Ecclesfield 1886

Ecclesfield Church/ Rotherham County cs 1903/ Ecclesfield Town cs 1904/ Worksop Town cs 1905
United: 24 Apr 1907 to cs 1909
Debut: 18 Jan 1908 United 2 Manchester United 0
Last game: 3 Apr 1909 Preston North End 1 United 1
New Brompton cs 1909/ Grimsby Town cs 1910/ Bolton Wanderers 1911–12

James Hobson spent two seasons at Bramall Lane, playing eight games in 1907–08 and seven the following season before moving on to New Brompton. He was a member of the Grimsby Town team who were Midland League champions in 1911 but didn't appear in the Bolton first team. He emigrated to Australia and coached the Alexandra team in Adelaide.

Appearances:		Apps	Gls
	FL	15	2
	Total	15	2

HOBSON Walter

CH 1889–90

Wednesday/Owlerton
United: cs 1889 to cs 1890
Debuts: 14 Sep 1889 Heeley 1 United 2 (Fr)
5 Oct 1889 Scarborough 1 United 6 (FAC)
Last games: 1 Feb 1890 Bolton Wanderers 13 United 0 (FAC)
22 Mar 1890 Rotherham Town 1 United 0 (SCC)
19 Apr 1890 Newcastle East End 2 United 0 (Fr)
Owlerton/ Rotherham Town

A powerful and skilful player, Walter Hobson had been Owlerton's captain and was one of the first three players—one report has him as the first—that United signed and was a regular member of the first team in the club's first season. He made his debut in United's second game and, as centre half, he played in 41 games, 27 of which were friendlies. During the season he played in what is still United's largest FA Cup victory (at Scarborough) and heaviest defeat (at Bolton).

When his playing career was virtually over, he made his FL debut with Rotherham Town on 28 December 1893 at Ardwick (now Manchester City). His last and twentieth FL appearance was in October 1895.

Appearances:		Apps	Gls
	FAC	7	0
	SCC	6	1
	WCC	1	0
	Total	14	1

HOCKEY Trevor

LH 1971–72 5' 6½" 10st 6
b. Keighley 1 May 1943
d. Keighley 1 April 1987

Keighley Central 1957/ Bradford City app May 1958, pro May 1960/ Nottingham Forest (£15k) Nov 1961/ Newcastle United (£25k) Nov 1963/ Birmingham City (£22.5k) Nov 1965
United: (£40k) 27/28 Jan 1971 to 20–22 Feb 1973
Debut: 30 Jan 1971 Oxford United 1 United 2
Last game: 30 Dec 1972 Newcastle United 4 United 1
Norwich City (exchange) Feb 1973/ Aston Villa (£38k) Jun 1973/ Bradford City (£12.5k) Jun 1974/ Athlone Town player-mgr Mar 1976/ San Diego Jaws Apr 1976/ Las Vegas Quicksilvers Apr 1977/ San Jose Earthquakes Jun 1977/ Stalybridge Celtic manager Aug 1977–78 / – / Keighley Town mgr Oct 1980

Trevor Hockey was born in Keighley where his Welsh father had moved to play Rugby League. He joined Bradford City and made his debut at the age of sixteen, on 2 April 1960 at Shrewsbury Town. A small, determined and energetic right winger, he was signed by Nottingham Forest for what was then a record fee for Bradford City. After two seasons, he moved to Birmingham City, where this extrovert character, who owned a custom built car with a velvet covered bonnet and a pink piano, became a hard tackling wing half and his six seasons with the club proved to be the longest of his nomadic career.

His move to Bramall Lane was a great success. United were fifth in Division Two but promotion looked to be slipping away and Trevor added steel, inspiration and energy to midfield. The instructions he received from John Harris, the United manager, were simple; his task was to win the ball and give it to Tony Currie and he did this admirably. Whilst with United, he won four Welsh caps, being the first player, known to have been born in England, to be capped by Wales, and he went on to win nine in total. Bearded and with long banded hair, his swashbuckling dynamic approach to the game added zest to the talented team that brought promotion and great enthusiasm to the club and supporters.

He lost his place in the team to Keith Eddy, mid-way through the 1972–73 season and moved to Norwich in a part exchange deal for Jim Bone with Trevor valued at about £40k. In total he made 521(2) FL appearances. In later years, he coached for a time in Germany and at Pontin's holiday camps and later ran a hotel in Keighley and died after playing in a five-a-side soccer match at the age of forty three.

Appearances:		Apps	Gls
	FL	68	4
	FAC	1	0
	LC	9	0
	TEX	2	0
	CC	1	0
	WC	3	0
	Total	84	4

HODGES Glyn Peter

LMF 1991–96 6' 0" 12st 10
b. Streatham 30 April 1963

Wimbledon app Feb 1981 pro Apr 1981/ Newcastle United (£300k) Jul 1987/ Watford ((£250/320k) Sep 1987/ Crystal Palace (£410k) Jun 1990
United: (L) 16/17 Jan 1991, (£410k) 15 Apr 1991 to 12/15 Feb 1996
Debut: 19 Jan 1991 Manchester City 2 United 0
Last games: 26 Dec 1995 United 1 Birmingham City 1
6 Jan 1996 Arsenal 1 United 1 (FAC)
20 Jan 1996 United1 Watford 1 (sub)
28 Jan 1996 United 0 Aston Villa 1 (sub FAC)
Derby County (free) Feb 1996 to cs 1996/ Sin Tao (Hong Kong) Jul 1996/ Nottingham F(trial)/ Hull City Aug 1997/ Nottingham Forest Feb 1998/ Scarborough Jan 1999/ Total Network Solutions (Welsh League) cs 1999/ United coaching staff Feb 2000/ Barnsley coach, caretaker mgr Oct to Nov 2001, acting mgr Oct 2002 to Jun 2003/ Wales U21 coach Mar to Nov 2004/ Blackburn Rovers reserve team coach Nov 2004 to present

Glyn Hodges joined Wimbledon from school in 1979 and made his FL debut as a substitute on 27 September 1980 at Halifax Town, his full debut coming on 11 October at home to Hartlepool United. He took part in Wimbledon's rise from Division Four to Division One, winning a Division Four championship medal in 1983 and in 1984 he became Wimbledon's first international when he came on as a substitute for Wales against Norway. He joined Newcastle United in 1987 but, 86 days later, he moved to Watford, signed by their new manager, and Glyn's former Wimbledon boss, Dave Bassett.

After becoming United's manager, Bassett tried to sign Glyn in the 1990 close season but it wasn't until early in 1991 that he came to the Lane on loan. His fine midfield play and vital goals helped to secure United's place in the top flight after relegation looked likely and in mid-April, the move was made permanent and he remained with the Blades until 1996, shortly after Howard Kendall's arrival as manager.

Glyn was one of those players frequently described as 'enigmatic' as he could delight and frustrate and was totally unpredictable. With a wonderful left foot, he had great touch, skill and vision but also, a certain lack of 'application, concentration and tolerance' (he was dismissed three times including being one of the three players sent off against Udinese). He found himself on the subs bench more often than a player with his talent should have done. Dave Bassett noted that it was 'stupid for a player of his talent to have achieved so little'.

A Welsh youth international, he won caps at U21 and B level and was awarded eighteen full caps, five whilst with United. After retiring he went into coaching with two spells as manager of Barnsley. In 2006 he represented United in the Yorkshire Masters.

Appearances:		Apps	Gls
	FL	116 (31)	19
	FAC	13 (3)	3
	LC	4 (3)	0
	AIC	1	0
	Total	134 (37)	22

HODGKINSON Alan (Hodgy) MBE

G 1954–71 5' 9½" 11st 2 to 12st 3
b. Laughton en le Morthen nr Rotherham 16 August 1936

Worksop Town 1951
United: Trial from Feb 1953, (£250) 17 Aug 1953 to 20 Dec 1971
Debuts: 6 Apr 1954 United 0 Clyde 1 (Fr)
28 Aug 1954 Newcastle United 1 United 2
Last games: 16 Jan 1971 Bolton Wanderers 2 United 1
23 Jan 1971 Chesterfield 1 United 0 (Fr)
10 May 1971 Swansea City 3 United 5 (sub BM)
Coaching staff 1971 to Nov 1975

Brought up in Thurcroft, near Rotherham, Alan Hodgkinson's first job was as a butcher's boy but, aged fifteen, he played in the tough Midland League for Worksop Town. Although Huddersfield Town showed an interest in Alan, it was United's manager Reg Freeman who secured a gentleman's agreement with the Worksop manager that Alan could have a trial with United reserves when he was sixteen and, if he joined the Blades on his seventeenth birthday, Worksop would receive £250.

Alan's early ability was remarkable. He played for the 'A' team and then for the reserves against Bury (11 April 1953 whilst still sixteen) and he was just eighteen when he made his FL debut. He gained a great deal of experience with Army and representative sides while serving in the Royal Signals during his National Service but this complicated his appearances for United and the first of his seven England U23 caps was sandwiched between appearances for United's third team. Because of Service commitments he did not become a regular in the first team until January 1956 and, in April 1957, he gained his first full England cap playing against Scotland after just 28 FL appearances. Four other caps came his way and he was never on the losing side.

He will be remembered as the goalkeeper behind the fine defence of Cec Coldwell, Graham Shaw, Brian Richardson, Joe Shaw and Gerry Summers. Moulded and coached by Joe Mercer, they were automatic selections between 1957 and 1963. Most memorable was the 1960–61 season when United were promoted and reached the FA Cup semi-final, losing at the third attempt to Leicester City.

Although on the small side for a 'keeper, Alan had a safe pair of hands, was strong, brave and agile and read the game well, making his work appear straightforward if not simple but above all, he was consistent and dependable and a blunder or 'soft' goal was virtually unknown. His judgement and anticipation were remarkable and between August 1957 and January 1971 he missed just 27 of a possible 571 FL games. It was only in the 1970–71 season that his reliability showed signs of wavering and, in January, he was replaced by John Hope, United going on to win promotion.

As well as Under 23 and full caps, Alan also played for the Football League and, as far as the Blades are concerned, only Joe Shaw has played more League games, with Alan playing a total 674 competitive games for the club. After retiring he was on the United coaching staff until November 1975 when he became Gerry Summers' assistant at Gillingham. Alan then became a specialist goalkeeping coach, eventually concentrating on assisting the Scottish national side. He gave up this role in 1999 but continued to coach at various clubs beyond his seventieth birthday. In January 2008 he was awarded the MBE.

Appearances:		Apps	Gls
	FL	576	0
	FAC	52	0
	LC	24	0
	CC	19	0
	WC	2	0
	ABD	1	0
	Total	674	0

HODGSON Douglas (Doug) John

CH/MF/WB 1994–97 6' 2" 13st 10
b. Frankston (Melbourne), Australia 27 February 1969

Dufftown (Victoria)/ Heidelberg Alex (Victoria)/ Dinalya Serbia (L) (W A)/ Hull C (trial) 1993

United: 18 May (trial), (£30k rising to £70k) 7 Jun, 4/22 Jul 1994 to 28 Feb 1997
Debuts: 18 May 1994 Northern NSW 1 United 1 (Fr)
24 Aug 1994 United 1 Udinese (Italy) 2 (AIC)
20 Sep 1994 Stockport County 1 United 5 (LC)
22 Oct 1994 United 1 Luton Town 3 (sub)
12 Sep 1995 United 2 Charlton Athletic 0
Last game: 22 Feb 1997 United 3 Grimsby Town 1
Plymouth Argyle (trial Jul), (L) 10 Aug 1995/ Mansfield T(L)/ Burnley(L) 17 Oct 1996
Oldham Athletic Feb 1997/ Northampton Town (L), (£20k) Oct 1998/ retired Dec 1999

Doug played against United for Western Australia and was invited by Dave Bassett to join the United party as a guest player on the close season tour and was signed ready for the start of the 1994–95 campaign. He played in just one League game during that season, coming on as a striker but for the following two, he frequently played in defence when the first choice players were unavailable.

Courage and determination were major factors in his character. Injured in a traffic accident when he was fifteen, he wore a neck brace for three years and a broken nose during the 1994–95 season led to three operations. Doug was not the most skilful of players but he was enthusiastic, direct, uncompromising in the tackle and good in the air. The single goal he recorded with United at Bradford City came shortly before his move to Oldham Athletic. He was transferred in an exchange deal involving Nick Henry valuing Doug at about £100k.

His playing career came to an early end at Northampton Town where a neck injury proved more serious than was first thought. He joined the United coaching staff in January 2000 but had to return to Australia in October when his father was ill and, in 2002, was coaching in Adelaide.

Appearances:		Apps	Gls
	FL	24 (6)	1
	FAC	2 (1)	0
	LC	3 (1)	0
	AIC	1	0
	Total	30 (8)	1

HODGSON William (Bill, Billy)

IL/OL 1957–63 5' 6½" 10st 7
b. Glasgow 9 July 1935

Dunoon Athletic/ St Johnstone cs 1954/ Guildford City (L) Sep 1956

United: (L) 15/24 May 1957, (£3,250) c4 Nov 1957 to 13/14/15 Sep 1963
Debut: 31 Aug 1957 Lincoln City 2 United 2
Last game: 31 Aug 1963 United 1 Chelsea 1
Leicester City (£20k) Sep 1963/ Derby County (£12k) Jun 1965/ Rotherham United, player-coach Sep 1967/ York City, player-coach Dec 1967, temporary manager Aug 1968 to Oct 1968/ United coach 8 Jul 1970 to Jul 1971/ Hamilton Academicals pl/coach 1971–72/ Irvine Victoria manager

Billy Hodgson began his playing career with St Johnstone and made 80 League and Cup appearances before his call up for National Service led to him being based in Southsea and playing as a guest with Guildford City. United's manager, Joe Mercer, signed Bill in 1957, initially on loan and after seven first team appearance he signed permanently.

Although small and lightweight, Bill was a tricky player, difficult to dispossess, with good ball control. He was a lively character who played with great commitment and energy and tackled well. He played mostly at outside left but when Ronnie Simpson was signed and took the left wing position, Billy played inside him. He could also perform an excellent man-to-man marking job, snuffing out, for instance, the threat of Danny Blanchflower in United's memorable 3–0 FA Cup victory over Spurs in 1958.

Bill was a key member of the United side for six years, including the 1960–61 promotion season when the club also reached the semi-final of the FA Cup. Injured in his final game when he collided with Peter Bonetti, the Chelsea goalkeeper, he moved on to Leicester City. He made 383 FL appearances and scored 62 goals.

Bill had a full FA coaching badge and assisted Joe Shaw when Joe was manager of York City, Bill taking over for a time when Joe resigned and he returned to the Lane to coach the juniors before, for family reasons, he returned to Scotland.

Appearances:		Apps	Gls
	FL	152	32
	FAC	18	1
	LC	6	2
	CC	7	2
	Total	183	37

HOGG John (Jack)

RH/CH 1904–05 5' 8" 11st 6 to 12st 7
b. Sunderland 22 May 1881
d. Newcastle-on-Tyne 2 August 1944

Sunderland/ Morpeth Harriers
United: 1/2 May 1903 to May 1905
Debut: 12 Mar 1904 Liverpool 3 United 0
Last games: 26 Mar 1904 Blackburn Rovers 3 United 0
29 Apr 1905 Woolwich Arsenal 2 United 3 (Fr)
Southampton May 1905 to cs 1907 / – / West Stanley May 1908/ Hartlepools United Nov 1909 to cs 1912

John Hogg had signed for Sunderland but lived to some extent in the shadow of his two older brothers who were both forwards with the north east club and he was never selected for the first team.

John's enthusiasm and grit were never in doubt but he froze when given a first team opportunity with United and, despite being at Bramall Lane for two seasons, he played just three FL games, all in March 1904. He played in the Southern League with Southampton before moving back to his native North East, United retaining his FL registration until 1915.

Appearances:		Apps	Gls
	FL	3	0
	Total	3	0

HOLDSWORTH David Gary

CD 1996–99 6' 1" 12st 4 to 12st 10
b. Walthamstow 8 November 1968

Watford from trainee to app Apr 1985, pro Nov 1986
United: (£300k rising to £500k) 3/4/8 Oct 1996 to 22/23 Mar 1999
Debut: 12 Oct 1996 United 0 Tranmere Rovers 0
Last game: 20 Mar 1999 United 3 Port Vale 0
Birmingham City (£1.2m) Mar 1999/ Walsall (L) Jan 2002/ Bolton Wanderers Sep 2002/ Scarborough Nov 2002/ Gretna Jul 2003 to May 2005, youth coach to Dec 2006/ media work/ Ilkeston T mgr May 2008

David Holdsworth, and his twin brother Dean, began their careers with Watford. David made his FL debut at West Bromwich Albion on 29 August 1988 and went on to make over 250 League appearances for the club in spite of serious injury problems. During his time at Vicarage Road, he had captained the England U17 team and gained England youth and U 21 caps.

When Howard Kendall became United's manager, he invested heavily in an attempt to take the club back to the Premiership and David was one of his signings early in the 1996–97 season. He was soon made captain, bringing stability and strength to the defence and forming a fine partnership with Michel Vonk and later Carl Tiler but, although the play-off final was reached, United lost to a last minute goal.

David was a very popular player; reliable, confident and consistent, he was good in the air, with good anticipation and always looking comfortable on the ball. He played steadfastly throughout the following season whilst Nigel Spackman and Steve Thompson came and went and he will be remembered for scoring the last minute goal against Coventry City in the FA Cup which resulted in United reaching the semi-final. He missed much of the following season through injury but, despite being as influential as before on his return, it was decided that he would be sold to Birmingham City in March 1999 although there were reports that he didn't want to move.

After leaving Birmingham City, he joined Bolton Wanderers, making a League Cup appearance, before moving into non-League football with Scarborough, having totalled 419(16) League appearances. He then moved to Scotland with the up-and-coming Gretna, where he continued to coach after he finished playing. He left to concentrate on his Soccer Schools and his Radio work as summariser on Radio Sheffield for United's games.

In May 2008 he became the manager of Ilkeston Town.

Appearances:		Apps	Gls
	FL	93	4
	PO	5	0
	FAC	13	3
	LC	7	0
	Total	118	7

HOLLAND Paul

MF 1995 5' 11" 12st 10
b. Lincoln 18 July 1973

Mansfield Town from jnr Jul 1991
United: (£200k+) 12/15/20 Jun 1995 to 5 Jan 1996
Debuts: 23 Jul 1995 Verdal(Norway) 0 United 2 (Fr, sub)
12 Aug 1995 Watford 2 United 1
Last game: 23 Dec 1995 Stoke City 2 United 2
Chesterfield (£150k) Jan 1996/ Bristol City (£200k) Sep 1999 / Mansfield Town coach, Jan 2002, very briefly caretaker mgr Dec 2006, asst mgr Dec 2007, mgr Mar 2008 to cs 2008

Paul Holland began his career with Mansfield Town, making his FL debut at Crewe Alexandra on 11 May 1991. He gained international honours for England at schoolboy, youth and Under 21 level before moving to Bramall Lane.

Paul was signed by Dave Bassett at the start of the Blades' second season in Division One after being relegated from the Premiership. A neat, stylish, attacking midfield player, he never made the progress expected of him. He was a regular member of the squad, either in the starting line-up or on the bench, until Howard Kendall's arrival when he found himself 'surplus to requirements'.

He moved on to Chesterfield for what may have been a record fee for the Derbyshire club and then to Bristol City where a knee injury ended his career in which he had made 295(18) FL appearances.

He then became a member of the Mansfield Town coaching staff, being caretaker manager for one game before Billy Dearden was appointed, with Paul as his assistant. Following Dearden's departure in March 2008, Paul was made acting manager to the end of the season but was unable to keep Town in the FL.

Appearances:		Apps	Gls
	FL	11 (7)	1
	LC	2	1
	Total	13 (7)	2

HOLMES Ian Michael

OL/OR 1968–73 5' 7½" 10st 8
b. Wombwell 8 December 1950

United: from 12 Dec 1967 and 16 Jan 1968 to May 1973
Debuts: 17 May 1968 Doncaster Rovers 3 United 1 (CC)
4 Apr 1972 United 1 Manchester United 1
Last games: 21 Oct 1972 United 0 Everton 1
26 Dec 1972 United 0 Liverpool 3 (sub)
3 Feb 1973 Carlisle United 2 United 1 (FAC)
York City Jul 1973/ Huddersfield Town (£10k) Oct 1977–Jun 1980/ Gainsborough Trinity player-coach

A skilful winger, Ian Holmes came to United from the De La Salle School but lacked the speed, power and determination to succeed at the top level of English football. He made ten first team appearances with United and his last was in a particularly dreadful team display in a cup-tie at Carlisle.

He was given a free transfer and went on to make 232 FL appearances for York City and later Huddersfield Town, scoring 51 goals. In particular, he was a key member of the York side which, in 1973–74, gained promotion to the old Second Division. He later moved into non-League football as a part timer and set up a business selling insurance to professional footballers.

Appearances:		Apps	Gls
	FL	4 (2)	0
	FAC	1	0
	LC	1 (1)	0
	CC	1	0
	Total	7 (3)	0

HOLMES James (Jimmy)

CH 1931–36 5' 11½" 11st 10 to 12st 6
b. Skelmersdale 27 December 1908
d. Chesterfield 1 November 1971

Sutton Commercial/ Sutton Parish/ amat with Liverpool and Wigan Borough 1925 / – / Prescot Cables 1928/ Chesterfield May 1930
United: (£1,750) 4/5 May 1931 to 16 Jun 1936
Debut: 3 Oct 1931 Manchester City 1 United 1
Last game: 26 Mar 1936 United 0 Fulham 1
West Ham United (£750) Jun 1936/ Reading Jul 1937 to Sept 1940
WW2 guest for Chesterfield (2 appearances Oct 1940)

Although he had played as a amateur with the Liverpool third team and Wigan Borough reserves, Jimmy Holmes came to the fore with Prescot Cables. A miner before joining Chesterfield, Jimmy made his FL debut on 6 December 1930 at Wigan Borough and after just 26 games he moved to Bramall Lane.

A strong and determined defender, his occasional more than robust approach to the game could get him into trouble and United left him out of a Boxing Day fixture at Highbury because of his treatment of Alex James which had shown little of the true spirit of Christmas. On another occasion, when a referee had denied him a 'goal', he shook him as a dog would a rat. He missed few games until the start of the 1935–36 campaign when Tom Johnson at last began to look more confident as a centre half and by December 1935 Johnson had become first choice.

In what turned out to be his last appearance for United, Holmes conceded a penalty which probably cost United promotion and, at the end of the season, he was transferred to West Ham United and subsequently Reading where he completed his 236 FL games.

Appearances:		Apps	Gls
	FL	135	0
	FAC	4	1
	CC	7	0
	Total	146	1

HOLMES John Thomas

OR 1901
b. Chesterfield AMJ 1880

Brunswick (Sheffield)/ Roundel (Sheffield) Aug 1901
United: 5/9 Oct 1901 to cs 1903
Debuts: 21 Oct 1901 United 2 Celtic 2 (BM)
26 Oct 1901 United 3 Derby County 0
Last game: 9 Nov 1901 United 3 Notts County 0
/ – / Fulham Aug 1904/ Southern United Aug 1905/ Fulham Dec 1905/ Tunbridge Wells Rangers Jul 1907 to at least 1912

Thomas Holmes made just four first team appearances, one a friendly, all shortly after his arrival. Although United held his FL registration seemingly until cs 1903, he appears to have left the club in the close season of 1902. He was even less successful when he eventually joined Fulham for he made just one first team appearance in his two spells with the Southern League club.

Appearances:		Apps	Gls
	FL	3	0
	Total	3	0

HOLMES S

OR 1918

United: WW1 guest
Only game: 16 Mar 1918 United 0 Wednesday 5 (WW1)

Reported as a 'young local' player, his single appearance was as a guest player during the First World War.

Appearances:		Apps	Gls
	WW1	1	0
	Total	1	0

HOOPER Harry Reed

RB/LB 1930–46 5' 9/5' 10" 11st 6 to 12st 2
b. Nelson 16 December 1910
d. Halifax 24 March 1970

Nelson Boys/ Nelson Trades/ Nelson amat 1927 to pro Nov 1928
United: (c£400) 15/17 Feb 1930 to 14 Jun 1947
Debut: 26 Dec 1930 United 5 Blackpool 1
Last games: 27 Dec 1938 Southampton 2 United 2
26 Jan 1946 Stoke City 2 United 0 (FAC)
13 Apr 1946 Blackburn Rovers 0 United 0 (WW2)
30 Apr 1947 Boston U 3 United XI 2 (CM)
WW2: Portsmouth (2 app) 1940–41
Hartlepool United 2 Aug 1947 to cs 1950/West Ham United trainer Nov 1950–57/ Halifax Town manager Oct 1957 to Apr 1962

Harry Hooper, who trained as a tailor in his youth and was always smart looking and well groomed, made his FL debut with Nelson in the old Third Division North on 7 September 1929 at Crewe Alexandra. He joined United along with Harry Tordoff for a joint transfer fee of £750.

A two-footed full-back, he could play on either flank; when he first arrived at Bramall Lane, he played reasonably regularly as left back but from 1933 to January 1939 he played at right back missing very few games. He was a fine kicker of the ball, a good tackler but his real strengths were his speed, his shrewd, calm play and his ability to keep an opponent on the touch-line, out of harms way. Harry captained United in the 1936 FA Cup final taking the post from Archie McPherson in November 1935 and holding it until the end of the following season when Tom Johnson took over.

Harry had an very good penalty record, shooting just inside the post with just enough power to beat the keeper and scoring nine of eleven taken in the FL and adding a further goal with a rebound off the 'keeper. He missed the end of the 1938–39 promotion season through injury and the next seven seasons because of the Second War. He served in the RAOC and rarely played for United. He did make a few appearances in 1945–46 but then played in the reserves until he moved to Hartlepool United, where his career total of FL games reached 356.

His son, Harry, played professional football and when he moved to West Ham United, Harry senior moved there as a trainer before returning north as the manager of Halifax Town.

A heavy cigarette smoker; he always had one at half-time, and Jack Smith, the United goalkeeper, was one of the few players who would share a room with him on away trips. Harry suffered from lung cancer and died aged fifty nine.

Appearances:		Apps	Gls
	FL	269	10
	FAC	23	1
	CC	8	0
	WW2	7	1
	Total	307	12

HOPE John William March

G 1971–74 6' 2" 13st 0 to 13st 7
b. Shildon 30 March 1949

Durham Boys/ Darlington from app May 1967/ Newcastle United (£8000) Mar 1969
United: 27 Jan 1971(player exchange) to 27 Jan 1975
Debut: 30 Jan 1971 Oxford United 1 United 2
Last game: 12 Mar 1974 United 0 Ipswich Town 3
Preston North End (L) Sep 1973
Pretoria(SA) trial Feb 1975/ Hartlepool United (free) Jul 1975/ Stockton coach Oct 1980/ Wingate manager cs 1986/ Whitby Oct 1988/ Willington manager cs 1989 to Jan 1991/ Hartlepool asst coach/ Darlington coach

John Hope had made his FL debut with Darlington at Brighton & Hove Albion, shortly after his sixteenth birthday, on 26 April 1965 and then joined Newcastle United as the number two to Willie McFaul playing in one FL game.

He joined United in an exchange deal. The Blades' promotion push was stuttering which led John Harris, the United manager, to sign John and David Ford from Newcastle with John Tudor moving the other way.

John's task was to replace Alan Hodgkinson whose outstanding playing career came to an end.

A large, agile 'keeper, John played a significant role in the final weeks of the season, which saw United promoted and he kept his place in the following season until the final four games. He had looked full of confidence as United swept to promotion and made a fine start in the former First Division but 'nerves', injuries and consequent operations, a gain in weight and a general loss of confidence meant he was replaced by Tom McAlister. John made just eight more appearances in 1974 before his contract was paid up.

John signed for Hartlepool where he managed to reach a career total of 101 FL appearances but it was a sad end to what might have been a glittering career. In later years, his son Chris became a professional footballer.

Appearances:		Apps	Gls
	FL	63	0
	FAC	1	0
	LC	5	0
	CC	2	0
	ABD	1	0
	Total	72	0

HORSFIELD Geoffrey (Geoff) Malcolm

Striker 2006 5' 10" 11st 0
b. Barnsley 1 November 1973

Worsborough Bridge Miners Welfare/ Scarborough trainee 1990, pro Jul 1992/ Halifax Town Mar 1994/ Guiseley cs 1994/ Witton Albion Nov 1995/ Halifax Town(free) Oct 1996/ Fulham (£325k) Oct 1998/ Birmingham City (£2m +) Jul 2000/ Wigan Athletic Sep 2003/ West Bromwich Albion (£1m) Dec 2003
United: (L) 13 Feb 2006, (undisclosed) 24 May 2006 to cs 2008
Debuts: 18 Feb 2006 Sheffield Wednesday 1 United 2 (sub)
25 Feb 2006 United 2 Queens Park Rangers 3
Last games: 11 Mar 2006 Coventry City 2 United 0 (sub)
24 Jul 2007 Longford Town 0 United 1 (Fr)
28 Aug 2007 MK Dons 2 United 3 (sub LC)
Leeds United (L) 3 Aug 2006 to 2 Jan 2007/ Leicester City (L) 31 Jan to 7 May 2007/ Scunthorpe United (L) 31 Jan to May 2008

Geoff Horsfield scored on his FL debut with Scarborough on 30 March 1993 at home to Barnet. After 12 appearances he moved into non-League football but 'rejoined' the FL when he helped Halifax Town regain their FL status. A strong, hard working forward, difficult to knock off the ball and able to bring other players into the game, he then moved up the Divisions and played in the Premiership with Birmingham City and later, West Bromwich Albion.

Having scored 74 goals in 272 League games, Geoff joined United, initially signing on loan for the remainder of the season, a fee having been agreed to make the move permanent in the summer. Neil Warnock said he had been after the player for some time and he arrived to help with United's promotion push. However, after three appearances, things went wrong. There were rumours that he had been 'in the reserves too long' and that he wasn't fit and, towards the end of the season, Geoff was not even training with the first team squad.

In the summer Geoff's move was made permanent and he and Neil declared that they had 'wiped the slate clean'. However he did not play in any pre-season fixtures and in August he went on loan to Leeds United. After returning to the Lane he was put on the transfer list in January and on the last day of the transfer window moved on loan to Leicester City for the remainder of the season.

It appeared that with Bryan Robson in charge, Geoff would perhaps play more regularly but this was not the case and he was restricted to two sub appearances in the League Cup, scoring in one, before moving on loan to Scunthorpe during the January transfer window. He was released in summer 2008.

Appearances:		Apps	Gls
	FL	1 (2)	0
	LC	0 (2)	1
	Total	1 (4)	1

HORWOOD Evan David

D 2005 6' 0" 11st 2
b. Billingham 10 March 1986

United: from trainee 12 Nov 2004 to 15 Jan 2008
Only game: 25 Oct 2005 Reading 2 United 0 (sub LC)
Stockport County (L) 11 Mar to 8 May 2005/ Scunthorpe United (L) 5 Aug to 6 Sep 2005/ York City (L) 24 Nov 2005 to Jan 2006/ Chester City (L) 31 Jan to Feb 2006/ Darlington (L) 12 Oct 2006 to 21 Oct injured, (L) 1 Jan 2007 to 6 May/ Gretna (L) 31 Aug 2007 to 12 Jan 2008
Carlisle United (free + sell on) Jan 2008

One of United's academy youngsters, Evan Horwood made his FL debut while on loan with Stockport County at home to Colchester United on 12 Mar 2005 and played in their final 10 games of the season.

He began the 2005–06 season by playing for United 'reserve' teams in pre-season fixtures against Parkgate, Matlock etc before a month on loan at Scunthorpe. He then made, what turned out to be, his only first team appearance for United, before various loan spells which included one, in August 2006 with Scottish Premier League newcomers Gretna. In January 2008 he made a permanent move to Carlisle, where he was a regular to the end of the season.

Appearances:		Apps	Gls
	LC	0 (1)	0
	Total	0 (1)	0

HOUSELEY John (Jack)

RB 1891
d. Sheffield 27 September 1908

Garrick/ Wednesday 1874–75 and 1881–82/ Exchange/ Lockwood Bros. 1883–85
United: see below
Only game: 28 Mar 1891 Long Eaton Rangers 2 United 3 (MCL)
United trainer 1889? 1890–93/ Liverpool trainer 1893–94/ United asst trainer cs1894 to 1908

In his playing days, Jack Houseley was described as 'one of the best footballers in Sheffield' and he represented the Sheffield Association on many occasions. He was probably United's trainer in their first season and certainly did the job from 1890 to 1893, returning one year later to assist George Waller. His appearance as a player in 1891 came about because both Teddy Cross and Harry Lilley missed their train but United, playing with nine men and their trainer, still managed a victory. Houseley died in 1908 after an operation following a fall while getting off a tram and slipping on a banana skin.

Appearances:		Apps	Gls
	MCL	1	0
	Total	1	0

HOUSTON Stewart Mackie

D 1980–83 5' 11" 12st 12
b. Dunoon 20 August 1949

Port Glasgow Rangers/ Chelsea Aug 1967/ Brentford (£15/17k) Mar 1972/ Manchester United (£55k) Dec 1973
United: (free) 1/7 Jul 1980 to 31 Jul 1983
Debuts: 31 Jul 1980 Chesterfield 1 United 0 (ASC)
16 Aug 1980 Carlisle U 0 United 3
Last game: 14 May 1983 Orient 4 United 1
Colchester United player-coach 8 Aug 1983/ Plymouth Argyle coach/ Arsenal coach and asst manager cs1987, caretaker mgr Feb to Jun 2005 and Aug to Sep 2005/ Queens Park Rangers mgr Sep 1996 to Dec 1997/ Ipswich Town coach cs1998/ Tottenham Hotspur asst mgr Feb 1999 to Mar 2001/ Walsall coach Aug to Sep 2002 / – / Arsenal scout c2006

Stewart Houston made his FL debut with Chelsea at home to Liverpool on 12 February 1968 but a series of injuries led to him being transferred to Brentford. His impressive displays brought him a transfer to

Manchester United where he was a member of the Second Division Championship side in 1975 and played in the 1976 F A Cup Final and was awarded a Scottish Cap.

Stewart who was thirty, was one of several new signings by United's manager, Harry Haslam in an attempt to secure promotion from Division Three. He read the game well, passed the ball accurately and was a fine organiser on the pitch from the back but he was not alone in finding the transition to a lower level of football far from easy. Appointed team captain, United, under his leadership, made a good start to the campaign but performances fell away and the Blades were surprisingly relegated. Stewart stayed on and made 27 FL appearances in the side which won the Fourth Division Championship but, after one further season, he moved to Colchester as a player-coach. During his time at Bramall Lane he averaged about 30 FL games a season, being captain in the promotion season and his single goal for the club came in his final appearance.

After various coaching jobs he became the assistant manager at Arsenal and was the caretaker manager when they reached the Cup Winners Cup Final in 1995.

Appearances:		Apps	Gls
	FL	93 (1)	1
	FAC	10	0
	LC	8	0
	ASC	2	0
	AMC	4	0
	CC	4	0
	Total	121 (1)	1

HOWARD Henry (Harry)

LH/RH 1895–1901
b. Rotherham 1871

Rotherham Town(trial)/ Wednesday (trial)
United: 30 Sep 1894 to cs 1901
Debuts: possibly, 20 Oct 1894 United 5 Chirk 1 (Fr)
16 Mar 1895 Third Lanark 4 United 1 (Fr)
18 Apr 1895 Nottingham Forest 0 United 1 (UCL)
5 Oct 1895 Everton 5 United 0
Last game: 30 Apr 1901 West Bromwich Albion 2 United 0
/ – / Small Heath (Birmingham) 29 Apr 1902/ Wisbech Town Aug 1906 to May 1907

Essentially a reliable reserve player, Harry Howard was at Bramall Lane for seven seasons and for all that time he was competing for a half back place with the legendary Ernest Needham and for much of the time with internationals Rab Howell and, from 1897, Harry Johnson.

Harry played quite regularly in his second season, 1895–96, and made a significant contribution in 1899–00 but otherwise, he generally played in the less important competitive games or friendlies, although he did play in the final two FL games which saw United clinch the League Championship in 1898. He was prone to injuries in his last three seasons and, although it was thought that he would sign again for United for the 1901–02 season, he failed to do so. A part time player, he may have taken time out from football but, eleven months later, he joined Small Heath (now Birmingham City) and made a further 48 FL appearances.

Harry's brother, Fred Howard joined United in 1895 and played for the reserves before later playing for Lincoln City (1 FL app) and Barnsley (49 FL app). Inevitably, the two were an occasional source of confusion to the FL's record keepers, contemporary journalists and football historians.

Appearances:		Apps	Gls
	FL	48	2
	FAC	5	0
	UCL	1	0
	BC	4	0
	ABD	3	0
	Total	61	2

HOWELL Rabbi (Rab)

CH/RH/CF 1890–98 5' 5½" 9st 8
b. Wincobank (Sheffield) 12 October 1869 or OND 1868
d. Preston July 1937

Ecclesfield 1887/ Rotherham Swifts 1889
United: 24 Mar 1890/cs 1890 to 7 Apr 1898
Debuts: 24 Mar 1890 United 1 Halliwell 1 (Fr)
13 Sep 1890 Burton Wanderers 1 United 1 (MCL)
4 Oct 1890 Derby Junction 0 United 1 (FAC)
3 Sep 1892 United 4 Lincoln City 2
Last game: 26 Mar 1898 West Bromwich Albion 2 United 0
Liverpool (£150/200) Apr 1898/ Preston North End Jun 1901

Rab Howell was occasionally spoken of as 'The Little Gypsy'. He was born, and lived as a boy, in a caravan in a wood in the Wincobank district of Sheffield where his father was a horse dealer who also sold pots and pans. It appears that his name was registered as Rabbi though this may have been a registrar's misunderstanding of a familiar form of 'Robert' and, in any case, he was always known as 'Rab'.

He began playing for United in a series of club (friendly) matches towards the end of March 1890 along with Arthur Watson and Mick Whitham, two other United stalwarts to be. All three had played as professionals for Rotherham Swifts and it seems probable, in view of the club's financial problems, that they were 'on trial' with United until the close season when a transfer fee of perhaps £200 would be negotiated.

Rab began at centre forward, scoring on his debut, and then moved to centre half but, when Billy Hendry was signed, Rab moved to right half where he continued to play until he was transferred to Liverpool in 1898. The famous United half-back line of Howell, Hendry (later Morren) and Needham were all small of stature but none doubted their individual qualities. Rab was 'as hard as nails', frequently playing without stockings or shin pads but he was rarely injured. A good ball winner, he could 'stick to an opponent like a leech' and was very fast into a tackle, even on the heaviest of grounds. Capped twice by England, once in 1895 and later in 1899 when with Liverpool, only his passing, shooting and discipline off the field let him down.

He faced the United Football Committee on several occasions on charges of 'misconduct' and a solution to the various crises that came his way wasn't easy but one was to give him extra money and he was usually asked 'to mend his ways'. Far more serious was the shadow of suspicion over his leaving. Perhaps there was no case to answer and the truth is unlikely to be ever known. On the 5 March 1898 with United seeking to become League Champions, they travelled to Sunderland who were their main rivals for the trophy. On two occasions, crosses passed in front of keeper Foulke and appeared to be going out of play but Howell intercepted them 'attempting to clear' and both finished in the net, one clearly an own goal. United lost the game and Rab played just one more game for the Blades before moving to Liverpool and later to Preston North End where he was a regular until a broken leg ended his career in September 1903. He had played 274 FL games and scored nine goals.

Appearances:		Apps	Gls
	FL	155	6
	TM	1	0
	FAC	22	0
	NL	19	0
	MCL	18	2
	UCL	11	0
	SCC	5	3
	WCC	3	0
	BC	4	0
	ABD	2	0
	Total	240	11

HOWITT Robert (Bobby) Gibb

IL/CF/IR 1955–58 5' 10" 11st 1 to 11st 7
b. Glasgow 15 July 1929
d. Carluke 31 January 2005

Vale of Clyde/ Partick Thistle 1948
United: (£8000) 15/21 Jul 1955 to 30 Apr 1958
Debut: 20 Aug 1955 Newcastle United 4 United 2
Last game: 28 Apr 1958 United 1 Fulham 1
Stoke City (£6500) Apr 1958 to cs 1963/ Morton coach 1963–65/ Motherwell manager Mar 1965 to Mar 1973

Bobby Howitt began his career with Partick Thistle, making his Scottish League debut at Motherwell on 12 March 1949. He had made 158 League appearances for the Glasgow club and one for the Scottish League when he joined United, apparently on the recommendation of a scout and in the period between the death of Manager Reg Freeman and the appointment of Joe Mercer as his successor.

Bobby could shoot with both power and accuracy but he had his critics, for his lack of pace was very obvious. He formed, however, a good left wing partnership with Colin Grainger, Bobby's passing being both astute and accurate. He missed few games during his and Mercer's first season, which ended in relegation but, after a spell out of the side and then playing at centre forward, he was never sure of a first team place. Although he had averaged an impressive goal every three games during his time at the Lane, he was transferred to Stoke City where he played mainly as a half back.

After leaving Stoke he returned to Scotland where he coached and then managed before scouting for Stoke.

Appearances:		Apps	Gls
	FL	89	31
	FAC	6	1
	CC	3	1
	Total	98	33

HOWLETT Charles (Charlie) Herbert

G 1889–94 5' 8"
b. Glanford, Brigg Aug or September 1864
d. Gainsborough 17 August 1906

Gainsborough Victoria/Gainsborough Trinity
United: cs 1889 to cs 1894
Debuts: 7 Sep 1889 Notts Rangers 4 United 1 (Fr)
5 Oct 1889 Scarborough 1 United 6 (FAC)
26 Nov 1892 United 8 Bootle 3
Last games: 7 Apr 1894 Preston North End 3 United 0
14 Apr 1894 Wednesday 1 United 1 (UCL)
Gainsborough Trinity 1894–1903

Charlie Howlett was living in Grenoside, near Sheffield, when United announced that they were forming a football team and, having applied, he became the club's first goalkeeper and the only one to wear spectacles. A 'very agile and daring' character, he played in the Blades' first game against Notts Rangers and the first FA Cup game when United recorded their biggest win in the competition. Unfortunately, and he was never allowed to forget it, he also played in the Club's heaviest FA Cup defeat and is the only United 'keeper to concede 13 goals in a game. That day at Bolton on the old wet and muddy Pikes Lane ground was not the best for a 'keeper who wore glasses and it was said that the poor keeper spent most of the time searching for them in the mud.

Charlie didn't like being charged and one consequence was that he frequently fisted away balls that others would catch and that included low ground shots! He was first choice keeper for United's first three seasons but for his last two, he shared the duties with Will Lilley and eventually played in 112 competitive and 118 club (friendly) games for United in his five seasons at the Lane.

A popular character, he was a talented musician and comedian; useful attributes on away trips. He returned to play for Gainsborough and then settled in Birmingham, only returning to the Lincolnshire town on the death of his wife.

Appearances:		Apps	Gls
	FL	38	0
	TM	1	0
	FAC	17	0
	NL	14	0
	MCL	19	0
	UCL	4	0
	SCC	13	0
	WCC	5	0
	ABD	1	0
	Total	112	0

HOYLAND Jamie William

MF/CD 1990–94 6' 0" 12st 8 to 13st 2
b. Sheffield 23 January 1966

Sheffield Throstles/ Manchester City from app Nov 1983/ Bury Jul 1986
United: (£250k) 8 Jun/4 Jul 1990 to 4 Nov 1994
Debuts: 27 Jul 1990 Kramfors A (Sweden) 1 United 5 (Fr)
25 Aug 1990 United 1 Liverpool 3
Last games: 22 Jan 1994 Sheffield Wednesday 3 United 1
24 Sep 1994 Port Vale 0 United 2 (sub)
27 Sep 1994 United 1 Stockport County 0 (LC)
5 Oct 1994 United 3 Ancona 3 (AIC)
Bristol City (L) 4 Mar 1994 to 4 Apr 1994
Burnley (L) 14 Oct 1994, (£130k) 4 Nov 1994/ Carlisle U (L) Nov 1997/ Scarborough Aug 1998 to cs 1999/ Altrincham Dec 1999/ Rochdale youth development officer Mar 2001, asst mgr Jun 2002 then coach/ Rossendale United Mar 2004 asst mgr/ Preston North End youth coach cs 2004

A Sheffield Boys and England youth International and the son of Tommy Hoyland, a former United half back, Jamie made his FL debut with Manchester City at home to Derby County on 26 November 1983 but he had cartilage problems and was released after making just two FL appearances. He then spent four seasons, making 172 FL appearances, with Bury before Dave Bassett signed him after United had been promoted to the top flight in 1994 and, for a month, he was the Blades' record signing until the arrival of Paul Beesley.

Jamie, who had been a ball-boy at the Lane, was generally regarded as a perceptive, constructive attacking mid-fielder but he came to accept that he was probably a better player in a deeper, more defensive role. He played around twenty League games a season during the time when United were in the top flight but moved to Burnley after relegation from the Premiership after rejecting a transfer offer from Blackpool.

Appearances:		Apps	Gls
	FL	72 (17)	6
	FAC	8 (2)	1
	LC	5 (3)	1
	FMC	2	1
	AIC	3	0
	Total	90 (22)	9

HOYLAND Thomas (Tommy)

RH/IR/RW 1949–61 5' 9" 10st 11
b. Sheffield 14 June 1932

Oaks Fold
United: from jnr to pro 25/27 Oct 1949 to 27/28 Oct 1961
Debuts: 5 Oct 1949 Western Command 0 United XI 2 (Fr at Lichfield)
18 Mar 1950 United 2 Leicester City 2
Last games: 27 Dec 1961 United 0 Sunderland 1
13 Sep 1961 Fulham 1 United 1 (LC)
19 Oct 1961 United 3 Eintracht Franfurt(WG) 1 (sub Fr)
Bradford City (£6500) Oct 1961 to cs 1963/ Retford Town Oct 1963/ Alfreton Town/ Chesterfield Sep 1964

A Southey Green and Sheffield Boys player, Tommy Hoyland played for the United nursery team, Oaks Fold and, playing at outside right, had the distinction of scoring on his FL debut at 17 years of age. The following season saw him play several games but his progress was then halted by injury problems and National Service in the Army.

From April 1954 however, for four seasons, Tommy was more or less a fixture in the side, first at inside right when Hagan was injured but then at right half when Joe Shaw took the number 5 shirt. Very quick in getting up and down the field and sharp in the tackle, he made an excellent link between Cec Coldwell at right back and Alf Ringstead on the wing.

Pressure on his place in the team came first in September 1957 when Joe Mercer, the manager, brought in Brian Richardson, a more defensive player. Tommy turned down a transfer to Plymouth Argyle in November 1958 and, a month later, returned to the first team when Richardson was injured and held the right half position until October 1959.

Tommy was transferred to Bradford City (27 FL appearances) in October 1961 and, after a period in non-League football, he played a few games with the Chesterfield reserve team before injuries ended his playing career. He acted as a scout for Fulham, had a shop in Greenhill and was later the licensee of the Sheldon on Hill Street. Tommy's son Jamie also played for United.

Appearances:		Apps	Gls
	FL	181	12
	FAC	15	2
	LC	2	0
	CC	11	4
	Total	209	18

HOYLAND Walter

IL/IR 1921–27 5' 9½" 11st 0
b. Sheffield 14 August 1901
d. Worksop April 1985

United: Jan 1920/23 Aug 1920 to 4 Mar 1927
Debuts: 14 May 1921 Barnsley 1 United 1 (CC)
21 Jan 1922 Blackburn Rovers 2 United 3

Last game: 26 Feb 1927 United 3 Cardiff City 1
Fulham (£500) Mar 1927/ Boston Town Aug 1928/ Loughborough Corinthians Jun 1929/Peterborough & Fletton United Jul 1930/ Mansfield Town Jun 1932/ Spalding United Sep 1933/ Seymour Cobley (Spalding) Aug 1934

In his eight seasons at Bramall Lane, Walter Hoyland was unable to establish himself as a regular in the first team but was good enough to be retained as a useful reserve player. His best run of games was the last seven of the 1925–26 season and the first two of the following one. His brother Herbert, a full back, joined United in 1922 but was released without playing in the first team and joined Wath Wanderers.

Walter moved to Fulham (22 FL apps) and after four seasons in non-League football he joined Mansfield Town (25 FL apps) before playing as an amateur in Spalding, latterly for a works team.

Appearances:		Apps	Gls
	FL	24	4
	CC	3	0
	Total	27	4

HUDSON Jack (John?)

HB 1889–91
b. 'local' 11 October 1860
d. Worksop 21 November 1941

Surrey (Sheffield)/ Heeley 1878–1884/ Providence 1879–80/ Owlerton 1880/ Sheffield Club 1880–1883 / Wednesday 1880–1889/ Walkley c1882/ Blackburn Olympic 1886/ Lockwood Brothers 1886–87 / – /
United: cMay 1889 to cs1891
Debuts: 7 Sep 1889 Nottingham Rangers 4 United 1 (Fr)
5 Oct 1889 Scarborough 1 United 6 (FAC)
Last games: 25 Oct 1890 Burton Swifts 2 United 1 (FAC)
24 Nov 1890 United 2 Warwick County 0 (MCL
14 Mar 1891 Attercliffe 1 United XI 4 (Fr)
Wednesday trainer

One of the most well known, admired and experienced local players, Jack Hudson was one of the first three players signed by United. An engraver by trade and also a semi-professional athlete, he was strong, tenacious and difficult to pass and had played for England against Ireland in 1883 and had made many appearances for the Sheffield Association. As was common in those days, he had played for many Sheffield teams but is mainly associated with the Wednesday where he had served as captain, committee man and temporary secretary and in the season prior to joining United, Hudson had taken his benefit.

Jack captained United in their first season and played in the club's first ever game at Notts Rangers. Playing at right or left half, he went on to play in 47 games that season, most of which were friendlies. He played in United's first FA Cup game and in the record FA Cup defeat (0–13) at Bolton Wanderers but in the following season, he appeared just six times. He later had a short period as Wednesday's trainer before becoming the licensee of the Castle Inn on Dykes Hall Road.

Appearances:		Apps	Gls
	FAC	7	0
	MCL	1	0
	SCC	6	3
	WCC	2	0
	Total	16	3

HUDSON William (Bill) Albert

OR 1953 5' 7½" 10st 9
b. Swansea 10 March 1928

Pembroke Dock/ Pembroke Borough/ (Manchester C (trial) 1950/ Leeds United May 1951
United: (free) 7/9 May 1952 to 17 May 1954
Only game: 5 Sep 1953 Chelsea 1 United 2
Mansfield Town May 1954 to May 1955

After leaving the armed forces, Bill Hudson played for Pembroke Borough where he gained a Welsh Amateur cap in 1951 and he then became a professional with Leeds United but made just four FL appearances before being given a free transfer.

Quite quick and clever, he was one of Teddy Davison's last signings but never looked powerful enough for top level football and, after just one first team appearance for the Blades, he was given another free transfer. He joined Mansfield Town where he played eight FL games in his one season and scored his only FL goal.

Appearances:		Apps	Gls
	FL	1	0
	Total	1	0

HUFTON Arthur Edward (Ted)

G 1913–18 5' 10½" 12st 0
b. Southwell 25 November 1892
d. Swansea 2 February 1967

Saxon Street (Lincoln)/ Atlas & Norfolk (Sheffield)
United: c23 Apr 1912 to 5 Mar 1919
Debut: 8 Feb 1913 Manchester City 3 United 0
Last games: 2 Jan 1915 Wednesday 1 United 1
9 Jan 1915 Blackpool 1 United 2 (FAC)
16 Feb 1918 United 0 Nottingham Forest 1 (WW1)
WW1 guest: West Ham United
West Ham United (£300) Mar 1919/ Watford Jun 1932 to cs 1933

Ted Hufton first made his mark as a goalkeeper at school in Lincoln and came to United's attention with the Atlas & Norfolk works team, United making a grant of £20. His fine performance in the 1912 practice match confirmed first impressions of his potential quality and he became a full-time professional in October. Although he conceded three goals on his first team debut, (he had let in seven goals, one week before, in a reserve match) few doubted his ability. Life has its pitfalls of course and an injury, sustained in a practice match at the start of the following season, meant Harold Gough became first choice keeper, and it was Gough who played in the 1915 FA Cup Final.

During the First World War, Ted was in the Coldstream Guards and was wounded in action in France. On recovering, he played regularly for West Ham United as a guest and he signed for the Hammers before the start of the first peacetime season. Brave and somewhat unorthodox, which may in part have been a reason for his many injuries, Ted went on to play 401 FL and Cup games for West Ham including the first Wembley Cup Final and also won six England caps.

He moved to Watford on a free transfer in the 1932 close season but after one season and just two games, he went into the motor trade in London. After the Second World War he returned to Upton Park, acting as press room steward on match days. Later, he was beset by ill health and after a road accident, he moved to Swansea where failing eyesight compounded his problems and he died there aged 74.

Appearances:		Apps	Gls
	FL	15	0
	FAC	1	0
	WW1	12	0
	Total	28	0

HUGHES Robert (Bobby)

OL 1922 5' 6" 10st 6
b. Pelaw (Newcastle on Tyne) 5 August 1892
d. Hull September 1955

Pelaw/ Northampton Town Mar 1910 to cs1915
WW1 guest: Hull C from Aug 1917/ Hull City Jul 1919
United: (£150) c10 May/7 Jul 1922 to cs 1923
Debut: 16 Sep 1922 United 2 Newcastle United 0
Last game: 18 Sep 1922 Blackburn Rovers 1 United 0
Brentford 7 Aug 1923/ Rochdale Jul 1924/ Wigan Borough Jun 1928 to cs1930/ Ashton National Sep 1930

Before the First War, Bobby Hughes had spent more than four seasons with Southern League Northampton Town and was almost ever present in the three seasons before the War, making over 100 appearances in total. Based in Hull for much of the War, he played regularly for the City and signed permanently for them at a record fee of close on £1000 in 1919. He made his FL debut on 30 August 1919 at Birmingham City and went on to play 66 games for Hull, on the left or right wing, before joining United.

It was a strange and unsuccessful move. Hughes had been a fast, tricky, goal scoring winger when he first played for Hull with David Mercer but now he was thirty, had injury problems, looked nervous and the level of football in the First Division was beyond him. He played just two first team games before moving on a free transfer to Brentford and there, and later with Rochdale and Wigan Borough, he scored seventy goals in 209 FL games.

Appearances:		Apps	Gls
	FL	2	0
	Total	2	0

HUGHES Walter Cyril Joseph

OR 1956 5' 8" 10st 10
b. Liverpool 15 March 1934

Winsford United/ Liverpool Oct 1954/ Stockport C/ Winsford United
United: (£600)19/21 Jan 1956 to 19 Oct 1956
Debut: 4 Feb 1956 United 3 Preston North End 1
Last game: 3 Mar 1956 Bolton Wanderers 2 United 1
Wisbech Town (£150) Oct 1956/ Bradford Park Avenue 23 Apr 1957/ Southport Feb 1958/ Crewe Alexandra Oct 1958/ Bangor City/ Prescot Cables 1961–62

Walter Hughes's first FL club was Liverpool but his FL debut came with United. Signed by Joe Mercer, he spent less than a year at the Lane and, though he had a hand in two of the goals on his debut, there never seemed the possibility of him making the grade. He made one other first team appearance for United but later played 20 games for Bradford PA and 11 for Southport but failed to score with all three clubs.

In 1973 he emigrated to New Zealand where he coached Dunedin City before becoming the national coach. After coaching in Dubai he returned to New Zealand, coaching Fiji in the 1982 World Cup before continuing to coach in New Zealand.

Appearances:		Apps	Gls
	FL	2	0
	Total	2	0

HULSE Robert (Rob) William

Striker 2006–08 6' 1" 12st 4
b. Crewe 25 October 1979

Crewe from trainee Jun 1998/ Hyde United (L)/ West Bromwich Albion (£750k+) Aug 2003/ Leeds United (L) Feb 2005 , (£1.1m) Aug 2005
United:: (£2.125m to £3m) 26 Jul 2006 to 21 Jul 2008
Debuts: 28 Jul 2006 Rotherham United 1 United 1 (Fr)
19 Aug 2006 United 1 Liverpool 1
Last games: 4 May 2008 Southampton 3 United 2
16 Jul 2008 KVK Tienen (Belgium) 1 United 3 (Fr)
Derby County (£1.75m Jul 2008)

Rob Hulse began his career with Crewe Alexandra where he made his FL debut as a substitute on 4 March 2000 at Norwich City. His full debut came the following season on 26 August at QPR. A move to West Bromwich Albion saw him experience the Premiership but he lost his place, in part due to the signing of Geoff Horsfield, and was transferred to Leeds United after an initial loan spell.

He moved to Bramall Lane, following United's promotion to the Premiership, for a fee of £2.125 million rising to a possible £3 million. He was an immediate hit, scoring the opening goal of the Premiership season (United's game had kicked off earlier than the rest), and he was a regular member of the side. An unselfish player, he worked very hard for the side, chasing and harrying, occasionally playing as a lone striker and bringing other players into play. In March he suffered a double leg fracture at Chelsea and his absence from the final eight games of the season may well have contributed to United's relegation, although he still finished as the top scorer.

Rob returned, earlier than expected, in late December 2007, partly due to other strikers being injured and was unlucky on several occasions not to score. Having played in one pre-season friendly in July 2008 he moved to Championship rivals Derby County.

Appearances:		Apps	Gls
	FL	38 (12)	8
	FAC	0 (3)	0
	Total	38 (15)	8

HUNT Herbert

OR/IR 1944–45

RASC
WW2 guest: Chesterfield (1940–42,19 app, 1gl)
United: 26/28 Aug 1944 to cs 1945
Debut: 26 Aug 1944 Sheffield Wednesday 1 United 1 (WW2)
Last game: 10 Mar 1945 Lincoln City 3 United 1 (WW2)

The Sheffield Telegraph reported that Herbert Hunt, who was stationed at the local RASC depot, was a former West Bromwich Albion player but, if so, he had never featured in the first eleven and he was not a registered player. Another possibility is that he was the Walsall forward who made six FL appearances in the 1936–37 season.

The first two of his five first team games (one was a friendly) were against Sheffield Wednesday and he scored the equalising goal on his debut and also scored in the 10–2 victory over Lincoln City.

Appearances:		Apps	Gls
	WW2	4	2
	Total	4	2

HUNT Jonathan (Jon) Richard

MF 1998, 1999–2000 5' 10" 11st 12
b. Camden 2 November 1971

Slough Town/ Barnet from jnr in 1989–90/ Southend United Jul 1993/ Birmingham City (£50k) Sep 1994/ Derby County (£500k) May 1997
United: (L)20 Aug 1998
Debut: 22 Aug 1998 United 0 Birmingham City 2
Last game: 8 Sep 1998 United 3 Crewe Alexandra 1 (sub)
Ipswich Town (L) Oct 1998
United: 12 Mar 1999 to 21 Jul 2000
Debut: 13 Mar 1999 Tranmere Rovers 2 United 3
Last games: 28 Dec 1999 United 2 Fulham 0
8 Jan 2000 Newcastle United 4 United 1 (FAC)
Cambridge United (L) 23 Mar 2000
Wimbledon (free) Sep 2000 to Jan 2001/ Reading trial/ Peterborough United (nc) Sep 2002 to cs 2003

Jon Hunt made his FL debut with Barnet as a substitute 21 Dec 1991 at home to Mansfield Town; his full debut coming on 8 January 1992 at Maidstone. Barry Fry, his manager, also signed him for Southend and Birmingham and Jon later played for Derby County in the Premiership.

Steve Bruce brought him to Bramall Lane as a mid-field playmaker, initially on loan. He then made a permanent move later in the season, along with Rob Kozluk and a cash adjustment, with Vassilis Borbokis moving to Derby County. He played fairly regularly in this midfield role under Bruce and later under Adrian Heath but with little success and never endeared himself to the fans.

After Neil Warnock's arrival, Jon played just six more games before being loaned to Cambridge United and at the end of the season, his contract was paid up and he was given a free transfer. He subsequently played a few games for Wimbledon but none during his time with Peterborough, ending his career with 160(67) League appearances.

Appearances:		Apps	Gls
	FL	20 (7)	2
	FAC	3	0
	LC	2 (2)	0
	Total	25 (9)	2

HURST Kevan James

MF 2002–07 6' 0" 11st 7
b. Chesterfield 27 August 1985

United: from trainee 24 Mar 2004 to 6 May 2007
Debuts: 3 Aug 2002 Linfield 1 United 5 (sub Fr)
23 Sep 2003 United 0 Queens Park Rangers 2 (sub LC)
25 Sep 2004 United 1 Coventry City 1 (sub)
24 Jul 2005 Hu Nan Xian Jung 1 United 1 (Fr)
Last game: 6 Jan 2007 United 0 Swansea City 3 (FAC)
Boston United(L) 25 Mar 2004 to 9May 2005/ Stockport County(L) 18 Feb 2005 to 8 May 2005/ Chesterfield(L) 18 Aug 2005 to 1 Jan 2006 and then to Apr/ Chesterfield (L) 18 Jul 2006 to 2 Jan 2007/ Scunthorpe United (L) 31 Jan to 6 May 2007
Scunthorpe United May (£200k + buy on)

A product of the United Academy, Kevan made his FL debut as a substitute at Bury whilst on loan with Boston United on 27 March 2004 and his full debut came three weeks later on 17 April at home to Yeovil. He had already made a League Cup appearance for the Blades and after three sub appearances at the start of 2004–05 he went on loan to Stockport County for three months. His opportunities at the Lane were limited, the staff feeling he was not potential PL quality and for most of 2005–06 he was on loan to Chesterfield and the following season he made just one FA Cup appearance for United between extended loan spells with Chesterfield and then Scunthorpe United.

In May 2007 he signed permanently for Scunthorpe and was a regular in the first team, bringing his total of FL appearances to over 100.

Appearances:		Apps	Gls
	FL	0 (1)	0
	FAC	1	0
	LC	0 (3)	0
	Total	1 (4)	0

HUTCHINSON George Henry

OR/OL/IF 1948–53 5' 7" 10st 8
b. Allerton Bywater 31 October 1929
d. Sheffield 30 July 1996

Huddersfield Town am May 1945 pro Jan 1947
United: (exchange) 11/13 Mar 1948 to 29 Jun 1953
Debut: 16 Oct 1948 Charlton Athletic 2 United 1
Last games: 3 Jan 1953 Huddersfield Town 1 United 1
10 Jan 1953 Newport County 4 United 1 (FAC)
Tottenham Hotspur Jun 1953/ Guildford City Jul 1954/ Leeds United Aug 1955/ Halifax Town Jul 1956/ Bradford City Jul 1958/ Skegness Town/ Worksop Town

George Hutchinson's single first team appearance for Huddersfield Town was his FL debut on 27 September 1947 at Aston Villa, just before his eighteenth birthday. He came to Bramall Lane, along with full back Graham Bailey and £1000 for Albert Nightingale, in what turned out to be a disappointing exchange deal.

He was a very talented young winger and most of the older players thought that he would have a great future. He was two footed, fast and nimble with good ball control and he had the ability to beat his opponents but those high opinions turned out to be incorrect. Perhaps National Service played a part, but attitude and character were the key to a disappointing career. He played only eight games in his first season at Bramall Lane and for the following three seasons he played in roughly half the games and, in United's promotion season of 1952–53, George played in only four games.

At the end of the season he moved to Spurs for a season as a possible reserve and later spent a season with Leeds United but he could never rise to the challenge of those new opportunities. It was only with Halifax Town that he played regularly, bringing his total FL appearances to 134. He lived latterly in the Gleadless area of Sheffield and died in rather sad circumstances.

Appearances:		Apps	Gls
	FL	73	10
	FAC	7	0
	CC	4	1
	Total	84	11

HUTCHINSON James (Jim) Arthur

IL/IR 1939–46 5' 8" 11st 0
b. Sheffield 28 December 1915
d. Sheffield 8 November 1997

Aqueduct(Sheffield)
United: 19/20 Nov 1937 to 4 May 1946
Possible debut: 13 May 1938 Halmstad B (Sweden) 2 United 5 (Fr)
Debut: 18 Nov 1939 Lincoln City 1 United 2 (WW2)
Last game: 26 Jan 1946 Stoke City 2 United 0 (FAC)
WW2 guest: Bradford PA (1939–40), Bradford City(1940–41), Portsmouth, Lincoln City (1944–45, 1945–46), Hull City (1944–45), Port Vale (1945–46)
Bournemouth (£350) 12 Jun 1946/ Lincoln City Nov 1946/ Oldham Athletic Feb 1949 to cs 1950/ Denaby United 1950

An Attercliffe lad, Jim Hutchinson was nearly twenty two when he joined United after a trial with the A team. An inside forward of real promise, United rejected an approach for him from Wolves early in 1938 but he was still without a first team appearance at the outbreak of war in 1939 other than a possible scoring debut on tour in 1938.

The War robbed Jim of the major part of his playing career. He made his war time United debut in 1939 but was called up to serve in the Royal Navy and took part in the very dangerous convoys to Malta on HMS Rodney. There were few opportunities to play football and Jim had turned out in only one other game for United and a handful of games as a guest player for other clubs before the summer of 1944.

A direct, effective player and difficult to dispossess, he was calm in front of goal with a strong shot and had a good goal scoring record. He returned in November 1945 and made ten appearances, scoring nine goals which included a vital hat trick at Middlesbrough as the Blades captured the League North Championship. Now thirty and never a fast player, he was released at the end of the season.

He finally made his FL debut with Bournemouth at Notts County on 31 August 1946. He then had a successful spell with Lincoln City, scoring 55 FL goals in 85 games and winning a Third Division Championship medal in 1948 but an injury, sustained in October 1949 ended his career.

In his career he scored 61 goals in 107 FL games, having lost seven seasons to the War when he would have been at his best as a player. His son Barry was also a professional footballer and scored over a century of goals.

Appearances:		Apps	Gls
	FAC	1	0
	WW2	14	9
	Total	15	9

HUTCHISON Donald (Don)

MF 1996–98 6' 1½" 11st 8
b. Gateshead 9 May 1971

Hartlepool United from trainee Mar 1990/ Liverpool (£175k) **Nov 1990/ West Ham United (£1.5m) Aug 1994**
United: (£1.2m) 11 Jan 1996 to 27 Feb 1998
Debut: 13 Jan 1996 Tranmere Rovers 1 United 1
Last games: 7 Feb 1998 United 1 Oxford United 0
13 Feb 1998 United 1 Reading 0 (FAC)
Everton (£1m plus a player) Feb 1998/ Sunderland (£2.5m) Jul 2000/ West Ham United (£5m) Aug 2001/ Millwall Aug 2005/ Coventry City(L) Nov 2005, (free) Jan 2006/ Luton Town Jul 2007 to cs 2008

Don Hutchison made his FL debut with Hartlepool United on 7 October 1989 at Scunthorpe United. He was quickly snapped up by Liverpool and then signed for West Ham United before becoming United's record signing.

He was one of Howard Kendall's early signings and Don worked hard in the battle to avoid relegation. Playing as a creative midfielder, he was composed on the ball with good passing skills and a powerful shot. Some fans felt that he didn't put himself about enough and that he had a tendency to drift in and out of games but he played an important role in the club's progress to the play-offs in 1997 but a broken wrist and a dislocated shoulder, early on in the final, may have cost United the match. This injury meant that he missed the start of the 1997–98 season but he was back in the team by November. In February however, he became yet another of several high profile players to be sold when he was transferred to Everton in an exchange deal for Jon O'Connor and one million pounds. Before arriving at Bramall Lane Don had gained a Scottish B cap and after leaving he gained 26 full caps, scoring six times.

After leaving United he played for various high profile clubs, including West Ham United where he was their record signing for a second time, before moving into the lower Leagues including troubled Luton, where, by the summer of 2008, he had brought is career total to 323(101) League games.

Appearances:		Apps	Gls
	FL	70 (8)	5
	PO	2 (1)	0
	FAC	5	1
	LC	3 (2)	0
	Total	80 (11)	6

IBBOTSON Ernest Edward

CF 1909 5' 11" 12st 3
b. Hathersage (Derbyshire) AMJ 1885

Hathersage
United: 1905–06 and FL registration 22 Aug 1906 to cs 1911
Only game: 1 Apr 1909 Woolwich Arsenal 1 United 0

Ernest Ibbotson was an amateur player registered by United with the League for five seasons but he rarely played for the reserves other than in the 1905–06 season and made just one first team appearance when he 'failed to do himself justice.' A commercial traveller by profession, he may have played for Mansfield Mechanics in the 1910–11 season and another 'Ibbotson' (probably a relative), played twice in club fixtures for United in November 1890 and January 1891.

Appearances:		Apps	Gls
	FL	1	0
	Total	1	0

IFILL Paul

RW 2005–06 6' 0" 12st 10
b. Brighton 20 October 1979

Millwall from trainee Jun 1998
United: (£800k rising to £1m) 20 May 2005 to 5/8 Jan 2007
Debuts: 11 Jul 2005 Worksop Town 0 United 1 (Fr)
6 Aug 2005 United 4 Leicester City 1
Last games: 16 Sep 2006 United 1 Reading 2
24 Oct 2006 United 2 Birmingham City 4 (LC)
Crystal Palace (£750k) Jan 2007

Paul Ifill's FL debut with Millwall was on 13 February 1999 at Lincoln City and he made more than 200 FL appearances for the London club. He scored against United in both matches in the 2002–03 season and played in the 2004 FA Cup Final and in June 2004, he gained two caps for Barbados in World Cup qualifying matches.

He was one of Neil Warnock's first signings after the United manager was given money to spend after the disappointing 2004–05 season. Two footed with a strong shot and described as 'direct, positive and unpredictable', Paul scored on his League debut with the Blades and was a key member of the promotion side. Playing mainly as a right winger, he took time to win over some of the fans, who felt he wasted too many opportunities but he worked hard, producing openings with his tricky play and scored some vital goals. He was less happy in the Premiership and after just three appearances he lost his place. While at the Lane, he added to his number of caps for Barbados, playing, in particular in the Caribbean Cup, in the autumn of 2006.

Paul moved to Crystal Palace during the January 2007 transfer window and soon was reunited with Neil Warnock when he became the Palace manager. By the summer of 2008 Paul was nearing 300 League appearances.

Appearances:		Apps	Gls
	FL	31 (11)	9
	FAC	1	0
	LC	2	0
	Total	34 (11)	9

ILEY James (Jim)

LH 1954–57 5' 10" 11st 9
b. South Kirkby 15 December 1935

Moorthorpe St Joseph's BC
United: 11/13 Jun 1953 to 31 Aug 1957
Debuts: (Trial) 22 Apr 1953 Buxton v United (BM)
27 Apr 1954 Northampton Town 1 United 1 (BM)
4 Dec 1954 Charlton Athletic 3 United 1
Last game: 24 Aug 1957 United 1 Notts County 1
Tottenham Hotspur (£16k) Aug 1957/ Nottingham Forest (£16k) Jul 1959/ Newcastle United (£17k) Sep 1962/ Peterborough United player-mgr Jan 1969 to Sep 1972 / – / Barnsley mgr Apr 1973/ Blackburn Rovers mgr Apr 1978 / – / Bury mgr Jul 1980 to Feb 1984/ Exeter City mgr Jun 1984 to Apr 1985/ Charlton Athletic coach

Jim Iley was working at Frickley Colliery when he joined United in June 1953 after a trial with United's Hatchard League team and a match against Buxton. A strong, wing half, predominantly left footed but with good ball control and distribution, he was a stern tackler and had a powerful shot. He undoubtedly benefited from the presence and advice of United's manager, Joe Mercer and in 1956 played for the Football League against the Irish League. His progress hadn't gone without notice and United, who needed new floodlights, felt that he had to be sold. Sheffield Wednesday were interested in him but he was transferred to Tottenham Hotspur just after the start of the season at the end of August in 1957.

Jim had not been happy with the move to London and had a difficult start as he continued to live in Sheffield and train with United but his form did improve and he won an U23 cap and played again for the Football League. He left White Hart Lane when he lost his place to Dave Mackay and was happy to move to Forest but was perhaps at his best as a player during his six seasons with Newcastle United, making nearly 250 senior appearances (he played 536 FL games in total). Thereafter he spent 16 years as a manger with various clubs, gaining a reputation for running clubs on a shoestring budget. In his time at Peterborough he became their first player to be sent off in the Football League. On retiring from football he lived in Bolton and for a time ran an Italian restaurant.

Appearances:		Apps	Gls
	FL	99	13
	FAC	7	0
	CC	6	0
	Total	112	13

IRVING David

Forward 1975 5' 9" 10st 8
b. Crosby Villa (nr Cockermouth) 10 September 1951

Aspartria/ Workington May 1970/ Everton (£28/35k) Jan 1973
United: (L) 5/6 Sep 1975 to 4 Oct 1975
Debut: 13 Sep 1975 United 0 Coventry City 1 (sub)
Last game: 20 Sep 1975 West Ham United 2 United 0 (sub)
Oldham Athletic Jun 1976/ Fort Lauderdale Strikers 1977–80/ Tulsa Renegades Jun 1980/ Atlanta Chiefs Jul 1980/ San Jose Earthquakes Jun 1981

A youth International, David Irving scored on his FL debut for Workington on 9 November 1970 at Cambridge United. His move to Everton, for a then record fee for Workington and one that has been beaten only once since, was not a great success and he played only 4(2) FL games. His loan spell with United in a disastrous relegation season was brief and similarly disappointing.

After a short time with Oldham Athletic, bringing his FL career to 79(15) games, he played for five seasons in the North American Soccer League. He still lives in America and was the coach of Wilmington Hammerheads for several years.

Appearances:		Apps	Gls
	FL	0 (2)	0
	Total	0 (2)	0

JACKSON

United: 1895
Only game: 25 Mar 1895 United 3 Leicester Fosse 2 (UCL)

Reported as 'Scotch', this was his only appearance in United's colours.

Appearances:		Apps	Gls
	UCL	1	0
	Total	1	0

JACKSON Ernest

RH/IR 1933–49 5' 9" 11st 0 to 11st 8
b. Sheffield 11 June 1914
d. Sheffield 6 February 1996

Atlas & Norfolk (Sheffield)/ Sheffield Wednesday amat Oct 1931 to cs 1932/ Grimsby Town (trial)/ Atlas & Norfolk
United: 1 Jul and 3/5 Sep 1932 to 31 Jul 1949
Debut: 11 Feb 1933 United 0 Wolverhampton Wanderers 0
Last game: 19 Apr 1949 Wolverhampton Wanderers 6 United 0
WW2 guest: Barnsley 1945–46 (1 app)
Boston United May 1949 player-coach
United trainer cs1950 to Aug 1955
Rotherham United trainer/ Chesterfield trainer

A Sheffield and Yorkshire Boys' player, Ernest Jackson joined United initially as a part time player and was still employed at the Atlas & Norfolk works when he made his FL debut. He was held back for a time by cartilage injuries but recovered after an operation in 1935.

A conspicuous figure with fair hair, a fresh complexion and a determined attitude, he became an outstanding right half. Quick and powerful in the tackle with good ball control, Ernest had a fine sense of anticipation and judgement and had a long throw. He was probably the fittest and certainly the strongest United player at that time as he once demonstrated by lifting a telephone pole washed up on a beach. He played in the 1936 FA Cup Final and he was among the players who won promotion to the top flight in 1939 and it was often said that he deserved international recognition.

During the War Ernest returned to his previous job and was available to play for United although he gave up playing for a short while due to travel difficulties and the long hours of work. He was a prominent member of the League North Championship team of 1945–46 and was still a fine player in the first two years after the War. Eyesight problems and advancing years led to his release in 1949 when United were relegated but, after a season with Boston United in the Midland League, he returned to the Lane as a member of the training staff.

When Reg Freeman became manager, Ernest became first team trainer and he was involved with the Second Division championship side of 1953 but he resigned in 1955, unable to establish a satisfactory working relationship with the new manager, Joe Mercer.

Appearances:		Apps	Gls
	FL	229	7
	FAC	21	0
	CC	11	0
	WW2	136	12
	39–40	3	0
	Total	400	19

JACOBSEN Anders

CD 1999 6' 3" 13st 7
b. Oslo (Norway) 18 April 1968

Asker SK 1985–88/ Valerengen 1989–93 ?/ Lillestrom Sportsklubb 1993 ?–94/ Skeid (Oslo) 1995–96/ IK Start 1997–98
United: trial Nov 1998, (£15k) 21 Dec 1998 to Aug 1999
Debuts: 23 Jan 1999 Notts County 3 United 4 (sub FAC)
6 Feb 1999 United 3 West Bromwich Albion 2 (sub)
27 Feb 1999 Norwich City 1 United 1
Last games: 9 May 1999 Ipswich Town 4 United 1
18 Jul 1999 East Fife 0 United 4 (sub Fr)
Stoke City (L) Jul, Transfer Aug 1999/ Notts County Sep 2000/Asker SK 2001/ Skeid 2001–03/ Stromsgodset coach 2004/ Skeid (Oslo) coach 2004

After playing part time for many years in his native Norway, Anders Jacobsen, a student at Oslo University, who had gained four Norwegian caps and was captain at IK Start, joined United for a small fee. When called upon he was a solid and reliable defender who played regularly at the end of the season after David Holdsworth's departure. At the end of the season he moved to Stoke City and, after a spell with Notts County, he returned, to Norway.

Appearances:		Apps	Gls
	FL	8 (4)	0
	FAC	0 (1)	0
	Total	8 (5)	0

JAGIELKA Philip (Phil or Jags) Nikodem

MF/CD/RWB 1999–2007 5' 11" 12st 8
b. Manchester 17 August 1982

Everton to 1996/ Stoke C
United: from trainee May 2000 to 4 Jul 2007
Debuts: 7 Dec 1999 Whitby Town 1 United XI 3 (sub Fr)
7 May 2000 United 2 Swindon Town 2 (sub)
26 Jul 2000 Bodmin 0 United 8 (Fr)
22 Aug 2000 United 6 Lincoln City 1 (LC)
21 Apr 2001 Grimsby Town 0 United 1
Last game: 13 May 2007 United 1 Wigan Athletic 2
Everton (£4m) Jul 2007

Phil Jagielka was a versatile and consistent player for United, gaining England youth and U21 caps and, shortly before his departure, an England B cap. He established himself as a permanent member of the side towards the end of the 2001–02 season, prior to which he had been in the squad but frequently used as a substitute. Fast, athletic, good in the air and with immense stamina, he played as a right wing back, a central defender and as an attacking midfielder. As a midfielder, he was dangerous going forward and at set pieces and yet was quick to get back to defend in his own penalty box. At the end of the 2004–05 season, there were bids for him from Premiership clubs but he chose to stay with United and played a vital role in the promotion campaign which was his second successive ever-present season.

He was again ever-present during United's season in the Premiership where he again played both in midfield and as a central defender, the position where he felt more at home at the higher level. His final appearance was in the final game of the season which saw United relegated and it was Phil who conceded the vital penalty with a handball in the area. It was his 137th successive League game for the Blades, a total surpassed by only Jack Smith and Alan Woodward. A clause in his contract meant he was able to leave following relegation and Phil moved to Everton, the club which had released him aged 14.

He was the supporters 'Young Player of the Season' in 2003 and 'Player of the Season' in 2005, 2006 and 2007, and will be particularly remembered for the explosive equalising goal from 25 yards against Leeds United in the 2002–03 League Cup. Phil also proved to be an excellent substitute keeper when United didn't have a goalkeeper on the bench. He fulfilled this role on four occasions, none more dramatically than when he kept a clean sheet for about 30 minutes against Arsenal in December 2006, helping United to a 1–0 win.

In May 2008 he was called up to the England squad for two friendlies and came on as a second half substitute against Trinidad and Tobago. Phil's elder brother, Steve, also played for United (2003–04); their grandparents were Polish.

Appearances:

	Apps	Gls
FL	231 (23)	18
PO	3	0
FAC	14	2
LC	16	2
Total	264 (23)	22

JAVARY Jean-Phillipe

MF 2002–03 6' 0" 12st 6
b. Montpellier (France) 10 January 1978

Montpellier 1995–98/ Espanyol 1998–99/ Valence 1999–200/ Raith Rovers Jan 2000/ Brentford Aug 2000/ Plymouth Argyle Feb 2001 / – / Partick Thistle Oct 2001/ Raith Rovers Nov 2001 to Mar 2002/ Bradford City trial Feb 2002
United: Mar (nc) 2002, signed 12/15 Apr 2002 to 1/2 Sep 2003
Debut: 19 Mar 2002 United 3 Millwall 2
Last game: 7 Apr 2003 Wimbledon 1 United 0
Walsall (L) 17 Jan 2003 (no apps)
SS Excelsior (French Reunion Islands) 2003/ Hamilton Academicals Jan–May 2005/ SS Excelsior 2005/ FC Les Avirons (Reunion) 2007

A French youth international captain, Jean-Phillipe Javary appeared to have a wonderful future ahead of him but an intended move to Barcelona broke down and his career failed to take off. He moved to the UK in January 2000, playing initially in Scotland but his FL debut came with Brentford as a substitute on 19 August 2000 at home to Swansea City and his full debut, a week later at Oxford United.

A box to box player with good technique, he joined United after a trial with the reserve team at Barnsley and impressed at first with his combative, hard working mid-field displays. He was given a two year contract but couldn't win a regular place in the side and his final appearance was in front of just 1325 spectators at Wimbledon. He left the club by mutual consent in September 2003.

He subsequently played in the French Reunion Islands apart from a brief return to Scotland.

Appearances:

	Apps	Gls
FL	8 (5)	1
FAC	0 (1)	0
Total	8 (6)	1

JEEVES J

LH/CH/RH 1890–91

Sheffield Club
United: occasional Apr 1890 to Jan 1891
Debuts: 7 Apr 1890 United 1 Crewe Alexandra 1 (Fr, abandoned)
4 Oct 1890 Derby Junction 0 United 1 (FAC)
Last game: 31 Jan 1891 United 3 Kilnhurst 3 (SCC)

Jeeves was one of the Sheffield Club amateur players who assisted United in the first years of the new football club and had played for the Sheffield Association as early as 1884.

Appearances:		Apps	Gls
	FAC	1	0
	MCL	2	0
	SCC	1	0
	Total	4	0

JEFFERY Alfred (Alf or Rabbit) Howard

OL 1920 5' 3½" 9 st 2
b. Sheffield March 1895
d. Sheffield 17 January 1921

Trinity Wesleyans
United: 19 Dec 1919 to Oct 1920
Debut: 7 Feb 1920 West Bromwich Albion 0 United 2
Last game: 10 Apr 1920 Bradford City 1 United 2
Retired

Alf Jeffery ('Jeffrey' in some reports) may have been United's smallest player but he certainly wasn't the luckiest. Fast, with good ball control, he scored on his debut (possibly twice but reports are unclear as to whether he or Bolam scored the second goal) and was never on the losing side in his four appearances but he was soon forced to retire and died four months later.

He had played for the reserve team at Scunthorpe in mid-September and complained of being shaken up but felt fit enough to play again a fortnight later at Gainsborough. That was his last appearance and 'he retired on medical grounds' and a post-mortem gave the cause of death as 'vascular disease of the heart'.

Appearances:		Apps	Gls
	FL	4	1
	Total	4	1

JEFFRIES Alfred (Alf)

OR 1939–43 5' 7½" 10st 0
b. Bishop Auckland 21 September 1914
d. Nottingham 28 January 2004

Willington/ Norwich City Aug 1934/ Bradford City May 1935/ Derby County Feb 1937
United: (£3,208) 8/9 Jun 1939 to 4 May 1946
Debuts: 19 Aug 1939 Sheffield Wednesday 2 United 4 (Fr)
26 Aug 1939 United 2 Liverpool 1 (1939–40 fixture*)
Last game: 6 Mar 1943 Barnsley 1 United 4 (WW2)
WW2 guest: Mansfield Town, Chesterfield, Nottingham Forest, Watford, Portsmouth, Basingstoke Town

Alf Jeffries began his FL career with Norwich City but his debut was with Bradford City on 7 September 1935 at Manchester United. He had a spell with Derby County but, though blessed with pace and good ball control, he had few first team opportunities because of the presence of the England international, Sammy Crooks.

In the summer of 1939, having scored 12 FL goals in 70 games, he was signed by Teddy Davison; the only significant addition to the promoted United team and he scored on his debut, a FL Jubilee charity fixture at Hillsborough against Wednesday.

The possibility of a war against Germany seemed ever more likely in August 1939 and sadly, the only peace-time FL appearances* that Alf made for United were deleted from most official records because the season was abandoned due to the outbreak of the Second World War.

He worked in Sheffield in the early years of the war and was able to play over fifty matches for United and scored in his final game at Barnsley. By then, called up in 1941, he was serving in the Royal Navy.

He later qualified as an accountant and lived at Eastwood, near Nottingham.

Appearances:		Apps	Gls
	CC	1	0
	WW2	47	10
	39–40	3	0
	Total	51	10

JENKINSON Frederick (Fred)

RB/LB 1940–43 5' 9" 11st 0
b. Chapeltown/ Sheffield 7 April 1910
d. Harrogate April 1990

Chapeltown/ Intake WMC/ United (trial)/ Huddersfield Town amat Aug 1929/Intake WMC/ Nottingham Forest (trial)/ Stockport County Dec 1930/ Bury Jun 1939
United: WW2 guest
Debut: 16 Mar 1940 United 1 Lincoln City 0 (WW2)
Last game: 10 Apr 1943 United 0 Sheffield Wednesday 0 (WW2)
WW2 guest: Nottingham Forest (1 app v Sheff Utd Sep 1942)

A Barnsley Grammar School boy, Fred Jenkinson had trials with United and Forest and a season as an amateur with Huddersfield Town before he signed for Stockport County. He made his FL debut at Doncaster Rovers on 29 August 1931 and was with the club until 1939, becoming one of their finest full backs, making 295 FL appearances (1 goal). He joined Bury, a few months before the outbreak of war in September 1939 but, because of the war, he made only one appearance in February 1942 at Chesterfield.

A neat, stylish player and a good tackler, his games for United were as a guest player during the early part of the war. His final game was at Hillsborough and was remarkable in that the attendance was the largest (43,718) of his career and he played most of the second half with a fractured ankle!

After retiring from football, he moved to Bournemouth and ran a guest house.

Appearances:		Apps	Gls
	WW2	62	0
	Total	62	0

JENKINSON Thomas Ioldo

OR 1896–98
b. Sheffield AMJ 1877
d. Sheffield 21/24 January 1949

Sheffield Heeley 1893–94/ Gainsborough Trinity
United: May 1895 to 31 May 1898
Debuts: 12 Dec 1896 Manchester City 1 United 3 (Fr)
20 Nov 1897 Blackburn Rovers 1 United 1
Last games: 11 Dec 1897 Stoke City 2 United 1
19 Apr 1898 Victoria United (Aberdeen) 1 United 0 (Fr)
Grimsby Town May 1898

Tom and Frederick William Jenkinson both played for Heeley and joined United in May 1895 but Tom was the only one to play for the first team. He played two competitive games for the club and both were in the season which saw United become League Champions. He was transferred (with Greenwood) to Grimsby Town for a token fee of £10 and scored 24 goals in 66 FL games before injury forced his retirement in 1901.

Appearances:		Apps	Gls
	FL	2	0
	Total	2	0

JESSOP Frederick (Fred) Samuel

LH/RH/CH 1937–39 5' 8½" 11st 0
b. Barrow Hill (Chesterfield) 7 February 1907
d. Chesterfield OND 1979

Barrow Hill/ Staveley Works/ Derby County am Jan 1926, pro Mar 1926
United: (£500) 16/17 Dec 1937 to 4 May 1946
Debut: 18 Dec 1937 United 5 Southampton 0
Last game: 25 Mar 1939 United 2 Tranmere Rovers 0
WW2 guest: Lincoln City (1939–41 and 1945), Chesterfield (1 app 1939–40)/
Atherstone Town 1945/ Norton Woodseats(coach)

Fred Jessop made his FL debut with Derby County in a 3–1 victory at Sunderland on 10 September 1930 when he was twenty three and went on to make 84 FL appearances for the club. A rough, tough, hard working, utility mid-field player, Fred never really had an established first team place either with Derby or United but was an excellent player to have in reserve, particularly on the heavy grounds in winter. One of the hardest tacklers in the game, he occasionally overstepped the mark. He was, for instance, cautioned and censured by the FA in February 1938 after an injudicious tackle on Eastham of Liverpool but it was often his team mates who suffered the consequences when opponents sought some form of retribution.

He was thirty when Teddy Davison, the United manager, brought him to the Lane but he was able to play a useful role in the 1938–39 season when United were promoted to the top Division.

An accident at work late in 1940 essentially ended his playing career though he did play for the reserve team in November 1943 and once for Lincoln in January 1945 when United defeated them 10–2. After the war, he became a shoe repairer in Dronfield.

Appearances:		Apps	Gls
	FL	25	1
	FAC	6	0
	Total	31	1

JOHN William (Roy) Ronald

G 1934–35 5' 11" 11st 7
b. Briton Ferry (Neath) 29 January 1911
d. Port Talbot 12 July 1973

Briton Ferry Athletic/ Swansea Town am. Feb 1927/ Walsall May 1928/ Stoke City Apr 1932/ Preston North End Jun 1934
United: (£1,000+£250) 21 Dec 1934 to 12 Jun 1936
Debut: 22 Dec 1934 United 1 Brentford 2
Last game: 14 Dec 1935 Bradford City 2 United 1
Manchester United (£600) Jun 1936/ Newport County Mar 1937/ Swansea Town Jul 1937 to Nov 1939
WW2 guest: Southport, Blackburn Rovers, Burnley, Bolton Wanderers

Roy John was a half back when he signed as an amateur for Swansea Town in 1927 but made no senior appearances. After trials with various clubs, including Manchester United, he signed for Walsall making his FL debut on 6 October 1928 at Fulham. His first appearance as a goalkeeper came when he volunteered to play there in an emergency in a reserve match. He saved a penalty kick and made his FL debut between the posts on 1 March 1930 at Watford and was capped a few weeks later.

After spells with Stoke and Preston, he joined United in December 1934 and missed just one match during the rest of the season but after playing in the first six games of the following campaign, he lost his place to Jack Smith and played just once more before he was transferred to Manchester United.

He was an agile keeper but prone to take risks by making 'hair raising sorties from goal' and he also had a reputation for making long kicks up-field. During his career he played 14 times for Wales (3 whilst with United) but later, he admitted to regretting becoming a keeper.

He returned to Wales, playing for Newport and then Swansea and planned to retire from football in October 1939 when he became a hotel manager but did make occasional appearances later and also worked for British Steel.

Appearances:		Apps	Gls
	FL	29	0
	FAC	2	0
	Total	31	0

JOHNS Nicholas (Nicky) Paul

G 1978 6' 2" 11st 5
b. Bristol 8 June 1957

Minehead/ Millwall (£2,000) Feb 1976/ Tampa Bay Rowdies (£150k) cs 1978
United: 1 Sep 1978 to 20 Dec 1978
Debuts: 12 Sep 1978 Norton Woodseats 0 United 2 (BM)
18 Sep 1978 United 4 Doncaster Rovers 1 (CC)
7 Oct 1978 United 3 Sunderland 2
Last games: 10 Oct 1978 United 1 Leeds United 4 (LC)
23 Oct 1978 Winterton Rangers 1 United 1 (Fr)
Charlton Athletic Dec 1978, (£135k) Aug 1979/ Queens Park Rangers (£40k) Dec 1987/ Maidstone United (L) Oct 1989, signed Mar 1990

Rejected by both Bristol City and Bristol Rovers after trials, Nicky joined Minehead and then Millwall, where he completed an engineering apprenticeship, and made his FL debut with the Lions on 20 November 1976 at Carlisle United.

He joined United after a short period (8 app) in the NASL but was not a success at Bramall Lane and had a particularly nervous FL debut against Sunderland.

His later career, after moving to Charlton Athletic, was far more successful and he played nearly 300 FL games for the club. Latterly he worked with Crystal Palace in the 'Football in the Community' area becoming part time after a car accident in 1998.

Appearances:		Apps	Gls
	FL	1	0
	LC	1	0
	CC	1	0
	Total	3	0

JOHNSON Arthur John

RH 1907 5' 9" c12st
b. Orsett, Grays (Essex) JFM 1885

Grays United (QPR and Woolwich Arsenal) 1905–06/ Southend United 1906–07
United: 15/16 May 1907 to Dec 1908
Debut: 16 Nov 1907 Bristol City 3 United 2
Last game: United 0 Notts County 1
Southend United/ New Brompton

Arthur Johnson became a professional player with Southern League Southend United, playing in their first ever game, and returned to the Essex club after just two first team outings with the Blades, United retaining his FL registration.

Appearances:		Apps	Gls
	FL	2	0
	Total	2	0

JOHNSON Charles (Charlie)

LB/RB 1905–10 5' 9" 11st 0 to 11st 7
b. North Shields 29 April 1884

Hylton Rov/ Wallsend Park Villa 1901/ Willington Athletic 1903
United: (£80) 12 Jan 1905 to cs 1910
Debuts: 29 Apr 1905 Woolwich Arsenal 2 United 3 (Fr)
10 Feb 1906 Everton 3 United 2
Last game: 12 Feb 1910 United 1 Nottingham Forest 4
South Shields cs1910/ Jarrow Caledonians player-mgr1912/ South Shields 1913

Charlie Johnson was a consistent, reliable full back with judgement in everything he did and a player who never suffered any significant injury. He helped manage a billiard saloon at Hillsborough while he was with United and later had another business in North Shields. He played four FL games in South Shields' first League season (1919–20).

Appearances:		Apps	Gls
	FL	71	0
	FAC	3	0
	Total	74	0

JOHNSON David Anthony

Striker 2005 5' 6" 12st 3
b. Kingston (Jamaica) 15 August 1976

Manchester United from trainee Jul 1994/ Bury Jul 1995/ Ipswich Town (£800k) Nov 1997/ Nottingham Forest (£3m+) Jan 2001-Sep 2006/ Sheffield Wednesday (L) Feb 2002/ Burnley (L) Mar 2002
United: (L) 11 Mar 2005 to May 2005
Debut: 12 Mar 2005 Stoke City 2 United 0 (sub)
Last game: 23 Apr 2005 Watford 0 United 0 (sub)
Hucknall Town Mar 2007

David Johnson made his FL debut with Bury on 23 September 1995 as a substitute at home to Barnet, his full debut coming four weeks later at Mansfield Town on 28 October. Quick and with an eye for goal, Neil Warnock signed him on a three month loan to add pace to the attack. The return to fitness of Steve Kabba and the signing of Danny Webber meant David was restricted to just four rather disappointing sub appearances before returning to Forest. A back injury brought his full time playing career to an end in September 2006, having totalled 112 League goals in 266(43) games. After a brief spell with Hucknall he was forced to retire completely.

Appearances:		Apps	Gls
	FL	0 (4)	0
	Total	0 (4)	0

JOHNSON Edward William

OL 1898–99 5' 8" 11st 8
b. c 1876

Rochdale Feb 1898
United: (£50–100) 17/20 Dec 1898 to cs 1899
Debut: 26 Dec 1898 United 2 Wednesday 1
Last game: 2 Jan 1899 United 0 Liverpool 2

E W Johnson played four consecutive games for United, in one of which, a friendly against Corinthians, he scored a hat trick.

Appearances:		Apps	Gls
	FL	3	0
	Total	3	0

JOHNSON Harry (Young Harry)

CF/OR/IR/IL 1916–31 5' 8" 10st 2 to 11st 0
b. Ecclesfield 4 January 1899
d. Sheffield 26? May 1981

Ecclesfield
United: amat 1915, pro Jun 1919 to 17 Jul 1931
Debuts: 4 Mar 1916 Hull City 5 United 2 (MG WW1)
20 Oct 1919 United 2 Blackburn Rovers 0
Last game: 2 May 1931 Sunderland 2 United 1
WW1 guest: Notts County (1916 v Utd), Birmingham (1917–18, 2 app), Rotherham County (1 app, Feb 1918)
Mansfield Town (£500) Jul 1931 to May 1936

Young and Old Harry

Harry Johnson, the son of 'Old Harry', the international right half and assistant trainer, joined United as an amateur, during the First War in 1915. A former Barnsley Grammar School boy, he scored on his debut in March 1916 and soon established himself in the wartime side, often appearing at outside right or inside forward. He missed most of the 1918–19 season serving in France with a special unit of the Royal Engineers (the 'gas mob') but, on his return, he became a regular in the side again, scoring 12 goals in 26 games.

United's record goal scorer, his success could be said to be a triumph for attitude over technique (apart from his heading). Harry was relatively small and slim and was forever hitching up his standard size shorts, which drew a plentiful supply of knicker elastic from female supporters. He was an opponent's nightmare: very fast, fearless and with seemingly inexhaustible energy. Many of his opportunities came through his speed, anticipation and courage and he was a fine header of the ball often seeming to fly 'horizontally' through the air. He chased lost causes, seizing on opponents' errors and confusion. He never shirked a challenge and, if knocked off his feet, he always seemed to hit the ground rolling before getting to his feet with a smile on his face. Despite being a part time player, working as a metallurgical chemist in a steel works, his scoring record is second to none. Harry Hammond is the only other United player who has scored five goals in a League game and Johnson scored four goals in a game a record seven times and a further twelve hat tricks (nine of his hat tricks or better were scored under the old off-side rule). He was even more prolific under the new rule which suited the United side of the time, and he was top scorer for nine successive seasons and his club record 201 FL goals is 43 more than second placed Alan Woodward.

Technically, Harry was not a great player. It was said that he missed more 'sitters' than he scored goals but that he 'was the greatest scorer of impossible goals'. His first touch often let him down ('still can't trap a ball' in a December 1928 match report) and he was neither a schemer nor a ball player. He explained that his attitude to the game was due to the fact that he worked during the week making each game something special to look forward to.

He played in United's 1925 FA Cup winning side (his father had won a medal with United earlier) and his brother Tom was on the losing side in 1936. He won one representative honour, playing for the Football League against the Irish League in 1927 and scored three goals (Dixie Dean however, scored four).

He was transferred to Mansfield Town in 1931 and scored 104 goals for the Stags, becoming their leading FL goal scorer, before retiring in 1936. He remains the leading goalscorer for both United and Mansfield. Harry had never been prone to injury but in 1934 he broke his wrist and a subsequent X-ray showed he had six previous breaks which he had never reported.

Appearances:		Apps	Gls
	FL	313	201
	FAC	27	20
	CC	10	6
	WW1	44	25
	ABD	1	0
	Total	395	252

JOHNSON Howard

CH/RB/CF 1951–57 5' 10" 11st 8 to 12st 8
b. Pitsmoor (Sheffield) 17 July 1925

Inland Revenue (Sheffield)/ Norton Woodseats
United: 1/3 Mar 1951 to 17 Aug 1957
Debut: 23 Mar 1951 Brentford 3 United 1
Last games: 1 Dec 1956 Liverpool 5 United 1
14 Jan 1957 Huddersfield Town 2 United 1 (FAC)
York City Aug 1957 to cs 1959/ Denaby United to cs 1962

A Firth Park Grammar School boy who had served in the Navy, Howard Johnson was twenty five when he came to Bramall Lane from local club Norton Woodseats, United making donations totalling £200 to the Dronfield club. A finance clerk, he trained as an accountant and later became a computer systems analyst.

A powerfully built part-time player, Howard was 'as hard as nails' and gave as good as he got in battles with the old fashioned centre forwards such as Trevor Ford and Nat Lofthouse. He was good in the air, strong, enthusiastic and fearless and his tackles were decisive, if at times, in the words of Lofthouse, 'mistimed'. Nat added that his 'zeal was misplaced on occasion' but then, Lofthouse didn't explain how Howard's

nose came to be broken when the pair clashed. He made intermittent appearances until season 1952 –53 when he had a run of games in the Second Division Championship side. The retirement of Harry Latham, who had done much to encourage him, meant a more regular place in the side in 1953–54 but he then found himself competing with Joe Shaw and for a while with Joe Mercer's curious signing, Malcolm Barrass. Although Howard played most of his games for United at centre half, his final four games were at centre forward and he scored in his final appearance.

He added 28 more FL appearances during his time at York.

Appearances:		Apps	Gls
	FL	92	0
	FAC	10	1
	CC	5	0
	Total	107	1

JOHNSON Martin James

IL 1927 5' 10" 11st
b. Windy Nook (Co Durham) 21 March 1906
d. North Shields 25 April 1977

Felling Colliery/ Sunderland trial/ Durham City Jul 1925/ Bradford PA Feb 1926
United: (£1,100) 30 Jun/1 Jul 1927 to Jul 1928
Debut: 8 Oct 1927 Sunderland 0 United 1
Last games: 12 Nov 1927 United 1 Huddersfield Town 7
28 Nov 1927 Sheffield Wednesday 3 United 1 (CC)
Durham City Jul 1928/ Wolverhampton Wanderers Oct 1928/ Spennymoor/ Murton CW Feb 1931/ North Shields Aug 1933/ Wardley CW Oct 1933

A scheming inside left, Martin Johnson made his FL debut with Durham City 29 September 1925. Later that season he moved to Bradford Park Avenue from where he joined United. At Bramall Lane, his seven appearances came within a spell of eight weeks. He was transfer listed with the FL at £500 but returned to Durham City who, by then, were a non-League club. In all Martin made 62 FL appearances and scored 10 goals.

Appearances:		Apps	Gls
	FL	6	0
	CC	1	0
	Total	7	0

JOHNSON Thomas (Tommy)

Striker 2005 5' 11" 12st 8
b. Newcastle on Tyne 15 January 1971

Notts County from trainee Jan 1989/ Derby County (£1.375m) Mar 1992/ Aston Villa (£1.45m) Jan 1995/ Celtic (£2.4m) Mar 1997/ Everton (L)Sep 1999/ Sheffield Wednesday Sep 2001/ Kilmarnock Dec 2001/ Gillingham Aug 2002
United: 10 Feb 2005 to Jun 2005
Only game: 26 Feb 2005 United 1 Rotherham United 0
Scunthorpe United Sep 2005/ Tamworth (L) Mar to cs 2006/ Rocester Sep 2006 / – / Notts County coach Oct 2007

Tommy Johnson made his FL debut with Notts County, coming on as a substitute at home to Preston North End on 24 September 1988. He made his full debut later in the season, at Cardiff City on 18 April after Neil Warnock had become County's manager and helped to take County to the first Division.

An U21 international with both Notts and Derby County and a record signing by the Rams, this quick and tricky forward's career was long but the number of appearances he managed each season dwindled away as injuries took their toll. Tommy left Gillingham by mutual consent, moving to Bramall Lane primarily as a coach but made just one FL appearance and in the close season moved to Scunthorpe United and then into non-League football.

During his League career, both North and South of the border, Tommy totalled 120 goals in 271(77) games.

Appearances:

	Apps	Gls
FL	1	0
Total	1	0

JOHNSON Tom

CH/LH/RB 1930–41 5' 11" 11st 9 to 12st 7
b. The Wheel, Ecclesfield (Sheffield) 4 May 1911
d. Sheffield 19 August 1983

Ecclesfield WMC/ Ecclesfield United
United: 5/7 Sep 1928 to 28 Feb 1946
Debut: 8 Mar 1930 United 2 Bolton Wanderers 3
Last games: 6 May 1939 United 6 Tottenham Hotspur 1
2 Sep 1939 Leeds United 0 United 1 (39–40)
24 May 1941 Everton 3 United 3 (WW2)
WW2 guest: Stockport County Jan 1940 (1 app), Sheffield Wednesday Apr 1941 (1), Chesterfield
Lincoln City (free) 11 Mar 1946 to Dec 1948

Educated at Barnsley Grammar School, Tom Johnson was a son of 'Old Harry' and younger brother of 'Young Harry' Johnson who were both Cup Winners with United. He signed for the club in 1928 as a part timer—following the example of his brother—but it wasn't until 1934–35 that he established himself as anything like a regular member of the side; in fact, his application, in 1934, to become full-time had been rejected.

Tom had the pressure that his father had been and his brother still was, a great player and both were immensely popular. Tom, moreover, was disappointingly slow to develop and wasn't even sure which position suited him best. He appeared to be more suited to the successful 'third back game' used by the Arsenal than Jimmy Holmes but the turning point in his career didn't come until Christmas Day 1935 when he returned to the first team after having been dropped.

Rapidly growing in confidence, he became strong, steadfast, decisive in the tackle and good in the air and missed very few games as the team began a long unbeaten run and reached the FA Cup Final. He remained the first choice centre half until the Second War, taking over the captaincy for the 1937–38 campaign and leading the side back to the top flight in the following season.

When the War began, he became an electrician at Whitwell Colliery but joined the RAF at the end of 1940 though he played regularly for United until May 1941. He served in East Africa but was discharged in 1943 with an ankle injury and played no serious football until March 1946. He had been in a dispute with United and was given a free transfer. He started playing for Lincoln City and went on to captain their 1948 championship side and made 75 FL appearances before retiring. He became Lincoln's Yorkshire area scout in 1949 and had an electrical business in Sheffield.

Appearances:

	Apps	Gls
FL	183	0
FAC	19	0
CC	7	0
WW2	45	0
39–40	3	0
Total	257	0

JOHNSON William Harrison (Harry)

RH/CH/LH/LB/RB 1895–1908 5' 8" 12st
b. Ecclesfield 4 January 1876
d. Ecclesfield 17 July 1940

Norfolk Works/ Ecclesfield Church/ Barnsley (trial)
United: 22 Oct 1895 to 30 Apr 1909
Debuts: 27 Dec 1895 United 1 Corinthians 0 (Fr)
10 Feb 1896 Walsall 2 United 5 (BC)
23 Oct 1897 United 2 Preston North End 1
Last game: 31 Oct 1908 United 1 Woolwich Arsenal 1
Asst trainer Aug 1909 to 1934

Turned down by Barnsley after asking for 10 shillings (50p) a week, Harry Johnson, whose sons Harry and Tom later played for United, moved to Bramall Lane in October 1895. He made his first team debut later that year in the same match as Tommy Morren but his FL debut wasn't until the Blades' Championship season, 1897–98, when he made 10 appearances. He became first choice towards the end of that season, essentially because of his own determined play but helped by the departure of Rab Howell, and remained as a regular first team player until 1905.

An excellent player in a fine team, he added three F A Cup medals (winners' in 1899 and 1902, losers' in 1901) to his League Championship medal of 1898 and was awarded six England caps. He was a consistent, hard-working clever player with tremendous stamina and 'scrupulously fair'. A fine tackler, he was difficult to dispossess and he was a good header of the ball, always trying to use it constructively.

In January 1906, playing at full-back in a match at Sunderland, he suffered a terrible injury, his leg being smashed just above the knee. It was thought his career had ended but he did make a few more appearances.

He took control of the reserves in September 1908 and in August 1909, he became assistant trainer and, a year later, also took on the duties of assistant groundsman. 'Old Harry', as he came to be known after his son became a United player, remained at the Lane until 1934. 'Young Harry', his eldest son, was a FA Cup winner in 1925 and United's record top scorer and Tom, a younger son was a losing Cup finalist in 1936 and captained the 1939 promotion team.

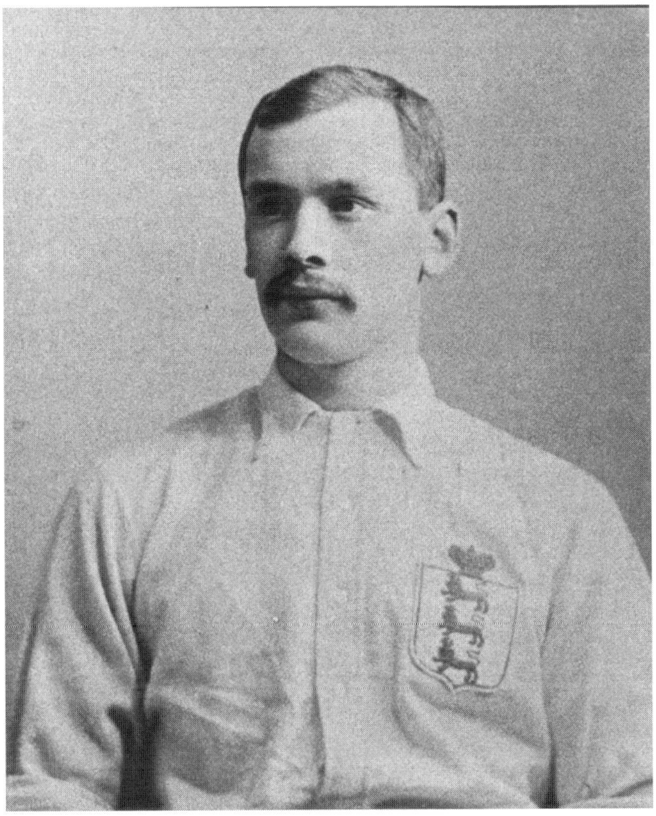

Appearances:

	Apps	Gls
FL	242	6
FAC	31	1
BC	1	0
ABD	1	0
Total	275	7

JOHNSTONE F J

IR 1945

Glasgow Rangers?
United: WW2 guest
Only game: 19 May 1945 United 1 Sheffield Wednesday 3 (WW2)

A totally incompetent guest player, ('Johnson' in one report) belonging to Glasgow Rangers in the FL match record, who made this one appearance for United. Reported to be serving in the RAF and married to a Sheffield girl, his first half 'display' so annoyed some of the United players that they insisted that he should play the second half even though it was obvious that he was totally unfit and suffering, so he complained, from a septic toe. He may have played 'as a joke' but may have changed his mind as he limped onto the field for the second half, some time after the kick-off!

Appearances:

	Apps	Gls
CC	1	0
Total	1	0

JOHNSTONE James (Jimmy or Jinky) Connolly

OR/IR 1975–77 5' 4" 9st 8
b. Viewpark, Uddingston (Glasgow) 30 September 1944
d. Glasgow 13 March 2006

Blantyre Celtic 1960/ Celtic Nov 1961/ Hamilton Academicals (L) Mar 1975/ San Jose Earthquakes Jun 1975
United: (free) 19 Nov 1975 to 7 May or Jun 1977
Debut: 22 Nov 1975 Stoke City 2 United 1
Last games: 23 Oct 1976 Charlton Athletic 3 United 2
13 Apr 1977 Grantham Town 0 United 3 (Fr)
Dundee 6 Jul 1977/ Shelbourne Nov 1977/ Elgin City 1978 to Aug 1979 / – / Blantyre Celtic player-coach Jul 1980 / – / Celtic coach to Nov 1980

One of Scotland's greatest footballers and voted as Celtic's greatest ever player by their fans, Jimmy represented the club for 12 years, winning many domestic League and Cup medals and was a member of the Celtic side which became the first British side to win the European Cup in 1967. Said to have been inspired by Stanley Matthews, he worked on his dribbling ability as a youngster and although small, he was strong and difficult to knock of the ball and could tackle well. He gained caps at U23 level and had 23 full caps as well as representing the Scottish League. Always vulnerable to drink problems, it still came as a surprise to many when he was awarded a free transfer in 1975.

He was past his best and the desire had gone when he was signed by fellow Glaswegian, Jimmy Sirrel for United. Rows between the two—unintelligible to most of the other players—were not uncommon and Jimmy's drinking remained a problem but he trained hard, helped the young players and there were occasional glimpses of the old magic such as the game against Fulham who included George Best and Bobby Moore. It could have been an inspired signing but it was always unlikely and, after seventeen months and thirteen competitive games for the first team, only one had ended with a victory for United.

Jimmy found life difficult after hanging up his boots but became an active charity campaigner when diagnosed with motor neurone disease in 2001. Sadly, he died in 2006.

Appearances:

	Apps	Gls
FL	11	2
FAC	1	0
CC	1	0
Total	13	2

JONES F or A

OL 1918

United: WW1 guest
Only game: 23 Feb 1918 Nottingham Forest 0 United 1 (WW1)

A 'local lad' according to one report, he appears as F Jones in the FL match records but an 'A Jones' is at outside left in a United reserve programme soon after and may have played for Rotherham County in the same period.

Appearances:

	Apps	Gls
WW1	1	0
WW1	1	0

JONES Garry Edwin

CF 1975 5' 9" 10st 2
b. Wythenshawe (Manchester) 11 December 1950

Bolton Wanderers from 1966 to app Jan 1968
United: (L) 3/7 Feb 1975 to 4 Mar 1975
Debut: 8 Feb 1975 Carlisle United 0 United 1
Last game: 22 Feb 1975 Burnley 2 United 1
Blackpool Nov 1978/ Hereford United Aug 1980/ Northwich Victoria cs 1981/ Prescot Bl

Garry Jones made his FL debut with Bolton Wanderers on 4 March 1969 at Huddersfield Town and went on to make over 200 FL appearances for the club. At the time of his loan period with United he had lost his place in the Wanderers' side but, despite scoring on his United debut at Carlisle, he didn't live up to the fee of £40k that Bolton required for his transfer. He ended his FL career with Hereford United, totalling 237(21) FL games and 51 goals, before moving into non-League football.

Appearances:		Apps	Gls
	FL	3	1
	Total	3	1

JONES George Henry

OL/OR/CF 1936–51 5' 6½" 9st 6 to 10st 10
b. Sheffield 27 November 1918
d. Sheffield 10 March 1995

Woodbourn Alliance
United: 8 May 1935(am), 29 Nov 1935 (pro) to 21 Feb 1951
Debut: 14 Sep 1936 United 2 West Ham United 0
Last games: 20 Jan 1951 United 2 Luton Town 1
31 Jan 1951 Mansfield Town 2 United 1 (FAC)
WW2 guest: Shorts Sports(Rochester) 1939–40, Aldershot (1941–45, 43 app, 8 goals), Gillingham 1944–45 (7 app, 3 gls), Fulham (1 app, 1944–45)
Barnsley (£2,500) Feb 1951

A Sheffield and Yorkshire Boys winger, George Jones made his United first team debut when he was seventeen. He played in half the games in the promotion season of 1938–39 but the Second War intervened. After initially working in Sheffield for the ESC, within a few weeks, he had taken a job in the Shorts aircraft factory near Rochester in Kent, playing for the works team and then with Aldershot. He had played in United's first war time game at Chesterfield but he made only four other appearances for United—which included a hat trick against Manchester United—before he returned to Sheffield in the summer of 1945.

George was two footed, fast and direct with a strong shot and centred well but he did well to play as a professional for he suffered from bronchial pneumonia and it was a common sight to see him bending over as he struggled to draw breath. He was a member of the 1945–46 League North Championship team playing mainly at outside right but later switched to the left wing for five more seasons before moving to Barnsley, but only in 1948–49 could it be said that he was an automatic choice in the side.

He spent just 15 months with Barnsley, making 26 FL appearances and had a news agency business in Page Hall Road.

Appearances:		Apps	Gls
	FL	141	36
	FAC	10	4
	CC	6	1
	WW2	30	18
	Total	187	59

JONES Glyn

IL/IR 1956–57 5' 8" 11st 10
b. Dalton (Rotherham) 8 April 1936

Rotherham United (amat)
United: pro 9 Jun 1954 to 28 Dec 1957
Debut: 28 Apr 1956 Tottenham Hotspur 3 United 1
Last game: 21 Dec 1957 Notts County 1 United 0
Rotherham United Dec 1957/ Mansfield Town Jul 1959 to cs1961/ Cheltenham Town

A former schoolboy international and Rotherham United amateur inside forward, Glyn was signed by Reg Freeman for United and made his first team debut in a match at White Hart Lane when the Blades were relegated.

A stylish player, Glyn had good ball control and passing ability but lacked speed and devil. An England youth international whilst at Bramall Lane, he had only one consistent run in the first team, playing 13 successive games towards the end of the 1956–57 season.

He made 97 FL appearances with his three clubs before moving into non-League football.

Appearances:		Apps	Gls
	FL	29	4
	CC	2	0
	Total	31	4

JONES John (Jack) Leonard

LH/RH/CH/OL/IL/OR 1894–97 5' 10" 12st 8
b. Rhuddlan 1869
d. Sunderland 24 November 1931

Bootle amat 1886 to 1890/ Stockton 1890/ Grimsby Town May 1893
United: 14 May 1894 to 10 May 1897
Debut: 1 Sep 1894 United 2 West Bromwich Albion 1
Last games: 13 Mar 1897 United 0 Preston North End 2
21 Apr 1897 Clowne 2 United 7 (Fr)
Tottenham Hotspur May 1897 to May 1904 / – / Worcester City Jun 1905

Jack Jones didn't play much football as a boy but he moved from Wales to Bootle and it was there that he learned to play cricket as well as football. He became a professional at both games with Stockton but moved to Grimsby Town when Stockton returned to being an amateur club. He made his FL debut on 2 September 1893 at home to Northwich Victoria and was ever present that season, playing at outside left.

On moving to the Lane, he played cricket for United and when the football season opened, he scored on his first two outings but, although he had many admirable qualities, he was short of speed and was usually regarded as a utility player, generally filling in when regular first team players were injured. A skilful, thoughtful but wholehearted player who revelled in the mud, his passing was excellent. He usually played as a half back or inside forward and although he was never a regular member of

the United side, his ability was appreciated and he gained nine Welsh caps in his time at the Lane.

After three seasons, he accepted an offer from Spurs who didn't have to pay a transfer fee because they were then in the Southern League. United were particularly annoyed because the Secretary, J B Wostinholm had secured a summer coaching position for Jones at Rugby School and, a year later, the player probably played a part when Bob Cain and Kenny McKay left United to join Spurs. To add to United's chagrin, Jones was a mainstay of the Tottenhaam side for seven seasons and was the captain of the Spurs side which beat United in the 1901 FA Cup Final.

He won twelve more Welsh caps (21 in total) and was Spurs' first capped player and whilst with Tottenham, he coached cricket and football at Rugby School and after retiring from the game he played and coached cricket at Leinster (1907) and in South Africa. In 1923, he became the coach and groundsman at Whitburn Cricket Club in Durham and, working as a pattern maker, he fell down a stairway and sustained fatal head injuries.

Appearances:		Apps	Gls
	FL	31	5
	FAC	4	0
	UCL	1	0
	BC	1	1
	Total	37	6

JONES Michael (Mick) David

CF/IL/IR 1963–67 5' 10½" 11st 11
b. Rhodesia, Worksop (Nottinghamshire) 24 April 1945

Dinnington Miners Welfare
United: 5 Apr 1961, app 16/17 Nov 1962 to 22 Sep 1967
Debut: 20 Apr 1963 Manchester United 1 United 1
Last game: 16 Sep 1967 Manchester City 5 United 2
Leeds United (£100k) Sep 1967 to Aug 1975

Mick Jones was brought up in Shireoaks and played for Worksop and Notts Boys. He had a trial with West Bromwich Albion but was playing with Dinnington Miners Welfare and working in a cycle factory when he was spotted by United and invited to train with the club for two nights a week. He scored freely in the excellent NIL side that United had at that time and made his first team debut four days before his eighteenth birthday and on his birthday, he scored twice against Manchester City.

He formed a very effective dual strike force, at first with Derek Pace and then with Alan Birchenall. Well built, brave, determined and hard working, Mick had a strong shot in both feet, was a fine header of the ball and led the line well, using his strength to hold the ball and distribute it well to supporting players. Whilst with United, he won nine U23 caps and two full caps.

His sale to Leeds United shocked Blades' fans but he did well with his new club. He won Championship medals in 1969 and 1974 and an FA Cup winners' medal in 1972, when he dislocated his elbow whilst making the cross from which Allan Clarke scored the winner, and gained one more full England cap. Serious knee problems came to a head in April 1974 and with the Championship secured, Mick stopped playing though his formal retirement was delayed until August 1975 after a season on the sidelines. He made 219 FL appearances for Leeds and scored 77 goals.

More recently Mick has been involved with the Corporate Hospitality at Bramall Lane.

Appearances:		Apps	Gls
	FL	149	63
	FAC	11	9
	LC	7	1
	CC	5	3
	Total	172	76

JONES Philip (Phil) Howard

MF/CB 1978–81 6' 0½" 12st 4
b. Mansfield 12 September 1961

United: from 3 Jul 1978, app 28 May/Jun 1979 to 26 May 1982
Debuts: 23 Oct 1978 Winterton Rangers 1 United 1 (sub Fr)
28 Feb 1979 Wrexham 4 United 0
Last games: 28 Mar 1981 United 2 Millwall 3
3 Aug 1981 Ayr United 1 United 0 (sub Fr)
Boston United 1982/ Matlock Town/ Gainsborough Trinity 1989–90

Phil Jones played for United's Reserves in September 1977 a few days before his sixteenth birthday. Jimmy Sirrel was the manager and Phil played for United at a difficult time for the club and the young player struggled to win a regular place in the side though he did have run of games in the fateful season which saw the club relegated to Division Four. A thoughtful, well built, mid-field player, he lacked the speed and determination to succeed at the top level of English football and his contract was cancelled in 1982.

Appearances:		Apps	Gls
	FL	25 (3)	1
	FAC	4	0
	ASC	3	0
	CC	1	0
	Total	33 (3)	1

JONES Vincent (Vinny to 1989, then Vinnie) Peter

MF 1990–91 6' 0" 11st 12
b. Watford 5 January 1965

Wealdstone/ Holmsund (Sweden) summer 1986/ Wimbledon (£10–15k) Nov 1986/ Leeds United (£650k) Jun 1989
United: guest app: 11 May 1990 Brentford 4 United XI 2 (BM)
(£650/£700k) 11/13 Sep 1990 to 29/30 Aug 1991
Debut: 15 Sep 1990 Southampton 2 United 0

Last game: 28 Aug 1991 Coventry City 3 United 1
Chelsea (£575k) Aug 1991/ Wimbledon (£700k) Sep 1992/ Queens Park Rangers (£500k) Mar 1998

Vinny Jones made his FL debut with Wimbledon, then managed by Dave Bassett, on 22 November 1986 at Nottingham Forest. During the game he punched the ball away to concede a penalty but things improved and he gained an FA Cup Winners' medal in 1988.

After a season with Leeds United, Bassett signed Jones to add leadership to the United side following the club's poor start to their first season back in the top flight. Jones had actually appeared in United's colours a few weeks earlier in a benefit match for Bob Booker, playing part of the second half in goal. He was made captain and, although United's first win came as late as December, they finished a respectable thirteenth.

A controversial figure, 'Vinnie', as he was now usually known, was a powerful player in mid-field; he was difficult to dispossess and he was a great ball winner, tackling really hard. Good in the air, his distribution was sound and his long throw was dangerous but he frequently came to the referee's attention and collected a much higher than average number of red and yellow cards. He was proud of being a 'hard man' and it brought him into conflict with the authorities. One yellow card was awarded after about five seconds against Manchester City and another, against United, after three seconds in a cup-tie in February 1992.

Shortly after the start of the following season, Vinny was sold to Chelsea to raise funds for new players. He went on to win nine caps for Wales during his second spell at Wimbledon and ended his League career with 377(9) appearances.

He went on to make a career in films, appearing in well over a dozen, starting with 'Lock, Stock and Two Smoking Barrels' and has appeared in various roles on TV.

Appearances:		Apps	Gls
	FL	35	2
	FAC	1	0
	LC	4	0
	FMC	1	0
	Total	41	2

JOSEPH Francis (Black Joe)

Striker 1988–89 5' 10" 12st 0
b. Kilburn 6 March 1960

Willesden/ Wealdstone/ Hillingdon Borough Jul 1979/ Wimbledon (£3,000) Nov 1980/ Honka (Finland) (L) summer 1981/ JYP77 (Finland) summer 1982/ Brentford (£40k) Jul 1982/ Wimbledon (L) Mar 1987/ HJK Helsinki(Finland) (L) May 1987/ Reading (£20k) Jul 1987/ Bristol Rovers (L) Jan 1988/ Aldershot (L) Mar 1988

United: (free) Jul 1988 to 25 Feb/Mar 1989
Debuts: **3 Aug 1988 Hagfors XI (Sweden) 1 United 12 (sub Fr)**
6 Aug 1988 Krylbo IF (Sweden) 0 United 7 (Fr)
13 Aug 1988 Bradford City 0 United 1 (YHC)
27 Aug 1988 Reading 1 United 3
Last game: 21 Jan 1989 United 4 Gillingham 2
Gillingham (£5,000) Mar 1989/ Crewe Alexandra Dec 1989/ Fulham Aug to Oct 1990/ Racing Ghent (Belgium) Nov 1990/ Tampa Bay Rowdies 1991/ Barnet Oct 1991/ Slough Town Nov 1991/ Wokingham Town/ Leatherhead Aug 1992/ Dulwich Hamlet Oct 1992/ Chertsey Town Jul 1993/ Walton & Hersham Aug 1994/ Chesham United Aug 1995/ Chertsey Town player-coach Nov 1995 / – / Wealdstone coach

Francis Joseph began his senior career with Wimbledon, scoring on his FL debut as a substitute on 6 December 1980 at home to Darlington, his full debut coming on 18 April 1981 at Bournemouth and he was voted their 'Player of the Year' in his first full season. He moved to Brentford and made a successful start but, after suffering a broken leg, he never repeated the same success and left after making over 100 FL appearances to join Reading.

Dave Bassett, who had been his manager a Wimbledon, signed Francis on a free transfer to help newly relegated United climb back into Division Two. He made an impressive start in United's pre-season friendlies, scoring in his first three games including a hat trick in his second appearance and he scored on his FL debut at Reading but unfortunately, he was injured. For the next game, Bassett played Deane and Agana as twin strikers and their prolific scoring and the form of Bryson, meant that Francis played only a minor role although he scored in his final game.

He ended his FL career having played 193(49) games, scoring 67 goals. Towards the end of his non-League career he moved into coaching with non-League clubs and carried on in this role once his playing career was over.

Appearances:		Apps	Gls
	FL	5 (8)	3
	FAC	0 (1)	0
	LC	0 (2)	0
	AMC	0 (1)	0
	YHC	3	1
	Total	8 (12)	4

JOYNER Francis (Frank) McNab

OL 1938–39 5' 10½" 11st 7
b. Strathkinness, St Andrews (Fife) 20 August 1918
d. Paisley 25 April 1997

St Andrews Univ/ Dundee (trial)/ Hamilton Academical (trial)/ Raith Rovers Apr 1937
United: (£1,800) 7/9 Apr 1938 to 6 May 1939
Debuts: **5 May 1938 Boston U 1 United XI 2 (Fr)**
31 Oct 1938 Doncaster Rovers 0 United 3 (CC)
2 Feb 1939 Norwich City 1 United 2
Last game: 4 Feb 1939 Plymouth Argyle 0 United 1
Kidderminster H. Aug 1939/ Third Lanark Nov 1941
WW2 guest: Third Lanark 1939?–41, Norwich City 1940–41, Raith Rovers 1941, Chelsea 1941
Dundee Mar 1946/ Raith Rovers 1949/ Hamilton Academicals 1950/ Kettering Town 1951/ Falkirk Oct 1952/ Forfar 1953/ Stirling Albion Aug 1954/ Third Lanark manager / – / Stirling Albion manager 1969 to Dec 1970

An all round athlete, Frank Joyner had an excellent season with Raith Rovers who were Scottish Second Division champions. Despite scoring on his United debut in a friendly match at Boston and in the County Cup, Frank played just twice more for the first team, and, although his appearances were all away from Bramall Lane, he was always on the winning side.

An army officer, he spent much of his war service in India. He spent most of his career, playing and managing, in Scotland and was also a businessman, journalist and accomplished golfer.

Appearances:		Apps	Gls
	FL	2	0
	CC	1	1
	Total	3	1

KABBA Steven

Striker 2002–06 5' 10" 11st 12
b. Lambeth 7 March 1981

Crystal Palace from YTS Jun 1999/ Luton Town (L) Mar 2002/ Grimsby Town (L) Aug 2002
United: (£250k) 15 Nov 2002 to 25 Jan 2007
Debut: 23 Nov 2002 Bradford City 0 United 5
Last games: 18 Apr 2006 United 1 Leeds United 1
21 Oct 2006 United 2 Birmingham City 4 (LC)
25 Nov 2006 West Ham United 1 United 0 (sub)
15 Jan 2007 United 1 Chengdu Blades (China) 1 (Fr)
Watford (£500k rising to £750k) 25 Jan 2007/ Blackpool (L) Jul 2008

Steven Kabba made his FL debut with Crystal Palace on 4 December 1999 at Crewe but was unable to go on and claim a regular place in the side. After two loan spells and having impressed against United for Grimsby Town, he moved to the Lane and made his debut alongside Dean Windass, both players scoring. Fast, strong, tricky and unpredictable but with an eye for goal and good in a one-on-one situation, Steven, after his arrival, was a regular member of the squad in the exciting 2002–03 season either in the starting line-up or coming on from the bench. The following eighteen months were a disaster for Steven, tendonitis in his knee kept him out until Christmas and 28 minutes into his first game back he broke his ankle and in April he ruptured his Achilles tendon in a reserve comeback fixture. He finally returned in February 2005 and was able to play an integral part in the promotion campaign of 2005–06.

Described by Neil Warnock as 'easily frustrated' and unable to make the starting line-up in the Premiership, he moved to Watford in the January window but has not been a regular in the starting line up. By the summer of 2008 he had made a total of 74(55) League appearances.

Appearances:

	Apps	Gls
FL	46 (32)	18
PO	1 (2)	1
FAC	6	4
LC	1	0
Total	54 (34)	23

KAMARA Christopher (Chris)

MF 1992–93, 1993–94 6' 1" 12st 3
b. Middlesbrough 25 December 1957

Portsmouth app to pro Dec 1975 or Jan 1976/ Swindon Town (£20k) Aug 1977/ Portsmouth (£50k) Aug 1981/ Brentford Oct 1981/ Swindon Town (£14.5k) Aug 1985/ Stoke City (£27.5) Jul 1988/ Leeds United (£150k) Jan 1991
United: guest app 11 May 1990 Brentford 4 United XI 2 (BM)
Luton Town (£150k) Nov 1991
United: (L) 11 Nov 1992 to 10 Feb 1993
Debuts: 21 Nov 1992 Norwich City 2 United 1 (sub)
26 Dec 1992 Manchester City 2 United 0
Last game: 6 Feb 1993 Manchester United 2 United 1
Middlesbrough (L) Feb 1993
United: (free) 26 Jun/23 Jul 1993 to 25 Jul 1994
Debuts: 27 Jul 1993 Bradford City 0 United 3 (Fr)
24 Aug 1993 United 2 Wimbledon 1
Last games: 13 Mar 1994 United 2 Leeds United 2
1 May 1994 Australian Olympic XI 1 United 1 (Fr)
Bradford City (free) Jul 1994 to May 1996, mgr Nov 1995 to Jan 1998/ Stoke City mgr Jan to Apr 1998

Chris Kamara came to Portsmouth's attention as a naval seaman and made his FL debut with them at the age of seventeen on 6 September 1975 at home to Luton Town. A combative midfielder who used the ball well, Chris, while playing for Swindon Town against Shrewsbury in February 1988 had been the first British player to be fined (£1200) in a court of law for an assault on another player (Jim Melrose)

He first played for United as a guest player from Leeds United with Vinnie Jones in Bob Booker's benefit match at Griffin Park in 1990 but his two spells at Bramall Lane came towards the end of his career. He came on a loan in 1992 which was extended to three months and, although there were suggestions that the move would become permanent, Bassett was reluctant to pay a fee, reported to be £125k, for a 35 year old player. He signed on a free transfer during the close season and played frequently in what would turn out to be the Blades last season in the top flight for some time.

He moved to Bradford City where his playing career ended, Chris having played over 750 first team games. He then had two spells in management, beginning as player manager at Bradford City and then moving to another former club, Stoke City. More recently he has been a TV presenter and can also be heard on the radio and as an after dinner speaker.

Appearances:

	Apps	Gls
FL	21 (3)	0
FAC	1	0
Total	22 (3)	0

KATCHOURO Petr (Peter)

Striker 1996–2000 6' 0" 11st 10 to 12st 6
b. Minsk (Belarus) 2 August 1972

Dinamo Minsk
United: Trial Mar 1996, (£650k) 12 Jul 1996 to 10/14 Mar 2000
Debuts: 23 Jul 1996 Sabah FC (Malaysia) 0 United 0 (Fr)
17 Aug 1996 Reading 1 United 0 (sub)
12 Sep 1996 Stockport County 2 United 1 (LC)
12 Oct 1996 United 0 Tranmere Rovers 0
Last game: 29 Jan 2000 Ipswich Town 1 United 1
Chengdu Wuniu (China) (free) Mar 2000/ Dinamo Minsk 2001/ Sokol Saratov (Russia) Jul 2002

Petr Katchouro (Piotr Kachuro) was signed by Howard Kendall after a trial with the club, making his debut and scoring against Derby County reserves on the 6 March. He took time to make his first League start and, although he played the full 90 minutes in only a third of the 43 League and play-off games in which he was involved, he was voted 'Player of the Year' in 1997, scoring a fine goal at Ipswich in the play-off game. The following season was not as successful. He was in and out of the side, failed to score a single goal and missed in the FA Cup penalty shoot-out against Coventry City although he did score for Belarus against Scotland in a World Cup qualifier. He began 1998–99 sidelined by a cartilage injury but made an instant impact on his return, scoring six goals in eight games but a damaged kidney more or less ended his season. Work permit problems almost delayed his start to the 1999–00 campaign and again he was frequently used as a sub. Once Neil Warnock became manager he played a few games, mainly as a sub, and then moved to play in China.

Petr was quick and, at his best, a dangerous striker but too often, he appeared to lack confidence and effectiveness. He played ten times for his country whilst with United and left holding the club record for most sub appearances in the League, FA Cup and in total. In due course he returned to his former club Dinamo Minsk and later played in Russia.

Appearances:		Apps	Gls
	FL	50 (45)	19
	PO	3	1
	FAC	2 (9)	0
	LC	8 (4)	3
	Total	63 (58)	23

KAY Alexander (Alex)

LB/RB 1901–02

St Bernards May 1899/ Partick Thistle Jun 1900
United: 16 May 1901 to Dec 1902/cs 1903
Debuts: 21 Dec 1901 United 1 Glasgow Rangers 0 (Fr)
8 Mar 1902 Notts County 4 United 0
Last game: 7 Apr 1902 United 2 Bolton Wanderers 0
West Ham United cs 1903 ?

Alex Kay made his Scottish League debut with St Bernards and later played with Partick Thistle. He was a full back but made his United, and FL, debut as a centre forward, although his other Blades' appearances were at full back. He proved to be too slow for English League football and after some disciplinary problems with United, he was suspended by the club early in December 1902 and transfer listed.

Appearances:		Apps	Gls
	FL	6	0
	Total	6	0

KAY(E) Harry

OL/IL 1915–16
b. Elsecar (Barnsley)?

United: WW1 guest
Debut: 25 Dec 1915 Grimsby Town 2 United 1 (WW1)
Last game: 24 Apr 1916 Wednesday 0 United 1 (WW1)
WW1 guest: Rotherham C, Barnsley 1916–17, 1917–18, Bradford(PA) Dec 1918 v United

Described as 'an Elsecar lad' and 'working in Sheffield', Harry Kaye played in all five forward positions in his eleven appearances for United in the 1915–16 season, scoring in his first four games. The Football League record this player as 'H Kaye' and both spellings appear in United's programmes. 'Harry Kaye' is generally used by the Sheffield Independent but the Telegraph refers to 'Kay' and the Green 'Un used 'Harry' and 'Frank'. He later made 49 appearances for Barnsley.

There is scope for confusion as a Harry Kay played for Elsecar 1906–07/ Barnsley 1907–11/ Rotherham T 1911–13/ Bristol R 1914/ Rotherham C cs1914 (and for Wombwell 1921?–23 and Mexborough cs1923) and one might assume he is the United guest player but the newspapers of 1915–16 never mention this football background. Note also that Harold Kaye (b. Chapeltown 1900) who came out of the army in 1920 and played for Barnsley, Southend, Barrow, Crewe and Mansfield would appear too young to have played for the Blades in 1915 but that assumes the year of birth is correct. One of them however, played for a United XI against the Wednesday in an unofficial fixture at Tankersley, 27 Dec 1918.

Appearances:		Apps	Gls
	WW1	11	7
	Total	11	7

KAZIM-RICHARDS Colin

Striker/MF 2006–07 6' 1" 10st 10
b. Leyton 26 August 1986

Wimbledon to c2001/ Bury from trainee Sep 2004/ Brighton & Hove Albion (£250k) Jul 2005
United: (£150k) 31 Aug 2006 to 13/15 Jun 2007:
Debuts: 9 Sep 2006 United 0 Blackburn Rovers 0 (sub)
19 Sep 2006 United 1 Bury 0 (LC)
23 Sep 2006 Arsenal 3 United 0
Last games: 5 May 2007 Aston Villa 3 United 0
13 May 2007 United 1 Wigan Athletic 2 (sub)
Fenerbahce (Turkey) (£1.275m, 25% to Brighton) Jun 2007

Colin Kazim-Richards had been with Wimbledon as a boy but joined Bury when he left school. He made his FL debut as a sub, with Bury on 2 October 2004 at home to Maidstone. After 14 more sub appearances he finally made his full debut on 8 February at home to Shrewsbury. In the summer of 2005 he signed for Brighton, with the money won by a Brighton supporter in the Coca Cola 'Win a Player' competition, and despite Brighton struggling in the Championship Colin finished as leading scorer.

He fell out of favour in the following season following disagreements with the manager and signed for United on the last day of the August window. Within a few weeks of playing for Brighton reserves he found himself playing at the Emirates stadium. He was unfazed by his move to the Premiership and he played mainly as a wide player. Tricky and strong with good ball control and awareness, he played with vision and often did the unexpected, as shown by his splendid goal against Bolton. Possessing an effective long throw, he did have a tendency to over-elaborate and, accused of having 'an attitude problem', he was used mainly from the bench.

In March he played for Turkey U21 (his mother was Turkish) and in early June he gained a full cap, coming on as a substitute. This prompted interest amongst Turkish clubs and a few days later he moved on giving United a profit of around £1m. He had made 50(50) League appearances in total and had scored 10 goals.

Known in Turkey as Kazim-Kazim, he played in the Champions League for Fenerbahce and in the 2008 European Championship competition.

Appearances:		Apps	Gls
	FL	15 (12)	1
	FAC	1	0
	LC	1	0
	Total	17 (12)	1

KEATING Patrick (Pat) Joseph

OL 1950–51 5' 8" 11st 0
b. Cork 17 September 1930
d. 1981

Cork Athletic
United: (£8000 joint purchase) 20 Feb/ 8 Mar 1950 to 30 Jun 1952
Debuts: 4 May 1950 Skegness Town 3 United XI 2 (Fr)
25 Nov 1950 Cardiff City 2 United 0
Last game: 23 Mar 1951 Brentford 3 United 1
Wisbech Town 31 Jul 1952/ Bradford PA Sep 1953/ Chesterfield Oct 1953 to May 1957

Pat Keating and Pat O'Sullivan were both signed—perhaps on the advice of a director—after playing for The League of Ireland but the pair failed to impress with United. Keating's four appearances, including one friendly, were all away from Bramall Lane and he was on the losing side each time. He was injured on his final appearance but said he would be 'all right as long as I can't see' (the injury). At that moment, he caught sight of the blood soaked sponge held by Ernest Jackson, the trainer, and collapsed.

Pat had speed and skill and could centre well but wasn't good enough and a £2000 transfer fee found no takers. Later and more mature, he went on to make 95 FL appearances for Chesterfield which brought his career total to 100.

Appearances:		Apps	Gls
	FL	3	0
	Total	3	0

KEELEY Andrew (Andy) James

MF/RB 1977–81 5' 10" 11st 4
b. Basildon 16 September 1956

Tottenham Hotspur app Sep 1972, pro Jan 1974
United: (free) 30 Dec 1977 to 31 Jul 1981
Debut: 14 Jan 1978 United 1 Bolton Wanderers 5
Last game: 3 Jan 1981 Newport County 4 United 0
Scunthorpe United Jul 1981 to cs 1983

An England youth international but always overshadowed by the success of his elder brother Glenn, Andy Keeley made his FL debut for Spurs at home to Birmingham City on 20 October 1976 but he managed only six FL appearances for the London club before moving to Bramall Lane.

Signed by caretaker manager, Cec Coldwell, Andy's first two appearances were 1–5 defeats which must be some sort of record. A hard working player, he lacked creativity and speed but he played regularly, mainly as a midfielder in both attacking and defensive roles, until November 1978 but thereafter, for two and a half seasons, he played only twice before his registration was cancelled.

He played 75(2) FL games for Scunthorpe and scored one FL goal.

Appearances:		Apps	Gls
	FL	28	0
	LC	1	0
	CC	2	1
	ASC	3	0
	Total	34	1

KEETON Frederick (Fred)

IR 1941–42 5' 8" 10st 10
b. c1921

Mosborough Trinity
United: 29 Sep 1941(amat), 21/22 Dec 1945(pro) to 14 Jun 1947
Debut: 6 Dec 1941 United 9 Lincoln City 0 (WW2)
Last games: 3 Jan 1942 United 2 Nottingham Forest 1 (WW2)
21 Aug 1943 United 3 Wednesday 2 (CM)

Fred Keeton played in six successive games around Christmas time 1941soon after he had been called up to serve in the Royal Artillery and he also played in a charity match which opened the 1943–44 season and scored in this final appearance for the first team. He served in Europe as the War drew to a close, returning to play for the reserve team but a cartilage operation in the spring of 1947 ended his career as a professional player. Fred had an elder brother who was a professional with Torquay United.

Appearances:		Apps	Gls
	WW2	6	3
	Total	6	3

KELLY Alan Thomas

G 1992–99 6' 2" 12st 8 to 14st 3
b. Preston 11 August 1968

Preston North End from app Sep 1985
United: (£150k rising to £200k + 20% sell-on clause)
Jul/1 Aug 1992 to 30 Jul 1999
Debuts: 25 Jul 1992 Offerdals (Sweden) 0 United 4 (sub Fr)
29 Jul 1992 Ljusne AIK (Sweden) 0 United 10 (Fr)
2 Sep 1992 Tottenham Hotspur 2 United 0 (sub)
19 Sep 1992 United 1 Arsenal 1
Last games: 9 May 1999 United 1 Ipswich Town 4
23 Jul 1999 United 0 Chelsea 2 (Fr)
Blackburn Rovers (£700k. £595k to United. £80k to PNE) Jul 1999 to cs2004/ Stockport County(L) Apr 2001/ Birmingham City (L) Aug 2001/ Tottenham H (L) 2001–02

Alan Kelly had played as a full back for Preston Boys and Preston North End youth teams, taking over in goal only when another player was injured. He trained as an electrician and his goalkeeping progress was hindered by a broken leg and head injuries suffered in a car accident and then another break in a testimonial game. He joined Preston North End, the club where his father, also Alan, had kept goal in 447 FL games, and made his FL debut on 8 March 1986 at home to Crewe Alexandra.

It was United manager Dave Bassett who brought Alan to the Lane and for seven seasons he and Simon Tracey vied for the first team goalkeeping spot but despite this rivalry they remained good friends. His United League debut came as a result of Simon Tracey being sent off, Alan coming on as substitute for Glyn Hodges and going in goal. Alan served United well, being a sound reliable goalkeeper and a model professional who was universally popular with the supporters. He will always be remembered for the three saves he made in the penalty shoot-out at Bramall Lane against Coventry City that took the Blades to the 1998 FA Cup semi-final.

Alan, who had gained caps at youth, U21 and U23 level for the Republic of Ireland, gained his first full cap in 1993 and went on to win 34 in total, 22 of them whilst with United (his father had gained 47 caps for the Republic). He left Bramall Lane at the start of the 1999–00 season, not because he asked for a transfer but because of United's financial problems and Simon Tracey was far more than a capable deputy. He retired in 2004 when he caught his finger in the turf and badly damaged his hand. He had made 402(4) League appearances. Alan, whose brother Gary subsequently made an appearance for United, continued to live in nearby north Derbyshire.

Appearances:

	Apps	Gls
FL	213 (3)	0
PO	2	0
FAC	22	0
LC	15	0
Total	252 (3)	0

KELLY David Thomas

Striker 2000–01 5' 11" 11st 10 to 12st 1
b. Birmingham 25 November 1965

Alvechurch/ Walsall Dec 1983/ West Ham United (£600k) Aug 1988/ Leicester City (£300k) Mar 1990/ Newcastle United (£250k) Dec 1991/ Wolverhampton Wanderers (£750k) Jun 1993/ Sunderland (£1m) Sep 1995/ Tranmere Rovers (£350k) Aug 1997
United: 21 Jul 2000 to 30 Jul 2001
Debuts: 24 Jul 2000 Hayle 0 United 9 (Fr)
12 Aug 2000 United 2 Portsmouth 0
Last games: 10 Mar 2001 United 1 Nottingham Forest 3
21 Apr 2001 Grimsby Town 0 United 1 (sub)
7 May 2001 United 11 All Stars XI 1 (BM)
Motherwell Jul 2001/ Stoke City (trial)/ Mansfield Town Jan 2002/ Derry C Jul 2002/ Tranmere R asst mgr Oct 2002
United: asst mgr 9 Jul 2003 to 23 Sep 2004
Preston North End Sep 2004 asst mgr to cs 2006 / – / Derby asst mgr Jul 2007

David Kelly made his FL debut with Walsall, as a sub, at Millwall on 14 April 1984, his full debut, and his first goal, coming at Burnley on 23 April. By the time he joined United he had played for seven League clubs and gained Republic of Ireland honours at U21, U23 and B level and 26 full caps.

He was signed by Neil Warnock on a one year deal after a trial and played a full part in the season, although, from February, he made most of his appearances from the bench. Despite his age—he was thirty four—David was very quick in and around the goal, a good finisher and he worked hard and used his experience and eye for goal to finish leading scorer in League games, albeit with only six goals. An unusual aspect of his play was the number of times he fell in the penalty area, tripped it often seemed, by himself.

After his one season, he moved on but returned to Bramall Lane as assistant manager in July 2003 following Kevin Blackwell's move to Leeds United. David remained with United for fourteen months before taking up a similar role at Preston North End and then Derby County. Including his time with Motherwell he scored 192 goals in 505(95) League games.

Appearances:

	Apps	Gls
FL	21 (14)	6
FAC	1	0
LC	4	2
Total	26 (14)	8

KELLY Gary Alexander

G 2003 5' 11" 13st 6
b. Preston 3 August 1966

Newcastle United from app Jun 1984/ Blackpool (L) Oct 1988/ Bury (£60k) Oct 1989/ Oldham Athletic (£10k) Aug 1996/ Northwich Victoria (nc)
United: 27 Mar to May 2003
Only game: 4 May 2003 Watford 2 United 0
Leigh RMI Sep 2003 to Sep 2004

Gary Kelly, elder brother of Alan, joined United in March 2003, from Northwich Victoria, on a non-contract basis as cover for Paddy Kenny and played in the final FL game of 2002–03. Kenny had been an ever-present until then but, with the important play-off games imminent, it was decided to rest him for the final League game, the result having no bearing on which club United would meet.

After leaving Newcastle United, where he made his FL debut at home to Wimbledon on 20 September 1986, Gary spent much of his time in the lower Divisions. He made well over 200 FL appearances for both Bury and Oldham Athletic, making 519(1) FL appearances in total, and gained Republic of Ireland caps at U21, U23 and B level.

Appearances:

	Apps	Gls
FL	1	0
Total	1	0

KEMP Samuel (Sammy) Patrick

OR 1957–58 5' 11" 11st 8 to 12st 7
b. Stockton 29 August 1932
d. Stockton 2 August 1987

Whitby Town/ Sunderland Mar 1952
United: (part exchange) 5/7 Feb 1957 to 16 May 1958
Debut: 9 Feb 1957 West Ham United 3 United 2
Last game: 12 Oct 1957 Doncaster Rovers 2 United 2
Mansfield Town (£1,500) May 1958/ Gateshead Oct 1958

Sammy Kemp made his FL debut with Sunderland, at home to Tottenham Hotspur, on 18 March 1953. He played only 17 FL games for Sunderland, acting as a reserve for international Billy Bingham.

Sammy came to the Lane as a minor part of an exchange deal when Joe Mercer, under pressure from the board of directors to sell a 'star player' accepted Sunderland's offer of Kemp and £17k in exchange for Colin Grainger. He was almost totally ineffectual and made little impact, neither at the Lane, nor at his two other clubs, making just 43 FL appearances in total.

Appearances:		Apps	Gls
	FL	16	1
	CC	1	0
	Total	17	1

KENDALL John (Jack) William

G 1930–34 5' 11½" 12st 0 to 13st 6
b. Broughton (Scunthorpe) 9 October 1905
d. Scunthorpe 9 October or 14 November 1961

Broughton Rangers/ Lincoln City Mar 1922/ Everton (£1,250) Apr 1924/ Preston North End May 1927/ Lincoln City Jul 1928
United: (£1,125) 12/15 Mar 1930 to 15 Jul 1934
Debut: 15 Mar 1930 Leeds United 2 United 2
Last game: 5 May 1934 Arsenal 2 United 0
Peterborough United Jul 1934 to cs 1938

Jack Kendall became a goalkeeper by accident when his junior team's regular 'keeper failed to turn up. Before becoming a professional footballer, he had worked as a labourer on Lord Yarborough's estate near his home town but he joined Lincoln after a trial in the reserves, making his FL debut on 2 September 1922 at home to Halifax Town. He was soon considered to be one of the best goalkeepers in the Third Division but his spells with Everton and Preston North End were affected by injury and he returned to Lincoln before signing for United.

He was first choice at the Lane for about a season but was inconsistent though capable of making brilliant saves and those with long memories would recall that an error by Kendall had brought United the winning goal in a Cup-tie against Everton in 1925. He was particularly good with high balls but a loss of confidence and mounting errors in the 1931–32 season eventually led to him losing his place to the up-and-coming Jack Smith. He had made 220 FL appearances before moving into non-League football.

Appearances:		Apps	Gls
	FL	80	0
	FAC	6	0
	CC	5	0
	Total	91	0

KENNEDY Andrew (Andy) John

Striker 1987 6' 1" 11st 10 to 12st 8
b. Stirling 8 October 1964

Sauchie Athletic/ Rangers Jul 1982 to Feb 1985/ Everton (trial)/ Seiko (Hong Kong) (L)/ Birmingham City (£50k) Mar 1985
United: (L) 19/20 Mar 1987 to 18 May 1987
Debut: 21 Mar 1987 Reading 2 United 0
Last game: 4 May 1987 Ipswich Town 0
Blackburn Rovers (£50k) Jun 1988/ Watford (part exchange, valued at £190k) Jul 1990/ Bolton Wanderers (L) Oct 1991/ Brighton & Hove Albion (£40k) Sep 1992/ Gillingham Sep 1994/ Hong Kong football cNov 1994/ Portadown (N Ireland) Jan 1995 to May 1995/ Witton Albion Nov 1995/ Hastings Town/ Hendon Mar 1996

A Scottish youth international, Andy Kennedy made his Scottish League debut with Rangers, coming on as a substitute at home to Motherwell on 6 November 1982; his full debut being at home to St Mirren on 18 December. His FL debut came with Birmingham City, on 8 April 1985, at home to the Blades, when he scored City's fourth goal.

Very fast for a big man, his brief loan spell with United, under Billy McEwan as manager, came at the end of the 1986–87 season and he scored a fine goal against Blackburn Rovers with a run of over 60 yards. It was with Blackburn that he was most successful but his technique and finishing were never quite good enough.

After his League career ended, with 56 goals in 160(54) games, he returned to the Brighton area in October 1995 and assisted former Brighton team mate Steve Foster in his insurance business.

Appearances:		Apps	Gls
	FL	8 (1)	1
	Total	8 (1)	1

KENNY Patrick (Paddy) Joseph

G 2002– 6' 1" 13st 8 to 14st 6
b. Halifax 17 May 1978

Ovenden/ Halifax T (trial)/ Bradford PA cs1997/ Birmingham C (trial)/ Bury (£10k) Aug 1998/ Whitby T (L) Mar 1999
United: (L) 16 Jul 2002, (£42k, £10k to Bradford) 15/16 Oct 2002mb
Debuts: 16 Jul 2002 Baslow 1 United XI 14 (Fr)
10 Aug 2002 Coventry City 2 United 1

Paddy Kenny made his FL debut with Bury, then managed by Neil Warnock, on 7 August 1999 at home to Gillingham and he made 133 FL appearances for the Lancashire club. It was Neil who brought him to Bramall Lane, United paying a reported fee of about £42k of which £10k went to Bradford.

Quickly losing a stone in weight, he was an instant success and became a favourite with the fans. An excellent shot stopper and very good in a one-on-one situation, he missed only two games in 2002–03, his first season at the Lane, those coming when he was rested for an FA Cup game and the final FL game prior to the play-offs. In total he played 59 competitive games during the season. An ankle injury kept him out for nearly four months in the autumn of 2003 but he was ever-present in the 2005–06 promotion season, during which he saved three penalties.

He nearly became the first Blades' goalkeeper to score in a competitive match when he took a penalty in a League Cup shoot-out against Watford but, sadly, he hit the post. Although remaining first choice in the Premiership season he was prone to the occasional error but in 2007–08, after a somewhat shaky start, he returned after injury to play impressively.

A Republic of Ireland international he won seven full caps before his international career was put on hold late in 2006 due to a mixture of injury and well publicised domestic problems. In the summer of 2007, Paddy ran from Skegness to Dinnington in three days to raise money for charity.

Appearances:		Apps	Gls
	FL	232	0
	PO	3	0
	FAC	17	0
	LC	14	0
	Total	266	0

KENT William Edward

(registered by the FL as E W Kent)

RB 1899–1900
b. Middlesbrough JFM 1875

Middlesbrough Grange/ North Eastern Railway/ Middlesbrough Grange/ Jarrow May 1897
United: 15 Aug 1899 to cs 1900
Debuts: 23 Oct 1899 United 7 Kaffirs 2 (Fr)
17 Apr 1900 Wolverhampton Wanderers 1 United 2
Last games: 23 Apr 1900 Burnley 1 United 0
30 Apr 1900 Workington & District XI 1 United 4
Glossop North End cs 1900

William Kent made just two FL appearances for United but he did play in a series of friendly games in April 1900. His last FL appearance for Glossop was in December 1900.

Appearances:		Apps	Gls
	FL	2	0
	Total	2	0

KENWORTHY Anthony (Tony) David

MF/LB 1976–86 5' 10" 10st 7 to 11st 2
b. Leeds 30 October 1958

United: app 7 Apr 1975, 1 Jun 1976 to 30 Jun 1986
Debuts: 2 Mar 1976 United 1 Rotherham United 1 (CC)
3 Apr 1976 Norwich City 1 United 3
Last games: 11 Jan 1986 Huddersfield Town 3 United 1
25 Jan 1986 United 0 Derby County 1 (FAC)
6 May 1986 United XI 3 Sheffield Wed 4 (BM)
Mansfield Town (L) March, (free) Jul 1986 to May 1989 / – / Huddersfield Town (trial) Aug 1990 / – / Chesterfield (trial) Mar 1991 / – / Ashfield United Feb 1993/ Oakham United cs1994/

Despite coming from Leeds and from a family of Elland Road regulars, Tony Kenworthy, who had captained Yorkshire Boys, had a trial at Bramall Lane and joined Sheffield United. He played for the reserves at sixteen and was only seventeen when he made his FL debut, becoming an England youth international later that year. Tony's few games at the end of the 1975–76 season were the only ones he played in the top flight as he was with the club as it sank from the First to the Fourth Division and rose again to the Second.

Throughout his time with United, he always played with one hundred per cent effort and determination, playing in a no-nonsense style relished by few opponents and he came through several career-threatening injuries. Primarily a left-footed midfielder, he tackled incisively with speed and directness and, although not tall, he was superb in the air and proved to be an excellent central defender, partnering John MacPhail, or full back when required. He scored some fine goals from free kicks and headers and he had an excellent penalty record, scoring twenty of twenty-two attempts in all competitions, including two at a vital time at Tranmere in the Fourth Division championship season. His final game with United was his own testimonial game when some of his colleagues could reflect on what his career might have been with a little more dedication to the game.

Following his move to Mansfield Town, where he made 98(2) FL appearances, he helped the Stags gain promotion in 1986 and scored the winning goal in the penalty shoot-out in the 1987 Freight Rover Trophy final.

Imprisoned after a traffic accident in 1990, he was later involved in Youth training in Scotland and, in 1998, was manager and coach with Grantham.

Appearances:		Apps	Gls
	FL	281 (5)	34
	FAC	17	1
	LC	21	1
	ASC	16 (2)	0
	AMC	7	1
	CC	8	2
	Total	350 (7)	39

'KERR' Pseudonym for Kenneth McKay (qv)

United: (trial) 4 Jan 1897 United 2 Corinthians 2 (Fr)

KETTLEBOROUGH Keith Frank

IR 1960–66 5' 8½" 10st 3
b. Rotherham 29 June 1935

Grimsby Town (trial)/ Rotherham YMCA/ Rotherham United Dec 1955
United: (£15k) 2/5 Dec 1960 to 6 Jan 1966
Debut: 3 Dec 1960 United 2 Bristol Roves 3
Last game: 1 Jan 1966 United 2 Northampton Town 2
Newcastle United (£22.5k) Jan 1966/ Doncaster Rovers (£10–12k) player-mgr Dec 1966, player Jun 1967/ Chesterfield (£6000) Nov 1967/ Matlock Town Jun 1969, then mgr Nov 1971 to Oct 1972

Small as a boy, Keith Kettleborough improved as a footballer when he served in the RAF and this led to a trial with Grimsby Town which Keith brought to a halt. He joined Rotherham United and made his FL debut with Rotherham United on 14 April 1956 at Plymouth Argyle.

After 118 games for the Millers, he was brought to Bramall Lane by John Harris and he was first choice at inside right for five seasons although he had several spells out with injury. Keith was a constructive inside forward passing the ball simply but effectively and he consistently did an excellent job in the difficult position of linking defence and attack. He was far from a robust player but was difficult to knock off the ball and dispossess and he could tackle hard.

In the autumn of 1963, with United top of the League Keith was chosen as reserve for a Football League side and called up for training with the England squad. Sadly an injury and cartilage operation, wrecked his progress.

After his move to Newcastle he was a member of Alf Ramsey's 'shadow' squad for the 1966 World Cup finals. He was player-manager at his next club, Doncaster, but was sacked in the 1967 close season, although retained as a player until his move to Chesterfield where he had a successful end to his FL career which totalled 403 games.

Injury ended his playing days at Matlock Town but he was manager there for a time before resigning. After a spell as a milkman in Rotherham he became a sports coach in a Sheffield school. Keith was also a very good professional club cricketer and played for both United and Rotherham in the Yorkshire League.

Appearances:		Apps	Gls
	FL	154	17
	FAC	15	4
	LC	10	1
	CC	4	2
	Total	183	24

KILGALLON Matthew (Matt) Shaun

CD 2007– 6' 1" 12st 5
b. York 8 January 1984

Leeds United from trainee Jan 2001/ West Ham United (L) Aug 2003
United: £1.75m) 8 Jan 2007
Debut: 31 Mar 2007 Bolton Wanderers 1 United 0

An England youth international, Matthew Kilgallon had joined Leeds United aged 11 and made his League debut as a sub, on 8 February 2003 at home to West Ham; his full debut coming whilst on loan with the Hammers on 30 August 2003 at Ipswich. It wasn't until 2004–05 that Matt became a frequent member of the Leeds first team and gained the first of his five U21 caps.

In the summer of 2007 he was a target for various clubs, including United, as Neil Warnock looked to strengthen the squad for the Premiership campaign. Matt finally signed in the January transfer window but an ankle injury sustained in November meant his debut was delayed and was made at left wing back. He reverted to the centre of defence for the final few games.

Matt became first choice under Bryan Robson and, as the season progressed, his performances improved significantly. He was impressive in the air, read the game well, was quick and accurate in the tackle and was a danger in the opposition's area at set pieces.

Appearances:		Apps	Gls
	FL	45 (1)	2
	FAC	3	0
	LC	3	0
	Total	51 (1)	2

KILLEEN Lewis

Striker 2002 5' 10" 10st 4
b. Peterborough 23 September 1982

United: from YTS 1 Aug 2001 to 3 Jun 2003
Only game: 13 Apr 2002 United 0 Walsall 1 (sub)
Halifax Town (L) 25 Mar 2003
Halifax Town (free) Jun 2003 to present

Lewis Killeen was a regular in the United reserve side but managed just one substitute appearance for the first team. When he moved to Conference team Halifax Town he became a regular member of the side.

Appearances:		Apps	Gls
	FL	0 (1)	0
	Total	0 (1)	0

KILLOURHY Michael (Mick)

IR/IL 1932–36 5'10" 10st 6 to 11st 6
b. New Springs (Wigan) 19 February 1911
d. Southport November 2002

Coldstream Guards/ Wigan Borough amat Jan 1930, pro Mar 1930
United: (£450) 3/16/20 Nov 1931 to 2 May 1936
Debut: 9 Apr 1932 Chelsea 1 United 1
Last games: 12 Oct 1935 Blackpool 3 United 0
16 Jan 1936 United 2 Burnley 1 (FAC)
Doncaster Rovers (£750) May 1936 to cs 1946
WW2 guest: Bradford City 1939–40, Rotherham United 1939–40, Watford 1941–42, Millwall 1941–42, York City 1943–44/
Denaby United cs 1946/ Goole Town 1948

Michael Killourhy (alternative spellings include Kilhourhy, Kilhoury) made his FL debut with Wigan Borough on 8 March 1930, scoring in the 1–3 defeat at home to Hartlepools United. He also played in Borough's final ever game on 24 October 1931, a 0–5 League defeat at Wrexham. On 26 October, Wigan Borough resigned form the Football League due to financial problems and soon disbanded and their playing record of 12 games was expunged. Michael's 7 games and 3 goals that season are not included in his career figures.

He then moved to Bramall Lane but, facing competition from Bobby Barclay and Jack Pickering, he was never able to win a regular first team place. A clever player with a good shot, he lacked both speed and industry.

A record signing by Doncaster Rovers, he scored 28 goals in 63 FL games before the war intervened. Mick was a Sergeant in the Guards during the Second War, subsequently became a teacher in Doncaster and was a County standard golfer.

Appearances:		Apps	Gls
	FL	27	6
	FAC	2	0
	CC	2	0
	Total	31	6

KING Jeffrey (Jeff)

OL/IL 1982–83 5' 8" 11st 0
b. Fauldhouse (Edinburgh) 9 November 1953

Fauldhouse United/ Albion Rovers Dec 1972/ Derby County (£7000) Apr 1974/ Notts County (L) Jan 1976/ Portsmouth (L) Mar 1976/ Walsall Nov 1977/ Sheffield Wednesday (£27.5k) Aug 1979 to Jan 1982/ Hibernian (L) Sep 1981

United: (free) 12 Jan 1982 to 10 Nov 1982
Debut: 16 Jan 1982 Rochdale 0 United 1
Last game: 2 Nov 1982 Newport County 3 United 1
Re-engaged 30 Dec 1982 to 28 May 1983
Debut: 1 Jan 1983 United 3 Orient 0
Last games: 29 Mar 1983 Bristol Rovers 2 United 1
18 Apr 1983 United XI 1 Ipswich Town 1 (BM)

Chesterfield (trial) Oct 1983/ Stafford Rangers Nov 1983/ Altrincham Feb 1984/ Burton Albion Aug 1984/ Kettering Town 1984/ Jubilee Sports/ Wadsley Bridge

Jeff King began his professional career with Albion Rovers, making his Scottish League debut on 23 December1972 at home to Stenhousemuir. His first English League club was Derby County, but Jeff made his FL debut at home to York City, on 10 January 1976 while on loan at Notts County. In November 1977 he followed his former Derby manager, Dave MacKay, to Walsall and from there, he moved to Hills borough where he had a successful season, playing a key role in Wednesday's promotion from the old Division Three in 1980. His career at Hillsborough then stalled and he asked for a transfer several times.

After an unsuccessful trial with Hibs, his contract was cancelled and Ian Porterfield, United's manager, who had played with Jeff at Hillsborough, brought him across the city to United.

Essentially a tenacious, right footed player, Jeff worked well down the left flank and was more or less ever-present as United became Fourth Division champions, contributing, in particular, a last minute winner at Crewe. He started in the side the following season but personal problems made it a nightmare and his contract was cancelled only for him to be re-engaged. He scored on his come-back but conceded a horrendous own goal at Reading and soon, his life as a professional player was all but over, having played 159(8) FL games. Later, he started work as a painter and decorator.

Appearances:		Apps	Gls
	FL	35 (2)	5
	FAC	2	0
	LC	1	0
	AMC	3	0
	Total	41 (2)	5

KING John (Jack)

G 1939–42 5' 8½"
b. Dalton (Rotherham) c1922

Rotherham YMCA

United: (amat) 12 May 1939 to cs 1945
Debuts: 7 Oct 1939 Leicester City 2 United 2 (Fr)
1 Jun 1940 Barnsley 3 United 1 (WW2)
Last game: 28 Mar 1942 Newcastle United 1 United 6 (WW2)
WW2 guest: Barnsley Nov 1940 v United

Jack King played six games in total during the Second War, two in the wartime League and four friendlies, and he failed to keep a clean sheet and failed to impress. He was also playing, in 1940–41, for Fulwood, a United 'nursery team.

Appearances:		Apps	Gls
	WW2	2	0
	Total	2	0

KING Seth

CH/LB/RB 1922–29 5' 8½" 11st 7
b. Penistone 14 February 1897
d. Leigh 8 February 1958

Penistone Church FC/ Huddersfield Town (reserves) amat during 1919–20/ Penistone Church

United: (£10) 18 Nov 1920 to 23 May 1929
Debut: 16 Sep 1922 United 2 Newcastle United 0
Last game: 1 Apr 1929 United 1 Leeds United 1

Oldham Athletic (£400) May 1929 to Feb 1932/ Denaby United Aug 1932 to Jul 1934

Seth King joined United in November 1920 and he had to wait nearly two years before he made his first team debut. For the following two seasons he made intermittent appearances at full back but an injury to centre half Jimmy Waugh in December 1924 gave him an opportunity which he seized.

Raven haired, wiry, agile and robust, he had been regarded as a useful utility player but now he looked faster, his passing had improved, his tackling was keener than ever and he reserved his finest performance for the 1925 Cup Final. Seth was not alone in finding the change in the off-side law for the 1925–26 season difficult but he held his place until September 1927 when he lost it to the newly signed Vince Matthews.

In May 1929 he moved to Oldham Athletic but his contract was cancelled in February 1932 after an injury, having made 91 FL appearances. Intending to retire from the game, he took over the tenancy of the Castle Inn at Hillsborough though he did play for a while with Denaby United. At the time of his death he had a newsagents shop in Leigh.

Appearances:		Apps	Gls
	FL	107	0
	FAC	8	0
	CC	3	0
	ABD	1	0
	Total	119	0

KITCHEN Joseph (Joe) Ernest

CF/OR/IR/IL 1908–20, 1920–21 5' 8" 11st 4 to 12st
b. Brigg 20 June?/JAS 1890
d. Enfield 23 November 1974

Ancholme United 1904/ Brigg Britannia/ Brigg Town/ Gainsborough Trinity 1906

United: (£600 for Kitchen and GG Brown)
26/27 Mar 1908 to 12/15 Aug 1920
Debut: 28 Mar 1908 United 1 Manchester City 2
Last game: 1 May 1920 Blackburn Rovers 4 United 1
WW1 guest: Grimsby T (12/10/1918)

Rotherham County (£650) Aug 1920

United: (£650) 16/18 Dec 1920 to cs 1921
Debut: 18 Dec 1920 Oldham Athletic 0 United 0
Last game: 2 Apr 1921 United 1 Arsenal 1

Hull City (£250) Sep 1921/ Scunthorpe & Lindsey United Aug 1922/ Gainsborough Trinity Sep 1924/ Shirebrook Sep 1925/ Gainsborough T Nov 1925/ Barton Town 1926

Joe Kitchen made his FL debut with Gainsborough Trinity on 29 December 1906 in a 0–7 defeat at Chesterfield. He was still only sixteen and he was only seventeen when he made his United debut. One of his main attributes was a tremendous burst of speed, putting the ball past an opponent on one side and swerving by with long strides on the other. Although he played mainly at centre forward, many thought he was even more dangerous at outside right, but this was not a position he enjoyed. He was an individualist, 'hard as nails' and noted for 'solo dashes' and first time shooting although, for a centre forward, his heading was judged as no better than adequate.

Although near to international selection in 1909 his form dropped away but he was back to his best by 1914 when United reached the FA Cup semi-finals and a year later when United won the Cup. Joe scored United's third goal with a typical individual burst.

He was selected for a 'victory international' in 1919 but was injured. In 1920, after a disagreement over terms, he was transferred to Rotherham County but he was not happy there and he returned to the Lane, United agreeing to pay the same fee, although the directors were not unanimous over this decision.

Joe's best days were over and he moved on to Hull City, after scoring on his final appearance for the Blades. United had accepted a cheque of £200 from Southend U but returned it after receiving one for £250 from Hull City. His FL career ended with 128 goals in 327 games and he finished his playing days with Barton Town where, although a non-smoker and teetotaller, he became the landlord of the Wheatsheaf Hotel.

Appearances:		Apps	Gls
	FL	248	105
	FAC	21	6
	WW1	71	58
	ABD	2	0
	Total	342	169

KITE Phillip (Phil) David

G 1990–92 6' 1" 13st 0 to 14st 7
b. Bristol 26 October 1962

Bristol Rovers from app Oct 1980/ Tottenham Hotspur (L) Jan 1984/ Southampton (£50k) Aug 1984/ Middlesbrough (L) Mar 1986/ Gillingham (L), signed Feb 1987/ Bournemouth (£55k) Aug 1989

United: (£20k–£25k) 6/10 Aug 1990 to 1 Jul 1993
Debuts: 7 Aug 1990 Skegness 0 United XI 4 (Fr)
13 Aug 1990 Barnsley 0 United 2 (sub Fr)
17 Aug 1990 Sheffield Wednesday 3 United 0 (SCCT)
29 Aug 1990 Derby County 1 United 1
Last games: 26 Oct 1991 Manchester City 3 United 2
15 Feb 1992 Chelsea 1 United 0 (FAC)
21 Jul 1992 Forfar Athletic 0 United 2 (Fr)

Mansfield Town (L) Nov 1991/ Burnley (L)/ Cambridge United (L)/ Plymouth Argyle (L) Sep 1992/ Rotherham United (L) Oct 1992/ Crewe Alexandra (L) Nov 1992/ Stockport County (L) Mar 1993
Cardiff City (free) Jul 1993/ Bristol City Aug 1994/ Bristol Rovers physio cs 1996

Phil Kite, who gained England caps at schoolboy and youth level made his FL debut with Bristol Rovers on 10 January1981 at Derby County and went on to make more than 100 appearances for the club. He then moved to Southampton as understudy to Peter Shilton and his opportunities were very limited but he had a more fruitful spell with Gillingham, making 70 FL appearances.

Phil moved to Bramall Lane, signed by Dave Bassett, at the start of United's first season back in the top flight and soon got his chance when Simon Tracey was injured in the first game against Liverpool. Phil played in the next nine games, half his total with United, but his only other significant run of games was in Autumn 1991. When Alan Kelly arrived in July 1992 Phil was then third choice goalkeeper and he spent much of the season on loan until moving on to Cardiff City.

When he retired from playing, having made 236 (2) FL appearances, Phil became physiotherapist at his first club, Bristol Rovers.

Appearances:		Apps	Gls
	FL	11	0
	FAC	1	0
	LC	5	0
	FMC	1	0
	Total	18	0

KNOTT Herbert (Bert)

CF 1945
b. Goole 5 December 1914
d. 1986

Goole Town/ Arsenal (Margate) 1935–36/ Brentford/ Brierley Hill Alliance/ Walsall Aug 1937/ Brierley Hill Alliance Aug 1938/ Hull City Oct 1940 to Feb 1947
WW2 guest: Norwich City 1941–42, Lincoln City 1941–44, Halifax Town 1941–42, Leicester City 1943–44, Millwall 1942–43, Nottingham Forest 1942–43, Derby County 1943–44, Notts County 1943–44, Bradford PA 1945–46 Clapton Orient 1945–46

United: WW2 guest
Debut: 1 Sep 1945 United 3 Newcastle United 0 (FLN)
Last game: 6 Oct 1945 United 1 Chesterfield 1 (FLN)

Bert Knott made his FL debut with Walsall on 28 August 1937 at Torquay United but was released (9 app, 2gl) in the close season. He joined Hull City during the Second War and was an impressive goal scorer in wartime competitions for a remarkable number of clubs.

He played five times as a guest player for United while serving in the RASC. Quick and alert in the penalty area, he scored in his first four appearances and contributed in a small way to United becoming champions of the Football League North in 1945–46.

He gained a first team place with Hull after the War but, now thirty one, was unable to make the transition to League football and was released in February 1947, his FL career being 3 goals in 15 games.

Appearances:		Apps	Gls
	FLN	5	5
	Total	5	5

KNOWLES Darren Thomas

RB 1989 5' 6" 10st 7 to 11st 6
b. Sheffield 8 October 1970

United: from trainee 1 Jul 1987 to 4 Sep 1989
Debuts: 31 Jul 1989 Skegness Town 4 United XI 0 (sub Fr)
10 Aug 1989 United 1 Rotherham United 1 (YH)
Last game: 14 Aug 1989 Halifax Town 1 United 0 (sub YH)
Stockport County (£3000 + £3000 after 10 games) Sep 1989/ Scarborough Aug 1993/ Hartlepool United Mar 1997/ Northwich Victoria cs 2001/ Gainsborough Trinity Jun 2002/ Stocksbridge Parks Steel cs 2003/ Ilkeston Town Feb 2004 to cs 2006/ Park & Arbour LFS

Although Darren failed to make a FL appearance for the Blades he did go on to make over 350 FL appearances for his three subsequent clubs, including over 100 consecutive appearances with Hartlepool. His FL debut came with Stockport County on 13 January 1990 when he came on as a sub at home to Burnley, his full debut coming on 10 February at Hartlepool (63 FL app with Stockport).

From the summer of 2001 he moved into non-League football, playing for several seasons.

Appearances:		Apps	Gls
	YHC	1 (1)	0
	Total	1 (1)	0

KOZLUK Robert (Rob)

LWB/RWB 1999–2007 5' 8" 11st 7
b. Sutton in Ashfield, Mansfield 5 August 1977

Notts C (school), Derby County from trainee Jan 1996
United: (exchange) 12 Mar 1999 to 4/7 Jul 2007
Debut: 13 Mar 1999 Tranmere Rovers 2 United 3
Last game: 17 Apr 2007 Manchester United 2 United 0
Huddersfield Town (L) Sep–Dec 2000/ Preston North End (L) Jan 2005
Barnsley (free) Jul 2007

Rob Kozluk began his career as a boy with Notts County, though he also had trials with Manchester United and Coventry. He became an apprentice with Derby County and made his debut in a FL Cup match at Southend and his League debut on 25 October 1997 at Liverpool and he gained two England U21 caps in the 1998 Toulon tournament.

Steve Bruce brought him to Bramall Lane, along with Jonathan Hunt, with Vas Borbokis moving the other way and Rob was by far the most successful of the three at his new club. He was a regular member of the side, playing as a right wing back for his first full season but was prone to error and went out on loan in September 2000. He returned a better player and regained his place until a serious knee injury in October 2001 sidelined him until the start of the following season. He lost his place to Phil Jagielka but then regained it, playing at left wing back, and in March he scored his first senior goal after well over 100 first team games. 2003–04 saw Rob back as a regular in the side playing equally well on left or right. A pre-season foot injury in July 2004 meant another long lay-off and a loan spell with Preston to regain fitness but he was back in the 2005–06 promotion season as a regular in the squad.

Renowned for his practical jokes in the dressing room and possessing an effective long throw, Rob played with enthusiasm, good anticipation and was quick to recover. Dangerous coming forward, his final ball was not always the best and his long range shooting could be wayward. Rob was placed on the transfer list at the end of the Premiership season and soon joined Barnsley where he enjoyed the club's FA Cup run to the semi final and has now exceeded 250 career League appearances.

Appearances:		Apps	Gls
	FL	193 (20)	2
	PO	3	0
	FAC	11	0
	LC	8 (1)	0
	Total	215 (21)	2

KUHL Martin

MF 1987–88 5' 11" 11st 13
b. Frimley (Surrey) 10 January 1965

Chelsea 1979/ Birmingham City app Jun 1981, pro Jan 1983
United: (exch for Steve Wigley) 19 Mar 1987 to 16 Feb 1988
Debut: 21 Mar 1987 Reading 2 United 0
Last games: 2 Jan 1988 United 0 Oldham Athletic 5
9 Jan 1988 United 1 Maidstone United 0 (FAC)
Watford (valued at £125k for Agana, Hetherston + £40k) Feb 1988/ Portsmouth (£125k) Sep 1988/ Derby County (£650k) Sep 1992/ Notts County (L) Sep 1994/ Bristol City (£330k) Dec 1994/ Happy Valley (Hong Kong) c 1996/ Farnborough Town/ Carshalton Ath 2000/ Aldershot Town 2001 player, coach caretaker mgr Mar to May 2007

Martin Kuhl made his FL debut with Birmingham City, at neighbours West Bromwich Albion on 19 March 1983 and his FL career eventually extended to 446(28) FL games.

He was brought to the Lane by Billy McEwan and made captain, going on to play 41 consecutive League and Cup games in a combative midfield role. When Dave Bassett became the new manager, Martin was almost immediately sold to Harry's previous club, Waford, with Tony Agana and Peter Hetherston coming to the Lane as part of the deal. He made minimal impact at Vicarage Road but went on to captain both Portsmouth and Derby County.

After a time in Hong Kong he returned to non-League football in England and became the coach and then caretaker manager of Aldershot Town.

Appearances:		Apps	Gls
	FL	38	4
	FAC	1	0
	LC	2	0
	FMC	1	0
	Total	42	4

KYLE Peter

IR/CF 1908–09 5' 8" 12st 0
b. Cadder (nr Glasgow) 21 December 1878
d. Glasgow 19 January 1957

Glasgow Parkhead Jun 1896/ Clyde Oct 1898 (West Ham United (trial)? Sep 1901)/ Aberdeen Sep 1902/ Cowdenbeath Jan 1903/ Heart of Midlothian (trial)? Aug 1903/ Royal Albert (Glasgow)// Larkhall Thistle/ Partick Thistle Apr 1905/ Tottenham Hotspur May 1905/ Woolwich Arsenal Apr 1906/ Aston Villa Mar 1908
United: **(£1100 for Evans & Kyle) 2/3 Oct 1908 to May 1909**
Debut: **10 Oct 1908 Manchester United 2 United 1**
Last game: **2 Jan 1909 Nottingham Forest 0 United 2**
Royal Albert/Ayr Parkhouse Nov 1909/ Watford Nov 1909 to Feb 1910/ Royal Albert Feb 1910–11

It is difficult to trace the nomadic career of this United player with confidence because it is probable that there were three contemporary Scottish inside forwards sharing the same surname* whose careers overlapped and two were called Peter. Moreover, the player signed by United, never carried a strong character reference but, because he was a talented player, clubs were willing to take a chance on him but the honeymoon period was usually of short duration.

What is not in doubt is that Peter Kyle was 'a bouncy, all action' forward with good ball control though a trifle slow and he made his Southern League debut for Spurs in September 1905 and scored in his first two games. He did quite well but discipline problems in March led to a move to Woolwich Arsenal where he made his FL debut, scoring twice in an away match against Manchester City. He scored 21 FL goals in 52 appearances for the Gunners and played in a trial match for Scotland in 1907 before joining the Villa.

Kyle moved to the Lane, a few months after signing for Aston Villa, as the lesser part of the transfer to United of Bob Evans. He scored on his first two appearances but, before the month had ended, he had been suspended for missing training. He promised to 'mend his ways' and played a few more times, scoring on his final appearance. United tried to sell him to Clyde and Ayr Parkhouse but he turned up with Watford and, yet again, he was soon sacked.

* There was probably another Peter Kyle who played for many clubs including: Clyde, Liverpool, Leicester Fosse, Wellingborough and Kettering and Archie Kyle, who played for Parkhead, Rangers, Blackburn Rovers, Boness, Clyde, St Mirren and Hamilton. One day, it will become clear.

Appearances:		Apps	Gls
	FL	10	4
	Total	10	4

LAKE Michael (Mike) Charles

MF 1989–93 6' 1" 12st 11 to 13st 6
b. Denton (Manchester) 16 November 1966

Curzon Ashton/ Macclesfield Town 1984/ Manchester C (trial)
United: **(£40k+ £10k + £10k) 11 Oct 1989 to 2 Mar 1993**
Debut: **25 Nov 1989 Newcastle United 2 United 0**
Last game: **27 Feb 1993 Southampton 3 United 2**
Wrexham (L) 25/26 Nov 1992
Wrexham (£60k) 3 Mar 1993 to Jun 1995 (retired)

Mike Lake, an elder brother of Manchester City's Paul, had a successful non-League career with Macclesfield Town. He became an England semi-professional International and helped the club gain promotion from the Northern Premier League to the Conference and also reach the FA Trophy final in 1989, where they lost to Telford United. A part-timer with the Silkmen, he was employed by British Rail and later British Telecom but had no hesitation in becoming a full time professional when joining United.

After a few appearances, he broke his leg at Ipswich in January 1990 and, although playing a few games the following season, it wasn't until September 1991 that he finally had a reasonable run in the side, scoring three fine goals. After making the starting line-up for the first five games of the 1992–93 campaign, he lost his place and moved on loan to Wrexham in November. He was recalled by Dave Bassett in February, but made just one more appearance before making a permanent move to the Racecourse Ground for the same fee as United had paid.

Mike played a major role in Wrexham's promotion to the Second Division in 1993 but he sustained a knee injury at the start of the 1994–95 season and this ended his career (58 FL app, 6 gl for Wrexham). He moved to his home town of Denton, working for the Royal Mail.

Appearances:		Apps	Gls
	FL	19 (16)	4
	FAC	5	1
	LC	3 (2)	0
	FMC	0 (1)	0
	Total	27 (19)	5

LAKING George Edward

LB 1942 5' 9" 12st 2
b. Harthill, nr Rotherham 17 March 1913
d. Staffordshire June 1997

Kiveton Park/ Dinnington/ Wolverhampton Wanderers May 1934/ Middlesbrough Oct 1936 to cs 1947
United: **WW2 guest**
Only game: **25 May 1942 Chesterfield 1 United 2**
WW2 guest: Sheffield Wednesday (1941–42), Doncaster Rovers (1942–44), Leeds United (1945)
Shrewsbury Town cs 1947 to 1949

George Laking made his FL debut with Wolves on 9 Nov 1935 at Grimsby Town. He moved to Middlesbrough and established himself as a robust right back. He was ever present the following season but, after losing his place, he later played at left back. He played as a guest for several clubs, including his one game for United, during the Second War and, having lost his best years to the War, he played just once more for the Boro in 1946. He moved to non-League Shrewsbury Town where he played Midland League football. George was also a good cricketer and played for Shropshire.

Appearances:		Apps	Gls
	WW2	1	0
	Total	1	0

LANG John

OR 1903–09 5' 6½" 11st 0
b. Kilbirnie (Ayrshire) 16 August 1881
d. Dinnington (S Yorks) 1 September 1934

Co-op United (Glasgow)/ Govan/ Barnsley Aug 1902
United: **(£75) 23/26 Mar 1903 to 15 Sep 1909**
Debut: **11 Apr 1903 United 3 Grimsby Town 0**
Last game: **9 Apr 1909 Aston Villa 3 United 0**
Leicester Fosse (£75) Sep 1909/ Denaby United cs 1910/ Dinnington Main Sep 1915

John Lang had won four Scottish Junior caps when he was signed by Barnsley, where he made his FL debut at home to Stockport County on 6 September 1902 but after less than a season, he moved to the Lane.

Fast, with a hard shot, he took over the outside right position from Walter Bennett in September 1904 and, in March 1905, he was near to winning a Scottish cap when chosen for the Anglo-Scots against the Home Scots. Unfortunately, he was injury prone and the 1904–05 season was the only one when he a regular member of the side though he did make over a hundred FL appearances in his six years with the Club and formed a fine wing with Jimmy Donnelly.

His move to Leicester Fosse was not straightforward as the initial cheque for £75 bounced. He was released at the end of the season and returned to South Yorkshire, resuming his work as a miner and playing with Denaby United until at least 1913.

Appearances:		Apps	Gls
	FL	103	13
	FAC	2	0
	Total	105	13

LARNER Keith D

IL 1978 5' 7" 10st 7
b. Bushey (Hertfordshire)

Stevenage and/or Letchworth
United: 30 Mar 1978 to 31 Jul 1980
Only game: 11 May 1978 United 2 Rotherham United 1 (CC)

One of the first players signed by Harry Haslam, Keith was a stylish, attacking, mid-field player but he broke his leg in the last minute of a reserve game against Coventry City in November 1978 and never played again for United.

Appearances:		Apps	Gls
	CC	1	0
	Total	1	0

LATHAM Harry (Scodger)

CH/HB/FB 1940–53 5' 11" 12st 7
b. Sheffield 9 January 1921
d. Rotherham 25 July 1983

Brightside & Carbrook Co-op
United: amat Oct 1937/ 28 May 1938, pro 15/17 Oct 1938 to 1953
Debuts: 29 Apr 1939 Rotherham U 2 United XI 1 (BM)
13 Jan 1940 Rochdale 2 United 0 (Fr)
6 Apr 1940 Notts County 3 United 0 (WW2)
5 Jan 1946 Huddersfield Town 1 United 1 (FAC)
31 Aug 1946 United 0 Liverpool 1
Last games: 29 Apr 1953 United 0 Hull City 2
2 May 1953 United 3 Barnsley 0 (CC)
17 May 1953 SV Sodingen (West Germany) 1 United 1 (Fr)
WW2 guest: Chesterfield 1941–42 (1)
trainer 1953 to 1974

Harry joined United before the Second War and was playing for the 'A' team in October 1937 but he didn't make his first team debut until 1940 although he had played for what was really a reserve eleven in April 1939 in a benefit match at Millmoor. He worked as a furnace man during the War and was able to play regularly for the Blades, first at full back and later at wing half. He first played at centre half in May 1945 when Bill Archer failed to turn up and played regularly at centre half in the League North championship season of 1945–46.

Harry was a first-rate professional and, although he could not be said to be an outstanding footballer, he more than held his own against the best centre forwards of his day. A 'stopper centre half', Harry was powerful and well built, good in the air and determined in the tackle and extremely difficult to pass. He always gave of his best and was a good dressing room man. Reliable and loyal, he was captain in 1946, 1949 and 1950–51. In 1952–53, his 25 appearances, in what was his final season as a player, contributed to United becoming Second Division champions.

Harry joined the training staff, as Ernest Jackson's assistant, in 1953 and took over the first team job in 1956 but he lacked confidence and would never attend coaching courses. Although he remained until 1974, as a loyal member of the training staff, others took on the more senior coaching roles.

Appearances:		Apps	Gls
	FL	190	1
	FAC	19	0
	CC	15	0
	WW2	203	0
	Total	427	1

LAUNDERS Brian Terence

MF 1999 5' 10" 11st 12
b. Dublin 8 January 1976

Cherry Orchard/ Crystal Palace Sep 1993/ Crewe Alexandra Aug 1996/ BV Veendam (Holland) cs 1997/ Derby County (L) Sep 1998/ Colchester United (L) Mar 1999, (free) Sep 1999/ Crystal Palace Oct 1999
United: trial, then 19 Nov 1999 to c 29 Nov 1999
Only game: 20 Nov 1999 Stockport County 1 United 1 (sub)

Brian Launders, a Republic of Ireland U21 International, made his League debut with Crystal Palace on 24 September 1994 at home to Chelsea but despite playing for five FL clubs Brian made only 24 League appearances in his career, 9 of which were as a substitute.

He joined United after a trial, signed by Adrian Heath and given a contract to the end of the season. His United career was brief. Less than ten minutes after he came on as a half time substitute, he had to be taken off, suffering from concussion, and, three days later, Heath resigned. Brian was judged unfit to take a medical and his contract was cancelled.

Appearances:		Apps	Gls
	FL	0 (1)	0
	Total	0 (1)	0

LAVERTY Patrick (Pat) James

IL/IR 1956–59 6' 0" 11st 0
b. Gorseinon (Swansea) 24 May 1934

Wellington Town
United: 12/16 May 1956 to 30 Jun/28 Jul 1960
Debut: 29 Dec 1956 United 5 Barnsley 0
Last game: 26 Dec 1959 Cardiff City 2 United 0
Southend United (£2,250) Jul 1960/ Wellington Town (Telford) Jun 1961

Pat Laverty was one of Joe Mercer's least successful signings. He had a strong left foot and scored twice at Hillsborough in a County Cup Final victory against the Wednesday but rarely looked likely to be anything better than a reserve team player whilst at the Lane.

He spent one season with Southend United making 21 FL appearances before returning to non-League football with his old club, Wellington Town. The club later became Telford and Pat, while still playing, was the assistant manager to World Cup hero, Geoff Hurst.

Appearances:		Apps	Gls
	FL	7	0
	CC	1	2
	Total	8	2

LAW Nicholas (Nicky)

MF 2005– 5' 10" 11st 6
b. Nottingham 29 March 1988

United: from trainee 17 Nov 2005
Debuts: 27 Jul 2005 Matlock 1 United XI 2 (Fr, scored)
25 Oct 2005 Reading 2 United 0 (sub LC)
19 Sep 2006 United 1 Bury 0 (LC)
28 Oct 2006 United 0 Chelsea 2 (sub)
4 Nov 2006 Newcastle United 0 United 1
Yeovil Town (L) 16 Feb 2007

The son of the former Chesterfield and Bradford City manager, Nicky Law made an impressive start to his career making quick, incisive runs and finishing well. His League debut came with United in the Premiership but later in the season he moved to Yeovil on loan.

Nicky failed to make the breakthrough into the first team in 2007–08 although he did score his first United goal at MK Dons in the League Cup.

Appearances:		Apps	Gls
	FL	2 (3)	0
	FAC	0 (1)	0
	LC	3 (1)	1
	Total	5 (5)	1

LEAFE Alfred Richard (Dicky)

CF/IR 1911–13, 1915
b. Boston 1891
d. Ramsgate 9 May 1964

Boston Town/ Grimsby Town amat May 1909 Boston Town c1910
United: 17/18 Nov 1911 amat, 20/22 Dec 1911 pro to May 1913
Debut: 16 Dec 1911 United 3 Liverpool 1
Last game: 1 Mar 1913 United 0 Wednesday 2
West Ham United May/ 6 Jun 1913 to retired cs 1922
United: WW1 guest 1915
Debut: 18 Sep 1915 Huddersfield Town 2 United 2 (WW1)
Last game: 2 Oct 1915 Notts County 3 United 0 (WW1)

Dicky Leafe joined Grimsby Town as an amateur and made his FL debut at home to Stockport County on 9 October 1909. This was his only appearance for the Mariners before he returned to Boston Town.

A prolific scorer, he was watched by Ernest Needham and joined United as an amateur, signing professional terms a few days after making his first team debut. He was at the Lane for two seasons, playing with plenty of energy and dash but he wanted to retain his job as a fish salesman in Boston and train there. He signed for West Ham United, members of the Southern League, who didn't have to pay the £250 FL transfer fee and United must have been far from amused when Leafe finished the new season as top scorer for his new club.

A sergeant in the army during the First War, he didn't play for the Hammers until November 1918, although he did make three appearances for United as a guest player. He returned to the Hammers after their election to the Football League in 1919 and made 31 FL appearances.

After retiring as a player, he became assistant secretary (and scout) at West Ham, a post which he held until the outbreak of the Second War when the club had to reduce the staff.

Appearances:		Apps	Gls
	FL	28	15
	WW1	3	0
	ABD	1	1
	Total	32	16

LEANING Andrew (Andy) John

G 1987–88 6' 0" 13st 0
b. Howden (Goole) 18 May 1963

York Railway Institute/ Rowntree Mackintosh York City amat 1984, pro Jun 1985/ Everton (trial) May 1987
United: (free) 22/28 May 1987 to 9 Nov 1988
Debuts: 25 Jul 1987 Chesterfield 1 United 1 (Fr)
15 Aug 1987 United 0 Bournemouth 1
Last game: 19 Mar 1988 Leeds United 5 United 0
Scunthorpe U (L) Aug 1988
Bristol City (L) 27 Sep, (£12k) Nov 1988/ Lincoln City Mar 1994/ Dundee Jul 1996/ Chesterfield Oct 1996 to Dec 1999, coach 2000/ United coach Sep 2002

Andy Leaning, a former British Rail joiner, became a York City professional in the summer of 1985 and made his FL debut at Newport County on 6 November 1985 but was surprisingly given a free transfer in May 1987.

He was signed by United manager Billy McEwan and saved a penalty kick on his League debut but he suffered ligament problems and was replaced by two loan keepers Roger Hansbury and Hans Segers and after Dave Bassett's arrival, he played just five more games before the new manager signed Graham Benstead.

Andy moved to Bristol City but his first team appearances were limited as he found himself competing for much of his time with ex-Blade Keith Waugh. Later, with Chesterfield, he was in competition with another former United keeper, Billy Mercer but an injury ended his playing career. He became a goalkeeping coach with Chesterfield, a role he filled at the Lane from September 2002.

Appearances:		Apps	Gls
	FL	21	0
	FAC	2	0
	LC	2	0
	Total	25	0

LEE David John

CD 1997–98 6' 3" 14st 7
b. Kingswood) Bristol 26 November 1969

Chelsea from trainee Jul 1988/ Reading (L) Jan 1992 Plymouth Argyle (L) Mar 1992/ Portsmouth (L) Aug 1994
United: (L) 19 Dec 1997 to 18 Jan 1998
Debut: 20 Dec 1997 Bury 1 United 1
Last game: 17 Jan 1998 United 1 Wolverhampton Wanderers 1
Bristol City (trial) Dec 1998/ Bristol Rovers Dec 1998 to May 1999/ Crystal Palace Oct 1999/ Colchester United Jan 2000/ Exeter City Feb 2000/ retired Mar 2000

David Lee, an England youth international, also won 10 England U21 caps whilst with Chelsea. He made his FL debut with the London club, as a substitute, on 1 October 1988 at home to Leicester City. His full debut came three days later at home to Walsall and he went on to help them win the Second Division title in 1989 and the League Cup in 1998. However, for much of his ten years at Stamford Bridge he was used mainly as a stand-in centre half or in midfield and played only 119(32) League games.

After a recovering from a broken leg and in an effort to regain match fitness, he had a loan spell with United, signed by his former team-mate Nigel Spackman. The heart of the defence had been wrecked by the loss of McGrath, Tiler and Vonk but Lee wasn't going to help solve that problem and he returned to Chelsea at the end of the loan period.

After leaving Chelsea he moved to various clubs but made only a few more League appearances, bringing his total to 155(35), before he was forced to retire.

Appearances:		Apps	Gls
	FL	5	0
	Total	5	0

LEE Kenneth (Ken)

CH 1942 6' 2" 13st
b. Sheffield 17 October 1922
d. Sheffield 3 November 2004

United: amat 8 Dec 1941 and 16 Oct 1942 to c1945
Only game: 14 Nov 1942 United 2 Chesterfield 2 (WW2)

A useful club cricketer who began playing for the United Cricket Club in 1937 and also appeared for Yorkshire's second eleven; Ken Lee had the physique for football but was slow on the turn and made just one first team appearance. A director of a Sheffield engineering company, Ken joined the United board as a director in June 1962.

Appearances:		Apps	Gls
	WW2	1	0
	Total	1	0

LEIGERTWOOD Mikele Benjamin

MF 2006–07 6' 1" 13st 11
b. Enfield 12 November 1982

Wimbledon from trainee Jun 2001/ Leyton Orient(L) Nov 2001/ Crystal Palace (£150k) Feb 2004
United: (c£600k) 4/5 Jul 2006 to 31 Aug 2007
Debuts: 17 Jul 2006 Worksop Town 0 United 5 (sub Fr)
5 Aug 2006 Sparta Rotterdam 1 United 1 (Fr)
19 Aug 2006 United 1 Liverpool 1 (sub)
26 Aug 2006 Fulham 1 United 0
Last games: 11 Aug 2007 United 2 Colchester United 2
25 Aug 2007 United 1 West Bromwich Albion 0 (sub)
29 Aug 2007 MK Dons 2 United 3 (LC)
Queens Park Rangers (£850/900k) Aug 2007

Mikele Leigertwood made his FL debut whilst on loan at Leyton Orient, at home to Oxford United on 20 November 2001. After moving to Crystal Palace, he played regularly in the second half of their 2004–05 season in

the Premiership. Although out of contract when joining United, compensation of £600k was paid to Crystal Palace because Mikele was under 24 years old.

A strong mid-field player, he made an excellent start to the new campaign tackling well, being able to hold the ball and possessing a good shot, although he took time to win over some of the fans. Just as he seemed to be settled in he was injured and was injured again on his comeback against Arsenal. By the time he recovered United were heavily involved in a relegation battle and Mikele played only occasionally.

Although he was involved in the pre-season games under Bryan Robson, he was allowed to leave in the August transfer window, as again sections of the crowd were 'on his back'. He was a regular in the QPR side for 2007–08.

Appearances:		Apps	Gls
	FL	17	4
	LC	2	0
	Total	19	4

LEMONS Charles (Charlie) F

OR 1945
b. Sheffield

St George's
United: 15 Jan 1945 amat to c1946
Only game: 17 Feb 1945 United 0 Doncaster Rovers 4 (WW2)
/ – / Weston Park (1951–52)

The son of a former professional footballer, Charlie Lemons was an amateur player with United who came out of the army and 'got in with the wrong crowd'. His only first team game proved to be 'an occasion too big' for him and he spent most of his last season with the 'A' team.

Appearances:		Apps	Gls
	WW2	1	0
	Total	1	0

LESTER Jack William

Striker 2003–04 5' 10" 11st 8
b. Sheffield 8 October 1975

Grimsby Town from jnr Jul 1994/ Doncaster Rovers(L) Sep 1996/ Nottingham Forest (£300k) Jan 2000
United: 1 Aug 2003 to 26 Nov 2004
Debuts: 15 Jul 2003 Frechville CA 0 United 9 (Fr)
9 Aug 2003 United 0 Gillingham 0
Last games: 18 Sep 2004 Wigan Athletic 4 United 0
26 Oct 2004 United 0 Watford 0 (LC)
13 Nov 2004 United 1 Watford 1 (sub)
Nottingham Forest (£50k) Nov 2004/ Chesterfield Jun 2007

An England schoolboy international, Jack Lester made his FL debut with Grimsby Town as a substitute on 27 August 1994 at home to Tranmere Rovers. His full debut finally arrived on 27 December at home to Oldham Athletic.

On joining United he quickly became a favourite with the fans. Whether playing as a striker or behind the front two, he worked hard and caused defenders problems particularly in the penalty area with his ability to turn quickly with the ball. Apart from a spell out with injury in February 2004 he was a regular member of the side and finished as top scorer although eight of his goals were from coolly taken penalties. His start to the following season was delayed by injury and he was unable to re-establish himself, the majority of his appearances being from the bench. He returned to Forest in November but unfortunately suffered a bad leg injury which sidelined him for nine months.

After two seasons being a regular member of the Forest squad he was released and joined Chesterfield where he had a very successful season scoring 25 goals and bringing his career tally to 89 League goals in 274(125) games.

Appearances:		Apps	Gls
	FL	26 (18)	12
	FAC	2	1
	LC	3 (1)	3
	Total	31 (19)	16

LEVICK Frank

IR/IL/CF 1907–08 5' 9" 11st 7
b. Eckington (north Derbyshire) JAS 1882
d. Tinsley (Sheffield) 1 February 1908

Eckington Juniors/ Tinsley 1901–06/ Wednesday 1902–03? Rotherham Town 1906–07
United: **(£50) 4/5 May 1907 to his death**
Debut: **7 Sep 1907 Chelsea 2 United 4**
Last game: **1 Jan 1908 United 1 Newcastle United 1**

Frank Levick had played one season with Wednesday's reserves but he came to the fore with Rotherham Town and that led to him coming to the Lane. He made an impressive debut in the opening game of the 1907–08 season and may have scored (reports credit a goal to him or Arthur Brown) against Chelsea who were playing their first fixture in the old First Division. Frank certainly scored in his second game and had a good run in the side. 'Full of dash, clever, with a good shot', he was probably United's best forward that season but sadly, soon after scoring on his final appearance, he broke his collar bone and died of pneumonia a few weeks later at his parents' home. United paid all the medical bills and funeral expenses and made a grant to his parents.

Appearances:		Apps	Gls
	FL	18	5
	Total	18	5

LEWINGTON Raymond (Ray)

MF 1985–86 5' 6½" 11st 6
b. Lambeth 7 September 1956

Chelsea app to pro 1974/ Vancouver Whitecaps (Canada) (£40k) Feb/Mar 1979/ Wimbledon (L) Sep 1979 Fulham (£50k) Mar 1980
United: **(£40k) 5/23 Jul 1985 to 3/18 Jul 1986**
Debuts: **30 Jul 1985 Skegness Town 0 United 3 (Fr)**
17 Aug 1985 Stoke City 1 United 3
Last game: **12 Apr 1986 United 2 Oldham Athletic 0**
Fulham (£25/30k) player-mgr Jul 1986, to club coach Jun 1990, caretaker-mgr Nov-Dec 1991, March-May 1994/ Crystal Palace coach May 1994, mgr Jun 1995–Feb 1996, coach/ Brentford coach Jul 1998 to Aug 2001, caretaker mgr Nov 2000/ Watford coach Aug 2001, mgr Jul 2002 to Mar 2005/ Fulham coach Jul 2005, caretaker mgr 2007 (3 games), asst-mgr

Ray Lewington made his FL debut with Chelsea as a substitute on 21 February 1976 at Notts County, his full debut being at Plymouth Argyle on 6 March and he was ever present in the side which won promotion from the Second Division in 1977. After brief spells in the NASL and with Wimbledon he moved to Fulham, playing an important role in their 1982 promotion.

Ray was a hard working, ball winning midfielder who used the ball well. Signed by Ian Porterfield, it was not a happy season at the Lane and poor team displays led to the termination of the manager's contract. Ray had worked hard and played regularly until an injury ended his season with six games to go. Appreciated by his colleagues, he failed to win the support of the majority of United's supporters and was no doubt happy to return south.

He accepted the position of player-manager with Fulham although still not thirty and he went on to have a long career in coaching and management with various clubs. During his playing career he made 369(9) FL appearances.

Appearances:		Apps	Gls
	FL	36	0
	FAC	2	0
	LC	3	0
	FMC	2	0
	Total	43	0

LEWIS Albert Edward Talbot (Tal)

or **Talbot-Lewis**

G 1902–03 6' 1" 12st 2 to 13st 10
b. Bedminster, Bristol, 20 January 1877
d. Southmead, Bristo,l 22 February 1956

Bedminster Jan 1896/ Gravesend U Sep 1896 Bedminster Oct 1896/ Woolwich Arsenal? Sep 1897 Bristol City Sep 1897/ Everton May 1898/ Bristol City 1899 Walsall Aug 1901
United: **2/3 May 1902 to 10 Jun 1904**
Debut: **29 Nov 1902 United 2 Liverpool 0**
Last game: **19 Dec 1903 Sunderland 2 United 1**
Sunderland (£75) Jun 1904/ Luton Town May 1905/ Leicester Fosse Jul 1906/ Bristol City Oct 1907 to 1908

In the early part of his career, he is frequently referred to as Talbot-Lewis but United registered him with the FL as Lewis and that name was used by the press. Popularly known as 'Tal', he played at both full back and goalkeeper for Bedminster in the Western League and had very brief periods with Gravesend and Arsenal. He made his Southern League debut with Bristol City at New Brompton on 9 October 1897 and played at left back. During his second spell with Bristol City, he made one appearance as a keeper but conceded six goals and he then joined Walsall who were members of the Midland League and played at left back on his debut. He wasn't a good full back as his tackling was poor and so, for his second game, which was at Bramall Lane, he played as a keeper and conceded eight goals! Surprisingly or not, he not only kept his place in the Walsall goal but was signed by United for the following season.

Tall and athletic, he came to Sheffield as the understudy to Billy Foulke and his first team appearances were inevitably limited. He played only four games for Sunderland before moving to Southern League Luton, but his FL career finally blossomed with 38 games for Leicester Fosse and 21in his third spell with Bristol City.

He then retired from football to concentrate on his cricketing career with Somerset. Between 1899 and 1914 he played 214 first class matches, scoring 7745 runs (including a double century) at an average of 21.4 and taking 515 wickets at an average of 23.0. After the First War he coached in India. He was also a highly skilled billiards player.

Appearances:		Apps	Gls
	FL	15	0
	FAC	2	0
	Total	17	0

LEWIS Kevin

OR 1957–60 5' 9½" 10st 12
b. Ellesmere Port 19 September 1940

United: jnr 1955, 24/ 6 Oct 1957 to 16/20 Jun 1960
Debut: 25 Dec 1957 Blackburn Rovers 1 United 0
Last games: 30 Apr 1960 United 2 Huddersfield Town 0
4 May 1960 United 2 Rotherham United 1 (CC)
7 May 1960 Basle (Switzerland) 1 United 1 (Fr)
Liverpool (£12k) Jun 1960/ Huddersfield Town (£18k) Aug 1963/ Port Elizabeth, South Africa Jul 1965 to Oct 1966/ Wigan Athletic Nov 1966

Kevin Lewis was still only fifteen when he made his CL debut for United's reserves against Everton. The son of a former professional player, Kevin was signed by manager Joe Mercer. A Wallasey Grammar School boy, Kevin was a superb young player; fast, strong, two footed and clever and soon to be an England youth international, he made his first team debut on Christmas Day 1957 at the age of seventeen and scored the following day in the game when Derek Pace made his debut. He had a good run of games, replacing the ageing Alf Ringstead and finished the season with 6 goals from 15 games. He again competed with Ringstead for the right wing spot during the following season but injury kept him out of the side for a while during the 1959–60 campaign.

He scored in his final FL appearance for United but, during the summer, he became one of Bill Shankley's first important signings—a record at the time for the Anfield club—and helped Liverpool win the Second Division championship in 1962.

When he moved to South Africa in 1965, he had a creditable career record of 75 goals in 178 FL appearances for his three clubs but the feeling remains that Kevin should have achieved far more than he did.

Appearances:		Apps	Gls
	FL	62	23
	FAC	14	6
	CC	4	0
	Total	80	29

LEYFIELD Charles (Charlie)

OL/OR 1937–38 5' 7" 10st 10
b. Chester 30 October 1911
d. Chester 1 April 1982

Chester Brickfields/ Everton Dec 1930/Apr 1934
United: (£2,500) 5/6 May 1937 to 8/9 Nov 1938
Debut: 28 Aug 1937 United 2 Nottingham Forest 1
Last game: 1 Oct 1938 United 0 Plymouth Argyle 1
Doncaster Rovers (£1,525) Nov 1938 to Jan 1945
WW2 guest: Chester 1939–40, 1941–42, 1943–44, Fulham 1942–45, Aldershot 1943–44, Brentford 1943–44, Millwall 1943–44

Charlie Leyfield made his FL debut with Everton on 29 August 1934 at home to Leicester City, scoring in this and the next two games. Strong, a good finisher and two footed, he began as an outside right but later moved to outside left but was unable to gain a regular place in the side.

Signed by the United manager, Teddy Davison, he was a regular in the side until March but then lost his place and moved to Doncaster Rovers in October. He scored 11 goals in 28 appearances for Rovers and scored two more in the opening game of the 1939–40 season which had to be abandoned because of the war. Serving in the army, he was a guest player for several clubs in the London area but his playing career was ended by an injury in January 1945 while playing for Fulham. Later, he was a member of the training staff at Wrexham, Everton (c1952–56) and Hull City's chief scout.

Appearances:		Apps	Gls
	FL	36	13
	FAC	3	0
	CC	1	0
	Total	40	13

LIDDELL Andrew (Andy) Mark

RW 2004–05 5' 7" 11st 6
b. Leeds 28 June 1973

Barnsley from trainee Jul 1991/ Wigan Athletic (£350k) Oct 1998
United: 7 Jul 2004 to 29 Jun 2005
Debuts: 13 Jul 2004 Matlock Town 4 United XI 3 (Fr)
7 Aug 2004 Burnley 1 United 1
Last games: 15 Apr 2005 United 0 Derby County 1
30 Apr 2005 United 0 Millwall 1 (sub)
Oldham Athletic (free) Jun 2005

A Scottish U21 international, Andy made his FL debut with Barnsley, coming on as a substitute at Portsmouth on 2 May 1992 and his full debut, was also at Portsmouth on 22 August 1992, at the start of the following season. He helped the Tykes gain promotion to the Premiership but he found his opportunities limited as Barnsley's top flight season progressed. In order to play first team football, he signed for Wigan Athletic and was a regular member of their side for nearly six seasons and became their all-time top League goal scorer with 70 goals.

Technically excellent in striking a ball, he was signed by Neil Warnock but he had injury problems at the start of the season. By October, he was a regular member of the United side, playing generally on the right wing. He created opportunities with his crosses but his goal tally was perhaps a little disappointing, although he did score twice against Aston Villa in the FA Cup. The signing of Paul Ifill during in May 2005 led to Andy's transfer to Oldham Athletic where he again played and scored regularly and at the end of the 2007–08 season, he had scored a total of 128 goals in 463(78) FL appearances.

Appearances:		Apps	Gls
	FL	26 (7)	3
	FAC	5	3
	LC	1	0
	Total	32 (7)	6

LIEVESLEY Joseph (Joe)

G 1904–12 5' 10" 12st 0 to 13st 0
b. Netherthorpe, Staveley 25 July 1883
d. New Rossington, Doncaster 13 October 1941

Ireland Colliery/ Poolsbrook 1899
United: amat 5 May 1901, pro 1/5 May 1903 to 28 Jun 1913
Debut: 17 Sep 1904 United 2 Small Heath 1
Last game: 19 Oct 1912 United 4 Everton 1
Woolwich Arsenal Jun 1913 to cs 1915/ Chesterfield Town 1915 to cs 1917 / – / Rossington Colliery cs 1921

Joe Lievesley (Joe preferred Leivesley) lived and worked in the Staveley area of north Derbyshire and signed for United, perhaps inspired by the fact that Ernest Needham, United's famous captain, also lived in the town. Having made his debut early in the 1904–05 season he soon took over the number one spot from the famous Bill Foulke. Joe then began a remarkable run of appearances missing just six competitive games from the end of November 1904 to the end of December 1911. He was ever present during seasons 1905–6, 1906–7 and 1908–9 and at one point, played in 130 consecutive FL and Cup games.

Joe was always described as dependable, calm and cool, a goalkeeper 'who always seemed to know exactly what advancing forwards intended to do' and 'who made his work look easy'. He saved a penalty in an England trial match in 1910 and played for the Football League against the Southern League and toured South Africa with the FA in 1911. He perhaps deserved more honours but he was a contemporary of another Chesterfield born keeper, the great Sam Hardy. Joe was also unlucky in that his career with United covered a period of disastrous FA Cup tie results, a fact not made easier by the knowledge that United won the Cup after he left.

Joe saved nine penalty kicks in a period when few were awarded and was the first United goalkeeper to save two penalties in one game, against Manchester City in 1906. Injured in what turned out to be his final game for United, he was supplanted by Joe Mitchell and was given a free transfer.

He joined the Arsenal and played there for two seasons, missing just three of 76 possible FL games and was ever-present in 1914–15. During the First War he served in the Royal Flying Corps and played for Chesterfield Town until the club was closed down by the FA for making illegal payments in 1917.

Joe's brothers, Fred and Wilf, were also professional footballers as were three of his sons, including Leslie, who was the Torino coach who perished in an air disaster in 1949. Joe was also a good cricketer, playing for Sheffield United and later Rossington and a nephew of United's full back, Harry Lilley.

Appearances:		Apps	Gls
	FL	278	0
	FAC	9	0
	ABD	1	0
	Total	288	0

LILLEY Edward Henry (Harry)

LB/RB 1890–94
b. Staveley JAS 1868
d. Worksop 30 August 1900

Staveley Lowgates 1887/ Staveley 1887
United: cs 1890 to cs 1894
Debuts: 1 Sep 1890 United 9 Sheffield Club 0 (Fr)
13 Sep 1890 Burton Wanderers 1 United 1 (MCL)
4 Oct 1890 Derby Junction 0 United 1 (FAC)
19 Nov 1892 Darwen 3 United 1
Last games: 20 Jan 1894 Sunderland 4 United 1
27 Jan 1894 Newcastle United 2 United 0 (FAC)
18 Apr 1894 Ardwick 0 United 2 (Fr)

Harry Lilley, a brother of United's Will Lilley, played regularly for United during the two seasons before the club joined the Football League, but his appearances were less frequent during the following two seasons. He shares with Mick Whitham, the honour of being United's first international; both played in the International trial of February 1892 and, one month later, Harry played for England against Wales at Wrexham on the same afternoon that Mick Whitham played against Ireland at Cliftonville. A 'wonderfully clean kicker' though a little slow, he was prone to knee injuries.

Appearances:		Apps	Gls
	FL	19	0
	FAC	12	0
	NL	18	0
	MCL	15	0
	ABD	1	0
	Total	65	0

LILLEY James William (Will)

G 1891–94
b. Staveley OND 1885

Staveley 1887 to Sep 1891
United: Nov 1891 to 13/20 Aug 1894

Debuts: 12 Dec 1891 Walsall Town Swifts 2 United 0 (Fr)
26 Dec 1891 Newcastle East End 1 United 2 (NL)
16 Jan 1892 Blackpool 0 United 3 (FAC)
3 Sep 1892 United 4 Lincoln City 2
Last games: 3 Feb 1894 United 3 Stoke 3
12 Feb 1894 United 0 Derby County 2 (UCL)
18 Apr 1894 Ardwick 2 United 0 (Fr)
Rotherham Town Aug 1894

Will Lilley had intended to sign for the Wednesday but, no doubt influenced by his brother Harry, he joined United. For all his time at Bramall Lane Will was competing for the goalkeeping role with Charlie Howlett and it was Charlie who played more games and was the better of the two although both had the same weakness in that they disliked being charged. Nevertheless, Will did play in United's first ever FL game and he was the goalkeeper who conceded the first FL goal scored against United. Will and his brother played together in their final first team game for United in April 1894 and Harry appears to have stopped playing but Will moved to Rotherham Town and played nine FL games in the 1894–95 season.

Appearances:		Apps	Gls
	FL	13	3
	FAC	3	0
	NL	12	0
	UCL	2	0
	Total	30	3

LINDLEY Frank Louis

OR 1912 5' 9 ½" 11st 8
b. Sheffield OND 1885

Midland Athletic (Sheffield)/ Dundee/ Motherwell cs 1911
United: May/13 Jul 1912 to cs 1913
Only game: 7 Sep 1912 United 1 Oldham Athletic 1
Newport County Aug 1913/ Luton Town cs 1914

Frank scored in Motherwell's first League game of season 1911–12 at Queens Park on 16 August. He played 26 League games that season but made just one FL appearance for the Blades. After one season he moved to Newport County and then Luton Town, both in the Southern League and subsequently he was wounded while serving in the army in France in the First War.

Appearances:		Apps	Gls
	FL	1	0
	Total	1	0

LIPSHAM Herbert (Bert) Broughall

OL 1900–08 5' 9½" 10st 12 to 11st 0
b. Chester 29 April 1878
d. Toronto (Canada) 22 March 1932

St Oswald's Ath, (Chester)/ Chester Jan 1896 Rock Ferry Aug 1897/ PSA 1897–98 Crewe Alexandra (pro) May 1898
United: 23 Feb 1900 to Apr 1908
Debut: 3 Mar 1900 Aston Villa 1 United 1
Last game: 8 Feb 1908 Birmingham 0 United 0
Fulham (£350) Apr 1908/ Millwall Athletic cs 1910 player, then player-mgr May 1911 to cs1913, manager 1913–18, advisory capacity cs1918–1920/ West Norwood coach cs 1920/ Northfleet United 1922–23 mgr

Educated at the King's School in Chester, Bert Lipsham was playing as a professional for Crewe Alexandra in the Lancashire League and working in the Chester office of the Official Receiver when he came to United's attention. John Nicholson, the United secretary, and Arthur Bingham, a director, went to Crewe to sign him but initially were unable to persuade him to join United. He did agree to accompany them to the railway station and, once there, they had to persuade a member of the railway staff to delay the train's departure before Bert finally agreed to sign.

Bert played all his competitive games for the Blades at outside left where he would twist and turn to deceive an opponent rather than dribble and he used his long raking stride, speed and ability to take the ball in his stride without hesitation. He was cool and composed and noted for fast—too quick on occasions—accurate crosses and shots with both feet. He played in both the 1901 and 1902 FA Cup Finals, gaining respectively losers' and winners' medals, gained an England cap against Wales in 1902, and twice played for the Football League.

At one time, Bert had a tobacconists shop near the Lane and two of his seven brothers had a trial with the United reserves in 1903. He represented the United players at the first meeting of the PFA in 1907 and played a leading role in the development of the Players' Union. In 1908, after being injured, he was selected for the reserves but refused to play, arguing that other senior players had returned immediately to first team duty after injury. He was suspended for seven days and quickly transferred to Fulham before moving to Millwall, first as a player and then, successfully as the manager. He had served on the PFA management committee between 1909 and 1911 and, during the First War, he worked for the Army Reserve Depot in Deptford.

After a few more years as a coach or manager, he emigrated in 1923 to Canada where he became a member of the Canadian FA. He lost his right hand in a timber yard accident and died of a heart attack in Toronto in 1932 at the age of 53.

Appearances:		Apps	Gls
	FL	235	29
	FAC	24	5
	Total	259	34

LITTLEJOHN Adrian Sylvester

Striker 1991–95, 2001 5' 9½" 10st 5
b. Wolverhampton 26 September 1970

West Bromwich Albion trainee/ Walsall May 1989
United: (free) 6 Aug 1991 to 12 Jul 1995
Debuts: 24 Aug 1991 United 0 Southampton 2 (sub)
31 Aug 1991 Crystal Palace 2 United 1
Last games: 29 Apr 1995 Barnsley 2 United 1
20 May 1995 Catania (Sicily) 1 United 0 (Fr)
Plymouth Argyle (£200k) Jul 1995/ Oldham Athletic (exchange) Mar 1998/ Bury (£75k) Nov 1998
United: (trial Aug), (free) (nc) 22 Oct 2001 to Dec 2001
Debut: 27 Oct 2001 United 1 Crewe Alexandra 0
Last game: 4 Nov 2001 Burnley 2 United 0 (sub)
USA/ China/ Barnsley trial/ Bradford City Jan 2003/Port Vale Feb 2003/ Lincoln City Aug 2004/ Rushden & Diamonds Jan 2005/ Mansfield Sep 2005 to Dec 2005/ Leek Town Mar 2006 to Oct 2006 / – / Retford United cs 2007/
United Football Development Officer Dec 2007

Adrian Littlejohn, an England School and Youth international, was offered a trial with United when a trainee at West Brom but signed for Walsall and made his FL debut at Huddersfield Town on 1 January 1990 but his scoring record of one goal in 26(18) FL appearances for the Third Division club was poor.

He was signed by Dave Bassett on a three month trial, after a disagreement over terms with Walsall. Very quick but sometimes lacking the necessary control and finishing skills, he made few appearances during his first season but in the following one, the first of the Premiership, Adrian played often alongside Brian Deane, his speed and direct approach creating problems for the opposition defences and he finished second top scorer with eight goals. For the rest of his time at the Lane he was in and out of the side, making many of his appearances from the bench.

He moved to Plymouth Argyle and then Bury, signed by Neil Warnock and it was Neil who brought him to the Lane for a second time as cover for injured strikers. He had a game (9 August) at Matlock and, although not fully match fit, he still showed impressive pace in his three appearances. After a spell at Port Vale he had short spells at three more League clubs, reaching a total of 301(124) League appearances, before moving into non-League football.

In late 2007 Adrian returned to the Lane, working as Football Development Officer, involved with the Club's work in the community.

Appearances:		Apps	Gls
	FL	45 (27)	12
	FAC	3 (2)	1
	LC	5 (1)	0
	FMC	1	0
	AIC	1	1
	Total	55 (30)	14

LOGAN Neil

CF/CH 1898 5' 11" 12st 6
b. Blantyre 16 December 1875
d. Swindon 8 June 1949

Blantyre/ Rutherglan Glencairn?
United: 10 Nov 1897 to May 1898
Debuts: 2 Feb 1898 Burslem Port Vale 2 United 1 (FAC)
5 Feb 1898 Liverpool 0 United 4
Last game: 26 Mar 1898 West Bromwich Albion 2 United 0
Swindon Town May 1898/ Blackburn Rovers Jun 1902/ Swindon Town cs 1903 to 1906 / – / Haydon St WMC (Swindon) amat 1909

Neil Logan made his United debut in the FA Cup but then scored twice in each of his next two appearances in FL games. Having played six successive games at centre forward as United advanced towards the First Division championship title, he then played his final game, four weeks later, at centre half. He had a strong shot but was slow and was happier, as his career progressed, playing as a centre half.

Appearances:		Apps	Gls
	FL	5	4
	FAC	1	0
	Total	6	4

LONGHORN Dennis

MF 1976–78 6' 0" 12st 0
b. Hythe nr Southampton 12 September 1950

Bournemouth app to pro Aug 1968/ Mansfield Town (£5,000) Dec 1971/ Sunderland (£20k + player) Feb 1974
United: (L) 18 Oct 1976, (£22.5k/£25k)18 Nov 1976 to 24 Feb 1978
Debut: 23 Oct 1976 Charlton Athletic 3 United 2
Last games: 21 Jan 1978 Sunderland 5 United 1
28 Jan 1978 Swindon Town 2 United 3 (Fr)
Aldershot (£20k) Feb 1978/ Colchester United May 1980/ Chelmsford City Jul 1983/ Halstead Town, mgr 1989/ Wivenhoe Town/ Braintree Town

Dennis Longhorn made his FL debut with Bournemouth on 23 March 1968 at home to Torquay United, five months before signing professional forms in August. Following a spell with Mansfield Town he moved to Sunderland where he was a marginal member of the squad which won the Second Division title in 1976.

Tall and slim, he was signed by Jimmy Sirrel during United's first season following relegation from the top flight and was a regular in the side for the remainder of the season. Dennis was a stylish player but he lacked aggression and determination and it was no surprise that he lost his place and when Harry Haslam arrived, he was transferred to Aldershot.

When he moved into non-League football, he had made 293(33) FL appearances. Latterly he was reported to be a football coach with Center Parcs.

Appearances:		Apps	Gls
	FL	34 (2)	1
	FAC	2	0
	LC	0 (1)	0
	ASC	4	1
	CC	1	0
	Total	41 (3)	2

LONGWORTH Bruce

RH 1924–26 5' 7½" 11st 6
b. Lanchester (Co Durham) AMJ 1898
d. Truro 12 March 1955

Hopley's All Blacks/ Army/ Bolton Wanderers WW1 guest and Jun 1919
United: (£2,500) 24 Oct 1924 to cs 1926
Debut: 25 Oct 1924 United 3 Preston North End 0
Last game: 6 Feb 1926 United 3 Bury 1
Darwen Sep 1926/ Clitheroe Sep 1927

A former inside forward, Bruce Longworth made his FL debut with Bolton Wanderers on Christmas Day 1920 at home to Sunderland, although he had played twice during the First War towards the end of the 1917–18 season. He was a regular in the side until September 1922 but injuries and the fine play of Harry Nuttall cost him his first team place.

He moved to Bramall Lane and played his first game with one knee swathed in bandages. He appeared in nine of the next ten games but a cartilage injury gave an opportunity to Harold Pantling, who returned to the team and won a Cup medal. Bruce scored in his final appearance for United but his playing days at a senior level were over. Later, he opened a toffee business in Bispham and became a hotel owner in Blackpool and then in Cornwall.

Appearances:		Apps	Gls
	FL	13	1
	FAC	1	0
	Total	14	1

LORD Gordon J

OR 1941

Rotherham junior football
United: 21 Apr 1941 amat to cs 1941
Only game: 26 Apr 1941 Leeds United 2 United 0 (WW2)

Gordon Lord was a player from Rotherham junior football.

Appearances:		Apps	Gls
	WW2	1	0
	Total	1	0

LOUKES Gordon

OL 1949–51
b. Sheffield 15 June 1928

Skelton's Works
United: 29 Nov 1946 amat, 27/30 Apr 1949 pro to 3 Jul 1951
Debuts: 5 Oct 1949 Western Command 0 United XI 2 (Fr, at Lichfield)
10 Feb 1951 Sheffield Wednesday 2 United 0 (CC)
Last game: 17 Feb 1951 United 1 West Ham United 1
Southend United (£500) Jul 1951/ Gravesend & Northfleet Jul 1952/ Dartford United/ Frickley Colly Aug 1958

A left winger with a strong shot, in his two seasons as a professional at the Lane Gordon Loukes made just two senior competitive appearances but played regularly in the reserves. After moving to Southend United he made two further FL appearances before moving in to non-League football.

Appearances:		Apps	Gls
	FL	1	0
	CC	1	0
	Total	1	0

LOVELL Stephen (Steve) William Henry

Striker 2002 5' 11"/ 6' 1" 11st 8/12st 7
b. Amersham 6 December 1980

Bournemouth Apr 1997 trainee, pro Jul 1999 Portsmouth (£250k) Aug 1999/ Exeter City (L) Mar 2000
United: (L) 19 Mar 2002 to cs 2002
Debut: 19 Mar 2002 Millwall 3 United 2
Last games: 13 Apr 2002 United 0 Walsall 1
21 Apr 2002 Birmingham City 2 United 0 (sub)
QPR Jul 2002/ Dundee Aug 2002/ Aberdeen (£250k) Jul 2005 to cs 2008/ Falkirk (free) Aug 2008

Steve Lovell made his FL debut with Bournemouth as a substitute on 6 April 1999 at home to Macclesfield Town, his full debut coming at home to Chesterfield on 24 April.

He joined United on loan from Portsmouth shortly before the transfer deadline in 2002 and made a few appearances before returning to Portsmouth. At the start of the following season he moved to Scotland where he played regularly, both for Dundee and then Aberdeen, scoring 48 goals in the Scottish League in just over 150 games, before being released in the summer of 2008.

Appearances:		Apps	Gls
	FL	3 (2)	1
	Total	3 (2)	1

LOWE David

OR 1922 5' 8" 11st 0
b. Darby End (Dudley) AMJ 1904
d. possibly Halesowen 26 March 1975

Cradley Heath
United: (£300) 20 Apr 1922 to cs 1923
Debut: 22 Apr 1922 Everton 1 United 1
Last games: 4 Sep 1922 United 1 Blackburn Rovers 1
11 Oct 1922 Hartlepools United 0 United 2 (BM)
Cradley Heath cs 1923/ Dudley T Aug 1933

David Lowe was quite fast and put across some good centres but he scored just two goals for the reserves and wasn't good enough for League football.

Appearances:		Apps	Gls
	FL	2	0
	CC	1	0
	Total	3	0

LOWE Richard (Dick) Ernest

CF 1938 5' 10½" 11st 12 to 12st 2
b. Cannock 13 July 1915
d. Cannock July 1986

Leeds United amat Nov 1934, pro Jan 1935
United: (£75) 3/5 May 1937 to 6/8 May 1939
Debut: 28 Mar 1938 United 1 Swansea Town 1
Last game: 29 Apr 1939 Rotherham U 2 United XI 1 (BM)
Hull City (£250) May 1939 to cs 1946

Dick Lowe failed to make a senior competitive appearance for Leeds United and in his two seasons at Bramall Lane, he made just one FL appearance. He moved to Hull City for a fee of £250 though United received a letter in the summer of 1943 informing them that the Humberside club were unable to pay for the player.

Dick made an immediate impact with Hull at the start of the 1939–40 season, scoring in a pre-season friendly and in Hull's two FL games played before the season was abandoned because of the outbreak of war. However, these two appearances and two goals do not 'count' in official FL records.

Appearances:		Apps	Gls
	FL	1	0
	Total	1	0

LUCAS Richard

LB 1989–91 5' 10" 11st 4
b. Chapeltown (Sheffield) 22 September 1970

United: trainee Apr 1987, pro 1 Jul 1989 to 19 Feb 1993
Debuts: 10 Aug 1989 United 1 Rotherham United 1 (YHC)
1 Dec 1990 Aston Villa 2 United 1
Last games: 8 May 1991 Leeds United 2 United 1
22 May 1991 Tulsa Renegades 1 United 4 (Fr)
7 Sep 1991 Oldham Athletic 2 United 1 (sub)
(L) Grebbstad (Swe) Apr 1990
Preston North End (L) Dec 1992, (£20k + £20k) Feb 1993/ Lincoln City (L) Oct 1994/ Scarborough Jul 1995/ Hartlepools United (L) Mar 1997, transfer/ Halifax Town Aug 1998/Boston United Jun 2000/ Hednesford Town Jun 2001/ Gainsborough Trinity Oct 2002/ Stocksbridge Parks Steel (L)/ Ilkeston Town Jun 2004 to cs 2005

A Sheffield and Yorkshire Boys player, Richard Lucas was unable to establish himself in United's first team, although all his League appearances for the Blades were in the top flight. A cruciate ligament operation in January 1992 held him back but he had more success at his subsequent clubs and had made 210(23) League appearances before he moved into non-League football.

Appearances:		Apps	Gls
	FL	8 (2)	0
	FAC	1	0
	FMC	0 (1)	0
	YHC	1	0
	Total	10 (3)	0

LUCKETTI Christopher (Chris) James

CD 2006–07 6' 0" 13st 6
b. Littleborough, nr. Rochdale 28 September 1971

Rochdale trainee/ Stockport County Jul 1990/ Halifax Town Jul 1991/ Bury (£50k) Oct 1993/ Huddersfield Town (£750k+) Jun 1999/ Preston North End (£750k) Aug 2001
United: (L) 8 Mar 2006, (£250k) 1/5 Jun 2006 to 4/5 Jul 2008
Debut: 18 Apr 2006 United 1 Leeds United 1
Last game: 29 Dec 2007 United 0 Crystal Palace 1
Southampton (L) 28 Mar 2008
Huddersfield Town (free) Jul 2008

Chris Lucketti made his FL debut with Rochdale on 22 April 1989 at home to Hartlepool United as a seventeen year old. It was his only senior appearance for the club before he moved to Stockport County but his next move, to Bury, saw him make 235 FL appearances. He also had a long spell with Preston North End where he made over 200 senior appearances.

When he joined United on loan towards the end of United's promotion campaign, rejoining Neil Warnock who had been his manager at Bury, he had amassed 571 FL appearances. He was signed as cover for the central defenders but was not called upon until promotion had been secured. His move was made permanent during the close season.

An injury delayed Chris' preparations for the 2006–07 season and with just one Carling Cup appearance by January he was offered a loan move. He decided to stay and in late January he made his Premier League debut at the age of thirty-five. He used his experience and anticipation to give a good account of himself but his brief run in the side was brought to an end by an injury at Liverpool although he appeared briefly afterwards. Acting on occasions as the captain and aged 35 he became United's oldest player to be captain for the first time.

2007–08 again found Chris on the fringe of the first team although he did score his first goal for the club at MK Dons in the League Cup. Towards the end of the season he moved on loan to Southampton and ended the campaign having totalled 579(13) League appearances. In July 2008 he was granted a free transfer, joining Huddersfield on a two year contract.

Appearances:		Apps	Gls
	Lge	14 (3)	0
	LC	3 (1)	1
	Total	17 (4)	1

LUDLAM Steven (Steve) John

IF/WH 1975–77 5' 6" 9st 11
b. Chesterfield 18 October 1955

Sheffield Throstles
United: 26 Apr 1971, pro Jan 1973 to 18 May 1977
Debut: 6 Dec 1975 United 1 Tottenham Hotspur 2
Last game: 3 May 1977 United 1 Millwall 1
Carlisle United (£16.2k) May 1977/ Chester C (£50k) Jul 1980/ Blackpool trial/ Tranmere Rovers trial/ FC Ilves (Finland) player-coach cs 1983–1984

Steve Ludlam made his FL debut as a First Division player in United's disastrous 1975–76 relegation season. He had a run of appearances at the start of the following season. Industrious and sharp in the tackle, he lacked height, pace and power and played only occasionally. He moved on to Carlisle United where he played regularly for three season and then played for a similar period with Chester before Achillies' tendon problems all but ended his playing career. He had made a total of 216(9) FL appearances.

After a spell in Finland he became a financial consultant and subsequently a licensee in Sheffield. His son Craig played for Wednesday's reserve team and Ryan for United's reserves.

Appearances:		Apps	Gls
	FL	26 (1)	1
	FAC	1 (1)	0
	LC	1	0
	ASC	3	0
	CC	2	0
	Total	33 (2)	1

LUKE George Baron

IL/CF 1954–55 5' 8" 10st 13
b. Lanchester 20 October 1932
d. Willington 10 December 2001

Esh Winning/ Ushaw Moor
United: (£50) 12/14 Jan 1952 to 16/26 May 1956
Debut: 16 Jan 1954 United 1 Chelsea 3
Last game: 19 Mar 1955 Tottenham Hotspur 5 United 0
Scunthorpe United May 1956/ Kings Lynn Jul 1957

Although George Luke was over four years at Bramall Lane, he played only a few first team games. Fast and direct, he was a regular in the reserve team but never looked good enough for regular first team football. After moving to Scunthorpe United he scored 6 goals in 18 games but after one season he moved into non-League football. He returned to the north-east working at the Royal Ordnance factory at Birtley. He lived in Esh Winning but died in a nursing home at Willington.

Appearances:		Apps	Gls
	FL	7	0
	CC	1	0
	Total	8	0

McALISTER Thomas (Tom) Gerald

G 1972–75 6' 0½" 11st 1 to 11st 7
b. Clydebank 10 December 1952

YMCA, Campsie Black Watch
United: app 22/25 Nov 1969, pro 13 May 1970 to 4 Mar 1976
Debuts: 2 Feb 1972 Israel XI 0 United 0 (Fr)
15 Apr 1972 Ipswich Town 0 United 0
Last game: 26 Dec 1975 United 1 Middlesbrough 1
Rotherham United (L) Jan, (£15k) Mar 1976/ Blackpool (£50k) Jul 1979/ Swindon Town May 1980/ Bristol Rovers (L) Feb 1981/ West Ham United May 1981 to cs 1989/ Colchester United (L) Feb 1989/ Harrow Borough player-mgr to Sep 1990

Tom McAlister had trials with Liverpool and Arsenal and was expected to sign for St Johnstone but came further south and joined United just before his seventeenth birthday. Alan Hodgkinson's career in the United goal was drawing to a close but, when Alan lost his place in January 1971, new signing John Hope took over. Hope occupied the goalkeeping spot for just over a year before a loss of confidence gave Tom his chance which he took impressively and, from his FL debut in April 1972 to October 1973, when he broke his leg in a collision with Manchester City's Rodney Marsh, he was ever-present.

Jim Brown had been signed and another fracture, in a pre-season friendly in 1974 at Altrincham, led to Tom losing his confidence and motivation. After nearly two years, during which he had played just a handful of first team games and United had rejected an offer of £35k from Wednesday, he moved to Millmoor. He went on loan to put him 'in the shop window' but United accepted an offer from Rotherham and he played 159 FL games for the Millers before moving on. He eventually signed for West Ham where, as a deputy to Phil Parkes, he made only 85 FL appearances in eight seasons, ending his career with 357 FL appearances.

After a time in non-League football, Tom became a cab driver.

Appearances:		Apps	Gls
	FL	63	0
	FAC	2	0
	LC	6	0
	TX	4	0
	CC	2	0
	WC	3	0
	Total	80	0

McALLE John Edward

CD 1981 6' 0" 11st 3
b. Liverpool 31 January 1950

Wolverhampton Wanderers app Jul 1965, pro Feb 1967
United: (£10k,tribunal) 1/20 Aug 1981 to 31 Mar 1982
Debut: 29 Aug 1981 United 2 Hereford United 2
Last games: 5 Dec 1981 United 2 Aldershot 0
29 Dec 1981 Poole Town 1 United 0 (Fr)
Derby County (L) 11 Feb 1982, transfer 1 Apr 1982/ Harrison's FC Apr 1984

John made his FL debut with Wolves on 29 April 1968 at home to Chelsea, and he went on to make over 400 FL appearances for the club and over 500 in total. He was on the winning side in the 1974 League Cup final and in the 1971 Texaco Cup final and was on the losing side to Spurs in the 1972 UEFA Cup final.

John was one of Ian Porterfield's first signings as United played their first ever season in Division Four. He played in United's first 24 competitive fixtures but then lost his place and soon moved, on loan, to Derby County, the move being made permanent two months later. He spent two seasons with Derby but left after a fall out with new manager Peter Taylor and moved into non-League football, having totalled 463(19) FL appearances.

After retiring from the game John was a groundsman and later set up a landscape gardening business.

Appearances:		Apps	Gls
	FL	18	0
	FAC	2	0
	LC	4	0
	Total	24	0

McCABE Arthur

OL 1893–94
b. Sheffield JAS 1871

Heeley and Rotherham Town 1891–92
United: 30 Jul 1892 to cs 1895
Debut: 30 Jan 1893 United 1 Stockton 3 (NL)
Last game: 31 Jan 1894 Lincoln City 1 United 0 (Fr)
Rotherham Town 27 Jul 1895/ Man C Jan 1896/ Ilkeston Town Jul 1896 to 1897

Arthur McCabe played as an inside forward as well as a winger but made only one competitive first team appearance for United in a period of three seasons before moving to Rotherham Town. He may have played for the Rotherham club against United in September 1894 though he was still appearing for the Strollers—the United reserve team—in April 1895.

He made his FL debut with Town on 7 September 1895 at home to Port Vale and in January, after 18 FL appearances, he moved to Manchester City where he played just one more FL game.

Appearances:		Apps	Gls
	NL	1	0
	Total	1	0

McCALL Andrew Stuart Murray

MF 2002–04 5' 7" 12st 0
b. Leeds 10 June 1964

Bradford City from app Jun 1982/ Everton (£850k) Jun 1988/ Glasgow Rangers (£1.2m) Aug 1991 Bradford City (free) Jun 1998
United: (free) 2 Jul 2002 to (as a player) cs 2006
Debuts: 22 Jul 2002 Bodmin 0 United 8 (Fr)
13 Aug 2002 United 1 Portsmouth 1 (sub)
24 Aug 2002 Burnley 0 United 1
Last games: 9 May 2004 Preston North End 3 United 3
21 Sep 2004 Wrexham 2 United 3 (LC)
First team coach Jul 2003/ Asst mgr Sep 2004 to 21 May 2007
Bradford City mgr May 2007

Stuart made his FL debut with Bradford City on 28 August 1982 at home to Reading. He went on to make nearly 250 FL appearances before joining Everton, where he played over 100 games and gained the first of his forty Scottish caps. After spending seven seasons with Rangers, during which time he won many Scottish League and Cup honours, he returned to Bradford City and captained them to promotion to the Premiership. After two seasons in the top Division, City were relegated and after one further season Stuart moved to Bramall Lane.

Neil Warnock signed Stuart, who was thirty eight, as a player coach but during his first two seasons at the Lane he played regularly and was a vastly influential figure. His energetic yet calm displays belied his age as he used his wide experience as a midfield player in front of the back four, holding and distributing the ball with 'simple' passes that brought the best out of the players around him. He was just over a month short of his 40th birthday when he made his final League appearance and over 40 when he played his final first team game.

During his career he totalled 763 Scottish and English League appearances and his goal against Preston North End in November 2003 made him the oldest player to score a League goal for United.

Whilst playing he was also in charge of the reserve side and after Kevin Blackwell's departure, he took on the role of first team coach. Later, when David Kelly moved to Preston North End, Stuart took over his role as assistant manager. When Neil Warnock left Bramall Lane Stuart left the Lane to become Bradford City's manager.

Appearances:		Apps	Gls
	FL	69 (2)	2
	PO	0 (1)	0
	FAC	9	0
	LC	8 (1)	0
	Total	86 (4)	2

McCARTHY Michael (Mick)

G 1934 5' 10"
b. Kunturk, County Cork 22 December 1913 (or c1910)
d. May 1973

Shamrock Rovers Nov 1931
United: 26/27 Jul 1934 to 4 May 1935
Debut: 27 Aug 1934 Bradford City 2 United 5
Last game: 15 Dec 1934 Nottingham Forest 2 United 1
Brideville Aug 1935

An Irish junior international, Mick McCarthy was awarded a full cap in 1932 when he played against Holland. He joined United in 1934, Shamrock Rovers agreeing to pay United's expenses if the receipts of a match between the clubs exceeded £150. At the start of the 1934–35 season, United's first choice keeper, Jack Smith, was out of action with a wrist problem and both Mick and Harry Wilkes were given their opportunity but in December, manager Davison signed Welsh international Roy John and Mick's brief FL career came to an end.

Appearances:		Apps	Gls
	FL	9	0
	Total	9	0

McCLELLAND Matthew L (see McLelland)

McCORMICK James

RH/CH 1905–07, 1910 5' 11" 11st 6 to 13st 4
b. Rotherham 28 April 1883
d. Canada January 1935

Thornhill United (Rotherham)/ Attercliffe
United: 4 Dec 1903 to cs 1907
Debut: 9 Sep 1905 United 3 Woolwich Arsenal 1
Last game: 29 Mar 1907 Blackburn Rovers 1 United 1
Plymouth Argyle cs 1907
United: Jun 21 1910 to Dec 1910
Only game: 3 Sep 1910 United 1 Sunderland 2
Plymouth Dec 1910 to cs 1920/ WW1 guest: Rotherham County 1918–19 / – / Ladysmith FC (Vancouver, Canada 1924)

James McCormick, a steel fitter by trade, had to wait nearly two years after joining United before making his FL debut, not surprisingly given that he was competing with Ernest Needham, Bernard Wilkinson, Walter Wilkinson and Harry Johnson for a place in the half-back line. Seventeen of his appearances came in the 1905–06 season and he played in the final thirteen FL games, the last two at right back. After playing in the first four games of the following season, once at centre forward, he lost his place and played just once more before moving to Southern League Plymouth Argyle.

He was a regular in their side before making a brief return to Bramall Lane, making just one appearance before moving back to Plymouth where he again played regularly until the First World War. A sergeant in the army, he was reported killed in action but was actually wounded and a prisoner of war in Germany. He played again for Plymouth in 1919–20, appearing in the club's last Southern League game before their election to the Football League.

Appearances:		Apps	Gls
	FL	23	1
	Total	23	1

McCORMICK James

OR 1956–57
b. Rotherham 1 April 1937

Rotherham local football
United: 9 Oct 1956 to 30 Jun 1957
Debut: 8 Dec 1956 United 2 Middlesbrough 1
Last game: 12 Feb 1957 Royal Signals Reg 1 United XI 4 (Fr at Lincoln)
Rotherham United Jun 1957

With a good record as a goal scorer in local football, James McCormick was signed by Joe Mercer and made his first team debut after just five games with the reserves but this was because of serious injury problems with first team players rather than the obvious talent of the new player. As it turned out, he was 'out of his depth' and he failed to make the first team when he moved to Millmoor.

Appearances:		Apps	Gls
	FL	1	0
	Total	1	0

McCOURT James (Jim)

CH 1921–24 6' 1" 13st 2
b. Bellshill (Glasgow) 23 October 1901

Army/ Bedlay Jun/ Third Lanark c1919
United: (£2,350) 22/23 Feb 1921 to 15 Aug 1924
Debut: 5 Mar 1921 Derby County 1 United 1
Last game: 12 Apr 1924 United 0 Birmingham 2
Manchester City (£1,000) Aug 1924/ Dykehead Oct 1925

United paid a very large fee to bring Jimmy McCourt to the Lane but there were immediate problems. He came on condition that United would find him a teaching post in a local school and missed his first match insisting that he had a cold. He settled down however and missed just three games in the 1921–22 season, many thinking that he would be capped. A clever attacking centre half with good footwork and passing, he would have been a much better player if he had been a full timer. He could also be moody and was let down by his lack of pace and his heading was poor when challenged.

After thirteen games of the following campaign, he lost his place, in part perhaps, through illness and returned to Scotland for 'a change of air' but, when he returned, Jimmy Waugh had taken the position and was playing with confidence.

Jimmy played just three more times before moving to Manchester City but, after one season and four games, he returned to Scotland joining the Third Division club, Dykehead.

Appearances:		Apps	Gls
	FL	62	4
	FAC	1	0
	CC	3	0
	Total	66	4

McDERMOTT John or Joseph?

IL/OR 1895–96
Perhaps Joseph McDermott b. Burnley OND 1876

Rossendale May 1895
United: 6/7 Dec 1895 to cs 1896
Debut: 21 Dec 1895 United 1 Derby County 1
Last game: 4 Feb 1896 Burnley 5 United 0
Tottenham Hotspur Sep 1896?

Little is known about this forward. He was registered by the FL as John McDermott but he could be the Joseph McDermott, born in Burnley in 1876. The United forward may also be the forward who played in two friendly matches for Spurs in September 1896.

Appearances:		Apps	Gls
	FL	3	0
	Total	3	0

McFADZEAN Kyle John

CD 2005 6' 1" 13st 4
b. Sheffield 20 February 1987

United: from jnr 7 Jul 2004 to 18 May 2007
Debut: 26 Jul 2005 Matlock T 1 United XI 2 (Fr)
Last game: 20 Sep 2005 Shrewsbury Town 0 United 0 (sub LC)
Alfreton Town Jun 2007

Kyle McFadzean was unable to make the breakthrough into United's first team, his one competitive appearance being in the League Cup where he was a 90 minute sub but played for the 30 minutes of extra time.

Appearances:		Apps	Gls
	LC	0 (1)	0
	Total	0 (1)	0

McGEADY John Thomas

OR 1975–76 5' 6" 10st 0
b. Glasgow 17 April 1958

St Francis Boys F C/ Third Lanark
United: app 15/17 Jun 1974, pro 26/28 Jan 1976 to 6 Apr 1978
Debuts: 14 Oct 1975 United 1 Sheffield Wednesday 2 (CC)
26 Dec 1975 United 1 Middlesbrough 1
Last games: 24 Aug 1976 United 2 Wolverhampton Wanderers 2
13 Nov 1976 Blackpool 1 United 0 (sub)
California Lasers (USA) (£500) 1978/ Newport County Oct 1978

A fast, tricky winger, John McGeady had a long history of knee injuries. They had begun before his FL debut in the 1975–76 relegation season but a major blow came in March when he was tackled by Manchester City's Willie Donachie and fractured his knee-cap. He played in the first few games of the following season but lost his place and, after a few substitute appearances, his career was all but over. After a spell in the USA he had a trial with Newport County but, after two games, he was released. He returned to Glasgow and became a schoolteacher. His son, Aiden, plays for Celtic and is an Irish international.

Appearances:		Apps	Gls
	FL	13 (3)	0
	ASC	2 (1)	0
	CC	3 (1)	0
	Total	18 (5)	0

McGEENEY Patrick (Paddy) Michael

D 1984–87 5' 10" 11st 0
b. Sheffield 31 October 1966

United: from app 6 Jun 1983, pro 31 Oct 1984 to 30 Jun 1987
Debuts: 2 May 1984 Hull City 1 United 0 (AMC)
23 Mar 1985 United 2 Leeds United 1
Last games: 5 Apr 1986 Hull C 0 United 0
15 Sep 1987 Sheffield Wed 3 United 1 (BM sub)
Rochdale (L) Nov 1986
Chesterfield Aug 1987/ Australian football Mar 1989/ Gainsborough Trinity Oct 1989/ Matlock Town Aug 1991/ Redmires 1992–93

Paddy McGeeney played in the Sheffield Boys championship team with Brian Smith and they both made their debuts with Lee Walshaw and Jeff Eckhardt at Hull in the Associate Member's Cup but Paddy failed to realise his potential. He had been due to make his FL debut in February but the match was postponed when a war-time unexploded bomb was discovered in nearby Lancing Road. He had a run in the side towards the end of the 1984–85 season and again in October but couldn't win a permanent place and, after a loan spell with Rochdale (3 FL app), he was given a free transfer.

He joined Chesterfield and made a positive impression, making over 50 first team appearances, before injury curtailed his career, having played 63(5) FL games. He moved into non-League football before running a pub and restaurant in Sheffield.

Appearances:		Apps	Gls
	FL	15 (1)	0
	LC	1	0
	FMC	2	0
	AMC	1	0
	Total	19 (1)	0

McGHIE Joseph (Joe)

CH 1908 5' 7½" 11st 7
b. Kilbirnie (Ayrshire) 22 March 1884
d. Largs (Ayrshire) 8 September 1976

Vale of Glengarnock Strollers 1905/ Sunderland May 1906
United: (£250) 4/5 Apr 1908 to Aug 1909
Debut: 12 Sep 1908 Sunderland 3 United 1
Last game: 7 Nov 1908 Notts County 3 United 1
Brighton & Hove Albion Aug 1909/ Stalybridge Celtic Jun 1913

Joe McGhie spent only part of a season with Vale of Glengarnock and won Scottish Junior International honours but that was sufficient to bring him to the attention of several leading clubs of the day, both north and south of the border. Sunderland were successful and he made his FL debut at home to Aston Villa on 8 September 1906.

Small but stocky, he played fairly regularly at centre half for two seasons with Sunderland before moving to United. It appeared to be a strange move as he seemed unlikely to take the centre half position from Bernard Wilkinson and so it proved and McGhie played in only six FL games and one friendly for the Blades, never being on the winning side. After just one season he moved to Brighton & Hove Albion where he had four very successful seasons, helping the club to the Southern League championship in 1910. In May 1913 he refused the terms offered him and moved to Stalybridge Celtic. On his retirement, he returned to Ayrshire where he lived till his death at the age of 92.

Appearances:		Apps	Gls
	FL	6	0
	Total	6	0

McGOVERN Jon-Paul

MF 2002 5' 9" 9st 6
b. Glasgow 3 October 1980

Heart of Midlothian jnrs/ Glasgow Celtic Jun 2000
United: trial 6 Aug, (L) 13 Aug 2002 to 15 Jan 2003
Debuts: 6 Aug 2002 Stocksbridge Steels 0 United XI 7 (Fr)
13 Aug 2002 United 1 Portsmouth 1 (sub)
17 Aug 2002 United 1 Walsall 1
Last games: 2 Nov 2002 Nottingham Forest 3 United 0
23 Nov 2002 Bradford City 0 United 5 (sub)
Livingston Jul 2003/ Sheffield Wednesday (free) May 2004/ Milton Keynes Dons (free) Jul 2006/ Swindon Town Aug 2007

Jon-Paul McGovern failed to make the first team with Celtic and joined United for a trial, which became a long term loan deal in August 2002. After a debut as a substitute, he became a regular member of the side, playing as an attacking right side midfielder. He scored on his full debut and showed a direct approach, possessing a good shot and the ability to cross the ball. However he lost some of his initial impetus and by November he was replaced by the previously out-of-favour Peter Ndlovu and he returned to Parkhead.

He subsequently joined Livingstone where he won a Scottish League Cup winner's medal. In 2004 he moved back to Sheffield and was instrumental and ever-present in Wednesday's promotion season. Injuries meant he made few appearances in 2005–06 but there followed successful seasons with MK Dons and Swindon and by the summer of 2008 he had made 136(20) FL appearances.

Appearances:		Apps	Gls
	FL	11 (4)	1
	FAC	1	1
	LC	2	1
	Total	14 (4)	3

McGRATH Paul

CD 1997 6' 2" 14st 0
b. Ealing 4 December 1959

St Patrick's Athletic (Dublin)/ Manchester United (£30k) Apr 1982/ Aston Villa (£400k) Aug 1989/ Derby County (£100k+) Oct 1996
United: (free)17/18 Jul 1997 one month trial extended to cs 1998
Debuts: 24 Jul 1997 Tistedalen (Norway) 1 United 4 (Fr)
10 Aug 1997 United 2 Sunderland 0
Last game: 9 Nov 1997 Ipswich Town 2 United 2
Retired 17 Apr 1998

Paul McGrath was born in Ealing but moved with his family to Ireland when he was a youngster. He was 22 years old when he began his professional career with Manchester United, making his FL debut on 13 November 1982 at home to Spurs. He gained an FA Cup winners' medal in 1985 but his knee problems began soon after. Despite this he moved to Aston Villa and, though unable to cope with the rigours of full time training, he became an outstanding central defender, being voted PFA 'Player of the Year' in 1993 and gaining League Cup winners' medals in 1994 and 1996. He won a total of 83 Republic of Ireland caps playing in both the 1990 and 1994 World Cup Finals. He signed for Derby County at the age of 36 and was instrumental in keeping the Rams up in their first Premiership season.

Paul was brought to United by acting manager Nigel Spackman, initially on trial and then on a one month contract, later extended until the end of the season. Despite his long-standing knee problems, Paul gave some masterful displays in the centre of the defence. Powerfully built, cool under pressure, he read the game superbly. He could move quickly but he rarely needed to, so impressive was his anticipation, and he was sorely missed when he finally had to call it a day, though the announcement of his retirement was delayed until April. He had played a total of 442(10) League games.

Paul returned to Ireland, assisting his old colleague, Frank Stapleton, in player development in Waterford but sadly, this magnificent player continued to struggle with the off-field problems which had been with him for the better part of his life.

Appearances:		Apps	Gls
	FL	12	0
	LC	2	0
	Total	14	0

McGUIRE James

RH/LH/CH 1906–12 5' 7" 10st 10
b. Wallsend 10 December 1883

North Shields Athletic amat/ Jarrow/ Barnsley cs 1903 North Shields Athletic cs 1905
United: 9 May 1906 to cs 1913
Debuts: 1 Oct 1906 Wednesday 3 United 0 (CM)
6 Oct 1906 Sunderland 1 United 2
Last game: 23 Nov 1912 Middlesbrough 4 United 1
North Shields Athletic Oct 1913

James McGuire, a plater in the ship building industry by trade, made his FL debut with Barnsley on 27 February 1904 at Woolwich Arsenal and after 34 FL games returned to the North East in 1905.

He joined United in 1906, Barnsley receiving a late and small fee. A small conscientious, hard working player who had captained the North Shields club, McGuire made his United debut in fortuitous circumstances. United were due to play at Sunderland and Jimmy travelled with the team so that he could have a short break back in the north east but Billy Wilkinson was declared unfit, James played and held his place in the team. He made 28 appearances in his first season but failed to keep his place thereafter and, in his following six seasons, only in 1910–11 did he reach double figures again.

Appearances:		Apps	Gls
	FL	61	1
	FAC	2	0
	ABD	1	0
	Total	64	1

McHALE Raymond (Ray)

MF 1982–84 5' 8" 12st 4
b. Sheffield 12 August 1950

Hillsborough B C/ Huddersfield Town amat/ Chesterfield amat, pro Aug 1970/ Halifax Town (£3000 + player ex) Oct 1974/ Swindon Town Sep 1975/ Brighton & Hove Albion (£100k) May 1980/ Barnsley (£60k) Mar 1981
United: (£20k/£30k) 5 Aug 1982 to 15 Jan 1985
Debuts: 7 Aug 1982 Falkirk 2 United 3 (Fr)
14 Aug 1982 United 1 Grimsby Town 3 (FLT)
28 Aug 1982 Portsmouth 4 United 1
Last game: 10 Nov 1984 United 1 Charlton Athletic 1
Bury (L) Feb 1983, Blackpool (L) Aug 1983
Swansea City Jan 1985/ Rochdale Aug 1986/ Scarborough Dec 1986/ Goole Town Feb 1988/ Northwich Victoria cs 1988/ Guiseley player mgr Oct 1988/ Scarborough asst mgr Jan 1989, mgr Nov 1989 to Mar 1993/ Guisely mgr May 1993/ Scarborough mgr Dec 1994 to Mar 1996, asst mgr Mar 1996, youth coach Sep 2001/ Oldham Athletic chief scout Nov 2001 to Feb 2002

Ray McHale, an apprentice plasterer, did not turn professional until the age of 20, signing for Chesterfield. He made his FL debut on 25 September 1971 at Bournemouth. He established a reputation as an industrious midfield player with an eye for goal with Swindon and had a few games in the top flight during his one season with Brighton.

He was signed by Ian Porterfield from Barnsley at the age of thirty two. The Blades were newly promoted from the old Division Four but McHale had a poor season, lacking commitment and went out on loan to Bury. Porterfield gave him another chance at the start of the 1983–84 season and he missed just four competitive games and was a tireless worker in midfield, influential in helping United gain promotion. He lost

his place in November 1984 however and was transferred to Swansea City.

After a spell at Rochdale he moved to Scarborough in December 1986 beginning a long though not continuous association with the Yorkshire club which finally ended in November 2000. At Seamer Road, he helped the club gain Football League status in 1987 and scored in their first ever FL game. He had two lengthy spells as manager, two spells as assistant manager and a period as youth coach.

Ray played in all four Divisions of the FL, making 589(10) appearances and scoring 88 goals.

Appearances:		Apps	Gls
	FL	66 (1)	2
	FAC	7	0
	LC	11 (1)	1
	AMC	6	0
	Total	90 (2)	3

McINTYRE Peter

CH/LH 1901 5' 9" 12st
b. Glenbuck, Muirkirk (Ayrshire) November 1875
d. Lanark Aug 1938

Preston North End/ Glasgow Rangers May 1895 to cs 1896 / – / Abercorn Mar 1897/ Wigan County Nov 1897/ Preston North End cs 1898–cs1901
United: (£200) 1 May 1901 to cs 1902
Debut: 16 Sep 1901 Aston Villa 1 United 2
Last game: 2 Nov 1901 Wednesday 1 United 0
Hamilton Academicals (£50) 4 Sep 1902/ Portsmouth Nov 1902/ Hamilton A 1903

Peter McIntyre made his FL debut with Preston North End, at home to Sunderland, on 3 September 1898 but he had been on Preston's books three years earlier and had returned to Scotland to gain experience. Originally a winger, he was converted to a centre half back and played regularly for Preston, joining United when Preston were relegated.

His move to the Lane was not a success and he played few games, all towards the start of the 1901–02 season. After a brief spell in Scotland he joined Southern League Portsmouth but his stay lasted less than a season.

Appearances:		Apps	Gls
	FL	3	0
	Total	3	0

McKAY Kenneth (Kenny)

also played as **'KERR'**

IR 1897–98 5' 5½" 10st 11
b. Larkhall, Lanarkshire 1877

Hamilton area
United: 4/5 Jan 1897 to May 1898
Debuts: 4 Jan 1897 United 2 Corinthians 2 (Fr) playing as 'Kerr'
20 Mar 1897 Bury 0 United 1
Last games: 26 Mar 1898 West Bromwich Albion 2 United 0
30 Apr 1898 Liverpool 1 United 0 (Fr)
Tottenham Hotspur May 1898/ Thames Ironworks May 1899/ Wishaw United Sep 1900/ Fulham Jan 1901 to Jun 1902/ Royal Albert Oct 1902

Kenny McKay's name was given as 'Kerr' when he played his first game for United on trial and the Independent, two days later, reported that he was McKie of Hamilton. A small, clever player, he kept the ball on the ground and although he made only one further first team appearance that season, he played in 25 of the 30 FL games in 1897–98 and was an integral part of United's First Division championship team. It was a blow when he moved, with Bob Cain, to Southern League Tottenham Hotspur and it was similarly surprising when, after a successful season, he moved again. After one more season he returned briefly to Scotland before joining Fulham and helping them to win the Southern League Division Two title in 1902.

Appearances:		Apps	Gls
	FL	26	5
	FAC	2	0
	Total	28	5

McKEE Stephen (Steve)

OL 1977–78 5' 9" 10st 4
b. Belfast 15 April 1956

Linfield cs 1974
United: (£25k) 1 Dec 1976 to 31 Jul 1979
Debut: 22 Jan 1977 United 0 Luton Town 3
Last games: 7 May 1977 United 1 Plymouth Argyle 0
14 May 1977 Bristol Rovers 3 United 1 (sub)
19 May 1977 United 0 Rotherham United 1 (CC)
6 Aug 1977 Oldham Athletic 2 United 3 (sub ASC)
10 Apr 1978 Worksop Town XI 0 United 0 (BM)
Linfield 31 Jul 1979/ Ballymena Utd 1986–87/ Bangor cs 1987 to cs1990

Steve McKee and Peter Dornan were both signed by United manager Jimmy Sirrel from Linfield at the beginning of December 1976. Dornan was a talented player who quickly discovered that he was not cut out for the life of a professional footballer and returned to Ireland. McKee, on the other hand, was just not good enough, lacking power and determination and never looked as if he could achieve a regular first team place.

He returned to Ireland and for a time was involved in coaching after he had finished playing. Subsequently he became a printer's sales representative near Belfast.

Appearances:		Apps	Gls
	FL	4 (3)	0
	FAC	1	0
	ASC	0 (1)	0
	CC	1	0
	Total	6 (4)	0

MACKENZIE Ian Stanley

CD/LH 1969–74 6' 0" 10st 10 to 11st 2
b. Rotherham 27 September 1950

United: from 1966 jnr, pro 24/29 Jun 1968 to 16/30 May 1975
Debuts: 24 Jan 1969 Barnsley 2 United 2 (CC)
15 Oct 1969 Leicester City 2 United 0 (LC)
31 Mar 1970 United 3 Millwall 1
Last games: 2 May 1973 United 3 Tottenham Hotspur 2
8 Oct 1973 West Bromwich Albion 2 United 1 (LC)
17 Aug 1974 United 1 QPR 1 (sub)
29 Oct 1974 United 0 Rotherham United 0 (CC)
(L) Southend United 13 Mar–13 Apr 1975/ trial South Africa Apr-May 1975?
Mansfield Town 30 May 1975

A defensive mid-fielder or centre half, Ian Mackenzie was a reliable full time professional with United for seven seasons. Nearly all his first team appearances came between December 1971 and May 1973, when he competed with John Flynn for the number 4 shirt to play alongside Eddie Colquhoun at the heart of the United defence. Flynn was generally regarded as the number one choice as he was quicker and more powerful, particularly in the air.

Ian played only three competitive games for United in his final two seasons and six FL appearances on loan with Southend before his three seasons at Mansfield where his 69(1) FL games included winning the Third Division Championship in 1977. He was later a licensee in Peterborough.

Appearances:		Apps	Gls
	FL	43 (2)	1
	FAC	1	1
	LC	2 (1)	0
	TEX	0 (1)	0
	CC	3	0
	WC	3	1
	ABD	1	0
	Total	53 (4)	3

McLAFFERTY Maurice

LB 1951–52 5' 10" 11st 7
b. Baillieston (Glasgow) 7 August 1922
d. Worthing January 1999

Glasgow Celtic/ Glenavon Aug 1947/ St Mirren cs 1950
United: (free) 7/10 Aug 1951 (trial), 4 Sep 1951 to 23 Jun 1952
Debut: 24 Nov 1951 United 2 Doncaster Rovers 1
Last game: 3 May 1952 United 1 Queens Park Rangers 2
Brighton & Hove Albion (£1000) Jun 1952/ Dartford Aug 1954/ Hastings United/ Newhaven player coach

After being stationed in Ireland with the RAF, Maurice McLafferty played for Glenavon and, in March 1949, for the Irish League against the League of Ireland and then played in the Scottish First Division for St Mirren.

Maurice joined United after a month's trial but he lacked pace and was awkwardly one footed and he moved, after just one season, to Brighton. It was later reported that a Brighton director had read about him in the Green'Un and that no one from the Sussex club had seen him play. However he did play 22 first team games in that season for Brighton but then faded from the scene, moving to Southern League Dartford. He later captained Hastings United and was player coach at Newhaven.

In the 1960s he returned to Brighton as a fund-raiser and was steward at the Champion House Club in Southwick until he retired.

Appearances:		Apps	Gls
	FL	18	0
	FAC	1	0
	Total	19	0

McLAREN Andrew (Andy) (Torrance?)

IR 1949–50 5' 7" 10st 7
b. Larkhall 24 January 1922
d. Chorley 16 December 1996

Larkhall Thistle c.Jan 1938/ Preston North End amat Jul 1938, pro Feb 1939
WW2 guest: Carlisle United(1939–40,1 app), Royal Albert, Hamilton Academicals, Liverpool, Bristol City, Blackburn Rovers
Burnley Dec 1948
United: (£12k) 2/3 Mar 1949 to 8 Feb 1951
Debut: 5 Mar 1949 Manchester City 1 United 0
Last games: 7 Oct 1950 United 1 Notts County 2
15 Nov 1950 Western Command 0 United XI 1
(Fr at Wrexham)
Barrow (£1800) 10 Feb 1951/ Bradford PA Oct 1954/ Southport Jun 1955/ Rochdale Nov 1955/ Fleetwood May 1957

A Scottish schoolboy international, Andy joined Preston North End's ground staff before the Second War and he and Tom Finney both made their first team debuts for Preston in the 1940–41season and played in the War Cup Final of that season defeating Arsenal. McLaren, though rather small had a real eye for goal and scored all six goals in a victory against Liverpool. He then spent three years with the RAF in Egypt and didn't make his FL debut until 28 December 1946 at Leeds. He soon formed a fine right wing partnership with Tom Finney and went on to win four Scottish caps. In 1947–48 he was Preston's leading scorer but, after an injury early in the following season, he was transferred to Burnley where he made just four appearances.

Signed by Teddy Davison for United, he went straight into the first team who were involved in a relegation battle. A small, neat, combination player with a good shot, he was given permission to live in Preston. Sadly, his addition to the team brought only modest reward and United were relegated along with his old club Preston, on the final day of the season. Early in the new season, he suffered a broken leg at Chesterfield and was out of the team for six months and though he returned, he never rediscovered with United, the form of his best years.

He moved to Barrow where the slower pace of Third Division football was more to his liking and he made 155 FL appearances, scoring 52 goals and eventually recorded 324 FL appearances and 106 goals. Later, Andy worked for Leyland Motors and scouted for Bury.

Appearances:		Apps	Gls
	FL	31	4
	CC	3	0
	Total	34	4

McLEARY Alan Terry

CD 1992 6' 1" 11st 12
b. Lambeth 6 October 1964

Millwall from app Oct 1981
United: (L) 23 Jul 1992 to 24 Aug 1992
Debuts: 25 Jul 1992 Offerdals IF (Sweden) 0 United 4 (Fr)
15 Aug 1992 United 2 Manchester United 1
Last game: 22 Aug 1992 Queens Park Rangers 3 United 2
Wimbledon (L) Oct 1992/ Charlton Athletic May 1993/ Bristol City Jul 1995/ Millwall Feb 1997, then asst mgr, then joint mgr May 1999 to Sep 2000

Alan McLeary began his career with Millwall, making his FL debut on 4 December 1982 at Lincoln City. He gained two England B caps as well as making U21 and youth appearances and had more than 300 first team appearances to his name when he joined United on loan, although Dave Bassett may have had the idea of a permanent move.

After being involved in the pre-season games, Alan played in United's first ever Premiership game, the 2–1 defeat of Manchester United, but after two more games he returned to Millwall stating that he did not want to stay at the Lane as cover for Gayle and Beesley.

After leaving the Den for Charlton Athletic and then Bristol City he returned and ended his playing career with the Lions, becoming assistant manager and later joint manager with Keith Stevens. He had made a total of 429(21) League appearances. He went on to have various roles with other clubs including assistant manager at Oxford United 2000–01. More recently he became chief scout with Gillingham.

Appearances:		Apps	Gls
	FL	3	0
	Total	3	0

McLELLAND Matthew L (also 'McClelland')

OL 1945

United: 7 May 1945 to cs 1945
Only game: 12 May 1945 Leeds United 4 United 1 (WW2)

A war-time mystery player, registered in the FL records as a United professional on 7 May 1945, the day before the war in Europe ended. He played in this one game as 'McLelland' in the programme but the FL used both ways of spelling in their records—but he does not appear in United's register of new players and no player of this name played for other FL clubs that season or later.

Appearances:		Apps	Gls
	WW2	1	0
	Total	1	0

McLEOD Izale (Izzie) Michael

Striker 2004 6' 0" 11st 2
b. Perry Bar, Birmingham 15 October 1984

Derby County from trainee Feb 2003
United: (L) 12 Mar 2004 to cs 2004
Debut: 13 Mar 2004 Watford 0 United 2 (sub)
Last game: 9 May 2004 Preston North End 3 United 3

MK Dons (£100k) Aug 2004/ Charlton Athletic (£1.1m) Aug 2007/ Colchester U (L) Feb 2008

Izzie McLeod made his FL debut with Derby County on 28 September 2002 at Ipswich Town, without having made a single start in the reserves, and made 20(9) FL appearances during his first season. A cartilage operation in October 2003 kept him out of action for a while and when Paul Peschisolido joined Derby, part of the deal was that Izzie moved to United on loan for the remainder of the season with the option to make the move permanent.

He produced some lively displays, using his speed but he made the starting line-up only once, in his final appearance.

He subsequently was a regular for MK Dons for three seasons before moving to Championship promotion hopefuls, Charlton. He was used mainly as a substitute and a loan spell with Colchester brought his total of FL appearances to 132(50), having scored 59 goals.

Appearances:		Apps	Gls
	FL	1 (6)	0
	Total	1 (6)	0

McNAB Samuel (Sammy)

OR/OL/IL 1952–54 5' 7" 10st 12
b. Glasgow 20 October 1926
d. Paisley 2 November 1995

Dalry Thistle
United: (£425) 9/11 Jan 1952 to 29 May 1954
Debuts: 5 May 1952 Sheffield Wednesday 1 United 3 (CC)
27 Sep 1952 Hull City 4 United 0
Last game: 26 Apr 1954 United 2 Aston Villa 1
York City (£1000) May 1954/ Cheltenham Town cs1956/ Hamilton Academicals cs1957

Sammy McNab was a clever player with an accurate shot but he was 'light', didn't work hard enough and was easily brushed off the ball. He paid United 10/6 (52½p) per week for his flat, of which it was written 'it was doubtful if any other player would care to go into'. Reported to be 'twenty three', his first two games for United were in the County Cup, both of which United won, giving him a medal on his second appearance but his FL appearances were rare and he was always on the periphery, standing in for injured players.

On moving to York City he soon found himself in a similar position, making only 19 FL appearances, but he did play, and play well, with another former United player, Arthur Bottom, in York's historic 1–1 FA Cup semi-final draw with Newcastle United at Hillsborough in 1955.

After a spell in non-League football he returned to Scotland but injury forced his retirement after just one appearance for the Accies.

Appearances:		Apps	Gls
	FL	11	4
	CC	3	1
	Total	14	5

McNAUGHT Hugh

RB 1906 6' 0" 12st 4
b. c1884

Edinburgh University/ Queens Park/ 1903–04/ Dundee Sep 1904/ Heart of Midlothian May 1905
United: 19 May 1906 to cs 1907
Only game: 8 Sep 1906 Bolton Wanderers 6 United 1
Heart of Midlothian (free) cs 1907 and cs 1910

Hugh's disastrous debut may have been the reason for the letter from his mother asking him to return home and to devote his time to the study of medicine. The dutiful young man, who had also played twice for the reserves, paid £40 to have his contract cancelled and returned north. It is believed that he never played for the Hearts first team before or after his short period with United and should not be confused with the man of the same name who was a Cup winner in 1906. United retained his FL registration until 1911.

Appearances:		Apps	Gls
	FL	1	0
	Total	1	0

McNAUGHT Kenneth (Ken)

CD 1985–86 6' 2" 13st 11
b. Kircaldy 11 November 1955

Everton app to pro May 1972/ Aston Villa (£200k) Aug 1977 West Bromwich Albion (£125k) Aug 1983/ Manchester City (L) Dec 1984 to Mar 1985
United: **(£10k) 5 Jun 1985 to 30 Sep 1986**
Debuts: **30 Jul 1985 Skegness Town 0 United 3 (Fr)**
17 Aug 1985 Stoke City 1 United 3
Last game: **22 Apr 1986 United 3 Leeds United 2**
Retired Sep 1986/ Dunfermline Athletic coach 1986–87/ Swansea City asst mgr1987–88/ Vale of Leven mgr 1988–89

Ken McNaught, who had earlier gained youth and amateur caps for Scotland, made his FL debut with Everton on 11 January 1975 at home to Leicester City. However it was with Aston Villa that he had most success, making over 200 FL appearances and winning League Championship, European Cup and Super Cup winners' medals.

He was brought to Bramall Lane by Ian Porterfield and was one of the few players to live up to his excellent reputation and impress in an extremely disappointing season. A strong, calm player at the heart of the defence, he was good in the air, tackled well and read the game well. Sadly for United, he was forced to retire through injury, having totalled 354(2) League appearances.

He subsequently spent some years in coaching and management before working in the Pro's Shop at Gleneagles golf course and then moved to Australia. Ken's father, Willie, was a Scottish international full back with Raith Rovers.

Appearances:		Apps	Gls
	FL	34	5
	FAC	1	0
	LC	4	1
	FMC	2	0
	Total	41	6

MacPHAIL John

CD 1979–83 6' 0½" 12st 3
b. Dundee 7 December 1955

St Columba's/ Dundee 1972
United: **(L) Dec 1978, (£30k) 14/15 Jan 1979 to 24 Mar 1983**
Debut: **6 Feb 1979 United 1 Fulham 1**
Last game: **28 Dec 1983 Chesterfield 3 United 1**
York City (L) 1/3 Feb, transfer Mar 1983/ Bristol City (£14k) Jul 1986/ Sunderland (£23k) Jul 1987/ Hartlepool United (L) Sep 1990, Dec 1990, player mgr Nov 1993–Sep 1994, player to Mar 1995/ South Tyneside United

John MacPhail began his professional career in Scotland, making his debut for Dundee at Ibrox in April 1976 and he had made 68 League appearances for the Dens Park club when he joined the Blades.

Harry Haslam brought him to the Lane on loan and signed him before giving him a first team debut but all the manager's many transfers in and out were not enough to prevent relegation. In the following two seasons, John missed few games and playing a tough and uncompromising role at the heart of the defence but United continued to decline and dropped into Division Four.

Strong in the air and a good tackler, MacPhail made 26 FL appearances in the Fourth Division championship side but the player and Ian Porterfield, the manager, did not have an easy relationship. John felt that he should have been given more guidance and help at the Lane and a parting became inevitable. Porterfield tried to transfer him to Darlington but he moved to York City, winning a further Division Four championship medal in 1984.

Following a losing Freight Rover Trophy final with Bristol City, he moved to Sunderland, winning a Third Division Championship medal and promotion in 1990 to the top flight though he played just one game in the First Division before losing his place.

He moved to Hartlepool where he helped the club gain promotion to Division Three and he later had a spell there as player manager. After being dismissed as manager he continued to play for a while.

When he finally retired he had made 591(5) FL appearances, scoring 58 goals and had made more than 100 appearances for all but Bristol City of his five English clubs. He played for a time in non-League football and was a partner in a South Shields kitchen installation business and a car salesman in Sunderland.

Appearances:		Apps	Gls
	FL	135	7
	FAC	8	1
	LC	9	0
	ASC	9	1
	AMC	5	0
	CC	3	0
	Total	169	8

McPHERSON Archibald (Archie)

LH 1934–37 5' 8½" 11st 0 to 11st 13
b. Alva, nr. Stirling 10 February 1910
d. 1969

Alva Albion Rovers/ Bathgate/ Rangers Mar 1928 Liverpool (£2,000) Nov 1929
United: **(£1,875) 20 Dec 1934 to 12 Jun 1937**
Debut: **22 Dec 1934 United 1 Brentford 2**
Last games: **2 Jan 1937 Newcastle United 4 United 0**
4 Feb 1937 United 1 Wolverhampton Wanderers 2 (FAC)
Falkirk (£350) 12/14 Jun 1937/ East Fife Dec 1938/ Dundee United Aug 1939 / – / Alloa Athletic mgr 1959–69 ?

Archie McPherson was an inside left who made his Scottish League debut with Rangers on 24 August 1929 at St Johnstone although he had made an appearance in a minor cup competition during the previous season. After just six League appearances, he signed for Liverpool and made his FL debut on 23 November 1929 at home to Leeds United. For the next three seasons, he missed very few games, being an ever-present in 1930–31 but he played less frequently in his final season at Anfield when he had a few games at left half.

Signed by Teddy Davison to play at left half, he was a regular for two seasons and played in the 1936 FA Cup Final. A constructive attacking wing half, his passing was excellent but he lacked pace and although he was strong and 'as hard as nails', he wasn't a good tackler but his skilful play lifted United to Wembley and near promotion.

He lost his place to Eddie Boot towards the end of September 1936 and returned to Scotland during the close season. He played for various Scottish clubs and after the Second War he managed Alloa Athletic.

Appearances:		Apps	Gls
	FL	57	1
	FAC	10	0
	CC	1	0
	Total	68	1

MACE Robert Stanley (Stan)

CH 1926–27 5' 10" 11st 7 to 12st 0
b. Cleethorpes 2 December 1895
d. Sheffield JAS 1974

Grimsby Rovers
United: (£75) 11 Feb 1922 amat, 3 Mar 1922 pro to May 1927
Debut: 11 Dec 1926 Bury 4 United 4
Last game: 1 Jan 1927 Manchester United 5 United 0
Brighton & Hove Albion (£150) Aug 1927 to May 1928

Stanley Mace joined United in 1922 and spent five seasons as a stalwart of the CL side—though he missed most of the 1924–25 season with cartilage trouble—and he was the extraordinary age of 31 when he made his FL debut. Despite making just five first team appearances, he was awarded a testimonial which, impressively, realised £350. He spent just one season and made five FL appearances with Brighton before knee problems ended his playing career.

During the First War, Stan served with the Sportsman's Battalion of the Royal Fusiliers. He later became a postmaster in the Sheffield suburb of Dore.

Appearances:		Apps	Gls
	FL	4	0
	CC	1	0
	Total	5	0

MACHENT Stanley (Stan) Charles

WH/IF 1939–47 5' 8" 11st 8
b. Chesterfield 23 March 1921

Chesterfield Ramblers
United: 8 Aug 1938 amat, 25/27 Oct 1938 pro to 22 Nov 1947
Debuts: 16 Dec 1939 Manchester United 1 United 2 (WW2 Fr)
5 Oct 1940 United 1 Chesterfield 0 (WW2)
7 Jan 1946 United 2 Huddersfield T 0 (FAC)
31 Aug 1946 United 0 Liverpool 1
Last games: 25 Oct 1947 United 2 Wolverhampton Wanderers 2
29 Oct 1947 Western Command 0 United XI 5
(Fr, at Oswestry)
WW2 guest: Bolsover Colly 1939–40, Chesterfield, Bath City, Distillery, 1945–46
Chesterfield (£1000 + player) Nov 1947/ Buxton cs 1949/ Hereford United Jul 1951/ Buxton 1952–53/ Chesterfield/ Stocksbridge BSC 1955–56

Stan Machent was an apprentice builder who played for Chesterfield Ramblers. Spotted by both United and Chesterfield, he chose Bramall Lane and was playing for the A team when the Second War intervened. He made his first team debut in 1939 and had a regular place in the 1940–41 season. He served in the RAF from the summer of 1942 being a Flight Sergeant wireless operator with over 400 flying hours but he never fired a shot in anger!

Originally a two footed inside forward with a strong shot, Stan became a hard working, reliable and constructive wing half. He returned to the Lane in 1945 replacing Ernest Jackson, who was injured, and had a significant role in United winning the League North championship but, unable to establish himself as a regular in the first team, he moved to Chesterfield with Dick Cushlow coming to United as part of the deal.

Good luck didn't follow the move: he broke his arm in his fourth match and a second break soon followed and after two seasons, and 21 FL games, he moved into non-League football though he returned to Saltergate to coach and play for their Yorkshire League side. Later he worked as a joiner and maintenance man at the Scarsdale Hospital and with the NCB.

Appearances:

	Apps	Gls
FL	22	2
FAC	3	0
CC	4	1
WW2	86	16
Total	115	19

MACK S

RH/LH/CH 1889–90

Notts Rangers Sep 1887/ Gainsborough Trinity cs? 1888
United: cs 1889 to 30 Apr 1890
Debuts: 7 Sep 1889 Nottingham Rangers 4 United 1 (Fr)
5 Oct 1889 Scarborough 1 United 6 (FAC)
Last games: 22 Mar 1890 Rotherham Town 1 United 0 (SCC)
19 Apr 1890 Newcastle East End 2 United 0 (Fr)
Crewe Alexandra May 1890 to 1892–93

Described as 'a rare good half back', Mack played in United's first ever game, a friendly against his former club and scored his only goal for United in the next, a friendly against Heeley, a goal which helped United to secure their first ever victory. He also played in the club's first FA Cup game. A regular in the side, mainly at wing half, he missed just six of the 57 games played in United's first season but he then moved on to Crewe Alexandra.

With Crewe, he played for two seasons in the Football Alliance but on 3 September 1892, playing at centre half, he made his FL debut at Burton Swifts but after playing in the next two FL games, his first team career with Crewe came to an end.

Appearances:

	Apps	Gls
FAC	7	0
SCC	6	0
WCC	2	0
Total	15	0

MADIN William (Billy)

OR/IR/CF 1889–90

Eckington/ Staveley Sep 1887
United: cs1889 to Apr 1890
Debuts: 7 Sep 1889 Nottingham Rangers 4 United 1
2 Dec 1889 United 1 Heeley 0 (SCC)
7 Dec 1889 Rotherham Town 2 United 2 (FAC)
Last games: 1 Feb 1890 Bolton Wanderers 13 United 0 (FAC)
22 Mar 1890 Rotherham Town 1 United 0 (SCC)
14 Apr 1890 Staveley 2 United 1 (Fr)
Staveley Apr 1890 to 1892/ Eckington 1892–93

Billy Madin played in United's first ever game and in the club's first season he made 21 appearances, 14 of them in friendly games. He played in all five forward positions but mainly at outside right or centre forward, and he was in the side which suffered the club's heaviest ever defeat, losing 0–13 at Bolton.

Appearances:

	Apps	Gls
FAC	3	0
SCC	3	0
WCC	1	0
Total	7	0

MALLENDER Kenneth (Ken)

CH/LB/RH/IR 1962–68 5' 9½" 11st 6
b. Thrybergh, Rotherham 10 December 1943

United: Dec 1959, app 6 Aug 1960, pro 20/25 Feb 1961 to 31 Oct 1968
Debut: 3 Apr 1962 Blackpool 2 United 4
Last game: 19 Oct 1968 Huddersfield Town 1 United 0
Norwich City (£38.5k) Oct 1968/ Hereford United player/coach Jul 1971 to 1973/ Telford United Jul 1974/ Minehead Jun 1977/ Gloucester City

A product of United's NIL side, Ken Mallender took time to establish himself in the first team. Regarded as a potential successor to Joe Shaw, he played just once in his debut season, once in the following season and twice in the next. 1964–65 saw greater involvement and in 1965–66 he moved to left back when Bernard Shaw was ill and, in a match against Arsenal, was the first United substitute to score. He kept that position in general for two seasons before reverting to centre half. Ken later admitted that he wished he had trained harder with United but he was a strong defender who tackled and read the game well and had the ability to play occasionally as a wing-half or inside-forward.

When Arthur Rowley became manager, he signed Colquhoun, Powell and Hemsley and Ken moved on to Norwich City. He then joined Hereford United, managed by his former Blades' team mate Colin Addison, and was a member of the side which famously beat Newcastle United in the FA Cup in February 1972. At the end of his first season the club was elected to the Football League, Ken playing in their first FL game in August 1972. He then moved into non-League football but continued to live in Hereford.

Appearances:

	Apps	Gls
FL	141 (2)	2
FAC	10	0
LC	9	0
CC	9	1
Total	169 (2)	3

MALLON Ryan

MF 2001 5' 9" 11st 8
b. Sheffield 22 March 1983

United: from jnr 13 Jul 2001 to 3 Jun 2003
Only game: 13 Oct 2001 United 3 Grimsby Town 1 (sub)
Halifax Town (L) 1 Aug 2002 to 15 Nov 2002, Scarborough (L) 22 Nov 2002 to 4 May 2003
Halifax Town Jun 2003/ Gainsborough Trinity (L) Jan to May 2005/ York City Aug 2005/ Gainsborough Trinity (L) Nov 2005, signed Jan 2006

Ryan made just one substitute appearance in the first team during is two seasons at Bramall Lane, coming on after 88 minutes giving him one of the shortest League careers for United. He had two loan spells at Conference sides Halifax and Scarborough and then moved into non-League football on a permanent basis, having a long spell with Gainsborough.

Appearances:		Apps	Gls
	FL	0 (1)	0
	Total	0 (1)	0

MARCELO CIPRIANO Dos Santos

Striker 1997–99 6' 0" 13st 8
b. Niteroi, Brazil 11 October 1969

Tirsense(Portugal)1993/ Benfica (Portugal) 1995 Deportivo Alaves (Spain)
United: Trial 1 Sep 1997, (£400k) 24/25 Sep/3/6 Oct 1997 to 25 Oct 1999
Debuts: 18 Oct 1997 United 2 Queens Park Rangers 2 (sub)
` 25 Oct 1997 West Bromwich Albion 2 United 0
Last game: 19 Oct 1999 United 0 Norwich City 0
Birmingham City (£500k) Oct 1999/ Walsall (free/£100k) Feb 2002/ Academica Coimbra (Portugal) Jul 2002

Born in Brazil of Portuguese parents, the family moved to Portugal when Marcelo was twelve. Signed by Nigel Spackman, he scored on his first outing with the reserves and made an immediate impact by scoring with a fine header on his first team debut after coming on as a substitute and secured a more permanent first team place after the departure of Brian Deane and Jan Aage Fjortoft.

Fast, enthusiastic and hard working and a good finisher, his first touch occasionally let him down but he gave United excellent service. Marcelo was a regular member of the side in 1998–99, finishing as top scorer with 16 League goals and four more in the FA Cup, including the equaliser in the sixth round at Coventry City. He started the following season as first choice but he was to be out of contract at the end of the season and wished to move abroad or to a Premiership club. He finally was sold to Birmingham City where he did well for a while but after a short spell with Walsall, he returned to Portugal, having scored 49 League goals in 103(49) games in England.

He later became became a players' agent in Portugal.

Appearances:		Apps	Gls
	FL	47 (19)	24
	PO	1 (1)	1
	FAC	10 (1)	6
	LC	3 (1)	2
	Total	61 (22)	33

MARKER Nicholas (Nicky) Robert Thomas

MF 1997–99 6' 0½" 12st 11 to 13st 0
b. Budleigh Salterton 3 May 1965

Budleigh Salterton/ Exeter C app May 1983 Plymouth Argyle (£95k) Oct 1987/ Blackburn Rovers (£500k) Sep 1992
United: (£400k-near £500k) 24/29 Jul 1997 to Oct 1999
Debuts: 28 Jul 1997 Lorenskoj (Norway) 0 United 4 (Fr)
10 Aug 1997 United 2 Sunderland 0
Last games: 26 Dec 1998 Birmingham City 1 United 0
2 Jan 1999 United 1 Notts County 1 (FAC)
27 Jul 1999 York City 0 United 3 (Fr sub)
Plymouth Argyle (L) 26 Feb 1999
Cheltenham T trial Oct 1999/ Tiverton Town Nov 1999

Nicky Marker made his FL debut with Exeter City as a sixteen years old on 17 October 1981 at Burnley and went on to make over 200 FL appearances for the club. He then moved to Plymouth Argyle, making 202 more FL appearances, before joining Blackburn Rovers where he began well but serious injuries cost him any chance of Premiership championship glory.

Signed by Nigel Spackman at the start of the 1997–98 season, he made his United home debut in a friendly match against his former club, Blackburn Rovers. He missed just three FL games during his first season at the Lane and his consistent and hard working performances, covering, passing shrewdly and reading the game well, earned him the 'Player of the Year' award. When Steve Bruce became the manager, Nicky was expected to sign for Reading but an injury to David Holdsworth saw him re-instated and he played regularly until January. After losing his place, he had a brief loan spell on loan with Plymouth Argyle before his contract was bought out for £70k and he returned to the south west, moving into non-League football. He later was involved with Tamarside FC in a coaching and managerial capacity.

Appearances:		Apps	Gls
	FL	60 (1)	5
	PO	2	0
	FAC	9	0
	LC	7	0
	Total	78 (1)	5

MARRISON Colin Ian

F 2005–06 6' 1" 12st 5
b. Sheffield 23 September 1985

United: from trainee 6 Jul 2005 to 31 May 2007
Debuts: 26 Jul 2005 Matlock T 1 United XI 2 (sub, Fr)
20 Sep 2005 Shrewsbury Town 0 United 0 (sub LC)
25 Oct 2005 Reading 2 United 0 (LC)
Last game: 19 Sep 2006 United 1 Bury 0 (sub LC)
Leigh RMI (L) 2005 Hinckley United (L) Dec 2005/ Bury (L) 12 Jan 2006 to May 2006/ Hinckley United (L) Mar to May 2007
Hinckley United cs 2007/ Tamworth Jan 2008/ Gainsborough Tr May 2008

Colin Marrison made his United first team debut in the League Cup at Shrewsbury, coming on after 89 minutes and scoring in the successful 4–3 penalty shoot-out. His FL debut came while on loan with Bury on 14 January 2006 at home to Torquay United and he made 8(8) FL appearances in total.

He was on loan at Hinckley for the latter part of 2006–07 and joined the club permanently after being released by United.

Appearances:

	Apps	Gls
LC	1 (2)	0
Total	1 (2)	0

MARROW Gary/Garry

MF 1980–81 5' 7" 10st 7
b. Worksop/Belper

United: app 8 Jun 1979, pro 1 Aug 1980 to 17 Mar 1982
Debut: 17 Nov 1980 United XI 8 Select XI 4 (Flynn BM)
Last game: 6 May 1981 United 0 Rotherham United 2 (sub CC)
Finland (L) Jul-Oct 1981
Finland 1982 and 1983/ Burton Albion (1983–84)/ Worksop T(1984–85)/ Gainsborough Tr/ Goole Town (1989–90)/ N Ferriby (1990–91)/ Harworth C I (1990–91)/ Worksop T asst mgr (1994–95)/ Matlock Town asst and mgr Mar 1999–Jan 2000/ Frickley Athletic asst mgr Sep 2000, caretaker mgr Sep 2001/ Belper mgr 2002–03/ Frickley Athletic mgr Jan 2004/ Grantham Town mgr Sep 2006 to Feb 2007 / – / Stocksbridge Park Steels mgr Jun 2007

Gary Marrow played for Worksop and Nottinghamshire Boys and was signed for United by Harry Haslam. A skilful, careful mid-fielder, he lacked speed and power and failed to develop. He scored in the John Flynn benefit match but his only other first team appearance in his three seasons at Bramall Lane was as a substitute in the County Cup. He then had two years in Finland before moving into non-League football, first as a player then as a manager.

Appearances:

	Apps	Gls
CC	0 (1)	0
Total	0 (1)	0

MARSDEN Alfred (Alf)

CF 1939–42
b. Rotherham c1921

Park Gate National
United: 2 Mar 1937 am, 19 Feb 1938 pro to 4 May 1946
Debut: 28 Oct 1939 Mansfield Town 4 United 2 (WW2)
Last game: 14 Nov 1942 United 2 Chesterfield 2 (WW2)

Alf signed for United before the Second War but made no first team appearances until wartime football was underway. Probably the fastest player on United's books, he had earned the nickname 'the Parkgate flier' in Rotherham local football. He played occasionally for four seasons, scoring on his debut but severe hernia problems all but ended his playing career though he did play again in the reserve team in November 1945.

Appearances:

	Apps	Gls
WW2	11	1
Total	11	1

MARSDEN Christopher (Chris)

MF 1987–88 5' 11" 10st 12
b. Sheffield 3 January 1969

United: YTS 1 Jul 1985, app 6 Jan 1987 to 5 Jul 1988
Debuts: 13 May 1987 Glossop 0 United XI 3 (Fr)
29 Aug 1987 United 3 Blackburn Rovers 0
Last games: 5 Dec 1988 United 2 Huddersfield Town 2
13 Feb 1988 United 0 Shrewsbury Town 1 (sub)
Huddersfield Town (£10k) Jul 1988/ Coventry City (L) Nov 1993/ Wolverhampton Wanderers (£250k) Jan 1994/ Notts County (£250k) Nov 1994/ Stockport County (£70k) Jan 1996/ Birmingham City (£500k) Oct 1997/ Southampton (£800k) Feb 1999/ Busan Icons (South Korea) Jan 2004/ Sheffield Wednesday (free) Jun 2004 to Mar 2005

Chris Marsden played regularly as an eighteen year old from the start of the 1987–88 campaign, his one goal coming on his FL debut. Billy McEwan was the manager but when Dave Bassett took over, Chris made just one appearance as a substitute and at the end of the season he was sold to Huddersfield Town.

It turned out to be a poor decision. After making more than 100 appearances for Huddersfield, Chris moved on to Wolves, United receiving about £75k from the transfer fee. After three further moves, he joined Southampton where he enjoyed the best years of his career,

playing more than 100 games in the Premiership as a hard working, hard tackling yet creative midfielder with a deft left foot.

After a brief time in South Korea, he moved back to Sheffield and joined Wednesday but he was plagued by injuries and after one season he retired having totalled 396(27) career League appearances.

Appearances:		Apps	Gls
	FL	13 (3)	1
	LC	1	0
	FMC	1	0
	Total	15 (3)	1

MARSH Cedric (Cecil?) Arnold

CF/IL 1917
b. Darnall (Sheffield) 15 July 1895
d. Sheffield December 1984

Beighton Rec
United: Feb 1916 and Jan-Feb 1917
Debut: 13 Jan 1917 United 1 Huddersfield Town 0 (WW1)
Last game: 24 Feb 1917 United 1 Nottingham Forest 4 (WW1)
Craven Sports 1918/Blackpool May 1919/ Nelson May 1921/ Fleetwood Oct 1922

Cedric (perhaps Cecil) Marsh who had played for Beighton Recreation, appeared for United's reserves against Barnsley in February 1916 and scored three goals. He made three appearances for the first team early in 1917 but United made no attempt to retain his services.

In 1919 he joined Blackpool and made his FL debut on 7 February 1920 at home to Spurs. He spent most of the season playing well with the reserves who won the CL championship but his second season was less satisfactory. He made five appearances for the first team and went on to make 17 further FL appearances for Nelson, bringing his total to 22, one of which was in the club's first ever FL game in 1921.

Note that the above player is often confused with Charles A Marsh, a full back who he played for Darnall Congregational, Shirebrook, Heeley Friends, United (pro16 Dec 1913 to cs 1915). In the 1915–16 season, he played for Heeley Friends and for Wednesday's reserves in December. The Green 'Un in December 1918 reported that Marsh, a United and Heeley Friends right back, had been severely wounded.

Appearances:		Apps	Gls
	WW1	3	0
	Total	3	0

MARSHALL Ernest (Ernie)

LH/RH 1937–38, 1942 5' 11½" 11st to 12st
b. Dinnington 23 May 1918
d. Pwllheli JAS 1983

Huddersfield T amat 1934/ Dinnington Athletic
United: 25/27 May 1935 to 6 May 1939
Debut: 20 Mar 1937 Nottingham Forest 1 United 1
Last games: 28 Mar 1938 United 1 Swansea Town 1
20 May 1938 Soedermanland XI (Swe) 1 United 5 (Fr)
Cardiff City May 1939
WW2 guest: Mansfield T (1940–41), Tottenham H (Oct 1942), Sheffield United (Nov-Dec 1942), Luton T (1942–43 to 1945–46), Aldershot (1943–45)
United: WW2 guest
Debut: 28 Nov 1942 Grimsby T 4 United 3 (WW2)
Last game: 5 Dec 1942 United 6 Mansfield Town 2 (WW2)
Yeovil Town/ Bath City Feb 1948

Ernest Marshall joined the Huddersfield Town ground staff soon after leaving school but this was contrary to FA regulations. He was at the Lane for four seasons but it was only towards the end of the 1936–37 season, after the transfer of Eddie Boot, that he had a run in the first team but he eventually lost his place to the more powerful Alf Settle.

He moved to Cardiff City and played in the three games in September 1939 before League football was abandoned due to the start of the Second World War. He served in the army as a sergeant PTI but returned to Bramall Lane as a guest, playing twice in 1942.

He made his one recognised FL appearance for Cardiff City at home to Notts County on 7 September 1946 (his 'first' FL appearance at Norwich on 26 August 1939 is not acknowledged in some quarters as the games at the start of the 1939–40 season were declared null and void). His playing career ended with Bath City and he later became the club Secretary.

Appearances:		Apps	Gls
	FL	13	3
	CC	1	0
	WW2	2	0
	Total	15	3

MARSHALL Scott Roderick

CD 1994 6' 1" 12st 5
b. Edinburgh 1 May 1973

Arsenal from trainee Mar 1991/ Rotherham United (L) Dec 1993/ Oxford United (L) Mar 1994
United: (L) 25 Aug 1994 to 22 Nov 1994
Debut: 27 Aug 1994 United 1 Notts County 3
Last game: 20 Nov 1994 Burnley 4 United 2
Southampton Aug 1998/ Brentford (£250k) Oct 1999 to cs2003/ Wycombe Wanderers Nov 2003 / – / Brentford Youth Team mgr Sep 2007

Scott made his League debut with Arsenal on 6 May 1993 at Sheffield Wednesday but although he was with the club for several seasons, he played only 24 League games.

His loan move to United came after the club's relegation from the Premiership and was as cover for the injured Paul Beesley. He played poorly on both his debut and final game but in general, in 17 successive League games during his 3 month loan, he was solid and sound at the centre of defence, being particularly good in the air. A Scottish schoolboy and youth international, his form with the Blades earned him an U21 cap against Russia.

He returned to Arsenal but it was only after moving to Brentford, where he made 75 appearances that he found a regular first team place. His time with Wycombe was significantly affected by injury and after one season he retired, having totalled 129(7) League appearances.

Appearances:		Apps	Gls
	FL	17	0
	Total	17	0

MARTIN Lee Robert

LMF/LW 2008 5' 10" 10st 3
b. Taunton 9 February 1987

Manchester United from trainee Feb 2005 Glasgow Rangers (L) Aug 2006/ Stoke City (L) Jan 2007 Plymouth Argyle (L) Oct 2007
United: (L) 10 Jan 2008 to May 2008
Debut: 19 Jan 2008 Sheffield Wednesday 2 United 0
Last games: 12 Feb 2008 West Bromwich Albion 0 United 0
16 Feb 2008 United 0 Middlesbrough 0 (FAC)
26 Apr 2008 United 2 Bristol City 1 (sub)
Nottingham F (L) Aug 2008

Lee Martin made his first team debut with Manchester United in a League Cup game in October 2005. His Scottish League debut came on 13 August 2005 whilst on loan to Rangers and after his loan move to Stoke he made his FL debut, on 30 January 2006, at home to Ipswich.

Bryan Robson brought Lee to the Lane to give more attacking options from the wide midfield players. Lee made his debut in the Sheffield derby and his performances steadily improved. Quick and tricky he was able to deliver searching crosses into the box but was susceptible to knocks and in his last two appearances (at Middlesborough in February and against Bristol City) he was injured after coming on as a sub.

Appearances:		Apps	Gls
	FL	5 (1)	0
	FAC	2 (1)	0
	Total	7 (2)	0

MARWOOD Brian

MF 1990–92 5' 7" 11st 6
b. Seaham Harbour 5 February 1960

Hull City app Jun 1976, pro Feb 1978/ Sheffield Wednesday
(£115k) Aug 1984/ Arsenal (£600k) Mar 1988
United: (£300k) 20 Sep 1990 to 7 Dec 1992
Debut: 23 Sep 1990 United 0 Leeds United 2
Last games: 29 Feb 1992 United 0 Queens Park Rangers 0
20 Apr 1992 Notts County 1 United 3 (sub)
10 Aug 1992 Cambridge United 1 United 2 (sub Fr)
Middlesbrough (L) 17 Oct 1991
Swindon Town (nc) Mar 1993/ Barnet Aug 1993 to cs1994

A clever winger who could put across some excellent centres, Brian Marwood made his FL debut with Hull City at home to Mansfield Town on 12 January 1980. He played over 154 FL games for Hull and was with Hull when they missed out on promotion to Division Two, beaten on goal difference by United in 1984. After a spell with neighbours Wednesday in the top flight, he moved to Arsenal where he had what was possibly his best season, winning a League Championship medal in 1989 and gaining his one England cap against Saudi Arabia in November 1988.

Signed by Dave Bassett, Brian played more of a mid-field role when he moved to the Lane but he was not a success and he rarely showed the skill and purpose for which he was renowned in his earlier days. Most of his appearances came in his first season but he played only a minor role thereafter.

After leaving United he played only 37 more games, including his spell at Middlesbrough, bringing his career total to 98 League goals in 372(25) games. He was chairman of the PFA for three years from November 1990 and subsequently worked for Nike and then moved into media work.

Appearances:		Apps	Gls
	FL	14 (8)	3
	FAC	0 (2)	0
	LC	3	0
	Total	17 (10)	3

MASON Clifford (Cliff) Ernest

LB/RW 1955–62 5' 8" 10st 9 to 11st 0
b. York 27 November 1929

York City (trial)/ RAF/ Sunderland Jan 1950 Darlington Jul 1952
United: (£6,500) 3 Jul/8 Aug 1955 to 9/13 Mar 1962
Debut: 1 Sep 1955 Charlton Athletic 3 United 2
Last games: 13 Jan 1962 Aston Villa 0 United 0
15 Jan 1962 United 2 Bury 0 (FAC at Hillsborough)
Leeds United (£7000) Mar 1962/ Scunthorpe United Jan-Feb 1964/
Chesterfield Jul 1964 to cs1967

Cliff Mason began his career as a part-timer with Sunderland but he failed to make the first team and his FL debut came with Darlington on 30 August 1952 at Crewe Alexandra.

Cliff had been the target of United's manager, Reg Freeman, to act as cover for Graham Shaw who had begun his National Service. Sadly, Freeman died but Cliff was signed just before Joe Mercer took up his first post as a manager. Cliff's debut was watched by Walter Winterbottom, the England manager who told Ernest Selwood, a United director, that the United left back would be chosen for the next England U23 international; Selwood didn't bother to tell him that Shaw hadn't played!

A shrewd and thoughtful player who covered and tackled well, his astute positional play compensated for his lack of pace. He was a regular in the side in his first season at the Lane and continued so until December 1956. For the rest of his time with United, Cliff played mainly in the reserves, getting a first team place only in the absence of Shaw or Cec Coldwell but he was a reliable player. He made 21 FL and Cup appearances in the 1960–61 promotion season, when United also reached the semi-final of the F A Cup, including a spell on the right wing and it was in his ten games in that position that he scored his three goals for the club.

After playing for Leeds and Scunthorpe, he finished his career as a part-timer, totalling 252 FL appearances, and then briefly as a coach and scout with Chesterfield. Trained as a printer, he had a printing and later, a specialised engineering business.

Appearances:		Apps	Gls
	FL	97	2
	FAC	11	1
	LC	1	0
	CC	9	0
	Total	118	2

MASTERMAN Wallace (Wally)

IL 1914–19 5' 10½" 11st 5 to 13st 0
b. Newcastle on Tyne 29 January 1888
d. Sheffield 24 January 1965

Stockton/ Gainsborough Trinity May 1910
United: (£800) 27 Apr/2 May 1914 to 20 May 1920
Debut: 5 Sep 1914 United 0 Wednesday 1
Last game: 27 Dec 1919 Chelsea 1 United 1
WW1 guest: West Ham United (1915–16), Gainsborough Trinity (1917), Rotherham County (Dec 1918)
Stoke City (£300) May 1920

Brought up in Stockton on Tees, family legend had it that he celebrated his birthday on a different January day to that on his birth certificate. Wally made his FL debut with Gainsborough Trinity on 3 September 1910 at home to Glossop North End. He played regularly for two seasons, making 42 FL appearances, but then Gainsborough fell out of the Football League and two seasons later, he joined United.

A strong, unselfish, hard working inside forward, he wasn't fast but dribbled, head down, as if the ball was tied to his feet and yet he had the ability to pass to a colleague at exactly the right moment or finish with a strong shot. He had a marvellous first season at Bramall Lane in what turned out to be the last FL campaign before the First World War. He was a regular in the side and played in the United team which defeated Chelsea 3–0 in the FA Cup Final.

He served in the Coldstream Guards until medically discharged when he returned to Sheffield. He played regularly in 1916–17 and 1918–19 and at the start of the first post-war season but received a serious knee injury against the Wednesday in March 1919 and he was never really fit again.

He moved to Stoke but never appeared in the first team and, after he returned to Sheffield, he worked for Hadfields (ESC) for over thirty years.

Appearances:		Apps	Gls
	FL	36	12
	FAC	6	2
	WW1	50	18
	Total	92	32

MATTHEWS John Barry

OL 1943–44
b. Sheffield 18 January 1926
d. 1995?

United: 28 Aug 1943 amateur to 23 Feb 1945 and 23 Jun 1947 to Oct 1949
Debut: 23 Oct 1943 Barnsley 3 United 2 (WW2)
Last game: 26 Dec 1944 United 3 Manchester United 4 (WW2)
Lincoln City (am) Oct 1949/ Corby Town cs 1952/ Peterborough United cs 1953/ Corby Town cs 1954/ Spalding United Jun 1955 to cs 1956

A sixth form student at Firth Park Grammar School, Barry Matthews began playing as an amateur for United in August 1943. He had asked United if he could play and the club agreed but his headmaster objected and, on occasions refused his permission, insisting that the boy should play for the school. Fast when he got into his stride and with a good left foot, he played most of his games for United in the 1943–44 season, which included the first leg of the County Cup Final against Rotherham United. He went to Birmingham University in 1944 and from 1945 to October 1949, his rare appearances in United's colours were limited to occasional games with the reserve or A team.

He joined Lincoln City playing mainly reserve football but he did make two FL appearances, his debut being on 12 November 1949 at home to Bradford City. He later played for several seasons in non-League football and worked in Peterborough.

Appearances:		Apps	Gls
	CC	1	0
	WW2	14	3
	Total	15	3

MATTHEWS John Melvin

MF/CD 1978–82, 1983 6' 0" 12st 6
b. Camden 1 November 1955

Arsenal app Jul 1971, pro Aug 1973
United: (£80 to £90k) 17/28 Aug 1978 to 19/24 Jul 1982
Debut: 23 Aug 1978 Leicester City 0 United 1
Last games: 15 May 1982 Darlington 0 United 2
19 May 1982 United 1 Everton 1 (Fr)
18 Apr 1983 United 1 Ipswich Town 1 (BM)
Mansfield Town Aug 1982/ Chesterfield Aug 1984/ Plymouth Argyle Aug 1985/ Torquay United Jul 1989/ Dorchester Town 1990

After spending his first season as a professional in the Arsenal reserve team, John Matthews made his FL debut on 17 August 1974 at Leicester City but couldn't establish himself as a regular in the first team, through a combination of injuries and stiff competition.

A strong, long striding player with a fierce shot and good passing ability, he was far from quick and slow to turn or recover. He joined United at the start of the 1978–79 campaign as Harry Haslam invested in several new players and scored on his debut. He played regularly and steadily as a defender in a poor United team that were relegated to the Third Division for the first time in their history.

They began the new season well only to fall away and worse was to follow. Matthews, now playing more in mid-field, had missed much of the 1980–81 campaign but played in the vital last match of the season against Walsall when a last minute penalty, awarded to United, was to decide which club would be relegated. It was subsequently reported that John had agreed to take any penalties but at the last moment, he found the responsibility too great and Don Givens was the one who accepted responsibility but missed.

Ian Porterfield, United's new manager, attempted to sell John to Brentford but the deal collapsed. John made twenty four appearances and played in the final game at Darlington which clinched the Division Four Championship but sensed that he wasn't wanted and was given a free transfer.

He joined Mansfield Town—returning once to play in the Les Tibbott's benefit match—and won a second Division Four championship medal with Chesterfield and then had a lengthy spell with Plymouth Argyle. He ended his career having played 397(21) FL games.

After retiring from the game, he ran soccer schools and also a furniture business in Plymouth.

Appearances:		Apps	Gls
	FL	98 (5)	14
	FAC	5	1
	LC	5	0
	ASC	8	1
	AMC	3	0
	CC	2	2
	Total	121 (5)	18

MATTHEWS Vincent (Vince)

CH 1927–31 6' 1" 13st 0
b. Oxford 15 January 1896
d. Oxford 15 November 1950

St Frideville/ Oxford City/ Boscombe (pro) Oct 1921 Bolton Wanderers (£1000) Jan 1923 Tranmere Rovers Jul 1925
United: (£2,300) 23/25 Jul 1927 to 1 May 1931
Debut: 8 Oct 1927 Sunderland 0 United 1
Last game: 7 Apr 1931 Leeds United 4 Leeds United 0
Shamrock Rovers 29 May 1931/ Shrewsbury Town Jun 1935/ Oswestry Town player-mgr Oct 1937/ Morris Motors coach

Vince Matthews made his FL debut with Bolton Wanderers on 12 March 1922 at Burnley but after just two more games, spread over two years, he moved to Tranmere Rovers.

He moved to the Lane and missed very few games, playing particularly well in the 1927–28 season when United reached the F A Cup semi-final and those displays earned him two England caps against France and Belgium. He was quick and strong but lacked confidence at times and wasn't consistent because he didn't adapted well to the changes in the off-side law which some clubs exploited to the full with quick breakaways using fast forwards.

He gave a fine display in the vital match at Old Trafford in 1930 but there were too many indifferent displays particularly at Bramall Lane and his distribution was poor. Despite this, he was a regular until December 1930 when Paddy Carrigan took the centre half spot. He asked for a transfer and Sunderland wanted to sign him but United wanted £5000 which Sunderland considered too much.

When he left United he moved to Ireland and then returned to England to play in non-League football.

Appearances:		Apps	Gls
	FL	125	2
	FAC	11	0
	CC	5	1
	Total	141	3

MATTHEWSON Reginald (Reg)

LH/CH/RH 1962–67 5' 11" 11st 11 to 12st 4
b. Sheffield 6 August 1939

Hillsborough B C/ Birley Carr
United: **amat, pro 20/21 Jun 1958 to 9/15 Feb 1968**
Debuts: **15 Jan 1962 United 2 Bury 0 (FAC at Hillsborough)**
17 Mar 1962 Fulham 5 United 2
Last games: **23 Sep 1967 United 2 Newcastle United 1**
28 Nov 1967 Barnsley 2 United 3 (CC)
23 Dec 1967 United 2 Coventry City 0 (sub)
Fulham (£30k) Feb 1968/ Chester Jan 1973/ Wrexhan coach 1976/ Bangor City player-coach 1978/ Shrewsbury Town asst mgr, coch 1980–81 / – / Kelsall FC coach 1993

Born near the Wednesday ground, Reg Matthewson improved as a player when he was serving in the RAOC, playing for various army teams. He was twenty two when he made his United debut in a replayed cup-tie at Hillsborough and he scored on his first FL outing though goals were rare in his playing career. He made only occasional appearances until January 1964 when he finally replaced Gerry Summers at left half. A solid, dependable and steady player, he missed very few games and moved to centre half in March 1966, taking over that position from Joe Shaw. He was injured in September 1967 and lost his place to Ken Mallender and after winning a County Cup medal in his final start for the Blades, Reg asked for a transfer.

He moved to Fulham where he made over 150 FL appearances in five seasons and finished his playing career with Chester after playing 388(6) FL games before moving into coaching. He later worked in Ellesmere Port and lives in the Chester area (2006).

Appearances:		Apps	Gls
	FL	146 (3)	3
	FAC	11	1
	LC	8	0
	CC	8	1
	Total	173 (3)	5

MAYCOCK Harry

IL 1918 5' 6"
b. Rotherham 16 April 1890
d. Rotherham AMJ 1978

Rotherham local football
United: **WW1 guest**
Debut: **30 Mar 1918 United 2 Barnsley 3 (WW1)**
Last games: **1 Apr 1918 Rotherham County 0 United 1 (WW1)**
13 Apr 1918 Wednesday 2 United 0 (Fr)
Parkgate Christ Church/ Scunthorpe & Lindsey United Apr 1921–cs1923/ Southend United Jul 1923/ Rotherham Town Oct 1924

Spotted playing in Rotherham local football, Harry made three first team appearances for United during the First War. He had two seasons with Scunthorpe before moving to Southend United where he made his FL debut, and scored, on 15 September 1923 at home to Newport County. He made just two more FL appearances before moving back to South Yorkshire.

Appearances:		Apps	Gls
	WW1	2	0
	Total	2	0

MELLOR William (Billy)

RB/LB/CH 1892–93 12st

Heywood Central/ Exchange (Sheffield) Melville (Sheffield)/ Darlington (Dec 1891) trial?
United: **2 Jul 1892 to 12 Dec 1893**
Debuts: **26 Oct 1892 Gainsborough Trinity 0 United 1 (Fr)**
23 Jan 1893 United 1 Northwich Victoria 1
Last games: **6 Feb 1893 United 3 Burton Swifts 1**
3 Apr 1893 Darlington 2 United 3 (NL)
11 Nov 1893 Newcastle United 5 United 1 (Fr)
Wednesday Dec 1893 to May 1895/ Loughborough Town May 1895/ Oldham County May 1896/ Swindon T May 1897/ Wigan County Jun 1898/ Darwen Dec 1899

Registered by the FL in 1892 as 'Mellors' and 1893–94 as 'Mellars' (the FA always used that spelling), Billy played six competitive games in 1892–93 and ten friendly fixtures and two more 'club' matches as they were then called, during the following season. During 1893–94 he made a FL appearance for the Wednesday thus becoming the first player to play a FL game for both Sheffield clubs. He later made three FL appearances for Loughborough Town during their first season in the Football League.

Appearances:		Apps	Gls
	FL	2	0
	FAC	1	0
	NL	2	0
	WCC	1	0
	Total	6	0

MELLORS Mark

G 1908 6' 1½" 12st 6 to 12st 10
b. Old Basford, Nottingham 30 April 1880
d. Otley 20 March 1961

Carrington/ Bulwell/ Nottingham Forest (amat) Notts County Nov 1902/ Brighton & Hove Albion May 1904
United: (£100) 14 May/24 Aug 1906 to Apr 8 1909
Only game: 29 Feb 1908 United 2 Woolwich Arsenal 2
Bradford City (£350) 7 Apr 1909 to Feb 1918

Mark Mellors made his FL debut with Notts County against United at the Lane on 10 April 1903, United winning 3–0. He moved to Southern League Brighton but County still held his FL registration and, when he joined United, the £100 transfer fee was paid to County. His opportunities were limited at the Lane due to the impressive form of Joe Lievesley and, after three seasons, he moved to Bradford City.

He played at Valley Parade in the greatest period of their history, helping them avoid relegation in 1909 and having an important role in winning the FA Cup in a replay in 1911. He lost his first team place, after 68 FL appearances, to Ewart in 1913 but played frequently during the war until February 1918 when he retired, eventually running his own textile business in Bradford.

Appearances:		Apps	Gls
	FL	1	0
	Total	1	0

MENDONCA Clive Paul

Striker 1986–88, 1991 5' 10" 10st 8 to 11st 7
b. Islington 9 September 1968

United: YTS 1 Jul 1985, app 9/10 Sep 1986 to 18/25 Mar 1988
Debuts: 15 Sep 1986 Sheffield Wednesday 3 United XI 1 (BM sub)
2 May 1987 Brighton & Hove Albion 2 United 0 (sub)
13 May 1987 Glossop 0 United XI 3 (Fr)
31 Oct 1987 United 2 Leeds United 2
Last game: 13 Feb 1988 United 0 Shrewsbury Town 1
Doncaster Rovers (L) 26 Feb 1988
Rotherham United (£20–£30k) Mar 1988
United: (£114k) 8 Jul/1 Aug 1991 to 13 Aug 1992
Debuts: 6 Aug 1991 Helsingborg IF (Sweden) 0 United 2 (Fr)
28 Aug 1991 Coventry City 3 United 1 (sub)
31 Aug 1991 Crystal Palace 2 United 1
Last game: 7 Dec 1991 Queens Park Rangers 1 United 0
Grimsby Town (L) 9 Jan 1992 and 19 Mar 1992
Grimsby Town (£85k) Aug 1992/ Charlton Athletic (£700k) May 1997 to Jan 2002

Brought up in Sunderland, Clive Mendonca scored over ninety goals in two seasons in the United Junior and Reserve teams. Quick in thought and movement, with a good shot and calm in the penalty area, Clive was a 'natural goal scorer'. Billy McEwan gave him his chance in the first team and he scored four goals in eleven FL appearances but facing relegation, new manager, Dave Bassett gave him just one appearance before moving him out on loan and then transferring him to Rotherham United. At Millmoor, he scored 27 goals in 84 appearances but, despite this success, it was a surprise when, with Dave Bassett still in charge, he returned to the Lane. Many felt that his chances were unnecessarily limited and he made just four FL starts before moving on loan to Grimsby Town. The move was made permanent at the end of the season.

Clive again showed he had the scoring touch, scoring 58 goals in 156 FL appearances and this continued after he moved to Charlton Athletic where his hat-trick in the 1998 Play-off Final helped take his final club into the Premiership. Despite problems with injuries, he managed 40 goals in 84 games before his last first team game in Dec 1999. He announced his retirement in 2002 and ended his career with 133 League goals in 324(35) games but only five of those goals were for the Blades.

In 2004 he won both the BBC's 'Grimsby's cult heroes' and 'Charlton's cult heroes' polls. He was the only player to win more than one club's poll.

Appearances:		Apps	Gls
	FL	12 (11)	5
	LC	0 (3)	0
	FMC	1 (1)	0
	Total	13 (15)	5

MENLOVE Bertram (Bert)

CF/IF 1922–26 5' 8½" 11st 6
b. St Albans 8 December 1892
d. Bridge (Kent) 3 July 1970

Army/ Southern Railway/ Barnet Aston Villa amat Oct 1919/ Crystal Palace Nov 1919
United: (£2,000) 9/11 Mar 1922 to 17 Jul 1926
Debut: 11 Mar 1922 United 0 Cardiff City 2
Last game: 1 Mar 1926 Blackburn Rovers 3 United 1
Boston Jul 1926/ Aldershot Town May 1928/ Worksop Town (trial) Dec 1928/ Bangor City Jan 1929/ Clapton Orient May 1929/ Connah's Quay cs1930/ Coleraine Dec 1930/ Ashford Town Dec 1931 (player-mgr) to cs1932

Bert Menlove, who served four years with the army in France, had at least three games with Aston Villa reserves before becoming a professional with Crystal Palace. He made his FL debut on 4 September 1920 at home to Merthyr Town in what was the club's third ever FL game and first victory.

A thoughtful, calculating player, he joined United and found himself competing with Harry Johnson for the centre forward spot. He was more robust than Johnson and a better shot but Harry was more effective and less injury prone. Menlove's talents were obvious however and United, in December 1923, rejected a bid of £3000 from Middlesbrough for his transfer but towards the end of his time at the Lane, he played only when Johnson was unavailable.

He scored on his final appearance before moving into non-League football, scoring fifty goals in his first season with Boston. He did sign later for Third Division Clapton Orient but never appeared in the first team and when he left the game, he became a mental health worker.

Appearances:		Apps	Gls
	FL	74	41
	FAC	3	0
	CC	4	2
	Total	81	43

MERCER Arthur Stanley

IR 1926–27 5' 8½" 10st 7
b. St Helens 28 December 1902
d. Chester 2 October 1994

Parr St Peters/ Wigan Borough Nov 1921, pro Apr 1922/ Bury (£750) Jun 1925
United: (£700) 28/29 Oct 1926 to cs1928
Debut: 30 Oct 1926 Leicester City 2 United 2
Last games: 19 Nov 1927 Tottenham Hotspur 2 United 2
28 Nov 1927 Sheffield Wednesday 3 United 1 (CC)
Rhyl Athletic cs1928/ Connah's Quay Dec 1928/ Bristol City (£425 to SUFC) 14 May 1930/ Chester Oct 1931/ Halifax Town Nov 1933/ Dartford Aug 1935/ Rhyl Athletic Jun 1936

Arthur Mercer was some nine years younger than his brother David, the United winger. Arthur made his FL debut with Wigan Borough, in their first season as a FL club, on 22 April 1922 at Barrow. After a brief spell with Bury, he moved to Bramall Lane where all his appearances were at inside right, the majority of them with his brother David at outside right. A strong, two footed, industrious player, he appeared regularly in the first team for about a year but eventually moved on, playing for a variety of clubs, both League and non-League, with a career total of over 218 FL appearances and 68 goals. He later became a newsagent.

Appearances:		Apps	Gls
	FL	35	14
	FAC	1	1
	CC	2	0
	ABD	1	0
	Total	39	14

David and Arthur Mercer

MERCER David William

OR 1920–28 5' 7" 10st 7 to 11st 4
b. Skelmersdale, St Helens 20 March 1893
d. Torquay 4 June 1950

Prescot Athletic/ Skelmersdale United/ Hull City Jan 1914
United: **(£4,250) 14/15 Dec 1920 to cs 1928**
Debut: **18 Dec 1920 Oldham Athletic 0 United 0**
Last game: **7 Apr 1928 Cardiff City 2 United 2**
Prescot Athletic/ Shirebrook Oct 1928/ Torquay United Jun 1929 to cs1930/ Dartmouth United 1931

David Mercer began his professional career with Hull City, making his FL debut on 18 April 1914 at Fulham. He then made 224 consecutive FL and Cup appearances for the club, mainly during the First World War, during which he played in every game. In January 1919 he had played against United in a game abandoned due to darkness with Hull leading 6–1 and David had scored all six goals. Perhaps recalling this, when United were involved in a relegation struggle in December 1920, he was one of two players who were signed, the other being Fred Tunstall. The fee paid for Mercer was probably a FL record at the time.

Although he had played many games at inside right for Hull, he played all but three games at outside right for United. David was fast and extremely skilful and contemporary references to 'twinkling feet' and 'dancing master' give some impression of a quick and tricky player. Stocky in build, he was difficult to knock off the ball—though he was never over-fond of a challenge—and he provided many a 'model centre' for his fellow forwards and some were long and intended for Fred Tunstall, racing in from the left wing. Initially, he seemed to lack confidence but the arrival of Tommy Sampy as inside right in March 1921 saw David blossom.

He was a member of the FA touring party to South Africa in 1920 and played for England against Ireland in October 1922 and later against Belgium. He played for the Football League against the Scottish League in 1924 and helped United win the FA Cup in 1925. His brother Arthur also played for United and the two played together more than 30 times.

After moving into non-League football in 1928, he later joined Torquay United for one season and then settled there, working for a time as a green-keeper at a local golf club. He ended his career with 48 FL goals (but none for Torquay) in 342 games. His son, also David, made 66 FL appearances for Torquay after the end of the Second World War.

Appearances:		Apps	Gls
	FL	223	22
	FAC	18	0
	CC	8	0
	ABD	1	0
	Total	250	22

MERCER William (Billy)

G 1994–95 6' 1½" 13st 5
b. Liverpool 22 May 1969

Liverpool from trainee Aug 1987 Rotherham United (£50k) Feb 1989
United: **(L) May, (£75k) 12 Oct 1994 to 11/12 Dec 1995**
Debuts: **13 May 1994 Western Australia 1 United 2 (Fr)**
12 Nov 1994 United 2 Derby County 1
Last game: **29 Aug 1995 United 2 Crystal Palace 3**
Nottingham Forest (L) 20 Mar 1995 (no apps)
Chesterfield (L) 5 Sep 1995, (£93k of which £6k to RUFC) 12 Dec 1995/ Bristol City (£300k) Oct 1999 to Jan 2003

Billy began his career at Liverpool but failed to make a first team appearance. He then moved to Rotherham, initially on loan, making his FL debut on 1 January 1990 at home to Bristol Rovers. After over 100 appearances for the Millers, he was invited to go on United's end-of-season tour of Australia in 1994 and he made a permanent move in October. Having to compete with both Simon Tracey and Alan Kelly, his opportunities were limited and he moved to Chesterfield, initially on loan, where he gave four years sterling service, being involved in the club's memorable FA Cup run to the semi-final in 1997.

Financial difficulties at Chesterfield prompted his move to Bristol City. His move was initially a success and he was voted 'Player of the Season' but then injuries brought a halt to his playing career in which he made 282 FL appearances. He became a goalkeeping coach and latterly filled this role with Sheffield Wednesday.

Appearances:		Apps	Gls
	FL	4	0
	Total	4	0

MILBURN John (Jackie) Edward Thompson

OR 1945 5' 11" 12st 9
b. Ashington 11 May 1924
d. Ashington 9 October 1988

Welfare Rangers/ REC Rovers/ Hirst East Old Boys/ Ashington YMCA/ Ashington ATC/ Newcastle United Aug 1943
WW2 guest: Sunderland, Sheffield United
United: **WW2 guest**
Only game: **26 May 1945 Sheffield Wednesday 4 United 2 (CC)**
Linfield player-mgr Jun 1957/ Yiewsley Nov 1960, player-mgr Dec 1960/ Carmel College, coach 1962/ Ipswich Town mgr Jan 1963–Sep 1964

Known to most Newcastle football followers as 'Wor Jackie', Milburn's only peacetime FL club was Newcastle United although he played as a guest for Sunderland as well as his one appearance for United. He had to wait until then end of the Second War to make his FL debut, which he did on 31 August 1946 at Millwall. Very fast, he had a lethal shot with both feet, could turn quickly but he also had good ball control and was a good tackler. He began his career with the Magpies in August 1943 while working as a pit apprentice but went on to win three FA Cup Winners medals, scoring in the first minute in the1955 final, and to play 13 times for England. Although known primarily as a centre forward he began his career at outside right and it was in that position that he surprisingly turned out for the Blades in an end of the season game after Newcastle had completed their fixtures.

After leaving Newcastle he spent two seasons with Linfield where he appeared in the European Cup. There followed a few years in non-League football before he tried his hand as a manager with Ipswich Town. After 18 months he returned to Tyneside and became a respected journalist with the News of the World for 20 years. He died of cancer at the early age of 64.

Appearances:		Apps	Gls
	WW2	1	0
	Total	1	0

MILLERSHIP Walter

CH 1942 5' 10" 12st 7
b. Warsop Vale, Nottinghamshire 8 June 1910
d. Brimington, nr Chesterfield 1978

Warsop Main 1926–27/ Welbeck Athletic 1926 Shirebrook FC Dec 1927/ Bradford Park Avenue (£10 donation) Jan 1928/ Sheffield Wednesday (£2,600)Mar 1930 WW2 guest: Doncaster Rovers, Sheffield Utd
United: WW2 guest
Only game: 25 May 1942 Chesterfield 1 United 2 (WW2)
Denaby United May 1946

Walter Millership began his FL career with Bradford Park Avenue as a centre forward, making his debut on 25 February 1928 at Nelson. His performance against Wednesday in a cup-tie persuaded them to sign him and, after three seasons playing mainly in the reserves, it was as a rough, tough, uncompromising centre half that he made his breakthrough to become a regular in the first team. He won an FA Cup winners' medal in 1935 and captained Wednesday throughout the Second War whilst working as a forge-man. It was in 1942 that he made his one guest appearance for United.

He became a licensee in Sheffield in 1944 and, after the War, played for Denaby where, playing against Lincoln City reserves, he came across Derek Dooley and immediately contacted his former club. After a period as landlord of the Bricklayer's Arms at Brimington, he returned to his first job as a miner until he retired in 1969.

Appearances:		Apps	Gls
	WW2	1	0
	Total	1	0

MILLS Henry (Harry)

CF/IL 1947 5' 11" 11st 12
b. Bishop Auckland 23 July 1922

Consett
United: 27 Jun 1946 to 16 Mar 1948
Debut: 29 Mar 1947 Sunderland 2 United 1
Last games: 7 Jun 1947 United 2 Arsenal 1
29 Oct 1947 Western Command 0 United XI 5 (Fr, at Oswestry)
Rotherham United (£500) Mar 1948 to cs1948/ Tonbridge/ Rochdale Apr 1950/ Halifax Town Aug 1952/ Wisbech cs1953

United made a donation of £100 to Consett when they signed Harry Mills but although he had some neat touches and scored in his first two appearances, he played just one more competitive game for United. He later managed three goals in six games for Rotherham United and made one appearance for Rochdale, thus ending his FL career with the impressive tally of five goals in ten games.

Appearances:		Apps	Gls
	FL	3	2
	Total	3	2

MILNES Fred Houghton

LB 1903–05
b. Wortley, nr Sheffield 26 January 1878
d. Leeds 1 July 1946

Wycliffe (Sheffield)
United: amat, occasional 5 May 1902 to 1 Feb 1907
Debut: 21 Mar 1903 United 3 Wolverhampton Wanderers 0
Last games: 8 Oct 1904 Stoke 2 United 1
4 Mar 1905 West Ham United 1 United 3 (Fr)
Sheffield Club/ West Ham United (Oct 1904)/ Tottenham Hotspur Dec 1905/ Manchester United Mar 1906/ Leicester Fosse (FL transfer) 1 Feb 1907/ St Mirren Mar 1907/ Reading/ Ilford cs1908/ Norwich City Sep 1908

Fred Milnes was a gifted amateur full-back, able and willing to offer his services to a wide variety of clubs. In Sheffield, he usually played for the strong Wycliffe club but he also assisted United—who held his FL registration—and Sheffield Club where he gained an FA Amateur Cup winners' medal and scored the third goal in 1904.

A businessman, who had no need to become a professional, he played twice for West Ham in the Southern League and, in September 1905, he sailed to North America as a member of the Pilgrims, a group of top amateur players attempting to popularise the game there. On his return he made two Western League appearances with Spurs and gained an amateur international cap against France in November 1906. He was reported to be assisting Manchester United and he continued to play briefly for a variety of clubs and made one FL appearance for Leicester Fosse after United had transferred his FL registration to the midlands club.

Appearances:		Apps	Gls
	FL	12	0
	Total	12	0

MILTON Ernest

LB/RB 1917–26 5' 8" 11st 0 to 11st 10
b. Kimberworth (Rotherham) 7 August 1897
d. Sheffield 2 September 1984

Kimberworth Wesleyans/ Parkgate Christ Church Kilnhurst Town
United: Dec 1916 to May 1927
Debuts: 13 Jan 1917 United 1 Huddersfield Town 0 (WW1)
30 Aug 1919 Manchester City 3 United 3
Last game: 23 Oct 1926 United 0 West Ham United 2
WW1 guest: Rotherham County (1918–19), Birmingham (1 app, 1918), Barnsley (1918–19), Kilnhurst Town (1917–19)

Ernest Milton, a miner with thinning fair hair and a younger brother of Albert, a Sunderland full-back (d. October 1917) and Alf (Rotherham C and Coventry), was playing for Kilnhurst Town early in the First War and was recommended to United by Bob Chantrey, a team-mate who had played a few games for the Blades. A strong, bustling, energetic player though hardly composed, he impressed sufficiently in his first games to be given further opportunities and at the end of the season signed amateur forms—signing professional was not allowed during the First War. After playing the first game of the 1918–19 season, he left the Lane, claiming that he had signed by 'misinterpretation'. He played for various clubs but in March 1919, he wrote to United, offering his services and hoping that there would be no 'ill-will' if he returned.

Ernest was fortunate when normal football was resumed for Jack English, the pre-war full back, stayed in Darlington and Milton missed just two games of the first post-war season and his form in 1920–21 was such that he was chosen for an FA XI. Ernest was a resolute player who tackled well and was difficult to beat. He was two two-footed and could kick the ball powerfully and at any angle but tended to clear wildly and he wasn't fast.

In October 1924, United signed Len Birks and Ernest lost his place for a while and, in 1925, a newspaper commented that he had 'hardly fulfilled early expectations' but he returned to the team and United went on to win the FA Cup.

He played only twelve more games after the Cup Final. The new offside law, which put an emphasis on speed, his long standing injury problems and an ankle operation, brought his career to an early end. After retiring he worked for a coal merchant, set up a business and also became a county standard bowl's player but he continued to live in Sheffield, less than a quarter of a mile from Bramall Lane.

Appearances:

	Apps	Gls
FL	203	3
FAC	17	1
CC	8	0
WW1	43	0
Total	271	4

MITCHELL Greg A

OL/MF 1982

United: 25 May 1981 to 30 Jun 1983
Only game: 21 May 1982 United 3 Sheffield Wednesday 2 (CC)
Buxton (1983–85)/ Matlock Town (1989–90)

Greg Mitchell's only first team game came in the County Cup in a season when the clubs were allowed to use their reserve players.

Appearances:

	Apps	Gls
CC	1	0
Total	1	0

MITCHELL Joseph (Joe) Thomas

G 1909–13, 1918 5' 11½" 11st 0
b. Darnall (Sheffield) 1 January 1886
d. Sheffield 20 December 1964

Darnall Congs/ Thorpe Hesley
United: 24 Apr 1908 to 19 Jun 1913
Debut: 11 Dec 1909 Notts County 1 United 2
Last games: 25 Jan 1913 United 3 Bradford City 2
1 Feb 1913 Clapton Orient 3 United 1 (Fr)
Luton Town (£50) cs 1913
WW1 guest: Barnsley (1918), United (1918), Rotherham County (1918–19)
United: WW1 guest
Debut: 7 Sep 1918 United 5 Huddersfield T 1 (WW1)
Last game: 12 Oct 1918 Birmingham 4 United 1 (WW1)
South Shields Jun 1919/ Coventry City Feb 1920/ Chesterfield Mar 1921/ Denaby U cs1922 to May 5 1923/ Eckington Works Aug 1923

Joe Mitchell spent much of his time at the Lane as second choice to Joe Lievesley who rarely missed a game and Joe's appearances were few until the latter part of the 1911–12 season. He played regularly for about a season but in January 1913 he was replaced by Ted Hufton.

He moved to Southern League Luton Town returning to make a few guest appearances for United in 1918 and after the war, he joined South Shields for their first season as a FL club, playing just once. He made more than 40 FL appearances for his two subsequent clubs, but reached only 78 in total. When his playing career was over, he became a widely respected groundsman in Sheffield and also played cricket for United.

Appearances:

	Apps	Gls
FL	36	0
FAC	2	0
WW1	5	0
ABD	1	0
Total	44	0

MONTGOMERY Nicholas (Nick) Anthony

MF 2000– 5' 9" 11st 8
b. Leeds 28 October 1981

United: trial age 15, appr 1998, pro 7 Jul 2000
Debuts: 21 Oct 2000 Norwich City 4 United 2 (sub)
24 Oct 2000 United 1 Stockport County 0

Nick Montgomery played with Leeds United as a schoolboy and also for Leeds Boys before moving to the Lane when he was fifteen. He came through United's junior ranks though hindered by injuries and illness and has played a full part in each season since making his first team debut in 2000.

Combative and committed, he can be relied on to give his all for the full 90 minutes of every game, running as enthusiastically at the finish as he was at the start. He played most of his games as a defensive midfielder, sometimes, and successfully, as a one-to-one marker when the situation demanded. His passing skills and shooting are disappointing although, when he did get his long range shooting on target, he could produce a spectacular goal. There were occasions when the influx of other players looked to have brought an end to Monty's United career and for much of the 2005–06 season he was on the transfer list but he always fought his way back. 2007–08 was a particularly disappointing season for after

recovering from the previous season's shoulder injury he suffered ligament problems, pleurisy and a broken foot.

He had spells when he was a regular on the bench and as a result, he holds the club record for the most substitute appearances and he has played for the Scotland Under 21 and 'Futures' teams

Appearances:		Apps	Gls
	FL	165 (62)	7
	FAC	13 (4)	0
	LC	11 (3)	2
	Total	189 (69)	9

MOONEY Thomas (Tommy) John

Striker 2003 5' 10½" 12st 7
b. Billingham 11 August 1971

Aston Villa from trainee Nov 1989/ Scarborough Aug 1990 Southend United (£100k) Jul 1993/ Watford Mar 1994 Birmingham City (free) Jul 2001/ Stoke City (L) Sep 2002/
United: (L) 17 Jan 2003 to c3 Mar 2003
Debuts: 21 Jan 2003 Liverpool 2 United 0 (sub LC)
25 Jan 2003 United 4 Ipswich Town 3 (FAC)
1 Feb 2003 Millwall 1 United 0
Last game: 22 Feb 2003 United 0 Norwich City 1
Derby County (L) Mar 2003/ Swindon Town (free) Jul 2003/ Oxford United Jul 2004/ Wycombe Wanderers Jul 2005/ Walsall Jul 2007/ UD Marbella (Spain) Jun 2008

Tommy Mooney began his career with Aston Villa but his FL debut had to wait until he joined Scarborough. He appeared as a substitute at Burnley on 8 September 1990 and his full debut was at Hereford United on 3 November. During his career he played for a variety of clubs, his longest spell being at Watford where he made 250 League appearances. During 2002–03 he fell out of favour at his then current club Birmingham City and had three loan spells, one of which was at the Lane.

United, being in the throes of two cup competitions and doing well in the League, had a shortage of fit strikers and Tommy was signed for a month. His first three games were in three different competitions but after differences with Neil Warnock and six hard-working appearances he returned to Birmingham.

He continued to move from club to club and by the end of 2007–08 had played 579(59) League games scoring 185 goals.

Appearances:		Apps	Gls
	FL	2 (1)	0
	FAC	2	1
	LC	0 (1)	0
	Total	4 (2)	1

MOORE Anthony (Tony) Peter

RB 1979–82 5' 9" 10st 12
b. Wolverhampton 19 September 1957

Burton Albion
United: 9 Jul 1979 to 8 Apr 1982
Debuts: 7 Aug 1979 Notts County 0 United 1 (ASC)
11 Aug 1979 United 1 Doncaster Rovers 1 (LC)
25 Aug 1979 Chester 1 United 1
Last game: 30 Jan 1982 United 0 Hull City 0
Crewe Alexandra Aug 1982/ Worksop Town Mar 1983/ Goole Town ?/ Rochdale Oct 1984/ Belper Town/ Sheffield Club mgr 1987–88

Tony Moore was signed by manager Harry Haslam and, although he put plenty of energy into his play, he never managed a consistent run in the first team during his three seasons with United. His best was a run of nine games in late 1981 and many supporters will chiefly remember him for a goal which cannoned in off his back-side after just 12 seconds of a match at Exeter in 1980. He fared no better at his two other League clubs, making a further 20 FL appearances in total. In more recent years, he has been a painter and decorator in Sheffield and involved with Wednesday's junior coaching system.

Appearances:		Apps	Gls
	FL	29	0
	LC	2	0
	ASC	2	0
	Total	33	0

MOORE John

MF 1989 6' 0" 11st 11
b. Consett 1 October 1966

Blackhall Juniors/Sunderland app May 1983, pro Oct 1984 St Patrick Athletic (L) Jan 1985/ Newport County (L) Dec 1985/ Darlington (L) Nov 1986/ Mansfield Town (L) Mar 1987 Rochdale (L) Jan 1988/ Hull City (£25k) Jun 1988
United: (L) 7 Mar 1989 to cs 1989
Debuts: 25 Apr 1989 United 1 Mansfield Town 2 (sub)
1 May 1989 United 1 Aldershot 0
Last game: 13 May 1989 Bristol City 2 United 0
FC Utrecht (£30k) (Holland) cs 1989/ Shrewsbury Town Jul 1990/ Crewe Alexandra Jan 1991/ FC Utrecht (Holland) Mar 1991/ Scarborough Aug 1991 to Apr 1992

John Moore made his FL debut with Sunderland as a substitute at home to Chelsea on 30 March 1985, his full debut coming four days later at home to Liverpool. After various loan moves and a transfer to Hull City, Dave Bassett brought John to Bramall Lane on loan to bolster up United's ultimately successful bid for promotion. There were rumours of a permanent move but he joined Utrecht instead. Normally an aggressive forward, Bassett used him more in mid-field but he was never a real success in either position.

John had a nomadic career but in the FL, he made just 48(22) appearances, some as an attacker, scoring eight goals.

Appearances:		Apps	Gls
	FL	4 (1)	0
	Total	4 (1)	0

MORAN Martin (Micky)

OR 1899–1900 5' 5" 10st to 10st 7
b. Bannockburn 19 December 1879

Benburb (Glasgow)/ Celtic Mar 1898/ Clyde Oct 1898
United: 5/6 Aug 1899 to 22 May 1900
Debut: 2 Sep 1899 Everton 1 United 2
Last games: 25 Dec 1899 Manchester City 1 United 2
19 Mar 1900 Northamton Town 0 United 3 (Fr)
Middlesbrough May 1900/ Millwall Athletic Aug 1902/ Heart of Midlothian May 1904/ Chelsea May 1905/ Glasgow Celtic May 1908/ Hamilton Academicals Jun 1909/ Albion Rovers Oct 1910

Martin Moran, a Scottish Junior international, played for Celtic 'on trial' against United at Bramall Lane in what was called 'the Championship of Great Britain' in March 1898. He played really well and signed as a professional for Celtic and made his Scottish League debut on 1 October 1898 at St Mirren but just over a year later, after a spell with Clyde, he joined United.

A very tricky winger who could put across some fine centres, he was quite fast but facing competition from 'Cocky' Bennett for the right wing spot, he played only a few games during his one season at the Lane.

After a successful spell with Middlesbrough he moved to Southern League Millwall Athletic and then back to Scotland before joining the newly formed club, Chelsea. Nicknamed 'the Muscular Midget', he played in their first ever FL game in September 1905, alongside the former United keeper Bill Foulke, and was a regular member of the side for that first season. In 1908, having reached 106 career FL games, he returned to his native Scotland.

Appearances:		Apps	Gls
	FL	7	0
	Total	7	0

MORDUE Thomas ('Tommy' or Tucker)

IL/CF/IR 1926–27 5' 7" 10st 8
b. Horden (Co. Durham) 22 June 1905
d. Sunderland OND 1975

Herrington Swifts/ Hull City Sep 1923/ Horden Athletic Jun 1924/ Newcastle United (£150) Nov 1925
United: (£500) 30 Sep/1 Oct 1926 to cs 1928
Debut: 16 Oct 1926 Tottenham Hotspur 3 United 1
Last game: 17 Dec 1927 Blackburn Rovers 1 United 0
Hartlepools United (£100) 6 Sep 1928/ Horden Colliery Welfare 1931/ Shotton CW Apr 1931/ Horden Coke Ovens

Brought up in Kimblesworth, near Durham City, Tommy Mordue made his FL debut with Hull City on 27 October 1923 at Stoke City but both at Hull and at Newcastle, where he made his debut against the Blades and scored, he was mainly a reserve player.

Small and aggressive, he distributed the ball well but was too slow for top class football and in nearly two seasons with United, he played only seven games and was put on the transfer list in May 1928.

He had much more success with Hartlepools United where he played 101 FL games, bringing his total to 119. In the 1930's he was a prominent handball player and played doubles with his brother Billy.

Appearances:		Apps	Gls
	FL	7	0
	Total	7	0

MOREMENT Ralph

LB/CF 1947–50 5' 10" 11st 7
b. Sheffield 24 September 1924
d. 1982?

Hampton's Sports
United: 7/8 Oct 1946 to 16 May 1950
Debuts: 29 Oct 1947 Western Command 0 United XI 5 (Fr, at Oswestry)
4 Feb 1950 United 3 Grimsby Town 1
Last games: 11 Feb 1950 United 0 Southampton 1
4 May 1950 Skegness Town 3 United XI 2 (Fr)
Chester May 1950/ Worksop T cs1953/ Rochdale Aug-Nov 1955

A solid, dependable player, who was good in the air though he lacked speed, Ralph Morement played for the reserves at full back, wing half or centre half in his four seasons at Bramall Lane. He also had a few games at centre forward and it was in that position that he made his two competitive first team appearances.

Given a free transfer in 1950, he joined Chester and made 121 FL appearances, scoring 19 goals, playing usually as a halfback but frequently at centre forward. He made one appearance for Rochdale.

Appearances:		Apps	Gls
	FL	2	0
	Total	2	0

MORGAN Christopher (Chris) Paul

CD 2003– 6' 1" 12st 5 to 13st 6
b. Barnsley 9 November 1977

Barnsley from trainee Jul 1996
United: (free) 1 Aug 2003
Debuts: 23 Jul 2003 Tavistock 0 United 4 (Fr)
9 Aug 2003 United 0 Gillingham 0

A Penistone lad, Chris Morgan played for Barnsley Boys before beginning his football career with Barnsley and became a defender at their Academy. He watched Barnsley's promotion season from the sidelines and made his first team debut in the Premiership on 10 January 1998 in a 0–6 defeat at West Ham United.

After 185 League appearances for Barnsley, he moved to Bramall Lane and immediately became a first choice central defender. A no-nonsense, uncompromising defender who always gave 100%, he did not shirk a challenge and showed good anticipation, and was excellent in the air and a danger at set pieces in the opposition penalty area. His distribution could be lacking at times and in his first seasons with United he was prone to losing his temper, being sent off four times, and suspended for a further incident 'caught on camera' against Arsenal.

Voted 'Player of the Year' at the end of his first season he was appointed captain for the 2004–05 campaign and, in 2006, led the team to the Premiership. He played in the opening few games before being replaced by Davis but returned on several occasions to make a significant contribution to the team. In 2007–08 he soon found himself out of favour after Gary Cahill's arrival on loan but again Chris returned to play a significant role in the club's revival under Kevin Blackwell. Chris's season ended early after he was sent off twice, both times somewhat unluckily, for two yellow cards, making him United's most 'sent-off' player with a total of six.

Appearances:		Apps	Gls
	FL	155 (6)	9
	FAC	10	1
	LC	9	1
	Total	174 (6)	11

MORREN Thomas ('Tommy')

CH 1895–1903 5' 5½" 10st 4 to 10st 10
b. Monkwearmouth, Sunderland AMJ 1871
d. Sheffield 30/31 January 1929

Middlesbrough Victoria?/ Middlesbrough Vulcan Middlesbrough Ironopolis/ Middlesbrough Vulcan Middlesbrough
United: 26 Nov 1895 to cs 1904
Debuts: 27 Dec 1895 United 1 Corinthians 0 (Fr)
28 Dec 1895 Burnley v United (abd 0–1)
30 Dec 1895 United 1 Bolton Wanderers 0
Last games: 31 Jan 1903 Everton 1 United 0
7 Feb 1903 Woolwich Arsenal 1 United 3 (FAC)
29 Apr 1903 Leeds Association XI 2 United 7 (Fr)
Leeds City 1904

Tommy Morren played as an amateur—probably with fairly generous expenses—for most of the senior clubs in the Middlesbrough area and won NL medals in 1894 and 1895 and an FA Amateur Cup winners' medal in 1895 with the Middlesbrough Football Club. The Middlesbrough captain, Phil Bache, had turned professional with Reading and Tommy, who had taken over the captaincy but was out of work, agreed to join him and become a professional.

Tom's train journey to Reading was via Sheffield and United heard of his plans from the Middlesbrough secretary. George Waller, the United trainer, who had played football and cricket in Middlesbrough and knew Tommy, was sent to the Midland station to persuade him to have a trial with United. George took positive action, grabbing his bag and making off to a waiting cab with poor Tommy in tow. He played that afternoon in a reserve match at the Lane and then returned to Middlesbrough, agreeing to sign for United if they would find him work in Sheffield as a moulder.

Tommy was the centre half in the famous 'midget' United half back line. He was 'better in defence than in feeding the forwards' according to Ernest Needham, always in the thick of the action, fighting to the last and talking incessantly in an attempt to unsettle his opponents. Difficult to knock off the ball, he was the centre half when United won the Championship in 1898 and played in two FA Cup finals, winning in 1899 and losing in 1901. He played once for England in 1898, but missed other opportunities through illness or injury, and twice for the Football League.

Injuries and finally sickness took their toll and he lost his place to Bernard Wilkinson though he finished with a flourish in his final first team appearance, perhaps scoring a hat trick though match reports are confusing.

After leaving United, he played a few friendly games for the newly formed Leeds City team before retiring and running a newspaper and general store in the Sharrow Vale district of Sheffield.

Appearances:		Apps	Gls
	FL	160	5
	FAC	26	1
	ABD	4	0
	Total	190	6

MORRIS Colin

OR 1982–88 5' 6½" 10st 5
b. Blyth 22 August 1953

Burnley app Aug 1969, pro Aug 1971/ Southend United (£7,000) Jan 1977/ Blackpool (exchange deal value £175k) Dec 1979
United: (£100k) 6 Feb 1982 to 1 Jul 1988
Debut: 9 Feb 1982 United 4 Stockport County 0
Last games: 30 Apr 1988 Reading 2 United 1
18 May 1988 United 1 Bristol City 1 (PO)
12 Sep 1988 United XI 1 Sheffield W 3 (BM)
Scarborough player coach Jul 1988, mgr Jan 1989 to Nov 1989/ Boston United/ Goole Town Feb 1990/ Bridlington Town player-mgr, Apr-Oct 1991

Colin Morris began his career with Burnley, making his FL debut on 11 January 1975 at Queens Park Rangers. After ten FL games he moved to Southend, where he made 133 FL appearances (25 goals) and he then spent two seasons at Blackpool (87 FL app, 25 gls).

In February 1982 United had high hopes of an immediate return to Division Three after the previous season's relegation and, although Ian Porterfield had brought in several new players at the start of the season, there had been some disappointing results. Colin was signed for what turned out to be a bargain price of £100k and he added that bit extra that meant United became Champions.

A small traditional tricky, two footed right winger, Colin was an instant success at Bramall Lane. His darting runs, combining speed and with fine ball control, provided many scoring opportunities for others and Keith Edwards in particular took full advantage. Colin was a good finisher himself and a very good penalty taker; more than half of his FL goals were scored from the spot. He took over 50 penalties in competitive games, failing with about a dozen and he holds the club record for both scoring and missing the most spot-kicks.

Colin was a fixture in the side, a consistent performer, providing skill and entertainment for more than six seasons. He played and scored in the unsuccessful play-off game against Bristol City but new manager Dave Bassett, brought down the curtain on Colin's United career.

He moved to Scarborough in the summer of 1988 though returning in September for his benefit match. He ended his FL career having scored 121 goals in 484(10) games. He succeeded Neil Warnock as Scarborough's manger but all too soon, he in turn was succeeded by Ray McHale and for a short time, he moved into non-League football. Colin's son, Lee, later played for United.

Appearances:		Apps	Gls
	FL	235 (5)	67
	PO	1	1
	FAC	16 (1)	5
	LC	19 (1)	7
	FMC	4	3
	AMC	5	1
	Total	280 (7)	84

MORRIS Hugh

IR/IL 1893–95 5' 4"
b. Chirk, Wrexham 1872
d. Chirk, 20 September 1897

Chirk FC 1888/ Ardwick Mar 1891
United: 1/2 Dec 1893 to 7/9 Nov 1895
Debut: 16 Dec 1893 Stoke 5 United 0
Last games: 19 Oct 1895 Wolverhampton Wanderers 4 United 1
23 Oct 1895 Gainsborough Trinity 2 United 0 (Fr)
Manchester City Nov 1895/ Grimsby Town May 1896/ Millwall Athletic May 1897

Hugh came to prominence with Chirk in Welsh Cup matches and joined Ardwick, then in the Football Alliance. The following season Ardwick joined the FL and Hugh made his debut, scoring twice in the club's first FL game at home to Bootle on 3 September 1892. He moved to United from Ardwick and would return there, nearly two years later, by which time Ardwick had become Manchester City.

A hard working little forward, he played regularly in his first season at Bramall Lane though several of his games were friendlies. He rejected an offer in September 1894 to play in the United States and he appeared in 20 of the 30 FL games of that 1894–95 season and was capped against Scotland. In September 1895, he and Joe Davies, both former Ardwick players, were suspended for 'lodging in a public house', contrary to their contracts and were transferred back to Manchester along with Bob Hill.

Hugh was capped again with City and gained his third with Grimsby Town and ended his FL career with 33 goals in 99 games. He moved on to Southern League Millwall Athletic but, before he could make his first team debut, he was taken ill and died of tuberculosis.

Appearances:		Apps	Gls
	FL	32	8
	FAC	1	0
	UCL	7	1
	WCC	1	0
	Total	41	9

MORRIS Lee

MF/OR/OL 1997–99 5' 10" 11st 2
b. Blackpool 30 April 1980

United: from trainee, pro 24 Dec 1997 to 14 Oct 1999
Debuts: 19 Aug 1997 United 0 Everton 4 (sub Fr)
17 Jan 1998 United 1 Wolverhampton Wanderers 0 (sub)
30 Jan 1999 Crewe Alexander 1 United 2
Last games: 9 May 1999 Ipswich Town 4 United 1
9 Oct 1999 Crewe Alexander 1 United 0 (sub)
Derby County (£900k rising to£3m?) Oct 1999/ Huddersfield Town (L) Mar 2001/ Leicester City (£120k) Feb 2004/ Yeovil Town Aug 2006 to Mar 2008

Lee Morris, a son of the former United winger Colin, was a quick and skilful player who appeared to have a first class future ahead of him but he was extremely unlucky with injuries. The first serious blow came when his leg was broken on tour with the juniors in France in 1996 but there would be many more.

He played for the England U18 team in October 1997 and made 16 FL and Cup appearances as a substitute before making his first start for United. His progress had been hindered by foot injuries but towards the end of the 1998–99 season, he had a run in the side scoring seven goals in sixteen FL and Cup starts. Another broken foot injury in the 1999 pre-season tour kept him out of the side but once he was fit again, he was transferred to Derby County, United receiving a club record fee, initially of £900k but rising to possibly £3 million.

He stated well for his new club but his foot problems recurred and although he did play nearly 100 games for the Rams, he moved on eventually to lower divisions of the Football League. Further injury (a cruciate ligament rupture) problems meant he left Yeovil by mutual consent in March 2008 by which time he had 29 League goals in 106(60) appearances.

Appearances:		Apps	Gls
	FL	14 (12)	6
	PO	0 (1)	0
	FAC	2 (5)	2
	Total	16 (18)	8

MORRIS Mark John

CD 1989–91 6' 1" 13st 8
b. Carshalton, Surrey 26 September 1962

Wimbledon from app, pro Sep 1980/ Aldershot (L) Sep 1985/ Watford (£37.5k) Jul 1987

United: **(£175k) 11 Jul 1989 to 26/31 Jul 1991**
Debuts: **23 Jul 1989 TuS Celle(W Germany) 2 United 2 (sub Fr)**
24 Jul 1989 TSV Havelese (West Germany) 0 United 6 (Fr)
9 Aug 1989 Scarborough 1 United 3 (YHC)
19 Aug 1989 West Bromwich Albion 3 United 0
Last games: **1 Dec 1990 Aston Villa 1 United 1**
22 May 1991 Tulsa Renegades 1 United 4 (Fr)

Bournemouth (£95–100k) Jul 1991/ Gillingham (L) Sep 1996/ Brighton & Hove Albion Oct 1996/ Hastings Town Dec 1997/ Dorchester Town Feb 1999 then mgr 2003 to Jul 2006

Mark began his career with Wimbledon making his FL debut on 31 October 1981 at home to Exeter City. He was a regular in the Wimbledon side which rose from Division Four to Division One and then followed Dave Bassett to Watford.

When Mark signed for United, for what was the club's record transfer fee at the time, it was the third time he had played under 'Harry' Bassett. A no nonsense, traditional central defender, known to the players as 'Guppy', his attitude was first class and he was a key member of the side which gained promotion to the top flight but, after 14 games in the old First Division, he lost his place and at the end of the season moved to Bournemouth where he had a long and successful time, being voted 'Player of the Year' in 1992–93.

After spells with Gillingham and Brighton he retired from League football, having played 501(9) League games. He moved to Dorchester Town first as a player and then as manager, being in charge when the club were promoted to the Conference South.

Appearances:		Apps	Gls
	FL	53 (3)	3
	FAC	5	0
	LC	5	0
	FMC	2	0
	YHC	1	1
	Total	66 (3)	4

MORRISON Andrew (Andy) Charles

CD 2001 6' 0" 14st 8
b. Inverness 30 July 1970

Plymouth Argyle from trainee Jul 1988/ Blackburn Rovers (£500k) Aug 1993/ Blackpool (£245k) Dec 1994 Huddersfield Town (£500k) Jul 1996/ Manchester City (£80k) Oct 1988/ Blackpool (L) Sep 2000/ Crystal Palace (L) Oct 2000

United: **(L) 22 Mar 2001 to cs 2001**
Debut: **14 Apr 2001 Gillingham 4 United 1**
Last game: **28 Apr 2001 United 2 Burnley 1**

Retired cs 2001 / – / Bury (trial) 2002 / – / Worcester City asst mgr Feb 2005 to Apr 2007

Andy Morrison made his FL debut with Plymouth Argyle, as a substitute, on 27 February 1988 at Aston Villa, his full debut coming a year later on 6 May at home to Oxford United. He was a popular player at Manchester City but his career was blighted by injuries, one keeping him out for over 12 months.

A hard player with few if any frills and with an admitted temper, he was towards the end of his career when he joined United on transfer deadline day in 2001. His debut was in a disappointing defeat at Gillingham but he had an excellent game at Grimsby before an injury in the next match ended his season early. He retired during the close season, having played 246(160) League games and a trial with Bury reserves in late 2002 was unsuccessful.

He became assistant manager of Worcester City in February 2005 where he had a successful time as coach. In July 2006 he was convicted of defrauding the Department of Work and Pensions and was fined and given 50 hours community service and in 2006–07, he was given a six match FA ban, in addition to a club ban and fine, following an incident at a friendly game against Kidderminster Harriers which was abandoned.

Appearances:		Apps	Gls
	FL	3 (1)	0
	Total	3 (1)	0

MORRISON John Owen

MF/W 2003 5' 8" 11st 12
b. Derry 8 December 1981

Sheffield Wednesday from trainee, pro Jan 1999 Hull City (L) Aug 2002

United: **(free) 21 Feb 2003 to 6 Aug 2003**
Debuts: **22 Feb 2003 United 0 Norwich City 1 (sub)**
22 Mar 2003 United 2 Brighton & Hove Albion 1
Last game: **26 Apr 2003 United 3 Wolverhampton Wanderers 3**

Stockport County (free) Aug 2003/ Bradford City Dec 2004/ Dunfermline Athletic Jul 2006/ Qingdao Zhongneng (China) (trial) Feb 2007/ Derry City Feb 2008

Owen Morrison began his career with neighbours Wednesday, making his League debut as a substitute on 26 December 1998 at home to Leicester City and his full debut on 16 September 2000 at Tranmere Rovers. He was seen as an outstanding talent, winning Northern Ireland caps at schoolboy, youth and Under 21 level but off-field problems affected his progress. The 2002–03 season was a disappointing one for him at Hillsborough and after a loan spell with Hull City, his contract was cancelled.

He moved to Bramall Lane on a short term contract. United had reached the League Cup semi-final and were still involved in the FA Cup and were also hoping for a play-off place and Owen was recruited as cover for injuries. His opportunities were limited but despite being an ex-Owl, he won over the crowd with some lively performances as an attacking left sided midfielder and he nearly scored against Brighton after a run from the half-way line. He won three more U21 caps whilst with United but at the end of the season, he was released.

After a spell with Bradford, he moved to Scotland and toyed with a move to China but decided to stay with Dunfermline. In February 2008 he moved back to Ireland having played just over 150 League games during his time in England and Scotland.

Appearances:		Apps	Gls
	FL	3 (5)	0
	Total	3 (5)	0

MORTIMER Dennis George

MF 1984–85 5' 10" 12st 4
b. Liverpool 5 April 1952

Coventry City from 1967, pro Sep 1969 Aston Villa (£175k) Dec 1975
United: (L) 27 Dec 1984 to 27 Feb 1985
Debut: 29 Dec 1984 United 4 Portsmouth 1
Last game: 23 Feb 1985 United 3 Barnsley 1
Brighton & Hove Albion Aug 1985/ Birmingham City Aug 1986/ Kettering Town Aug 1987/ Redditch United player-mgr 1988

Dennis Mortimer began his career with Coventry City making his FL debut as a substitute 11 October 1969 at home to West Ham United; his full debut coming on 31 January at home to Arsenal. Having won England caps at youth and U23 level, he moved to Aston Villa where he had nine successful seasons, playing over 300 FL games. A superb mid-field player with vision and control, he gained a League Cup winner's medal and later captained Villa to the League Championship in 1981 and the following season, to victory in the European Cup. He captained England B and was considered by many to be unlucky never to gain a full cap.

Dennis moved to United on loan, signed by Ian Porterfield and was immediately influential in midfield but his loan ended after seven games following a serious off-the-ball facial injury against Barnsley which was soon followed, after a further foul, by the dismissal of Rodger Wylde.

After finishing his FL career with Birmingham City, having totalled 575(15) FL appearances, he had a spell in non-League football. He moved to West Bromwich Albion, in 1992, as Community Officer, then coach and assistant manager until October 1994. More recently, he has worked for the PFA.

Appearances:		Apps	Gls
	FL	7	0
	Total	7	0

MORTON David

IR/CF 1897 5' 10" 12st 3
b. Alva, Clackmanna 1871?

Berryhill (Stirling)/ Millwall Athletic Mar 1897
United: 14/15 Jun 1897 to Nov 1897
Debut: 1 Sep 1897 United 2 Derby County 1
Last game: 2 Oct 1897 Wolverhampton Wanderers 1 United 1
Camelon FC (nr. Falkirk) May 1898/ Wishaw Nov 1899/ Falkirk May 1900/ Camelon Mar 1902

Having played eight games and scored four goals for Southern League Millwall Athletic in the 1896–97 season, David Morton moved to Bramall Lane but the Sheffield newspapers made no comment on his play or the reason for his early departure in the season which ended with United crowned as champions.

Appearances:		Apps	Gls
	FL	2	0
	Total	2	0

MOSFORTH William (Billy)

OL/IL 1889–90 5' 3½" 11st 0
b. Sheffield 2 January 1858
d. Sheffield 11 July 1929

Sheffield Albion 1872–73 to 79/ Ecclesfield Wednesday 1875–88/ Norfolk 1876/ Crookes 1876 Exhange 1879/ Providence 1879/ Hallam Nov 1879 Walkley 1884/ Heeley 1884/ Lockwood Brothers 1886 Owlerton 1889
United: cs 1889 to cs 1890
Debuts: 7 Sep 1889 Nottingham Rangers 4 United 1 (Fr)
5 Oct 1889 Scarborough 1 United 6 (FAC)
Last games: 21 Dec 1889 United 2 Rotherham Town 1 (FAC)
22 Mar 1890 Rotherham Town 1 United 0 (SCC)

Billy Mosforth, an engraver by trade, was an all-round sportsman, running in both flat and hurdle races and playing cricket for Hallam C.C. but it was as a footballer that he excelled. He possessed great speed, marvellous dribbling ability where he used both feet and became famous for his left footed, accurate, 'screw' shots, occasionally catching a keeper unaware from near the corner flag. Popularly known as 'the Little Wonder' or the 'Sheffield Dodger', he played for several of the local sides but particularly for the Wednesday who were becoming the leading team in the town. He probably first played for them in 1875 and, two years later, he gained the first of his nine England caps and played in most of Wednesday's more important games for thirteen years though as an amateur, he also played for other local teams.

Billy was 31 years old when he joined the newly formed United in 1889, one of the first three players to be signed and all his twenty eight appearances—nineteen friendly games—came in the club's first season. He played in United's first ever game and in the first FA Cup tie at Scarborough where he scored. He could also claim to be the first United player to be substituted when he played the first few minutes of the friendly against Bolton Wanderers on 18 November 1889. When the selected player, Aizlewood, arrived Billy left the field.

He later became a licensee in Sheffield and died in Fir Vale Hospital.

Appearances:		Apps	Gls
	FAC	4	2
	SCCetc	3	0
	WCC	2	2
	Total	9	4

MUGGLETON Carl David

G 1996 6' 2" 13st 4
b. Leicester 13 September 1968

Leicester City from app Sep 1986/ Chesterfield (L) Sep 1987/ Blackpool (L) Feb 1988/ Hartlepool **United** (L) Oct 1988/ Stockport County (L) Mar 1990/ Liverpool Sep 1990/ Stoke City (L) Aug 1993/ United (L) 25/26 Nov 1993/ Glasgow Celtic (£150k) Jan 1994/ Stoke City (£150k) Jul 1994/ Rotherham United (L) Nov 1995
United: **(L) 28 Mar 1996 to c30 Apr 1996**
Only game: **27 Apr 1996 Reading 0 United 3 (sub)**
Mansfield Town (L) Sep 1999/ Chesterfield (L) Dec 1999/ Cardiff City (L) Mar 2001/ Cheltenham Town (free) Jul 2001/ Bradford City (L) Dec 2001/ Chesterfield (free) Jul 2002/ Mansfield Town (free) Jul 2006 to May 2008/ Notts County goalkeeping coach Jul 2008

A Leicester City player, Carl Muggleton made his FL debut on loan at Chesterfield on 12 September 1987 at home to Port Vale. In 1990, despite several loan moves and not having an established place in a club side, he gained an England U21 cap.

He joined United on loan in November 1993 and, although on the bench for 10 games, he didn't make an appearance. Carl continued on his travels and then returned to Bramall Lane, again on loan, for the end of the 1995–96 campaign. Having been on the bench for six games, his chance finally came as a substitute for the final two minutes of a game at Reading. It was kit-man, John Greaves who suggested he should get his chance but not in goal but as a forward; he came on for the injured Chris Short but sadly, he never touched the ball.

He has continued to play for a variety of clubs, clocking up over 444(3) League appearances including his time with Celtic.

Appearances:		Apps	Gls
	FL	0 (1)	0
	Total	0 (1)	0

MULLIGAN Gary Thomas

Striker 2005 6' 1" 12st 3
b. Dublin 23 April 1985

Wolverhampton Wanderers from trainee, pro Jul 2002 Rushden & Diamonds (L) Oct 2004 to Jan 2005
United: **(free) 6 Jul 2005 to 13 May 2006**
Debuts: **11 Jul 2005 Worksop Town 0 United XI 1 (sub. Fr)**
23 Aug 2005 United 1 Boston United 0 (sub LC)
Last game: **20 Sep 2005 Shrewsbury Town 0 United 0 (LC)**
(L) Port Vale 22 Sep 2005 to 22 Dec 2005/ Gillingham (L) 13 Jan 2006 to 7 May 2006
Gillingham May 2006

Gary Mulligan made his League debut with Wolves as a substitute on 21 August 2004 at Burnley. His full debut came whilst he was on loan at Rushden & Diamonds when he scored in the 1–1 draw at Wycombe Wanderers.

He joined United on a free transfer and made just three appearances, one in a pre-season friendly and the other two in the League Cup. After his appearance at Shrewsbury, he spent most of the remainder of the season on loan, latterly at Gillingham where he moved permanently in the summer.

He was a regular in the squad and had totalled over 100 League appearances by the end of 2007–08.

Appearances:		Apps	Gls
	LC	1 (1)	0
	Total	1 (1)	0

MUNKS David

RH/FB 1964–69 5' 9½" 11st 8
b. Sheffield 29 April 1947

United: **from 1962, app Sep 1963, pro 28 Jul/1 Aug 1964 to 19 May 1969**
Debuts: **28 Nov 1964 United 3 Barnsley 2 (CC)**
21 Aug 1965 United 1 Aston Villa 0
Last game: **25 Mar 1969 Charlton Athletic 2 United 1**
Portsmouth (£20/25k) May 1969/ Swindon Town Dec 1973/ Exeter City (L) Dec 1974, signed Mar 1975 to 1976/ Waterlooville mgr/ Havant coach

A pupil of the Rowlinson School at Meadowhead, David Munks played for Sheffield and Yorkshire Boys. He came through the United junior ranks and made his first team debut in a County Cup fixture and became an England youth international in April 1965. He went on the end of season tour to New Zealand during which United played Blackpool 12 times and began the 1965–66 season as first choice right half but unluckily broke his leg at Highbury. He re-established himself towards the end of the season and played quite regularly during the following campaign.

A hard working right sided, mid-field player, particularly in a defensive role, David covered and tackled well and could also play at full back or inside forward. In 1967–68 he played in every match but during the next season, he was replaced by Ted Hemsley and at the end of the season, he was sold to Portsmouth by manager Arthur Rowley.

With Pompey, he was voted 'Player of the Year' in 1970–71 and although David scored only three FL goals, one of those was against the Blades in September 1970 though the result was 5–1 in United's favour. After spells at Swindon and Exeter, David moved into non-League football having made 281(9) FL appearances.

Appearances:		Apps	Gls
	FL	108 (4)	1
	FAC	4 (1)	0
	LC	7	1
	CC	5	0
	Total	124 (5)	2

MUNRO (MUNROE) Harry

RH/LH 1890–91
b. Scotland

Somerton Athletic or Summerfield Athletic
United: Dec 1890 to 1891–92
Debuts: 8 Dec 1890 United 3 Middlesbrough Ironopolis 2 (Fr)
23 Mar 1891 United 2 Burton Wanderers 2 (MCL)
Last game: 23 Apr 1891 Wednesday 2 United 1 (WCC)
Gainsborough Trinity Mar 1892 to cs 1899/ South Shields 1899

The Sheffield newspapers differed as to where Harry Munro had played before joining United and the Independent referred to him initially as 'Monroe'. He played in eleven friendly fixtures as well as his two competitive games for United before moving to Gainsborough Trinity. An amateur with the Lincolnshire club—and presumably with United—he captained the team and made 89 FL appearances scoring twice. Described as 'Scottish' and a 'bag of tricks', by 1896, his name in the Gainsborough newspaper is given as 'Munroe'.

Appearances:		Apps	Gls
	MCL	1	1
	WCC	1	0
	Total	2	1

MURPHY Shaun Peter

CD 1999–2003 6' 1" 12st 0
b. Sydney, Australia 5 November 1970

Blacktown City/ Heidelberg/ Perth Italia, Australia 1990 Notts County Sep 1992/ West Bromwich Albion (£500k) Dec 1996/ Sorrento, Perth 1999
United: (free) 22 Jul 1999 to cs 2003
Debuts: 16 Jul 1999 Doncaster Rovers 0 United 1 (Fr)
7 Aug 1999 Portsmouth 2 United 0
Last game: 26 Apr 2003 United 3 Wolverhampton Wanderers 3
(L) Crystal Palace 1 Feb 2002
Perth Glory 2003–04

Shaun's family moved to Perth when he was two and it was there that he began an engineering degree and having played for various clubs in Australia he was a member of the Australian Olympic squad in 1992. He was signed by Neil Warnock for Notts County and he made his FL debut as a substitute on 5 September 1992 at home to Barnsley. His full debut came a week later at Watford but it wasn't until March 1994, after Neil's departure, that Shaun established himself as a regular in the side. A bronze medal winner in the 1996 Olympics, he won his first full cap in that same year and was transferred to West Bromwich Albion.

He joined United, signed by Adrian Heath, with a record of 180 FL appearances and 12 goals under his belt and immediately became a

fixture in the centre of defence. This continued after the arrival of Neil Warnock, despite Shaun's reported concerns that he might be thought to be not good enough.

He was a player of great commitment, good anticipation, excellent in the air as a defender and at set pieces in the opposition's penalty area and a strong decisive tackler. Only his distribution, which could be wayward, let him down. He missed just four FL games during his first season but was at his best in the second (2000–2001) when he played in every game, was 'Player of the Year' and, in June, scored the winning goal for Australia against Brazil.

His 2001–02 season was disrupted by international call-ups, in particular the Australia v Uruguay World Cup play-off. On his return, there were problems over his agreeing a new contract and he was placed on the transfer list and went on loan to Crystal Palace. He returned to United but, in April 2003, due to his wife's serious illness, his contract was cancelled and he returned to Australia where he played one season with Perth Glory, captaining them to the NSL Championship. With United, he had won 10 international caps for Australia. His brother Peter joined United in July 2001 and performed well for the reserves but was never given an opportunity with the first team.

Appearances:		Apps	Gls
	FL	157 (1)	10
	FAC	6	1
	LC	18	1
	Total	181 (1)	12

MYERS Martin

F 1989

United: trialist Aug 1989
Only game: 14 Aug 1989 Halifax Town 1 United 0 (YHC)

Martin Myers played just one game as a trialist in the pre-season competition.

He is possibly the player (b. Birmingham 10 January1966) who began his career as a schoolboy with Birmingham C, moved to Shrewsbury (no FL app), then to Tamworth 1984 (with whom he won the FA Vase in 1989)/ Telford U Jul 1990/ Solihull Borough (£11k) Jul 1996/ Strourbridge cs 1998/ Redditch U c1999/ Moor Green cs 2001/ Redditch U cs2003/ ?/ Tamworth/ Halesowen Mar 2006/ Evesham U cs 2006/ Tipton Town Sep 2006.

Appearances:		Apps	Gls
	YHC	1	0
	Total	1	0

NADE Christian

Striker 2006–07 6' 1" 12st 8
b. Montmorency (France) 18 September 1984

Troyes (France) Jul 1999/ Le Havre (France((L) Jan to May 2005/
Derby C trial May 2006
United: 27 Jun 2006 to 31 Aug 2007
Debuts: 28 Jul 2006 Rotherham United 1 United 1 (sub Fr)
8 Aug 2006 Ado den Haag 2 United 2 (Fr)
22 Aug 2006 Tottenham Hotspur 2 United 0 (sub)
19 Aug 2006 United 1 Bury 0 (LC)
28 Nov 2006 Watford 0 United 1
Last game: 13 May 2007 United 1 Wigan Athletic 2
Hull City (trial) Jul 2007
Hearts (£400k) Aug 2007

Christian made his French League debut in the 2002–03 season with Troyes. An U21 international, he was recommended to Neil Warnock by former Blade, Laurent D'Jaffo and signed a three-year deal on his arrival at the Lane, United paying nominal compensation to Troyes.

A strong, quick striker, with the ability to hold the ball, described by Neil as a 'raw talent', his first appearances were from the bench as it was felt he was lacking the necessary fitness. Having scored on his club debut in a friendly, he scored with superb strikes on his full debut in the League Cup and against Arsenal in December. He was a difficult opponent to handle and though United had an excess of strikers, many supporters were surprised when he was sold to Hearts, where he was a regular member of the side, though a proposed transfer to Hull City collapsed over 'fitness problems'.

Appearances:		Apps	Gls
	FL	7 (18)	3
	FAC	1	0
	LC	1 (1)	1
	Total	9 (19)	4

NALIS Lilian Bernard Pierre

MF 2005–06 6' 1" 13st 3
b. Nogent sur Marne/ Paris (France) 29 September 1971

Meaux/ Auxerre 1992/SM Caen 1993/ Laval cs 1995 Guingamp cs 1997/ Le Havre cs 1998/ Bastia cs 1999 Chievo(Italy) cs 2002/ Leicester City Jul 2003
United: (free) 17 May/6 Jul 2005 to 13 Jan 2006
Debuts: 11 Jul 2005 Worksop Town 0 United 1 (Fr)
6 Aug 2005 United 4 Leicester City 1
Last games: 13 Aug 2005 Queens Park Rangers 2 United 1
17 Sep 2005 Watford 2 United 3 (sub)
7 Jan 2006 United 1 Colchester United 2 (FAC)
Coventry City (L) 14 Oct 2005
Plymouth Argyle Jan 2006 to Jun 2008/ Swindon Town Jul 2008

Lilian made his League debut in France, playing for Caen in August 1993. He played for several French clubs and was on the losing side with Bastia in the 2002 French Cup Final. He moved to Italy for a season and then to England, joining Leicester City, newly promoted to the Premiership, making his League debut as a substitute on 16 August at home to Southampton, his full debut coming a week later at Chelsea.

He joined United to play as a holding midfielder and was fully involved in the pre-season games but, after an injury in the third League game of the season, he lost his place to an improving Nick Montgomery. Following a loan spell with Coventry City, he was released from his contract and joined Plymouth Argyle where, by the end of 2007–08, he had played over 100 FL games bringing his total to 145(26).

Appearances:		Apps	Gls
	FL	3 (1)	0
	FAC	1	0
	LC	1	0
	Total	5 (1)	0

NAYLOR Bernard

OL 1920 5' 8" 11st 4
b. Sheffield AMJ 1897
d. Sheffield 15 March 1950

Darnall Old Boys
United: Apr/1 May 1920 to cs 1921
Debut: 4 Oct 1920 United 2 Everton 0
Last game: 16 Oct 1920 United 0 Liverpool 1
Doncaster Rovers cs 1921 to cs 1922

United made a £25 donation to the Darnall team when they signed Bernard Naylor. He made three first team appearances in successive games but was released at the end of the season and moved to Doncaster Rovers who were then playing in the Midland League.

Appearances:		Apps	Gls
	FL	3	0
	Total	3	0

NAYSMITH Gary Andrew

LWB 2007– 5' 7" 11st 8
b. Edinburgh 16 November 1978

Whitehill Welfare/ Heart of Midlothian Jun 1996 Everton (£1.75m) Oct 2000
United: (£1m) 5 Jul 2007
Debuts: 17 Jul 2007 Alfreton Town 0 United 2 (Fr)
11 Aug 2007 United 2 Colchester United 2

Gary Naysmith, a Scottish schoolboy, youth and U21 international, made his Scottish League debut with Hearts on 21 September 1996 at home to Motherwell, and won the first of his full caps. After 92(5) Scottish League appearances he moved to Everton, making his English League debut, as a substitute, on 21 October 2000 at Newcastle United. His full debut came at home to Villa on 5 November. He went on to make 113(21) League appearances and win 33 more caps before moving to the Lane.

Gary, one of Bryan Robson's first signings, was looking for regular first team football and signed a three year contract with United. He made his debut (both friendly and League) as captain, in the absence of Chris Morgan, and apart from missing a few games through injuries, mainly early in the season, he was a regular at left wing back. Concentrating on his defensive role he used his experience well although there were the occasional lapses. The arrival of Kevin Blackwell and United's revival saw Gary finish the season strongly, an he continued to play regularly for Scotland having won 40 caps by the cs of 2008.

Appearances:		Apps	Gls
	FL	38	0
	FAC	3	0
	LC	2	0
	Total	43	0

NDLOVU Peter

MF/Striker 2001–04 5' 8" 10st 2
b. Bulawayo (Zimbabwe) 25 February 1973

Highlanders (Zimbabwe)/ Coventry City (£10k) Aug 1991 Birmingham City (£1.6m) Jul 1997/ Huddersfield Town (L) Dec 2000
United: 2 Feb 2001 to cs 2004
Debut: 4 Feb 2001 Fulham 1 United 1
Last games: 17 Apr 2004 United 0 Stoke City 1
30 Apr 2004 United 1 Ipswich Town 1 (sub)
Mamelodi Sundowns (South Africa) Aug 2004

Peter began his football career in his native Zimbabwe and then joined Coventry City, making his FL debut as a substitute on 24 August 1991 at Queens Park Rangers. After six further substitute appearances, he made his full debut at Everton on 21 September. After over 150 FL appearances for Coventry and over 100 for Birmingham City he signed for United, where, again, he passed a century of League games.

From his arrival at the Lane, Peter was a regular member of the first team squad, usually in the starting line up but having spells on the bench. These were sometimes as a result of a dip in form but often because of his travels to and from Africa to represent his country. In his first part season with United he was sometimes used as a striker but from then on he played as an attacking midfielder, usually on the right but not infrequently on the left. He gradually became more accustomed to his defensive duties and worked hard in this role.

Speedy, with the ability to beat an opponent, his decision as to when to pass or cross the ball was not always the best. He did have an eye for goal both from a distance and close in and one of his most memorable goals was in the last minute against Leeds United in a dramatic League Cup victory in November 2002.

During his time at the Lane he was capped 25 or possibly 26 times for Zimbabwe, some as captain, making him the club's most capped player alongside, or ahead of Billy Gillespie. Peter also scored 21 goals in those international matches, a record for United. On occasions, because of his international commitments, he had to leave immediately after a United game, or he arrived back in Sheffield just before a match and this was perhaps one reason why he returned to play in South Africa. Certainly, in Zimbabwe, he was seen as a soccer hero and at one stage he had decided to retire from international football but he carried on due to public demand. During his time in England he scored 88 League goals in 339(86) games.

Appearances:		Apps	Gls
	FL	114 (21)	25
	PO	3	0
	FAC	7	2
	LC	6 (3)	2
	Total	130 (24)	29

NEAVE Robert A

CH 1912–13 5' 7" 11st 0
b. c1890 or Lochee, Dundee 23 May 1894?
d. Glasgow 3 July 1951

Glasgow Perthshire
United: 13/15 Apr 1912 to Aug 1913
Debut: 28 Sep 1912 Bradford City 3 United 1
Last game: 8 Feb 1913 Manchester City 3 United 0
Chesterfield Aug 1913/ Rochdale Jun 1914/ Clyde Oct 1915/ Kilmarnock Feb 1918/ Johnstone Aug 1922/ Helensburgh Aug 1925

Robert Neave, a Scottish junior international, was reported to be twenty-two years of age when he was signed by United. Terrier like and strong, his passing was unsatisfactory and United soon realised that he wasn't good in the air. He played intermittently during his one season with United before spending a season as the captain of Chesterfield.

His best seasons were with Kilmarnock where he won a Scottish Cup winners medal in 1920. A brother played for Clyde.

Appearances:		Apps	Gls
	FL	11	0
	Total	11	0

NEEDHAM Archie

IL 1903–05 5' 8" 11st 10
b. Ecclesall (Sheffield) August 1881
d. Brighton 29 October 1950

United: 6 May 1901/17 Nov 1902 to cs 1905
Debut: 14 Feb 1903 West Bromwich Albion 3 United 3
Last games: 23 Apr 1904 West Bromwich Albion 2 United 2
29 Apr 1905 Woolwich Arsenal 2 United 3 (Fr)
Crystal Palace cs 1905/ Glossop North End 29 May 1909/ Wolverhampton Wanderers Jul 1910/ Brighton & Hove Albion Jul 1911 to cs 1915

Archie came to United after playing for Sharrow Lane and Sheffield Schools. A hard working, bustling player, he spent four seasons with United but, although scoring on his debut and finishing with a good goals to games ratio, he never commanded a regular place in the side.

Transfer listed in 1905, he joined Crystal Palace who were just starting their first season in the Southern League and he had four good seasons there, helping them to win their League's Second Division. He return to the FL with Glossop and then Wolves and finished his career with four more seasons in the Southern league with Brighton, under the same manager that he had had at Palace. By now a utility player, he played in every position but goalkeeper for the Seagulls and ended his playing career having made 262 FL and Southern League appearances and scored more than sixty goals.

Archie was an early First World War volunteer, serving in the Footballer's Battalion and, on his return, he ran a haberdashery business in Hove where he lived until his death.

Appearances:		Apps	Gls
	FL	16	6
	Total	16	6

NEEDHAM C L

G 1915

Darfield United
United: WW1 guest
Only game: 4 Sep 1915 Lincoln City 7 United 3 (WW1)
Walh Athletic cs 1919

C L Needham's one appearance in goal for United's first team was a rather unhappy affair. It was the first fixture of 'war-time' football and United had a very weak team—five players were making their debut—and though it was reported that the new keeper 'performed very creditably' and was injured in the second half, he conceded seven goals.

He played for the reserves and probably for Mexborough before joining the Coldstream Guards.

Appearances:		Apps	Gls
	WW1	1	0
	Total	1	0

NEEDHAM Ernest (Nudger)

LH/F/D 1891–1910 5' 5" 10st 6 to 11st
b. Newbold Moor, Chesterfield (20th?) 21 January 1873
d. Chesterfield 8 March 1936

Staveley Wanderers (boys) 1889/ Staveley Oct 1889
United: Feb 1891 to 29 Mar 1910/ cs 1914
Debuts: 5 Sep 1891 Woolwich Arsenal 0 United 2 (Fr)
26 Sep 1891 United 7 Darlington 1 (NL)
24 Oct 1891 United 4 Lincoln City 1 (FAC)
3 Sep 1892 United 4 Lincoln City 2
Last games: 22 Jan 1910 Bolton Wanderers 1 United 0
5 Feb 1910 Oldham Athletic 3 United 1 (Fr)

It may be argued that Ernest Needham was Sheffield United's greatest ever player. He was described by Fred Spiksley, a contemporary fellow international as, taking all aspects of the game into consideration, 'the greatest player association football has ever seen'.

Born in Newbold Moor, a district of Chesterfield, Ernest moved to nearby Staveley at the age of six and at the age of sixteen, he began to play for Staveley, a club of standing in those days. His extraordinary talents were clear and he played for the Sheffield Association in 1890 and, a year later, against Glasgow,

When he signed for United, the club was an average team in the MCL but, during his time at the Lane, United advanced to become Football League Champions and FA Cup winners. Ernest had signed shortly after his eighteenth birthday and was already being spoken of as a fine player but his development was helped by the advice and encouragement he would receive from Billy Hendry, the United captain and George Waller who was a player-coach and then trainer.

United had joined the NL and initially, Ernest played at outside right but he soon moved to left half and that position became his favourite and normal one for the rest of his career. The club joined the FL in 1892 and, at the end of the season, became a First Division team while Ernest, was selected for the 1893 International Trial and for the League against the Scottish League and, a year later, for England against Scotland.

It would later be written that there was 'no better player in the Kingdom' and yet he would always lack pace and height. He was the smallest yet heaviest player in United's famous half-back line of 'midgets' but he could and did play anywhere and frequently moved into the forward line if United were seeking a vital goal and he scored a good number. A clever, tenacious player, he was here, there and everywhere on the field and one criticism of his play was that he often tried to do too much. As with all great players, he had a superb sense of anticipation and the ability to read the game, watching the ball like a hawk and playing apparently without a moment of hesitation over the next move. He tackled keenly but fairly, he dribbled superbly, seeming to drag the ball along as if it was tied to his feet and he finished well.

Known by his contemporaries as 'the Prince of half backs' and described as a 'faultless football machine', Ernest was United's captain when the club were League Champions in 1898, FA Cup winners in 1899 and 1902, and runners up in 1901 and for eight years he was, when fit, an automatic choice for England, winning 16 caps and he was one of the first professionals to captain England.

He was a fine captain; a commander on the field, changing tactics and the formation of the team during a game, though he would later write that the post was 'a proud one' but not always 'pleasant'.

His place as a first team player had ended in 1910 but he continued to coach and play occasionally for the reserves until 1912 when his FL registration ended. United changed their mind and his registration remained until 1914 though it was said that he was not expected to play again. He did however, serve as a scout for many years and worked at Staveley Works for sixteen years.

Ernest had another string to his bow and from 1901 to 1912, he played County cricket for Derbyshire, playing 186 matches and heading the batting averages in 1908 and had an average overall of 20.2.

Appearances:		Apps	Gls
	FL	464	49
	TM	1	0
	FAC	49	12
	NL	22	4
	UCL	9	0
	SCC	1	0
	BC	3	0
	ABD	5	0
	Total	554	65

NEEDHAM Ernest Godfrey

LH 1912 5' 6½" 11st.
b. Staveley 5 March 1892
d. Staveley 14 March 1975

Staveley Church
United: 29 Mar 1909, 9Apr/12 May 1910 to cs 1913
Only game: 30 Nov 1912 United 2 Notts County 0
Staveley Town 1913/ Luton T 26 May 1914 to cs 1915/ Chesterfield T to 1916–17/ – / Staveley T/ Rossington Colly

EG Needham was the son of Wright Needham, the elder brother of 'Nudger' and Chesterfield trainer. The youngster played occasionally with his uncle for United's reserve team but he made only one FL appearance for the Blades and any hope of a career with Luton Town was ended by the 1914–18 war. He was one of the Chesterfield players suspended for accepting 'boot money' (illegal payments) and so he joined the army. The suspension was lifted in January 1919. His younger brother, George played for Gillingham and Northampton Town.

Appearances:		Apps	Gls
	FL	1	0
	Total	1	0

NELSON George

LH 1944–45
b. Mexborough 5 February 1925

Sheffield Wednesday Reserves?/ Denaby Rovers
United: 28/31 Aug 1943 to 4 May 1946
Debut: 29 Apr 1944 Rotherham United 1 United 0 (CC)
Last game: 26 May 1945 Sheffield Wednesday 4 United 2 (CC)
Lincoln City Sep 1946 to cs 1948/ Denaby Utd?

George Nelson played regularly for United's first team during the 1944–45 wartime season and for the reserves in the next before moving to Lincoln City where he made just one FL appearance on 23 November 1946 at New Brighton.

Appearances:		Apps	Gls
	CC	4	0
	WW2	20	0
	Total	24	0

NESBITT W

RH 1891–92

United: cs 1891 to cs 1892
Debuts: 1 Sep 1891 United 5 Middlesbrough Ironopolis 1 (Fr)
12 Sep 1891 Sunderland Albion 2 United 4 (NL)
16 Jan 1892 Blackpool 0 United 3 (FAC)
Last games: 30 Jan 1892 Wolverhampton Wanderers 3 United 1 (FAC)
27 Feb 1892 Kilnhurst 0 United 4 (SCC at Carbrook)
12 Mar 1892 United Strollers 2 Wednesday Wanderers 1 (SCC)

Nesbitt ('Nisbitt' in some reports) played in 19 friendly fixtures as well as the ten competitive games, all during the 1891–92 season. A clue as to his style of play came after a game at Middlesbrough when a newspaper stated that 'United played a very foul game, Nesbitt especially.' He was a Sheffield Challenge Cup winner in his final 'senior' appearance although both United and Wednesday played reserve teams who, in those days, were referred to as the Strollers and the Wanderers.

Appearances:		Apps	Gls
	FAC	2	0
	NL	5	0
	SCC	3	0
	Total	10	0

NETTLESHIP Reginald (Reg)

F 1943
b. Warsop 23 February 1925
d. 2001

Welbeck Colliery/ Warsop
United: 29 May/2 Jun 1943 to 4 May 1946
Only game: 18 Sep 1943 United 2 Halifax Town 0 (WW2)
WW2: guest Mansfield Town (1943–44)
Mansfield Town Jul 1946/ Welbeck Colliery cs 1947

Reg was a war-time reserve inside forward but he played at centre forward in his one first team appearance for United and 'was out of his depth'. After the War, he moved to Mansfield Town and made one FL appearance on 12 October 1946 at Leyton Orient. His father was a good non-League player and his brother Bob, a schoolboy international.

Appearances:		Apps	Gls
	WW2	1	0
	Total	1	0

NETTLETON Ernest (Ernie)

OL/OR/IR 1944–45 5' 4"
b. Sheffield 7 January 1918

Norfolk Juniors/ Army/ Hartlepools U (1944)
United: guest, 30 Dec 1944–45 Jan 1945 to Jul 1946
Debut: 25 Dec 1944 Sheffield Wednesday 1 United 2 (WW2)
Last game: 6 Jan 1945 United 0 Rotherham United 1 (WW2)
WW2 guest: York City (1944 and 1945), Hartlepools Utd (1945–46)
York City Jul 1946 to cs 1947/ Fulwood Amateurs (Sheffield) player and coach

Ernest was serving in the army when he first appeared as a guest player for Hartlepools United towards the end of the 1943–44 season. He signed as a professional and when he first played for United, he was guest player and on leave over the period of Christmas and the New Year. United secured his transfer but he returned to his duties, becoming a sergeant in the army, after making four appearances.

He played fairly regularly as a guest player for York City and they signed him in the close season of 1946. He made his FL debut with York on 31 August 1946 at home to Chester, scoring City's first post War League goal and made six more appearances before his professional career was ended by a broken leg.

Appearances:		Apps	Gls
	WW2	4	0
	Total	4	0

NEVILLE Steven (Steve) Francis

Striker/OR 1980–82 5' 9½" 11st 0
b. Walthamstow 18 September 1957

Southampton from 1973 app, pro Sep 1975 Exeter City (£25k) Sep 1978
United: (£70k) 23 Oct 1980 to 31 Jul 1983
Debut: 25 Oct 1980 Millwall 1 United 4
Last games: 27 Feb 1982 United 2 Port Vale 1
17 Apr 1982 Aldershot 1 United 1 (sub)
21 May 1982 United 3 Sheffield Wednesday 2 (CC)
4 Aug 1982 Heart of Midlothian 4 United 2 (Fr)
13 Oct 1982 United 2 Manchester City 2 (sub Fr)
Exeter City (L) 19 Oct 1982 to May 1983, Transfer (£15k) 31 Jul 1983/ Bristol City Nov 1984/ Exeter City Jul 1988/ Sun Valley (Hong Kong) Aug 1991 player-coach/ S China (Hong Kg)/ Dorchester T Feb 1993

Steve made his FL debut with Southampton on 12 November 1977 at home to Blackpool. After a spell with Exeter he became one of Harry Haslam's last signings for United, then in their second season in Division Three.

Fast and direct, Steve scored on his United debut (he may have scored twice but his second 'goal' was classed as an own goal by some) but his scoring record at the Lane was disappointing. He played fairly regularly as a striker but missed the last few games of the season which saw United relegated. New manager Ian Porterfield used him on the right wing but the arrival of Colin Morris effectively brought an end to Steve's United career although he did win a County Cup medal in his final competitive appearance.

He finished his FL career having scored 135 goals in 493 appearances but sadly, his poorest scoring return came with United.

Appearances:		Apps	Gls
	FL	40 (9)	6
	FAC	5 (1)	0
	LC	4	0
	AMC	3	0
	CC	2 (1)	1
	Total	54 (11)	7

NEWBY Jonathan (Jon) Philip Robert

Striker 2000 6' 0" 12st 0
b. Warrington 28 November 1978

Liverpool from jnr May 1997/ Carlisle United (L) Dec 1999 Crewe Alexandra (L) Mar 2000
United: (L) 4 Aug 2000 to 5 Nov 2000
Debuts: 4 Aug 2000 Rotherham United 1 United 2 (Fr)
12 Aug 2000 United 2 Portsmouth 0 (sub)
9 Sep 2000 Birmingham City 1 United 0
Last game: 4 Nov 2000 United 1 Gillingham 2
Bury (L) Feb 2001, (£100k) Mar 2001/ Huddersfield Town (free) Aug 2003/ York City (L) Mar 2004/ Bury (free) Aug 2004/ Kidderminster H (L) Mar 2006/ Wrexham Aug 2006/ Southport 2007/ Morecambe (free) Jul 2007

Jon Newby made his League debut with Liverpool, appearing as a substitute on 22 January 2000, at home to Middlesbrough. His full FL debut came whilst on loan at Crewe on 4 March 2000 at home to Norwich City.

He moved to Bramall Lane at the start of the following season on a three month loan when Patrick Suffo was unavailable. Appearing mainly as a substitute he was undoubtedly quick but ineffective.

After a brief return to Anfield he moved into the lower Divisions but his progress was hindered by injuries. In July 2007 he moved to Morecambe and was a regular member of the squad for the club's first season in the FL, although many of his appearances were as a substitute. He did play as a sub in Morecambe's first FL game and he scored the club's first ever FL goal in their second game.

By the end of 2007–08 he had totalled 167(72) League appearances.

Appearances:		Apps	Gls
	FL	3 (10)	0
	Total	3 (10)	0

NEWTON Willis

OR/IL 1945

Treeton
United: 12/14 Mar 1945 to 4 May 1946
Debut: 12 May 1945 Leeds United 4 United 1 (WW2)
Last game: 26 May 1945 Sheffield Wednesday 4 United 2 (CC)
/ – / Wombwell?

Willis Newton played in a few reserve team games in March 1945 and then made two first team appearances at the end of the 1944–45 wartime season. Retained for a further year, he made a few appearances in the CL but never scored.

Appearances:		Apps	Gls
	CC	1	0
	WW2	1	0
	Total	2	0

NIBLOE John ('Joe') Allister

IR/IL 1959–60 5' 8" 11st 0
b. Sheffield 1 June 1939
d. Stocksbridge 29 November 1964

United: am Jul 1955, pro 15/19 Aug 1958 to 19 Oct 1961
Debut: 14 Mar 1959 Derby County 2 United 1
Last game: 10 Dec 1960 Derby County 2 United 0
Stoke City (£5,000) 21 Oct 1961/ Doncaster Rovers (£5000) Oct 1962/ Stockport County Jul 1964

The son of Joe Nibloe, a Kilmarnock, Aston Villa, Wednesday and Scotland full back, John, a very promising youngster, played in only six reserve matches before his first team debut. A strong player with a good shot, his National Service in the RAOC was detrimental to his football career at the Lane but he had a good run in the side from April to November 1960 and he has the record of scoring the Blades' first ever League Cup goal (at Bury). John Harris, the manager, was not satisfied however and signed Keith Kettleborough and that effectively saw an end to John's career with United.

John had totalled 103 FL appearances with his various clubs when he was tragically killed at the early age of 25 in a car accident returning home after a game at Newport.

Appearances:		Apps	Gls
	FL	25	4
	LC	1	1
	CC	3	2
	Total	29	7

NICHOLL Terence (Terry) John

F/MF 1973–75 5' 9" 10st 8
b. Wilmslow 16 September 1952

Crewe Alexandra app to pro Feb 1972
United: (£20k) 6/7 Mar 1973 to May 1975
Debuts: 30 May 1973 Panionios (Greece) 1 United 1 (Fr sub)
2 Feb 1974 United 1 Everton 1 (sub)
16 Mar 1974 Manchester City 0 United 1
Last games: 28 Dec 1974 United 1 Arsenal 1
25 Jan 1975 Aston Villa 4 United 1 (FAC)
28 Mar 1975 Coventry City 2 United 2 (sub)
8 Apr 1975 Barnsley 1 United 1 (BM sub abd)
Southend United (£5555) May 1975/ Gillingham (£6000) Oct 1976–cs 1981 / – / Wichita Wings (USA) Oct 1981/ Memphis (USA) coach 1987/ Dayton (USA)

A former Stockport Boys player, Terry Nicholl made his FL debut with Crewe Alexandra on 5 February 1972 at home to Darlington.

A younger brother of Chris, the more famous Northern Ireland international, Terry was a neat and tidy, constructive forward or midfield player but he lacked the power and determination of his brother. He moved to the Lane at the end of the 1972–73 season, one of John Harris' last signings and played in an end of season friendly fixture. It was February, after Ken Furphy had taken the position of manager, that he made a competitive first team appearance and it was only after seven successive substitute appearances that he finally made his first start. He then played regularly until the end of the season but only intermittently after that.

He moved on to Southend United and played regularly with Gillingham for five seasons before moving to the USA where he played and later coached in the American Indoor League for several years. During his Football League career he made 292(10) appearances.

Appearances:		Apps	Gls
	FL	12 (10)	1
	FAC	2	0
	TX	1 (1)	0
	CC	1	0
	Total	16 (11)	1

NICHOLSON Shane Michael

LWB/MF 2001–02 5' 10" 12st 6
b. Newark 3 June 1970

Lincoln City from trainee Jul 1988/ Derby County (£100k) Apr 1992/ West Bromwich Albion (£150k) Feb 1996 / – Chesterfield (free) Aug 1998/ Stockport County (free) Jun 1999
United: (free) 1/18 Jul 2001 to 15/17 Jul 2002
Debuts: 17 Jul 2001 Sheffield FC 0 United 7 (Fr)
11 Sep 2001 Grimsby Town 3 United 3 (LC)
15 Sep 2001 United 0 Coventry City 1
Last games: 1 Apr 2002 United 0 Wimbledon 1
6 Apr 2002 Watford 0 United 3 (sub)
Tranmere Rovers (free) Jul 2002/ Chesterfield (free) Jul 2004/ Lincoln City (L) Nov and Dec 2006/ Boston Utd (L) Jan 2007

Shane was the youngest player to make a FL appearance for Lincoln City when he made his debut on 22 November 1986 at Burnley at the age of 16 years 172 days. A promising career stalled when he was with West Bromwich Albion and was accused of drug taking. Suspended by the FA and sacked by his club, he was helped by the PFA and allowed to return to the game.

He arrived at the Lane in the summer of 2001and played in the pre-season games but, due to a previous suspension, was unavailable for the first FL games. A reliable, essentially left footed defender, solid in the tackle and creating openings when coming forward, Shane made his debut in the League Cup at Grimsby, where he successfully converted in the penalty shoot-out, which United lost. He was then a regular until January, playing mainly as a left wing back but occasionally in midfield and he became the club's penalty taker. He lost his place through injury in January and played only occasionally when fit again.

He moved on after one season and was the Chesterfield 'Player of the Year' (2004–5). He retired in the summer of 2007, having played 485(38) League games and became the fitness and rehabilitation coach at Chesterfield.

Appearances:		Apps	Gls
	FL	21 (4)	3
	LC	1	0
	Total	22 (4)	3

NIGHTINGALE Albert

IR/CF 1941–48 5' 8" 10st 8
b. Thrybergh, Rotherham 10 November 1923
d. Liverpool 26 February 2006

Thurcroft Colliery
United: 8 Mar 1941, pro 28/30 Jun 1941 to 11/13 Mar 1948
Debuts: 14 Apr 1941 Sheffield Wednesday 3 United 1 (WW2)
5 Jan 1946 Huddersfield Town 1 United 1 (FAC)
31 Aug 1946 United 0 Liverpool 1
Last game: 21 Feb 1948 Burnley 0 United 0
WW2 guest: Chesterfield (2 app)
Huddersfield Town (£10k + 2 players) Mar 1948/ Blackburn Rovers (£12k) Oct 1951/ Leeds United (£10k) Oct 1952 to cs 1957

From a football family, Albert was working as a miner during the second War when United spotted him playing for Thurcroft Colliery. He had a trial on Easter Monday 1941at Hillsborough and a second with the reserves in September at Denaby. In November he played for the Blades at Rotherham, scoring United's goal, and held his place in the team. In the following four wartime seasons he averaged a goal every other game, playing at centre forward or inside right.

Albert was perhaps a little on the small side but he was strong, tenacious and aggressive. Hard as nails and terrier like in his determination, he was difficult to knock off the ball and had the ability to weave and wriggle his way through a packed defence with the ball seemingly glued to his feet. He scored 22 goals when United won the 1945–46 FL North championship but when League football resumed in 1946–47, he continued to work as a miner because of the post-war economic problems.

He asked for a transfer in February 1948 and moved to Huddersfield Town a month later in an exchange deal which turned out to be unsatisfactory for United with Graham Bailey and George Hutchinson moving to the Lane. Perhaps his most satisfying season was his last full one with Leeds United when he helped the club gain promotion to the top flight. Sadly, he suffered a bad knee injury in the first game of the 1956–57 season and never played again. However, despite his late start, he has totalled 346 FL appearances and scored 88 goals.

After his retirement he worked in the Huddersfield Parks Department for many years. He lived in Huddersfield but was taken ill and died while visiting his daughter in Liverpool.

Appearances:

	Apps	Gls
FL	62	15
FAC	10	2
CC	8	4
WW2	145	67
Total	225	88

NILSEN Roger

LB/CD 1993–99 5' 11" 12st 6
b. Tromso, Norway 8 August 1969

Tromso 1987/ Viking Stavanger 1989 Koln (Germany) (L) 1993
United: (£400k rising to £550k/£660k) 4 Nov 1993 to 25/26 Mar 1999
Debut: 6 Nov 1993 United 1 Norwich City 2
Last game: 6 Feb 1999 United 3 West Bromwich Albion 0
Tottenham Hotspur (free) Mar 1999/ Grazer AK Jun 1999/ Molde (Norway) 2000/ Byrne (L) 2002/ Stavanger IF/ 2003

Roger, who, apart form a loan spell in Germany with Cologne, had played all his football in Norway was signed by Dave Bassett during what turned out to be the season United were relegated from the Premiership. Before arriving at the Lane, Roger had gained 16 Norwegian caps and had won the Norwegian championship and cup competition with Viking.

Roger had played in the left centre of defence and that was the position he preferred but frequently played at left back for United. A strong player, he tackled firmly and was good in the air and had a powerful shot and this made it all the more surprising that he never scored a goal from open play, despite having a good scoring record in Norway. He did score in the penalty shoot-out against Coventry City in the quarter final FA Cup replay at the Lane but that was the only penalty he took.

Although his standards were high, he did have the occasional amazing lapses which usually left the goalkeeper exposed and were amusing in retrospect if United had got away with it! He won a further 15 caps whilst at the Lane and went with the Norwegian squad to the 1994 World Cup but sadly, he did not play.

His contract ended in 1999 and following talks with Steve Bruce he was aware that it would not be extended so he spent the final few months with Tottenham Hotspur as emergency cover. After a brief time in Austria, he returned home to play for several years in Norway. His final and 32nd cap came whilst with Molde. In his first season as manger of Stavanger the club were promoted to the Second Division.

Appearances:

	Apps	Gls
FL	157 (9)	0
PO	2 (1)	0
FAC	9 (2)	0
LC	9 (1)	0
Total	177 (13)	0

NIX Kyle Ashley

MF 2005 5' 6" 9st 10
b. Sydney (Australia) 21 January 1986

Manchester Utd 2002/ Aston Villa from trainee Jan 2003
United: Apr 2005 to cs 2006
Debut: 20 Sep 2005 Shrewsbury Town 0 United 0 (sub LC)
Last game: 25 Oct 2005 Reading 2 United 0 (sub LC)
Barnsley (L) 28 Feb 2006 to end of season
Peterborough United (trial)/ Grimsby Town (trial)/ Buxton/ Parkgate/ Bradford City trial Jul 2007, signed Jul 2007

Born in Australia but brought up in Rotherham, Kyle, an England youth international, was given an academy contract in the summer of 2005 after a trial. He played for England U20 in August but, after just two League Cup appearances for the Blades, he was released at the end of the season and had made no FL appearances whilst on loan at Barnsley.

After two unsuccessful trials, during the second of which he damaged his ankle he spent some of 2006–07 playing non-league football. In the summer of 2007, with Stuart McCall now in charge, Kyle was given a trial with Bradford City where he was successful and given a short term contract, later extended. He made his FL debut on the 18 August 2007, coming on as a substitute at Shrewsbury Town's first game at their new ground. His full debut came a week later at home to Wrexham and he went on to be a regular in the side making 31(9) FL appearances.

Appearances:

	Apps	Gls
LC	0 (2)	0
Total	0 (2)	0

NORTH James Thomas (Tommy)

CH 1907–08 5' 8" 12st
b. Codnor Park, Derbys 7 August 1882

Constitutional 1900/ Linby 1903–04/ Constitutional (1904–05)/ Mansfield Mechanics 1905?–1907
United: 29 Apr 1907 to cs 1909
Debut: 7 Dec 1907 United 2 Preston North End 0
Last game: 18 Jan 1908 United 2 Manchester United 0
Huddersfield Town cs 1909 to cs 1910

Tommy North was a miner who joined United in 1907. The Independent was not impressed, reporting that his tackling was 'weak' but his career was all but ended soon after when he was seriously injured in what turned out to be his final FL match. He broke down in training and claimed compensation but the insurance company declared that United were not liable. He recovered sufficiently to play for the reserves in the Wharncliffe Charity Cup in November 1908 but was released at the end of the season.

Tommy moved on to Huddersfield Town who had joined the Midland League and made a dozen first team appearances but was not retained.

Appearances:		Apps	Gls
	FL	4	0
	Total	4	0

NOTMAN Alexander (Alex) McKeachie

Striker 2000 5' 7" 10st 11
b. Edinburgh 10 December 1979

Manchester United/ Aberdeen (L) Feb 1999
United: (L) 20/21 Jan 2000 to 20/21 Mar 2000
Debut: 22 Jan 2000 United 1 Manchester City 0
Last games: 7 Mar 2000 United 3 Barnsley 3
21 Mar 2000 Bolton Wanderers 2 United 0 (sub)
Norwich City (£250k) Nov 2000 to Nov 2003 / – / Kings Lynn Jan 2004 briefly then Aug 2006 / – / Wroxham Oct 2007/ Boston United Oct 2007/ Wroxham cDec 2007

Alex, a Scottish schoolboy, youth and U21 international, began his career with Manchester United but his only first team appearance was as a substitute in the League Cup. He made two substitute appearance in the Scottish League with Aberdeen in the Spring of 1999 but his FL debut came with the Blades.

Small but quick, he was Neil Warnock's first loan signing and he played alongside Marcus Bent in attack. He showed ability to hold and distribute the ball well and he scored three goals but he looked far from the finished article though his one month loan was extended to two.

He later joined Norwich City but damaged ankle ligaments rules him out of much of the 2002–03 season and he failed in a comeback attempt in Autumn 2003. He retired from the professional game, with just 25(39) League appearances to his credit, joining Kings Lynn in January 2004 but found he was not fit enough for competitive action. He re-joined Lynn in August 2006 and subsequently played for various non-League clubs.

Appearances:		Apps	Gls
	FL	7 (3)	3
	Total	7 (3)	3

O'CONNOR Jonathan (Jon)

RB/MF 1998–2000 5' 10" 11st 3
b. Darlington 29 October 1976

Everton from trainee Oct 1993
United: 10 Feb (trial), 26 Feb 1998 to Jun 2000
Debuts: 28 Feb 1998 United 2 Bradford City 1 (sub)
16 Jul 1998 Sheffield FC 0 United XI 2 (Fr)
5 Dec 1998 Bristol City 2 United 0
Last games: 20 Dec 1998 United 1 Ipswich Town 2
23 Jan 1999 Notts County 3 United 4 (FAC)
28 Mar 2000 United 0 Latvia XI 1 (Fr)
Cambridge U (trial) Oct 1999/ Scunthorpe U (trial)/ Chester(trial) 2000/ Darlington (L) Mar 2000
Lincoln City (trial)/ Blackpool Oct 2000 to Jun 2002

Jon O'Connor had been one of the boys who had attended the ill fated England School of Excellence at Lilleshall. Signed by Everton, he made his League debut in the Premiership on 21 February 1996 at Manchester United but made only four more appearances though he did win England caps at youth and U21 levels.

He had a trial with United against Blackpool Reserves and moved to the Lane as part of the deal which took Don Hutchison to Goodison. Jon played for a FL Under 21 team against an equivalent Italian League side in March 1998 but, lacking pace and injury prone, he found his opportunities with United very limited. He eventually moved on to Blackpool but he managed only 10(1) FL appearances in his two seasons.

Appearances:		Apps	Gls
	FL	2 (2)	0
	FAC	1	0
	Total	3 (2)	0

OGDEN Alan

LB 1971–74 5' 10" 11st 11
b. Thrybergh, Rotherham 15 April 1954

United: from app 17 Jul 1969, pro 10/12 May 1971 to 25 Nov 1974
Debuts: 10 May 1971 Swansea City 3 United 5 (BM)
12 Feb 1972 United 3 Manchester City 3
Last games: 23 Feb 1974 Leicester City 1 United 1
10 Aug 1974 United 1 Blackpool 2 (TX)
York City (L) Oct, free transfer Nov 1974/ Huddersfield (Trial) Mar 1975

Alan Ogden made his FL debut with United whilst still 17 years of age but, competing with Ted Hemsley for the left back role, he made few competitive appearances. He moved on a one month loan to York City in October 1974 and returned after three games but signed on a permanent basis shortly afterwards. Although he played only nine games before his contract was cancelled in March, they did include two FA Cup games against Arsenal.

Forced to retire, he later worked for British Steel and British Rail as a crane driver but has suffered from heart problems.

Appearances:		Apps	Gls
	FL	6 (6)	0
	TX	2	0
	CC	1	0
	WC	0 (1)	0
	Total	9 (7)	0

OLDACRE Percival (Percy)

CF 1921–23 5' 9" 11st 8
b. Stoke 25 October 1892
d. Stoke 26 January 1970

Stoke C 1910? / – /
WW2 guest: Sheffield Wednesday 1916–17 (2 app) Exeter City Jun 1919/ Castleford T Nov 1920
United: (£1000)+(£100 to Exeter C) 27 Apr 1921 to 1 Aug 1923
Debuts: 14 May 1921 Barnsley 1 United 1 (CC)
17 Sep 1921 Liverpool 1 United 1
Last game: 27 Jan 1923 United 2 Bolton Wanderers 2
Halifax T (£150) Aug 1923/ Crewe Alexandra Nov 1924 to cs 1925/ Mid Rhondda Oct 1925/ Shrewsbury T Dec 1925/ Port Vale (£150) Aug 1926 to cs 1927/ Hurst Nov 1927

Percy Oldacre may have been a Stoke City player at some time before the First War but he doesn't appear to have turned out for the first team. A sergeant in the army during the war, he joined Exeter City who were members of the Southern League but when the club were elected to the new Third Division of the FL, Percy was suspended and he moved north to play for Castleford scoring twenty eight goals that season.

He joined United in April 1921 and made his debut in the club's first ever County Cup game. He had a fine shot but he was slow and, facing competition from Harry Johnson, Menlove and Rawson, he had few opportunities and played just once in his final season leaving United with a record of having scored five goals in six FL matches.

He eventually retired after scoring 18 goals in 40 games but it was only with Crewe that his appearances reached double figures.

Appearances:		Apps	Gls
	FL	6	5
	CC	2	0
	Total	8	5

ONUORA Iffem (Iffy)

Striker 2002 6' 1½" 13st 13
b. Glasgow 28 July 1967

Bradford University/ Huddersfield Town Jul 1989 Mansfield Town (£75k) Jul 1994/ Gillingham (£12.5k) Aug 1996/ Swindon Town (£120k) Mar 1998/ Gillingham (L) for 2 days then (£100k) Jan 2001

United: (free) 4 Jul 2002 to 24 Oct 2003
Debuts: 16 Jul 2002 Baslow 1 United 14 (Fr)
10 Aug 2002 Coventry City 2 United 1
Last game: 14 Sep 2002 United 1 Rotherham United 0
Wycombe Wanderers (L) 20 Aug 2003/ Grimsby Town (L) 19 Sep 2003
Grimsby T Oct 2003/ Tranmere Rovers Feb 2004/ Huddersfield Town Mar 2004/ Walsall player-coach to Oct 2004 / – / Swindon Town asst to mgr Oct 2005 to May 2006/ radio work/ Gillingham coach Jun 2007, joint caretaker mgr Sep to Nov 2007/ Lincoln City asst mgr and caretaker mgr Feb 2008

Having gained a degree at Bradford University, Iffy made his FL debut as a substitute with Huddersfield Town at home to Swansea City on 19 August 1989 and his full debut came at home to Brentford on 16 September. After making 414 FL appearances and scoring 112 goals for his various clubs, the big striker was signed for United by Neil Warnock, his former manager at Huddersfield.

He started the season as first choice target man but ruptured his achilles tendon when falling awkwardly and it was soon clear that his season had ended. The following season, after two loan spells, Iffy moved to various clubs before retiring, having scored 116 league goals in 350(102) games.

Iffy moved into coaching with Walsall and then Swindon Town where he became manager for the 2005–06 season. More recently he commentated on Gillingham matches on Radio Kent before taking a coaching role with the Gills. He then had a two month stint as caretaker manager alongside Mick Docherty. In February 2008 he joined Lincoln in part to act as manger whilst Peter Jackson was ill with throat cancer.

Appearances:		Apps	Gls
	FL	7	1
	LC	1	0
	Total	8	1

ORR Henry (Harry)

LH 1959–62 5' 9½" 10st 12
b. Lisburn 30 June (Oct?) 1936

Distillery
United: 24 Oct/1 Nov 1958 to 20 Jul 1964
Debuts: 7 Apr 1959 Distillery 1 United 3 (Fr)
20 Apr 1959 United 5 Bristol Rovers 2
Last game: 14 Mar 1962 United 1 Everton 1
Peterborough United Jul 1964 to May 1967

A Northern Ireland school and youth international, Harry was one of Joe Mercer's last signings though there were stories that Chairman Blacow Yates and a scout made the decision; United paying £9000 for Harry and Dennis Shiels and also playing an expenses paid match in Belfast.

A calm, skilful player though lacking power and speed, Harry was competing with Gerry Summers for the left half spot and had few opportunities in his nearly six years at the Lane but was always a competent reserve player.

He moved to Peterborough with Shiels for a combined fee of £5000 and in his first season he was a regular in the first team but his opportunities were less frequent after that and he was released after three seasons, having made 47(1) FL appearances for the Posh.

Appearances:		Apps	Gls
	FL	10	1
	LC	3	0
	CC	1	0
	Total	14	1

OSWALD Robert (Bert) Raymond Broome

OL/IL 1930–34 5' 7" 10st 7
b. Bo'ness/Linlithgow 20 December 1904
d. Rochford, Essex. AMJ 1961

Linlithgow Rose/ Heart of Midlothian Nov 1924 Bo'ness Feb 1926/ Reading (£400) Jun 1928
United: (Oswald and Percy Thorpe, £4,000) 12/13 Jun 1930 to 4/5 May 1934
Debut: 1 Nov 1930 West Ham United 4 United 1
Last game: 5 May 1934 Arsenal 2 United 0
Southend United (£500) May 1934

Bert began his career in Scotland with Hearts but he made only one League appearance before moving to Bo'ness who were the Scottish Second Division champions in 1927. He made his FL debut with Reading—their manager had been in charge at Bo'ness—at home to Middlesbrough on 25 August 1928 but after two seasons, during which he missed just two games, Bert moved to the Lane.

Small, sturdy and fast, with good ball control and a strong shot, Bob must have been aware that his task would be to replace the great but ageing Fred Tunstall and shortly after the start of the following season, he took over the left wing spot. No one could replace the great winger of course but Oswald was a regular for three seasons and gave United reasonable service although his final season saw the Blades relegated for the first time.

In the summer of 1934 he moved to Southend United where he played until the outbreak of the Second War by which time he had reached 311 FL appearances.

Appearances:		Apps	Gls
	FL	106	23
	FAC	5	1
	CC	4	0
	Total	115	24

OVER Eric

OL 1954–55 5' 10½" 11st 10
b. Sheffield 5 July 1933

Sheffield FC
United: 15/18 Nov 1954 to 25/28 Jan 1956
Debuts: 30 Nov 1954 United 7 Esjberg (Denmark) 0 (sub Fr)
14 Mar 1955 United 1 Sunderland 0
Last game: 19 Mar 1955 Tottenham Hotspur 5 United 0
Barrow (£400) Jan 1956/ Oldham Athletic (£450) Dec 1957 to Jun 1958

Eric had a good turn of speed but didn't look good enough for First Division football in his three first team outings though he scored after coming on as a substitute in his first appearance.

He moved to Barrow, reportedly the offer of a house clinching the deal but a broken leg restricted his progress. He secured a regular first team place with Oldham Athletic and it was a surprise when it was announced that he was retiring at the end of the season. He had played 42 FL games in total but recorded only three goals. He joined the Grimsby Borough Police and continued to play for the police team.

Appearances:		Apps	Gls
	FL	2	0
	Total	2	0

OWENS Maurice R

CF/IL 1941–44

Clipstone CW
United: amateur 3 Oct 1941 to cs 1944. 1 Dec 1944 to cs 1945
Debut: 25 Oct 1941 Sheffield Wednesday 1 United 3 (WW2)
Last game: 23 Dec 1944 Mansfield Town 4 United 1 (WW2)
WW2 guest: Rotherham U (1942–43 1 app) Mansfield T (1944–45 1 app)
Ollerton Colliery (1946–47) / – / Shirebrook (1950–51)

Maurice Owen was one of a large number of miners who played for United during the Second World War. He scored on his debut for the reserve team in September 1941 but his five games for the first team were spread over three years. Unusually, all were away fixtures and included two games at Field Mill and one against Manchester United.

Appearances:		Apps	Gls
	WW2	5	1
	Total	5	1

OXLEY Bernard (Bunny)

OR/IR/IL 1928–34 5' 9" 11st 0
b. Whitwell 16 June 1907
d. Worksop 7 January 1975

Whitwell Old Boys/ Chesterfield am Oct 1925, pro Dec 1925
United: (£1,350) 11 May 1928 to 4 May 1934
Debut: 24 Nov 1928 Huddersfield Town 6 United 1
Last games: 14 Apr 1934 United 0 West Bromwich Albion 1
16 Apr 1934 Doncaster Rovers 1 United 1 (CC)
Sheffield Wednesday (£1,000) May 1934/ Plymouth Argyle (£600) Sep 1935/ Stockport County Jun 1936/ Worksop Town player-sec-mgr cs 1938/ Scunthorpe & L United player-coach Nov 1938/ ADO Den Haag coach 1939 / – / Firbeck (1945)/ Wombwell Ath player-coach cs 1946 ?/ Denaby Utd coach Aug 1946/ Worksop Town mgr 1947

A younger brother of Cyril Oxley, the Chesterfield and Liverpool player, Bernard made his FL debut with Chesterfield on 2 April 1926 at Grimsby Town.

A strong, enthusiastic and fast winger, he could centre well at speed but his goal scoring record was poor. He came as a right winger but later played in all the forward positions for United except outside left.

He began the 1929–30 season playing well with Jack Pickering as his partner but missed most of the games after an appendicitis operation. He returned to the first team and his crosses provided many goals for Jimmy Dunne but he rarely scored, he gained a reputation as inconsistent and

lost the right wing position in October 1932 to Bertie Williams. He had opportunities to win a regular first team place at inside and centre forward but failed to grasp them and so, after nearly six seasons at the Lane, he became one of the few players to move directly between United and Wednesday.

The thinking behind the move is not clear: a reserve with United, he became a Wednesday reserve player but his career was revived by a move to Stockport County where he won a Third Division (North) Championship medal before moving into non-League football. In total, he made 249 FL appearances but scored only 35 or 36 goals.

In 1939 he moved to Holland, coaching football and cricket but he and his wife had to flee the country in 1940 when the Germans invaded the Netherlands. During the War he worked for the Worksop Fire Service and carried on in this role after the War. He had a spell as the Worksop Town manager, later scouting for Leyton Orient and he also played cricket for Langwith.

Appearances:		Apps	Gls
	FL	116	11
	FAC	7	0
	CC	6	3
	Total	129	14

PACE Arthur

OL 1918
b. Newcastle on Tyne 1885
d. 1968

Hebburn Argyle am Aug 1904/ Hull City Nov 1907 Rotherham Town Jul 1910/ Croydon Common Sep 1911 Worksop Town Sep 1915
United: WW1 guest
Only game: 19 Jan 1918 Hull City 2 United 4
WW1 guest: Hull City and Worksop T

Arthur Pace made his FL debut with Hull City at Gainsborough Trinity on 28 November 1908 but made only five appearances before moving into non-League football. However, he returned to play for Hull as a guest player during the First War and made his one guest appearance for United against the Tigers when Albert Sturgess missed the train to Hull.

Appearances:		Apps	Gls
	WW1	1	0
	Total	1	0

PACE Derek (Doc) John

CF 1957–65 5' 10" 11st 7
b. Essington (Wolverhampton) 11 March 1932
d. Essington 17 October 1989

Bloxwich Strollers/ Aston Villa Sep 1949
United: (£12k) 26 Dec 1957 to 11 Dec 1964
Debut: 26 Dec 1957 United 4 Blackburn Rovers 2
Last game: 29 Aug 1965 United 2 Burnley 0
Notts County (£5,500) Dec 1964/ Walsall Jul 1966 to May 1967/ Walsall Wood mgr Jul 1968 to May 1970

Derek Pace made his FL debut with Aston Villa on 17 March 1951, scoring at home against Burnley. He served in the Royal Army Medical Corps whilst doing his National Service and it was this that earned him the nickname 'Doc'. Although he had scored 40 goals in just 98 FL appearances for Villa, Derek was unable to establish himself as regular in the Villa first team and was twelfth man when they won the FA Cup in 1957, missing out because of a groin strain. He had however, always played well against United and scored a hat trick in April 1956 and United's manager, Joe Mercer, had made more than one attempt to sign him before he finally 'got his man' in December 1957. Derek made his United debut on Boxing Day and, having registered with the FL at 2pm, he scored at eight minutes past three.

Derek wasn't a big man but he was dedicated, brave and fearlessly determined to reach the ball in the penalty area and difficult to knock off it. Quick thinking and two footed with awareness in front of goal, he timed his runs perfectly and his finishing, particularly with his head, was superb. He was United's leading goal scorer for seven successive seasons, twice reaching a total of 26 FL goals and that tally in 1960–61 helped United to win promotion to the top flight and reach the FA Cup semi-final. He scored seven hat tricks, including four goals against Charlton Athletic, and none of his goals came from the penalty spot.

After playing three games at the start of the 1964–65 season he had a stomach operation and was transferred to Notts County after a fitness test in a Sheffield Senior Cup tie (won 7–0) at the Ball Inn on 5 December. The agreed fee of £7000 was reduced by United because County had financial problems. After retiring, with 196 FL goals in 384 games, he worked as a representative and coached a local amateur side in Walsall. He died after a heart attack aged fifty seven.

Appearances:

	Apps	Gls
FL	253	140
FAC	31	18
LC	10	5
CC	7	12
Total	301	175

PAGE Robert John

CD 2001–04 6' 0" 12st 5
b. Llwynypia 3 September 1974

Watford from trainee Apr 1993
United: (L) 6 Aug 2001, (£350k) 11/13 Sep 2001 to 2 Jul 2004
Debut: 11 Aug 2001 Nottingham Forest 1 United 1
Last game: 9 May 2004 Preston North End 3 United 3
Cardiff City Jul 2004/ Coventry City Feb 2005/ Huddersfield Town Jan 2008/ Chesterfield May 2008

Robert Page made his FL debut with Watford, on 16 October 1993 at Birmingham City and went on to make over 200 League appearances for the club. At Watford, he gained U21, B and full caps to add to those he won at schoolboy and youth level.

In the summer of 2001 he was discarded by the new Watford manager, Gianluca Vialli and joined United, initially on a one month's loan but, after a brief return to Watford, the move was made permanent. He soon settled in, partnering Shaun Murphy and then Keith Curle in the centre of defence. Although perhaps lacking in pace he showed good anticipation, he was commanding in the air and a good tackler and made few mistakes. At the end of his first season he was voted the supporters 'Player of the Year'

During the three seasons with United, he was a regular in the side; the games he missed being through injury and he made 13 appearances for Wales. The arrival of Chris Morgan meant Robert was not certain of a regular place and he moved to Cardiff City, the club he had supported as a boy but, not being a regular in the side, he soon moved on to Coventry City.

By the end of 2007–08, by which time he was at Huddersfield, Robert had totalled 410(10) League appearances and in May he agreed to join Chesterfield.

Appearances:

	Apps	Gls
FL	106 (1)	1
PO	3	0
FAC	11	0
LC	7	0
Total	127 (1)	1

PALIN Frank

OR/IL/CH 1898–99
b. Whitwick (Leicestershire) AMJ 1876

Hucknall St Johns/ Hucknall Torkard
United: 5 May 1898 to cs1899
Debut: 26 Nov 1898 West Bromwich Albion 3 United 0
Last game: 1 Apr 1899 Blackburn Rovers 2 United 1
Newstead Byron (Notts) Aug 1899

A Notts miner, Fred Palin made two of his appearances at outside right, two at outside left and three at centre half.

Appearances:		Apps	Gls
	FL	7	0
	Total	7	0

PANTLING Harry Harold

RH/LH/FB 1915–26 5' 9½" 11st 6
b. Leighton Buzzard 16 May 1891
d. Sheffield 21 December 1952

Watford 1908 am, pro Jul 1911
United: 25 Apr/3 May 1914 to 9 Aug 1926
Debut: 6 Feb 1915 Bradford City 1 United 1
Last games: 19 Dec 1925 United 3 Liverpool 1
30 Jan 1926 United 1 Sunderland 2 (FAC)
WW1 guest: Watford
Rotherham United (£50) Aug 1926 to cs 1927 / – / Heanor Town Nov 1927

Having played regularly for Southern League Watford, mainly at right back or right half, Harold moved to the Lane, along with Ashbridge, an inside forward, United paying £850 for the two.

Although he had joined United in 1914, it wasn't until the Wartime season of 1915–16 that he claimed a regular first team place but he then became a regular for nine seasons. Only three players made more appearances during the First War and during those four seasons he played in both wing half and both full back positions but he eventually established himself at right half.

For the first six seasons after the war he missed few games and was awarded an England Cap against Ireland in October 1923 and for a time was a member of the PFA's management committee. He lost his place in the autumn of 1924 to Bruce Longworth but an injury to the new man restored Pantling to the team and his season closed with an appearance at Wembley and a FA Cup winner's medal. Never quick, he lost his place to Tommy Sampy during the following season and signed for Rotherham United (12 app).

Harold was not a stylish player but his all round defensive qualities were good. Utterly reliable, consistent and stout hearted, his tackling was both resolute and shrewd and his heading was sound. It could be said that Harold was one of football's 'hard men', but many of his misdemeanours were due to his seeking retribution for fouls committed on other United players. He was sent off twice in 1917–18 and again in 1920–21 although press reports suggest this latter decision was harsh. It was another 54 years before another United player, Len Badger, suffered a third dismissal.

Pantling is also remembered for his part, in August 1923, in what was Manchester City's first game at Maine Road. United's goalkeeper, Gough, was injured and Pantling went in goal and his first touch of the ball was to save a penalty kick. Harold became a licensee, keeping the Ecclesall Tavern and the Burgoyne Arms on Langsett Road.

Appearances:		Apps	Gls
	FL	224	1
	FAC	20	0
	CC	11	0
	WW1	113	1
	Total	368	2

PARKER Paul Andrew

RWB/LWB 1996 5' 7" 11st 11
b. West Ham 4 April 1964

Fulham from app Apr 1982/ Queens Park Rangers (£300k) Jun 1987/ Manchester United (£2m) Aug 1991 Derby County (free) Aug 1996
United: (free) 7/8 Nov 1996 to 6 Jan 1997
Debuts: 16 Nov 1996 Port Vale 0 United 0 (sub)
30 Nov 1996 Queens Park Rangers 1 United 0
Last game: 26 Dec 1996 Bradford City 1 United 2
Fulham (free) Jan 1997/ Chelsea (free) Mar 1997/ Heybridge Swifts Aug 1997/ Farnborough Town Dec 1997/ Sunderland (trial) Jan 1998/ Ashford Town director of football 199–Jan 2000/ Chelmsford City asst mgr Apr 2000, mgr Jun 2001 to May 2003/ Welling United mgr 2003 to Dec 2004 / – / Folkestone Invicta asst mgr Sep 2005 / – / Queens Park Rangers commercial & communications director, temporary appointment Jun 2007

Paul Parker, an England youth International, made his FL debut with Fulham, at home to Reading, about three weeks after his seventeenth birthday on 25 April 1981. He made over 100 League appearances with each of his first three clubs and gained 19 full caps as well as those at U21 and B level. Whilst with Manchester United he won FA Cup, League Cup and two Premier League Championship winners' medals.

Struggling with injuries, he was released by Manchester United in the summer of 1996 and, after a brief spell with Derby, he was signed by Howard Kendall but after two months he moved on. At the end of the season, having made 376(28) League appearances, he moved into non-League football in a variety of roles.

More recently he has worked on television covering, in particular, Conference football.

Appearances:		Apps	Gls
	FL	7 (3)	0
	Total	7 (3)	0

PARKER William (Billy) Edwin

LH/RH 1900–09 5' 9" 12st
b. Sheffield 5 April 1880
d. 1/2 June 1940

St John's Wesleyans, Malin Bridge (Sheffield)
United: May 1895 (FL), Oct 1898 (amat), 7 Nov 1898 (FL), 10 May 1899 (pro) to Jun 1909
Debuts: 16 Apr 1900 Corinthians 0 United 4 (Fr)
22 Mar 1902 Manchester City 4 United 0
27 Mar 1902 United 1 Derby C 0
(FAC s/f 2nd replay at Nottinghsm)
Last games: 9 Apr 1909 Aston Villa 3 United 0
12 Apr 1909 Stoke 0 United 1 (Fr)

Billy Parker played for Sheffield Schools and his early promise led to United registering him with the FL. He made his First Division debut in March 1902 and five days later played a fine game in a second replay of an FA Cup semi-final. Although he was at the Lane for ten seasons, he faced competition for the left half position from England international Ernest Needham and his FL appearances reached double figures only twice—in 1905–06 and 1908–09.

A strong player and speedy, he frequently captained the reserves and took his benefit (a guarantee of £150) against Wednesday's second team on Boxing Day 1907. A steel analyst at Hadfields and a prominent mason, he later became a United director and his son, WS Parker, a winger and a Cambridge blue, played for the reserves, Christmas 1928.

Appearances:		Apps	Gls
	FL	75	2
	FAC	7	1
	ABD	1	0
	Total	83	3

PARKIN Frederick (Fred) William

G 1943–44

Folkestone Town?/ Derby County May 1936? Mansfield T?/ Notts C (amat) 1942–43
United: pro 30 Jun/ 3 Jul 1943 to 15/17 Jan, 13 Feb 1945
Debut: 27 Dec 1943 United 4 Rotherham United 1 (WW2)
Last game: 6 May 1944 United 2 Rotherham United 3 (CC)
WW2 guest: Lincoln C (1 app, Jan 1944)
Sheffield Wed Mar 1945/ Lincoln City Aug 1945/ Scarborough cs 1946

Fred Parkin made 4 wartime appearances for Notts County before joining United. He made two first team appearances and one other as a guest for Lincoln City and then appeared on 10 occasions 'on trial' for the Owls. During his one season with Lincoln City he played 19 first team matches including four games in the FA Cup.

United's Fred is probably the same one who played one FL game for Derby County on 29 March 1936 at home to Huddersfield. Town and he may have been on Mansfield Town's books at some time.

Appearances:		Apps	Gls
	WW2	1	0
	CC	1	0
	Total	2	0

PARKIN Harold (Harry)

RB/LB 1944–45

United: 7 Oct 1943 (amat), 31 Oct/2 Nov 1944 to 31 Jul 1948
Debut: 26 Dec 1944 United 3 Manchester United 4 (WW2)
Last game: 12 May 1945 Leeds United 4 United 1 (WW2)
Beighton MW

Tall and slim and from the Handsworth area of Sheffield, Harold Parkin made two known wartime first team appearances for United though he may also have made his first team debut as a second half substitute in the 21 August 1943 charity match against the Wednesday.

Appearances:		Apps	Gls
	WW2	2	0
	Total	2	0

PARKIN Herbert (Bert) Buttery

LB/LH/RB 1942–51 5' 9" 11st 4
b. Sheffield 10 April 1920
d. July 1992

Atlas & Norfolk
United: 12 Mar 1942 am, 25/27 Apr 1942 pro to 31 Jul 1951
Debuts: 25 Apr 1942 United 3 Sheffield Wednesday 0 (CC)
20 Dec 1947 United 1 Charlton Athletic 1
Last game: 28 Apr 1951 United 0 Manchester City 0
Chesterfield (£1,500) 3 Aug 1951/ Buxton cs 1953/ Stocksbridge Works Aug 1954

Strong and fearless with two good feet, Herbert Parkin made his United debut near the end of the 1941–42 season and was a regular in the wartime side for the following two seasons. A serious injury in September 1944 at the City Ground in Nottingham almost brought his playing career to an end. His right leg had been broken five inches above the knee and left him with one leg shorter than the other and he didn't play again until he appeared for the third team in January 1946.

Herbert was competing with Eddie Shimwell and Albert Cox for the left back position in the first team and it was not until late in 1947 that he made his FL debut and he was never assured of a regular place in the team. He moved on to Chesterfield and made 55 FL appearances in his two seasons at Saltergate.

Appearances:		Apps	Gls
	FL	35	0
	CC	7	0
	WW2	54	1
	Total	96	1

PARKINSON Andrew (Andy) John

MF 2003–04 5' 8" 10st 12
b. Liverpool 27 May 1979

Liverpool (trainee)/ Tranmere Rovers Apr 1997
United: (free) 18 Jul 2003 to 30 Jul 2004
Debuts: 15 Jul 2003 Frechville CA 0 United XI 9 (sub Fr)
21 Jul 2003 Penrhyn Athletic 0 United XI 6 (Fr)
9 Aug 2003 United 0 Gillingham 0 (sub)
23 Sep 2003 United 0 Queens Park Rangers 2 (LC)
24 Feb 2004 Crewe Alexandra 0 United 1
Last games: 2 Mar 2004 United 2 Millwall 1
7 Mar 2004 Sunderland 2 United 0 (FAC)
Notts County (L) 15 Jan 2004, (L) 19 Mar 2004
Grimsby Town (free) Jul 2004/ Notts County Jun 2006 to Jun 2008/ Cambridge U Jul 2008

Andrew Parkinson made his FL debut with Tranmere Rovers as a substitute at Wolverhampton Wanderers on 22 October 1997, his full debut coming on 31 January at home to Manchester City. After over 150 FL appearances he was signed by Neil Warnock but found his opportunities limited. He had two loan spells with Notts County, the first for one month and then later until the end of the season.

At the end of the season, he moved to Grimsby and later to Notts County continuing to have a successful career in the lower Divisions having made 241(97) FL appearances by the end of 2007–08, when he was released by County.

Appearances:		Apps	Gls
	FL	3 (4)	0
	FAC	1 (1)	0
	LC	1	0
	Total	5 (5)	0

PARKS John (Jack) Alfred

CF 1963–64 5' 10" 13st 1
b. Wath-on-Dearne 14 September 1943

United: amateur to app 30 Jul 1960, pro 4/7 Nov 1960 to 23 Sep 1966
Debut: 25 Sep 1963 United 1 Bolton Wanderers 2 (LC)
Last game: 29 Feb 1964 Ipswich Town 1 United 0
Halifax Town (£1,000) Sep 1966/ Weymouth (1967–69)

Jack Parks was one of a group of young players who came to the Lane from the Don & Dearne Schools. He was broad and strong but was unable to make the breakthrough into United's first team. However he did go on to make 40 FL appearances for Halifax Town (14 goals) at the Shay.

Appearances:		Apps	Gls
	FL	1	0
	LC	1	0
	Total	2	0

PARTRIDGE Albert (Bert) Edward

OR/RB 1923–29 5' 7½" 11st 6
b. Birmingham 10 August 1901 or 13 February 1901
d. Shipley 11 November 1966

Newcastle United Aug 1921/ Redditch Town Aug 1922
United: (£150 to Red T, £50 to Newcastle U) 3 May/14 Aug 1923 to 31 May 1929
Debut: 1 Sep 1923 United 3 Manchester City 0
Last game: 13 Apr 1929 Manchester City 3 United 1
Bradford City (£425) 31 May 1929/ Northampton Town Sep 1933 to May 1934

Bert Partridge scored on his debut for the Blades but though he could be regarded as a first team player in his six seasons at the Lane, he spent most of those competing unsuccessfully with David Mercer for the outside right role. He was clever and very fast—this earned him the

nickname 'Mumtaz' after a racehorse—and had a good run in the side in 1924–25 but he was 'hit or miss' and 'sometimes left the ball behind'. United decided to release him in 1928 but kept him on and he played his final ten games at right back, before moving on to Bradford City.

He played 55 FL matches (7 goals) with City but only twice for Northampton during his one season there and, for some years, he was the landlord of the Angel Hotel in Baildon.

Appearances:		Apps	Gls
	FL	90	17
	FAC	11	3
	CC	2	2
	Total	103	22

PATON Thomas

IL/IR 1906–07 5' 8½" 11st
b. E. Kilbride 8 November 1881

Larkhall Thistle/ Hamilton Academicals 1901/ Royal Albert Aug 1902/ Rangers cs1903/ Derby County May 1904
United: (£275) 8 Mar 1906 to cs 1907
Debut: 17 Mar 1906 United 1 Bury 1
Last game: 26 Jan 1907 United 2 Stoke 0
St Mirren cs 1907 to cs 1908/ Airdrie May 1912/ Cowdenbeath Jul 1914

Thomas Paton made his Scottish League debut for Rangers on 2 January 1904 at home to Partick Thistle and, after one further League appearance, he moved south, joining Derby County. He made his FL debut on 1 September 1904 at Stoke but managed only four goals in his 38 appearances for the Rams. Following his move to the Lane, fifteen of his competitive appearance came in the first sixteen games of 1906–07 season and he showed 'delightful touches' but at the end of that season he returned to Scotland and played for St Mirren ending on the losing side in the 1908 Scottish FA Cup final.

Appearances:		Apps	Gls
	FL	21	4
	Total	21	4

PATTERSON Mark Andrew

MF 1995–97 5' 6" 11st 4
b. Darwen 24 May 1965

Blackburn Rovers from app May 1983/ Preston North End (£20k) Jun 1988/ Bury Feb 1990/ Bolton Wanderers (£65k) Feb 1991
United: **(exchange, valued at £300k/£500k) 21/22 Dec 1995 to 11 Dec 1997**
Debut: **23 Dec 1995 Stoke City 2 United 2**
Last game: **2 Dec 1997 United 3 Stoke City 2**
Southend United (L) 27 Mar 1997
Bury (£125k) Dec 1997/ Blackpool (L) Dec 1998/ Southend United (free) Mar 1999/ Leigh RMI May 1999/ Accrington Stanley Aug 2000–Feb 2001/Darwem Mar 2001to May 2001/ Rossendale United 2001/ Scarborough player-coach Nov 2001/ Rossendale United Dec 2002/ Leigh RMI player-mgr Dec 2002/ Chorley player-mgr Nov 2003–Apr 2004/ Scarborough mgr Jul 2006 / – / Hednesford asst mgr Oct 2007 to Feb 2008

Mark Patterson made his FL debut with Blackburn Rovers as a substitute on 17 September 1983 at Manchester City, his full debut coming a week later at home to Brighton & Hove Albion but it was perhaps with Bolton Wanderers where he played his best football, making over 160 League appearances.

Mark was one of Howard Kendall's early signings, valued at c£400k. He moved from Bolton with, surprisingly to many, Nathan Blake moving the other way. Mark scored vital goals in his first two games and his energetic displays and no nonsense tackling helped United move up the table. He took over the captaincy and in the following season, he was more or less ever present until Nick Henry's arrival made Mark's position less certain. He had a spell on loan at Southend but rejected moves to the Essex team and Burnley. After starting as a regular in 1997–98 he failed to agree terms for a new contract and moved to Bury.

After retiring from League football, having made 458(30) League appearances, he played, coached and managed with a variety of non-League clubs. Between such engagements he worked as a landscape gardener with his brother and later worked in the construction industry and was also involved in Pro-Active Soccer Schools. In August 2007 he was declared bankrupt and in February he was sacked as assistant manager at Hednesford due to financial restrictions at the club.

Appearances:		Apps	Gls
	FL	72 (2)	4
	FAC	3	0
	LC	9	0
	Total	84 (2)	4

PATTERSON W H (or 'Pattison')

FB/WH
b. Scotland

United: **Dec 1891 to Dec 1892**
Debuts: **12 Dec 1891 Walsall Town Swifts 2 United 0 (Fr)**
26 Dec 1891 Newcastle East End 1 United 2 (NL)
16 Jan 1892 Blackpool 0 United 3 (FAC)
10 Sep 1892 Bootle 2 United 0
Last game: **31 Oct 1892 United 2 Rotherham Town 6 (Fr)**
Gainsborough Trinity Dec 1892

WH Patterson who came to United 'from Edinburgh', was not short of speed and played in a variety of positions (left and right back, left and right half back and inside left) in his brief time at the Lane. On his final appearance he scored both goals in the 2–6 defeat.

Appearances:		Apps	Gls
	FL	1	0
	NL	3	0
	SCC	1	0
	WCC	1	0
	Total	6	0

PATTINSON John Bouch

OR/IR 1905–07 5' 10" 11st 4
b. Worksop OND 1886
d. Gainsborough 29 November 1918

Gainsborough Trinity 1903
United: **15 May 1905 to 13 Jun 1907**
Debuts: **13 Sep 1905 Gainsborough Trinity 0 United 8 (Fr)**
10 Feb 1906 Everton 3 United 2
Last games: **15 Dec 1906 Aston Villa 5 United 1**
6 Apr 1907 Brighton & Hove Albion 1 United 2 (Fr)
Grimsby Town Jun 1907/ Doncaster Rovers (£10 to United) Oct 1908/ Gainsborough Trinity Dec 1908/ Manchester City Sep 1911–cs 1912/ Doncaster Rovers Sep 1912/ Rotherham County cs 1913

John Pattinson made his FL debut with Gainsborough Trinity on 12 September 1903 at home to Woolwich Arsenal and, after just 6 FL appearances (3 gl), he joined United.

In his time at the Lane he was unable to establish himself as a regular in the first team but he did score the winning goal in the only one of his four competitive games which United won. Although signing for various clubs (115 FL appearances for Gainsborough, United and Grimsby), it was during his second spell with Gainsborough Trinity (1908–1911) that he was most successful, scoring 16 goals in 86 FL appearances.

Described as 'fast, tricky with a fair shot', he was a professional sprinter and a pawnbroker.

Appearances:		Apps	Gls
	FL	4	1
	Total	4	1

PEAKE William (Billy) Edward

IR/IL 1910–12 5' 10½" 11st 7
b. Prestwich (Manchester) c1888
d. Manchester 12 March 1960

St John's College, Battersea/ Northern Nomads Eccles Borough
United: **4 Jan 1910 to 12 Jul 1912**
Debut: **22 Jan 1910 Bolton Wanderers 1 United 0**
Last game: **10 Feb 1912 Everton 3 United 2**
Bury (£250) Jul 1912/ Newcross cs 1922/ Macclesfield/ Manchester North End 1922–24

Trained as a teacher, Billy Peake became a professional when he signed for United though he continued to teach and live in Manchester. A hard working player who passed the ball well, Billy was a useful reserve player but he never played more than six successive games.

Transferred to Bury, he became their captain and made 168 FL appearances. He also played occasionally during the First World War for Bury and as a guest for Spurs. He became a lieutenant in the artillery and in later years, a head teacher in Manchester.

Appearances:		Apps	Gls
	FL	27	6
	Total	27	6

PEARS John (Jack)

OL 1934–35 5' 8½" 11st 8
b. Ormskirk 23 February 1907

Skelmersdale United Jun 1926/ Burscough Rangers Dec 1926/ Liverpool Aug 1927/ Rotherham United Aug 1928/ Accrington Stanley May 1929/ Oldham Athletic Jul 1930/ Preston North End Mar 1934
United: (£1,500) 7 Nov 1934 to 4 May 1935
Debut: 10 Nov 1934 United 5 Newcastle 1
Last game: 6 Apr 1935 Blackpool 1 United 0
Swansea Town (£350) 30 Jul 1935/ Hull City (£100) Jun 1937/ Rochdale Jun 1938/ Mossley Sep 1938/ Workington

The much travelled Jack Pears began his FL career at Liverpool but his FL debut did not come until he moved to Rotherham United, on 28 August 1928 at Bradford City when he scored.

He came to the Lane facing competition for the left wing position from Spooner and Williams as United tried to solve the problem of finding 'another Tunstall'. Fast, with a good shot, he scored twice on his United debut and played in the following 14 games but after one more game, later in the season, he was put on the transfer list. United accepted an offer of £500 from Cardiff City but they were unable to proceed with the transfer and he moved to Swansea Town.

His best seasons had been with Oldham Athletic where he scored 33 goals in 92 FL games but despite his nomadic career he eventually played 245 FL games—none with Liverpool and Rochdale—and scored an impressive 74 goals.

Appearances:		Apps	Gls
	FL	13	3
	FAC	2	1
	CC	1	0
	Total	16	4

PEARSON Albert (Bert) Victor

IL/OL 1912–14 5' 8½" 11st
b. Tynemouth 6 September 1892
d. Newcastle under Lyme 24 January 1975

Hebburn Argyle
United: 26/29 Apr 1912 to cs 1914
Debut: 28 Sep 1912 Bradford City 3 United 1
Last game: 14 Feb 1914 Everton 5 United 0
Port Vale cs 1914/ Liverpool (£100 to United) Mar 1919/ Port Vale May 1921/ Llanelly cs 1922/ Rochdale May 1923/ Stockport County Nov 1925/ Ashton National Jun 1929

A clever ball player, Bert Pearson joined United a few days after his Hebburn colleague, Bill Cook but he played only the occasional game during his two seasons at the Lane. He moved to Port Vale for a season before the club went into abeyance due to the First War and then returned to the north east working as a boilermaker. He returned to Port Vale in 1917 but was sold to Liverpool in 1919. United claimed successfully that he was still registered with the FL as a United player and received some of the small fee.

Bert was at his best with Liverpool (44 app, 4 gl) and also with Rochdale (52 app, 12 gl), and despite missing four seasons due to the War he had a career record of 190 FL appearances for his various clubs. He later acted as a scout for Wolves and kept a shop in Hanley.

Appearances:		Apps	Gls
	FL	6	0
	Total	6	0

PEART John (Jack) George

CF 1908–10 5' 10½" 11st 10
b. South Shields 3 October 1888
d. Paddington, London 3 September 1948

South Shields Adelaide 1905/ Treharris? am 1906 S Shields Adelaide
United: (£20) 27/30 Apr 1907 to 6 Jun 1910
Debut: 11 Mar 1908 Manchester City 0 United 2
Last game: 26 Mar 1910 United 4 Bristol City 0
Stoke Jun 1910/ Newcastle United (£600) Mar 1912/ Notts County (£600) Feb 1913
WW1 guest: South Shields, Leeds City (107 app), (Stoke (1), Rochdale, Chesterfield (1), Barnsley (1)
Birmingham Nov 1919/ Derby County (£2000) Jan 1920 / Ebbw Vale player mgr Jul 1920/ Port Vale Jan 1922/ Norwich City Jul 1922/ Rochdale player mgr Mar 1923, mgr May 1924/ Bradford City mgr Jul 1930/ Fulham mgr May 1935 to Sep 1948

Jack Peart was a man of many clubs and injuries. A strong, bustling and tenacious centre forward, he was United's regular centre forward for much of the 1908–09 season before being replaced, in February, by Joe Kitchen. He made just two more appearances, a year later, but was regarded as 'cumbersome' and put on the transfer list.

He signed for Stoke, who were then members of the Southern League. A broken leg, a few months later proved to be the first of many injuries but he had a long career as a player and a good scoring record and represented the Southern League on three occasions and the Football League against the Southern League in 1914. He never stayed long as a player with any club and as the player manager of Ebbw Vale, he negotiated his own transfer back into the FL

As a club secretary-manager, he served two FL clubs for a total of 18 years. He was in charge of Fulham when they were beaten by United in the FA Cup semi-final in 1936 and he built the side which reached the top flight eight months after his death. In 1945 he was awarded the Football League's long service medal.

Appearances:		Apps	Gls
	FL	27	7
	FAC	1	0
	Total	28	7

PEATTIE Donald (Don) Simpson

F/MF 1984–85 5' 11½" 11st 10
b. York 5 April 1963

Gretna
United: 10 Aug 1984 to 31 Dec 1986
Debuts: 13 Aug 1984 Skegness Town 0 United 3 (sub Fr) ?
15 Aug 1984 Mansfield Town 2 United 1 (Fr)
1 Dec 1984 United 0 Huddersfield Town 2 (sub)
6 May 1985 United 1 Blackburn Rovers 3
Last games: 13 May 1985 Huddersfield Town 2 United 2
5 Aug 1985 United 0 Leicester City 2 (Fr)
Doncaster Rovers (L) Jan 1986
Newcastle Blue Star/ Spennymoor/ Blyth Spartans/ Bedlington Terriers 1995

Don Peattie's family had moved to Scotland when he was ten. Educated at Dumfries High School, he had played for Scotland's Boys and U18's and was a Sports student at Newcastle Polytechnic.

Following his move from Gretna, he scored well in the reserves but, lacking in speed and determination, he was unable to make the breakthrough into the first team at the Lane. He made four more FL appearances whilst on loan at Doncaster.

Appearances:		Apps	Gls
	FL	3 (2)	0
	Total	3 (2)	0

PEDEN John

OL 1894
b. The Maze Racecourse, Lisburn 12 July 1863
d. Belfast 15 September 1944

Linfield 1886/ Newton Heath Feb/cs 1893
United: (£30?) 6 Jul 1894 to Feb 1895
Debut: 1 Sep 1894 United 2 West Bromwich Albion 1
Last games: 8 Dec 1894 United 2 Liverpool 2
27 Dec 1894 United 3 Corinthians 7 (Fr)
Distillery Jul 1895/ Linfield 1900–06 player and coach

John Peden played in Linfield's first fixture in 1886 and was thought to be the first Irish professional player when he joined Newton Heath (now Manchester United). He made his FL debut at home to Burnley on 2 September 1893 and joined the Blades in the close season.

George Waller, the United trainer and a fine judge of players, described Johnny as 'a great outside left' but he was also 'difficult, temperamental, unreliable and homesick'. He became the father of twins towards the end of 1894 and, early in February 1895, he returned to Belfast.

He was a popular player in Ireland winning 24 caps and scoring 7 goals. First capped in 1887 with Linfield, before he played for Newton Heath and United, his final nine caps came with Distillery. Ireland, in those days, didn't use men who were playing in England but the final three of Johnny's fifteen caps earned while playing for Linfield, came after he had been registered by the FL (23 Feb 1893) with Newton Heath.

Appearances:

	Apps	Gls
FL	8	2
UCL	1	0
Total	9	2

PEEL Nathan James

Striker 1991–92 6' 1" 12st 7
b. Blackburn 17 May 1972

Preston North End from trainee Jul 1990
United: (£75/50k) 8 Jul/1 Aug 1991 to 25 Oct 1993
Debut: 23 Nov 1991 Tottenham Hotspur 0 United 1 (sub)
Last games: 4 May 1992 United XI 2 Ex-Blades Select XI 3 (BM Brian Smith)
10 Aug 1992 Cambridge United 1 United 2 (sub Fr)
Halifax Town (L) 3/5 Feb 1993
Burnley (L) 28 Sep, Transfer (£60/35k) 25 Oct 1993/ Rotherham United (L) Mar 1995/ Mansfield Town (L) Oct 1995/ Doncaster Rovers (L) Feb 1996/ Rotherham United (free) Jul 1996/ Macclesfield Town (free) Jan 1997/ Winsford United Dec 1997/ Stevenage Borough (L)/ Northwich Victoria Jan 1999/ Barrow Feb 2000/ Droylsden cDec 2000/ Barrow Jan 2001/ Clitheroe Mar 2001

Nathan Peel made his FL debut with Preston North End as a substitute on 25 August 1990 at Grimsby Town but only began one FL game for Preston (10 FL app), scoring at Reading on 3 September.

He joined United at the start of the club's second season in the top flight. He scored twice in his first appearance in United's colours against a Midland Bank team but sadly suffered a cruciate ligament injury. He was one of Dave Bassett's 'gambles' that did not come off and other than his one 'last five minute' substitute appearance, he played only in friendlies.

He then played for several clubs, including Macclesfield Town where he played twice during the season in which they gained promotion to the Football League. After a few FL appearances with the Silkmen he moved into non-League football, having totalled 57 FL appearances, 26 as a substitute.

Appearances:

	Apps	Gls
FL	0 (1)	0
Total	0 (1)	0

PEMBERTON John Matthew

RWB/ CD 1990–93 5' 11" 12st 2
b. Oldham 18 November 1964

Chadderton Aug 1983/ Rochdale Sep 1984/ Chadderton Crewe Alexandra (£1,000) Mar 1985/ Crystal Palace (£80k) Mar 1988
United: (£300k) 23/27 Jul 1990 to 12/16 Nov 1993
Debuts: 27 Jul 1990 Kramfors A (Sweden) 1 United 5 (Fr)
25 Aug 1990 United 1 Liverpool 3
Last games: 18 Sep 1993 Leeds United 2 United 1
21 Sep 1993 Blackpool 3 United 0 (LC)
Leeds United (£250k) Nov 1993/ Crewe Alexandra (free) Aug 1997 player-coach/ Nottingham Forest coach

John Pemberton was a striker as a youth but was converted to a defensive role. He made his FL debut with Rochdale on 2 October 1984 at home to Aldershot and then played for Crewe and Crystal Palace where he featured in the 1990 FA Cup Final.

He was signed by Dave Bassett for United who were newly promoted to the top flight. Strong and determined, he used his speed both in defence and coming forward but was prone to making occasional errors. His League debut with the Blades came in the opening fixture against Liverpool and was particularly memorable because, after about 15 minutes, he went into goal following an injury to Simon Tracey but unfortunately conceded two goals in the second half. For the next three seasons he was in and out of the side, playing more as a central defender in his final season (when he was also played in goal in a friendly match at Bideford).

John's move to Leeds United was something of a surprise and he was restricted to 53 League appearances in his time there largely because of injuries. His return to Crewe was as a player coach but, after two appearances, injury struck again and he retired from playing having made 305(17) League appearances.

In due course he took on a coaching role with Nottingham Forest, initially with the academy but subsequently with the reserves.

Appearances:

	Apps	Gls
FL	67 (1)	0
FAC	4	0
LC	4	0
FMC	1	0
Total	76 (1)	0

PERICARD Vincent de Paul

Striker 2005 6' 1" 13st 8
b. Efok (Cameroon) 3 October 1982

St Etienne (France)1999/ Juventus (Italy) 2000 Portsmouth (L) 2002, (£400k) Jul 2003

United:	**(L) 16 Sep 2005 to Dec 2005**
Debuts:	**24 Sep 2005 United 2 Derby County 1 (sub)**
	18 Oct 2005 Millwall 0 United 4
Last games:	**26 Nov 2005 Leicester City 4 United 2**
	3 Dec 2005 United 1 Sheffield Wednesday 0 (sub)

Plymouth Argyle (L) Feb 2006/ Stoke City (free) Jun 2006/Southampton (L) Mar 2008 to May 2008

Having played for Juventus in the Champions League, Vincent Pericard moved to Portsmouth on loan, making his FL debut, and scoring, on 10 August 2002 at home to Nottingham Forest. At the end of the season, Portsmouth, having been promoted to the Premiership, made the move permanent but two serious injuries then limited his appearances and he missed the entire 2004–05 season in rehabilitation.

He moved to Bramall Lane on a three-month loan, Neil Warnock wishing to ensure he had plenty of striking options as United started the 2005–06 campaign in impressive form. Due to the form of the strikers already playing, Vincent was never given a real chance to impress but he did show he had the speed to be potentially dangerous.

He returned to Portsmouth a few days early but went on loan Plymouth. Released at the end of the season he joined Stoke. However, his start to 2007–08 season was delayed due to a four month prison sentence given for various motoring offences. He returned in October 2007 but was re-arrested after problems with his electronic tag. He was released after about 2 weeks and in March moved to Southampton on loan.

Appearances:		Apps	Gls
	FL	3 (8)	2
	Total	3 (8)	2

PESCHISOLIDO Paulo(Paul or Pesch) Pasquale

Striker 2001, 2001–04 5' 7" 10st 12
b. Scarborough (Canada) 25 May 1971

Toronto Blizzards (Canada)/ Birmingham City (£25k) Nov 1992/ Stoke City (£400k) Aug 1994/ Birmingham City (£400k) Mar 1996/ West Bromwich Albion (£600k) Jul 1996 Fulham (£1.1m) Oct 1997/ Queens Park Rangers (L) Nov 2000

United:	**(L) 16/18 Jan 2001 to 20 Mar 2001**
Debut:	**20 Jan 2001 West Bromwich Albion 2 United 1**
Last games:	**24 Feb 2001 United 1 Crystal Palace 0**
	17 Mar 2001 Huddersfield Town 2 United 1 (sub)

Norwich City (L) Mar 2001

United:	**(£150k) 6 Jul 2001 to 12 Mar 2004**
Debuts:	**17 Jul 2001 Sheffield FC 0 United 7 (Fr)**
	11 Aug 2001 Nottingham Forest 1 United 1
Last games:	**21 Feb 2004 United 1 West Bromwich Albion 2**
	28 Feb 2004 Reading 2 United 1 (sub)
	7 Mar 2004 Sunderland 2 United 0 (sub FAC)

Derby County Mar 2004, (player-coach) Feb 2006/ Luton Town Jul 2007 to May 2008

Paul Peschisolido had Italian parents and had a trial with Juventus when he was sixteen. He was recommended to Birmingham by the Canadian National coach and made his FL debut as a substitute on 21 November 1992 at Barnsley; his full debut coming on 9 January at home to Luton Town. He played for several clubs and had scored 79 goals in around 250 League appearances when he made his loan move to the Lane.

Signed by Neil Warnock, he was terrier-like in his attitude, a handful for any defender and an excellent finisher. Scoring on his debut, his energetic displays meant he quickly became popular with the fans and he would probably have been signed on a permanent basis immediately but the fee being asked by Fulham, said to be £1m, was too high. He returned there while United waited, hoping for the fee to fall, which it did.

He returned in the summer, making a slow start in terms of goals but, after returning from injury, he scored five goals in six games and continued to produce some excellent performances full of commitment, selfless running and anticipation. The following injury ravaged season saw Paul used mainly as a substitute in which role he scored four of his seven goals, none more dramatic than the equalising goal against Forest in the play-off semi-final.

Paul had gained caps for Canada at youth and U23 level and whilst at the Lane added four more to his tally of full caps. He made more starts for United in 2003–04 and it was a surprise when he was allowed to move to Derby County in March. One reason given was Paul's travelling from Birmingham (he was married to the Birmingham City managing director Karren Brady). During his time at Derby he was again frequently used as a substitute bringing tremendous energy to the task but his managers had also realised that few players studied their potential opponents more closely than Paul while sat on the bench.

He moved to Luton in the summer of 2007 but an ankle injury in September ended his season early when it was decided an operation was needed and he was released in the summer. By then, Paul had scored 118 League goals in 295(152) games and had exceeded 50 international caps. It was reported that he was hoping to open some soccer schools in Canada.

Appearances:		Apps	Gls
	FL	39 (45)	19
	PO	0 (2)	1
	FAC	3 (5)	2
	LC	3 (5)	2
	Total	45 (57)	24

PETERS Martin Stanford MBE

See 'Managers' section

Appearances:		Apps	Gls
	FL	23 (1)	4
	LC	2	0
	ASC	2	0
	Total	27 (1)	4

PHELAN Terence (Terry) Michael

LWB 2001 5' 8" 10st 6
b. Manchester 16 March 1967

Leeds United from app Aug 1984/ Swansea City (free) Jul 1986/ Wimbledon (£100k) Jul 1987/ Manchester City (£2.5m) Aug 1992/ Chelsea (£900k) Nov 1995 Everton (£850k) Jan 1997/ Crystal Palace (L) Oct 1999 Fulham (free) Feb 2000

United: trial, 9/10 Aug 2001 to Nov 2001
Debuts: 3 Aug 2001 Brighton & Hove Albion 2 United 3 (Fr)
11 Aug 2001 Nottingham Forest 1 United 1
Last game: 30 Oct 2001 United 0 Watford 2
Charleston Battery(USA) Jan 2001 / – / Otago United (New Zealand) coach Oct 2005

Terry Phelan made his FL debut with Leeds United on 7 September 1985 at Shrewsbury Town. He went on to play over 400 League games for his various clubs, winning 42 full caps for the Republic of Ireland as well as caps at youth, U21, U23 and B level. He was a member of the Wimbledon 'Crazy Gang' team that won the FA Cup in 1988.

He moved to Bramall Lane, signed by Neil Warnock, after being released by Fulham and played in the first six games of the season before being replaced by Shane Nicholson. He made three further appearances in October before his release in January. He then moved to the United States, playing and coaching youngsters, and then moved on to coach in New Zealand.

Appearances:		Apps	Gls
	FL	8	0
	LC	1	0
	Total	9	0

PHILIP George

CF/IF 1918–19 5' 9" 12st 10
b. Newport (Fife)

Dundee 1911/ Sunderland (£2,000) Apr 1914
United: WW1 guest
Debut: 7 Sep 1918 United 5 Huddersfield Town 1 (WW1)
Last game: 21 Dec 1919 Bradford P A 3 United 0 (WW1)
Dundee Jun 1920–21

George Philip made his Scottish League debut with Dundee on 2 December 1911 at home to Clyde. In his time with Dundee he played mainly at centre half and switched to centre forward shortly before his move to Sunderland for a record fee for the two clubs. His FL debut was on 2 September 1914 at home to United and he had an excellent first season scoring 22 FL goals in 37 games.

A corporal in the army, his ten appearances for United were as a guest player during the First World War and after the war, he returned to Sunderland but was reported as intending to return to Scotland and he played one more season with Dundee (27 app), mainly at centre forward.

Appearances:		Apps	Gls
	WW1	10	2
	Total	10	2

PHILLIPSON Thomas (Tom) William

IL/IR/CF 1928–30 5' 6½" to 5' 9" 11st 4
b. Ryton on Tyne 31 October 1898
d. Wolverhampton 19 November 1965

Scotswood 1914/ Newcastle United (£500) Dec 1919 Swindon Town (£500) May 1921 Wolverhampton Wanderers (£1,000) Dec 1923
United: (£2,600) 15/16 Mar 1928 to cs 1930
Debut: 17 Mar 1928 United 4 Middlesbrough 1
Last games: 18 Jan 1930 Birmingham 2 United 1
25 Jan 1930 Huddersfield Town 2 United 1 (FAC)
Bilston United player-mgr Jul 1930/ Walsall (£500?) Aug 1931 to Feb 1932

Tom Phillipson, who gained England schoolboy caps, served with the Western Regiment as a sergeant in Russia during the First War. On his return, he joined Newcastle United, making his FL debut on 24 January 1920 at Everton but had few first team opportunities and moved, via Swindon, to Wolves where he was a great success. He scored 111 FL and Cup goals in 159 appearances and captained the team when they won the Third Division (North) championship in 1924.

Well built with good ball control and a fine shot, his move to the Lane was something of a surprise but, playing alongside Harry Johnson, he scored a goal in nearly every other game in spite of the fact that he was rather slow. In his final season with United, he lost his place in February because of illness and couldn't win it back. He returned to the Midlands to non-League Bilston before playing one season with Walsall.

On retiring, Tom, who had totalled 162 FL goals in 308 games, concentrated on his business interests in Wolverhampton and became the mayor and a director of the Wanderers.

Appearances:		Apps	Gls
	FL	56	26
	FAC	3	0
	CC	2	1
	Total	61	27

PHILLISKIRK Anthony (Tony)

Striker 1983–88 6' 1" 11st 3
b. Sunderland 10 February 1965

Sunderland
United: appr 8/16 Aug 1983 to 30 Jun 1988
Debuts: 17 Aug 1983 Mansfield Town 1 United 2 (Fr)
22 Oct 1983 United 0 Brentford 0
Last games: 19 Apr 1988 United 1 Plymouth Argyle 0
7 May 1988 Huddersfield Town 0 United 2 (sub)
15 May 1988 Bristol City 1 United 0 (sub PO)
Rotherham United (L) 16 Oct 1986

Oldham Athletic (£25k) Jul 1988/ Preston North End (£50k) Feb 1989/ Bolton Wanderers (£50k) Jun 1989/ Peterborough United (£85k) Oct 1992/ Burnley (£80k)Jan 1994/ Carlisle United (L) Oct 1995/ Cardiff City (£60k) Dec 1995/ Halifax Town (L) Dec 1997/ Macclesfield Town (L) Feb 1998/ Oldham Athletic youth coach 1998, asst mgr cs2002, youth coach Dec 2003

An England schoolboy international, Tony Philliskirk made his FL debut in 1983–84, his 8 goals in 20(1) FL appearances helping United gain promotion to the Second Division. Tony had good ball control and used the ball well but he didn't make the progress that many had anticipated, partly because of injuries but also, he lacked pace, determination and physique. He scored some exceptional goals but was unable to become a regular member of the side for the following three seasons but played regularly in 1987–88 until Dave Bassett's arrival and at the end of that season he left the Lane.

After leaving United he played briefly for Oldham and Preston before moving to Bolton where he had the most successful part of his career, scoring 51 goals in 139(2) FL appearances. On the move again, he eventually signed for Cardiff City where he had a successful 1996–97 season, playing in a more defensive role, but he was surprisingly out of favour during the following one. After two loan spells, one with Conference side Halifax, he went into coaching with Oldham Athletic, although he had considered refereeing and had taken the relevant examinations.

He was youth team coach for four seasons and became assistant manager on Iain Dowie's arrival as manager. When Iain left for Crystal Palace, Tony could have followed but for family reasons he remained with Oldham.

During his playing career Tony had played for ten League clubs, scoring for all of them and totalling 110 FL goals in 352(56) appearances.

Appearances:		Apps	Gls
	FL	62 (18)	20
	PO	0 (1)	0
	FAC	5	1
	LC	4 (1)	1
	AMC	3	0
	FMC	0 (1)	0
	Total	74 (21)	22

PICKERING John (Jack)

IL/IR/OR 1927–48 5' 10½" 11st 6
b. High Green, Chapeltown 18 December 1908
d. Bournemouth 10 May 1977

Mortomley St Saviours
United: 27 Apr/4 May/Dec 1925 to 31 Jul 1948
Debut: 7 Feb 1927 United 1 Liverpool 4
Last game: 1 Jan 1948 United 1 Portsmouth 2
Poole Town Jul 1948 mgr-coach

Educated at Barnsley Grammar School, United gave Jack Pickering a trial with the reserves on Cup Final Day in April 1925 against Burnley Reserves and he scored. He was sixteen but it was nearly two years before he made his first team debut. Because of his intelligence and ability, United's idea was to groom Jack as a successor to Billy Gillespie but it took time for the idea to come to fruition. The young man also wanted to follow the example of Harry Johnson in being a part-time player and obtained an 'office job'. United discovered that the job was with a turf accountant and encouraged him to train as a chartered accountant.

Tall and slim with a long stride, good ball control and a football brain, he was a player, similar in many ways to United's midfield general, Billy Gillespie. Jack 'let the ball do the work' and he rarely dribbled, saying, that if he had to, he had made a mistake. He found space, called for the ball and had the ability, following the example of Gillespie, to send out long, accurate passes and Jack could also shoot with power and accuracy. Other forwards regarded him as the perfect partner but his temperament was a problem and he tended to play well 'only in flashes' and at his own pace. His ability was obvious however and he played for the Football League in 1932 and was capped for England against Scotland in 1933. A few months later, and not for the first time, he was relegated to the reserves only to score six goals against Preston North End.

Several clubs sought his services: United rejected offers from Arsenal, Liverpool, Birmingham and Everton and the player turned down a move to Plymouth. United had been relegated in 1934 but Jack

remained a vital player, particularly in 1936 when United lost to Arsenal in the FA Cup final and narrowly missed promotion and he was a leading player in the club's promotion in 1939. He captained United through much of the Second War, his calm demeanour and advice helping the development of several young players.

When he made his final appearance at the age of 39 on New Year's Day 1948, he had represented United for nearly 21 years. He moved to the south coast, coaching and managing Poole Town and later becoming a hotelier in Bournemouth for 27 years.

Appearances:		Apps	Gls
	FL	344	102
	FAC	23	9
	CC	20	8
	39/40	1	0
	WW2	173	72
	Total	561	191

PIKE Martin Russell

LB 1986–89 5' 11" 11st 7
b. South Shields 21 October 1964

West Bromwich Albion from app Oct 1982 Peterborough United Aug 1983
United: (c£20k) 5/22 Aug 1986 to 5 Feb 1990
Debuts: 5 Aug 1986 Skegness Town 1 United 11 (Fr)
23 Aug 1986 United 1 Shrewsbury Town 1

Last games: **23 Sep 1989 United 0 Hull City 0**
7 Nov 1989 United 1 Wolverhampton Wanderers 0 (sub ZDS)
4 Dec 1989 Bourne Town 0 United XI 2 (Fr)
11 May 1990 Brentford 4 United XI 2 (guest, sub, BM)
Tranmere Rovers (L) 10 Nov 1989/ Bolton Wanderers (L) 14 Dec 1989
Fulham (£60/65k) 8 Feb 1990/ Rotherham United Jul 1994/ Durham City Aug 1996/ Blyth Spartans/ Bedlington Terriers cs 1998

Starting his career as a midfield player, Martin Pike had to wait until he moved to Peterborough to make his FL debut on 27 August 1983 at home to Hartlepool United. He finally established himself as a regular in the side after moving to left back, being 'Player of the Season' in 1984–85, and missed just one game during his final two seasons with Peterborough.

A quick, committed and determined defender, he was a popular player in spite of his shortcomings. Signed by Billy McEwan, Martin was ever-present during his first season and missed just six FL games during the first three, being an integral part of the side which gained promotion to Division 2 in 1989. During that campaign he scored his first United goal (at Blackpool) after 89(1) FL appearances. During the following season, he lost his place to David Barnes and Wilf Rostron and after two loan spells he moved to Fulham.

He made nearly 200 FL appearances for Fulham, missing just two games during his first three campaigns but he lost his place through injury and moved to Rotherham United. His two seasons at Millmoor were blighted by injury and in the summer of 1996 he moved into non-League football, having played 447(14) FL games, and later played at Wembley for Bedlington in the FA Vase final in 1999. Subsequently he worked at the Sunderland youth academy and then as scout for Fulham.

Appearances:		Apps	Gls
	FL	127 (2)	5
	PO	1 (1)	0
	FAC	12	0
	LC	10	0
	FMC	2 (1)	0
	AMC	2	0
	YHC	6	0
	Total	160 (4)	5

PILGRIM James (Jim) Ernest

LB/RB 1898–99 5' 10" 12st 0
b. Holmes (Rotherham) JAS 1874

Parkgate/ Thornhill United/ Rotherham T
United: **8/9 Oct 1896 to 8 Jul 1999**
Debut: **10 Sep 1898 Notts County 2 United 2**
Last game: **29 Apr 1899 Sunderland 1 United 0**
Chesterfield Town Jul 1899/ Thornhill United Sep 1901/ Rotherham Town Oct 1902 to c1907

Jim Pilgrim may also have played for the original Rotherham United team in March 1894 and then for Rotherham Town's second team. A turner and fitter by trade, he made all but two of his appearances at the start of the 1898–99 season. A report on his debut at Nottingham was unpromising, commenting that he was 'ungainly' and that he had 'much to learn' in his tackling. He was replaced by Peter Boyle and moved to Chesterfield, playing in their first FL fixture at the new Owlerton ground of the Wednesday and making a total 54 FL appearances for the Spireites.

Appearances:		Apps	Gls
	FL	15	0
	Total	15	0

PLANT James (Jim) Edward

RH/LH 1920–23 5' 9" 11st 7
b. Whitwell (Worksop) JAS 1898 or 1900

Whitwell/ Cresswell Colliery/ Whitwell Discharged Soldiers
United: **6 Jan 1920 to cs1925**
Debut: **9 Feb 1920 United 0 Derby County 0**
Last game: **3 Sep 1923 Bolton Wanderers 4 United 2**
/ – / Macclesfield Town Jun 1926/ Worksop Town Jun 1927/ Ripley Town Jul 1927/ Whitwell OB (amat) Feb 1929/ Whitwell Colliery Jan 1931

A former soldier, wounded while serving with the Sherwood Foresters, Jim Plant spent over two seasons at the Lane without really establishing himself, although he made a big impression in United's first two County Cup games, scoring the one goal in the first game and all three in the second. His kicking was strong and he 'passed the ball with judgement' but United were unsure of his best position until, in season 1922–23, he played regularly at wing half. Injured at the start of the following season, he was replaced by George Green and was released in 1925 on medical grounds. After a period out of the game, he returned, signing for Macclesfield Town. In later years, he may have used his mother's name of 'Heath'.

Appearances:		Apps	Gls
	FL	55	1
	FAC	10	0
	CC	5	4
	Total	70	5

POOLE Cyril John

LB 1945 5' 9" 10st 7
b. Forest Town, Mansfield 13 March 1921
d. Balderton, Nottinghamshire 11 February 1996

Annesley Colliery Welfare cs 1935/ Mansfield Town cs 1936, am/ Wolverhampton Wanderers Dec 1937/ Mansfield Town cs 1938 am, pro Feb 1944
United: **WW2 guest**
Only game: **24 Mar 1945 United 2 Bradford City 2 (WW2)**
WW2 guest Chesterfield (3), Nottingham Forest (1), United, Gillingham (2)
Gillingham Jun 1946/ Mansfield Town Jun 1949/ Mansfield Colliery cs1951–58/ Clipstone M W 1959–60

Cyril Poole made his FL debut, and his only pre-war appearance, with Mansfield Town, at home to New Brighton, on 27 February 1937 at the age of 15 years 351 days, making him one of the youngest players ever to play League football. He made no FL appearances during his time with Wolves and then returned to Mansfield.

During the 1939–46 War, he played over 70 games for Mansfield but he didn't play well on his single guest appearance for United. He then joined Gillingham, who were a non-League club whilst he was there, before returning again to League soccer at Field Mill and so there was a twelve year gap before he made his second FL appearance. In total, he played in 17 FL matches in his time with Mansfield. His elder brother George, played twice for Mansfield Town during the 1944–45 season.

Cyril was also a very good cricketer, graduating from Mansfield Colliery in the Bassetlaw League to Nottinghamshire CCC and England. He made his first class debut in 1948 at the age of 27 and went on to play in 3 Test matches and in 383 first class matches, averaging 32.5 with the bat.

Appearances:		Apps	Gls
	WW2	1	0
	Total	1	0

POOLE George

OR 1944 5' 6½" 10st 8
b. Sheffield 11 August 1926

Thurcroft Colliery
United: 23 Sep 1944 amat to cs1945
Debut: 16 Dec 1944 United 4 Mansfield Town 1 (WW2)
Last game: 23 Dec 1944 Mansfield Town 4 United 1 (WW2)
WW2 guest: Mansfield T
Rotherham United 1946–48/ Grantham Town 1948–49/ Wath Wanderers/ Wolverhampton W (reserve team trial)/ Worksop Town/ Stocksbridge/ Chesterfield Dec 1952 trial/ Frickley/ Buxton

A Bevin Boy, who later served in the RAF, George Poole's two first team appearances for United were in successive games against Mansfield during the Second War. He later played as a guest for Mansfield and featured in six FA Cup-ties in the two legged affairs in the 1945–46 season. Despite spending time at Rotherham and having trials with other FL clubs he never made a FL appearance.

Appearances:		Apps	Gls
	WW2	2	0
	Total	2	0

POOLE John (Jack) Smith

CH 1916–19 5' 11" 12st 10
b. Codnor OND 1892
d. Mansfield 21 March 1967

Sutton United/ Sutton Junction/ Sherwood Foresters Nottingham Forest 1914
United: WW1 guest
Debut: 22 Jan 1916 Bradford Park Avenue 0 United 1 (WW1)
Last game: 8 Mar 1919 Leeds City 2 United 1 (WW1)
Sunderland May 1919/ Bradford City May 1924, player coach reserves Oct 1927, ass trainer 1930–1935/ Mansfield Town trainer Jul 1935, mgr May 1938/ Notts County trainer Aug 1944/ Derby County trainer 1945 to 1956/ Sutton T trainer 1956

A Nottingham Forest reserve player from 1914, Jack Poole began to play for the United reserve team as a guest player during the First War season of 1915–16. He had a painful debut at Bradford; knocked out when he was hit by the ball, he was badly kicked and had a cut under his eye and he used to recall walking 18 miles in the snow to play for United at Chesterfield on Xmas day 1917. A strong and intelligent half back, he played regularly until March 1917 when he made his first team debut with Forest.

He joined the Sherwood Foresters and may have played once or twice for Sunderland as a guest towards the end of the final war-time season before signing for them and making his FL debut on 30 August 1919 at home to Aston Villa. After playing for Bradford City, he retired having made 241 FL appearances, scoring once. He carried on as a reserve player and coach and for many years acted as trainer, coach or manager at various clubs.

Appearances:		Apps	Gls
	WW1	25	1
	Total	25	1

POOLE Terence (Terry)

G 1980 6' 1" 13st 0
b. Chesterfield 16 December 1949

Manchester United from jnr Feb 1967/ Huddersfield Town Aug 1968/ Bolton Wanderers Jan 1977
United: (L) 13 Mar 1980 to 10 May 1980
Debut: 25 Mar 1980 Barnsley 0 United 0
Last game: 26 Apr 1980 United 2 Wimbledon 1

Although he began his professional career with Manchester United, Terry Poole's FL debut came after his move to Huddersfield Town, on 14 September 1968 at home to Cardiff City. He was ever present for the Terriers in 1969–70 and stayed with the club for nearly nine seasons having long spells in and out of the side. He had played 207 FL games before he moved to Bolton Wanderers but his 29 FL appearances there were after his brief loan spell at the Lane.

For United, he played just seven games towards the end of the disappointing 1979–80 season, being the third goalkeeper United had tried—Ramsbottom and Richardson were the other two—following the injury to Steve Conroy.

Appearances:		Apps	Gls
	FL	7	0
	Total	7	0

POWELL Clifford (Cliff) George

RB/LB 1988–89 5' 11' 11st 3
b. Watford (Harlesdon?) 21 February 1968

Gadeside Rangers/ Watford app Jul 1984, pro Feb 1986 Hereford United (L) Dec 1987
United: 8 Mar 1988 to Nov 1991
Debuts: 19 Mar 1988 Leeds United 5 United 0 (sub)
9 Apr 1988 Birmingham City 1 United 0
Last games: 1 May 1989 United 1 Aldershot 0
13 May 1989 Bristol City 2 United 0 (sub)
14 Aug 1989 Halifax Town 1 United 0 (YHC)
Doncaster Rovers (L) Mar 1989/ Cardiff City (L) Nov 1989
Retired 1991

Cliff Powell failed to make a FL appearance with Watford, his FL debut coming with Hereford United on 12 December 1987 at Burnley. He was at Watford during Dave Bassett's brief time as manager there and when Dave took charge of United, Cliff was one of his several new signings and he played in the final seven games of the season which ended in relegation. After this disappointing start to his career with United, Cliff featured little due to injuries and although he had two loan spells, breaking a leg in his only appearance with Cardiff City was the last straw and he was forced to retire in 1991 after several operations. He had made only 22 FL appearances in total.

Appearances:		Apps	Gls
	FL	7 (3)	0
	PO	2	0
	LC	1	0
	YHC	4	0
	Total	14 (3)	0

POWELL David

LH/RH 1968–71 5' 10" 11st 0
b. Dolgarrog 15 October 1944

Gwydir Rovers/ Wrexham groundstaff Jan 1962, pro 14 May 1963
United: (£28.5k) 11/12 Sep 1968 to 21/22 Sep 1972
Debut: 21 Sep 1968 Blackburn Rovers 1 United 0
Last game: 13 Mar 1971 Queens Park Rangers 2 United 2
Cardiff City (free) Sep 1972/ retired cs 1974

Slim, fair haired, David Powell, gained youth caps for Wales whilst with Gwydir and made his FL debut with Wrexham on 11 May 1963 at Bristol Rovers. In the following four seasons he stood out in what was, for much of the time, a struggling side but Dave won U23 caps and in May 1968, he became Wrexham's first player since 1939 to win a full cap.

Quick into the tackle, always in the thick of the action, and good in distribution, he moved to the Lane, signed by Arthur Rowley, after 134 appearances for the Welsh club. He played impressively for United, both at left half or in a more central defensive role alongside Eddie Colquhoun and was a regular in the side for three seasons, winning 10 Welsh caps and being an integral part of the side which gained promotion to the top flight in 1971. Towards the end of that campaign however, he had badly injured his knee at Queens Park Rangers and that was to be his final game for United.

In September 1972 he joined Cardiff City, along with Gil Reece, Alan Warboys moving to the Lane. Dave continued to have problems with his knee and retired after two seasons, having gained a Welsh Cup winners' medal in 1973. He joined the South Wales Police, working at their Bridgend training centre and managing the Police football team. After retiring from the police he continued to live in the Cardiff area.

Appearances:		Apps	Gls
	FL	89	2
	FAC	2	0
	LC	5	0
	CC	1	0
	WC	2	0
	ABD	1	0
	Total	100	2

PRICE A

IR 1918

United: WW1 guest
Only game: 6 Apr 1918 Barnsley 1 United 1 (WW1)

An unknown player though possibly the same man who had played a month earlier for the Wednesday at Huddersfield. It is not the well known Sheffield born Leeds City forward as he played for Leeds on both occasions.

Appearances:		Apps	Gls
	WW1	1	0
	Total	1	0

PRIDMORE William (Bill) H

LB 1944–45

Atlas & Norfolk
United: 24/26 Aug 1944 to 21 Mar 1946
Debut: 14 Oct 1944 Doncaster Rovers 3 United 0 (WW2)
Last game: 27 Jan 1945 United 10 Lincoln City 2 (WW2)
Gainsborough Trinity cs 1946/ Retford Aug 1949/ Gainsborough Trinity cs1951

A 'native of Sheffield', Bill Pridmore played on five occasions during the 1944–45 wartime season; his final appearance, a 10–2 defeat of Lincoln City. He played regularly for the reserves until his release in 1946.

Appearances:		Apps	Gls
	WW2	5	0
	Total	5	0

PRIEST Alfred (Fred) Ernest

OL/IL/CF/LB 1896–1905 5' 8½" 12st 8
b. South Bank JAS 1875
d. Hartlepool 6 May 1922

South Bank (1889–1890 to 1896)
United: 19 Feb 1896 (registered FL), cs 1896 to Aug 1906
Debuts: 18 Apr 1896 Newcastle United 3 United 1 (Fr)
5 Sep 1896 United 1 Burnley 0
Last game: 28 Oct 1905 Nottingham Forest 4 United 1
Middlesbrough (free) trainer-player Aug 1906/ Hartlepool United 1908 player-mgr 1908 to 1912

Fred Priest was a regular in the side for six seasons, playing mainly at outside or inside left, although he had the occasional game at centre forward and a spell at left back. Scoring on his FL debut, he went on to score an average of a goal in every third game. He won a Championship medal in 1898 and appeared in five FA Cup finals (two of them replays) scoring in three of the games and gaining two winners' medals and one losers' medal. In 1900 he gained a full England cap against Ireland.

Fred was a popular player with a sunny temperament but he was determined, tenacious and difficult to knock off the ball and a player who never failed when the pressure was great. He had the ability to collect a pass on the run and was a fine crosser of the ball. The signing of Bert Lipsham in 1900 and injuries cost Fred his place but he returned at inside left, partnering Lipsham. His final season was essentially 1904–05 although his final game, at right back, came the following season.

He moved to Middlesbrough on a free transfer to act as trainer but with permission to play occasionally and made 12 appearances. In 1908, he was appointed player manager of the newly formed Hartlepools United playing in the North Eastern League and under his leadership they were twice winners of the Durham Senior Cup. He gave up playing during the first season and gave up the managerial position in 1912 to keep the Market Hotel in Hartlepool where he died in reduced circumstances in 1922. United played a benefit game for his widow and children with his old colleague, Alf Common, acting as referee.

Appearances:		Apps	Gls
	FL	209	68
	FAC	37	18
	ABD	2	0
	Total	248	86

PRIEST Harry

CF 1956–57 5' 11" 11st 13
b. Clay Cross 26 October 1935

Clay Cross Works
United: 26/27 Feb 1954 to 14 Jan 1958
Debuts: 15 Oct 1956 United 5 Barnsley 3 (CC)
2 Feb 1957 United 0 Blackburn Rovers 2
Last game: 9 Feb 1957 West Ham United 3 United 2
Halifax Town (£1500) Jan 1958

Despite scoring on his United debut and in his final game Harry Priest was unable to make the breakthrough into the first team on a regular basis. Strong, with a good shot, he spent two seasons with Halifax Town, scoring 12 FL goals in 30 appearances.

Appearances:		Apps	Gls
	FL	2	1
	CC	1	1
	Total	3	2

PUNTON William (Bill) Hamilton

OL 1966–67 5' 8½" 11st 8
b. Glenkindrie (E Lothian) 9 May 1934

Bredalbane/ Portadown 1953/ Newcastle United Feb 1954 Southend United Jul 1958/ Norwich City Jul 1959
United: (£7500?) 18 Nov 1966 to 26 Jan 1968
Debut: 19 Nov 1966 Chelsea 1 United 1
Last games: 9 Sep 1967 United 2 Arsenal 4
13 Sep 1967 Millwall 3 United 2 (LC)
Scunthorpe United (£3000) Jan 1968/ Yarmouth Town player-mgr Jun 1969, player to May 1974, mgr to May 1990/ Diss Town mgr May 1990

Bill Punton joined Portadown after being spotted playing in the Highland League. Scoring freely in his first season, several clubs were keen on signing him, Newcastle United being the successful one. He made his FL debut on 3 April 1954 at home to Manchester City but the likelihood of replacing Bobby Mitchell in the first team was remote and, after completing his National Service, he moved to Southend United where he made 38 FL appearances and scored six goals. He had played well against Norwich City and they soon signed him and he went on to make 219 FL appearances for the Canaries and won a League Cup winners' medal in the competition's second season.

He joined United in 1966 when Gil Reece's leg was broken. United allowed him to live and train in Norwich and travel to Sheffield before

matches. With good ball control and the ability to beat his man, he will be best remembered for his one FL goal fore the Blades, scored in front of the Kop, giving United a 1–0 victory in the Sheffield derby.

Initially he had the same arrangement with Scunthorpe United but in due course he returned to Norfolk after a FL career of 34 goals in 345 games. He became the manager of Yarmouth Town for 21 years followed by a stint as manager of Diss Town where he won the FA Vase Trophy at Wembley in 1994. He also could be heard as a pundit on local radio.

Appearances:		Apps	Gls
	FL	16	1
	FAC	3	2
	LC	1	0
	CC	1	0
	Total	21	3

PYE Reginald

RH 1917–18 5' 8" 10st 2
b. Woodhouse JAS 1898

Beighton
United: **Nov 1917 to cs1920**
Debut: **3 Nov 1917 Birmingham 4 United 1 (WW1)**
Last game: **12 Oct 1918 Birmingham 4 United 1 (WW1)**
Beighton/ Rotherham County May 1924/ Loughborough Corinthians cs1925/ Staveley Town Jun 1928/ Loughborough C cs1929?/ Dinnington Main Ath Nov 1929/ Hurst cs1931?

By a strange coincidence, Reg's debut and final appearance produced identical results at Birmingham. He appears as 'Bye' in the Independent on his debut and the same newspaper refers to him in 1924 as the former Brighton (rather than Beighton) player. When the First War was over, he played in the United reserve team but he did eventually make his FL debut, making one appearance at right back for Rotherham County at home to Lincoln City on 13 December 1924.

Appearances:		Apps	Gls
	WW1	7	0
	Total	7	0

QUINN Alan

MF 2004–07 5' 9" 10st 6
b. Dublin 13 June 1979

Lourdes Celtic/ Cherry Orchard/ Sheffield Wednesday Nov 1997/ Sunderland (L) Oct 2003
United: **1 Jul 2004 to 23 Jan 2008**
Debuts: **13 Jul 2004 Matlock Town 4 United XI 3 (Fr)**
10 Aug 2004 United 0 Stoke City 0 (sub)
20 Aug 2004 Preston North End 0 United 0
Last games: **27 Oct 2007 Hull City 1 United 1**
3 Nov 2007 United 0 Burnley 0 (sub)
Ipswich Town (£400k rising to £600k) Jan 2008

Alan Quinn joined Sheffield Wednesday after impressing whilst playing against an Owls youth side. He came for a trial and quickly signed, making his League debut as a substitute against Everton on 25 April 1998. He gained Eire U18 caps at the end of that season and made his full League debut at Wimbledon on 19 September 1998 and by December 1999 he had become a first team regular, winning U21 caps and later four full caps. Alan broke his leg playing against United in April 2001 but bounced back, being voted 'Player of the Year' in 2003. A downturn in form and two sendings-off in 2003–04 resulted in his being released (147(10) League app, 16 gl) and signed by Neil Warnock for United.

His energetic play and tackling and his willingness to run at defenders caused problems for the opposition and he was a regular in his first season at the Lane and prominent in 2005–06 and scored some vital goals. Alan achieved a unique record when he became the first player to score for both United and Wednesday in derby games and was capped four times with United. He played regularly in United's Premiership side and played alongside his younger brother Stephen for the first time in September 2006. Garry, another brother on United's books in 2005 had returned to Ireland but a fourth brother, Keith had joined United's Academy but the family connection was broken when Alan lost his first team place under Bryan Robson and was transferred to Ipswich.

Appearances:		Apps	Gls
	FL	76 (21)	11
	FAC	3 (1)	0
	LC	6 (2)	0
	Total	85 (24)	11

QUINN Stephen

MF 2005– 5' 6" 9st 8
b. Dublin 4 April 1986

United: from trainee, 6 Jun 2005
Debuts: 27 Jul 2005 Matlock Town 1 United XI 2 (sub Fr)
20 Sep 2005 Shrewsbury Town 0 United 0 (LC)
2 Dec 2006 United 2 Charlton Athletic 1
Milton Keynes Dons (L) 23 Sep to 23 Oct 2005, (L) 11 Nov 2005 to Jan 2006/ Rotherham United (L) 19/21 Jan to 22 Apr 2006

Stephen Quinn, brother of Alan and Keith, was a product of the United Academy. He made his debut at Matlock, replacing his brother at half time and scored a penalty in the shoot-out at the end of his League Cup debut. He was loaned out during the 2005–06 season, making his FL debut with MK Dons (13(2) app) on 24 September 2005 at Blackpool and had a further loan period with Rotherham (16 FL app).

Stephen and Alan first appeared together in a competitive fixture in September 2006 against Bury and Stephen made his Premiership debut in December 2006, almost scoring in the opening minutes, and immediately established himself as a regular in the side. He played with energy and was always looking to produce a creative pass. A good striker of the ball he scored with a superb free kick against Portsmouth and has played for Ireland at U18 and U21 levels. Seemingly out of favour for much of the time under Bryan Robson he seemed set for a regular place under Kevin Blackwell until an unnecessary sending off in added time against Charlton. He ended the season scoring two goals including a quality volley against Hull.

Appearances:		Apps	Gls
	FL	30 (4)	4
	FAC	4 (1)	0
	LC	4 (1)	0
	Total	38 (6)	4

QUINN Wayne Richard

LWB/MF 1993–2001, 2003 5' 10" 11st 10
b. Truro 19 November 1976

United: from apprentice cs 1993 to 21 Feb 2001
Debuts: 15 Nov 1993 Sutton Utd 3 United XI 2 (sub, BM)
17 Jul 1995 Boston United 2 United 2 (sub Fr)
18 Jul 1997 Sheffield FC 0 United 3 (Fr)
10 Aug 1997 United 2 Sunderland 0
Last games: 23 Dec 2000 Portsmouth 0 United 0
1 Jan 2001 Tranmere Rovers 1 United 0 (sub)
Newcastle U (L) 10 Jan 2001, (£750/800k) 21 Feb 2001
United: (L) 4 Jan 2003 to 5 Mar 2003
Debuts: 8 Jan 2003 United 2 Liverpool 1 (LC)
13 Jan 2003 Portsmouth 1 United 2
Last game: 22 Feb 2003 United 0 Norwich City 1
West Ham United (L) Sep 2003/ released May 2004 / – / Penzance/ Hoyle

Wayne Quinn played in occasional first team friendly fixtures but he was twenty years old before he made the break into the first team at the start of the 1997–98 season. For three an a half seasons, he missed very few games, gaining England caps at youth, U21 and B level. Playing mainly as a left wing back, but occasionally in midfield, he used his speed particularly when coming forward and could centre well. His defensive work improved under Neil Warnock and he played with calm authority, using the ball well and avoiding mistakes and looked to have a fine future in the game.

To the surprise of many, in January 2001, he moved to Premier League side Newcastle United but was unable to become a regular in the side and, in January 2003, he returned to the Lane on loan. United were involved in demanding League and Cup campaigns and Wayne replaced Jon Harley, whose loan spell had come to an end. Wayne's first game was a League Cup semi-final against Liverpool and a highlight of his return was his scoring the decisive penalty in the shoot-out against Coventry City, taking United to the FA Cup semi-final but, after ten games and lacking his old pace and enthusiasm, he returned to St James Park.

In 2003 he moved to West Ham United on an extended loan and had a run in the first team until displaced by John Harley. He returned to Newcastle but was released in the summer of 2004, moving into non-League football with Penzance. It does seem that Wayne had the potential to achieve far more in the professional game than was the case.

Appearances:		Apps	Gls
	FL	137 (8)	6
	PO	2	0
	FAC	14 (1)	0
	LC	16 (1)	0
	Total	169 (10)	6

RADFORD Bernard

IL 1929–31 5' 9½" 11st 4
b. West Melton, nr Rotherham 23 January 1908
d. Basingstoke 2 October 1986

Dearne Valley OB/ Wath Ath Feb 1925/ Wombwell Jun 1926 Darfield Aug 1927/ Nelson Dec 1927
United: **(£850) May 1929 to 13 Jul 1931**
Debut: **26 Oct 1929 United 4 Sunderland 2**
Last games: **25 Apr 1931 Middlesbrough 4 United 1**
28 Apr 1931 Grimsby Town 6 United 0 (CM, at Spalding)
Northampton Town (£350) Jul 1931/ Royal Navy Depot (Chatham) Oct 1932/ Banstead Mental Hospital Dec 1934

Bernard Radford made his FL debut with Nelson on 17 December 1927 and did really well scoring 41 goals in 55 FL appearances, playing frequently at centre forward.

At Bramall Lane, he found the gap between the Third and First Divisions difficult to bridge and looked 'fragile' and he was not a good team player. He made 15 appearances during his first season but he played little during the second though he did score on his final FL appearance. He moved to Northampton (8 FL app) but failed to make a significant impact.

Appearances:		Apps	Gls
	FL	20	7
	FAC	1	0
	CC	1	0
	Total	22	7

RAINE James Edmundson

OR 1905 5' 11" 12st 8
b. Newcastle March 1886
d. Davos, Switzerland 4 September 1928

Sheffield University/ Scotswood 1903/ Newcastle U (amat)
United: **amat, 2 Aug 1904 to 14 Jan 1906**
Debut: **4 Mar 1905 West Ham United 1 United 3 (Fr)**
Last game: **18 Mar 1905 Aston Villa 3 United 0**
Newcastle United (amat 1904–07), (FL) Jan 1906/ Sunderland Dec 1906/ Bohemians (Newcastle) Mar 1908/ Reading Mar 1908/ Glossop Sep 1908/ Percy Park (rugby)

A graduate of Sheffield University, James Raine was a top amateur player with ten caps. He scored on his United debut in a friendly fixture but made just one FL appearance before moving to Newcastle (4 FL app, 1 gl) and then to Sunderland (25, 6), where he represented the Football League against the Irish League, and Reading (1 SL app). His FL career ended with Glossop (52, 4). During 1905 he toured North America with the amateur Pilgrims touring team and in 1910 he toured with an England amateur side to South Africa.

During the First War he served with the Durham Light Infantry and achieved the rank of major. He was also the managing director of an iron and steel firm.

Appearances:		Apps	Gls
	FL	1	0
	Total	1	0

RAMSBOTTOM Neil

G 1979 6' 1" 13st 0
b. Blackburn 25 February 1946

Bury from jnr Sep 1964/ Blackpool (£13k + player exch) Feb 1971/ Crewe Alexander (L) Jan 1972/ Coventry City (£10k) Mar 1972/ Sheffield Wednesday (£12.75k) Aug 1975 Plymouth Argyle Jul 1976/ Blackburn Rovers Jan 1978 New Jersey Americans (USA)
United: **6 Oct 1979 to 31 Jul 1980**
Debut: **22 Oct 1979 Brentford 1 United 2**
Last games: **8 Dec 1979 Wimbledon 1 United 1**
15 Dec 1979 Grimsby Town 2 United 0 (FAC)

New Jersey Americans cs 1980/ Bradford City Aug 1980/ Bournemouth Aug 1983/ Chorley

Neil Ramsbottom made his FL debut with Bury on 15 January 1966 at home to Leyton Orient and made 174 FL appearances before moving on, playing for a variety of clubs including neighbours Wednesday.

Neil was signed by Harry Haslam for United, initially on a month contract but it was extended. Steve Conroy was first choice goalkeeper and Neil had the opportunity of a regular first team spot when Conroy broke his arm but, after the FA Cup defeat at Grimsby, he was replaced by Derek Richardson. All four of Neil's first team appearances were in away fixtures.

He moved on to Bradford City at the end of the season and later ended his FL career at Bournemouth having amassed 386 FL appearances

On retiring Neil qualified as a financial consultant and later was employed as quality controller for an insurance consultancy business.

Appearances:		Apps	Gls
	FL	2	0
	FAC	1	0
	ASC	0 (1)	0
	Total	3 (1)	0

RANKINE Simon Mark

MF 2003–04 5' 8" 12st 1
b. Doncaster 30 September 1969

Doncaster Rovers from YT Jul 1988/ Wolverhampton Wanderers (£70k) Jan 1992/ Preston North End (£100k) Sep 1996
United: **(L) 27 Mar 2003, 15 Jul 2003 (free) to 2 Jul 2004**
Debuts: **5 Apr 2003 Crystal Palace 2 United 2 (sub)**
7 Apr 2003 Wimbledon 1 United 0
Last games: **9 Apr 2004 Sunderland 3 Unit**
24 Apr 2004 Walsall 0 United 1 (sub)
Tranmere Rovers (free) Jul 2004

Mark Rankine made his FL debut with his home-town club Doncaster Rovers on 15 August 1987 at home to Grimsby Town whilst still 17 years old. He followed his 160(4) FL appearances for Rovers with 112(20) for Wolves and 217(16) for Preston.

A neat, hard working player, he was signed by Neil Warnock on loan towards the end of the arduous 2002–03 campaign and played in most of the final ten games in place of Stuart McCall but failed to shine against his old club in the Play-Off Final against Wolves. Signing permanently in the summer, he didn't play well and McCall again played the majority of the games. In the close season Mark moved on to Tranmere Rovers where he brought his total of League appearances to 561(52) before retiring in April 2006.

Appearances:

	Apps	Gls
FL	11 (8)	0
PO	3	0
FAC	0 (2)	0
LC	1	0
Total	15 (10)	0

RAWSON Albert Noble

CF 1919–22 5' 9" 11st.
b. West Melton/ Rotherham OND 1896
d. Sheffield 10 August 1949

Darnall Old Boys
United: Amateur 1918–19, pro May 1919 to 14/17 Feb 1923
Debut: 11 Oct 1919 Burnley 2 United 2
Last game: 14 Oct 1922 United 0 Chelsea 2
Birmingham £1500 Feb 1923/ Barnsley (£500) Sep 1924 to cs 1925/ Worksop T Aug 1925

Gassed and wounded during the First World War, Albert Rawson never had the stamina that was necessary to compete consistently at the top level of English football. He had several games with the reserves during the final year of war-time football before becoming a professional in 1919 but then faced competition for the centre forward spot from Harry Johnson. He had a good scoring ratio but, with few opportunities due to the form of Johnson and Bert Menlove, he was sold to Birmingham.

He played a similar number of games at his two other clubs, finishing with 22 FL goals in 52 appearances but his playing career came to a premature end after a severe injury with Worksop Town. A successful businessman in Sheffield and a Class 1 referee, his application in 1935 to the FA to become a football club director was successful but doesn't appear to have been put into practice.

Appearances:

	Apps	Gls
FL	18	7
FAC	1	0
CC	1	1
Total	20	8

RAWSON Colin

LH/IL/IR 1953–55 5' 8" 11st
b. Shirebrook 12 November 1926

Welbeck Colliery Welfare/ Nottingham Forest Sep 1944 Peterborough United Aug 1947/ Rotherham United Jul 1948
United: (£5,500) 16/17 Mar 1953 to 28/31 Oct 1955
Debuts: 9 May 1953 Altona 93 (West Germany) 2 United 2 (Fr)
22 Aug 1953 Portsmouth 3 United 4
Last games: 17 Sep 1955 Cardiff City 3 United 2
24 Oct 1955 United 4 Frank Swift's XI 1 (Fr)
Millwall (£4,500) Oct 1955/ Torquay United Jul 1959/ Taunton Town player/coach 1961–62

A miner towards the end of the war, Colin Rawson played for Forest in two wartime seasons before making his FL debut on 4 January 1947 at Newport County but with little chance of a place in the first team, he moved, via non-League Peterborough United, to Rotherham.

After 113 FL appearances and 12 goals for the Millers, he was signed for the Blades by his old manager, Reg Freeman, and was ever present in the 1953–54 First Division campaign when United fought a successful battle to escape relegation. A studied, careful player, he covered and tackled well and made good use of the ball but he lacked speed and the advent of new manager Joe Mercer and his introduction of the more powerful Jim Iley brought Colin's days at the Lane to an end.

He played 159 FL games for Millwall, captained Torquay and played over 400 FL games in his career. He later worked and played for the East Midlands Electricity Board and worked as a window cleaner.

Appearances:

	Apps	Gls
FL	70	1
FAC	2	0
CC	4	0
Total	76	1

RAYNOR George

OR 1931 5' 6" 10st 6
b. Hoyland 13 January 1907
d. Buxton 11 January 1985

Elsecar Bible Class/ Mexborough Athletic Wombwell Town cs 1929
United: 18 Apr 1930 to May 1932
Only game: 12 Oct 1931 Sheffield Wednesday 4 United 1 (CC)
Mansfield T (free) May 1932/ Rotherham United Jul 1933/ Bury Feb 1935/ Aldershot Jul 1938, asst trainer 1945/ AIK Sweden coach 1946/ Sweden National coach 1947/ Roma Italy coach 1951/ Lazio Italy coach 1953/ Coventry City coach Jun 1955, mgr Jan to Jun 1956, coach Jun 1956/ Lincolnshire Schools coach Aug 1956/ Sweden National coach Dec 1956/ Skegness Town mgr c1960/ Doncaster Rovers mgr May 1967to Dec 1968/ AIK Stockholm coach

George Raynor was a tricky and fast winger who made over 150 FL appearances for his four clubs after leaving the Lane. During the Second War he made guest appearances for Doncaster, Bournemouth, Hull and Crystal Palace as well as his then current club Aldershot and he served in the Middle East, organising football in Baghdad.

However, it was as a coach that he made his name. He coached at club level in Italy and Sweden as well as for a short time with Coventry City where he was briefly manager but he had great success as the National coach of Sweden. They won the Olympic gold medal in 1948, finished third in the World Cup in 1950 and were finalists in 1958, losing to Brazil. For his services to Swedish football he became a Knight of the order of Vasa.

George later managed Skegness during which time he worked as a stores manager at Butlin's Holiday Camp before returning to League football with Doncaster.

Appearances:

	Apps	Gls
CC	1	0
Total	1	0

READ C W (see REED Charles (Chick) William)

REAY Edwin (Ted) Peel

RB 1937 5' 9" 11st 7
b. Tynemouth 5 August 1914

Washington Colliery/ W'ton Chemical Works/ Ferryhill Newcastle U (amat) May 1935/ North Shields
United: 27 Dec 1936 ama, 12/13 Mar 1937 pro to 12 Nov 1937
Only game: 18 Oct 1937 Doncaster Rovers 5 United 1 (CC)
Queens Park Rangers (£300) 15 Nov 1937 to 1950

Ted Reay had no success with United but made his FL debut with Queens Park Rangers at Watford on 2 April 1938. Although he was with Rangers for six seasons either side of the Second War he was limited to 37 FL appearances, but he did win a Division 3(S) Championship medal in 1948.

During the war he toured Italy with an Army XI and was a guest player for Brentford, Chelsea, Fulham and Millwall.

Appearances:		Apps	Gls
	CC	1	0
	Total	1	0

REDFERN Levi

LH 1935 5' 9" 11st 10
b. Denaby 18 February 1905
d. Ferndown (Dorset) 18 September 1976

Conisbrough Discharged Soldiers/ Denaby U Doncaster R (trial)/ York City Oct 1926/ Huddersfield Town May 1927/ Bradford City Dec 1932/ Rochdale Jun 1934
United: 29/30 Aug 1935 to 20/29 Oct 1935
Debut: 28 Sep 1935 Norwich City 0 United 1
Last game: 12 Oct 1935 Blackpool 3 United 0

Levi Redfern made his FL debut with Huddersfield Town at home to Leicester City on 17 December 1927. Although with Town for five seasons (52 app) and described as a 'polished footballer', he was never a regular in the side and neither did he establish himself in Bradford City's first team. After a relatively successful season with Rochdale he joined United but his contract was cancelled by mutual consent and his career ended with 4 FL goals in 85 appearances.

A schoolmaster by profession, it was reported in 1937 that he was a 'sweepstake winner' and also a racing and betting man and racehorse owner.

Appearances:		Apps	Gls
	FL	2	0
	Total	2	0

REECE Gilbert (Gil) Ivor

OL/OR/CF 1965–72 5' 7" 9st 9
b. Cardiff 2 July 1942
d. Cardiff 20 December 2003

Cardiff City amat, pro May 1961/ Ton Pentre (L) Pembroke Borough 1962/ Newport County Jun 1963
United: (£10k) 17/22 Apr 1965 to 21 Sep 1972
Debuts: 3 May 1965 Doncaster Rovers 0 United 4 (CCF)
21 Aug 1965 United 1 Aston Villa 0
Last game: 2 Sep 1972 United 3 Southampton 1
Cardiff City (c£20k + players) Sep 1972/ Swansea City Jul 1976/ Athlone Town/ Barry Town Aug 1977

Gil Reece was a Welsh schoolboy international and a keen boxer but, having failed to make the grade with Cardiff City where he was a part-timer, he signed for Newport County. He made his FL debut on 21 October 1963 at home to Workington and after just 32 FL games, he signed for United.

Gil was one of John Harris' rare excursions into the transfer market but he was a shrewd buy and scored twice on his debut for United at Doncaster in the County Cup.

Fast, clever and tough, he was a good finisher, a fine header, a hard tackler with the will to succeed and he shrugged off injuries. Difficult to mark, he won the first of his 29 Welsh caps (16 with United) in 1965. Gil broke his leg and missed much of the 1966–67 season but he played an important role in United's promotion season of 1970–71 but lost his place to Stewart Scullion. Gil was stubborn and proud. Resenting being a substitute, he walked out of the Welsh squad in 1970 and he was suspended by United when he refused to travel to Workington for a FL Cup-tie.

In 1972, he joined Cardiff City with Dave Powell in an exchange deal with Alan Warboys moving to the Lane. Gil was made captain and took part in their 1975 relegation and the 1975–76 promotion campaigns but he was then given a free transfer and he became a part-timer with Swansea. He continued to live in Wales setting up a plumbing and central heating business and later becoming a hotelier running the Clare Court Hotel in Cardiff. In April 2000, he had to have part of a leg amputated and he died a few years later.

Appearances:		Apps	Gls
	FL	197 (14)	59
	FAC	7 (1)	1
	LC	11 (1)	2
	CC	7	4
	WC	2	1
	ABD	1	0
	Total	225 (16)	67

REED (READ) Charles (Chick) William

CF 1931 5' 8" 11st 0
b. Holbeach 21 March 1912
d. Spalding/ Holbeach 28 July 1964

Little London Vics/ Spalding Institute Spalding United cs 1929
United: (£50) 24/29 Oct 1930 to Aug 1932
Debuts: 28 Apr 1931 Grimsby Town 6 United 0 (CM, at Spalding)
19 Sep 1931 Birmingham 1 United 3
Last game: 17 Oct 1931 United 0 Huddersfield 2
Lincoln City (£125) Aug 1932/ Southport Mar 1935/ Chesterfield (£200) Feb 1936/ Spalding United May 1937/ Mansfield Town (L) Dec 1937/ Notts County (£250) May 1938/ Pinchbeck/ Crowland/ Spalding United 1946

Registered with the FL and known during his career as 'Read', his birth and death certificates confirm he was 'Reed'.

Tricky and enthusiastic but small for a centre forward, Chick Reed was at the Lane for nearly two seasons and, although scoring on his debut, was never likely to take over the first team centre forward position from Jimmy Dunne. He was a good third Division player however and despite his career being shortened due to the Second War, he went on to play 187 FL games, scoring over 50 goals. He gained a Division 3(N)

Championship medal with Chesterfield and later in his career he was converted to wing half.

During the War he served with the Royal Army Service Corps in North Africa and was mentioned in despatches for bravery. He returned to Notts County after the War and later played in non-League football before serving on the Spalding United Committee and playing in an occasional reserve match.

Appearances:		Apps	Gls
	FL	2	1
	Total	2	1

REED John Paul

MF 1990–96 5' 9" 10st 11
b. Rotherham 27 August 1972

United: from Jul 1988, YTS Jul 1990 to 21 Jul 1997
Debuts: 11 Aug 1990 Altrincham 1 United XI 1 (sub Fr)
6 Mar 1992 Kilmarnock 0 United 0 (Fr abd)
2 May 1992 Wimbledon 3 United 0 (sub)
10 Sep 1994 United 3 Bolton Wanderers 1
Last games: 18 Mar 1995 United 2 Charlton Athletic 1
4 May 1996 United 1 Port Vale 1 (sub)
27 Aug 1996 United 4 Sheffield Wednesday 1 (sub SCCT)
Scarborough (L) Jan 1991/ Darlington (L) Mar 1993/ Mansfield Town (L) Sep 1993, Chesterfield (trial) cs 1996
Blackpool Jul 1997 to cs 1998/ Bury nc Aug 1998/ Gainsborough Tr/Leek T/ Ethnikos Perez (Greece)/ Gainsborough Tr Sep 1999/ Matlock T/ Frickley Ath/ Ilkeston T Oct 2003

John Reed spent seven seasons as a professional at the Lane managed by Dave Bassett but lacked power and speed and was unable to establish himself as a regular member of the first team squad. He made his FL debut whilst on loan at Scarborough on 12 January 1991 away to Chesterfield and made more FL appearances whilst on loan from United (43 app, 10 gl) than for the Blades. His move to Blackpool was not successful and he made just 3 substitute appearances.

With good ball skills, his playing career was ruined by knee injuries. He later played for various non-League teams and also had a spell in Greece.

Appearances:		Apps	Gls
	FL	11 (4)	2
	LC	1	0
	AIC	1	1
	Total	13 (4)	3

REES Melvyn (Mel) John

G 1992 6' 2" 12st 12
b. Cardiff 25 January 1967
d. Derby 30 May 1993

Cardiff City (nc) Aug 1983, pro Sep 1984/ Watford (£63k) Jul 1987/ Crewe Alexandra (L) Aug 1989/ Southampton (L) Nov 1989/ Leyton Orient (L) Jan 1990/ West Bromwich Albion (£45k) Sep 1990/ Norwich City (L) Jan 1992
United: £25k, 26 Mar 1992 until his death
Debut: 28 Mar 1992 United 2 Liverpool 0
Last game: 26 Apr 1992 United 2 Leeds United 3
Chesterfield (L) Jan 1993

Few players have become so popular with the Bramall Lane crowd in such a short time as Mel Rees. The Wales youth international made his FL debut with his hometown club, Cardiff City, on 8 September 1984 at home to Brighton. Having moved to Watford he bided his time as Tony Coton's understudy but found himself superseded by a young David James but, because of his loan spells, he had played in all four Divisions of the FL before he was 21.

United were Mel's eighth League club, although he had not played at first team level for Southampton and Norwich. He made an excellent debut at home to Liverpool but what turned out to be his final game for United (and the last of his 75 FL appearances) came just a month later when Leeds United visited the Lane and their 3–2 win made them Champions. Mel was injured in that game but carried on and one of Leeds goals was a Brian Gayle lob which went over Mel's head. At the time, Mel had been included in the Welsh squad to play Austria but had to withdraw.

During the summer it was revealed that Mel had cancer. At one stage it seemed that he had recovered and he went on loan to Chesterfield and was a substitute for United at Villa Park in January 1993 although he did not play. He led out the United team at Wembley for the FA Cup semi final against Wednesday in 1993 but shortly afterwards he died.

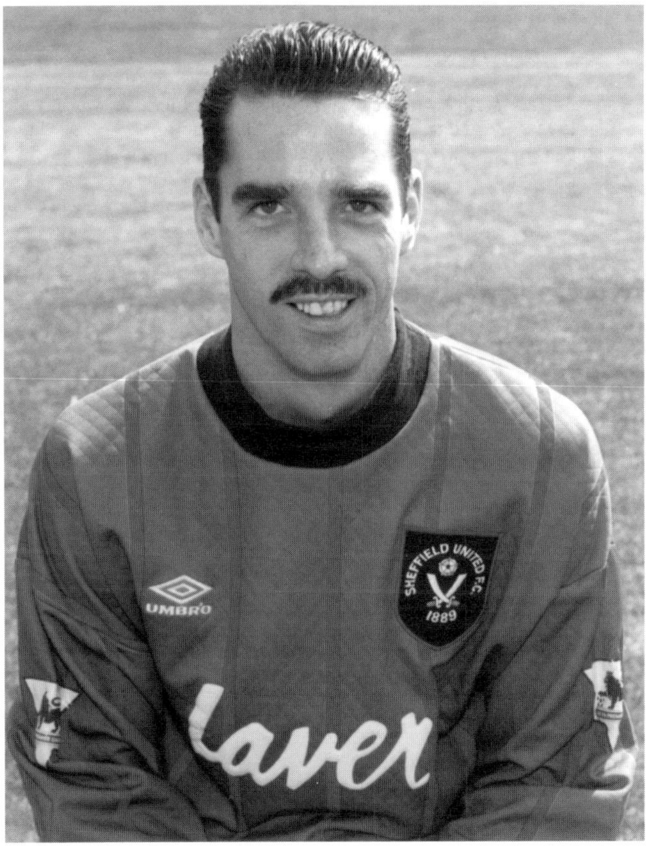

Appearances:		Apps	Gls
	FL	8	0
	Total	8	0

REGAN Robert (Bobby) Hunter

IR 1944
b. Falkirk

Linlithgow Rose/ Partick Thistle Jan 1933 Manchester City Aug 1936/ Dundee Jul 1937
WW2 guest: Chesterfield (1940–41)
United: 31 Aug 1944 to cs 1945
Only game: 2 Sep 1944 United 0 Sheffield Wednesday 1 (WW2)

Robert Regan made his Scottish League debut with Partick Thistle on 18 November 1933. He played for three seasons, becoming a regular member of the side in 1935–36 and moved to Manchester City where he made his FL debut on 3 October 1936 at Stoke City. He played just three more games before returning to Scotland where he played one season for Dundee.

He served and played locally with the RASC during the Second World War turning out as a guest for Chesterfield (1940–41, 13 app) and he appeared in an army representative team at Hillsborough in May 1941. In 1944, he was surprisingly signed by United and made this one first team appearance.

Appearances:		Apps	Gls
	WW2	1	0
	Total	1	0

REID Robert (Bobby)

OL 1939–46 5' 7½" 10st 11
b. Hamilton 19 February 1911
d November 1987

Ferniegar Violet/ Hamilton Academicals Dec 1932 Brentford (c£4,200) Jan 1936
United: (£5,500) 22/24 Feb 1939 to 1/2 Nov 1946
Debut: 25 Feb 1939 United 1 Manchester City 0
Last game: 14 Sep 1946 United 1 Grimsby Town 1
Hamilton Academicals (L) 9 Dec 1939 to cs 1941, Airdrie (L) Apr 1943
Bury (£1,050) Nov 1946/ Third Lanark 1947

Bobby Reid played for Hamilton Academicals, twice representing the Scottish League, before making his FL debut with Brentford on 18 January 1936 at home to Middlesbrough. He had played over 100 games for the London club and had gained two Scottish Caps when he moved to the Lane.

United were involved in a promotion battle early in 1939 but an injury to Jack Pickering and the knowledge that Jock Dodds wanted a transfer led manager Davison into the transfer market to strengthen the forward line and one of his targets was Bobby Reid. He was fast, two footed with a powerful shot and had excellent ball control; he also had the ability when running with the ball at top speed, to suddenly stop dead in his tracks leaving his opponent floundering. He played in the final 13 games of the season and his fast direct runs, fine centres and valuable goals helped to achieve promotion. The Second World War then intervened and United saw virtually nothing of Reid; his leg was broken in December 1939 but he did play once for United in 1942 and he was given permission to play for Airdrie in April 1943.

He returned to Sheffield for the FLN championship season of 1945–46 when he made 16 appearances (6 gl) but by the time League football resumed, he was 35 and played just one more game before moving to Bury. He finished with a total of 134 FL appearances (39 gls).

Bobby returned to Scotland at the end of the season, joining Third Lanark. He later had spells as the trainer of Aidriconians and Hamilton and subsequently as physiotherapist of Hamilton Academicals.

Appearances:		Apps	Gls
	FL	14	4
	CC	2	0
	WW2	17	6
	1939–40	3	0
	Total	36	10

RENWICK Craig

D 1978–80 5' 10" 11st 2
b. Lanark 22 September 1958

Darvel FC/ East Stirling
United: (£20k) 24 Apr 1978 to 6 Nov 1980
Debuts: 11 May 1978 United 2 Rotherham United 1 (CC)
9 Sep 1978 Fulham 2 United 0 (sub)
18 Nov 1978 United 0 Preston North End 1
Last game: 19 Apr 1980 Plymouth Argyle 4 United 1
East Stirling Nov 1980 to cs 1983?

One of Harry Haslam's least successful transfers, Craig Renwick moved to the Lane from East Stirling, where he made his Scottish League debut on 26 February 1977 at home to Forfar Athletic. He won a County Cup winners' medal in his first game with United and although playing a few games in various defensive positions during season 1978–79 he was clearly not good enough for the first team. He returned to East Stirling where he played regularly for nearly three seasons.

Appearances:		Apps	Gls
	FL	8 (1)	0
	CC	1	0
	Total	9 (1)	0

REVILL James (Jimmy) W

OL/OR 1910–16 5' 7" 9st 10
Sutton in Ashfield c1892
d. 9 April 1917

Sutton Junction/ Tibshelf
United: 22/29 Apr 1910 until his death in Apr 1917
Debut: 10 Sep 1910 Woolwich Arsenal 0 United 0
Last games: 16 Jan 1915 United 2 WBA 0
22 Jan 1916 Bradford Park Avenue 0 United 1 (WW1)
WW1 guest: Sutton T 1915–16/ New Hucknall Colliery 1915–16

Spotted by Ernest Needham, Jimmy Revill spent his five seasons of peacetime football at the Lane as second choice to outside left Bob Evans and so Jimmy rarely had a consistent run in the side. A fast and tricky winger, nicknamed 'old aeroplane legs' by the crowd, he also occasionally 'filled in' at outside right. He had a powerful shot but his crosses could be too strong and were not as measured as those of Evans.

He joined the army early in 1916 and served in France in the Royal Engineers but towards the end of the 1916–17 season, the news arrived that he had been severely wounded and had died in France though later, his death was reported as having occurred in an English hospital. In January 1918, a benefit match was held at the Lane in aid of his widow and child.

Appearances:		Apps	Gls
	FL	60	3
	FAC	8	1
	WW1	3	0
	Total	71	4

RHODES Philip

RH 1942–43
b. Sheffield 2 May 1922
d. 12 July 2002

Cambridge University
United: amat, 26/29 Dec 1942 to cs1945
Debut: 26 Dec 1942 Grimsby Town 3 United 3 (WW2 at Scunthorpe)
Last game: 9 Jan 1943 United 1 Chesterfield 2 (WW2)

An old boy of King Edward VII School (Sheffield) and a captain of Cambridge University FC, Philip Rhodes was a medical student at Clare College and made just two guest appearances for United during the Second World War. He played occasionally for Corinthian Casuals and subsequently became a Professor of Obstetrics and Gynaecology.

Appearances:		Apps	Gls
	WW2	2	0
	Total	2	0

RHODES Stanley (Stan)

IL 1951
b. Sheffield 19 April 1929

Leeds United May 1948/ Worksop Town
United: 17 Nov 1951 to 30 Jun 1952
Only game: 24 Nov 1951 United 2 Doncaster Rovers 1
Worksop Town cs 1952

A constructive type of player, he scored on his reserve team debut for United and was given an immediate first team opportunity but, although he had earlier been on the books of Leeds United, his FL appearance for United was the only one of his career.

Appearances:		Apps	Gls
	FL	1	0
	Total	1	0

RIBEIRO Bruno Miguel Fernandes

MF 1999–2000 5' 8" 12st 2
b. Setubal (Portugal) 22 October 1975

Vitoria Setubal/ Leeds United (£500k) Jul 1997
United: (£500k) 22 Oct 1999 to Mar 2001?
Debut: 23 Oct 1999 Swindon Town 2 United 2
Last games: 28 Oct 2000 Wimbledon 0 United 0
1 Nov 2000 Sheffield Wednesday 2 United 1 (LC)
11 Nov 2000 Burnley 2 United 0 (sub)
(L) Uniao Leiria (Portugal) Nov 2000
SC Beira Mar 2001/ Santa Clara 2002/ Setubal 2004

Signed by George Graham, Bruno Ribeiro, a Portuguese U21 creative midfield player, made his League debut with Leeds United on 9 August 1997 at home to Arsenal. He was a regular in the side during his first season but, injured at the start of the following season, he was unable to re-establish himself and, having made 35(7) League appearances, moved to the Lane, brought in by Adrian Heath shortly before he resigned.

Playing in midfield he showed some nice touches but too often was not as fully involved as was needed and Neil Warnock thought that he was not suitable for English relegation battles and was never fully fit. Bruno shocked his manager by forgoing £12k in wages rather than travelling to Trinidad and Tobago in a close season tour and, often on the bench, he returned to Portugal.

Appearances:		Apps	Gls
	FL	12 (13)	1
	FAC	1 (1)	0
	LC	3	0
	Total	16 (14)	1

RICHARDSON Brian

RH 1955–65 5' 9½" 11st 10
b. Sheffield 5 October 1934

United: 17/24 Dec 1954 to 7/8 Jan 1966
Debuts: 30 May 1955 Union Krefeld (W Germany) 4 United 1 (Fr)
27 Dec 1955 Luton Town 2 United 1
Last games: 24 Apr 1965 United 0 Leeds United 3
2 Jun 1965 Blackpool 2 United 1 (Fr at Invercargill, NZ)
Swindon Town (£3,000) Jan 1966/ Rochdale Jul 1966

Brian Richardson spent three seasons as an amateur playing for the United nursery club Oaks Fold but it was not until Jack Smith, United's former goalkeeper, spotted him playing for the local S&HFA Youth team that he was offered the chance of turning professional and he was nearly twenty three years old before he became a regular first team player. He was not a stylish player but hard work and determination made him a successful First Division player.

It was written of him when he was fifteen that he was 'a good strong tackler, making up for his lack of constructive ability by determination and tirelessness'. This summed up Brian's time at Bramall Lane. He played most of his games at right half, although he played at centre half in his early days in the first team, where his primary role was defensive, rarely being seen in the oppositions penalty area. Good in the air, his strengths were close marking, razor-sharp tackling and covering and the ability to steer opponents into less dangerous areas.

It was Joe Mercer in September 1957 who gave Brian his opportunity and he owed much of his success to Mercer's coaching. Brian took over the right half position from Tommy Hoyland and he formed part of the famous defence which played so many games together between September 1957 and August 1963 and which took United to the 1961 FA Cup semi finals and promotion to the top flight. A colleague summed up Brian: 'He was all heart and guts and strength … and greatly under-rated by his opponents'.

Between September 1957 and May 1965, when he lost his place to David Munks, he missed few games. He was ever present in 1961–62 and 1962–63 and made 118 consecutive FL appearances. He moved to Swindon Town and later Rochdale where he brought his career total of FL appearances to 321. He scored just 10 goals.

Appearances:		Apps	Gls
	FL	291	9
	FAC	28	0
	LC	10	0
	CC	7	0
	Total	336	9

RICHARDSON Derek

G 1979–81 6' 1" 14st 0
b. Hackney 13 July 1956

Chelsea from app Feb 1974/ Queens Park Rangers Apr 1976
United: (£50k) 18/19 Dec 1979 to 15 Mar 1982
Debut: 21 Dec 1979 United 2 Southend United 0
Last games: 14 Feb 1981 Swindon Town 5 United 2
18 Aug 1981 Grimsby Town 2 United 0 (GC)
Coventry City Mar 1982/ Maidstone United 1982/ Welling c1987

Derek Richardson, who was capped at youth level for England, joined four FL clubs but played only for two. He made his debut with Queens Park Rangers on 8 March 1977 at home to Leeds United but spent much of his time as an understudy to Phil Parkes. He played in the final 18 games of the 1978–79 season when Rangers were relegated but lost his place when Rangers signed Chris Woods from Nottingham Forest.

He was signed by Harry Haslam, following Steven Conroy's injury and Neil Ramsbottom being found unsatisfactory. Sadly for the new man, he was far from impressive, making a poor start in the derby match at Hillsborough and was replaced by the on-loan Terry Poole towards the end of the season completing a poor year in United's history as far as goalkeepers are concerned. He returned to the side at the start of the following season but Conroy took his place as soon as he was fit.

Derek played only a few more games before moving to Coventry where he did not make the first team. Having totalled 73 FL appearances he moved into non-League football, winning two semi-professional England caps in 1984–85 with Maidstone.

Appearances:		Apps	Gls
	FL	42	0
	FAC	3	0
	LC	2	0
	ASC	3	0
	AMC	2	0
	CC	3	0
	Total	55	0

RICHARDSON George

IR/IL 1936–38 5' 10" 11st 4
b. Worksop 12 December 1912
d. Worksop 24 March 1968

Manton Colliery/ Worksop Town Huddersfield Town Apr 1933
United: 7/9 May 1934 to 24/25 Nov 1938
Debuts: 25 Jan 1936 Preston North End 0 United 0 (FAC)
1 Feb 1936 United 3 Norwich City 2
Last game: 1 Oct 1938 United 0 Plymouth Argyle 1
Hull City (£500) Nov 1938 to Jun 1948
WW2 guest: Barnsley (1 app), Ransome & Marles to Aug 1947, Firbeck Colliery (1944–45)
Bangor City player-mgr Jun 1948/ Worksop T mgr cs 1961

George Richardson's FL debut came in his only appearance for Huddersfield Town on 24 February 1934 at Leicester City.

Signed by Teddy Davison, he joined United with Jock Dodds in May 1934 but was unlucky to break his leg in September after playing a few reserve team games and it was 18 months before he made a first team appearance. Very clever, he promised more than he achieved for he was neither strong nor fast enough and it was only in season 1937–38, after United had sold Bobby Barclay, that he played a significant number of games (25 FL appearances), helping the Blades to finish third in the Second Division.

In November of the following season, he moved to Hull where he scored 15 goals in 36 FL games before the Second War brought an end to League football. Hull could only afford to pay half the fee and the final £250 was possibly never paid. He made 20 FL appearances for the Tigers before the advent of the 1939–46 war and a further 16 in the 1947–48 season before being released in 1948 to become player-manager of Bangor City. He spent most of the war as a guest player with Ransome & Marles, the strong works team who played in the Midland League and was allowed to play for them in the first post-war season, only returning to Hull in the summer of 1947.

Appearances:		Apps	Gls
	FL	32	9
	FAC	5	0
	Total	37	9

RICHARDSON George William Richard

LH/RH 1921–23 5' 10" 10st 10
b. Gainsborough JFM 1899
d. Boston 13 November 1963

Gainsborough Wednesday/ Lincoln City Feb 1920
United: (£1,225) Nov, 8 Dec 1921 to Jun 1924
Debut: 10 Dec 1921 United 1 Tottenham Hotspur 0
Last game: 31 Mar 1923 West Bromwich Albion 4 United 0
Bournemouth & Boscombe Ath (£200) Jun 1924/ Boston Jun 1925 to c1929

George Richardson joined Lincoln City whilst they were in the Midland League, having failed to gain re-election to the Football League in 1920. George was instrumental in City being Midland League champions and they were re-elected to the Football League, George making his FL debut on 27 August 1921 at home to Walsall.

After just 12 FL games, the auburn haired, tough tackling half back moved to the Lane but he wasn't good enough for the First Division and, eighteen months later, he moved to Bournemouth where he made ten first team appearances and then he returned to non-League football with Boston where he later kept a pub.

Appearances:		Apps	Gls
	FL	13	0
	CC	1	0
	Total	14	0

RICHARSDSON J W (Pussy)

OR 1895 5' 8"

South Bank 1889/ Middlesbrough 1894–95
United: 2 Aug 1895 to 1896
Only game: 30 Sep 1895 United 2 Preston North End 1
South Bank 1896

JW Richardson had played against United for South Bank in the NL and would be well known by player/trainer George Waller but, despite scoring on his United debut, this proved to be his only first team game for the club and the only FL appearance of his career.

Appearances:		Apps	Gls
	FL	1	1
	Total	1	1

RICHARDSON Paul

MF 1981–83 5' 11" 12st 0
b. Shirebrook 25 October 1949

Nottingham Forest from app Aug 1967 Chester (£13k) Oct 1976/ Stoke City (£50k), Jun 1977
United: (£20k), 20 Aug 1981 to 20 Jul 1983
Debut: 26 Sep 1981 United 1 Scunthorpe United 0
Last game: 14 May 1983 Orient 4 United 1
Blackpool (L) Jan 1983
Swindon Town (£10k) Jul 1983/ Swansea City (nc) Sep 1984/ Gloucester C manager/ Fairford T manager 1988

A youth international who never quite fulfilled his early promise, Paul Richardson made his FL debut with Forest as a sub at Sunderland on 4 November 1967, his full debut coming at Chelsea on 14 August. An attacking midfield player, he had a regular first team place by 1969. Forest were relegated in 1972 and he played in a more central role and had a spell at full back under Brian Clough. He was in the Stoke promotion team of 1979 and had a career record of 378 FL appearances when he was signed by Ian Porterfield.

Paul was 31 and still tackled hard and didn't waste the ball and he had a useful part to play in securing the Fourth Division championship but his lack of pace was more obvious in the Third Division and, after a loan spell, he was sold. He ended his FL career with 409(27) appearances.

Appearances:		Apps	Gls
	FL	35 (1)	2
	FAC	4	0
	LC	4	1
	CC	1	0
	Total	44 (1)	3

RICHARDSON Tom ('Needham')

RB/LB 1913–16 5' 9½" 12st
b. Worksop JAS 1891

Worksop Town c1908/ Retford Town cs 1910
United: 28 Apr 1911 to cs 1916
Debut: 15 Feb 1913 United 1 West Bromwich Albion 0
Last games: 4 Apr 1914 United 5 Burnley 0
29 Apr 1916 United 0 Grimsby Town 0 (WW1)
6 May 1916 United 3 Wednesday 0 (CM)
Worksop Town 1919/ Worksop West End (amat)1929–30

Tom Richardson made just two first team appearances during his three peace-time seasons with United and also played occasionally during the First World War season of 1915–16. An assured and intelligent full back, he had enlisted in the army after working at Manton Colliery and returned to play for Worksop in April 1919 and captained them from 1920 to at least 1925–26.

The 'Green'Un' in October 1914 reported that he rejoices in the very appropriate name of 'Needham'.

Appearances:		Apps	Gls
	FL	2	0
	WW1	5	0
	Total	7	0

RICKETT Walter

OR/OL/CF 1939–47 5' 6" 10 to 11st (1947)
b. Sheffield 20 March 1917
d. Kettering 25 July 1991

Kiveton Park Wire Works/ Aqueduct (Sheffield)
United: Apr (trial) and 10/11 May 1939 to 2/3 Jan 1948
Debuts: 29 Apr 1939 Rotherham U 2 United XI 1 (BM, scored)
13 Jan 1940 Rochdale 2 United 0 (Fr)
9 Mar 1940 Chesterfield 5 United 0 (WW2)
5 Jan 1946 Huddersfield T 1 United 1 (FAC)
31 Aug 1946 United 0 Liverpool 1
Last game: 22 Nov 1947 United 3 Chelsea 1
WW2 guest: Huddersfield T (1 app, 1942–43), Chesterfield (1 app, Dec 1943), Mansfield Town (4 app, 1944–45)
Blackpool (player exch) Jan 1948/ Sheffield Wednesday (£6,000) Oct 1949/ Rotherham United (£2,450) Sep 1952/ Halifax Town Aug 1953/ Ballymena United player-mgr, Aug 1954/ Dundalk/ Ards player-mgr/ Sittingbourne mgr 1956–Feb 1959/ Ramsgate mgr Mar 1959 to Mar 1963/ Gravesend mgr Jun 1963/ coach, asst mgr Leyton Orient 1966

Walter Rickett came to United as a centre forward but was used for most of his time at the Lane as a winger, usually at outside left. Because he had a reserved occupation he was able to play for United during the Second World War. He made his debut on the same day as Harry Latham and only Harry played more games during that time.

He was a lively character, irrepressible, two-footed and dangerous when cutting in and he was a regular goal scorer. He did have his limitations, being an instinctive player. Schemes worked out in training were forgotten and 'he needed the ball in front of him' and 'he was no

good if he had time to think'. As hard as nails, fearless and rarely injured—'must have broken his leg' was the only comment from the trainer when it was pointed out to him that Walter was limping—and the little winger was also the United player who would take it upon himself to 'sort out' an opponent when he felt it was necessary.

His two best seasons at the Lane were 1945–46, when United won the FLN Championship and the first post-war season when his goal in the final game robbed Stoke City of the Championship.

He moved to Blackpool in an unexplained and what turned out to be a disastrous, from United's point of view, exchange for George Farrow. Walter, on the other hand, came well out of the move and played well for Blackpool against Manchester United in the 1948 FA Cup final defeat. He returned to Sheffield where he assisted Wednesday in two promotion campaigns—and a relegation—and also won an England B cap. He later spent time playing and managing in Ireland before returning to England, where he moved into non-League football as a manager and his career in football ended in 1966 with a six week stint as assistant manager at Leyton Orient. He returned to Kent working for a cable manufacturing firm before moving to Corby. He died in Kettering hospital.

Appearances:		Apps	Gls
	FL	57	16
	FAC	9	0
	CC	11	3
	WW2	199	55
	Total	276	74

RIDGE Roy

LB/RB 1953–62 5' 7" 11st 10 to 12st
b. Ecclesfield/ Sheffield 21 October 1934

Ecclesfield Boys Club/ Oaks Fold 1949
United: 21/23 Nov 1951 to 10 Aug 1964
Debut: 5 Dec 1953 Manchester United 2 United 2
Last games: 21 Jan 1961 United 4 Stoke City 1
5 Nov 1962 Heart of Midlothian 2 United 2 (BM)
Rochdale (£1,000) Aug 1964/ Worksop T cs1966

Roy Ridge became famous for being an almost permanent reserve. Quick and a good tackler, he spent 13 years as a professional with United and yet made only 15 first team appearances and nine of his eleven FL appearances were in his debut season. A part-time professional, working as a turner for the English Steel Corporation until 1955, the consistent excellence of Cec Coldwell and Graham Shaw and Cliff Mason when they were absent, made first team opportunities for Roy very rare and he made no FL or FAC appearances whatsoever between November 1954 and January 1961.

He was then transferred to Rochdale and in his two seasons there, he made 85 FL appearances.

Appearances:		Apps	Gls
	FL	11	0
	FAC	2	0
	CC	2	0
	Total	15	0

RINGSTEAD Alfred (Alf)

OR/IR 1950–59 5' 7" 10st 7
b. Dublin 14 October 1927
d. Sheffield 15 January 2000

Everton jnr/ Ellesmere Port/ Northwich Victoria (£200) 1950
United: (£2,500) 17/20 Nov 1950 to 1 Jul 1959
Debut: 2 Dec 1950 United 2 Coventry City 0
Last game: 27 Apr 1959 United 1 Cardiff City 1
Mansfield T (£2,850) Jul 1959/ Frickley Colliery Aug 1960/ Buxton/ Macclesfield Town

Alf Ringstead, the son of a well known jockey, was born in Dublin but lived in Ellesmere Port from the age of two. He joined Everton at the age of fourteen but did not feel part of the club and rejected a trial with Bolton Wanderers feeling that he would be happier playing local football with Ellesmere Port. He became an upholsterer and coach fitter before serving with the Army in India. In 1950 he joined Northwich Victoria and after a handful of games during which he scored eleven goals, he joined United a few days after he had been watched in a game at Buxton.

Signed by Teddy Davison, it was immediately obvious that he had a great future in the game and after two games with the reserves, he made his first team debut. He scored in his first three games and won the first of his 20 Republic of Ireland caps at the end of the season. His first team debut was the first FL game he had ever seen.

Playing at outside right, he scored 100 goals in his first 208 games and proved to be one of the most dangerous wingers of his time. He was fast and direct, able to shoot with power and accuracy with both feet (although he failed with three of his penalties) and he was a fine header of the ball, scoring a notable hat-trick of headers against Scunthorpe in October 1958. Added to those attributes was his superb sense of anticipation and his ability to lose his marker.

Injuries and loss of speed coupled with the fact that he was unhappy playing under Joe Mercer led to him losing his place to Kevin Lewis. He was transferred to Mansfield Town (3 gl in 27 FL app) and subsequently returned to non-League football.

Appearances:		Apps	Gls
	FL	247	101
	FAC	13	4
	CC	11	4
	Total	271	109

RIOCH Bruce David

MF 1979 5' 11" 12st 5
b. Aldershot 6 September 1947

Luton Town from app Sep 1964/ Aston Villa (£100k) Jul 1969 Derby County (£200k) Feb 1974/ Everton (£180k) Dec 1976 Derby County (£150k) Nov 1977/ Birmingham City (L) Dec 1978
United: (L) 29 Mar to 26 Apr 1979
Debut: 31 Mar 1979 United 1 Bristol Rovers 0
Last game: 25 Apr 1979 Sunderland 6 United 2
Seattle Sounders (USA) (L) Mar to Sep 1980/ Torquay United player-coach Oct 1980 (Seattle Sounders Mar to Jun 1981)/ Torquay United mgr Jul 1982 to Jan 1984/ Seattle Sounders coach Jul 1985/ Middlesbrough asst mgr Jan 1986, mgr Feb 1986 to Mar 1990/ Millwall mgr Apr 1990 to Mar 1992/ Bolton Wanderers mgr May 1992/ Arsenal mgr Jun 1995 to Aug 1996/ Queens Park Rangers asst mgr Sep 1996 to Nov 1997/ Norwich City mgr Jul 1998 to Mar 2000/ Wigan Athletic mgr Jun 2000 to Feb 2001 / – / Odense BK (Denmark) Jun 2005 to Mar 2007

Bruce Rioch made his FL debut with Luton Town on 28 November 1964 at home to Southend United. A commanding, skilful, midfield player with a powerful shot, he made over 100 FL appearances for each of his first three clubs and 548(14) in total, scoring 129 goals. He was the first English born player to captain Scotland and was awarded 24 Scottish caps whilst with Derby and Everton and captained his country to the 1978 World Cup.

Harry Haslam brought him to the Lane as United struggled in Division Two and he played with calm authority before returning to Derby. It was later reported that he had not been asked if he was willing to extend the loan period and, despite his efforts, the Blades were relegated. Bruce then spent some time playing in the USA before moving into management. He was particularly successful with Middlesbrough being in charge as they moved from Division 3 to Division 1. In his short time at Arsenal he was responsible for bringing Dennis Bergkamp to Highbury.

Appearances:		Apps	Gls
	FL	8	1
	Total	8	1

RITCHIE Duncan

OR/OL 1912–13 5' 8½" 11st 7
b. Renton 1886

Renton Jul 1905/ Hibernian/ Dumbarton? Raith Rovers cs 1911
United: (£375) 8/19 Apr 1912 to Jul 1913
Debut: 14 Sep 1912 Chelsea 4 United 2
Last game: 22 Feb 1913 Tottenham Hotspur 1 United 0
Derby County (£300) Jul 1913/ Renton May 1914

United were refused permission to play Duncan Ritchie in the final two FL games of the 1911–12 season as the opponents were involved in relegation problems but he played 11 successive games (including a friendly) soon after the start of the 1912–13 season. A 'native of Renton', Duncan was sturdy with good ball control. He came with a big reputation and had played in a Scottish international trial but he lacked determination. He made three more appearances at outside left later in the season and then was put on the transfer list. The fee was cut and he moved to Derby County where he made two further FL appearances.

Appearances:		Apps	Gls
	FL	13	1
	Total	13	1

ROBERTS Alan

OR 1988–89 5' 9" 10st 4
b. Newcastle 8 December 1964

Middlesbrough app Apr 1981, pro Dec 1982 Darlington Sep 1985
United: (£15k) 7 Jul 1988 to c14 Oct 1989
Debuts: 26 Jul 1988 Skegness Town 1 United 8 (Fr)
13 Aug 1988 Bradford City 0 United 1 (YHC)
27 Aug 1988 Reading 1 United 3
Last games: 26 Sep 1989 United 2 Oldham Athletic 1
30 Sep 1989 Sunderland 1 United 1 (sub)
Lincoln City (£63.5k) Oct 1989

Alan Roberts began his career with Middlesbrough, making his FL debut as a substitute on 30 October 1982 at Rotherham. His next appearance and full debut was at Portsmouth on 27 August 1983 and later that season, he scored after 15 seconds against Manchester City. After 38 FL appearances (2 gls) for the Boro but never sure of a first team place, he moved to Darlington where he made 119 FL appearances, scoring 19 goals.

He was brought to the Lane by Dave Bassett following United's relegation and he played a key role in the subsequent promotion. Slight but tricky and tenacious, he was a good crosser of the ball and much of the time he played as an outside right, although he was regularly substituted towards the end of a game. He was first choice at the start of the following season but he was replaced by Carl Bradshaw who was more powerful and aggressive. Alan later made it known that he did not like Dave Bassett's 'style of football'.

He moved to Lincoln for what was, at the time, a club record fee but was injured in an FA Cup tie and, although he returned to first team action, his knee gave way again and he had to retire in November 1990, having scored 23 goals in 185(18) FL appearances. United were Lincoln's opponents in a benefit match for him in April 1991.

Appearances:		Apps	Gls
	FL	31 (5)	2
	FAC	4	0
	LC	7	0
	AMC	2 (1)	0
	YHC	2	0
	Total	46 (6)	2

ROBERTSON W

CF/IR/IL/other 1889–91
b. Scotland

Boys of Dundee/ Dundee Strathmore
United: cs 1889 to cs 1891
Debuts: 7 Sep 1889 Notts Rangers 4 United 1 (Fr)
5 Oct 1889 Scarborough 1 United 6 (FAC)
13 Sep 1890 Burton Wanderers 1 United 1 (MCL)
Last games: 6 Dec 1890 United 6 Loughborough 1 (FAC)
13 Apr 1891 Burslem PV 3 United 1 (MCL)

It is frustrating and a great pity that so little is known about W Robertson for he will always hold so many United records. He was the first player to score for the club (7 Sep 1889 in the first fixture against Nottingham Rangers); the first to record a hat-trick (19 October 1889); the first to be an ever present through a season (1889–90) and the first to be sent off (22 Mar 1890).

It was reported that he 'hails from Dundee' and was one of several players United recruited from Scotland for the club's first season. He then proceeded to play in all United's 57 first team games during that season, 42 of them being friendlies. He played in all the forward positions but mainly at centre forward or inside right, scoring 19 goals. He went on to play in the first 27 games of the following season, thus playing in United's first 84 first team games.

As the 1890–91 season progressed, he steadily played fewer games and at the end, he left and the contemporary local newspapers never reported why or whether he would play for another team! At some time however, he certainly went to Canada as there was a report in September 1908 that he was coaching in Haileybury, a remote part of Ontario.

Appearances:		Apps	Gls
	FAC	11	4
	MCL	16	3
	SCC	9	5
	WCC	2	0
	Total	38	12

ROBINS Arthur

OR 1909–10, 1916 5' 5" 10st
b. Northampton c1888
d. Pontefract 12 March 1924

Raunds St Peters (Rushden)/ Gainsborough Tr (trial)
United: 5 Feb (amat), 11 Feb (pro) 1908 to cs 1910
Debuts: 6 Mar 1909 Woolwich Arsenal 0 United 0 (Abd)
20 Mar 1909 Newcastle United 4 United 0
Last game: 2 Apr 1910 Bury 2 United 0
Castleford Town cs 1910, player-mgr from 1911–12 to cs 1915
WW1 guest: Goole T 1915/United 1915–16/ Luton T
United: WW1 guest
Debuts: 29 Jan 1916 United 4 Leeds U 1 (WW1)
4 Mar 1916 Hull City 5 United 2 (WW1)
Castleford T Player-mgr 1919–20, Manager to 1924

Arthur Robins had two FL debuts as his first game was abandoned. A very quick winger, he played intermittently for United for two seasons and made three appearances as a guest player (and for the reserve team on Xmas Day) from December 1915 to March 1916.

Appearances:		Apps	Gls
	FL	7	0
	WW1	3	0
	ABD	1	0
	Total	11	0

ROBINSON Albert (Arthur in some records)

G 1924 5' 11" 12st
b. Sheffield c1901

Hillsborough Ex Servicemen/ Shirebrook Nov 1921 Rotherham County Jul 1922
United: 23/25 Aug 1924 to cs 1925
Debuts: 18 Sep 1924 United 2 Wednesday 2 (BM)
20 Sep 1924 Arsenal 2 United 0
Last game: 27 Sep 1924 United 0 Manchester City 5
Worksop T Aug 1925/ Bilsthorpe Colliery Sep 1929/ Ilkeston 1932–33/ Alfreton Welf/ Heanor T/ Ranleigh Ath/ Ilkeston/ S Normanton W

Although he was with Rotherham County for two seasons, Albert Robinson made no FL appearances because of the consistency of Charles Sutcliffe.

United faced a goalkeeping crisis in August 1924: Harold Gough had broken his contract and Ernest Blackwell had been recommended to retire with abdominal problems. Robinson was taken on trial and his first appearance was in the public Practice Match (23 Aug) when he saved a Fred Tunstall penalty kick. He was signed after the game but, sadly, one swallow doesn't make a summer and in is his four first team appearances, including a benefit match, he conceded ten goals. In his final FL game, when he was slow to move, he was blamed by the press for three of the five goals.

Appearances:		Apps	Gls
	FL	3	0
	Total	3	0

ROBINSON Carl Philip

MF 2004 5' 10" 12st 10
b. Llandrindod Wells 13 October 1976

Wolverhampton Wanderers from trainee Jul 1995 Shrewsbury Town (L) Mar 1996/ Portsmouth (free) Jul 2002 Sheffield Wednesday (L) Jan 2003/ Walsall (L) Feb 2003 Rotherham United (L) Sep 2003/
United: (L) 30 Jan 2004 to Mar 2004
Debut: 31 Jan 2004 Norwich City 1 United 0
Last game: 2 Mar 2004 United 2 Millwall 1
Sunderland (L) Mar 2004, (free) Jun 2004/ Norwich City (L) Nov 2005, (£50k) Jan 2006/ Toronto Lynx (free) Jan 2007

Carl Robinson, a Welsh youth international, made his FL debut, as a substitute, whilst on loan to Shrewsbury Town, on 30 March at home to Hull City, his full debut coming 3 days later at York. He returned to Wolves and went on to make 165 appearances in his seven seasons at Molineux. He was less successful at Portsmouth, spending much of his time on loan including spells at both Hillsborough and later at the Lane. During his month with United he played in midfield showing some neat touches.

He went on to play a big part in Sunderland's promotion to the Premiership in 2005 and after a spell with Norwich he moved abroad to Toronto Lynx. During his career, of 267(52) League games, he won Welsh U21 and 39 full caps, some with each of his four permanent clubs.

Appearances:		Apps	Gls
	FL	4 (1)	0
	Total	4 (1)	0

ROBINSON Ernest (Ernie) George

RB 1933 5' 9½" 11st 8
b. Shiney Row 21 January 1908
d. Vancouver (Canada) 1991

Shildon Jun 1926/ Houghton Colliery?/ York City (amat) Aug 1927, pro Aug 1928/ Notts C May 1929 Shiney Row Swifts/ Nelson Jun 1930/ Northampton Town (trial) Mar 1931/ Tunbridge Wells Rangers Jul 1931 Barnsley Jul 1932
United: (£500+ £250) 4/5 May 1933 to 5 May 1934
Debut: 4 Sep 1933 United 2 Leicester City 1
Last game: 23 Dec 1933 United 1 Arsenal 3
Carlisle United (£175) Aug 1934/ Lincoln City Aug 1935 to cs 1939

Ernest Robinson, a former miner, made his FL debut with Nelson on 30 August 1930 and had made 50 FL appearances when he was signed by Teddy Davison. Robust and quite fast, he spent one season at the Lane, playing all his games in succession just after the start of the campaign. He tackled hard and gave of his best but he struggled in the First Dividion and was dropped. The season ended in relegation and he was transferred to Carlisle at a reduced fee.

He was released by Lincoln just before the start of the Second War having totalled 169 FL appearances. After the War, he worked as a trainer in Holland and, in 1985 emigrated to Canada where he died a few years later though some reports mention his death in Sheffield in 1990 or 1991.

Appearances:		Apps	Gls
	FL	17	0
	CC	1	0
	Total	18	0

ROBINSON John

OR/IL 1938–39 5' 8" 10st 12
b. Leeds AMJ 1914 or 1 April 1913
d. Leeds June 1989?

Huddersfield Town (amat)
United: 4/14 May 1936 to 6 May 1939
Debut: 9 Apr 1938 United 0 Aston Villa 0
Last games: 4 Feb 1939 Plymouth Argyle 0 United 1
29 Apr 1939 Rotherham U 2 United XI 1 (BM)
Hull City May 1939 to cs 1946

John Robinson was reported to be 21 when he joined United. He had few first team opportunities but both games in which he played in the 1938–39 promotion season were won. Released in May 1939, he moved to Hull City. He played 50 games for the Tigers during the Second War, although they did not compete in every season. He was released in the summer of 1946 before League football began again so his three FL appearances with United were the only ones of his career.

Appearances:		Apps	Gls
	FL	3	0
	CC	1	0
	Total	4	0

ROGERS Kristian Raleigh John

G 2003 6' 3" 12st 6
b. Chester 2 October 1980

Chester City jnr/ Wrexham Aug 1998
United: (free) 11 Jul 2003 to Jun 2004
Debuts: 15 Jul 2003 Frechville CA 0 United XI 9 (sub Fr)
21 Jul 2003 Penryn Athletic 0 United XI 6 (Fr)
Last game: 23 Sep 2003 United 0 Queens Park Rangers 2 (LC)
(L) Macclesfield Town 25 Mar 2004
Worksop Town Jun 2004/ Wrexham/ Northwich Victoria Mar 2005/ Port Talbot Aug 2006

England schoolboy international Kristian Rogers made his FL debut with Wrexham on 24 April 2000 at home to Colchester United and in his five seasons there he made 39(1) FL appearances. He moved to the Lane as cover for Paddy Kenny but when Paddy was injured, requiring a lengthy lay-off, United signed Paul Gerrard on loan and later Lee Baxter and Alan Fettis. Kirstian's one competitive appearance for the Blades was in the Carling Cup defeat to Queens Park Rangers and although he moved on loan to Macclesfield at the end of the season, he made no appearances.

After leaving United he played in non-League football, reportedly having a brief return to Wrexham but again making no appearances. From 2006–08 he was a regular with Port Talbot in the Welsh League.

Appearances:		Apps	Gls
	LC	1	0
	Total	1	0

ROGERS Paul Anthony

MF 1992–95 6' 0" 12st 0
b. Portsmouth 21 March 1965

Sutton United
United: (£50k) 20/29 Jan 1992 to 29 Dec 1995
Debuts: 17 Feb 1992 United 4 New Zealand 2 (sub Fr)
22 Feb 1992 Luton Town 2 United 1
Last game: 26 Dec 1995 United 1 Birmingham City 1
Notts County Dec 1995 (£25k + C Short)/ Wigan Athletic (L) Dec 1996, signed (£50k) Mar 1997/ Brighton & Hove Albion (free) Jul 1999/ Sutton U cs 2003/ Worthing Aug 2003/ Pease Pottage Village

A City commodity investment broker, Paul Rogers, who won 6 semi professional England caps whilst with Sutton, was brought to the Lane by Dave Bassett with United in the top flight. He went immediately into the side, scoring on his friendly debut and was a regular for nearly four seasons. He played with energy and enthusiasm as an attacking midfielder, his all action style and strong running typifying a Bassett player.

Shortly after Howard Kendall's arrival, Paul moved on to Notts County. Later, with Wigan, he scored the winning goal in the Auto Windscreen Shield final, and with Brighton he was involved in two successive promotions.

Despite beginning his senior professional career late, he still ended with a career total of 338(28) League appearances. He then moved into non-League football with Worthing, later becoming their coach. In 2007 he played for Pease Pottage Village, coached by Bob Booker, in the Sussex Intermediate Cup and gained a Winners' medal, being 'man of the match' in the final.

Appearances:		Apps	Gls
	FL	120 (5)	10
	FAC	4	0
	LC	8 (1)	1
	AIC	1	0
	Total	133 (6)	11

ROONEY Robert (Bobby)

IL/IR 1958–60 5' 8" 11st 7
b. Stirling 8 July 1938

Bathgate Thistle/ Clydebank (a Scottish junior team)
United: (£300) 26/28 Jun 1958 to 30 Oct 1962
Debuts: 27 Oct 1958 United 0 Hibernian 1 (Fr)
31 Mar 1959 United 3 Brighton & Hove Albion 1
Last game: 23 Apr 1960 Stoke City 1 United 2
Doncaster Rovers (£5,000) 31 Oct 1962/ Lincoln City (player exc Broadbent) Jan 1963/ Cambridge City 1964/ Gainsborough Trinity cs 1965/ Spalding United Dec 1967 to May 1968/ Ruston Hornsby

A former miner, Bobby Rooney was signed for United by Joe Mercer. He could dribble and use the ball but he lacked speed and his football career almost certainly suffered by having to spend much of his National Service in Germany. With a reputation as a 'hard man', he lost his way and despite scoring on his final appearance he spent two further years at the Lane under John Harris before moving on.

In his six seasons as a professional, Rooney played just 48 FL games, scoring 7 goals. After leaving Lincoln he spent several seasons in non-League football and worked for 25 years on the railways.

Appearances:		Apps	Gls
	FL	15	3
	FAC	1	0
	Total	16	3

ROSS Ian

MF 2004–07 5' 11" 11st 10
b. Sheffield 23 January 1986

United: from trainee 1 Jul 2003 to 9 Jan 2008
Debuts: 16 Jul 2004 Weymouth 3 United 5 (sub Fr)
23 Aug 2005 United 1 Boston United 0 (LC)
Last games: 25 Oct 2005 Reading 2 United 0 (LC)
17 Jul 2007 Alfreton Town 0 United XI 2 (Fr scored)
(L) Boston United 26 Aug to Nov 2005/ Bury 23 Mar to May 2006/ Notts County 17 Jul 2006 to Jan 2007, 26 Jan to cs 2007/ Rotherham U (L) 8 Nov 2007
Rotherham U Jan 2008 to cs 2008/ Gainsborough Trinity (trial) Jul 2008

Ian Ross, an England Youth international, spent much of his time with United on loan to other clubs. A thoughtful, midfielder with a strong shot, he perhaps lacked the necessary fire and determination. He scored on his competitive debut for the Blades in the Carling Cup against Boston, the club he joined on loan a few days later. It was with the Pilgrims that he made his FL debut as a substitute on 27 August 2005 at home to Mansfield. His full debut, and his first FL goal, came two days later at Northampton.

Most of 2006–07 was spent on loan at Notts County and he made no first team appearances for United. Neil Warnock announced his release at the end of the season but changed his mind. Further loan spells followed before he was transferred to Rotherham but with a sell-on clause in the contract, but he was released at the end of the season despite making 9 (8) FL appearances, bringing his total to 54 (20).

Appearances:

	Apps	Gls
LC	2	1
Total	2	1

ROSS William

OL/IF 1895–97 5' 11" 11st 8
b. Kiveton Park (or Chesterfield) 1874

Kiveton Park/ Chesterfield Town Aug 1894
United: 29 May/ Jun 1895 to 25 May 1897 and 23 Aug to 2 Nov 1897
Debuts: 11 Sep 1895 Grimsby Town 2 United 3 (Fr)
2 Nov 1895 Stoke 4 United 0
Last games: 20 Feb 1897 United 0 Nottingham Forest 3
29 Apr 1897 Colchester & District 1 United 5 (Fr)
Lincoln City Nov 1897/ Gravesend United May 1898/ Reading May 1899/ Notts County May 1900/ Grimsby Town (£25) Jun 1904/ Glossop May 1905 to 1908

After beginning his career with Chesterfield Town, William Ross moved to the Lane, scoring on his friendly debut whilst playing at centre forward. He played at outside right on his FL debut and then at inside forward before moving to outside left where he played regularly for over half the season. Quick with a good shot, he was hard working and had 'plenty of dash and ability'.

His opportunities were limited during the following campaign and during the summer it was reported that he had moved to Gainsborough Trinity for £50 but the move did not come about. He joined Lincoln and played for five other clubs before ending his career with 234 FL appearances (62 gl), of which over 100 were for Notts County, and other appearances in the Southern League.

He was a useful cricketer being on the groundstaff of Nottinghamshire CCC in 1902. After retiring from football he was a hotel keeper in Derbyshire for a time and in 1914 he tried to join the board of Glossop but was refused permission as, at the time, former professional players were not allowed to become directors.

Appearances:

	Apps	Gls
FL	19	3
BC	4	0
ABD	1	0
Total	24	3

ROSS Trevor William

MF 1982–83, 1984 5' 9" 11st 10
b. Ashton under Lyne 16 January 1957

Arsenal 1973, pro Jun 1974/ Everton (c £170k) Nov 1977 Portsmouth (L) Oct 1982
United: (L) Dec 1982 to Jan 1983
Debut: 4 Dec 1982 Wigan Athletic 3 United 2
Last game: 1 Jan 1983 United 3 Orient 0
AEK Athens (free) cs 1983
United: 23 Jan 1984 to 15 Jun 1984
Debut: 31 Jan 1984 Preston North End 2 United 2
Last game: 11 Feb 1984 Wigan Athletic 3 United 0
Bury Aug 1984 to cs 1987/ Hyde United/ Altrincham Jan 1988

An England schoolboy international, Trevor Ross began his career with Arsenal and made his FL debut at home to Liverpool on February 1975. For two seasons, he was a regular in the side and gained a Scottish U21cap but he lost his place at the start of the 1977–78 season and joined Everton where he spent six seasons making more than 120 FL appearances. After loan spells with Portsmouth and United he joined AEK Athens on a free transfer but after six unhappy months he returned to United on a permanent basis.

Signed by Ian Porterfield, Ross returned with a reputation as a hard working player who could pass the ball with accuracy but he didn't play well and after four more appearances, he was replaced by Ray McHale. At the end of the season he joined Bury where he had three successful seasons, ending his career in England with 286(7) FL appearances.

Appearances:

	Apps	Gls
FL	8	0
Total	8	0

ROSS William Bernard

IR/IL 1948 5' 7½" 11st
b. Swansea 8 November 1924
d. 1999

Towey United/ Cardiff City Mar 1943
United: (£4,000) 7/13 May 1948 to 31 Jul 1949
Debut: 28 Aug 1948 Derby County 2 United 1
Last game: 2 Oct 1948 Aston Villa 4 United 3
Southport Aug 1949/ Bangor City cs 1951/ Llanelli cs 1952/ Gloucester City cs 1953/ Llanelli Dec 1953/ Haverfordwest cs 1955/ Caernarvon 1957/ Rhyl 1958

A Welsh schoolboy international, Bernard Ross joined Cardiff City during the Second World War but didn't make a first team FL appearance until his debut on 17 May 1947 at Exeter City.

Signed by Teddy Davison, he moved to the Lane after only eight FL appearances and he made only three more with United despite scoring on his debut. Thick set and constructive with good ball control, he lacked speed and was more successful in his two seasons with Southport, making 43 FL appearances, before moving into non-League football, mainly in Wales. He was a trainer with Bethesda in the mid 1960s.

Appearances:

	Apps	Gls
FL	3	1
Total	3	1

ROSSINGTON Kenneth (Ken)

RH 1941–45

Treeton/ Denaby United 1940–41
United: 18/23 Jun 1941 to 14 Mar 1946
Debuts: 30 Aug 1941 Sunderland 7 United 1 (WW2)
17 Apr 1943 Barnsley 4 United 1 (CC)

Last game: 3 Feb 1945 United 2 Grimsby Town 2 (WW2)
WW2 guest: Mansfield Town (1944–45), Lincoln City, (1944–45), Notts County (1945)
Denaby United/ Scarborough 1947–48/ Grantham T 1948–49/ Beighton MW

A strong, hard tackling wing half, Ken Rossington played occasionally for four seasons during the Second War and was a useful man to bring into the first team.

Appearances:		Apps	Gls
	CC	3	0
	WW2	15	0
	Total	18	0

ROSTRON John Wilfred (Wilf)

LWB/MF 1989–90 5' 6½" 11st 11
b. Sunderland 29 September 1956

Arsenal app May 1973, pro Oct 1973/ Sunderland (£40k) Jul 1977/ Watford (£150k) Oct 1979/ Sheffield Wednesday (free) Jan 1989
United: (L) 19 Sep–20 Nov 1989, (free) 28 Nov 1989 to Jan 1991
Debut: 26 Sep 1989 United 2 Oldham Athletic 1
Last game: 22 Dec 1990 United 3 Nottingham Forest 2
Brentford player coach, Jan 1991–cs 1953/ Gateshead player-coach, then caretaker-mgr Oct 1993/ Ryhope C W Dec 1993–1994

Wilf Rostron, a schoolboy international, began his career with Arsenal as a winger and made his FL debut, and scored, at home to Newcastle United on 18 March 1975. He moved to Sunderland and then, after two seasons, to Watford where he was converted from a winger to full back. He was with Watford for nearly ten seasons and made over 300 FL appearances for the Hornets, helping them rise to the First Division and the 1984 FA Cup final, which he missed through suspension.

After a half a season at Hillsborough he moved on loan to United, newly promoted to Division Two, returning briefly to Hillsborough before singing permanently for the Blades. He was a regular in Dave Bassett's side for a few months but David Barnes then became first choice and the following season, now in Division One, Wilf was in and out of the side fulfilling a variety of roles. Ironically his final game in December was United's first win of the season.

He moved to Brentford where he later became a coach and then returned to the North East. He had played 467 (28) League games, scoring 46 goals.

Appearances:		Apps	Gls
	FL	33 (3)	3
	FAC	0 (2)	0
	LC	2 (1)	0
	Total	35 (6)	3

ROTHERY Harry

OL 1905–06 5' 11" 11st 5
b. Royston, Barnsley AMJ 1881

Wath Ath (1900–01)/ Mexborough West End (1903–04) Mexborough Town
United: 2 Dec 1904 to 19 Apr 1906
Debut: 14 Oct 1905 Derby County 1 United 0
Last game: 27 Jan 1906 Sunderland 2 United 0
Nottingham Forest (£225) Apr 1906 to May 1908/ Rawmarsh Albion Sep 1908

Tall for a winger, Harry Rothery was strong and could put across some fine centres. He made just four appearances for United and five with Nottingham Forest where his career was upset by a broken leg.

His son, a half back, had a few months on United's books in 1935.

Appearances:		Apps	Gls
	FL	4	0
	Total	4	0

ROXBURGH John (Johnny, Jack) A

CF/IR/IL 1925–26 5' 7" 11st
b. Granton (Edinburgh) 10 November 1901
d. Scotland 1965

(Amateur): Edinburgh Emmett/ Rugby Town Leicester City Jun 1920/ Aston Villa Oct 1922 Stoke Feb-Apr 1924/ Sheffield FC
United: Amateur Aug? 1925 to cs 1927
Debut: 21 Nov 1925 United 2 Leeds United 0
Last game: 9 Oct 1926 Cardiff City 3 United 0
Sheffield FC

Educated at Rugby (School), John Roxburgh was an amateur forward, employed at a senior level in the foundry industry in the Midlands. He made his FL debut with Leicester City on 9 October 1920 at home to West Ham United and went on to make 48 FL appearances for the club. His elder brother Andrew, also played for City and is thought to be the only man to have also played for Leicester Rugby Club.

After playing for Aston Villa and Stoke, he moved to Sheffield, working at Brightside and played for Sheffield Club and then played in the August 1925 United Public Practice match and signed amateur forms for United.

He was fast, direct and clever and scored on his debut but wasn't quite good enough. He was chosen to play for the England Amateur side in 1926 but had to point out his place of birth and he did later play for the Scottish amateur team and also again for Sheffield Club. His final FL career tally consisted of 79 games and 8 goals.

Appearances:		Apps	Gls
	FL	5	2
	Total	5	2

RUSH Ian James

Striker 1998 6' 0" 12st 6
b. Flint 20 October 1961

Chester from app Sep 1979/ Liverpool (£300k) May 1980 Juventus (Italy) (£3.2m) Jul 1986/ Liverpool (L) Jul 1986 to cs 1987/ Liverpool (£2.8m) Aug 1988/ Leeds United May 1996/ Newcastle United Aug 1997
United: (L) 23 Feb 1998 to 22 March 1998
Debut: 25 Feb 1998 Queens Park Rangers 2 United 2
Last game: 21 Mar 1998 Manchester City 0 United 0
Wrexham player-coach Aug 1998–99

Ian Rush had an illustrious career, mainly associated with Liverpool. He had been a Welsh schoolboy and U21 international and went on to win 73 full caps. He had made his FL debut with Chester City, on 28 April 1979 at home to Sheffield Wednesday, and moved to Anfield after 34 FL games.

He left Liverpool for Juventus but was immediately loaned back for the 1986–87 season and returned permanently in 1988. During his time at Anfield, he scored 228 goals in 469 League appearances and won many League, Cup and European honours.

After a season with Leeds he had short spell with Newcastle during which time he moved on loan to Bramall Lane, signed by Nigel Spackman, who resigned during Ian's month with United. The veteran striker failed to find the net for the Blades, Newcastle and Wrexham but did finish his career having made 536 (34) League appearances scoring 245 goals.

Appearances:		Apps	Gls
	FL	4	0
	Total	4	0

RUSSELL George Henry

LB 1934 5' 9" 12st 5
b. Atherstone JAS 1902

Atherstone Town/ Portsmouth May 1925/ Watford (free) Jun 1926/ Northampton Town (free) May 1927/ Bristol Rovers (£110) Jan 1931/ Atherstone Town Aug 1932 Cardiff City Dec 1932 to cs 1934

United: one week trial 30 Apr 1934
Debut: 30 Apr 1934 United 6 Shamrock Rovers 4 (DC)
Last game: 2 May 1934 Doncaster Rovers 2 United 1 (CC)
Newport County (free) Aug 1934/ Stafford Rangers 1935/ Bangor City player mgr 1936/ Cradley Heath Feb 1937/ Stafford Rangers Aug 1938

Impressing whilst playing against Watford for Portsmouth reserves, George Russell moved to Vicarage Road where he made his FL debut on 4 September 1926 at Bristol City. He played 12 FL games for Watford and over 50 for each of his next three FL clubs before having a trial with United at the end of the 1933–34 relegation season.

In view of his age and lack of first class experience, a trial seems strange but, in any case, he wasn't offered a contract and, after a season with Newport County and reaching a total of 192 FL appearances, he moved into non-League football.

Appearances:		Apps	Gls
	CC	1	0
	Total	1	0

RUSSELL William (Billy)

IL/IR/OR 1957–63 5' 8 10st 7
b. Hounslow 7 July 1935

Rhyl (amat)/ Man C (trial)/ Bishop Auckland (amat 1app) Rhyl (pro) 12 Nov 1957
United: 21 Aug am, (£1000 +) 14/16 Nov 1957 to 23 Mar 1963
Debut: 29 Aug 1957 Charlton Athletic 3 United 1
Last games: 24 Nov 1962 Everton 3 United 0
16 Mar 1963 Southampton 1 United 0 (FAC)
Bolton Wanderers (£20k) 26 Mar 1963/ Rochdale Jul 1966/ Scarborough (1968–69)/ Chorley (1970)

Billy Russell was playing for Rhyl, where his father, a former professional with Chelsea and Hearts, was the manager, when Joe Mercer signed him. Billy was training to be a teacher and initially signed as an amateur (he had played and scored for Bishop Auckland in the Amateur Cup Final that year). He was still an amateur when he played, scoring twice, for United reserves at Bolton and he scored again on his first team debut.

He won four Amateur England caps whilst with United but then, in November 1957, he signed as a professional for Rhyl thus allowing Rhyl to capitalise on his transfer. United, for their part, were able to pay Rhyl £1000 plus the total receipts from two games between the clubs and an additional fee at a later date. Billy completed his studies at Loughborough and remained a part-time player with United while teaching, initially in a secondary school and later as Head of Languages at a Further Education College in Altrincham.

During his time at the Lane, Billy had an impressive goal scoring record. He was fast and direct with a sharp crisp and accurate shot. He had good ball control and worked assiduously in midfield before breaking forward at speed, having the ability to move the ball accurately and quickly to his colleagues. He missed much of the 1959–60 season with a broken leg, sustained playing at outside right, and he briefly continued in this role after his return but was then moved to inside right and had an impressive run. He scored eleven goals in ten games as United moved towards promotion and in every round of the FA Cup through to round six where he scored a hat-trick in the first eighteen minutes at Newcastle.

Billy played well in the First Division but by 1963, he was less effective. He moved to Bolton and then Rochdale, reaching a career total of 65 FL goals in 226(1) games and continued playing in non-League football until he broke his leg in a pre-season friendly with Chorley.

Appearances:		Apps	Gls
	FL	144	55
	FAC	23	15
	LC	4	0
	CC	4	3
	Total	175	73

RYAN John Gilbert

RB/MF 1980–82 5' 11" 11st 8
b. Lewisham 20 July 1947

Tonbridge/ Maidstone United/ Arsenal Oct 1964 Fulham Jul 1965/ Luton Town Jul 1969/ Norwich City (£60k) Aug 1976/ Seattle Sounders (£70k) Mar to Aug 1979 and Mar to Sep 1980
United: (£25/70k) 17/24 Sep 1980 to 7 Jan 1982
Debut: 27 Sep 1980 United 1 Rotherham United 2
Last game: 2 Jan 1982 United 2 Halifax Town 2
Manchester City (£10k? + a match) Jan 1982/ Stockport County player-coach Aug 1983/ Chester City player-coach Sep 1983/ Cambridge United player-mgr Oct 1984 to Feb 1985/ Maidstone United player-coach 1985, asst mgr 1986/ Sittingbourne Town mgr Sep 1991/ Dover Athletic mgr Feb to Sep 1995/ Dulwich Hamlet mgr Mar 1997 to Feb 1998/ FA School of Excellence 1999

John Ryan had been under the guidance of Harry Haslam at Tonbridge and Harry was responsible for him joining Fulham, Luton and United. John spent a year in the reserves at Arsenal before moving to Fulham where he made his FL debut on 12 December 1965 at Stoke City.

He arrived at the Lane in September 1980 with United in Division Three and his debut perhaps summed up his days at the Lane: he scored with a superb shot from 35 yards and United lost. Ryan covered a lot of ground, played with enthusiasm, passed the ball reasonably well and had a hard shot and he missed just one of the remaining games that season but he also missed two vital penalties and United were relegated. He played in a variety of positions, mainly as a right wing back or in midfield but occasionally at centre forward. He was ever present the following season, playing at right back, until his surprise move to Manchester City but he did play sufficient games to gain a Division Four Championship medal.

He spent several seasons with various clubs as player-coach or player manager. His spell as the manager of Cambridge United was something of a disaster but when he finally finished his involvement with FL clubs, he had played 504(11) games. He later went into management in non-league Football and spent time as a coach at the FA School of Excellence.

Appearances:		Apps	Gls
	FL	56	2
	FAC	6	0
	LC	4	0
	AMC	3	0
	CC	2	0
	Total	71	2

RYAN Vaughan William

RWB 1989 5' 8" 10st 12
b. Westminster 2 September 1968

Wimbledon from app Aug 1986
United: (L) 10 Jan 1989 to Feb 1989
Debut: 14 Jan 1989 Bristol Rovers 1 United 1
Last games: 21 Jan 1989 United 4 Gillingham 2
11 Feb 1989 Cardiff City 0 United 0 (sub)
Leyton Orient Aug 1992 to cs 1995

Vaughan Ryan, a skilful and determined midfield player, had captained the English Schools U15 and Wimbledon youth teams and was a tremendous prospect. He made his FL debut with Wimbledon on 22 April 1987 at home to Spurs and had made 33 FL appearances for the Dons when Dave Bassett, who has been his manager at Wimbledon, signed him on loan. United were looking for promotion from Division 3 but Ryan, who had lost his place in the Wimbledon team, looked far from impressive and, after one month, he returned. Later, after three seasons with Leyton Orient where he was troubled by injuries, he retired from League football with a career total of 109(20) appearances.

Appearances:		Apps	Gls
	FL	2 (1)	0
	AMC	1	0
	Total	3 (1)	0

SABELLA Alejandro (Alex)

IL/OL 1978–80 5' 8" 10st 13
b. Buenos Aires (Argentina) 5 November 1954

River Plate (Argentina)
United: (£160k?) 21 Jul 1978 to 9 Jun 1980
Debut: 19 Aug 1978 United 1 Orient 2
Last games: 3 May 1980 Grimsby Town 4 United 0
8 May 1980 Sheffield Wednesday 1 United 2 (cc)
Leeds United (£400k) Jun 1980/ Estudiantes (Argentina) (£120k) Jan 1982/ Gremio of Port Alegre (Brazil) 1986–87/ Ferro Carril Oeste (Argentina) cs 1987

'Alex' Sabella was signed from Argentina by manager Harry Haslam after the 1978 World Cup for a reported United record fee of £160,000 (the actual amount may be less than half that figure for United took the receipts from a match v River Plate) but his first appearance was delayed until a work permit had been secured. Alex had magnificent ball control with clever jinking runs but there was little end product. He disliked the training, the preparation and the physical demands of English football, particularly the close marking. His English remained poor which didn't help and he came to be regarded as more of an entertainer than a useful team man. He played regularly in his two seasons at the Lane but United were relegated at the end of his first season when he rejected a reported £600k transfer to Sunderland. Sabella was no more influential in his second season although he did score in his final appearance, winning a County Cup winners' medal.

After that season in the Third Division, he moved to Leeds United (22(1) app, 2 gl) but after one and a half seasons at Elland Road, he returned to South America and went on to win eight full caps.

In 1989, he went into coaching as the assistant to the former national team captain, Daniel Passarella. The teams included: R Plate/ Argentine national/ Uruguayan national/ Parma (Italy) 40 days/ Monterey (Mex) and Corinthians (Sao Paulo) before returning to Argentina.

Appearances:		Apps	Gls
	FL	76	8
	FAC	4	0
	LC	2	0
	ASC	3	0
	CC	3	2
	Total	88	10

SALMONS Geoffrey (Geoff)

IR/IL/OL 1966–74 and 1977 5' 11" 11st 12
b. Mexborough 14 January 1948

United: from jnr 31 Jan/2 Feb 1966 to 9 Jul 1974
Debuts: 26 Oct 1966 United 2 Walsall 1 (LC)
23 Sep 1967 United 2 Newcastle United 1 (sub)
30 Sep 1967 West Bromwich Albion 4 United 1
Last games: 27 Apr 1974 Ipswich Town 0 United 1
15 Jun 1974 Levski Spartak (Bulg) 2 United 0 (CIT)
Stoke City (£160k–£180k) Jul 1974
United: (L) 13 Sep to 12 Oct 1977
Debut: 17 Sep 1977 United 0 Crystal Palace 2
Last game: 8 Oct 1977 Mansfield Town 1 United 1
Leicester City (£42.5k) Oct 1977/ Chesterfield (£35k) Aug 1978

Geoff Salmons was one of several Don and Dearne Boys who came to the Lane during the 1960s. He began at outside left but moved to inside left and later into midfield. His pace and stamina meant he could cover a good deal of ground during a game and long-striding surging runs from deep were a feature of his play. A mainly left footed player, his work rate was

appreciated by supporters and he was deservedly a popular player and only his poor goal scoring record let him down.

Geoff played intermittently during 1968–69 and steadily became more of a regular and featured in every game in United's first season back in the top flight in 1971–72. When he was sold to Stoke, his manager Ken Furphy, stated that it was for 'purely financial reason'.

Tony Waddington, Stoke City's manager was reported as saying that Geoff, when he played for United, 'was a player who gave us a lot of trouble'. During his three seasons with Stoke, Geoff returned to the Lane on loan for a month in 1977. He played five games and although there was talk of a permanent move, United were in turmoil towards the end of Jimmy Sirrel's time as manager and he returned to Stoke.

He was transferred to Leicester City before ending his FL career with a successful time at Chesterfield who played a club record fee for his services. He helped the Spirerites win the Anglo Scottish Cup but injuries hastened the end of his playing career. He had played 434 (15) FL games but with a low tally of 41 goals. He continued to live in South Yorkshire as a successful licensee and restaurant owner.

Appearances:		Apps	Gls
	FL	175 (10)	8
	FAC	7	1
	LC	10 (2)	0
	TX	2	0
	CC	9	1
	WC	3	0
	ABD	1	0
	Total	207 (12)	10

SALT Harold

IL 1918 5' 9" 11st 7
b. Ecclesfield 20 November 1899
d. Banstead 16 November 1971

Ecclesfield United
United: trial 23 Mar 1918
Only game: 23 Mar 1918 Wednesday 2 United 1 (WW1)
WW 1 Guest: Wednesday (1917–18, 1918–19) and Barnsley (1918–19)
Brighton & Hove Albion Jun 1921/ Mexborough May 1922/ Peterborough & Fletton United/ Port Vale Dec 1925/ Queens Park Rangers May 1926/ Grays Thurrock, Sep 1927/ Crystal Palace Jan 1928/ Brentford May 1929/ Walsall May 1932//Yeovil & Petters United cs 1933

Harold Salt made just one guest appearance for United during the First War, scoring the Blades' only goal. He also appeared few times on trial as a guest for Wednesday and Barnsley. While serving in the army, he had played at centre half and it was in that position that he made his first FL appearance with Brighton at home to Southend United on 27 August 1921 but, during the season, he was converted from centre half to inside forward. He went on to play for a variety of FL and non-League clubs, playing a total of 141 FL games with Brighton, Queens Park Rangers, Crystal Palace, Brentford, where he had the most successful period of his career, and Walsall.

Appearances:		Apps	Gls
	WW1	1	1
	Total	1	1

SAMPY Thomas (Tommy)

RH/IR 1921–34 5' 6½" 10st 9
b. Backworth 14 March 1899
d OND Sheffield 1978

Choppington/ Seaton Delaval/ South Shields cs 1919 Chopwell Colliery Institute 1920
United: 15/17 Nov 1920 to 5 May 1934
Debut: 12 Feb 1921 United 1 Blackburn Rovers 1
Last games: 30 Sep 1933 Huddersfield Town 6 United 1
16 Apr 1934 Doncaster Rovers 1 United 1 (CC)
Barnsley player coach cs 1934/ Sheffield Wednesday coach May 1936 to cs 1938

Tommy Sampy was an engineer by trade who played his early football in the North East. He began his United career at inside right, scoring on his debut but in the autumn of 1925 he moved to right half where he played regularly until 1931. Tommy was a clever, hard working, terrier like player and a good header of the ball. He took over the United captaincy from Billy Gillespie in 1930–31 but in the following season, he lost his place to Harry Gooney although he played frequently in 1932–33.

In 1934, after 14 seasons at the Lane he moved to Barnsley, where he acted mainly as a coach, playing just one FL game, and he then moved onto the coaching team at Hillsborough. He had owned a gentleman's outfitters shop on Abbeydale Road and during the war, he returned to engineering as a production manager.

Tommy's big disappointment was missing out on the 1925 FA Cup Final. He had played in the previous two rounds but Tommy Boyle had been more effective in the games prior to the final, scoring six goals in the five games in which he played. Half an hour before the kick-off, it was announced that Boyle was to play. Tommy Sampy was later quoted as saying that it was the right decision but it must have remained a bitter memory and in 1940 he was quoted as saying that his twenty years in football 'were wasted years'. Perhaps he was also recalling the occasion in a Portsmouth hotel when he asked the United Secretary if he could have cheese and biscuits rather than the sweet. There was no problem, John Nicholson replied, as long as Sampy paid the extra 3d.

His brother Bill (qv) also played for United.

Appearances:		Apps	Gls
	FL	340	27
	FAC	31	5
	CC	12	1
	Total	383	33

SAMPY William (Bill) Albert

RB 1922–26 5' 8½" 11st 10
b. Backworth 22 January 1901
d. Coventry JFM 1973

Chopwell Colliery Institute
United: (£250 for Sampy and J Waugh) 26 Apr/1 May 1921 to 28 Feb/1 Mar 1927
Debuts: 11 Oct 1922 Hartlepools United 0 United 2 (BM)
4 Oct 1924 Bury 1 United 0
Last game: 23 Oct 1926 United 0 West Ham United 2
Swansea Town (£500) Mar 1927/ Waterford C Aug 1930, player manager 1931/ Newbiggin West End (trial) Sep 1933/ Nelson Oct 1933

Bill Sampy joined United from the same club as his elder brother Tommy (qv) but he was generally regarded as a reserve player and his progress was slow. A vigorous, first-time tackler, it was two years after making his debut in a benefit match that he finally made his FL debut and it was not until October 1925 that the brothers played together and Bill had a significant run in the side.

Part way through the following season he moved to Swansea (41 FL app) but again spent much of his time in the reserves. The FL gave him a free transfer in February 1930 and he moved to Ireland with Waterford, becoming their player manager for a time before playing for Nelson, by then a non-League club.

Appearances:		Apps	Gls
	FL	34	0
	FAC	2	0
	CC	1	0
	Total	37	0

SANDFORD Edward (Ted) Albert

IL 1939 5' 9½" 12st 12
b. Handsworth (Birmingham) 22 October 1910
d. Sandwell 14 May 1995

Tantany Athletic/ Overend Wesley Birmingham Carriage Works/ Smetwick Highfield West Bromwich Albion amat Oct 1929, pro May 1930
United: (£1,500) 16/17 Mar 1939 to 10 Jan 1946
Debut: 18 Mar 1939 Chesterfield 1 United 1
Last games: 8 Apr 1939 United 1 Bury 1
29 Apr 1939 Rotherham U 2 United XI 1 (BM)
Morris Commercial/ retired 1943

Ted Sandford had a splendid career with West Bromwich Albion. He made his FL debut, and scored, on 15 November 1930 at Preston North End and went on to make 266 FLappearances and scored 67 goals. He won a FA Cup winners' medal and one England cap whilst at the Hawthorns.

A strong inside forward, he joined United towards the end of the 1939 promotion season when Jack Pickering was injured but it was a poor signing by Teddy Davison for Ted was 'crippled'. His legs had gone and in the previous season he had played at centre half. Fortunately for United, after just five appearances, his place at inside left was taken by a young Jimmy Hagan, who had been playing on the right wing until that point, and promotion was secured.

During the Second World War, Ted played in local football in the Midlands but had to give up in 1943; remarkably, he remained on United's retained list until 1946. He became a coach with West Brom in the 1950's and later was a scout for the club.

Appearances:		Apps	Gls
	FL	5	1
	Total	5	1

SANDFORD Lee Robert

CD/LWB 1996–2002 6' 1" 13st 4
b. Lambeth 22 April 1968

Portsmouth from school, app Dec 1985 Stoke City (£140k) Dec 1989
United: (£450+50k) 15/22 Jul 1996 to 27 May 2002
Debuts: 18 Jul 1996 Sarawak (Malaysia) 1 United 2 (Fr)
17 Aug 1996 Reading 1 United 0
Last games: 8 Dec 2001 West Bromwich Albion 0 United 1
26 Jan 2002 Preston North End 2 United 1 (FAC)
9 Feb 2002 United 4 Portsmouth 3 (sub)
Reading (L) 5 Sep 1997, Stockport County (L) Oct 2001
Woking Aug 2002 (retired)

An England youth international, Lee Sandford began his career with Portsmouth, making his FL debut as a substitute on 26 October 1985 at Millwall, his full debut coming on 16 November at Grimsby Town. In 1988 a spinal injury meant he was out of the side and the following season he moved to Stoke where he was a regular in the side for over six seasons.

Lee was signed by Howard Kendall who appreciated his reliable qualities, his ability to read the game and that he was not afraid to have the ball. During his first season, he played at left wing back but when Kendall resigned, he began the following season on loan at Reading and was then injured. On his return, he played alongside David Holdsworth forming a solid central defence. Looking to the future, Lee had a BSc in Sports Science and Coaching and was a regular in the side for nearly three seasons and, although lacking pace, he used his anticipation and experienced to produce a series of reliable performances.

A neck problem sidelined him in February 2001 and, although he recovered, he made few appearances in his final season at the Lane spending time on loan at Stockport. Lee's contract was cancelled in May by mutual agreement and he moved to Woking in the summer but retired after just a few weeks, having played 475(18) FL games in his career. He subsequently had an interest in property and Commodity Trading.

Appearances:		Apps	Gls
	FL	142 (9)	4
	PO	3 (1)	0
	FAC	16 (1)	1
	LC	12 (1)	0
	Total	173 (12)	5

SANTOS Georges

MF/CD 2000–02 6' 3" 14st 0
b. Marseilles (France) 15 August 1970

Toulon (France)/ Tranmere Rovers Jul 1998 West Bromwich Albion (£25k) Mar 2000
United: **(free) 5 Jul 2000 to 27 Sep 2002**
Debuts: **18 Jul 2000 Tideswell 0 United 8 (Fr)**
12 Aug 2000 United 2 Portsmouth 0
Last games: **1 Jan 2002 United 1 Manchester City 3**
16 Mar 2002 United 0 West Bromwich Albion 3 (sub)
Kilmarnock trial Jul 2002/ Grimsby Town (free) Sep 2002/ Ipswich Town (free) Aug 2003/ Queens Park Rangers (free) Aug 2004/ Brighton & Hove Albion (free) Aug 2006 to May 2007/ Oxford United (L) Jan 2007/ Chesterfield (trial) Sep 2007/ Rotherham U (trial) Nov 2007/ Lincoln C (trial) Nov 2007/ Alfreton T Dec 2007/ Farsley Celtic Jan 2008

Georges Santos made his FL debut in England after joining Tranmere Rovers on 8 August 1998 at Wolves. He went on to play for six more FL clubs in the following eight seasons, Queens Park Rangers being where he stayed longest and played most games.

He was signed by Neil Warnock at the start of Neil's first full season at the Lane and Georges was a regular in the squad filling a variety of roles but playing mainly in midfield. In March 2001 he suffered a serious facial injury in a clash with Andy Johnson (Forest) involving damage to his eye socket and there were initial fears that he could have lost the sight in the eye. He had a titanium plate inserted in his skull and was fit for the start of the following season and the big, hard-working no nonsense performer was once again a regular in the squad, being either in the starting line-up or coming off the bench.

In March 2002 he came on as a substitute against West Bromwich Albion at the Lane and within minutes, was sent off for a tackle on the player with whom he had clashed the previous season when sustaining his serious injury. In the resultant melee Patrick Suffo was dismissed and eventually the game was stopped because United were down to six men.

Georges did not play again for the Blades but in September 2002, he became a Cape Verde international and his career in English football continued. He reached a total of 214(47) FL games before moving into non-League football.

Appearances:		Apps	Gls
	FL	37 (24)	6
	FAC	1 (1)	0
	LC	2 (3)	0
	Total	40 (28)	6

SAUL Charles Ernest

CH 1900
b. Kimberworth AMJ 1878

Kimberworth/ Thornhill Utd
United: **8 May 1900 to cs 1901**
Only game: **26 Dec 1900 United 1 Manchester City 1**
Thornhill Utd Oct 1901

A part-timer (15/- per week), Charles Saul made just one first team appearance for United and it was the only FL appearance of his short career. He was the elder brother of Percy (144 app, 10 gl with Gainsborough Tr and Liverpool) who also played for Coventry C, Rotherham Town and County and Arthur Saul who played for Thornhill and Rotherham County.

Appearances:		Apps	Gls
	FL	1	0
	Total	1	0

SAUNDERS Dean Nicholas

Striker 1997–98 5' 8" 10st 6?
b. Swansea 21 June 1964

Swansea City from app Jun 1982/ Cardiff City (L) Mar 1985 Brighton & Hove Albion (free) Aug 1985/ Oxford United (£60k) Mar 1987/ Derby County (£1m) Oct 1988 Liverpool (£2.9m) Jul 1991/ Aston Villa (£2.3m) Sep 1992 Galatasary (Turkey) (£2.35m) Jul 1995/ Nottingham Forest (£1.5m) Jul 1996
United: **(free) 2/5 Dec 1997 to 7/10 Dec 1998**
Debut: **6 Dec 1997 Norwich City 2 United 1**
Last game: **21 Nov 1998 Queens Park Rangers 1 United 2**
Benfica (Portugal) (£500k, Dec 1998)/ Bradford City (free) Aug 1999 to Jul 2001/ Blackburn Rovers coach 2001 to 2003/ Newcastle United coach Sep 2004 to 2006/ Wales asst mgr cs 2007

Dean Saunders, the son of a former Liverpool and Swansea player, made his FL debut with Swansea City, as a substitute, on 22 October 1983 at Charlton Athletic and his full debut came on 18 January 1984 at home to Huddersfield Town. He went on to have an impressive career, winning 75 Welsh caps, the FA Cup and League Cup and when he retired he had scored 170 goals in 540(34) games in English League Football, many in the top flight, as well as playing in Turkey and Portugal.

Dean moved to the Lane whilst Nigel Spackman was in charge, his contract with Nottingham Forest having been terminated and, although nearing the end of his career, he delighted the supporters with his skill, work rate, unselfish running and positive demeanour. He will be particularly remembered for his goal against Port Vale in March 1998. He and the Vale keeper chased a through ball to the touchline level with the

opposition's penalty area. The ball went out for a United throw but with no United players anywhere near, Dean threw the ball at the retreating keeper's back and kicked the ball into the net from the rebound. A clause in his contract meant the club were powerless to prevent his return to Benfica after a season at the Lane during which he had gained five more Welsh caps.

He subsequently returned to play for Bradford City and on his retirement in the summer of 2001, he began coaching at Blackburn Rovers.

Appearances:		Apps	Gls
	FL	42 (1)	7
	PO	2	0
	FAC	6	2
	LC	4	3
	Total	54 (1)	12

SAVAGE Harry

OL 1920 5' 7½" 11st
b. Frodsham JFM 1897
d. Runcorn OND 1968

Army football/ Crewe Alexandra 1919
United: (£750) 16/18 May 1920 to 15 Jun 1921
Debut: 28 Aug 1920 United 1 Sunderland 1
Last game: 23 Oct 1920 Aston Villa 4 United 0
Watford (£250) Jun 1921 to cs 1922/ Frodsham 1922?/ Connah's Quay Jan 1924/ Mold T Jul 1925/ Frodsham Sep 1926

Harry Savage had played amateur football before the First War and for the army during it. After a season with Crewe who were then a CL club and where he played quite regularly, he moved to the Lane. Several players had been tried at outside left in the previous season and Harry played in the first nine games of the 1920–21 season. His crosses were good but he was unreliable and clearly not good enough and when, a few weeks later, Fred Tunstall was signed, Harry played no more.

He moved to Watford for what was, at the time, their record fee but played only seven games before rejecting the offer of a new contract and returning home to non-League football.

Appearances:		Apps	Gls
	FL	10	0
	Total	10	0

SAYER Andrew (Andy or 'Leo') Clive

Striker 1991 5' 9" 10st 2
b. Park Royal, Brent 6 June 1966

Wimbledon app 1982, pro Jun 1984/ Cambridge United (L) Feb 1988/ Fulham (£70k) Aug 1988/ Leyton Orient (£70k) Feb 1990
United: (L) 26 Mar 1991 to 31 May 1991
Debuts: 1 Apr 1991 Nottingham Forest 2 United 1 (sub)
23 Apr 1991 Lincon City 2 United 1 (BM)
Last games: 11 May 1991 United 2 Norwich City 1 (sub)
22 May 1991 Tulsa Renegades 1 United 4 (Fr)
Slough Town Aug 1992/ Enfield (£11k) cs 1995/ Walton & Hersham Apr 1996–May 1999 / – / Leatherhead 2000/ Egham Town/ Tooting & Mitcham Jan 2001/ Chertsey Town/ Tooting & Mitcham United Aug 2001/Molesey Aug 2003

Andy Sayer made his FL debut with Wimbledon on 27 August 1983 at Bolton Wanderers. Never a regular in the side, he moved to Fulham but after an impressive start, a loss of form resulted in a move to Orient where injuries meant he never settled at the club.

Signed by his former Wimbledon manager Dave Bassett, Andy appeared only as a sub in his three FL games. There was a suggestion that he might make the move permanent but after going on United's brief tour to the USA, he returned to Orient.

He left Brisbane Road in 1992, having made 115(34) career FL appearances, and had a lengthy spell in non-League football. Later, he was reported to be working as a customs officer at Heathrow and subsequently managing a restaurant in Surbiton.

Appearances:		Apps	Gls
	FL	0 (3)	0
	Total	0 (3)	0

SCOTT Andrew (Andy)

Striker/MF/LWB 1993–97 6' 1" 11st 5
b. Epsom 2 August 1972

Sutton United/ Cambridge U (trial)
United: (£50k+ £50k) 23 Nov/ 1 Dec 1992 to 21 Nov 1997
Debuts: 21 Apr 1993 Sheffield Wednesday 1 United 1 (sub)
8 May 1993 United 4 Chelsea 2
Last games: 13 Sep 1997 United 1 Nottingham Forest 0
23 Sep 1997 United 4 Watford 0 (LC)
25 Oct 1997 West Bromwich Albion 2 United 0 (sub)
Chesterfield (L) 17 Oct 1996/ Bury (L) 21 Mar 1997
Brentford (£75k) Nov 1997/ Oxford United (£75k) Jan 2001–cs 2003/ Leyton Orient (free) Mar 2004 to Apr 2005, coaching, youth team mgr/ Brentford asst mgr May 2007, caretaker mgr Dec 2007, mgr Jan 2008

Dave Bassett had rejected Andy Scott when he was the manager of Wimbledon but signed him and his brother Rob from Sutton United when United were in the Premiership. Andy had previously rejected an offer from Cambridge United and he had to wait some time to make his first team debut which was as a substitute in a 1–1 draw at Hillsborough and he scored on his full debut about 2 weeks later.

An attack of glandular fever meant that he was in and out of the side in the following season, playing mainly as a striker, but in 1994–95, with United now in Division One, he played more regularly but as a left wing back or attacking midfielder. Andy's opportunities were then limited by cruciate ligament problems and after two loan spells and four appearances together with his brother, he moved to Brentford.

Andy played for seven seasons in the lower divisions although troubled by injuries towards the end of his career. Heart problems prompted his retirement in April 2005, having played 276(72) League games but after a spell coaching with Orient, he returned to Brentford as assistant manager and subsequently became manager.

Appearances:		Apps	Gls
	FL	39 (36)	7
	FAC	2 (1)	0
	LC	5	2
	AIC	3 (1)	3
	Total	49 (38)	12

SCOTT John ('Jack' or 'Jock') C

CF 1891–92 5' 10" 'over 12st'
b. Leith 7 Aug 1873 or Edinburgh 1 January 1872

Cameron Highlanders/ Leith Athletic
United: Dec 1891 to early Dec 1892
Debuts: 12 Dec 1891 Walsall Town Swifts 2 United 0 (Fr)
19 Dec 1891 United 5 Newcastle West End 1 (NL)
16 Jan 1892 Blackpool 0 United 3 (FAC)
17 Sep 1892 United 2 Small Heath 0
Last games: 19 Nov 1892 Darwen 3 United 1
21 Nov 1892 United 1 Wednesday 3 (Fr)
Gainsborough Trinity by 13 Dec 1892 to cs 1900/ Leith Ath 1900?

Jack Scott, a centre forward, was described by George Waller, the United trainer and an excellent judge of a player, as 'one of the best'. He scored on his competitive debut in the NL, on his FA Cup debut and then on his FL debut. He played regularly in the side and was one of the very few players in those early years who played as a substitute, replacing Fred Davies in a friendly game at the Lane (substitutes were not allowed in competitive games).

Transferred to Gainsborough Trinity (92 FL app, 20 goals), he became one of their most popular players. His final FL appearance came in September 1899 when, as an army reservist, it was reported that he would be called-up because of the war in South Africa.

Appearances:		Apps	Gls
	FL	5	2
	FAC	2	1
	NL	12	3
	SCC	3	5
	Total	22	11

SCOTT Lawrence (Laurie)

LB 1944 5' 9" 11st 4
b. Sheffield 23 April 1917
d. 22 July 1999

Edgar Allen/ Bolton Woods/ Bradford City (am 1931), pro 1934/ Arsenal (player exch) Feb 1937
United: WW2 guest
Debut: 23 Sep 1944 Barnsley 2 United 1 (WW2)
Last game: 2 Dec 1944 Chesterfield 1 United 1 (WW2)
Crystal Palace player manager Oct 1951 to Oct 1954/ Hendon Town mgr late 1954 to cs 1957/Hitchin Town coach Aug 1957/ Finchley Jul 1968 to Oct 1969

Laurie Scott made his FLdebut with Bradford City on 8 February 1936 at home to Charlton Athletic, but after 39 games he joined Arsenal. He played in the reserves for two seasons, then the Second War intervened and he served as a PT instructor in the RAF. He became a fine full back; two footed with speed, a good positional sense and distribution and he gained 16 Wartime England caps.

During the war, United had tried to develop their own players and avoided, as far as possible, using guest players but injuries and other problems in 1944 meant that more guests were used and Laurie, on leave, was one of these.

In 1946, he finally made his Arsenal FL debut and went on to win 17 England caps, an FA Cup winners' medal and a League Championship medal. In a career of distinction, he made over 200 war-time and 182 FL appearances but never scored a goal. He later had a rather unsuccessful time as manager of Crystal Palace and in due course worked on the sales side of a hardware business and retired to Hoylandswaine in South Yorkshire.

Appearances:		Apps	Gls
	WW2	2	0
	Total	2	0

SCOTT Robert (Rob)

Striker 1993–95 6' 1" 11st 10
b. Epsom 15 August 1973

Dorking/ Sutton United 1989
United: (£20k) 1 Aug 1993 to 8 Jan 1996
Debuts: 10 Oct 1993 Brunei 1 United 4 (sub Fr)
18 May 1994 Northern NSW(Australia) 1 United 1 (Fr)
6 Sep 1994 Piacenza 2 United 2 (AIC)
25 Oct 1994 United 1 Bolton W 2 (sub LC)
27 Dec 1994 Swindon Town 1 United 3 (sub)
12 Aug 1995 Watford 2 United 1
Last games: 19 Aug 1995 United 0 Tranmere Rovers 2
14 Oct 1995 Southend United 2 United 1 (sub)
Scarborough (L) 22 Mar 1995/ Northampton Town (L) 24 Nov 1995
Fulham (£30k) 10 Jan 1996/ Carlisle United (L) 18 Aug 1998/ Rotherham United (£50k) 17 Nov 1998/ Oldham Athletic (free) Jul 2005/ Macclesfield Town Sep 2006/ Halifax T Aug 2007

Rob Scott was signed by Dave Bassett from Sutton United, joining his elder brother Andy and they played together on Rob's full United FL debut at Watford. He had few opportunities at the Lane and he was on the losing side in his six FL outings. He had two spells on loan, and it was at Scarborough, on 25 March 1995 at Colchester United, that he had made his full FL debut.

After two and a half seasons with United, he joined Fulham where he had more success and scored some important and spectacular goals. Transferred to Rotherham United, he converted to a defender, spending nearly seven seasons at Millmoor. Latterly he was troubled by a shoulder problem and a cruciate ligament injury and was released in the summer of 2005. In 2006–07, after a spell at Oldham, he helped Macclesfield maintain their FL status and reached a total of 288(43) FL appearances before moving into non-League football.

Appearances:		Apps	Gls
	FL	2 (4)	1
	LC	0 (1)	0
	AIC	2 (1)	0
	Total	4 (6)	1

SCULLION Stewart McNab Adam

OL/IR/OR 1971–73 5' 7½" 10st 6
b. Bo'ness 18 April 1946

Chesham United/ Charlton Athletic amat Dec 1964, pro Mar 1965/ Watford (part exch) Feb 1966
United: (£25k) 7 May 1971 to 3/6 Dec 1973
Debuts: 1 Aug 1971 NAC Breda (Holland) 0 United 1 (sub Fr)
4 Aug 1971 KV Malinois (Belgium) 2 United 1 (Fr)
14 Aug 1971 United 3 Southampton 1
Last game: 3 Nov 1973 United 1 Birmingham City 1

Watford (£15k) Dec 1973/ Tampa Bay Rowdies (USA) (L) May to Aug 1975, (£8,000) Feb 1976/ Wimbledon Sep 1976/ Portland Timbers (USA) Apr to Aug 1977/ Hayes c Nov 1977/ Portland Timbers (USA) Mar 1978 to Aug 1979

An airline clerk, Stewart Scullion began his career with Charlton Athletic but his FL debut came with Watford when he scored on 5 February 1966 at Exeter City and he went on to play 225 FL games with the Hornets.

For most Unitedites, their first sight of Scullion came when he smashed the ball against the United cross-bar in the last and vital game of the 1970–71 promotion season. He was signed by John Harris at the end of that week and played an important role in the club's impressive start to the 1971–72 campaign. Two footed, strong with good ball control, in his first season he missed few games and played mainly at outside left though he was moved to inside right towards the end of the season. During his following one and a half seasons at the Lane, he was in and out of the side and played in every forward position at least once.

He returned to Watford where he brought his FL appearances for Watford to over 300 and in his career to 357(12), scoring 56 goals. He later spent several summers in the USA, representing 'Team America' against England, and the winters in non-League football in London. He was subsequently reported to be working at Heathrow Airport.

Appearances:		Apps	Gls
	FL	53 (4)	7
	FAC	2	0
	LC	5	0
	TXAS	1	0
	CC	2	0
	WC	3	0
	ABD	1	0
	Total	67 (4)	7

SEGERS Johannes (Hans) C A

G 1987–88 5' 11½" 12st 10
b. Eindhoven (Holland) 30 October 1961

PSV Eindhoven/ Nottingham Forest (£50k) Aug 1984 Stoke City (L) Feb 1987
United: (L) 19 Nov 1987 to Feb 1988
Debut: 21 Nov 1987 United 4 Reading 1
Last game: 20 Feb 1988 United 1 Barnsley 0
Dunfermline Athletic (L) Mar 1988/ Wimbledon (£180k) Sep 1988/ Wolverhampton Wanderers (free) Aug 1996/ Woking 1 Feb 1997/ Wolverhampton Wanderers 27 Mar 1997/ Tottenham Hotspur Aug 1998 to cs 1999, coach to Oct 2007

Hans Segers made his FL debut with Nottingham Forest on 17 November 1984 at Coventry City. He could not fully establish himself in the first team and he had three loan spells whilst at the City Ground including his time with United. An agile goalkeeper, he was popular at the Lane but after three months he returned to Forest.

He moved to Wimbledon where he spent eight years, playing 265(2) League games, including being in goal in May 1992 at Goodison Park where Everton's 3–2 victory, thought by many at the time to be an unlikely result, helped keep them in the Premiership and meant United were relegated.

Later, in 1994, he was accused, along with Bruce Grobbelaar, John Fashanu and a Malaysian businessman of match fixing but all four defendants were found not guilty at Winchester Crown Court. After spells with Wolves and Spurs, bringing his career total to 346(2) League games, he became goalkeeping coach with Tottenham.

Appearances:		Apps	Gls
	FL	10	0
	FMC	1	0
	Total	11	0

SENIOR James

OL 1895
b. Grantham JFM 1873

Grantham Rovers
United: 3 May 1894 to May 1895
Only game: 19 Jan 1895 United 1 Wolverhampton Wanderers 0
Grantham Rovers May 1895 to c1901

James Senior made just one first team appearance for the Blades, the only FL appearance of his career, and his time with United passed without comment in the Sheffield newspapers.

Appearances:		Apps	Gls
	FL	1	0
	Total	1	0

SESTANOVICH Ashley

MF 2003–04 6' 3" 13st 0
b. Lambeth (London) 18 September 1981

AFC Lewisham/ Manchester City 1999/ Mullingar Town (Eire)/ Royal Antwerp (Belgium)/ Metz (France)/ Hampton & Richmond Borough Jul 2002/ Stockport C (trial)
United: (£10k) 5 Mar 2003 to Feb 2005
Debuts: 15 Jul 2003 Frechville CA 0 United XI 9 (sub Fr)
3 Apr 2004 Nottingham Forest 2 United 1 (sub)
Last game: 9 Apr 2004 Sunderland 3 United 0 (sub)
31 Oct 2003 (L) Scarborough/ Grimsby Town (L) 6 Jul 2004
Chester City Feb 2005/ Gravesend & Northfleet Aug 2005/ Farnborough Town Sep 2005/ Grays Athletic Jun 2006 to Jul 2006

Ashley had a chequered football career and failed to fulfil his potential. Having been on Manchester City's books, he played in the Republic of Ireland, Belgium and France before joining Hampton & Richmond and it was from there that he joined United after he had been spotted on trial with Stockport County.

He spent much of his first season with non-League Scarborough where he played a big part in their FA Cup run and eventual defeat by Chelsea. Tall but with good ball control, he used the ball well but was too laid back and casual. He returned to the Lane making his FL debut as a substitute but his full FL debut came during the following season while on loan with Grimsby Town and, although he was due to be there for the full season, he returned early due to various disputes.

After a move to Chester City, where again he left 'early', he moved into non-League football having played 20(11) FL games.

One of his 'claims to fame' was his acting as Thierry Henry's body double in various adverts but his football career had come to an end in June 2006 when he was arrested. He was later found guilty and subsequently sentenced to eight years in prison for his part in planning a robbery during which a man was killed.

Appearances:		Apps	Gls
	FL	0 (2)	0
	Total	0 (2)	0

SETTLE Alfred (Alf)

LH/RH 1936–43 5' 10" 11st 6
b. Barugh Green, Barnsley 17 September 1912
d. Warwickshire January 1988

Wooley Colliery/ Barugh Green
United: 4/15 Dec 1934 to 10 Jan 1946
Debut: 30 Apr 1936 Hull City 2 United 2
Last games: 6 May 1939 United 6 Tottenham Hotspur 1
2 Sep 1939 Leeds U 0 United 1 (FL competition abandoned)
3 Oct 1942 United 4 Rotherham United 2 (WW2)
21 Aug 1943 United 3 Sheffield Wednesday 2 (CM)
WW2 guest: Barnsley 1 app v United Oct 1941
Lincoln City Feb 1946 to cs

Chance brought Alf Settle to United. Manager Davison had gone to watch the Barugh Green winger, Eric Bray but discovered on arrival that he had signed for Barnsley. The Secretary told Davison that Settle was their best player and Bray's father agreed and so the fair haired left half became a United player.

Alf became a full-time pro in January 1935 and made his FL debut in April 1936 but he had to wait until August 1937 for his next appearance and it was not until October that he became a regular member of the side. A 'grafter', he was strong and powerful and an ever present at left half in the 1938–39 promotion season. He played regularly during the first two seasons of the Second War but, working as a miner, he found travelling was difficult and an injured ankle—a broken bone was found later—restricted further appearances after October 1942 to just his last senior game in August 1943. He made a few appearances for the reserves in the first half of the 1945–46 season but then asked for his release before playing 16 games for Lincoln City.

Appearances:		Apps	Gls
	FL	70	2
	FAC	4	0
	CC	3	0
	WW2	58	1
	1939/40	3	0
	Total	138	3

SEVERN Jack C

LB/RB 1919

Mexborough T (1915–16)/ Wath/ Denaby U
United: WW1 Guest Jan 1919
Debut: 1 Jan 1919 Barnsley 2 United 2 (WW1)
Last game: 4 Jan 1919 Hull City 6 United 1 (WW1, abandoned)
Mexborough Town cs1919/ Barnborough Main (amat) Aug 1922

Jack Severn played his two games for United within a space of four days and the second game was abandoned with 10 minutes remaining due to darkness, the game having started late.

Appearances:		Apps	Gls
	WW1	2	0
	Total	2	0

SHANKLY James (Jimmy) Blyth

CF 1926–28 5' 10½" 12st 8
b. Glenbuck 19 June 1901
d. Muirkirk 31 January 1978

Glenbuck Cherrypickers/ Bedlington Utd/ Guildford United cs 1923/ Halifax Town Jun 1924/ Nuneaton Town Aug 1925 Coventry City Feb 1926/ Carlisle United cs 1926
United: (£500 to Carlisle, £100 to Cov C) 28 Oct/ 2/4 Nov 1926 to 4 Jun 1928
Debuts: 13 Dec 1926 Barnsley 3 United 0 (CC)
12 Feb 1927 United 2 Newcastle United 1
Last game: 10 Mar 1928 Birmingham 4 United 0
Southend United (£270) Jun 1928/ Barrow May 1933/ Carlisle United Aug 1935

Jimmy Shankly was the second eldest of the five famous Shankly brothers who were all professional footballers. The most well known of course was Bill who was a Preston and Scotland wing half and the manager of Liverpool. Nevertheless, Jimmy was a successful centre forward but mainly in the lower divisions and he finished his career with 253 FL appearances and 155 goals. He had made his FL debut with Halifax Town at Grimsby on 11 October 1924 but had never settled long with any club.

He was 'as strong as a bull' with a powerful shot in his left foot but was lacking in speed. A useful reserve, during his time at the Lane, he was competing for the centre forward position with the prolific Harry Johnson and so Jimmy had few opportunities.

He had a more successful time in the Third Division with Southend United (147 FL app, 97 gl) and then with Barrow (78 FL app, 47 gl) and after a second period with Carlisle, he became a coal merchant.

Appearances:		Apps	Gls
	FL	7	4
	CC	1	0
	Total	8	4

SHARP(E) Arthur

OL/IR 1918

Barlborough/ Retford T/ Rotherham T 1910 S Normanton 1912–Jan 1913/ Shirebrook Feb 1913–Dec 1915/ Retford T/ Harthill 1916–17/ Manton Colliery
United: WW1 guest Mar 1918 to Apr 1918
Debut: 30 Mar 1918 United 2 Barnsley 3 (WW1)
Last game: 13 Apr 1918 Wednesday 2 United 0 (Fr)
Gainsborough Tr 1919–20/ Doncaster R 1920–21/ Chesterfield/ Clowne T 1921–22

Arthur Sharp(e), a 'native of Barlborough', probably played for the United reserve team in the 1915–16 season. Normally a centre forward, he made two guest appearances for United, one a friendly game, scoring on his debut with 'a splendid 15 yard shot'.

A potential cause of confusion, particularly during the war period 1915–19 (with guest players) lies in the fact that there are other contemporary forwards called Sharp or Sharpe playing in the locality. Examples include Chesterfield (G Sharp), Rotherham C. (G Sharp), Nottingham F (W Sharp) and, to cap it all, the Green 'Un (April 1918) hinted that Sharpe was not his correct name.

Appearances:		Apps	Gls
	WW1	1	1
	Total	1	1

SHARP William (Billy) Louis

Striker 2004–05, 2007– 5' 8" 12st 2
b. Sheffield 5 February 1986

Rotherham U (schoolboy)
United: (c£15k) from trainee 7 Jul 2004 to 18 Aug 2005
Debuts: 13 Jul 2004 Matlock Town 4 United XI 3 (sub Fr)
13 Nov 2004 United 1 Watford 1 (sub)
Last game: 8 May 2005 Wolverhampton Wanderers 1 United 1 (sub)
Rushden & Diamonds (L) 21 Jan 2005
Scunthorpe United (£100k) Aug 2005
United: (undisclosed) 18 Jul 2007
Debuts: 24 Jul 2007 Longford Town 1 United 0 (Fr scored)
11 Aug 2007 United 2 Colchester United 2

Billy Sharp joined the Rotherham United Academy as a schoolboy but then moved to United who paid a small fee when he made his FL debut. A good finisher, he was a prolific scorer with the youth and reserve sides at Bramall Lane and many wondered why he was not given more opportunities in the first team. He made his FL debut as a substitute with United but his full debut came whilst he was on loan with Rushden & Diamonds on 22 January 2005 at home to Leyton Orient. Despite playing only 16 games he finished as Diamonds' leading scorer and at the end of the season, he was sold by Neil Warnock to Scunthorpe United where Billy hoped he would have more regular first team football, United insisting on 25% of any sell-on fee.

Billy was Scunthorpe's leading scorer in his first season (23) and his tally of 31 the following season helped the club to become League One champions.

To the delight of the vast majority of the Blades' supporters Billy returned to the Lane in the summer of 2007, signed by Bryan Robson for an undisclosed fee. Scoring twice in pre-season games and in the League Cup, it was March before he scored his first League goal but, despite this, he remained a favourite with the crowd. Under Robson, he had played more of a wide role but under his successor, Kevin Blackwell, he was encouraged to get into the penalty area and he finished as United's second leading League goal scorer, albeit with only four goals.

Appearances:		Apps	Gls
	FL	21 (10)	4
	FAC	2 (2)	0
	LC	3	2
	Total	26 (12)	6

SHAW Bernard

LB 1963–69 5' 7½" 11st 10
b. Sheffield 14 March 1945

United: from amat Aug 1961, app 29 Oct 1962 to 14/17 Jul 1969
Debut: 26 Apr 1963 United 2 Leyton Orient 0
Last games: 12 Apr 1969 United 3 Blackburn Rovers 0
9 May 1969 Doncaster Rovers 0 United 0 (CC)
Wolverhampton Wanderers (£15k) Jul 1969/ Sheffield Wednesday (£34.2k) Jun 1973/ Worksop Town Jul 1976/ Baslow cs 1977 to cs 1980

Bernard Shaw, ten years younger than his brother Graham, had been rejected by Sheffield Boys as being too small but he joined United and he and fellow full back, Len Badger (born June 1945), soon gained England youth caps and played for the team which won the 1963 European Championship.

His first team debut came when he replaced his brother Graham at left back for one game towards the end of the 1962–63 season (Badger made his full FL debut in the same game) and during the following season, Bernard played more often than Graham in the left back position. He missed much of the following two campaigns with a heart problem but returned in April 1966 and thereafter, was a regular in the side. In 1968 he won two U23 caps, playing alongside Len Badger for part of one game. He played all but four of his games for United at left back and in three of those he was at right back with Graham as his partner.

United were relegated in 1968 and, after one strained season with Arthur Rowley in Division Two, he was transferred to Wolves. There he was a regular in the side, playing at right back for the second two of his three seasons and helping them to the 1972 UEFA Cup final and to win the Texaco Cup in 1971. He then returned to Sheffield, joining Wednesday, where he played for three seasons missing very few games. He was one of the Owls' more consistent players but after being in the side which beat Southend United to avoid the drop into Division Four, he was given a free transfer. He had played over 100 FL games for each of his three clubs and played a total of 348(8).

He played in non-League football for three seasons before retiring and ran a public house in Baslow for many years and has other business interests in the area.

Appearances:		Apps	Gls
	FL	135 (1)	2
	FAC	10	0
	LC	7	1
	CC	9	0
	Total	161 (1)	3

SHAW Bernard L

OR 1890–91

Hallam, Wednesday and Sheffield FC
United: amateur who assisted United 1890–91
Debuts: 1 Sep 1890 United 9 Sheffield Club 0
13 Sep 1890 Burton Wanderers 1 United 1 (MCL)
4 Oct 1890 Derby Junction 0 United 1 (FAC)
Last games: 17 Jan 1891 United 1 Notts County 9 (FAC)
21 Feb 1891 United 0 Derby Midland 1 (MCL)
21 Mar 1891 Royal Arsenal 1 United 1 (Fr)

Bernard Shaw was one of the leading Sheffield amateur players who assisted and usually captained United when he was available to play during the 1890–91 season. A son of John Shaw, a founder member of the Hallam Club, he had also assisted the Wednesday. As well as his competitive matches, he played 16 friendly games, his appearances being at outside right but for three as wing half and one at outside left.

Business reasons took him to London in 1891 and he made very occasional appearances for Woolwich Arsenal for two seasons.

Appearances:

	Apps	Gls
FAC	5	2
MCL	11	0
SCC	2	2
Total	18	4

SHAW Graham Laurence

LB 1952–67 5' 8" 11st 8
b. Sheffield 9 July 1934
d. Sheffield 12 May 1998

United: from jnr 11 Jul 1951, pro 9 Jul 1951 to Sep 1967
Debut: 5 Jan 1952 Sheffield Wednesday 1 United 3
Last games: 1 Oct 1966 United 4 West Bromwich Albion 3
26 Apr 1967 United XI 3 Sheffield Wednesday 2 (BM)
Doncaster Rovers Sep 1967/ Scarborough player manager Mar 1968 to Jan 1969/ Bradway U (coach)

Graham Shaw was an all-round athlete as a boy, being excellent at cricket, football and boxing (ABA junior champion). While at school, he played football both as a goalkeeper and centre half before moving to left back with Sheffield Boys, the position he played during his United career.

He was invited to train at Bramall Lane by the United coach, Duggie Livingstone and to play for the nursery club, Oaks Fold, quickly moving on to the A team and the reserves when he was sixteen. He signed as a professional on his seventeenth birthday; three days later he had a cartilage operation and soon made a remarkable first team debut, playing in the Sheffield derby at Hillsborough in front of 65,000 fans. Earlier in the season, United had beaten Wednesday 7–3 but by January, the defence was leaking goals. Graham had only played about a dozen games for the reserves but the young, black haired full back, displayed all the calm authority that would always be a feature of his play as United won 3–1.

Graham became a regular first team player early in the following season when United were Division Two champions and continued until September 1955 when National Service with the Royal Signals led to absences from the team which were covered by securing Cliff Mason from Darlington. Graham played in some excellent army teams and for the England U23 side but in September 1956, Joe Mercer, to the distress of the fans, tried to sell him to Stoke City (Graham refused to go), played him at right back and then at outside right. Mercer later apologised for his treatment and Graham became a regular member of the famous defence, along with Hodgkinson, Coldwell, Richardson, Joe Shaw and Summers which served United so well for so long.

Naturally right footed, Graham played at left back displaying rare composure, authority and style. His tackling was perfectly timed, being both swift and accurate and his distribution, both long and short, was made with care. Ten of his goals came from the penalty spot but one of his misses came in the FA Cup semi final second replay against Leicester City. He won five U23 caps and five full caps, the first being against Russia in 1958. He also represented the Football League on four occasions and went on an FA Tour of the Far East, New Zealand and the USA in 1961. In March 1965 he played three times alongside his younger brother Bernard.

He had a brief time with Doncaster Rovers, playing 22 FL games, and then was appointed player-manager of Scarborough though injuries quickly brought his career to an end. He ran a snack bar in the Castle market and was landlord of the Sportsman Inn. He was also chairman of the Future Blades and served as captain and president of the Dore & Totley Golf Club. He died of cancer in the Weston Park Hospital.

Appearances:

	Apps	Gls
FL	439	14
FAC	37	0
LC	9	1
CC	12	0
Total	497	15

SHAW Joseph (Joe)

CH/RH/LH/IF 1945–66 5' 8" 11st 8
b. Murton (Co Durham) 23 June 1928
d. Sheffield 18 November 2007

Upton Colliery
United: amat 30 Mar 1945, 19/20 Jul 1945 to 19 Jan 1967
Debuts: 2 Apr 1945 United 3 Huddersfield Town 1 (WW2)
15 Apr 1946 Sheffield Wednesday 0 United 0 (CC)
30 Aug 1948 United 1 Liverpool 2
Last game: 19 Feb 1966 West Ham United 4 United 0
United coaching staff Apr 1966/ York City mgr Oct 1967 to Aug 1968/ United scout/ Fulham chief scout 1972 / – / Chesterfield mgr Sep 1973 to Oct 1976

Joe Shaw, one of United's greatest players, was a sixteen year old inside forward railway fireman, playing for Upton Colliery when he was spotted by United. Before he had done any training with the club, he received a postcard: 'You are selected to play v Huddersfield Town at Bramall Lane Ground, on Easter Monday next, 2 April 1945. Report at Dressing Room at 2.15 pm'. Joe had an uneventful debut and, after one more first team appearance that season and four the following one, he spent three seasons in the reserves.

Although energetic and full of enthusias, he was not equipped to play at inside forward for his passing and shooting were not First Division quality but he did eventually make his FL debut at the start of the 1948 season. Joe was soon given a game at left half (2 October) but it was in February 1949 in a County Cup match at Hillsborough that it really became apparent that he was a better half back than a forward; his anticipation and swift and decisive tackling winning him a permanent first team place.

He was an ever present in the 1952–53 Second Division Championship season and took over the captaincy in 1954 for three seasons and it was in August 1954 that Reg Freeman began to play him regularly at centre half and eventually, this would become his best position. He had played there earlier when United's centre half was injured and he used to the full, his tackling skills and exceptional ability to anticipate the opposition's moves though, in those early days, he was not always successful in dealing with some of the big and burly centre forwards.

When Joe Mercer became manager in 1955, Joe was never sure of his place, Mercer preferring a more robust centre half, firstly Howard Johnson and then the unfortunate signing of Malcolm Barrass. Mercer eventually acknowledged his mistake, restoring Joe to centre half in January 1957 and putting together and coaching as a unit the memorable defence of Hodgkinson, Coldwell and Graham Shaw, Richardson, Joe Shaw and Summers which played together from September 1957 until August 1963.

Between 1957–58 and 1963–64, Joe missed just 13 out of a possible 252 FL games. The tall opponent was no longer a problem; he was left unbalanced, on the wrong foot and looking rather foolish as Joe strode away with the ball. When he had played his final game, Joe had made 632 FL appearances for the Blades; 56 more than any other United player and only Alan Hodgkinson has played more FA Cup games. Many thought Joe should have been capped for England but his only representative honours were two appearances for the Football League and an FA Tour to Australia in 1952. However those who saw him at his best could not fail to be delighted by his play. One former manager described him as 'the greatest game reader I have ever seen. He seems to know what's going to happen to the ball as soon as it leaves the opposition's penalty area'.

After his retirement from playing, he coached United's youngsters and was the reserve team trainer (cs 1967) before becoming York City's manager. He resigned in 1968 but became the manager at Chesterfield in 1973.

Appearances:		Apps	Gls
	FL	632	7
	FAC	51	0
	LC	7	0
	CC	21	1
	WW2	2	0
	Total	713	8

SHAW Paul

Striker 2004–05 5' 11" 12st 4
b. Burnham 4 September 1973

Arsenal from trainee Sep 1991/ Burnley (L) Mar 1995 Cardiff City (L) Aug 1995/ Peterborough United (L) Oct 1995 Millwall (£250k) Sep 1997/ Gillingham (£450k) Jul 2000
United: (£75k) 12 Jan 2004 to 20 Jan 2006
Debuts: 17 Jan 2004 United 3 West Ham United 3 (sub)
28 Jan 2004 Derby County 2 United 0
Last games: 26 Feb 2005 United 1 Rotherham United 0
20 Aug 2005 United 2 Preston North End 1 (sub)
23 Aug 2005 United 1 Boston United 0 (LC)
Rotherham United (L) 6 Aug 2004
Rotherham United (free) Jan 2006/ Chesterfield Jun 2006 to Aug 2007/ Oxford U (nc) Sep 2007 to Oct 2007/ Ferencvaros (Hungary) Oct 2007

Paul Shaw made his League debut, as a substitute in the Premiership, with Arsenal on 3 December 1994 at Nottingham Forest; his full debut coming while he was on loan at Burnley when he scored at home to Port Vale on 28 March 1995. After two further loan spells, he joined Millwall and then Gillingham where he played regularly.

His move to the Lane was not successful though many felt that, despite scoring on his debut, he was not really given a chance, making just four starts in his first half season with United. A thoughtful player with a good shot, he was better playing behind the front players but the following season he was used more as a striker. Described by his manager as 'a poor man's Dennis Bergkamp', Neil Warnock never solved the problem as to whether he was worth a regular place and where to play him.

In 2004–05 he spent a time on loan with Rotherham and in January 2006 he made a permanent move to Millmoor helping the Millers to avoid relegation but he was unable to do the same at Chesterfield the following season. He had totalled 300(74) League appearances scoring 81 goals. After a brief spell with Oxford, he moved, on an 18 month contract, to Ferencvaros, the club with which United have a close association.

Appearances:		Apps	Gls
	FL	20 (15)	8
	FAC	1 (1)	0
	LC	1 (2)	0
	Total	22 (17)	8

SHAW Richard (Dick)

CF 1917 5' 9" 11st 6
b. Kilnhurst?

Highthorne and amat United 1914–1915 Mexborough (from 1915–16)
United: amat 1914–1915 and 1916–1917
Debut: 13 Jan 1917 United 1 Huddersfield Town 0 (WW1)
Last game: 7 Apr 1917 United 2 Barnsley 0 (WW1)
Mexborough 1919/ Rotherham County c1920/ Wath A cs 1922/ Denaby cs 1923/ Wombwell cs 1924/ Wath A cs 1926/ Mexborough A Aug 1927

Dick Shaw was an amateur on United's books and played for the reserves in the 1914–15 season. When war-time football started, he played for Highthorne and Mexborough but assisted the United reserves in November 1916 and made four appearances for the first team during the early part of 1917, scoring on his debut and also hitting the woodwork twice. He continued playing for Mexborough with at least one appearance for Rotherham County (1917–18) and he later played in the FL with Rotherham County, making his debut on 4 September 1920 at Coventry City and going on to make 29 FL appearances in his two seasons there.

Appearances:		Apps	Gls
	WW1	4	2
	Total	4	2

SHEARMAN Benjamin (Ben) W

OL 1915–18 5' 9½" 10st 12
b. Lincoln 2 December 1884
d. October 1958

Attercliffe 1899/ High Hazels 1900/ Worksop T Rotherham Town Aug? 1905/ Bristol City Apr 1909 West Bromwich Albion (£100) Jun 1911
United: WW1 guest: Sep 1915 to cs 1918
Debut: 4 Sep 1915 Lincoln City 7 United 3 (WW1)
Last games: 6 Apr 1918 Barnsley 1 United 1 (WW1)
4 May 1918 United 2 Everton 2 (Fr)
WW1 guest: Rotherham C (Xmas 1918)
Nottingham Forest (£2,500) Jun 1919/ Gainsborough Trinity Jun 1920 to c 1924/ Norton Woodseats player and coach to May 1938

Ben Shearman played for Sheffield Schools and came to the fore with Rotherham Town*. A speedy and elusive left winger, he could deliver accurate crosses. He made his FL debut with Bristol City on 4 September 1909 at Bradford City and after two seasons he moved to West Bromwich Albion and gained a FA Cup losers' medal in 1912 when Albion lost to Barnsley in the replay at Bramall Lane.

He returned to Sheffield to work at Tinsley during the First World War and played regularly as a guest for United for three seasons before joining the army. Only five players played more times for the club during the First War.

Despite missing four seasons of League football due to the War, Ben ended his career with 217 FL appearances. He spent many years as a part time player with Norton Woodseats and was their trainer and coach when they reached the Amateur Cup semi-final in 1938.

* Rotherham County had a player called 'Sherman' from c1904–08 and he and Shearman both played for Town 1908–09.

Appearances:		Apps	Gls
	WW1	75	12
	Total	75	12

SHEEN John (Jock)

LH/CF 1938–46 5' 9½" 10st 10
b. Baillieston (Airdrie) 30 August 1920
d. Sheffield 5 July 1997

Baillieston Juniors
United: am 24 May 1937, pro 31 Aug/ Sep 1937 to 4 May 1946
Debuts: 5 May 1938 Boston United 1 United XI 2 (Fr)
16 Sep 1939 Chesterfield 2 United 0 (WW2)
Last game: 15 Apr 1946 Sheffield Wednesday 1 United 0 (CC)
WW2 guest: Bradford (PA) 1939–40/ Linfield 1940–42/ Queens Park Rangers 1943–44/ Bath C 1944/ Lovell's Ath 1945/ Scunthorpe U/ Notts C 1945–46
Hull City (£250) Jul 1946/ Kettering Town Oct 1946, player-mgr Mar 1947/ Shrewsbury Town Jul 1947–cs 1949/ Worksop T Aug 1949 trainer-coach to 1952–53

Jock Sheen joined the ground staff as a sixteen year old and played in the final A team game of the 1936–37 season. A stocky, powerfully built centre forward with a good left foot, he used the ball well but was a bit short of speed. He made no peace time competitive appearances for United but played occasionally in the war-time season 1939–40 at centre forward.

He had joined the RAF in 1940 and played for Linfield where he won the Irish Cup and two League Championships before returning to United for a few months in December 1942. By now, he usually played a sound game at left half but his lack of pace held him back from playing at the top level.

Transfer listed in November 1945, he joined Hull City in the close season and was made captain, leading the team out for their first FL match at Boothferry Park on his FL debut on 31 August 1946 at home to Lincoln City but after just five appearances and unhappy with the manager's 'monkey gland treatment', he moved into non-League football.

Appearances:		Apps	Gls
	CC	2	0
	WW2	45	7
	Total	47	7

SHELTON Luton

Striker 2007–08 5' 11" 11st 11
b. Jamaica 11 November 1985

Harbour View (Jamaica) Jul 2005/ Burnley trial Jul 2006/ Helsingborgs (c£100k) (Sweden) Aug 2006
United: (£1.85/2m) 25 Jan 2007 to 24 Jul 2008
Debuts: 31 Mar 2007 Bolton Wanderers 1 United 0 (sub)
17 Apr 2007 Manchester United 2 United 0
Last games: 12 Feb 2008 West Bromwich Albion 0 United 0
4 May 2008 Southampton 3 United 2 (sub)
Valerenga (Norway) Jul 2008 (£1m minimum + sell on)

Jamaican international Luton Shelton was signed by Neil Warnock, mainly as a future prospect but also to add the option of speed in attack. During the summer of 2005 he had a pre-season trial with Burnley but was unable to obtain a work permit and was signed by the Swedish club Helsingborgs. There he played alongside Henrik Larsson and scored nine goals in 14(5) appearances.

Luton impressed on his full United debut at Old Trafford, where he had space to attack, but often disappointed in his other appearances. Lacking a good first touch and with uncertain ball control, his speed caused defences problems. Despite being in and out of the side during 2007–08 he scored an impressive goal at Colchester and an unusual one against Manchester City when the ball deflected off a balloon. A regular member of the Jamaican squad, he also played for the FIFA XI against a China/ Hong Kong side in July 2007.

Appearances:		Apps	Gls
	FL	7 (12)	1
	FAC	2 (1)	1
	LC	1 (2)	2
	Total	10 (15)	4

SHEPHARD George

LB/RB 1943–45 5' 7½" 11st 8
b. Denaby

Denaby amateurs
United: 7/9 Sep 1943 to 4 May 1946
Debut: 11 Sep 1943 Halifax Town 2 United 2 (WW2)
Last game: 25 Aug 1945 Newcastle United 6 United 0 (WW2)
WW2 guest: Hull City Oct 1944 (1)
Gainsborough Tr cs 1946/ Scarborough (1946–47–)/ Grantham T?

Short and stocky, George Shephard played a few games at right back near the start of the 1943–44 season and more frequently and at left back during following campaign. His younger brother Roy was on United's books 1949–51.

Appearances:

	Apps	Gls
CC	2	0
WW2	23	0
Total	25	0

SHEPHERD Harry

RH 1945

(amat) Rotherham United cs 1943–cs 1945
United: WW2 guest: May 1945
Only game: 9 May 1945 United 2 Wednesday 0 (WW2)
Hull C 1946–47/ Goole T cs 1947/ Selby T (1949–50)

A Rotherham United's reserve amateur half back during the war, Harry Shepherd made no senior appearances for the club but he made one guest appearance for the Blades in a match arranged to celebrate the end of the war in Europe. He became a professional with Hull City but his only first team appearance came in a friendly match.

Appearances:

	Apps	Gls
WW2	1	0
Total	1	0

SHIELS Dennis Patrick

CF/OR 1958–64 5' 8" 11st 10
b. Belfast 24 August 1938

Distillery
United: 24 Oct/1 Nov 1958 to 20 Jul 1964
Debut: 1 Nov 1958 Fulham 4 United 2
Last games: 14 Dec 1963 United 1 Blackpool 0
28 Jan 1964 Swansea Town 4 United 0 (FAC)
Peterborough United Jul 1964/ Notts County Jul 1965/ Retford Jul 1966/ Sligo Rovers Feb 1967

A schoolboy international and Ulster Cup winner with Distillery in 1958, Dennis Shiels moved to the Lane, along with Harry Orr, for a combined fee of £9,000 and an expenses paid game. He signed on condition that he could continue his studies as an accountant and played mainly at outside right or centre forward although he did play in all forward positions at some time. Although he was at the Lane for six seasons, he was never more than a good reserve forward who offered plenty of entertainment for those who watched the reserves. It was only in 1959–60 that he played a significant number of first team games (18 app, 5 gl) and gained two Northern Ireland B caps.

He left United for Peterborough with Orr for a much reduced fee of £5,000 but, after one season, he joined Notts County, initially playing alongside Derek Pace. He became County's first substitute, coming off the bench against Lincoln City on 5 February 1966 and ended his FL career with 72(1) appearances and 18 goals.

Appearances:

	Apps	Gls
FL	32	8
FAC	1	0
CC	2	2
Total	35	10

SHIMWELL Edmund (Eddie)

LB/RB 1940–46 5' 11½" 12st 5
b. Birchover, Matlock. 27 February 1920
d. Blackpool 3 October 1988

Birchover
United: amat 26 Apr 1938, pro 7/10 Jan 1939 to 20 Dec 1946
Debuts: 28 Dec 1940 United 0 Rotherham United 2 (WW2, at Millmoor)
1 Sep 1945 United 3 Newcastle U 0 (LN)
26 Jan 1946 Stoke City 2 United 0 (FAC)
31 Aug 1946 United 0 Liverpool 1
Last game: 30 Nov 1946 Aston Villa 2 United 3
WW2 guest: York C 1942–43 (1 app)/ Lincoln 1943–44 (1 app)/ Southampton 1943–44 (15 app)
Blackpool (£7,500) Dec 1946/ Oldham Athletic May 1957/ Burton Albion Jul 1958, retired Dec 1958

Eddie Shimwell signed for United before the Second World War began but apart from one game in 1940, played at Millmoor because of the German blitz attack on Bramall Lane, his war-time appearances were limited to the 1945–46 season. He had served in the Royal Engineers and returned to the Lane in the summer of 1945 and was able to play a significant part in the 1945–46 FLN Championship success.

A strong, two footed player with the confidence to dwell on the ball and distribute it with care, his kicking was powerful and accurate and he used his weight to good effect in shoulder charging and when using the sliding tackle.

He began the first post-war season (1946–47) playing well and was chosen as the reserve when England played Ireland in 1946 but after just 14 games, to the astonishment of the supporters, Eddie was sold to Blackpool. He had broken his contract by seeking to take over the license of the Plough Inn at Two Dales, near Matlock, from his mother-in-law. The directors may have seen the decision as a matter of principle but they had made a major error in selling him.

He spent more than ten seasons with Blackpool, appearing in three FA Cup finals and gaining one England cap in 1949. He scored from the penalty spot in the 1948 final, which Manchester United won, but he gained a winners' medal in the 1953 'Matthews' final. A dislocated shoulder caused problems in his final three seasons at Bloomfield Road and he played little first team football.

His free transfer to Oldham was not a success and he played only seven games, bringing his career total to 307 and after a brief spell with Burton Albion, he became a licensee in Clay Cross and then in Matlock.

Appearances:

	Apps	Gls
FL	14	0
FAC	2	0
WW2	35	1
Total	51	1

SHIPPERLEY Neil Jason (Shipps)

Striker 2005–06 6' 1" 13st 12
b. Chatham 30 October 1974

Chelsea from trainee Sep 1992/ Watford (L) Dec 1994 Southampton (£1.25m) Jan 1995/ Crystal Palace (£1m) Oct 1996/ Nottingham Forest (£1.5m) Sep 1998 Barnsley (£700k) Jul 1999/ Wimbledon (£750k) Jul 2001 Crystal Palace Jul 2003

United: (undisclosed fee) 20 Jul/ 3 Aug 2005 to 15 Jan 2007
Debuts: 26 Jul 2005 Matlock T 1 United XI 2 (sub, Fr)
30 Jul 2005 United 1 Sunderland 0 (sub Fr)
6 Aug 2005 United 4 Leicester City 1 (sub)
9 Aug 2005 Burnley 1 United 2
Last game: 30 Apr 2006 United 1 Crystal Palace 0
Brentford 23 Jan 2007 to cs

The son of a former Plymouth, Gillingham, Charlton and Reading defender, Neil Shipperley made his League debut with Chelsea as a substitute on 10 April 1993 at Southampton, his full debut coming two days later when he scored at home to Wimbledon. He gained seven England U21 caps and went on to play for a variety of clubs, many in the Premiership and when he hung up his boots, he had made 394(52) League appearances scoring 120 goals.

'Shipps' was not the fastest nor the most mobile of players and when he arrived at the Lane, he had been written off by his many critics on numerous occasions but he was a good front man with a powerful shot, was cool in front of goal and had a good goal scoring record.

Signed by Neil Warnock at the start of the 2005–06 season, he was expected to play a supporting role but he was involved in 39 of the 46 League games. He was used as a target man, playing alongside Danny Webber, Steven Kabba or Ade Akinbiyi and was a key figure in United's promotion to the Premiership, scoring on his League debut and finishing as top scorer with 11 goals.

The following season Neil was troubled by injuries and was unable to make an appearance for United in the Premiership. He was allowed to leave in January and played for Brentford until the end of the season but announced his retirement in April 2007.

Appearances:		Apps	Gls
	FL	34 (5)	11
	Total	34 (5)	11

SHIRTLIFF Norman

CF 1941

United: amat 1 Apr 1941 to cs
Only game: 24 May 1941 Everton 3 United 3 (WW2)

An unknown amateur player, Norman Shirtliff made one wartime appearance for United in the game at Everton, played to the accompanying noise of a German air-raid, when Fred Furniss made his debut.

Appearances:		Apps	Gls
	WW2	1	0
	Total	1	0

SHORT Christian (Chris) Mark

RWB 1996–98 5' 10" 12st 2
b. Munster (West Germany) 9 May 1970

Pickering Town/ Scarborough Jul 1988/ Notts County (£100k) Sep 1990/ Huddersfield Town (L) Dec 1994

United: (player exch + £25k) 29 Dec 1995 to 20 Jun, 1/2 Jul 1998
Debuts: 6 Jan 1996 Arsenal 1 United 1 (FAC)
13 Jan 1996 Tranmere Rovers 1 United 1
Last game: 3 May 1998 Stockport County 1 United 0
Stoke City (free) Jul 1998 to cs 2000
United: Sep/Oct 2000 (nc)
Scarborough Jul 2001/ Hinckley United Oct 2001

Chris Short made his FL debut with Scarborough on 29 Apr 1989 at Wrexham, alongside his established brother Craig, who also later played for United. When Chris moved to the Lane, he was one of Howard Kendall's early signings in an exchange deal for Paul Rogers and £25k. Chris was initially a regular but was in an out of the side during the following season due to injuries. Very fast, he tackled well and, playing as a right wing back, he was impressive coming forward, producing searching crosses. He missed much of season 1997–98 through injury and in the summer he joined Stoke City.

Again he had problems with injuries but more seriously for a man who had been a great athlete, he found he had an unusual illness (intestinal fungal infection) which threatened to end his playing career.

He returned to the Lane in September 2000 to train and played twice with the reserves before it was reported that his League career was over after having played 198(24) League games.

He had a trial period in non-League football and then trained as a physiotherapist and worked with Blackburn as a fitness coach before returning to Bramall Lane as a physio in 2006. It was in that year that he successfully rowed across the English Channel, raising money for charity, despite bad weather cutting short his first attempt. In the autumn of 2007 he moved to Derby County.

Appearances:		Apps	Gls
	FL	40 (4)	0
	PO	1 (1)	0
	FAC	7	0
	LC	3 (1)	0
	Total	51 (6)	0

SHORT Craig Jonathan

CD 2005–06 6' 3" 14st 6
b. Bridlington 25 June 1968

Pickering Town/ Scarborough Oct 1987/ Notts County (£100k) Jul 1989/ Derby County (£2.5m) Sep 1992 Everton (£2.4m) Jul 1995/ Blackburn Rovers (£1.7m) Aug 1999

United: 29 Jun/1 Aug 2005 to cs 2007
Debuts: 11 Jul 2005 Worksop Town 0 United 1 (Fr)
30 Jul 2005 United 1 Sunderland 0 (sub, Fr)
13 Aug 2005 Queens Park Rangers 2 United 1 (sub)
20 Aug 2005 United 2 Preston North End 1
Last games: 30 Apr 2006 United 1 Crystal Palace 0
24 Oct 2006 United 2 Birmingham City 4 (LC)
Retired cs 2007

Craig Short lived in Germany, where both his parents were teachers, until he was ten. An England schoolboy international, he began his professional career with Scarborough, making his FL debut, as a substitute, on 21 October 1987 at Hereford United. His full debut came at Swansea City on 16 January 1988. During the following season his brother Chris, who later played for United, made his debut alongside Craig. His manager at the time was Neil Warnock, under whom Craig and Chris played at Notts County and United and it was Neil who had switched him from midfield to centre half. Having left Scarborough, Craig had a long and distinguished career making over 100 League appearances for three of his clubs and 90(9) for Everton, gaining a League Cup winners' medal whilst at Blackburn.

In June 2005, he joined Neil Warnock for the third time to add experience to the back four. Injuries meant he was in and out of the side but, although lacking pace, he was a 'born leader' who used his physical presence, calm authority and anticipation to advantage, particularly in the final nine games, as United were promoted to the Premiership.

Craig had earlier announced his retirement but he was persuaded to stay for a further year. He played in just two League Cup games but his professional attitude and experience were valuable in the dressing room. He then retired, having made 548(17) League appearances, scoring 31 goals, to concentrate on his sailing school in the Lake District.

Appearances:		Apps	Gls
	FL	20 (3)	1
	LC	2	0
	Total	22 (3)	1

SIMMONS James (Jimmy) William

IR/OR/IL 1909–20 5' 7" 10st 11
b. Blackwell JAS 1889 (registered Mansfield as 'Simmonds')

Blackwell
United: 18/19 Nov 1908 to c8 May 1920
Debut: 10 Apr 1909 United 2 Middlesbrough 0
Last game: 24 Apr 1920 Bolton Wanderers 1 United 0
West Ham United (£1,000–£1,400) cs 1920 to 1922

United made a donation of £50 to the Blackwell club when they signed Jimmy Simmons. A nephew of Bill Foulke and from the same village, he filled a variety of roles during his time at Bramall Lane. He began at inside right and scored on his debut but was just as happy at inside left. He later played on the right wing but he preferred to play at inside right.

He was a quick, clever and elusive player, described as a 'will o' the wisp' and a prolific goal scorer. He had a big heart but was prone to

injuries and he was injured in the first few minutes of the 1914 FA Cup semi final which United drew and wasn't able to play in the re-play. In 1915, he and Joe Kitchen both played on the right wing but as United made progress in the Cup, a decision was finally made to play Simmons on the wing and Kitchen at centre forward. Jimmy may not have been happy with the decision but he scored the first goal in the semi-final and was outstanding in the Cup Final at Old Trafford and scored the first of United's three goals.

During the First War, he initially worked at Blackwell Colliery and was able to play for United, filling all five forward positions at some time or other. In September 1916 he made one guest appearance for Blackpool while on honeymoon and in 1918, he joined the services as an Air Mechanic but returned in 1919 when League football resumed. He still showed much of his old brilliance but spent much of the season injured and United were happy to receive a transfer fee from West Ham United. After two seasons (27 FL app, 1 gl), injury forced his retirement and he returned north, eventually becoming a licensee in Matlock.

Appearances:		Apps	Gls
	FL	204	43
	FAC	18	6
	WW1	78	18
	ABD	1	0
	Total	301	67

SIMONS Henry Thomas (Tommy)

CF/IR 1910–12 5' 9" 12st 4
b. Hackney OND 1887
d Stoke Newington 26 August 1956

Peel Institute/ Clapton Orient Mar 1906/ Leyton c Sep 1906 Tufnell Park 1907/ Leyton pro May 1908/ Doncaster R Nov 1909
United: (exchange) 7 Jul 1910 to cs 1912
Debuts: 3 Oct 1910 Wednesday 2 United 0 (CM)
8 Oct 1910 Manchester City 0 United 4
Last games: 6 Jan 1912 Bolton Wanderers 0 United 3
13 Jan 1912 Chelsea 1 United 0 (FAC)
Halifax Town Aug 1912/ Merthyr Town (£25 to United) Nov 1912/ Brentford Aug 1913/ Fulham Apr 1914/ Queens Park Rangers Nov 1914 to 1917/ WW1 guest: Tottenham Hotspur 1918 (3)/ Norwich City Sep 1920/ Margate Nov 1920

Tommy Simons was a much respected London amateur player who made his FL debut with Clapton (now Leyton) Orient on 24 March 1906 at Gainsborough Trinity. He became a professional with Leyton and moved north to join Doncaster Rovers.

He joined United soon after in an exchange deal for Billy Bromage and spent two seasons with United but, despite scoring on his FL debut and on his final appearance, he was never more than a useful reserve.

He played most of his career in the Southern League but made 28 FL appearances, scoring 7 goals, for Clapton Orient, United, Fulham and Norwich (who were under the impression he was aged 28, not 33, when they signed him).

Appearances:		Apps	Gls
	FL	9	2
	FAC	1	0
	Total	10	2

SIMPSON George Robert

LB/RB 1897–1900
b. Chesterfield AMJ 1876
d. Chesterfield 29 August 1955

Sheepbridge
United: Aug/14 Sep 1897 to Oct 1900
Debuts: 27 Nov 1897 Corinthians 2 United 0 (Fr)
29 Jan 1898 United 1 Burslem PV 1 (FAC)
3 Sep 1898 United 1 Everton 1
Last games: 14 Apr 1900 Stoke 1 United 1
19 Apr 1900 Aberdare 2 United 1 (Fr)
Doncaster Rovers Oct 1900/ Chesterfield cs 1903/ Rotherham Town cs 1904

George Simpson, a cousin of Ernest Needham, made only twelve competitive first team appearances for United and seven in friendlies during his more than three seasons at the Lane but he was a valuable reserve player, happy to play in both full back positions. Employed by the Midland Railway, he may have been an amateur with United until early in 1898 when he became a part-timer on £1 per week. His first competitive appearances were in the two humbling FA Cup ties against Burslem Port Vale but he occasionally played after a Cup-tie so that Harry Thickett could be rested.

He was transferred to Doncaster Rovers in 1900 who were members of the Midland League and had the honour in 1901 of captaining them when they played their first FL game. Rovers took over the fixtures of New Brighton Tower at the last minute and paid United £15 for Simpson's registration. George went on to play FL games for Chesterfield, making a career total of 95 appearances, before moving to Midland League Rotherham Town.

Appearances:		Apps	Gls
	FL	10	0
	FAC	2	0
	Total	12	0

SIMPSON Paul David

MF 1996 5' 7" 11st 11
b. Carlisle 26 July 1966

Manchester City from app Aug 1983/ Oxford United (£200k) Oct 1988/ Derby County (£500k) Feb 1992
United: (L) 2 Dec 1996 to 2 Jan 1997
Debut: 7 Dec 1996 United 1 Portsmouth 0
Last games: 14 Dec 1996 Oxford United 4 United 1
28 Dec 1996 United 2 Oldham Athletic 2 (sub)
Wolverhampton Wanderers (£75k) Oct 1997/ Walsall (L) Sep 1998, Dec 1998/ Blackpool (free) Aug 2000/ Rochdale (free) Mar 2002, mgr May 2002 to May 2003/ Carlisle Aug 2003, player-mgr Dec 2003, mgr May 2006/ Preston North End mgr Jun 2006 to Nov 2007/ Shrewsbury T mgr Mar 2008

Paul Simpson's long career as a player began with Manchester City where he made his FL debut as a substitute at Bramall Lane on 17 November 1984. His full debut and first goal came on 30 March 1985 at home to Cardiff City. With a superb left foot, Paul played well over 100 League games for his first two clubs and nearly 200 games for Derby County, ending his playing career with 550(121) League appearances as well as gaining five U21 England caps to add to those gained at youth level.

He joined United on a one month loan, signed by Howard Kendall and made two starts and four sub appearances but only played well in the last game. Later he took on managerial responsibilities and was in charge of Carlisle when the club were relegated to the Conference. They regained their FL status the following season and were promoted the next. He has continued his managerial career with other clubs.

Paul's uncle, Ron Simpson, played for United 1958–64.

Appearances:		Apps	Gls
	FL	2 (4)	0
	Total	2 (4)	0

SIMPSON Ronald (Ronnie)

OL/IL 1958–64 5' 9" 10st 9
b. Carlisle 25 February 1934

Holme Head Works/ Huddersfield Town 1950, pro Feb 1951
United: (£6,000 + player) 29/30 May 1958 to 9 Dec 1964
Debut: 23 Aug 1958 Charlton Athletic 1 United 1
Last game: 26 Aug 1964 United 0 Stoke City 1
Carlisle United (£4,950) 11 Dec 1964/ Queen of the South 1966

Ronnie Simpson went to Huddersfield with a friend (who had been invited for a trial) to keep him company but was offered a game and a place on the ground staff. Ronnie had played for Carlisle and Cumberland Boys and made his FL debut on 20 October 1951 at Bolton Wanderers but he did not become a regular member of the first team until February 1956.

Joe Mercer, the United manager, tried to sign him in 1957 but Bill Shankly, the Town boss, wanted £20k and refused a bid of £10k but, six months later, agreed to an exchange deal for Derek Hawksworth and £6000. Ronnie began his time with United at inside left, the position he had usually played at Huddersfield, but he soon moved to outside left, the position he grew to prefer. He had pace and a strong left foot and provided well struck centres, taken at full stride on the run and Derek Pace in particular, turned many of these into goals. Ronnie was an important member of the promotion side of 1961 which also reached the FA Cup semi final. He might perhaps have been an even better player had he been more forceful but he did score one of United's quickest goals, finding the net with his right foot after about 8 seconds against Burnley in October 1963.

After six seasons with United and having lost his place to Barry Hartle, he joined Carlisle, helping them to become Division Three champions in 1965. Having made 359 FL appearances, scoring 74 goals he had a spell with Queen of the South before working for Pearl Insurance and in the family retail business. His nephew, Paul Simpson, later played for the Blades.

Appearances:

	Apps	Gls
FL	203	44
FAC	26	2
LC	7	1
CC	3	0
Total	239	47

SLOAN Joseph (or Joshia/Josiah?) (Paddy) Walter

IR/RH 1948 5' 9" 11st 6
b. Lurgan 30 April 1920
d. Victoria (Australia) 7 January 1993

Glenavon/ Manchester United (£200) Sep 1937 Tranmere Rovers May 1939 WW2 guest: Man U (3 app) May 1944 and May 1945/ Fulham 1944–45 Brentford 1945–46/ Arsenal May 1946
United: (£6,000) 23/26 Feb 1948 to 19 Aug 1948
Debut: 28 Feb 1948 Sunderland 1 United 1
Last games: 1 May 1948 United 2 Manchester City 1
17 May 1948 Sheffield Wednesday 2 United 2
(played Isle of Man, Fr)
Milan (£7,000) Aug 1948/ Turin Aug 1949/ Udinese Aug 1950/ Brescia Aug 195/ Cardiff C trial Sep 1951/ Norwich C (£4,000) Dec 1951/ Peterborough United 1952/ Malta 1953, Rabat Ajax FC (Malta) player-coach Jul 1954/ Bath City Jul 1955/ Hastings United player-coach Sep 1955/ Lockheed Leamington Spa player-mgr Jan 1956/ Bath City player coach Aug 1956/ Woodford Town coach 1962

Spotted by Arsenal when he was 15, his mother refused to let him leave home. He began his career in England with Manchester United junior teams before moving to Tranmere Rovers in May 1939 but the following seven seasons were essentially lost due to the Second War, although he did play in the three FL games at the start of the 1939–40 season, games which were later discounted in players' records. Serving in the RAF during the War, he was in Canada (1941–1943) but played 22 games for Rovers and in two Wartime Victory Internationals for Ireland.

He eventually made his FL debut after his move to Arsenal, on 31 August 1946 at Wolverhampton. Whilst at Highbury he won two caps for Northern Ireland and one for the Republic of Ireland. After 18 months and 33 appearances, he moved to the Lane with Alex Forbes joining Arsenal.

Paddy was a player with an eye for space and the shrewd pass, better at wing half, where he had more time, than inside forward but he wouldn't live in Sheffield and Tom Whittaker, the Arsenal manager, helped negotiate his transfer to Milan at the end of the season, but not before he had scored in his final FL appearance and against Wednesday in a friendly.

Paddy spent over three seasons in Italy before returning to England, spending a brief time with Norwich (6 FL app) and Peterborough and three years in Malta before playing, coaching and managing in non-League football. Eventually he moved to Australia where he coached and became a sports teacher. He died in Australia after suffering a series of strokes.

Appearances:

	Apps	Gls
FL	12	2
CC	1	0
Total	13	2

SMEETS Axel

MF 1999 5' 10" 12st 1
b. Karawa (Congo) 12 July 1974

Bosvoorde/ RSC Anderlecht/ Standard Liege (Belgium) 1993–94/ AA Ghent (Belgium) 1994–97 Salamanca (Spain) 1997–98/ KV Kortrijk (Belgium) 1998–99
United: (free) 12 Jul 1999 to cs 2000
Debuts: 16 Jul 1999 Doncaster Rovers 0 United 1 (Fr)
7 Aug 1999 Portsmouth 2 United 0
Last games: 14 Aug 1999 United 1 Walsall 1
14 Sep 1999 United 2 Preston North End 0 (LC)
6 Nov 1999 Barnsley 2 United 0 (sub)
12 Dec 1999 United 1 Rushden & Diamonds 1 (sub FAC)
Lierse SK (Belgium) 2000–03/ Ankaragüçü (Turkey) 2003–04/ Torino Jan 2004 ?/ Ham Kam (Norway) 2004 to at least Dec 2005

Belgian U21 international Axel Smeets was one of new manager Adrian Heath's first signings. He was sent off for two yellow cards on his FL debut playing as an attacking right sided midfielder. He found the transition to English football difficult and after playing in the first three games, his only other start was in the League Cup.

After Neil Warnock's arrival Axel made just one substitute appearance in the FA Cup and in the summer of 2000 was released but continued to play in various countries.

Appearances:

	Apps	Gls
FL	2 (3)	0
FAC	0 (1)	0
LC	2	0
Total	4 (4)	0

SMITH A or J

CH/LB 1918

Wycliffe BC
United: WW1 guest Mar to Apr 1918
Debut: 30 Mar 1918 United 2 Barnsley 3 (WW1)
Last game: 27 Apr 1918 Everton 1 United 1 (Fr)
Silverwood Colliery Aug 1919

'A Smith' in the FL records but 'J Smith' in the United programme, a 'Hillsborough youth', made two guest appearances for United during the First War, the second being in a friendly fixture.

Appearances:

	Apps	Gls
WW1	1	0
Total	1	0

SMITH Andrew (Andy) William

Striker 2000–01 5' 11" 11st 10
b. Lisburn 25 September 1980

Ballyclare Comrades
United: 8/11 Sep 1999 to 19/ 20 Feb 2002
Debuts: 18 Jul 2000 Tideswell 0 United 8 (sub Fr)
5 Sep 2000 Lincoln City 1 United 0 (sub LC)
9 Sep 2000 Birmingham City 1 United 0 (sub)
Last games: 11 Nov 2001 Burnley 2 United 0 (sub)
17 Jul 2001 Sheffield FC 0 United 7 (sub Fr)
Bury (L) 30 Nov 2000/ Glenavon (L) 22 Nov 2001
Glentoran (free) Feb 2002/ Preston North End (£130k to £150k) Sep 2004/ Stockport County (L) Nov 2004/ Motherwell (L) Aug 2005/ Cheltenham Town (L) Nov 2006/ Bristol City (free) Feb to May 2007

Andy Smith was signed, after a trial against Scarborough Reserves (8 Sep), by Adrian Heath during his short reign as manager but had to wait a year to make a first team appearance. Although a regular with the reserves and producing promising performances, all his senior appearances, including eight friendlies, were as a substitute and all but one during season 2000–01. His 6 appearances as a sub in League games without a start and 10 such appearances in all competitive games are both records for United. He made his full FL debut whilst on loan at Bury on 2 December 2000 at Bristol City and the following season he had a spell on loan with Glenavon before signing for Glentoran.

In 2003 he was capped by Northern Ireland and then moved to Preston. He failed to become a regular at Deepdale and had several spells on loan before a move to Bristol City. By the end of 2006–07, he had 18 caps and made 14(28) FL appearances but had failed to score.

Appearances:		Apps	Gls
	FL	0 (6)	0
	LC	0 (4)	0
	Total	0 (10)	0

SMITH Brian

MF/RB/LB 1984–89 5' 9" 11st 2
b. Sheffield 27 October 1966

United: from YTS Jun 1983, app Oct 1984 to Mar 1992
Debuts: 2 May 1984 Hull City 1 United 0 (AMC)
24 Nov 1984 Shrewsbury Town 3 United 3
Last game: 8 Apr 1989 United 3 Preston North End 1
Scunthorpe United (L) Mar 1987
Retired

Brian Smith, whose brother Paul also played for the Blades, played in a variety of positions for United, starting at left back, then moving to midfield and right back. He used his pace well and had good powers of recovery. The brothers first played together in the FL in April 1985 and Brian had established himself in the first team during season 1988–89 when United were promoted to Division Two. Sadly, just before the end of the season he broke his leg and the injury (three breaks, a stress fracture when he recommenced training and further infection complications) forced his retirement.

He did play once more at the Lane on 4 May 1992. A benefit match was held and Brian played in goal for the ex-Blades Select XI against a United side. During his brief loan spell with Scunthorpe (6 FL app) Brain scored the only FL goal of his career.

Appearances:		Apps	Gls
	FL	81 (3)	0
	FAC	9 (1)	0
	LC	6 (1)	0
	FMC	2	0
	AMC	2	0
	YHC	3 (1)	0
	Total	103 (6)	0

SMITH Frederick (Jock) Adamson

IR 1951–52 5' 5½" 11st 0
b. Aberdeen 14 February 1926

Hall Russell's FC/ Aberdeen (amat to c1946) Aug 1948 Hull City Oct 1949
United: (£4,000) 1/3 May 1951 to 27 Jan 1953
Debut: 5 May 1951 Doncaster Rovers 1 United 1
Last game: 27 Sep 1952 Hull City 4 United 0
Millwall (£2,500) Jan 1953/ Chesterfield Jul 1956/ Montrose Nov 1956

The son of a former professional player, Jock Smith served in the navy during the 1939–46 war and made two Scottish League appearances with Aberdeen, his debut being on 12 February 1948 at home to Rangers. His FL debut came with Hull City on 4 March 1950 at Preston North End but he failed to command a regular place in the side.

A clever, hard working and shrewd player, he was signed by United's manager, Teddy Davison in May 1951 and played in the final game of the season. He was a regular at inside right during the following campaign but then lost his place as Jimmy Hagan moved to inside right and Harold Brook took Hagan's inside left position. He was often referred to as 'Little Fred Smith' because he played with United at the same time as the centre forward 'Big Fred Smith'.

Perhaps his best years were with Millwall where he played quite regularly for over 3 seasons, scoring 20 goals in 92 FL appearances. After a brief time with Chesterfield, bringing his career total to 156 FL appearances, he returned to Scotland.

Appearances:		Apps	Gls
	FL	40	11
	FAC	4	0
	Total	44	11

SMITH Frederick (Fred) Edward

CF 1948–52 6' 0½" 12st 10
b. Draycott 7 May 1926

Draycott/ Derby County Jun 1947
United: (player exch) 16/17 Mar 1948 to 10 May 1952
Debut: 17 Apr 1948 United 0 Huddersfield Town 1
Last games: 29 Dec 1951 United 1 Barnsley 2
10 May 1952 Rotherham United 1 United 3 (CC)
Manchester City (£4,000) May 1952/ Grimsby Town (£4,000) Sep 1952/ Bradford City (player exch) Jul 1954/ Frickley Colliery Dec 1954

Fred Smith made his FL debut with Derby County, his only FL appearance for the Rams, on 3 September 1947 at home to Burnley.

He was at the Lane for a little over four seasons but only in season 1949–50 was Fred a regular in the first team and he appeared to be blossoming into a fine player. He was often referred to as 'Big Fred Smith', because he played with United at the same time as 'Little Fred (Jock) Smith', but was troubled by injuries and fibrositis and, for the following two seasons, he was never sure of a place in the first team and he lost it for certain when United bought Len Browning from Leeds United.

He scored on his final appearance with United, securing a County Cup winners' medal in the defeat of Rotherham United and signed for Manchester City after the game. The tale that the City Secretary and a director had gone to the game with instructions to sign F A Smith and got the wrong man is probably true!

After a brief time with City, Fred made 50 FL appearances for Grimsby Town, scoring 24 goals, before playing a few games for Bradford City, bringing his career total to 115 FL appearances.

Appearances:		Apps	Gls
	FL	53	18
	FAC	5	0
	CC	5	5
	Total	63	23

SMITH G/J (see also Thomas Smith)

LH 1890–91

United: 1890–91
Debut: 27 Sep 1890 United 0 Long Eaton Rangers 1 (MCL)
Last game: 4 Apr 1891 United 5 Staveley 0 (MCL)

Smith, whose initial is in doubt, may have played just two MCL fixture for United. The Independent uses the initial G in September and J in April. The player may have been Thomas Smith (qv).

Appearances:		Apps	Gls
	MCL	2	0
	Total	2	0

SMITH Grant Gordon

LMF/Striker 2001–03 6' 1" 12st 7
b. Irvine 5 May 1980

Wycombe Wanderers trainee/ Reading Aug 1998 Heart of Midlothian (free) Mar 1999/ Livingston (free) Jul 2000/ Clydebank (free) Dec 2000
United: (free) 9/13 Jul 2001 to 25 Jul 2003
Debuts: 17 Jul 2001 Sheffield FC 0 United 7 (sub Fr)
19 Mar 2002 United 3 Millwall 2 (sub)
21 Apr 2002 Birmingham City 2 United 0
Last games: 26 Oct 2002 United 1 Wimbledon 1
4 Jan 2003 United 4 Cheltenham Town 0 (sub FAC)
Halifax Town (L) 6/7 Sep to Nov 2001/ Plymouth Argyle trial,(L) 11 Mar to 4 May 2003
Swindon Town Jul 2003/ Bristol City (free) Jul 2005/ Walsall (L) Jan 2006/ Barnsley trial Aug/ Dundee United Sep 2006/ Helsinki Apr 2007/ Klubi On (L) (Finland)/ Carlisle United Feb 2008

Grant Smith, the son of the former Brighton forward, was with his fourth club before he made a first team League appearance. His debut was as a substitute with Livingston on 26 August 2000 at Alloa but his full debut came after his move to Clydebank, on 16 December 2000. He played regularly till the end of the season when he joined United.

He played in one pre-season game before spending two months on loan at Halifax, making his FL debut on 8 September 2001 at home to Macclesfield Town and after 11 straight appearances, he returned to the Lane. He had a good left foot and made several sub appearances and one start towards the end of the season but was unable to make the breakthrough into the first team squad.

Grant continued to move from club to club and his two more successful spells were with Swindon Town, 23(10) FL appearances and 10 goals and Walsall. In 2006 he returned to Scotland and, after a time in Finland, returned to England with Carlisle United. By the summer of 208 he had made 72(31) FL appearances.

Appearances:		Apps	Gls
	FL	2 (8)	0
	FAC	0 (1)	0
	Total	2 (9)	0

SMITH Guy Rex

(RB)/CF 1921 5' 7" 11st 4

Bakewell
United: 28 May 1920 to cs1922
Only game: 17 May 1921 Barnsley 2 United 3 (CC at Hillsborough)

Rex Smith was a right back who had a trial with United towards the end of the 1919–20 season. He failed to impress but was given a game at centre forward, playing in United's second ever County Cup game. The experiment failed and Jim Plant, a half back, took the position at half time and scored a hat trick. Surprisingly, Smith was retained for a further year.

Appearances:		Apps	Gls
	CC	1	0
	Total	1	0

SMITH Harry R

LH 1943

Sheffield Twist Drill
United: amat 26 Apr 1943, pro 22 Aug 1944 to cs 1947
Only game: 24 Apr 1943 United 2 Barnsley 1 (CC)

Harry Smith was given a trial in a war-time County Cup match and then signed amateur and, later, pro forms. He appears to have been retained until the close season of 1947 (perhaps by mistake or because he was in the armed forces overseas) but made no further appearances.

Appearances:		Apps	Gls
	CC	1	0
	Total	1	0

SMITH Jeffrey (Jeff) Edward

LB/OL 1956–57 5' 9" 11st 0
b. Macclesfield? 8 December 1935

United: 11/13 Jun 1953 to 27 Feb 1958
Debut: 1 Dec 1956 Liverpol 5 United 1
Last games: 14 Jan 1957 Huddersfield Town 2 United 1 (FAC at Maine Road)
12 Feb 1957 Royal Signals 3 TA Regt 1 United XI 4 (Fr)
15 May 1957 Enschede (Hol) 3 United 3 (sub Fr)
Lincoln City (£2,500) Feb 1958 to May 1967

Jeff Smith was brought up in Warren, part of Ecclesfield and may have been born there. He came to the Lane after playing for Oaks Fold, a United nursery club, but in nearly five years, he made just four first team appearances, two of them in friendlies. Left footed, his only FL appearance was at Anfield when manager, Joe Mercer, selected an extraordinary team with Jeff on the left wing and Graham Shaw, another full back, on the right.

He moved to Lincoln City in 1958 and in his ten seasons at Sincil Bank, he proved to be a consistent and efficient defender making 315 FL appearances and scoring twice.

Appearances:		Apps	Gls
	FL	1	0
	FAC	1	0
	Total	2	0

SMITH John (Jack)

IR 1910–11 5' 7" 11st 2
b. Wardley (Newcastle on Tyne) 15 September 1886
d. France, September1916 (killed in action)

Hebburn Argyle/ Hull City Jun 1905
United: (£500) 14/15 Nov 1910 to 16 Mar 1911
Debut: 19 Nov 1910 Middlesbrough 3 United 1
Last game: 25 Feb 1911 United 0 Wednesday 1
Nottingham Forest (£350) Mar 1911/ Nelson Aug 1911 / – / York City Aug 1912/ Hebburn Argyle Jan 1913/ Heckmondwike 1915

Jack Smith joined Hull City as a teenager and scored prolifically in the reserves. He made his FL debut on 23 September 1905 at Leeds City and established himself in the first team towards the end of that season. Described at the time as possessing a big heart and being willing to take on bigger opponents with relish, he scored 31 goals in 37 FL appearances in 1907–08, earning him a place in the Football League side against the Scottish League, and 32 in 35 outings two seasons later.

Smith had not played well at the start of the 1910–11season and United may have taken a risk in signing him but he began well. He had come with a reputation as 'a born comedian' however and was soon facing a charge that he had not been 'in attention to training orders'. He was sold to Forest but only made three appearances before the Nottingham Secretary was reported as saying that they hadn't seen him play and accused United of misleading them as to his ability and character. He later retracted the statement but Forest did make an unsuccessful appeal to the FL.

Smith's career as a FL player, perhaps through injuries or for other reasons, was over and he moved into non-League football where he eventually played at full back. In the second year of the First War, he enlisted in the York & Lancaster Regiment and was killed in action in early September 1916; he left five children, the eldest eight.

Appearances:		Apps	Gls
	FL	12	6
	FAC	1	0
	Total	13	6

SMITH John (Jackie or Tiny)

IR 1944 5' 2½" 9st 9
b. Littletown (Co Durham)

Sherburn Hill/ West Stanley/ Barnsley 1932 Plymouth cs 1935 to cs 1946
United: WW2 guest
Only game: 28 Oct 1944 United 0 Derby County 2 (WW2)

It seems too good to be true that 'Tiny' Smith, who played one game as a guest for United and was one of our smallest ever players, was born in Littletown. John Smith had played non-League football in the North East before joining Barnsley where he played regularly for three seasons, following his debut on 1 October 1932 at home to Doncaster R. A clever inside forward, he moved to Plymouth and again played regularly for his first two seasons there but then less frequently. He played in Argyle's last two games before the outbreak of the Second War and during the rest of that season, which was the final one for Plymouth until 1945–46.

After the War, he retired, having totalled 35 FL goals in 185 appearances, but acted as a scout for Plymouth for a time.

Appearances:		Apps	Gls
	WW2	1	0
	Total	1	0

SMITH John (Jack, Smithy, Smiler) Clayton

G 1931–50 5' 10½" 11st 4
b. Stocksbridge nr. Sheffield 15 September 1910
d. Sheffield 7 April 1986

Bolsterstone/ Sheffield Wednesday amat 1929–30/ Worksop Town 1929–30
United: amat 26 Sep 1930, pro 9/10 Oct 1930 to 31 Jul 1951
Debut: 4 Apr 1931 United 4 Liverpool 1
Last games: 24 Sep 1949 Grimsby Town 4 United 0
4 May 1950 Skegness Town 3 United XI 2 (Fr)
WW2 guest: West Bromwich Albion 1942–43 (2)/ Grimsby T 1942–43 (15)/ Sheffield Wednesday 1942–44 (3)/ Lincoln 1943–44 (14)/ Fulham ?/ Nottingham Forest 1944–45 (2)/ Tranmere Rovers 1944–45 (1), Southport ? 1944–45 (1)
Training staff 1949 to 1952
Worksop T 18 Oct 1952 (1)

Over the years, United have had many excellent goalkeepers and Jack Smith was one of the very best. He was born near Sheffield but, when he was ten, his family emigrated to Pittsburgh in the United States where school meant baseball, basketball and American football and real life drama—he witnessed a man being shot. He introduced soccer to his school in Pittsburgh and was appointed coach but also had to play in goal as the other boys thought the position was a 'cissy' job.

Jack returned to England with his family when he was in his mid-teens and played inside forward with Bolsterstone in the Penistone & District League. An injury to the goalkeeper meant Jack took up the position again and decided to make it a permanent 'move'. Spotted by

Sheffield Wednesday, he signed as an amateur, playing in midweek games and he played Saturday games with Worksop. Wednesday showed no real interest in Jack and he jumped at the chance of trial with United, the club he and his father supported.

After two games with the reserves, the first a 0–4 defeat at Goodison Park, he was offered terms. He made his first team debut later that season and from 1932 onwards 'Smiler' was regarded as United's first choice keeper. He initially missed games through injury and in 1933–34, when United were relegated, he suffered a 'loss of confidence' but when a troublesome wrist was investigated in the close season, it was discovered that he had at some stage fractured it and it had reset itself incorrectly. Once the problem was solved 'Smithy' became the very best of goalkeepers.

On and off the field, Jack always looked smart and that was the way he played. In many ways, he was similar to Alan Hodgkinson; his judgment and technique were both excellent and efficient but he did things the simple orthodox way and without extravagance. Agile and reliable, he played with great confidence and his catching of a high ball was superb. Cheerful, with an endearing smile and popular with the other players, he had one superstition that he had to be the first player out after the captain. He also had a cap which appeared to have been used by several generations and looked filthy but it was carried to every goalmouth—and occasionally worn.

Jack was unlucky not to win international honours; he played in the 1936 FA Cup Final and was ever present in the 1938–39 promotion side. From 21 December 1935 to the outbreak of the Second War on 3 September 1939 Jack played in every game—League, Cup and friendlies—a total of 190 games. He continued playing after the War and holds the club record of 203 consecutive FL appearances, or 206 if the three games at the start of the 1939 season are included. Had he not missed seven FL seasons (294 possible games) due to the War, his total FL appearances for United may well have been a record too.

During the War, Jack served in the RAF but played quite frequently for United, although rarely between 1941 and 1944, as well as for other clubs as a guest. He was still an excellent keeper after the war but it seemed that he had made his final appearance for United on 14 May 1949 when he was chaired from the field after a County Cup match at Oakwell but an injury crisis in the September of the following season meant he made two more FL appearances. His final first team appearance came in a friendly at Skegness and he appeared in the CL team in the early part of the 1950–51 season, 20 years after he had made his first team debut. His appearance for Worksop in 1952 was an emergency response to their injury problems.

Appearances:		Apps	Gls
	FL	347	0
	FAC	31	0
	CC	13	0
	WW2	104	0
	1939–40	3	0
	Total	498	0

SMITH Joseph (Joe)

RB/LB 1910–12 5' 10½" 12st
b. Sutton-on-Trent c1888
d. Burton on Trent January 1928

Worksop NE/Kiveton Park
United: amat 26 Apr 1907, pro cs 1907 to May 1913
Debuts: 19 Feb 1910 Leeds City 0 United 2 (Fr)
12 Mar 1910 United 1 Bradford City 2
Last game: 21 Sep 1912 United 1 Woolwich Arsenal 3
South Shields May 1913/ Derby County May (£200 to United) Aug 1914

Joe Smith spent some time in the reserves before playing for the first team. Totally devoid of fear, he was reckless, going for the ball with arms and legs flying and 'if he does not kill someone first, he will end up by killing himself'. Nicknamed 'old aeroplane', his play did become more effective and he gave some fine displays but he was frequently injured—on four occasions in the Public Practice matches!—and broke his collar bone in 1911 on the day he learned he had been chosen for the Football League. In and out of the team, he lost his place to Bill Cook and was placed on the transfer list.

After a season with South Shields, he moved to Derby but after six FL appearances, he lost his place and set up a business in Burton.

Appearances:		Apps	Gls
	FL	48	0
	FAC	2	0
	Total	50	0

SMITH Mark Cyril

CF 1980 5' 11" 12st 0
b. Sheffield 19 December 1961

United: semi-pro 10 Dec 1979, 14 Aug 1980 to 10 Mar 1982
Debuts: 26 Jan 1980 United 2 Leeds United 1 (sub Fr)
5 May 1980 United 6 Doncaster Rovers 1 (CC)
Last games: 8 May 1980 Sheffield Wednesday 1 United 2 (CC)
8 Dec 1980 United 4 Doncaster Rovers 2 (sub CC)
Worksop Town/ Gainsborough Trinity/ Scunthorpe United Sep 1985/ Kettering Town/ Rochdale Jul 1988/ Huddersfield Town (£50k) Feb 1989/ Grimsby Town (£55k) Mar 1991/ Scunthorpe United (£20k) Aug 1993/ Boston United Jun 1995/ Gainsborough Trinity Sep 1995/ Matlock Town/ Sheffield FC/ Hallam Jul 2000/ Buxton Jul 2002

Mark Smith was a quick centre forward but he never featured in the FL for United. He did gain a County Cup winners' medal in 1980 and scored on what is thought to be his final appearance. He may have also played 7 December 1981 in a friendly match at Barrow.

After a spell in non-League football he made his FL debut, as a substitute, with Scunthorpe United on 28 September 1985 at Aldershot. This was his only first team appearance at the time but he made his full debut after moving to Rochdale, on 27 August 1988 at Burnley.

Mark went on to play for several clubs, finally returning to Scunthorpe where his FL career came to an end having played 198(65) games. He continued to play for several seasons in non-League football.

Appearances:		Apps	Gls
	CC	2 (1)	1
	Total	2 (1)	1

SMITH Martin Geoffrey

MF 1999–2000 5' 11" 12st 6
b. Sunderland 13 November 1974

Sunderland from trainee, pro Sep 1992
United: (free) 5/6 Aug 1999 to 3 Feb 2000
Debuts: 7 Aug 1999 Portsmouth 2 United 0 (sub)
14 Aug 1999 United 1 Walsall 1
Last game: 15 Jan 2000 Walsall 2 United 1
Huddersfield (£300k) Feb 2000/ Northampton Town (free) Aug 2003/ Darlington Jun 2006 to Mar 2008

England schoolboy and youth international Martin Smith, who also gained one U21 cap, made his FL debut with Sunderland, scoring at home to Luton Town on 20 October 1993. Although a regular in the side for this and the following season, his appearances became less frequent and after declining a new deal at Sunderland, he joined United on a one-year contract.

Martin was as an immediate hit with two goals in the League Cup when coming on as a substitute. He played as an attacking midfielder behind the front two for much of his time at the Lane but still amassed 12 goals in his first 17 games although having a tendency to 'disappear' for spells in the game and from mid-October his tally dropped significantly.

Unhappy with the new contract he was offered under Neil Warnock, Martin was sold to Huddersfield Town and continued to play successfully in the lower Divisions. In March 2008 injuries prompted Martin to leave Darlington by mutual consent. He had totalled 93 FL goals in 313(55) games.

Appearances:		Apps	Gls
	FL	24 (2)	10
	FAC	3	1
	LC	3 (1)	4
	Total	30 (3)	15

SMITH P (see Beaumont)

CH 1918

United: WW1 guest
Debut: 5 Oct 1918 United 1 Birmingham 3 (WW1)
Last game: 9 Nov 1918 United 6 Lincoln City 1 (WW1)

'P. Smith' appears in the United programme of 26 October and played five games according to the local war-time newspapers and was described as 'stylish'. The Green 'Un commented 'there are lots of Smiths, some rightly named and some not' and later mentioned a pseudonym. The FL take their information from their clubs and record his appearances under P. Beaumont—the two never played together—and there can be no doubt that 'P. Smith' was Percy Beaumont (qv).

Appearances:		Apps	Gls
	WW1	5	0
	Total	5	0

SMITH Paul Michael

RB/MF 1981–86 5' 11" 10st 9
b. Rotherham 9 November 1964

Throstles (Sheffield)
United: from app 25 May 1981, pro 10 Nov 1982 to 28 Jul 1986
Debuts: 7 Dec 1981 Barrow 0 United XI 1 (Fr)
17 May 1982 Barnsley XI 0 United XI 0 (CC)
26 Mar 1983 Southend United 3 United 1
Last games: 3 May 1986 Crystal Palace 1 United 1
15 May 1986 Jersey XI 1 United XI 5 (Fr)
Stockport County (L) Aug 1985
Port Vale (£10k) Jul 1986/ Lincoln City (£48k) Sep 1987 to cs 1995/ Kettering Town (L) Oct 1994/ Halifax T Sep 1995 to cs 1996

Paul Smith, the elder brother of Brian who also played for United, looked very promising as a youngster but he was in and out of the side, playing in a variety of roles from full back to striker. His best run of games was at the end of the 1985–86 season when Paul played at right back but, in the close season, Billy McEwan, the manager, sold him to Port Vale.

After one season he signed for Lincoln City. The Imps were then in their first season in the Conference and paid a club record fee of £48k which was also a non-League record transfer and he helped City return to the FL at the first attempt. Initially signed as a striker, he soon reverted to defence and he spent eight seasons at Sincil Bank. He ended his FL career having made 297(22) appearances, scoring 40 goals.

Appearances:		Apps	Gls
	FL	29 (7)	1
	FAC	2	0
	CC	2	0
	Total	33 (7)	1

SMITH Thomas

OR/IR 1891–92
b. Ecclesfield 1869

Ecclesfield (1889–90)
United: Nov 1891 to cs 1892
Debut: 5 Nov 1891 United 1 Bootle 3 (Fr)
Last game: 27 Feb 1892 Kilnhurst 0 United XI 4 (SCC)
Barnsley cs 1892 to c1900

Thomas Smith made two definite first team appearances for United and also played for the reserves but there is a very slight possibility that he might have played 1890–91 (see G/J Smith). We know he was a small man for he was quoted, many years later, as saying 'I'm not big enough to be awkward' and he left the 'bumping' to other players.

He had more success after moving to Barnsley, playing regularly for several seasons and he made his FL debut in Barnsley's first home FL game against Luton Town on 10 September 1898, making 11 FL appearances in total.

Appearances:		Apps	Gls
	SCC	1	1
	Total	1	1

SMITH Thomas (Tommy) Edgar

F 1979 5' 10" 12st 9
b. Wolverhampton 30 July 1959

Bromsgrove Rovers
United: 30 Mar/ 1 Apr 1978 to 29 Mar 1979
Debut: 6 Feb 1979 United 1 Fulham 1
Last game: 24 Feb 1979 United 0 Millwall 2
Huddersfield Town Mar 1979/ Emley FC Jul 1981 / – / Witton A (1983–85)/ Leigh RMI (1989–90)

Tommy Smith and Brian McGarry were both signed on the same day from Bromsgrove Rovers but neither proved successful. Both probably made their debuts for United in a friendly match (25 Sep 1978) at Bromsgrove arranged as part of the transfer deal. Tommy's three FL appearances for United were in successive games, and he scored on his debut.

His one substitute appearance for Huddersfield came in April 1979, although he made a League Cup appearance during the following season.

Appearances:	Apps	Gls
FL	2 (1)	1
Total	2 (1)	1

SMITH William (Bongo)

IF 1967 5' 6½" 10st 4
b. Cumnock (Ayrshire) 12 October 1942

Carlisle U Mar 1963/ Preston NE/ Cumnock Juniors
United: 20 Jun, 6 Jul 1965 to 6/9 Jan 1968
Debut: 11 Feb 1967 West Bromwich Albion 1 United 2
Last games: 25 Feb 1967 United 2 Southampton 0
12 Aug 1967 Norwich C 3 United 1 (Fr)

A Scottish Junior and Amateur international, Willie Smith had brief spells with Carlisle and PNE but was spotted by United playing in New Zealand when United toured there in 1965. He was a clever player but not top quality. He made his three competitive appearances for United within a fortnight, scoring on his debut and made one appearance on the club's tour of South America. He returned to Scotland when he secured a job there outside of football but, much later, he did some coaching with Ayr United.

Appearances:	Apps	Gls
FL	2	1
FAC	1	0
Total	3	1

SOMMEIL David

RB 2006–07 5' 10½" 12st 12
b. Point a Pitre (Guadeloupe) 10 August 1974

St Lo/ Caen 1993/ Rennes cs 1998/ Bordeaux cs 2000 Manchester City (£3.5m) Jan 2003/ Marseilles (L) Feb 2004
United: (free) 24 May 2006 to 19(?) Jul 2007
Debuts: 17 Jul 2006 Worksop Town 0 United 5 (Fr)
22 Aug 2006 Tottenham Hotspur 2 United 0
Last games: 23 Sep 2006 Arsenal 3 United 0
6 Jan 2007 United 0 Swansea City 3 (FAC)
Valenciennes (France) Jul 2007

David Sommeil made his French League debut in 1993–94 with Caen and gained a French B cap with Bordeaux. His League debut in England came after his move to Manchester City on 29 January 2003 at home to Fulham and the following season he became the first City player to score at their new City of Manchester Stadium. Following a loan spell in France, injuries and loss of form restricted his appearances for City but he became one of Neil Warnock's first summer signings after United's promotion to the top flight.

Injured in his first pre-season game he returned for the second League game but was soon replaced by Leigh Bromby and subsequently played in just two cup games. At the end of the season he was placed on the transfer list and returned to France.

Appearances:	Apps	Gls
FL	4 (1)	0
FAC	1	0
LC	1	0
Total	6 (1)	0

SPACKMAN Nigel James

See 'Managers' section

Appearances:	Apps	Gls
FL	19 (4)	0
PO	1	0
FAC	1	0
LC	2	0
Total	23 (4)	0

SPEED Gary Andrew

MF 2008– 5' 10" 12st 10
b. Deeside 8 September 1969

Leeds United from trainee Jun 1988/ Everton (£3.5m) Jul 1996/ Newcastle United (£5.5m) Feb 1998 Bolton Wanderers (£750k) Jul 2004
United: (L) 1 Jan 2008, signed Jan 2008
Debut: 1 Jan 2008 Wolverhampton Wanderers 0 United 0

Gary Speed made his FL debut with Leeds United on 6 May 1988 at home to Oldham Athletic. By March of the following season he became a regular in the side and missed just one FL game in 1991–92 when Leeds were Champions of the old Division One and went on to have an impressive career as an influential midfielder in the Premiership. He played and scored in every Premiership season including 2006–07 and was capped 85 times for Wales. On leaving Bolton he had made 610(30) League appearances, scoring 98 goals and had played more Premiership games than any other player.

He joined United, on a two and a half year contract, on the opening day of the January transfer window. During the first 18 months he was to concentrate on playing but was given carte blanche to pass on his knowledge to the less experienced players. He quickly adjusted to the different demands of the Championship and was an influential figure on the pitch both in his own play and his effect on others.

Appearances:	Apps	Gls
FL	20	3
FAC	2	0
Total	22	3

SPEIGHT Michael (Mick)

M 1971–80 5' 10½" 11st 7
b. Upton 1 November 1951

United: 10 Dec 1967, app 2 Jan 1968, 7/17 May 1969 to 17 Jul 1980
Debuts: 6 Nov 1971 West Ham United 1 United 2 (sub)
12 Feb 1972 United 2 Manchester City 3
Last games: 3 May 1980 Grimsby Town 4 United 0
8 May 1980 Sheffield Wednesday 1 United 2 (CC)
Blackburn Rovers (£40k) Jul 1980/ Grimsby Town (£25k) Aug 1982/ Bury (L) Mar 1983/ Chester City Aug 1984 player-coach, player-mgr to Jul 1985, player to Nov 1985 / – / coaching in Norway

Mick Speight was sixteen when he joined United from Don and Dearne boys but was twenty before he made his first team debut as a last minute substitute at West Ham. He continued to make occasional appearances until October 1973 when he became a regular member of the side for the following six seasons, although missing much of the 1975–76 relegation season and most of the following one through injury. He was made captain in 1978–79 but in the summer of 1980, following relegation to Division Three, he was transferred to Blackburn.

Mick was unfortunate to spend most of his time at the Lane when the club was in decline. He described himself as a 'workhorse' but he was a first-class professional, offering total dedication, loyalty and a will to win. There were few frills to his game and he was often given a specific man-marking task and, although lacking pace, he could read the game well. In the summer of 1978 he toured New Zealand, Singapore and Malaysia with the England B side, gaining four caps and scoring one goal.

He spent two seasons at both Blackburn and Grimsby, and a loan spell at Bury where he made no appearances, before moving to Chester City, firstly as player coach and then as player manager. His time as manger was successful but short lived due to some outspoken comments about the running of the club. In his FL career Mick totalled 21 goals in 309(19) games before he began a career in coaching and management in Norway.

Appearances:		Apps	Gls
	FL	184 (15)	14
	FAC	7 (2)	1
	LC	7 (1)	1
	TX	3	0
	ASC	13	1
	CC	9	0
	Total	223 (18)	17

SPENCER John Raymond

IL/IR/OL 1954–57 6' 0" 10st 7
b. Bradfield/Stannington 20 November 1934
d. Sheffield 22 August 2007

United: amateur then pro 8/9 Jun 1954 to Feb 1960
Debuts: 26 Oct 1954 United 1 Barnsley 0 (CC)
18 Dec 1954 Everton 2 United 3
Last games: 27 Apr 1957 United 0 Nottingham Forest 4
22 May 1957 Ajax Amsterdam (Holland) 1 United 2 (Fr)
Retired

An England youth international with five caps, John Spencer played for the reserves as an amateur but became a part time player with United, training as an accountant. He played mainly as an inside forward but filled other forward positions during his time at the Lane but it was only in his final season that he secured a regular first team place. A constructive, thoughtful player, he had good ball control, positional sense and an accurate shot but after three seasons, he was forced by injuries to retire.

Appearances:		Apps	Gls
	FL	24	10
	FAC	4	1
	CC	2	1
	Total	30	12

SPICER Walter

IR 1930 5' 10" 11st 10
b. Sheffield 7 May 1909
d. Henley on Thames AMJ 1981

Norton Woodseats
United: Amat Aug 1925, pro 17/24 May 1929 to cs 1931
Debuts: 3 Nov 1930 Sheffield Wednesday 1 United 2 (CC)
6 Dec 1930 United 3 Aston Villa 4
Last game: 25 Dec 1930 Blackpool 2 United 1
Rotherham United free cs 1931 to Jan 1934/ Sheffield FC to 1944

After studying at the Central School, Walter Spicer came to the Lane as both a promising forward and batsman. He was a fine cricketer, playing for United for many years. He was a Yorkshire colt in 1931 but decided to concentrate on business. United allowed him to play football as a teenager for Norton Woodseats and he played for the North in an Amateur International trial match in 1928 at Stamford Bridge.

A clever player, Walter made just four first team appearances during his two seasons at the Lane but he was more successful after his move to Rotherham United. He was a regular for two seasons, making 66 FL appearances, before he decided to concentrate on business and revert to amateur status with Sheffield Club.

Appearances:		Apps	Gls
	FL	3	0
	CC	1	0
	Total	4	0

SPOONER Peter Goodwill

OL 1933–35 5' 8" 10st 10
b. Hepscott, Morpeth 30 August 1907 (or 1910)
d. Newcastle upon Tyne January 1987

Newbiggin Utd/ Ashington Aug 1929/ Newcastle United (1929 trial)/ Bradford Park Avenue May 1930 York City Jun 1931
United: (£500) 8/9 May 1933 to 4 May 1935
Debut: 2 Sep 1933 Liverpool 3 United 2
Last game: 4 May 1935 Brentford 3 United 1
York City (£100) Jul 1935 to May 1939/ Gateshead Jul 1939

Rejected by Newcastle United after a trial, Peter Spooner made his FL debut with Bradford PA on 30 August 1930 at Oldham Athletic, moving to York after one season. Fast with a good shot and ball control, Peter's success at York prompted a move to the Lane.

Signed by Teddy Davison, Peter was the first of six outside lefts bought before the 1939–45 war who weren't fully satisfactory. Spooner found the jump in class difficult to bridge and, although he scored on his debut, he lost his place after six games. United were relegated to Division Two at the end of his first season but Peter played only 11 games in the following campaign.

In the summer of 1935 he returned to York where he was ever present during 1935–36 and missed only six games during the following two seasons. In and out of the side during 1938–39 he moved to Gateshead in the summer of 1939, playing in their three games of the 1939–40 season, scoring twice. Peter made 214 FL appearances and scored 47 goals and also made some wartime appearances for Gateshead.

Appearances:		Apps	Gls
	FL	17	2
	CC	1	0
	Total	18	2

SPRATT Herbert (Bert)

OL 1918

United: WW1 guest: Feb 1918
Only game: 16 Feb 1918 United 0 Nottingham Forest 1 (WW1)
WW1 guest: Rotherham C (20 app, 1916–17)Wednesday (25 app, Nov 1917–Nov 1918), Leeds C Mar 1918 (1)

Herbert Spratt made one appearance for United as a guest during the First War after appearing regularly with Rotherham County and the Wednesday. He also played at the Lane for Leeds City when they were a man short and may have played for the reserves towards the end of 1916.

Appearances:		Apps	Gls
	WW1	1	0
	Total	1	0

STACEY Alexander (Alec)

RH 1933–37 5' 8½" 12st 4
b. London 3 June 1904
d. Leeds September 1993

Grove House Lads Club (Manchester)/ New Mills Northwich Victoria/ Leeds United Oct 1927
United: (£2,000) 22 Nov 1933 to 1 May 1937
Debut: 25 Nov 1933 United 1 Blackburn Rovers 0
Last game: 23 Jan 1937 Barnsley 1 United 1
Kidderminster Harriers cs 1937/ Workington Jul 1938

Alec Stacey made his FL debut with Leeds United on 10 March 1928 at Oldham Athletic. He played infrequently in the first team (51 FL app), being the backbone of Leeds reserve side but he had a run of games in the senior team at the start of the 1932–33 and 1933–34 seasons.

A sturdy, hard working 'grafter', he lacked speed but passed the ball well. When he joined United, the Blades were a Division One club and Alec was a regular in the side until, at Blackburn in April 1934, soon after the start and not having touched the ball, he went to take a throw-in and fell awkwardly and broke his leg. By the time he returned, United were in Division Two. He re-established himself in the side in January 1935 but twelve months later he lost his place to Ernest Jackson and played only a handful of games the following season before moving into non-League football with Kidderminster. In his first season with the Harriers, he helped them win their League and Cup competitions.

Appearances:		Apps	Gls
	FL	64	3
	FAC	5	0
	CC	2	0
	Total	71	3

STAINROD Simon Allan

Striker/OL 1976–79 6' 0" 11st 12
b. Grenoside, Sheffield 1 February 1959

United: app Jul/28 Sep 1975, pro 1 Jun/Jul 1976 to Mar 1979
Debuts: 2 Mar 1976 United 1 Rotherham United 1 (sub CC)
27 Mar 1976 Tottenham Hotspur 5 United 0
Last game: 28 Feb 1979 Wrexham 4 United 0
Oldham Athletic (£60k) Mar 1979/ Queens Park Rangers (£250/275k) Nov 1980/ Sheffield Wednesday (£250k) Feb 1985/ Aston Villa (£250k) Sep 1985/ Stoke City (£90k) Dec 1987/ RC Strasbourg (France) (L)/ Rouen (France) (£70k) Jun 1989/ Falkirk (£100k) Aug 1990/ Dundee player asst mgr Feb 1992, player mgr May 1992, director of football May 1993/ Ayr United player mgr Dec 1993 to Sep 1995

England youth international Simon Stainrod, made his FL debut for United towards the end of the disastrous 1975–76 relegation season and played the rest of his games for the Blades in Division Two as the club gradually declined. A self confident, flamboyant player with plenty of skill but he wouldn't 'graft'—Ken Furphy said the 16 year old would never make a footballer—he was in and out of the side under Jimmy Sirrel but fared better when Harry Haslam arrived. However it was Haslam, who disliked his 'moaning', who sold Simon to Oldham.

He subsequently had a long and successful time at Queens Park Rangers where he gained a losers' medal in the 1982 FA Cup Final. After a brief spell at Hillsborough he had another successful time with Aston Villa. After a time in France he moved to Scotland where he played a starring role in Falkirk's Division 1 Championship success in 1991and scored a 60 yard goal straight from the kick-off. The following season he repeated this promotion success with Dundee.

Simon had two seasons as manager of Ayr and a brief spell coaching in Scotland before going into TV work. He was a founding partner of Match Day Media TV. He became a licensed football agent in 1996 and is based in Cannes.

Appearances:

	Apps	Gls
FL	59 8)	14
FAC	1 (1)	0
LC	1 (1)	0
ASC	4	0
CC	3 (2)	1
Total	68 (12)	15

STANCLIFFE Paul Ian

CD 1983–90 6' 2" 12st 13
b. Sheffield 5 May 1958

Rotherham United Aug 1974, app Mar 1976
United: 19 Jul, completed c30 Dec 1983 to Nov 1990
Debuts: 2 Aug 1983 Grantham Town 1 United 5 (Fr)
27 Aug 1983 United 4 Gillingham 0
Last game: 1 Sep 1990 Crystal Palace 1 United 0
Rotherham United (L) 10 Sep 1990
Wolverhampton Wanderers (L) 8 Nov, (free) 17 Dec 1990/ York City Jul 1991 to cs 1995 then coach and head of youth development to May 2005/ Doncaster R youth coach summer 2005

Paul Stancliffe had signed schoolboy forms with Sheffield Wednesday but after the manager Danny Williams was sacked, Paul was released and joined Rotherham. He made his first team debut and scored in the County Cup at home to Barnsley on 1 May 1975, just before his seventeenth birthday and his FL debut was on 16 August 1975 at Brighton & H A. He made 285 FL appearances for the Millers and was a member of the side which won the Division Three championship in 1981. He was injured in September 1982 and was out of the side for seven months as Rotherham were relegated.

Paul had asked for a transfer and was ready to join Barnsley when Ian Porterfield, his former manager at Millmoor, brought him to the Lane for a reported fee of £100k but which was actually an extended exchange deal which involved Mike Trusson.

For his seven full seasons with United he was first choice at the centre of the defence and the games he missed were through injury. 'Stan the Man' was an instant success and soon became captain. A 'true professional', Paul was dedicated, composed and loyal and players, managers and supporters were all well aware of his qualities and he provided stability through his first five seasons when lack of money and other off-field problems formed a permanent background to events at the Lane.

He was quoted as saying 'I've always played to my limitations' and in so doing, he used the attributes he had and the skills he had developed to the full. He was good in the air, had two good feet, could resist a challenge, read the game well and had good anticipation. He covered well, marshalled his fellow defenders and his tackling was well timed and determined. Above all else his conduct, both on and off the field did him and the game great credit.

Paul was one of the few who retained his position when Dave Bassett arrived on the scene and, after the initial relegation, he missed few games during the following two campaigns as United were promoted twice and back to the top flight. He captained the side against Liverpool on the opening day of the new season but after three games he lost his place as Bassett decided he needed younger players in the defence. Paul was given a free transfer as a gesture to reward his loyal service. After a brief loan spell back at Millmoor, he spent the remainder of the season at Wolves before moving to York where he played until 1994–95 by which time he had played in 674(2) FL games during his career. In 1993 Paul, who had been voted 'Clubman of the Year', played at Wembley when York were promoted via the play-offs

After playing, Paul was head of youth development at York City until May 2005 when cash restraints brought his time there to an end. In the summer of 2005 he became youth coach with Doncaster Rovers.

Appearances:

	Apps	Gls
FL	278	12
PO	2	0
FAC	24	3
LC	21	4
FMC	7	0
AMC	4	0
YHC	5	1
Total	34 1	20

STANIFORTH David Albry

CF/OL/IR 1968–74 5' 11½" 11st 7
b. Chesterfield 6 October 1950

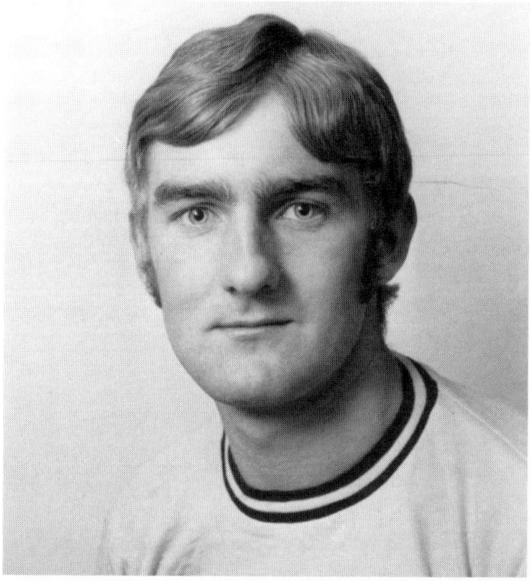

United: app 27 Apr 1966, pro 9/15 May 1968 to Mar 1974
Debuts: 13 May 1968 Chester 2 United 3 (BM)
8 Apr 1969 United 1 Hull City 1
Last game: 9 Feb 1974 Norwich City 2 United 1
Bristol Rovers Mar 1974/ Bradford City Jun 1979/ Halifax Town Jul 1982/ Burton Albion cs1984?/
Crookes player-coach 1984 to 1990s

David Staniforth had played for Nottingham Boys before he joined United but although he was a professional at the Lane for nearly six years, he never established himself as a regular in the first team. He played in a variety of forward roles but was primarily a hard working striker. He scored on his (friendly) debut and twice in his second FL appearance but after losing his place because of an injury, he scored just one more competitive goal and it was no surprise when he moved on in March 1974.

David met with more success at his three other clubs, particularly at Bradford City where he played most regularly. He ended his FL career with 80 goals in 330(33) games.

Appearances:		Apps	Gls
	FL	22 (4)	3
	LC	4	0
	TX	1	0
	CC	3	2
	Total	30 (4)	5

STANIFORTH Harold

OL 1943

United: amateur 30 Apr 1943 to 12 Jan 1945
Only game: 1 May 1943 Manchester United 2 United 1 (WW2)

Harold Staniforth was an amateur from the Kilnhurst and Swinton area of south Yorkshire who was chosen to make his debut in April 1943 against Manchester United at the Lane but the match was cancelled. He did play one week later at Maine Road where Manchester United were playing after their ground had been bombed. He may also have played in the late 1940's for Scunthorpe's reserves and for Grantham Town.

Appearances:		Apps	Gls
	WW2	1	0
	Total	1	0

STANIFORTH Joseph J

RB 1894

United: 24 Oct 1893 to cs 1894
Only game: 14 Apr 1894 Wednesday 1 United 1 (UCL)

Joseph Staniforth made this one first team appearance for United. A utility player, he played for the 'Strollers' (reserves) in the half back line and as a forward.

Appearances:		Apps	Gls
	UCL	1	0
	Total	1	0

STARBUCK Philip (Phil) Michael

Striker/MF 1994–96 5' 10" c12st?
b. Nottingham 24 November 1968

Nottingham Forest from app Aug 1986 Birmingham City (L) Mar 1988/ Hereford United (L) Feb 1990 Blackburn Rovers (L) Sep 1990/ Huddersfield Town (£100k) Aug 1991
United: (L) 28 Oct 1994, £150/158k 3 Jan 1995 to cs 1997
Debuts: 29 Oct 1994 Millwall 2 United 1 (sub)
2 Nov 1994 Stoke City 1 United 1
Last games: 21 Sep 1996 Wolverhampton 1 United 2
1 Oct 1996 Southend United 3 United 2 (sub)
Bristol City (L) 15 Sep 1995/ RKC Waalwijk (Netherlands) (L) 11 Nov 1996/ Oldham A (L) Feb 1997 (injured)
Oldham Athletic (nc) Jan 1998/ Plymouth Argyle Mar 1998 to May 1998/ Cambridge City Sep 1998 / – / Burton Albion 1999 to May 2002/ Hucknall Town mgr to Jun 2003/ Leigh RMI player asst mgr then mgr Jul 2003 to Nov 2004/ Arnold Town mgr/ Hednesford Town mgr Jun 2006 to May 2008

Phil Starbuck made his FL debut with Nottingham Forest scoring at Newcastle United on 13 December 1986. Unable to establish himself in the first team he had three loan spells before moving to Huddersfield Town where he played 137 FL games, scoring 36 goals.

Phil was signed for United by Dave Bassett but though constructive, he never looked a Bassett type of player. He played as a striker for much of his first season and then in a more midfield role before a spell on loan. After Bassett's departure Phil's opportunities were severely limited and after a loan spell in the Netherlands he was released.

He joined Oldham but a knee injury sustained on the training pitch kept him out until January and shortly afterwards he moved to Plymouth but niggling injuries curtailed his appearances and he was released in the summer. He then went into non-League football, firstly as a player and

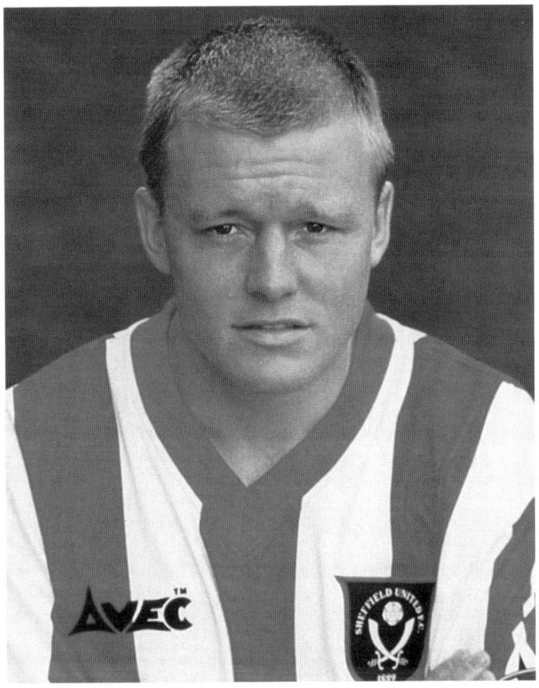

then as a manager. Phil joined 'Christians in Sport' in 1998, supporting players in the top two professional divisions, co-ordinating bible studies between players and organising other events, whilst continuing his non-League career.

Appearances:		Apps	Gls
	FL	26 (10)	2
	FAC	1 (1)	0
	LC	0 (2)	0
	Total	27 (13)	2

STEAD Jonathan (Jon) Graeme

Striker 2007– 6' 3" 11st 7
b. Huddersfield 7 April 1983

Huddersfield Town from trainee 30 Nov 2001 Blackburn Rovers (£1.2m) Feb 2004/ Sunderland (£1.8m) Jun 2005/ Derby County (L) Oct 2006
United: (£750k) 11 Jan 2007
Debut: 13 Jan 2007 United 1 Portsmouth 1

Jon Stead represented Yorkshire at swimming and joined Huddersfield as a trainee making his FL debut as a substitute on 10 August 2002 at home to Brentford. His full debut came on 26 August at Tranmere Rovers and the following season he scored 16 goals. This prompted a move to Blackburn Rovers and his goals played a big part in Rovers avoiding relegation from the Premiership. The following season was not so successful and nor was his time with Sunderland as they struggled in the top flight although he did win eleven U21 England caps whilst with the two clubs.

Signed by Neil Warnock in the January transfer window as United fought to stay in the Premiership, the tall speedy striker always gave of his best and Jon's five goals nearly did the trick, particularly his brave header against Wigan Athletic in the final game. With a good football brain and the ability to run the channels, there remained uncertainty as to his best role and he was in and out of the team and his Championship season was disappointing.

Appearances:		Apps	Gls
	FL	24 (14)	8
	FAC	4	1
	LC	3	2
	Total	31 (14)	11

STEANE Nigel Brian

F 1980
b. Nottingham 18 January 1963

United: from app 15 Oct 1979, pro Jan 1981 to 19 Mar 1981
Only game: 26 Apr 1980 United 2 Wimbledon 1 (sub)
Finland

Nigel Steane's one first team appearance for United, at the age of seventeen, was as a substitute for fifteen minutes and it was the only FL appearance of his career.

Appearances:		Apps	Gls
	FL	0 (1)	0
	Total	0 (1)	0

STEELE Frederick (Freddie) Charles

CF 1940 5' 10" 10st 12
b. Hanley 6 May 1916
d. Newcastle under Lyme 23 April 1976

Stoke City am Jul 1931/Downing Tileries Stoke City Aug 1933
United: WW2 guest Aug 1940
Only game: 31 Aug 1940 Rotherham United 3 United 3 (WW2)
WW2 guest: Notts County, Leicester City, Northampton Town, Nottingham Forest, Bradford PA, Doncaster Rovers, Leeds United, Fulham and Arsenal Mansfield Town (£1,000) player mgr Jun 1949/ Port Vale (£1,500) Dec 1951 player mgr to Dec 1952, mgr to Jan 1957 / – / Port Vale mgr Oct 1962 to Feb 1965

Freddie Steele was one of the best centre forwards of the 1930s. He had made his FL debut with Stoke City on 22 December 1934 and had an impressive goal scoring record, many of which were scored with his head but he was fast, shrewd and powerful. He played twice for the Football League and gained six full England caps. Just before the Second War he badly injured his knee in a collision with a goalkeeper and although he played until 1953 it continued to cause problems.

United was one of many clubs for whom he played as a guest during the Second War. Temporarily stationed in south Yorkshire, he scored on his only appearance and was posted away before he could play again for the Blades.

He was the player manager at Mansfield when they 'knocked' United out of the Cup and manager of Port Vale in 1954 when they took the Third Division (North) Championship and reached the semi-final of the FA Cup.

Despite seven seasons lost to the War, Freddie had still reached 301 FL appearances on his retirement, scoring 191 goals.

Appearances:		Apps	Gls
	WW2	1	1
	Total	1	1

STEVENS Harold (Harry, Ham)

RH 1937–40 5' 9" 11st 4
b. Morton (Derbys) 27 March 1917
d. Chesterfield January 1998

Stretton Inst
United: am 24 Sep 1935, pro 14/15 Nov 1935 to 8 Oct 1945
Debut: 11 Sep 1937 United 2 Luton Town 0
Last games: 9 Oct 1937 United 1 Blackburn Rovers 1
31 Aug 1940 Rotherham United 3 United 3 (WW2)
WW2 guest: Bolsover Colliery (1939–40)
Clay Cross Park House

Harold Stevens' birth and death were both registered in Chesterfield. He first played for the reserves in November 1935 and made his first team debut in 1937 with seven FL appearances in successive games for United. He lost his place to the more powerful Alf Settle and Fred Jessop and those games proved to be the only senior ones of his career other than two war-time games (one was a friendly at Bury) in 1940.

Appearances:		Apps	Gls
	FL	7	0
	WW2	1	0
	Total	8	0

STEVENSON Arthur Brown

OL 1925–28 5' 8½" 11st 2
b. Padiham 24 August 1896?
d. Padiham JFM 1976

Accrington Stanley Sep 1919/ Darwen Jun 1921/ Wigan Borough May 1922/ Middlesbrough (£1100) Oct 1923/ Wigan Jan 1924/Mid Rhondda United (£750) cs 1924
United: (£600) 12 Feb 1925 to 14 May 1930
Debut: 4 Apr 1925 United 2 Tottenham Hotspur 0
Last game: 9 Apr 1928 Portsmouth 4 United 1
Bristol City (£400) May 1930/ – / Wigan Borough cs 1931/ Chorley/ Stalybridge C Jun 1932

The son of a former Millwall captain, Arthur Stevenson rarely stayed more than one season with any club other than United. He made his FL debut with Wigan Borough on 26 August 1922 at home to Ashington and was a regular in the side until October in the following season when he moved to Middlesbrough and then to Mid Rhondda, a Welsh Southern League team, before joining United.

Arthur came to Sheffield knowing that United wanted him as an adequate reserve for those occasions when Fred Tunstall was injured or was playing for England against Scotland and the new man soon discovered that Tunstall hardly ever missed a game. As a consequence, he made just four first team appearances, including one friendly, in five seasons though he played and scored regularly for the reserves.

He moved to Bristol City but soon went home to Padiham. He joined Wigan Borough but, after 12 games of the 1931–32 season, the club resigned from the FL and disbanded. Arthur had played in four of those games including their final home and penultimate game.

Appearances:		Apps	Gls
	FL	3	0
	Total	3	0

STEWART R

CF 1918

United: WW1 guest
Only game: 25 Dec 1918 Wednesday 4 United 0 (WW1)

Stewart's one first team appearance for United was during the First World War but he had a poor game. He was reported to be a 'Sheffielder' and a private in the army who had assisted Millwall. A man of that name had played twice at outside left, earlier in the month for the London club and also played on New Year's Day at centre forward. A player reported as 'Stewart' played twice for Lincoln City at centre forward in April 1919 but City gave his name to the FL as 'I Little'.

Appearances:		Apps	Gls
	WW1	1	0
	Total	1	0

STEWART Thomas

RB/LB 1904–05

Wycliffe (Sheffield)
United: amat.19 May 1903, pro cs 1904 to cs 1906
Debuts: 29 Dec 1904 United 1 Corinthians 2 (BM)
25 Nov 1905 Preston North End 1 United 1
Last game: 16 Dec 1905 United 1 Liverpool 2

Thomas Stewart made four first team appearances for United, two in friendlies, during his time at the Lane but played regularly for the reserves.

Appearances:		Apps	Gls
	FL	2	0
	Total	2	0

STONE Jack

IL/CF/IR 1941–44 5' 9" 10st 7
b. c1921

Norton Woodseats 1937–39
United: 5/6 Apr 1939 to 27 Sep 1946
Debut: 20 Sep 1941 Mansfield Town 2 United 3 (WW2)
Last game: 12 Feb 1944 Lincoln City 0 United 0 (WW2)
WW2 guest: York City and Bradford City (1943–44), Watford 1943–45, Hull City (1944–45)
Boston United (L) Feb, (£315) Sep 1946 to 1951–52

Jack Stone went to Burngreave School and played for Sheffield Boys. He joined Norton Woodseats and played for them in the 1938 Amateur FA Cup semi-final before signing for United a few months before the outbreak of the Second War and he played occasionally during the following seasons while serving in the RAF. In December 1942 he played in United's 6–2 defeat of Mansfield Town and scored 5 of the goals equalling the United individual record held by Harry Hammond and Harry Johnson.

He also made guest appearances for York City (3 games), Bradford City (10), Watford (21), who wanted to sign him, and Hull City (6). Despite his wartime connections with five FL clubs and scoring for most of them, he never played a FL game and went into non-League football with Boston United. His career was brought to an end by injuries but he stayed in Boston keeping the Station Hotel.

Appearances:		Apps	Gls
	WW2	6	6
	Total	6	6

STRINGER E (Ned)

RB/LB 1889–92

Ecclesfield and Lockwood Bros
United: cs 1889 to cs 1892
Debuts: 7 Sep 1889 Nottingham Rangers 4 United 1 (Fr)
5 Oct 1889 Scarborough 1 United 6 (FAC)
Last games: 1 Feb 1890 Bolton Wanderers 13 United 0 (FAC)
28 Feb 1891 Derby Junction 1 United 3 (MCL)
12 Mar 1892 United XI 2 Wednesday XI 1 (SCC)
14 Mar 1892 Chesterfield 4 United 3 (Fr)

Ned Stringer was a well known local player with Ecclesfield but he also played for Lockwood Bros., the Sheffield works team, in their FA Cup run of 1886–87 when they played Nottingham Forest and West Bromwich Albion and also in 1887–88.

He was a regular in United's first ever season, playing in 51 of the 57 games, most of which were friendlies. He played in the club's first ever game, the first FA Cup game (and biggest victory in the competition) and also in the club's heaviest FA Cup defeat, 0–13 at Bolton.

During the following two seasons he appeared mainly in friendly games and also for 'the Strollers' (reserve team) and occasionally with two other Stringers, one certainly a brother. During his time at the Lane, he played mainly at right back, sometimes at left back and very occasionally at half back. Ned remained at the Lane in one minor capacity or another for some years; in December 1897, he was the United linesman at a reserve match in Halifax but played the second half and scored and was also paid 7shillings (35p) per week as a scout.

Appearances:		Apps	Gls
	FAC	7	0
	MCL	5	0
	SCC	13	0
	WCC	2	0
	Total	27	0

STUART Graham Charles

MF 1997–99 5' 9" 11st 6
b. Tooting 24 October 1970

Chelsea from trainee Jun 1989/ Everton (£850k) Aug 1993
United: (player exch + £500k)) 28 Nov 1997 to 23/25 Mar 1999
Debut: 29 Nov 1997 United 1 Crewe Alexandra 0
Last games: 19 Feb 1999 United 2 Bradford City 2
23 Feb 1999 Arsenal 2 United 1 (FAC)
Charlton Athletic (£1.1m) Mar 1999/ Norwich City (Free) Jan 2005/ retired cs 2006

England youth international Graham Stuart, made his FL debut with Chelsea, scoring at home to Crystal Palace on 16 April 1990 and soon won his five U21 caps. By season 1992–93 he had secured a regular place in the side and then moved to Everton.

Graham was a regular in the Everton side for his four and a half seasons there, gaining a FA Cup winners' medal in 1995. On the final day of the 1992–93 season, he scored twice in Everton's defeat of Wimbledon which kept the club in the Premiership and saw United relegated.

A quick, intelligent player with a very professional attitude, he was signed by Nigel Spackman in exchange for Mitch Ward, Carl Tiler and around £500k. Playing on the left side of midfield, Graham took time to win over the United crowd but he steadily became more influential until a wrist injury meant that he played only as a substitute in the second of the play-off games against Sunderland. The following season, he again played in midfield but occasionally in a more forward position which he preferred, until he was injured in the 'replayed' FA Cup game against Arsenal.

He was transferred to Charlton in March 1999 where he enjoyed over five seasons, although he missed most of 2002–03 through a cruciate ligament injury and he ended his career with a short spell at Norwich, finishing with 381(51) League appearances. Subsequently he became involved in TV work.

Appearances:

	Apps	Gls
FL	52 (1)	11
PO	0 (1)	0
FAC	10 (1)	0
LC	4	0
Total	66 (3)	11

STURGESS Albert (Hairpin or Ike)

LH/RB/LB/RH/CH 1908–23 5' 11½" 11st 7 to 12st 10
b. Etruria, Stoke-on-Trent 21 October 1882
d. Sheffield 16 July 1957

Tunstall Cresswells 1901/ Stoke 1902
United: (£50 including another player) 9 Jun 1908 to 21 Jul 1923
Debut: 1 Sep 1908 Bury 1 United 2
Last game: 10 Feb 1923 Huddersfield Town 2 United 1
Norwich City Jul 1923 to Feb 1925

Albert Sturgess began his senior career with the original Stoke club, making his FL debut on 4 October 1902 at Grimsby Town. He established himself as a regular in the first team in March 1905 and missed just one game in each of the following three seasons. This reliability was a feature of his career. Stoke became bankrupt in 1908 and the players were offered for sale and Albert and George Gallimore joined United for a total of £50.

Sturgess immediately became a regular in the United first team and remained there until the early part of the 1922–23 season. Available during the First War he made more appearances for United during those four seasons than any other player.

In appearance Albert was tall and slim, being 'all arms and legs' and was nicknamed 'Hairpin'. Not a 'brilliant' player, he was a calm, diligent professional, providing 90 minutes of consistency, honesty and reliability. His tackling and anticipation were excellent and being two-footed he could play on the right on the left or in the centre. He rarely missed a game and was prepared to play anywhere. He would play in spite of injuries but that was in part because he feared that he might lose his place if another, probably younger player, took his place. He was chosen to play in all five outfield defensive positions and gained an FA Cup winners medal in 1915, toured South Africa with the FA in 1910 and gained two full England caps (1911 and 1914).

On seven occasions, three during the First War, he went into goal when the goalkeeper was injured, conceding a total of eight goals in around 325 minutes of play and twice spent 70 or more minutes as keeper.

Despite being the oldest player to make a League appearance for United, Albert did not finish his career at the Lane but joined Norwich City at the age of 40 and is still the oldest player to make his debut and to captain the Canaries. After retiring in 1925, having played 524 FL games in total, he returned to live in Sheffield running a crockery shop in Ecclesall Road.

Appearances:

	Apps	Gls
FL	353	5
FAC	22	0
CC	6	0
WW1	130	0
ABD	1	0
Total	512	5

STURRIDGE Dean Constantine

Striker 2004 5' 8" 12st 1
b. Birmingham 27 July 1973

Derby County from trainee Jul 1991/ Torquay United (L) Dec 1994/ Leicester City (£350k) Jan 2001/ Woloverhampton Wanderers (£375k) Nov 2001
United: (L) 2 Jan 2004 to Feb 2004
Debuts: 3 Jan 2004 Cardiff City 0 United 1 (FAC)
17 Jan 2004 United 3 West Ham United 3 (sub)
28 Jan 2004 Derby County 2 United 0
Last game: 7 Feb 2004 United 0 Crystal Palace 3
Queens Park Rangers (free) Mar 2005/ Kidderminster Harriers Jun 2006/ retired 2007

Dean Sturridge was, at his best, a fast and powerful striker. He made his FL debut with Derby County on 11 January 1992 at Southend United. He went on to make 142(48) League appearances for the Rams, scoring 53 goals and was a regular in the side for five season. He subsequently had two good seasons (2001–03) with Wolves but injury meant a slow start to 2003–04.

His short loan spell with United was disappointing due to his lack of match fitness and a knee problem. He returned early when he sustained a hamstring injury and although he later had a knee operation, he failed to play on a regular basis thereafter. When he moved into non-League football with Kidderminster, he had made 231(88) League appearances but his time with the Harriers was brought to an early end by injury. He has since worked on BBC Radio Derby as a summariser for Derby County's matches.

Appearances:		Apps	Gls
	FL	2 (2)	0
	FAC	1	0
	Total	3 (2)	0

SUFFO Kengne Herve Patrick

Striker 2000–02 5' 9" 12st 2
b. Ebolowa (Cameroon) 17 January 1978

Tonerre Yaounde/ Nantes 1995/ Barcelona (L) 1996–97/Nantes
United: trial Apr 2000, (£150k + £30–50k) 9 Jun/ 20 Nov 2000 to 6 Jun 2002
Debuts: 21 Nov 2000 United 1 Fulham 1 (sub)
25 Nov 2000 United 1 Bolton Wanderers 0
Last games: 29 Dec 2001 Wolverhampton Wanderers 1 United 0
16 Mar 2002 United 0 West Bromwich Albion 3 (sub)
Numancia (Spain) (L) Apr 2002, signed May 25, 5 Jun 2002/ Al Hilal Saudi Arabia) Sep 2002 to May 2003/ Coventry City (free) Jul 2003/ Dubai Club Jan 2005/ Odd Grenland (Norway) Jul 2005/ Maccabi Petah Tikva (Israel) Feb 2006/ Dundee United (trial) Sep 2007/ FC Ashod (Israel)/ UD Puertollano (Spain) Jan 2008/ Walsall (trial) Jul 2008

Patrick Suffo had spent much of the 1999–2000 season under suspension at Nantes for his behaviour towards a referee. He appeared for his country, Cameroon, in the 2000 Sydney Olympic Games, winning a gold medal although not appearing in the final. A fast striker and strong on the ball with a powerful shot, he made more than half his United appearances from the bench.

Patrick seemed to be adjusting to English football with a run of starts in the autumn of 2001 and scoring a fine goal against Rotherham but an injury brought these to an end. At the turn of the year he was away for two months with Cameroon in the African Nations' Cup, where he gained a winners' medal, scoring in the penalty shoot-out in the final. On his return, his second appearance was also his last for the club. Coming on as a substitute against West Bromwich Albion, he became involved with the fracas following Georges Santos' foul and was sent off for head butting, two minutes after coming on.

He was placed on the transfer list and joined the Spanish club Numancia, initially on loan and has subsequently played in various countries.

Appearances:		Apps	Gls
	FL	16 (20)	5
	FAC	0 (1)	0
	LC	0 (1)	1
	Total	16 (22)	6

SUMMERS Gerald (Gerry) Thomas Francis

LH 1957–64 5' 9" 11st 6
b. Small Heath, Birmingham 4 October 1933

Erdington Albion/ West Bromwich Albion amat Aug 1950, pro Aug 1951
United: (£3,000) 28/30 May 1957 to 14/16 Apr 1964
Debut: 29 Aug 1957 Charlton Athletic 3 United 1
Last games: 18 Jan 1964 Sheffield Wednesday 3 United 0
25 Jan 1964 United 1 Swansea Town 1 (FAC)
Hull City (£13k) Apr 1964/ Walsall (£10k) Oct 1965 to May 1967, coach from Feb 1967/ Wolverhampton Wanderers coach Aug 1967/ FA staff coach/ Oxford United mgr Jul 1969/ Gillingham mgr Oct 1975 to May 1981/ Southampton scout/ West Bromwich Abion chief coach Oct 1981 to Apr 1982 Leicester City asst mgr, coach Oct 1982–Dec 1986/ Derby County youth development coach 1986 to Oct 1998

Gerry Summers joined West Bromwich Albion as a youngster and, although given a taste of reserve team football at the age of sixteen it wasn't until 24 Dec 1955 at home to Manchester United that he made his FL debut. Gerry realised that first team opportunities at the Hawthorns would be limited as the left half position was occupied by English International Ray Barlow and so he accepted the transfer deal offered by the United manager, Joe Mercer, a former England wing half.

It was Joe Mercer who put together and coached the famous United defence of Hodgkinson, Coldwell, Graham Shaw, Richardson, Joe Shaw and Summers which served United well so many seasons in both FL and Cup.

Gerry was a two footed, constructive midfield player and 'the brain of the side, a player of real perception, imagination and flair'. He played with determination, providing a link between defence and attack, always being available to receive a pass from a fellow defender and pass it forward with accuracy.

He missed few games and was ever present throughout a season on three occasions. In 1961, he went on an FA tour of the Far East, New Zealand and the USA. An all-round sportsman, he also played cricket for United.

He was injured in what proved to be his final game for United and, shortly afterwards, he moved to Hull City and then Walsall where he did some coaching. He had long been interested in that aspect of the game and was a qualified FA coach and, after spells coaching, he became the manager of Oxford and later Gillingham before returning to coaching. He ended his playing career with 382(3) FL appearances.

Appearances:		Apps	Gls
	FL	260	4
	FAC	32	3
	LC	6	0
	CC	7	0
	Total	305	7

SUTCLIFFE Charles Spencer

G 1924–27 5' 11½" 11st 8
b. Bradford 7 September (October?) 1891
d. Bradford 18 August 1964

Halifax FC (1910–11)/ Halifax T 1911/ York cs 1913/WW1guest: Bradford C (1 app, 1916), Grimsby T (Dec 1916 to Nov 1917), Leeds City (Apr and May 1919)/ Leeds C cs 1919?/ Rotherham County (by Dec 1919)
United: (£2,400) 2 Oct 1924 to cs 1927
Debut: 4 Oct 1924 Bury 1 United 0
Last games: 22 Jan 1927 Arsenal 1 United 1
4 May 1927 Bradford Park Avenue 4 United XI 1 (BM)

Charles Sutcliffe came from a large family and his eldest brother played for England at both rugby and soccer. Charles may have been a part-time professional forward as early as sixteen but he switched to goalkeeping. A sergeant instructor in the Royal Engineers during the First World War, he played as a guest for Grimsby Town and won a West Riding Senior cup medal in May 1919 with Leeds City but after they were disbanded, he moved to Rotherham County, making his FL debut on 2 October 1920 at home to South Shields. He became their first choice keeper towards the end of season 1921–22 and was ever-present for the following two seasons.

He joined United when the club face a goalkeeping crisis; Harold Gough, the first choice keeper, had broken his contract by taking licensed premises and reserve Ernest Blackwell, had been forced to retire on medical grounds. A new signing, Arthur Robinson had proved to be totally inadequate and so United turned to a well known local player with Rotherham United. It was a curious signing and the new man was regarded as something of a stop-gap for he was probably 33 years old, had no experience of First Division football and no reputation of note other than 'reliable'.

It could be said that he was fortunate and the United players had no great faith in his ability. He was nervous and United's trainer let him smoke his pipe before a game but he did his job, saving a penalty kick in the FA Cup semi-final and doing everything that was required—very little as it turned out—in the FA Cup final. The following season Jack Alderson was signed—the same age as Sutcliffe but United's Secretary was too polite to ask—and Charles lost his place and, after two more seasons during which he played only 12 competitive matches, he retired, at first managing a furniture business and then becoming a sub-postmaster.

Appearances:

	Apps	Gls
FL	45	0
FAC	6	0
CC	2	0
Total	53	0

'SWIFT'

OR 1918

United: WW1 guest Feb 1918
Only game: 23 Feb 1918 Nottingham Forest 0 United 1

Nothing is known of 'Swift' who was reported in the Sheffield papers as having played this one game for United during the First War. The FL record Jimmy Simmons as the United outside right.

Appearances:

	Apps	Gls
WW1	1	0
Total	1	0

SWIFT Humphrey (Hugh) Mills

LB 1945 5' 11" 11st 8
b. Sheffield 22 January 1921
d. Sheffield 24 January 1979

Burngreave Old Boys/ Lopham Street WMC1939 Sheffield Wednesday WW2 trial 1942, amat 1942, pro 1944
United: WW2 guest Mar 1945
Only game: 31 Mar 1945 Bradford City 4 United 3 (WW2)
Retired Aug 1951

A fervent Wednesday supporter, Hugh Swift trained at Hillsborough as a youngster but was told he was too frail and he stopped attending. However in February 1942 he made a guest appearance for the Owls and soon signed amateur forms. He was near ever present in 1942–43 and towards the end of the season played as an emergency left back (he was a left winger at the time) and did so well he played there for the rest of his career and it was as a left back that he made his one guest appearance for United.

He made 136 wartime appearances for Wednesday and finally made his FL debut on 31 August 1946 at Luton Town. He missed just one FL game in the first three post-war seasons and captained Wednesday to promotion in 1950. He gained an England B cap in January 1950 but knee problems, possibly due to rheumatic fever as a youth, brought his career to an early end.

Always a part time professional he worked as a department manager at Turners Limited, owned a general dealer's shop and scouted and coached for Wednesday until his death.

Appearances:

	Apps	Gls
WW2	1	0
Total	1	0

SYKES William

RH 1920 5' 10" 10st 4
b. Sheffield

Atlas & Norfolk
United: 1918–19, pro Jun 1919 to 13 Sep 1920
Only game: 1 Jan 1920 United 2 Preston North End 1

William Sykes's one appearance for United was the only FL appearance of his career. He had played for the reserves in 1918–19 and may have played for Barnsley reserves 1921–22 before joining Wombwell.

Appearances:

	Apps	Gls
FL	1	0
Total	1	0

TALIA Francesco (Frank)

G 2001 6' 1" 13st 6
b. Melbourne (Australia) 20 July 1972

Sunshine G C (Australia)/ Blackburn Rovers (free) Aug 1992 Hartlepool United (L) Dec 1992/ Swindon Town (L) Sep 1995, (£150k) Nov 1995/ Wolverhampton Wanderers (trial) Aug 2000/
United: Trial Sep 2000, (free) 26 Sep 2000 to cs 2001
Debut: 10 Apr 2001 United 1 Norwich City 1
Last game: 6 May 2001 Bolton Wanderers 1 United 1
Royal Antwerp (Netherlands) cs 2001/ Reading Mar 2002/ Wycombe Wanderers (free) Aug 2002 to May 2007

Frank Talia, an Australian schoolboy and U21 international began his career in the National Soccer League in 1990–91. He spent three seasons with Blackburn Rovers but made no League appearances for the club, his FL debut coming when on loan to Hartlepool on 9 January 1993 at Leyton Orient. Transferred to Swindon, he had a successful time, making over 100 FL appearances.

He joined United as cover for Simon Tracey, making his debut for the reserve team (25 Sep) against Rochdale but he had to wait for his first team debut which came towards the end of the season when he played in the final seven games. Released at the end of the season he spent a time with Antwerp before joining Wycombe where he made 132 FL appearances, bringing his total to 259.

Appearances:		Apps	Gls
	FL	6	0
	Total	6	0

TALBOT LEWIS Albert Edward (see LEWIS T A L)

TAYLOR Charles Stanley

CF 1924 5' 8" 11st 7
b. Sheffield JAS 1897
d. Sheffield OND 1963

Norfolk Amateurs Oct 1919/ Wednesday Feb 1920 Norton Woodseats cs 1921
United: 27 Feb 1924 to cs 1925
Only game: 7 Apr 1924 United 3 Notts County 1
Denaby United cs 1925/ Mexborough Athletic Mar 1926/ Worksop Town cs 1926/ Mexborough Ath May 1927/ Worksop T Dec 1927

During the First World War Stanley Taylor was in the Marines and then the Army, regularly playing in representative service games. After the War he spent most of his career in local football whilst being employed in a Sheffield lawyer's office but he had spells as a professional with both Sheffield clubs.

He made his FL debut with neighbours Wednesday on 7 February 1920 at home to Preston North End and played seven games at inside forward during the rest of the season but failed to score. He then reverted to amateur status with Norton Woodseats where his success led to a chance with United and though he scored in his only appearance, he soon returned to local football.

Appearances:		Apps	Gls
	FL	1	1
	Total	1	1

TAYLOR Gareth Keith

Striker 1996–98 6' 2" 13st 8
b. Weston-super-Mare 25 February 1973

Southampton trainee/ Bristol Rovers Jul 1991 Crystal Palace (£750k) Sep 1995
United: (player exch) 6/8 Mar 1996 to 26 Nov 1998
Debut: 9 Mar 1996 United 0 Stoke C 0
Last game: 17 Oct 1998 United 1 Barnsley 1
Manchester City (£400k) Nov 1998/ Port Vale (L) Jan 2000/ Queens Park Rangers (L) Mar 2000/ Burnley (L) Feb 2001, (free) Jun 2001/ Nottingham Forest (£500k) Aug 2003/ Crewe Alexandra (L) Jan 2006/ Tranmere Rovers (free) Jul 2006/ Doncaster R (L) Jan, (free) Feb 2008

Gareth Taylor began his career with Southampton but made his FL debut after his move to Bristol Rovers, on 28 February 1992 at Cambridge United. At the time he appeared as a defender but his next FL appearance, at the start of the 1994–95 season, was as a striker. After just over a season in this role, during which time he gained Welsh U21 caps, Gareth joined Crystal Palace, gaining his first full cap, but soon moved to the Lane.

He was signed by Howard Kendall; David Tuttle and Carl Veart moving to Selhurst Park with a cash adjustment making the reported fee to be equivalent to £750k. Gareth was a good header of the ball and held the ball up well under pressure though some questioned his overall contribution. He was a regular in the squad throughout his time at the Lane but he scored a goal in fewer than every four games though a significant number of his appearances were from the bench. He scored nine of his FL goals when appearing as a substitute, the most by any United player.

In December 1997, it appeared that United were trying to sell him and he worked hard to win the support of the fans and it was somewhat of a surprise when he was sold to Manchester City. With United, he had gained six more caps (he gained 15 in all).

He continued to move from club to club, his most successful time perhaps being with Burnley. Despite never reaching the 100 League appearance mark with any of his clubs he had, by the summer of 2007–08, made 379(97) League appearances, scoring 121 goals.

Appearances:		Apps	Gls
	FL	56 (28)	24
	PO	1 (2)	0
	FAC	5 (2)	0
	LC	8 (3)	2
	Total	70 (35)	27

TAYLOR M or R or S

LH/RB 1918

United: Apr to Nov 1918
Debuts: 6 Apr 1918 Barnsley 1 United 1 (WW1, FL 'R Taylor' at RB)
13 Apr 1918 Wednesday 2 United 0 (WW1, Fr, at LH)
20 Apr 1918 United 1 Wednesday 1 (WW1, Fr, programme 'M Taylor', LH)
27 Apr 1918 Everton 1 United 1 (sub, Fr)
Last game: 2 Nov 1918 Lincoln City 2 United 1 (WW1, FL 'M Taylor' at LH)

'Taylor' confusion! The Telegraph reported in August 1915 that Samuel C Taylor, the Gainsborough left half was willing to assist United during the war. Perhaps he never did though he did turn out for Rotherham County in 1916–17 and 1917–18. Players recorded or reported with the surname did play for United and the games are listed above.

SC Taylor signed for Rotherham C in 1920 though he never made a FL appearance and in 1923 played for Turton Platts Sports.

Appearances:		Apps	Gls
	WW1	2	0
	Total	2	0

TEBILY Oliver

CD 1999 6' 1" 13st 4
b. Abidjan, Ivory Coast 19 December 1975

Niort/ Chateauroux
United: (£200k) 24 Mar 1999 to 8 Jul 1999
Debuts: 26 Mar 1999 United 1 Oxford United 2 (sub)
3 Apr 1999 Barnsley 2 United 1
Last game: 9 May 1999 Ipswich Town 4 United 1
Celtic (£1.25m) Jul 1999/ Birmingham City (£700k) Mar 2002 / – / Toronto FC Apr 2008

Oliver Tebily gained U21 caps for France whilst playing in the French second division and it was from there that he joined United, signed by Steve Bruce. In his brief time at the Lane he produced some promising and determined performances as a central defender and he gained a full cap for the Ivory Coast in the close season.

In July, after just over three months with United, he joined Celtic (38 SL app) and then he moved to Birmingham City (83 FL app) where, partly through injuries, he was unable to hold a regular place in the side. He made around 18 appearances for the Ivory Coast.

In January 2008 he was released by Birmingham and subsequently moved to Canada.

Appearances:		Apps	Gls
	FL	7 (1)	0
	Total	7 (1)	0

TEN HEUVEL Laurens

Striker 2002–03 6' 0" 12st 3
b. Duivendrecht (Netherlands) 6 June 1976

FC Den Bosch (Netherlands) / Barnsley (£75k) Mar 1996/ Northampton Town (L) Feb 1998/ First Vienna FC (Austria) cs 1998/ DCG Amsterdam cs 2000 / (Netherlands) cs 2001
United: (200k euro) 9 Jul 2002 to 10 Sep 2003
Debuts: 16 Jul 2002 Baslow 1 United 14 (sub Fr)
17 Aug 2002 United 1 Walsall 1 (sub)
Last games: 9 Nov 2002 United 0 Ipswich Town 0 (sub)
21 Jan 2003 Liverpool 2 United 1 (sub LC)
Bradford City (L) 27 Mar 2003/ Grimsby Town (L) 8 Aug 2003
De Graafschap (Netherlands) (free) Sep 2003/ HFC Haarlem (Netherlands) cs 2004/ RBC Roosendaal (Netherlands) cs 2006/ Stormvogels Telstar (L) Jan 2008

Laurens Ten Heuvel made his professional debut in December 1995 with Den Bosch. He moved to Barnsley, making his English League debut as a substitute on 27 April 1996 at Luton and made his full debut on 4 May at home to Grimsby Town. He made few first team appearances whilst at Oakwell although he did play in the Premiership. He made no appearances in his loan spell with Northampton and then moved to Austria and the Netherlands, playing regularly as a part-timer with Telstar before joining United.

As at Barnsley. Laurens found it difficult to break into the first team and all his appearances were from the subs bench, although he did score twice on his friendly debut at Baslow. Two loan spells produced a few appearances before he returned to the Netherlands.

Once again, he played regularly for his various clubs, scoring, on average, a goal every three games.

Appearances:		Apps	Gls
	FL	0 (5)	0
	FAC	0 (1)	0
	LC	0 (3)	0
	Total	0 (9)	0

THACKER Francis (Frank) William

IR 1898 5' 8" 11st 4
b. Sheepbridge, Chesterfield 1876
d. Chesterfield 8 August 1949

Sheepbridge Red Rose/ Sheepbridge Works Jul 1897
United: 4 Feb/Apr 1898 to 8 Jul 1899
Debuts: 26 Feb 1898 United 1 Wednesday 4 (Fr)
12 Sep 1898 United 1 Wolverhampton Wanderers 0
Last game: 17 Sep 1898 United 1 Stoke 1
Chesterfield Town (£10) Jul 1899/ Clapton Orient Sep 1906/ Rotherham Town cs 1907/ Chesterfield Town cs 1909/ Sheepbridge Works cs 1912/ Chesterfield Town player-trainer cs 1913 to 1915 / – / Chesterfield trainer 1921to May 1925

Frank Thacker, a former worker at the Sheepbridge Forge, made his United debut on trial in a friendly match against the Wednesday and was promptly signed in spite of the discouraging result. He played in three friendly games at the end of the 1897–98 season and two FL games at the start of the next and that was the total of his first team appearances for United but he became a mainstay of Chesterfield's side for seven seasons.

Signed as a scheming inside forward he soon converted to left half. Sturdy and hard working he was fiercely competitive and hard as nails and was quite prepared to 'mix it' if there was any dirty play. After 228 FL appearances he failed to agree terms and joined Clapton (now Leyton) Orient for a season. In due course, via Rotherham Town, he returned to Chesterfield Town, now in the Midland League as both player trainer and, after the First War, when the new Chesterfield club was formed, he was the trainer until 1925.

In 1910 he found himself on a charge of stealing pig's trotters, half a stone of tripe and vinegar from a cart. He conducted much of his own defence, reduced the court to helpless laughter and was acquitted. After football he worked in the Corporation Cleansing Department and as a canteen attendant at Sheepbridge Works.

Appearances:		Apps	Gls
	FL	2	0
	Total	2	0

THETIS Jean-Manuel (Manu)

CD (Striker) 2001 6' 3" 14st 12
b. Dijon (France) 5 November 1971

Racing Club Paris 1988/ Montpellier 1990–94 Marseilles 1994–95/ Montpellier 1995/ Seville (Spain) 1997 Ipswich Town (£50k) Sep 1998/ Wolverhampton Wanderers (L) Aug 2000
United: (free) trial 20 Mar, 22 Mar 2001 to cs 2001
Only game: 14 Apr 2001 Gillingham 4 United 1 (sub)

After spending much of his career in France and latterly in Spain, Jean-Manuel Thetis made his FL debut in with Ipswich Town on 12 September 1998 at Oxford United. He played regularly for the remainder of the season but his appearances during the following season became less frequent.

Following a loan spell with Wolves he joined United on transfer deadline day on a match-by-match basis after playing for the reserves. Despite being a central defender his one appearance was as a half time substitute playing as a striker in a poor team display at Gillingham. At the end of the season he was released and returned to France having totalled 47(4) league appearances in England.

Appearances:		Apps	Gls
	FL	0 (1)	0
	Total	0 (1)	0

THICKETT Henry (Harry)

RB 1891, 1893–1904 5' 9½" 12st 10 to 14st 7
b. Hexthorpe nr Doncaster 28 March 1873
d. Trowbridge 15 November 1920

Hexthorpe Wanderers 1890
United: trial Jan to Mar 1891
Debut: 31 Jan 1891 Grimsby Town 5 United XI 2 (Fr)
Last game: 27 Mar 1891 Rotherham Town 1 United 0 (MCL)
Doncaster Rovers (trial?) Apr 1891/ Rotherham Town 1891
United: (£30) 24 Nov 1893 to May 1904
Debuts: 2 Dec 1893 Notts County 0 United 0 (UCL)
9 Dec 1893 United 0 Everton 3
Last game: 23 Apr 1904 West Bromwich Albion 2 United 2
Bristol City May 1904, mgr Mar 1905 to Oct 1910

Harry Thickett first appeared for United in 1891 as a seventeen year old on trial. His debut was on a day when United had two first team games and he played in the friendly fixture. He played four more games, including one appearance at left back—virtually all his other appearances for United were as a right back—and he returned to Doncaster to play for the Rovers though United had not forgotten him. He quickly became a professional with Rotherham Town and on 2 September 1893, he made his FL debut at Lincoln City in Town's first ever FL game.

United had kept an eye on him and in November 1893 he moved to the Lane and went straight into the first team and in February 1894 was selected to play for the Football League for the first of two such appearances. He played regularly for over ten years during which time United were one of the top clubs in the country. He won a League Championship medal (1898), two FA Cup winners' medals (1899, 1902) and a runners' up medal (1901) and in 1899 won two England caps. His one goal for United came in February 1898 in the FA Cup surprise defeat by Burslem Port Vale.

Harry was a big, sturdy man but was surprisingly quick. His kicking, a quality needed by full backs in those days, was fine but his outstanding qualities were his willingness and hard work. His honesty was exemplified when he offered to take a pay cut in 1895 because he had missed so many games due to typhoid fever. He frequently played when he should not have done and this led to the often repeated tale that he had been injured prior to the 1899 FA Cup final and had played swathed in forty yards of bandages and fortified by copious amounts of whisky to kill the pain. The story had been given to the press by a Manchester doctor who specialized in treating injured players but a few days after the final, he said he had spoken 'in jest'.

Harry joined Bristol City in the summer of 1904 and then became the club's manager. He was very successful, gaining promotion to the top Division in 1906 and finishing second the following season. He also took City to the FA Cup final in 1909 where they lost 0–1 to Manchester United. Just over a year later, in October 1910, he was sacked and became a licensee in Trowbridge and died there aged 47.

Appearances:		Apps	Gls
	FL	259	0
	FAC	40	1
	MCL	1	0
	UCL	7	0
	ABD	3	0
	Total	310	1

THIRLWELL Paul

MF 2004–05 5' 11" 11st 4
b. Washington 13 February 1979

Sunderland from trainee Apr 1997/ Swindon Town (L) Sep 1999/
United: (free) 30 Jul 2004 to 5 Aug 2005
Debuts: 16 Jul 2004 Weymouth 3 United 5 (Fr)
14 Aug 2004 United 0 Reading 1
Last games: 23 Apr 2005 United 0 Watford 0
11 Jul 2005 Worksop Town 0 United 1 (sub Fr)
Derby County (nominal)Aug 2005/ Carlisle United (L) Sep 2006, (free) Jan 2007

England U21 international Paul Thirlwell made his FL debut with Sunderland, as a substitute, on 22 August 1997 at home to Tranmere and his full debut came on 1 November at Bolton W. He made 55(22) appearances for the club and had been captain in 2004–05 but a series of injuries limited his appearances.

Out of contract with Sunderland, Neil Warnock brought him to the Lane and he played for United as a trialist in some pre-season games and, as a result, signed permanently. He was a regular in the side until December playing as a defensive midfielder, winning, holding and distributing the ball. When Phil Jagielka moved into midfield from defence, Paul lost his place and made only occasional appearances thereafter.

After one season he moved to Derby County where he failed to make an impact, partly through injury, and he moved to Carlisle U, where he was made captain for 2007–08 and reached a career total of 144(39) League appearances with his only League goal being for the Blades.

Appearances:		Apps	Gls
	FL	24 (6)	1
	FAC	2 (1)	0
	LC	2 (1)	0
	Total	28 (8)	1

THOMAS James Alan

Striker 2000–01 6' 1" 13st 2
b. Swansea 16 January 1979

Blackburn Rovers from trainee Apr 1995, Jul 1996 West Brom A (L) Aug 1997/ Blackpool (L) Mar 2000
United: (L) 24 Nov 2000 to cs 2001
Debuts: 25 Nov 2000 United 1 Bolton Wanderers 0 (sub)
29 Nov 2000 Nottingham Forest 2 United 0
Last games: 13 Jan 2001 United 0 Watford 1
28 Apr 2001 United 2 Burnley 0 (sub)
7 May 2001 United XI 11 All Stars 1 (sub BM)
Bristol Rovers (L) Mar 2002/ Swansea City (free) Jul 2002 to May 2005

James Thomas, a Welsh youth international, made his FL debut as a substitute while on loan at West Bromwich Albion on 3 September 1997 at Stoke City; his full debut coming 10 days later at Queens Park Rangers. After various loan spells he eventually made his senior debut for his club, Blackburn, against United at the Lane in September 2000.

In November 2000, Marcus Bent left the Lane for Blackburn and, as part of the deal, James moved to the Lane on loan for the remainder of the season. He had plenty of pace but the striker made most of his appearances from the subs bench and he was injured for a time later in the season.

James returned to Ewood Park but continued to find his opportunities limited although he brought his total of Welsh U21 caps to 2. He eventually signed for Swansea and during his time there was called up for the full Welsh squad but did not make the team. After three seasons, the last of which was curtailed by knee problems requiring an operation, James retired, having made 42(15) League appearances for the Swans and 63(27) in his career.

Appearances:		Apps	Gls
	FL	3 (7)	1
	FAC	0 (1)	0
	Total	3 (8)	1

THOMAS John William

OR 1891
b. Wales
d. March 1920

Gainsborough Trinity (1889–90)
United: 5 May 1891 to Oct(?) 1891
Debuts: 1 Sep 1891 United 5 Middlesbrough Ironopolis 1 (Fr)
12 Sep 1891 Sunderland Albion 2 United 4 (NL)
Last game: 19 Sep 1891 Middlesbrough Ironopolis 2 United 2 (Fr)
Gainsborough Trinity (Dec 1891 to 1892–93)

'The Welshman' came to United after Trinity had won the MCL. 'Very fast', he played in the first seven games at the start of the 1891–92 season, all at outside right. Six of the games were friendly fixtures and despite scoring on his debut and United's first goal in the NL, he was replaced by the young Ernest Needham and returned to Gainsborough.

Appearances:		Apps	Gls
	NL	1	1
	Total	1	1

THOMPSON Charles (Charlie) Maskery

CF/CH/WH 1940–47 6' 0" 11st 7
b. Arkwright Town, Chesterfield 19 July 1920
d. August 1997

Bolsover Colliery
United: amat 18 Dec 1936, (£225) pro 19/21 Jul 1937 to 18 Aug 1947
Debuts: 27 Apr 1940 Rotherham United 0 United 3 (WW2)
5 Jan 1946 Huddersfield Town 1 United 1 (FAC)
9 Sep 1946 United 2 Chelsea 2
Last game: 31 May 1947 United 1 Charlton Athletic 3
WW2 guest: Bolsover Colliery (1939–40), Hereford U, Lovells Ath, Bath C
Hereford United Aug 1947 to 1958

Charlie Thompson became a United professional on his seventeenth birthday and the club knew by 1939 that they had a young player who could play equally well at centre half or centre forward. He was used as a centre forward and scored on his first team debut in a 1940 wartime game and held his place to the end of the season.

Fast and tough with a great shot and a fine header of the ball, he was full of enthusiasm and seemed destined to do very well. He joined the RAF in 1940 and United didn't see much of him until April 1942 but from then, playing mainly at centre forward, he scored freely, averaging 0.8 goals per game. Sadly, for Charlie and United, his leg was broken in April 1944 in the War Cup North semi-final at Villa Park and though he returned a year later, he had lost some of his speed. He made fifteen appearances in the 1945–46 FLN championship campaign and finally made his FL debut in 1946 and of his seventeen FL appearances that season, six were at centre forward, six at centre half and the others at wing half with one at right back.

United gave him a free transfer in August 1947 because he had the offer of a job in Hereford and he moved into non-League football with Hereford United. He became an idol of the crowd, a much respected player and no-one did more for the development of the club. He played over 450 competitive game s for the club, many after a terrible head and eye injury and against medical advice, and is still their record goal scorer with a total of 184. In 1947–48 he scored a club record eight goals in the 11–0 FA Cup defeat of Thynnes Athletic.

Appearances:		Apps	Gls
	FL	17	3
	FAC	1	0
	CC	6	3
	WW2	80	64
	Total	104	70

THOMPSON Dennis

OR/IL/OL/IR 1941–51 5' 6½" 10st 7
b. Sheffield 2 June 1925
d. June 1986

United: amat 29 Mar 1939, pro 10/14 Aug 1942 to 21 Jul 1951
Debuts: 13 Sep 1941 United 1 Mansfield Town 2 (WW2)
5 Oct 1946 Stoke City 3 United 0
Last game: 28 Apr 1951 United 0 Manchester City 0
WW2 guest: Rotherham U (1 app, 1942–43), Lincoln City (7 app, 1943–44), Crystal P (1 app)
Southend United (£1,500) Jul 1951/ Clacton Town Jul 1954 to cs 1957/ Matlock T Aug 1957/ Denaby United

A Sheffield Schoolboy international winger, small but with perfect ball control, a box of tricks and described as 'full of football', Dennis—often 'Denis' in the press—joined the groundstaff from school and played with the United nursery teams, Woodbourn Alliance and Fulwood in the early years of the Second World War.

He became the youngest ever United first team player when he made his debut in 1941 (16 years, 103 days) but joined the Durham Lt Infantry in 1943. He played occasionally for United but was wounded in Germany in 1945. He made his FL debut in his one appearance of 1946–47 but after he came out of the army in the summer of 1947, he played fairly regularly in the first team for the next three seasons. He was very clever with a fair turn of speed but many supporters felt that he lacked aggression and determination and subsequent barracking led to a transfer request in September 1949. He had a spell at inside forward but in 1950–51, with the signing of Hawksworth and Ringstead, his appearances became less frequent and he moved to Southend United.

He spent three seasons at Southend, making 51 FL appearances before moving into non-League football but his life, without top class football, 'went into a decline'.

Appearances:		Apps	Gls
	FL	96	20
	FAC	9	2
	CC	3	0
	WW2	10	2
	Total	118	24

THOMPSON Desmond (Des)

G 1955–62, 1963 5' 11" 12st 10
b. Southampton 4 December 1928

Scunthorpe United/ Gainsborough Trinity (1949–50) Dinnington/ York City Jan 1951/ Burnley (£7,350) Nov 1952
United: (£4,250) 9/11 May 1955 to 30 Jun 1963
Debut: 8 Oct 1955 United 1 Manchester City 1
Last games: 17 Mar 1962 Fulham 5 United 2
23 Oct 1962 Bury 3 United 1 (LC)
Buxton Jun 1963
United: 23 Nov 1963 to 8 Jan 1964
Debut: 23 Nov 1963 Fulham 3 United 1
Last game: 28 Dec 1963 United 1 Nottingham Forest 2

Des Thompson came from a goalkeeping family. His father George played for York City and played League football for Southampton and his brother George made over four hundred FL appearances for four clubs. Des made his FL debut with York City on 10 February 1951 at Halifax Town. Strong and athletic, good in the air in a crowded goalmouth, he missed just three FL games following his debut before moving to Burnley where he made 59 consecutive appearances before losing his place to Colin McDonald.

He joined United as an understudy to Ted Burgin and Alan Hodgkinson, who was in the army. Des soon had a run of six FL games but, when 'Hodgy' returned from National Service in January 1957 and proved to be rarely injured, Des, never played more than five FL games in a season although he did play regularly in the reserves. He moved into non-League football in the summer of 1963.

In November 1963 Hodgkinson broke his thumb and reserve goalkeeper Bob Widdowson had a dislocated shoulder so Des was recalled. He made seven successive FL appearances, his longest run of games for the club, before returning to non-League football.

Appearances:		Apps	Gls
	FL	25	0
	LC	1	0
	CC	4	0
	Total	30	0

THOMPSON George Alexander

OR 1907–08 5' 6½" 10st 7
b. South Shields 23 March 1884

South Shields Bertram 1904–05/ South Shields Adelaide 1905–06/ North Shields
United: 13 Oct 1906 to Sep 1908
Debut: 19 Jan 1907 Manchester United 2 United 0
Last game: 5 Sep 1908 United 1 Nottingham Forest 2
Derby County (£350)/ Newcastle United 1911 / – / Luton Town mgr Feb to Oct 1925

United paid a fee of £135 to secure George Thompson and Jim McGuire from North Shields. After making his United debut, George was a regular in the side for the remainder of the season. Noted for his quick 'dashes', he played a significant role during the following season but after playing the first two games in September 1908, he moved to Derby County.

George played regularly in his first season with Derby but he steadily became less involved and made no first team appearances whilst at Newcastle. He later became the first manager (as opposed to a secretary-manager) of Luton Town but lasted only a short time.

Appearances:		Apps	Gls
	FL	40	5
	FAC	2	0
	Total	42	5

THOMPSON Harold John

LH 1899

United: 16 Aug 1898, (FL) 22 Nov 1898 to cs? 1899
Debut: 31 Mar 1899 Burnley 1 United 0
Last game: 1 Apr 1899 Blackburn Rovers 2 United 1

A £1 per week part-time reserve player, Harold Thompson's two first team appearances for United were both away from the Lane and ended in defeat. Both appearances were in place of Ernest Needham in the two games between the FA Cup semi final and the final.

Appearances:		Apps	Gls
	FL	2	0
	Total	2	0

THOMPSON John (Jack) L

OR 1914–20 5' 8½" 10st 4 to 11st 7
b. Redcar 22 July 1892
d. Bath September 1969

South Bank/ Scunthorpe & L United (1913–14)
United: 6 May, 8 Jul 1914 to 9/12 Nov 1920
Debut: 26 Sep 1914 Chelsea 1 United 1
Last game: 11 Sep 1920 Bradford Park Avenue 2 United 0
Bristol City (£500) Nov 1920 to cs 1922/ Bath C cs 1922/ JS Fry FC 1924

Jack Thomson was never able to establish himself as a regular in the United first team. Making his debut in the final season before League football was suspended due to the First War, he was quite fast and 'a trier' but lacked 'devil' and wasn't able to win a regular place in the Cup winning season. The first United player to volunteer for army service, he joined the Royal Engineers. He played a few games in 1918–19 and occasionally during the first two seasons after the War before asking for a move to the south of England for domestic reasons.

He moved to Bristol City and later played for Bath City. He became a cinema manager in Treharris until 1939, worked for Fry's, the chocolate manufacturer and trained their football team. He died following a car accident.

Appearances:		Apps	Gls
	FL	21	2
	FAC	1	0
	WW1	4	1
	Total	26	3

THOMPSON Norman

CF/IR 1936
b. West Moor, Monkseaton 5 October 1915
d. North Tyneside April 1991

Whitley Bay & Monkseaton
United: amat 30 Jul 1936, pro 28/30 Sep 1936 to 1 May 1937
Debut: 20 Mar 1937 Nottingham Forest 1 United 1
Last game: 3 Apr 1937 Coventry City 2 United 0
Hartlepool United Jun to 2 Oct 1937/ Ashington Oct 1937/ Blyth Spartans May 1938/ Jarrow/ West Stanley Jun 1939

Norman Thompson made four first team appearances for United, in successive games. He then spent a few weeks with Hartlepool making one further FL appearance before moving into non-League football.

Appearances:

	Apps	Gls
FL	4	1
Total	4	1

THOMPSON Philip (Phil) Bernard

CD 1984–86 6' 0" 11st 8
b. Liverpool 21 January 1954

Liverpool from app, pro Feb 1971
United: (L) 13 Dec 1984, signed 13 Mar 1985 to 11 Jul 1986
Debut: 22 Dec 1984 Cardiff City 1 United 3
Last games: 15 Mar 1986 United 1 Grimsby Town 1
5 Apr 1986 Hull City 0 United 0 (sub)
Liverpool coaching staff Jul 1986 to 1992 / – / Liverpool coach 1998–2004

Phil Thompson, who had stood on the Liverpool Kop as a youngster, made his FL debut with Liverpool as a substitute on 3 April 1972 at Manchester United. His full debut came on 28 October 1972 at Norwich and he was a regular in the side from 1973–74 to 1982–83. He won many honours with both his club and country. An England youth international, he gained caps at U23 level and 42 full caps and he also represented the Football League. With Liverpool he won winners' medals in the European Cup, the UEFA Cup, the FA Cup and League Cup and he also gained five FL Championship medals.

A gangling looking player, he began his career as a midfielder but found his niche when he moved to the centre of the defence. A hard tackler and a good reader of the game he played with authority and was Liverpool's captain for a while during which time they won the European Cup.

Losing his place in 1983–84, he was signed by United's manager Ian Porterfield, initially on loan, in December 1984. During his time at the Lane, he suffered a lung injury and despite playing for much of the 1985–86 season, he looked slow and seemed incapable of adjusting to a different level of football. Unpopular with the supporters and also the players who were made very aware of his wealth, he returned to Anfield as a member of the coaching staff.

Dismissed six years later by Graeme Souness, he then spent several years as a public speaker and as a media pundit before returning to Anfield as Houllier's assistant. Phil spent several months in charge when Houllier was absent having had heart surgery but when Houllier left the club so did Phil and he returned to his media work and the speaking circuit.

Appearances:

	Apps	Gls
FL	36 (1)	0
FAC	3	0
LC	4	0
FMC	1	0
Total	44 (1)	0

THOMPSON Steven (Steve) Paul

See 'Managers' section

Appearances:

	Apps	Gls
FL	20	1
FAC	2	0
AMC	1	0
Total	23	1

THOMPSON Tyrone

MF 2000–03 5' 9" 11st 2
b. Sheffield 8 May 1982

United: from trainee, pro 10 Jul 2000 to 24 Jul 2003
Debuts: 22 Aug 2000 United 6 Lincoln City 1 (sub LC)
5 Sep 2000 Lincoln City 1 United 0 (LC)
Last game: 25 Jan 2003 United 4 Ipswich Town 3 (FAC)
Lincoln City (L) 18 Oct 2002/ Doncaster Rovers (L) 27 Mar 2003
Huddersfield Town Jul 2003/ Scarborough Jun 2004/ Halifax Town Aug 2005/ Crawley Town Jun 2007/ Torquay United May 2008

Tyrone thought hard about giving up ideas of being a professional footballer in 1999 but spent three seasons as a professional at the Lane. Though he made three appearances in the two major Cup competitions, he failed to make a League appearance. He was very fast and played regularly in the reserves with occasional appearances in friendly matches but his team play and finishing were disappointing and he wasn't powerful enough. He did finally make his FL debut as a substitute, whilst on loan to Lincoln City at home to Bury on 29 October 2002.

After moving to Huddersfield Town, he made his full FL debut on 9 August 2003 at home to Cambridge United but he made only one more FL appearance before dropping down into non-League football. More at home at this level, Tyrone played in every Conference game for Scarborough in 2004–05 but scored only two goals.

Appearances:

	Apps	Gls
FAC	1	0
LC	1 (1)	0
Total	2 (1)	0

THORPE John (Jack)

OL 1895
b. Heanor JAS 1875

Heanor Town/ Kettering Town cs 1894
United: Jun, 2 Jul 1895 to cs 1896
Debuts: 11 Sep 1895 Grimsby Town 2 United XI 3 (Fr)
7 Oct 1895 United 1 Sunderland 2
Last game: 14 Oct 1895 United 0 Celtic 1 (Fr)
Heanor Town Jul 1896/ Huddersfield FC (Dec 1898?)

Jack Thorpe's chief claim to fame as a footballer was that he had only one arm though the truth may be that he had one hand. He made just three first team appearances for United, two of them friendlies. His one FL appearance was the only one of his career.

Appearances:	Apps	Gls
FL	1	0
Total	1	0

THORPE Percy

RB 1930–33 5' 8½" 11st 12
b. Nottingham 18 July 1899
d. Ashton u Lyne JFM 1972

Sutton Town/ Blackpool May 1924/ Connah's Quay Aug 1928 Reading (£100) Oct 1928
United: 12/13 Jun 1930 to 6 May 1933
Debut: 30 Aug 1930 Birmingham 3 United 1
Last game: 6 May 1933 United 3 Arsenal 1
West Ham United (£415) 7/10 Jun 1933/ Accrington Stanley Sep 1934/ Port Vale Nov 1934 to cs 1935

Percy Thorpe made his FL debut with Blackpool on 30 August 1924. After four seasons and over 100 games he failed to agree terms and moved into non-League football before joining Reading. Again he missed few games in his nearly two seasons at the club.

Percy moved to the Lane along with Bert Oswald for a total fee of £4000 (Thorpe valued at £1750). Short and stocky, he was a cool, determined and hard working defender and in his three seasons, as at his previous clubs, he missed very few games. A colleague in the defence commented that he wasn't a good back but United certainly missed him when he left in the summer of 1933 and were relegated twelve months later. On the other hand, although he had totalled 293 FL appearances with his first three FL clubs, probably due to injury problems, he managed only six with his final three.

Appearances:	Apps	Gls
FL	103	0
FAC	8	0
CC	3	0
Total	114	0

THORPE Samuel (Sam)

RH 1944–48
b. Sheffield 2 December 1920
d. Sheffield 6 August 2002

Norton Woodseats
United: amat 31 Jul 1944, pro 6/9 Apr 1945 to 31 Jul 1949
Debuts: 23 Dec 1944 Mansfield Town 4 United 1 (WW2)
30 Apr 1947 Boston U 3 United XI 2 (CM)
27 Mar 1948 Derby County 1 United 1
Last games: 6 Sep 1948 United 2 Sunderland 5
24 Nov 1948 Western Command 0 United XI 3 (Fr, at Lichfield)
WW2 guest: Liverpool (1943–44, 2 app, 1944–45 (1), Tranmere R (1943–44, 4 app), Southport (1944–45, 15? app, 1945–46 8 app)
Frickley Colliery Oct 1949/ Gainsborough Tr/ Wisbech T/ Buxton player-mgr (1952–53)

Fair haired Sam Thorpe was an outside right with Norton Woodseats and played for United reserves in October 1942 and also played cricket for United. He joined the RAF during the Second World War and, playing in service teams with former professionals, his ability as a footballer improved but he was never quick and never looked as if he would become anything better than a steady, hard working reserve wing half. He was at the Lane for several seasons but made just seven first team appearances, three of them in friendlies. His two FL appearances for United were the only ones of his career.

Appearances:	Apps	Gls
FL	2	0
WW2	2	0
Total	4	0

TIBBOTT Leslie (Les)

LB/MF 1979–81, (1983) 5' 10" 11st 10
b. Oswestry 25 August 1955

Ipswich Town pro Mar 1973
United: (£100k) 27 Mar 1979 to 31 Oct 1982
Debut: 31 Mar 1979 United 1 Bristol Rovers 0
Last games: 12 Sep 1981 United 1 Colchester United 0
15 Sep 1981 York City 1 United 1 (LC)
29 Dec 1981 Poole T 1 United 1 (Fr)
18 Apr 1983 United XI 1 Ipswich Town 1 (BM)
TP Seinajoki (Finland) 1985

Les Tibbott came through the ranks at Ipswich, making FL his debut on 17 January 1976 at home to Coventry City. He gained two Welsh U21 caps but he didn't win a regular place in the Town side until season 1977–78.

He moved to the Lane, with United in Division Two, but his presence could not prevent relegation. He was a regular in the side in the following season but in 1980–81 he played in a variety of roles both in defence and and midfield. United were again relegated and Les began in midfield for the club's first season in Division Four. Injuries meant his career was coming to a premature end and, after September, he played in just two friendly games and his benefit match against his old club, towards the end of the following season.

Later he played in Finland and was the player manager for a time.

Appearances:		Apps	Gls
	FL	78	2
	FAC	4	0
	LC	5 (1)	0
	ASC	9	0
	AMC	2 (1)	0
	CC	2 (1)	1
	Total	100 (3)	3

Li TIE

MF 2006 6' 0" 11st 0
b. Liaoning (China) 18 September 1977

Liaoning Youth 1992/ Jianlibao (Brazil) 1993/ Liaoning Fushen 1998/ Everton (L) Aug 2002 signed (c£1m) Aug 2003
United: 27 Jul/1 Aug 2006 to c Jan 2008
Debut: 28 Jul 2006 Rotherham United 1 United 1 (Fr)
Last game: 19 Sep 2006 United 1 Bury 0 (LC)
Chengdu Blades c Jan 2008

Between 1993 and 1998 Li Tie spent five years in Brazil on a sponsored training programme and made his Chinese league debut with Liaoning Bodao in the 1998–99 season. He moved to Everton on loan in 2002 and had an impressive first season, making his English League debut at home to Spurs on 17 August 2002. He faded towards the end of the campaign following 12 months of continuous football, having represented China in the 2002 World Cup. In August 2003 he signed for Everton for a fee reportedly between £500k and 1.5m but his season was spoilt by injuries culminating in a broken leg whilst on international duty in February. Sidelined for 18 months he was unable to re-establish himself in the first team.

Signed by Neil Warnock, after training with Cheng Du, in preparation for the Premiership campaign, he was again troubled by injuries and made just one first team appearance in the League Cup. He did however continue to add to his 80+ Chinese caps and it was reported that his wages were covered by sponsors in the Far East.

He returned to China, playing for Chengdu Blades for the opening of their season in the top flight.

Appearances:		Apps	Gls
	FL	0	0
	LC	1	0
	Total	1	0

TILER Carl

CD 1997 6'2" 13st 10
b. Sheffield 11 February 1970

Barnsley from YTS, pro Aug 1988/ Nottingham Forest (£1.4m) May 1991/ Swindon Town (L) Nov 1994 Aston Villa (£750k) Oct 1995
United: (£650k) 26 Mar 1997 to 28 Nov 1997
Debut: 31 Mar 1997 Huddersfield Town 2 United 1
Last game: 22 Nov 1997 Port Vale 0 United 0
Everton (exchange) Nov 1997/ Charlton Athletic (£700k) Sep 1998/ Birmingham City (L) Feb 2001/ Portsmouth (£250k) Mar 2001/ retired Jun 2003

Carl Tiler, the son of a former Chesterfield, Brighton and Rotherham professional, made his FL debut with Barnsley as a substitute in the final

game of the season on 7 May 1988 at West Bromwich Albion, three months before he became a full professional. His full debut came on 11 March 1989 at home to Leeds United and having established himself as a regular in the side by 1990–91 he made an expensive move to Nottingham Forest. With his first two clubs, Carl had gained 13 England U21 caps but his injury prone career had not proved to be as successful as was once thought.

Carl was signed by Howard Kendall as United pushed for promotion and had made 153 League appearances. He made an excellent partner for David Holdsworth in the centre of defence and United reached the play-off final but were defeated by Crystal Palace. Carl had played in every competitive game since his arrival but financial restraints led to his transfer to Everton in November 1997 along with Mitch Ward, in an exchange deal, with Graham Stuart moving to the Lane. In September 1998, it was reported that he wanted to return to the Lane but with United cash strapped, he was transferred to Charlton Athletic.

Carl had more problems with injuries and had to retire at the age of 34. He had played 245(18) League games.

Appearances:		Apps	Gls
	FL	23	2
	PO	3	0
	LC	5	0
	Total	31	2

TILLOTSON Arthur

RB 1918–19 5' 10" 11st 10
b. Hunslet JFM 1894

United: WW1 guest
Debut: 26 Dec 1918 United 3 Wednesday 0 (WW1)
Last game: 15 Mar 1919 United 1 Leeds City 0 (WW1)
WW1 guest: Chelsea (2 app, Nov 1918), Bradford C (2app, Mar-Apr 1919)
Castleford Town Aug 1919/ Leeds United Jul 1920/ Castleford Town Sep 1920

A sturdy skilful full back and a corporal in the First War, Arthur Tillotson had played army football and for Chelsea with United's Stanley Fazackerley who brought him to the Lane when they were on leave.

He joined Castleford when the war was over and had a brief spell at Elland Road, playing in the newly formed club's first two FL games, his debut being at Port Vale on 28 August 1920, but he soon returned to Castleford.

Appearances:		Apps	Gls
	WW1	5	0
	Total	5	0

TODD Mark Kenneth

MF 1987–91 5' 6½" 10st 0
b. Belfast 4 December 1967

Manchester United YTS, pro Aug 1985
United: (free) 8 Jun, 1 Jul 1987 to 14 Nov 1991
Debuts: 28 Jul 1987 Skegness Town 0 United 7 (sub Fr)
25 Nov 1987 Leeds United 3 United 0 (sub SM)
1 Jan 1988 Blackburn Rovers 4 United 1 (sub)
2 Jan 1988 United 0 Oldham Athletic 5
Last games: 2 Feb 1991 United 4 Southampton 1
23 Apr 1991 Lincoln City 2 United 0 (BM)
Wolverhampton Wanderers (L) 14 Mar 1991
Rotherham United (L) 11 Sep, (£35k) 14 Nov 1991/ Mansfield T (trial cs 1995)/ Cambridge U (trial cs 1995)/ Scarborough (free) Aug 1995/ Mansfield Town (free, (nc)) Feb 1996/ Telford United/ Stalybridge Celtic to Nov 1996/ Blyth Spartans Nov 1996 player-asst mgr/ Ilkeston Oct 1997/ Blyth Sp/ Worksop T Mar 1998/ Stocksbridge Steels Jan 1999/ retired

Mark Todd, a Northern Ireland schoolboy and youth international, was an apprentice with Manchester United but failed to make a first team appearance. Brought to the Lane by Billy McEwan, Mark made his full debut in the 0–5 home defeat by Oldham which prompted McEwan's resignation.

An energetic, creative midfielder and a good man to have around the dressing room, he had a good run in the side under new manager Dave Bassett and was a key player during the following season as United won promotion from Division Three. United won promotion again but his appearances were now more limited and although he played a few times in the top flight, he moved on to Rotherham after a brief loan spell at Wolves.

He joined Scarborough but financial constraints meant he had to leave and after a dozen games with Mansfield and having totalled 161(15) FL appearances, he moved into non-League football, including a period with Blyth Spartans, managed by John Burridge.

In 1999 he returned to Millmoor and the Football in the Community programme and in December 2007, he returned to the Lane as Community Development Manager.

Appearances:		Apps	Gls
	FL	62 (8)	5
	FAC	10 (1)	1
	LC	5 (1)	0
	FMC	3 (1)	0
	AMC	2	0
	YHC	5	0
	Total	87 (11)	6

TOMLINSON Paul

G 1982–86 6' 2" 13st 12
b. Rotherham 4 February 1965

United: trainee 30 Jun 1980, pro 1 Jun 1983 to 22/23 Jun 1987
Debuts: 13 Oct 1982 United 2 Manchester City 2 (Fr)
19 Nov 1983 Wrexham 1 United 5 (FAC)
26 Nov 1983 United 5 Southend United 0
Last game: 29 Nov 1986 United 0 Brighton & Hove Albion 1
Birmingham City (L) 20 Mar 1987
Bradford City (£47.5) Jun 1987 to cs 1995

Paul Tomlinson was a full back when he played in the NIL and CL teams (1980–81) but played in goal for the Juniors in November 1981 and the reserves in May 1982 and showed a great deal of promise. He made two appearances in friendly games during the 1982–83 season and in November, he replaced Keith Waugh and saved a penalty kick on his FL debut and played capably for the rest of the season as United were promoted. Waugh regained his place at the start of the new season and in October, John Burridge was signed and though Paul spent three more seasons at the Lane, he played few competitive games. He did however score a goal during a friendly fixture in Dallas in May 1985 when he came on as an outfield substitute.

After a brief loan spell with Birmingham, Paul joined Bradford City where he played regularly until 1994–95, playing more games than any other Bradford City keeper (293 FL appearances) and ending his career with 341 FL appearances at his three clubs.

Appearances:		Apps	Gls
	FL	37	0
	FAC	5	0
	LC	1	0
	AMC	3	0
	Total	46	0

TONER William (Bill)

CH/LH/RH/CF/FB 1951–54 5' 11" 12st 4
b. Shettleston, Glasgow 18 December 1929
d. Glasgow 16 March 1999

St Paul's Boys' Guild Shettleston/ Queens Park Strollers amat 1947/ Celtic Feb 1948
United: (free) 5 May 1951 to 2/3 Nov 1954
Debut: 25 Aug 1951 United 4 Hull City 1
Last games: 26 Apr 1954 United 2 Aston Villa 1
19 May 1954 Hamburger SV (W Germany) 3 United 2 (Fr)
Guildford City Oct 1954/ Kilmarnock (£2,000) Nov 1954/ Hibernian (£750) Apr 1963/ Ayr United player-coach Nov 1963/ Dumbarton mgr Oct 1964 to Sep 1967/ Shettleston Juniors mgr

Bill Toner joined Celtic just before his National Service, making his Scottish League debut on 18 February 1950 but was given a free transfer.

A cool, stylish but strong centre half who always attempted to use the ball and was good in the air, he could fill in anywhere in the defence and was an emergency goalkeeper in a match when Ted Burgin was injured. This ability and willingness to play in any position probably turned out not to be to his advantage for as a 'utility player', he never held a regular place in the side although he played quite frequently during his three seasons at the Lane, winning a Second Division Championship medal in 1953. In the First Division, he had a spell at centre forward and did quite well until he missed a vital penalty against Wednesday in the FA Cup.

He left the Lane in a dispute over terms and took a van driving job in Glasgow and travelled to play for Guilford at the weekend. In due course he joined Kilmarnock and his career blossomed. He won two Scottish caps, played five times for the Scottish League and was on the losing side in three Cup Finals. In 1962 we became chairman of the Scottish Footballers' Association and he had a spell coaching and later in management before working for British Rail.

Appearances:		Apps	Gls
	FL	55	2
	FAC	5	1
	CC	1	0
	Total	61	3

TONGE Michael William

MF 2001– 6' 0" 11st 10
b. Manchester 7 April 1983

United: from trainee 16 Mar 2001
Debuts: 17 Apr 2001 United 0 Wimbledon 1 (sub)
6 May 2001 Bolton Wanderers 1 United 1

Michael Tonge began his career at Old Trafford but was rejected by Manchester United at the age of 16. He moved to the Lane and was a regular in the squad from 2001–02. He was ever present during 2003–04 but his best season was 2002–03 where he produced some splendid performances alongside Michael Brown in midfield.

Though naturally right footed, he was particularly dangerous when attacking down the left flank. Playing either in the centre of midfield or wide on the left, he had the ability to hold the ball and produce openings for others. Possessing a good shot, his overall goal tally has been a little disappointing although his goal against Wednesday at Hillsborough in 2005–06 was magnificent. There have been times when he 'disappeared' from the game but his enthusiasm and determination returned in 2008 under Kevin Blackwell and by the end of the 2007–08 season, he was the current United player with most appearances for the club.

Appearances:		Apps	Gls
	FL	230 (28)	21
	PO	3	0
	FAC	17 (2)	0
	LC	14 (3)	3
	Total	264 (33)	24

TOOTILL George (Alf) Albert

CH/WH 1938–45 6' 0½" 11st 13
b. Walkden 20 October 1913
d. Sheffield July 1984

Chorley (1934)/ Plymouth Argyle May 1936
United: (£1,300) 3/6 Jan 1938 to 14 Jun 1947
Debuts: 5 May 1938 Boston United 1 United XI 2 (Fr)
27 Aug 1938 Nottingham Forest 0 United 2
Last games: 11 Mar 1939 United 1 Swansea Town 2
24 Nov 1945 United 2 Bolton Wanderers 3 (FLN)
30 Apr 1947 Boston U 3 United XI 2 (CM)
WW2 guest: Rotherham U (Nov 1939 v United), Aldershot (1942–43), Hartlepool United 1943–46, Bournemouth (1945–46)
Hartlepool United Jul 1947 to cs 1948

'Alf' Tootill made his FL debut with Plymouth Argyle on 3 April 1937 at home to Tranmere Rovers but only made nine first team appearances.

He was signed by Teddy Davison, the United manager, as a reserve centre half and played in the first ten FL games of the following season when Tom Johnson was injured but Johnson replaced him as soon as he was fit. 'Alf' was quick and constructive but lacked power and was prone to error. A sergeant in the army, he played occasionally during the Second War but, after a poor display against Nat Lofthouse in November 1945, he never played for the first team again.

He played with Hartlepool for one season, 1947–48, ending his career, which had been disrupted by the War, with a total of 39 FL appearances and became a licensee in Aston.

Appearances:		Apps	Gls
	FL	12	0
	CC	1	0
	WW2	27	0
	Total	40	0

TOWNER Antony (Tony, Tiger) James

OR/OL 1983 5' 7" 9st 11
b. Brighton 2 May 1955

Lower Bevendean/ Brighton & Hove Albion app Dec 1970, pro Oct 1972/ Millwall (£65k) Oct 1978/ Rotherham United (£180k inc other player, Towner estimated at over £100k) Aug 1980
United: (L) 24 Mar 1983 to 14 May 1983
Debut: 26 Mar 1983 Southend United 3 United 1
Last game: 14 May 1983 Orient 4 United 1
Wolverhampton Wanderers (£100k) Aug 1983/ Charlton Athletic (£15k) Sep 1984/ Rochdale Nov 1985/ Cambridge United Mar 1986/ Gravesend & Northfleet Sep 1986/ Fisher Ath cs 1987/ Crawley Town cs 1989/ Worthing cs 1990/ Gravesend & Northfleet Oct 1990/ Crawley T Jan 1991/ Lewes Sep 1991/ Crawley Town Nov 1991/ Newhaven and Saltdean United Dec 1992 player and coach

Tony Towner made his FL debut with Brighton at home to Luton Town on 10 February 1973 and it was with the Seagulls that he enjoyed the most successful part of his career making over 150 FL appearances. His move to Millwall brought Brighton their then record fee but he moved to Rotherham two seasons later as Millwall were in need of the money.

A traditional tricky winger, he made over 100 FL appearances for Rotherham and gained a Division Three Championship medal in 1981. Tony was about to sign for Wolves when he was persuaded by his former Rotherham manager Ian Porterfield to join United on loan. He played regularly for two months before returning to Rotherham and then signing for Wolves.

Tony made 397(22) FL appearances and had a long career in non-League football before becoming a lorry driver.

Appearances:		Apps	Gls
	FL	9 (1)	1
	Total	9 (1)	1

TRACEY Simon Peter

G 1988–2002 (2003) 6' 0" 13st 0
b. Woolwich 9 December 1967

Wimbledon app to pro Feb 1986
United: (£12.5k) 14/19 Oct 1988 to cs 2002
Debuts: 5 Dec 1988 Wrexham 1 United 1 (SVT)
11 Mar 1989 United 5 Huddersfield Town 1
Last games: 23 Apr 2002 Birmingham City 2 United 0
2 Aug 2003 United 2 Middlesbrough 3 (BM)
Manchester City (L) 27 Oct 1994/ Norwich City (L) 31 Dec 1994/ Wimbledon (L) 2 Nov 1995
Retired cs 2002/ Rotherham U coach 2005

Simon Tracey was the understudy to Dave Beasant who had a long injury free run whilst at Wimbledon and Simon had to wait until Beasant moved to Newcastle before he made his first team debut. This was at Wembley in the Charity Shield against Liverpool. Simon's FL debut came a week later on 27 August 1988 at home to Arsenal and he conceded five goals. This was his last first team game for the Dons until his one 'on loan' appearance in 1995.

Dave Bassett had been Simon's manger for a time at Wimbledon and it was he who brought Simon to the Lane in October 1988. Initially Simon played second fiddle to Graham Benstead and his United FL debut came when Graham was suspended. Bassett took supporters by surprise when he replaced Benstead with Tracey for the last six games of the 1988–89 promotion season but he took his opportunity and he was ever present during the following season as United gained promotion to the top flight. A regular for the following two seasons, the possibility arose that Simon might play for Ireland but the family links didn't satisfy the regulations and he was robbed of the chance to train with the England squad in 1992 by a shoulder injury which kept him sidelined for the end of the 1991–92 campaign and for much of the next one.

By this time, Alan Kelly had arrived at the Lane and Simon played mainly only when Kelly was unfit though he did have three loan spells in the mid 1990s. Tracey had the misfortune to be in goal when United were relegated at Stamford Bridge in 1994 and he also conceded the last minute play-off goal against Crystal Palace at Wembley in 1997.

When Kelly left in the summer of 1999, Simon regained his place and played in 126 (out of a possible 138) League games in the following three seasons before retiring, although he did make one further appearance in his benefit match.

An agile and brave goalkeeper, he could kick long and accurate to his forwards but was occasionally prone to the odd 'rush of blood to the head' when challenging an onrushing opponent and this resulted in him being dismissed five times. He was the first United player to be sent-off in the notorious abandoned game against West Bromwich Albion but in Simon's case, it was for handling the ball outside the area. His first dismissal, at Tottenham in September 1992, resulted in an outfield player being withdrawn and Alan Kelly coming on as a substitute, the first time this had happened in a United game. His total of 335 League appearances for the Blades placed him 18th in the all-time appearance list for the club.

Appearances:		Apps	Gls
	FL	329 (3)	0
	PO	3	0
	FAC	18	0
	LC	22	0
	FMC	4	0
	AMC	1	0
	AIC	2	0
	YHC	1	0
	Total	380 (3)	0

TROTH Joseph (Joe) William

LB 1946 5' 10" 11st 0
b. 1926

Whittington Moor YC
United: 8/11 May 1945 to 4 May 1946
Only game: 12 Jan 1946 United 2 Middlesbrough 7 (WW2)
Boston United (1946–47)

Joe Troth played just one first team game for United during the transitional season at the end of the War. He had played reasonably well for the reserves but had a totally disastrous first team debut against Johnny Spuhler, the Boro outside right, who went past him at will, and the Middlesbrough centre forward, Fenton, scored five goals.

Appearances:		Apps	Gls
	WW2	1	0
	Total	1	0

TRUEMAN Albert (Nigger) Harry Cowell

LH/IL/CH 1911–13 5' 7" 11st 0
b. Leicester AMJ 1882
d. Leicester 24 February 1961

Leicester Fosse amat 1899/ Grasmere Swifts (Coalville) Hinckley Town cs 1902/ Coalville Town 1903/ Leicester Fosse Aug 1905/ Southampton May 1908
United: 28/31 Mar 1911 to Jun 1913
Debut: 1 Apr 1911 Preston North End 1 United 1
Last game: 22 Feb 1913 Tottenham Hotspur 1 United 0
Darlington Jun 1913/ South Shields/ Leicester Imperial 1914
WW1 guest: Leicester F (1 app, 1916), Clydebank 1917
Clydebank 1919

Albert Trueman was an amateur with Leicester Fosse (now City) and re-joined them as a professional and made his FL debut on 2 September 1905 at home to Clapton Orient. He had three successful seasons with Southern League Southampton, representing the Southern League on four occasions and scoring the winning goal against the Football League in November 1910 but in 1911, unsettled with Southampton, he asked for a transfer and moved to the Lane.

A strong, determined, stocky player, he played well in his first full season of 1911–12 and many felt he was worth a cap and he continued to play regularly at left half. His lack of height was a disadvantage and in 1913, he was put on the transfer list. He moved into non-League football with Darlington but soon after the outbreak of war in 1914, he returned to work in Leicester then, in 1917, went to work in Glasgow.

Appearances:		Apps	Gls
	FL	55	0
	FAC	2	0
	ABD	1	0
	Total	58	0

TRUSSON Michael (Mike) Sydney

MF 1980–83 5' 11" 12st 4
b. Northolt 26 May 1959

Plymouth Argyle Aug 1975, app Jan 1977/ Stoke City (L) Dec 1979
United: (£60k) 7 Jul 1980 to 29 Dec 1983
Debuts: 31 Jul 1980 Chesterfield 1 United 0 (ASC)
9 Aug 1980 Sheffield Wednesday 2 United 0 (LC)
16 Aug 1980 Carlisle United 0 United 3
Last games: 22 Oct 1983 United 0 Brentford 0
25 Oct 1983 United 2 Shrewsbury Town 0 (LC)
Rotherham United Dec 1983/ (free) Brighton & Hove Albion Jul 1987/ Gillingham (£20k) Sep 1989/ Hong Kong/ Bournemouth coaching Aug 1992/ Stamco FC (Hastings) Aug 1994

Mike Trusson made his FL debut with Plymouth Argyle whilst still a trainee, on 23 October 1976 at Bristol Rovers, aged 17. For the following three seasons he played frequently, if not regularly, before moving to the Lane.

Signed by Harry Haslam, Mike was a regular in the side for over three seasons, missing 23 of a possible 149 FL games whilst at the Lane. He experienced the last minute relegation in 1981 but played a significant role in the Division Four Championship season. The strong, attacking midfielder missed just two games that season and scored some valuable goals. He enjoyed his time with the Blades and was popular with the fans but was 'persuaded' to move to Millmoor as a belated part of the deal which brought Paul Stancliffe to the Lane.

Mike spent a productive time with Rotherham before spells with Brighton and Gillingham where injury cut short his career which came to a close after having played 417(17) FL games and scoring 74 goals. He then became involved in coaching. Later he was involved with various sports' promotions and was a marketing executive with the PFA.

Appearances:

	Apps	Gls
FL	125 (1)	31
FAC	11	0
LC	12	0
ASC	3	0
AMC	3	1
CC	1	0
Total	155 (1)	32

TUDOR John Arthur

Striker 1968–71 5' 10½" 12st 2
b. Ilkeston 25 June 1946

Stanley Common Welfare/ Cotmanhay Utd/ Middlesbrough amat/ Ilkeston Town/ Coventry City Jan 1965
United: (£58.5k) 14 Nov 1968 to 27 Jan 1971
Debut: 16 Nov 1968 Bury 0 United 2
Last games: 16 Jan 1971 Bolton Wanderers 2 United 1
23 Jan 1971 Chesterfield 1 United 0 (Fr)
Newcastle United (player exch) Jan 1971/ Stoke City (£25/30k) Oct 1976/ AC Ghent (£10k) Aug 1977 to cs 1978. retired/ North Shields coach, mgr Oct 1979/ Gateshead Dec 1980/ Bedlington Terriers Nov 1982 to 1983/ Derbyshire coaching/ Minnesota (USA) coaching

John Tudor had unsuccessful trials with several clubs as a youngster including United where he was unlucky in that his 'team' lost 10–1 and as a result, he was a late developer in football. He had worked as a welder, truck driver and tile maker before becoming a professional with Coventry City and it was with the Midlands club that he made his FL debut on 24 September 1966 at home to Bury and played a significant role in their promotion to the top Division. Unable to maintain his early goal scoring success and facing competition from Tony Hateley and Neil Martin, he moved to the Lane.

Signed by John Harris, John scored twice in each of his first two games. He continued to have a very good goal scoring record, being particularly good in the air, timing his jumps to perfection but he did not always see eye to eye with Harris and he was convinced that the manager didn't like him. To boost United's flagging, but eventually successful, promotion push, David Ford and goalkeeper John Hope were signed from Newcastle with John moving the other way.

After a stuttering first season at St James Park, his career took off when he played alongside Malcolm MacDonald and he was a member of the 1974 Cup final team. A change of manager and MacDonald's departure led to John's move to Stoke but he had knee problems which caused his eventual retirement. He had a spell in non-League football before becoming a publican, firstly in the North East and then back in his native Derbyshire before moving to the United States and then setting up a business in Canada.

Appearances:

	Apps	Gls
FL	64 (7)	30
FAC	2	1
LC	5	2
CC	6	4
ABD	1	0
Total	78 (7)	37

TUMMON Oliver

OR/OL 1915–20 5' 6½" 11st to 12st 2
b. Sheffield 3 March 1884
d. Sheffield October 1955

South St. New Connection (Sheffield)/ Gainsborough Tr 1901/ Wednesday amat Mar 1902, pro Feb 1903 Gainsborough Trinity (£40) Jun 1910/ Oldham Athletic (£300) Jul 1912
United: WW1 guest 1915–18, pro Aug 1919 to cs 1920
Debuts: 16 Oct 1915 Wednesday 0 United 0 (WW1)
1 Sep 1919 United 3 Notts County 0
Last game: 3 Apr 1920 United 0 Bradford City 0
Barnsley Aug 1920/ Sir Albert Hawkes FC amat Aug 1922/ Nether Edge (Sheffield) amat Aug 1924

Oliver Tummon made his FL debut with Wednesday on 23 April 1906 at home to Everton. Due to the form of other players he was unable to become a regular in the first team and moved to Gainsborough where he had two ever-present seasons, and then Oldham where he missed six games in three seasons in Athletic's most successful period in their history.

A short and powerful player, he favoured a direct approach in his wing play; not afraid to cut in on goal, he had a powerful shot with either foot. On the outbreak the First War he returned to Sheffield to work in a munitions factory and played frequently for United as a guest during the first three seasons of the War. He played mainly at outside right, sometimes on the left wing and very occasionally at inside forward or wing-half and scored a comical goal against the Wednesday in May 1916, collecting an intended back pass to the keeper who had chosen the wrong moment to bend down to fasten his boot laces. Tummon played for both Oldham and United in 1917–18 and then joined the army, returning in 1919 to sign for United. He began the first post-War season at outside left but eventually lost his place and moved to neighbours Barnsley where his one FL appearance brought his total to 248, despite the loss of four seasons due to the War.

On leaving Barnsley he reverted to amateur status and continued to play in local football beyond the age of 40 and later became a bowls player with Brincliffe Oaks.

Appearances:		Apps	Gls
	FL	23	2
	WW1	78	23
	Total	101	25

TUNSTALL Frederick (Fred) Edward

OL 1920–32 5' 7½" 11st 6
b. Newcastle under Lyme 28 May 1897
d. Boston, Lincolnshire July 1971

Darfield St George/ Scunthorpe United May 1920
United: (£1,000) 1/4 Dec 1920 to 3 Feb 1933
Debut: 4 Dec 1920 Tottenham Hotspur 4 United 1
Last games: 19 Mar 1932 United 2 Leicester City 2
27 Apr 1932 Darlington 1 United 6 (BM)
Halifax Town (£400) Feb 1933/ Boston United player, coach, mgr, groundsman Jul 1936 to 1967

Fred Tunstall was brought up in Low Valley near Darfield in south Yorkshire after his parents moved there from Staffordshire when he was a child. Fred worked as a miner at Houghton Main Colliery and had played little football until he joined the Royal Horse Artillery in 1915.

After being demobbed in 1919, he played for Darfield St George and came to United's attention but the scout sent to watch him was not impressed and neither were Barnsley who didn't think he was worth the £10 signing-on fee. Fred joined Midland League Scunthorpe United and his potential ability soon became obvious and after only 19 games United paid what was then reported as a post-war record fee for a non-League player. There was little publicity about the move and while Fred was making his United debut at White Hart Lane, the Spurs manager was at Scunthorpe hoping to watch the brilliant young prospect.

Fred played regularly for United for the next ten years, rarely missing a game and being ever present for two successive seasons 1925–27. He played every game at outside left and for nearly all of that time he had Billy Gillespie as his partner at inside left and George Green behind him at left half and they combined superbly.

Fred didn't look like an athlete and couldn't head a ball for toffee but he was two footed, fast and strong, with a long raking stride and he could do the unexpected at speed and pass an opponent on either side. He advocated first time shooting and crossing, both of which were usually struck with awesome power and many contemporary players thought he had the hardest shot seen in football for thirty years whether on the run or with a dead ball. Harry Johnson said he often hesitated before putting his head to a Tunstall centre knowing the speed of the ball and the headline 'Tunny-Dunne-it' became a standard in the Sheffield sports pages as Jimmy Dunne, like Johnson, took advantage of Tunstall's centres. Fred had a good record from the penalty spot, converting 31of 38 attempts (only Colin Morris has taken more).

His most famous goal came in the 1925 FA Cup Final from a cross-field ball though opinions were divided as to who provided the pass and which foot was used to score. The pass wasn't a particularly good one but Tunstall spotted hesitancy by a Cardiff player—ironically called Wake—and scored from just inside the penalty area with a typical hard cross-shot into the far corner of the net securing United a 1–0 victory. Only one other United player has since scored for the Blades at Wembley.

Because of the Cup final Fred had to miss the 1925 FA Tour of Australia but he did tour Canada the following season. He also played for the Football League and won 7 England caps. He remains eighth on United's League appearances list.

After a short time with Halifax, he joined Boston United where he became a legendary figure, spending 30 years in a variety of roles. He became the player-manager in 1937, played in emergency as late as 1950–51 at both Grantham and Peterborough and was the trainer and groundsman from the mid 1950s until 1967.

Appearances:		Apps	Gls
	FL	437	129
	FAC	35	5
	CC	18	1
	ABD	1	0
	Total	491	135

TURLEY John William

CF 1957 5' 9½" 10st 13
b. Bebington 26 January 1939

Wolves 1954/ Ellesmere Port 1955
United: 11/15 May 1956 to 6 Jul 1961
Debuts: 12 Feb 1957 Royal Signals 3rd Training Regt 1 United XI 4 (Fr at Lincoln)
16 Sep 1957 United 2 West Ham United 1
Last game: 25 Dec 1957 Blackburn Rovers 1 United 0
Peterborough United (£1600) Jul 1961/ Rochdale May 1964/ Cambridge U

John Turley was signed by Manager Joe Mercer from his old home town club. John was seventeen and had been on the Wolverhampton Wanderers ground staff for two years and had played with Ellesmere Port for about six months.

He played centre forward for the NIL side and looked a tremendous prospect for he was good in the air, had a strong shot and good ball control and those opinions were confirmed when he scored in each of his first three FL appearances for United. Despite this, for whatever reason, John, after one more game lost his form, his enthusiasm and his place and only made one more appearance for the first team. This was on Christmas Day 1957, the day before Derek Pace was signed and Pace held the number nine shirt for several years. Turley never seemed likely to recapture his early promise and after three more seasons in the reserves, he was put on the transfer list and joined Peterborough United, then in their second season as a FL club. He was not a regular member of the side but was cover for the regular strikers and scored 14 goals in 32 appearances and after one season with Rochdale (22 app, 5 gl), he moved into non-League football, spending two seasons with Cambridge United.

Appearances:		Apps	Gls
	FL	5	3
	Total	5	3

TURLEY Roy David OBE

OR 1954 5' 8" 10st 7
b. Sheffield 1936

Woodbourn Ath/ Wath W/ RAF
United: part-time 20 Jul 1953 to 30 Jun 1955
Only game: 26 Oct 1954 United 1 Barnsley 0 (CC)
Stocksbridge Works 1955/ Retford T 1962/ Biggleswade T/ Matlock T 1967/ Stalham T

Roy Turley was a trainee teacher who turned down manager Reg Freeman's offer of a full-time contract. A tricky winger, he concentrated on his teaching career. He first taught at Greystones and other posts included Matlock College and Stalham High School in Norfolk where, in 1986, he was awarded the OBE for services to education. His brother, Mike, played four games for Sheffield Wednesday.

Appearances:		Apps	Gls
	CC	1	0
	Total	1	0

TURNBULL George

G 1927 5' 10" 11st 4
b. Douglas (Lanark) c1906

Stakeford United (Northumberl'd)/ Blyth Spartans cs 1926
United: (£300) 24/26 Mar 1927 to cs 1928
Only game: 29 Aug 1927 Leicester City 3 United 1
Blyth Spartans Aug 1928

Brought up in Blyth, Northumberland, George Turnbull, apart from his season with one first team game with United, played all his football with non-League teams.

Appearances:		Apps	Gls
	FL	1	0
	Total	1	0

TURNBULL Thomas

RB 1900 5' 11" 12st 10
b. Scotland c1877

Falkirk Dec 1893/ East Stirling May 1898/ Celtic May 1899
United: 13/22 Sep 1900 to 1901
Debut: 29 Sep 1900 United 1 West Bromwich Albion 1
Last games: 17 Nov 1900 Wolverhampton Wanderers 3 United 0
27 Dec 1900 Aston Villa 5 United 1 (BM)
/ – / Stenhousemuir Mar 1903/ Partick Thistle Oct 1903

Tommy Turnbull spent the whole of his career in Scotland other than a few months with United. He had joined United with Pat Gilhooly from Celtic for a joint fee reported as £150. He was signed as a promising reserve full back for he had played in an international trial in 1897 but after he had played a couple of games with the first team, he was chosen to play centre half in a benefit match at Villa Park. Sadly for the young Scot, his leg was broken and United were unhappy when they were told that no ambulance was available and George Waller, the United trainer, had to make some very makeshift arrangements in order to get the player to hospital.

He returned to Scotland and eventually played again but he never became a regular first team player. His younger brother Jamie was a Championship and FA Cup winner with Manchester United.

Appearances:		Apps	Gls
	FL	2	0
	Total	2	0

TUTTLE David Philip

CD 1993–96 6' 1" 13st
b. Reading 6 February 1972

Tottenham Hotspur from trainee Feb 1990 Peterborough United (L) Jan 1993
United: (£400k) 1/6 Aug 1993 to 6/8 Mar 1996
Debuts: 9 Aug 1993 United 0 Sheffield Wednesday 1 (Dooley BM)
14 Aug 1993 United 3 Swindon Town 1
Last game: 28 Feb 1996 Norwich City 0 United 0
Crystal Palace (player exch + cash)Mar 1996/ Charlton A (L) Mar 1999/ Barnsley (£150k) Aug 1999/ Millwall (£200k) Mar 2000/ Wycombe Wanderers (L) Feb 2002/ Millwall coaching, Dec 2005 acting mgr to Apr 2006 / – / Swindon, coaching and scouting Jun 2006, caretaker mgr 23–24 Oct 2006, to Nov 2006 / – / Dorking player + advisor Jun 2007/ MK Dons chief scout Jul 2007

England youth international David Tuttle made his FL debut with Spurs on 1 December 1990 at Chelsea but was unable to hold down a regular first team place.

He moved to the Lane, signed by Dave Bassett, at the start of United's second season in the Premiership. A regular in the side as a central defender he hurt his knee in the last home game of the season against Newcastle United but the victory in that game meant United looked fairly certain to stay up. It was not to be and David did not play again for nearly 12 months. He did play regularly in 1995–96 but in March, under new manager Howard Kendall, he moved to Selhurst Park with Carl Veart in exchange for Gareth Taylor and around £400k.

After a successful time with Palace, his career stalled and during 2002–03 a recurring back problem meant he had to give up first team football, having played 187 (16) League games, and he became involved with the Millwall academy. In December 2005 he was made caretaker manager, with Millwall bottom of the Championship. Unable to avoid relegation, David resigned just before the end of the season. Taking a scouting and coaching role at Swindon he accepted the caretaker manager's job on 23 October but 24 hours later decided to revert to his former role. He left the club when a new manager was appointed and after a month with Dorking, where he also signed as a player, he moved to MK Dons as chief scout.

Appearances:

	Apps	Gls
FL	63	1
FAC	3	0
LC	2	0
Total	68	1

TWEDDLE Frederick (Freddie)

OR 1910–11 5' 6" 11st
b. Middlesbrough JFM 1887
d. Middlesbrough

Darlington St Augustine 1907–08/ Saltburn 1907–08 Hartlepools United cs 1908
United: (£75) 19 Apr/ 4 May 1910 to cs 1911
Debut: 19 Sep 1910 United 2 Liverpool 0
Last game: 17 Apr 1911 Oldham Athletic 3 United 0
Hartlepools United Aug 1911/ Shildon Athletic cs 1912

Reported to be 'a Middlesbrough lad', Freddie Tweddle (whose birth was registered as Tweddell) had a good turn of speed and was a useful reserve when Joe Walton was unavailable. An intelligent player, United used him as a scout when he was injured. His brother Samuel played with him for Hartlepools.

Appearances:

	Apps	Gls
FL	10	0
Total	10	0

TWISS Michael John

MF 1998–99 5' 11" 12st 8
b. Salford 26 December 1977

Manchester United from 1994, pro Jul 1996
United: (L) 1/6 Aug 1998 to 10 Mar 1999
Debut: 3 Oct 1998 United 2 Portsmouth 1
Last games: 9 Jan 1999 Swindon Town 2 United 2
27 Jan 1999 United 4 Cardiff City 1 (FAC)
9 Mar 1999 Portsmouth 1 United 0 (sub)
Preston North End (L) Mar 2000/ Port Vale Jul 2000/ Leigh RMI Sep 2001/ Chester City May 2002/ Morecambe May 2004

Michael Twiss began his career with Manchester United but he made only one FA Cup substitute appearances for the club. Signed on a long term loan by manager Steve Bruce, Michael made his FL debut with United but was lightweight and unable to win a regular place in the side.

Returning to Old Trafford he then moved to Port Vale for a season before moving into non-League football. In 2006–07 he was a regular member of the Morecambe side which gained promotion to the FL for the first time in the club's history and continued as such in 2007–08. By the summer of 2008 he had made 44(22) FL appearances.

Appearances:

	Apps	Gls
FL	2 (10)	1
FAC	2 (3)	0
Total	4 (13)	1

UHLENBEEK Gustav (Gus) Reinier

RWB/LWB 2000–02 5' 10" 12st 6
b. Paramaibo, Surinam 20 August 1970

Ajax (Netherlands) 1990/ Cambuur Leeuwarden (Netherlands) cs 1992/ Newcastle U (trial) Aug 1993 TOPS SV(Netherlands) cs 1994/ Ipswich Town (£100k) Aug 1995/ Fulham (free) Sep 1998
United: (free) 10 Aug 2000 to Jun 2002
Debuts: 18 Jul 2000 Tideswell 0 United 8 (sub Fr)
24 Jul 2000 Hayle 0 United 9 (Fr)
12 Aug 2000 United 2 Portsmouth 0
Last game: 23 Mar 2002 United 3 Burnley 0
Walsall (L) 28 Mar 2002

Bradford City (free, (nc)) 9 Aug 2002/ Chesterfield (free) Aug 2003/ Wycombe Wanderers (free) Jul 2004/ Mansfield Town (free) Aug 2005/ Halifax Town Aug 2006 to May 2007

Gus Uhlenbeek made two League appearances for Ajax before moving to less well known clubs in the Netherlands. He joined Ipswich Town after trials in the summer and made his FL debut on 12 August 1995 at Birmingham City.

After a spell with Fulham, he moved to the Lane, signed by Neil Warnock at the start of his first full season in charge. Gus was quick and capable of delivering good crosses but at times wayward; he played mainly at right wing back, the position he had converted to from right wing in his early days with Ipswich, and was a regular in the side until losing his place to Rob Kozluk. He then played in a variety of positions, on both flanks or in the centre of defence and was on the transfer list at the start of his second season. He played in the reserves until Kozluk was injured and Gus was again first choice until his deadline day loan move to Walsall.

He then had four successive seasons each with a different club, mainly in the lower Divisions, each time playing regularly, before moving into non-League football, for one season, with Halifax Town. He made 293(52) FL appearances.

Appearances:		Apps	Gls
	FL	47 (4)	0
	FAC	3	0
	LC	5	0
	Total	55 (4)	0

ULLATHORNE Robert (Rob)

LWB 2000–01, 2001–02 5' 8" 11st 3
b. Wakefield 11 October 1971

Norwich City from trainee, pro Jul 1990/ CA Osasuna (Spain) cs 1996/ Leicester City (£600k) Feb 1997/ trials with Huddersfield Town, Real Zaragoza, Tenerife, Newcastle United

United: (free) 1 Dec 2000 to Jun 2001
Debut: 2 Dec 2000 Stockport County 0 United 2
Last games: 6 May 2001 Bolton Wanderers 1 United 1
7 May 2001 United XI 11 All Stars 1 (Whitehouse BM)
/ – /
United: 23 Nov 2001 to cs 2003
Debuts: 5 Jan 2002 United 1 Nottingham Forest 0 (FAC)
12 Jan 2002 Gillingham 0 United 1
Last game: 19 Oct 2002 Brighton & Hove Albion 2 United 4

Trials with: Stoke City, Walsall, Derby County/ Northampton T Feb 2004/ Notts County (free) Jul 2004/ Kidderminster Harriers trial cs 2006/ Goole Town/ Tamworth Jul to Aug 2007

Raised in Goole, England, youth international Rob Ullathorne made his FL debut with Norwich City on 22 April 1991 at Nottingham Forest. Season 1995–96 saw him make most appearances but, being a free agent in the summer he moved to Spain. He returned to join Leicester City but his leg was broken in his first game. He appeared on the losing side in the League Cup final of 1999 but shortly afterwards broke his leg again, an injury which threatened his career. After trials with various clubs, including games with Newcastle reserves, Rob joined United, initially on a one month's contract.

He played as a left wing back using his pace and anticipation well but he was in and out of the side through injury. Out of contract at the end of the season he could not agree terms for an extension but, after various trials, he continued to train at the Lane. He rejoined United following an injury to Shane Nicholson and had a good run in the side until the notorious game against West Bromwich Albion. It was an injury to Rob that finally reduced United to six players, causing the game to be abandoned.

A regular for the start of 2002–03, Rob had a hernia operation which ended his season and he left in the summer. After more trials he ended his League career with two productive seasons at Notts County, finishing with 231(16) career FL appearances, before moving into non-League football. Subsequently, based in Nottingham, he worked for a company that offering advice to sportsmen.

Appearances:		Apps	Gls
	FL	39 (1)	0
	FAC	2	0
	LC	2	0
	Total	43 (1)	0

UNDERWOOD George Ronald

RH/CH 1949–50 5' 9" 11st
b. Sheffield 6 September 1925

(United amateur 4 Sep 1943–cs 1945), Owler Lane Evening School

United: amat 5 Sep 1946, pro 10/14 May 1947 to 31 Jul 1951
Debuts: 5 Oct 1949 Western Command 0 United XI 2 (Fr at Lichfield)
25 Mar 1950 Bury 1 United 5
Last game: 23 Dec 1950 United 1 Southampton 2

Buxton/ Sheffield Wednesday (£1000) 28 Oct 1951/ Scunthorpe United Jun 1953/ Rochdale Jun 1954

An amateur on United's books towards the end of the war, George was playing for Owler Lane Evening School when he returned to the Lane as a part-timer, working in the offices of the Arthur Lees factory where he eventually became a company director. With United for four seasons, George was a reliable, composed reserve but his first team appearances were limited to the end of the 1949–50 season, when he replaced the injured Harry Latham as United made a determined late attempt to win promotion only to miss out by one goal, and for part of the first half of the following one.

He made no first team appearances for Wednesday but added 27 FL appearances to his career total with one season at Scunthorpe and another with Rochdale.

Appearances:		Apps	Gls
	FL	17	0
	FAC	2	0
	CC	2	0
	Total	21	0

UNSWORTH David Gerald

LWB 2005–06 6' 1" 14st 2
b. Chorley 16 October 1973

Everton from trainee Jun 1992/ West Ham United (£1m +) Aug 1997/ Aston Villa (£3m) Jul 1998/ Everton (£3m) Aug 1998/ Portsmouth (free) Apr 2004/ Ipswich Town (L) Jan 2005
United: 22 Aug 2005 to 5 Jan 2007
Debut: 27 Aug 2005 United 2 Coventry City 1
Last games: 16 Sep 2006 United 1 Reading 2
24 Oct 2006 United 2 Birmingham City 4 (LC)
Wigan Athletic 5 Jan 2007 to May 2007 / – / Burnley Aug 2007

England youth international David Unsworth made his FL debut as a substitute with Everton scoring at Tottenham on 25 April 1992. His full debut came at home to Chelsea on 2 May. After over 100 League appearances, and having gained U21 caps and one full cap, he moved to West Ham but after one season he moved to Villa—for about three weeks. Realising that Everton were keen to have him back, Villa allowed him to return to Goodison without kicking a ball for them, Everton paying Villa the same fee that they had paid West Ham. He remained at Goodison Park for six seasons and after two further clubs he joined United.

He was brought to the Lane—for a fee dependant on promotion—to add defensive experience and, despite his lack of pace, he used all his strength, skill and experience and was a key player in the successful campaign. He scored a penalty on his debut and his four goals, including one direct from a corner, all earned United valuable points. After playing the first few games in the Premiership he lost his place to the speedier Chris Armstrong and was one of two players to miss a penalty against Blackburn.

In the January transfer window, he left for Wigan and returned to the Lane on 'survival Sunday'. This time he was successful from the penalty spot and Wigan's 2–1 victory relegated United and saved the visitors. That was his last game for Wigan and he was released in the summer. The goal, his only one for Wigan, was his 50th in League and Cup games. By the summer of 2008 he had made 405(40) League appearances.

Appearances:		Apps	Gls
	FL	38 (1)	4
	LC	1	0
	Total	39 (1)	4

URWIN Thomas A

LH 1913 5' 7" 11st 10
b. Scotswood (Newcastle on Tyne)

Newburn
United: (£50) 22 Apr 1913 to cs 1915
Debut: 8 Sep 1913 Tottenham Hotspur 2 United 1
Last game: 13 Sep 1913 United 1 Manchester City 3
Luton Town (£60) May 1919

Normally a right half, Thomas Urwin's two first team appearances were at left half and came within five days of each other. A former miner, he returned to the north east in 1915 because of the First War.

When the war came to a close, Norwich City and Luton Town sought his transfer and he signed for the Bedfordshire club and played regularly for Luton in season 1919–20 in the Southern League but he wasn't retained after the club had joined the FL in the following season.

Appearances:		Apps	Gls
	FL	2	0
	Total	2	0

UTLEY George

LH/IL 1913–22 5' 10½" 13st 0
b. Elsecar 16 May 1887
d. Blackpool 8 January 1966

Wentworth Mar 1904/ Wednesday (trial) cs 1906 Elsecar 1906/ Barnsley Sep 1907
United: (£2000) 17/18 Nov 1913 to 20 Sep 1922
Debut: 22 Nov 1913 United 2 Manchester United 0
Last game: 11 Mar 1922 United 0 Cardiff City 2
WW1 guest: Barnsley Feb 1919
Manchester City Sep 1922/ Bristol City Nov 1923 coach & trainer/ Wednesday May 1924 trainer/coach/ Fulham cs 1925 trainer to 1928

George Utley had a trial with Wednesday but was injured and heard nothing more. He joined Barnsley and made his FL debut on 24 October 1908 at Stockport County. George played an important role in the club reaching the FA Cup final of 1910 and winning the trophy, in a replay at the Lane, in 1912. He remains the only Barnsley player to be capped by England and a few days after joining United, he played for England against the South in the international trial.

United's record in the League since about 1905 had not been impressive and the club had an even worse record in the FA Cup. In those days, when the captain played a very significant role on the pitch, it was thought that George would be the man to change the club's fortunes. He was in no hurry to sign, for initially, he would be worse off but United were not to be put off and, as well as equalling the FL record fee of the time, United gave him a five year contract and the promise of a future benefit.

A commanding and inspiring figure on the field, George did change the club's fortunes and United reached the semi-final of the Cup in 1914 and won the trophy a year later. He scored a splendid goal in the 1915 semi-final and 'was a tower of strength, particularly in a cup-tie, and a clever leader of men'.

George was a big, bustling, strong midfield player with the longest throw of his time; the United players knew that he threw one handed 'but he got away with it'. He could play up front and 'was a good dribbler for

a big man' and possessed a hard shot. He was a fighter, determined to win, playing with both strength and intelligence and he used his role as captain to plan and dictate the pattern of play on the field. He could also use his weight to good effect (charging was much more part of the game in those days) although he felt that referees penalised him unfairly.

Only Albert Sturgess made more appearances for United during the First War and when League football resumed, George had still not had his benefit match. A problem arose because others (Gillespie, Cook, Gough and Fazackerley) had all given longer service. The matter was eventually resolved but not without some ill-feeling for George took the huge proceeds from a FL game against Sunderland, which meant he received almost twice as much as the others. As a consequence, the FL abandoned the system of benefit matches.

George also played cricket for United but, by 1921, he was no longer an automatic choice at football. He accepted an offer to captain and coach Manchester City but made just one appearance, bringing his total to 278 in the FL, and after 12 months he moved on, taking various coaching jobs, including a spell at Hillsborough, before leaving the game in 1928. George had taken over trainer George Waller's sports shop in Bramall Lane but he moved to the Fylde area of Lancashire to run a poultry farm and to coach both cricket and football at Rossall School.

Appearances:		Apps	Gls
	FL	107	4
	FAC	15	5
	WW1	118	15
	Total	240	24

VARADI Imre

Striker 1978–79 5' 9" 10st 6
Paddington 8 July 1959

Letchworth Garden City
United: 30 Mar/ 1Apr 1978 to Mar 1979
Debuts: 10 Apr 1978 Worksop Town XI 0 United 0 (sub BM)
30 Aug 1978 United 1 River Plate (Arg) 2 (sub, Fr)
2 Sep 1978 United 0 Crystal Palace 2
Last games: 30 Dec 1978 United 3 Cambridge United 3
15 Jan 1979 Aldershot 1 United 0 (FAC)
Everton (£80k) Mar 1979/ Benfica (trial) Jul 1981/ Newcastle United (£125k) Aug 1981/ Sheffield Wednesday (£150k + player) Aug 1983/ West Bromwich Albion (£285k) Jul 1985/ Manchester City Oct 1986/ Sheffield Wednesday (player exch) Sep 1988/ Leeds United (£50k) Feb 1990/ Luton Town (L) Mar 1992/ Oxford United (L) Jan 1993/ Rotherham United Mar 1993–Apr 1994 / – / Mansfield Town (nc 1 app) Aug 1995/ Boston United Aug 1995/ Scunthorpe United Sep 1995/ Matlock Town player-mgr Nov 1995 to May 1996/ Guiseley player-coach 1996/ Denaby United player-coach Jan 1997/ Stalybridge Celtic asst mgr Dec 1997/ Sheffield FC Feb to cs 1999

Imre Varadi, the son of an Hungarian father and Italian mother, began, what was to be a lengthy, productive and much travelled career with United. He had been playing non League football whilst training two nights a week with Luton. He had trials with Spurs and Cambridge United but was rejected by both but when Harry Haslam took over at the Lane, he contacted Imre who jumped at the chance to join a FL club.

He was only 19 when, after one season with United, he was sold to pay the wages of the other staff and moved to Goodison Park. After Everton (26 app, 6 gl), he had a trial game with Benefica before joining Newcastle where he had what was probably the best spell of his career, scoring 39 goals in 81 FL games. His surprise move to Hillsborough brought further success (33 gl in 72(4) games) as he was leading scorer as the Owls were promoted. He returned to Hillsborough later in his career, in a player exchange—Carl Bradshaw moved to Manchester City—but did not see eye to eye with manager Peter Eustace. He played for a variety of clubs, including a two year spell with Rotherham, and eventually moved into non-League football.

A fast, keen striker with a powerful shot, Imre was popular with the fans at all his clubs and ended his FL career with 151 goals in 366(53) games. He finished playing non-League football just before he reached forty and set up a company in Sheffield coaching youngsters. He later became a football agent.

Appearances:		Apps	Gls
	FL	6 (4)	4
	FAC	2	0
	Total	8 (4)	4

VAUGHTON Willis

RH/LH 1934 5' 9½" 12st 2
b. Sheffield 20 January 1911

Chapel en le Frith/ Atlas & Norfolk/ Huddersfield Town amat Jul 1929, pro 1932
United: (£200)17/18 May 1934 to 4 May 1935
Debut: 15 Sep 1934 United 0 Burnley 0
Last game: 15 Dec 1934 Nottingham Forest 2 United 1
Boston United Aug 1935 player coach/ New Brighton Aug 1936, retired cs 1939 (injury)

Willis Vaughton made his FL debut with Huddersfield Town on 30 December 1933 at Sunderland. His one other FL appearance for Town was later that season at the Lane when he scored the only FL goal of his career in a 4–1 victory.

An astute player who had played for Sheffield Boys, he moved to the Lane at the end of the season to captain the reserves. Willis was too slow and 'wooden' in the first team and in the summer he moved into non-League football with Boston. After one season he returned to League football with New Brighton and missed few games, making 110 FL appearances, before a badly broken leg in February 1939 eventually ended his career. As he was being placed on the stretcher he reportedly said 'Don't forget lads, I like black grapes best'. He returned to Sheffield and worked at Firth Brown's and Vickers. In 2008 he was United's oldest surviving player.

Appearances:		Apps	Gls
	FL	3	0
	CC	2	0
	Total	5	0

VEART Thomas Carl

Striker/MF 1994–96 5' 11½" 12st 8
b. Whyalla, Australia 21 May 1970

Whyalla Croatia/ Salisbury/ Adelaide City (Australia)
United: (£250k) 4/22 Jul 1994 to Mar 1996
Debuts: 28 Jul 1994 Stord (Norway) 1 United 3 (sub Fr)
1 Aug 1994 Fyllingen (Norway) 1 United 1 (Fr)
24 Aug 1994 United 1 Udinese 2 (AIC)
27 Aug 1994 United 1 Notts County 3 (sub)
3 Sep 1994 Tranmere Rovers 2 United 1
Last games: 20 Feb 1996 United 1 West Bromwich Albion 2
24 Feb 1996 United 1 Barnsley 0 (sub)
Crystal Palace (player exch +cash) 8 Mar 1996/ Millwall (£50k) Dec 1997/ Adelaide City cs 1998/ Adelaide United 2003–04/ Adelaide City 2004/ Adelaide United 2005–07

Carl Veart was signed following United's close season tour of Australia, one game of which was against Adelaide when he played and scored. He was not expected to be a regular in the side initially, but he gave some promising displays and contributed 11 goals despite playing some games in midfield due to injuries to others. Carl played with commitment and enthusiasm and one memorable goal was the one which beat Arsenal in the FA Cup replay at the Lane.

Shortly afterwards he—valued at £200k—moved to Crystal Palace with David Tuttle in exchange for Gareth Taylor and a cash adjustment. After one successful season he moved to Millwall and then returned to Adelaide, playing with both City and United. At the start of the 2005 season he scored the first ever goal in the newly formed Hyundai A League. He retired from playing in May 2007. During his career he gained 23 Australian caps, two whilst with United, and was a schoolboy and U23 international and played in the 1992 Olympics in Barcelona.

Appearances:		Apps	Gls
	FL	47 (19)	16
	FAC	2 (1)	1
	LC	2 (1)	1
	AIC	2	0
	Total	55 (21)	18

VERDE Pedro Andres

Striker 1979–80 5' 11" 12st 2
b. Buenos Aires, Argentina 12 March 1952

Estudiantes/ Las Palmas/ Hercules Alicante (Spain)
United: 6 Jul 1979 to 3 Jul 1981
Debuts: 11 Aug 1979 United 1 Doncaster Rovers 1 (LC)
8 Mar 1980 Millwall 1 United 1
Last games: 29 Apr 1980 United 0 Chesterfield 2
8 May 1980 Sheffield Wednesday 1 United 2 (sub CC)
Argentina

Pedro Verde was one of Harry Haslam's signings at the start of the 1979–80 season, the club's first in the Third Division. An international with three caps when a teenager, he played in two League Cup games against Doncaster and was surprised, thinking they were friendly matches, to finish with loose teeth and other injuries. He found it difficult to adjust to the pace of the game in England and his signing also had a foolish aspect as the FL limited clubs to two foreigners and United usually played De Goey and Sabella.

He made his FL debut in March, scoring in this and his next game and displayed an eye for goal and good positional play. He was in the side until the end of the season and on his final appearance, as a substitute in the County Cup final, he gained a winners' medal. He made no appearances during his second season and returned to Argentina.

Appearances:		Apps	Gls
	FL	9 (1)	3
	LC	2	0
	CC	0 (2)	0
	Total	11 (3)	3

VONK Michel Christian

CD 1995–97 6' 3" 13st 3
b. Alkmaar (Netherlands) 28 October 1968

AK 67 Alkmaar (Netherlands)1968/ SVV Dordrecht (Netherlands) 1991/ Manchester City (£300k) Mar 1992 Oldham Athletic (L) Nov 1995
United: (£350k) 19/21 Dec 1995 to c25 Jul 1998
Debut: 23 Dec 1995 Stoke City 2 United 2
Last game: 13 Dec 1997 United 2 Swindon Town 1
MVV Maastricht (Netherlands) (£100k) cs 1998 to cs 2001/ PSV Eindhoven youth coaching/ Sparta Rotterdam asst coach

Michel Vonk made his League debut in the Netherlands with AK 67 Alkmaar during the 1968–69 season. After playing more than 150 league games in Holland he moved to Manchester City, making his FL debut as a substitute at Nottingham Forest on 21 Mar 1992. His full debut came a week later at home to Chelsea. He played most of the time alongside Keith Curle in his time at City but when Alan Ball arrived as the new manager, he found himself out of favour. He moved to Oldham on loan and a fee had been agreed to make the move permanent but personal terms could not be agreed.

Michel was Howard Kendall's first signing for United. Particularly good in the air, he was a regular in the side playing at the centre of defence, until he damaged his cruciate ligament in November 1996. A year later, he played again, conceding an own goal and being sent off in his first game but the knee problem quickly re-occurred and it was decided to cancel his contract at the end of the season.

He returned to the Netherlands, having made 139(4) League appearances in England, playing for Maastricht but he was one of several players released after the club was relegated in 2001. Michel subsequently moved into coaching, and was at Sparta Rotterdam when United played a friendly there in 2006.

Appearances:		Apps	Gls
	FL	37	2
	FAC	2	0
	LC	4	2
	Total	43	4

WAGSTAFF Barry

LH/RH 1964–69 5' 11" 11st 5
b. Wombwell 28 November 1945

United: from Mar 1961, app 1/3 Apr 1963 to 10 Jul 1969
Debut: 7 Oct 1964 Liverpool 3 United 1
Last games: 30 Nov 1968 Cardiff C 4 United 1
21 Dec 1968 United 0 Huddersfield T 0 (sub)
9 May 1969 Doncaster R 0 United 0 (CCF)
7 Jun 1969 Verona (It) 0 United 2 (Fr)
Reading (£22k for Barry and Tony) 12 Jul 1969/ Rotherham United (£10k) Mar 1975/ Worksop Town 1977/ Barnsley youth mgr 1996 and Academy head coach to at least c2004

Barry Wagstaff was one of a group of Don & Dearne and other local boys 'discovered' by Archie Clark who would play for United in the mid 1960s. A year younger than his brother Tony who had made his first team debut in 1961, Barry captained the successful NIL team and made his senior debut in 1964 in the same game as Alan Woodward.

He became a regular first team player in September 1965 playing mainly at left half but some times at right half and occasionally at inside forward or centre half. Barry was a good reader of the game and passed the ball well but he lacked pace. Bigger and more forceful than Tony, the two played together on more occasions than any other United brothers. When Arthur Rowley became United's manager, Barry lost his place and he and his brother moved to Reading.

They continued to play together until 1974, when Tony moved into non-League football. Barry stayed another season at Reading before returning to South Yorkshire and after two seasons with Rotherham, where he brought his career total of FL appearances to 246(19), he moved into non-League football and then into coaching with Barnsley.

Appearances:		Apps	Gls
	FL	107 (10)	5
	FAC	7	0
	LC	5 (1)	0
	CC	7 (1)	0
	Total	126 (12)	5

WAGSTAFF Tony

IL/IR/OR/et al 1961–69 5' 8" 9st 7
b. Wombwell 19 February 1944

United: ground staff 1959, app 30 Jul 1960, pro 6/9 Mar 1961 to 10 Jul 1969
Debut: 29 Apr 1961 United 4 Middlesbrough 1
Last games: 19 Apr 1969 Oxford United 1 United 0
4 Jun 1969 Bologna (Italy) 0 United 0 (Fr)
Reading (£22k for Tony and Barry) 12 Jul 1969/ Cheltenham Town Apr 1974/ Hillingdon Borough Mar 1975/ Hounslow Dec 1976

Tony Wagstaff joined the United ground staff after playing for Don & Dearne Boys. One of the youngest United players to make his first team debut, he became a regular first team player in March 1963 replacing Kettleborough who was injured. Tony played regularly during the following season but thereafter, his appearances became a little more intermittent until Kettleborough was sold in January 1966.

Tony was United's first substitute, replacing Alan Birchenall at Fulham in September 1965 and in that same month, Barry Wagstaff, Tony's younger brother, began to play regularly. They first played together in the FL in November 1965 and they appeared together on more occasions than any other brothers for United.

Tony played most of his games at inside forward and perhaps never fulfilled his early promise whilst at the Lane. He was nervous before a game and, upset by crowd criticism, preferred to play away from the Lane. He had good ball control and distribution and a fine positional sense but he was never fast and, being slight in frame, he lacked power and his scoring record was disappointing.

In the relegation season of 1967–68, Carlin and Currie were signed and Tony played only twice in the FL and asked for a transfer and though he played more frequently under new manager Arthur Rowley, they were in a variety of roles including centre forward and on the wing.

Tony moved to Reading at the same time as Barry and only in 1974, when Tony moved into non-League football, did they go their separate ways. He had made 304(10) FL appearances. He later worked for over twenty years at Heathrow airport in baggage handling and security.

Appearances:		Apps	Gls
	FL	138 (3)	19
	FAC	12	1
	LC	7	1
	CC	7	2
	Total	164 (3)	23

WAGSTAFF(E) Edward (Teddy) Herbert

CH 1911–12 5' 10½" 13st 3
b. Bethnal Green 2 Mar 1885
d. Hillingdon 12 September 1965

Walthamstow Grange/ South Weald Feb 1907 Norwich City Aug 1907/ West Ham United May 1909 Doncaster Rovers cs 1910
United: 20?/24 Aug 1911 to cs 1912
Debut: 16 Dec 1911 United 3 Liverpool 1
Last game: 16 Mar 1912 United 4 Bury 0
Halifax Town cs 1912/ Scunthorpe United Nov 1912

Teddy Wagstaffe had played Southern League football for both Norwich City (25 app) and West Ham (3 app) before spending a season with Midland League Doncaster. United made grants of £50 to both Doncaster and West Ham for the player. With United, he was too slow though good in the air and, after one season, he returned to the Midland League with Halifax.

Appearances:		Apps	Gls
	FL	2	0
	Total	2	0

WAGSTAFFE Russell

MF 1989

United: 1989–90
Debut: 10 Aug 1989 United 1 Rotherham United 1 (YHC)
Last game: 14 Aug 1989 Halifax Town 1 United 0 (sub YHC)

Russell Wagstaffe played as a trainee in the pre-season Cup competition and although a regular in the youth team and playing for the reserves he failed to win a professional contract.

Appearances:		Apps	Gls
	YHC	1 (1)	0
	Total	1 (1)	0

WAINWRIGHT Harry

OR 1925–26 5' 10" 11st 8
b. Sheffield JAS 1899

Highfields/ Port Vale amat Dec 1919, pro Jan 1920 Doncaster Rovers cs 1920/ Brodsworth Main cs 1922 Frickley Colliery 1923
United: (£300) 18 Oct 1924 to cs 1926
Debut: 11 Apr 1925 Bolton Wanderers 3 United 1
Last game: 1 Mar 1926 Blackburn Rovers 3 United 1
Boston Town Aug 1926/ Scunthorpe & L United Jun 1927/ Newark Town May 1928/ Scarborough?/ Scunthorpe & L Utd Sep 1930

Harry Wainwright made his FL debut with Port Vale on Boxing Day 1919 at Barnsley. An amateur at the time, he turned professional but after playing a total of four successive games he lost his place and moved to Midland League Doncaster Rovers in the summer and was playing with Frickley.Colliery when he joined United.

During his time with United he made just two first team appearances and gave a particularly poor display in the second. He was put on the FL transfer list at £250 but returned to non-League football.

Appearances:		Apps	Gls
	FL	2	0
	Total	2	0

WALDOCK Ronald (Ronnie, Polly)

IL/OR/CF 1954–57 5' 7½" 11st 4
b. Heanor 6 December 1932

Loscoe Youth Club/ Coventry City 1949, pro Feb 1950
United: (£5–6k) 7/8 May 1954 to 28 Jan 1957
Debut: 21 Aug 1954 United 2 Everton 5
Last game: 19 Jan 1957 Bristol City 5 United 1
Scunthorpe United (£2450) 1 Feb 1957/ Plymouth Argyle (£5000) Sep 1959/ Middlesbrough (£5000) Jan 1960/ Gillingham (£6000) Oct 1961/ Margate Jul 1964 to Dec 1966/ Halifax Town trial/ Selby Town Jun 1966 player-mgr

Ronnie Waldock made his FL debut with Coventry City in a Third Division match at Millwall on 27 September 1952 and had scored nine goals in 29 League and Cup games when he was signed by United manager, Reg Freeman.

It was a strange signing for United were in the top flight and Ronnie was replacing the accomplished Harold Brook who had been sold to Leeds United on mistaken medical advice. The United players were not impressed with the new player although he lacked nothing in enthusiasm. Not the most skilful of players, Ronnie was honest and hard working but a poor finisher. He played in various positions in the forward line in his time with United but never looked good enough even when United dropped into the Second Division.

He left the Lane and was more at home in the lower divisions winning Championship medals with Scunthorpe (Division 3N) and Gillingham (Division 4). He had joined Gillingham for what was then a club record fee, leaving Middlesbrough after a dispute over money.

When he moved into non-League football he had scored 91 FL goals in 294 games.

Appearances:		Apps	Gls
	FL	52	10
	FAC	4	0
	CC	4	0
	Total	60	10

WALKER Andrew (Andy) Francis

Striker 1996–97 5' 8" 11st 5
b. Glasgow 6 April 1965

Baillieston Juniors/ Motherwell (free) Jul 1984 Celtic (£350k) Jul 1987/ Newcastle United (L) Sep 1991 Bolton Wanderers (L) Jan 1992, (£160k) Feb 1992 Celtic (£550k) Jul 1994
United: (£500k) 23 Feb 1996 to 30 Jun 1998
Debut: 24 Feb 1996 United 1 Barnsley 0
Last games: 31 Mar 1997 Huddersfield Town 2 United 1
19 Aug 1997 United 0 Everton 4 (Fr)
13 Sep 1997 United 1 Nottingham Forest 0 (sub)
Hibernian (L) Dec 1997/ Raith Rovers (L) Mar 1998
Walsall (trial)/ Ayr United (free) Jul 1998/ Carlisle United (free) Aug 1999/ Partick Thistle Sep 1999 to Oct 1999 / – / Alloa Athletic Jan 200 to May 2000

Andy Walker made his Scottish League debut with Motherwell on 29 December 1984 at Kilmarnock. He then had a successful time with Celtic, winning U21 and his first full Scottish caps, before making his FL debut during his brief loan spell with Newcastle United on 21 September

1991 at Millwall. After a second spell with Celtic, winning two more full caps, he was brought to the Lane by Howard Kendall as he rebuilt the United side.

Andy was ever present for the remainder of the season and was a regular in the side during the following one, albeit frequently from the bench. Quick around the penalty area and two footed, his scoring ratio was excellent and included the late equaliser at Ipswich in the second leg of the play-off semi final when he came off the bench. When Nigel Spackman became manager, Andy found himself out of favour and made just one competitive substitute appearance before spending time on loan back in Scotland.

In the summer of 1998 he returned to Scotland and, apart from a brief spell with Carlisle, ended his career there having scored 143 goals in 328(85) League games both sides of the border. Following his retirement he has worked as a TV presenter on Scottish Television and writes a newspaper column.

Appearances:		Apps	Gls
	FL	32 (20)	20
	PO	0 (2)	1
	FAC	1	0
	LC	2	2
	Total	23 (22)	22

WALKER James (Jimmy) Frederick

LH/CH 1949–55 5' 11½" 12st 8
b. Sheffield 1 July 1931

Hanover YC
United: 6 May 1947 amat, 9/11Nov 1948 pro to 30 Jun 1955
Debuts: 5 Oct 1949 Western Command 0 United XI 2 (Fr, Lichfield)
24 Dec 1949 Luton Town 1 United 4
Last games: 26 Sep 1953 Aston Villa 4 United 0
7 Feb 1955 United 4 Grazer SK (Austria) 0 (Fr)
Huddersfield Town (£600) Aug 1955/ Peterborough United cs 1956 to 1965 / – / Peterborough United trainer-coach to 1972 / – / Peterborough youth team mgr 1993

Jimmy Walker spent eight seasons at the Lane and only made four FL appearances. A part-timer, he was only happy using his left foot and he wasn't quick but he was a careful, reliable player in the reserves.

He had one season at Huddersfield without making a FL appearance but success came when he joined Peterborough who were a Midland League side when Jim moved to London Road. He helped them to win four more Midland League titles, resulting in the club's election to the Football League. He played in Posh's first ever FL game and missed only three during the first two FL seasons, ending his playing career with 125 FL appearances for Peterborough. He later had a spell there as trainer/coach and much later as youth team manager.

Appearances:		Apps	Gls
	FL	4	0
	Total	4	0

WALLACE Alexander (Sandy)

OR/IR/F 1891–93

Abercorn
United: Dec 1891 to cs 1893
Debuts: 25 Dec 1891 United 3 Woolwich Arsenal 0 (Fr)
26 Dec 1891 Newcastle East End 1 United 2 (NL)
16 Jan 1892 Blackpool 0 United 3 (FAC)
3 Sep 1892 United 4 Lincoln City 2
Last games: 22 Apr 1893 Accrington 0 United 1 (TM at Nottingham)
27 Apr 1893 Rotherham Town 0 United 1 (Fr)
Middlesbrough Ironopolis cs 1893

Sandy Wallace had an intensive start to his United career, playing seven games in eleven days, most of them friendlies. He scored in his first competitive (NL) game and twice in his first FA Cup game for the club. A quick and clever player and an accurate shot, he was 'a bit on the light side'. At the end of his first season, United were elected to the Football League and Sandy played and scored in the club's first ever FL game against Lincoln City. He played frequently during the season, mainly at inside right (he had played at outside right the previous season) but he played in every forward position at least once. Sandy's final competitive appearance for the club was the Test Match, which United won thus gaining promotion to the First Division.

He then moved to Middlesbrough Ironopolis, newly elected to the FL in place of Accrington who had been defeated by United in the Test Match and resigned from the FL. Ironopolis lasted just one season before ground and financial problems caused them to disband.

(It is possible that he is the Alexander (Alec) Wallace (b. Darwen 1872, d. Bolton 1950) who played for Blackpool Feb 1894, Ardwick (June1894, 6 FL app), Baltimore October 1894, Small Heath, now Birmingham (Nov 1897, 2 FL app) and Hereford Thistle 1898).

Appearances:		Apps	Gls
	FL	16	3
	FAC	2	2
	NL	13	6
	WCC	1	0
	ABD	1	0
	Total	33	11

WALLER George

HB/G 1892–96 5' 10" 11st 12
b. Pitsmoor, Sheffield 3 December 1864
d. Ecclesfield, Sheffield 10 December 1937

Pitsmoor Christ Church/ Pyebank 1883–84 Wednesday 1885/ Middlesbrough cs 1890
United: 6 Aug 1892 to 1896 (FL registration to cs 1915)
Debuts: 12 Sep 1892 United 1 Woolwich Arsenal 0 (Fr)
31 Dec 1892 Middlesbrough 2 United 1 (NL)
1 Apr 1893 Burton Swifts 0 United 3
Last games: 16 Nov 1895 Aston Villa 2 United 2
25 Apr 1896 Walsall 1 United 0 (BC final, at Perry Bar)
22 Sep 1896 Notts County 1 United 0
(Fr at Fartown, Huddersfield)
Training staff May 1894 to cs 1930

George Waller's claim to fame with United was not as a player but as the club's trainer during the time when United were League Champions in 1898 and FA Cup winners in 1899, 1902, 1915 and 1925 and finalists in 1901.

He began his professional career with Wednesday and played for three seasons, his final game being in the FA Cup final of 1890, which Wednesday lost 1–6 to Blackburn Rovers. He and three other of the Wednesday players intended to join United but the forms they signed were obsolete and so George joined Middlesbrough where he played both cricket and football for two seasons.

He returned to Sheffield in 1892 to captain United's reserve team ('Sheffield Strollers') but, during his first two seasons, he often played for the first team, mainly in friendly games but occasionally in competitive matches if the need arose. In March 1894 he played in goal on three occasions due to a goalkeeping crisis, the first being a First Division game at Newton Heath (Man Utd) which United won 2–0 and he remains as the only United outfield player to be selected in goal for a competitive game. Subsequently he played infrequently although, playing in borrowed boots, he did score on his final FL appearance, as he had done on his FL debut.

George had taken over the duties of trainer in the close season of 1894. He drew on his great experience in the fields of both football and cricket and his willingness and eagerness to learn that he became one of the most respected—what we would term—'physiotherapists' in the game. The players thought he had 'magic hands' and he was often consulted by dancers, athletes and the like.

United had no football manager in those days but were run by the decisions of the Football Committee. However, they were enormously dependent on George's advice aided by that of the captain and no greater tribute can be given to him than to reflect on the honours that came to the club. The First Division Championship was won in 1898, the F A Cup in 1899 and 1902—United were finalists in 1901—and the club could soon field a team of internationals.

George was also a tactical innovator; he and captains Hendry and Needham introduced the idea of using one inside forward, capable of accurate passing, in a deeper constructive way, bringing fast raiding wingers into play, often with long cross-field balls. This style remained a feature of United's play into the 1930s.

With a cheerful personality, he was also an expert in what we today would term 'man management' for 'he seemed to know instinctively how to bring the best out of every man in his care' and he was 'a guide, philosopher and friend to all'.

United continued to be run by their Football Committee and advised by George until 1932. They retained their proud record of continuous top level football and the F A Cup was won again in 1915 and 1925. George had continued as trainer and physio at the Lane for a record thirty six years until 1930 and also ran a sports shop near Bramall Lane.

He had also played cricket for United and Yorkshire. He had played for the County as early as 1893 but in his three Championship games, he averaged just 4.25 with the bat but he took four wickets at an average of 17.5. More typical of his ability were the 2,000 runs and 198 wickets in the Yorkshire Council in 1896.

Appearances:		Apps	Gls
	FL	6	2
	NL	3	0
	UCL	1	0
	BC	1	0
	WCC	1	0
	Total	12	2

WALLS George

CF 1896–97
b. Edinburgh 20 January 1874

Heart of Midlothian
United: Jun 1896 to cs 1897
Debuts: 2 Sep 1896 Lincoln City 0 United 1 (Fr)
5 Sep 1896 United 1 Burnley 0
Last games: 13 Mar 1897 United 0 Preston North End 2
30 Apr 1897 Combined Suffolk XI 1 United 4 (Fr)

George Walls arrived at the Lane from the Scottish First Division club Hearts. He scored on his friendly debut for United and on his final appearance—again a friendly—but he made a poor start to the season and rarely looked the answer to United's centre forward problem. Three of his four FL goals came as a hat-trick in the 7–0 defeat of Blackburn Rovers and, despite having appeared in half United's games during the season, he left in the summer.

Appearances:		Apps	Gls
	FL	16	4
	FAC	1	0
	Total	17	4

WALSHAW Lee

MF 1984–87 5' 9" 11st 5
b. Sheffield 20 January 1967

United: from YTS 6 Jun 1983, app 20 Jan 1985 to 30 Jun 1987
Debuts: 2 May 1984 Hull City 1 United 0 (AMC)
6 May 1985 United 1 Blackburn Rovers 3
Last game: 14 Mar 1987 Huddersfield Town 1 United 1
Worksop Town cs 1987/ Gainsborough Tr/ Crookes 1989–90/ Aurora/ Alfreton Town Oct 1992/ Armthorpe Welfare 1994–95/ Arnold T 1996–/ Maltby/ Sheffield FC June 2001 asst mgr to May 2008 then Community and Schools mgr

Lee Walshaw captained Sheffield Boys in their Championship year and spent several seasons at Bramall Lane but he was very unlucky with injuries, breaking a leg on three occasions. He failed to progress in the first team, although his one goal was the winner in an end of season game against Leeds United.

He left United and has a long career in non-League football particularly with Arnold Town and Sheffield Club.

Appearances:		Apps	Gls
	FL	8 (1)	1
	AMC	1	0
	Total	9 (1)	1

WALTON Joseph (Joe)

OR 1909–11 5' 11" 12st 7
b. Preston 8 January 1881

Preston North End 1898/ Tottenham Hotspur May 1903
United: 27 May 1909 to cs 1911
Debut: 1 Sep 1909 Middlesbrough 0 United 2
Last game: 29 Apr 1911 Bury 1 United 1
Stalybridge Celtic Jul 1911

Joe Walton made his FL debut with Preston North End on 29 March 1902 at home to Stockport County and he made eighteen appearances in the following season before moving to Spurs where he took time to settle. He did become a regular in the side and attracted the attention of the international selectors but, despite three trial matches, he failed to gain an England cap. Spurs were a Southern League club for all but Joe's final season at White Hart Lane and he played in their first ever FL game in 1908 and helped them to gain promotion to Division One.

He moved to United in 1909 and was a regular in the side for two seasons. On his day, the auburn haired winger could be superb; a ball juggler and real box of tricks who could supply good centres but he could be selfish and hang on to the ball too long. He was also moody and unreliable, missing a train and a match at Liverpool and suffering from 'financial problems'. Warned as to his future conduct, United paid his near £25 debts.

He was transfer listed in 1913 at £200 but there were no takers and he moved to the Lancashire Combination side Stalybridge Celtic in their first season as a professional club.

Appearances:		Apps	Gls
	FL	60	5
	FAC	2	1
	Total	62	6

WARBOYS Alan

OL/CF 1972 6' 0½" 13st 7
b. Goldthorpe 18 April 1949

Doncaster Rovers from app Apr 1967/ Sheffield Wednesday (£12k) Jun 1968/ Cardiff City (£42k) Dec 1970
United: (£27.5k) 21 Sep 1972 to 3 Mar 1973
Debut: 23 Sep 1972 Liverpool 5 United 0
Last game: 26 Dec 1972 United 0 Liverpool 3
Bristol Rovers (£38,888) Mar 1973/ Fulham (£25k) Feb 1977/ Hull City (£20k) Sep 1977/ Doncaster Rovers (£12.5k) Jul 1979 to Oct 1982/ Burton Albion

Alan Warboys made his FL debut with Doncaster Rovers three days before his 18th birthday on 15 April 1967 at Leyton Orient. After some good performances during the following season, he was transferred to Sheffield Wednesday (71 app, 13 goals) but he came to prominence with Cardiff City, who paid their record fee, scoring 27 goals in 60 FL games. He helped City win the Welsh Cup in 1971 and 1972 and played in the European Cup Winners' Cup.

Alan was signed by John Harris in a complicated exchange deal for Gil Reece and David Powell. An old fashioned swashbuckling striker who could play down the left flank, it was thought that he could add height and power to United's attack but it didn't work out that way and he failed to score a goal in his short stay with United. At his best in and around the penalty area, Alan didn't enjoy the idea that he should offer more in mid-field, doing the work that the injured Geoff Salmons had done, and he was happy to move on.

He found his scoring touch again alongside Bruce Bannister at Bristol Rovers, scoring 53 FL goals in 144 appearances but found goals hard to come by with his next two clubs. He returned to Doncaster and helped them win promotion in 1981 but a back injury forced his retirement and he ended his FL career with 136 goals in 462(17) games. He later became a publican in Swinton (South Yorkshire) and subsequently, an HGV driver.

Appearances:		Apps	Gls
	FL	7	0
	TEX	1	0
	Total	8	0

WARD Ashley Stuart

Striker 2003–05 6' 2" 13st 10
b. Manchester 24 November 1970

Manchester City from trainee Aug 1989/ Wrexham (L) Jan 1991/ Leicester City (£80k) Jul 1991/ Blackpool (L) Nov 1992/ Crewe Alexandra (£80k) Dec 1992/ Norwich City (£500k) Dec 1994/ Derby County (£1m) Mar 1996/ Barnsley (£1.3m) Sep 1997/ Blackburn Rovers (£4.25m) Dec 1998 Bradford City (£1.5m) Aug 2000

United: 7 Aug 2003 to 11 May 2005
Debuts: 9 Aug 2003 United 0 Gillingham 0 (sub)
12 Aug 2003 Macclesfield Town 1 United 2 (LC)
16 Aug 2003 West Ham United 0 United 0
Last games: 18 Sep 2004 Wigan Athletic 4 United 0
5 Feb 2005 United 0 Ipswich Town 2 (sub)

Retired Jul 2005

Ashley Ward made his FL debut as a substitute for Manchester City on 9 December 1989 at Southampton. His full debut came whilst he was on loan at Wrexham, Ashley scoring twice at home to Doncaster Rovers on 12 January 1991. His career made a slow start and it was only when he moved to Crewe that he played regularly. He had productive spells with all his subsequent clubs but he was past his best when he moved to the Lane.

Strong and powerful, he worked hard as a target man but his first touch could be disappointing and he was troubled by injuries. It was a knee injury that ended his first season and, after another knee injury at Wigan early in the following season, he made just one more appearance as a substitute before retiring. He ended his career with 110 League goals in 348(40) appearances.

Appearances:		Apps	Gls
	FL	25 (8)	5
	FAC	2	0
	LC	2	0
	Total	29 (8)	5

WARD Mark Steven

Striker 2001 6' 0" 11st 2
b. Sheffield 27 January 1982

Sheffield Colleges

United: 7 Jul 2000 to Jun 2002
Debut: 6 May 2001 Bolton Wanderers 1 United 1 (sub)
Last game: 27 Oct 2001 United 1 Crewe Alexandra 0 (sub)
Aldershot T (L) 8 Feb 2002

Stocksbridge Pk S Jun 2002/ Belper Town Sep 2002/ Worksop Town (L)/ Hucknall Town Nov 2003/ Frickley Athletic Mar 2006/ Grantham Town Dec 2006/ Bradford Park Avenue Mar 2007/ Stocksbridge Park Steels Jul 2007

Mark Ward, an England schoolboy international, spent two seasons at the Lane but, although a regular in the reserves, he managed only two substitute appearances for the first team. After his release, he moved into non-League football after trials with Lincoln City and Boston United.

Appearances:		Apps	Gls
	FL	0 (2)	0
	Total	0 (2)	0

WARD Mitchum (Mitch) David

MF/RWB 1989–97 5' 8" 11st 3
b. Sheffield 19 June 1971

United: from school 1985, YTS 1987, pro 1 Jul 1989 to 27/28 Nov 1997
Debuts: 31 Jul 1989 Skegness Town 0 United XI 4 (sub Fr)
10 Aug 1989 United 1 Rotherham United 1 (YHC)
7 Nov 1989 United 1 Wolverhampton Wanderers 0 (sub ZDS)
8 Sep 1990 United 1 Manchester City 1
Last game: 22 Nov 1997 Port Vale 0 United 0
Crewe Alexandra (L) 1 Nov 1990
Everton 25 Nov 1997 (L), (£750k) 28 Nov 1997/ Barnsley (£200k) Jul 2000/ York City Aug 2003/ Alfreton Town May 2004 to cs 2005

Mitch Ward scored on his first reserve appearance when he was sixteen but he made a slow start with United's first team playing in several minor games before his FL debut. After two FL appearances, he had a loan spell with Crewe where he scored his first FL goal.

It wasn't until season 1992–93 that he became a regular in the United side. During that season, Mitch contributed memorably to United's FA Cup defeat of Blackburn Rovers; he came on as a substitute and scored twice to force a shoot-out and then scored one of the penalty kicks and went on to play in the subsequent semi-final at Wembley.

He was a regular for the following four seasons, playing in midfield or as a right wing back. Hard working and consistent, Mitch had good ball control and could produce excellent crosses. He fell out of favour when Nigel Spackman became manager and joined Everton, along with Carl Tiler, with Graham Stuart moving to the Lane.

Mitch was never a fixture in the Everton first team but he had a successful time at Barnsley before a season at York where he failed to recover his form after an injury. When he moved into non-League football he had played in 252(38) League games and scored 12 goals, all of which, apart from his first with Crewe, had been scored with United. Retired and living in north Derbyshire, he works as a plasterer.

Appearances:		Apps	Gls
	FL	135 (19)	11
	PO	3	0
	FAC	7 (2)	2
	LC	8 (3)	2
	FMC	0 (1)	0
	AIC	2	1
	YHC	2	0
	Total	157 (25)	16

WARHURST Roy

OL/IL 1944–50 5' 7" 10st 12
b. Handsworth, Sheffield 18 September 1926

Atlas & Norfolk (Huddersfield Town amat 1943 Sheff Wed amat 1944)
United: 10 May 1944 amat, 23/25 Sep 1944 pro to 15 Mar 1950
Debuts: 23 Sep 1944 Barnsley 2 United 1 (WW2)
16 Nov 1946 United 3 Wolverhampton Wanderers 1
Last game: 11 Mar 1950 Bradford Park Avenue 1 United 1
Birmingham City (£5500) Mar 1950/ Manchester City (£10k) Jun 1957/ Crewe Alexandra Mar 1959/ Oldham Athletic Aug 1960/ Banbury Spencer player-mgr Aug 1961 to May 1964

Roy Warhurst began his career with United at outside left. Very dependent on his left foot, he made little progress and missed most of the years from 1946 to 1948 while serving in the army. His eight appearances in the 1948–49 season were mainly at inside left and he became a full-time pro in August 1949. Never more than a useful hard working, reserve player with United, he asked for a transfer and joined Birmingham.

For more than a season, Roy was no more successful at St Andrews than he had been in Sheffield but, in September 1951, he began to find his feet at left half and established himself as a hard tackling wing half. With Birmingham, he was a Second Division championship winner and he helped them reach the 1956 Cup Final though he missed the game through injury. In May 1956 he became the first United player to subsequently play in a European competition when Birmingham entered the Inter Cities Fairs Cup.

Roy had short spells at two further clubs before ending his FL career having totalled 330 games and after a spell in non-League football, he became a scrap metal dealer.

Appearances:		Apps	Gls
	FL	17	2
	FAC	2	1
	WW2	10	2
	Total	29	5

WARNER Thomas (Tom)

LH 1919 5' 11"
b. Sheffield 28 February 1895
d. Sheffield 22 August 1972

United: Aug/ 4 Sep 1919 to cs 1920
Debut: 26 Dec 1919 Bradford Park Avenue 1 United 0
Last game: 27 Dec 1919 Chelsea 1 United 0

Tom Warner served in the army during the Great War and had played for several local clubs prior to joining United. His first team appearances for United were on successive days, neither at Bramall Lane. He was released at the end of the season.

Appearances:		Apps	Gls
	FL	2	0
	Total	2	0

WARREN Harry

CH 1929 6' 0½" 12st 6
b. Newhall 1 April 1902
d. Leigh on Sea 4 April 1968

Gresley Rovers Jan 1924/ Blackpool cs 1924 Exeter City May 1927/ Merthyr Town Jun 1928

United: (£300) 17 May 1929 to 4 Jul 1930
Debut: 7 Sep 1929 Leicester City 3 United 3
Last game: 9 Sep 1929 United 1 Middlesbrough 3
Notts County Jul 1930/ Folkestone Apr 1931 player-mgr, Jun 1931 mgr to Mar 1939/ Chelmsford C sec-mgr Apr 1939/ Chelmsford-Southend sec-mgr 1939–45/ Southend U sec-mgr Aug 1945 to cs 1956/ Coventry C mgr Jun 1956 to Sep 1957

The son of Ben Warren, one of England's finest wing halves, Harry Warren was a very ordinary player but a good manager. He made his FL debut with Blackpool on 7 February 1925 at home to Barnsley but with only five appearances in three seasons he moved to Exeter City where he played just once. After a season with Merthyr (26 FL games) who were all but bankrupt, he must have thought that his luck had changed when he joined United in the First Division.

Harry was a big fellow but far too slow for the new off-side law at the top level of English football and was soon relegated to the reserves and after another unsuccessful season at Notts County (no appearances) he moved into non-League football and a fine career as a manager.

Appearances:		Apps	Gls
	FL	2	0
	Total	2	0

WATSON Arthur

IL/OL/IR 1890–96 5' 6½" 11st 3
b. Ecclesfield JFM 1870
d. Sheffield 3 or 4 June 1931

Ecclesfield by 1887/Rotherham Swifts cs 1889
United: Mar 1890 to 14 Aug 1896
Debuts: 29 Mar 1890 Doncaster Rovers 1 United 1 (Fr)
13 Sep 1890 Burton Wanderers 1 United 1 (MCL)
4 Oct 1890 Derby Junction 0 United 1 (FAC)
12 Sep 1891 Sunderland Alb 2 United 4 (NL)
10 Sep 1892 Bootle 2 United 0
Last games: 7 Apr 1896 Small Heath 2 United 1
25 Apr 1896 Walsall 1 United 0 (CM)
West Bromwich Albion Aug 1896 to 1898/ Lincoln C 1898?
United: 23 Oct 1899 to cs 1900

Arthur Watson joined United along with Rab Howell and Mick Whitham towards the end of the club's first season from Rotherham Swifts who were in severe financial difficulties. All three had previously played for Ecclesfield.

Watson was small, fast and clever with a hard shot and he could also put across fine centres and was equally at home on the wing or at inside forward. He was a regular in the side during the following three seasons; the first and second in the MCL and NL and the third in the new Second Division of the Football League. Arthur did not play in the first FL fixture but made his FL debut at Bootle in United's first away FL game and first League defeat. He played in 15 of the 22 FL fixtures and scored six goals and he also played in the Test Match against Accrington which secured promotion to the First Division. Injuries meant that he missed all the League matches of 1893–94 but he was again a regular for the following two campaigns.

He played for West Bromwich Albion (1896–98) and made 28 FL appearances (2 goals)and when he returned to the Lane in 1899, he agreed to play for the reserves without pay if United would grant him a benefit match and that took place in January 1900. During his first spell with United, as well as the 127 competitive games, he also played in 120 friendly matches.

Appearances:		Apps	Gls
	FL	59	14
	TM	1	0
	FAC	15	6
	NL	15	7
	MCL	19	10
	UCL	8	3
	SCC	5	3
	BC	3	0
	Abd	2	0
	Total	127	43

WATT-SMITH Donald (Don) Stephen

IR/CF 1940–44 10st 7 (1939)
b. July 1920
d. 2002

Sheffield University
United: cs 1939 amat, 11 Apr 1941 to cs 1945
Debut: 23 Mar 1940 Rotherham United 0 United 4 (WW2)
Last game: 8 Apr 1944 Newcastle United 3 United 1 (WW2)
WW2 guest: Luton Town 1942–43
Yorkshire Amateurs (1946–50)/ Old Centralians

Don Watt-Smith, a product of High Storrs Grammar School, was training as a dentist at Sheffield University at the outbreak of the Second War. An all-round sportsman he represented the University at soccer, athletics and cricket and played occasionally for United as an amateur during the Second War, making 12 of his appearances during season 1942–43. Tall and slim, he occasionally played at centre forward but preferred the role of an inside forward and his final appearance for the first team was at Newcastle in a war cup game before a crowd of over fifty two thousand spectators.

He had qualified as a dentist in 1943 and served in the Royal Navy in Wales. On being demobbed he received offers to turn professional from United, Leeds United and Derby County but declined, continuing to work as a dentist. He had played for the Corinthians and had been a reserve for the England amateur side and after the war, he captained Yorkshire Amateurs for several years and also played for and eventually captained Hallam Cricket Club, being their President at the time of his death. He was also a keen golfer and one time Captain and President of Abbeydale Golf Club.

Appearances:		Apps	Gls
	WW2	17	7
	Total	17	7

WAUGH James (Jimmy)

CH 1921–26 5' 9" 11st 4
b. Chopwell 12 August 1898
d. Darlington 26 March 1968

Durham City Aug 1920/ Chopwell Institute
United: (£250 for Waugh and W Sampy) 26 Apr, 1 May 1921 to 21 Jan 1927
Debut: 26 Dec 1921 United 2 Aston Villa 3
Last game: 4 Dec 1926 United 2 West Bromwich Albion 1
Darlington Jan 1927, player-coach Jul 1927 to 1933, coach

After a slow start to his career with United, Jimmy Waugh became the regular first team centre half in November 1922 and missed just one of the following 103 FL and Cup games, including being ever present in 1923–24. Tireless and reliable, Jimmy was a good tackler and 'never beaten' and he was also a good attacking centre half in the old style. He lacked speed however and this caused him problems when the off-side rule was changed in 1925. A neck injury meant that he was very unlucky to miss the 1925 FA Cup final and after a run of games in the following season, he lost his place to Seth King.

He was chosen for the 1926 FA tour of Canada but was transferred to Darlington in January 1927 on the same day that the Quakers sold Mark Hooper, their star right winger to the Wednesday. Waugh was a success with his new club and he was a regular member of their side until 1933, being ever present in 1929–30. He made 236 FL appearances for the Quakers before joining their coaching staff. United played a benefit game for him in April 1932 and he acted as a United scout from 1934.

Appearances:		Apps	Gls
	FL	126	2
	FAC	12	1
	CC	5	0
	Total	143	3

WAUGH Keith

G 1981–84 6' 1" 12st 0
b. Sunderland 27 October 1956

Sunderland from 1973, app Jul 1974 Peterborough United (free) Jul 1976
United: (£90k) 26 Aug 1981 to 31 May 1985
Debut: 29 Aug 1981 United 2 Hereford United 2
Last games: 13 Oct 1984 United 0 Middlesbrough 3
15 Oct 1984 Gretna 1 United 3 (Fr)
Cambridge United (L) Nov 1984/ Bristol City (L) Dec 1984
Bristol City (free) Jul 1985/ Coventry City (£40k) Aug 1989/ Watford (L) Dec 1990, (free) Feb 1991to May 1993, youth team mgr Aug 1993 to May 1994

Keith Waugh failed to make a first team appearance with Sunderland and his FL debut came with Peterborough on 16 October 1976 at Brighton. He spent five seasons with the Posh, missing just one game in his final three seasons before moving to the Lane.

Keith was signed by new manager Ian Porterfield as United began their first season in Division Four. He missed just one game and kept two clean sheets against his former club as United twice beat promotion rivals, Peterborough, 4–0 in capturing the championship title. A good shot stopper but less sure when dealing with crosses, he competed with Steve Conroy for the goalkeeping spot during the following season and in 1983–84 with Paul Tomlinson but John Burridge's arrival in October 1984 saw the end of Keith's career at the Lane.

He moved to Bristol City and made two Wembley appearances in the Freight Rover Trophy finals of 1986 and 1987. He made one appearance for Coventry, his only one in the top Division, before a short time at Watford and ended his career with 476 FL appearances. He spent 1993–94 as youth team coach at Vicarage Road before joining the police force and becoming a CID officer.

Appearances:		Apps	Gls
	FL	99	0
	FAC	6	0
	LC	12	0
	AMC	4	0
	Total	121	0

WEATHERSPOON Charles William

CF 1951
b. Newcastle 3 October 1929
d. 1986

Sunderland from jnr Aug 1947/ Annfield Plain
United: (£750) 3/6 Jan 1951 to 30 Jun 1952
Only game: 5 May 1951 Doncaster Rovers 1 United 1
Hartlepool United Aug 1952/ Hexham Hearts

Charlie Weatherspoon began his career with Sunderland but failed to make a first team appearance. After a spell in non-League football he joined United and was given one game in the final fixture of the 1950–51season. He never looked first team quality and, one year later, he joined Hartlepool United and, despite scoring twice in three early League fixtures, he soon returned to non-League football.

Appearances:		Apps	Gls
	FL	1	0
	Total	1	0

WEBBER Daniel (Danny) Vaughn

Striker/MF 2005– 5' 9" 10st 8
b. Manchester 28 December 1981

Manchester United from trainee Jan 1999/ Port Vale (L) Nov 2001/ Watford (L) Mar 2002, (L) Aug 2002, (nominal fee) Jul 2003
United: (L) 24 Mar 2005, (£500k) 1 Jun 2005
Debuts: 2 Apr 2005 Reading 0 United 0 (sub)
5 Apr 2005 Leeds United 0 United 4

Danny Webber began his career with Manchester United, but failed to make a League appearance, although he did make a substitute appearance in the European Cup at Deportivo in March 2003. His FL debut came while on loan at Port Vale as a substitute at home to Huddersfield Town on 24 November 2001. His full debut came a week later at home to Blackpool. After two subsequent loan spells at Watford he signed permanently for the Hornets.

During the 2004–05 season, he dislocated his shoulder and, unable to gain his place on recovering, he joined United on loan on deadline day with an agreement to a permanent move. He was an immediate success, scoring three goals in seven appearances before the end of the season. A fast, tricky player, willing to run at opponents and with an eye for goal, Danny played a significant role in the promotion season 2006–07 despite having a delayed start due to injury and a ligament problem in January. His goal at Cardiff in April effectively clinched promotion.

Despite being first choice at the start of 2006–07, subsequent injuries meant Danny's contribution in the Premiership was limited and he had the agony of seeing his shot hit the post in the final relegation game against Wigan and injuries ruined his 2007–08 season.

Appearances:		Apps	Gls
	FL	43 (21)	16
	FAC	1	0
	LC	3	0
	Total	47 (21)	16

WEBER Nicolas

LWB 2000 6' 0" 12st 10
b. Metz (France) 28 October 1970

Sochaux 1988/ Chateauroux 1995/ Le Harve (£400k) cs 1998
United: (L) 9 Aug 2000 to 19 Oct 2000
Debuts: 26 Jul 2000 Bodmin 0 United 8 (Fr)
12 Aug 2000 United 2 Portsmouth 0
Last games: 28 Aug 2000 Watford 4 United 1
5 Sep 2000 Lincoln City 1 United 0 (LC)
12 Sep 2000 Wolverhampton Wanderers 0 United 0 (sub)
Grenoble cs 2001/ Nimes Olympique 2003–05

Nicolas Weber had played in France for over 10 years before moving to the Lane, initially on trial, his club, Le Havre, having been relegated. He played in some pre-season games and was signed on a three month loan. He began the season as first choice left wing back, showing a good turn of speed but, soon lost his place to Wayne Quinn who had been playing a more forward role. Injury meant Nicolas had difficulty regaining his place and he returned to Le Havre, moving to Grenoble at the end of the season.

Appearances:		Apps	Gls
	FL	3 (1)	0
	LC	2	0
	Total	5 (1)	0

WEBSTER Richard (Dick)

LH/RH 1942 5' 9" 11st 8
b. Accrington 6 August 1919
d. Blackburn 11 October 1979

Baxenden Rovers/ Woodnook Amateurs/ Accrington Stanley amat May 1937, pro Nov 1937
United: (£750) 13/14 Jan 1939 to 8 Nov 1945
Debut: 10 Jan 1942 Huddersfield Town 3 United 1 (WW2)
Last game: 9 May 1942 Barnsley 5 United 1 (CC)
WW2 guest: Accrington Stanley 1939–42 (22 app) and 1945 (10)/ Blackburn Rovers (2)/ Rochdale 1941–42 (7)/ Burnley 1942–45 (81)
Accrington Stanley (£800) Nov 1945 to Jul 1951

Richard Webster made his FL debut with Accrington Stanley on 22 January 1938 and was immediately a regular in the side, mainly playing at left half. Signed by United in 1939, his immediate career prospects as a player were wrecked by the outbreak of war. He worked in Lancashire and made just five appearances for the Blades, all in 1942, but was able to play as a guest for Accrington and other clubs in that area of Lancashire.

In 1945, now playing for Stanley as a guest at left back, he decided that he would be better off as a part-time player and was transferred back to his old club and he became a regular first team player. A persistent groin injury forced his retirement in 1951 and Dick subsequently ran a local plumbing business and later worked as a technician for a local council.

Appearances:		Apps	Gls
	CC	2	0
	WW2	3	0
	Total	5	0

WEBSTER Simon Paul

MF/CD 1988–90 6' 0" 11st 7
b. Earl Shilton, Hinckley 20 January 1964

Tottenham Hotspur app May 1980, pro Dec 1981 Barnet (L) Dec 1982/ Exeter City (L) Nov 1983, (L) Jan 1984 Norwich City (L) Jan 1985/ Huddersfield Town (L) Feb 1985, (£15k) Mar 1985
United: (L) 18 Mar, (£35k) 22 Mar 1988 to 28 Aug 1990
Debut: 19 Mar 1988 Leeds United 5 United 0
Last games: 18 Apr 1990 Leeds United 4 United 0
28 Apr 1990 United 4 Bournemouth 2 (sub)
11 Aug 1990 Altrincham 1 United XI 1 (Fr)
Charlton Athletic (L) 13 Aug 1990, (£120k) 28 Aug 1990/ West Ham United (£525k) Jun 1993/ Oldham Athletic (L) Mar 1995/ Derby County (L) Aug 1995/ retired Nov 1995/ St Albans City

Simon Webster made his FL debut with Tottenham Hotspur on 3 January 1983 at home to Everton but made only three FL appearances for Spurs. After a successful loan spell at Exeter his career progressed with a successful time at Huddersfield.

He moved to the Lane as one of Dave Basset's early signings and was a regular in the side for the few remaining games and at the start of the following season. Strong and enthusiastic, in November of 1988 he suffered a double fracture in a leg at Mansfield in the FA Cup which sidelined him for year. After a run of games he lost his place, becoming a regular substitute and he moved for a very successful time at Charlton.

Simon's chance to become a Premiership player came with his move to West Ham but after 14 days, he suffered an horrendous broken leg in training and it took nearly two years to make his Hammers debut. He then had a brief successful loan spell at Oldham where it seemed he had recovered from his injury but after a three games on loan at Derby the following season he was forced to announce his retirement. Despite his injuries he managed 309(17) League appearances, topping the 100 mark with both Huddersfield and Charlton.

During his battle for fitness he studied A levels and, after retiring, he qualified in physiotherapy at East London University. He rejoined West Ham on a part-time basis but in 2003 became the first team physio. In March 2004 he moved to Gillingham, leaving in October 2006.

Appearances:		Apps	Gls
	FL	26 (11)	3
	PO	2	0
	FAC	5 (1)	0
	LC	5	0
	FMC	1 (1)	0
	YHC	4	0
	Total	43 (13)	3

WEBSTER Walter (Wally) George

RB 1925–30 5' 9" 12st 4
b. West Bromwich 22 May 1895
d. Sheffield 15 September 1980

Kingsbury Colliery/ West Bromwich United/ Walsall 1921 Lincoln City Jun 1925
United: (£1650) Oct 1925 to cs 1930
Debut: 19 Dec 1925 United 3 Liverpool 1
Last game: 19 Apr 1930 United 3 Aston Villa 3
Scunthorpe & Lindsey United Aug 1930/ Torquay United (free) Aug 1931/ Rochdale Aug 1933/ Stalybridge Celtic Aug 1934/ Barrow Oct 1934 to 1935/ Workington cs 1935

Walter Webster made his FL debut with Walsall on 21 January 1922 at Ashington and missed just six FL games before his move to Lincoln in the summer of 1925. He was made captain on joining Lincoln and gained considerable praise from his contemporaries for his full back play. After a few games he moved to the Lane for what was at the time a record fee for Lincoln.

Never more than a useful reserve player, he was unable to establish himself in the first team and the most games he played in one season was 14 in 1928–29.

After leaving United he had spells with various clubs, including non-League Scunthorpe and Stalybridge, and ended his FL career with 249 appearances, 132 being for Walsall.

Appearances:		Apps	Gls
	FL	35	0
	CC	1	0
	Total	36	0

WESLEY Fred

IL 1919 5' 11" 12st 10
b. Derby 21 April 1898
d. Derby September 1992

Derby Midland Railway Carriage Dept
United: guest Apr 1919, pro May 1919 to cs 1920
Debut: 12 Apr 1919 Wednesday 0 United 1 (WW1 Fr)
Last game: 26 Apr 1919 Rotherham County 0 United 4 (WW1)
Long Eaton May 1920/ Chesterfield Aug 1921/ Long Eaton Feb 1922

Fred Wesley played for United in the last month of the final First War season and signed as a professional. He scored a few goals for the reserves in the early part of the season but never played again for the first team and left at the end of the season to play for Long Eaton. A year later he joined Chesterfield and played two FL games, his debut being on 8 October 1921 at home to Crewe Alexandra and, a week later, he made his final FL appearance in the return fixture. Later in the season, he returned to Long Eaton.

Appearances:		Apps	Gls
	WW1	1	0
	Total	1	0

WEST Gary

CD 1980–85 6' 2" 13st 0
b. Scunthorpe 25 August 1964

United: from 25 Aug 1980, app 25 Aug 1982 to 5 Aug 1985
Debuts: 17 Nov 1980 United 8 Select XI 4 (sub BM)
17 May 1982 Barnsley 0 United 0 (CC)
23 Oct 1982 Exeter City 0 United 3
Last game: 20 Apr 1985 Manchester City 2 United 0
Lincoln City (£34k) Aug 1985/ Gillingham (£50k) Jul 1987/ Port Vale (£70k) Feb 1989/ Gillingham (L) Nov 1990/ Lincoln City (L) Jan 1991/ Lincoln City (£25k) Aug 1991/ Walsall (L) Sep 1992/ Boston United Mar to cs 1993/ Kings Lynn during 1993–94 Gainsborough Tr 1994 / – / Spalding U coach 1998

Signed by Harry Haslam, Gary West was a tall, stylish, defender who attempted to use the ball but he could look a little awkward. He gained England youth caps whilst at the Lane and played a significant role in the promotion side of 1984 and was a regular during the following season. Ian Porterfield then decided that he needed a more experienced central defender and brought in Ken McNaught and Gary was transferred to Lincoln City.

Whilst he was at Sincil Bank the Imps were relegated out of the Football League in 1987 but Gary was voted player of the season. He moved Gillingham where he had a successful first season but thereafter, with permanent injury problems, he found difficulty in commanding a regular first team place despite his various moves. After a loan spell at Walsall, where he reached 250(8) career FL appearances, he moved into non-League football.

Appearances:		Apps	Gls
	FL	75	1
	FAC	7	0
	LC	3	0
	AMC	2	0
	CC	2	0
	Total	89	1

WHARTON Arthur

G 1894–95 5' 11" 12st 7
b. Accra (Gold Coast) 28 October 1865
d. New Edlington, Doncaster 12 December 1930

Cannock FC and Cannock White Cross 1883–84 Cleveland College and Darlington 1885–86 Preston North End & Darlington 1886–88 Rotherham Town Aug 1889
United: 25 Aug 1894 to cs 1895
Debuts: 24 Nov 1894 Linfield Athletic 1 United 5 (Fr)
23 Feb 1895 Sunderland 2 United 0
Last games: 25 Mar 1895 United 3 Leicester Fosse 2 (UCL)
16 Apr 1895 Rotherham Town 3 United 2 (Fr)
Rotherham Town 27 Jul 1895/ Stalybridge Rovers 30 Dec 1895/ Ashton North End Feb 1897/ Stalybridge Rovers Jul 1899/ Stockport County 3 May 1901 to cs 1902

Arthur Wharton was the first black footballer to play in the Football League. His grandfathers were Scottish and his grandmothers of African descent and in those days, before the current ideas of political correctness, Arthur was often referred to in the press as 'Darky'. He completed his education in England and played soccer in Cannock and Darlington and then from 1886–88 for both Darlington and Preston North End as an amateur, playing for the latter in the FA Cup semi-final of 1887. An agile goalkeeper who attracted publicity ('the goalkeeper with the

prodigious punch'), his fame began to spread for he was also an outstanding sprinter. In February 1888, he appeared at Bramall Lane for Sheffield Wednesday in Billy Mosforth's benefit game (Billy also later played for United). Sadly, he let in eight goals against Preston.

He never appeared for Preston in their first FL season and in 1889, he joined Midland League side Rotherham Town as a professional, usually playing as an outfield player to lessen the risk of injury affecting his running career. He soon reverted to goalkeeping and when Town were elected to Division Two, Arthur made his FL debut on 26 September 1893 at Walsall.

Arthur was athletic but by now, his reputation as a goalkeeper was becoming increasingly eccentric; faced by onrushing Wednesday forwards, he had hung from the cross-bar and caught the ball between his knees but this factor didn't put United off when they sought a deputy for Bill Foulke.

His opportunities were inevitably limited and his weaknesses were exposed. He was found wanting in his single First Division game at Sunderland and in his other competitive fixture, he hung from the bar as the ball sailed into the back of the net!

He returned to Rotherham Town but quickly moved across the Pennines having a successful and popular spell with Stalybridge and a longer spell with Ashton where, because of his erratic form, he played occasionally as an outfield player but without success. His playing days ended with a brief return to League football with Stockport. During this period, he acted as a trainer as well as a player and was to the fore in negotiating contracts and standing up for 'players' rights'.

Arthur was also a first class sprinter, winning the AAA 100 yard championship in 1886 and 1887 when his time of 10 seconds was the first recorded 'even time' run in those championships and, from 1888, he ran as a professional in handicap races for money. He was also a professional cyclist and a good cricketer, playing in local Leagues in Lancashire and then in South Yorkshire well into his 50s.

Arthur ended his days as a haulage hand at Yorkshire Main Colliery, Edlington and died of cancer in relative obscurity and was largely forgotten. However he now has a marked gravestone in Edlington cemetery and was the subject of the book 'The First Black Footballer, Arthur Wharton 1865–1930' by Phil Vasili.

Appearances:		Apps	Gls
	FL	1	0
	UCL	1	0
	Total	2	0

WHARTON Clarence Norman

G 1928–30 6' 1" 12st 2
b. Askham in Furness 28 July 1903
d. Askham in Furness 13 July 1961

Askham/ Barrow May 1922/ Preston North End Aug 1925 Barrow Sep 1927
United: (£700) 8/10 May 1928 to cs 23 Jul 1931
Debut: 6 Oct 1928 United 1 Aston Villa 3
Last games: 26 Apr 1930 Everton 3 United 2
5 May 1930 United 3 Sheffield Wednesday 1 (CC)
Norwich City (£100) Jul 1931/ Doncaster Rovers May 1935/ York City May 1936/ Leeds United Aug 1939

Norman Wharton had seven brothers who played rugby. He made his FL debut with Barrow on 22 December 1924 at home to Rochdale. Following two years at Preston where he played few games he returned to Barrow before moving to the Lane.

Capable of brilliant saves, he was strong when challenging for a centre but he preferred to punch rather than catch the ball. He was also prone to error and had poor games and his confidence wasn't helped because he took life very seriously. He played the first 67 of his 70 FL games for United in succession and his final appearance saw him win a County Cup winners' medal against Wednesday. During his second season, his confidence declined and he was replaced by Jack Kendall and made available for transfer.

He moved to Norwich and played in every match in their promotion season of 1933–34 and made over 100 FL appearances, as he did at York where he produced many outstanding displays.

In August 1939 he moved to Leeds and played in two of their three FL games, his final appearance coming against United before League football was suspended due to the outbreak of War. He retired during the War and returned to his trade of an electrician.

Appearances:		Apps	Gls
	FL	70	0
	FAC	3	0
	CC	4	0
	Total	77	0

WHELAN Michael

OR/IR 1898–99
b. Port Clarence, Middlesbrough c1876

Middlesbrough Ironopolis?/ South Bank/ Whitby Millwall May 1895
United: 3 May 1898 to cs 1899
Debut: 3 Sep 1898 United 1 Everton 1
Last game: 22 Apr 1899 Derby County 1 United 0
Bedminster 18 May 1899 (merged with Bristol City cs 1900) to cs1901

Michael Whelan played for Southern League Millwall for three seasons, scoring 30 goals in 89 League and Cup games. He had helped them win the Southern League and had played for the Southern League before moving to the Lane.

Fast and clever, he played intermittently throughout the season but as United drew nearer to their first FA Cup success, Billy Beer became the preferred choice and Whelan was not retained and joined the Bristol team of Bedminster who merged with Bristol City a year later.

Appearances:		Apps	Gls
	FL	13	1
	ABD	1	0
	Total	14	1

WHITAKER William (Bill)

CH 1944 6' 0" 12st 3
b. Chesterfield 7 October 1923
d. Chesterfield 29 August 1995

Tapton School Old Boys/ Chesterfield amat Dec 1941, pro Aug 1942
United: WW2 guest
Only game: 4 Nov 1944 United 3 Grimsby Town 1 (WW2)
Middlesbrough (£9500) Jun 1947/ Kings Lynn ?/ Gainsborough Trinity cs 1955/ Creswell Colliery Jul 1957

Bill Whitaker worked as a 'Bevin Boy' (miner) during the Second World War and was able to play regularly for Chesterfield from December 1941. He made one guest appearance for United who wanted to have a look at him. An exchange was arranged with Albert Nightingale playing for Chesterfield and it also gave the Derbyshire club a chance to give Ken Booker a game as he was home on leave.

Bill made his FL debut with Chesterfield on 31 August 1946 at home to Bradford PA but lost his place through injury. However he showed enough promise to be signed by Middlesbrough and in his eight seasons there, he made 177 FL appearances despite being hampered by knee ligament and cartilage problems. He represented the Football League in 1950.

On moving into non-League football, he returned to his job as a coal miner.

Appearances:		Apps	Gls
	WW2	1	0
	Total	1	0

WHITE David

MF/W 1995–97 6' 1" 13st 9
b. Urmston, Manchester 30 October 1967

Manchester City from app Nov 1985/ Leeds United (£2m) Dec 1993
United: (L) 17 Nov, (£500k) 29 Dec 1995 to Jul 1998
Debuts: 18 Nov 1995 Sunderland 2 United 0 (sub)
21 Nov 1995 United 1 Grimsby Town
Last games: 4 May 1997 Charlton Athletic 0 United 0
26 May 1997 Crystal Palace 1 United 0 (PO - Wembley)
23 Aug 1997 United 2 Portsmouth 1 (sub)
26 Aug 1997 United 3 Wrexham 1 (LC)
Retired Jul 1998

David White made his FL debut with Manchester City as a substitute on 27 September 1986 at Luton, his full debut coming a week later at home to Leicester City. A youth international, he went on to gain U21, B and one full cap and made 273(12) League appearances for City before a move to Leeds but for much of his time there he was troubled by injuries.

Dave Bassett's last signing for the Blades, David moved to the Lane initially on loan and the move was made permanent after Howard Kendall's arrival. David played for much of the season with a groin problem but showed glimpses of his potential with forceful runs from midfield down the right flank. He had a powerful shot and scored his 100th league goal whilst with United. He was again troubled with niggling injuries the following season though he missed few games but 1997–98 saw David's retirement when an ankle injury against Wrexham in the League Cup ended his season early.

David's father was a United director, coinciding with David's time at the Lane.

Appearances:		Apps	Gls
	FL	55 (11)	13
	PO	3	0
	FAC	4	0
	LC	3 (1)	1
	Total	65 (12)	14

WHITE Frederick (Fred)

G 1939–49 6' 1" 12st 5
b. Wolverhampton 5 December 1916
d. Sheffield 13 January 2007

Wolverhampton W 1931/ Everton May 1935
United: (£10) 5/6 May 1937 to 12 Jun 1950
Debuts: 29 Apr 1939 Rotherham U 2 United XI 1 (BM)
2 Dec 1939 Sheffield Wednesday 2 United 3 (WW2)
7 Jan 1946 United 2 Huddersfield Town 0 (FAC)
18 Oct 1947 Aston Villa 2 United 0
Last game: 5 Nov 1949 United 4 Bury 4
WW2 guest: Wrexham (2 app, 1939)/ Rotherham U (1 app,1939–40)/ Grimsby Town (1 app, 1942–43)/ Mansfield Town (4 app,1944–45)/ Sheffield Wednesday (8 app,1944–45)/ Nottingham Forest (2 app,1945–46)
Lincoln City (£200) Jun 1950/ Gainsborough Trinity Aug 1951 to cs 1952

Fred White played for Wolverhampton Boys when they reached the English Schools Final in 1931 and signed for the Wolves and then Everton but he made no FL appearances for the two clubs.

He joined United whilst Jack Smith was in his record breaking sequence of over 200 consecutive FL appearances for United and so Fred had to wait until the outbreak of War to make his first team debut and over 10 years to make his FL debut. Fred worked for his father in the building trade on essential construction during the war and was one of only nine players to make over 100 appearances for United during the Second War and he also made guest appearances for several other clubs including Wednesday.

Tall and brave, he suffered more than his fair share of injuries including a cracked skull playing for Wednesday in February 1945. His FL career at the Lane lasted only two seasons, Fred losing his place to the young Ted Burgin. He then moved to Lincoln City for a season and had to retire through injury after one season with Gainsborough.

After retiring he worked as a salesman in the building trade and was a part-time member from 1955 to 1971 of the United training staff and then acted as a scout. He subsequently scouted for Leeds United and various clubs managed by Jim Smith, formerly on United's books.

Appearances:		Apps	Gls
	FL	44	0
	FAC	2	0
	CC	9	0
	WW2	124	0
	Total	179	0

WHITE Henry

CF 1897 5' 8" 11st 4

Hibernians Sep 1895/ Hamilton A Mar 1896
United: 4 Jul 1897 to 27 Jan 1898, 27 Feb to cs 1898
Debut: 1 Sep 1897 United 2 Derby County 1
Last games: 23 Oct 1897 United 2 Preston North End 1
27 Nov 1897 Corinthians 2 United 0 (Fr)

Henry White was the first of six centre forwards who played for United in their Championship season of 1897–98. Henry played in the first five games and in one further competitive game but he was slow and failed to score. His final appearance was in a friendly game and it was the only time that he was on the losing side for United.

Everton were interested in signing him and he was transferred to them at the end of January subject to him measuring up but he failed his trial, didn't play for the first team and returned to the Lane until the end of the season.

Appearances:		Apps	Gls
	FL	6	0
	Total	6	0

WHITE James (Jack) H

G (1941)

United: amat 30 Apr 1939 to cs 1944

Jack White played for Fulwood, a United 'nursery' team in 1940. The Football League record him as playing at Everton 25 May 1941 and at Mansfield on the 20 September 1941 but these appear to be an error with Fred White appearing in both games.

WHITEHOUSE Dane Lee

MF/OL/LB 1988–97 5' 10" 12st 8
b. Sheffield 14 October 1970

United: from 1985, YTS 1 Jul 1987, pro Jul 1989 to 21 Dec 1999
Debut: 15 Oct 1988 Blackpool 1 United 2
Last game: 22 Nov 1997 Port Vale 0 United 0
Retired 1999

Dane Whitehouse joined United when he was fourteen and, after only six full reserve appearances, he made his FL debut the day after his eighteenth birthday. He initially played on the left flank but, facing competition from Ian Bryson, Dane's opportunities were limited and it as not until the 1991–92 season that he became a regular in the firs team, some times playing more in midfield or even in defence.

In October 1992 he broke his shin and on his return he played as a defender, including the FA Cup semi final against Wednesday at Wembley but he soon reverted to his more attacking midfield role on the left.

Dane was a reliable and consistent performer with a 'good engine' and a good touch who could defend and attack. Strong on the ball and in the tackle, he was skilful and could beat an opponent, put in dangerous crosses and had a strong shot with his left foot and an eye for goal.

There were rumours of him leaving the Lane but he wanted to stay to play for the Blades. Sadly his career came to a premature end at Port Vale in November 1997 as a result of a tackle by Gareth Ainsworth which wrecked his knee. After a year of rehabilitation and two operations he attempted a comeback in some reserve fixtures, both pre-season friendly

and competitive games at the start of the 1999–2000 season, but it was to no avail. A benefit match was played at the Lane in May 2001.

Dane continues to live in Sheffield.

Appearances:		Apps	Gls
	FL	204 (27)	38
	PO	3	0
	FAC	14 (3)	2
	LC	20 (1)	8
	FMC	2	2
	AMC	1	0
	YHC	2 (1)	1
	Total	246 (32)	51

WHITEHURST William (Billy)

Striker 1990–91 6' 1" 13st 0
b. Thurnscoe 10 June 1959

Hickleton Colliery/ Retford Town Aug 1978 Bridlington Trinity Jul 1979/ Mexborough Town Aug 1980 Hull City (£2,500) Oct 1980/ Newcastle United (£232k) Dec 1985/ Oxford United (£188k) Oct 1986/ Reading (£120k) Feb 1988/ Sunderland (£100k) Sep 1988/ Hull City (£150k + player exchange) Dec 1988

United: (£30k) 31 Jan/ Feb 1990 to 21 Mar 1991
Debut: 24 Feb 1990 United 1 Newcastle United 1
Last games: 19 Jan 1991 Manchester City 2 United 0
22 Jan 1991 United 0 Manchester City 2 (ZDS)
26 Jan 1991 United 1 Derby County 0 (sub)
Stoke City (L) Nov 1990
Doncaster Rovers (L) Feb, (free) Mar 1991/ Crewe Alexandra (L) Jan, (free) Feb 1992/ Hatfield Main/ Kettering Town/ Goole Town (Oct)/ Stafford Rangers/ South China (Hong Kong) Nov 1992/ Glentoran Jan 1993/ Frickley Athletic Aug 1993, pl-mgr Nov 1994 to Nov 1995

Billy was a bricklayer after leaving school but played as a part-timer in non-League football. He made his name with Hull City and his first spell with the Tigers was the longest he spent with any club, making 176(17) FL appearances following his debut on 25 October 1980 at Gillingham. He rarely spent more than a season at any of his subsequent clubs, plain speaking losing him his place at Newcastle and at Oxford during their time in the top flight, leaving Reading because of a reported incident in a night club and returning to Hull when he failed to impress at Sunderland.

An old fashioned centre forward who no-one enjoyed playing against, he was signed by Dave Bassett as United fought for promotion to the top flight. A fearless, enthusiastic, hard but fair player, Billy was a regular in the side for the last two months of the successful campaign. He made the occasional appearance the following season in Division One but then moved on to Doncaster and subsequently a variety of non-League clubs and a brief spell abroad. He scored 77 goals in 351(37) FL appearances.

Billy tried his hand at management with Frickley and was a publican at the Cricketers' Arms in Bramall Lane. In 2006 he was working at the BP refinery in Hull.

Appearances:		Apps	Gls
	FL	12 (10)	2
	FMC	1	0
	Total	13 (10)	2

WHITELUM Clifford (Cliff)

CF/OR/IL/IR 1947–49
b. Farnworth 2 December 1919
d. Kings Lynn August 2000

Doncaster Co-op Society/ Bentley Colliery Welfare Sunderland Dec 1938
WW2 guest: Doncaster R (1939), Barnsley (1 app, 1940–41)
United: (£7000) 24/27 Oct 1947 to 31 Jul 1949
Debut: 1 Nov 1947 Everton 2 United 0
Last game: 4 May 1949 Man Utd 3 United 2
Kings Lynn Jul 1949, player-coach 1950/ Stowmarket (1954–55)

Cliff Whitelum was born in Lancashire but his family moved to Doncaster when he was five months old. He played no football after leaving school until he was asked to turn out for the local Co-operative Society Sports Club (he was working in the grocery department) and he progressed so rapidly that he was offered a trial with Sunderland and signed as a professional before the month was up. He made his FL debut on 25 January 1939 at Blackpool but the Second War brought League football to a close. Cliff served in the Royal Artillery for over six years but was still able to score goals. He scored 142 in 165 games for Sunderland during the hostilities and resumed as first choice centre forward after the War.

In 1947 he joined United, for what was, at the time, a record fee for the Blades and, although signed as a centre forward, Cliff played in four forward positions during his time at the Lane but United hadn't realised that he had knee injury problems. A nice story but perhaps apocryphal has Cliff arriving at Sheffield's Midland station and asking how far away the ground was. Told that it was a 'ten minutes walk', he is said to have replied 'not with my knees' and taken a taxi. Nevertheless, he was quick and elusive and able to shoot with either foot. He played in the first 29 competitive games after his arrival but his appearances during the following two campaigns were less frequent.

He then moved into non-League football with Kings Lynn, managed by former Blade, Joe Cockroft. Because of the War he managed only 84 FL games in total but scored 32 goals.

Appearances:		Apps	Gls
	FL	41	14
	FAC	1	0
	CC	1	0
	Total	43	14

WHITHAM Frank

RB 1941

Lopham St
United: 24 Sep 1936 amat to 10 Apr 1937 as 'Witham' (FL), 17 Feb 1941 to cs 1941
Only game: 1 Mar 1941 Hull City 1 United 0 (WW2)
Same player ?: Sheff Wed Reserves Oct 1941/ Rotherham U Apr 1945/ Gainsborough Tr/ Wombwell Jan 1949

Frank 'Witham' is recorded by the Football League as a United amateur for the 1936–37 season. He may be the Frank 'Whitham' who made one first team appearance in 1941.

Appearances:		Apps	Gls
	WW2	1	0
	Total	1	0

WHITHAM Michael (Mick)

RB/LB/CH/RH 1890–97 5' 9" 12st 11
b. Ecclesfield 6 November 1867 (or 1869)
d. London 5 May 1924

Atlas Rovers, Thorpe Hesley, Rawmarsh (all 1886–87) Ecclesfield (1887–88 and Sep 1890)/ Lockwood Brothers 1887–88/ Sheffield Wed (1 app, 1887–88) Rotherham Swifts 1889–90
United: guest Mar 1890. Signed by 5 Apr 1890 to cs 1899
Debuts: 24 Mar 1890 United 1 Halliwell 1 (Fr)
13 Sep 1890 Burton Wanderers 1 United 1 (MCL)
4 Oct 1890 Derby Junction 1 United 0 (FAC)
3 Sep 1892 United 4 Lincoln City 2
Last game: 4 Oct 1897 United 5 Blackburn Rovers 2
Rotherham Town trainer c1908/ Gainsborough Trinity trainer 1910–11, mgr 1911–12/ Huddersfield Town trainer cs 1912/ Brentford trainer cs 1914 until his death in 1924

Mick Whitham was baptised as 'Witham' and occasionally appeared in press reports in his early years as 'Whittam'. A file cutter by trade, he played for several local clubs as a fast but robust midfield player. He had joined Rotherham Swifts with Rab Howell and Arthur Watson: all three were former Ecclesfield players but in March 1890, their new club was close to folding. United stepped in and gave Mick and Howell a trial against Halliwell. Watson played a few days later and all three were signed.

Mick began his career with United in 1890 as a full back playing in United's first MCL game and, in September 1891, he played in the club's first NL fixture. He had moved to left half and in March 1892, he and Harry Lilley became United's first internationals, both representing England. Mick played against Ireland at Cliftonville, and Harry in Wrexham against Wales, both games being played on the same afternoon.

In September 1892, Mick played at right back in United's first FL game and that was his position for most of his playing career, though he also played at centre half in the period after Billy Hendry's serious injury until Tommy Morren was signed. He had also played in the Test Match which clinched promotion to Division One and then played in the opening game in the top flight. Mick was a regular for most of the following three campaigns and his final appearance was his only one in the Championship season of 1897–98.

Mick was impulsive in his early days but he 'improved with keeping', he was quick and learned to kick with judgement and to keep the ball low and he tackled well. He was as 'strong as a horse' and a master of the hefty shoulder charge. Hard as nails with a 'reputation for roughness', he was never popular with opposition supporters. After a particularly rough game at Middlesbrough, the supporters were threatening violence and as the players walked back to the pub where they had changed, they passed a duck pond. Here Mick made his stand, rolled up his sleeves and invited the 'best man of Middlesbrough' to step forward. None did.

After ending his playing days, he became a trainer and whilst with Brantford, he worked for Wilkinson Sword as a grinder. Massively overweight and in poor condition, he died in 1924.

Appearances:

	Apps	Gls
FL	86	1
TM	1	0
FAC	17	0
NL	16	0
MCL	21	0
UCL	8	0
SCC	4	0
WCC	2	0
BC	3	0
ABD	2	0
Total	160	1

WHITING (J?)

CF 1916

WW1 guest: Worksop T (Dec 1915? Jan and Mar 1916), Gainsborough Tr (Mar 1916),
United: WW1 guest 1916
Debut: 22 Apr 1916 Lincon City 1 United 1 (WW1)
Last game: 30 Sep 1916 United 1 Rotherham County 0 (WW1)
WW1 guest: Blackpool Nov 1916, Chesterfield ? Apr 1917, QPR? Feb-Apr 1917,

Lieutenant Whiting came from the East Riding of Yorkshire and had been promoted to captain in the month prior to first playing for United and was probably serving in the RAMC. Stationed near Gainsborough, he may have scored on his debut, some reports giving him as scorer, others credit Masterman with the goal, but he did score in a charity match against the Wednesday in the final game of that season. His brother, CP Whiting played cricket for Yorkshire in 1914 and 1915.

Appearances:

	Apps	Gls
WW1	2	0
Total	2	0

WHITLOW Michael (Mike) William

CD/LWB 2003–04 6' 0" 12st 12
b. Northwich 13 January 1968

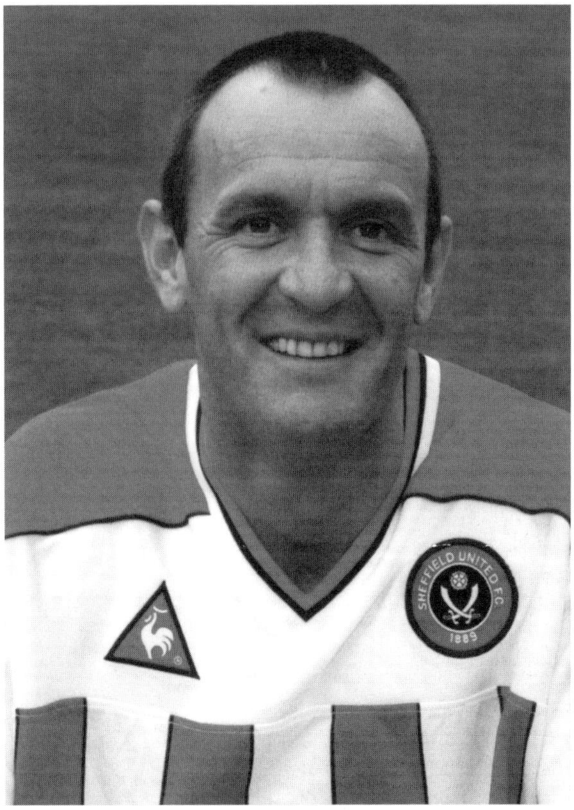

Witton Albion Aug 1988/ Leeds United Nov 1988 Leicester City (£250k) Mar 1992/ Bolton Wanderers (£500k) Sep 1997

United: (free) 22 Jul 2003 to 30 Jun 2004
Debuts: 19 Jul 2003 Cheltenham Town 2 United 2 (sub Fr)
21 Jul 2003 Penryn Athletic 0 United 6 (Fr)
26 Aug 2003 Crystal Palace 1 United 2 (sub)
20 Sep 2003 United 5 Cardiff City 3
Last game: 2 Mar 2004 United 2 Millwall 1
Notts County Jun 2004, player coach cs 2005 to May 2007

Mike Whitlow made his FL debut with Leeds United on 26 November 1988 at home to Stoke City and went on make 10 appearances in the Leeds Championship season of 1991–92. He then had two lengthy spells at Leicester and then Bolton before, being out of contract, he joined United as defensive cover.

He played in the pre-season games and made his FL debut after an injury to Chris Armstrong and a Chris Morgan red card. During a run of nine games at left wing back or central defence, Mike showed his experience and positional sense in compensating for his lack of pace.

At the end of the season he joined Notts County, playing for a season and then continuing as a player coach, although making no further appearances, until the summer of 2007. He finished his career three games short of 400 League appearances.

Appearances		Apps	Gls
	FL	13 (4)	1
	FAC	1 (1)	0
	LC	1	0
	Total	15 (5)	1

WHITTLE

RH/CH 1889–92

Ecclesfield

United: guest 1889, United 1891–92
Debuts: 9 Nov 1889 Staveley 7 United XI 0 (Fr)
1 Jan 1892 United 4 Rotherham 3 (Fr)
Last game: 27 Feb 1892 Kinhurst 0 United 4 (SCCSF at Carbrook)

Whittle was one of four Ecclesfield guest players who played for United in a club fixture at Staveley in United's first season. He played regularly for the reserves in the 1891–92 season but his one competitive appearance came on the day when the club had two games, the other being a friendly at Everton.

Appearances:		Apps	Gls
	SCC	1	0
	Total	1	0

WIDDOWSON John Robert (Bob)

G 1960–68 6' 0" 11st 8
b. Loughborough 12 September 1941

British Ropes

United: 27/31 Jul 1959 to 23 Jun 1968
Debuts: 12 May 1960 Lucerne (Switzerland) 0 United 7 (Fr)
3 Apr 1962 Blackpool 2 United 4
Last games: 4 May 1968 Burnley 0 United 2
13 May 1968 Chester 2 United 3 (BM)
York City May 1968 to May 1970/ Portsmouth (L) Nov 1969/ Gainsborough Trinity Aug 1970

Despite spending nine seasons at the Lane Bob Widdowson made only 12 competitive appearances and never made more than two in succession. This was due the reliability of first choice goalkeeper Alan Hodgkinson and an unfortunate number of injuries.

Bob moved on to York City, managed by Joe Shaw, where he made 30 appearances though he had missed the end of his first season with a dislocated elbow. He played four games on loan at Portsmouth and after a spell in non-League football, Bob was a rep for Rowntrees.

Latterly he was involved in coaching at Bramall Lane having previously been involved in Football in the Community and coaching at Barnsley.

Appearances:		Apps	Gls
	FL	7	0
	FAC	1	0
	CC	4	0
	Total	12	0

WIGGAN Trenton Ashton

OR/CF 1979–82 5' 10"
b. Jamaica 20 September 1962

United: from 5 Jun 1979, pro 1 Aug 1980 to 31 Jul 1982
Debuts: 14 Aug 1979 Doncaster Rovers 3 United 1 (sub LC)
3 May 1980 Grimsby Town 4 United 0
Last games: 19 Sep 1981 Hull City 2 United 1
21 Sep 1981 Stockport County 2 United 1 (sub)
27 Oct 1981 Arsenal 2 United 0 (LC)
21 May 1982 United 3 Sheffield Wednesday 2 (CC)
Gainsborough Trinity cs 1982/ Scarborough cs 1983 to 1986/ Frickley A/ Gainsborough Tr/ Bishop Aukland Feb 1991/ Buxton Oct 1992

An England Schoolboy international, Trenton Wiggan made his first team debut in the League Cup about 5 weeks before his 17th birthday. Very quick with good ball control, his FL debut came in the final game of the season and in 1980–81 he was frequent if not regular member of the first team as United were relegated to Division Four. He played a few games at the start of the 1981–82 promotion season under new manager Ian Porterfield but soon lost his place, United feeling that he lacked dedication.

In his final appearance he won a County Cup winners' medal and then moved into non-League football. More recently Trenton has been involved in the Barnsley Black and Ethnic Minority Initiative.

Appearances:		Apps	Gls
	FL	20 (4)	3
	LC	5 (1)	0
	ASC	3	0
	CC	5	2
	Total	33 (5)	5

WIGLEY Steven (Steve)

MF/OL 1985–87 5' 9" 10st 5
b. Ashton under Lyne 5 October 1961

Curzon Ashton/ Nottingham Forest Mar 1981
United: (£90k) 21 Oct 1985 to 19 Mar 1987
Debuts: 2 Nov 1985 United 3 Hull City 1 (sub)
21 Dec 1985 Wimbledon 5 United 0
Last game: 17 Mar 1987 United 1 Crystal Palace 0
Birmingham City (exchange) Mar 1987/ Portsmouth (£350k) Mar 1989/ Exeter City Aug 1993/ Bognor Regis Town cs 1994/ Aldershot T Feb 1995, Sep 1996 to cs 1997 mgr/ Nottingham Forest coaching/ Southampton director of coaching cs 2001, caretaker-mgr Feb 2004 (2 games), coaching, mgr Aug 2004 to Dec 2004//Manchester City 2006 to May 2007 coaching, asst-mgr

Steve Wigley was signed by Nottingham Forest manager Brian Clough where he had what was probably his most successful spell as a player. He made his FL debut as a substitute on 23 October at home to Arsenal, his full debut coming the following year on 16 September at Norwich.

His arrival at United, brought in by Ian Porterfield, coincided with Colin Morris's return to form and Steve had few opportunities during his first season though he did score his only United goal, a brilliant individual effort, on his second appearance. Fast and clever on either flank but lacking determination and strength, he had a run in the side in the following season under Billy McEwan but, in March, Steve was transferred to Birmingham in exchange for Martin Kuhl. Two years later, he moved to Portsmouth where he played over 100 games.

When Steve's playing days came to an end, having made 302(38) FL appearances, he had three years as manager of non-League Aldershot before moving into coaching with Nottingham Forest, Southampton and Manchester City as well as an involvement with the England U21 squad. Whilst at Southampton he was caretaker manager after Gordon Strachan's departure and was made manager when Paul Sturrock left but, after 14 games with only one win, Steve was dismissed and he moved to Maine Road.

Appearances:		Apps	Gls
	FL	21 (7)	1
	FAC	1	0
	LC	1 (1)	0
	FMC	1	0
	Total	24 (8)	1

WIGMORE Walter

RB/LB/CF/HB 1893, 1894–96 5' 9" 12st
b. Chipping Sodbury 25 February 1873
d. Worksop 8 September 1931

Kiveton Park/ Worksop Town 1889
United: 12 Jun 1892 to cs 1893
Debut: 30 Jan 1893 United 1 Stockton 3 (NL)
Last game: 29 Apr 1893 Bolton W 3 United 0 (Fr)
Worksop T 1893–94
United: cs 1894 to cs 1896
Debuts: 10 Sep 1894 United 4 Rotherham T 2 (Fr)
18 Apr 1895 Nottingham F 0 United 1 (UCL)
4 Feb 1896 Burnley 5 United 0
Last games: 10 Feb 1896 Walsall 2 United 5 (BC)
25 Mar 1896 Devon XI 1 United XI 4 (Fr, at Plymouth)
Worksop?/ Gainsborough Trinity Aug 1896/ Sheffield Wed Feb 1899/ Small Heath (now Birmingham C) (£180) Mar 1899/ Brierley Hill Alliance Aug 1912 to May 1913

Walter Wigmore may have been born in the Cotswolds but he was brought up in Kiveton Park. He joined United from Worksop Town and, although he was at the Lane for three seasons, he played only occasionally. In his first season, he played mainly for the Strollers (reserves). He made his first team debut at centre forward but his two other appearances were at full back before he returned to Worksop for one season. He was no more successful in his second period with United; all his few appearances were at full back and they included an unhappy First Division debut at Burnley.

Walter made his name after leaving the Lane. In brief, he was an opponent to avoid though he claimed, 'I'm not a foul player, I'm a rough player' and I 'never believed football a matter for the drawing room'. A hard working centre forward, he rarely headed the ball, preferring to kick it at any possible height. He played for Gainsborough Trinity, starting at centre half but moving to centre forward, scoring 41 FL goals in 79 games and, after a month with the Wednesday, he joined Small Heath. There he began at centre forward but soon moved to centre half where he played most of his 329 FL games for the club.

Appearances:		Apps	Gls
	FL	1	0
	NL	1	0
	UCL	1	0
	BC	1	0
	Total	4	0

WILDER Christopher (Chris) John

RWB 1986–92, 1998 5' 11" 10st 10 to 12st 8
b. Wortley 23 September 1967

Southampton from 1983, pro Sep 1985
United: (free) 13/20 Aug 1986 to 28 Aug 1992
Debuts: 15 Sep 1986 Sheffield Wednesday 3 United 1 (sub BM)
10 Jan 1987 United 0 Brighton & Hove Albion 0 (FAC)
24 Jan 1987 Shrewsbury Town 1 United 0
Last games: 21 Sep 1991 Arsenal 5 United 2
24 Sep 1991 Wigan Athletic 2 United 2 (LC)
8 May 1992 Frickley A 4 United XI 4 (sub, BM)
Walsall (L) 2 Nov 1989/ Charlton Athletic (L) 12 Oct 1990/ Charlton Athletic (L) 28 Nov 1991/ Leyton Orient (L) 27 Feb 1992
Rotherham United (L) 30 Jul, (£50k) 28 Aug 1992/ Notts County (£130k) Jan 1996/ Bradford City (£150k) Mar 1997
United: (£150k) 25/26 Mar 1998 to 31 Jul 1999
Debut: 28 Mar 1998 United 2 Port Vale 1
Last game: 20 Oct 1998 United 1 Stockport County 1
Northampton Town (L) 6 Nov 1998/ Lincoln City (L) 25 Mar 1999
Brighton & Hove Albion (monthly) Jul 1999/ Halifax Town Oct 1999/ Alfreton Town player-mgr Sep 2001, mgr/ Halifax Town mgr Jul 2002/ Bury asst mgr cs 2008

A ball-boy at the Lane, Chris began his career at Southampton but he failed to make the first team. The south coast club had signed Gerry Forrest from Rotherham and it was Forrest who tipped off United manager Billy McEwan that Wilder might be available.

Chris was quick and clever on the ball and tackled hard. He had a run of games early in 1987 and then competed for the right back spot with Andy Barnsley in the season when United were relegated. They bounced back under Dave Bassett and Chris played regularly until he suffered a stress fracture and, although he played in the promotion game at Leicester which took United back in the top flight, he had only made eight League appearances. Chris moved on loan early in the 1990–91 season but played quite regularly on his return. He faced increasing competition from Hill, Pemberton and Gage and after four loan spells, he was transferred to Rotherham.

Chris had a successful three and a half years at Millmoor making well over 100 appearances before moving on and it was something of a surprise when he returned to the Lane. Nigel Spackman had resigned as manager and Steve Thompson was temporarily in charge and Chris was one of three signings on deadline day. He appeared nine times that season but played little after Steve Bruce arrived in the summer. He had been a good servant to United but, as he admitted later, 'I should have done a little more as a player'.

After two loan spells he moved to Brighton and then to Halifax where a back injury eventually ended his playing days in 2001. In total he made 398(16) FL appearances. Later in 2001 he became manager of Alfreton Town, where he played a few games. However, when Halifax were relegated from the Football League in 2002 and went into administration, Chris was chosen as their new manager and retained the post until the club went into administration again in 2008.

Appearances:		Apps	Gls
	FL	100 (5)	1
	PO	2	0
	FAC	7	0
	LC	8 (2)	0
	FMC	1	0
	AMC	1	0
	YHC	4 (2)	0
	Total	123 (9)	1

WILKES Harry Theodore

G 1934 5' 11" 12st 2
b. Sedgeley, Wolverhampton 24 June 1907
d. Derby 5 April 1984

Sedgley Congs/ Wellington T May 1926/ Aston V (trial) Derby County Feb 1927
United: (£700) 15/16 Mar 1934 to 4 May 1935
Debut: 17 Mar 1934 United 4 Newcastle United 0
Last game: 8 Dec 1934 Hull City 4 United 3
Rhyl Athletic Oct 1935/ Heanor Town Aug 1936

Harry Wilkes had a trial with Aston Villa but he successfully joined Derby County where he made his FL debut at home to Arsenal on 24 September 1927. The agile keeper went on to make 208 FL appearances for the Rams before moving to the Lane.

He joined United when Jack Smith suffered a loss of confidence, although it was later discovered that he had been playing with a broken wrist which had not reset itself satisfactorily. Harry played a few games at the end of the 1933–34 season when United were relegated but it was obvious that he was past his best. At the start of the following season McCarthy was initially first choice in goal before Harry had a run of 12 games but he was then replaced by new signing Roy John. Released by United at a fee of £200, He moved into non-League football.

Appearances:		Apps	Gls
	FL	13	0
	CC	3	0
	Total	16	0

WILKINSON Bernard

CH/LH/RH 1900–13 5' 6" 10st 6
b. Thorpe Hesley 12 September 1879
d. Sheffield 28 May 1949

Thorpe Hesley Parish Church/ Shiregreen/ Atlas & Norfolk Thorpe Hesley
United: 19 Jul 1899 to May 1913
Debuts: 19 Mar 1900 Northampton Town 0 United 3 (Fr)
24 Mar 1900 United 1 Preston North End 0
Last game: 7 Apr 1913 Blackburn Rovers 3 United 1
Rotherham Town Jun 1913 to 1914–15

Bernard Wilkinson—the family name had been 'Pickles'—was one of United's most popular players but, like another later great favourite, Harry Johnson, he was a part time player. Bernard was asked by his employer in 1901 to give up football and he handed in his notice but he was soon employed by Tom Bott, a United director who had a fish and poultry business.

A cheerful and energetic player, he was often referred to as a 'pocket Hercules' because he was also small in stature but he could get up well to head the ball. He had joined United as a nineteen year old and made his debut nearly a year later. He finally became a regular in the side in October 1901 and remained so until the end of 1911–12. He played most of his games at centre half with the occasional appearance at half back. 'Thick set' with 'broad shoulders', he 'was always in the right spot' but his speed, strength and tackling were excellent and he was renowned for his long sweeping passes to the wings. His shooting, on the other hand, was poor and often over the bar.

At the end of his first regular season he gained an FA Cup winners' medal and two years later he played for England against Scotland but, although England were successful, Bernard was not selected again. He was captain of United from 1910–11 until he resigned in January 1912. He was transfer listed at £350 but within a few weeks, the amount was scrapped and he moved to Rotherham Town.

Bernard was also a very good cricketer and was offered a contract with Yorkshire CCC but turned it down because of his work. He did play as a professional for Sheffield United CC and was a mighty hitter, delighting the spectators by despatching the ball into Bramall Lane. His brother Billy, who signed for United on the same day, did play cricket for Yorkshire as well as football for United.

Appearances:		Apps	Gls
	FL	373	14
	FAC	23	0
	ABD	1	0
	Total	397	14

WILKINSON Charles (Charlie) Edward

LB 1933–38 5' 9½" 11st 4
b. Medomsley, Co Durham 7 May 1907
d. Medomsley OND 1975

Wallsend/ Consett Aug 1927/ Leeds United Sep 1928
United: (£2,000) 19 Oct 1933 to 6 May 1938
Debut: 21 Oct 1933 Sheffield Wednesday 0 United 1
Last games: 2 Apr 1938 Bradford Park Avenue 5 United 1
5 May 1938 Boston United 1 United XI 2 (Fr)
Southampton (£250) 28 Jun 1938/ Bournemouth & Boscombe Athletic Aug 1939 player-coach

Charlie Wilkinson, a former Durham miner, made his FL debut with Leeds United on 26 March 1932 at Preston but he was unable to win a regular first team spot, making just three appearances.

Charlie contracted pneumonia soon after his arrival at the Lane but recovered and was a regular at left back for that and the following two seasons. Reliable, cool with sound judgement, he appeared in the 1936 FA Cup final but he lost his place to the emerging Albert Cox in December 1936.

He moved to Southampton in the summer of 1937 but he received a serious knee injury in his second game for the Saints and failed to regain his place after recovering from a cartilage operation, playing just once more. He joined Bournemouth as player coach just before the Second War and played in one of the three games prior to the suspension of League football. During the war, he served in the RASC.

Appearances:		Apps	Gls
	FL	120	0
	FAC	9	0
	CC	4	0
	Total	133	0

WILKINSON Jack

CF 1956–57 6' 1" 12st 0
b. Middlewich 17 September 1931
d. Winsford 10 April 1996

Middlewich Ath Rangers/ Man Utd amat/ Witton Albion Arsenal Oct 1953
United: (£5,000) 28 Feb/2 Mar 1956 to 5 Jun 1957
Debut: 3 Mar 1956 Bolton Wanderers 2 United 1
Last games: 27 Apr 1957 United 0 Nottingham Forest 4
15 May 1957 Enschede SC (W Germany) 3 United 3 (Fr)
Port Vale (£2,000) 21 Jun 1957/ Poole T/ Exeter City £2,500) Oct 1959/ Wellington Town cs 1961/ Witton Albion?/ Winsford U/ Mossley/ Murgatroyds

Jack Wilkinson made just one FL appearance for Arsenal on 19 February 1955 at home to Leicester City. A year later, he was signed by Joe Mercer, the United manager, as the Blades faced a relegation battle but Jack's six goals in a dozen appearances which included a hat-trick at Everton, were not enough to prevent a fall into the Second Division. He started the following season as first choice and scored ten goals in seventeen games but he played very little after Christmas.

Jack was an unusual player; tall and slim, he didn't look like a traditional centre forward but there were occasions when he distributed the ball well and he had a good scoring record wherever he played. He was transferred to Port Vale in the summer and scoring 39 goals in 80 FL games and helped them win the initial Fourth Division championship in 1959. He then scored 26 goals in 48 FL games for Exeter before he moved into non-League football; a record that any forward would be proud of.

Appearances:		Apps	Gls
	FL	29	16
	CC	1	1
	Total	30	17

WILKINSON William (Billy) Herbert

WH/IL/others 1902–08 5' 9" 11st 0
b. Thorpe Hesley, Sheffield 12 March 1881
d. Winson Green, Birmingham 4 June 1961

Shiregreen?/ Thorpe Hesley
United: 19 Jul 1899 to cs 1909
Debut: 5 Apr 1902 Liverpool 1 United 0
Last game: 7 Nov 1908 Notts C 3 United 1
Bolton Wanderers (£150) Oct 1909 to cs 1910

Billy Wilkinson—the family name changed from Pickles—was the younger brother of Bernard though they both signed for United on the same day. In his 10 seasons at the Lane Billy was rarely more than a reserve player who 'filled in' when the first choice players were unavailable. Billy made his first team debut at centre forward and then played as an inside forward but by 1904, he was generally regarded as a half back. Two footed, he occasionally looked capable of winning a regular place in the team but he was injured and lost his place to McGuire in 1906 and in 1908 he was replaced by Sturgess. United placed him on the transfer list and he joined Bolton Wanderers in 1909. An 'H Wilkinson' made two first team appearances for Wanderers in 1909–10 and this may have been Billy.

Billy was also a first class cricketer with Yorkshire; capped in 1907, he took part in 127 matches, scoring 3912 runs at an average of 21.7 and taking 31 wickets at an average 31.3. He later played league cricket in the Birmingham area.

Appearances:		Apps	Gls
	FL	58	7
	FAC	5	0
	Total	63	7

WILLIAMS Bertram (Bertie)

OR/OL 1932–37 5' 6" 10st 7
b. Merthyr Tydfil 4 March 1907
d. Sheffield 1968

Cyfartha Stars/ Merthyr Town 1926/ Bristol City Dec 1927
United: (£1400) 30 Jan 1932 to 1 May 1937
Debut: 30 Jan 1932 United 1 Birmingham 0
Last game: 17 Apr 1937 Fulham 4 United 0

Bertie Williams had been on the books of Merthyr Town before joining Bristol City but had never appeared for them in the FL. He made his FL debut with City on Christmas Eve 1927 at South Shields and went on to make over 103 FL appearances, mainly at inside forward or at outside left, and had won one Welsh cap before joining United.

It was soon clear that although he was very tricky, two footed and an elusive player, he was erratic and lacked determination and speed but he was a regular in the side, mainly on the right wing but sometimes on the left, for two seasons.

In the summer of 1934 United, who had been relegated for the first time in their history, signed Harold Barton from Liverpool to play at outside right but couldn't find an adequate left winger. Williams, who preferred to play on the right, faced competition for the position from Spooner, Pears, Dryden and Bird but all were found wanting. United made a strong challenge in the 1935–36 season for promotion and reached the FA Cup final. Bird had played and scored in the semi-final but it was Williams who was surprisingly chosen for the Cup Final and he had a poor day.

In the following season, he played only four games, refused a transfer to a Third Division club and retired to work as a foreman in a tool factory at Millhouses and as a sub-postmaster on Abbeydale Road.

Appearances:		Apps	Gls
	FL	113	16
	FAC	7	0
	CC	5	2
	Total	125	18

WILLIAMS George Robert (Bobby)

LH 1954 5' 9½" 11st
b. Felling 18 November 1932

Rotherham United Jul 1950
United: (£1,000) 7/10 May 1954 to 30 Jun 1955
Debut: 26 Oct 1954 United 1 Barnsley 0 (CC)
Last game: 30 Nov 1954 United 7 Esbjerg (Denmark) 0 (sub Fr)
Wisbech Town cs 1955/ Bradford C Jun 1956/ Mansfield T Jul 1957 to cs 1962

Bobby Williams had made four FL appearances with Rotherham, scoring on his FL debut at home to West Ham United on 24 August 1953 and again in his final game, before his old manager, Reg Freeman, now with the Blades, brought him to the Lane. Composed on the ball but slow, he moved into non-League football with Wisbech Town. He returned to League football with Bradford C (6 app) and Mansfield (154 app, 5 gl).

Appearances:		Apps	Gls
	CC	1	0
	Total	1	0

WILLIAMS Gordon

CF 1949 5' 9½" 11st
b. Wardley, Newcastle 22 February 1929
d. Gateshead June 2002

South Shields ex Boys FC
United: 12/16 Sep 1949 to 12 Jun 1950
Debut: 1 Oct 1949 United 1 Queens Park Rangers 1
Last game: 5 Nov 1949 United 4 Bury 4
Darlington Jun 1950 to cs 1951

Gordon Williams was an electrician from Hebburn and a relation of former United defender, Dick Young. Gordon had been playing for what was, in effect, South Shields Reserves and he never looked good enough in his five games for United which came in a six weeks spell. At the end of the season, he moved to Darlington where he made just five FL appearances and scored one goal.

Appearances:		Apps	Gls
	FL	5	0
	Total	5	0

WILLIAMS Nigel L

OL 1974 5' 8" 9st 8
b. Rossett (Wrexham) c1956

United: app 28 Jul/1 Aug 1970, pro 30 Oct 1972 to Feb 1975
Debuts: 1 May 1974 Algeria XI 0 United 0 (sub Fr)
3 May 1974 Algeria XI 3 United 1 (Fr)
Last game: 29 Oct 1974 United 0 Rotherham United 0 (CC)
S Africa/ Mexborough T 1978

A former Welsh schoolboy international, Nigel Williams made his first team debut on United's brief tour of Algeria in May 1974 and played a few days later in Alan Woodward's benefit match against Sheffield Wednesday. He made one competitive appearance in the County Cup in the following season, gaining a winners' medal as United won on penalties.

Drink related behavioural problems ruined his football career and his contract was cancelled later in the season and he emigrated to South Africa only to return and make an attempt to play non-League football.

Appearances:		Apps	Gls
	CC	1	0
	Total	1	0

WILLIAMS Paul Andrew

Striker 1988–89 6' 3" 12st 9
b. Sheffield 8 September 1963

Distillery/ Leeds U c1982/ Grenaker Rangers (S Africa) Nuneaton Borough/ Preston North End (free) Dec 1986 Carlisle United (free) Jul 1987/ Newport County (free) Aug 1987
United: (£17k) 6/7 Mar 1988 to May/ 10 Oct 1989
Debut: 19 Mar 1988 Leeds United 5 United 0
Last games: 14 Jan 1989 Bristol Rovers 1 United 1
17 Jan 1989 Wrexham 2 United 1 (SVT)
South Africa/ PNE ?/ Hartlepool United (free) 10 Oct 1989/ Stockport County (free) Aug 1990/ West Bromwich Albion (£250k) Mar 1991/ Coventry City (L) Oct 1992/ Stockport County (£25k) Jan 1993/ Rochdale (free) Nov 1993 to cs 1996/ Doncaster Rovers (L) Mar-May 1996

Paul Williams was born in Sheffield but his mother moved to Northern Ireland when he was a baby. She set up the NI Peace movement in 1975 and became a Nobel Prize winner. Paul became an NI youth international and made his FL debut with Preston North End on 21 March 1987 at Cambridge United, this being his only FL appearance for the club. He played well for Newport County and prompted Dave Bassett to bring Paul to the Lane as United struggled (unsuccessfully) to avoid relegation.

He was sent off on his home debut against Ipswich for striking an opponent who was pulling his shirt and was always a willing, enthusiastic and fearless player but, in part because of injuries, he only made two FL appearances when United were promoted from Division Three and was released.

He moved to Hartlepool and then Stockport where he scored 14 goals in 24 FL games and it was something of a surprise when West Brom paid £250k for his services. Whilst at the Hawthorns he won a full cap for Northern Ireland. He subsequently had a brief spell of success at Rochdale before falling out of favour. When he retired from League football he had scored 33 goals in 121(48) FL appearances.

Appearances:		Apps	Gls
	FL	6 (2)	0
	PO	1	0
	AMC	1 (1)	0
	YHC	1 (2))	0
	Total	9 (5)	0

WILLIAMS Victor

RH 1926–27 5' 9½" 11st 3
b. Bordesley Green, Birmingham 27 October 1901

Redditch U Jan 1924
United: (£200) Mar/ 1 Apr 1925 to cs 1928
Debut: 2 Oct 1926 United 2 Burnley 2
Last game: 1 Jan 1927 Manchester United 5 United 0
Redditch Aug 1928

Victor Williams joined United from Redditch, just a few weeks after his colleague Harry Green but neither were successful.

Appearances:		Apps	Gls
	FL	3	0
	Total	3	0

WILSON Alfred Royle

RB/LB/OR 1915–19 5' 10" 12st 4
b. Wortley, Sheffield JFM 1890

Malin Bridge/ Sheffield Wed Apr 1912 Rotherham Town cs 1913 to 1915
United: WW1 guest
Debut: 18 Sep 1915 Huddersfield Town 2 United 2 (WW1)
Last game: 1 Mar 1919 United 1 Nottingham F 1 (WW1)
WW1 guest: United, Notts C (1 app v Utd) Dec 1916, Birmingham (8 app, 1917–18, 2 app 1918–19)
Birmingham Apr 1919/ Rotherham Town cs 1920

Alfred Wilson had never played for the Wednesday first team but they still held his FL registration when he played as a guest for United and Birmingham during the First War. He played for United in all four of the wartime seasons but after the war, he signed for Birmingham who paid a nominal sum to Wednesday. He made his FL debut on Christmas Day 1919 at Leicester City but his only other appearance for the Blues was on the following day.

Appearances:		Apps	Gls
	WW1	43	1
	Total	43	1

WILSON Andrew (Andy)

OR 1960 5' 6" 9st 10
b. Rotherham 27 September 1940

United: amateur, part-time pro 6/7 Jan, full Jul 1960 to Jun 1961
Debut: 5 Mar 1960 United 3 Lincoln City 2
Last game: 27 Dec 1960 United 0 Sunderland 1
Scunthorpe United (£750) Jun 1961/ Doncaster Rovers Jul 1965/ Chesterfield Jul 1966/ Aldershot Jul 1968/ Gainsborough Trinity cs 1969/Boston United (1969–70)/ Worksop Town/ Matlock Town Feb 1971, mgr Oct 1972–May 1974

Andy Wilson was a quite promising reserve outside right but the signing, by John Harris, of John Docherty and Len Allchurch in United's push for promotion in the spring of 1961 meant that Andy would have few first team opportunities and he was not retained.

Transfer listed at £2000, he was sold to Scunthorpe for £750 and was more successful in the lower divisions. He made 112 FL appearances for Scunthorpe and 225(4) and 28 goals in his career. He moved into non-League football and managed Matlock Town for a while before working as a milkman in Rotherham.

Appearances:		Apps	Gls
	FL	4	0
	CC	1	0
	Total	5	0

WILSON H

OR 1918

United: WW1 guest 1918
Debut: 6 Apr 1918 Barnsley 1 United 1 (WW1)
Last game: 27 Apr 1918 Everton1 United 1 (Fr WW1)

Wilson played in one First War League game for United and two subsequent friendlies at the end of the 1917–18 season. Described as a 'local' and 'army' player, he took a penalty in his last match but it was saved. He could be the man who played from August 1918 with Rotherham Town or the 'E Wilson' who played for Silverwood Colliery at the same time.

Appearances:		Apps	Gls
	WW1	1	0
	Total	1	0

WILSON Stuart Kevin

MF/Striker 2000 5' 8" 9st 12
b. Leicester 16 September 1977

Leicester City from trainee Jul 1996
United: (L) 23 Mar 2000 to 8 May 2000
Debuts: 25 Mar 2000 United 1 Birmingham City 2 (sub)
28 Mar 2000 United 0 Latvia XI 1 (Fr)
1 Apr 2000 Blackburn Rovers 5 United 0
Last game: 29 Apr 2000 Norwich City 2 United 1
Cambridge United Dec 2000 to May 2001/ Shepshed Dynamo Sep 2001/ Grantham Town Sep 2001/ Nuneaton Borough cs 2004/ Coalville Town cs 2005/ Shepshed Dynamo Mar 2006/ Stamford cs 2006 to Jul 2007 / – / Barrow Town (Leicestershire) Aug 2007

Stuart Wilson spent over four seasons with Leicester City but never held a regular place in the first team and 21 of his 22 League appearances were as a substitute. He made his League debut on 22 February 1997 at home to Derby County and his one League start and final League appearance for City was at home to Manchester United on 16 January 1999.

He came to the Lane on loan at the end of Neil Warnock's first part season in charge, playing as an attacking midfielder or alongside Marcus Bent but returned to Leicester at the end of the season. After six months with Cambridge United 3(3) FL app he moved into non-league football.

Appearances:		Apps	Gls
	FL	4 (2)	0
	Total	4 (2)	0

'WILSON T'

IR 1890

United: trialist
Only game: 18 Jan 1890 United 2 Burnley 1 (FAC)

'T Wilson' was the pseudonym that appeared in the Sheffield newspapers for a player who scored for United while on trial and no mention was ever made that he had been signed. What seems extraordinary is that the game was an FA Cup tie. It may be however, that his correct name was given to the FA.

Appearances:		Apps	Gls
	FAC	1	1
	Total	1	1

WINDASS Dean

Striker 2002, 2003 5' 10" 12st 6
b. Hull 1 April 1969

Hull City (YTS) Jul 1986/ Junior football Jul 1988 North Ferriby United Aug 1990/ Hull City (free) Oct 1991 (£700k) Aberdeen Dec 1995/ Oxford United (£475k) Aug 1998 Bradford City (£950k+) Mar 1999/ Middlesbrough (£600k) Mar 2001/ Sheffield Wednesday (L) Dec 2001
United: (L) 14 Nov 2002 to 17 Dec 2002
Debut: 23 Nov 2002 Bradford City 0 United 5
Last game: 14 Dec 2002 Reading 0 United 2
United: (free) 16 Jan 2003 to 14 Jul 2003
Debut: 17 Jan 2003 United 3 Sheffield Wednesday 1
Last games: 4 May 2003 Watford 2 United 0
15 May 2003 United 4 Nottingham Forest 3 (PO)
Bradford City Jul 2003/ Hull City (L) Jan 2007 to May 2007, (£150k) Jun 2007

A much travelled striker, Dean Windass was a trainee with Hull City but was released and moved into local football, working as a bricklayer. He was spotted by a new Hull management team some time later and re-signed, making his FL debut, as a defender, on 11 October 1991 at Swansea City but he soon became a striker. He went on to score a career total 197 League goals in 550(62) appearances, including his time in Scotland, to the end of the 2007–08 season.

Hard running, physical and fearless, but quick to react, Dean always gave 100% commitment and he was once given three red cards in the same game. Playing for Aberdeen in November 1997, the first red followed the award of a second yellow; the second awarded for his comments to the referee and the third for hurling a corner flag to the ground as he left the field!

He was a key figure as the top scorer in keeping Bradford City in the Premiership in their first season but his time at Middlesbrough was less successful and his loan spell with Wednesday was cut short by injury.

Dean moved to the Lane, initially on loan, as United were coping with the heavy League and Cup commitments. He scored three times in four appearances, including a debut goal at Bradford City before he was recalled by Middlesbrough. One month later, he signed for United on a permanent basis and, although he was in and out of the side, his wholehearted displays endeared him to the supporters. Involved in the play-off semi-finals he was disappointed at his omission from the final and his contract was cancelled by mutual consent.

There followed a long successful spell back at Bradford before a return to Hull City where he played a massive part in their reaching the Premier League, in particular scoring the only goal in the play-off final against Bristol City.

Appearances:		Apps	Gls
	FL	20	6
	PO	2	0
	Total	22	6

WINDLE William (Billy) Henry

IL/OL 1940 5' 3"/ 5' 4½" 10st 0
b. Maltby 9 July 1920 ?

Thrybergh
United: cs 1939 to cs 1940, amateur 9 Aug 1940 to cs 1940
Debuts: 17 May 1940 Bury 2 United 2 (Fr)
18 May 1940 United 3 Grimsby Town 0 (WW2)
Last game: 28 Sep 1940 Doncaster Rovers 1 United 0 (WW2)
Denaby United/ Leeds United Oct 1947/ Lincoln City Feb 1948/ Chester (£2000) Oct 1951/ Caernarvon T/ New Brighton Nov 1955

Billy Windle was a colliery worker and a small and skilful forward who made his debut in a friendly match and then added four more appearances for United at the end of the 1939–40 season and one more early the next season but wasn't retained.

He may be the player who signed for Leeds United from Denaby for a small fee after the war, making his FL debut on 22 November 1947, at he age of 27. After one more game, he moved to Lincoln where he was troubled by cartilage problems but he overcame these and went on to play regularly for Chester for nearly four seasons, reaching a total of 227 FL appearances before moving in to non-League football.

Appearances:		Apps	Gls
	WW2	5	0
	Total	5	0

WINSTANLEY Dennis A

CF 1941

Clipstone Colliery
United: 13/17 Sep 1941 am, 27/29 Sep 1941 pro to cs 1944
Debut: 20 Sep 1941 Mansfield Town 2 United 3 (WW2)
Last game: 1 Nov 1941 United 3 Sheffield Wednesday 3 (WW2)
WW2 guest: Mansfield Town (1942–43, 2 app)

Dennis Winstanley was an enthusiastic and aggressive centre forward who worked during the war at Clipstone Colliery near Mansfield. He signed for United in September 1941 after first playing for the reserves at Stocksbridge and for the first team at Mansfield and Chesterfield and scoring in all three games. He scored again in his first appearance at the Lane but after three more appearances for United and two for Mansfield, he faded from the scene.

Appearances:		Apps	Gls
	WW2	6	3
	Total	6	3

WINTER Julian

MF 1989–92 6' 0" 11st 10
b. Huddersfield 6 September 1965

Huddersfield Town from app Sep 1983/ Scunthorpe United (L) Aug 1988
United: (£50k) Jul 1989 to 26 Mar 1992
Debuts: 23 Jul 1989 TuS Celle (West Germany 2 United 2 (Fr)
9 Aug 1989 Scarborough 1 United 3 (sub YHC)
Last games: 10 Aug 1989 United 1 Rotherham United 1 (YHC)
17 Mar 1992 Leek T 3 United XI 1 (Fr)
Bury (free) Mar to cs 1992 (no app)

Julian Winter made his FL debut with Huddersfield Town on 25 August 1984 at home to Oxford United. He was a regular in the side during the 1986–87 campaign and also after his loan spell at Scunthorpe in 1988.

He moved to the Lane, United having been promoted to Division Two but, having played in the pre-season games, he suffered a serious knee injury in his first reserve team game and, after one more reserve game, his career was essentially over.

He completed a degree in Recreational Management and subsequently worked for Grimsby Town (Community Officer), Sheffield Wednesday (Community Manager) and as a Regional Director for Football in the Community Programme. In April 2006, he joined Watford and became Community Director.

Appearances:		Apps	Gls
	YHC	1	1
	Total	1	1

WINTERHALDER Herbert Tirrell

OR 1902–03
b. Kettering AMJ 1879
d. Kettering 28 September 1946

Kettering Athletic/ Kettering Town
United: amat May, pro 25 Aug 1902 to cs 1903
Debuts: 29 Sep 1902 Kettering T 2 United 1 (Fr)
8 Nov 1902 Middlesbrough 0 United 2
Last game: 10 Apr 1903 United 3 Notts County 0
Plymouth Argyle cs 1903/ Wellingborough May 1904/ West Ham United Jul 1905/ Kettering T Oct 1906 to 1907

Herbert Winterhalder and full back W H Clarke came to United's attention during the1900–01 season with Midland League club Kettering Town and both were signed at the end of the following season; United playing a match at Kettering rather than a fee. Herbert was fast but facing competition for a place from Walter Bennett, he moved to Southern League Plymouth Argyle for their first ever season. He then returned to Northamptonshire, playing for Wellingborough Town but it was a bad move because the club folded due to lack of funds. He then moved to Southern League West Ham for some two seasons but wasn't a great success. On retiring Herbert ran a photographic and art shop in Kettering until his death.

Arthur Winterhalder, another winger, who played for West Ham, Everton, Preston and Accrington Stanley from 1905 to 1912 was probably not related but he and Herbert are often confused with each other.

Appearances:		Apps	Gls
	FL	11	2
	Total	11	2

WIRMOLA Jonas

CD 1993
b. Vaxjo (Sweden) 17 July 1969

Kalmar FF/ Vackelsangs IF/ Vederslöv/Dänningelanda IF/ Sparvagens FF (Sweden)
United: (£50k) 9 Aug 1993 to 27 Jan 1994
Debut: 9 Aug 1993 United 0 Sheffield Wed 1 (sub Dooley BM)
24 Aug 1993 United 2 Wimbledon 1
Last game: 29 Dec 1993 Arsenal 3 United 0
Malmo FF (£50k)/ Dundee United Jan 1997/ Skeid/ Malmo IFK, to mgr 2002/ Hollvikens GIF mgr 2003/ Hogaborgs BK mgr 2004/ BK Näset/Höllviken mgr 2006/ Halmstads BK asst mgr

Jonas Wirmola had played all his football in Sweden before joining the Blades though he had spent three weeks training with United in the 1992–93 season and had played in one reserve match at Maine Road. He returned for United's second season in the Premiership. He made an encouraging debut playing very well against John Fashanu and subsequently against other high profile strikers, however after a few months he returned to Sweden where he played and then managed, apart from one month (January 1997) spent with Dundee United.

Appearances:		Apps	Gls
	FL	8	0
	LC	1	0
	Total	9	0

WISHART James Walker McNab

CH 1909–10 5' 11" 11st 7
b. London 1886

Kilmarnock Jan 1906/ Carlisle United Aug 1907
United: 11/14 Aug 1909 to May 1910
Debut: 30 Oct 1909 Bradford City 2 United 0
Last game: 23 Apr 1910 Blackburn Rovers 3 United 1
Carlisle United

McNab Wishart had played as a forward for Kilmarnock but moved to centre half. United paid Carlisle United £227.50p for McNab and Alf Robinson though Robinson never played for the first team and Wishart only twice before he returned to captain Carlisle.

Appearances:		Apps	Gls
	FL	2	0
	Total	2	0

WITHE Peter

Striker 1985–88 6' 1" 13st 2
b. Toxteth, Liverpool 30 August 1951

Smiths Coggins (Liverpool)/ Southport amat Nov 1970, pro Aug 1971/ Skelmersdale (L)/ Barrow (free) Dec 1971 Port Elizabeth City (S Africa) 1972/ Arcadia Shepherds (S Af) 1973/ Wolverhampton W (£13.5k) Nov 1973 Portland Timbers (USA) May 1975/ Birmingham City (£40k) Aug 1975/ Nottingham Forest (£42k) Sep 1976 Newcastle United (£200k) Aug 1978/ Aston Villa (£500k) May 1980
United: 17 Jun/1 Jul 1985 to 30 Jun 1988
Debut: 17 Aug 1985 Stoke City 1 United 3
Last games: 7 May 1988 Huddersfield Town 0 United 2
15 May 1988 Bristol City 1 United 0 (PO)
Birmingham City (L) Sep 1987
Huddersfield Town player, asst-mgr Jul 1988/ Aston V coaching staff/ Wimbledon mgr Oct 1991–Jan 1992/ Evesham Utd Feb 1992/ Football in Community 1993/ Aston Villa youth development 1995, chief scout 1996/ Thailand national team mgr 1998–2002 / – / Indonesia national team mgr 2004-Jan 2007

Peter Withe was an apprentice electrician in Liverpool who made a slow start to his football career. He had made his FL debut with Southport on 4 December 1970 at home to Scunthorpe United and had spent time in South Africa and the United States. He came to the fore when he teamed up with Brain Clough at Nottingham Forest, helping them to the First Division championship. He then played in the Second Division with Newcastle but, after two seasons without gaining promotion, he moved to Aston Villa. There he helped them win the First Division title and scored the winning goal when Villa beat Bayern Munich in the European Cup final and won his 11 England caps.

An 'old fashioned' centre forward, he was a strong and determined target man who led the line well and was particularly good in the air. He was signed by Ian Porterfield for United and was a regular in the side for two seasons but this was an unhappy period for the club and Porterfield was replaced by Billy McEwan. Peter played few games in 1987–88, partly due to his loan spell at Birmingham during which he played eight games and scored 2 goals, both at the Lane in City's 2–0 win over United. When he returned, United, with Bassett in charge, were relegated.

Peter subsequently went into coaching, firstly as a player with Huddersfield and then with Wimbledon. He had a brief, unsuccessful, time as manager of Wimbledon before returning to Villa in various roles and he was also involved in media work. More recently he had successful spells as manager of Thailand and Indonesia. His younger brother, Chris, was a defender with Newcastle, Bradford City and Notts County and his son, Jason has also played as a FL professional.

Appearances:		Apps	Gls
	FL	70 (4)	17
	PO	1	0
	FAC	4	1
	LC	6 (1)	2
	FMC	4	0
	Total	85 (5)	20

WOOD Alexander M

LB 1900–02
b. Edinburgh

Cowdenbeath? Aug 1895 to Jun 1896 / – / St Bernards (Edinburgh) Apr 1897/ Hibernia/ St Bernards Feb 1900
United: 1 May 1900 to cs 1902
Debuts: 27 Dec 1900 Aston Villa 5 United 1 (BM)
19 Jan 1901 United 0 Stoke 4
Last game: 22 Mar 1902 Manchester City 4 United 0
/ – / St Bernards Jan 1904

Alexander Wood had two seasons at Bramall Lane occasionally deputising at left back for Peter Boyle before he returned to Scotland.

Appearances:		Apps	Gls
	FL	6	0
	FAC	1	0
	Total	7	0

WOOD Paul

MF 1988
b. Uppermill (Oldham) 20 March 1970

United: from YTS 31 May 1984, pro Sep 1988 to Mar 1989
Only game: 23 Apr 1988 United 0 West Bromwich Albion 0 (sub)
IFK Varnamo (Swe, L) cs 1988/ Rochdale (L) Nov 1988
Hyde United ? / – / Denaby U (1993–94) / – / Buxton (1998–99)/ Denaby U 1999–

Dave Bassett gave Paul Wood his FL debut as a substitute in a vital relegation match but his full debut came during his loan spell at Rochdale on the 3 December 1988 at Peterborough. His 2(3) appearances with Rochdale brought his FL career to an end and he moved into non-League football.

Appearances:		Apps	Gls
	FL	0 (1)	0
	Total	0 (1)	0

WOOD Paul Anthony

OR/Striker 1990–91 5' 9" 11st 3
b. Saltburn, Cleveland 1 November 1964

Guisborough 1980/ Portsmouth from app Nov 1982 Brighton & Hove Albion (£80k) Aug 1987
United: (£90k) 9 Feb 1990 to 3 Nov 1991
Debuts: 10 Feb 1990 United 1 Plymouth Argyle 0 (sub)
24 Feb 1990 United 1 Newcastle United 1
Last game: 3 Sep 1991 United 0 Chelsea 1
Bournemouth (L) 31 Jan 1991
Bournemouth (L) Oct, (£40k) Nov 1991/ Portsmouth Feb 1994 to cs 1995/ Happy Valley (Hong Kong) Jun 1997/ Andover/ Havant and Waterlooville Sep 1998 to 2003

Paul Wood made his FL debut with Portsmouth at Middlesbrough on 14 January 1984. His career was restricted by a pelvic injury and he never fully established himself at Fratton Park. He moved to Brighton where he was a regular in the side for two seasons helping the club to gain promotion.

He was signed for United by Dave Bassett. Tricky, skilful and quick, Paul played 15(2) FL games towards the end of the season which saw United gain promotion to the top Division. He scored in a 2–2 draw against his old club Brighton and he opened the scoring in the dramatic vital victory at Leicester City on the final day of the season. He found it difficult to keep his place in the First Division and his few appearances were mainly as a substitute. He returned to the Lane for the start of the 1991–92 campaign after a loan spell at Bournemouth but soon made the move permanent having a successful spell with the club.

Paul had an injury troubled time during his second spell with Portsmouth, where he ended his FL career with 38 goals in 239(59) appearances, before spending some time in Hong Kong and later in non-League football.

Appearances:		Apps	Gls
	FL	19 (9)	3
	LC	1	0
	FMC	1	0
	Total	21 (9)	3

WOOD William (Bill)

LB 1952 5' 8" 11st 4
b. Barnsley 28 December 1927

Spen Juniors/ Sunderland Oct 1948/ Hull City (£5000) Jul 1951
United: 18/20 Jun 1952 to 30 Jun 1953
Debut: 23 Aug 1952 Swansea Town 1 United 2
Last game: 6 Sep 1952 Plymouth Argyle 5 United 2
Wisbech Town cs 1953

Bill Wood served in the navy as the Second War drew to a close and then had three seasons at Roker Park but only made one FL appearance for Sunderland on 1 April 1950 at home to Aston Villa. He moved to Hull City for what was, at the time, a sizeable fee, but made no competitive first team appearances.

He moved to the Lane and played in the first five games of what was to be a championship season, but it was soon obvious that he was slow and one footed and he quickly lost his place to the young Graham Shaw.

Appearances:		Apps	Gls
	FL	5	0
	Total	5	0

WOODHOUSE Curtis

MF/WB 1997–2001 5' 8" 11st 0
b. Beverley 17 April 1980

York C to c1994
United: (£2,000 + £15k + £13.75k) from trainee, pro 28 Nov 31 Dec 1997 to 2 Feb 2001
Debuts: 29 Nov 1997 United 1 Crewe Alexandra 0 (sub)
6 Dec 1997 Norwich City 2 United 1
Last game: 20 Jan 2001 West Bromwich Albion 2 United 1
Birmingham City (£1m) Feb 2001/ Rotherham United (L) 31 Jan 2003/ Peterborough United (free) Oct 2003/ Hull City (£25k) May 2005/ Grimsby Town (free) Jan 2006 to cs 2006/ boxing/ Rushden & Diamonds Nov-Dec 2006/ boxing/ Rushden & Diamonds Mar 2007

Curtis Woodhouse was a York City schoolboy but his friendship with Lee Morris drew him towards United who made an initial grant of £2000 to bring him to the Lane and further amounts were paid in 1999 and 2002.

Having made his first team debut in November 1997, Curtis made nine appearances and, after a cartilage operation, he became a regular member of the first team in the following season and remained so, particularly after Neil Warnock's arrival. Curtis played mainly in midfield for United where he produced enthusiastic and combative performances but he occasionally played as a wing-back. In December 1999 he was made captain against Rushden & Diamonds, making him the youngest captain in United's history (19 years 239 days). He had also made 89 first team appearances whilst a teenager, a total bettered by only one United player. A youth international, Curtis gained four U21 England caps whilst with United.

His performances were less convincing in 2000–01 and he had a tendency to be involved in various off-field incidents. His name was circulated to other clubs resulting in his move to Birmingham, with Peter Ndlovu, and c£1m moving to the Lane.

Eventually he moved to Grimsby (16 FL app) and after a few months announced his retirement from football to become a professional boxer. He had played 226(32) League games. He made his boxing debut on 8 September 2006 beating Dean Marcantonio on points in a welterweight contest. He returned to football with Rushden & Diamonds when he received a Community Service Order for assaulting a police officer whilst drunk and was not allowed to box. He returned to boxing but, in the summer of 2007, he signed a two year deal with Rushden but continued his new career as a boxer.

Appearances:		Apps	Gls
	FL	92 (12)	6
	FAC	10	0
	LC	5 (3)	0
	Total	107 (15)	6

WOODWARD Alan

OR/OL/IR 1964–78 5' 9" 11st 10
b. Chapeltown, Sheffield 7 September 1946

United: app 18 Mar/19 Apr 1962, pro 20 Sep 1963 to 7 Oct 1978
Debuts: 29 Apr 1964 Rotherham United XI 0 United XI 2 (CC)
7 Oct 1964 Liverpool 3 United 1
Last games: 9 Sep 1978 Fulham 2 United 0
12 Sep 1978 Norton Woodseats 0 United 2 (BM)
Tulsa Renegades Oct 1978–81

Born in Chapeltown, Alan Woodward was raised in Silkstone Common and played for Barnsley Boys. He was one of the fine group of essentially local youngsters, spotted by Archie Clark and signed by John Harris, who played together in the United NIL side in the early 1960s and then in the First Division.

Alan was sixteen when he first played for the reserve team at Maine Road in April 1963 and his 'first team' debut came in a County Cup game which, for that season, was restricted to 'reserve players'. His FL debut was at Anfield in September (with Barry Wagstaff) and he was a regular in the side for the next 14 years. He is third in United's all time FL appearances list and made 148 consecutive FL appearances between 1968 and 1972 and only goalkeeper Jack Smith has played more. During that time, he was an ever present for three successive seasons and was ever present twice more. Playing the vast majority of his games on the right wing, Alan is the club's second highest goal scorer, only Harry Johnson has scored more and Alan was the leading scorer on seven occasions.

The facts and figures are impressive but do not tell the full story. Alan was a player of the very highest quality and thrilling to watch. He was fast, clever and two footed and could beat defenders on either side. He had a powerful and accurate shot and he could deliver pinpoint crosses and his corner kicks were a defender's nightmare. They were struck hard but with precision and with just the right weight and height. Some were straight and others, delivered with the outside of his right foot, had a vicious swerve.

Alan scored three competitive hat tricks, including his four goals against Ipswich Town in November 1971 and his penalty record was 20 successes from 24 attempts in League and major Cup games. He was also a very capable stand-in goalkeeper, a task he undertook on five occasions. In a total of about 160 minutes as the 'keeper', he conceded just one goal and his clean sheet in a challenging game against Leeds at the Lane in 1967 was impressive.

He was an England youth international but the only other honours to come Alan's way were two appearances for the Football League. It was the time of Alf Ramsey's 'wingless wonders' and Alan never had the chance that many thought he deserved but there may be another reason for his lack of recognition and that was his lack of self belief. John Harris, United's manager, said of Alan, 'he simply has no conception of how much talent he has'. This lack of confidence was evident at an early age. If he made a simple mistake early in the game, perhaps failing to control a pass, his play suffered but if he scored, he was a totally different player and he would often play better in the second half after a half time roasting from John Harris. A superb player but probably not a player for the big occasion and during his time at the Lane, sadly, United had few 'big occasions'.

Alan was United's captain in 1976 but because of domestic issues, he moved to the United States where he played for Tulsa Renegades for three seasons. 'Woody' then played a season of 'grid-iron' football with Oklahoma Thunder as a goal kicker, an activity which on occasions required just two minutes of action. He stayed in the States, doing some coaching and ran a sports store and worked for American Airlines.

Appearances:		Apps	Gls
	FL	536 (2)	158
	FAC	25	3
	LC	30 (2)	14
	TX	6	2
	ASC	12	2
	CC	24	9
	WC	5	4
	ABD	2	1
	Total	640	193

WOODWARD Andrew (Andy) Stephen

RWB 2000–01 6' 0" 13st 6
b. Stockport 23 September 1973

Crewe Alexandra from trainee Jul 1992 / Bury Mar 1995
United: (£35k) 22/23 Mar 2000 to Jun 2001
Debuts: 25 Mar 2000 United 1 Birmingham City 2 (sub)
28 Mar 2000 United 0 Latvia XI 1 (Fr)
1 Apr 2000 Blackburn Rovers 5 United 0
Last games: 8 Apr 2000 United 0 Grimsby Town 0
5 Sep 2000 Lincoln City 1 United 0 (LC)
21 Mar 2001 Scarborough 1 United 0 (sub Fr)
Scunthorpe United (L) 23 Sep 2000, (L) 22 Dec 2000
Halifax Town (free) Jul 2001/ Northwich Victoria Aug 2002 to May 2003

Andy Woodward made his FL debut with Crewe as a substitute, on 17 April 1993. After five further substitute appearances he made his full debut at Bury on 28 August but, failing to gain a regular first team place,

he moved to Bury where he had his most successful spell making 95(20) FL appearances, some when Neil Warnock was manager.

Andy moved to the Lane just before the transfer deadline in 2000, a few months after Neil had taken charge at United. He was wholehearted and enthusiastic but he had few opportunities and went out on loan with Scunthorpe. He totalled 147(33) FL appearances before moving into non-League football.

Appearances:

	Apps	Gls
FL	2 (1)	0
LC	1	0
Total	3 (1)	0

WRAGG Peter

IL/IR/CF 1953–56 5' 8" 10st 11
b. Rotherham 12 January 1931
d. Plymouth 24 June 2004

Rotherham Boys' Welfare/ Rotherham United May 1948
United: 31 Dec 1952/ 2 Jan 1953 to 11 Aug 1956
Debuts: 4 Feb 1953 Birmingham City 3 United 1 (FAC)
7 Feb 1953 Lincoln City 3 United 2
Last games: 24 Mar 1956 United 0 Arsenal 2
10 May 1956 Doncaster Rovers 4 United 0 (CC)
York City (£3400) Aug 1956/ Bradford City Jul 1963 to May 1965/ Frickley Colliery 1965 to 1967?

An English schoolboy international, Peter Wragg made his FL debut with Rotherham United on 26 March 1949 at Chester. A part-time player, he made only 31 appearances (4 goals) during his four seasons at Millmoor and didn't play in any of the FL games when the Millers were promoted in 1951.

Reg Freeman, his former manager at Millmoor, brought him to the Lane but couldn't persuade him to become a full-time professional. Peter was given two early outings in United's championship season but played more frequently in the following season as United narrowly escaped relegation from the top Division.

Peter looked rather slight and wasn't particularly quick but he was two footed, his positional play and ball control were good and he had a good shot. He became a full-time player in August 1954, United making a donation of £500 to Rotherham United but there was no obvious improvement in his play. Soon after the start of the 1955–56 season, United's centre forward, Jack Cross took a job in the south and Wragg, a most unlikely choice, was given the position and scored in seven successive League games but he soon lost his unexpected form. He had an awful game in his last FL game for United and during the summer, he moved to York City.

He had seven successful seasons with York, scoring 78 FL goals in 264 appearances. Top scorer in 1958–59, he captained the side to promotion. He ended his career with Bradford City, bringing his career total to 424 FL games and 106 goals.

When he stopped playing, he worked for the probation services and managed Haxby FC before retiring to the West country.

Appearances:

	Apps	Gls
FL	56	17
FAC	6	3
CC	3	1
Total	65	21

WRIGHT

OR 1918

United: WW1 guest
Only game: 14 Sep 1918 Huddersfield Town 1 United 0 (WW1)

Wright was described as an 'air mechanic' when he played for United as a guest in the First War fixture. He may have been Grayson Wright (qv).

Appearances:

	Apps	Gls
WW1	1	0
Total	1	0

WRIGHT Alan Geoffrey

LWB/MF 2003–06 5' 4" 9st 9
b. Ashton under Lyne 28 September 1971

Blackpool from trainee Apr 1989/ Blackburn Rovers (£400k) Oct 1991/ Aston Villa (£1m) Mar 1995/ Middlesbrough (free) Aug 2003
United: 31 Oct 2003 (L), free 12 Jan 2004 to May 2007
Debut: 1 Nov 2003 Stoke City 2 United 2
Last game: 23 Sep 2006 Arsenal 3 United 0
Derby County (L) 23 Feb 2006/ Leeds United (L) 12 Oct 2006/ Cardiff City (L) 23 Nov 2006/ Doncaster Rovers (L) 16 Feb 2007/ Nottingham Forest (L) 16 Mar 2007
Oldham A (trial) Jul 2007/ Cheltenham T Oct 2007

An England schoolboy and youth international, Alan Wright made his FL debut with Blackpool, aged 16 as a substitute on 2 May 1988 at home to Chesterfield. His full debut came on the opening day of the following season, 27 August, at Chester. After his move to Blackburn, Alan won

two U21 caps in 1993 and was part of the Premiership winning squad in 1995. Towards the end of that campaign he moved to Villa Park where he spent eight seasons.

After a brief spell at Middlesbrough where his appearances were limited, Alan moved, initially on loan, to the Lane and became a regular in the side at left wing back, allowing Phil Jagielka to move to centre back. Quick and tenacious in the tackle and coming forward, he was very small but could climb high for the ball and with a fine left foot, he used the ball well.

He had a brief spell in midfield before reverting to left wing back. He began the following season as first choice but after being sidelined for a while through injury he damaged his cruciate ligament in January 2005 shortly after his return. Alan made a few appearances in 2005–06 and his final appearance for the club came at the Emirates Stadium in the Premiership.

He spent time on loan with four clubs and played for Forest in the play-off semi-finals before being released by United. In October 2007 he joined Cheltenham, initially on a non-contract basis and by the end of the season had made a total of 510(26) League appearances.

Appearances:		Apps	Gls
	FL	36 (6)	1
	FAC	3 (1)	0
	LC	3 (1)	0
	Total	42 (8)	1

WRIGHT Grayson

IR 1910 5' 11" 12st 0
b. Sheffield AMJ 1890

Darnall Cong/ Worksop Town
United: 24 Apr 1909 to cs 1910
Debut: 16 Mar 1910 Sunderland 1 United 0
Last game: 19 Mar 1910 Wednesday 1 United 3
Rotherham Town cs 1910 and 1911–12/ Worksop T ? to cs 1913/ Rotherham C cs 1913
WW1: Rotherham T and County

Grayson Wright's two first team appearances were both away from Bramall Lane. He may have also appeared or United 14 September 1918 at Huddersfield. It is understood that he was killed in an industrial accident c1925.

Appearances:		Apps	Gls
	FL	1	0
	Total	1	0

WRIGHT Reginald (Reg)

RB 1940 5' 8½" 11st 9
b. Dronfield 17 January 1901
d. Chesterfield 24 January 1973

Mosborough Trinity/ Sheffield Wednesday amat Jun 1921, pro Jan 1922/ Worksop Town 1924/ Mansfield Town (trial) Blackpool May 1925/ Bournemouth & Boscombe Athletic Jun 1928/ Chesterfield (£50) Jun 1931/ Frickley Colliery cs 1932/ Worksop Town/ Buxton trainer coach c1934
United: 1 Aug 1936 trainer-coach to 1957
Only game: 28 Sep 1940 Doncaster Rovers 1 United 0 (WW2)

Reg Wright was a United trainer for 21 years but he also played one wartime game for the first team. A quick, two footed full back, his first senior club was the Wednesday but he never played for the first team. He made his FL debut with Blackpool on 2 September 1925 at Middlesbrough and went on to play for Bournemouth and Chesterfield and make a total of 73 FL appearances.

After a spell in non-League football, he became a trainer and coach and joined United in 1936 to supervise the third ('A') team who played at Woodhouse. During the war, he worked at High Storrs Boys' Grammar School but on match days, was still a United trainer and was pressed into service as an emergency full-back for United for this one appearance in 1940 at Doncaster at the age of 39.

He continued to train the A team after the war, taking over the reserves in 1948 and the first team from October 1949 until 1952. He then reverted to the A team but he worked as a physio for all the players until 1957 when he moved to Chesterfield as a trainer and physio. Reg was a Methodist lay-preacher.

Appearances:		Apps	Gls
	WW2	1	0
	Total	1	0

WRIGHTSON H

OR 1916

United: WW1 guest
Only game: 2 Dec 1916 Leeds City 2 United 0 (WW1)

The Sheffield newspapers reported that Wrightson ('Wrighton' in the Telegraph/Green 'Un) was a Sheffield Schools and Sheffield Loco diminutive 16 year old who had gone to Leeds to watch United after working all night and offered to play as the club were a man short. The newspapers added that although he was 'plucky', he was also 'more or less a passenger'.

Appearances:		Apps	Gls
	WW1	1	0
	Total	1	0

YATES James (Jimmy)

OR/IR 1893–97 5' 6" 10st 8
Tunstall (Staffs) 2 November 1869
d. Southampton 5 September 1922

Staffordshire Lads/ Ardwick Nov 1892
United: 1/2 Dec 1893 to cs 1897
Debut: 9 Dec 1893 United 0 Everton 3
Last games: 16 Apr 1897 Bolton Wanderers 0 United 2
30 Apr 1897 Combined Suffolk XI 1 United 4 (Fr)
Southampton St Mary's cs 1897/ Gravesend U/ Southampton Mar 1899/ Hastings & St Leonards United cs 1901/ Southampton Wanderers Sep 1902/ Copenhagen 93 FC coach 1903/Southampton 1905/ Gravesend United 1905/ Hastings & St Leonards/ Coaching in Brazil & USA 1906/ Salisbury City Oct 1906–09

Jimmy Yates made his FL debut with Ardwick (now Manchester City) at Lincoln City on 24 December 1892 during the club's first season in the FL.

A clever winger capable of putting across fine centres, he was signed by United to replace Jack Drummond and to consolidate their first season in the top Division. His fine displays put him in line for a cap and United turned down an offer of £75 for him from Celtic in January 1894 and the player rejected an offer in October to play in the United States. He was a regular in the United side at outside right for three seasons but he lost form in February 1896 and in the summer of 1897, facing competition from the more dynamic Walter Bennett, he accepted an offer from Southern League Southampton.

He played regularly until March 1898 for his new club who went on to win the championship and reached the semi-final of the FA Cup but he was dogged by ill-health. After a short spell with Gravesend, he returned to Southampton and helped them to win the Southern League Championships of 1899 and 1901. There followed a varied career including coaching in Europe and North and South America and a brief one-game return to the Saints making him the only player to sign for the club three times.

In 1907 he returned to Southampton to work in the Docks but ill health led to unemployment, and sadly, he committed suicide.

Appearances:		Apps	Gls
	FL	80	7
	FAC	7	0
	UCL	11	2
	SCCetc	5	0
	ABD	1	0
	Total	104	9

YATES Stephen (Steve)

RWB/CD 2002–03 5' 11" 12st 2
b. Bristol 29 January 1970

Bristol Rovers from trainee Jul 1988/ Queens Park Rangers (£650k) Aug 1993/ Tranmere Rovers (free) Aug 1999
United: **(free) 1/4 Jul 2002 to 7 Aug 2003**
Debuts: **16 Jul 2002 Baslow 1 United 14 (Fr)**
10 Aug 2002 Coventry City 2 United 1
Last game: **22 Feb 2003 United 0 Norwich City 1**
Huddersfield Town (free) Aug 2003/ Scarborough Jan 2006 / – / Halifax Town Jan 2006/ Morecambe Aug 2006/ Caernarfon Town Sep 2006

Steve Yates made his FL debut with Bristol Rovers, aged 17, on 3 March 1987 at Darlington. After 196(1) FL appearances for Rovers he went on to play over 100 games for both his next two clubs, so was very experienced when he joined United.

Initially playing at right wing back he also had a spell in the centre of defence. He produced a series of battling performances, being calm under pressure and good in the air. A training ground injury kept him sidelined for three months and a hamstring injury on his return saw an end to his career at the Lane.

After two productive seasons with Huddersfield, where he was made captain, he moved into non-League football with Scarborough, having reached 488(20) career FL appearances. After a spell out of the game he played for other non-League clubs but injuries limited his appearances.

Appearances:		Apps	Gls
	FL	11 (1)	0
	LC	1	0
	Total	12 (1)	0

YOUNG Alexander (Alan) Forbes

Striker 1982–83 6' 0" 12st 10
b. Kirkcaldy 26 October 1955

Kirkcaldy YMCA/ Oldham Athletic Jul 1974 Leicester City (£250k) Jul 1979
United: **(£160k) 25/31 Aug 1982 to 11 Aug 1983**
Debuts: **31 Aug 1982 United 3 Hull City 1 (LC)**
4 Sep 1982 United 2 Preston North End 1
Last games: **7 May 1983 United 0 Lincoln City 1**
2 Aug 1983 Grantham T 1 United 5 (Fr)
Brighton & Hove Albion (£140k) Aug 1983/ Notts County (£55k) Sep 1984/ Rochdale (£10k + player exch) Aug 1986/ Shepshed Charterhouse player-coach Mar 1988/ Ilkeston Town 1989–90/ Alfreton T Dec 1990/ Notts County coach then Football in the Community Officer/ Chesterfield Youth development Jul 1998/ Leeds United Academy coach

Alan Young was a former Scottish schoolboy international who made his FL debut with Oldham Athletic, scoring after coming on as a substitute, on 24 September 1974 at Portsmouth. He scored again on his second appearance as a substitute and on his full debut on 26 October at Cardiff City. He made sufficient progress to move to Leicester where he gained a Division Two Championship medal, but two seasons later, with Gary Lineker coming to the fore and with a new manager at Leicester, Alan moved to the Lane.

Signed by Ian Porterfield, Alan was a tall and powerful forward, always prepared to challenge for the ball. He scored twice on his debut in the League Cup and, on average, scored a goal every 2.5 games but he suffered a remarkable number of injuries; some as a direct result of his forceful play but also because of a nagging back ailment and, after one season, he moved on.

He played for three more clubs and when injuries ended his career, he had scored 90 goals in 315(34) FL games.

He moved into non-League football but also took courses in business management and sports' injuries and added FA coaching badges.

Appearances:		Apps	Gls
	FL	23 (3)	7
	FAC	2	3
	LC	4	3
	Total	29 (3)	13

YOUNG Charles **Stuart** Robertson

G 1952
b. Falkirk 23 August 1929

Stalybridge Celtic
United: 24 May 1951 to 30 Jun 1952
Debuts: 23 Feb 1952 Southend United 1 United 2 (FAC)
22 Mar 1952 United 5 Leicester City 0
Last game: 5 Apr 1952 United 1 Brentford 4

United had no capable deputy goalkeeper in 1951 if Ted Burgin was injured and manager Teddy Davison didn't solve the problem when he signed Stuart Young who was a Manchester glazier and football part-timer. Stuart was agile but weak when challenged in the air and he made just four first team appearances for United.

Appearances:		Apps	Gls
	FL	3	0
	FAC	1	0
	Total	4	0

YOUNG Richard (Dick) Harker

RB/CH/LB/WH 1936–49 6' 0" 12st 2
b. Wardley, Gateshead 17 April 1918
d. Carlisle 31 January 1989

Reyrolle's FC (Hebburn)/ Hebburn St Cuthbert's/ Wardley Colliery
United: 1 Oct amat, 14/15 Nov pro 1935 to 16 Mar 1949
Debuts: 7 Jun 1936 Nykoebing Falster XI (Denmark) 1 United 5 (Fr)
1 May 1937 West Ham United 1 United 0
Last game: 5 Mar 1949 Manchester City 1 United 0
WW2 guest: Northampton T (1941–42, 6 app), Luton T (1942–44, 47 app)
Lincoln City (£2000) Mar 1949, player-coach 1951–52, trainer cs 1954/
Carlisle United trainer 1955, mgr Nov 1975 to Nov 1976, asst mgr 1976 to 77 and 1980 to 1982

Dick Young's career was badly affected by the Second War. A two footed, slim but strong and determined defender, he was difficult to beat both on the ground and in the air. He played occasionally in 1937–38 at left back and had a run of games in the following promotion season at right back. He was chosen for the first three FL games of 1939–40 but the League programme was then abandoned. Playing anywhere in the defence and occasionally as a forward, Dick was a regular member of the first team for the following two war-time seasons. He joined the RAF in 1941 and served as a PTI playing occasionally for United and Northampton Town and then for Luton before he was moved to Italy in 1945.

His versatility continued after he came out of the RAF and he played regularly from April 1947 to October 1948 but, after a few more games, he was transferred to Lincoln City where he made 100 FL appearances. He spent seven seasons with the Imps as a player, coach and trainer. He moved on to Carlisle where he spent over 25 years in various roles including a spell as manager.

Appearances:		Apps	Gls
	FL	71	0
	FAC	6	0
	CC	6	0
	1939–40	3	0
	WW2	56	5
	Total	142	5

LATE TRANSFERS

The following players left United, either permanently or on loan, on or before 1 September 2008, but the transfers are not mentioned above:

ARMSTRONG Christopher
Joined Reading (£500k to a possible £800k) 26 August 2008

STEAD Jonathan
Joined Ipswich Town on 1 September on loan until January 2009

TONGE Michael
Joined Stoke City (undisclosed fee) on 1 September 2008

The following players signed for United during the close season of 2008:

HABER Justin b. Floriana (Malta) 9 June 1981
Signed (free) 31 July 2008

HALFORD Gregory (Greg) b. Chelmsford 8 December 1984
Signed on a season-long loan from Sunderland on 2 July 2008

HENDERSON Darius Alexis b. Sutton 7 September 1981
Signed from Watford for £2m on 22 July 2008

SPRING Matthew John b. Harlow 17 November 1979
Signed from Luton Town on a season-long loan on 31 July 2008

SUN Jihai b. Dalian China 30 Sep 1977
Signed from Manchester City (free) on 2 July 2008

Other United Players

Players who made no first team appearances in competitive fixtures but have played in friendly games–formerly known as 'club' games–or were United players who made Football League, Scottish League or pre-First World War Southern League appearances for other clubs. A few other significant players who were linked in some way to United have also been included.
Career coverage is not comprehensive and tends to concentrate on their connection with United.
Appearances (App) refer to Football League fixtures and include those as a substitute.

ABDI Liban
b. Burco (Somalia) 5 Oct 1988
Striker. Played: Newport Pagnell T, Buckingham T, United (Academy). He played:
25 Mar 2008 Ferencvaros (Hung) 0 United XI 1 (Fr, scored)
Ferencvaros (L) cs 2008.

ADAMS Michael (Micky)
b. Sheffield 8 Nov 1961
United junior released Jan 1978 by Harry Haslam. Played for Gillingham, Coventry C, Leeds U (£110k), Southampton (£250k), Stoke C, and Fulham (total 438 app). Later managerial appointments have included Leicester and Coventry City.

AIZLEWOOD George H
A Sheffield Club amateur forward who had earlier played for Park Friendly (1882), Attercliffe and Collegiate. He can be regarded as United's first substitute as he arrived late for his debut and Mosforth played until he arrived. He played twice:
18 Nov 1889 United 0 Bolton W 2 (Fr, sub):
9 Dec 1889 United 1 Everton 10 (Fr).

ALDRIDGE Steven
b. Armthorpe 2 Nov 1957
Apprentice signed Dec 1975. He made one appearance for Doncaster Rovers as a non-contract player in 1981.

ALEKSIC Milija
b. Newcastle-u-Lyme 14 April 1951
The Tottenham keeper joined United 21 March 1979 on a one month loan.
(138 app, for Plymouth, Luton, Spurs).

ALLFORD W
b. Woodhouse Mill
A Swallownest player signed after a trial in February 1913 and who appears on the 1913–14 team photograph but was transfer listed at the end of that season.

ALLISON J J (Joe)
b. Consett 17 Nov 1913
A Linfield centre forward who joined United in Jan 1936 and was released cs1937.
He later played for Workington, Barnsley (1939–40) and made 13 FL appearances for Hartlepools U (1946–47).

ANDISON Gary
b. Gateshead 12 Dec 1976
A defender who made two appearances on trial with the reserve team and also played:
21 Dec 1995 Worksop 2 United XI 4 (Fr).
He later played for several non-League clubs in the North East of England.

ANNERSON Jamie
b. Sheffield 21 June 1988
England Youth and U19 keeper with United from age 16. He played:
29 July 2006 Scunthorpe U 1 United 0 (sub, Fr)
15 Jan 2007 United 1 Chengdu Blades 1 (Fr)
Ilkeston Town (L) Oct 2006/ Rotherham U (L) Sep 2007 where he played in a Johnstone's Paint Trophy fixture/ Chesterfield (L) Mar 2008.

ARBLASTER Brian M
b. London 6 June 1943
A United amateur goalkeeper who became a part-time professional in July 1962 working as a miner and later as a lorry driver.
Transferred to Chesterfield (55 apps) in Dec 1964, he later played for Scunthorpe Utd (10 app), Barnsley (111 app), Boston U and Matlock T.

ARCHER Frederick John
b. Aston on Trent 28 Feb 1900
An inside left who played for Rotherham County in 1919–20 (2 app), Walsall (29 app 10 g).
Archer joined United at the end of Feb 1925 leaving at the end of that season.

ARCHER Paul
A forward who played on trial for the Reserves and:
2 Apr 1990 Combined Services 0 United XI 0 (Fr at Catterick Camp).

ARCHER Phillip
b. Rotherham 25 Aug 1952
A United apprentice who joined Reading, August 1971 (17 app).

ARMESON Lawrence Raymond
b. Rotherham.
Half-back who joined United in 1934 from Rotherham YMCA.
Released in 1935, he played for Rotherham U (2 app) and Coventry C (7 app).

ARNOTT J
A Glasgow Clyde full back who was among the 1889 list of new United players but it is likely that he never came.

ASHBRIDGE Thomas Edwin
b. Maryport c1890
A Watford inside right who joined United 25 April 1914 (£350) with Harold Pantling.

ASHMAN George **Alan**
b. Rotherham 30 May 1928
A United amateur centre forward who played for Nottingham F (13 app, 3 goals), Carlisle U (207/208 app, 98 goals). He later was the manager of Carlisle U, WBA, etc. Died 2002.

ASHMORE Jamie
b. Sheffield 2 March 1986
Midfield player released by Neil Warnock cs 2007 but recalled by Bryan Robson. He played:
16 July 2007 Worksop T 0 United XI 2 (Fr).
(L) Macclesfield.Jan 2008 (8 app)/ Ferencvaros cs 2008.

ASHTON Jonathan (Jon) F
b. Plymouth 4 Aug 1979
Full back. Played Plymouth A (34 app), Exeter (13). United trial:
17 July 2001 Sheffield FC 0 United XI 7 (sub, Fr).

ATKINSON Brian
b. Sheffield 16 Nov 1934
A half-back signed by United June 1953 from Oaks Fold. Transferred Halifax T 2 June 1956 (67 app).

ATKINSON Dalian R
b. Shrewsbury 21 Mar 1968
The Ipswich, Aston V and Wednesday forward who had a trial with the reserves, February 1998.

ATKINSON Patrick D
b. Singapore 22 May 1970
United apprentice 1986–88. He played for Hartlepool U (21 app, 3 goals), York C (41 app) and Scarborough (27).

ATKINSON Tim
He played:
2 Apr 1990 Combined Services 0 United XI 0 (Fr at Catterick Camp).

ATKINSON Wm Henry
Registered with the FL 10 Dec 1898, he may have played:
27 Dec 1898 United 5 Corinthians 3 (E Needham BM).
Reported pre-match to be 'a local centre (forward) of some note', he is referred to as 'Mellor'(qv) in match reports.

ATTREE Albert
A Doncaster Rovers defender who played over 300 games for the club. He turned out for United against his own club when another United player failed to arrive:
28 Dec 1889 Doncaster R 2 United 0 (Fr, abandoned).

BABAYARO Emmanuel
A Nigerian international keeper who had a trial with the Reserves, April 1996.

BACH Philip (Phil)
b. Ludlow 1872
A full back who played for Middlesbrough and Reading before joining Sunderland in June 1897. Sunderland had tried to sign him earlier but found to their dismay that his FL registration for 1896–97 was held by United. Capped in 1899, he later became a Middlesbrough director and served both the FA and the League.

BAILEY Alf
Reported to be from Kettering, he was probably the Raunds Town amateur forward who resisted offers from several League clubs. He played in two friendly games for United:
26 Feb 1894 United 7 Rotherham Town 1 (scored)
12 Mar 1894 United 0 Woolwich Arsenal 2.

BAILEY Ian (see Secretaries, Trainers section)
He played:
23 Nov 1986 Hallam 3 United XI 5 (Fr).

BAKEWELL George
A Derby County forward (49 app, 9 gl) from 1884, he played and scored as a guest for United:
9 Dec 1889 United 1 Everton 10. (Fr).

BANNISTER Keith
b. Sheffield 13 Nov 1930

A Sheffield Boys inside forward, he signed for United May 1945 (amateur) and in May 1948 as a pro. A Youth international in that year, he was released July 1950.
He then played for Birmingham (22 app), Wrexham (14 app), Chesterfield (21 app, 1 gl), Norwich C (7 app) and several non-league clubs.

BARBER Eric
b. Stockport 25 Mar 1926
An amateur centre forward who had made three war-time appearances with Manchester City. He had a trial with United and signed 5 Feb 1947 after scoring a hat-trick for the reserves. He played:
24 Nov 1948 Western Command 0 United XI 3 (Fr)
Released in Jan 1949, he played for Macclesfield, Bolton W and Rochdale (17 app, 2 gl).

BARKER Jeffrey (Jeff)
b. Glanford, Brigg 16 Oct 1915
A Goole T and Scunthorpe U full-back, he signed for United 6 Oct 1934 to 4 May 1935. He then played for Scunthorpe U, Aston V (3 app), Huddersfeld T (67 app) and Scunthorpe again (73 app, 1 goal). A fine player, he made many more appearances for Scunthorpe in their Midland League days and for other clubs in war-time football.

BARRICK Dean
b. Hemsworth 30 Sept 1969
The Sheffield Wednesday, Rotherham and Cambridge U player who had a 1995 trial with United. He played:
25 July 1995 Wokingham v United XI
27 July 1995 Aylesbury U v United XI
He then played for PNE 1995–8 and Bury. (Total 357 app).

BASSETT David (Dave) (see Managers section)
He played:
16 Mar 1992 United XI 1 Malmo (Sweden) 6 (Stancliffe BM).

BASSETT Graham
b. Sunderland 6 Oct 1984
A Sunderland apprentice forward given a trial with United Reserves in April 1982. He later played for Hartlepool U (7 app).

BATES Ernest
A wing half signed 13 April 1949 and released cs 1952. He played:
4 May 1950 Skegness 3 United XI 2 (Fr).

BEACOCK Gary
Signed 30 July 1976.
Released 22 Jan 1978. He may have played:
13 Apr 1977 Grantham v United XI as a substitute.
Subsequently played in Holland and for Grimsby T (17 app) and Hereford U (27 app).

BEARDSHAW William F (Baltic) (see Directors section)
b. Sheffield 1858
Sheffield Club goalkeeper who had also played for Attercliffe and Collegiate. He played;
14 Apr 1890 Staveley 2 United 1 (Fr).

BEAUMONT Christopher
b. Sheffield 5 Dec 1965
A hard working United apprentice forward/midfield player. He later played for Denaby U, Rochdale (34 app 7 gl), Stockport (258 app 39 gl) and Chesterfield (72 app 2 gl).

BECKRAM John George
b. Sunderland Aug 1881
An inside forward signed by United in November 1901. He is incorrectly credited in FL records with 3 appearances. His only first team appearance was in an Ibrox Disaster match:
3 May 1902 Wednesday 3 United 0 (CM)
He was transferred to Bradford C July 1903 and played in their first season in the FL (25 app, 6 gl).

BENNETT George R
An inside left, signed 6/12 June 1946 from Dundee North End and released May 1947. He played:
30 April 1947 Boston U 3 United XI 2 (CM).
He joined Dundee U but never played a senior game.

BENNETT William
b. Leyland 1896
A centre forward who joined United 2 Feb 1921 from Leyland Motors. Released cs 1922, he made one FL appearance for Nelson.

BENNISON Thomas John (Jack)
b. Barrow Hill (Chesterfield) JAS 1874
A wing half, he played for Poolsbrook and Chesterfield Town before joining United in May 1899. His only first team game was:
19 Mar 1900 Northampton T 0 United 3 (Fr)
He rejoined Chesterfield in Sep 1900 (2 app) and then played for Poolsbrook Rangers and Royston Colliery.

BENTLEY
An amateur full back who played:
22 Feb 1890 Middlesbrough 6 United 4 (Fr)
He may be Willis Bentley, a Channing Rovers, Owlerton and former Wednesday player, born Sheffield 1863.

BENTLEY W
He played in goal for United and may be the player recorded above:
5 Apr 1890 United 2 Staveley 1 (Fr).

BERNARD Olivier
b. Paris (Fr) 14 Oct 1979
French full back who played for Newcastle U (102 app), Darlington, Southampton and Glasgow R. He had a trial making his debut:
24 July 2006 Morton 1 United 3 (Fr).

BINNION Travis
b. Derby 10 Nov 1986
Defensive midfield Academy player who has played for the Republic of Ireland U19 team.
Debut: 6 Aug 2007 Stocksbridge 0 United XI 4 (Fr)
IFK Mariehamn (Finland) Apr 2008.

BIRCH Jeffrey
b. Sheffield 21 Oct 1927
An outside left, he joined United in September 1947 from Selby Town. Released one month later, he played for Scarborough but returned to the Lane in May 1948. He played:
24 Nov 1948 Western Command 0 United 3 (Fr at Lichfield)
Released July 1949, he joined York C (7 app, 1 gl) and later worked as a fitter in Stannington.

BIRKHEAD Alfred
b. Deepcar (Sheffield) c1909
An amateur United goalkeeper (Dec 1931), he joined Rotherham United and became a professional (64 app). He died in 1978.

BISHOP Peter J
b. Sheffield 4 Jan 1944
A United England Youth forward, he signed amateur forms Aug 1961 and became a part-time pro 12 April 1963 to May 1965. He joined Chesterfield in June 1965 (81 app, 8 gl).

BLACKSHAW Herbert (Bert) K
b. Altrincham 1916
United gave this outside left a two month trial from 10 July 1936. He joined Oldham (62 app, 15 gl) and was the player-manager of Wisbech T from January 1946.

BLACKWELL Kevin P (see Managers section)
b. Luton 21 Dec 1958
He played:
14 May 2000 Tobago XI 1 United XI 3 (Fr, sub).

BONNYMAN Phil
b. Glasgow 6 Feb 1954
A very useful mid-field player whose clubs included Carlisle, Chesterfield and Grimsby Town (total 459 app). He made a guest appearance for United:
8 May 1986 Chesterfield 2 United XI 1 (BM for E Moss).

BOURNE George
An 'Attercliffe lad' and probably the brother of Richard, he joined United in Oct 1895 after serving with the Y&L regiment. He played:
6 Apr 1896 Mexborough 3 United XI 6 (Fr)
13 Apr 1896 Celtic 2 United 2 (Fr, scored)
Released cs1897, he played for Attercliffe and Roundel.

BOWN(E)S George H
b. Sheffield c1859
A wing half who played for the Wednesday as 'Bown', then for Pye Bank and Clinton. He played once for United, perhaps as a guest:
25 Jan 1890 United 3 Derby Midland 1 (Fr).

BRAND Andrew S
b. Edinburgh 8 Nov 1957
An Everton goalkeeper (2 app) with loan appearances for Crewe A (15 app). He had a month loan with United from 23 Aug 1979, playing for the reserves and was a non-playing sub v Dundee (ASC). He joined Hereford U (54 app) in 1980 and then Wrexham (1 app) and Blackpool (3 app).

BREWSTER Craig
A Forfar Athletic mid-field player who was a member of the 1989 United tour of Germany but the Scottish club refused to let him play.

BRIND Henry
b. Sheffield.
Left footed forward, signed March 1910, released cs 1911. He played for Chesterfield 1911–12 (15 app) in the Midland League and Shirebrook.

BROMAGE Enos
b. Mickleover 22 Oct 1898
Sturdy outside left. Son of the Derby C trainer, his brother George also played for United and five other brothers were professionals. Enos signed for United in 1922 and was transferred to Derby C November 1923 (4 app, 2 gl). He also played for Gillingham, WBA and Nottingham Forest (total 36 app). A nephew (Sidney) played for United reserves 1937–38.

BROUGHTON
An outside left who may have made a substitute appearance in a charity match:
21 Aug 1943 United 3 Sheffield Wednesday 2.

BROWN Alfred
b. Sheffield c1899
A Sheffield Boys and Carbrook Reform forward, he played:
20 Apr 1918 United 1 Wednesday 1 (Fr)
Rotherham T, half back with Blackpool (9 app), Barnsley (12 app), Swindon (14 app), Nelson (2 app), Barnsley, Manchester Central.

BROWN Jonathan
b. Barnsley 8 Sept 1966
Denaby U full back who had a trial with the Reserve team in January 1990. He played for Exeter City 1990–95 (164 app, 3 gl).

BROWNLOW L
A local half back who had played for Clinton and Ecclesfield. His first appearance for United may have been as a guest:
9 Nov 1889 Staveley 7 United 0 (Fr)
In the 1890–91 season he made seven appearances in club games. The first was:
30 Dec 1890 United 7 Casuals 0 (Fr) and the last:
21 Mar 1891 Royal Arsenal 1 United 1 (Fr)
He then (cs1891) played for Gainsborough Trinity.

BUBB Alvin R
b. Paddington 11 Oct 1980
A striker, he was released by QPR (1 app), and was given a trial by Neil Warnock and played:
16 July 2006 Baslow 1 United XI 14 (Fr)
He later played for Bristol R (13 app).

BUCKLEY Delron or Deiron
A South African international midfielder who had played for Armenia Bielefeld and Dortmund in Germany. He trained with United and played:
8 Aug 2006 ADO Den Haag (Holland) 2 United 2 (Fr).

BULLIVANT Thomas
b. Sheffield 1876
A goalkeeper who played in the FL with Gainsborough Trinity (11 app, season 1901–02). He was on United's books 1904–05.

BUNYAN Charles
A goalkeeper with Old Horns (Chesterfield), he played for Hyde United and conceded a record 26 goals against PNE in a 1887 FA Cup-tie. He moved to Derby C (9 app) and in Aug 1892 to Chesterfield Town. He played once for United, as a 'guest':
28 Nov 1892 United 1 Bolton W 0 (Fr).
He played again for Derby C, Ilkeston, Walsall (44 app), New Brompton, Newcastle U, Ripley and in Brussels where he died in 1922.

BURGIN Eric
b. Sheffield 4 Jan 1924
An amateur on United's books from Aug 1940, he served in the RAF and became a pro 18 Dec 1946. He played centre half for the Reserves until cs 1949. He had been asked to play at centre forward at Highbury in January 1949 but turned it down! He played for York City (23 app) until cs 1951.
A Yorkshire fast-medium pace bowler (1952–53), he played and served the United Cricket Club for many years.

BURKE Paul
b. Doncaster 17 July 1981
English schoolboy striker who joined United at sixteen and played:
16 July 1998 Sheffield Club 0 United XI 2 (Fr, sub)
Loaned to Whitby Town, he was released and played in non-league football.

BURLEY Benjamin
b. Sheffield 1912
Joined United as an amateur (Nov 1931), he became a pro Oct 1932 but was released at the end of the season. An outside left, he played for Southampton (2 app), Grimsby T (22 app, 5 gl), Norwich C (35 app, 4 gl) and Darlington (35 app, 7 gl).

BURRIDGE Crofton ('Charles')
A Sheffield Club amateur forward, he played:
28 Dec 1893 United 7 Casuals 0 (Fr, scored 2)
and in three further club matches that season. He played twice more in April 1896 scoring twice against Dundee (Fr) at home and finally appearing:
18 April 1896 Newcastle U 3 United 1 (Fr).

BURROWS Lycurgus
b. Ashton under Lyne 26 June 1875
An amateur full back who had played for Woolwich Arsenal (10 app) and for Spurs in the Southern League. He was working in Sheffield and played:
26 Feb 1898 United 1 Wednesday 4 (Fr)
He was hoping to receive a free transfer from the Arsenal but United didn't pursue matters. He died in Gosforth in Aug 1952.

BURTON (-GODWIN) 'Sagi'
b. Birmingham 25 Nov 1977
A defender with Crystal P (25 app, 1 goal) and Colchester U (9 app), he had a trial with the reserves (Nov 1999) and was signed by Adrian Heath. He was a non playing substitute at Stockport but failed a medical and his contract was cancelled and after a trial with Sunderland, he joined Port Vale (86 app, 2 gl). Crewe A (1 app), Peterborough U (96 app, 4 gl), Shrewsbury T(44 app, 5 gl) and Barnet (30 app, 1gl).

BUTTERFIELD Timothy (Tim)
b. Sheffield 18 Oct 1974
United first year apprentice who played:
12 Dec 1994 Staveley XI 3 United XI 4 (sub, BM).

BYRNE
A goalkeeper given a trial:
14 Dec 1992 Worksop T 3 United XI 1 (BM Substituted at half time).

BYRNE David
b. Dublin 28 April 1905
A prolific scorer with Shamrock Rovers, he had a brief spell with Bradford City (3 app, 1 goal) before returning to Ireland. He played for Shelbourne and then returned to Shamrock Rovers. He signed for United 27 Oct 1932 and played two days later for the Reserves but was injured and he was released (23 Nov). He had a brief period with Man Utd (1933–34. 4 app, 3 gl) and was awarded three Republic of Ireland caps.

CAGALJ Adrian
b. Australia 16 Feb 1976
A goalkeeper who played for N Geelong Warriors, Carlton, Adelaide City. He played as a United trialist 22 July 2000 with the reserves at Alfreton and:
1 Aug 2000 Notts C 3 United 3 (Fr).
He saved a penalty kick but it was twice retaken. He returned to Adelaide and also played for Melbourne Knights and Oakleigh Commons.

CALVERT James W
An inside forward, possibly b. Chesterfield OND 1873, who played for Worksop (1891–93) and Bury. Signed by United cs1895, he made one first team appearance, scoring twice:
11 Sep 1895 Grimsby T 2 United 3 (Fr).

CARTER Sydney
b. Chesterfield 28 July 1916
A centre forward who joined United 7 Nov 1936 from Bolsover Colliery and was released at the end of the season. He played for Wolves, Macclesfield and Mansfield T (1938–47. 39 app, 10 gl) and was a trainer and physio at Field Mill for over twenty years.

CASE Norman
b. Prescot 1 Sept 1925
An outside right who signed for United 19 Aug 1948 and played in the public practice match. His contract was soon cancelled and he signed for Leyton O, Rochdale, Ards, Sunderland (4 app, 2 gl), Watford (10 app, 4 gl), Yeovil, Rochdale (2 app), Cheltenham and Canterbury C.

CATLIFF Herbert
b. 9 July 1889
Signed 2 Nov 1911 from Hartshead Friends. A full back, he joined Doncaster Rovers cs 1912 and emigrated to Australia in 1927.

CHAMBERLIN Thomas
A goalkeeper 'from Lowestoft' who signed for United in Oct 1899. His only first team appearance came in the Arthur Watson benefit match:
15 Jan 1900 United 5 International XI 1 (BM).

CHANOT Maxime
b. Nancy (France) 21 Nov 1989
Central defender who joined the Academy from Reims July 2007. He played:
25 Mar 2008 Ferencvaros 0 United XI 1 (Fr).

CHAPMAN Adam
b. Doncaster 29 Nov 1989
A Northern Irish grandmother provided the qualification that led to this defender winning U19 and U21 caps. He played:
10 Oct 2007 Sheffield Club 1 United XI 5 (Fr).

CHARLESWORTH
Played at outside left in a game for the 'FA War Fund' and described as 'slow' and couldn't beat his man':
3 May 1919 Manchester City 1 United 0 (CM)
He may have played in the following season for Scunthorpe U. Other nearby contemporary players with that surname played for Sutton T, Chesterfield, Hull C, Worksop, Doncaster R and Wombwell.

CHARLTON J
An unknown forward who made one appearance in the first season and scored:
29 Mar 1890 Doncaster R 1 United 1 (Fr).

CHEFFINS
An Owlerton forward who scored on a trial:
18 Apr 1891 Matlock 3 United XI 2 (Fr).

CHERRILL Matthew
b. Sheffield 10 Oct 1973
A United Youth team midfield player who played:
14 Dec 1992 Worksop T 3 United XI 1 (sub, BM).

CIRCUIT Steven
b. Sheffield 11 Apr 1972
A United junior from 1988–89 and pro Sep 1990, he played:
2 Apr 1990 Combined Services 0 United XI 0 (Fr at Catterick)
He went out on loan in Norway before his release in 1991. He then played for Stockport C, Stafford R, Halifax T (1 sub app), Boston U and other non-league clubs.

CLAPHAM Jamie
b. Lincoln 7 Dec 1975
Left side midfielder who began with Spurs but made his name with Ipswich (207 app, 10 gl). He moved to Birmingham (84 app, 1 gl) before coming to United on trial. He played:
28 July 2006 Rotherham U 1 United 1 (Fr)
He joined Wolves (26 app) in August 2006 and later played for Leeds (13 app) and Leicester (11 app).

CLARK Graham J
b. Aberdeen 20 Jan 1961
A schoolboy international and United midfield junior, June 1977 to Oct 1978. A Youth international, he played:
23 Oct 1978 Winterton R 1 United 1 (Fr)
He joined Darlington (Aug 1979, 6 app) and then Montrose but lost a leg in a motorbike accident.

CLARKE
Perhaps a newspaper error for Calder but may have played and scored:
14 Apr 1890 Staveley 2 United 1 (Fr).

CLARKE
He played:
2 April 1990 Combined Services 0 United XI 0 (Fr at Catterick Camp).

CLARKE Michael
b. Sheffield 28 Nov 1944
A United apprentice and pro, 3 July 1960 to 30 June 1964. A mid-field player, he played for Aldershot (5 app) and Halifax T (51 app, 1 gl).

CLARKE Richard
A 23-year-old mid-fielder with Newry City He had a trial with Bury before his trial with United:
28 July 2007 Portadown 0 United 2 (Fr).

CLOETE George
Cloete and Cyril Mitchley were South African players from Johannesburg signed by Joe Mercer early in January 1959. Cloete was released at the end of the season after four games with the 'A' team.

COLGAN Nicholas Vincent
b. Drogheda (Ireland) 19 Sept 1973
An international keeper (Youth, U21 and B) who played for Drogheda, Chelsea (1 app) and other clubs on loan but had made that one single FL appearance when he played on trial for United:
24 July 1997 Arjang (Sweden) 1 United 8 (Fr)
He came on as a sub, five days later at Odds BK (Norway) but returned to Chelsea. After ten games on loan with Brentford and Reading, he joined Bournemouth and then Hibs (121 SL app), Stockport ((L) 15 app), Barnsley (101 app), Dundee (1 SL app), Ipswich and Sunderland.

COLLEY Karl
A Sheffield born Newcastle United reserve defender signed by United 4 July 2002. Released in March 2003, he has since played for Kettering, Frickley Ath, Halifax, Stocksbridge, Retford and Sheffield Club.

COLLINS Eric
b. Newcastle on Tyne 5 Jan 1976
YTS keeper who played:
6 Sep 1993 Mansfield T 1 United 2 (Dearden BM).

CONLEY Brian
b. Thurnscoe 21 Nov 1948
A United apprentice defender from 20 Apr 1964, he was transferred to Bradford PA 19 Dec 1968 (13 app).

CONNELL Thomas E
b. Newry (NI) 25 Nov 1957
A Coleraine U21 international defender, he was given a trial in the Central League team (1 March 1978). He made one substitute full international appearance for Northern Ireland before joining Manchester United (2 app). He signed for Glentoran cs 1982.

CONROY Martin
b. Kilsyth
A small forward who joined United 30 June 1972. He played:
28 July 1974 ROW Rybnik (Pol) 0 United 1 (Fr, substituted after 25 mins).
Released at the end of the season, he later played for Stenhousemuir (9 SL app) and Worksop Town.

CONTEH Denni
b. Denmark
A player from Strasbourg who played on trial:
21 July 1999 Raith R 1 United 0 sub, (Fr)
23 July 1999 United 0 Chelsea 2 (Fr).
He was released as United couldn't guarantee first team football.

COOKE
An unidentified player—perhaps A Cook—who played at inside left and scored in what was probably an unofficial charity fixture:
27 Dec 1918 United XI 2 Wednesday XI 2 (CM at Tankersley).

COOKSEY Scott A
b. Birmingham 24 June 1972
A Derby C, Shrewsbury and Bromsgrove R goalkeeper, given a trial with the reserves in October 1991. He joined Peterborough U in Dec 1993 (15 app), Hednesford T and Shrewsbury (1 app).

COPELAND
Perhaps Peter Coupland who played for Spalding United.
A 'Lincolnshire' goalkeeper given a trial:
25 Jan 1969 United XI 5 Port Vale 1 (Fr).

COPELAND Simon D
b. Sheffield 10 Oct 1968
A defender who signed YTS July 1985 and played:
8 May 1986 Chesterfield 2 United XI 1 (Ernie Moss BM).
Given a free transfer cs1988, he joined Rochdale (28 app) and later played for Alfreton. His life deteriorated with drug and criminal activities.

COPESTAKE William Henry
b. Stoke on Trent JFM 1871
A winger who joined United from Worksop Town in June 1894.
He played:
2 Mar 1895 Stoke 3 United 2 (Fr)
He appeared in two other club matches away at Luton (25 Mar) and Grimsby (12 Apr) before rejoining Worksop in September.

COULE John (Jack)
A tall outside left, born in Stockport but brought up in Regina, Canada. He joined United 28 Oct 1920, 'age 23', after working with the Royal Mounted Police Force and played for the reserves but was released in the close season. He made one FL appearance for Crewe A.

COULIBALY Dramane
A French striker from Marseilles. He scored twice:
18 July 2000 Tideswell 0 United XI 8 (Fr)
and appeared as a sub in three more friendly games the last being
1 Aug 2000 Notts County 3 United 3 (sub Fr).

COXON David
Signed for the Blades 20 July 1970 and released 1974. He had a loan spell with Southend (Apr 1974) and signed for Chester City but made no League appearances. He was a Sheffield publican and was the chief executive of Stockport County.

CRESSWELL Ryan
b. Rotherham 22 Dec 1987
A central defender from the Academy who first played:
6 Aug 2007 Stocksbridge 0 United XI 4 (Fr)
He was loaned to Halifax (Jan 2007), Rotherham (Sep 2007 and played in a JPT tie), Morecambe (Nov 2007) and Macclesfield (Jan 2008). (Total 24 app). Transferred to Bury July 2008.

CRETCHLEY
Described in a Luton newspaper as 'a Cockney', this may be Copestake, a United player, or the 'Vampires' amateur forward.
He played:
25 Mar 1895 Luton T 1 United XI 2 (Fr).

CROISSANT Benoit
b. Vitriy le Francois 9 Aug 1980
A French midfield Youth international from Troyes. He signed 8 Aug 2001 after a trial matches:
17 July 2001 Sheffield FC 0 United XI 7 (Fr) and four further pre-season games, the last being:
31 Jul 2001 Burton Albion 2 United 4 (sub Fr)
He was loaned for the 2002–03 season to Tel Star (Holland) and later played in various countries.

CROOKES Ronald Graham
b. Sheffield 22 Mar 1931
A Hillsborough BC keeper who played for the United A team from 1948. An ABA boxer in the army, he signed pro forms for United in Sep 1952 and made his debut in the first floodlight game:
16 March 1954 United 2 Rotherham U 1 (Fr)
and also played against Hibs (3–3) a week later. He played for King's Lynn and worked for the London police.

CROSSAN John A
b. Derry (NI) 29 Nov 1938
A Derry City amateur international forward, he was recommended to Joe Mercer by Billy Gillespie, our former Irish international. The plan was that Crossan would become a Derry professional and then sign for United but other contacts warned Mercer against signing the future star inside forward. Banned by the Irish FA for illegal payments, he first played abroad but eventually made 232 FL appearances, scoring 70 goals, with Sunderland, Manchester City and Middlesbrough and was awarded 24 caps.

CURRIE Darren
b. Hampstead 29 Nov 1974
A nephew of Tony Currie, he was a trainee with West Ham but made his League debut with Shrewsbury Town. He trained with United (Jan 1998) but was signed by Plymouth, later playing for a host of clubs in a career of over 500 League appearances.

CURRY Robert E
A United midfielder who came through the junior ranks. Signed in January 1956, he played:
26 Sep 1956 Worksop T 1 United 0 (CM) and in February at Lincoln against a Royal Signals team before his release in June 1958.

CUSHLOW Richard (Dick)
b. Shotton 15 June 1920
A Chesterfield centre half (34 app) who joined United 28 Nov/1 Dec 1947 and was transferred to Derby C (2 app) as part of an exchange deal for Fred E Smith. He moved to Crystal Palace (28 app) but his career was ended in 1952 by injury.

DALEY Tony (see Secretaries, Trainers section)
He played:
19 July 2004 Tavistock 2 United XI 5 (sub, scored, Fr).

DALTON Paul
b. Middlesbrough 25 April 1967
A midfield player who had played for Hartlepool (151 app, 37 gl) and Plymouth (98 app, 25 gl). He played on trial and scored:
17 July 1995 Boston U 2 United 2 (Fr)
He joined Huddersfield T. (98 app, 25 gl) and then Carlisle U ((L) 3app, 1 gl).

DASHPER E E (or A E)
An amateur full back who played for the Crouch End Vampires and was registered by United with the League in Oct 1894. He played:
23 March 1895 Corinthians 1 United 2 (Fr).

DAUGHTREY J T
('Dawfry' in the Independent). A Rotherham Town (13 FL apps) player who played as a guest for United:
1 April 1895 game Rotherham T 1 Sheffield United and District XI 2 (Fr).

DAVIES Colin
b. Shrewsbury 12 Apr 1936
Had a trial at left half with the Central League team in April 1957.
He played for Port Vale 1958 to 1961 (13 app).

DAVIES Gareth
b. Chesterfield 4 Feb 1983
With United as a schoolboy before playing as a midfielder for Buxton, Chesterfield (116 app), Stalybridge and Halifax.

DAVIES Kevin
b. Sheffield 15 Nov 1978
Sheffield Boys and United apprentice midfield-striker, pro Apr 1997.
His first senior appearance may have been:
21 Dec 1995 Worksop T 2 United XI 4 (sub, Fr)
He played:
16 July 1998 Sheffield Club 0 United XI 2 (Fr)
7 Dec 1999 Whitby T 1 United XI 3 (Fr)
He was released June 2000 and played for Worksop T.

DAVIES Kevin Cyril
b. Sheffield 26 March 1977
A United schoolboy forward, he was released and joined Chesterfield April 1994, later winning England Youth and U21 honours and having an excellent career in the game with Southampton, Blackburn and Bolton W. (total 441 app, 80 gl by cs 2008).

DAVISON Thomas
A forward from the Middlesbrough area, he had a trial with the reserves in Sep 1899 and signed in October. He played:
15 Jan 1900 United 5 International XI 1 (Arthur Watson BM).

DAW Edwin (Teddy)
b. Doncaster 23 Jan 1875
A Hexthorpe Wanderers goalkeeper, he had an unsuccessful trial with United before signing for Grimsby Town (2 app) and later played for Barnsley, Rushden, Luton (34 app), Leicester (56 app), New Brompton, Doncaster (2 app), Bradford City (16 app) and Oldham.

DAYKIN Andy (see Secretaries, Trainers and Other Staff section)
He played:
12 May 1986 Guernsey XI 1 United XI 9 (sub, Fr).

DEAKIN
A 'local' inside right who played:
20 Apr 1918 United 1 Wednesday 1 (Fr)
He may be Henry (Harry) Deacon, born Sheffield 25 April 1900 who had played for Hallam and later made over 470 FL appearances and scored 146 goals (mainly with Swansea and Crewe).

DEAKIN A
An Edinburgh player, he was listed in May 1889 as one of the new United players but he never came to Sheffield.

DEMPSEY Paul
b. Wirral 3 Dec 1981
A defender given a free transfer to Northampton Town 22 Mar 2001 (6 app). He joined Scarborough and then played for Leonidas (Holland), Worksop T, Hucknal T and Worksop again.

DEY Geoffrey
b. Chesterfield 11 Jan 1964

A midfielder who signed June 1980 and was an apprentice from Jan 1982 and a Youth international. He played:
17 Nov 1980 United XI 8 Select XI 4 (sub, Flynn BM) and
18 Apr 1983 United 1 Ipswich T 1 (sub, Tibbott BM)
Released in 1983, he joined Scunthorpe U (17 app, 1 gl).

DIBBLE Andrew (Andy) Gerald
b. Cwmbran 8 May 1965
A keeper with many clubs, he was released by Glasgow Rangers and signed by United 8 Aug 1997. He played:
19 Aug 1997 United 0 Everton 4 (Fr)
and was a non playing substitute against Sunderland before moving to Luton 15 Sep 1997 and further transfers.
He made 391(4) appearances for his 16 clubs, including Rangers and Aberdeen.

DICKENS (DICKINS) Matthew (Matt)
b. Sheffield 3 Sep 1970

A YTS pro keeper, signed July 1987, he played:
2 Apr 1990 Combined Services 0 United XI 0 (Fr, at Catterick).
He had loan spells which ended with a transfer to Lincoln City in 1991 (27 app). Sold to Blackburn (£250k., 1 app), he made a guest appearance 4 May 1992 in the Brian Smith Benefit match. Loan spells included Blackpool (19 app) and Rochdale (4 app) before he was transferred to Stockport (13 app). He moved into non-league retiring with Sheffield Club in 2000.

DICKMAN Lewis
b. Hexham 15 Jan 1977

An apprentice 1993–95, he played:
15 May 1994 Adelaide C 3 United 0 (sub, Fr)
21 May 1994 Australian Olympic XI 1 United 1 (sub Fr at Gold Coast, Queensland).

DINGWALL Wm Norman
b. Gateshead 29 July 1923

A wing half with United Aug 1945 who signed pro March 1946.
He played:
30 April 1947 Boston U 3 United XI 2 (CM)
Released June 1947, he signed for Halifax T (9 app).

DODDS Gerald
b. Sheffield 4 Jan 1935

A forward with Oaks Fold, he became a United professional 14 Feb 1952 and played:
22 April 1953 Buxton v United XI (BM)
He signed for Chesterfield 13 June 1955 (4 app) and later played for Worksop, South Shields, Scunthorpe U and Sutton Town.

DOHERTY Alan
An 18 year old 'from Dublin' who played on trial:
6 April 1992 Immingham 0 United 0 (sub Fr).

DONACHIE William
(see Secretaries, Trainers section)

b. Glasgow 5 Oct 1951

United coach. He played:
30 July 1997 Forde IL (Nor) 0 United 4 (Fr, sub).

DONAGHY Mal
b. Belfast 13 Sep 1957

The famous Northern Ireland defender with 91 caps. He was playing with Larne Town when Harry Haslam gave him, and other young players, an opportunity in a reserve match against Aston Villa (Feb 1978) which resulted in a 10–0 defeat. In June, Donaghy joined Luton Town, later playing for Manchester United and Chelsea. (Total 572 app).

DONALDSON Alexander
b. Gateside (Renfrewshire) 4 Feb 1892

A small, slight but tricky winger, he signed for United from Ripley Athletic 30 March 1911. George Waller, the trainer, seeing him for the first time in the dressing room, sent him out, saying 'boys aren't allowed in here', and he wasn't retained. He joined Bolton (Dec 1911, 139 app) and later played for Sunderland (43 app) and Manchester City (1 app) winning six Scottish caps.

DOWIE Iain
b. Hatfield 9 Jan 1965

Northern Ireland international with 49 caps. A forward with Hendon, he had trials with the United Central League team in 1988 scoring twice on his September debut. Iain had a good job and Dave Bassett wasn't able to persuade him to move north and he joined Luton Town. He made 323 app for his six League clubs.

DONOWA B Louis (Louie)
b. Ipswich 24 Sep 1964

A Norwich (62 app, 11 gl) and England U21 outside left, sold to Real Deportivo, loaned to Stoke C (4 app, 1 gl), transferred to Willelm 11 and released. Dave Bassett gave him a trial and he played:
23 July 1989 TuS Celle (W Gy) 2 United 2 (Fr) and in two further games in West Germany and:
31 July 1989 Skegness T 0 United 4 (Fr, scored).
He signed for Ipswich T and also played for six other FL clubs (205 more app) and Ayr U.

DUKE Matt
b. Sheffield 16 July 1977

A 6ft 5in keeper, signed by United in Aug 1999 from Alfreton Town.
He played:
28 Mar 2000 United 0 Latvia XI 1 (Fr, sub).
He went out on loan to Bury (reserves) and was transferred (7 Sep 2000) to Burton A. Sold to Hull City in 2004 he has made 16 app including loans at Stockport and Wycombe. In January 2008 he had an operation for cancer.

DUNCAN Alexander (Ronnie)
b. 21 March 1951

A Raith Rovers outside left (182 SL app, 27 goals) who played on trial:
10 May 1976 United 0 Sheff Wed 0 (Harry Latham BM).

DUNGWORTH John H
b. Rotherham 30 Mar 1955.

A forward who played mainly in the lower divisions; he made over 486 FL appearances (115 goals) for nine clubs but mainly for Aldershot and Rotherham. A United coach, he made occasional appearances for the reserves and played:
8 May 1992 Frickley A 4 United XI 4 (BM)
14 Dec 1992 Worksop T 3 United XI 1 (BM, sub)
He joined the coaching staff at Huddersfield T and Leeds U (Sep 1997).

DYER Liam
b. Doncaster 2 May 1978

A United trainee who played:
12 Dec 1994 Staveley XI 3 United XI 4 (BM, sub, scored)
He had a trial with Bury in the 1996–97 season and then was released.

DZODIC Nenad
b. Belgrade 4 Jan 1977

Serbian & Montenegrin international defender. Played: FK Zemun (Belgrade) and Montpellier. Trial with United:
29 July 2004 Boston U 0 United XI 0 (Fr).
He returned to Ajaccio and then Montpellier.

EASON William D
A wing half from United's nursery club, Oaks Fold, he was signed 12 May 1950 and released cs1952. He played:
4 May 1950 Skegness T 3 United XI 2 (Fr).

EBETO
An Albanian player who played:
18 May 1995 Viterbese (It) 3 United 1 (Fr, sub).

EDWARDS Edmund (Eddie)
b. Thurcroft AMJ 1912
Educated at Rotherham Grammar School, he played for Dinnington before joining United 24 Mar 1933. Released cs 1934, he played for Worksop, Bury (No FL app), Clapton Orient (1 app), Hull C (10 app, 1 gl), Mossley and Carlisle(2 app). He acted as a scout for Reg Freeman at Rotherham and came with Reg to the Lane taking charge of the NIL team. He was a scout for several clubs and was a fine spin bowler for the United cricket team.

ELLIMAN A R
An amateur who played at outside right:
26 Jan 1891 United 0 Grimsby T 1 (Fr)
and in three further club games, the last at outside left:
9 Feb a1891 United 6 Heanor T 4 (scored).
He played for Notts C (1891–92) and then Mansfield T. It is possible that he was Alan R Elleman, a Cliftonville Irish international.

ELLIOTT Charles
An inside forward who joined United in December 1920, he then played for Rotherham Town and by February 1922 was with Rotherham County (5 app, 1goal).

ELLIS Paul
b. Dinnington 16 Nov 1957
A United apprentice, signed 24 April 1974. A probable late addition to the May-June 1975 tour party, he may have played:
28 May 1975 Otago (NZ) 1 United 4 (Fr, sub)
and in two fixtures as a sub in New Caledonia. He was released in December 1975.

ELLIS Reg
A winger signed by United from Boston in March 1939 who joined Reading but may never have featured in their first team, perhaps as a consequence of the war.

EMMERSON J E
A full back from the Heeley Club who played:
25 Dec 1889 Lincoln C 5 United 1 (Fr).

ENSOR
A centre forward from Blackwell FC who had also played for Chesterfield. He played on trial:
27 Dec 1894 United 3 Corinthians 7 (Fr).

EVANS G Cameron
b. Stevenston
A Glasgow Rangers reserve player, he joined United in November 1968 but returned to Glasgow two days later after playing one CL game because he was homesick. He later signed for Kilmarnock (10 SL app).

EVANS Jethro
b. Irchester 2 Jan 1887
An inside forward from Raunds (Rushden) St Peters, he joined United February 1908 and was put on the transfer list cs1909. He played for Sutton Junction and Watford (1912–13, 11 app SL, 1 gl).

EVANS Thomas
b. Doncaster 31 Dec 1976
A United YTS player and Northern Ireland Youth goalkeeper, he was on the substitutes bench in September 1994 at Reading but didn't play. He became a professional July 1995 and played:
21 Dec 1995 Worksop T 2 United XI 4 (Fr).
He then joined Crystal Palace Jun 1996, Harrow B (L), Coventry C (L), Scunthorpe Aug 1997 where he made his FL debut (247 app), York C 2006, Alfreton T cs 2008.

FAGAN Stephen
b. Attercliffe (Sheffield) 28 Oct 1886
A full back registered with the FL by United from April 1905 to cs1911 though he continued to play in local football (Rawmarsh Athletic 1906–07) for a while. A moulder, he played regularly for the reserve team until August 1909 when he signed for the SL team, Plymouth Argyle. He later played for Bristol C (34 app) and Stockport C (109 app) and played for United Reserves, Rotherham C, Barnsley, Bradford C, and Huddersfield during the First World War.

FAIRBURN Arthur Millward
b. Sheffield AMJ 1870
A forward who may also have played for the Wednesday Reserves (Sep 1890) and Owlerton (1890–91). He played for the United reserve team from December 1890 and also:
14 Mar 1891 Attercliffe 1 United XI 4 (Fr)
He played for Rotherham T (1893–94, 12 app, 3 gl) and may have played for Sheffield Club and Doncaster in the previous season.

FALANA Wade
b. Westminster 7 Jan 1970
A forward from Tooting & Mitcham, he had a trial with United playing:
10 Aug 1992 Cambridge U 1 United 2 (Fr, sub).
He made 10 nc appearances with the reserves but failed to score and moved on to Doncaster R (4 app), Scarborough and Chesterfield (5 app).

FAULKNER Michael
b. Conisborough 3 Jan 1950
A half back with United from school, he became a pro Dec 1967. Given a free transfer, he signed for Oldham A., July 1969 (1 app) and Morecambe (Mar 1970).

FEATHERSTONE Lee P
b. Chesterfield 20 July 1983
A United midfield player from school. He played:
6 Aug 2002 Stocksbridge Pk St 0 United XI 7 (sub Fr, scored).
Loaned to Scunthorpe, he was given a free transfer and signed for them (32 app).

FENWICK Ashley
A trainee who played:
27 July 1988 Skegness 1 United 8 (sub Fr, scored 2)
but was released 1990.

FERRIDAY Leslie
b. Manchester 3 June 1929
A Buxton half back given a trial in the Central League Jan 1952.
He signed for Walsall (32 app, 1 gl) in May 1954.

FIRBY George
A Hallam half back signed by United (1910–13). He played for Rotherham Town and broke his leg playing for the Wednesday in 1917.

'FISHER'
An unknown player given a trial at centre forward:
6 Nov 1897 United 2 Corinthians 2 (Fr).

FLOWER Johannes (John) G
b. Northampton 9 Dec 1964
A tall centre half, signed by United from Corby T 22 Aug 1989 for £15k after trial games with the reserves, late in the previous season.
He played:
2 April 1990 Combined Services 0 United XI 0 (Fr, at Catterick).
Aldershot took him on loan Oct 1990 and signed him (£10k) Jan 1991 (32 app, 2 gl). He later played for Aylesbury and Rushden & D.

FOULKE
A son of Bill Foulke. Either (John) Robert, born Blackwell June 1897 or Redvers, born Sheffield c1900. He played at outside right:
13 Apr 1918 Wednesday 2 United 0 (Fr).

FOWLER John (Jack) Barry
b. Sheffield 13 Apr 1935
A United junior outside right from 1951, he played:
22 April 1953 Buxton v United XI (BM)
He signed 4 May 1953 and (pro)10 July 1954 and played:
7 Feb 1955 United 4 Grazer SK (Austria) 0 (Fr, sub)
and 4 Apr 1955 United 3 St Mirren 1 (Fr).
He joined Halifax T on a free transfer in June 1956 (19 app, 3 gl) and later, had a cutlery business in Sheffield.

FOX
An outside right with the Scots Guards who played as a guest:
19 Feb 1894 Crouch End 2 United 3 (Fr, scored).

FOX W Stanley
b. Sheffield 6 July 1906
A Sheffield Club midfield player who had played with Reading reserves (1926–27) and joined United June 1927. He played frequently for the CL team before moving to Bury (Aug 1930). He made his League debut with York City (1931–38, 136 app, 4 gl).

FRANCIS Albert
b. Arlesey (Beds) 15 July 1902
His real name was Albert Francis Albon. A centre forward, he joined United in May 1923 from Spalding Utd. Released, a year later he had a season with Watford (1 app).

FRANCIS Dexter
A local player who played as a trialist:
15 May 1993 Trinidad & Tobago XI 1 United XI 1 (Fr)

FRIEDMANN Gall
Played for United on trial:
17 July 2001 Sheffield FC 0 United XI 7 (sub Fr).

FRITH Robert William
b. Hassop JAS 1892
A half back who joined United April 1909. He moved to Derby C (1 app) in 1910, Luton T (59 SL app) in 1913, South Shields (18/20 app) in 1919 and Rotherham County in 1920 (21 app). He also played for Mid Rhondda and Rochdale. His son, Billy was a player and manager.

FROST Brian P
b. Sheffield 5 June 1938
A United amateur forward from May 1956, he played:
26 Sep 1956 Worksop T 1 United 0 (CM)
and 12 Feb 1957 Royal Signals Rgt 1 United XI 4 (Fr at Lincoln).
He played for Oswestry before joining Chesterfield (103 app, 20 gl) in May 1959. A part-timer, building an accountancy business, he played non-League football from 1965.

FURPHY Keith
b. Stockton 30 July 1958
Son of the United manager, he became an apprentice in Aug 1974.
An outside left, he played:
6 May 1975 Watford 2 United 2 (BM, sub)
and in four matches on the tour of New Zealand and New Caledonia in May/June 1957. Released in Feb 1976, he joined QPR and then played in the USA and for Plymouth A (6 app, 1 gl) and Bath City.

FURPHY Ken (see Managers section)
He played:
1 June 1975 Taranaki XI (NZ) 0 United 5 (Fr, sub).

GEORGE Liam
b. Luton 2 Feb 1979
A Luton (102 app, 20 gl) and Ireland U21 striker, released in March 2002. He had had a trial with United Reserves in January 2002 and with Clydebank but joined Stevenage Borough. He returned to the Lane for a further trial and played:
16 July 2002 Baslow 1 United XI 14 (Fr, scored twice)
20 July v Bristol R at Clevedon and at Bodmin and Saltash.
He left Stevenage in Aug 2002 and made 32 FL appearances for Bury Boston and York.

GEORGE Matt
A goalkeeper who made a few appearances for the youth team (1996–97) and eight for the reserves (1997–98) and played:
19 Aug 1997 United 0 Everton 4 (Fr, sub)
He was released at the end of the season.

GIBBINGS Gary
A guest midfielder on trial who played:
14 May 2000 Tobago XI 1 United XI 3 (Fr).

'GIBSON'
An unknown inside left who played:
4 Jan 1897 United 2 Corinthians 2 (Fr).

GILLIGAN Alex (Sandy)
A Dundee forward who made one appearance for Bolton W in April 1894. His FL transfer from Bolton to United was registered (1 May 1894) but he appears to have returned to Dundee (40 SL app, 12 goals) before playing again with Bolton (98 app, 17 gl).

GLEESON Alan
United's Kitman who played:
14 May 2000 Tobago XI 1 United XI 3 (Fr, sub).

GLEW Joseph
b. Chapeltown (Sheffield) 24 Oct 1903
An Elsecar forward, signed by United in September 1923. Released at the end of the season, he played for Frickley Colliery before joining Rotherham County who became Rotherham United (1924–26, 4 app).

GODFREY Joseph (Joby)
b. Waleswood, Sep 1894
A forward who played for Beighton Rec and for Nottingham Forest in 1916. He played once for United:
28 Apr 1917 United 4 Rotherham C 0 (Fr, scored).
He was signed by Forest and later made 25 FL appearances (4 gl) for Birmingham, Coventry C, Manchester C and Merthyr. He returned to south Yorkshire, playing for Rotherham T, Denaby and Mexborough.

GODWIN Jon B
A trainee keeper, released cs 1992, who played:
16 Mar 1992 United XI 1 Malmo (Swe) 6 (Stancliffe BM)
17 Mar 1992 Leek T 3 United 1 (Fr).

GOMEZ S
A local striker who played on trial:
12 May 2000 Joe Public FC 0 United XI 0 (Fr).

GORDON Leslie William
b. Barking (Essex), July 1903
A midfield player signed by United in May 1923 from Grimsby Rovers. Released by United (cs1925), he then played for Crystal Palace, Shirebrook, Nottingham Forest (2 app) and Brighton (18 app).

GORDON Michael Alexander
b. Tooting 11 Oct 1984
An Arsenal trainee, he played or Wimbledon (19 app) but was released cs 2004. United trial:
13 July 2004 Matlock T 4 United XI 3 (sub, Fr)
He then played Waterlooville, Aldershot T and Crawley Town.

GORDON Robert
One of United's first players. A Scottish full back who had played for Glanfield (Glasgow) and had captained Northern(Glasgow) and Ayrshire. His only appearance was in the first fixture:
7 Sep 1889 Notts Rangers 4 United 1 (Fr).

GOUGH
An unidentified forward who played:
1 Apr 1895 Rotherham T 1 Sheffield United & District XI 2 (Fr).

GRAHAM Alister (Ally)
b. Glasgow 11 Aug 1966
A tall forward on trial from Albion Rovers. He played:
31 July 1989 Skegness T 0 United 4 (Fr)
1 Aug 1989 Notts C 0 United 1 (Fr).
He joined Ayr U in Sep 1990 and played for several other SL clubs, scoring over 100 goals in over 500 appearances..

GRAHAM William
Signed by United in October 1895, he was transferred seven weeks later to Bacup. He is perhaps the forward with Burnley (1891–93, 24 app, 3 gl) and Lincoln City (1893–94, 19 app, 2 gl).

GRANT Alexander (Alick) F
b. Camerton Peasdown (Somerset) 11 Aug 1916
An amateur goalkeeper with Doncaster and United (Feb 1937), he became a pro with Bury and then played for Aldershot (1938–39, 5 app), Leicester City (1941–46, 2 app), Derby C (12 app), Newport C (20 app) Leeds U., York (3 app) Worksop and Corby T.

GRAY Roland (Ron)
b. N. Shields 25 June 1920
A Bolden Colliery half back who joined United in May 1938. Released, a year later he was signed by Lincoln City. He joined Watford in 1945 (16 app) but his playing career was soon ended by injury. He became a trainer at Watford and then the manager and also managed both Lincoln and Millwall.

Roland Gray

GRAYSON Simon
b. Sheffield 21 Oct 1968
Signed YTS July 1985. He played:
5 Aug 1987 United 0 Wednesday 3 (CM, sub)
He was loaned to Chesterfield (Nov 1987, 8 app) and transferred to Hartlepool U, April 1988 (£10k, 44 app, 13 gl). Troubled with knee injuries, he later played for Sheffield Club, Gainsborough, Halifax, Boston and Ilkeston.

GREAVES John
Kitman appointed by Dave Bassett. He played:
2 Aug 1992 Bracke (Swe) 0 United 9 (Fr, sub, scored) and
18 Jan 1993 Jersey XI 3 United 3 (Fr, sub).

GREGORY Harry
An Ecclesfield FC half back who played as a guest:
9 Nov 1889 Staveley 7 United XI 0 (Fr)
United registered him with the FL 2 July 1892 (United's first FL season) and he played:
31 Oct 1892 United 1 Rotherham T 0 (Fr).

GROVES Fred
b. Lincoln 6 May 1892
An inside forward with Lincoln C (7 app, 1 gl) and Worksop T, he joined United in June 1911. He was sold to Huddersfield T (4 app) for £50 in August 1912 and also played for Pontypridd, Tranmere R (12 app, 7 gl), Stoke (£1,000, 41 app, 13 gl) Crystal P., Rhyl and Sutton Town.

GYAKI Ryan
b. Toronto (Canada) Dec 1985
A Canadian U20 midfielder and a member of the United Academy from 2003. He played:
26 Jul 2005 Matlock 1 United XI 2 ((sub Fr)
21 Jul 2006 Inverness CT 0 United 3 (sub Fr)
and three more sub appearances in Jul/Aug 2006 in the friendly games at Greenock Morton, Notts C and Matlock
and 15 Jan 2007 United 1 Chengdu Blades 1 (sub Fr). He was released cs 2007 and joined Hansa Rostock in Germany.

HABER Justin
b. Floriana 9 June 1981.
A Maltese international keeper who played for Floriana and Birkirkara in Malta, Dobrudzha Dobrich (Bulg), le Petit-Quevilly (France), Virton (Belgium). He played as a United trialist:
17 July 2006 Worksop T 0 United XI 5 (sub, Fr).
He then played: Marsaxlokk (Malta), Haidari (Greece). He joined United on 31 July 2008.

HAIGH Maurice
b. Sheffield 1877–78
A son of David Haigh, a United committee member, Maurice was a Sheffield Club winger who played for United's reserves in April 1895 and:
27 Nov 1897 Corinthians 2 United 0 (Fr).
He began playing for Gainsborough Trinity in September 1899 (26 app, 5 gl) and, a year later, for Chesterfield Town (6 app, 2 gl). He studied at and played for St. Mark's College (Chelsea) and then for Rotherham Town.

HALL George W
b. Shildon
A Darlington player (21 app, 4 gl) who was a guest substitute for Tunstall:
27 April 1932 Darlington 1 United 6 (BM for Jimmy Waugh), sub.
He had begun his professional career with Huddersfield Town and later played for Spennymoor.

HANCOX David
b. Conisborough 2 Oct 1947
A United apprentice forward (Sep 1965), released cs1967 who signed for Chester (19 app, 4 gl) in July 1967.

HANSON Frederick
b. Sheffield 23 May 1915
A forward, Fred joined United May 1933 playing in the third team and scoring on his CL debut. Released one year later, he had short spells with Bradford C, Mexborough T, Wolves, Crystal Palace (1 app) and Spurs before moving in March 1936 to Rotherham United. He gave the Millers fine service (97 app, 28 gl) before the war and played frequently during the war when he moved to left back and 9 app in the 1946-47 season when he was forced to retire after a serious injury.

HARKUS Joseph C

A half back (Harkuss or Harkins in some reports) who joined United in March 1931 from the Co Durham team, Chopwell Inst. He was the twelfth man on the day that John Nicholson, the United Secretary was knocked down by a lorry outside the Midland Station and went with him in an ambulance to the Royal Hospital. Released at the end of that season, he signed for York City. Later, he became a clergyman and achieved the rank of Squadron Leader in the RAF during the Second World War.

HARPER Adrian
b. Dublin 4 May 1985
Academy midfielder who played:
13 July 2004 Matlock T 4 United XI 3 (sub, Fr)
Scarborough (L, 4 app), Grimsby T (L, Aug 2005). Released May 2006.

HARPER Ronald E
An inside left, signed April 1950 from Parkgate OB. He made one senior appearance:
15 Nov 1950 Western Command 0 United 1 (Fr at Wrexham).
He was released at the end of that season.

HARRIS Terry
Made nine appearances with the reserves (1990–91) and played:
11 Mar 1991 Harrogate Railway 1 United 5 (Fr, sub, scored).
He went out on loan to Finland, played again in the reserves (1991–92) and was released. He then played in non-League football.

HARRISON Charles
A goalkeeper registered with the League Feb 1894 to cs1895. He could be CE Harrison who played for Bolton W 1888–90 (24 app).

HARRISON John G
b. Worksop 18 May 1946
A winger signed for a small fee from Worksop Town January 1967 and transferred to Lincoln City (4 app) July 1968. A knee injury in April 1969 ended his career.

HARRISON Richard
b. Sheffield 11 Jan 1972
A United goalkeeper (trainee pro 1990) who played:
2 Apr 1990 Combined Services 0 United XI 0 (Fr, sub at Catterick)
9 Aug 1990 Notts C 2 United 0 (Fr)
and in four other friendly fixtures that season, the last being:
23 Apr 1991 Lincoln City 2 United 0 (sub BM).
He was given a free transfer (cs 1991) and moved into non-league football.

HASSALL Harry
(also 'Hatsell' and 'Hansell') A left side forward who joined United (1892–93) from Kiveton Park FC. His only first team appearances were:
9 Feb 1893 Grimsby T 0 United 2 (CM played at Hull) and:
29 Apr 1893 Bolton W 3 United 0 (Fr)
His death was reported in Feb 1894.

HEALD Paul A
b. Wath on Dearne 20 Aug 1968
Joined United from school May 1984, YTS June 1986. He played:
3 Aug 1987 Scunthorpe U 1 United 2 (Fr)
26 July 1978 Skegness T1 United 8 (Fr)
He went to Leyton O (L) Oct 1988, transfer November £2,500 (176 app), Coventry (L, 2 app), Swindon (L, 2 app), Wimbledon (£125k, half to United, 20 app), Wednesday (L, 5 app). He retired Feb 2004.

HELLEWELL Craig
b. Doncaster 9 July 1975
A defensive midfielder, he played:
14 Dec 1992 Worksop T 3 United XI 1 (BM, sub) and made eleven appearances for the reserves before his release in 1994.

HENDERSON James
A right half 'from Burnley', signed Feb 1895 who played:
16 April 1895 Rotherham T 3 United 2 (Fr)
but was not retained.

HENSON Philip M (see Secretaries, Trainers section)
b. Manchester 30 Mar 1953
United coach. He played:
23 Nov 1986 Hallam 3 United XI 5 (Fr).

'HERBERT S'
An unknown outside right who played in United's first private practice match in Aug 1889 and also:
28 Oct 1889 Sheffield FC 1 United 1 (Fr).

HERITAGE Paul
b. Sheffield 17 Apr 1979
United trainee keeper who played:
27 Aug 1996 United 4 Wednesday 1 (SCCT, sub) and:
18 July 1997 Sheffield FC 0 United 3 (Fr, Don Valley Stadium).
He joined Barnsley and Carlisle U but didn't appear in a League fixture.

HERNANDEZ Stephen
b. Doncaster 17 Aug 1989
A goalkeeper who moved from Wednesday to United's Academy.
He played:
15 Jan 2007 United XI 1 Chengdu Blades 1 (sub, Fr).
He turned pro cs 2007 and moved to Worksop T (L) from September.
He was released cs 2008 and joined Worksop T.

HEYWOOD Colin
An apprentice who played:
2 April 1990 Combined Services 0 United XI 0 (Fr at Catterick).

HIBBERT Henry C (Harry) (Hibberd)
b. Dore (nr Sheffield) c1887
He had played for Hathersage, Sheffield Wednesday (2 app), Stockport C (1 app), Lincoln C (4 app, 1 gl) and Rotherham County before he joined United in April 1913. A reserve half back, he returned to the Rotherham club in Feb 1914 and was reported to have signed Aug 1914 for Scunthorpe. In October he was playing for Halifax T and for Chesterfield later during the war.

HILL Haydn H C (Aitch)
b. Cresswell, Derbys, 4 July 1913
A Sheffield University amateur goalkeeper who played for the reserves in October 1932. His FL registration was transferred to the Wednesday 19 Dec 1934 (4 app) and he also played for Yorkshire Amateurs and the Corinthians, won five amateur caps and was a member of the 1936 British Olympic team. He became a teacher in Dorset signing as an amateur for Bournemouth and playing for Weymouth and in 1939 for Dulwich Hamlet.

HILL S (George?)
A Sheffield outside right who played for the Simplex Motor Works and for United:
4 May 1918 United 2 Everton 2 (Fr)
and as a guest player for Birmingham and Grimsby at Bramall Lane.
He later probably played for Rotherham Town and Leeds United (7 app).

HINCHCLIFFE William B
A small inside forward signed June 1958 from Sauchie FC. Given a free transfer a year later, he joined Raith Rovers.

HOBSON Reg
A local centre forward, signed Mar 1933 from City Surveyors.
He played:
3 April 1935 Sheffield Wed 0 United 0 (BM).
Released in 1937, he died in Sheffield c1991.

HOCKING Matthew (Matt) J
b. Boston 30 Jan 1978
A trainee defender, he played:
17 July 1995 Boston U 2 United 2 (Fr, sub)
5 Aug United 1 Wednesday 3 (SCCT, sub)
19 Aug 1997 United 0 Everton 4 (Fr).
He signed for Hull C Sep 1997 £25k. (57 app, 2 gl), York C (97 app, 2 gl) and Boston U (67 app, 1 gl).

HODGSON
An unknown full-back who played:
28 Dec 1889 Doncaster R 2 United 0 (Fr, abandoned).

HODGSON Fred
b. Lytham St Annes JAS 1901
Fred was a promising Rotherham County left back (1923–24, 43 app, 2 gl). On 1 Nov 1924, John Nicholson, the United Secretary left a signed cheque, 'sufficient to buy the ground' in the Millmoor office and watched Hodgson play what was to be his last game for the Millers before signing for United. A few minutes before the end, his leg was broken and his League career was over.

HODGSON Lawrence (Laurie)
b. Birkenhead 19 Jan 1917
A full back, signed on amateur forms by United in August 1936, he was not retained but played later for Tranmere Rovers (1939–51, 78 app).

HOLMES 'Fred'
b. New Tupton, Chesterfield 1892?
A right half, signed from Shirebrook (£70) in April 1914 but not retained cs1915. He joined Chesterfield Town in October but was one of the players suspended by the FA for 'illegal payments'.

HOLMES Luther
A Wombwell keeper who played for the reserves 1900–03 and subsequently for Doncaster Rovers.

HOLT Arnold Andrew
A schoolboy international winger who played for Kidderminster and Denaby before joining United in May 1911. Released at the end of the season, he played for Newport C, Cardiff C, Merthyr, Linfield, Distillery, Sutton T, Chesterfield Municipal, Gillingham (1920–21, 6 app), Mansfield T and Wath A.

HOOLEY Joseph (Joe)
b. Hoyland, Barnsley 26 Dec 1938
A Barnsley (1 app) forward, he signed for the Blades 5 Dec 1957 but was transferred (£500) to Workington (6 app, 2 gl) in June 1958, later playing for Holbeach, Bradford PA (13 app, 4 gl), Bedford and Accrington Stanley.

HOOST Darwin
Dutch midfielder. Trial:
17 July 2001 Sheffield FC 0 United XI 7 (sub, Fr).

HOPKIN David
b. Greenock 21 Aug 1970
Red haired midfielder with Morton (48 SL app, 4 gls) who had a trial with United:
6 May 1992 Barrow XI 0 United 3 (BM)
8 May 1992 Frickley A 4 United 4 (BM)
Signed by Chelsea (£300k, 40 PL app, 1 goal) and Crystal P (£850k, 83 app, 21 gls), where he scored the last minute winning goal in the play-off final against United, the Scottish international then moved on to Leeds U (£3.25m, 73 app, 6gl), Bradford C (11 app) and Crystal P again (29 app,4 gl). He returned to Morton playing briefly before he retired with an ankle injury.

HOSEY Edward (Ted)
b. Whittington (Chesterfield) JAS 1876
A United reserve centre half (May 1898 to cs 1899) who then played for Chesterfield (41/42 app) and Denaby Utd.

HOWARD Frederick
b Blacker Hill, Hoyland, Barnsley JFM 1877.
A right sided player and the brother of Harry Howard, United registered him with the FL in May 1895. Lincoln C (1 app) signed him in Oct 1897 and he was with Barnsley (49 app, 1 gl) Jan 1898 to perhaps cs1901 and may have played later for Leeds C (1904–05) and Wombwell Main from Jan 1907.

HOWEY Stephen (Steve) N
b. Sunderland 26 Oct 1971
An England defender with 4 caps who played for Newcastle U (191 app, 6gl), Man City (£2m, 94 app, 11 gl), Leicester C £300k (13 app, 1 gl), Bolton W (3 app). He had a United trial:
19 July 2004 Tavistock 2 United XI 5 (Fr).
He then played briefly in the USA and with Hartlepool U (1 app).

HOYLAND Herbert
A right back, born c1903 and with United Jan 1922 to cs1923 when he joined Wath Athletic. Credited by the FL with an appearance against Sunderland in April 1922, this is an error confusing him with his brother Walter.

HUGHES James
Signed in August 1893, he made one first team appearance:
23 March 1894 Grimsby T 2 United 2 (Fr).

HUMBERSTONE S P
A Sheffield Club player reported 25 May 1889 to be among those who would also play for United but he was never used by the new club at the Lane.

HUMPHRIES ROBERT (Bob)
b. Hindhead 4 July 1933
A Spurs amateur midfielder who had been playing for Eastbourne.
He joined United as a pro in Jan 1956 and played:
14 Dec 1955 Royal Signals 1 United 7 (Fr, at Catterick, scored).
He was transferred to Brighton, Nov 1956 (10 app, 2 gl) and then played for Millwall (47 app,4 gl).

HUNT
Played at inside left:
16 Apr 1895 Rotherham T 3 United 2 (Fr, scored)
He may be Sam Hunt (Barnsley St Peters) and a former United trainer or the Darwen player of the same name.

HUNT George S
b. Barnsley 22 Feb 1910

An inside forward and future English international, rejected by Barnsley who also had a trial with United. One tale is that he played in Tommy Sampy's boots, having left his own at home and was hopeless; a second, and more well known, is that he scored four goals. Perhaps they were separate occasions but he signed for Chesterfield in September 1929 (14 app, 9 gl) and Spurs (185 app, 125 gl) and also played for Arsenal (18 app, 3 gl), Bolton (48 app, 25 gl) and post-war for the Wednesday (32 app, 8 gl).

HUNTER Albert Edward
b. Sheffield Aug 1902
A Norton Woodseats right back with United from April 1924 to cs1925. He then played for Brighton, Denaby, Scarborough, Bradford (PA), Walsall (35 app), Doncaster R (58 app), Accrington S (38 app, 1 gl), Barrow (35 app, 1 gl) and Frickley Colliery.

HUNTER Les
b. Middlesbrough 15 Jan 1958
A centre half who had three spells with Chesterfield between 1975 and 1988 (295 app, 20 gl) and two with Scunthorpe (110 app, 13 gl).
He played:
8 May 1986 Chesterfield 2 United XI 1 (Moss BM, as a guest).

HUTTON
A forward who played:
3 Jan 1895 Raith R 2 United 4 (Fr).

HYDE Micah A
b. Newham 10 Nov 1974
Experienced Jamaican international midfielder who played for Cambridge U (107 app, 13 gl), Watford (£225k, 253 app, 24 gl).
United trial:
13 July 2004 Matlock T 4 United XI 3 (Fr)
He then joined Burnley (102 app, 1 gl) and Peterborough (55 app to cs2008).

IBBOTSON E E
An amateur winger who played:
17 Nov 1890 United 2 Bolton W 1 (Fr)
31 Jan 1891 Grimsby T 5 United 2 (Fr).

INCE Clayton
b. Trinidad 13 July 1972
The keeper had made one appearance for Crewe A when he played on trial with a £75k fee required:
4 Aug 2000 Rotherham U 1 United 2 (Fr).
After making 123 app for Crewe he joined Coventry C (Jul 2005, 1 app) then Walsall (91 to cs 2008).

INNES Gary
b. Consett 7 Oct 1977
A United apprentice and England Youth forward who had followed his elder brother Lee to the Lane. He was transferred to Darlington in July 1996 appearing in 15 (14 as a sub) League games and scoring once, before moving into non-League football.

INNES Lee
b. Newcastle 28 Feb 1976
Released by Manchester United, Lee joined United in 1993. He played on loan in New Zealand in 1995 and:
21 Dec 1995 Worksop 2 United XI 4 (Fr, sub).

IORFA Dominic
b. Lagos 1 Oct 1968
A Nigerian international forward who had played for Royal Antwerp; he had a trial in January 1990 with the reserve team. He later played for QPR (8 app), Peterborough (60 app, 9 gl) and Southend (12 app, 1 gl).

JAMES George
A forward who played:
9 Apr 1894 Woolwich Arsenal 0 United 1 (Fr)
11 Apr 1894 Swindon T 1 United 1 (Fr).

JANI
Played on trial:
23 July 1998 Romagna XI (It) 1 United 1 (Fr).

JARDINE Robert
An amateur forward who played:
26 Jan 1891 Grimsby T1 United 0 (Fr).
He may be the Notts County forward who played for several other Notts and Derbyshire clubs.

JOHNSON Ernest L
b. Sheffield 27 Jan 1917
A half back who became a pro with United in May 1936 and was transferred to Forest in August 1937, joining New Brighton (8 app) in October of the same year. He served in the army during the war and played a few games for Ayr United.

JOHNSON George W
A forward signed in 1906 from an Eckington team. He was transferred to Chesterfield (3 app) in June 1907 and joined Rotherham County in May 1908.

JONES Benjamin
A Rotherham centre forward who joined United from Goldthorpe Institute in April 1906. He quickly moved on to Rotherham Town, Aston Villa, and Doncaster Rovers before joining Barnsley (1908–09, 16 app, 5 gl). He later played for Denaby U, Doncaster R and Worksop.

JONES Glyn
A Welsh amateur international half back on United's books Jan-April 1913 while working as a chemist at Beighton Colliery. He later played for Beighton Rec.

JONES Herbert
b. St Helens 1915
A goalkeeper, who joined Bradford (PA) (10 app, 1936–37) from Warrington. He was with United June 1937 to May 1938.

JONES J
A left half who played:
29 Sep 1890 United 1 Nottingham F 2 (Fr).

'JONES W'
A fine pseudonym for a fast Scottish forward who played:
23 Nov 1889 United 1 Rotherham T 1 (Fr)
25 Nov 1889 United 2 Nottingham F 0 (Fr, scored).
'Jones' may have been Billy Calder who signed a few days later.

JOWETT Sylvester James (Jim)
b. Sheffield 27 Jan 1946
A small winger on United's books as an amateur from September 1941 to cs1946 when he joined York City (1 app).

KEEGAN J Kevin OBE
The renowned Liverpool and England forward was playing for Scunthorpe when their chairman, Bill Archer, a former United player during the 1939–45 war, informed the Blades that they ought to have a look at this nippy, enthusiastic youngster. The first United report was in favour but John Harris and John Short were not impressed and the opportunity was lost.

KELK Charles G
A Sheffield YMCA full back who joined United in May 1949 and played:
4 May 1950 Skegness T 3 United XI 2 (Fr)
15 Nov 1950 Western Command 0 United XI 0 (Fr at Wrexham).
Released July 1952, he later played for Gainsborough Trinity and in Northern Rhodesia.

KEMP David M
b. Harrow Feb 1953
The former Crystal Palace, Portsmouth, Carlisle, Plymouth, Gillingham and Brentford forward (total 256 app, 104 gl) who played:
11 May 1990 Brentford 4 United XI 2 (Booker BM, sub).

KENNEDY John (Jack)
A '22-year-old' inside forward signed from Blyth Spartans (Jan 1928, £175). Played regularly in the CL, transfer listed cs1930 at £300. He moved to Tranmere R in August (65app, 45 gl) and later played for Exeter C (16 app, 3 gl), Torquay (19 app. 1 gl) and Watford.

KENNEDY Steven
b. Mansfield 24 Feb 1976
United midfield-defender apprentice who played:
6 Sep 1993 Mansfield T 1 United XI 2 (sub Dearden BM)
He then played for Worksop T and Belper T (for about 10 seasons).

KERKAR Karim
b. Givors (France) 3 Jan 1977
A French forward from Le Havre who played on trial:
31 July 2002 Scarborough 0 United 0 (Fr)
3 Aug 2002 Linfield 1 United 5 (Fr)
He had a season with Manchester C (no app) and also played for Clyde (2 SL app), Dundee U (10 SL).

KERLEY Michael
Played on trial:
23 April 1991 Lincoln C 2 United 0 (Alan Roberts BM)
and in four reserve fixtures.

'KERR'
Pseudonym for Kenny McKay when he played on trial:
4 Jan 1897 United 2 Corinthians 2 (Fr).

KERRY Lloyd
b. Chesterfield 22 Jan 1988
A midfield apprentice who made his FL debut on loan with Torquay U 17 Feb 2007 (7 app, 1 gl). He played for United:
6 Aug 2007 Stocksbridge 0 United XI 4 (Fr, sub)
10 Oct 2007 Sheffield Club 1 United XI 5 (Fr)
In February 2008, he went to Chesterfield (L, 13 app, 2 gl) and was transferred June 2008.

KETTLING
Reported as United's outside left at Stockton, 2 April 1891. Probably a newspaper error for Getliffe.

KEY Lance W
b. Kettering 13 May 1968
A Sheffield Wednesday goalkeeper who made one substitute appearance in a FA Cup tie during his six years at Hillsborough though he did make 28 FL appearances out on loan with five clubs. He played for Dundee Utd and Linfield before joining United in March 1997 as an nc player. He was soon given a contract to the end of the season before moving to Rochdale (19 app), one of his previous 'loan' clubs.

KIDGER Edward Albert
b. Derby 16 July 1892
A forward who signed for United 28 Aug 1913 and played regularly for the reserves that season. He joined Worksop T in August 1914 and 'returned to Worksop' in the cs1919 after serving in the army. He was transferred to Norwich City 27 Aug 1920 (4 app).

KUHNEL Donald
A Goole centre forward who joined Aldershot cs1939. He played as a war guest for United:
26 Dec 1939 Huddersfield T 5 United 0 (Fr)
30 Dec 1939 United 3 Leeds U 0 (Fr).
He also played once for Doncaster Rovers.

LAMINE Mohamed
From the Ivory Coast. He played for Chengdu Blades and then moved to Fernecvaros Played as a guest:
25 Mar 2008 Ferencvaros 0 United 1 (sub Fr).

LANCASTER Darren
A United YTS apprentice, signed 1 July 1985. He played:
8 May 1986 Chesterfield 2 United XI 1 (Ernie Moss BM, sub).

LAYTON Arthur Edward
b. Gornall (Staffordshire) Feb 1885
A full back, and younger brother of the famous Wednesday player, with United from May 1903 to May 1904. He later played for Rotherham T, Aston V (16 app), Middlesbrough (7 app), Cardiff C (63 SL app, 2 FL) and Stockport C (59 app).

LEATHER Robert (Bob)
A forward from Northwich Victoria who came to Rotherham c1891 playing for Rotherham Town, Rotherham United (no connection with the modern team), Rotherham Town (1 app). He played:
1 Apr 1895 Rotherham T 1 Sheffield United & District XI 2 (Fr, scored).

LEE Garth
b. Sheffield 30 Sep 1943
An amateur forward who became a United pro in May 1961. A Youth international, he joined Chester in Sept 1963 (28 app, 7 gls) and then played for New Brighton.

LEHTINEN Ville
b. Jyvaskyla (Finland) 17 Dec 1978
He played with HJK Helsinki. A Finnish U21 midfield-forward and captain, he had a trial with United 15 Oct 1997 with the reserves, returning to Finland. He returned to sign c2 Jan 1998 (c£50k) and played:
16 July 1998 Sheffield FC 0 United XI 2 (sub, Fr).
Released 14 Dec 1998, he then played for: FC Jazz, Pallo-Iirot, Tampere U, AC Allianssi, Atlantis FC, and Ac Oulu in Finland, then Bodo Glint (Nor). He had trials with Roma, Tranmere *et al* and with Barnsley Dec 2006.

LEIGHTON James (Jim)
The most capped (91) Scottish keeper who totalled over 600 SL and FL appearances, Jim had played for Aberdeen, Manchester United, Reading (loan). He was with Dundee when he came to the Lane on loan in March 1993 and played for the reserves and was an unused sub for 8 League games. He was transferred to Hibs in July and later played again for Aberdeen.

LEVITT Frank
A Barnsley schoolboy international forward who joined Sheffield Wednesday and was transferred to United 1 Nov 1950. He played:
15 Nov 1950 Western Command 0 United XI 1 (Fr, scored, at Wrexham).
He was released cs 1952.

LIVINGSTONE Wm Edmund
A left back, signed Aug 1910 from S Kirkby. Released cs1911, he played for Rotherham T and made two war-time appearances for Bradford C (1916–17).

LLOYD David
b. Gateshead 1 June 1928
A Sunderland amateur midfielder, he joined United in August 1949 from N Fenham (Newcastle) and played:
15 Nov 1950 Western Command 0 United XI 1 (Fr at Wrexham).
Released Feb 1951, he played for York C (1 app) and Swindon T.

LUDLAM Ryan
b. Carlisle 12 May 1979
The son of Steve, he became a pro in April 1997. He played:
19 Aug 1997 United 0 Everton 4 (sub Fr)
31 July 1998 Notts C 0 United 0 (sub Fr).
He had a trial with Carlisle (Nov 1998) and then played non-league football.

LYNE John Henry
An outside left signed June 1951 from Beighton MW. He played:
15 Nov 1950 Western Command 0 United XI 1 (Fr, at Wrexham)
26 Sep 1951 Gainsborough Tr v United XI (BM).
He was released cs1952.

MABBERLEY Ivor
b. Newnham (Glos) June 1889

A forward, he had worked in Swindon for the GWR and played as an amateur for Swindon T, 1910–11. He signed for United, Dec 1912 from Yoker Athletic, a Glasgow team but was released at the end of the season. Reported to have joined Third Lanark and then Clyde, he played for Barrow in 1914 and joined Chesterfield (cs1919) and later played for Bath City.

MACARI Paul
b. Manchester 23 Aug 1976
Son of the Scottish international and United scout, he made three substitute appearances for Stoke City. A forward, he had a trial with United's reserves in November 1998, was released cs2000 and joined Huddersfield Town (11 sub app).

McAUGHTRIE Craig
b. Burton on Trent 3 Mar 1981
A United apprentice 1997–98, he was released June 2000 and joined Carlisle U (10 app, 1 gl).

McAULEY Sean
b. Sheffield 23 June 1973
A Manchester Utd trainee, he had a trial with United and played:
16 Mar 1992 United XI 1 Malmo 6 (Stancliffe BM, sub)
17 Mar 1992 Leek T 3 United XI 1 (Fr, sub).
He joined St Johnstone (£100k, 62 SL app), Chesterfield (L) , Hartlepool, Scunthorpe, Scarborough (L) and Rochdale (total 198 app, 3 gl) and became the manager of the Wednesday Academy.

McCARTHY Anthony Paul
b. Dublin 9 Nov 1969
A UDC (Dublin) defender who played on trial Aug 1990 for United XI's against Frecheville, Skegness T and Altrincham. He joined Shelbourne and then Millwall (21 app, 1 gl), Crewe (L, 2 app) and Colchester (89 app, 1gl).

McCARTHY Michael (Mick)
b. Barnsley 7 Feb 1959
The Worsborough Bridge and Barnsley Boys Club defender had a trial with United before becoming a Barnsley apprentice, Irish international and manager.

McDONALD John
A Scottish player 'from Newcastle', signed July 1896. He played at left half:
4 Jan 1897 United 2 Corinthians 2 (Fr).
He could be the Newcastle U inside left (6 app, 2 gl, 1895–96) who later played for Lincoln City.

McEWAN William (Billy) (see Managers section)
The United coach and manager who played:
8 May 1986 Chesterfield 2 United XI 1 (BM)
and in other games that year against GuernseyXI, Jersey XI and Hallam.

McFARLANE Andrew
b. Wolverhampton, 30 Nov 1966
A forward with Portsmouth (2 app), Swansea (55 app, 8 gl) who had a trial with United Reserves in April 1995. Signed later by Scunthorpe (60 app, 19 gl) and Torquay (56 app, 11 gl).

MacFARLANE Edison
A local international striker who played on trial:
14 May 2000 Tobago XI 1 United 3 (Fr, scored 2).

McGAHEY Charles P
A well known amateur full back from Essex who had also assisted Spurs. He played:
25 Mar 1895 Luton T 1 United 2 (Fr).
United registered him with the League in October but it was cancelled later. Charlie also played county cricket for Essex (437 matches) and 2 Tests.

McGARRY Brian
A wing half, signed by Harry Haslam, 30 March 1978 from Bromsgrove Rovers, he played well for the reserves and also appeared:
25 Sept 1978 Bromsgrove 2 United XI 4 (Fr).
He was released 31 July 1980.

McINTOSH Martin W
b. E Kilbride 19 Mar 1971
A Tottenham Hotspur junior and St Mirren defender (4 app) who played four trial games with United Reserves (1990–91). He later played for Clydebank, Hamilton A, Stockport C, Hibs, Rotherham and Huddersfield T in a career of 450 League games and 37 goals.

McNULTY Joseph
b. Dundalk 17 July 1923
Ards goalkeeper who joined Burnley (8 app) and moved to United in June 1952. He played:
22 April 1953 Buxton v United XI (BM)
Released cs 1953, Bangor (NI).

MALICKI Gregory
b. France 23 Nov 1973
A Rennes goalkeeper who played on trial for United:
17 July 2001 Sheffield FC 0 United XI 7 (Fr).
He later joined Lille.

MARADONA Diego
In July 1978, Harry Haslam, the United manager secured the transfer of Alex Sabella and played a part in the transfer of the Argentine internationals, Ardiles and Villa to Spurs. He may also have attempted to secure the transfer of Maradona – who was fifteen – and another young player but was stopped, partly by the intervention of the Argentine FA.

MAREGGINI Mario
A Fiorentina keeper with over 300 appearances to his credit who played a United trial (45 minutes for both teams):
17 July 1997 Sheffield FC v United (Fr).

MARKLEW Roger
b. Sheffield 30 Jan 1940
An outside left from Penistone Church, Roger signed amateur forms for United in May 1957 and joined the Wednesday, a year later. He moved to Accrington Stanley and Grimsby T (6 app, 1 gl).

MARKOS Dimitri
A Greek Panathinakos midfielder given a short contract cs 1997.
He played:
19 Aug 1997 United 0 Everton 4 (Fr).
He appeared in six reserve team games and joined Kalamata (Greece) in Jan 1998 and later played for Aris Thessaloniki, AEK Athens and PAOK.

MARASS Tommy
An Australian keeper who had been playing in Hong Kong. He had a trial:
18 May 1994 Northern NSW Australia 1 United 1 (Fr).

MARSH Fred W
A full back signed from Oxspring June 1947. He played:
5 Oct 1949 Western Command 0 United XI 2 (Fr, at Lichfield).
Released cs 1951, he played for Worksop Town.

MARSHALL Frank
b. Sheffield 26 Jan 1929
An amateur inside right who had played for Fulwood. He made his debut in the CL team in December 1949 but United wouldn't offer him professional terms and he signed for Scarborough in December 1950. He joined Rotherham in May 1951 (117 app, 5 gls) and became an excellent right half back, later playing for Scunthorpe (80 app) and Doncaster R (35 app).

MARTIN John (Jack)
A half back from Whittington Exchange(Chesterfield), he signed for United 30 April 1904 and was transfer listed a year later. He joined New Brompton in May 1905 (92 Southern L app), playing from the end of that year as a goalkeeper before moving to Chesterfield (Sept 1908–cs1910) and Castleford.

MARTNEZ Juan Manuel
b. Viedma (Argentina) 25 Oct 1985
A River Plate (Argentine) U23 defender had a trial with the reserves Feb 2002.

MEIJER Hennie I
b. Paramaribo (Surinam) 17 Feb 1962
A Netherlands Surinam forward who had been playing for Gronigen, he played:
16 Aug 1993 Matlock T 3 United XI 4 (Fr, scored 2)
and scored on his reserve team debut, three days later. Later he played in Japan.

MELLIS Jacob
b. Nottingham 8 Jan 1991
United Academy forward and England U16 international. Made his United debut aged 15:
11 Aug 2006 Matlock T 0 United XI 2 (sub, Fr).
His debut for the reserves was at Grimsby in Nov 2006. Transferred to Chelsea 4 June 2007 for a fee of £400k that could rise to £1.3m.

'MELLOR W'
A player who probably made two appearances for Chesterfield Dec and Jan 1894–95. Signed May 1898 and reported to be a centre forward from Whittington Moor or Brampton Works (Chesterfield), he may have played (qv Atkinson WH):
27 Dec 1898 United 5 Corinthians 3 (Needham BM).
He was transferred cs1899 to Wellingborough.

MERCER Joe (see Managers section)
Joe made nine appearances for United in Friendly and Benefit matches:
14 Nov 1955 Reading 0 United 2 (Fr)
and eight other away victories against Royal Signals: at Catterick (7–1, 14 Dec 1955), and at Lincoln (4–1, 12 Feb 1957); against Coventry (6–0, 6 Nov 1956), Eintracht Braunschweig (W Gy, 3–2, 19 May 1957), Rhyl (6–2, 21 Oct 1958) and three (BM) games against Wisbech (4–0, 17 Apr 1957), Rhyl (4–1, 6 Nov 1957) and Hereford (3–2, 26 Mar 1958).

METCALF Ian
b. Gateshead 22 Sep 1977
Left side defender who played:
18 May 1995 Viterbese (It) 3 United 1 (Fr) and
21 May 1995 Marsala (It) 1 United 1 (Fr).
Released cs 1996.

METHVEN A Harold
b. Derby 9 Oct 1908
A centre forward and the son of one of Derby County's greatest players, he joined Portsmouth (2 app) in 1929 and United in August 1931 but was playing for Scunthorpe in September. He joined Loughborough Corinthians (1932) and Mansfield Town (1933–34, 10 app, 9 gl).

MILLER
A left back who played:
15 April 1892 United 3 Millwall 0 (Fr)
'Said to hail from Dumbarton... gave so eccentric a display of alleged football as to excite the amusement of the spectators.'

MILLER
An unknown inside left (possibly from Heanor) who played:
6 Nov 1897 United 2 Corinthians 2 (Fr).

MILLER Lumley Robert (Bob)
b. Blaydon 3 Aug 1938
A winger, signed July 1962, he moved to Hartlepool U (9 app, 2 gl) in November.

MILLS Thomas W
b. Washington (Co Durham) 16 Sep 1908
A goalkeeper, he joined United in April 1929 from Washington Colliery (£200) and returned to his old club a year later before moving to Bury (1931–33, 62 app).

MIMMS Robert (Bobby) A
b. York 12 Oct 1963
Rotherham, Everton, Spurs and England U23 keeper, released by Blackburn Rovers. He came to the Lane on trial and played:
7 Aug 1996 Glenavon 0 United 4 (Fr) and
12 Aug 1996 Stocksbridge 0 United 3 (Fr, sub).
He played once for Crystal P and then joined PNE, Rotherham, York and Mansfield. Including his three loan clubs he made 471 app.

MITCHELL Greg A

An apprentice midfielder, signed May 1981 who played:
21 May 1982 United 3 Wednesday 2 (CCF, competition restricted to 'reserves').
Released cs1983, he later played for Buxton and Matlock T.

MITCHELL Neil N
b. Lytham 7 Nov 1974
A Blackpool midfielder (pro, Nov 1992, 67 app, 8 gls), he played on trial with United:
23 July 1995 Verdal (Nor) 0 United 2 (Fr)
and in four further games on that tour. After a loan spell with Rochdale (4 app), he joined Macclesfield (6 app).

MITCHLEY Cyril J
b. 4 July 1939 (S Africa)
A Marist Brothers (Jo'burg) South African inside forward recommended (with George Cloete) to the United manager, Joe Mercer. He signed December 1958. Unfortunately, Mercer resigned a day or two later. Critchley played twice for the reserves and had 10 games with the third team before his release. He later became a cricket umpire (26 Tests) and was the first to give a player out from the pavilion basing his decision on a television screen.

MITE Robert (Bob)
b. Kimberworth (Rotherham) May 1889
A forward, signed from Rotherham County June 1911; released, a year later. He later played for Rotherham T, Goole, Rotherham C, Coventry C (1919–20, 7 app), Rotherham T and Mansfield Town.

MOLLI(N)SON Alexander
A 20/21 year old right half who had spent three seasons with Arbroath. He joined United Aug 1902 but was not retained.

MONKOU Kenneth (Ken) J
b. Surinam 29 Nov 1964
The former Chelsea, Southampton and Dutch international defender moved in 1999 to Huddersfield T and had a trial with United's reserves in March 2001.

MOODY John (Jack)
b. Heeley (Sheffield) 10 November 1903
A Hathersage goalkeeper reported as having failed a trial with United, he joined Norton Woodseats and then moved to the Arsenal in 1925 (6 app) and made 287 further FL appearances with Bradford (PA), Doncaster, Manchester Utd and Chesterfield.

MOON WR (Billy)
b. Maida Vale 27 June 1868
Famous Corinthians and England amateur keeper who also played cricket for Middlesex. A guest player:
21 Mar 1891 Royal Arsenal 1 United XI 1 (Fr, at Kennington Oval).

MOORCROFT Maurice
b. Chesterfield 4 Nov 1929
A United amateur goalkeeper from Sep 1945, he played for a Mosborough club but became a United part-time pro in July 1948 and played:
26 Sep 1951 Gainsborough Tr v United XI (BM)
Released cs1952, he joined Gillingham (8 app).

MOORE Peter (Phil?)
A forward who joined United Aug 1980. He played:
7 Dec 1981 Barrow 0 United XI 1 (Fr, sub, scored)
He was released cs 1982.

MORE
A right back from Linlithgow who played:
27 Dec 1898 United 5 Corinthians 3 (E Needham BM).

MORGAN Laurence (Lol)
b. Rotherham May 1931
A nephew of Albert Nightingale, he was a United amateur half back from June 1947. He moved to Huddersfield Town (7 app) in March 1949 and to Rotherham U in Aug 1954 (291 app) where he developed into a fine full back. Later, he was the player-manager of Darlington (31 app) and managed Norwich City.

MORGAN William (Bill) A
b. Rotherham Sept 1926
An amateur wing half with Wolves, he made 4 appearances (c1943) and joined United in September 1947. He played at least once for the reserves in September 1947. Given a free transfer (July 1948), he moved to Halifax T (108 app, 3 gl) and played for Rochdale (1953–54, 28 app).

MORRIS Andrew D (Andy/'Bruno')
b. Sheffield 17 Nov 1967
An apprentice at Millmoor, Chesterfield paid £500 for the 6ft 4in striker in Jan 1988 (266 app, 56 gl) and. He played with Exeter (L, 7app, 2gl). He played a trial:
6 May 1992 Barrow 0 United XI 3 (BM)
He later played for Rochdale (32 app, 7 gl).

MORRIS Lee
An apprentice forward who played:
2 April 1990 Combined Services 0 United XI 0 (sub Fr, at Catterick).

MULRENAN Bernard William
b. Bolsover April 1912
England amateur international outside right who played for Huddersfield, Wednesday, Chesterfield (1 app) and for United Reserves (Sep 1936). He became a member of the FA Council in 1963.

MURPHY Kevin
b. Perth 4 Sep 1980
A younger brother of Shaun. (qv). Trial debut:
31 July 2002 Scarborough 0 United XI 2
Similar to his brother, a powerful central defender, he signed and spent one season with the reserves.

MURPHY Neil
Possibly born Carlisle JFM 1879 or Blaydon c1880.
Joined United at the end of December 1901 from Darlington St Augustine. A centre forward, he played:
1 April 1902 Tottenham H 3 United 2 (Fr)
3 May 1902 Wednesday 3 United 0 (CM Ibrox disaster).
He later played for QPR (51 SL app, 11 gl, 3 Irish caps), Aston V. Luton T, Gainsborough Tr. (19 app, 3 gl) and Shildon.

MURPHY Peter M
b. Dublin 27 Oct 1980
A midfield-defender with Blackburn R and Halifax T (L, 21 app, 1 gl), he had a United trial:
17 July 2001 Sheffield FC 0 United XI 7 (sub Fr).
He joined Carlisle U (199 app, 11 gl).

MUSCAT Kevin
b. Crawley 7 Aug 1973
Tough tackling international defender, brought up in Australia. Played for South Melbourne and captained the Olympic team. Dave Bassett gave him a trial in 1995 including a reserve match against Notts C Aug 23) and:
13 Dec 1995 Sheffield Club 0 United XI 5 (Fr, scored)
21 Dec 1995 Worksop T 2 United XI 4 (Fr)
Bassett wanted to sign him but the board of directors said 'no'. Muscat joined Crystal P (Aug 1996, £35k) and played all but three games that season and was in the team that defeated United in the Play-off Final. Subsequently made 256 app for Wolves, Rangers and Millwall.

MUSE Robert
United's first Australian player. Born in Queensland, he came to England c1910 and played Army football and then signed for Annfield Plain and Newcastle United. An inside forward, United signed him April 1922 from Leadgate Park but he was not retained cs 1923.

NASH Herbert
b. Sheffield Aug 1893
An outside right with Clapton Orient (1914), Fulham (1919, 3 app), Gillingham (1919, 13 SL app) and Northfleet (Aug 1920). He joined United in Nov 1920 and his final move as a professional player was 1 April 1921 to Rotherham T.

NAUGHTON Kyle
b. Sheffield 11 Nov 1988
United Academy midfield-defender. Played:
29 July 2006 Scunthorpe U 1 United 0 (Fr)
1 Aug 2006 Notts C 0 United 0 (sub Fr)
17 Jul 2007 Alfreton T 0 United 2 (sub Fr).
He went out on loan 9 Jan 2008 to SPL side Gretna (18 app) and played in United's pre-season tour in July 2008.

NEWTON Robert (Bob)
b. Chesterfield Nov 1956
A forward with Huddersfield, Hartlepool U, Port Vale and Chesterfield. He had a second spell with Hartlepool and was on loan with Stockport C when he played:
8 May 1986 Chesterfield 2 United XI 1 (E Moss BM).
He later played for Bristol Rovers with a FL career record of 343 appearances and 109 goals.

NORTH Ernest Joseph (Joe)
b. Burton on Trent 23 September 1895
After achieving the rank of lieutenant in the Tank Corps and winning the Military Medal, he was playing for Atlas & Norfolk, a Sheffield works team and turned out for a United reserves team in October 1919 against Heeley Friends. He joined Arsenal a month later and became a professional in December. He also played for Reading, Gillingham, Norwich and Watford with a FL career record of 128 appearances and 36 goals. He played County Cricket for Middlesex (27 matches).

NORTON Paul
b. Mexborough Sept 1969
A United apprentice goalkeeper, he played for the reserves in 1985 and had one season (1988–89) with Hartlepool U (5 app), before moving into non-League football.

NUTTALL John (Jack)
A centre half, signed by United cs1910 from the local All Saints club and released a year later. He joined Doncaster Rovers and Millwall cs1914 (27 SL app, 1 goal). Note that United had also a 'Jas. Nuttall' registered with the League 1908–11.

OAKLEY Colin
A young goalkeeper who was a non-playing substitute 31 July 1979 against Mansfield (A/Scot). He became an apprentice in April 1980 and was released Nov 1981.

OAKTON Albert Eric
b. Kiveton Park, Dec 1906
An amateur winger with Grimsby T (1924–25, 2 app), Dinnington, Rotherham U pro, cs 1926 (7 app, 3 gl), Worksop T. Signed United (Nov 1927, £700). Transfer listed cs1930. He then played for Scunthorpe U, Bristol Rovers (May 1931, £200, 40 app, 9 gl), Chelsea (107 app, 27 gl), Nottingham F (1937–38, 7 app, 1 gl) and Boston (1938–39).

O'BRIEN Patrick G (Paddy)
b. Edinburgh 1873
A forward who had played for Hibs and Middlesbrough Ironopolis. He joined United June 1894 and played:
5 Nov 1894 United 5 Linfield Ath 0 (Fr).
Transferred 13 Dec 1894 to Newcastle U (9 app, 2 gl), he also played for St Bernards and Hebburn Argyle.

OGHANI George W
b. Manchester Sept 1960
A young winger given several opportunities in the CL side at the beginning of the 1976–77 season by Jimmy Sirrell but probably never an apprentice pro. He joined Bury in Feb 1978 and played with Hyde U before joining Bolton W in Oct 1983 (99 app, 27 gl). He was loaned to Wrexham (7 app) and then played for Burnley. His other FL clubs were Stockport, Hereford, Scarborough and Carlisle with a final League tally of 299 appearances and 85 goals.

OGILVIE John F
b. Motherwell, 28 October 1928
A full back, given a free transfer by Hibernian in 1955, he had an unsuccessful trial with the United CL side in August of that year. He signed for Leicester City (1955–59, 82 app, 2 gl) and also played for Mansfield T (1960–61, 24 app, 1 gl).

OSCROFT Harry
b. Warsop, Notts, 10 March 1926
A forward who signed amateur forms with United in June 1943. He played for a United reserve team in August 1943 but United didn't keep in touch when he joined the navy. Demobbed in 1947, he joined Mansfield Town (113 app, 41 gl) and then played for Stoke (326 app, 100 gl) and Port Vale (47 app, 12 gl).

O'SULLIVAN Patrick Christopher
b. Cork 1 Jan 1926
He played for Cork Athletic and was watched by a United director, so the story goes, playing for the League of Ireland against the Football League. True or not, he signed for United (15 February / 8 March 1950) in a deal that also involved Pat Keating for a joint fee of £8,000. 'Paddy' was a clever inside forward but lacked speed and determination and was released at the end of July 1951. United came to an agreement with the Cork club (March 1952) that he could play for them subject to a fee if he was re-transferred.

Patrick O'Sullivan

OVERFIELD Jack
b. Leeds, May 1932
An outside left who had a trial with the reserves (12 April 1952) and with Bolton before signing for Leeds U (159 app, 20 gl). He joined Sunderland in 1960 (65 app, 5 gl), Peterborough (1 app) and Bradford City (11 app).

PACHE (K) O (see Pochenko)

PALMER Keith
Reported to have played: 11 May 1990 Brentford 4 United XI 2 (Bob Booker BM, sub).

PARKER G? A
A Sheffield Club half back who played for the Sheffield Club in their first MCL fixture in September 1889. He played once for United:
11 Jan 1890 Derby Midland 2 United 1 (Fr).

PARKINSON Robert
b. Preston April 1873
A Rotherham Town midfield player (14 app, 1 gl) who played:
1 April 1895 Rotherham Town 1 United and District XI 2 (Fr).
Previously with Newton Heath, he also played for Blackpool (8 app, 1 gl), Nottingham F (2 app), Newton Heath (15 app, 8 gl) and Watford.

PARTRIDGE Cyril
b. York Oct 1931
An outside left, he played for the reserves and signed amateur forms with United in December 1951 while serving in the Army. He joined QPR in 1954 and Rotherham United in 1957 (7 app, 2 gl).

PASHLEY Robert W
b. Sheffield 9 Sep 1937
A Wednesday amateur wing half, he signed for United (pro Jan 1956) and was released cs1958. He played for Gainsborough Trinity, Scunthorpe (3 app, 1 gl) and Barrow (26 app, 2 gl).

PATERSON Steven (Steve) W
b. Nairn, 8 April 1958
A Man U (pro Jan 1975, 6 app) midfield player, he came to the Lane, 17 July 1980 (£65k) but was released because of injury problems 27 September. He played overseas for some years and returned to Scotland to play and manage in the Highland League and to manage Aberdeen (2002–05).

PAUCKSTADT Gasper
A Swedish midfield player on trial from the Swiss club Yveardon while United were on tour in Sweden. He played:
27 July 1990 Kramfors A 1 United 5 (sub, Fr)
and in the three subsequent games. the last being:
1 Aug 1990 HBK Kronby (Finland) 0 United 7 (Fr).

PEAKE George
b. Blackwell (Derbys) 8 May 1902
A goalkeeper who played for Blackwell and South Normanton Colliery. He joined United September 1924, was released cs1927 and then played for South Normanton, Chesterfield (1928–30, 23 app), Ilkeston U and Sutton T.

PEARSON Gary
b. Sunderland 7 Dec 1976
United apprentice 1993. A midfield player, he played:
21 Dec 1995 Worksop 2 United XI 4 (Fr)
and had a few games with the reserves. Released in 1996, he joined Gateshead.

PEARSON James
A YTS player, signed July 1984. He may have played:
25 April 1985 Welbourn 0 United XI 7 (sub? Fr)
He was released at the end of February 1986.

PECK Roger S
A midfielder or full back, apprentice 13 Oct 1964 who played in the CL 1967–68 and:
10 Oct 1968 United 2 Wednesday 2 (sub, Hodgkinson BM)
25 Jan 1969 United XI 5 Port Vale 1 (Fr)
He was released 10 Oct 1969 to assist with his father's business.

PEPPER
An unknown player who played at right back
27 Dec 1918 United XI 2 Wednesday XI 2 (CM at Tankersley).

PEPPER Francis (Frank)
b. Sheffield 1875–76
A half back who joined United from Greasborough (Rotherham) in May 1898. Transferred to Newton Heath on 24 November 1898 (7 app), Barnsley (1899–1901, 57 app), Doncaster R (1 app).

PERRIER-DOUMBE Jean-Joel
b. Paris (France) 27 Sep 1978
A Cameroon international defender with 15 caps. He played in France with Auxerre and Rennes and with Celtic (L) Jan 2007 and later signed and scored the winning goal in the Cup Final. He played on trial with United:
17 July 2007 Alfreton T 0 United XI 2 (Fr).

PERRY Colin
A forward who joined United in May 1933 from Kiveton Park and played occasionally in the CL. Released in May 1934, he was later on the books of Wolves, Wrexham, Gainsborough, Aston Villa and Forest but never appeared in an FL fixture other than 3 for Forest (2 gl) at the start of the abandoned 1939–40 season.

PLATTS Mark
b. Sheffield 23 May 1979
A Sheffield and England Boys and U18 outside left and an outstanding prospect for the Wednesday as a youngster. He became their youngest outfield player when he made his debut as a substitute (16 years, 263 days) but he only made one other substitute appearance. He had a trial with United in January 1999 and then signed for Torquay (34 app, 1 goal) and left the game after a short period with Worksop Town.

POCHENKO (or PACHE(K)O) Antonio
Reported to be a Portuguese international midfielder, he had a trial with United in Scandinavia playing:
24 July 1997 Tistedalen (Nor) 1 United 4 (Fr)
25 July 1997 Arjang (Swe) 1 United 8 (Fr).

POLOSEI (Polosel?) Stephano
An 23 year old Italian midfield player reported as signed in August 1998 from Venezia (£400k) after a trial 6 Aug 1998 in a United XI against Lincoln United but he returned home a few days later as permission had not been granted for him to play in competitive games.

PORIC Adem
b. Kensington April 1973
Midfield. Played in Australia and had a trial for United against Newcastle U Reserves in November 1991. He returned to Australia, but later played for Sheffield Wednesday (14 app), Southend U (7 app), Rotherham U (4 app) and Notts C (4 app).

PORTER Ernest W
b. Annfield Plain JFM1901
He joined United April 1924 from Birtley but wasn't retained cs1925. A winger, he played for Boston, Reading (15 app, 3 gl), Norwich City (130 app, 30 gl) and Tunbridge Wells Rangers.

PORTERFIELD (Ian) John (see Managers section)
b. Dunfermline 11 Feb 1946
He played:
31 May 1985 Dallas Americans (USA) 0 United 2 (Fr, sub).

PORTMAN Horace
An amateur left back from High Green Swifts; he made three appearances for the United reserve team He returned to the Swifts but later played for Rotherham United (1927–30, 20 appearances), mainly at centre half.

POWELL Craig
b. Doncaster 10 June 1977
United apprentice forward from 1993, he played:
21 May 1994 Australian Olympic XI 1 United 1 (sub Fr at Gold Coast, Queensland)
21 Dec 1995 Worksop T 2 United XI 4 (Fr).
He had a trial with Doncaster Rovers and a loan spell with Stalybridge (March 1996) before his release.

PRATT Eric Johnson
A Whitby Road Schoolboy, Eric played for Oaks Fold, United (amat, usually at centre half). Worksop T, United (trial):
5 October 1949 Western Command 0 United 2 (Fr at Lichfield).
He signed for United 25 October 1949, released 30 June 1952.

PRATT Richard
b. 1876
An inside forward who joined United in October 1897. He was released at the end of the season and after a period with South Bank, he joined Middlesbrough (16 app, 1 gl).

PREGET Antoine
b. Sete 5 Dec 1972
French defender with Nimes, Chateauroux and Toulouse. After a trial with Southampton he played for Raith R (2 SL app), Dundee (4 SL app) and in Greece. He had a trial with United at left back:
31 July 2001 Burton A 2 United XI 4 (Fr)
before returning to France with Cannes and Marseilles.

PROCTOR Edward (Ted)
b. Barlaston 1870
An army sergeant and forward, registered by United with the FL in January 1894. He appeared for the reserves and:
14 March 1894 Woolwich Arsenal 0 United 2 (Fr, sub).
He then played for Leek, Stoke (3app 1895–96, 2 gl) and Burslem Port Vale.

PYE Jesse
b. Treeton 22 Dec 1919
An inside forward. United (amat December 1938 to cs 1939). Released possibly because of the problems caused by a speech impediment. Army football, Notts County 1945, Wolves (£12k) May 1946, Luton T and Derby County. An international (1 cap), he made 310 FL appearances and scored 146 gls.

RAE Peter
A midfielder who played for Burton Swifts (1 app), Northwich Victoria (9 app, 2 gl), Rotherham Town (19 app, 5 gl) in November 1893. He played as a guest:
1 April 1895 Rotherham Town 1 Sheffield United and District XI 2 (Fr).
He returned to the Swifts in 1896 (48 app, 5 gl).

RAISBECK Luke
An inside left from Slamannan, he joined United in March 1899 and made his debut in the Midland League a few days later. He asked for a transfer six weeks later but United refused and he returned to Scotland to play for Third Lanark. In September United offered him to Middlesbrough (19 app, 1 goal) and accepted £10 for his transfer. His cousin Alex, was one of Liverpool's greatest centre halves.

RAYNES John (Jacky)
b. Sheffield Nov 1928
A Wybourn YC winger, he played in the 1945 Public Practice match and became a United pro in November. He played:
30 April 1947 Boston U 3 United XI 2 (Fr).
Released cs 1948. He joined Rotherham United Mar 1949 (5 app, 1 gl) and later played for Worksop, Northampton T and Stocksbridge.

READ Paul C
b. Harlow Sept 1973
Played Arsenal, Orient (11 app), Southend (4 app, 1 gl) and Wycombe W (41 app, 8 gl) and Sweden before having a trial with a United Reserve side in January 2000. He later played for Luton T (no app), Exeter C (26 app, 1 gl).

RHODES Irvin(e)/ Irwin
b. Rotherham JAS 1916
An amateur full back with United (April 1934), Rotherham and Accrington Stanley and PNE, he returned to Rotherham where he became the first full back to score on his debut in March 1937 (2 app, 1 gl). He became a pro with Accrington (5 app) and also played for Boston.

RICHARDS William
A half back who joined United in August 1920 but wasn't retained. He then played for Scunthorpe, Exeter, Frickley, York and Mansfield T.

RICHARDSON Joseph A S
b. Sheffield 17 Mar 1942
An inside forward with Birmingham and Winsford U, he joined United January 1960. He was transferred to Rochdale in October for 'family reasons' (115 app, 31 gl) and also played for Tranmere R.

RIEPER Marc J
b. Denmark 5 June 1968
An Aarhus defender who had a trial with the reserves in January 1991. Signed by Brondby, the Danish international was sold to West Ham (90 app, 5 gl) for £500k in December 1994.

RITCHIE Paul S
b. Kirkcaldy 21 Aug 1975
An experienced defender who had played for Hearts (133 app, 5 gl), and 86 appearances (1 gl) for Bolton W, Manchester C, Portsmouth, Derby C and Walsall. He played as a trialist:
29 Jul 2004 Boston U 0 United 0 (sub Fr).
He subsequently joined Dundee United (45app), Nicosia and Dundee.

ROBERTS
Played:
31 Jul 2001 Burton A 2 United 4 (sub Fr).

ROBERTS Charles (Charlie)
b. Darlington 6 Apr 1883
The Darlington St Augustine's defender had a trial with United in 1900. One of England's finest central defenders, he played for Bishop Aukland, Grimsby T (31 app, 4 gl), Manchester U (271 app, 22 gl) and Oldham A (72 app, 2 gl) and was a founder member of the Players Union.

ROBERTS William
An outside left, signed by United in January 1904 from Grangemouth Athletic. Transfer listed at the end of the season, he was sold two years later for £35 to Middlesbrough (12 app).

ROBERTSON
A Newcastle W End half back who played as a guest:
19 Apr 1890 Newcastle E End 2 United 0 (Fr).

'ROBERTSON'
Had a trial at left back:
4 Jan 1897 United 2 Corinthians 0 (Fr).

ROBERTSON Christopher (Chris)
b. Dundee 11 Oct 1985
A trainee who signed pro in Oct 2005 he played:
13 Jul 2004 Matlock T 4 United 3 (sub Fr)
11 Aug 2006 Matlock T 0 United XI 2 (sub Fr)
15 Jan 2007 United 1 Chengdu Blades 1 (Fr)
In Jan 2006 he moved to Chester C (L, 1 app) and after his release in March 2007 he joined Torquay (9 app, 1 gl) and continued at Torquay in the Conference in 2007–08.

ROBERTSON Jordan
b. Sheffield 12 Feb 1988
The trainee striker signed pro in July 2006 and had a loan spell with Torquay U (Nov 2006, 9 app 2 gl), and Northampton T (Jan 2007 17 app, 3 gl). He played:
17 Jul 2007 Alfreton T 0 United 2 (sub Fr scored)
31 Jul 2007 Rotherham U 0 United 0 (sub Fr).
During 2007–08 he was on loan with Dundee U (Aug 2007, 14 app, 2 gl) and with Oldham A (Feb 2008, 3 app, 1 gl).

RODGERS W 'Ronnie'
b. Sheffield 14 Dec 1911
A Norton Woodseats outside left who played for Rotherham U (1932–33, 10 app, 1 gl). He signed amateur forms for United in August 1933 but was released at the end of the season and returned to Norton Woodseasts. He was their Secretary for many years and United played a benefit game for him in 1978.

ROLLINSON Frank
b. June 1884 Ecclesall (Sheffield)
An inside forward who joined United in September 1904 and was transferred to the Wednesday in June 1905 (1905–11, 41 app, 15 gl). He later played for Leicester Fosse (17 app, 2 gls), Portsmouth (32 SL app, 9 gl) and Luton (59 SL app, 28 gl).

ROMA Dominic M
b. Sheffield 29 Nov 1985
A trainee who signed as a pro in July 2004. In February 2005 he was loaned to Boston U (2 app). Following subsequent loan spells with Hinckley U and Tamworth he played:
15 Jan 2007 United 1 Chengdu Blades 1 (Fr)
Released in the summer 2007 he joined Hinckley U.

ROSE Gordon
b. Sheffield 22 Mar 1935
A winger, signed June/pro Oct 1956. He played:
26 Sep 1956 Worksop T 1 United XI 0 (CM) and
12 Feb 1957 Royal Signals Rgt 1 United XI 4 (Fr, at Lincoln).
Released cs 1958, he played for Halifax T (8 app, 1 gl), Gainsborough Tr, Sutton T, Skegness T and Selby T.

ROSS N
A Clyde half back and one of the first of United's players (May 1889). He reported for training but quickly returned to Scotland without appearing in any fixture.

ROTHERY Harry
A wing half on United's books for a year from May 1934. He joined Frickley Colliery FC in October 1935 and was a guest player for Bournemouth with four appearances during the 1940–41 season.

RU(S)NAK Stefan
A Czech forward on trial:
20 May 1995 Catania (It) 1 United 0 (Fr)
21 May 1995 Marsala (It) 1 United 1 (Fr).

RUSSELL Craig S
b. Jarrow 4 Feb 1974
He was Sunderland's leading striker in 1995–96. Having scored 31 goals in 150 games he moved on to Manchester City with loan spells at Tranmere, Port Vale and Darlington before playing for United's Reserve team in a trial in January 2000. After a loan spell at Oxford, he played for St Johnstone, Carlisle and Darlington with a final League record of 306 appearances and 42 gls.

RYAN George
b. Glasgow 29 Dec 1931
A centre forward who, while in the RAF, had played for Andover and had been on Hull City's books as an amateur. He joined United in May 1952 from a Glasgow junior side. Released a year later, he joined Third Lanark and then played for Chesterfield (3 app), Wisbech and Kings Lynn.

SANJUAN J G
Spanish midfielder ex R Zaragoza, on trial who played:
18 July 1997 Sheffield FC 0 United XI 3 (Fr)
He then played for Wolves (L, 4 app) for three months. He subsequently played in Spain and in Scotland for Aidrie (22 SL app, 5 gl) and Kilmarnock (31 SL).

SCOTTER
(Initials HA or HC or SC) A left back, perhaps from Norwich, who played:
21 Sep 1889 Lincoln C 0 United 1 (Fr).

SECK Mamadou
b. Rifisque, Dakar (Senegal) 23 Aug 1979
The Senegal international defender (6 caps) joined United on a free transfer from Le Havre on 15 Jan 2007. He had previouslty played in France(Toulouse, Nimes, Ajaccio), and in Turkey (Erciyesspor).
He played:
15 Jan 2007 United 1 Chengdu Blades 1 (Fr)
In Jan 2008 he moved to Scunthopre U (L, 1 app).

SHAW Robert
Played at outside left:
26 Feb 1898 United 1 Wednesday 4 (Fr).

SHEFFIELD Jonathon (Jon)
b. Bedworth 1 Feb 1969
A goalkeeper who came to the Lane on loan from Cambridge United in January 1992. In a career with eight clubs and loan periods, he made 316 FL appearances, 155 for Plymouth.

SHELTON John Arthur
b. Wakefield 15 July 1889
A Rotherham T centre half who joined United in Sept 1908. He played:
12 Apr 1909 Stoke 0 United 1 (Fr).
He returned to Rotherham T cs 1910.

SHENTON John
A Wednesday reserve wing half signed by United 1 September 1924. Due to 'an oversight', the United Secretary hadn't realised that he was a Wednesday player and the 'transfer' took place in November, United paying a £50 fine. The player was released at the end of the season.

SHEPHARD Roy
A younger brother of United's George Shephard (qv), Roy signed for the Blades in February 1949 from Mexborough Tech Old Boys. Nicknamed 'the professor' as his nose was always buried in a book when travelling, he was released in July 1951. He later played for Gainsborough, Bury and Worksop.

SHEPPARD J Barry
A Sheffield born keeper signed Nov 1965. He played:
19 May 1966 Atlas (Mexico) 1 United 0 (Fr, sub)
He may have played in other games on that tour. He joined Torquay United in July 1968.

SHUFFLEBOTTOM Frank
b. Chesterfield 9 Oct 1917

A full back, he joined United in September 1934 from Norton Woodseats and was released in May 1936. He played (amat) for Margate, Ipswich (pro 1938, 2 app) and Nottingham Forest June 1939 (2 app). He joined the army but from 1942 he played again for Forest and as a guest for the Orient and as 'A Newman' for Kilmarnock, then October 1946 to Bradford City (56 app) where he later acted as the trainer.

SIMMONITE Horace
A Rotherham Town player (6 app) who played at left back as a guest:
1st April 1895 Rotherham T 1 Sheffield United and District XI 2 (Fr).

'SIMPSON'
Outside left who played:
13 Apr 1903 Distillery 1 United 2 (Fr)
May be a misprint for Lipsham.

SINCLAIR Ronald
b. Stirling 19 November 1964
A Nottingham Forest reserve goalkeeper who made his League debut on loan with Wrexham. He came to United on loan in August 1985 and saved a penalty kick on his debut with the reserves. He moved to Leeds U in 1986 and his other clubs included Halifax, Bristol C, Stoke and Chester. He made a total of 237 FL appearances.

SINGLETON Stephen Smith
b. Earby OND 1896
A full back with the old Accrington club, he made four appearances in the first season of the League and may have played earlier for Aberdeen University. Signed by United September 1894, released cs 1895.

SLAVKOVSKI Goran
b. Sweden 8 Apr 1989
The youngest player to play for Inter Milan (May 2006) and a Swedish international Youth forward. He joined United on loan Feb 2008 to May 2008.
Only appearance:
25 Mar 2008 Ferencvaros 0 United 1 (Fr, substituted after 75 min).
He signed for Hajuk Split cs 2008.

SMELT Lee A
b. Edmonton 13 Mar 1958
A Colchester keeper who had been playing for Gravesend when he came on trial and played:
2 Aug 1977 Exeter C 1 United 4 (Fr)
He joined Nottingham Forest in 1980 (1 app) and also played for Peterborough (5), Halifax (119), Cardiff (37) and Exeter. (13).

'SMITH'
Played left half:
22 Feb 1890 Middlesbrough 6 United 4 (Fr).
This is probably the Sheffield Club half back who was among those who had offered to assist the new club. See also G/J and T Smith and note that a J F Smith had played for the amateurs in the 1890 Public Practice match and that Montrose (Sheffield) had a half back of that name 1890–91.

SMITH Daniel S
b. Sheffield 8 Jan 1975
A Manchester C associate schoolboy who came to the Lane 1991 and played:
10 Oct 1993 Brunei XI 1 United 4 (Fr).
He was released cs 1993 and played for Boston U.

SMITH George
An inside forward from Staveley who joined United in July 1897. Released at the end of the season, he signed for Chesterfield Town in the Midland League.

SMITH James (Jim) Michael
b. Sheffield 17 October 1940
A United junior, signed as a part time player January 1959. A wing half, he had a 'football brain' but was painfully slow and after one appearance for the reserves in early 1961, he was transferred to Aldershot and later played for Halifax, Lincoln C, Boston as player-manager and Colchester in a League career of 250 appearances and 8 goals, all in the Fourth Division.
A comparatively humble playing career but later, he became more well known as a manager with Colchester, Birmingham, Oxford, QPR, Newcastle, Portsmouth and Derby County.

'SMITH W'
A Scottish full back who played:
23 Sep 1889 United 1 Rotherham T 1 (Fr)
25 Sep 1889 United 2 Nottingham F 0 (Fr).
He 'was a decided success' but wasn't signed.

SNEDDON Scott
The East Stirling (1 SL app) central defender who played a trial:
17 July 1995 Boston U 2 United 2 (Fr).
He later played for Cowdenbeath (71 SL app, 3 gl) and Montrose (2 SL app).

SOLOMON Keith
b. Truro
Truro City keeper, signed Aug 1980 who played:
23 Jan 1981 United 1 Leeds U 0 (Fr).
He died 19 Feb 1981 during a training session at the Ball Inn ground and United played, 22 March, a Truro City XI (9–1) in aid of a Memorial Fund.

SPANN Silvio
b. Couva 21 Aug 1981
A Trinidad & Tobago international midfielder. He played for W Connection (T & T), in Italy (Perugia, Sambenedettese Calcio), Dinamo Zagreb, Yokohama (Japan). He played as a trialist:
16 Jul 2007 Worksop T 0 United 2 (Fr).
He joined Wrexham in Sep 2007 (9 app, 1 gl).

SPEIGHT Jake
b. Sheffield 28 Sept 1985
United youth attacking midfielder. He played for Gainsborough T (L) Dec 2004, Scarborough (L), Scarborough Sep 2005, Bury 2006 (30 app, 2 gls), Northwich Victoria (cs 2007).

SPOUNCER William A (Alf)
b. Gainsborough 1 July 1877
Played Gainsborough Tr at outside left, United October 1895 to cs, Gainsborough (28 app, 15 gl), Nottingham Forest (1897–1910, 300 app, 47 gl). He won one cap and was one of the first League players to coach on the continent.

STANLEY Paul
b. Chesterfield April 1966
A United apprentice forward, July 1982 to June 1984. He joined Scunthorpe U in July 1984 and played twice in the FA Cup but then moved on to Buxton in January 1985.

STAROSTA Ben M
b. Sheffield 7 Jan 1987
Spotted on a coaching course and joined the United Academy and had a loan spell with Tamworth (Feb 2006). He played:
15 Jan 2007 United 1 Chengdu Blades 1 (sub Fr).
In the summer of 2007 he played for Poland (grandparents) in the U20's World Cup. He spent Sep 2007 to Jan 2008 at Brentford (21 app) and the second half of the season at Bradford C (15 app). In Jul 2008 he joined Aldershot Town on loan playing in their opening FL game and in September he moved on loan to Lechia Gdansk (Poland).

STEELE David M (see Secretaries, Trainers section)
The United trainer coach) played at inside left:
3 April 1935 Wednesday 0 United 0 (Craig Memorial match).

STEVENSON John
A half back transferred to United 3 Sep 1895. He played:
11 Sep 1895 Grimsby T 2 United 3 (Fr) and in two away defeats in friendly matches that season against Third Lanark and
23 Oct 1895 Gainsborough Tr 2 United 0 (Fr).
Probably the former Bolton W half back (2 app, 1894–95).

STEWART Demar
b. Jamaica 15 Dec 1984
The defender began his career with Portmore United in Jamaica before moving to White Star Woluwe in Belgium. He played:
10 Oct 2007 Sheffield FC 1 United 5 (sub Fr).
In Jan 2008 he moved to Chengdu Blades.

STEWART Alexander
b. Perth
A centre forward. Played for Queens Park, St Johnstone, St Mirren and Rhyl before joining United in April 1932. He returned to St Johnstone in February 1933 (£600) then Rhyl, and played for Motherwell (1936–38) and the Scottish League against the FL.

STEWART Graham
b. Birkenhead (Hoylake?) 8 Mar 1938
An amateur centre forward with Everton, he became a pro with United in Aug 1958. He played:
27 Oct 1958 United 0 Hibernian 1 (Fr).
Transferred to Chesterfield 25 May 1959 (5 app, 2 gl), he joined Alfreton T cs 1960.

STOREY Brett
b. Sheffield 7 July 1977
United YTS July 1995 but was soon released. He played for Lincoln C (nc March 1996, 2 sub apps, 1 gl).

STRICKLAND Robert P
b. Hull 16 Dec 1979
A Trainee midfielder who played:
19 Aug 1997 United 0 Everton 4 (Fr, sub).
Released 1998. Subsequently he was a youth coach in the USA.

STUPART P
A forward who had played for the Glanfield (Glasgow) Club. He was one of United's first signings in the spring of 1889 but was released without ever playing for the new United team.

SWANNACK Paul
b.Guilford 10 May 1969.
Midfielder, released by Oxford U. United trial:
31 July 1989 Skegness T 0 United 4 (Fr, sub)
He signed for Wokingham and then Newbury Town.

SWINBURNE Trevor
b. E Rainton (Co Durham) 20 June 1953
A Sunderland goalkeeper (10 app) from June 1970 who joined United for one month (L) in the reserve team (23 Dec 1976). He then played for Carlisle U (May 1977, 248 app), Brentford (45 app), Leeds U (2 app), Doncaster (L, 4 app) and Lincoln City (34 app).

SYLVESTER (Silvester) Walter
Probably a guest or on trial at inside right:
27 April 1893 Rotherham T 1 United 2 (Fr)
He may be the Rotherham T inside forward (1893–94, 6 app, 1 goal) and Sheffield Club had a player of that name.

TAHAR Aymen
b. Algiers 2 Oct 1989
An attacking midfielder, he joined the United Academy at the end of 2005–06 and played:
6 Aug 2007 Stocksbridge parks Steel o United XI 4 (sub Fr).

TAYLOR Albert H
b. Worksop 2 May 1924
A goalkeeper with Worksop and Bury (October 1945, 4 app).
Signed for United (May 1948) and played for the reserves but was released in July 1951. He then played for Halifax T (8 app) and Worksop.

TAYLOR G Barry
b. Sheffield 3 Dec 1939
Amateur outside left, part-time pro April 1958. Converted to full back, he was transfer listed (£1000) cs1963. He then played for Oldham A, June 1963 (40 app), Chesterfield (35 app, 2 gl) August 1964 and Worksop T. cs1967.

TAYLOR Geoffrey J
Wimbledon midfield trainee. Trial:
6 Apr 1994 Immingham 0 United 0 (Fr).
Released by Wimbledon 1994.

THOMPSON
A teacher from Ackworth College who played at inside left as a guest:
27 Dec 1894 United XI 3 Corinthians 7 (Fr, scored).

THOMPSON LEE J
b. Sheffield 25 Mar 1983
Schoolboy international trainee who played:
7 May 2001 United 11 Blades All Stars 12 (sub, Whitehouse BM)
17 July 2001 Sheffield Club 0 United XI 7 (sub, Fr).
He moved to Boston U (L) Oct 2002—he scored on his debut and hit a hat trick in the next game—transfer Nov 2002 (95 app, 12 gl), Worksop T 2005 and Boston U 2007.

THOMPSON Martin
b. Bradford 3 Oct 1974
Trainee defender who played:
12 Dec 1994 Staveley XI 3 United XI 4 (BM).
He joined Sheffield FC.

THOMPSON Robert
A Sheffield Schoolboy international winger (and a Powderhall sprinter). A United reserve from Jan 1916 and scored four goals on his debut. He played for Wednesday against United in April, Rotherham C (1916–17), Barnsley 1916–18).

THORPE
One of four Ecclesfield guest players who played:
9 Nov 1889 Staveley 7 United XI 0 (Fr).

TORDOFF Harry
b. Barnsley Nov 1905
A half back who played for Nelson (9 app),, joining United (£350, Feb 1930). Unlucky in that, almost immediately, he was found to be suffering from appendicitis. He was transfer listed cs1931.
Played: Rotherham United June 1931 (2 app), Boston (1932–33), Barnsley July 1933.

TRACEY Richard S
b. Dewsbury 9 July 1977
Became a United apprentice February 1995. He played:
18 July 1997 Sheffield Club 0 United XI 3 (sub Fr, scored and broke his wrist).
Given a free transfer in March 1998 he played for Rotherham U (3 app), Carlisle U (53 app, 11 gl), Macclesfield (33 app, 5 gls), Scarborough, Bradford PA, Ossett T, Frickley A and Belper T.

TRAJANOWSKI Kris
b. Australia 19 Feb 1972
An international striker given a trial:
17 July 2001 Sheffield Club 0 United XI 7 (sub Fr).

TRAVERS Mervyn
b. Dublin 22 Nov 1982
An Academy goalkeeper. He played in Dane Whitehouse's benefit match:
7 May 2001 United XI 11 All Stars XI 0.
He subsequently returned to Ireland.

TRAVIS Nicholas (Nicky) V
Sheffield 12 Mar 1987 A midfielder/defender and product of the Academy he played:
11 Aug 2006 Matlock T 0 United 2 (sub Fr)
15 Jan 2007 United 1 Chengdu Blades 1 (sub Fr).
In Aug 2007 he joined Chesterfield (L) and made two League appearances as a sub.

TRUEMAN Frederick S
Better known as the Yorkshire and England fast bowler than the amateur centre forward registered by United with the Football League in late September 1949. Fred first played cricket for United during the summer of 1948 and for Yorkshire in 1949.

TURNER Alan
b. Sheffield 22 Sept 1935
An inside forward playing for Hallam. United registered him as an amateur with the FL Dec 1956 and he began playing for the reserves. He turned pro September 1957 but was released at the end of the season. He played for Halifax T (7 app), Worksop, Retford, Goole, Sutton T and Ilkeston and managed Heanor and Hallam.

TURNER Raymond
A Mortomley St Saviours forward who scored for United in his first reserve outing in March 1951. He signed as a pro in May and played in two benefit matches for United at Gainsborough in September and at Buxton, where he was on loan, in April 1953. Released cs 1953.

VALENTINO
Romanian who played on trial:
18 May 1995 Viterbese(Italy) 3 United 1 (Fr) and
20 May 1995 Marsal (Italy) 1 United 1 (Fr).

VERVEER Etienne E
b. Surinam 22 Sept 1967
A midfielder who played for Ajax, in Switzerland, Millwall (Dec 1991, 56 app, 7 gl). He had a trial with United in the CL in September 1994, then Bradford City (L, 9 app, 1 gl), Aberdeen and Ischia (Italy).

VEYSEY Kenneth J
b. Hackney 8 June 1967
A goalkeeper who played for Dawlish T, Torquay (72 app), Oxford United (57 app), United (L) November 1992 and played for the reserves, Reading, Exeter C (12 app), Dorchester T, Torquay (37 app) and Plymouth A (6 app).

VILANAKIS Angelos
A Greek forward who played with United on trial:
18 July 1999 East Fife 0 United 4 (sub Fr)
23 July 1999 United 0 Chelsea 2 (sub Fr)
27 July 1999 York C 0 United 3 (Fr).

VINE Darren
b. Sheffield 22 Dec 1976
A United trainee striker who played:
21 December 1995 Worksop T 2 United XI 4 (Fr)
Released cs 1996 he played for Stalybridge, Gainsborough (L), Blyth Spartans (L), Matlock Jan 1998.

VLACHOS Michail
b. Athens Sept 1967
Greek international midfielder or left wing back. He had a United trial with reserves in January 1998 and later played for Portsmouth (57 app), Walsall (11 app, 1 gl) and in Greece.

WAINWRIGHT Danny
United trainee keeper who played:
6 May 1992 Barrow XI 0 United XI 3 (BM)
8 May 1992 Frickley A 4 United XI 4 (BM)
and was on the subs bench for a PL fixture.

WAINWRIGHT Lee
b. Sheffield 9 Jan 1975
Trainee defender who played:
14 Dec 1992 Worksop 3 United 1 (BM, sub).
Later he played in New Zealand and for Buxton, Hallam, Ashfield U, Matlock T, Alfreton T and Stocksbridge Park Steels.

WAINWRIGHT Thomas
b. Ecclesfied (Sheffield) JAS 1897
He played for Thorpe Hesley, joining United in September 1922 but not retained cs1923. He then played: Rotherham Town, Notts C, Boston, Cardiff C, Exeter (13 app), Tunbridge Wells R, Shirebrook, Loughborough Corinthians before returning to Thorpe Hesley.

WALKER Kyle
b. Sheffield 28 May 1990
A versatile player, playing mainly at full back, he joined the Academy at the age of seven. He played:
25 Mar 2008 Ferencvaros 0 United 1 (Fr).

WALKER Leigh
b. Sheffield 12 Feb 1981
A Sheffield Boys keeper on the books of Doncaster R before joining United. Son of Philip Walker (qv), he played:
16 July 1998 Sheffield FC 0 United XI 2 (Fr) and
7 Dec 1999 Whitby T 1 United XI 3 (Fr).
He was released later that month. He played for Barnsley Dec 1999, Emley, Stalybridge C, Scarborough, Lincoln U, Worksop T, Sheffield FC and has a semi-pro England Cap.

WALKER Philip
b. Sheffield 27 Nov 1956
A United apprentice goalkeeper registered July 1972 to November 1974. Father of Leigh (qv). He played: Luton T (trial), Cambridge United Feb 1975 (19 app) and Rotherham U Sep 1977.

WALKER Stephen
b. Sheffield 16 Oct 1914
Gainsborough Trinity wing half who joined United May 1937. Released cs 1938. He then played for: Exeter C (1938–50, 141 app, 3 gl), Portsmouth (1 war guest app), Minehead player coach 1950.

WALKER Willis (Willie)
b. Gosforth 24 Nov 1892
A goalkeeper who may have played for Clayworth (Notts). He joined United in August 1911 after a trial. Released cs 1912. He then played for: Doncaster R (cs1912), Leeds City (22 FL app, 70 war-time), South Shields (206 app), Bradford PA (34 app) and Stockport C (19 app) and war-time appearances for Crystal P and Hartlepools. A fine cricketer, he scored more than eighteen thousand runs for Notts.

WALTON David Lee
b. Bedlington 10 April 1973
A tall central defender. Joined United from Ashington 13 Mar 1992.
He played:
6 Apr 1992 Immingham 0 United XI 0 (Fr)
and in three pre-season friendly games in July and Aug of 1992.
He also played:
7 Aug 1993 Glenavon 0 United 2 (Fr).
He then played for Shrewsbury T (L) Nov, £25k Dec 1993, (128 app, 10 gl), Crewe A £500k Oct 1997 (155 app, 3 gl), Derby C (2003–04, 5 app), Stockport C (L, Feb 2004, 7 app), Shrewsbury T (2004–05, 38 app, 4 gl).

WALTON James B
He had a United trial 20 Aug 1956, registered (FL) 22 September.
He played right half:
26 Sep 1956 Worksop T 1 United XI 0 (CM)
and was released 17 October.

WARD Darren
b. Worksop 11 May 1974
Welsh U21 and B and full (5 caps) international goalkeeper. He played for Mansfield T (81 app), Notts C (251 app), Forest (123 app) and Norwich City (1 app). Out for a long period with a knee injury, he had a United trial:
24 July 2006 Morton 1 United 3 (Fr).
He 'appeared nervous' and wasn't given a contract but joined Sunderland (33 app).

WARD Peter
b. Rotherham 20 Oct 1954
A United apprentice full back October 1972 and a member of the 1973–74 Youth Cup Semi-Final team. Released cs 1974. Played for: Workington July 1974 (43 app, 2 gl), Huddersfield T July 1976.

WARD William
A full back who joined United in September 1909. He signed for Castleford and then was transferred (£10) to Glossop in August 1914 (19 app).

WARNOCK Neil (see Managers Section)
b. Sheffield 1 Dec 1948
He played and scored:
7 May 2001 United 11 All Stars XI 1 (sub Whitehouse BM).

WARREN Mark W
b. Clapton 12 Nov 1974
Played: Leyton Orient utility player 1992 (152 app, 5 gl) and was an England Youth player. He had a loan spell with West Ham and a United trial with the reserves in October 1994. He later played for: Oxford (L, 4 app), Notts C (84 app, 1 gl), Colchester (20 app), Southend U (32 app, 2 gl), Fisher A and Kings Lynn.

WATFORD Albert
b. Halfway 12 Feb 1917
A Mosborough, United and Chester (1938–39, 1 app) amateur half back. He later played for: Chesterfield (Feb 1944 to 1946), Lincoln C (guest 1944–45, 1946–47 14 app), Scunthorpe U and Boston U.

WATKINS Dale A
b. Peterborough 4 Nov 1971
United 1989–90 YTS midfielder who then played for: Grimsby T, Rotherham U, Peterborough (Mar 1990, 10 app), Wisbech T, Grantham T, Rushden & Diamonds, Gloucester C, Cheltenham T (9 app), Kettering where he gained England semi professional honours, Chelmsford C, Grantham T, Kings Lynn, Stamford, Blackstones and Yaxley.

WATSON James (Jimmy, 'Daddy Long Legs')
b. 4 October 1877 Larkhall (Lanark)
A full back who played for Burnbank (Lanark) and Clyde (Dec 1897) before coming to United for a trial.
He joined Sunderland (Jan 1900) and was there for eight seasons winning a championship medal in 1902 and later played for Middlesbrough. Capped six times by Scotland, he made 313 FL appearances.

WATTS Grant S
b. Croydon 5 Nov 1973
A forward who played for Crystal Palace (4 app) and Colchester United (L, 12 app, 2 gl). Released by Palace, he signed nc forms with United and played and scored:
6 Aug 1994 Lincoln United 3 United XI 6 (Fr).
He then moved to Gillingham (3 app) and various non-League clubs including Dulwich Hamlet, Sutton U, Croydon, Egham T, Erith T, Banstead A and Bromley.

WEBSTER Terence (Terry)
b. Retford 27 Sept 1941
A small (5' 5") wing half. A United pro October 1958, released cs 1959. He joined Accrington S Nov 1959 and Barrow July 1960 (4 app).

WEDGBURY Sam
b. Oldbury 26 Feb 1989
A midfielder with Worcester City. He had a United trial with the reserves Jan 2006 at Grimsby. Signed 31 Jan 2006 though he continued to play for Worcester that season. Played:
6 Aug 2007 Stocksbridge 0 United XI 4 (Fr)
10 Oct 2007 Sheffield FC 1 United 5 (sub Fr) and
25 Mar 2008 Ferencvaros 0 United 1 (Fr).

WELLS Ernest
An Ackworth College amateur left back who played as a guest:
27 Dec 1894 United XI 3 Corinthians 7 (Fr).
He probably never played again for any United team but he was registered with the FL for the 1894–95 and 1902–03 seasons. He played for the Oxfordshire FA and may be the Leeds and Christ's College (Camb) full back who played in the 1901–02 varsity match.

WEST Enoch (Knocker) J
b. Hucknall Torkard (Notts) 31 March 1886
United made a grant of £5 to Linby FC when they signed West in November 1903 but, after scoring four goals in six games for the reserves, he was put on the transfer list at the end of the season. He played for Hucknall Constitutional and was to become one of the most celebrated centre or inside forwards.

Nottingham Forest paid United £5 for West (cs1905) and he repaid them by scoring 93 goals in 168 FL appearances before moving to Manchester U (166 app, 72 gl) where he won a Championship medal in 1910. His career ended in disgrace in 1915 when he received a life suspension for 'match fixing'.

WHELAN Noel D
b. Leeds 30 Dec 1974
The England U21 and youth international had made 274 appearances and scored 51 goals for Leeds U, Coventry C, Middlesbrough, Crystal P, Millwall and Derby C before he played as a trialist:
13 Jul 2004 Matlock T 4 United 3 (sub, Fr)
19 Jul 2004 Tavistock 2 United XI 5 (sub Fr)
21 Jul 2004 Bodmin 0 United 1 (sub Fr).
He subsequently played for Aberdeen (20 app, 5 gl), Boston U (15 app, 4 gl) and Livingstone (8 app, 1 gl) and Dunfermline (1 app).

WHITE Mark I
b. Sheffield 26 Oct 1958
Sheffield Boys left side player. Joined United in July 1975, released by Jimmy Sirrel in Oct 1976. He joined Reading Mar 1977 (278 app, 11 gl) and later he played for Cape Town Spurs and Henley T.

WHITEHALL Steven C
b. Bromborough, 8 Dec 1966
A striker who played for non-league Southport. He had a trial with United reserves in May 1990 but wasn't signed. He subsequently played for Rochdale (238 app, 75 gl), Mansfield T (43 app, 24 gl) and Oldham A (76 app, 13 gl), Chester C, Nuneaton B and Southport again.

WHITNEY Michael
A friend of Neil Warnock , living in Cornwall, who played:
23 Jul 2003 Tavistock 0 United XI 4 (sub Fr).

WHITTLE
An Ecclesfield left half who played:
9 Nov 1889 Staveley 7 United 0 (Fr).

WHITTLE Alan
b. Liverpool 10 Mar 1950
England U23 and Everton forward (1967–72, 74 app, 21 gl), Crystal P Dec 1972 £80k, (108 app, 19 gls). He joined United in July 1976 on a free transfer subject to a medical examination and played:
30 July 1976 RC de Lens (Belgium) 4 United 2 (Fr)
and in two other games on tour at Eindhoven and Charleroi. The contract was cancelled on medical grounds but he was taken on by the Orient Sep 1976 (50 app, 6 gl), Persepolis (Iran), Bournemouth (9 app).

WILBOURN Henry (Harry)
b. Eckington (Derbys) 10 Feb 1905
Outside left. Played: Anston Ath, United Oct 1924 played frequently for the reserves until released cs1927. He then played for Watford (2 app), Halifax T (7 app), Gainsborough Tr, Mexborough and Grantham.

WILCOCK
The name given in Scottish newspapers for the centre half who played:
3 Jan 1895 Raith Rovers 2 United 4 (Fr).
Sheffield reports have Harry Hammond.

WILKINSON Algernon (Algie)
Greasborough born keeper who played for Rotherham Town (1913–14), Rotherham County and Bradford City during the First World War.
He also played:
27 Dec 1918 United XI v Wednesday XI (Fr at Tankersley).
He played for Rotherham County (May 1919) and signed (FL) Bradford City (12 app) and Liverpool.

WILKINSON Eric
b. Sheffield 6 Mar 1931
A midfielder who played: Bradford City 1951, United Aug 1953 though he had played for the reserves in March of that year. Released cs1955, he made his FL debut with Bournemouth (4 app).

WILKINSON Howard
b. Sheffield 13 Nov 1943
An outside left and United amateur August 1961 to Jan 1962. He subsequently played for: Hallam, Wednesday June 1962 (22 app, 2 gl) and Brighton in 1966 (129 app, 19 gl). A youth international, he later managed Boston U, Notts C, Sheffield Wed (1983–88) and Leeds U (1983–96) and became the Technical Director of the FA, twice taking the England manager's job on a temporary basis. He moved back into club management with Sunderland but was unsuccessful.

WILKINSON Joseph H
b. Darfield c1906
Half back. Played: Wombwell, Mexborough A and Southampton (trial). United (Mar 1927). He played:
4 May 1927 Bradford PA 4 United XI 1 (BM).
Transfer listed cs 1928, he joined Doncaster R (25 June, 12 app (6 in goal), 1 gl).

WILLIAMS Daniel (Danny)
b. Maltby 20 Nov 1924
One of Rotherham United's greatest players, Danny played for Silverwood Colliery but began evening training with United in the winter of 1942. The war-time traveling involved was difficult and he was also told that United had 'too many half backs'. He joined the Millers and made a record 461 full League appearances for them before becoming a manager with Rotherham, Swindon, Sheffield Wednesday and Mansfield before returning to Swindon.

WILLIAMS Jan-Michael
b. Trinidad and Tobago 26 October 1984
A goalkeeper from Connection FC (Trinidad) given a trial:
17 July 2007 Alfreton T 0 United XI 2 (Fr).
He played for White Star Woluwe (Belgium, L, 2007–08) and joined Ferencvaros in July 2008 after he had failed to get a work permit to play for United.

WILLIAMSON
A defender who played:
4 Apr 1890 Rotherham T 1 United 2 (Fr)
5 Apr 1890 United 2 Staveley 1 (Fr).

WILSON Kevin J
b. Banbury, 18 Apr 1961
A Banbury FC forward who had a United trial September 1979. Harry Haslam and Banbury agreed terms for a transfer but they were never finalized. Later played: Derby C (Dec 1979, 122 app, 30 gl), Ipswich T (98 app, 34 gl), Chelsea (152 app, 42 gl), Notts Co (69 app, 3gl), Bradford C (L, 5 app), Walsall (125 app, 98 gl) and Northampton T (31 app, 2 gl) and was awarded 42 Northern Ireland caps.

WILSON Peter
Rhyl FC amateur outside left who played for United on trial:
6 Nov 1957 Rhyl 1 United 4 (Fr, scored).
He later played for Whitley Bay 1958–59 (awarded 3 English amateur caps).

WINDRIDGE David H
b. Atherstone 7 Dec 1961
An Atherstone forward who joined United 24 Jan 1979. He was named substitute on at least three occasions but didn't play. He later played for: Chesterfield 14 Mar 1980 (FL debut May 1981, 78 app, 14 gl), Blackpool (101 app, 18 gl), Turkey, Northwich V, Bury (1 app), Rochdale (5 app) before playing non-League football for some years in northern Lancashire.

WINTER John G A (Jack)
b. Stoke Newington 6 Aug 1928

Gleadless Town End centre forward signed Aug 1948 (amat) and Nov (pro). Played:
4 May 1950 Skegness T 3 United XI 2 (Fr).
He signed for Walsall £500 Jan 1951 (42 app, 12 gl).

WOOD(S) Fred
Scots Guards soldier who played for Woolwich Arsenal (29 Oct 1892) in a FA Cup tie. He made five appearances in goal for United in club matches. His debut was:
10 Nov 1892 Casuals 1 United 2 (Fr, at Leyton).
Two days later, he played at Swindon and a month later, at Bramall Lane against the Wednesday. United registered him with the FL (23 Nov 1892 and 14 Nov 1893) and he played at Newcastle and finally:
24 Mar 1894 Corinthians 4 United 1 (Fr).
He was registered with the League by Derby C in Aug 1897 and may have appeared for a 'Halifax FC' 1897–98.

WOOD S
An unknown inside right who played:
26 Jan 1891 United 0 Grimsby T 1 (Fr).

WRIGHT John (Jack)
b. Swallownest
Centre forward. Played for Woodhouse Brunswick, United (amateur February 1930, pro May/Oct 1931). Released in May 1933, he joined Rotherham United (11 app) and made his debut in the first game of the season but his final ten games were as a goalkeeper. He later played for Dinnington Ath and Mexborough.

WRIGHT Nicholas (Nick) J
b. Derby 15 Oct 1975
A forward with: Derby C 1994, Carlisle U 1997 (25 app, 5 gl), Watford (37 app, 6 gl).
Injury prone, he had a trial with United reserves in Feb 2002 and scored but his playing career soon came to an end.

WRIGHT Stephen
b. Bellshill 27 Aug 1971
Scotland right back with: Aberdeen (147 app, 2 gls), Rangers (7 app), Wolves (L, 3 app), Bradford C (22 app). United trial:
18 July 2000 Tideswell 0 United 8 (Fr).
Subsequently with: Sheff W (trial), Dundee U (trial), Scunthorpe U 2002 (2 app), Dundee (coach).

WYLDE Gordon
b. Glasgow 12 Nov 1964
A strong, hard tackling East Stirling midfield player (124 app, 5 gl). On loan for a month with United March 1987 and played for the reserves. Transferred to Kilmarnock (Sep 1987, £12k, 59 app, 1 gl), his future career was placed in jeopardy by a severe injury but he did play for Queen of the South (6 app), Clyde (69 app, 1gl) and Kilbirnie Ladeside.

YATES John
b. Rotherham 18 Nov 1929
An Aughton Juniors outside right who joined United Oct 1950 after a two month trial. Released cs 1951 he signed for Chester (2 app).

ZIVKOVIC B Lee
b. Doncaster 27 Nov 1975
A United apprentice who played:
7 Aug 1993 Glenavon 0 United 2 (sub Fr).
12 Dec 1994 Staveley XI 3 United XI 4 (sub BM).

The following Chinese players made guest appearances for United in China, all as substitutes.

TMENG YE
24 Jul 2005 Hu Nan Star United 1 United 2 (Fr).

JIANG/ZHANG XIAOYU
22 Jul 2005 Combined XI 3 United 1 (Fr at Wulihe Stadium).
24 Jul 2005 Hu Nan Star United 1 United 2 (Fr).

TANG JINKAI
22 Jul 2005 Combined XI 3 United 1 (Fr at Wulihe Stadium).
24 Jul 2005 Hu Nan Star United 1 United 2 (Fr).

Secretaries, Trainers Other Staff and United People

ARCE Oscar
Youth coach May 1978–cs 1979
A former Argentine footballer and coach who joined United from Millwall and enabled Harry Haslam to make contact with Antonio Rattin, the 1966 World Cup captain and open negotiations with Argentine FA officials, Alex Sabella etc during his 1978 visit to Argentina. Arce moved on to Sunderland.

BAILEY Ian
Physiotherapist 1986–88
A former full back with Middlesbrough and Wednesday, who suffered a series of terrible injuries which, coupled with arthritis, brought his playing career to an end. He trained as a physiotherapist and was engaged by Billy McEwan and, more recently, worked at Millmoor.
He played for United:
23 Nov 1986 Hallam 3 United XI 5 (Fr).

BAILEY John
Assistant Coach
The former Blackburn, Everton and Newcastle full-back who joined Howard Kendall's training staff in March 1996.

BAMFORD Alan
A former Director of the Henry Boot Construction Company, he assisted the Board in the development of Bramall Lane during his tenure which lasted from 1999 to 2005. He was also instrumental in the purchase of the Shirecliffe Academy site and the work which took place there in readiness for its opening.

BARKER Reg
Head groundsman November1964–75
Reg worked for United for twenty years. He took over from Tom Parkin and was at the Lane when the cricket area was closed and the South Stand was built. He died in 1979.

BARLOW Sam
Sam Barlow (senior) was a gateman at the Lane with 70 years service, retiring when he was 92. His son, Sam junior, worked on match days for 65 years until he was 79.

BEATTIE Andrew (Andy)
Assistant Manager 1967–68
A former Preston NE and Scottish international full back who was the assistant manager to John Harris from October 1967. It was Harris who suggested to the United directors that he should become a General Manager with Andy, who was nearly four years older than Harris, in charge of team affairs. The board took up the idea of moving Harris 'upstairs' and appointed Arthur Rowley as team manager.

BELL Matthew
Editor 'Flashing Blade'
Sheffield-born Matthew has been editor of the long-running fanzine 'Flashing Blade' since issue 6 (May1989). A Blades fan since 1968, he took over from founders **Jamie Pigott, Brian Exford** and **Jon Middleton** and, with their help, Matthew, **Kate Gibb, Clive Porter, Karen Knight, Darren Reid, Paul Anderson, Kevin Titterton, Richard Guest, Lindon Colley** and many regular contributors, he has guided FB well past 100 issues. He also writes the 'Fanscene' section of 'Blades Notes' in the *Green 'Un.*

BELLAMY Bernard
The maintenance foreman who began work at the Lane c1961 and retired in the mid 1980s.

BERGARA Daniel (Danny) Alberto
Assistant manager 1978–1981
A Uruguayan forward who was a youth coach with Luton Town and England. Harry Haslam made him Assistant Manager and Director of Coaching with United in February 1978. He was released in August 1981 after relegation to Division Four and became the first foreign born manager of a Football League team when he took that post at Rochdale in 1988. He was very successful with Stockport County and also managed Rotherham and Doncaster Rovers. He died in July 2007.

BRIGGS Neville
Neville was appointed as Chief Scout by Jimmy Sirrel in January 1976.

CAPPER David
Club Secretary1989–99
David succeeded George Smith as the United Secretary in January 1989. Prior to coming to the Lane, he had worked for eleven years with Stoke City and was a leader in the move to introduce Family Enclosures. He left United in June 1999 to become Head of Administration with Hull City though the move proved to be ill-judged.

CHESTER Richard (Dick)
Club Secretary January 1979 to October 1983
He was the Secretary of Lincoln City for seven years but left in 1978 to move into industry for a short period before joining United. He had worked for Reg Brealey in Lincoln and it was Chester who suggested that Brealey might be a useful newcomer to the United board. He resigned in October 1983 and moved to Hillsborough.

CIRCUIT Denis
Assistant Physiotherapist 1986 to November 1997
He joined United from Rotherham United in 1986 and left to work in Germany before returning to Millmoor.

CLAREBROUGH Denis
The Club historian, Denis was born in Sheffield in 1932 and brought up in Greenhill. He first watched United in the late 1930s and has been a season ticket holder since 1946. He began writing articles on United's history for the programme in 1983 and was the author of *The First 100 Years* and the *Complete Record* and three later titles.

CLARK Archibald (Archie)
Scout, Caretaker Manager and Assistant Manager
Oct 1958 to Jan 1967
Born in Leeds in 1902, Archie was a half-back with Brentford, Arsenal, Luton, Everton, Tranmere and Gillingham. He was the manager of the Kent club when they entered the Football League in 1950 but resigned in 1958.

Just two months after being appointed chief scout by his former Everton colleague, Joe Mercer, Archie found himself caretaker manager but he stayed on and proved to be an invaluable help to the next manager, John Harris. Clark was an excellent judge of young players, building close relationships with local school Football Associations and a steady flow of boys made their way to Bramall Lane and into the

United First Division side of the mid 1960s. By then, Clark was regarded as the Assistant Manager and his death in 1967 was a major blow to United.

COOKSON Kevin

A Worksop-born former journalist, Kevin joined the United staff in June 1998. He has assisted Media Manager Andy Pack and now works on editing the programme as well as involving himself in other aspects of the media operation.

DALEY Anthony (Tony)

Fitness coach 2003–2007

Born in Birmingham 18 Oct 1967, Tony was a winger with Aston Villa (233 apps, 31 gl),), Wolves (21, 3) Watford (12, 1), Walsall((7) and Forest Green Rovers who won 7 England caps. After an injury troubled career, Tony took a Sports Science degree course and was working with Forest Green as a fitness coach when Neil Warnock brought him to the Lane in July 2003. He had little experience but he worked with enthusiasm. He played and scored for United:
19 Jul 2004 Tavistock 2 United 5 (sub Fr).
He lost his position in August 2007 after Bryan Robson became the new United manager and he moved to Wolverhampton Wanderers.

DANES Adrian

Adrian had worked for Leicester City before he was appointed at the end of September 1999 as Commercial Manager replacing Shaun O'Toole. He left in the spring of 2001.

DAVIES Alf

Alf Davies replaced Andy Daykin in July 1998 as Commercial manager after working at Bolton and Headingley. He left after less than a year and set up a consultancy business.

DAYKIN Andy

Commercial Manager

Andy joined the Club in August 1982 initially as Marketing Executive before taking the position of Commercial Manager in April 1983. Instrumental in securing many of the key sponsorship deals involving the business down the years, he is the only member of the non-footballing staff to have appeared for the first team:
12 May 1986 Guernsey XI 1 United XI 9 (sub, Fr).
Andy had short spells with Hull City and Barnsley before returning to United in June 2001. He is Chairman of the Federation of Commercial Managers.

DEEHAN John

Assistant Manager1998–99

A successful striker with Aston Villa, West Brom, Norwich City and Ipswich and then a coach and manager, he joined United in July 1998 as assistant manager to Steve Bruce. Less than a year later he moved with Bruce to Huddersfield Town. In 2006 he was Director of football with Lincoln City.

DIXON Jim

Coach and physiotherapist cs 1981 to Jan 1986

A player with Sunderland and Gateshead, Jim Dixon came to the Lane with manager Ian Porterfield from Rotherham United and left when Porterfield was dismissed. It was said that he acted as the manager's 'ears' on the training ground or in the dressing room and the mere sight of him entering the physio room was sufficient to make many 'unfit' players feel fit again.

DONACHIE William (Willie)

Chief Coach July 1997 to Feb 1998

The former Manchester City, Oldham and Scotland full-back, was brought to the Lane by acting manager, Nigel Spackman.
He made one appearance for United:
30 Jul 1997 Forde IL (Norway) 0 United 4 (sub, Fr).
Disillusioned by boardroom, financial and managerial problems, he left to work with Joe Royle at Oldham. He was the chief coach at Millwall until October 2007.

DUCKWORTH Richard (Dick)

Chief scout cs 1956 to cs 1957 and from March-Oct 1967

A former strong, forceful wing half and manager of York City and Stockport County, Dick was appointed chief scout to assist new manager Joe Mercer. He left to manage Darlington and Scunthorpe but returned to assist John Harris following the death of Archie Clark.
He died in Sheffield in April 1983.

DUNGWORTH John (see Other Players section)

A Youth team coach

EADIE Bill

Bill trained the 'A' team in the late 1930s though his background was in athletics.

ELLIS Samuel (Sam)

Assistant manger to Kevin Blackwell from 14 February 2008

Born in Ashton-under-Lyne 12 Sep 1946, he played as a centre half for Wednesday (157 app, 1 gl) in the 1966 Cup Final and for Mansfield T (64 app, 7 gl), Lincoln C (173 app, 33 gl) and Watford (34 app, 4 gl) where he became assistant manager to Graham Taylor as Watford climbed through the divisions. He spent seven years as manager of Blackpool, a brief time managing Bury before becoming Peter Reid's assistant at Manchester City. After a brief spell managing Lincoln, he was assistant to Stan Ternent at Bury and then Burnley. He first worked with Kevin Blackwell at Leeds and later at Luton.

ELMS E John (Jack)

Assistant Groundsman and cricket coach

An all rounder, United registered Elms with the FL in 1898 but he was far more successful playing for the United Cricket Club from 1899 after playing previously for Pitsmoor. Born in 1876, he retired in 1945 and died in 1951.

EYRE Fred

Chief scout and 'assistant manager' 1997–98

A journeyman footballer, Fred became a successful businessman, author and after dinner speaker. Appointed by Nigel Spackman as chief scout, he became caretaker manager Steve Thompson's assistant when United reached the FA Cup semi-final and play-offs after Spackman and Willie Donachie resigned.

FLETCHER Donna
Company Football Secretary
Donna began work in the United ticket office in 1990 and has held several posts in an administrative capacity including that of personal assistant to Derek Dooley. She has been the Football Company Secretary since 2002.

FOGG Kevin
Assisted John Warnock from January 2000 as Director of Youth Development and U17 team manager.

FRENCH Derek. (Frenchie)
Physiotherapist Feb 1988 to July 1996
'Frenchie' had been part of Dave Bassett's management team at Wimbledon and Watford and soon followed him north to the Lane. He left soon after Bassett's resignation to concentrate on private practice though he did rejoin his old boss for a short period at Barnsley.

GARRETT John
Player Liaison/Education and Development Officer
John joined the Club in 1998 and took in hand the collating, collection and preservation of items connected with United's history, many of which are displayed in the ground's 'Legends of the Lane' facility. John is responsible for educational visits, mascots and liaison work between club administration and the playing staff which is non media based.

GOODALL Geoff
Physiotherapist 1962 to 1981
United's first appointed physiotherapist though some earlier trainers such as George Waller could be said to have had basic qualifications and great ability. Goodall chose to be 'part-time' from 1964.

GOODCHILD Norman
Steward etc
Norman retired after a fifty-nine year association with the club. A former Trade Union general secretary, he worked for United as a programme seller, steward and latterly was in charge of the Abbeydale training ground. He died in 2001, aged eighty four.

GREEN A. Charles
Chief Executive February 1996 to March 1998
Appointed in 1996, Green had been doing the work since September 1995 following Mike McDonald's take over of the club from Reg Brealey. A former professional footballer, he had worked in engineering but moved into the managerial and financial side of business and was essentially McDonald's day to day man at the Lane.

Green began to take decisions over a wider area than previously and staff, players and supporters grew increasingly unhappy as it was felt that Nigel Spackman's managerial authority was seriously threatened and in decline. Early in March 1998, Spackman resigned and a few days later, Green stood down as chief executive though for a short period, he remained a member of the plc before leaving with McDonald.

HARTLEY George
George worked as an assistant groundsman and handyman at the Lane from 1889 until at least 1957, retiring at the age of 78.

HATCLIFFE Claire
Customer Services Manager
Claire joined United's staff in 1992, working on the Commercial side of the business acting as Personal Assistant to Andy Daykin. She then became Corporate Care manager in 2003 before taking on the role of Customer Services Manager in 2008.

HAWKINS Richard
Fitness Coach 2007–08
A specialist sports, exercise science and fitness coach with the FA and with West Bromwich Albion from 2005, he joined his former manager, Bryan Robson at the Lane in September 2007. Shortly after Robson's resignation, he moved to Old Trafford.

HAWLEY Howard Vincent
Assistant Secretary 1932–52
Howard was a director for two years before taking the position in June 1932 as the assistant to Teddy Davison, the secretary manager. Illness led to his retirement in March 1952 and the appointment of Arnold Newton as club secretary.

HENSON Phil
Coach
The former Manchester City, Wednesday, Stockport and Rotherham United player was brought to the Lane in July 1986 by United's manager Billy McEwan to assist the senior coach, Danny Bergara. He played:
23 Nov 1986 Hallam 3 United XI 5 (Fr).
He left United early in 1988 when Dave Bassett took over and returned to Millmoor as McEwan's assistant. He became the Rotherham manager in 1991 and took the post of Chief Executive in 1994.

HOLLAND Frank
Groundsman 1983–88
A Yorkshire county athlete from Barnsley, he had been a groundsman at Oakwell and Blackpool and also at the Dorothy Hyman Stadium.

HOUSELEY Jack (see Players section)
Player and Trainer

HOWARD Peter
Journalist
Born in Stockport in 1937 but brought up in Sheffield, Peter joined the local newspaper group in 1952 and was the United corespondent from 1960 to 1973. He died in 2007.

HOWARTH John
Football Club Secretary June 1999 to April 2002
John became the Football Club Secretary following the departure of David Capper in June 1999, a role he stayed in until April 2002. Howarth had been one of the youngest secretaries in the history of the Football League when he assumed the role at Blackburn Rovers in 1970. He now fulfils a similar role with Shrewsbury Town F.C.

HUNT Sam
Trainer
A forward with Doncaster Rovers, Lincoln City (1889) and Barnsley (1889–cs 93, Hunt was a United trainer 1893–94. In 1894, he appears in a photograph as 'Hurst'. He returned to play for Barnsley and may have played for Darwen but he returned to Barnsley and became their trainer; making one League appearance, presumably in an emergency in 1899.

JONES Mick
Mick worked as an assistant to Neil Warnock, 2003 to 2007. A central defender with Derby C, Notts C and Peterborough (188 FL app), he worked as an assistant for Warnock at Notts C, Huddersfield, Plymouth, United and Crystal Palace, where he is assistant manager.

KEEN Frederick (Fred)
Groundsman
Fred Keen (Kean) joined United from the Hull Club as head groundsman and caretaker in June 1920 at the age of 33. Fred will chiefly be remembered for the major drainage system introduced at the outbreak of war in 1939 and the relaying of the cricket area which had been wrecked by the 'blitz' in December 1940. Fred retired in 1949 when he was succeeded by Tom Parkin.

KELLY David (see Players section)
Assistant manager cs 2003 to Sep 2004
David was the former Republic of Ireland forward who played for United in the 2000–01season. He was the assistant manager of Tranmere Rovers from Oct 2002 until the close season of 2003 when he returned to the Lane as Neil Warnock's assistant following the departure of Kevin Blackwell to Leeds United. In September 2004, David took a similar position at Preston North End.

KIDD Brian
Coaching staff 2006–07, Assistant Manager July 2007 to 14 Feb 2008
Born in Manchester, 29 May 1949, the former Manchester United and England forward—he also played for Arsenal, Manchester C, Everton and Bolton W—moved into management and coaching with Barrow and Preston before returning to Old Trafford. He has also been the manager of Blackburn Rovers (1998–99), the head coach at Leeds and a member of the England coaching staff. He resigned along with Bryan Robson in February 2008.

KILNER Dave
Radio Hallam presenter who became closely linked to the club from the 1980s.

KIRKHAM Andrew L
The club statistician, who was born in Whiston, Rotherham in 1945. A United supporter since 1953, following the example of his father and grandfather, his daughter Sarah has followed in his footsteps. He has written for United's programme since 1984 and was co-author of *A Complete Record of Sheffield United Football Club 1889–1999.*

LIVINGSTONE Dugald (Dug, Duggie)
Trainer coach (1936–49)

A Scottish full back, born in 1898, who played for Celtic, Everton, Plymouth and Tranmere Rovers before beginning his successful coaching career with the Jersey FA and Exeter City. He succeeded David Steele as the United coach and trainer in June/July 1st 1936 and saw United return to the First Division in 1939 and win the 1945–46 League North championship. He accepted the position as Sheffield Wednesday's manager in January 1947 but changed his mind but was sacked in October 1949 believing he was the scapegoat for poor results.

Later posts included Sparta (Rotterdam) coach, national coach of Eire and Belgium and manager of Newcastle United, Fulham and Chesterfield. He died in January 1981.

MACARI Lou
The former Manchester United and Scottish international forward and football manager was appointed chief scout by Steve Bruce in September 1988 and also assisted with coaching.

McCABE George
A goalkeeper on the books of Wolves and the Wednesday, George became a referee during the war while serving in the RAF and rose to become a FIFA World Cup referee and was in charge of the 1969 Cup Final. A Youth Officer at Hillsborough, Harry Haslam brought him to the Lane where he worked with both the Junior and Senior Blades and in other capacities until 1992. He died in January 2001 at the age of 77.

McCALL Stuart (see Players section)
Player-coach July 2002, first team coach July 2003, assistant mgr Sep 2004 to 21 May 2007
Stuart was signed by Neil Warnock to bring some calm authority to the United mid-field and to gain coaching experience. He was successful on both counts and became the assistant manager when his predecessor, David Kelly, moved to Preston North End. When Warnock left, McCall was not offered his job but became the manager of Bradford City.

McCORMICK Jimmy
Coach/Asst Trainer 1952–53
Born in Rotherham in 1912, Jimmy played for Spurs and Fulham and coached overseas before becoming United's reserve team trainer. He left after one season to become the manager of York City.

McGUIGAN Jim
Coach 1983–84
Born in Glasgow in 1924, Jim became a shrewd coach and manager with Crewe, Grimsby, Chesterfield, Rotherham and Stockport. He joined United in November 1983 as first team coach and helped the team win promotion but left before the start of the new season, perhaps in part because his influence with the players was becoming rather more than manager Porterfield and his assistant, John McSeveney, had expected or desired. A 'player's man', Jim died in March 1988.

McSEVENEY John
Assistant Manager June 1981 to March 1986
Born in Scotland, McSeveney was a wing forward before switching to coaching with Hull City. He managed Barnsley but was more successful as a coach with Nottingham Forest, in the Republic of Ireland and further overseas. He assisted Ian Porterfield at Millmoor and came to the Lane with Porterfield in the close season of 1981and left, just a few days after the manager.

MATHEWS Dr William (Bill)
Club Doctor 1925–65
Bill Mathews had a practice on London Road for forty years and was the club doctor from 1925 to 1965. He died in February 1992 at the age of 92.

MERRY Reg
Groundsman 1905–20
Born in Somerset, Reg joined United as Head Groundsman in October 1905 after previously working at Hunslet (Parkside) and left in April 1920 to take over a similar position at Park Avenue, Bradford. His son played for United's reserve team from 1914 to 1917.

MINCHER Keith
Youth Coach 1988–96
Keith was brought to the Lane by Dave Bassett after working with Huddersfield Town. He had a brief spell in 1999 as the manager of Carlisle United and was a Watford coach 2007–08.

MUGGLETON Dr Robert
Club Doctor
He joined Sheffield United as Club Doctor in November 1997 and has worked with the first team at the Club ever since.

NEWTON Arnold
Secretary 1952–72

Born in Rotherham in 1912, he worked at Brown Bayley's for twenty years and joined United in 1949 to assist Teddy Davison, the Secretary-Manager and Howard Hawley, the assistant Secretary. He was appointed as the club's Secretary at the beginning of April 1952 when Hawley was ill and Teddy Davison gave up his secretarial duties shortly before he stood down from the position of manager.

NICHOLSON John
Secretary 1899–1932

A lawyer's clerk who had been born in Attercliffe, John Nicholson took the post of Secretary when United became a limited company in 1899. He had a sound knowledge of football's rules, laws and regulations and had previously acted as the secretary of the Attercliffe Football Club and assistant secretary of the Sheffield & Hallamshire FA.

Honest and conscientious, he could grasp the essentials in the most complicated affairs and became one of the most respected men in football and served numerous other organizations such as the Midland League and the Yorkshire (cricket) Council. He is occasionally referred to as the 'manager' of Sheffield United and he did reject a post of that wording with Manchester City in 1926 but Nicholson was always essentially an administrator with limited football managerial responsibilities. He was for instance, a shrewd intermediary and buffer between the board and players and the United Football Committee could always make use of his wide knowledge of people within the game when, for instance, signing players.

Finance was not his strong suit and auditors dreaded opening the drawer in a huge roll-top desk where bills, receipts and so forth were stored and queries as to 'perhaps missing' petty cash were stopped in their tracks by money from Nicholson's wallet. He could be also be shrewd when signing players rejecting what he regarded as excessive demands—Gillespie for example—but seems to have been reluctant to check a player's declared age even when requested to do so by the directors. He was respected by the players but he was a man of his age. Tommy Sampy never forgot asking if he could have cheese and biscuits (3d extra) in a Portsmouth hotel. 'Certainly' said Nicholson, 'if you pay for them'.

Nicholson died on the 23rd of April 1932 at the age of 68 when he was knocked down by a lorry outside the Midland Station while on his way to a match at Villa Park. It was estimated that six thousand people attended the funeral service and a memorial programme was issued for the next United home match against Newcastle United.

NIGHTINGALE Lawrence (Lol)
Training Staff 1946–49

An elder brother of United's inside forward, Albert Nightingale, 'Lol' had been an assistant trainer at Millmoor when he moved to the Lane in the close season of 1946. He took responsibility for the reserve team but he switched positions in 1948 with Reg Wright, becoming the 'A' team trainer.

NORRIS Andrew

Andrew celebrated 25 years service as the Treasurer of the Supporters Club in 2007.

NORTHCLIFFE Glenn
Groundsman

Glenn joined the ground staff in 1987 and became the Head Groundsman in 1989 at the remarkably young age of twenty.

PACK Andy
Media Manager

Formerly a sports teacher at a local comprehensive school, Andy became the programme editor in 1990 and also assisted Radio Sheffield. He became United's full-time publicity officer in 1995 and subsequently media manager.

PADLEY George
Bramall Lane Ground Secretary 1855?–1862

George Padley was the first Ground Secretary and held the post until he was replaced by Joseph Wostinholm in 1862. He was then Secretary of the Yorkshire (cricket) Match Fund and the first Secretary of the new Yorkshire County Cricket Club until 1864 when he became the Sheffield Borough Accountant.

PARKIN Thomas (Tom)
Groundsman 1911–64

Born in nearby Queens Road, Tom Parkin joined the United groundstaff in 1911 and took over the position of head groundsman and caretaker from Fred Keen in 1949. He was probably the last groundsman to use horses for mowing and rolling. Trained as a (horse) shoeing-smith, his favourites were 'Darby', an ex-fire brigade horse who wouldn't work without a feed when the cricket pavilion clock reached 12 o'clock and 'Monty' who needed an old cap or a shovel handle between his teeth before he would work. Tom died in February 1968 aged 79.

PETTITT Dennis
Physio 1998–
Dennis was fifty three when he joined United in 1998. He had previously served five years with both Mansfield Town and Notts County.

PRITCHETT Tony
Journalist 1973–99
A reporter in Ilkeston and Nottingham, Tony was the Sheffield Wednesday reporter for the local Star and Green'Un from 1968 before switching to write about United in 1973. The chief Star sports reporter, he retired in 1999 and died in 2001.

RAMSAY Ian
A disc jockey and stadium announcer from March 1963 who perhaps first used the phrase 'beautiful down-town Bramall Lane' and played two songs ('Rose Garden' and 'You can do magic') which will always be linked by supporters in the early 1970s with the Tony Currie era.

RANDALL Kevin
The former Chesterfield, Notts County, Mansfield and York inside-forward joined Neil Warnock's coaching staff working for part of the time as reserve team manager and assisting Neil by watching opponents. He continued with this latter role when Neil joined Crystal Palace.

RATCLIFFE Tom
Trainer 1930–32
A trainer with Arsenal, Brentford and Notts County, Ratcliffe had also assisted with the English football and cricket teams. He joined United in the close season of 1930 but was not re-engaged for the 1932–33 season when Bill Brelsford was given the position. He returned to Notts County in 1936.

RATTIN Antonio
Agent and Scout 1978
The captain of the 1966 Argentine World Cup team, Rattin played a part in Alex Sabella signing for United and made a surprise appearance at the Lane in that summer of 1978 but no further players followed.

REID Ronald Eric
Youth coach, Education officer Jan 2000, Academy Manager 2004
A PE master and non-league striker with Worksop, Boston, Scarborough etc, Ron also made seven appearances for Chesterfield (1967–68). He was a manager and coach with non-League teams and also managed the England semi-pro team and was a coach with Neil Warnock at Oldham and Bury before moving to the Lane.

RIDDLE Dean
Performance Manager
In March 2008 Dean began his second spell as fitness 'Guru' for Sheffield United FC having first worked with Neil Warnock and Kevin Blackwell. He re-joined the backroom staff following the return of Blackwell in 2008 in a part time capacity whilst working with both Yorkshire County Cricket Club and Castleford Tigers. Dean became full time fitness consultant once more during the summer of 2008.

ROBINS David
Groundsman from 1975–83
He succeeded Reg Barker and set up his own business when he left.

ROOKER Mick
Promotions Manager
Mick joined United in 1987 on the promotions side and also worked on the organisation of coach travel for United's supporters. He had a brief spell with Hull City in June 1999 but quickly returned to the Lane.

RUMSEY Harold
Commercial Manager
Rumsey was United's first Commercial Manager and promised an annual income of £100k but delivered only £15k. He later became the Secretary of Gillingham, retiring in 1989.

SELLARS Scott
Academy coach Sep 1994 and mgr U18 and reserves to Feb 2008
Born in Chapeltown, near Sheffield in November 1965, Scott played for Leeds, Blackburn, Newcastle and Bolton Wanderers and won three Under 21 caps. Prior to coming to the Lane, he had also assisted Huddersfield T, Aarhus (Denmark) and Mansfield Town and made 531 FL appearances. He moved to Chesterfield as the assistant manager in February 2008.

SHIELD James
Journalist
Born in St Alban's but brought up in Fulham, James began reporting on United in the *Star* and *Green 'Un* in December 2001. He had moved from the Hull Daily Mail where he reported on Hull City and Hull KR.

SHORT John
Coach, assistant manager and scout 1961–78

Born in Gateshead in January 1921, John was a forward with Leeds United who made his name in war-time football. He moved to Millwall (245 FL appearances) and played mainly at wing half before joining their training staff and later moved to Huddersfield Town.

He applied for the position of coach and physio with United in January 1960 but it was a year later when John Harris made him United's chief coach and he became Assistant manager and chief scout in 1969. Jimmy Sirrel moved him to Youth Team Manager in 1976 and he was sacked when Haslam became the Manager in 1978. A hard working and valuable coach but sadly for the Blades, when on scouting duty, he dismissed Kevin Keegan as too small. After leaving United, he acted as Gillingham's chief scout and died in 1986.

SINCLAIR Gary

Gary joined the commercial staff in 2001 and though now self employed, he has remained at the Lane as the match day stadium announcer.

SLADE Russell

Coach, assistant and caretaker-manager 1996–99

A former teacher, Russell was a Notts County reserve and youth team coach and acted as caretaker-manager in the autumn of 1994. He was retained as assistant-manager at Meadow Lane when Howard Kendall took over and joined United's staff in May 1996, soon after Kendall became United's manager. He remained at the Lane when Nigel Spackman took over and was the caretaker manager for a couple of games when Adrian Heath resigned in November 1999. Slade wanted the post of manager and resigned when Neil Warnock took over. Since then, Russell has had managerial jobs with Scarborough, Grimsby Town and Yeovil Town.

SMITH Geoff

Company Secretary 1984–88

Born in Sheffield, Geoff Smith joined United in 1974 as the Office manager and became the Company Secretary early in 1984, replacing Dick Chester. He retired in 1988.

SMITH George

Gateman (1946–88)

Head gateman from 1973; he retired without ever seeing a complete game at the Lane.

SMITH George C

Coach 1955, 1960–61

Born in Bromley-by-Bow in 1915 and a former centre half with Charlton, Brentford, QPR and Ipswich Town and a war-time international, George Smith built up a reputation as a first class coach. He was working with the England Youth team when Joe Mercer, the United manager, brought him to the Lane in September 1955 but he left in January 1956. He returned to the Lane in March 1960 when John Harris was the manager but left to take over the position of manager at Portsmouth in April 1961. He died in 1983.

SMITH Mark

Coach

The Wednesday U21central defender (b. Sheffield 1960) had been a ball-boy at the Lane. He made 350 FL and Cup appearances for the Owls (1978–87). His coaching and assistant managerial career began in 1994 with Lincoln and he has worked for Notts County, Barnsley and Wednesday before joining United's Academy in October 2007.

SPARLING Richard (Dick)

Journalist

A Sheffield football journalist from the 1920s, Dick Sparling became the senior football writer for the *Sheffield Telegraph* and was made an honorary life member of the council of the S&H FA. He was the author (1926) of *The Romance of the Wednesday*—which also covers United's history—and also wrote a brief history of United, issued in 1948, which was one of a series of booklets of club histories. He died in April 1972.

SPRINGETT Peter J

Born in Fulham in 1946, the former QPR, Wednesday and Barnsley goalkeeper (508 FL app in total) was the Community policeman at the Lane for fifteen years. After a serious illness, he died in Sheffield in September 1997.

STEELE David

Coach and Trainer from 9th August 1934 to 30th April 1936

Born in Carluke, Lanarkshire in 1894, Steele had been a fine international half-back with Huddersfield Town before coaching at Bury and in Denmark. In his second and final year with United, the team had lost 1–0 to Arsenal at Wembley and narrowly missed out on promotion. Steele then accepted the position of manager of Bradford (Park Avenue). He later managed Huddersfield and Bradford City.
He made one appearance for United:
3 April 1935 Wednesday 0 United XI 0 (BM).

STONES Henry Herbert 'Harry'

Assistant Secretary 1889

Born in 1860, he played occasionally for the Wednesday, Oxford and Albion clubs in Sheffield. He began working at the age of thirteen for Wostinholm & Stevenson, who were stockbrokers, accountants and estate agents in Norfolk Row. JB Wostinholm was also the Secretary of the Bramall Lane Ground Committee and the Yorkshire County Cricket Club and made Harry Stones his assistant but when the United Football Club was formed in 1889, Wostinholm concentrated on cricket and general affairs at the Lane, leaving football to Stones.

'Zealous and painstaking', he 'put his whole heart into his work' and the club's early successes owe a great deal to him. When John Nicholson became the Secretary in 1899, Stones dealt mainly with cricket matters and he was made a director of the club. He died in May 1922.

TAYLOR Geoff

Coach and Assistant Manager 1988–95

Geoff Taylor, eleven years older than Dave Bassett, played with him for Hayes, the Athenian League amateur team. Geoff became the manager of Southall and Ruislip Manor before Bassett offered him the position of Youth Coach at Wimbledon. Taylor became an invaluable assistant to Bassett at both Wimbledon and Watford and followed him to Sheffield even though, for a few months, Bassett was paying his salary and expenses. Strange to relate, Taylor came as a coach and it was not until perhaps 1991 that his position as the assistant manager was officially recognized.

TAYLOR Richard (Dick)

Coach 1957–58

Born in Wolverhampton in 1918, Dick Taylor was a centre-half with Grimsby Town and Scunthorpe United. He became the trainer-coach with Scunthorpe and joined Joe Mercer at the Lane in June 1957. He followed Mercer in December 1958 to Villa Park and took over Mercer's position as the manager in 1964 but was sacked in 1967 when the club were relegated. He died in Birmingham in 1995.

THURMAN John

Chief Executive/Managing Director 1999–2002

John Thurman was appointed in June 1999. The former Royal Marines officer and businessman left in April 2002.

TOWNSEND Ian

Chief Executive 1998–99

Took over the position of Chief Executive from Charles Green and resigned in March 1999.

TURNER Arthur O

Chief Scout 1979–81

Born in April 1915 Arthur Turner was a player with Stoke, Birmingham and Southport and manager of Crewe, Birmingham and Oxford United. Appointed by Harry Haslam, he was United's chief scout from August 1979 to February 1981 and later had the same job at Millmoor.

TURNER David

Youth Coach 1974–78

Born in Retford in 1943 and a former Newcastle, Brighton and Blackburn wing half, he lost his position with United when Harry Haslam became the manager.

ULYETT John (Jack)

Groundsman 1892–1905

Born in Pitsmoor in Sheffield, 'Happy Jack' was the elder brother of George, the famous Yorkshire cricketer. A big man, he became Head Groundsman in November 1892 following the death of Henry Wright. He lost his position in 1905 to Reg Merry but remained on the staff until his death in December 1915.

VOWDEN Geoff

Coach 1979–81

The former Forest, Birmingham and Villa forward became the Saudi Arabian national coach before moving to join Harry Haslam and Danny Bergara at the Lane in September 1979. He left in the close season of 1981 after United descended into the Fourth Division.

WALKER Keith

Secretary 1973–78

A former part-time professional player with Manchester City and then a local government officer, Keith Walker became a Football League and FIFA referee before joining United in January 1973 at the time that the South Stand development began. He left United at the end of 1978 and worked on the development of soccer in the United States. Later, he was the Chief Executive at Millmoor and had become a director at Mansfield Town when his death was announced in May 1995.

WALLER George (see Players section)

Player and Trainer

WALTERS Fred

Journalist

A Sheffield journalist from the 1930s associated in the main as the chief soccer writer for *The Star* and *Green 'Un*. He was the author of the centenary history of the Sheffield Club and he died in 1970.

WARNOCK John

Director of Coaching at the Centre of Excellence and Academy (1988–2004)

Born in Frecheville and the brother of manager, Neil Warnock, John was virtually always involved in sport and physical education including student football at an international level and was responsible for FA coaching in South Yorkshire. The period with United coincided with the huge development of the Shirecliffe coaching site.

WHITHAM William (Billy)

Match card producer

Billy produced, printed and sold match cards (forerunner of the match programme) for games at Bramall Lane. Born in Sheffield c1833, Billy Whitham printed and sold cricket scorecards as early as 1857 with the agreement of the Bramall Lane Ground Committee and he later sold his cards at the other Yorkshire County grounds. He also produced football match cards for games played in Sheffield—only a handful appear to have survived—prior to United (1897) and Wednesday (1900) producing official programmes. Popularly known as 'Donner' or 'Donnie', Whitham died in 1910.

WHITNEY Beryl & Peter

Long service members of the Supporters Club, Peter celebrated 25 years as Chairman in 2007 and Beryl 20 years as Secretary before she retired from the post in 2008.

WIGLEY Peter
Programme editor 1986–90
Peter was born in Sheffield in 1931 and educated at High Storrs Grammar School. He was the senior Public Relations Officer in Sheffield and was succeeded as programme editor by Andy Pack.

WILLEY Alf
Physiotherapist 1955–60
A hospital remedial gymnast, Alf helped United on a part-time basis becoming full-time in the summer of 1957.

WINNILL A G
Secretary 1892–93
A principal of Upperthorpe School, Winnill became United's Football Secretary in September 1892 when United became members of the Football League though Joseph Wostinholm, who dealt with cricket matters, remained in overall charge. Winnill gave up his post in November 1893.

WOSTINHOLM Joseph Beckett
Secretary 1862–99

Born in Sheffield in 1836, JB Wostinholm took the position in December 1862 of Secretary of the Bramall Lane Cricket Ground. In 1864, he replaced George Padley as the Secretary of the recently established Yorkshire County Cricket Club and no man did more, other than perhaps Lord Hawke, to establish Yorkshire as the leading county cricket club.

A chartered accountant, stockbroker and estate agent, working from Norfolk Row and Bramall Lane, he watched over the building of the walls, pavilion and other structures, the expansion of the ground, the enclosure of the Shoreham Street side, the growth of the Yorkshire County Cricket Club and the establishment of the United Football and Cricket Clubs.

He gave up the position of Secretary of the Football Club in 1892, resuming the position in 1893 and continued in his role as Secretary of the Sheffield United and Yorkshire Cricket Clubs until 1902. He died in April 1909.

WRIGHT Harry
Groundsman 1855?–92
Harry Wright was a well known Sheffield and Yorkshire cricketer who was a member of the committee who drew up the plans for the new cricket ground at the Lane and he played in the first match in 1855. He may have been the first groundsman and certainly held the responsibility from 1866 until his death in 1892.

WRIGHT 'Reg' (see Players section)
Trainer 1936–57

He made one emergency appearance for the United first team (28 Sep 1940) at Doncaster.

THE SUBSCRIBERS

Trevor P Allison
Mike Arthur
Kurtis Ash HAPPY BIRTHDAY KURTIS XX
Robert Ash HAPPY BIRTHDAY ROBERT
Stewart Atkinson
Gordon Edward Badger
Paul Philip Badger
Andrew G Barnett
Gerry Beardsmore
Jack Daniel Bedford
John Bell
David A Bennett
Andrew Billard
Benjamin Bird
Paul Bolt
Kevin John Booth
Phil Bottomley
Hannah Louise Bowen
Gary Bower
John Charles Bradford
Michael Richard Bradley
Scott Andrew Bradley
Stephen Paul Bradley
Ian Brown
Richard Burgin
Ben Burkinshaw 100% BLADE
Tony Burkitt
Paul Charles 100% BLADE
Catherine Clareborough
Denis & Maureen Clareborough
Thomas Fragel Clareborough
John, Alice & Ava Clark
Philip Claxton
Lindsey Clayton
Trevor & Robert Coleman
Alan Colton
Martin James Cornish
John Cressey
Alexander Crossland
Gavin Crossland
Lee Crossland
Peter Crossland
Steve Cryan
Eric Dawson 70 YEARS A BLADE
David Dooks
Gareth Kevyn Dunn
Keith Ecklid
Fiona Elcoat
Anna Eleftheriou
Sophia Eleftheriou
Ian Emmingham
Richard W Evans EEZABLADE
Dr Frances Fermer
Alan J Fidler CRESWELL BLADE
Jamie Fleet
David & Margaret Fletcher
Brian Flower
Arthur Foreman 1915–2002
Martin Fox
Stephen Fox
Brian Garbett
Martin Garbett
Carl J Garnham
Daniel Garrett
Liam Garrett
Helen Gill
Richard Gilson
Hollie Claire Godbehere
Derek Goodison TRUE BLADE
Shaun Goodman SHAUN IS A TRUE BLADE
David James Joe Goodwin
Steve Goulding

Richard WH Grafton

Kevin Greathead

Ricky, Luke & Max Greaves

Andrew Green (Greeny)

Leonard Green

Ryan Green

Linda Griffiths

Mick Hallam

Josh L Hancock BLADE 4 LIFE

Christopher Paul Hardy

Graham Harvey

Bob Hill

Hillsborough Labour Party

Robert Hogg

Howard Holmes

John Flirtog Hough

Jon Hough

Stephen Ibbotson 23RD JULY 1971

Keith William Jackson

Peter Alec Jackson

Brian (Tenpints) Jessop

Andrew Alan Johnson

Andrew Jones

Carnley Jones

Danny Jones

Geoff Jones

Tom Keeton

The Keenan Family

Joe Kelly

John Joseph Kennelly

Kent Family, Caistor

Andrew James Kilner

Richard John Kilner

Stewart (Kit Kat) Kitridge

Korklin Family, Stanmore

Michael Laughton

Adam Lawson

Ken Lawson

Malcolm Leary UP THE BLADES

Adrian John Marriott

John Alan Marriott

Dave Masters YEOVIL BLADE

Gordon Matthews

Graham Matthews .doc.pace.fan

WH, ST, BR & RH Mattock

Steve & Charlie May

Peter May STOCKYBLADE

Charles Patrick McCabe

Kevin McCabe

Sandra McCabe

Scott McCabe

Simon McCabe

Sophia Alice McCabe

Aaron Peter McDonagh

Alan McKenna BORN A BLADE

Andrew McWhirter

Stephen Metham

Gary Meynell

Oscar Miller

Neil Moncrieff

Steve Moore

Chris Myers BLADE 4 LIFE

Andrew Peter Needham

Andrew Nelson

Simon Newsum

Gerald Oliver

Gordon Osborne

Roger Osbourn

Harry James Owen 31ST MAY 2008

Andrew Parker

Sarah Parkinson

Katie Pass

Duncan Payne

Keith Plowman

Richard (Dicky) Price

Margaret Proctor

George Rands

Andrew Michael Reeves

Dennis Richards

Paul Rickus A BLADE

Neil Robertson HAPPY 60TH

Donald Ryalls

John David Ryalls

Keiron Salt

Robert Matthew James Saxby

Jon-Peter Schofield

Peter Schofield

Gordon Scothern

James Scribley 100% BLADE

Peter, Rebecca & Bobby Sharpe

James M Slack

John Gerrard Slater

Martin Slater

Ade Alex Oliver Smalley

Alan Smith SUSC KIVETON

Christopher Smith

Richard James Smith

Roland Smith

Ella Somerset

Mark Somerset

Roger Somerset

John Stancliffe

John Stannard

Charlie Norman Stephenson

Robert Stockley 100% BLADE

Steven Storrs

In Memory of Alan Douglas Straker

Malcolm Styan

Hanspetter Syversen

Mats-Henrik Nygren Syversen

Philip Taylor

Ross Taylor 23RD AUGUST 2001

Paul Thackeray

John Patrick Thurston

Roger Tingle

Stephen Titterton

Andrew J Treherne

Bob Uttley

John Vaughan

Brian & Mavis Vickers

Luke Walker

Matthew Walker

Bryan Ward

Sarah & Alan Warrington

George Watson HEELEY RED

Bradley Mark Weaver

Charlie Webster

John M Webster

Michael J Webster

Danny Whelan

Adam & Laura Whitaker

Andrew Whitham

Roger Widdison KIVETON BLADE

Jake Barry George Wilkinson

George Wood

Jayne L Woodhead

Ian J Woodruff

David Wright

Frank Yates SEN BLADES